Lecture Notes in Computer Science 2681
Edited by G. Goos, J. Hartmanis, and J. van Leeuwen

Springer
Berlin
Heidelberg
New York
Barcelona
Hong Kong
London
Milan
Paris
Tokyo

Johann Eder Michele Missikoff (Eds.)

Advanced Information Systems Engineering

15th International Conference, CAiSE 2003
Klagenfurt/Velden, Austria, June 16-20, 2003
Proceedings

Volume Editors

Johann Eder
Universität Klagenfurt, Institut für Informatik-Systeme
Universitätsstr. 65-67, 9020 Klagenfurt, Austria
E-mail: eder@isys.uni-klu.ac.at

Michele Missikoff
Istituto di Analisi dei Sistemi ed Informatica - CNR
Viale Manzoni, 30, 00185 Roma, Italy
E-mail: misskoff@iasi.rm.cnr.it

Cataloging-in-Publication Data applied for

A catalog record for this book is available from the Library of Congress

Bibliographic information published by Die Deutsche Bibliothek
Die Deutsche Bibliothek lists this publication in the Deutsche Nationalbibliografie; detailed bibliographic data is available in the Internet at <http://dnb.ddb.de>.

CR Subject Classification (1998): H.2, H.4-5, H.3, J.1, K.4.3-4, K.6, D.2, I.2.11

ISSN 0302-9743
ISBN 3-540-40442-2 Springer-Verlag Berlin Heidelberg New York

Springer-Verlag Berlin Heidelberg New York
a member of BertelsmannSpringer Science+Business Media GmbH

http://www.springer.de

Printed in Germany

Typesetting: Camera-ready by author, data conversion by PTP Berlin GmbH
Printed on acid-free paper SPIN 10927595 06/3142 5 4 3 2 1 0

Preface

CAiSE 2003 was the 15th in the series of International Conferences on Advanced Information Systems Engineering. This edition continues the success of the previous conferences, a success largely due to that fact that, since its first edition, this series has been able to evolve in parallel to the evolution of the information system methods and technologies. CAiSE has been able to follow, and often to anticipate, the deep changes that have occurred since the late 1970s when the first CAiSE conference was organized by Arne Sølvberg and Janis Bubenko.

In all these years, the mission of information systems has been inherently the same, but it is not too excessive if we say that nothing seems to be the same. This edition of the conference, the CaiSE 2003, falls into a very special historical contingency. The incredible expansion of the Internet and the Web has contributed to make our planet smaller – probably we are actually in the process of building the Global Village, as prophesized by Marshall McLuhan. From personal digital assistants to global broadcasting systems over the Internet, information systems, with all its possible variations and derivatives, represents one of the key elements of this increasingly connected society. Researchers have been challenged by all these changes, and the CAiSE conferences represent important occasions for presenting and debating important scientific results. In fact, the CAiSE series has been able to build a strong tradition, while being ... *non-traditional,* in the sense that CAiSE is positioned in the middle of this tumultuous process, hosting new emerging ideas and fostering innovative solutions, but always being subject to rigorous scientific selection.

In CaiSE 2003, we decided to select a theme, a sort of "fil rouge," aimed at giving a more comprehensive perspective to the scientific event. We also intended to stimulate a reflection about our work, after putting so much energy into it. The theme we suggested is: "Information Systems for a Connected Society." A connected society is the goal of the confluence of information systems, telecommunication systems and their application in business, government, and everyday life. The scenario is complex from a technological point of view. As already stated in the Call for Papers, the pervasiveness of infrastructures for modern information systems greatly extends the demands on engineering information systems, in terms of scalability, quality, dependability and adaptability. Information Systems for a Connected Society will be multimedial, multimodal, multilingual, and multicultural. Situation and location awareness will allow users to cope with the complexity of these systems.

The challenge has been accepted, as witnessed by the significant number of submissions, 219, out of which the PC was able to select 45 top-quality papers. The selection was very hard, due to the very high standard of the submitted papers. Here it is mandatory to thank all the authors and, on the "other side of the fence," all the PC members who did tremendous work (indeed, their workload was heavier than expected ... this is the "cost" of the success of the conference!). Another remarkable aspect was the high profile of the co-located events, workshops, panels, keynote addresses, demo and poster sessions, that we collectively grouped into the CAiSE forum: a new space for confronting emerging ideas. We wish to thank collectively all colleagues who accepted working hard to support all these initiatives.

We wish to devote a special thanks to our young colleagues who dedicated great amounts of energy to support the local organization, the PC activities, and the organization of the publishing of this volume.

Finally, we wish to thank our sponsors who helped with their support, and the organization for offering a nice environment and enjoyable services, while keeping the fees in a reasonable range.

A final word, to remind us, is due to the city of Velden that is hosting the conference, with its magic lake and the atmosphere of Carinthia. Another word is due to the University of Klagenfurt that promoted and made possible the whole event.

April 2003
Klagenfurt and Rome

Johann Eder and Michele Missikoff

CAiSE 2003 Conference Organization

Advisory Committee

Arne Sølvberg
NTNU Trondheim, Norway

Janis Bubenko
KTH Stockholm, Sweden

General Chair

Johann Eder
Università Klagenfurt
Austria

Program-Committee Chair

Michele Missikoff
IASI-CNR
Italy

Program Committee

Breiteneder, C.	Austria	Orlowska, M.	Australia
Brinkkemper, S.	The Netherlands	Ozsu, T.	Canada
Bubenko, J.	Sweden	Panagos, T.	USA
Bussler, C.	USA	Panti, M.	Italy
Castano, S.	Italy	Papazoglou, M.	The Netherlands
Catarci, T.	Italy	Pastor, O.	Spain
D'Atri, A.	Italy	Paton, N.	UK.
Fugini, M.	Italy	Pernici, B.	Italy
Geppert, A.	Switzerland	Pirotte, A.	Belgium
Giorgini, P.	Italy	Plexousakis, D.	Greece
Hainaut, J.L.	Belgium	Pohl, K.	Germany
Jajodia, S.	USA	Rabinovich, M.	USA
Jarke, M.	Germany	Rabitti, F.	Italy
Jeffery, K.	UK	Reich, S.	Austria
Jensen, C.S.	Denmark	Rolland, C.	France
Jeusfeld, M.	The Netherlands	Scholl, M.	France
Kangassalo, H.	Finland	Sellis, T.	Greece
Kappel, G.	Austria	Sernadas, A.	Portugal
Karagiannis, D.	Austria	Siau, K.	USA
Kerschberg, L.	USA	Sølvberg, A.	Norway
Lenzerini, M.	Italy	Studer, R.	Germany
Leonard, M.	Switzerland	Sutcliffe, A.	UK
Loucopoulos, P.	UK	Thalheim, B.	Germany
Maiden, N.	UK	Torlone, R.	Italy
Mylopoulos, J.	Canada	Vargas-Solar, G.	Switzerland
Neuhold, E.	Germany	Vassiliou, Y.	Greece
Norrie, M.	Switzerland	Wand, Y.	Canada
Olivé, A.	Spain	Wangler, B.	Sweden
Opdahl, A.	Norway	Yu, E.	Canada

Additional Referees

Adão, P. (PT)
Aiello, M. (IT)
Amato, G. (IT)
Analyti, A. (GR)
Arazy, O. (CA)
Atzeni, P. (IT)
Aufaure, M.A. (FR)
Backlund, P. (SE)
Balinska, K. (PL)
Barbini, F. (IT)
Berardi, D. (IT)
Bernauer, M. (AT)
Binemann-Zdanowics, A. (DE)
Blanzieri, E. (IT)
Bolchini, D. (CH)
Bolici, F. (IT)
Borghese, A. (IT)
Bounif, H. (CH)
Bresciani, P. (IT)
Cappiello, C. (IT)
Casalino, N. (IT)
Chen, L. (CA)
Chen, S. (US)
Christophides, V. (GR)
Contenti, M. (IT)
Cullot, N. (FR)
Dahchour, M. (MA)
Dahlstedt, A. (SE)
Damm, D. (CH)
D'Andrea, V. (IT)
D'Antona, O. (IT)
De Giacomo, G. (IT)
Debole, F. (IT)
Drozdowski, M. (PL)
Eidenberger, H. (AT)
Erickson, J. (US)
Evermann, J. (CA)
Fabi, T. (IT)
Fankhauser, P. (DE)
Felici, G. (IT)
Ferrara, A. (IT)
Feyer, T. (DE)
Gennaro, C. (IT)
Gounaris, T. (UK)
Gouveia, P. (PT)
Griffiths, T. (UK)
Gross, D. (CA)
Gruber, R. (US)
Hakimpour, F. (CH)
Handschuh, S. (DE)
Hartmann, S. (NZ)
Henrard, J. (BE)
Hotho, A. (DE)
Huemer, C. (AT)
Jankiewicz, K. (PL)
Janssen, M. (NL)
Jouanot, F. (CH)
Jurk, S. (DE)
Karvounarakis, S. (GR)
Kaschek, R. (NZ)
Khadraoui, A. (CH)
Klarlund, N. (US)
Klement, T. (DE)
Kotsis, G. (AT)
Koubarakis, M. (GR)
Kramler, G. (AT)
Krolikowski, Z. (PL)
Kuehn, H. (AT)
Kuper, G. (IT)
L'Abbate, M. (DE)
Le, T. (CH)
Lembo, D. (IT)
Li, Y. (US)
Link, S. (NZ)
Luu, H. (CH)
Maedche, A. (DE)
Maetzel, C. (DE)
Makkonen, P. (AT)
Marchetti, C. (IT)
Matera, M. (IT)
Mateus, P. (PT)
Maurino, A. (IT)
Mecella, M. (IT)
Melchiori, M. (IT)
Missier, P. (IT)
Missikoff, O. (IT)
Muratidis, H. (UK)
Nawrocki, J. (PL)
Newman, J. (AT)
Oria, V. (US)
Pagani, E. (IT)
Parent, C. (CH)
Parsons, J. (CA)
Pedersen, T.B. (DK)
Peim, M. (UK)
Pelechano, V. (ES)
Penserini, L. (IT)
Perini, A. (IT)
Persson, A. (SE)
Pham, T. (CH)
Plebani, P. (IT)
Putz, W. (DE)
Ralyte, J. (CH)
Ramos, J. (PT)
Ravara, A. (PT)
Retschitzegger, W. (AT)
Rizzi, S. (IT)
Ronchetti, M. (IT)
Sajkowski, M. (PL)
Sanchez, J. (ES)
Savino, P. (IT)
Scannapieco, M. (IT)
Schewe, K.D. (NZ)
Schiappelli, F. (IT)
Simitsis, A. (GR)
Sindoni, G. (IT)
Snene, M. (CH)
Sobaniec, C. (PL)
Soederstroem, E. (SE)
Soffer, P. (IL)
Sotnykova, A. (CH)
Spalazzi, L. (IT)
Stojanovic, N. (DE)
Strand, M. (SE)
Stumme, G. (DE)
Sure, Y. (DE)
Taglino, F. (IT)
Tarantino, L. (IT)
Theodoratos, D. (US)
Thiel, U. (DE)
Thiran, P. (BE)
Tian, Y. (US)

Tininini, L. (IT)
Tretiakov, A. (NZ)
Turki, S. (CH)
Urbaniak, A. (PL)
van den Heuvel, W.J. (NL)
Vassiliadis, P. (GR)
Vestenicky, V. (DE)
Virgillito, A. (IT)
Vituzzi, A. (IT)
Volz, R. (DE)
Wang, L. (US)
Wijesekera, D. (US)
Wombacher, A. (DE)
Wrembel, R. (PL)
Yang, J. (NL)
Yetongnon, K. (FR)
Zezula, P. (CZ)
Zhu, S. (US)

Organizing Committee

Local Organization, Web-site and Communication

Institut für Informatik-Systeme, Universität Klagenfurt, Austria

Wöllik, U. Samonig, C. Pichler, H.
Koncilia, C. Gruber, W.

Program-Committee Assistant

Formica, A., LEKS, IASI-CNR (IT)

Publishing Assistants

De Nicola, A., Wang, X.F., LEKS, IASI-CNR (IT)

Sponsoring Organizations

Academic Sponsors

Universität Klagenfurt
www.uni-klu.ac.at

LEKS, IASI-CNR
leks.iasi.rm.cnr.it

Gold Sponsors

Sun Microsystems, Inc.
www.sun.com

Silicon Alps
www.siliconalps.com

S-Innovationscenter
www.s-innovationscenter.at

Silver Sponsors

Siemens AG Austria
www.siemens.at

ilogs - information logistics, Austria
www.ilogs.at

CAiSE 2003 Panels, Tutorials and Posters

Panel and Tutorial Chair

Hannes Werthner
Università degli Studi di Trento, Italy

Martin Hitz
Universität Klagenfurt, Austria

Evaluation, Assessment and Certification of Dependable Information Systems

Hans-Ludwig Hausen, Germany

Developing Maintainable Systems – Roundtrip Engineering with Metrics

Leszek A. Maciaszek, Australia
Bruc Liong, Australia

Poster Chair

Tatjana Welzer
Univerza v Mariboru, Slovenia

CAiSE 2003 Pre- and Postconference Workshops

Workshop Chair

Barbara Pernici
Politecnico di Milano, Italy

Roland Mittermeir
Universität Klagenfurt, Austria

10th Doctoral Consortium

Eva Söderström	Sweden
Joerg Evermann	Canada
Julia Kotlarsky	The Netherlands

Evaluation of Modeling Methods in Systems Analysis and Design (EMMSAD 2003)

Keng Siau	USA
John Krogstie	Norway
Terry Halpin	USA

9th International Workshop on Requirements Engineering: Foundation For Software Quality (REFSQ 2003)

Björn Regnell	Sweden
Camille Salinesi	France
Erik Kamsties	Germany

Requirements Engineering for Business Process Support (REBPS 2003)

Ian Alexander	UK
Ilia Bider	Sweden
Gil Regev	Switzerland

Ubiquitous Mobile Information and Collaboration Systems (UMICS 2003)

Luciano Baresi	Italy
Sara Comai	Italy
Schahram Dustdar	Austria
Harald Gall	Austria
Maristella Matera	Italy

Decision Systems Engineering (DSE 2003)

Jacky Akoka	France
Isabelle Comyn-Wattiau	France
Nadira Lammari	France
Elisabeth Métais	France
Nicolas Prat	France
Samira Si-Saïd	France

Semantic Web for Web-Based Learning (SW-WL 2003)

Marie-Noelle Bessagnet	France
Michel Sala	France

Development of Product Software (DoPS 2003)

Sjaak Brinkkemper	The Netherlands
Hans van Vliet	The Netherlands

Web Services, e-Business, and the Semantic Web (WES 2003)

Jian Yang	The Netherlands	Christoph Bussler	USA
Dieter Fensel	Austria	Maria Orlowska	Australia

Table of Contents

Methods & Models for Information Systems – II

Internet Business & Social Modeling

Peer2Peer

Ontology-Based Methods

Advanced Design of Information Systems

Knowledge Management

Web Services

Data Warehouse

Electronic Agreements & Workflow

Requirement Engineering

Metrics & Method Engineering

Agent Technologies and Advanced Environments

Towards Self-Managing Large Scale Information Systems

Marek Rusinkiewicz

Department of Computer Science
The University of Houston
marek@uh.edu

Abstract. Information systems and the IT infrastructure that is used to support them are becoming too complex to design, maintain, and evolve using traditional approaches. To realize the visions of ubiquitous and adaptive computing, the responsibility for the management of the complexity must be shifted from the designers and operators of the systems, to the systems themselves.

Current work in this area goes in the direction of creating systems that are capable of reacting without human intervention to the new requirements and to the changes in the operating environments. In this talk we will review several examples of technologies that bring us closer to achieving this goal. First, we will review the model of policy-based network management, using as examples automatic network configuration and policy-based network security enforcement. We will show how security objectives, formulated using high-level specifications can be automatically translated into appropriate network settings. The network can be then continuously monitored to detect violations, and appropriate adjustments can be made, as needed to enforce the security policies.

In the second part of the talk, we will discuss information exploitation applications developed as communities of collaborating software agents. We will review agent communication standards, including communication languages and agent conversation templates. We will also discuss various methods of creating agent communities, both facilitated, based on brokering/matchmaking, and self-organizing, based on market concepts. We will illustrate this with examples drawn from the InfoSleuth agent system.

J. Eder and M. Missikoff (Eds.): CAiSE 2003, LNCS 2681, p. 1, 2003.

Autonomous Semantic Web Services

Katia P. Sycara

School of Computer Science
Carnegie Mellon University
katia@cs.cmu.edu
http://www.cs.cmu.edu/~softagents

Abstract. Web Services are defining a new paradigm for the Web in which a network of computer programs become the consumers of information. The growing infrastructure for Web Services is based on SOAP and WSDL and assumes XML as unifying language to guarantee Web Services interoperability. XML guarantees syntactic interoperability by providing a standard for a common syntax that is shared across the Web, with the result that Web Services can parse each other's messages, verify whether they adhere to the expected formats, and locate each piece of information within the message. Unfortunately, current Web Services do not have any means to extract the meaning of the messages exchanged. The Web Services understand the structure of each other's message, but do not understand the content of those messages. This limitation requires programmers to hard-code Web Services with information about their interaction partners, the messages that they exchange and the interpretation of those messages; moreover, current Web Services cannot reconfigure dynamically to adapt to changes without direct human intervention.

Ideally, we would like Web Services to act autonomously. Web Services should be able to register autonomously with infrastructure Registries such as UDDI, use the infras-tructure Registries to locate providers of services that they need, and they should be able to transact with these Web Services sending them information formatted in a way that they can understand. Correspondingly, Web Services should be able to interpret the information that they receive. Autonomous Web Services not only minimize the human intervention by automating interaction with other Web Services, allowing programmers to concentrate on application development, but also are able to recover from failures more efficiently by automatically reconfiguring their interaction patterns. For example, if one of their partners fails, or becomes unreliable, they may be able to find other more reliable partners; similarly, if a new, cheaper, or higher quality provider comes on line, Web Services should be able to dynamically find the new partner and interact with it in peer to peer fashion. In order to find partners, Autonomous Web Services need to be able to semantically describe and automatically register their own capabilities with public registries. Semantically meaningful capability descriptions are crucial to automated partner discovery so that discovery is based on the service semantics of the partners, rather than on matching keywords, such as service name or name of the company that deploys the Service. In addition, a Web Service should have information on how to interact with another Web Service, which means that it should know the interaction protocol and binding information. Most crucially, this information should allow the re-

J. Eder and M. Missikoff (Eds.): CAiSE 2003, LNCS 2681, pp. 2–3, 2003.

questing Web Services as well as the provider to decode the information exchanged, so it should specify not only the format of the messages to exchange or the remote procedures to call, but also the semantic type of the information.

This view is embraced by DAML-S (The Darpa Agent Markup Language for Services) which defines a DAML ontology for the description of Web Services. DAML-S attempts to bridge the gap between an infrastructure of Web Services based essentially on WSDL and SOAP, and the Semantic Web. In other words, DAML-S bridges the gap between the specification of the format of the information to be exchanged and the specification of its meaning. DAML-S assumes that a transaction between Web Services involves at least three parties: a provider of the service, a requester of the service, and some infrastructure component such as UDDI that facilitates the location of the provider and possibly facilitates the transaction between provider and requester. Furthermore, DAML-S allows for a flexible assignment of roles in which a Web Service can be both a provider in one transaction and a requester in another, and it also allows for a role switch within the same transaction.

DAML-S has three modules that provide a description of different aspects of Web Services. The first one, called Profile, is an abstract description of the Web Service described as a transformation from the inputs the Web Service requires to the outputs it generates. The second module is the Process Model that characterizes the Web Service, specifically, it describes the interaction flow with the Web Service. The third module, called Grounding, specifies how the inputs/outputs of each step are mapped on WSDL specifications of messages that the two Web Services exchange.

In this talk, I will describe in depth the vision of Autonomous Semantic Web Services, the requirements it imposes, and the research challenges it presents. I will also present DAML-S, contrast it with current industrial proposed standards for Web Services and present a roadmap to get us from today's Web service technology to the future of Autonomous Semantic Web Services.

Managing an XML Warehouse in a P2P Context*

Serge Abiteboul**

INRIA-Futurs, LRI and Xyleme
Serge.Abiteboul @inria.fr

Abstract. The paper is about warehousing XML content in a P2P environment. The role of an XML warehouse is to offer a centralized entry point to access a variety of information in an enterprise and provide functionalities to acquire, enrich, monitor and maintain this information. We consider a number of reasons to use a P2P approach to such warehouses, e.g., reducing the cost or sharing the management of information. We mention research issues that are raised.

1 Introduction

Enterprises and more generally communities centered around some common interest may benefit from the construction, enrichment, monitoring and maintenance of large repositories of information with methods to access, analyze and annotate this information. We propose to use XML and Web services as the basis for such a warehouse. A warehouse is typically a server that centralizes and manages all the relevant information. In this paper, we consider as an alternative the management of such a warehouse in a Peer to Peer (P2P) environment.

Let us first see the main aspects of these two concepts:

Warehouse. [24] The goal of a warehouse is to provide an integrated access to heterogeneous, autonomous, distributed sources of information. The information is acquired in advance, transformed, filtered, cleaned, and integrated. Queries are then evaluated without access to the original sources.

Peer to Peer. There are many possible definitions of P2P systems. We mean here that a large and varying number of computers cooperate to solve particular tasks (here warehousing tasks) without any centralized authority. In other words, the challenge is to build an efficient, robust, scalable system based on (typically) inexpensive, unreliable, computers distributed on a wide area network. This leads in particular to complex communication and information discovery schemes.

The combination of the two may seem a bit confusing, so let us try to articulate it more precisely. The data sources are heterogeneous, (very) autonomous

* The research was partly funded by EC Project DBGlobe

** Gemo Team, PCRI Saclay, a joint lab between CNRS, Ecole Polytechnique, INRIA and Université Paris-Sud

J. Eder and M. Missikoff (Eds.): CAiSE 2003, LNCS 2681, pp. 4–13, 2003.

and distributed. The warehouse presents a unique entry point to this information. Thus, the warehouse is logically homogeneous and centralized; and a P2P XML warehouse should logically not be distinguishable from a centralized one - to some extent, it is *only* an implementation issue. Now, the physical resources of the P2P warehouse consist of distributed peers. So, the physical organization also consists of heterogeneous, autonomous, and distributed machines, although a higher level of trust may possibly be achieved in this setting.

It is important to keep in mind that the warehouse is *logically centralized* with all peers acting as entry-points and *physically distributed.*

To see an example, consider the management of a very large collection of preprints. Any registered user is allowed to publish preprints. Other preprints may be found, say by a Web crawler. The warehouse is implemented over several peers that store replicas of the preprints. It may be the case that a site (say INRIA) is a source of preprints and is, as well, one of the peers in the warehouse. These two roles should not be confused. In principle, an INRIA preprint may be replicated, from the warehouse viewpoint, at several peers and possibly not even be on the INRIA peer.

The paper is organized as follows. In Section 2, we discuss the functionalities of the warehouse. In Section 3, we consider advantages of implementing it in a P2P environment. In Section 4, we mention research issues that are raised. In place of a conclusion, we briefly present Active XML as a candidate infrastructure for such a warehouse.

2 XML Warehouse

In this section, we present the main functionalities of an XML warehouse. We will consider why to implement it in a P2P system and issues that this raises in the following sections.

We are concerned here with a *warehousing of content* to provide a unified view over distributed, autonomous and heterogeneous information sources.

The focus is on warehousing. One typically distinguishes between a mediation approach (the integration remains virtual) and a warehouse approach (the data is materialized and possibly transformed). Both approaches present advantages. In a warehousing approach, we fetch information ahead of time from information sources. In contrast to a mediation approach, the information may be cleaned, enriched, integrated before the arrival of any query.

The focus is on a warehouse of "content" ("qualitative information") rather than typical warehouses that are more concerned with "quantitative information" typically organized in relations. Content has less structure; one sometimes say it is semi-structured. This motivates the use of XML. With XML, one can capture plain text, as well as text with some structure, all the way to very structured information such as tuples. Clearly, the management of meta-data is here an essential component, as advocated in Tim Berners-Lee's view of the Semantic Web [9].

Let us make more precise this notion of content.

Content: physical and logical. For us, content is information in its most general form. The primary unit of information is the *content element.* Content elements may be documents, fragments of documents, files, relational tuples, and similar information. We will use XML, the standard for data exchange, as a core data model. Content elements will be transformed, when possible, into XML so that their structure becomes available. Some may stay in their original formats, e.g., pdf files. However, meta information about pieces of information will always be in XML. A content element is a physical notion, but also a logical notion. Typically, a content element may be a portion of a document in its XML incarnation, such as the Subject field of an email, or a collection of such multiple content elements, such as an email folder.

Another essential component of the warehouse is the *global schema* of the warehouse, i.e., the organization that a user would see, for instance, while browsing the warehouse. This aspect will not be considered here.

The main functionalities of such a warehouse are as follows:

Acquisition. A goal is to locate content elements in source information systems and load them in the warehouse (pull mode). This is typically based on Web services, Web crawlers or general LTE tools[1] to obtain data from virtually any system, e.g., LDAP, newsgroup, emails, file systems, database systems, etc.

Content may also be acquired from users in *push* mode. This may involve document or meta-data editing (achieved, e.g., via the WebDAV protocol) or explicit publication in the warehouse.

Enrichment. The goal is to enrich the warehouse or, in other words, add value to its content. This may involve for instance translation to XML (XML-izer of various forms), structural transformations (e.g., via XSL/T processor), classification, summarization, concept tagging, etc. Enrichment may act at different levels:

1. enriching the meta-data, e.g., document classification;
2. enrichments inside the document, e.g., extraction and tagging of concepts inside the document; and
3. enriching the relationships between documents, e.g., creation of tables of content.

Repository. The warehouse should be able to store massive amounts of XML, up to terabytes. It should also support indexing (of data and meta-data) and processing of queries over XML data. Finally, it should provide standard repository functionalities such as recovery and access control.

Change control. It is often the case, that users are particularly interested in changes (e.g., a new release of software or the newly published newspaper articles on a particular topic). This leads to issues in versioning and the support of continuous queries [11]. Of particular importance is the monitoring of the loading of information in the warehouse.

[1] LTE stands for load, transform and extract.

View and Integration. The system should provides tools for building user views, e.g., by restructuring documents via XSL/T transformations and integrating collections of heterogeneous XML documents. One should also consider proposing automatic or semi-automatic tools to analyze a set of XML schemas and, using some ontologies of the domain, integrate them and then support queries on the integration view.

Exploitation. The exploitation of the warehouse primarily involves functionalities such as: querying, browsing, annotating content, generation of complex parameterized reports, and on-line analysis of content.

Administration. The warehouse has to be administered. This includes in particular the means to register acquisition and enrichment tasks, the management of users and of their access privileges, as well as the control on-going tasks such as backup and failure recovery.

The functionalities of the warehouse should be available via GUI or via programs. When we move to a Web context, HTTP and Web services are clearly the natural candidates for the interface.

The advantages of such a warehouse approach are discussed in more details in [5].

3 Why a Distributed Warehouse?

In many contexts (e.g., in an enterprise), the best physical architecture for such a warehouse is a centralized server, or a cluster of machines as proposed by Xyleme [26]. In others (e.g., in a large consortium), a P2P organization may be preferable, e.g., to share the cost of the warehouse as well as its management. This is what we consider here. A main difference is that there is no (or less) centralized authority. In contrast with the machines involved in a cluster implementing an XML warehouse, the machines involved in a P2P warehouse are imposed little constraints; they are typically heterogeneous, less reliable and connected via a much slower network.

Although the architecture is very different, observe that the functionalities remain the same. However, because of the P2P aspect, they take a slightly different flavor. For instance, discovery of data and services becomes a central issue, whereas it was not really an issue in the centralized case (except for the feeding part). For instance, consider a P2P warehouse of pre-prints involving thousands of actors. Finding a particular preprint may require more work since we cannot rely on a single trusted peer to maintain it.

As mentioned in the introduction, this may seem a bit confusing since one typically think of a warehouse as centralized. We would like to stress again the fact that the warehouse is *logically centralized* with all peers acting as entry-points and *physically distributed.* It is also important to see the difference with a mediation approach. In a P2P approach, the content is copied to the warehouse and pre-processed (enriched).

Since the data in a P2P warehouse is distributed between the peers, query processing involves distributed computation (as in the mediation setting). It is, in general, natural to consider hybrid approaches merging warehousing and mediation. Indeed, it is even much more natural to think in these terms in the P2P setting since both now involve distributed computations. The following table tries to picture the various possibilities:

Integrator is:	Centralized server	Cluster of machines	Machines in P2P
data in integration system	warehouse	Xyleme warehouse	P2P warehouse
Hybrid			
data in source systems	mediation		P2P mediation

In the following of the section, we consider advantages of P2P warehouses. There are first the standard advantages of distribution:

- Performance. Better performance may be achieved by avoiding the bottleneck of a centralized server and using data replication and caching.
- Ownership. Each peer may keep full control over its own information. This does not have to be the rule but in some cases, this may allow to let the responsibility of access control to the owner of information.
- Cost. This avoids the cost of a centralized server and enables taking also advantage of local unused resources (storage and processing). Also, with this approach the costs may be shared between the peers, e.g., the peers that participate in a topic-driven crawl of the Web may share the network cost.
- Dynamicity. Peers may enter and leave the system in a transparent manner whereas it is typically difficult to add/remove new sources of data in a centralized setting.

These advantages come at some cost:

- Performance. Complex queries over distributed collections may get real expensive, in particular, communication cost may become high.
- Consistency maintenance. It is much more complicated to keep data consistent in a P2P setting. In particular, this is not the right framework for OLTP applications.
- Quality. Quality may be more easily controlled in a centralized setting. However, for some aspects of quality such as reliability and availability, the distributed approach has very good answers based on replication.
- Complexity. There is the extra complexity of managing distribution, e.g., replication of documents.

Example 1. Distributing a warehouse of preprints. Each peer contains some preprints. Each peer knows about other peers that are part of the preprint P2P warehouse. They do not need to use the same physical organization. One can query any peer to find information about preprints. Peers know how to route queries to the appropriate peers. All are willing to use some common tools to make this work. Installation and linking of these tools should be 0-effort.

Based on the previous discussion, one may try to sketch the main lines of a typology of P2P warehouses vs. centralized ones:

- decentralized organizations: the P2P approach may be more appropriate for a loose consortium, in absence of any centralized authority and centralized accounting.
- lower end applications: the P2P approach allows developing warehouse applications at zero cost when information quality and access control is not critical.
- upper end applications: the P2P approach may be appropriate to provide better performance, more availability and reliability.

Observe that the two approached may be combined. One company may, for instance, decide to use "content marts" implemented on clusters of machines in local area networks. These marts are then made to cooperate in a global P2P environment. This is in the spirit of grid of clusters.

4 Some Issues

From a technical viewpoint, the main issue is *distributed data management*, by no means a novel issue [22]. However, in a P2P environment, the context and in particular, the absence of central authority and the number of peers (possibly thousands to possibly millions), change the rules of the game. Typically, problems that have long been studied take a different flavor here.

In this section, we illustrate the problem with some issues that are raised. This is certainly not meant as a comprehensive survey of all the research issues in the area. It is voluntarily biased by the interests and recent works of the author.

Information and service discovery. This is the most classical technical problem and research has already been considering it in the global setting of the Web, see, e.g., Object Globe [10]. An important feature is that communications may be slow or blocking and query processors should be built with that in mind.

The core problem is perhaps that of "look-up". Given a piece of information specified by a key or just some attribute value, find the relevant information in a P2P system over a changing set of nodes. Starting from centralized techniques such as the one used by Napster, there have been a lot of work in this area, in particular around dynamic hash tables, see, e.g., [8,17].

Note that such indexing may be used to discover data, but also services of interest. This is related to emerging world-wide efforts to publish services, e.g.,

UDDI. UDDI is promoting a centralized repository of Web services. It would be interesting to consider systems that would provide the same functionalities in a P2P setting.

Web crawling and page ranking. Web crawlers such as Google crawl the Web and rank pages according to certain criteria. A community may want to organize its own crawl to adapt it to its needs: (i) be able to crawl private portions of the Web or (ii) guide discovery and refresh of pages based on the precise interest of the community.

Some Web crawlers are implemented on clusters of PCs (e.g., Google or Xyleme). In some sense, the cooperation between different peers is similar to the cooperation between the PCs in a cluster with different Web sites a priori distributed between the various machines. Communications are then needed between peers to send to other peers the list of discovered URLs they are responsible for. The computation of page rank in this setting is more challenging. We are investigating this issue starting from an algorithm that does not require storing the graph of the Web [6].

P2P mediation. In a centralized setting, one usually assumes that the semantics of the integration is known in advance, e.g., by some mapping rules from the different sources to a global schema or via ontologies that describe the correspondences. See, e.g., [19] for a survey on semantic integration. In some communities, such well accepted ontology may exist. However, in many cases, there may be several related ontologies with bridges between them that should be used to derive the mappings between the sources. This challenging problem is, for instance, the topic of [16,14,18].

Monitoring. We developed a monitoring system for the Web based on a centralized warehouse [21]. It would be interesting to "move" such functionalities to a P2P setting. This will best illustrate various aspects of P2P warehousing. So, more precisely, consider a very large collection of documents and a very large number of users who want to be notified when some particular documents they are interested in change. For sources that are willing to participate in this monitoring (willing to be peers in the system), it definitely makes sense to let them monitor their own information. Other information sources may not be able to support such monitoring or may not be willing to participate in the P2P system. Then, the various peers have to share the task of monitoring the information of such sources, thereby avoiding the bottleneck of a centralized server and possibly taking advantage of "network locality".

5 Advertisement: Active XML

We believe that peer to peer data management will become more and more popular. Research projects are already addressing some aspects of the problem, e.g., Piazza [23,15] at U. Washington, PlanetP [12] at Rutgers U. Active XML

[2] at INRIA, P-grid [1] at EPFL Lausanne or the P2P project at ETH Zurich [13].

We next consider Active XML (AXML for short), a language and a system under construction at INRIA as the basis for developing such a P2P warehouse. A more detailed description of AXML may be found in [20] whereas some essential extensions of AXML to support the distribution and replication of portions of a document may be found in [3].

An Active XML document is an XML document where some of the data is given explicitly while other parts consist of calls to Web services that may be used to obtain more data or request some particular processing. We can see such documents as *intentional*, since parts in them are defined by programs that are used to obtain data when needed. We also view them as dynamic in the sense of dynamic Web pages that possibly return different documents when called at different time. An *AXML peer* consists of a repository containing (A)XML documents. It is a client in that activations of the calls inside the documents use Web services. It is a server in the sense that it provides queries to the repository as Web services.

A key aspect of the approach is that AXML peers exchange AXML documents, i.e., document with embedded service calls. Of particular importance is the process of *materializing* some or all the calls in a document and replacing them by their results.

We believe that the AXML approach is an appropriate infrastructure for the development of a P2P warehouse for a number of reasons:

1. AXML is based on a P2P architecture and uses the standards of the Web, and in particular, XML and Web services.
2. Each AXML peer provides an XML repository and an XML query processor.
3. Web services may be called from virtually anywhere, so warehouse functionalities may be published and used in a transparent manner.

Indeed, a first step in that direction is the SPIN project [7] that aims to constructing a warehouse from resources found on the Web using AXML. A lot of works is still needed in particular to incorporate aspects such as cooperative crawl or dynamic hash tables.

Acknowledgments. I want to thank A. Milo for discussions on content warehouses, G. Cobena, A. Poggi B. Nguyen for discussions on SPIN, T. Milo for discussions on the ideas described in this paper, and P. Valduriez, T. Priol for general discussions on P2P data management. Last but not least, I would like to thank the entire AXML team for the fun we share in developing the language and the system.

References

1. K. Aberer, P-Grid: A Self-Organizing Access Structure for P2P Information Systems, CoopIS, 179–194, 2001.

2. The AXML project, INRIA, http://www-rocq.inria.fr/verso/Gemo/Projects/axml.
3. S. Abiteboul, A. Bonifati, G. Cobéna, I. Manolescu, T. Milo, Active XML Documents with Distribution and Replication, ACM SIGMOD, 2003.
4. S. Abiteboul, P. Buneman, and D. Suciu, Data on the Web, Morgan Kaufmann Publishers, 2000.
5. S. Abiteboul, S. Cluet, G. Ferran and A. Milo, Xyleme Content Warehouse, Xyleme whitepaper, 2003.
6. S. Abiteboul, M. Preda, G. Cobena, Adaptive On-Line Page Importance Computation, WWW Conference, 2003.
7. S. Abiteboul, G. Cobena, B. Nguyen, A. Poggi, Construction and Maintenance of a Set of Pages of Interest (SPIN), Conference on Bases de Donnees Avancees, 2002.
8. H. Balakrishnan, M. F. Kaashoek, D. Karger, R. Morris, I. Stoica, Looking up data in P2P systems, CACM 46(2): 43–48, 2003.
9. T. Berners Lee, O. Lassila, and R. R. Swick, The semantic Web, Scientic American, vol. 5, 2001.
10. R. Braumandl, M. Keidl, A. Kemper, D. Kossmann, A. Kreutz, S. Seltzsam, K. Stocker, ObjectGlobe: Ubiquitous query processing on the Internet, The VLDB Journal, 10:48, 2001.
11. Gregory Cobéna, Serge Abiteboul, Amélie Marian, Detecting Changes in XML Documents, Proceedings of the Int'l ICDE Conference, 2002.
12. F. M. Cuenca-Acuna, C. Peery, R. P. Martin, T. D. Nguyen, PlanetP: Using Gossiping to Build Content Addressable Peer-to-Peer Information Sharing Communities, Department of Computer Science, Rutgers University, 2002.
13. T. Grabs, K. Böhm, H.-J. Schek, Scalable Distributed Query and Update Service Implementations for XML Document Elements, IEEE RIDE Int. Workshop on Document Management for Data Intensive Business and Scientific Applications, 2001.
14. F. Goasdoue and M.-C. Rousset, Querying Distributed Data through Distributed Ontologies: a Simple but Scalable Approach, 2003.
15. S. Gribble, A. Halevy, Z. Ives, M. Rodrig, D. Suciu, What can databases do for peer-to-peer? WebDB Workshop on Databases and the Web, 2001.
16. A. Y. Halevy, Z. G. Ives, D. Suciu, I. Tatarinov, Schema Mediation in Peer Data Management Systems, ICDE, 2003.
17. M. Harren, J. Hellerstein, R. Huebsch, B. Thau Loo, S. Shenker, I. Stoica, Complex Queries in DHT-based Peer-to-Peer Networks, Peer-to-Peer Systems Int. Workshop, 2002.
18. A. Kementsietsidis, M. Arenas, and R. Miller, Mapping Data in Peer-to-Peer Systems: Semantics and Algorithmic Issues, ACM SIGMOD, 2003.
19. M. Lenzerini, Data Integration, A Theoretical Perspective, ACM PODS 20'02, Madison, Winsconsin, USA, 2002.
20. T. Milo, S. Abiteboul, B. Amann, O. Benjelloun, F. Dang Ngoc, Exchanging Intensional XML Data, ACM SIGMOD, 2003.
21. B. Nguyen, S. Abiteboul, G. Cobena, M. Preda, Monitoring XML Data on the Web, ACM SIGMOD, 2001.
22. M.T. Özsszu, and P. Valduriez, Principles of Distributed Database Systems, Prentice-Hall, 1999.
23. The Piazza Project, U. Washington, http://data.cs.washington.edu/p2p/piazza/
24. J. Widom, Research Problems in Data Warehousing, In Proceedings of the 4th Int'l Conference on Information and Knowledge Management (CIKM), 1995.

25. F. M. Cuenca-Acuna, C. Peery, R. P. Martin, T. D. Nguyen, Using Gossiping to Build Content Addressable Peer-to-Peer Information Sharing Communities, Department of Computer Science, Rutgers University, 2002.
26. Xyleme Web site, http://www.xyleme.com

Multivalued Dependencies and a 4NF for XML

Millist W. Vincent and Jixue Liu

School of Computer and Information Science
University of South Australia
{millist.vincent, jixue.liu}@unisa.edu.au

Abstract. While providing syntactic flexibility, XML provides little semantic content and so the study of integrity constraints in XML plays an important role in helping to improve the semantic expressiveness of XML. Functional dependencies (FDs) and multivalued dependencies (MVDs) play a fundamental role in relational databases where they provide semantics for the data and at the same time are the foundation for database design. Since XML documents are closely coupled with relational databases in that XML documents are typically exported and imported from relational databases, the study of FDs and MVDs in XML is of fundamental significance in XML research. In this paper we define multivalued dependencies in XML (XMVDs). We then propose a normal form for XML documents in the presence of XMVDs and justify our normal form by showing that it ensures the elimination of redundancy.

1 Introduction

XML has recently emerged as a standard for data representation and interchange on the Internet [22,1]. While providing syntactic flexibility, XML provides little semantic content and as a result several papers have addressed the topic of how to improve the semantic expressiveness of XML. Among the most important of these approaches has been that of defining integrity constraints in XML [5]. Several different classes of integrity constraints for XML have been defined including key constraints [5,6], path constraints [8], and inclusion constraints [9] and properties such as axiomatization and satisfiability have been investigated for these constraints. However, one topic that has been identified as an open problem in XML research [22] and which has been little investigated is how to extended the traditional integrity constraints in relational databases, namely *functional dependencies* (FDs) and *multivalued dependencies* (MVDs), to XML and then how to develop a normalisation theory for XML. This problem is not of just theoretical interest. The theory of normalisation forms the cornerstone of practical relational database design and the development of a similar theory for XML will similarly lay the foundation for understanding how to design XML documents. In addition, the study of FDs and MVDs in XML is important because of the close connection between XML and relational databases. With current technology, the source of XML data is typically a relational database [1] and relational databases are also normally used to store XML data [13]. Hence, given that FDs

J. Eder and M. Missikoff (Eds.): CAiSE 2003, LNCS 2681, pp. 14–29, 2003.

and MVDs are the most important constraints in relational databases, the study of these constraints in XML assumes heightened importance over other types of constraints which are unique to XML [7]. The only papers that have specifically addressed the problem of FDs in XML are the recent papers [3,19,20]. Before presenting the contributions of [3,19,20], we briefly outline the approaches to defining FD satisfaction in incomplete relational databases.

There are two approaches, the first called the *weak satisfaction* approach and the other called the *strong satisfaction* approach [4]. In the weak satisfaction approach, a relation is defined to weakly satisfy a FD if there exists *at least one* completion of the relation, obtained by replacing all occurrences of nulls by data values, which satisfies the FD. A relation is said to strongly satisfy a FD if *every* completion of the relation satisfies the FD. Both approaches have their advantages and disadvantages (a more complete discussion of this issue can be found in [19]). The weak satisfaction approach has the advantage of allowing a high degree of uncertainty to be represented in a database but at the expense of making maintenance of integrity constraints much more difficult. In contrast, the strong satisfaction approach restricts the amount of uncertainty that can be represented in a database but makes the maintenance of integrity constraints much easier. However, as argued in [11], both approaches have their place in real world applications and should be viewed as complementary rather than competing approaches. Also, it is possible to combine the two approaches by having some FDs in a relation strongly satisfied and others weakly satisfied [10].

The contribution of [3] was, for the first time, to define FDs in XML (what we call XFDs) and then to define a normal form for an XML document based on the definition of an XFD. However, there are some difficulties with the definition of an XFD given in [3]. The most fundamental problem is that although it is explicitly recognised in the definitions that XML documents have missing information, the definitions in [3], while having some elements of the weak instance approach, are not a strict extension of this approach since there are XFDs that are violated according to the definition in [3] yet there are completions of the tree that satisfy the XFDs (see [19] for an example). As a result, it is not clear that there is any correspondence between weak satisfaction of FDs in incomplete relations and XFD satisfaction in XML documents as defined in [3].

In [19,20] a different and more straightforward approach was taken to defining XFDs. The definition in [19,20] is based on extending the strong satisfaction approach to XML. The definition of an XFD given in [19] was justified formally by two main results. The first result showed that for a very general class of mappings from an incomplete relation into a XML document, a relation strongly satisfies a unary FD (only one attribute on the l.h.s. of the FD) if and only if the corresponding XML document strongly satisfies the corresponding XFD. The second result showed that an XML document strongly satisfies an XFD if and only if every completion of the XML document also satisfies the XFD. The other contributions in [19] were firstly to define a set of axioms for reasoning about the implication of XFDs and show that the axioms are sound for arbitrary XFDs. The final contribution was to define a normal form, based on a modification of the one proposed in [3], and prove that it is a necessary and sufficient condition for the elimination of redundancy in an XML document.

In this paper we extend the work in [19] and investigate the issue of multivalued dependencies and normalisation in XML, a topic which to the best of our knowledge has not been investigated previously. We firstly give a definition of MVDs in XML (what we call XMVDs) using an extension of the approach used in [19]. We note that in an allied paper [21], we formally justify the definition by proving that, for a very general class of mappings from relations to XML, a relation satisfies a MVD if and only if the corresponding XML document satisfies the corresponding XMVD. Thus there is a natural correspondence between MVDs in relations and XMVDs in XML documents. We then propose a normal form for XML documents in the presence of XMVDs. We then justify our normal form by showing that it ensures the elimination of redundancy. Finally, we note that in contrast to [19], in the present paper we assume that XML documents do not have missing information and leave the problem of how to extend the approach to the case of missing information for future research.

The rest of this paper is organised as follows. Section 2 contains some preliminary definitions. Section 3 contains the definition of an XMVD. In Section 4 we define a 4NF for XML and prove that it eliminates redundancy. Finally, Section 5 contains some concluding comments.

2 Preliminary Definitions

In this section we present some preliminary definitions that we need before defining XFDs. We model an XML document as a tree as follows.

Definition 1. *Assume a countably infinite set* $\mathbf{E}$ *of element labels (tags), a countable infinite set* $\mathbf{A}$ *of attribute names and a symbol* S *indicating text. An* XML tree *is defined to be* $T = (V, lab, ele, att, val, v_r)$ *where* V *is a* finite *set of nodes in* T*;* lab *is a function from* V *to* $\mathbf{E} \cup \mathbf{A} \cup \{S\}$*;* ele *is a partial function from* V *to a sequence of* V *nodes such that for any* $v \in V$*, if* $ele(v)$ *is defined then* $lab(v) \in \mathbf{E}$*;* att *is a partial function from* $V \times \mathbf{A}$ *to* V *such that for any* $v \in V$ *and* $l \in \mathbf{A}$*, if* $att(v, l) = v_1$ *then* $lab(v) \in \mathbf{E}$ *and* $lab(v_1) = l$*;* val *is a function such that for any node in* $v \in V, val(v) = v$ *if* $lab(v) \in \mathbf{E}$ *and* $val(v)$ *is a string if either* $lab(v) = S$ *or* $lab(v) \in \mathbf{A}$*;* v_r *is a distinguished node in* V *called the root of* T *and we define* $lab(v_r) = root$*. Since node identifiers are unique, a consequence of the definition of* val *is that if* $v_1 \in \mathbf{E}$ *and* $v_2 \in \mathbf{E}$ *and* $v_1 \neq v_2$ *then* $val(v_1) \neq val(v_2)$*. We also extend the definition of* val *to sets of nodes and if* $V_1 \subseteq V$*, then* $val(V_1)$ *is the set defined by* $val(V_1) = \{val(v) | v \in V_1\}$*.*

For any $v \in V$*, if* $ele(v)$ *is defined then the nodes in* $ele(v)$ *are called* subelements *of* v*. For any* $l \in \mathbf{A}$*, if* $att(v, l) = v_1$ *then* v_1 *is called an* attribute *of* v*. Note that an XML tree* T *must be a tree. Since* T *is a tree the set of ancestors of a node* v*, is denoted by* $Ancestor(v)$*. The children of a node* v *are also defined as in Definition 1 and we denote the parent of a node* v *by* $Parent(v)$*.*

We note that our definition of *val* differs slightly from that in [6] since we have extended the definition of the *val* function so that it is also defined on element nodes. The reason for this is that we want to include in our definition paths that do not end at leaf nodes, and when we do this we want to compare element nodes by node identity, i.e. node equality, but when we compare attribute or text nodes we want to compare them by their contents, i.e. value equality. This point will become clearer in the examples and definitions that follow.

We now give some preliminary definitions related to paths.

Definition 2. *A* path *is an expression of the form* $l_1.\cdots.l_n$, $n \geq 1$, *where* $l_i \in \mathbf{E} \cup \mathbf{A} \cup \{S\}$ *for all* $i, 1 \leq i \leq n$ *and* $l_1 = root$. *If* p *is the path* $l_1.\cdots.l_n$ *then* $Last(p) = l_n$.

For instance, if $\mathbf{E}$ = {`root, Division, Employee`} and $\mathbf{A}$ = {`D#, Emp#`} then `root, root.Division, root.Division.D#,` `root.Division.Employee.Emp#.S` are all paths.

Definition 3. *Let* p *denote the path* $l_1.\cdots.l_n$. *The function* $Parnt(p)$ *is the path* $l_1.\cdots.l_{n-1}$. *Let* p *denote the path* $l_1.\cdots.l_n$ *and let* q *denote the path* $q_1.\cdots.q_m$. *The path* p *is said to be a* prefix *of the path* q, *denoted by* $p \subseteq q$, *if* $n \leq m$ *and* $l_1 = q_1, \ldots, l_n = q_n$. *Two paths* p *and* q *are equal, denoted by* $p = q$, *if* p *is a prefix of* q *and* q *is a prefix of* p. *The path* p *is said to be a* strict prefix *of* q, *denoted by* $p \subset q$, *if* p *is a prefix of* q *and* $p \neq q$. *We also define the intersection of two paths* p_1 *and* p_2, *denoted but* $p_1 \cap p_2$, *to be the maximal common prefix of both paths. It is clear that the intersection of two paths is also a path.*

For example, if $\mathbf{E}$ = {`root, Division, Employee`} and $\mathbf{A}$ = {`D#, Emp#`} then `root.Division` is a strict prefix of `root.Division.Employee` and `root.Division.D#` ∩ `root.Division.Employee.Emp#.S` = `root.Division`.

Definition 4. *A* path instance *in an XML tree* T *is a sequence* $\bar{v}_1.\cdots.\bar{v}_n$ *such that* $\bar{v}_1 = v_r$ *and for all* $\bar{v}_i, 1 < i \leq n, v_i \in V$ *and* $\bar{v}_i$ *is a child of* $\bar{v}_{i-1}$. *A path instance* $\bar{v}_1.\cdots.\bar{v}_n$ *is said to be* defined over the path $l_1.\cdots.l_n$ *if for all* $\bar{v}_i, 1 \leq i \leq n$, $lab(\bar{v}_i) = l_i$. *Two path instances* $\bar{v}_1.\cdots.\bar{v}_n$ *and* $\bar{v}'_1.\cdots.\bar{v}'_n$ *are said to be* distinct *if* $v_i \neq v'_i$ *for some* i, $1 \leq i \leq n$. *The path instance* $\bar{v}_1.\cdots.\bar{v}_n$ *is said to be a* prefix *of* $\bar{v}'_1.\cdots.\bar{v}'_m$ *if* $n \leq m$ *and* $\bar{v}_i = \bar{v}'_i$ *for all* $i, 1 \leq i \leq n$. *The path instance* $\bar{v}_1.\cdots.\bar{v}_n$ *is said to be a* strict prefix *of* $\bar{v}'_1.\cdots.\bar{v}'_m$ *if* $n < m$ *and* $\bar{v}_i = \bar{v}'_i$ *for all* $i, 1 \leq i \leq n$. *The set of path instances over a path* p *in a tree* T *is denoted by* $Paths(p)$

For example, in Figure 1, $v_r.v_1.v_3$ is a path instance defined over the path `root.Dept.Section` and $v_r.v_1.v_3$ is a strict prefix of $v_r.v_1.v_3.v_4$

We now assume the existence of a set of legal paths P for an XML application. Essentially, P defines the semantics of an XML application in the same way that a set of relational schema define the semantics of a relational application. P may be derived from the DTD, if one exists, or P be derived from some other source which understands the semantics of the application if no DTD exists. The advantage of assuming the existence of a set of paths, rather than a DTD, is that it allows for a greater degree of generality since having an XML tree conforming to a set of paths is much less restrictive than having it conform to a DTD. Firstly we place the following restriction on the set of paths.

Definition 5. *A set P of paths is* consistent *if for any path $p \in P$, if $p_1 \subset p$ then $p_1 \in P$.*

This is natural restriction on the set of paths and any set of paths that is generated from a DTD will be consistent.

We now define the notion of an XML tree conforming to a set of paths P.

Definition 6. *Let P be a consistent set of paths and let T be an XML tree. Then T is said to* conform *to P if every path instance in T is a path instance over some path in P.*

The next issue that arises in developing the machinery to define XFDs is the issue is that of missing information. This is addressed in [19] but in this we take the simplifying assumption that there is no missing information in XML trees. More formally, we have the following definition.

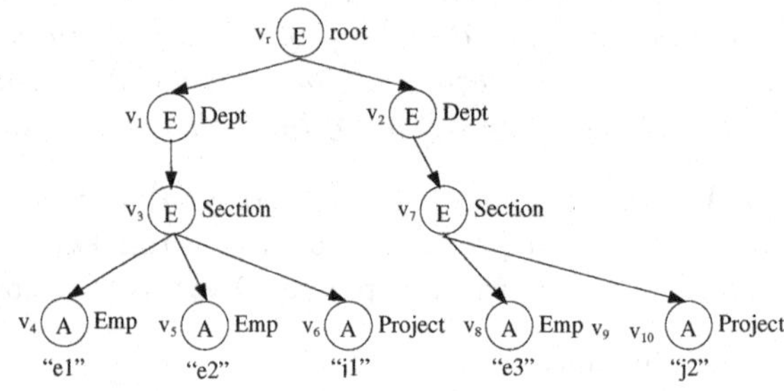

Fig. 1. A complete XML tree.

Definition 7. *Let P be a consistent set of paths, let T be an XML that conforms to P. Then T is defined to be* complete *if whenever there exist paths p_1 and p_2 in P such that $p_1 \subset p_2$ and there exists a path instance $\bar{v}_1.\cdots.\bar{v}_n$ defined over p_1, in T, then there exists a path instance $\bar{v}'_1.\cdots.\bar{v}'_m$ defined over p_2 in T such that $\bar{v}_1.\cdots.\bar{v}_n$ is a prefix of the instance $\bar{v}'_1.\cdots.\bar{v}'_m$.*

For example, if we take P to be {`root`, `root.Dept`, `root.Dept.Section`, `root.Dept.Section.Emp`, `root.Dept.Section.Project`} then the tree in Figure 1 conforms to P and is complete.

The next function returns all the final nodes of the path instances of a path p in T.

Definition 8. *Let P be a consistent set of paths, let T be an XML tree that conforms to P . The function $N(p)$, where $p \in P$, is the set of nodes defined by $N(p) = \{\bar{v}|\bar{v}_1.\cdots.\bar{v}_n \in Paths(p) \land \bar{v} = \bar{v}_n\}$.*

For example, in Figure 1, $N(\texttt{root.Dept}) = \{v_1, v_2\}$.
We now need to define a function that returns a node and its ancestors.

Definition 9. *Let P be a consistent set of paths, let T be an XML tree that conforms to P. The function $AAncestor(v)$, where $v \in V \cup \mathbf{N}$, is the set of nodes in T defined by $AAncestor(v) = v \cup Ancestor(v)$.*

For example in Figure 1, $AAncestor(v_3) = \{v_r, v_1, v_3\}$. The next function returns all nodes that are the final nodes of path instances of p and are descendants of v.

Definition 10. *Let P be a consistent set of paths, let T be an XML tree that conforms to P. The function $Nodes(v,p)$, where $v \in V \cup \mathbf{N}$ and $p \in P$, is the set of nodes in T defined by $Nodes(v,p) = \{x|x \in N(p) \land v \in AAncestor(x)\}$*

For example, in Figure 1 , $Nodes(v_1, \texttt{root.Dept.Section.Emp}) = \{v_4, v_5\}$. We also define a partial ordering on the set of nodes as follows.

Definition 11. *The partial ordering $>$ on the set of nodes V in an XML tree T is defined by $v_1 > v_2$ iff $v_2 \in Ancestor(v_1)$.*

3 XMVDs in XML

Before presenting the main definition of the paper, we present an example to illustrate the thinking behind the definition. Consider the relation shown in Figure 2. It satisfies the MVD `Course` $\to\to$ `Teacher|Text`. The XML tree shown in Figure 3 is then a XML representation of the data in Figure 2. The tree has the following property. There exists two path instances of `root.Id.Id.Id.Text`, namely $v_r.v_{13}.v_{17}.v_{21}.v_9$ and $v_r.v_{16}.v_{20}.v_{24}.v_{12}$ such that $val(v_9) \neq val(v_{12})$. Also, these two paths have the property that for the closest `Teacher` node to v_9, namely v_5, and the closest `Teacher` node to v_{12}, namely v_8, then $val(v_5) \neq val(v_8)$ and for the closest `Course` node to both v_9 and v_5, namely v_1, and for the closest `Course` node to both v_{12} and v_8, namely v_4, we have that $val(v_1) = val(v_4)$. Then the existence of the two path instances $v_r.v_{13}.v_{17}.v_{21}.v_9$ and $v_r.v_{16}.v_{20}.v_{24}.v_{12}$ with these properties and the fact that `Course` $\to\to$ `Teacher|Text` is satisfied in the relation in Figure 2 implies that there exists two path instances of `root.Id.Id.Id.Text`, namely $v_r.v_{15}.v_{19}.v_{23}.v_{11}$ and $v_r.v_{14}.v_{18}.v_{22}.v_{10}$, with the following properties. $val(v_{11}) = val(v_9)$ and for the closest `Teacher` node to v_{11}, v_7, $val(v_7) = val(v_8)$ and for the closest `Course` node to v_{11} and v_7, namely v_3, $val(v_3) = val(v_1)$. Also, $val(v_{10}) = val(v_{12})$ and the closest `Teacher` node to v_{10}, v_6, $val(v_6) = val(v_5)$ and for the closest `Course` node to v_{10} and v_6, namely v_2, $val(v_2) = val(v_4)$. This type of constraint is an XMVD. We note however that there are many other ways that the relation in Figure 2 could be represented in an XML tree. For instance we could also represent the relation by Figure 4 and this XML tree also satisfies the XMVD. In comparing the two representations, it is clear that the representation in Figure 4 is a more compact representation than that in Figure 3 and we shall see later that the example in Figure 4 is normalised whereas the example in Figure 3 is not.

Course	Teacher	Text
Algorithms	Fred	Text A
Algorithms	Mary	Text B
Algorithms	Fred	Text B
Algorithms	Mary	Text A

Fig. 2. A flat relation satisfying a MVD.

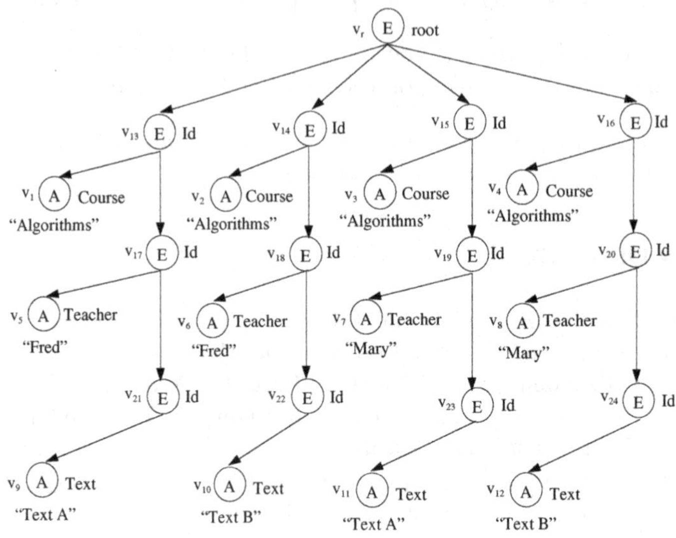

Fig. 3. An XML tree

This leads us to the main definition of our paper. In this paper we consider the simplest case where there are only single paths on the l.h.s. and r.h.s. of the XMVD and all paths end in an attribute or text node.

Definition 12. *Let P be a consistent set of paths and let T be an XML tree that conforms to P and is complete. An XMVD is a statement of the form $p \to\to q|r$ where p, q and r are paths in P. T satisfies $p \to\to q|r$ if whenever there exists two distinct paths path instances $\bar{v}_1.\cdots.\bar{v}_n$ and $\bar{w}_1.\cdots.\bar{w}_n$ in $Paths(q)$ such that:*

(i) $val(\bar{v}_n) \neq val(\bar{w}_n)$;

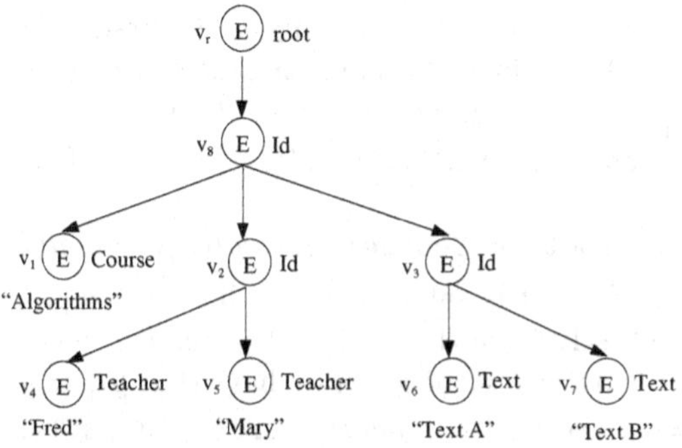

Fig. 4. An XML tree

(ii) there exists two nodes z_1, z_2*, where* $z_1 \in Nodes(x_{1_1}, r)$ *and* $z_2 \in Nodes(y_{1_1}, r)$ *such that* $val(z_1) \neq val(z_2)$*;*

(iii) there exists two nodes z_3 *and* z_4*, where* $z_3 \in Nodes(x_{1_{1_1}}, p)$ *and* $z_4 \in Nodes(y_{1_{1_1}}, p)$*, such that* $val(z_3) = val(z_4)$*;*

then:

(a) there exists a path $\bar{v}'_1.\cdots.\bar{v}'_n$ *in* $Paths(q)$ *such that* $val(\bar{v}'_n) = val(\bar{v}_n)$ *and there exists a node* z'_1 *in* $Nodes(x'_{1_1}, r)$ *such that* $val(z'_1) = val(z_2)$ *and there exists a node* z'_3 *in* $Nodes(x'_{1_{1_1}}, p)$ *such that* $val(z'_3) = val(z_3)$*;*

(b) there exists a path $\bar{w}'_1.\cdots.\bar{w}'_n$ *in* $Paths(q)$ *such that* $val(\bar{w}'_n) = val(\bar{w}_n)$ *and there exists a node* z'_2 *in* $Nodes(x'_{1_1}, r)$ *such that* $val(z'_2) = val(z_1)$ *and there exists a node* z'_4 *in* $Nodes(x'_{1_{1_1}}, p_l)$ *such that* $val(z'_4) = val(z_4)$*;*

where $x_{1_1} = \{v | v \in \{\bar{v}_1, \cdots, \bar{v}_n\} \wedge v \in N(r \cap q)\}$ *and* $y_{1_1} = \{v | v \in \{\bar{w}_1, \cdots, \bar{v}_n\} \wedge v \in N(r \cap q)\}$ *and* $x_{1_{1_1}} = \{v | v \in \{\bar{v}_1, \cdots, \bar{v}_n\} \wedge v \in N(p \cap r \cap q)\}$ *and* $y_{1_{1_1}} = \{v | v \in \{\bar{w}_1, \cdots, \bar{w}_n\} \wedge v \in N(p \cap r \cap q)\}$

and $x'_{1_1} = \{v | v \in \{\bar{v}'_1, \cdots, \bar{v}'_n\} \wedge v \in N(r \cap q)\}$ *and* $y'_{1_1} = \{v | v \in \{\bar{w}'_1, \cdots, \bar{v}'_n\} \wedge v \in N(r \cap q)\}$ *and* $x'_{1_{1_1}} = \{v | v \in \{\bar{v}'_1, \cdots, \bar{v}'_n\} \wedge v \in N(p \cap r \cap q)\}$ *and* $y'_{1_{1_1}} = \{v | v \in \{\bar{w}'_1, \cdots, \bar{w}'_n\} \wedge v \in N(p \cap r \cap q)\}$.

We note that since the path $r \cap q$ is a prefix of q, there exists only one node in $\bar{v}_1.\cdots.\bar{v}_n$ that is also in $N(r \cap q)$ and so x_1 is always defined and is a single node. Similarly for $y_1, x_{1_{1_1}}, y_{1_{1_1}}, x'_{1_1}, y'_{1_1}, x'_{1_{1_1}}, y'_{1_{1_1}}$. We now illustrate the definition by some examples.

Example 1. Consider the XML tree shown in Figure 4 and the XMVD `root.Id.Course` $\rightarrow\rightarrow$ `root.Id.Id.Teacher|root.Id.Id.Text`. Let $\bar{v}_1.\cdots.\bar{v}_n$ be the path instance $v_r.v_8.v_2.v_4$ and let $\bar{w}_1.\cdots.\bar{w}_n$ be the path instance $v_r.v_8.v_2.v_5$. Both path instances are in *Paths*(`root.Id.Id.Teacher`) and $val(v_4) \neq val(v_5)$. Moreover, $x_{1_1} = v_8$, $y_{1_1} = v_8$, $x_{1_{1_1}} = v_8$ and $y_{1_{1_1}} = v_8$. So if we let $z_1 = v_6$ and $z_2 = v_7$ then $z_1 \in Nodes(x_{1_1}, \texttt{root.Id.Id.Text})$ and $z_2 \in Nodes(y_{1_1}, \texttt{root.Id.Id.Text})$. Also if we let $z_3 = v_8$ and $z_4 = v_8$ then $z_3 \in Nodes(x_{1_{1_1}}, \texttt{root.Id.Course})$ and $z_4 \in Nodes(y_{1_{1_1}}, \texttt{root.Id.Course})$ then $val(z_3) = val(z_4)$. Hence conditions (i), (ii) and (iii) of the definition of an XMVD are satisfied.

If we let $\bar{v}_1'^i.\cdots.\bar{v}_n'^i$ be the path $v_r.v_8.v_2.v_4$ we firstly have that $val(\bar{v}_n'^i) = val(\bar{v}_n^i)$ as required. Also, since the path instances are the same we have that $x_{1_1} = x'_{1_1}$ and $x_{1_{1_1}} = x'_{1_{1_1}}$. So if we let $z'_1 = v_7$ then

$z'_1 \in Nodes(x'_{1_1}$,root.Id.Id.Text) and $val(z'_1) = val(z_2)$ and if we let $z'_3 = v_8$ then

$z'_3 \in Nodes(x'_{1_{1_l}}$,root.Id.Course) and $val(z'_3) = val(z_3)$. So part (a) of the definition of an XMVD is satisfied. Next if we let $\bar{w}_1'^i.\cdots.\bar{w}_n'^i$ be the path $v_r.v_8.v_2.v_5$ then we firstly have that $val(\bar{w}_n'^i) = val(\bar{w}_n^i)$ since the paths are the same . Also, since the paths are the same we have that $y_{1_1} = y'_{1_1}$ and $y_{1_{1_1}} = y'_{1_{1_1}}$. So if we let $z'_2 = v_6$ then $z'_2 \in Nodes(y'_{1_1}$,root.Id.Id.Text) and $val(z'_2) = val(z_1)$ and if we let $z'_4 = v_8$ then $z'_4 \in Nodes(x'_{1_{1_l}}$,root.Id.Course) and $val(z'_4) = val(z_4)$. Hence part (b) on the definition of an XMVD is satisfied and so T satisfies root.Id.Course $\rightarrow\rightarrow$ root.Id.Id.Teacher|root.Id.Id.Text.

As explained earlier, the tree in Figure 4 also satisfies
root.Id.Course $\rightarrow\rightarrow$ root.Id.Id.Teacher|root.Id.Id.Text.

Example 2 Consider the XML tree shown in Figure 5 and the XMVD root.Project.P# $\rightarrow\rightarrow$ Root.Project.Person.Name|root.Project.Part.Pid. For the path instances $v_r.v_1.v_5.v_{13}$ and $v_r.v_2.v_8.v_{16}$ in

Paths(Root.Project.Person.Name) we have that $val(v_{13}) \neq val(v_{16})$. Moreover, $x_{1_1} = v_1$, $y_{1_1} = v_2$, $x_{1_{1_1}} = v_1$ and $y_{1_{1_1}} = v_1$. So if we let $z_1 = v_{17}$ and $z_2 = v_{18}$ then

$z_1 \in Nodes(x_{1_1}$,root.Project.Part.Pid) and

$z_2 \in Nodes(y_{1_1}$,root.Project.Part.Pid). Also if we let $z_3 = v_4$ and $z_4 = v_7$ then $z_3 \in Nodes(x_{1_{1_1}}$,root.Project.P#) and

$z_4 \in Nodes(y_{1_{1_1}}$,root.Project.P#) and $val(z_3) = val(z_4)$. Hence conditions (i), (ii) and (iii) of the definition of an XMVD are satisfied. However, for the only other path in

Paths(Root.Project.Person.Name), namely $v_r.v_3.v_{11}.v_{19}$ we have that $x'_{1_1} = v_3$ and so $Nodes(x'_{1_1}$,root.Project.part.Pid) $= v_{21}$ and since $val(v_{21}) \neq val(z_2)$ and so it does not satisfy condition (a) and thus
root.Project.P# $\rightarrow\rightarrow$ Root.Project.Person.Name|root.Project.part.Pid is violated in T.

Consider then the XMVD XMVD root.Project.Person.Name
$\rightarrow\rightarrow$ Root.Project.Person.Skill |root.Project.P# in the same XML tree. For the path instances $v_r.v_1.v_5.v_{14}$ and $v_r.v_3.v_{11}.v_{20}$ in

Paths(Root.Project.Person.Skill) we have that $val(v_{14}) \neq val(v_{20})$. Moreover, $x_{1_1} = v_1$, $y_{1_1} = v_3$, $x_{1_{1_1}} = v_{13}$ and $y_{1_{1_1}} = v_{19}$. So if we let $z_1 = v_4$ and $z_2 = v_{10}$ then $z_1 \in Nodes(x_{1_1}$,root.Project.P#) and $z_2 \in Nodes(y_{1_1}$,root.Project.P#). Also if we let $z_3 = v_{13}$ and $z_4 = v_{19}$ then $z_3 \in Nodes(x_{1_{1_1}}$, root.Project.Person.Name) and

$z_4 \in Nodes(y_{1_{1_1}}$,root.Project.Person.Name) and $val(z_3) = val(z_4)$. Hence the conditions of (i), (ii) and (iii) of the definition of an XMVD are satisfied. However there does not exist another path instance in *Paths*(Root.Project.Person.Skill) such that *val* of the last node in the path is equal to *val* of node v_{14} and so part (a) of the definition of an XMVD is violated.

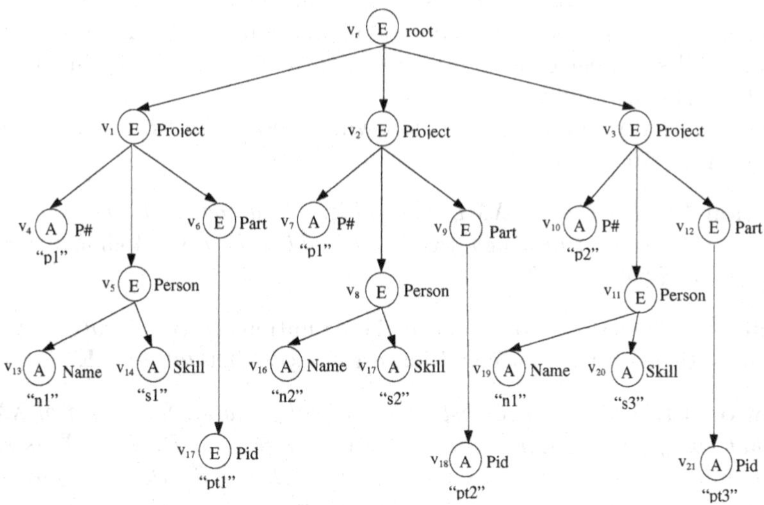

Fig. 5. An XML tree

4 A Redundancy Free 4NF for XML Documents

In this section we propose a 4NF for XML documents. We also provide a formal justification for the normal form by showing that it ensures the elimination of redundancy in the presence of XMVDs. This approach to justifying the definition of a normal form is an extension of the approach adopted by one of the authors in some other research which investigated the issue of providing justification for the normal forms defined in standard relational databases [14,15,16,12].

The approach that we use to justifying our normal form is to formalise the notion of redundancy, the most intuitive approach to justifying normal forms, and then to try to ensure that our normal form ensures there is no redundancy. However, defining redundancy is not quite so straightforward as might first appear. The most obvious approach is, given a relation r and a FD $A \to B$ and two tuples t_1 and t_2, to define a value $t_1[B]$ to be redundant if $t_1[B] = t_2[B]$ and $t_1[A] = t_2[A]$. While this definition is fine for FDs in relations, it doesn't generalise in an obvious way to other classes of relational integrity constraints, such as *multi-valued dependencies* (MVDs) or *join dependencies* (JDs) or *inclusion dependencies* (INDs), nor to other data models. The key to finding the appropriate generalisation is based on the observation that if a value $t_1[B]$ is redundant in the sense just defined then every change of $t_1[B]$ to a new value results in the violation of $A \to B$. One can then define a data value to be redundant if every change of it to a new value results in the violation of the set of constraints (whatever they may be). This is essentially the definition proposed in [16] where it was shown that BCNF is a necessary and sufficient condition for there to be no redundancy in the case of FD constraints and fourth normal form (4NF) is a necessary and sufficient condition for there to be no redundancy in the case of FD and MVD constraints.

The definition we propose is the following which is an extension of the definition given in [16].

Definition 13. *Let T be an XML tree and let v be a node in T. Then the change from v to v', resulting in a new tree T', is said to be a* valid change *if $v \neq v'$ and $val(v) \neq val(v')$.*

We note that the second condition in the definition, $val(v) \neq val(v')$, is automatically satisfied if the first condition is satisfied when $lab(v) \in \mathbf{E}$.

Definition 14. *Let P be a consistent set of paths and let Σ be a set of XMVDs such that every path appearing in an XMVD in Σ is in P. Then Σ is said to* cause redundancy *if there exists a complete XML tree T which conforms to P and satisfies Σ and a node v in T such that* every *valid change from v to v', resulting in a new XML tree T', causes Σ to be violated.*

The essential idea is that if a value is redundant, then it is implied by the other data values and the set of constraints and so any change to the value causes a violation of the constraints. For example, consider Figure 3 and the set Σ of XMVDs

{`root.Id.Course` $\to\to$ `root.Id.Id.Teacher|root.Id.Id.Id.Text`}. Then Σ causes redundancy because the tree shown in Figure 3 satisfies Σ yet every valid change to any of the `Text` nodes (or `Teacher` nodes) results in the violation of Σ.

Before presenting our definition of 4NF we place restrictions on XMVDs associated with an XML document. As shown in the full length version of this paper, these restrictions are not essential but they do simplify and shorten the presentation. The first restriction is on the structure of the XMVDs. In relations and nested relations, MVDs which have a hierarchical structure occur naturally and seem to correspond most closely to real world MVDs [11,17]. Given the close relationship between nested relations and XML documents we believe that the case is similar for XML documents and propose the following definition.

Definition 15. *A set Σ of XMVDs is said to be* hierarchical *if for every XMVD $p \to\to q|r \in \Sigma$, $Parnt(p)$ is a strict prefix of both q and r.*

For instance, in Example 2 the XMVD `root.Project.P#` $\to\to$ `Root.Project.Person.Name|root.Project.Part.Pid` is hierarchical but not the XMVD `root.Project.Person.Name` $\to\to$ `Root.Project.Person.Skill|root.Project.P#`.

Next, we define the notion of a key.

Definition 16. *Let P be a consistent set of paths, let T be an XML tree that conforms to P and is complete and let $p \in P$. Then T satisfies the key constraint p if whenever there exists two nodes v_1 and v_2 in $N(p)$ in T such that $val(v_1) = val(v_2)$ then $v_1 = v_2$.*

This leads us to the normal form definition and the main result of the paper.

Definition 17. *Let Σ be a hierarchical set XMVDs. Then Σ is in* XML fourth normal form *(4XNF) if either of the following conditions hold:*
(A) q and r are both keys;
(B) p is a key and $q \cap r = p$.

We now illustrate the definition by some examples.

Example 3. Consider the tree T in Figure 3 and assume that the only constraint is the XMVD
`root.Id.Course` $\rightarrow\rightarrow$ `root.Id.Id.Teacher|root.Id.Id.Id.Text`. T satisfies Σ and is complete. However Σ is not in 4XNF since `root.Id.Course` is not a key and `root.Id.Id.Teacher` is not a key and `root.Id.Id.Id.Text` is not a key. Consider then the tree shown in Figure 4 and assume that the only XMVD is `root.Id.Course` $\rightarrow\rightarrow$ `root.Id.Teacher|root.Id.Text`. If `root.Id.Course` is a key, which would be the case if `Course` was specified as type `ID` in the full DTD, then Σ is in 4XNF since `root.Id.Course` is a key and `root.Id.Teacher` $\cap$ `root.Id.Id.Id.Text` = texttroot.Id.Course.

This leads to the main result of this section.

Theorem 1. *If Σ is in 4XNF then Σ does not cause redundancy.*

Proof. Assume that (A) holds, i.e. q and r are both keys, and suppose to the contrary that Σ causes redundancy. Then by definition there exists an XML tree T which satisfies Σ and a node v in T such that *every* valid change from v to v', resulting in a new XML tree T', causes some XMVD $p \rightarrow\rightarrow q|r \in \Sigma$ to be violated. We firstly claim that $v \in N(q)$ or $v \in N(r)$. Suppose that this is not the case and that $v \notin N(q)$ and $v \notin N(r)$ and $v \notin N(p)$. Then obviously T' satisfies Σ and so Σ does not cause redundancy which is a contradiction. Suppose then that v in $N(p)$. If $lab(v) \in \mathbf{E}$ then by definition the new node v' is distinct in T' and so by definition of an XMVD T' satisfies Σ and so Σ does not cause redundancy which is a contradiction. If instead $lab(v) \in \mathbf{A}$ then if we choose a change such that $val(v')$ does not appear anywhere else in T, the XMVD $p \rightarrow\rightarrow q|r$ is not violated after the change and so T' satisfies Σ and so Σ does not cause redundancy which is a contradiction. Hence $v \in N(q)$ or $v \in N(r)$. We suppose firstly that $v \in N(q)$.

So since $p \rightarrow\rightarrow q|r$ in T' is violated, there exist path instances $\bar{v}_1.\cdots.\bar{v}_n$ (where $\bar{v}_n = v'$) and $\bar{w}_1.\cdots.\bar{w}_n$ in $Paths(q)$ in T' such that:
(i) $val(\bar{v}_n) \neq val(\bar{w}_n)$;
(ii) there exists two nodes z_1, z_2, where $z_1 \in Nodes(x_{1_1}, r)$ and $z_2 \in Nodes(y_{1_1}, r)$ such that $val(z_1) \neq val(z_2)$;

(iii) there exists two nodes z_3 and z_4, where $z_3 \in Nodes(x_{1_{1_1}}, p)$ and $z_4 \in Nodes(y_{1_{1_1}}, p)$, such that $val(z_3) = val(z_4)$.

and:

(a.1) there does not exist a path $\bar{v}'_1.\cdots.\bar{v}'_n$ in $Paths(q)$ such that $val(\bar{v}'_n) = val(\bar{v}_n)$ and there does not exist a node z'_1 in $Nodes(x'_{1_1}, r)$ such that $val(z'_1) = val(z_2)$ and there does not exist a node z'_3 in $Nodes(x'_{1_{1_1}}, p)$ such that $val(z'_3) = val(z_3)$;

or

(b.1) there does not exists a path $\bar{w}'_1.\cdots.\bar{w}'_n$ in $Paths(q)$ such that $val(\bar{w}'_n) = val(\bar{w}_n)$ and there does not exist a node z'_2 in $Nodes(x'_{1_1}, r)$ such that $val(z'_2) = val(z_1)$ and there does not exist a node z'_4 in $Nodes(x'_{1_{1_1}}, p_l)$ such that $val(z'_4) = val(z_4)$;

where

$x_{1_1} = \{v|v \in \{\bar{v}_1, \cdots, \bar{v}_n\} \wedge v \in N(r \cap q)\}$ and $y_{1_1} = \{v|v \in \{\bar{w}_1, \cdots, \bar{v}_n\} \wedge v \in N(r \cap q)\}$ and $x_{1_{1_1}} = \{v|v \in \{\bar{v}_1, \cdots, \bar{v}_n\} \wedge v \in N(p \cap r \cap q)\}$ and $y_{1_{1_1}} = \{v|v \in \{\bar{w}_1, \cdots, \bar{w}_n\} \wedge v \in N(p \cap r \cap q)\}$

and $x'_{1_1} = \{v|v \in \{\bar{v}'_1, \cdots, \bar{v}'_n\} \wedge v \in N(r \cap q)\}$ and $y'_{1_1} = \{v|v \in \{\bar{w}'_1, \cdots, \bar{v}'_n\} \wedge v \in N(r \cap q)\}$ and $x'_{1_{1_1}} = \{v|v \in \{\bar{v}'_1, \cdots, \bar{v}'_n\} \wedge v \in N(p \cap r \cap q)\}$ and $y'_{1_{1_1}} = \{v|v \in \{\bar{w}'_1, \cdots, \bar{w}'_n\} \wedge v \in N(p \cap r \cap q)\}$.

Next, because $\bar{v}_1.\cdots.\bar{v}_n$ and $\bar{w}_1.\cdots.\bar{w}_n$ satisfy (ii), it follows that since only node $\bar{v}_n$ is changed in T, then $z_1, z_2, z_3, z_4, x_{1_1}, x'_{1_1}, y_{1_1}, y'_{1_1}, x_{1_{1_1}}, x'_{1_{1_1}}, y_{1_{1_1}}$ and $y'_{1_{1_1}}$ are the same in T and T'. So there exist two nodes z_1, z_2, where $z_1 \in Nodes(x_{1_1}, r)$ and $z_2 \in Nodes(y_{1_1}, r)$ in T such that $val(z_1) \neq val(z_2)$. Also, since q is a key it follows that $val(v) \neq val(\bar{w}_n)$ in T. Consider then the path instances $\bar{v}_1.\cdots.v$ and $\bar{w}_1.\cdots.\bar{w}_n$ in $Paths(q)$ in T. As we have already noted, $val(v) \neq val(\bar{w}_n)$ so (i) of the definition of an XMVD is satisfied. Then since only node v is changed, if we let z_1, z_2 be as defined we have that $z_1 \in Nodes(x_{1_1}, r)$ and $z_2 \in Nodes(y_{1_1}, r)$ and $val(z_1) \neq val(z_2)$ and so (ii) of the definition of an XMVD is satisfied. Similarly, if we let z_3 and z_4 be as defined, then $z_3 \in Nodes(x_{1_{1_1}}, p)$ and $z_4 \in Nodes(y_{1_{1_1}}, p)$ and $val(z_3) = val(z_4)$ and so (iii) of the definition of an XMVD is satisfied. Hence by definition of XMVD satisfaction and since $p \to\to q|r$ is satisfies in T:

(a) there exists a path $\bar{v}'_1.\cdots.\bar{v}'_n$ in $Paths(q)$ in T such that $val(\bar{v}'_n) = val(\bar{v}_n)$ and there exists a node z''_1 in $Nodes(s'_{1_1}, r)$ such that $val(z''_1) = val(z_2)$ and there exists a node z''_3 in $Nodes(s'_{1_{1_1}}, p)$ such that $val(z''_3) = val(z_3)$ where $s'_{1_1} = \{v|v \in \{\bar{v}'_1, \cdots, \bar{v}'_n\} \wedge v \in N(r \cap q)\}$ and $s'_{1_{1_1}} = \{v|v \in \{\bar{v}'_1, \cdots, \bar{v}'_n\} \wedge v \in N(p \cap r \cap q)\}$;

and

(b) there exists a path $\bar{w}'_1.\cdots.\bar{w}'_n$ in $Paths(q)$ in T such that $val(\bar{w}'_n) = val(\bar{w}_n)$ and there exists a node z''_2 in $Nodes(t'_{1_1}, r)$ such that $val(z''_2) = val(z_1)$ and there exists a node z''_4 in $Nodes(t'_{1_{1_1}}, p_l)$ such that $val(z''_4) = val(z_4)$ where $t'_{1_1} = \{v|v \in \{\bar{v}'_1, \cdots, \bar{v}'_n\} \wedge v \in N(r \cap q)\}$ and $t'_{1_{1_1}} = \{v|v \in \{\bar{v}'_1, \cdots, \bar{v}'_n\} \wedge v \in N(p \cap r \cap q)\}$.

We claim that $\bar{v}'_1.\cdots.\bar{v}'_n$ must be distinct from $\bar{v}_1.\cdots.v$. Suppose that it is not. Consider then the result of the change to v. If we let the path $\bar{v}''_1.\cdots.\bar{v}''_n$

in T' be the same as the path instance $\bar{v}_1.\cdots.\bar{v}_n$, and $\bar{w}''_1.\cdots.\bar{w}''_n$ be the same as $\bar{w}_1.\cdots.\bar{w}_n$ then as we have seen $\bar{v}''_1.\cdots.\bar{v}''_n$ and $\bar{w}''_1.\cdots.\bar{w}''_n$ satisfy (i), (ii) and (iii) of the definition of an XMVD. However, if we let $z'_1 = z''_1$ and $z'_3 = z''_3$ then z'_1 in $Nodes(s'_{1_1}, r)$ and $val(z'_1) = val(z_2)$ and z'_3 in $Nodes(s'_{1_{1_1}}, p)$ and $val(z'_3) = val(z_3)$ so (a) of the definition of an XMVD is satisfied. Similarly, if we let $z'_2 = z''_2$ and $z'_4 = z''_4$ then z'_2 in $Nodes(t'_{1_1}, r)$ and $val(z'_2) = val(z_1)$ and z'_4 in $Nodes(t'_{1_{1_1}}, p)$ and $val(z'_4) = val(z_4)$ so (b) of the definition of an XMVD is satisfied. This contradicts the earlier fact that either (a.1) or (b.1) is satisfied since $p \twoheadrightarrow q|r$ is violated in T' and so we conclude that $\bar{v}'_1.\cdots.\bar{v}'_n$ must be distinct from $\bar{v}_1.\cdots.v$. However, by (a) above $val(\bar{v}'_n) = val(\bar{v}_n) = val(v)$ which contradicts the fact that q is a key.

Similarly, if $v \in N(r)$ then using the same arguments we contradict the fact that r is a key and so we conclude that Σ does not cause redundancy if (A) of the definition of 4XNF holds.

Assume next that (B) holds, i.e. p is a key and $q \cap r = p$, and suppose to the contrary that Σ causes redundancy.. Then, as before, there exists an XML tree T which satisfies Σ and a node v in T such that *every* valid change from v to v', resulting in a new XML tree T', causes some XMVD $p \twoheadrightarrow q|r \in \Sigma$ to be violated. Using the same arguments as in (A), it follows that $v \in N(q)$ or $v \in N(r)$. We suppose firstly that $v \in N(q)$. So since $p \twoheadrightarrow q|r$ in T' is violated, there exist path instances $\bar{v}_1.\cdots.\bar{v}_n$ (where $\bar{v}_n = v'$) and $\bar{w}_1.\cdots.\bar{w}_n$ in $Paths(q)$ in T' such that:

(i) $val(\bar{v}_n) \neq val(\bar{w}_n)$;

(ii) there exists two nodes z_1, z_2, where $z_1 \in Nodes(x_{1_1}, r)$ and $z_2 \in Nodes(y_{1_1}, r)$ such that $val(z_1) \neq val(z_2)$;

(iii) there exists two nodes z_3 and z_4, where $z_3 \in Nodes(x_{1_{1_1}}, p)$ and $z_4 \in Nodes(y_{1_{1_1}}, p)$, such that $val(z_3) = val(z_4)$.

and:

(a.1) there does not exist a path $\bar{v}'_1.\cdots.\bar{v}'_n$ in $Paths(q)$ such that $val(\bar{v}'_n) = val(\bar{v}_n)$ and there does not exist a node z'_1 in $Nodes(x'_{1_1}, r)$ such that $val(z'_1) = val(z_2)$ and there does not exist a node z'_3 in $Nodes(x'_{1_{1_1}}, p)$ such that $val(z'_3) = val(z_3)$;

or

(b.1) there does not exists a path $\bar{w}'_1.\cdots.\bar{w}'_n$ in $Paths(q)$ such that $val(\bar{w}'_n) = val(\bar{w}_n)$ and there does not exist a node z'_2 in $Nodes(x'_{1_1}, r)$ such that $val(z'_2) = val(z_1)$ and there does not exist a node z'_4 in $Nodes(x'_{1_{1_1}}, p_l)$ such that $val(z'_4) = val(z_4)$;

Consider then the paths $\bar{v}_1.\cdots.v$ and $\bar{w}_1.\cdots.\bar{w}_n$ in $Paths(q)$ in T. Since p is a key and $q \cap r = p$, then $x_{1_1} = x'_{1_1} = y_{1_1} = x'_{1_1}$ and $x_{1_{1_1}} = x'_{1_{1_1}} = y_{1_{1_1}} = y'_{1_{1_1}}$. Hence if T' violates $p \twoheadrightarrow q|r$ then so will T which is a contradiction. The same argument applies if $v \in N(r)$ and so we conclude that Σ does not cause redundancy. □

5 Conclusions

In this paper we have investigated the issues of multivalued dependencies and 4NF in XML. We firstly gave a definition of XMVDs in XML using an extension of the approach used in [19,20]. We then proposed a normal form for XML documents in the presence of XMVDs and justified it by showing that it ensures the elimination of redundancy for an important class of XMVDs, namely what we call *hierarchical MVDs*. Hierarchical XMVDs are a natural extension of hierarchical multivalued dependencies that appear in relational and nested relational models.

There are several other issues related to the ones addressed in this paper that warrant further investigation. The first is the need to generalise the main result of this paper. We need to show that 4XNF we proposed is also a necessary condition for the elimination of redundancy and also to extend the definition of 4XNF to the case where the XMVDs are not hierarchical. Secondly, we need to investigate the problem of developing an axiom system for reasoning about the implication of XMVDs. In [19] an axiom system for reasoning about the implication of XFDs was developed and the system was shown to be sound for arbitrary XFDs. Later [18], the axiom system was shown to be complete for unary XFDs and a polynomial time algorithm was developed for determining if a unary XFD is implied by a set of unary XFDs. Similarly, we need to develop an axiom system and algorithm for the implication problem for XMVDs. Thirdly, we need to develop algorithms for converting unnormalised XML documents to normalised ones. In the relational case, the equivalent procedure is performed using a decomposition algorithm based on the projection operator. However, at the moment there has been no commonly agreed upon algebra defined for XML, let alone a projection operator, so the development of procedures for normalising XML documents is likely to be more complex than in the relational case. Fourthly, it is necessary to consider the case where both XFDs and XMVDs exist in a document. It is interesting to note that unlike the situation for the relational case, 4XNF is not a straightforward generalisation of the normal form for XFDs (XNF). This means that, in contrast to the relational case where 4NF implies BCNF in the case where both MVDs and FDs are present, in XML a different normal form from 4XNF is needed when the constraints on an XML document contain both XFDs and XMVDs. The situation is further complicated by the fact that XMVDs and XFDs interact, in the sense that there are XMVDs and XFDs implied by a combined set of XMVDs and XFDs which are not implied by either the XMVDs or XFDs considered alone. This situation parallels that of relational databases [2].

References

1. S. Abiteboul, P. Buneman, and D. Suciu. *Data on the Web.* Morgan Kauffman, 2000.
2. S. Abiteboul, R. Hull, and V. Vianu. *Foundations of databases.* Addison Wesley, 1996.

3. M. Arenas and L. Libkin. A normal form for xml documents. In *Proc. ACM PODS Conference*, pages 85–96, 2002.
4. P. Atzeni and V. DeAntonellis. *Foundations of databases.* Benjamin Cummings, 1993.
5. P. Buneman, S. Davidson, W. Fan, and C. Hara. Reasoning about keys for xml. In *International Workshop on Database Programming Languages*, 2001.
6. P. Buneman, S. Davidson, W. Fan, C. Hara, and W. Tan. Keys for xml. *Computer Networks*, 39(5):473–487, 2002.
7. P. Buneman, W. Fan, J. Simeon, and S. Weinstein. Constraints for semistructured data and xml. *ACM SIGMOD Record*, 30(1):45–47, 2001.
8. P. Buneman, W. Fan, and S. Weinstein. Path constraints on structured and semistructured data. In *Proc. ACM PODS Conference*, pages 129–138, 1998.
9. W. Fan and J. Simeon. Integrity constraints for xml. In *Proc. ACM PODS Conference*, pages 23–34, 2000.
10. M. Levene and G. Loizu. Axiomatization of functional dependencies in incomplete relations. *Theoretical Computer Science*, 206:283–300, 1998.
11. M. Levene and G. Loizu. *A guided tour of relational databases and beyond.* Springer, 1999.
12. M. Levene and M. W. Vincent. Justification for inclusion dependency normal form. *IEEE Transactions on Knowledge and Data Engineering*, 12:281–291, 2000.
13. J. Shanmugasundaram, K. Tufte, C. Zhang, G. He, D. J. DeWitt, and J. F. Naughton:. Relational databases for querying xml documents: Limitations and opportunities. In *VLDB Conference*, pages 302–314, 1999.
14. M. W. Vincent. A corrected 5nf definition for relational database design. *Theoretical Computer Science*, 185:379–391, 1997.
15. M. W. Vincent. A new redundancy free normal form for relational database design. In B. Thalheim and L. Libkin, editors, *Database Semantics*, pages 247–264. Springer Verlag, 1998.
16. M. W. Vincent. Semantic foundations of 4nf in relational database design. *Acta Informatica*, 36:1–41, 1999.
17. M. W. Vincent and M. Levene. Restructuring partitioned normal relations without information loss. *SIAM Journal on Computing*, 39(5):1550–1567, 2000.
18. M.W. Vincent and J. Liu. The implication problem for unary functional dependencies in xml. Submitted for publication, 2002.
19. M.W. Vincent and J. Liu. Strong functional dependencies and a redundancy free normal form for xml. Submitted for publication, 2002.
20. M.W. Vincent and J. Liu. Functional dependencies for xml. In *Fifth Asian Pacific Web Conference*, 2003.
21. M.W. Vincent and J. Liu. Multivalued dependencies for xml. In *20th BNCOD Conference*, 2003.
22. J. Widom. Data management for xml - research directions. *IEEE data Engineering Bulletin*, 22(3):44–52, 1999.

Query Processing and Optimization for Regular Path Expressions

Guoren Wang and Mengchi Liu

School of Computer Science, Carleton University
Ottawa, Ontario, Canada K1S 5B6
{wanggr, mengchi}@scs.carleton.ca

Abstract. Regular path expression is one of the core components of XML query languages, and several approaches to evaluating regular path expressions have been proposed. In this paper, a new path expression evaluation approach, *extent join*, is proposed to compute both parent-children ('/') and ancestor-descendent ('//') connectors between path steps. Furthermore, two path expression optimization rules, *path-shortening* and *path-complementing*, are proposed. The former reduces the number of joins by shortening the path while the latter optimizes the execution of a path by using an equivalent complementary path expression to compute the original path. Experimental results show that the algorithms proposed in this paper are much more efficient than conventional ones.

1 Introduction

With the rapid development of advanced applications on the Web, numerous amount of information becomes available on the Web and almost all the corresponding documents are semi-structured. As the emerging standard for data representation and exchange on the Web, XML has been adopted by more and more applications as their information description mean. Even though XML is mainly used as an information exchange standard, storing, indexing and querying XML data have become research hotspots both in the academic community and in the industrial community.

To retrieve XML data, many query languages have been proposed so far, such as Quilt [3], XQuery [4], XQL [5], XPath [6], and Lorel [7]. Because one of the common features of these languages is the use of regular path expressions (RPE), query rewriting and optimization for RPE is becoming a research hotspot and some research results have been obtained recently. A usual way to optimize the execution of RPE expressions is to first rewrite RPE queries into simple path expressions (SPE) based on schema information and statistics about XML data, and then translate these SPE queries into the language of the database used to store the XML data, for example, into SQL. In the Lore system, three basic query processing strategies are proposed for the execution of path expressions, *top-down*, *bottom-up* and *hybrid*. The *top-down* approach navigates the document tree from the root to the leaf nodes while the *bottom-up* approach does from the

J. Eder and M. Missikoff (Eds.): CAiSE 2003, LNCS 2681, pp. 30–45, 2003.

leaf nodes to the root. In the *hybrid* way, a longer path is first broken into several sub-paths, each of which is performed with either *top-down* or *bottom-up*. The results of the sub-paths are then joined together. In the VXMLR system [1], regular path expressions containing '//' and/or '*' operators are rewritten with simple path queries based on schema information and statistics. The paper in [2] presents an *EE-Join* algorithm to compute '//' operator and a *KC-Join* algorithm to compute '*' operator based on their numbering scheme.

In this paper, we propose a new path expression evaluation approach, called *extent join*, to compute both parent-children ('/') and ancestor-descendent ('//') connectors between path steps. In order to support the *extent join* approach, we introduce indexes preserving parent-children and ancestor-descendent relationships. Furthermore, we propose two path expression optimization rules, *path-shortening* and *path-complementing*. The Path-shortening rule reduces the number of joins by shortening the path while the path-complementing optimizes the execution of a path by using an equivalent complementary path to compute the original path. The performances of the query processing and optimization techniques proposed in this paper are fully evaluated with four benchmarks, *XMark*, *XMach*, *Shakes* and *DBLP*.

The remainder of this paper is organized as follows. Section 2 presents some preliminaries for XML query processing, including XML data tree, XML schema graph and path expression. Section 3 describes the *extent join* algorithm along with indexes and rewriting algorithm for '//'. Section 4 presents two query optimization rules for regular path expressions. Section 5 gives the experimental results and the performance evaluation. Finally, Section 6 concludes the paper.

2 Preliminaries

In this section we review some concepts and definitions used throughout the paper.

2.1 XML Data Tree

XML is proposed by W3C as a standard for data representation and exchange, in which information is represented by elements that can be nested and attributes that are parts of elements. Document Object Model (DOM) is an application programming interface (API) for XML and HTML documents, which defines the logical structure of documents and the way a document is accessed and manipulated. In DOM, XML data are abstracted into entities, *elements* and *attributes*, and these entities are organized together via parent-children and element-attribute relationships to form a data tree, i.e. DOM tree. In this paper, we model XML data as a node-labelled tree in the following.

Definition 1. Formally, an XML data is represented as an XML data tree $T_d = (V_d, E_d, \delta_d, \Sigma_d, root_d, oid)$, where V_d is the node set including element nodes and attribute nodes; E_d is the set of tree edges denoting parent-children relationships between two elements and element-attribute relationships between elements and attributes; δ_d is the mapping function from nodes to nodes that are actually the relationship constraints. Every node has a unique name that is a string-literal of Σ_d and a unique identifier in set *oid*. Finally, every XML data tree has a root element $root_d$ that is included in V_d.

Figure 1 shows part of an XML document proposed in the XML Benchmark project [11], it is represented as an XML data tree. There are two kinds of nodes, *elements* denoted by *ellipses* and *attributes* by *triangles*. The numeric identifiers following "&" in nodes represent *oids*. The solid edges are tree edges connecting nodes via the δ_d function. In this model, the parents can actually be reached via the δ_d^{-1} function from the children. Node "&*1*" labelled "*site*" is the $root_d$ of this XML data tree and all other nodes can and only can be reached by $root_d$. Note that in Figure 1, there are two directed dashed lines between some nodes (&*23* and &*18*, &*28* and &*18*), representing the referencing-referenced relationship between elements.

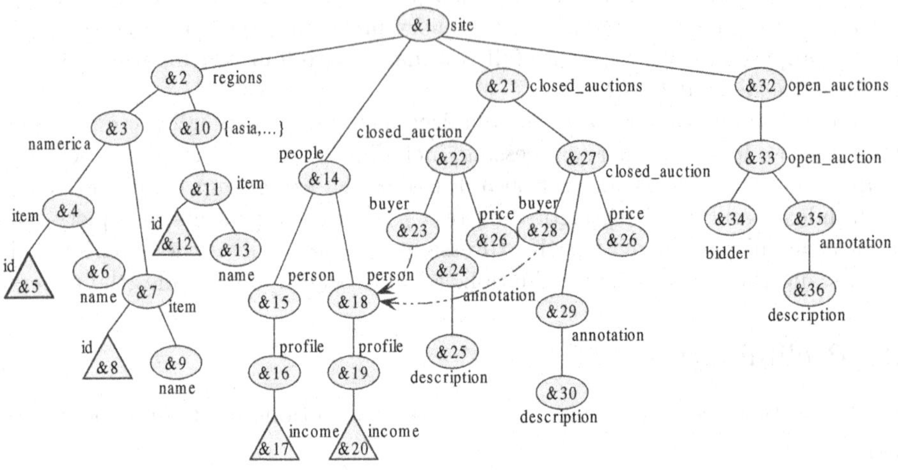

Fig. 1. Sample XML data tree

2.2 XML Schema Graph

Although XML data is self-descriptive, Document Type Definition (DTD) is proposed by W3C to further and explicitly constrains XML data, for example, an element should contain what kind of and/or how many sub-elements. XML mainly defines the parent-children relationship between XML elements and the order between the sub-elements of an element. In this paper, we model XML DTD as a directed, node-labelled graph.

Definition 2. Formally, an XML schema graph is defined as a directed, node-labelled graph $Gt = (V_t, E_t, \delta_t, \Sigma_t, root_t)$, where V_t is the node set including element type nodes; E_t is the set of graph edges denoting element-subelement relationships. Attributes are parts of elements; δ_t is the mapping function from nodes to nodes that actually constrains which element can contain which sub-elements. Every node has a unique name that is a string-literal of Σ_t and this name is actually element type name. Finally, every XML schema graph has a root element $root_t$ that is included in V_t, which is defined as the node with only outgoing edges and without any incoming edges.

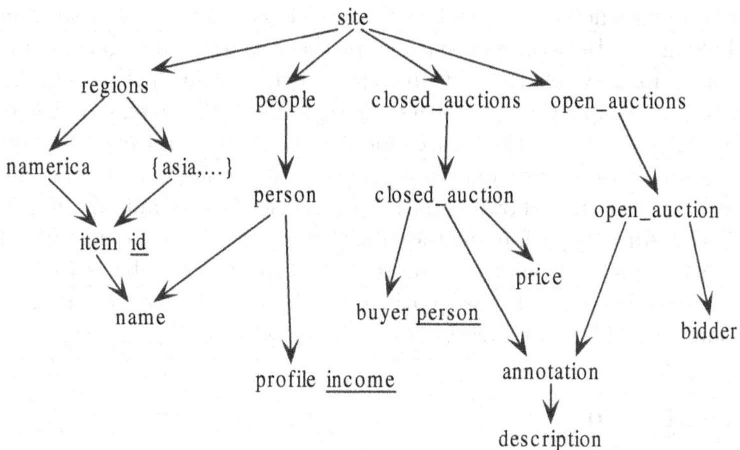

Fig. 2. XML Schema Graph

Figure 2 shows part of the XML schema graph that constrains the XML data tree in Figure 1, it is represented as an XML schema graph. The nodes are element types and the solid edges are graph edges connecting nodes via the δ_t function. In this model, the parent elements can actually be reached via the δ_t^{-1} function from the children elements and the corresponding reverse edges are omitted in Figure 2. The node labelled "*site*" is the $root_t$ of this XML schema graph. The attributes of element types are listed besides the nodes with underline, for example, *income*.

2.3 Path Expression

Path expressions can be straightforwardly defined as a sequence of element type names connected by some connectors such as '/' and '//' and wildcard '*'. For example, path expression "*/site//item*" can be used to find all items of the database whose root element $root_d$ is "*site*". The syntax definition of path expression is shown in Figure 3.

Path expressions mainly consist of two parts, *path steps* and *connectors.* Every path expression must begin from the root, that is, begins with a connector '/' or '//'. There are two basic kinds of path steps, *Name* and *wildcard* '*'. Path

```
PathExpression ::= CONNECTOR PathSteps
                 | PathSteps CONNECTOR PathSteps
PathSteps ::= Name | Name '|' PathSteps | (PathStemps) | '*'
CONNECTOR ::= '/' | '//'
```

Fig. 3. BNF syntax of path expression

step *Name* means that in this step only the element instances with the tag name *Name* will be matched and '*' will match any element instances no matter which type it belongs to. Between two path steps there must be a connector to specify the relationship between them. Connector '/' appearing in the beginning of a path expression means that the path expression begins from exactly the root and the following path step is the root element type, while connector '//' appearing in the beginning of a path expression means that the path expression begins from the root and the following path step is the descendant of the root, that is, '//' covers for sub-path-expressions with any length. A connector appearing between two path steps specifies the relationship between them. Connector '/' constrains that between the two path steps there must exist a parent-children relationship and '//' is an ancestor-descendant relationship constraint.

3 Extent Join

In this section, we discuss the *XML element extent* concept and the *extent join* algorithm. We present some indexes as well in this section to support the concept and the algorithm.

3.1 XML Element Extent

Given an XML data tree $T_d = (V_d, E_d, \delta_d, \Sigma_d, root_d, oid)$ and a corresponding XML schema graph $G_t = (V_t, E_t, \delta_t, \Sigma_t, root_t)$, we have the following definitions.

Definition 3. *pcpair(pid, cid)* is a pair of oids, in which *pid*, *cid* $\in$ *oid* and *pid* is the parent of *cid*, for example, *pcpair(&1, &2)*.

Definition 4. *adpair(aid, did)* is a pair of oids, in which *aid*, *did* $\in$ *oid* and *aid* is the ancestor of *did*, for example, *adpair(&1, &3)*.

A *pcpair* is a special case of an *adpair*. Additionally, ε is defined to act as any element instance, so *adpair(*ε*,&3)* can be used to represent *adpair(&1, &3)* or *adpair(&2, &3)*. Both *adpair* and *pcpair* can also act as logic operators, for example, if there exists an ancestor-descendent relationship between two element instances e_1 and e_2, then *adpair(*e_1*,* e_2*)* returns true. Otherwise, it returns false.

Definition 5. The set of all *pcpairs* of a given tag name *Tag*, called *parent-child element extent*, is represented by *Ext(any, Tag)* = {*pcpair(pid, cid)* | *cid is an instance of Tag* $\wedge$ *pcpair(pid, cid) is true*}. Similarly, the set of all *adpairs* of two given tag names *an* and *dn*, called *ancestor-descendant element extent*, is represented by *Ext(an,dn)* = {*adpair(aid, did)* | *pcpair(*ε*, aid)* $\in$ *Ext(any, an)* $\wedge$ *pcpair(*ε*, did)* $\in$ *Ext(any, dn)* $\wedge$ *adpair(aid, did) is true*}.

For examples, *Ext(any,name)*={*(&4, &6), (&7, &9), (&11, &13)*} and *Ext(site, annotation)* = {*(&1, &24), (&1, &29), (&1, &35)*}.

Definition 6. For two given elements, *an* and *dn*, and a given path *P*, the *path constrained element extent* is defined as *PCExt(an, dn, P)* = { *adpair(aid, did)* | *adpair(aid, did)* ∈ *Ext(an, dn)* ∧ *did* ∈ *P(aid)*}, where *P(aid)* is the element instance set that can be reached from *aid* via path *P*.

In the query processing, *PCExt* may be more useful than the basic XML element extents. A *PCExt* is actually an element extent with a path constraint and is a subset of the corresponding extent. For example, in *PCExt(site, annotation, "/site/closed_auctions/closed_auction/annotation")*, the third parameter is the path constraint on *Ext(site, annotation)*. This constraint regulates that in this *PCExt*, the instances of element *annotation* must be the ones that can be reached from the corresponding instances of element *site* via the path expression. As a result, *PCExt(site,annotation, "/site/closed_auctions/closed_auction/annotation")* = {*(&1, &24), (&1, &29)*}.

3.2 Indexes

Neither the DOM interface nor the XML data tree provides the extent semantic for XML data, so we introduce three structural indexes to support it, *ancestor-descendant index (ADX)*, *parent-children index (PCX)* and *path index (PX)*. We also propose *reference index (RX)* to support operations on references.

ADX is used to index *Ext(Pname, Cname)* where *Pname* is the ancestor of *Cname*. Actually, *ADX* indexes the ancestor-descendant relationship between specified elements. For example, *ADX(site, item)* = {*(&1, &4), (&1, &7), (&1, &11)*}. *PCX* is used to index *PCExt(Pname, Cname, "Pname/Cname")* where *Pname* must be the parent of *Cname*. For example, *PCX(namerica, item) is* {*(&3, &4), (&3, &7)*}. If the parent element name is not specified, *PCX(any, item)* indexes *Ext(any,item)* = {*(&3, &4), (&3, &7), (&10, &11)*}, written as *PCX(item)*. $PX(E_1/P/E_2)$ is used to index $PCExt(E_1, E_2, \text{"}E_1/P/E_2\text{"})$. For example, *PX(closed_auctions/closed_auction/buyer)* = {*(&21, &23), (&21, &28)*}. *RX* is used to support the reference semantics between XML elements. For example, *RX(buyer, person, person) is* {*(&23, &18), (&28, &18)*}.

For the indexes above, only the principles are introduced. Their implementations are relatively simple as they have no special demands on the index structures. The traditional index structures, e.g. B+ tree, are suitable for these indexes.

3.3 Extent Join Algorithm

The basic idea of the *extent join* algorithm is to replace the tree traversal procedures with join operations. Before the whole path expression is evaluated, the intermediate result sets to be joined must be first computed. Then the ancestor-descendant/parent-children relationship based multi-join operation is then performed to evaluate the whole path expression. The most special characteristic of these indexes is that they maintain the parent-children and ancestor-descendant relationship by the index results.

Consider the path expression *"/site//closed _auction/annotation/description"* that contains four path steps and three connectors. As shown in Figure 4, each path step corresponds to an intermediate results set, i.e. an element extent; each connector is transformed into a join operation, and the results of joins are the path constrained element extents. For example, the join between *Ext(any, site)* and *Ext(site, closed_auction)* is *PCExt(site, closed_auction, "/site/closed _auc-tions/closedc _auction")*, and the *PCExt* acts as an intermediate result used to perform another join with *Ext(closed_auction, annotation)* to get another *PCExt*. Path expressions must be transformed into evaluation plans to get evaluated. The art of transformation is focused on the path steps to corresponding extents, and the following shows the full transformation rules.

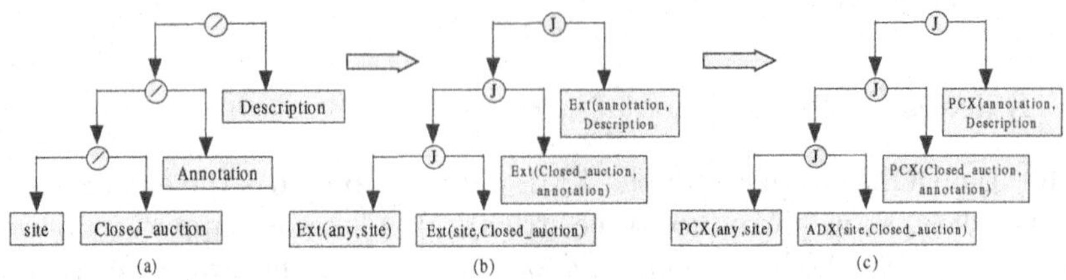

Fig. 4. (a) path expression, (b) extent join tree, and (c) execution tree

(1) Connectors ('/' and '//') are transformed into joins between two sets.
(2) Path step '*' is rewritten with element types using the mapping function δ_t. For example, δ_t*(site)* = {*regions, people, closed_auctions, ope_auctions*} and path expression *"/site/*/person"* is rewritten as *"/site/(regions | people | closed_auctions | open_auctions)/person"*.
(3) Path steps following connector '//' are transformed into a corresponding *ADX* operator. For example, path step S_2 in "$S_1//S_2$" is transformed into *ADX*(S_1, S_2).
(4) Path steps following connector '/' are transformed into a corresponding *PCX* operator. For example, path step S_2 in "S_1/S_2" is transformed into *PCX*(S_1, S_2).
(5) Path steps containing '|'s are transformed into the unions of corresponding indexes. For example, path step $(S_2|S_3)$ in "$S_1/(S_2|S_3)$" is transformed into $PCX(S_1, S_2) \cup PCX(S_1, S_3)$.

The third transformation rule transforms the '//' connectors into *ADXs*. However, to build this index for every element type pair with ancestor-descendent relationship will take too much time and space overhead. So in the case of no corresponding *ADX* available, the '//' connectors must be rewritten into path expressions connected only with '/'. This procedure should be achieved with the knowledge of the schema information, e.g. DTD of XML documents. For the XML schema graph is a directed graph, the rewriting algorithm is actually to find all possible paths between two nodes in a graph. Before introducing the details of the algorithm for rewritting '//' connector, we first define an important data structure *reverse path tree (RPT)* as follows.

Definition 7. A *reverse path tree* is defined as a node-labelled tree $T_r = (V_r, E_r, \Sigma_r, root_r)$, which organizes several path expressions with a same end path step together, where V_r is the node set that are actually the set of corresponding path steps; the edges contained in the edge set E_r are connector '/'; Σ_r is the same as Σ_t in G_t and $root_r$ is the root of this tree and is just the common end path step. We define *RPT(E)* as a *reverse path tree* rooted E which contains all path expressions from $root_r$ to E, and define $RPT(E_1, E_2)$ as a reverse path tree rooted E_2 which contains all path expressions from E_1 to E_2 and some path expressions from $root_r$ to E_2.

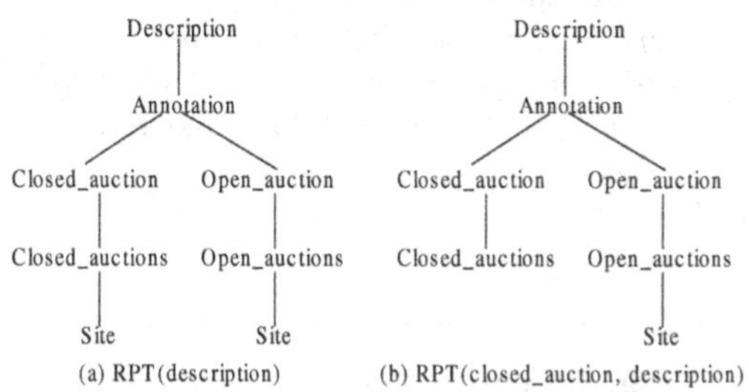

Fig. 5. Reverse path trees

For example, Figure 5 (a) shows *RPT(description)* and (b) shows *RPT(closed_acutions, description)*. We can easily retrieve path expressions with specified starting path step by traversing up through the *RPT* from the tree leaves with the given label. For example, if we only want path expressions beginning with *closed_acutions* from *RPT(closed_acutions, description)*, we can just traverse up from the most left leaf node of Figure 5(b) to the root. So, the connectors rewriting algorithm is just the *RPT* constructing algorithm, shown as in Figure 6. With the proposed transformation rules and the algorithm, we have the *extent join* algorithm, details are shown in Figure 7.

4 Optimizing Regular Path Expressions

In Section 3, we have introduced the basic idea of *extent join* that uses joins over sets to evaluate path expression queries. Its performance depends largely on the number of joins and the size of joining sets. In this section, we present two path expression optimization techniques to reduce the number of joins and the execution cost of path expressions when evaluating a path expression. Meanwhile, the general cost based optimization procedure is also introduced in this section.

4.1 Path-Shortening

Most of the existing algorithms proposed for path expressions are based on the entire paths. Actually, a path expression can sometimes be computed with relative path rather than absolute path, depending on DTD or schema information. A simple example is path *"/site/closed_auctions/closed_auction/price"*. From the XML schema graph in Figure 2, we know that only through this path we can find price elements, so the result of this path is exactly all elements tagged *price*, i.e. *Ext(any, price)*. This principle can be summarized as follows.

```
Problem: construct a RPT (rewrite "n1//n2")
Input: XML Schema Graph Gt = (Vt, Et, δt, Σt, roott),
       two graph nodes n1, n2
Output: result RPT rpt.
Algorithm body:
(1)    rpt.rootr = n2; // set the root of rpt
(2)    currentnode = rpt.rootr; // set the current node
(3)    currentnode.children = δt^-1(currentnode); // set children of current node.
(4)    For every node ccinδt^-1(currentnode) do // recursively construct the RPT
(5)       if cc! = n1 and cc! = roott
(6)       currentnode = cc
(7)      goto (3)
(8)    endfor
```

Fig. 6. Constructing RPT Algorithm

```
InputPath Expression Query P
Output: Result Set R
Algorithm body
(1) Checking the ADX and rewrite the no-index-supported '//' connectors
    using the algorithm in Figure 6.
(2) Transforming the rewritten path P into joins and indexes and organized
    as a simple query plan.
(3) Executing the query plan including indexes and joins.
```

Fig. 7. Extent join Algorithm

Definition 8. Suppose that $/P/E$ be a path starting from the root element. If $(\forall e)(pcpair(p,e) \in Ext(any, E) \rightarrow adpair(\varepsilon, p) \in R(P))$, then P is a *unique path* from the root to E, written as $UP(E_n) = P$, where P is a path expression and *R(P)* means the result set of path P.

Rule 1. *Path-shortening*: if $UP(E) = P$, then $R(/P/E) = Ext(E)$.

However, the situation that the end node is in the unique path does not happen very often, for example, the end node in the path

"/site/closed _auctions/ closed_auction/annotation/description" can also be reached by path *"/site/openauc-tions/open _auction/annotation/description"*. The characteristic of this path expression is that its head segment is unique, for example, *"/site/closed _auctions/ closed_auction"* is a unique path. In this case, we can shorten the long path into a relative shorter one *"closed_auction/annotation/description"*. Then we can get the general *path-shortening* rule.

Rule 2. *General Path-shortening*: if $P_1/E/P_2$ is a path expression starting from the root and $UP(E) = P_1$, then $R(P_1/E/P_2) = R(E/P_2)$.

This optimization technique is heuristic one because it reduces the sets to be joined by shortening the path expressions, and its key problem is how to determine if a path expression is the unique path of a given element type. Actually we can shorten a path expression step by step till the most optimal case. The algorithm in Figure 8 shows how to shorten a path expression. For the simplicity of algorithm description, we assume that the path steps of the path expression to be shortened do not include '*' for they can easily be rewritten to paths not containing '*' using function δ_t. In this algorithm, the path expression is shortened from the head to the tail, and if one path step could not be shortened, the rests then do not need to be checked any more. The reverse path tree is used to help to shorten path steps with connector '//'.

Input: Path expression P = $\Sigma_{i=1}^{n} S_i C_i$, XML schema graph $G_t = (V_t, E_t, \delta_t, \Sigma_t, root_t)$

Output: Shortened path expression P'

Algorithm body:

```
For i = 1 to n-1 do
    If S_i == '/' && δ_t^{-1}(S_{i+1}) = {S_i} then
        cs = i+1;
        continue;
    else break;
    end if
    If S_i == '//' then
        construct RPT(S_i, S_{i+1})
        if all leaves of RPT(S_i, S_{i+1}) are S_i then
            cs = i+1;
            continue;
        else break;
        end if
    end if
End for
P' = Σ_{i=cs}^{n} S_i C_i
```

Fig. 8. Path Shortening algorithm

4.2 Path-Complementing

Path-shortening reduces the cost of evaluating a path expression by optimizing the path itself. For example, consider the query "find all the names of items of all regions" that can be expressed as "/site/regions/*/item/name". From the XML schema graph in Figure 2 we know only elements *item* and *person* have element *name*, so these *name* element instances in database are either item names or person names. Actually all item names can be reached by path *"/site/regions/*/item/name"* , and all person names can be reached by path *"/site/people/person/name"* . So for element *name*, these two path expressions are complementary paths; that is, the former path can be evaluated by subtracting the results of the latter from the element extent *Ext(any, name)*. This gives us an alternative way to compute path expressions and we can choose the better one to get better performance.

Definition 9. Let E_1 and E_2 be element names, if $(\forall e_2)(pcpair(\varepsilon, e_2) \in Ext(any, E_2) \rightarrow (\exists e_1)(pcpair(\varepsilon, e_1) \in Ext(any, E_1) \wedge adpair(e_1, e_2)))$, then E_1 is a *key ancestor* of E_2.

Definition 10. Let E_1 is a key ancestor of E_2 and there exist path expressions P_1, P_2, $\cdots$, P_n from E_1 to E_2, if $(\forall e_2)(pcpair(\varepsilon, e_2) \in Ext(any, E_2) \rightarrow adpair(\varepsilon, e_2) \in \cup_{i=1}^{n} P(p_i))$, then $\cup_{j=1}^{i-1} p_j + \cup_{j=i+1}^{n} p_j$ is the complementary paths of P_i with respect to E_1 and E_2 .

Rule 3. *Path complementing*: if $\cup_{j=1}^{i-1} p_j + \cup_{j=i+1}^{n} p_j$ is the complementary paths of $P_i (1 \leq i \leq n)$ with respect to E_1 and E_2, then $R(P_i) = Ext(E_2)$ - $(\cup_{j=1}^{i-1} p_j + \cup_{j=i+1}^{n} p_j)$.

Obviously, reverse path tree is very helpful to determine the key ancestors of a given element type by checking the names of leaves and finding the complementary paths. Actually with reverse path tree the procedure is quite simple, so for saving the space, the details of this algorithm are omitted in this paper.

4.3 Querying and Optimizing Path Expressions

In the above subsections, two optimization techniques are proposed for path expression. We have mentioned that the *path-shortening* rule is heuristic, while the *path-complementing* technique is not suitable for all cases. Therefore, a cost based query plan selection is used for the path optimization procedure. In this subsection, we show how to use them in path expression query processing procedure. The selectivity of path expression and cost estimation are not the focuses of this paper, so the details of these issues are ignored.

Given a path expression query P and an XML schema graph $G_t = (V_t, E_t, \delta_t, \Sigma_t, root_t)$, the general steps of querying and optimizing path expression queries are shown as follows.

Step 1. Rewriting of '*'. With the XML schema graph, path steps '*' are rewritten to the unions of all possible sub-paths via function δ_t.

Step 2. Complementary path selection. With the XML schema graph, the complementary paths of user query are found and their costs are estimated.

Check if the cost of complementary paths is lower than that of the original path. If does, the complementary approach is chosen. Otherwise, the original path is chosen.

Step 3. *Path shortening.* Using the algorithm in Figure 8 to shorten the selected path expressions.

Step 4. Rewriting of connector '//'. Checking if there exists '//' connectors with no *ADX* support. If does, they are rewritten using the algorithm in Figure 6.

Step 5. Index selection and query plan construction. Select correct indexes and transform the path expressions into query plans.

Step 6. Query plan execution. Executing the query plan including indexes and joins.

5 Experiments

5.1 Overview

In this section, we discuss the performance evaluation of the extent join path expression evaluation strategy and the path-shortening and path-complimenting path expression optimization rules in terms of four benchmarks. The experiments were made on a single 800MHz CPU PC with 184MB main memory. We employed a native XML management system called XBase [8] as the underlying data storage, which stores XML documents into an object database with an ODMG-binding DOM interface. The testing programs were coded with MS VC++ 6.0 and ODMG C++OML 2.0 [9]. The datasets used are described as follows.

XMark is from the XML benchmark project [11]. The scale factor selected is 1.0, and the corresponding XML document size is about 100MB. The structure of the document is modelled for a database as deployed by an Internet auction site. The hierarchical schema is the same as in Figure 2. XMark focuses on the core ingredient of XML benchmark including the query processor and its interaction with the database. XMark totally specifies 20 queries that cover a wide range including exact match, ordered access, casting, regular path expressions, chasing references, construction of complex results, join on values, reconstruction, full text, path traversals, missing elements, function application, sorting and aggregation. *XMach* is a scalable multi-user benchmark to evaluate the performance of XML data management systems proposed by Rahm and Bohme [10]. It is based on a web application and considers different types of XML data, in particular text documents, schema-less data and structured data. The database contains a directory structure and XML documents. It is a multiple DTD and multiple document benchmark that totally consists of 11 queries, 8 retrieval and 3 update queries. *Shakes* is the Bosak Shakespeare collection available at `http://metalab.unc.edu/bosak/xml/eg/shakes200.zip`. 8 queries are designed over *Shakes* data set [12]. *DBLP* is from the DBLP bibliography web site, available at ftp://ftp.informatic.unitrier.de/pub/users/Ley/bib/records.tar.gz. 8 queries are defined over the *DBLP* data set [12].

In order to full explore the performance of the *extent join* algorithm and query optimization techniques proposed in this paper, we implemented 4 different query evaluating strategies: *DOMTR*, *EJX*, *EJPX* and *EJOPX*. *DOMTR* evaluates path expressions by traversing the XML date tree from top to down with no index support, which is similar to the *top-down* approach. *EJX* is implemented as an *extent join* approach with all indexes except path indexes, including *ADX*, *PCX* and *RX*. Path indexes are optional for they must be specified explicitly by users, while other indexes are indispensable to *EJX*. *EJPX* is a full *extent join* algorithm with all indexes used to explore the performance of path indexes. In the extreme cases where all indexes are available, EJX and EJPX do not need to access the XML data trees. *EJOPX* is an all query optimization rule applied *extent join* algorithm. It follows the optimizing steps in Section 4 to select the most optimal query execution plan.

5.2 Extent Join

Figure 9 shows the performance comparison of *DOMTR*, *EJX* and *EJPX* in terms of XMark. *Extent join* algorithm is much better than DOMTR in most cases. The *extent join* is about 2 $\sim$ 20 times, sometimes hundreds of times faster than *DOMTR*. However, there are some exceptions. (1) For Q2, Q3, Q13 and Q14, the performance of *extent join* is similar to *DOMTR*. The reasons are different: a) Q2 and Q3 are order accesses to elements. In this case, even *extent join* needs to traverse the XML data trees; b) Q13 is result reconstruction and needs to traverse a relative big sub-tree to get all results; c) Q14 is a full text query, which also needs to traverse the whole sub-tree to check if elements are right. (2) For Q15 and Q16 containing very long path traversals, *DOMTR* outperformed *extent join* by about 30%. Due to the much smaller selectivity of path expression *DOMTR* does not need to traverse the whole XML data tree, whereas *extent join* must do many join operations (e.g. Q15: 12, Q16: 14). Then we can get a conclusion: *extent join* is better than *DOMTR* in most cases except it needs to traverse a large XML data tree like *DOMTR* or the path queries are very long which *extent join* must do too many join operations.

There are only some queries in XMark can be evaluated using *EJPX* (Q8$\sim$Q11, Q15$\sim$Q17 and Q19) due to their characteristics. From Figure 9, we can see *EJPX* can improve the query performance by about 10%$\sim$30 times over *EJX*. In the extreme case, such as Q15, *EJPX* can be thousands times faster than *EJX*. However, for some queries like Q11, Q12, Q14, and Q18, which either have join on values or are full text queries, the benefit of path indexes are drowned.

Figure 10 shows the update performance with and without indexes in XMach. Since only XMach has specified update queries, the test has not been done on other benchmarks. The total size of indexes is about 0.1 to 0.2 times of the size of the original XML document, and the response times of the update operations are decreased by only about 10% to 20%. Thus, these indexes are much efficient and effective both in space utilization and supports for queries.

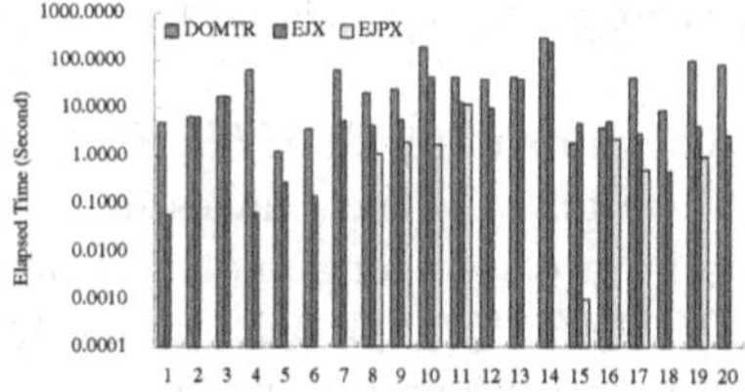

Fig. 9. Extent join (XMark)

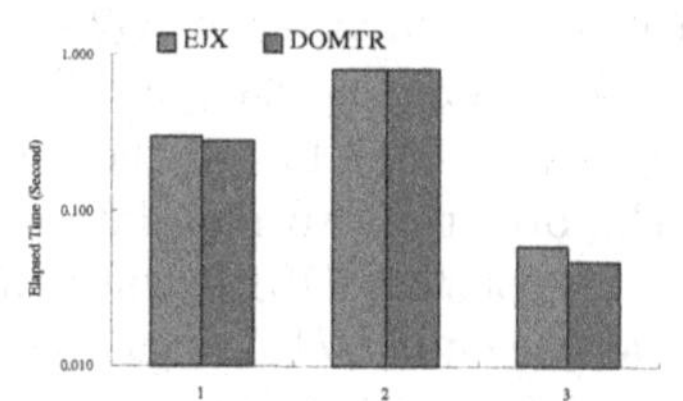

Fig. 10. Update queries (XMach)

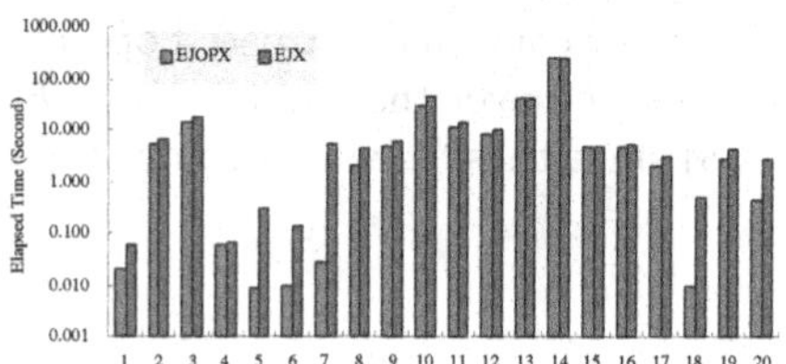

Fig. 11. Query optimization(XMarh)

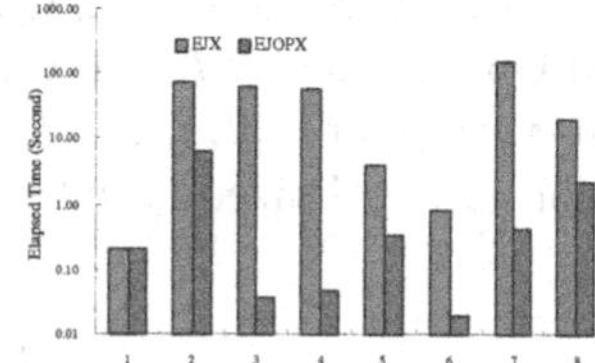

Fig. 12. Query optimization(XMach)

5.3 Query Optimization

Figures 11 and 12 show the performance comparison of *EJX* and *EJOPX* on XMark and XMach respectively. *EJOPX* is the winner in all query results, and queries are divided into several categories. (1) Query performance is improved greatly. Examples are Q5~Q7, Q18 and Q20 of XMark, whose path expressions are shortened to a very short one, and these queries have no predicates or the predicates are at the last step of the paths. In these cases, *EJOPX* can be 10~200 times faster than *EJX*. (2) Query performance is improved moderately. Q1~Q4, Q8~Q12 and Q17 belong to this category. They are either queries that can only be shortened a little by *path-shortening* rule and the saved *extent join* operations take relative small costs (Q1), or queries have some other high cost operations, such as join on values, ordered access and references chasing, in which the benefits of query optimization rules cannot be seen clearly (Q2~Q4, Q8~Q12), or queries whose complementary paths are still very complex (Q17). For queries of this category, *EJOPX* can save the evaluating time by about 10%~400%. Most queries fall in this category. (3) Query performance is improved slightly. Q13~Q15 and Q16 of XMark fall in this category and the benefit of

EJOPX on them is only 0.3%∼8%. The reasons are that these queries have very high cost operations (Q13: complex result reconstruction, Q14: full text scanning) or they are very long path expressions and can only be shortened very little (Q15: 2 out of 12, Q16: 2 out of 14). The XMach results in Figure 12 also indicates the similar result (Q2∼Q7 belong to category 1, Q8 belongs to category 2 and Q1 belongs to category 3).

Figures 13 and 14 are the performance comparison of *DOMTR*, *EJX* and *EJOPX* over the two real data sets, DBLP in Figure 13 and Shakes in Figure 14. First, consider DBLP where most of queries are very long and have predicates at the end. *EJX* is much better than *DOMTR* (Q2, Q3, Q4, Q5 and Q6). There exists a containing operator in Q1 and the path expressions in it are relatively short, all these factors cause *DOMTR* is better than *EJX* in this query. The performance of *EJX* on Q7 and Q8 is very bad and we cannot get their performance results, the reason should be they all contain several (4 or 5) long path expressions with more than 10 steps. Nevertheless, *EJOPX* performs very well on all queries of DBLP. For some queries of Shakes (Q2, Q3, Q5, Q6, Q7 and Q8), the performance of *EJX* is not very good since they either have long and complex path expressions (Q2, Q3, Q7 and Q8) or contain order based operators (Q5 and Q6). However, *EJOPX* performs very well over the queries where *EJX* performs very poor (Q2, Q3, Q4, Q7 and Q8) since these long and complex path expression are optimized largely.

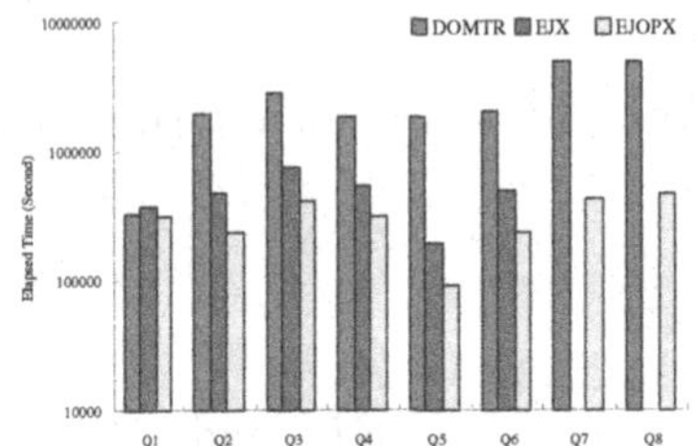

Fig. 13. Performance comparison(DBLP)

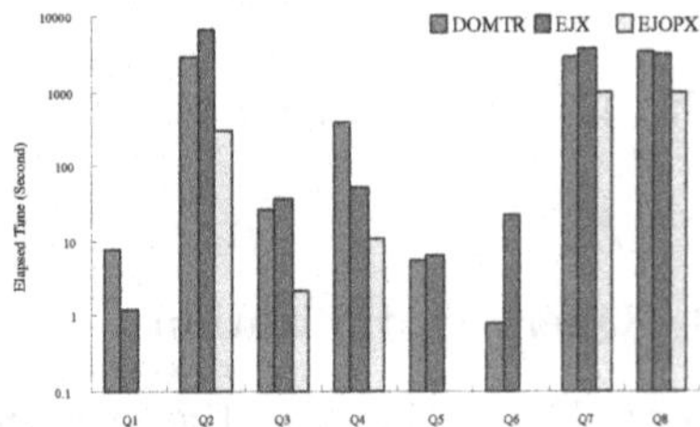

Fig. 14. Performance comparison(Shake)

6 Conclusions

In this paper, we have proposed the *extent join* approach to evaluating regular path expressions. In order to further improve the query performance, we also proposed two novel query optimization techniques, *path-shortening* and *path-complementing*. The former reduces the number of joins by shortening the path while the latter is a technique that uses an equivalent complementary path expression to compute the original path specified in a user query. They can reduce the path computing cost by decreasing the length of paths and using equivalent complementary expressions to optimize long and complex paths. From our experimental results, 80% of the queries can benefit from these optimization rules, and path expression evaluating performance can be improved by 20% $\sim$ 400% on average.

Acknowledgement. Guoren Wang's research is partially supported by the Teaching and Research Award Programme for Outstanding Young Teachers in Post-Secondary Institutions by the Ministry of Education, China (TRAPOYT) and National Natural Science Foundation of China under grant No. 60273079. Mengchi Liu's research is partially supported by National Science and Engineering Research Council of Canada.

References

1. Zhou, A., Lu, H., Zheng, S., Liang, Y., Zhang, L., Ji, W., Tian, Z.: VXMLR: A Visual XML-Relational Database System. In: Proceedings of the 27th VLDB Conference. Morgan Kaufmann. Roma, Italy (2001) 719–720
2. Li, Q., Moon, B.: Indexing and querying XML Data for regular path expressions. In: Proceedings of the 27th VLDB Conference. Morgan Kaufmann. Roma, Italy (2001) 361–370
3. Chamberlin, D., Robie, J., Florescu, D.: Quilt: An XML Query Language for Heterogeneous Data Sources. In: Proceedings of 3rd International Workshop WebDB. Lecture Notes in Computer Science Vol 1997. Dallas (2000) 1–25
4. Fankhauser, P.: XQuery Formal Semantics: State and Challenges. SIGMOD Record. **3** (2001) 14–19
5. Robie, J., Lapp, J., Schach, D.: XML Query Language (XQL). `http://www.w3.org/TandS/QL/QL98/cfp` (1998)
6. Cark, J., DeRose, S.: XMP Path Language (XPath). Technical Report REC-xpath-19991116, W3C (1999)
7. Abiteboul, S., Quass, D., McHugh, J., Widom, J., Wiener, J.: The Lorel Query Language for Semistructured Data. Int'l J. Digital Libraries. **1** (1997) 68–88
8. Lu, H., Wang, G., Yu, G., Bao, Y., Lv, J., Yu, Y.: Xbase: Making your gigabyte disk queriable. In Proceedings of the 2002 ACM SIGMOD Conference. ACM Press. Madison, Wisconsin (2002) 630–630
9. Cattel, R.G.G, Barry, D., Berler, M., et al.: The object data standard: ODMG 3.0. Morgan Kaufmann (2000)
10. Rahm, E., Bohme, T.: XMach-1: A Multi-User Benchmark for XML Data Management, In: Proceedings of 1st VLDB Workshop on Efficiency and Effectiveness of XML Tools, and Techniques. Lecture Notes in Computer Science Vol 2590. Springer-Verlag, Berlin Heidelberg. Hong Kong, China (2002) 35–46
11. Schmidt, A., Waas, M., Kersten, M.L., Carey, M.J., Manolescu, I., Busse, R.: XMark: A Benchmark for XML Data Management. In: Proceedings of 28th VLDB Conference. Morgan Kaufmann. Hong Kong, China (2002) 974–985
12. Jiang, H., Lu, H., Wang, W., Yu, J.X.: Path Materialization Revisited: An Efficient Storage Model for XML Data. In: Proceedings of Thirteenth Australasian Database Conference. Australian Computer Society Inc. Melbourne, Victoria (2002)

An Adaptive Document Version Management Scheme

Boualem Benatallah[1], Mehregan Mahdavi[1], Phuong Nguyen[1], Quan Z. Sheng[1], Lionel Port[1], and Bill McIver[2]

[1] School of Computer Science and Engineering
The University of New South Wales
Sydney, NSW 2052, Australia
[2] School of Information Science and Policy
University at Albany, State University of New York
Albany, New York 12222, USA
{boualem,mehrm,ntp,qsheng,lionelp}@cse.unsw.edu.au, mciver@albany.edu

Abstract. This paper addresses the design and implementation of an adaptive document version management scheme. Existing schemes typically assume: (i) *a priori* expectations for how versions will be manipulated and (ii) *fixed* priorities between storage space usage and average access time. They are not appropriate for all possible applications. We introduce the concept of document version pertinence levels in order to select the best scheme for given requirements (e.g., access patterns, trade–offs between access time and storage space). Pertinence levels can be considered as heuristics to dynamically select the appropriate scheme to improve the effectiveness of version management. We present a testbed for evaluating XML version management schemes.

1 Introduction

In several applications (e.g., digital government applications) there is a need for processing an increasing amount of data usually formatted using mark-up languages such as HTML and XML. In these applications, the issue of document content evolution is very important. For example, during a legislative mark-up process (i.e, the process of creating bills that will be proposed as laws), an initial document (i.e, the draft bill) is presented [1]. Legislators then begin a process of suggesting changes to the document, which ultimately voted out or are reconciled in a final document (i.e, the final bill).

1.1 Background

The work described in this paper focuses on the issue of managing multiple versions in document management systems such as file systems, HTML, and XML repositories. A variety of version management schemes has been developed for various data models including object, XML, HTML, text document models [2, 3,4,5,6,7,8,9,10,11,12,13,14,15,16,17]. Indeed, some these schemes can be used to

J. Eder and M. Missikoff (Eds.): CAiSE 2003, LNCS 2681, pp. 46–62, 2003.

manage versions in different document representation models. However, existing schemes typically assume: (i) *a priori* expectations for how versions will be manipulated and (ii) *fixed* priorities between storage space usage and average access time. Consider the following schemes as examples [18,17,2]:

- **Scheme 1 - Store last version and backward deltas:** In this scheme, only the most recent version is stored. In order to be able to generate other versions, backward deltas (i.e, changes from a version to the previous one) are stored. The generation of recent versions is rather efficient (e.g., access to the last version is immediate). However, this scheme is not appropriate for applications which require access to historical information (i.e, temporal queries).
- **Scheme 2 - Store all versions:** In its simplest form, this scheme stores all versions. Thus, this solution is appropriate for applications which require access to historical information. The main drawback of this scheme is storage overhead. In addition, extra processing is needed to generate deltas which makes this solution inappropriate for change queries.

Clearly, a fixed scheme is unlikely to be appropriate for requirements (e.g., access to multiple versions may not necessarily follow predictable patterns, priorities between storage space usage and average access time may vary) of all possible applications. For example, once a legislative process has been completed, historical search may be performed across different versions of bills, by academics and citizens alike. Access to bills and versions thereof may be highly unpredictable. Some bills may have greater social significance or be more controversial than others. In addition, researchers may engage in different types of analyses across versions. The co–existence of all these situations in this type of document management system calls for an adaptive versioning scheme.

1.2 Contributions

In this paper, we propose an adaptive document version management scheme, which supports different version management schemes. Our work aims at providing a unified framework that can be used to combine several document versioning schemes. More precisely, the salient features of our approach are:

- A version is *stored* only if its existence is justified on performance, information–loss avoiding, or trade–offs between access time and storage space grounds, for example. Otherwise, it is generated on–demand. We refer to the latter as a *calculated version*. For example, a version may be kept as a stored version when it is intensively requested. However, when it is rarely requested, it may be kept as a calculated version. Furthermore, our approach features the deletion of old versions that are no longer useful.
- To decide if a version is to be stored, calculated, or deleted, we introduce the concept of document version pertinence levels. A version may be *pertinent*, *relevant*, or *obsolete*. Intuitively, the pertinence level of a version is a means to characterise the importance of the availability of a version in the history of a document with regard to application needs [8]. A version is:

  - pertinent if its availability is deemed highly important (e.g., intensively requested). Maintaining such a version as a stored version may, e.g., help increasing access performance.
  - relevant if its availability is not deemed highly important, but its existence is still necessary (e.g., rarely requested). Maintaining such a version as a calculated version may not have, e.g., any major negative impact on the overall access performance.
  - obsolete if its availability is deemed useless (e.g., no longer needed by applications, not expected to be requested in the future). The deletion of an obsolete version may, e.g., help improving performance and reducing the volume of a document history.

  This classification is based on a number of criteria, including past user access patterns, storage space and processing time trade–offs.
- We propose a technique that continuously adjusts the history of a document to match the intensively requested versions. We show that transformations of a document history over time, result in offering better alternatives of its content. Our approach helps in reducing the volume of a document history by enabling deletion of obsolete versions and replacement of stored versions by calculated versions when their status changes from pertinent to relevant. We give experimental results which demonstrate the effectiveness of the proposed technique.

The remainder of this paper is organised as follows. Section 2 presents the adaptive document versioning scheme. Section 3 discusses the refreshing of a document history. Implementation and evaluation issues are discussed in Sect. 4. Section 5 gives some conclusions.

2 Adaptive Document Versioning Scheme

The adaptability of our approach lies in the following features. Firstly, the history of a document is continuously adjusted to provide an effective versioning scheme based on criteria such as estimation of future usage of versions. Secondly, our approach allows explicit tuning of: (i) the used criteria and (ii) how such criteria contribute to the selection of a given versioning scheme.

We propose the concept of *pertinence agent* to facilitate the adaptability of a versioning scheme. The role of this agent is to continually gather and evaluate information about versions and recommend changes to a document history. A pertinence agent is an extensible object that can be attached to a document[1]. It contains operational knowledge such as number of versions, number of times a version is requested, size of versions, and change control policies related to the document history (e.g., a pertinence agent can be programmed to periodically refresh versions). It also provides operations for refreshing a document history (e.g., deleting versions, generating new versions).

[1] Note that a pertinence agent can be attached to several documents (e.g., documents of an XML repository).

A pertinence agent is extensible in the sense that it is possible to change its operational knowledge, e.g., tuning certain parameters in order to provide applications with ability to dynamically adjust the version management scheme to their precise needs. The remainder of this section is organized as follows. Section 2.1 presents the document version model used in our approach. Section 2.2 discusses the usage of the pertinence agent to determine version pertinence levels.

2.1 Basic Concepts and Definitions

In this section, we present the version model used in our approach. In this model, a document is associated to the set of its versions. This set can be regarded as the physical representation of the document itself. At the system level, a document is represented by a pair `(d,vers)`, where `d` is the document identifier (e.g., name) and `vers` is the set of its versions. A version is identified by a pair `(d,num)`, where `d` is the identifier of the document and `num` is the number that the system associates to the version, at its creation time. We use the notation $v_i(d)$ to denote the ith version (i.e, version number i) of the document d. We designate the latest version of a document as the *current version*. A *historical version* of a document is any of its versions which is not the current version.

As we already mentioned before, our approach differentiates between stored and calculated versions. A calculated version is generated on–demand. To generate a calculated version $v_i(d)$, a sequence of change operations is applied to stored version $v_j(d)$, called the *generation root* of $v_i(d)$. In Section 4, we will discuss how to determine a generation root. A version is represented by a tuple:

$$(v_i(d), i, status, p_i(d))$$

where *status* can be either "`stored`" or "`calculated`". $p_i(d)$ is a pointer by which the content of the version can be obtained. In particular, if *status* is "`stored`" then $p_i(d)$ refers to the document associated to $v_i(d)$. Otherwise, $p_i(d)$ refers to a sequence of change operations which allows to generate the version $v_i(d)$ from its generation root.

In order to generate a version from another one, we maintain changes between versions. We use the term *delta* to refer to the sequence of changes between two versions of a document. It should be noted that our versioning model does not target a specific model such as XML or HTML. Instead, it uses concepts that are common in any document model.

Below, we introduce some notations that will be used in the remainder of the paper. We denote by:

- $A(t,d)$ the set of version numbers i such that $v_i(d)$ is accessible at time t,

$$A(t,d) = \{i : v_i(d) \text{ is accessible at time } t\}$$

- $D(t,d,i,j)$ the distance between $v_i(d)$ and $v_j(d)$ at time t,

$$D(t,d,i,j) = \begin{cases} \#\{l : l \in A_t(d), i < l \leq j\} & \text{if } i < j \\ \#\{l : l \in A_t(d), i > l \geq j\} & \text{if } i \geq j \end{cases}$$

- $L(t, d, i)$ the distance between $v_i(d)$ and its generation root at time t.
- $Z(t, d)$ the average of the distance between a calculated version and its generation root at time t (taken over all existing calculated versions).
- $N(t, d, i)$ the number of accesses to $v_i(d)$ at time t since the last refreshing.
- $S_c(t, d)$ the average size of calculated versions of document d at time t. If none of the versions is calculated at time t, a default value is assigned to $S_c(t, d)$. Since maintaining a calculated version requires 2 deltas, the size of a calculated version is approximated using the size of deltas associated with it.
- $S(d, i)$ the size of $v_i(d)$.
- $S_s(t, d)$ the average size of stored versions of document d at time t.

2.2 Pertinence Criteria

As mentioned before, the pertinence level of a version is determined based on a number of criteria including user access patterns, storage space and processing time trade–offs. Based on these criteria, the pertinence agent uses a scoring function to determine the pertinence levels. $Score(t, d, i)$ is a number between 0 and 1 that represents the score given by the pertinence agent to $v_i(d)$ at time t. Higher value of $Score(t, d, i)$ means that $v_i(d)$ is more likely to be pertinent. The pertinence agent sorts versions according to their scores. A version is classified obsolete if its score is less than certain threshold τ. The top p % ($0 \leq p \leq 100$) of non–obsolete versions are classified pertinent. The remaining versions are classified relevant. p is a pre–defined parameter (e.g., set by an administrator). For some applications, it may not be practical to delete any existing version. To avoid deleting versions, τ should be set to a negative number (e.g., -1). Calculation of the scores is based on the following parameters: *storage space saving* and *average access time saving*.

Storage Space Saving. Since a version $v_i(d)$ can be maintained as either stored or calculated version, the storage space saving is measured as the difference between the storage space requirement of these two possibilities, i.e, $S(d, i) - S_c(t, d)$. Let $\delta_S(t, d, i)$ be the difference between $S(d, i)$ and $S_c(t, d)$ (i.e, $\delta_S(t, d, i) = S(d, i) - S_c(t, d)$). The scoring function associated with storage space saving parameter is defined as follows:

$$Score_S(t, d, i) = \begin{cases} 1 & : \text{ if } \delta_S(t, d, i) < 0 \\ k_S/(k_S + \delta_S(t, d, i)) & : \text{ otherwise} \end{cases}$$

$Score_S(t, d, i)$ represents the score given to the storage space saving of maintaining $v_i(d)$ as a stored version at time t. If it takes less space to maintain $v_i(d)$ as a stored version than as a calculated version, then $Score_S(t, d, i)$ is 1, otherwise $Score_S(t, d, i)$ takes a value between 0 and 1. The higher $\delta_S(t, d, i)$ is, the lower is $Score_S(t, d, i)$, and the more likely is $v_i(d)$ going to be kept as a calculated version. k_S is a positive constant that is used to scale the measurement unit of the storage space (e.g., if space is measured in K-bytes, k_S can be 1, but if space is measured in bytes, then k_S should be 1000).

Total Average Access Time Saving. The scoring function associated with this parameter takes into account both *version popularity* and *version extraction time.*

Version Popularity. User interest in a version $v_i(d)$ is reflected by the number of accesses to it since the last refreshing time. Higher number of accesses to $v_i(d)$ implies higher popularity of this version.

If $v_i(d)$ is an old version (i.e., created before last refreshing), its popularity may be measured by $N_t(d, i)$, i.e., the number of accesses to it since last refreshing time. On the other hand, since a new version is created after last refreshing time (i.e., it is created after we started recording number of accesses to versions), the number of accesses to a new version $v_i(d)$ is "scaled up" to $\nu N(t, d, i)/(D(t, d, i, n) + 1)$ where n is the version number of the current version. Here, ν is called the *youth factor* which is used to account for the possible low number of accesses to younger versions (e.g., there may be only few accesses to recently created versions). Choosing an appropriate value of the youth factor depends on the number of new versions. More specifically, the value of ν should be greater than or equal to the number of new versions.

For example, assume that: (i) there are 20 new versions at each refreshing time, (ii) the average number of accesses to the 10 most heavily accessed old versions is 10000, and (iii) $\frac{1}{20}\sum_{v_i(d)}$ is new $\frac{N(t,d,i)}{D(t,d,i)+1} = 200$.

Let's assume that the new versions should be as popular as the 10 most heavily accessed old versions (i.e., the average number of accesses to new versions is equals to the average number of accesses to the 10 most heavily accessed old versions), then ν can be set to $10000/200 = 50$.

The number of accesses to a version $v_i(d)$ since the last refreshing time is computed using the following function:

$$M(t, d, i) = \begin{cases} N(t, d, i) & : \text{ if } v_i(d) \text{ is an old version} \\ \nu N(t, d, i)/(D(t, d, i, n) + 1) & : \text{ otherwise} \end{cases}$$

A straightforward way to compute the popularity of a version $v_i(d)$ is to use the function $M(t, d, i)$. A potential limitation of this approach is that versions are considered in isolation (i.e., the popularity of versions is computed independently of each other). However, if we consider the history as a whole, it may be beneficial, e.g., to maintain a $v_k(d)$ as a calculated if the version $v_{k-1}(d)$ is maintained as a stored version. affect the decision of whether or not to keep $v_k(d)$ as a stored version. Thus, it is important to consider correlation between versions when computing the popularity metric. For instance, if $v_{k-1}(d)$ is the generation root of $v_k(d)$, then accessing $v_k(d)$ requires accessing $v_{k-1}(d)$ first. The correlation between these two versions can be reflected in their popularity. Clearly, the effect of correlation between versions decreases as distance between them increases. Based on the above discussion, the popularity $P(t, d, i)$ of $v_i(d)$, at time t, can be approximated using the following function:

$$P(t, d, i) = M(t, d, i) + \sum_{j \in A(t,d), j \neq i} \frac{\mu M(t, d, j)}{(D(t, d, i, j) + 1)^2}$$

We measure the contribution of correlation between $v_i(d)$ and $v_j(d)$ to the popularity of $v_i(d)$ at time t using:

$$\frac{\mu M(t,d,j)}{(D(t,d,i,j)+1)^2}$$

The predetermined constant μ is called the *correlation factor* ($\mu \geq 0$). Here the expression $\mu/(D(t,d,i,j)+1)^2$ represents the effect of distance between versions on their correlation. Normally, storing the XML document of $v_i(d)$ has more effect on the pertinence level of $v_j(d)$ if $v_j(d)$ is closer to $v_i(d)$ (i.e., $D(t,d,i,j)$ is small). If $\mu = 0$ there is no effect of correlation between versions on their popularity. The higher μ is, the higher is the effect of correlation between versions on their popularity.

Version Extraction Time. Suppose that $v_i(d)$ is to be kept as a stored version, then the processing time for extracting it is proportional to its size:

$$T(d,i) = \lambda_1 S(d,i)$$

Here λ_1 is a constant called *direct access factor*, which accounts for costs such as CPU processing time and disk access. On the other hand, if $v_i(d)$ is to be maintained as a calculated version, then its XML document needs to be generated on–demand. Recall from Section 2.1 that this is done by applying the change operations specified in the deltas to the generation root of $v_i(d)$. Therefore, the processing time to extract $v_i(d)$ at time t is approximated using the following function:

$$T_c(t,d) = \lambda_2 Z(t,d) S_c(t,d) + \lambda_1 S_s(t,d)$$

where $\lambda_2 Z(t,d) S_c(t,d)$ is the approximated time for obtaining the deltas and applying the change operations on them, and $\lambda_1 S_s(t,d)$ is the approximation of access time to the root of generation.

Here λ_2 is a constant called *indirect access factor*, which accounts for costs such as CPU processing time and disk access as well as the time required for applying change operations. λ_1 and λ_2 should not be seen as tuning parameters. Their values depend only on the characteristics of the computing environment (e.g., CPU speed, memory size).

As pointed out before, the scoring function associated with the total average access time saving parameter incorporates both version popularity and extraction time. Let $\delta_T(t,d,i)$ be the difference between $T_c(t,d)$ and $T(d,i)$ (i.e, $\delta_T(t,d,i) = T_c(t,d) - T(d,i)$). The scoring function associated with the total average access time saving is defined as follows:

$$Score_T(t,d,i) = \begin{cases} 0 & : \text{ if } \delta_T(t,d,i) < 0 \\ P(t,d,i)\delta_T(t,d,i)/(k_T + P(t,d,i)\delta_T(t,d,i)) & : \text{ otherwise} \end{cases}$$

$Score_T(t,d,i)$ returns a score measuring the contribution of the average access time parameter in the decision of whether to keep $v_i(d)$ as a stored version. The higher the value of $Score_T(t, d, i)$ is, the more likely $v_i(d)$ is to be kept as a stored version. If it takes less time to access $v_i(d)$ as a calculated version than as a stored version, then $Score_T(t, d, i)$ is 0, otherwise $Score_T(t, d, i)$ takes a value between 0 and 1. The higher $P(t, d, i)\delta_T(t, d, i)$ is, the higher is $Score_T(t, d, i)$. k_T is a positive constant that is used to scale the measurement unit of access time.

Combined Weighted Score. The decision function $Score(t, d, i)$ combines the scores of storage space saving and total average access time saving. It can be tuned to capture trade–offs between space and access time. This is done by assigning weights to the importance of storage space saving and average access time saving. The combined score of a version $v_i(d)$ is computed as follows:

$$Score(t, d, i) = \lambda Score_S(t, d, i) + (1 - \lambda) Score_T(t, d, i)$$

where $\lambda \in [0, 1]$ is a the weight assigned to the importance of storage space saving and $1 - \lambda$ is the weight assigned to the importance of average access time saving.

3 Document History Refreshing

In this section, we present the algorithm that adapts the history of a document. During the refreshing: (i) a previously pertinent version may become relevant or obsolete, and (ii) a previously relevant version may become obsolete or pertinent.

In the adaptation process, the system needs to determine which of the versions need to be:

- Deleted, i.e, obsolete versions.
- Converted from stored versions to calculated versions, i.e, versions whose status changes from pertinent to relevant.
- Converted from calculated versions to stored versions, i.e, versions whose status changes from relevant to pertinent.

In the remainder of this section, we will consider the adaptation of a sequence of versions $v_k(d), \ldots, v_n(d)$. First, we introduce the basic operations used to convert or delete versions. We then present the history refreshing algorithm.

3.1 History Refreshing Operations

Some refreshing operations involve composing deltas. Before formally introducing these operations, we briefly discuss the composition of deltas[2]. The advantage of composing deltas is that: given $\Delta_{i,j}(d)$ and $\Delta_{j,l}(d)$, it is possible to generate $\Delta_{i,l}(d)$ without accessing any version of d.

[2] Note that the focus of this paper is not on composing deltas. We mention this aspect here for completeness

We will use the following notations. We denote by $\otimes$ the composition of deltas (i.e., $\Delta_{i,l}(d) = \Delta_{i,j}(d) \otimes \Delta_{j,l}(d)$), c_c the average time for processing the composition, c_g the average time for generating a version $v_j(d)$ from $v_i(d)$ and $\Delta_{i,j}(d)$, and c_d the average time for obtaining the changes between two versions (i.e., getting $\Delta_{i,j}(d)$ from $v_i(d)$ and $v_j(d)$).

Recall that $D(t,d,i,j)$ represents the distance between $v_i(d)$ and $v_j(d)$. If some versions between $v_i(d)$ and $v_j(d)$ have been deleted, then $D(t,d,i,j) < |j-i|$. For clarity, in the following discussion we assume that numbers associated to available versions (i.e, identifiers of versions) are always consecutive natural numbers. This can be achieved by a temporary renumbering of versions $v_k(d), \ldots, v_n(d)$.

Conversion from Calculated to Stored Version. Suppose that, the status of $v_i(d)$ changes from relevant to pertinent. In this situation, $v_i(d)$ needs to be converted to a stored version. As we already mentioned in Section 2.1, the generation of a stored version requires the identification of its generation root. The generation root of $v_i(d)$ is its nearest stored version $v_j(d)$. In case $v_i(d)$ has two nearest stored versions, the youngest one is selected.

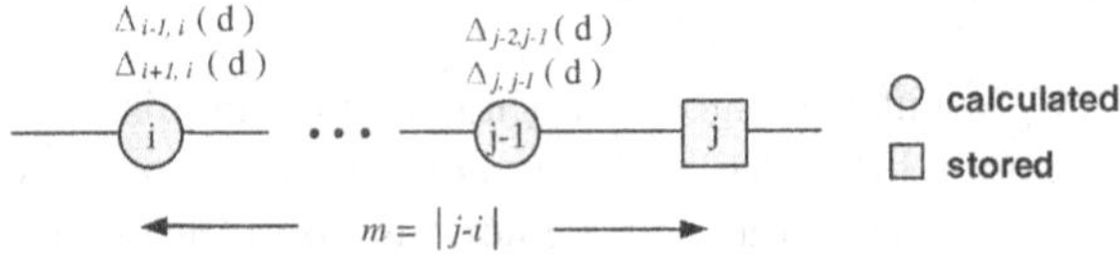

Fig. 1. Generating $v_i(d)$

$v_i(d)$ is generated by applying $\Delta_{j,i}(d)$ to $v_j(d)$. We use composition of deltas to get $\Delta_{j,i}(d)$:

$$\Delta_{j,j-2}(d) = \Delta_{j,j-1}(d) \otimes \Delta_{j-1,j-2}(d)$$
$$\Delta_{j,j-3}(d) = \Delta_{j,j-2}(d) \otimes \Delta_{j-2,j-3}(d)$$
$$\ldots$$
$$\Delta_{j,i}(d) = \Delta_{j,i+1}(d) \otimes \Delta_{i+1,i}(d)$$

It should be noted that the deltas $\Delta_{j,l}(d)$ $(i \leq l < j-1)$ are discarded after $v_i(d)$ has been generated. Let $m = L(t,d,i) - 1$, then the time needed to generate the stored version is $mc_c + c_g$.

Conversion from Stored to Calculated Version. Suppose that the status of $v_i(d)$ changes from pertinent to relevant. In this situation, $v_i(d)$ needs to be converted to a calculated version. Before the conversion, $p_i(d)$ refers to the XML document of $v_i(d)$. After the conversion, $p_i(d)$ should refer to $\Delta_{i-1,i}(d)$ and

$\Delta_{i+1,i}(d)$. Thus, it is necessary to generate $\Delta_{i-1,i}(d)$ and $\Delta_{i+1,i}(d)$. In order to do this, we need to get $v_{i-1}(d)$ and $v_{i+1}(d)$).

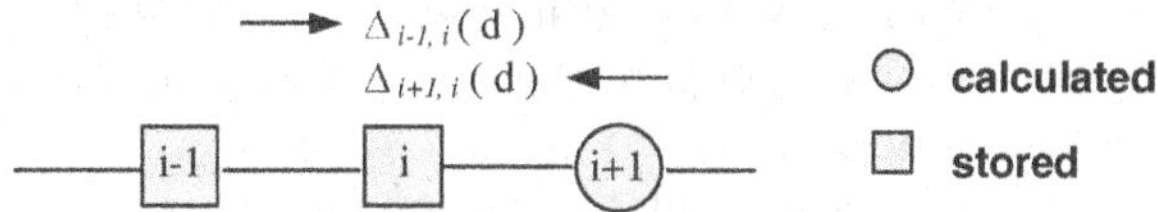

Fig. 2. Converting $v_i(d)$ into a calculated version

Suppose that among the versions $v_{i-1}(d)$ and $v_{i+1}(d)$, s versions are stored where $s \in \{0, 1, 2\}$. The average processing time for generating $v_{i-1}(d)$ and $v_{i+1}(d)$ is $(2-s)c_g$. The average processing time of the conversion is $(2-s)c_g+2c_d$.

Deletion of Versions. A version can be deleted when it becomes obsolete. This section discusses the deletion of a number of consecutive versions $v_i(d), \ldots, v_j(d)$ $(k \leq i \leq j \leq n)$.

If $v_{i-1}(d)$ and $v_{j+1}(d)$ are stored versions, then the deletion is simply done by removing $v_i(d), \ldots, v_j(d)$. However, if either $v_{i-1}(d)$ or $v_{j+1}(d)$ is a calculated version, then the situation becomes more complex. The following cases need to be considered:

Case 1. $v_{i-1}(d)$ is a stored version, $v_{j+1}(d)$ is a calculated version (Fig. 3)

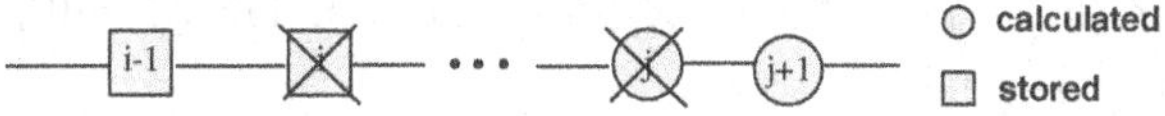

Fig. 3. Deleting $v_i(d), \ldots, v_j(d)$ (case 1)

Before the deletion, $p_{j+1}(d)$ refers to $\Delta_{j,j+1}(d)$ and $\Delta_{j+2,j+1}(d)$. After the deletion, $p_{j+1}(d)$ should refer to $\Delta_{i-1,j+1}(d)$ and $\Delta_{j+2,j+1}(d)$. Thus $\Delta_{i-1,j+1}(d)$ needs to be generated. There are two possible alternative strategies.

A first strategy is to generate $v_{j+1}(d)$ and $\Delta_{i-1,j+1}(d)$. The generation of $v_{j+1}(d)$ is done as discussed above. The generation processing time is $mc_c + c_g$, where $m = L(t, d, j+1) - 1$. The overall deletion average processing time is $mc_c + c_g + c_d$. Here we have $L(t, d, j+1) \leq 2 + D(t, d, i, j)$ and thus $m \leq D(t, d, i, j) + 1$.

A second strategy is to generate $\Delta_{i-1,j+1}(d)$ from other deltas, i.e.,

$$\Delta_{i-1,i+1}(d) = \Delta_{i-1,i}(d) \otimes \Delta_{i,i+1}(d)$$
$$\ldots$$
$$\Delta_{i-1,j+1}(d) = \Delta_{i-1,j}(d) \otimes \Delta_{j,j+1}(d)$$

The average processing time of the compositions in this strategy is $(D(t, d, i, j) + 1)c_c$. However, if not all of the deltas $\Delta_{i-1,i}(d), \ldots, \Delta_{j-1,j}(d)$ are available (i.e., some of $v_i(d), \ldots, v_j(d)$ are stored versions), then the generation of these deltas requires additional processing.

In the algorithm which is presented in Section 4.2, there is a preprocessing phase where we estimate and compare the costs of the two strategies, and then select the most efficient one.

The case where $v_{i-1}(d)$ is a calculated version and $v_{j+1}(d)$ is a stored version, is handled similarly.

Case 2. $v_{i-1}(d)$ and $v_{j+1}(d)$ are both calculated versions (Fig. 4).

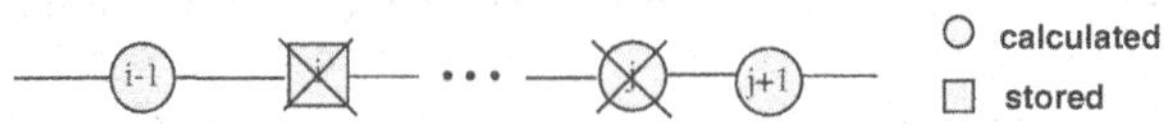

Fig. 4. Deleting $v_i(d), \ldots, v_j(d)$ (case 2)

Before the deletion, $p_{j+1}(d)$ refers to $\Delta_{j,j+1}(d)$ and $\Delta_{j+2,j+1}(d)$, while $p_{i-1}(d)$ refers to $\Delta_{i-2,i-1}(d)$ and $\Delta_{i,i-1}(d)$. After the deletion, $p_{j+1}(d)$ should refer to $\Delta_{i-1,j+1}(d)$ and $\Delta_{j+2,j+1}(d)$, while $p_{i-1}(d)$ should refer to $\Delta_{i-2,i-1}(d)$ and $\Delta_{j+1,i-1}(d)$. Thus $\Delta_{i-1,j+1}(d)$ and $\Delta_{j+1,i-1}(d)$ need to be generated.

Similar to case 1, this case can be handled using two different strategies. A first strategy is to generate $v_{i-1}(d)$, $v_{j+1}(d)$, $\Delta_{i-1,j+1}(d)$, and $\Delta_{j+1,i-1}(d)$. The average processing time of generating $v_{i-1}(d)$ and $v_{j+1}(d)$ is $(m_1 + m_2)c_c + 2c_g$ (where $m_1 = Z_t(d, i-1) - 1, m_2 = Z_t(d, j+1) - 1$). The overall processing time is $(m_1 + m_2)c_c + 2c_g + 2c_d$.

A second strategy is to compose $\Delta_{i-1,j+1}(d)$ using $\Delta_{i-1,i}(d), \ldots, \Delta_{j,j+1}(d)$ and $\Delta_{j+1,i-1}(d)$ using $\Delta_{j+1,j}(d)$,
$\ldots, \Delta_{i,i-1}(d)$. In this strategy, the overall processing time is $2(D_t(d, i, j) + 1)c_c$. However, similarly to the second strategy in case 1, if $\Delta_{i-1,i}(d), \ldots, \Delta_{j-1,j}(d)$ and $\Delta_{j+1,j}(d), \ldots, \Delta_{i+1,i}(d)$ are not available, the generation of these deltas requires additional processing. The most efficient strategy is selected at the preprocessing phase of the refreshing algorithm.

3.2 Refreshing Technique

This section describes the history refreshing algorithm. In this algorithm, operations for converting calculated versions to stored versions are scheduled in order to avoid repetition in generating deltas. For example, suppose that $v_i(d)$ and $v_l(d)$ are calculated versions which need to be converted to stored versions, and which have the same root of generation $v_j(d)$. Suppose also that: (i) $v_l(d)$ is located between $v_i(d)$ and $v_j(d)$ (i.e., either $i < l < j$ or $i > l > j$) and (ii)

$D(t, d, l, j) < D(t, d, l, i)$ (i.e, $v_j(d)$ is closer to $v_l(d)$ than $v_i(d)$). In this situation, $v_l(d)$ is converted before $v_i(d)$ in order to avoid repetition in composing deltas.

The detailed description of the algorithm is given in [18]. We summarise here the different phases of the algorithm, namely, *preprocessing*, *generation of versions*, and *history update*.

- **Preprocessing**: This phase consists of three main steps. In the first step, pertinence levels of versions are determined. In the second step, for each deletion, a strategy is selected based on the cost analysis discussed in 2. In the third step, the versions which need to be generated are identified. A sorted linked list, called L, is created. This list contains pairs (i, j), where $v_i(d)$ is a version which needs to be generated and $v_j(d)$ is the generation root of $v_i(d)$. L is sorted by $L(t, d, i)$ (i.e., $D(t, d, i, j)$).
- **Generation of versions:** In this phase, versions identified in the previous phase are generated. In order to optimise the processing cost, the version $v_i(d)$ which has the smallest value of $L(t, d, i)$ is generated first. In other words, the algorithm avoids repetition in generating the deltas. Thus, the algorithm minimises the overall generation processing time as well as the storage space.
- **History update:** In this last phase, pertinent versions which were relevant (before the refreshing) are stored, obsolete versions are deleted, and relevant versions which were pertinent (before the refreshing) are converted to calculated versions.

It can be seen that following this algorithm, all the documents which needed to be generated are identified in the first phase and generated in the second phase. After that, they are updated in the last phase. The processing time for the generation of documents is minimized by always generating the documents with smallest distance to its generation root first. This is because the processing time for generating the document of a calculated version $v_i(d)$ is $mc_c + c_g$, where $m = L(t, d, i) - 1$ and $L(t, d, i)$ is the distance from $v_i(d)$ to its root of generation.

4 Experiments and Analysis

In order to evaluate the performance of different XML version management schemes, we built a simulation testbed. In this section, we first present the architecture and implementation of the testbed. Then, we present the experimental results for evaluating the performance of different schemes.

4.1 Testbed Architecture

Figure 5 shows the generic architecture of the testbed. This testbed consists of the following components: *Simulator*, *VersionGenerator*, *RequestGenerator*, and *StrategySimulator*. The `Simulator` is used to initialise the experimental environment using configuration information (e.g., p, λ, μ, ν). The `VersionGenerator`

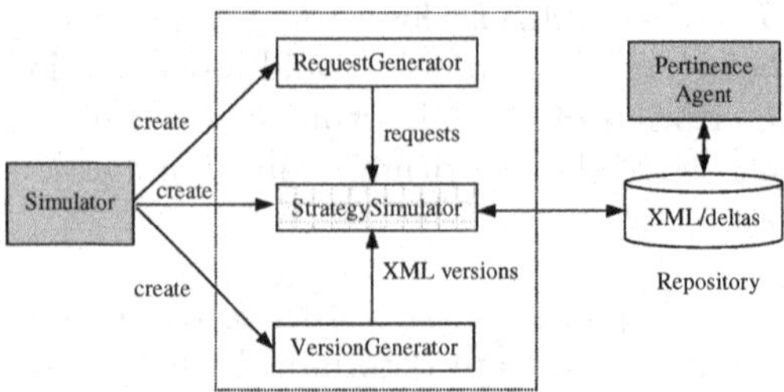

Fig. 5. Architecture of the testbed

acts as an XML document change simulator. Document versions are generated by randomly applying `deleteNode`, `updateText` and `insertElement` operations on each node of the XML document[3]. The `RequestGenerator` periodically generates requests (i.e., retrieving specific XML versions) based on a specific user's access pattern. Currently, the testbed supports three access patterns: (a) *recent* access in which younger versions (i.e., most recent versions) are intensively requested; (b) *early* access in which older versions are intensively requested; and (b) *uniform* access in which user's access does not depend on the age of versions. The `StrategySimulator` is used to either insert a new version or retrieve an existing version to/from the repository according to a versioning scheme. Currently, three versioning schemes are supported: *Store All Versions* (SAV for short), *Store Last Version And Backward Deltas* (SLVBD for short) and the *Adaptive Scheme* (AS for short). AS is the scheme proposed in this paper.

All the components of the testbed have been implemented in Java 2. In the current implementation, a PostgreSQL 7.1 database server is used as XML repository. For each scheme, versions are stored in separate tables as `text` fields in PostgreSQL tables. Each table has specific attributes to maintain version-specific meta–data. For example, in the adaptive scheme, these attributes include status, previous access frequency, etc. Document-specific meta–data is stored in another table. For example, in the adaptive scheme, these attributes include youth factor, correlation factor, etc. The storage of deltas is dealt with in the same way as stored versions because deltas are maintained as XML documents.

4.2 Experiments and Discussions

In this section, we first compare different strategies, namely SAV, SLVBD and AS. Then we show the effect of varying the refreshing interval on the performance of AS. A PC with Pentium III processor and Windows NT 4.0 operating system has been used to run the testbed.

Storage Space vs. Access Time. In the first experiment, we study the effect of changing the value of p on the average access time and storage space usage

[3] Taxonomy of XML change operations can be, e.g., found in [17,19,18]

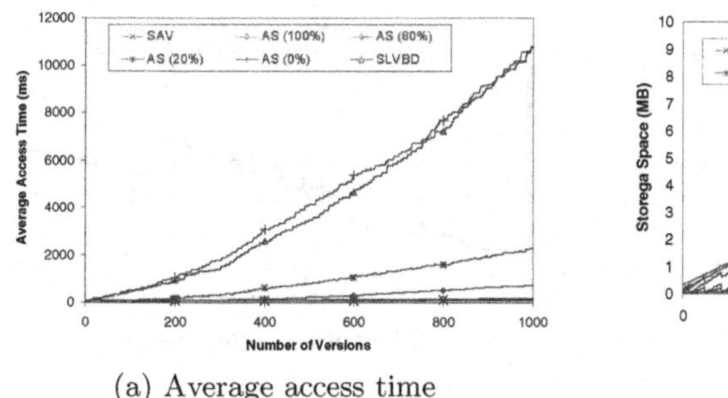

(a) Average access time

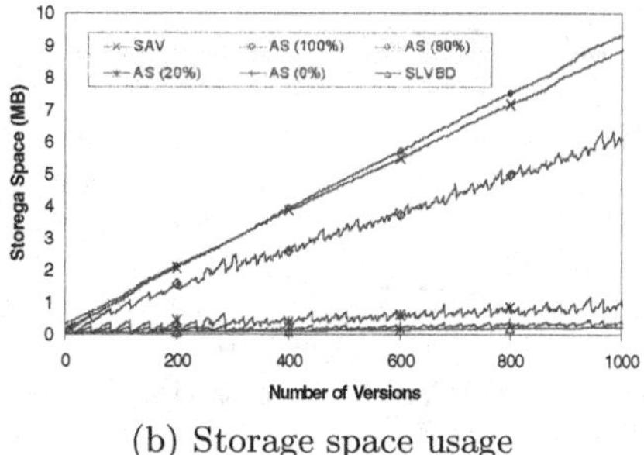

(b) Storage space usage

Fig. 6. Tuning AS using p

of AS. We use SAV (time optimal) and SLVBD (space optimal) as baselines for comparison. We use the following experimental settings:

- An average size of 80 K-bytes for versions
- An average size of 2 K-bytes for deltas
- A uniform access pattern on the history of versions
- λ is set to 0.5. ν is set to 50 (the average number of accesses to new versions is equal to the average number of accesses to the 10 most heavily accessed old versions, as in the example of section 3.4.2). μ is set to 1.

Figure 6(a) shows the average access time for the three schemes. We can see that SAV has the smallest average access time which remains almost constant (i.e., around 100 ms) even when the number of available versions increases. When p is equal to 100, the average access time for AS is close to those of SAV. The difference is due to the additional computation costs in AS (e.g., updating the meta–data). The average access time in SLVBD increases dramatically as the number of versions increases. When p is equal to 0, the access time results for AS are closer to those of SLVBD. When maintaining 20% of versions as stored versions (i.e., $p = 20$), the average access time decreases by a factor of 4.7. By maintaining more versions as stored versions, e.g., p equal to 80, the average access time is reduced.

Similarly, Fig. 6(b) shows the storage space usage. We can see that SLVBD has the least storage space usage. By choosing p equal to 0, the storage space usage of AS is slightly higher than SLVBD. This is due to the fact that more meta–data is stored in AS. It can also be seen that SAV consumes more space than the other schemes. When p is equal to 100, storage space usage results of AS are closer to those of SAV.

In the second experiment, we study the effect of changing the value of λ. We use the same settings as in the previous experiment except that p is set to 50 and λ varies. Figure 7(a) shows the resulting average access times. It confirms that small values of λ result in less access time. Similarly, Fig. 7(b) confirms that large values of λ result in less storage space usage.

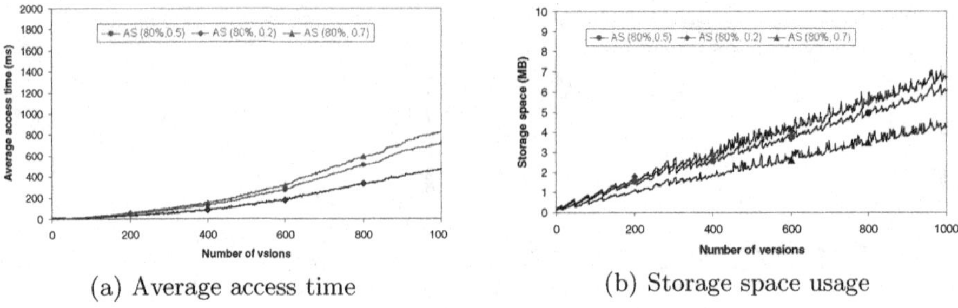

(a) Average access time

(b) Storage space usage

Fig. 7. Fine–tuning AS using λ

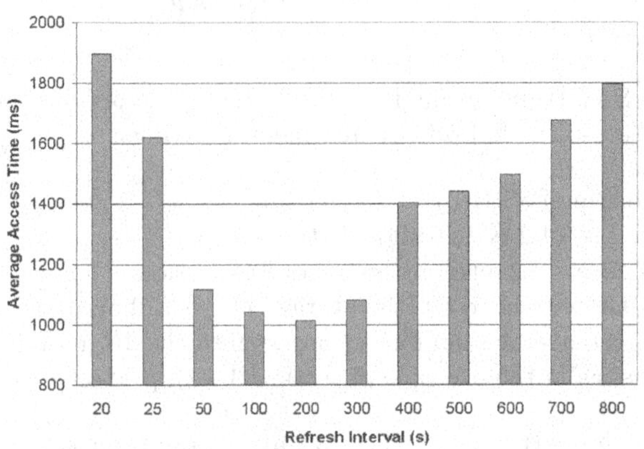

Fig. 8. Varying refreshing interval

Effect of Varying Refreshing Interval. This experiment studies the effect of changing the value of the refreshing interval on performance of AS. We use the same settings as the previous experiments except that $p = 20$ and $\lambda = 0.5$. The results are shown in Fig. 8. We can see that the length of the refreshing interval can significantly affect the average access time. When the interval value is too small, there is a performance degradation because the system does not have sufficient time to gather realistic information about usage patterns (e.g., number of accesses). On the other hand, when the interval value is too large, there is a performance penalty because changes in access patterns are not dealt with immediately. For example, an old version may remain calculated for a long time even if it should have been transformed into a stored version because of changes in its access patterns.

5 Conclusions

In summary, we have proposed an adaptive technique for continuously adjusting and improving the effectiveness of a versioning scheme taking into account both performance and storage space requirements. We also conducted simulation experiments to gauge the behaviour of few schemes. The comparison results show clear indications of the potential of the adaptive scheme. They show the viability of the adaptive scheme in depicting the behaviour of an effective versioning scheme for given requirements (e.g., access patterns, trade–offs between access time and storage space).

References

1. Bach, S.: The Committee Markup Process in the House of Representatives. `http://www.house.gov/rules/crs_reports.htm` (1999)
2. Chien, S.Y., Tsotras, V.J., Zaniolo, C.: Efficient Management of Multiversion Documents by Object Referencing. In: Proc. of 27th Int. Conf. on Very Large Data Bases (VLDB), Rome, Italy (2001)
3. Chien, S.Y., Tsotras, V.J., Zaniolo, C.: XML Document Versioning. SIGMOD Record **30** (2001) 46–53
4. Sommerville, I., Rodden, T., Rayson, P., Kirby, A., Dix, A.: Supporting information evolution on the WWW. World Wide Web **1** (1998) 45–54
5. Douglis, F., Ball, T.: Tracking and Viewing Changes on the Web. In: Proc. of the 1996 USENEX Technical Conference, Berkekey, CA (1996) 165–176
6. Vitali, F., Durand, D.G.: Using Versioning to Support Collaboration on the WWW. World Wide Web Journal (1995)
7. Benatallah, B.: A Unified Framework for Supporting Dynamic Schema Evolution in Object Databases. In: 18th Int. Conf. on Conceptual Modeling - ER'99, Paris, France, Springer-Verlag (LNCS series) (1999)
8. Benatallah, B., Tari, Z.: Dealing with Version Pertinence to Design an Efficient Object Database Schema Evolution Mechanism. In: The IEEE Int. Database Engineering and Applications Symposium – IDEAS, Cardiff, Wales, (UK) (1998)
9. Ra, Y., Rundensteiner, E.: A Transparent Object-Oriented Schema Change Approach Using View Evolution. Technical Report CSE-TR-211-94, Dept. of EECS, Univ. of Michigan (1994)
10. Monk, S., Sommerville, I.: Schema Evolution in OODBs Using Class Versioning. SIGMOD RECORD **22** (1993)
11. Ferrandina, F., Meyer, T., Zicari, R.: Schema and Database Evolution in the O2 system. In: Proc. of 21th Int. Conf. on Very Large Data Bases (VLDB), Zurich (1995)
12. Tichy, W.F.: RCS - A System for Version Control. Software Practice and Exprience **15** (1985) 637–654
13. Rochkind, M.J.: The Source Code Control System. IEEE Transactions on Software Engineering **1** (1975) 255–265
14. Chien, S.Y., Tsotras, V.J., Zaniolo, C.: Copy-Based versus Edit-Based Version Management Schemes for Structured Documents. In: RIDE-DM'2001, Heidelberg, Germany (2001)
15. Chawathe, S.S., Abiteboul, S., Widom, J.: Representing and Querying Changes in Semistructured Data. In: Proc. of Int. Conf. on Data Engineering (ICDE). (1998) 4–13
16. Chien, S.Y., Tsotras, V.J., Zaniolo, C.: Version Management of XML Documents. In: WebDB (Informal Proceedings). (2000) 75–80

17. Marian, A., Abiteboul, S., Cobena, G., Mignet, L.: Change-Centric Management of Versions in an XML Warehouse. In: Proc. of 27th Int. Conf. on Very Large Data Bases (VLDB). (2001) 581–590
18. Port, L.: Managing Changes in XML Documents and DTDs. Honour's thesis, Computer Science and Engineering, The University of New South Wales, Australia (2001)
19. Tatarinov, I., Ives, Z.G., Halvey, A.Y.: Updating XML. In: SIGMOD Conference. (2001)

Integrating Security and Systems Engineering: Towards the Modelling of Secure Information Systems

Haralambos Mouratidis[1], Paolo Giorgini[2], and Gordon Manson[1]

[1]Department of Computer Science, University of Sheffield, England
{h.mouratidis, g.manson}@dcs.shef.ac.uk
[2]Department of Information and Communication Technology,
University of Trento, Italy
paolo.giorgini@dit.unit.it

Abstract. Security is a crucial issue for information systems. Traditionally, security is considered after the definition of the system. However, this approach often leads to problems, which translate into security vulnerabilities. From the viewpoint of the traditional security paradigm, it should be possible to eliminate such problems through better integration of security and systems engineering. This paper argues for the need to develop a methodology that considers security as an integral part of the whole system development process. The paper contributes to the current state of the art by proposing an approach that considers security concerns as an integral part of the entire system development process and by relating this approach with existing work. The different stages of the approach are described with the aid of a case study; a health and social care information system.

1 Introduction

Information systems (IS) become more and more critical in every aspect of human society from the health sector to military. As the use of Information Systems arises, the demand to secure those systems also arises. This is true since many information systems contain private data that must be available only to authorised viewers. Take as an example a health and social care information system containing health data of different individuals. Security in such a system, as in any health and social care information system, is very important since security breaches might result in medical history to be revealed, and revealing a medical history could have serious consequences for particular individuals.

Software Engineering considers security as a non-functional requirement [1]. Non-functional requirements introduce quality characteristics, but they also represent constraints under which the system must operate [2,3]. Although software designers have been recognized the need to integrate most of the non-functional requirements, such as reliability and performance, into the software development processes [4] security still remains an afterthought.

Thus the usual approach towards the inclusion of security within a system is to identify security requirements after the definition of a system. However, considering security as an afterthought often leads to problems [7], since security mechanisms

J. Eder and M. Missikoff (Eds.): CAiSE 2003, LNCS 2681, pp. 63–78, 2003.

have to be fitted into a pre-existing design, therefore leading to serious design challenges that usually translate into software vulnerabilities [8].

There are at least two reasons for the lack of support for security engineering [5]. Firstly security requirements are generally difficult to analyse and model. A major problem in analysing non-functional requirements is that there is a need to separate functional and non-functional requirements yet, at the same time, individual non-functional requirements may relate to one or more functional requirements. If the non-functional requirements are stated separately from the functional requirements, it is sometimes difficult to see the correspondence between them. If stated with the functional requirements, it may be difficult to separate functional and non-functional considerations. Secondly developers lack expertise for secure software development. Many developers, who are not security specialists, must develop systems that require security features. Without an appropriate methodology to guide those developers on the development processes, it is likely that they will fail to produce effective solutions [6].

We believe that security should be considered during the whole development process and it should be defined together with the requirements specification. By considering security only in certain stages of the development process, more likely, security needs will conflict with functional requirements of the system. Taking security into account along with the functional requirements throughout the development stages helps to limit the cases of conflict, by identifying them very early in the system development, and find ways to overcome them. On the other hand, adding security as an afterthought not only increases the chances of such a conflict to exist, but it requires huge amount of money and valuable time to overcome it, once they have been identified (usually a major rebuild of the system is needed).

However, current methodologies for IS development do not meet the needs for resolving the security related IS problems [9], and fail to provide evidence of integrating successfully security concerns throughout the whole range of the development process.

In this paper we present an approach that integrates security and systems engineering, using the same concepts and notations, throughout the entire system development process. This work falls within the context of the Tropos methodology [10] in which security requirements are considered as an integral part of the whole development process.

The paper is structured as follows. Section 2 provides an introduction to the Tropos methodology describing briefly the methodology stages and its concepts, while Section 3 describes a health and social care information system that is used as a case study throughout the paper. Section 4 illustrates how our approach integrates security and systems engineering within the Tropos development process and Section 5 relates our work to the literature by providing an overview of related work. Finally, Section 6 concludes the paper.

2 Tropos Methodology

Tropos is a development methodology tailored to describe both the organisational environment of a system and the system itself. Tropos is characterised by three key aspects [11]. Firstly, it deals with all the phases of system requirements analysis and system design and implementation[1] adopting a uniform and homogeneous way. Secondly, Tropos pays great deal of attention to the early requirements analysis that precedes the specification of the perspective requirements, emphasizing the need to understand the how and why the intended system would meet the organisational goals. This allows for a more refined analysis of the system dependencies, leading to a better treatment not only of the system functional requirements but also of its non-functional requirements, such as security, reliability, and performance [11]. Thirdly, Tropos is based on the idea of building a model of the system that is incrementally refined and extended from a conceptual level to executable artefacts, by means of a sequence of transformational steps [12].

Tropos adopts the *i** modelling framework [13], which uses the concepts of actors, goals, tasks, resources and social dependencies for defining the obligations of actors (dependees) to other actors (dependers). Actors have strategic goals and intentions within the system or the organisation and represent (social) agents (organisational, human or software), roles or positions (represent a set of roles). A goal represents the strategic interests of an actor. In Tropos we differentiate between hard (only goals hereafter) and soft goals. The latter having no clear definition or criteria for deciding whether they are satisfied or not [13]. A task represents a way of doing something. Thus, for example a task can be executed in order to satisfy a goal. A resource represents a physical or an informational entity while a dependency between two actors indicates that one actor depends on another to accomplish a goal, execute a task, or deliver a resource. Figure 1 shows the graphical representation of the above-mentioned concepts.

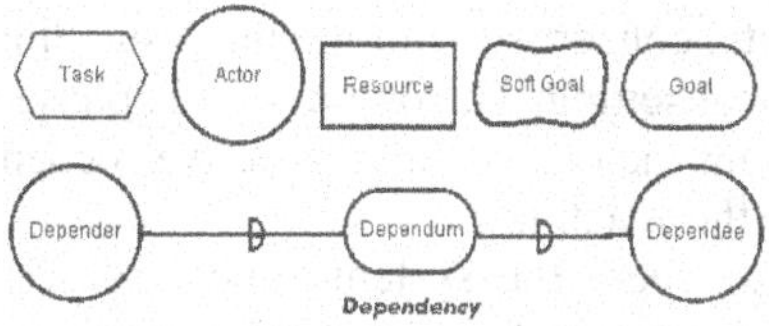

Fig. 1. Graphical Representation of Tropos Concepts

Although Tropos was not conceived with security on mind, a set of security concepts, such as *security constraint*, *secure entities* and *secure dependencies* have been proposed [14] to enable it to consider security aspects throughout the whole development process. A *security constraint* is defined as a constraint that is related to the security of the system, while *secure entities* represent any secure goals/tasks/resources of the system. *Secure goals* are introduced to the system to help in the achievement of a *security constraint*. A *secure goal* does not particularly define how the *security constraint* can be achieved, since (as in the definition of goal, see [13]) alternatives can be considered. However, this is possible through a *secure task*, since a task specifies a way of doing something [13]. Thus, a *secure task* represents a particular way for satisfying a *secure goal*. For example, for the secure goal *Authorise Access,* we might have secure tasks such as *Check Password* or *Check Digital*

[1] In this paper we do not consider the implementation stage. Readers interested in this stage can refer to [10].

Signatures. A resource that is related to a *secure entity* or a *security constraint* is considered a *secure resource*. For example, an actor depends on another actor to receive some information and this dependency (resource dependency) is restricted by a constraint *Only Encrypted Info*.

A *secure dependency [14]* introduces *security constraint*(s), proposed either by the depender or the dependee in order to successfully satisfy the dependency. For example a *Doctor* (depender) depends on a *Patient* (dependee) to obtain *Health Information* (dependum). However, the *Patient* imposes a *security constraint* to the *Doctor* to share *health information only if consent is obtained*. Both the depender and the dependee must agree in this constraint (or constraints) for the secure dependency to be valid. That means, in the depender side, the depender expects from the dependee to satisfy the *security constraints* while in the dependee side, a secure dependency means that the dependee will make an effort to deliver the dependum by satisfying the *security constraint*(s). The above-mentioned security concepts are illustrated in Figure 2.

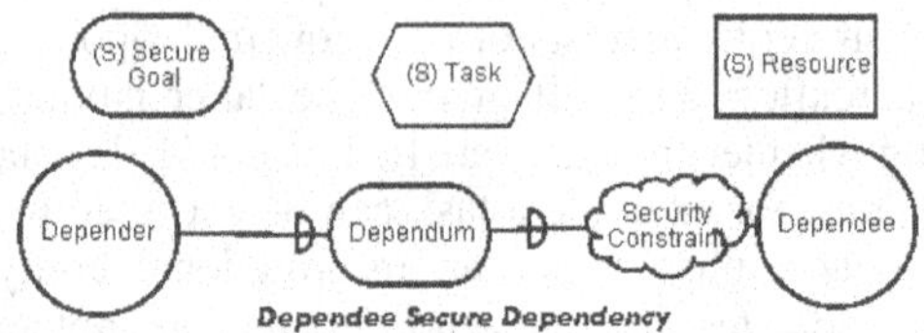

Fig. 2. Graphical Representation of the Security Concepts

Tropos covers four main software development phases:

Early Requirements, concerned with the understanding of a problem by studying an existing organisational setting. The output of this phase is an organisational model, which includes relevant actors, their respective dependencies and the security constraints imposed to those actors.

Late requirements, where the system-to-be is described within its operational environment, along with relevant functions and security requirements; this description models the system as a (small) number of actors, which have a number of dependencies and security constraints. These dependencies define the system's functional requirements, while the security constraints define the system's security requirements.

Architectural design, where the system's global architecture is defined in terms of subsystems, interconnected through data and control flows. Within the framework, subsystems are represented as actors and data/control interconnections are represented as (system) actor dependencies. In addition, during this stage, different architectural styles are analysed taking into account security and other non-functional requirements of the system and secure capabilities are identified and assigned to the different actors of the system to satisfy the secure entities.

Detailed design, where each architectural component is defined in further detail in terms of inputs, outputs, control, and the security aspects analysed in the previous stages. For this stage, *Tropos* is using elements of UML [15] to complement the features of *i**.

3 Case Study

This section introduces the case study that will be used in the rest of this paper to describe the security analysis process throughout the different stages of the Tropos methodology.

We consider the electronic Single Assessment Process (eSAP) system [16], an integrated health and social care information system for the effective care of older people. Security in the eSAP is an important concern, since security breaches of such system might result in personal and health information to be revealed and this could lead to serious consequences.

It must be noticed that, in our example, many functionalities of the system are omitted, since our aim is not to explore the complexity of the system, but rather to demonstrate how the Tropos methodology integrates security and systems engineering.

Throughout our case study, the security policy principles identified in [7] are used. In addition, some more principles are added: (1) System Authorisation, only authorised professionals and patients can access the system; (2) Access Control, each Care Plan shall be marked with an access control list naming the people or groups who may read it and append data to it. The system should prevent anyone not on the list from accessing the record in any way; (3) Care Plan Opening, a professional may open a care plan with themselves and the older person on the access control list. When an older person has been referred, the professional might open a record with themselves, the older person, and the referring professional on the access control list; (4) Control, only one of the professionals (most likely the professional responsible for the older person) may alter the control list, and add other professionals; (5) Information Flow, information derived from care plan A may be appended to care plan B if and only if B's Access control list is contained in A's; (6) Availability, the information must be available whenever a person included in the access control list requires any information.

4 The Development Process

4.1 Early Requirements

During the early requirements stage, the goals, dependencies and the security constraints between the stakeholders (actors) are modeled with the aid of an actors' diagram [11]. Such a diagram involves different actors, represented as nodes, and dependencies, represented as links, between the different actors that indicate that one depends on the other to accomplish some goals and also that some security constraints must be satisfied for the dependencies to be valid.

For the eSAP case study, we consider the following actors (Figure 3)

- *Professional*: the health and/or social care professional;
- *Older Person*: the Older Person (patient) that wishes to receive appropriate health and social care;
- *DoH*: the English Department of Health;

- *R&D Agency*: a Research and Development Agency interested in obtaining medical information;
- *Benefits Agency*: an agency that helps the older person financially.

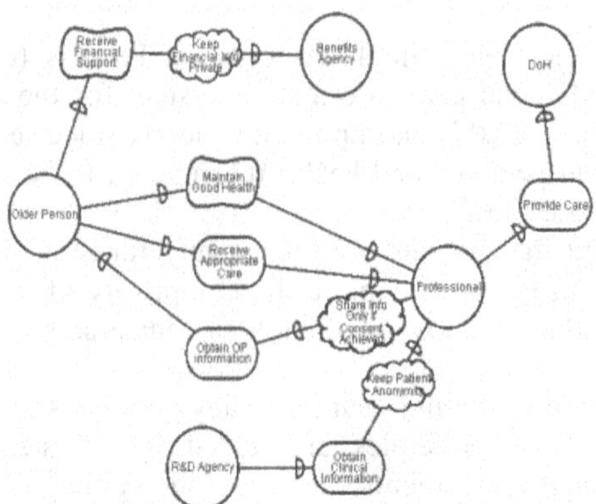

Fig. 3. Actors Diagram

The main goal for the *Older Person* actor is to *Maintain Good Health*[2] and a secondary goal is to *Receive Appropriate Care.* Since the *Older Person* cannot guarantee either of those goals alone, they depend on the *Professional* to help them satisfy them. In addition, the *Older Person* depends on the *Benefits Agency* to *Receive Financial Support.* However, the *Older Person* worries about the privacy of their finances so they impose a constraint to the *Benefits Agency* actor, to keep their financial information private. The *Professional* depends on the *Older Person* to *Obtain (Older Person) OP Information.* However one of the most important and delicate matters for the older person is the privacy of their personal medical information, and the sharing of it. Thus, most of the times, the Professional is imposed a constraint to *share this information if and only if consent is obtained.* On the other hand, one of the main goals of the *R&D Agency* is to *Obtain Clinical Information* in order to perform tests and research. To get this information the *R&D Agency* depends on the *Professional.* However, the *Professional* is imposed a constraint (by the *Department of Health*) to *Keep Patient Anonymity.*

When the stakeholders, their goals, the dependencies between them, and the security constraints have been identified, the next step of this phase is to analyse in more depth each actor's goals and the *security constraints* imposed to them. In addition, *secure entities* are introduced to help towards the satisfaction of the imposed *security constraints.* In this example, due to lack of space, we focus only in the analysis of the *security constraints,* and not in the goal or task analysis of each individual actor.

The analysis of the *security constraints* starts by identifying which goals of the actor they restrict. The assignment of a *security constraint* to a goal is indicated using a *constraint link* (a link that has the "restricts" tag). In addition, different alternatives

[2] It is captured as a soft goal since we cannot precisely define what "good health" means for different individuals.

can be considered for achieving the goals and the *security goals* of the stakeholders. For example, during the previous step (Figure 3), the *Professional* actor has been imposed two *security constraints* (*Share Info Only If Consent Achieved* and *Keep Patient Anonymity*). By analyzing the *Professional* actor (Figure 4) we have identified the *Share Medical Info* goal. However, this goal is restricted by the *Share Info Only If Consent Obtained* constraint imposed to the *Professional* by the *Older Person*. For the *Professional* to satisfy the constraint, a *secure goal* is introduced *Obtain Older Person Consent*. However, this goal can be achieved with many different ways, for example a *Professional* can *obtain the consent personally* or can *ask a nurse* to obtain the consent on their behalf. Thus a sub-constraint is introduced, *Only Obtain Consent Personally*. This sub constraint introduces another *secure goal Personally Obtain Consent*. This goal is divided into two sub-tasks *Obtain Consent by Mail* or *Obtain Consent by Phone*. The *Professional* has also a goal to *Provide Medical Information for Research*. However, the constraint *Keep Patient Anonymity* has been imposed to the *Professional*, which restricts the *Provide Medical Information for Research* goal. As a result of this constraint a *secure goal* is introduced to the *Professional*, *Provide Only anonymous Info*.

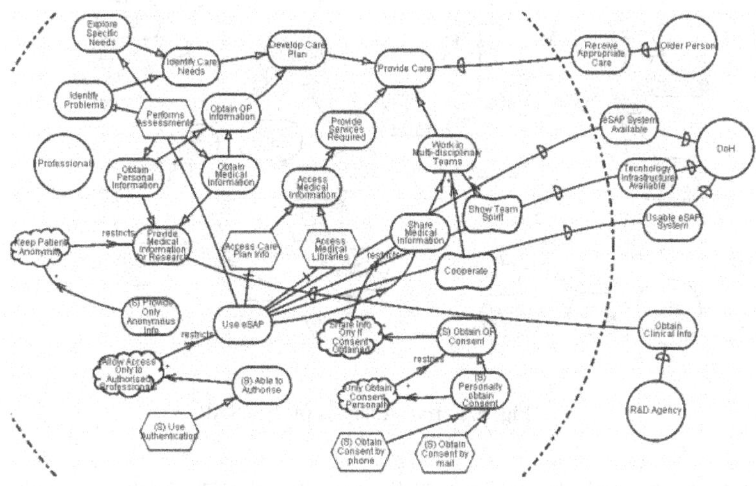

Fig. 4. Partial Analysis of the Professional Actor

4.2 Late Requirements

In the late requirements stage, the functional, security, and other non-functional requirements for the system-to-be are described. The system-to-be is introduced as one or more actors who have a number of dependencies with the other actors of the organization (defined during the early requirements stage) and it (the system) contributes to the goals of the stakeholders.

In our case study, one of the main aims of the *Department of Health* is to allow older people to get more involved in their care and also help professionals provide more efficient care. For this reason, the *Department of Health* depends on the *electronic Single Assessment Process* (eSAP) system to automate care. Thus, the eSAP system is introduced as another actor and it is analysed using the same concepts used for the analysis of the other actors.

Figure 5 shows a partial analysis of the *eSAP* System. To automate care the *eSAP* system must provide services. This goal can be decomposed into two different goals, *Provide Services to Professionals* and *Provide Services to Older People.* Both those sub-goals must be achieved for the top goal to be achieved. In addition, each of those goals can be decomposed to a number of alternative tasks. For example, the *Provide Services to Professionals* goal can be alternatively fulfilled by tasks *Assist Schedule Meetings*, *Assist with Assessment Procedures*, or *Assist with Care Plan Management.*

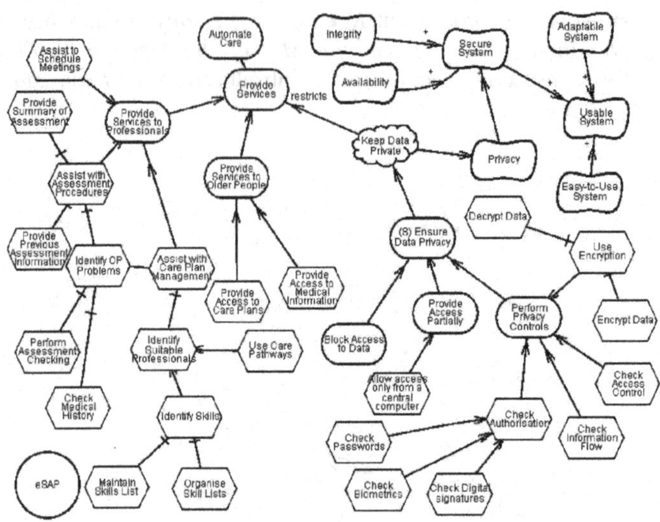

Fig. 5. Partial Analysis of the eSAP

In addition, to satisfy the security of the system, different *security constraints* are imposed to the system (according to the security policy defined in the previous section). In our case study, due to lack of space, we only consider the *Keep Data Private* security constraint that is imposed in order to contribute towards the privacy of the system. To satisfy this constraint, a secure goal *Ensure Data Privacy* is introduced to the system. This goal can be achieved either through the sub-goal *Block Access to Data* that blocks any access to the system (obviously not desirable); or provide access partially, which allows access only from a central computer; or perform privacy controls. The latter sub goal is fulfilled by the tasks *Use Encryption*, *Check Access Control*, *Check Information Flow*, and *Check Authorisation.* Each of those tasks can be achieved by considering different alternatives. For example, in order to *check authorisation* different alternatives can be considered such as *check passwords*, *check biometrics* or *check digital signatures.* An approach to evaluate the different alternatives could be to use the measures of *complexity* and *criticality* [17].

Complexity represents the effort required from an actor for achieving a (security) task, while *criticality* represents how the (security) goals of the actor will be affected if a (security) task is not achieved. Thus, by knowing how complex and how critical the different alternatives are, we can decide which alternative is the best solution.

4.3 Architectural Design

The architectural design phase defines the system's global architecture. During architectural design the first step is to identify the overall architectural organization by selecting among alternative architectural styles[3] using as criteria the non-functional requirements of the system identified in the previous stage.

However, quality characteristics (non-functional requirements) are difficult to measure since it is difficult to get empirical evidence during the design stages. For this reason, we employ an analysis process based on an independent probabilistic model, which uses the measure of *satisfiability* proposed by Giorgini et al [18]. In our example, *satisfiability* represents the probability that the non-functional requirement will be satisfied. Thus, the evaluation results in contribution relationships from the architectural styles to the probability of satisfying the non- functional requirements of the system identified in the late requirements stage. We use a weight to express the contribution of each style to the *satisfiability* of the non-functional requirements. Weights take a value between 0 and 1. For example, 0.1 means the probability that the architectural style will satisfy the requirement is very low (the style is not suitable for satisfying the requirement), while 0.9 means the probability that the architectural style will satisfy the requirement is very high (the style is suitable for satisfying the requirement).

The analysis involves the identification of more specific non-functional requirements, by refining the ones identified during the late requirements stage, and the evaluation of different architectural styles against those requirements. It must be noticed that the refinement of the security requirements took place during the late requirements analysis with the identification of secure tasks, so from the security point of view, the alternative architectural styles are evaluated against those tasks.

The weights of the contribution links reported in Figure 6, of each architectural style to the different non-functional requirements of the system, have been assigned after reviewing different studies [19,20], evaluations [21], and comparisons [22] involving the architectural styles. We must note that Figure 6 represents a partial illustration of the comparison process. For example, from the security point of view, we only consider privacy as in the previous stages of this example development. However, when the approach is employed in a complete comparison, all the security issues must be taken into account. In addition, we have omitted, in order to keep the figure simple and easy to understand, the contributions and the conflicts amongst the different non-functional requirements. For example, although privacy contributes negative to the mobility requirement, this is not shown in the figure.

We consider two architectural styles, a hierarchical style – *client/server* – and a mobile code style *-mobile agents*. We decided to consider those two since *client/server* is the most frequently encountered of the architectural styles for

[3] To avoid confusion we must note that architectural styles differ from architectures in that " a style can be thought of as a set of constraints on an architecture" [19, p. 25]

network-based applications [21], while *mobile agents* form a growing and quite different architectural style. In *client/server* style, a node is acting as a server that represents a process that provides services to other nodes, which act as clients. The server listens for requests upon the offered services. The basic form of *client/server* does not constrain how application state is partitioned between client and server components [21]. *Client/server* architectural style is also referred to by the mechanisms used for the connector implementation such as Remote Procedure Call (RPC) [21]. RPC is appropriate for *client/server* architectural styles since the client can issue a request and wait for the server's response before continuing its own processing. On the other side, in *mobile agents* style, mobility is used in order to dynamically change the distance between the processing and source of data or destination of results. The computational component is moved to the remote site, along with its state, the code it needs and possibly some data required to perform the task [21].

As shown in Figure 6, each of the two styles satisfies differently each of the non-functional requirements of the system. For instance, the *mobile agents* style allows more scalable applications (weight 0.8), because of the dynamic deployment of the mobile code. For example, a doctor wishes to access a large number of medical information, filtered according to the content. In the (pure) *client/server* architectural style (weight 0.4), the doctor would access the server data (medical information) and all the retrieved information would be transferred to the client. Then the filtering would be performed at the doctor site. In the *mobile agents* architectural style, such a filtering can be performed in the server site, where redundant information can be identified early and thus does not have to be transferred to the client. The latter approach is more scalable since the required filtering is distributed and can be performed close to the information sources.

On the other side, *mobile agents* style offers a greater opportunity for abuse and misuse, broadening the scale of security issues significantly [23]. This is due to the fact that mobility is involved. Thus, although protection of a server from mobile agents, or generally mobile code, is an evolution of security mechanisms applied in other architectural styles, such as *client/server*; the mechanisms focused on the protection of the *mobile agents* from the server cannot, so far, prevent malicious behaviour from occurring but may be able to detect it [23]. For example, the information flow property is easier to be damaged by employing mobile agents (weight 0.4) since possible platforms that a mobile agent could visit might expose sensitive information from the agent [23]. In the case of the *client/server* style (weight 0.8) sensitive information is stored in the server and existing security measures could be taken to satisfy the information flow attribute.

When the contribution weights for each architectural style to the different non-functional requirements of the system have been assigned, the best-suited architectural style is decided. This decision involves the categorization of the non-functional requirements according to the importance to the system and the identification of the architectural style that best satisfies the most important non-functional requirement using a propagation algorithm, such as the one presented by Giorgini et al [18]. In our example, security is the number one concern for the eSAP system and thus the architectural style that satisfies most the privacy (since we only consider privacy in this example) requirements of the system is the *client/server* style

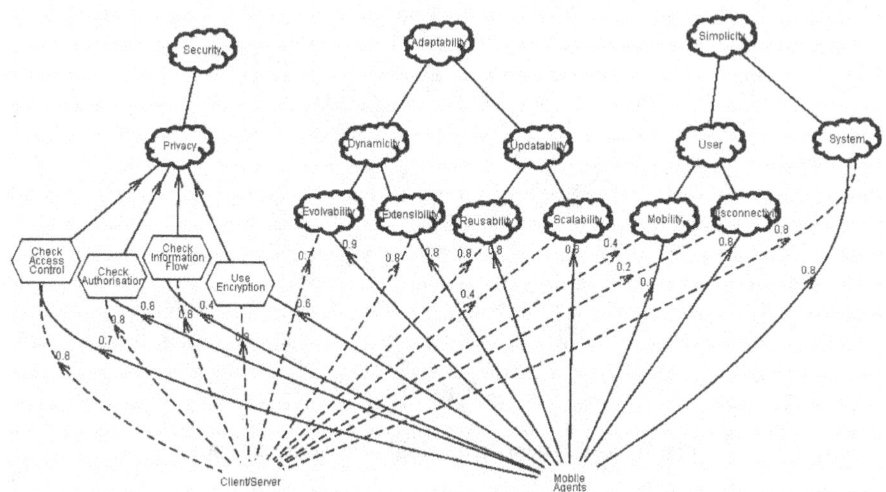

Fig. 6. Deciding for the system's architecture

(figure 6). In the case that two or more non-functional requirements are of the same importance, the presented approach can be integrated with other analysis techniques, such as the SAAM [24], to indicate which architectural style is best suited for the system-to-be.

As mentioned by Castro et al [10], an interesting decision that comes up during the architectural design is whether fulfillment of an actor's obligations will be accomplished through assistance from other actors, through delegation, or through decomposition of the actor into component actors. Thus, when various architectural styles have been evaluated, and one has been chosen, the next step of the architectural design stage involves the introduction of new actors and their dependencies, as well as the decomposition of existing actors into sub-actors and the delegation of some (security) responsibilities from the existing actors to the introduced sub-actors.

Figure 7 shows a partial decomposition of the *eSAP* system. In this example, focused on privacy, the *eSAP* system delegates responsibility for the *Ensure Data Privacy* secure goal to the *Privacy Manager*. The *Privacy Manager*, in order to efficiently fulfill the *Ensure Data Privacy* secure goal, delegates responsibility to the *Authorisation Manager* (to fulfill the *check authorisation* secure sub-goal), the *Access Control Manager* (to fulfill the *check access control* secure sub-goal), the *Information Flow Manager* (to fulfill the *check information flow* secure sub-goal) and the *Cryptography Manager* (to fulfill the *use cryptography* secure goal).

The last step of the architectural design is to identify capabilities for each of the actors by taking into account dependency relationships of the actors. A capability represents the ability of an actor of defining, choosing and executing a plan for the fulfillment of a goal, given certain world conditions and in presence of a specific event [11]. For example, the *Authorisation Manager* should have capabilities such as obtain authorisation details and provide authorisation clearance. However, the process of identifying capabilities for each actor has been extensively described in the literature [11,25] and thus it is not described here.

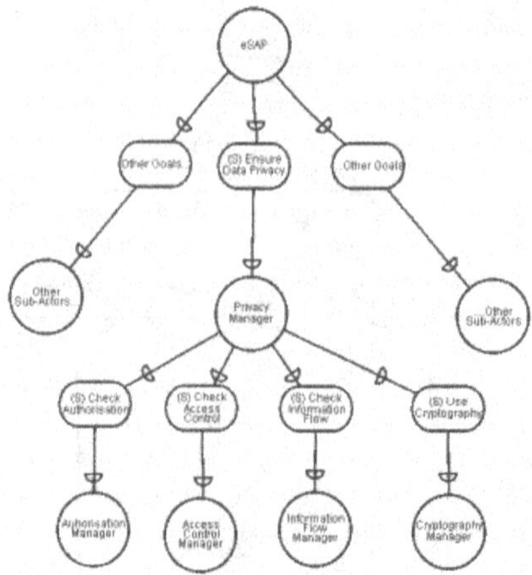

Fig. 7. eSAP system decomposition to ensure data privacy

4.4 Detailed Design

During the detailed design each component of the system, identified in the previous stages, is further specified. In Tropos the detailed design stage is based on the specifications resulted from the architectural design stage, and the reasons for a given component can be traced back to the early requirements analysis.

From the security point of view, during the detailed design the developers specify in detail the actors' capabilities and interactions taking into account the security aspects derived from the previous steps of the analysis.

For the detailed design stage, Tropos adopt a subset of UML [15] diagrams. In our example, a professional might request to view a care plan. The sequence diagram (simplified) for this request is shown in figure 8. However, it would be useful to denote under what constraints the authorisation is granted. For our example, the professional is allowed to access a care plan if and only if the professional's name is included in the care plan access table. For this purpose, we introduce security rules. These are similar to the business rules that UML has for defining constraints on the diagrams. Graphically, security rules are placed on Notes and attached to the related structure as shown in figure 8.

5 Related Work

As stated in the introduction, very little work has taken place in considering security requirements as an integral part of the whole software development process. However, literature provides some approaches towards this direction. In the current state of the art, security properties are, within the requirements engineering process, supported by a qualitative reasoning rather than a formal reasoning. Existing formal methods support the verification of a protocol, which has already been specified [26], while qualitative directions provide a process-oriented approach [1].

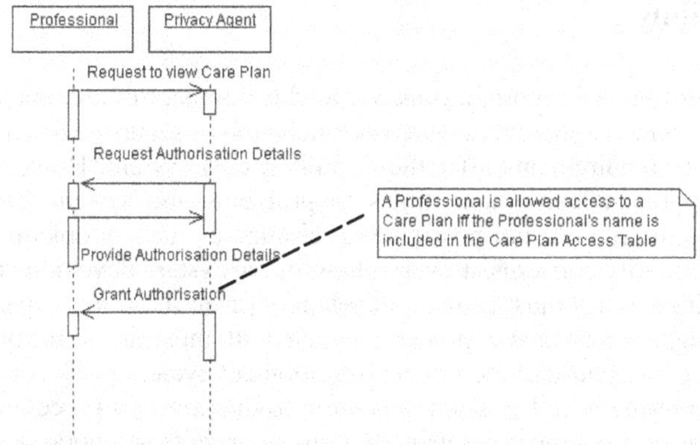

Fig. 8. Simplified sequence diagram including security rule notation

Chung applies a process-oriented approach [1] to represent security requirements as potentially conflicting or harmonious goals and using them during the development of software systems [1]. Rohrig [27], proposes an approach to re-use existing business process descriptions for the analysis of security requirements and the derivation of necessary security measures, while Liu et al [28] explore the explicit modeling of relationships among strategic actors in order to elicit, identify and analyse security requirements. The concept of obstacle is used in KAOS framework [29] to capture undesired properties of the system, and define and relate security requirements to other system requirements.

In addition, Jurgens proposes UMLsec [30], an extension of the Unified Modelling Language (UML), to include modeling of security related features, such as confidentiality and access control. Lodderstedt et al present a modeling language, based on UML, called SecureUML [31]. Their approach is focused on modeling access control policies and how these (policies) can be integrated into a model-driven software development process.

McDermott and Fox adapt use cases [6] to capture and analyse security requirements, and they call the adaption an abuse case model [6]. An abuse case is defined as a specification of a type of complete interaction between a system and one or more actors, where the results of the interaction are harmful to the system, one of the actors, or one of the stakeholders of the system [6]. Also, Guttorm and Opdahl [32] define the concept of a misuse case, the inverse of a use case, which describes a function that the system should not allow. In their approach security is considered by analysing security related misuse cases.

These above-mentioned approaches only guideline the way security can be handled within a certain stage of the software development process. Differently than them, our approach covers the whole development process. As mentioned in the introduction, it is important to consider security using the same concepts and notations during the whole development process.

6 Conclusions

Although Security is an important issue in the development of computerised systems, currently the common approach towards the inclusion of security within a system is to identify security requirements after the definition of a system. However, as pointed earlier, this approach leads many times to problems and systems full of security vulnerabilities. It should be possible to eliminate such problems through the integration of security concerns at every phase of the system development. To achieve this goal, methodologies must provide developers (even those not expert on security) guidance through a systematic process, which will integrate security and systems engineering at every phase of the system development cycle.

The main contribution of this paper is the introduction of a process that integrates security and systems engineering, using the same concepts and notations, in the entire system development process. The integrated security process in Tropos is one of analysing the security needs of the stakeholders and the system in terms of security constraints imposed to the system and the stakeholders, identify secure entities that guarantee the satisfaction of the security constraints and assign capabilities to the system to help towards the satisfaction of the secure entities. This process is characterized by five key ideas. Firstly by considering the overall software development process it is easy to identify security requirements at the early requirements stage and propagate them until the implementation stage. This introduces a security-oriented paradigm to the software engineering process. Secondly, *Tropos* allows a hierarchical approach towards security. Security is defined in different levels of complexity, which allows the software engineer a better understanding while advancing through the process. Thirdly, iteration allows the re-definition of security requirements in different levels therefore providing a better integration with system functionality. Fourthly, consideration of the organisational environment facilitates the understanding of the security needs in terms of the security policy. In addition, functional and non-functional requirements are defined together however a clear distinction is provided.

Future work includes applying our process to different case studies to refine it and also integrate our extensions to the Formal Tropos [33] specification language to enable us to formally evaluate it. The formal part of the work will also allow us to prove and check the properties of the system.

References

1. L. Chung, B. Nixon, "Dealing with Non-Functional Requirements: Three Experimental Studies of a Process-Oriented Approach", Proceedings of the 17th International Conference on Software Engineering, Seattle- USA, 1995
2. I. Sommerville, "Software Engineering", sixth edition, Addison-Wesley, 2001
3. E. Yu, L. Cysneiros, "Designing for Privacy and Other Competing Requirements", 2nd Symposium on Requirements Engineering for Information Security (SREIS' 02), Raleigh, North Carolina, 15–16 November, 2002
4. A. Dardenne, A. Van Lamsweerde, S. Fickas, "Goal-directed Requirements Acquisition. Science of Computer Programming", *Special issue on 6th Int. Workshop of Software Specification and Design*, 1991.

5. B. Lampson, "Computer Security in the real world", *Annual Computer Security Applications Conference* 2000.
6. J. McDermott, C. Fox, "Using Abuse Care Models for Security Requirements Analysis", Proceedings of the 15th Annual Computer Security Applications Conference, December 1999.
7. R. Anderson, "Security Engineering: A Guide to Building Dependable Distributed Systems", Wiley Computer Publishing, 2001
8. W. Stallings, "Cryptography and Network Security: Principles and Practice", Second Edition, Prentice-Hall 1999.
9. T. Tryfonas, E. Kiountouzis, A. Poulymenakou. "Embedding security practices in contemporary information systems development approaches", Information Management & Computer Security, Vol 9 Issue 4, 2001, pp 183–197
10. J. Castro, M. Kolp and J. Mylopoulos. "A Requirements-Driven Development Methodology," In *Proc. of the 13th Int. Conf. On Advanced Information Systems Engineering (CAiSE'01)*, Interlaken, Switzerland, June 2001.
11. A. Perini, P. Bresciani, P. Giorgini, F. Giunchiglia, J. Mylopoulos. "Towards an Agent Oriented Approach to Software Engineering. In A. Omicini and M.Viroli, editors, WOA 2001 – Dagli oggetti agli agenti: tendenze evolutive dei sistemi software, Modena-Italy, September 2001.
12. P. Bresciani and P. Giorgini. "The Tropos Analysis Process as Graph Transformation System". In Proceedings of the Workshop on Agent-oriented methodologies, at OOPSLA 2002, Seattle, WA, USA, Nov, 2002.
13. E. Yu, "Modelling Strategic Relationships for Process Reengineering", PhD thesis, Department of Computer Science, University of Toronto, Canada, 1995.
14. H. Mouratidis, P. Giorgini, G. Manson, I. Philp, "A Natural Extension of Tropos Methodology for Modelling Security", In the Proceedings of the Agent Oriented Methodologies Workshop (OOPSLA 2002), Seattle-USA, November 2002.
15. B. Bauer, J. Müller, J. Odell, "Agent UML: A Formalism for Specifying Multiagent Interaction". In *Agent-Oriented Software Engineering*, Paolo Ciancarini and Michael Wooldridge (eds), Springer, Berlin, pp. 91–103, 2001.
16. H. Mouratidis, i. Philp, G. Manson, "Analysis and Design of eSAP: An Integrated Health and Social Care Information System", in the Proceedings of the 7th International Symposium on Health Information Managements Research (ISHIMR2002), Sheffield, June 2002
17. M. Garzetti, P. Giorgini, J. Mylopoulos, F. Sannicolo, "Applying Tropos Methodology to a real case study: Complexity and Criticality Analysis", in the Proceedings of the Second Italian workshop on "WOA 2002 dagli oggetti agli agenti dall'informazione alla conoscenza", Milano, 18–19 November 2002
18. P. Giorgini, J. Mylopoulos, E. Nicchiarelli, R. Sebastiani. "Reasoning with Goal Models", in the Proceedings of the 21st International Conference on Conceptual Modeling (ER2002), Tampere, Finland, October 2002.
19. L. Bass, P. Clements, R. Kazman, "Software Architecture in Practice", SEI Series in Software Engineering, Addison – Wesley, 1998.
20. J. Bosch, "Design and Use of Software Architectures: adopting and evolving a product-line approach", ACM Press, Addison – Wesley, 2000.
21. R. T. Fielding, "Architectural Styles and the Design of Network-based Software Architectures", Doctoral dissertation, University of California, Irvine, 2000
22. A. Puliafito, S. Riccobene, M. Scarpa, ``Which paradigm should I use?: An analytical comparison of the client-server, remote evaluation and mobile agents paradigms'', *IEEE Concurrency and Computation: Practice & Experience*, vol. 13, pp. 71–94, 2001.
23. Kotz, D.; Mattern, F. (Eds.): Agent Systems, Mobile Agents, and Applications. Proceedings of the Second International Symposium on Agent Systems and Applications and Fourth International Symposium on Mobile Agents, ASA/MA 2000, pp. 57–72. LNCS 1882, Springer-Verlag, 2000

24. R. Kazman, G. Abowd, L. Bass, M. Webb, "SAAM: A Method for Analyzing the Properties of Software Architectures", Proceedings of ICSE-16, Sorrento – Italy, May, 1994.
25. H. Mouratidis, P. Giorgini, G. Manson, I.Philp, "Using Tropos Methodology to Model an Integrated Health Assessment System", Proceedings of the 4th International Bi-Conference Workshop on Agent-Oriented Information Systems (AOIS-2002), Toronto-Ontario, May 2002
26. C. Meadows, "A Model of Computation for the NRL protocol analyser", *Proceedings of the 1994 Computer Security Foundations Workshop*, 1994.
27. S. Rohrig, "Using Process Models to Analyze Health Care Security Requirements", International Conference Advances in Infrastructure for e-Business, e-Education, e-Science, and e-Medicine on the Internet, January 2002, L'Aquila, Italy
28. L. Liu, E. Yu, J. Mylopoulos, "Analysing Security Requirements as Relationships Among Strategic Actors", 2nd Symposium on Requirements Engineering for Information Security (SREIS'02). Raleigh, North Carolina, October 16, 2002.
29. Dardenne, A. van Lamsweerde, S. Fickas, "Goal-directed Requirements Acquisition. Science of Computer Programming", *Special issue on 6th Int. Workshop of Software Specification and Design*, 1991.
30. Jan Jürjens, "Towards Secure Systems Development with UMLsec", Fundamental Approaches to Software Engineering (FASE/ETAPS) 2001, International Conference, Genoa 4–6 April 2001
31. T. Lodderstedt, D. Basin, J. Doser, "SecureUML: A UML-Based Modelling Language for Model-Driven Security", in the Proceedings of the 5th International Conference on the Unified Modeling Language, 2002.
32. S. Guttorm, A. L. Opdahl, "Eliciting Security Requirements by Misuse Cases", Proceedings of TOOLS Pacific 2000, November 2000.
33. A. Fuxman, M. Pistore, J. Mylopoulos, P. Traverso, "Model Checking Early Requirements Specification in Tropos", Proceedings of the 5th Int. Symposium on Requirements Engineering, RE' 01, Toronto, Canada, August 2001

IBIS: Semantic Data Integration at Work

Andrea Calì[1], Diego Calvanese[1], Giuseppe De Giacomo[1], Maurizio Lenzerini[1], Paolo Naggar[2], and Fabio Vernacotola[2]

[1] Università di Roma "La Sapienza"
Dipartimento di Informatica e Sistemistica
via Salaria 113, I-00198 Roma, Italy
lastname@dis.uniroma1.it
[2] CM Sistemi
via N. Sauro 1, I-00195 Roma, Italy
firstname.lastname@gruppocm.it

Abstract. In this paper we present IBIS (*Internet-Based Information System*), a system for the semantic integration of heterogeneous data sources, which adopts innovative and state-of-the-art solutions to deal with all aspects of a complex data-integration environment, including query answering under integrity constraints and limitations on source access. IBIS is based on the global-as-view approach, using a relational mediated schema to query the data at the sources. Sources are wrapped so as to provide a relational view on them. A key issue is that the system allows the specification of integrity constraints (modeling constraints in the domain of interest) in the global schema. Since sources are autonomous, the extracted data in general do not satisfy the constraints. IBIS adapts and integrates the data extracted from the sources making use of the constraints in the global schema, so as to answer queries at best with the information available. IBIS deals with limitations in accessing data sources, and exploits techniques developed for querying sources with access limitations in order to retrieve the maximum set of answers. In particular, it may use integrity constraints available on the sources to improve the efficiency of the extraction process.

1 Introduction

The goal of a data integration system is to provide a uniform access to a set of heterogeneous data sources, freeing the user from the knowledge about how data are structured at the sources and how they are to be reconciled in order to answer queries. In this paper we present IBIS (*Internet-Based Information System*), a system for the semantic integration of heterogeneous data sources, studied and developed in the context of a collaboration between the University of Rome "La Sapienza" and CM Sistemi. IBIS adopts innovative and state-of-the-art solutions to deal with all aspects of a complex data integration environment, including query answering under integrity constraints, limitations on source access, and source wrapping. Despite there are several mediation systems for data integration (see e.g., [7,6,11,18,22,21,12,9,1]), IBIS is the first system that fully exploits

J. Eder and M. Missikoff (Eds.): CAiSE 2003, LNCS 2681, pp. 79–94, 2003.

all available information (including integrity constraints) for query answering. Thus, to the best of our knowledge, IBIS is the first system actually devoted to semantic data integration.

The problem of designing effective data integration systems has been addressed by several research and development projects in the last years. Data integration systems are based on a unified view of data, called *mediated or global schema*, and on a software module, called *mediator* that collects and combines data extracted from the sources, according to the structure of the mediated schema. A crucial aspect in the design and the realization of mediators is the specification of the relation between the sources and the mediated schema. Two basic approaches have been proposed in the literature, called *global-as-view* (or simply GAV) and *local-as-view* (or simply LAV) [19,10,14]. In the GAV approach, a view over the sources is associated to each element of the global schema, describing how to populate such an element using the data at the sources. Most data integration systems adopt the GAV approach, e.g., TSIMMIS [7], Garlic [6], COIN [9], *Squirrel* [23,22], and MOMIS [1].

IBIS follows the GAV approach, using a relational mediated schema to query the data at the sources. The system is able to cope with a variety of heterogeneous data sources, including data sources on the Web, relational databases, and legacy sources. Each non-relational source is wrapped to provide a relational view on it. Also, each source is considered incomplete, in the sense that its data contribute to the data integration system. A key issue is that the system allows the specification of integrity constraints (modeling constraints in the domain of interest) in the global schema. Since sources are autonomous and incomplete, the extracted data in general do not satisfy the constraints. To deal with this characteristic, IBIS adapts and integrates the data extracted from the sources making use of the constraints in the global schema, so as to answer queries at best with the information available. In this way, the intensional information in the constraints over the global schema allows one to obtain additional answers that would not be provided by the standard unfolding strategy associated with GAV data integration systems. Indeed, current GAV data integration systems, such as the above mentioned ones, answer a query posed over the global schema by unfolding each atom of the query using the corresponding view [19]. The reason why unfolding is sufficient in those systems is that the GAV mapping essentially specifies a single database conforming to the global schema. Instead, due to the presence of integrity constraints over the global schema there are several potential global databases conforming to the data in the sources, and hence query answering has to deal with a form of incomplete information [20,3,4].

A characterizing aspect of IBIS is the ability to deal with limitations in accessing data sources, and in particular Web sources, e.g., those requiring filling at least one field in a form. IBIS exploits and implements techniques developed for querying sources with binding patterns in order to retrieve the maximum set of answers [17,8,15,16]. Since the extraction process is the major bottleneck in the integration of data over the Web, specific optimization techniques have been developed. These allow one to take into account intentional knowledge holding on the sources (in particular, integrity constraints) to limit the number of source accesses.

In this paper we give an overview of IBIS, showing how the recent theoretical results on query answering and optimization have been implemented in the system. In particular, we first illustrate the data integration framework adopted in IBIS. We then describe the query processing phase. After a brief overview of the system architecture, we give some details on the data extraction techniques that have been crucial for the actual deployment of the system. Finally, we discuss the mechanisms provided by IBIS for the user interaction, and we conclude the paper.

2 Framework for Data Integration in IBIS

The formal framework of IBIS is based on the relational model with integrity constraints. As usual, a *relational schema* is constituted by a set of relation symbols, each one with an associated arity, denoting the number of its attributes, and a set of integrity constraints. Given a database $\mathcal{DB}$ and a relation symbol r, we denote with $r^{\mathcal{DB}}$ the set of tuples associated to r in $\mathcal{DB}$. In IBIS, we deal with four kinds of constraints (the notion of satisfaction is the usual one for the first three):

1. *Key constraints.* Given a relation r in the schema, a key constraint over r is expressed in the form $key(r) = \mathbf{X}$, where $\mathbf{X}$ is a set of attributes of r.
2. *Foreign key constraints.* We express a foreign key constraint in the form $r_1[\mathbf{X}] \subseteq r_2[\mathbf{Y}]$, where r_1, r_2 are relations, $\mathbf{X}$ is a sequence of distinct attributes of r_1, and $\mathbf{Y}$ is a sequence formed by the distinct attributes forming the key of r_2.
3. *Functional dependencies.* A functional dependency over a relation r has the form $r : \mathbf{A} \rightarrow \mathbf{B}$, where $\mathbf{A}$ and $\mathbf{B}$ are subsets of the set of attributes of r.
4. *Simple full-width inclusion dependencies.* A simple full-width inclusion dependency between two relations r_1 and r_2 is denoted by $r_1 \subseteq r_2$; it is satisfied in a database $\mathcal{DB}$ if $r_1^{\mathcal{DB}} \subseteq r_2^{\mathcal{DB}}$.

A data integration application in IBIS is modeled through a triple $\mathcal{I} = \langle \mathcal{G}, \mathcal{S}, \mathcal{M} \rangle$, where

- $\mathcal{G}$ is the *global schema*, expressed as a relational schema with key and foreign key constraints.
- $\mathcal{S}$ is the *source schema*, constituted by one relation for each source. The schema of each source relation is a relational schema with simple full-width inclusion dependencies and functional dependencies.
- $\mathcal{M}$ is the *mapping* between $\mathcal{G}$ and $\mathcal{S}$. The mapping is of type GAV: to each relation r in the global schema, $\mathcal{M}$ associates a query $\rho(r)$ over the source schemas. The query $\rho(r)$ is expressed in the language of union of conjunctive queries, and specifies how to retrieve the data satisfying r in terms of a view over the sources. In fact, such a query is also *annotated* by a description of

the additional processing to be carried out on the data retrieved in order not to violate the key constraint of r using a technique similar to that in [5]. That is, IBIS currently assumes that it is the responsibility of the designer to specify suitable data cleaning methods in such a way as to guarantee that the data retrieved for r satisfies its key constraint.

Finally, queries over the global schema are also unions of conjunctive queries.

In order to assign semantics to a data integration application $\mathcal{I} = \langle \mathcal{G}, \mathcal{S}, \mathcal{M} \rangle$, we start with the data at the sources, and specify which data satisfy the global schema. A *source database* $\mathcal{D}$ for $\mathcal{I}$ is a relational database constituted by one relation $r^{\mathcal{D}}$ for each source r in $\mathcal{S}$. A source database is said to be *legal* for $\mathcal{S}$ if it satisfies all the constraints in $\mathcal{S}$. A *global database* $\mathcal{B}$ for $\mathcal{I}$, or simply database for $\mathcal{I}$, is a database for $\mathcal{G}$. Given a legal source database $\mathcal{D}$ for $\mathcal{S}$, a global database $\mathcal{B}$ is said to be *legal* for $\mathcal{I}$ with respect to $\mathcal{D}$ if:

- $\mathcal{B}$ satisfies the integrity constraints of $\mathcal{G}$, and
- $\mathcal{B}$ satisfies the mapping $\mathcal{M}$, that is, for each relation r in $\mathcal{G}$, we have that the set of tuples $r^{\mathcal{B}}$ that $\mathcal{B}$ assigns to r contains the set of tuples $\rho(r)^{\mathcal{D}}$ that the query corresponding to r retrieves from the source database $\mathcal{D}$, i.e., $\rho(r)^{\mathcal{D}} \subseteq r^{\mathcal{B}}$.

Observe that the previous assertion amounts to consider any view $\rho(r)$ over $\mathcal{S}$ as *sound*, i.e., the tuples provided by $\rho(r)$ are sound but not necessarily complete. Although other assumptions are possible [14], the sound views assumption is usually considered the most natural in the context of data integration [10].

Given a data integration system $\mathcal{I} = \langle \mathcal{G}, \mathcal{S}, \mathcal{M} \rangle$ and a legal source database $\mathcal{D}$, the *semantics* of $\mathcal{I}$ is the set of global databases that are legal for $\mathcal{I}$ wrt $\mathcal{D}$. If such a set is not empty, the source database $\mathcal{D}$ is said to be *consistent* with $\mathcal{I}$.

The fact that the semantics of a data integration system needs to be defined in terms of a *set* of databases rather than a single one has a deep influence on the nature of query answering in IBIS, which indeed needs to deal with incomplete information [20]. In particular, IBIS aims at computing the *certain answers* of the query. Given a query q over the global schema of a data integration application $\mathcal{I}$, and a legal source database $\mathcal{D}$, the *certain answers* $q^{\mathcal{I},\mathcal{D}}$ of q to $\mathcal{I}$ wrt $\mathcal{D}$ are the tuples that satisfy the query in every database that belongs to the *semantics* of $\mathcal{I}$, i.e., in every global database that is legal for $\mathcal{I}$ wrt $\mathcal{D}$.

3 Query Processing

Query processing in IBIS is separated in three phases: (1) the query is *expanded* to take into account the integrity constraints in the global schema; (2) the atoms in the expanded query are *unfolded* according to their definition in terms of the mapping, obtaining a query expressed over the sources; (3) the expanded and unfolded query is *executed* over the retrieved source database, to produce the answer to the original query (see Section 5).

Query unfolding and execution are the standard steps of query processing in GAV data integration systems, while the *expansion* phase is the distinguishing feature of the IBIS query processing method. IBIS takes fully into account the integrity constraints over the global schema, which reflect the semantics of the application domain, and allows for retrieving *all* data that belong to the certain answer.

Let $\mathcal{I}$ be a data integration system and $\mathcal{D}$ a source database. In order to show how integrity constraints in the global schema are taken into account, we make use of the notion of *retrieved global database* for a query q. Such a database is obtained by populating each relation r in the global schema according to the retrieved source database $\mathcal{D}_q$ for q and the mapping, i.e., by populating r with the tuples obtained by evaluating the associated query $\rho(r)$ on $\mathcal{D}_q$. Note that, in general, integrity constraints may be violated in the retrieved global database.

Regarding key constraints, IBIS assumes, as mentioned before, that the query that the mapping associates to a global schema relation r is such that the data retrieved for r do not violate the key constraint of r. In other words, the management of key constraints is left to the designer.

On the other hand, the management of foreign key constraints cannot be left to the designer, since it is strongly related to the incompleteness of the sources. Moreover, since foreign keys are interrelation constraints, they cannot be dealt with in the GAV mapping, which, by definition, works on each global relation in isolation. Indeed, IBIS provides full support for handling foreign key constraints in an automated way.

The assumption of sound views asserts that the tuples retrieved for a relation r are a subset of the tuples that the system assigns to r; therefore, we may think of completing the retrieved global database by suitably adding tuples in order to satisfy foreign key constraints, while still conforming to the mapping. When a foreign key constraint is violated, there are several ways of adding tuples to the retrieved global database to satisfy such a constraint. In other words, in the presence of foreign key constraints in the global schema, the semantics of a data integration system must be formulated in terms of a *set* of databases, instead of a single one.

Since we are interested in the certain answers $q^{\mathcal{I},\mathcal{D}}$ to a query q, i.e., the tuples that satisfy q in all global databases that are legal for $\mathcal{I}$ wrt $\mathcal{D}$, the existence of several such databases complicates the task of query answering. To deal with this problem, IBIS expands the query q by taking into account the foreign key constraints on the global relations appearing in the atoms. The expansion technique exploits the fact that foreign key constraints can be rewritten as Datalog programs with suitable Skolem functions in the head and is based on partial evaluation of logic programs, see [3,4] for details. The expansion $exp_{\mathcal{G}}(q)$ of q is a union of conjunctive queries, and it is possible to show that the evaluation of $exp_{\mathcal{G}}(q)$ over the retrieved source database produces exactly the set of certain answers of q to $\mathcal{I}$ wrt $\mathcal{D}$ [4]. Notably, the expanded query can be exponential in the original query and the foreign key constraints, however it can still be evaluated in polynomial time in the size of the data. As the construction of the retrieved global database is computationally costly, in IBIS it is not constructed explicitly. Instead, $exp_{\mathcal{G}}(q)$ is unfolded and the unfolded query $unf_{\mathcal{M}}(exp_{\mathcal{G}}(q))$

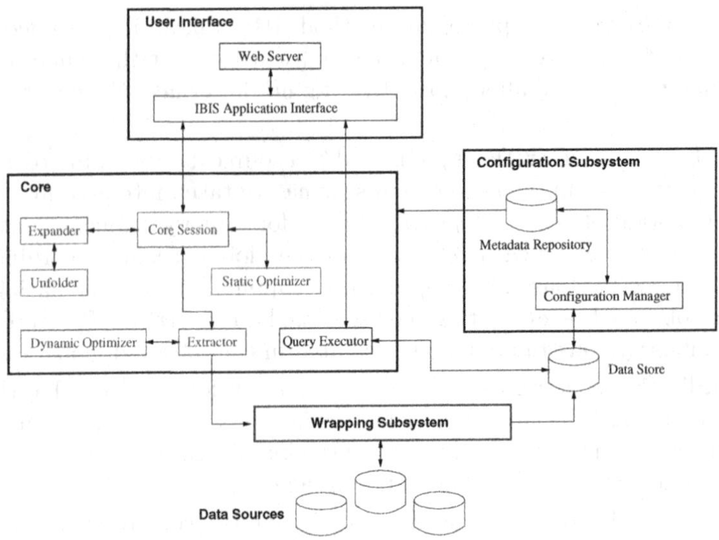

Fig. 1. Architecture of IBIS

is evaluated over the retrieved source database, whose data are extracted by an Extractor module (see next section). As shown in [4], this produces exactly the same results. Observe that in this way the query expansion is decoupled from the rest of the processing.

4 Architecture of IBIS

The system architecture of IBIS is shown in Figure 1. Four subsystems can be identified:

- the *wrapping subsystem*, which provides a uniform layer for all the data sources by presenting each source as a set of relations.
- the *configuration subsystem*, which supports system management and configuration of all the meta-data;
- the *IBIS core*, which implements the actual data integration algorithms and controls all the parts of the system;
- the *user interface*, which is divided in a Web interface and an application interface.

In addition to these subsystems, a *data store* is used to store temporary data which are used during query processing, and cached data extracted from the sources during the processing of previous queries. We detail below the wrapping subsystem and the IBIS core, which are the distinguishing elements of the IBIS architecture. The user interface and the interaction with the user are described in Section 6.

Wrapping Subsystem. The task of the wrapping subsystem is to provide a layer in which all data stored at the sources are presented to the other components of the system in a uniform way. Therefore, each component of IBIS sees the sources represented in the relational model. The wrappers in IBIS also take into account the limitations in accessing the sources; in fact, certain sources require a set of fields to be bound to constants in order to be accessed. A typical example is that of data accessible through Web forms, in which at least one field has to be filled with a value. Except for access limitations, wrappers do not need to expose any specific source behaviour. A set of properties, which can be configured by means of the configuration subsystem, allows the designer to specify the behavior of the wrapper according to source-dependent parameters such as throughput or reliability. Wrappers accept multiple requests which are buffered in a queue; thus the wrapping subsystem works asynchronously: each request is managed assigning it a wrapper taken from a pool. Several wrappers can work independently according to the capabilities of the source and of the server system.

IBIS Core. The IBIS Core is the set of components that take care at runtime of all the aspect of query processing. User queries are issued to the IBIS core by the application interface; the core performs evaluation of a query by (1) extracting data from the sources and (2) executing the query over such extracted data. *Data extraction*, which in IBIS is quite sophisticated because each source may present access limitations, is discussed in detail in Section 5. *Query processing* is performed according to the technique discussed in Section 3; an important feature is that the Expander module, which computes the expanded query, can operate independently from the Unfolder and the Executor modules, which respectively unfold the expanded query and evaluate it over the retrieved source database.

5 Data Extraction

The extraction of the data from the sources to build the retrieved source database for a given query is a key process in IBIS, and is complicated by the fact that limitations exist in accessing the sources. This is typical of Web data sources that are accessible through forms: usually a certain set of fields has to be filled with values in order to query the underlying database. Also, very often legacy databases have a limitation of this kind. To improve efficiency in data extraction IBIS exploits specific techniques to deal with access limitations, and implements several types of optimizations to avoid accesses that would produce already retrieved data. In the following we describe in some detail these features of IBIS.

5.1 Dealing with Access Limitations

In the presence of access limitations on the sources, simple unfolding is in general not sufficient to extract all obtainable answers from the sources [17,8,16]. IBIS

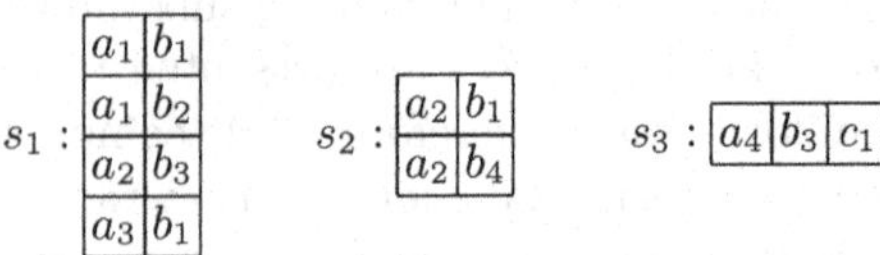

Fig. 2. Extension of sources of Example 1

exploits techniques developed specifically for dealing with access limitations [16], and extends them to make them deployable in practice. The extraction of data according to such techniques is performed as follows: starting from the set of initial values in the query, IBIS accesses as many sources as possible, according to their access limitations. The new values in the tuples obtained (if any), are used to access the sources again, getting new tuples, and so on, until there is no way of doing accesses with new values. At each step, the values obtained so far are stored in the data store.

In the following, without loss of generality, we assume that for each attribute of a relation an *abstract domain* with the same name is defined. An abstract domain is based on an underlying concrete domain, but represents information at a higher level of abstraction, e.g., to distinguish, strings representing person names from strings representing plate numbers. We call *binding tuple* a tuple of values that match with the attributes that must be bound to values; we call *binding values* the values of a binding tuple. For example, for a source $s(A^\star, B^\star, C)$, where the attributes that must be bound are starred, binding tuples are pairs of values (a, b), where a and b belong to the abstract domains D_A, D_B respectively, and D_A and D_B in turn characterize attributes A, B respectively.

Example 1. Consider the following source relations:

$$s_1(A^\star, B)$$
$$s_2(A, B^\star)$$
$$s_3(A, B^\star, C)$$

where, for the sake of simplicity, we have the same attribute names A, B, C for all attributes that belong to the abstract domains D_A, D_B, D_C respectively. Suppose we have the following conjunctive query over the sources:

$$q(C) \leftarrow s_1(a_1, B),\ s_3(A, B, C)$$

Now, assume the sources have the extension shown in Figure 2. Starting from a_1, the only constant in the query, we access s_1 getting the tuples (a_1, b_1) and (a_1, b_2). Now we have b_1 and b_2 with which to access s_2 and s_3; from s_2 we get (a_2, b_1), while from s_3 we get nothing. With the new constant a_2 we access s_1 getting (a_2, b_3). Finally, we access s_3 with b_3 getting (a_4, b_3, c_1) (with b_3 we do not get any tuple from s_2). At this point, we have populated the retrieved source database, on which we evaluate the query. The answer to q is therefore the tuple

(c_1). Observe that (a_3, b_1) and (a_2, b_4) could not be extracted from s_1 and s_2 respectively.

Although the extraction algorithm is straightforward, in order to make it efficient in practice, its implementation requires to take into account several technological aspects. The way the data extraction process is realized in IBIS is depicted in Figure 3, where the following elements can be identified:

- The *retrieved source database* (RSD) stores tuples retrieved during the data extraction for a certain query. It consists of physical tables, one for each source table defined in the source schema of IBIS.
- *Domain tables* store values that are used to produce binding tuples. There is one table for each abstract domain, containing all the values belonging to it. The values in the domain tables are contained in the set of values stored in the retrieved source database. The domain tables, although containing redundant data, are kept for efficiency reasons; indeed, experimental results have shown that the time needed for the generation of the binding tuples decreases significantly when domain tables are used.
- *Binding tables* are used to store binding tuples before submitting them to the sources; there is a binding table for each source with limitations.

To avoid wrappers to be overloaded with a number of binding tuples (i.e., access requests) that exceeds the capacity of the wrappers, they are fed with batches of binding tuples that do not exceed a prefixed maximum size. For each wrapper, according to its capabilities, the system manager assigns the maximum size of the batches it can accept.

Furthermore, the extraction strategy of IBIS tries to keep working as many wrappers as possible. In order to do so, the IBIS Core constructs the binding tuples to be sent to the wrappers independently from the order in which the values have been delivered to the retrieved source database. In doing so, it tries to generate the same amount of binding tuples for each wrapper.

Also, the new values in the tuples that are stored in the retrieved source database are not immediately "poured" in the domain tables, so as not to cause an excessive production of binding tuples: the transfer (see the arrow labeled with "Leaking" in the figure), controlled by the Core, is such that the values are

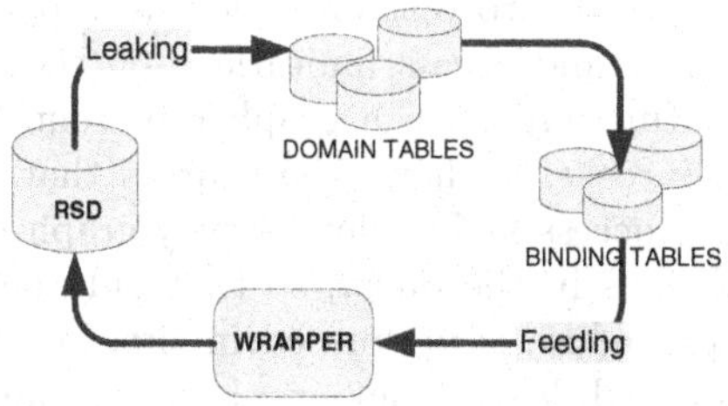

Fig. 3. Extraction process in IBIS

homogeneously distributed among the different abstract domains to which they belong.

The limitations in accessing the sources make the issue of data extraction inherently complex and costly. Our experimentations have shown that the time needed for the extraction of all obtainable tuples can be quite long. On the other hand, experiments have also shown that the system retrieves tuples (and values) that are significant for the answer in a time that is usually very short, compared to the total extraction time. This is due to the recursive nature of the extraction process, which obtains new values from the already retrieved ones; hence, a lower number of steps is required to obtain values extracted earlier, and these values have shown to be more likely part of the answer to the query.

5.2 Static Optimization

In general, having extracted a number of values at a certain point of the query answering process, and given a source s to be accessed using the values extracted so far as binding values, not all the possible accesses to s are necessary in order to calculate the answer to the query. This is illustrated in the following example.

Example 2. Let $\mathcal{S}$ be a source schema with $\mathcal{S} = \{s_1, s_2, s_3\}$; the sources are defined as follows:

$$s_1(A^\star, B) \qquad s_2(B^\star, C) \qquad s_3(C^\star, B)$$

For simplicity, suppose again we have distinct abstract domains D_A, D_B, D_C, one for each attribute name. Consider the following query:

$$q(C) \leftarrow s_1(a_0, B), s_2(B, C)$$

We easily observe that it is not useful to use the values obtained from s_2 to access s_3 in order to obtain new values of D_C with which to access s_2 again. In fact, due to the join condition between s_1 and s_2, the only tuples extracted from s_2 which can be used to construct a tuple of the answer to q are those obtained by binding the attribute B of s_2 with a binding value extracted from s_1.

In order to avoid unnecessary accesses, IBIS incorporates the optimization techniques presented in [2]. The optimization is as follows. Given an unfolded query on the sources, in order to optimise the query plan, information about the structure of the query and access limitations on the sources is encoded in a *dependency graph*. Intuitively, such a graph represents dependencies among sources, i.e., for any source s, it shows the sources that may provide binding values that are useful to access s. The dependency graph is pruned, taking into account the join conditions in the query, so that only necessary dependencies are left; the pruning procedure is performed in time polynomial in the size of the graph. From the pruned dependency graph, an optimized query plan is derived, which guarantees that only necessary accessed are performed during its execution.

Notice that the static optimisation of [2] is applicable for conjunctive queries, while an expanded and unfolded query in IBIS is a union of conjunctive queries. To this regard, IBIS offers the system manager two different strategies for processing a UCQ. The CQs can be either processed one by one, as if they were independent, or they can be *chained* in an ordered sequence, so that, in the extraction process for a CQ q, we can use as binding values the values extracted while processing the CQs preceding q in the chain.

5.3 Dynamic Optimization

The Dynamic Optimizer of IBIS is capable of avoiding useless accesses to the sources by exploiting already extracted tuples and integrity constraints on the sources. Dynamic optimization based on integrity constraints comes into play when a data source is accessible in several ways, i.e., the same underlying data can be accessed with different limitations. The most relevant case is that of Web sources, where the same form can be submitted by filling in different sets of fields, but not by leaving all fields empty (see for example Amazon[1] or the ACM Sigmod Antology[2]). The different access patterns for a source s are represented in IBIS as different sources $s_1, \ldots, s_n$ with different access limitations. To capture the fact that the sources $s_1, \ldots, s_n$ have the same extension, simple full-width inclusion dependencies $s_1 \subseteq s_2$, $s_2 \subseteq s_3$, ..., $s_{n-1} \subseteq s_n$, $s_n \subseteq s_1$ are used. More generally, the situation in which the extension of a source s is contained in that of another source s' is captured by the simple full-width inclusion dependency $s \subseteq s'$. Note that the abstract domains of s and s' must match.

Simple full-width inclusion dependencies, together with functional dependencies (which capture also key constraints), allow IBIS to performs runtime optimization during data extraction, taking into account the tuples already extracted from the sources. We introduce the technique adopted in IBIS with an example.

Example 3. Consider two sources

$$s_1(\mathit{Code}, \mathit{Surname}, \mathit{City}^\star)$$
$$s_2(\mathit{Code}^\star, \mathit{Surname}^\star, \mathit{City})$$

where s_1 stores identification code, surname and city of birth of employees, and s_2 stores the same information about persons. Assume that the simple full-width inclusion dependency $s_1 \subseteq s_2$ holds and that the functional dependency *Code* → *Surname*, *City* holds on s_2.

Suppose that s_1 and s_2 have both the following extension:

Code	*Surname*	*City*
2	*brown*	*sidney*
5	*williams*	*london*
7	*yamakawa*	*tokyo*
9	*peretti*	*rome*

[1] `http://www.amazon.com/exec/obidos/ats-query-page/`

[2] `http://www.informatik.uni-trier.de/~ley/db/indices/query.html`

If our set of initial values is *rome* and *tokyo*, at the first step we access s_1 and we get the following tuples:

Code	*Surname*	*City*
7	*yamakawa*	*tokyo*
9	*peretti*	*rome*

Now we have four new values: the three codes 7 and 9, and the two surnames *yamakawa* and *peretti*. With these values we could access source s_1 to try and get new values. But we can easily observe that, because of the functional dependency on s_2, if we bind the *Code* attribute with one of the known values, we get a tuple we had already obtained from s_2. Therefore the access to s_1 is useless in this case. Instead, if we get 2 as a code and *brown* as a surname from another source, we could access s_1 and get new tuples.

To consider the general case, let $\mathbf{B}_1$ and $\mathbf{B}_2$ the set of attributes that must be bound in s_1 and s_2 respectively; let the dependency $s_1 \subseteq s_2$ hold. If a functional dependency $s_2 : \mathbf{C} \rightarrow \mathbf{D}$ holds, with $\mathbf{C} \subseteq \mathbf{B}_1$ and $\mathbf{D} \supseteq \mathbf{B}_2$, then if we access s_1 with a binding tuple ϑ such that $\vartheta = t[\mathbf{B}_1]$, where t is a tuple previously extracted from s_2, then the access with ϑ is useless, because it provides only tuples that have been already extracted from s_2 [2]. IBIS exploits this technique by selecting only the binding tuples that are potentially useful from the binding tables, just after their generation.

Another optimization is performed by IBIS when a key constraint holds on a source s. Let $\mathbf{K}$ be the key of s, with $\mathbf{K} \subseteq \mathbf{B}$, where $\mathbf{B}$ is the set of attributes of s that must be bound. Then, if we access s_1 with a binding tuple ϑ such that $\vartheta = t[\mathbf{B}]$, where t is a tuple previously extracted from s, then the access with ϑ is useless, because it provides only tuples that have been already extracted from s. This is again exploited by IBIS, by a suitable selection on the binding tuples.

6 Interaction with the User

IBIS is equipped with a user-friendly Web interface. In practice, the time required for answering a query may be significantly long; the bottleneck is constituted by the extraction phase, which has to cope with the usually very long response time of remote sources (Web sources and legacy systems) and with the intrinsic complexity of dealing with access limitations. Therefore, the traditional "submit-and-wait" interaction with Web-based systems is not suitable for IBIS. In order to offer the user a suitable form of interaction, IBIS has been designed with the following capabilities:

- the capability of incrementally presenting answers while they are computed;
- the capability of enhancing the query answering process by using additional data provided by the user together with the query;
- the capability of chaining queries to each other.

Incremental Generation of Answers. While one of the goals of IBIS is to provide the maximum set of answers, in practice this often requires an amount of time that could be unacceptable for a user operating in an interactive Web session. In order to cope with this problem, IBIS provides two strategies. The first one consists in showing tuples to the user as soon they are obtained, while the answering process is going on. In fact, the asynchronous extraction process allows evaluating the query over the source retrieved database before the end of the process itself. In this way, the user will see a continuous upgrade of the result set. Moreover, the user has the opportunity to stop the process at any time, when he is satisfied with the answers obtained so far. The second feature is the ability to continue the answering process also while a user is logged off, and present the obtained answers as soon as the user logs on again. E-mail and pager alerts are also available, to signal the user that a query has been completed.

Use of Domain-related Values. When a user query is processed, the set of constants appearing in the query is crucial, because at the beginning of data extraction such values represent the only way to access the sources. Therefore, adding values before starting the extraction process may significantly alter the extraction process itself. IBIS offers the user the possibility of expanding the set of initial values according to his knowledge of the domain of the global schema.

These constants influence the process in two ways: first, they may enlarge the set of tuples in the answer, because it is possible that the additional values lead to the generation of binding tuples for accessing the sources that would not be generated starting from the original set of values. Furthermore, in our experimentations of the system, the addition of domain-related values has shortened the time required for retrieving significant answers in most cases. This is due to the "proximity" that in many cases exists between the added values and the tuples in the answer. Obviously, the effectiveness of this feature depends on the user knowledge of the domain. Experiments have been carried out with non-expert users, unaware of the underlying sources, with data sources coming from the context of Government Institutions; the addition of initial values has proven to be useful in the majority of cases.

Chainable Queries. IBIS offers the possibility of using tuples extracted while answering a set of queries (the retrieved source databases of the queries) to answer another query related to the previous ones. When the freshness of data is not required by the user, the retrieved source databases obtained while answering previous queries can be seen as a cache for the new query. With this feature, queries can be *chained*, in the sense that each query uses the retrieved source databases of all the queries preceding it in the chain. IBIS is able to avoid producing binding tuples which have already been issued to the sources during the extraction of previous queries.

At the interface level, before submitting the query to the system, the user can choose if he wants to tie it to a particular set of already executed queries. At the end of the answering process he can also choose to save the extracted tuples or to discard them. This feature can also be used in a multi-user context:

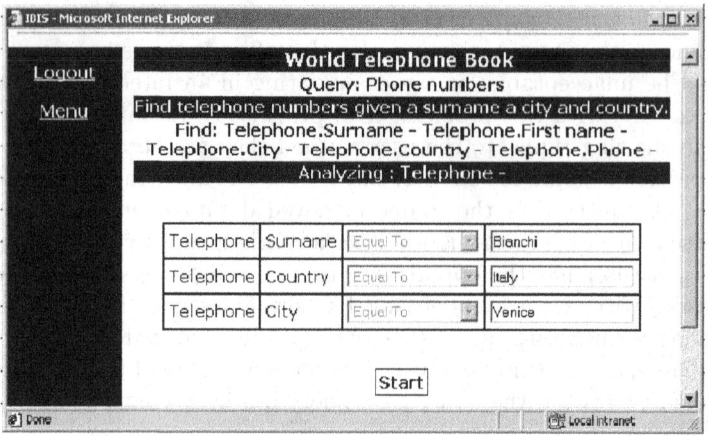

Fig. 4. Query interface in IBIS

the user who has issued a query q can allow a set of other users to use the data extracted from the sources while processing q.

Figure 4 shows a screen-shot of the IBIS Web interface to a stored query Phone numbers, and Figure 5 shows the result of evaluating such a query over a set of Web sources.

7 Conclusions

We have presented IBIS, a system for the semantic integration of heterogeneous data sources based on the GAV approach, adopting various innovative and state-of-the-art solutions to deal with source wrapping, source incompleteness, and limitations in accessing data sources. In particular, to the best of our knowledge, IBIS is the only data integration system capable of fully exploiting integrity constraints over the global schema and the sources in query answering.

IBIS - Microsoft Internet Explorer

Logout
Menu
Save

The query is: COMPLETED

Found 3 records

surname	first name	country	city	phone
Bianchi	Mario	Italy	Venice	+39367892
Bianchi	Fabio	Italy	Venice	+39365410
Bianchi	Laura	Italy	Venice	+39434245

Done Local intranet

Fig. 5. Query result in IBIS

IBIS has been already released as a beta version and its final release is currently under active development. We are working on extending the system in various directions. In particular, we are studing techniques to deal with the problem of key constraint violations without requiring intervention of the designer. A first step in this direction is based on a weaker non-monotonic semantics for the mapping, based on suitable preference criteria in case of key constraint violations [13].

References

1. Sonia Bergamaschi, Silvana Castano, Maurizio Vincini, and Domenico Beneventano. Semantic integration of heterogeneous information sources. *Data and Knowledge Engineering*, 36(3):215–249, 2001.
2. Andrea Calì and Diego Calvanese. Optimized querying of integrated data over the Web. In *Proc. of the IFIP WG8.1 Working Conference on Engineering Information Systems in the Internet Context (EISIC 2002)*, pages 285–301. Kluwer Academic Publisher, 2002.
3. Andrea Calì, Diego Calvanese, Giuseppe De Giacomo, and Maurizio Lenzerini. Accessing data integration systems through conceptual schemas. In *Proc. of the 20th Int. Conf. on Conceptual Modeling (ER 2001)*, pages 270–284, 2001.
4. Andrea Calì, Diego Calvanese, Giuseppe De Giacomo, and Maurizio Lenzerini. Data integration under integrity constraints. In *Proc. of the 14th Conf. on Advanced Information Systems Engineering (CAiSE 2002)*, volume 2348 of *Lecture Notes in Computer Science*, pages 262–279. Springer, 2002.
5. Diego Calvanese, Giuseppe De Giacomo, Maurizio Lenzerini, Daniele Nardi, and Riccardo Rosati. Data integration in data warehousing. *Int. J. of Cooperative Information Systems*, 10(3):237–271, 2001.
6. M. J. Carey, L. M. Haas, P. M. Schwarz, M. Arya, W. F. Cody, R. Fagin, M. Flickner, A. Luniewski, W. Niblack, D. Petkovic, J. Thomas, J. H. Williams, and E. L. Wimmers. Towards heterogeneous multimedia information systems: The Garlic approach. In *Proc. of the 5th Int. Workshop on Research Issues in Data Engineering – Distributed Object Management (RIDE-DOM'95)*, pages 124–131. IEEE Computer Society Press, 1995.
7. Sudarshan S. Chawathe, Hector Garcia-Molina, Joachim Hammer, Kelly Ireland, Yannis Papakonstantinou, Jeffrey D. Ullman, and Jennifer Widom. The TSIMMIS project: Integration of heterogeneous information sources. In *Proc. of the 10th Meeting of the Information Processing Society of Japan (IPSJ'94)*, pages 7–18, 1994.
8. Daniela Florescu, Alon Y. Levy, Ioana Manolescu, and Dan Suciu. Query optimization in the presence of limited access patterns. In *Proc. of the ACM SIGMOD Int. Conf. on Management of Data*, pages 311–322, 1999.
9. Cheng Hian Goh, Stéphane Bressan, Stuart E. Madnick, and Michael D. Siegel. Context interchange: New features and formalisms for the intelligent integration of information. *ACM Trans. on Information Systems*, 17(3):270–293, 1999.
10. Alon Y. Halevy. Answering queries using views: A survey. *Very Large Database J.*, 10(4):270–294, 2001.
11. Joachim Hammer, Hector Garcia-Molina, Jennifer Widom, Wilburt Labio, and Yue Zhuge. The Stanford data warehousing project. *Bull. of the IEEE Computer Society Technical Committee on Data Engineering*, 18(2):41–48, 1995.

12. Matthias Jarke, Maurizio Lenzerini, Yannis Vassiliou, and Panos Vassiliadis, editors. *Fundamentals of Data Warehouses.* Springer, 1999.
13. Domenico Lembo, Maurizio Lenzerini, and Riccardo Rosati. Source inconsistency and incompleteness in data integration. In *Proc. of the 9th Int. Workshop on Knowledge Representation meets Databases (KRDB 2002).* CEUR Electronic Workshop Proceedings, `http://ceur-ws.org/Vol-54/`, 2002.
14. Maurizio Lenzerini. Data integration: A theoretical perspective. In *Proc. of the 21st ACM SIGACT SIGMOD SIGART Symp. on Principles of Database Systems (PODS 2002)*, pages 233–246, 2002.
15. Chen Li and Edward Chang. Query planning with limited source capabilities. In *Proc. of the 16th IEEE Int. Conf. on Data Engineering (ICDE 2000)*, pages 401–412, 2000.
16. Chen Li and Edward Chang. Answering queries with useful bindings. *ACM Trans. on Database Systems*, 26(3):313–343, 2001.
17. Chen Li, Ramana Yerneni, Vasilis Vassalos, Hector Garcia-Molina, Yannis Papakonstantinou, Jeffrey D. Ullman, and Murty Valiveti. Capability based mediation in TSIMMIS. In *Proc. of the ACM SIGMOD Int. Conf. on Management of Data*, pages 564–566, 1998.
18. Yannis Papakonstantinou, Hector Garcia-Molina, and Jennifer Widom. Object exchange across heterogeneous information sources. In *Proc. of the 11th IEEE Int. Conf. on Data Engineering (ICDE'95)*, pages 251–260, 1995.
19. Jeffrey D. Ullman. Information integration using logical views. In *Proc. of the 6th Int. Conf. on Database Theory (ICDT'97)*, volume 1186 of *Lecture Notes in Computer Science*, pages 19–40. Springer, 1997.
20. Ron van der Meyden. Logical approaches to incomplete information. In Jan Chomicki and Günter Saake, editors, *Logics for Databases and Information Systems*, pages 307–356. Kluwer Academic Publisher, 1998.
21. Jennifer Widom (ed.). Special issue on materialized views and data warehousing. *Bull. of the IEEE Computer Society Technical Committee on Data Engineering*, 18(2), 1995.
22. Gang Zhou, Richard Hull, Roger King, and Jean-Claude Franchitti. Data integration and warehousing using H20. *Bull. of the IEEE Computer Society Technical Committee on Data Engineering*, 18(2):29–40, 1995.
23. Gang Zhou, Richard Hull, Roger King, and Jean-Claude Franchitti. Using object matching and materialization to integrate heterogeneous databases. In *Proc. of the 3rd Int. Conf. on Cooperative Information Systems (CoopIS'95)*, pages 4–18, 1995.

Towards a Generic Model for Situational Method Engineering

Jolita Ralyté[1], Rébecca Deneckère[2], and Colette Rolland[2]

[1]CUI, University of Geneva, 24, bd. du Général Dufour, CH-1211 Geneva, Switzerland
ralyte@cui.unige.ch
[2]CRI, University of Paris Sorbonne, 90 rue de Tolbiac, 75013 Paris, France
{denecker, rolland}@univ-paris1.fr

Abstract. The work presented in this paper is related to the area of Situational Method Engineering (SME) which focuses on project-specific method construction. We propose a generic process model supporting the integration of different existing SME approaches. This model shall help the method engineer either selecting one SME approach or combining several approaches that best fit the situation of the method engineering project at hand. The generic model presented in this paper already contains three SME techniques: (1) to assemble method chunks (2) to extend an existing method and (3) to generate a method by abstraction/instantiation of a model/meta-model. The paper presents and illustrates these three techniques and show how other SME techniques could be integrated in the model.

1 Introduction

The need for a better productivity of system engineering teams, as well as a better quality of products motivates the development of solutions to adapt methods to the project situation at hand. This is known as *Situational Method Engineering* (SME). Whereas SME promotes the construction of a method by assembling reusable method fragments stored in some method base [9, 3, 18, 19, 23, 29, 26], in this paper we propose a *generic process model* to capture a large variety of approaches supporting "on the fly" method construction.

As the selection of the suitable method engineering approach for the project at hand is not easy, our generic process model guides the method engineer in the definition of his/her project method engineering goal and in the selection of the approach which best allow him/her to achieve it. Besides, as in some cases a combination of several approaches could be the most suitable engineering solution in order to construct or adapt a method, the generic process model guides the method engineer in selecting the appropriated set of approaches.

We use a strategic process meta-model called Map [1, 27] to represent our generic SME process model. Map provides a representation system based on a non-deterministic ordering of *intentions* and *strategies*. A map is a labeled directed graph with intentions as nodes and strategies as edges between intentions. A triplet <*source intention, target intention, strategy*> in the map is called a *section*. Each section is defined by an *intention achievement guideline,* which provides advice to fulfil the target intention following the strategy given the source intention has been achieved.

J. Eder and M. Missikoff (Eds.): CAiSE 2003, LNCS 2681, pp. 95–110, 2003.

The directed nature of the graph shows which intentions can follow which one. Since, many strategies can be used for achieving an intention, Map allows us to integrate different approaches as different method engineering strategies in the same SME process model and to combine the application of these approaches in the construction of a new method or the adaptation of a given one.

In previous papers we presented a process model for assembly based situational method engineering [19], an approach for method extension based on the use of patterns [5, 6] and more recently, an abstraction based approach [24] responding to the needs of a large method engineering project in industry. All these approaches use different techniques for method construction but their objective is the same – to support the construction of a method matching the requirements of a given situation.

Our belief is that it will be useful to investigate the problem of integrating different approaches in a single SME process model. This is the objective we aim at in this paper. We propose a generic SME process model which integrates the three above-mentioned approaches. We also show that this model is flexible enough to integrate other approaches than the three that are integrated and illustrated in this paper.

The paper is organised as follows: section 2 describes our generic process model for SME. Sections 3, 4 and 5 present and illustrate respectively three method engineering approaches, namely *Assembly-based, Extension-based* and *Paradigm-based,* all being integrated in our generic model. Section 6 considers the similarities and the differences of these approaches and the possibility of their parallel use in the construction of a single method whereas section 7 draws some conclusions and discuss about our future work.

2 Generic Process Model for Situational Method Engineering

We consider that any SME process is made of two main tasks: setting the method engineering goal and then, constructing a method that matches this goal. In other words, there are two core intentions that the method engineer has in mind:

1. *Set Method Engineering Goal* that is to identify the kind of method he/she needs,
2. *Construct a Method* allowing him/her to satisfy this goal.

These intentions are the nodes of the map presented in Fig.1. As shown in this figure, the Map representation formalism allows us to propose several different strategies to support the realisation of these intentions.

The achievement of the first intention, namely *Set Method Engineering Goal,* depends on the method situation of the project at hand. In one project situation the method engineer may perhaps consider that a specific method could be applicable but requires some adaptations whereas in other situations, he or she may be convinced that any of the available methods is suitable for the project. In the first case, the method engineering (ME) goal refers to the adjustments of the selected method: enhancement, extension or restriction. We call the corresponding strategy the *Method-based strategy*. In the second case, it is necessary to construct a completely new method and the corresponding strategy is called the *From scratch strategy*.

The achievement of the intention *Construct a Method* depends on the applied method construction technique. Thanks to the map structure it is easy to integrate in the same model different method construction techniques as different strategies to reach the intention *Construct a Method.* The map of Fig. 1 proposes three SME techniques. The first one is based on the reuse of method components extracted from existing methods and stored in some method base. This technique helps to select and assemble different method components in order to construct a new method or to enrich an existing one. As a consequence, the corresponding strategy is called *Assembly-based strategy*. The second technique is used for extending a method by applying extension patterns and therefore it is referred in the map by the *Extension-based strategy*. Finally, the third technique is relevant when a new fresh method must be constructed either by abstracting from a given model or by instantiating a meta-model. This new method is based on some paradigm model or meta-model and this is why the corresponding strategy is called the *Paradigm-based strategy*. It is obvious that these three strategies can be combined in order to construct the method best fitting the situation of the project at hand.

Once the required method has been constructed it is necessary to validate it. For this, we propose the *Evaluation strategy* which implements different method evaluation techniques. Our *Generic Process Model* for SME is shown in Fig. 1.

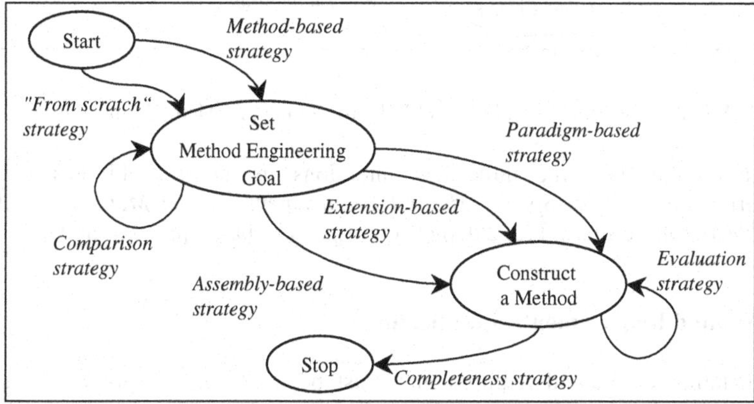

Fig. 1. Generic Process Model for Situational Method Engineering

It is obvious, that other SME techniques could be integrated in our generic SME process model as other strategies to achieve the intention *Construct a Method*. In this paper we concentrate on the three method construction techniques introduced in the map above and we present and illustrate them in the following sections.

3 Assembly-Based Method Engineering

Our approach for assembly-based SME aims at constructing a method 'on the fly' in order to match as well as possible the situation of the project at hand. It consists in the selection of method components (that we call method chunks) from existing methods that satisfy some situational requirements and their assembly.

Our approach is requirements-driven, meaning that the method engineer must start by eliciting requirements for the method. Next, the method chunks matching these requirements can be retrieved from the method base. And finally, the selected chunks are assembled in order to compose a new method or to enhance an existing one.

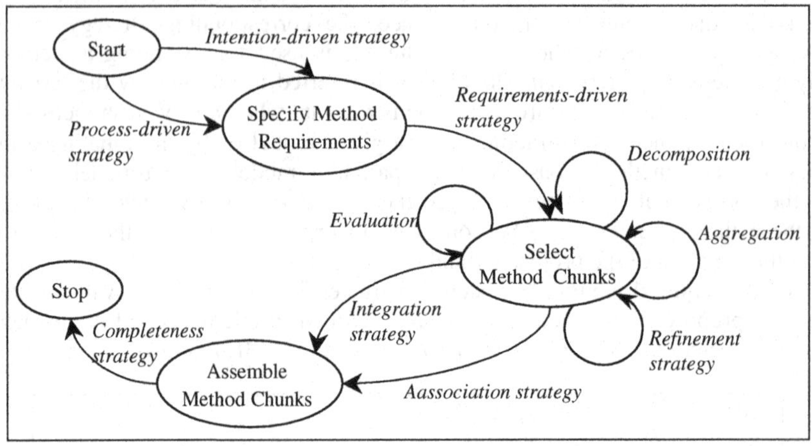

Fig. 2. Assembly-Based Process Model for Situational Method Engineering

As a consequence, the three key intentions in the assembly-based method engineering process are: *Specify Method Requirements*, *Select Method Chunks* and *Assemble Method Chunks*. Fig. 2 depicts our assembly-based process model for SME.

3.1 Method Requirements Specification

The elicitation of method requirements must be done in the light of the method engineering goal set previously (see Fig.1) that might be to adapt an existing method or to construct a new one. We identified two different strategies for requirements elicitation, namely *Intention-driven strategy* and *Process-driven strategy* (Fig. 2).

The first strategy is suitable for method adaptation. There are different types of method adaptation. The method in use can be strong in terms of its product model but weak with respect to its process model, which will be the subject of adaptation and enhancement. The adaptation can be to simply add a new functionality to the existing method, which is relevant in its other aspects. Vice versa, the project at hand could not need some functionality offered by the method. In all these cases, the requirements elicitation process is driven by the identification of the ME intentions such as 'add event concept', 'complete completeness checking step' etc., which will allow to complete, enhance or limit the method initially selected. For this reason, wee call this strategy *Intention-driven strategy* (Fig. 2).

The second strategy is relevant in the case of a new method construction. In such ME situation the requirements is not only to produce the list of ME intentions that will permit to adapt the selected method but to identify the full set of engineering intentions that shall be fulfilled by the new method. For this reason we call the corresponding strategy *Process-driven strategy.*

Both of these strategies lead to a set of requirements expressed as a map that we call the *requirements map*. More information about the guidelines supporting these two strategies to *Specify Method Requirements* can be found in [21].

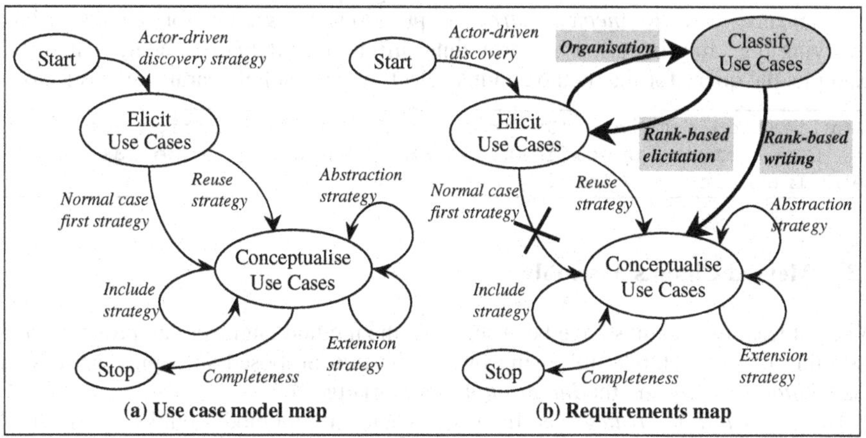

Fig. 3. Requirements Map for the Use Case Model Enhancement

As an example, let's assume that the goal of the method engineer is to enhance the use case approach proposed by Jacobson in [11] by some scenario classification & authoring guidelines in order to improve the quality of use case conceptualisation. This is a case of method adaptation and therefore, the *Intention-driven strategy* is the most suitable one. This strategy supports the identification of adaptation requirements expressed as intentions and strategies as shown in Fig. 3. The initial map for use case construction is shown in Fig. 3 (a) whereas Fig. 3 (b) highlights the requirements for enhancement expressed through three new sections (in colour) and the deletion of the *Normal case first strategy* which is replaced by the added features.

3.2 Method Chunks Selection

Once the method requirements have been specified, the selection of the method chunks matching these requirements can start. The *Requirements-driven strategy* helps the method engineer to select the best fitting chunks. The chunk selection queries must be formulated by giving values to the attributes of the descriptors and interfaces of method chunks (see [15, 23]). The validation of the retrieved chunks is supported by the *Evaluation strategy which* helps in evaluating the degree of matching of the candidate chunk to the requirements. This is done by applying similarity measures between the requirements map and the process model of the selected chunk. More details about these similarity measures could be found in [19].

The *Decomposition, Aggregation* and *Refinement* strategies help to refine the candidate chunk selection by analysing more in depth if the chunk matches the requirements. If the selected method chunk is an aggregate one, i.e. it is composed of several chunks, the *Decomposition strategy* drives the selection of the relevant sub-chunks and the elimination of the inadequate ones. Vice-versa, the *Aggregation strategy* is applicable when the retrieved chink matches partly the requirements. This strategy proposes to look for an aggregate chunk containing the candidate one based on the assumption that the aggregate chunk might provide a solution for the missing requirements. The *Refinement strategy* proposes to search for another chunk satisfying the same intention but providing different guidelines to achieve it. In our example, the query for the method chunk selection will include parameters as follows:

```
Application domain = 'Information System' AND Design activity
= 'Requirements specification' AND Situation = 'Use cases'
AND Intention = 'Classify use cases'
```

3.3 Method Chunks Assembly

When at least two chunks have been selected, the method engineer can progress in the assembly of these chunks following one of the two proposed strategies, namely the *Association strategy* and the *Integration strategy* (Fig. 2).

The *Association strategy* is relevant when the method chunks to assemble correspond to two different system engineering functionalities, i.e. they allow to achieve different engineering intentions and the result of one chunk is used as a source product by the second one. Such method chunks generally do not have common elements in their product and process models and the assembly process is therefore mainly dealing with making the bridge between the two chunks. More precisely, the product models of the chunks must be connected by defining links between their different concepts whereas the connection of their process models consists in defining their execution order. The connection of the product model is possible thanks to the ADD_LINK and ADD_CONCEPT operators [22]. The MERGE_INTENTION operator is applied to connect the process models and consists in identifying in the first chunk the intention producing the source product for the second chunk. Some method chunk adaptation could be required before their assembly in order to avoid concepts name ambiguity. This may be done by applying different RENAME operators. For example, the chunk producing use cases and the chunk constructing the system object structure can be assembled to get a method with a larger coverage than any of the two initial ones.

The *Integration strategy* is relevant to assemble chunks that have similar engineering goals but provide different ways to satisfy it. In such a case, the process and product models are overlapping, that is containing the same or similar elements. The assembly process consists in identifying the common elements in the chunks product and process models and merging them. Therefore, the integration process is mainly based on the application of different MERGE operators as MERGE_ INTENTION, MERGE-SECTION for the integration of process models and MERGE_CONCEPT, MERGE_LINK for the integration of product models. Each of these operators deals with the integration of similar elements belonging to the initial chunks into a new one in the integrated chunk. The SPECIALISE and GENERALISE operators define respectively the specialisation and generalisation links between the concepts of the chunks product models. Their application is useful to build a model of the integrated method chunk that is richer than those of the initial chunks.

Like in the previous case, the adaptation of the method chunks must precede their integration. Besides the RENAME operators, OBJECTIFY_LINK and OBJECTIFY_PROPERTY may be required for performing more complex transformation tasks.

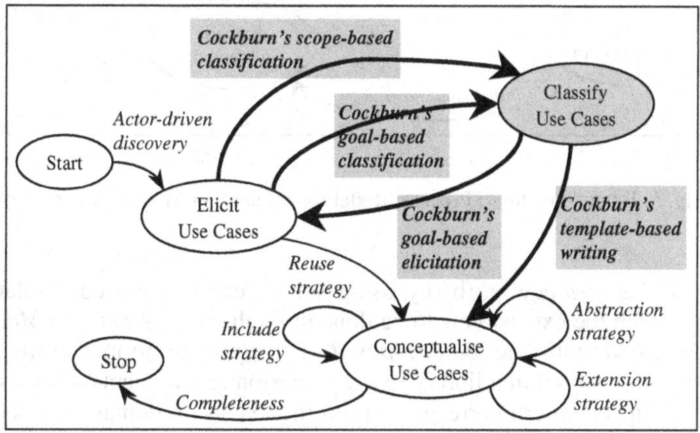

Fig. 4. The Enhanced Use Case Model Map.

For instance, the *Integration strategy* will be necessary to satisfy the method requirements defined in Fig. 3 as the method engineering objective is to enhance the use case conceptualisation process by new way of working. Let's suppose that the method engineer selects the use case conceptualisation guidelines proposed by Cockburn [4]. This approach proposes two complementary use case classification techniques: one is based on a three level goal hierarchy; other defines a design scope to capture in a use case typology. These two techniques cover the section <*Elicit Use Cases, Classify Use Cases, Organisation strategy*> in the requirements map. The guidelines supporting elicitation of other use cases of the lower or higher abstraction level are also provided by this approach and cover the section <*Classify Use Cases, Elicit Use Cases, Rank-based elicitation strategy*. Moreover, this approach proposes different templates for use case writing as well as the content guidelines depending on the use case goal level and design scope. It covers the section <*Classify Use Cases, Conceptualise Use Cases, Rank-based writing strategy*>. The obtained method (Fig. 4) will provide guidelines richer than those of each chunk used separately.

4 Extension-Based Method Engineering

Our approach for extension-based SME [5, 6] corresponds to a ME goal to adapt locally a method to the contingency of the project at hand. The approach guides method engineer by providing extension patterns that help identifying typical extension situations and provide advises to perform the required extension.

Fig. 5. shows the map representing the process underlying this approach. It can be seen that we advocate two different ways to extend a method: (a) directly through the

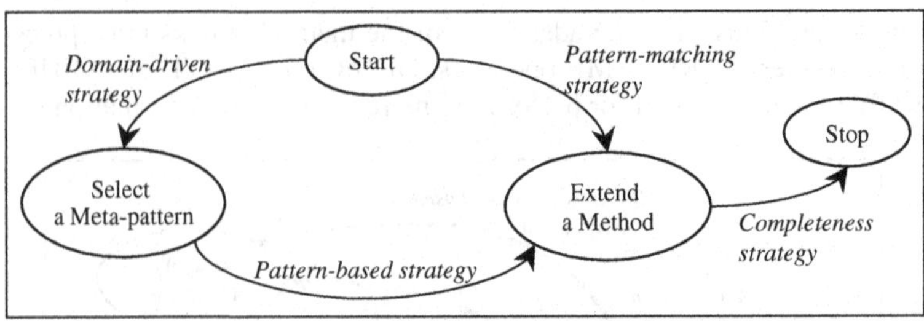

Fig. 5. Extension-Based Process Model for Situational Method Engineering

Pattern-matching strategy or (b) by using some generic knowledge related to the domain for which the extension is to be done through the path *Select a Meta-pattern*, *Extend a Method* with the *Pattern-based strategy*. The former helps to match extension patterns stored in a library to the extension requirements whereas the latter selects first, a meta-pattern corresponding to the extension domain and then, guides the method extension by applying the patterns suggested by the meta-pattern.

Both ways-of-working use a library of *extension patterns* but do it in different ways. The domain centric way exploits the fact that a set of patterns and their use can be embodied in a meta-pattern that is suitable for method extension in this domain (e.g. temporal data structures). If the required extension does not clearly correspond to a certain type of extension, a well-identified extension domain, then the pattern matching approach shall be selected by the method engineer.

4.1 Domain-Driven Adaptation

This path in the process of Fig. 5 comprises to *Select a Meta-pattern* with the *Domain-driven strategy* and then, to *Extend a Method* with the *Pattern-based strategy*. The guideline to *Select a Meta-pattern* helps the method engineer in recognising if the extension he/she has in mind corresponds to one of the so-called extension domains. A representative example of such domain is *temporal data structures*. The adaptation of a method to this domain includes different extensions such as the integration into the method product model the selected time model defining the appropriated calendar(s) (Gregorian, week-based, working-day-based etc.), the integration of temporal events and temporal expressions for defining event occurrence conditions etc. These extensions are captured in different patterns and organised in a meta-pattern. Meta-patterns for the different domains, for which knowledge about the extension and how to perform it has been defined, are stored in a repository together with the corresponding patterns.

Once the method engineer has selected the meta-pattern relevant for the extension domain at hand, the pattern-based strategy guides him/her in the systematic application of the patterns associated to the meta-pattern. Table 1 shows the meta-pattern guiding method extension with temporal data structures.

Table 1. Meta-pattern "Extend a method with temporal concepts"

Concept	Pattern	Arguments
Temporal Event	Extend a method with temporal events	Applications often need to trigger operations following a specific time data. This pattern allows the insertion of temporal events in the method. They use a time model and the temporal domains in order to define the specific moment to trigger the operations.
Time model with discrete time point	Extend a method with a discrete time point data structure	Temporal databases need to use precise knowledge on events. This pattern allows defining a time model (linear or having a tree structure) defined as a set of time points (or instants). These points have an asymmetric and transitive time precedence relationship.
Time model with interval	Extend a method with temporal types	Some applications need to manage fuzzy or imprecise temporal data. This pattern allows defining a time model seen as a set of intervals. It helps to describe three temporal types: *instants*, *intervals*, and *periods*, defined to manipulate the time.
Temporal domain	Extend a method with temporal domains	Classic methods mostly use the *Date*, *Time* and *Time zone* domains linked to an attribute. However, these domains are very poor and do not allow the representation of *relative* or *periodic* attribute. This pattern aims at supporting the generation of these temporal domains. The time used may be *valid*, *transaction* or *user-defined* [30].
Object history	Extend a method with temporal classes for object histories	Histories are sometimes required by applications in order to look at the data evolution and to execute the *replay* functions required for tracking decisional process of an organization. Therefore, the application should provide information for each object state when it is/was true as well as when it is/was exploitable. This pattern permits to integrate time management into the class definition and to group properties that evolve at the same time and that are linked to the same temporal dimension.
Object versioning	Extend a method with temporal classes for object versioning	*Rollback* operations are required in order to come back to previous states of the database. This pattern permits the creation of object histories supporting the application of rollback operations without endangering the database coherency. Documentation operations help the engineer to keep track of the different versions.
Time constraint	Extend a method with time constraint	The necessity to handle time introduces another problem that is to constrain data evolution. Models must include concepts helping to define which constraints are related to the time in order to keep the data coherency. This pattern proposes two constraints classification: (1) *intra-object* and *inter-object* constraints [7] and (2) *intra-time* and *inter-time* constraints [2].

4.2 Pattern-Matching Based Extension

The *Pattern-matching strategy* to *Extend a Method* (Fig. 5) helps in the selection of the extension patterns which better match requirements. Therefore, the process map representing this approach (Fig. 6) is centred around two core intentions: *Specify Extension Requirements* and *Select & Apply a Pattern.*

The *Requirement elicitation strategy* helps the method engineer to construct a map representing the method extension requirements. This map is called *requirements map. Introduce time model* could be an intention (a requirement) in the requirements map; *Interval based* could be a strategy to achieve this intention. *Discrete time point* could be another strategy to reach the same intention. These two manners to *Introduce*

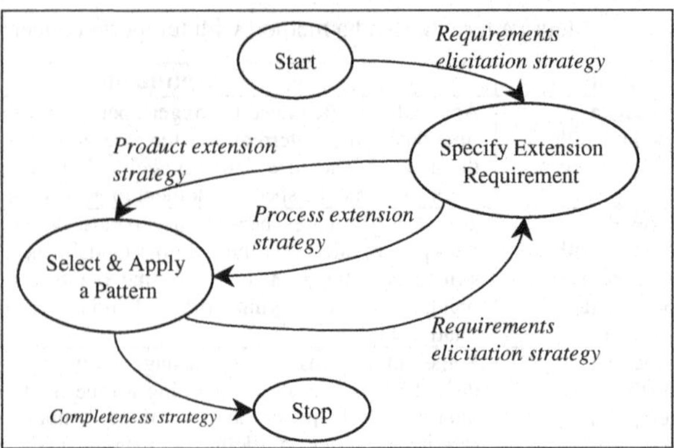

Fig. 6. Process Model for Pattern-Matching Based Method Extension

time model can be defined in two different requirements maps or can be captured in the same map meaning that the method extension will handle both of them.

Our extension patterns are divided into product extension patterns and process extension patterns. The former indicate how to extend a product model whereas the latter deal this the process model extension. This is reflected in the map of Fig. 6 by two strategies to *Select & Apply a Pattern* namely the *Product extension strategy* and the *Process extension strategy.* Both of them are supported by the guidelines which help to match the requirements map intentions and strategies with the pattern situation. Some of the similarity measures introduced in section 3 are applicable here to help in finding the 'best' fit between the requirements and the pattern situation.

5 Paradigm-Based Method Engineering

This approach uses *meta-modelling* as its underlying method engineering technique. It is the most generic of the three approaches to *Construct a Method* that we propose in our generic model shown in Fig. 1. The hypothesis of this approach is that the new method is obtained either by abstracting from an existing model or by instantiating a meta-model. We call this starting model the paradigm model.

Meta-modelling is known as a technique to capture knowledge about methods. It is a basis for understanding, comparing, evaluating and engineering methods. One of the results obtained by the meta-modelling community is the definition of any method as composed of a product model and a process model [16]. The product model defines the set of concepts, their properties and relationships that are needed to express the outcome of the process. The process model comprises the set of goals, activities and guidelines to support process goal achievement and action execution. Therefore, method construction following the meta-modelling technique is centred on the definition of these two models. This is reflected in the paradigm-based process map by the two core intentions *Construct a Product model* and *Construct a Process model* (Fig. 7). A number of product meta-models [8, 10, 17, 28] as well as process meta-models [12, 25, 27] are available and our approach is based on some of them.

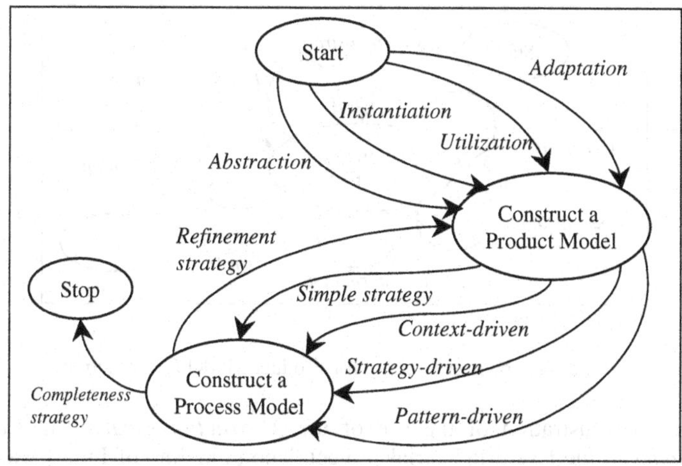

Fig. 7. Paradigm-Based Process Model for Situational Method Engineering

The construction of the product model depends of the method engineering (ME) goal. For example, the ME goal could be to construct a method:

- by raising (or lowering) the level of abstraction of a given model,
- by instantiating a selected meta-model,
- by adapting a meta-model to some specific circumstances,
- by adapting a model.

Each of these cases defines a strategy to *Construct a Product model*, namely the *Abstraction*, *Instantiation*, *Adaptation* and *Utilisation* strategies. Each of them is supported by a guideline. For example, the map of Fig. 8 expresses the guideline supporting the *Abstraction strategy*. According to this guideline, the product model construction consists in defining different product model elements such as objects, links and properties. It starts by the abstraction of some elements from the paradigm model. After that, the model under construction is refined thanks to the *Generalisation*, *Specialisation*, *Aggregation*, *Decomposition* and *Transformation* strategies.

The process model definition must conform to the product model. This is the reason why in the map of Fig. 7 the intention *Construct a Process model* follows the one to *Construct a Product model*. We know that a process model can take multiple different forms. It could be a simple informal guideline, a set of ordered actions or activities to carry out, a set of process patterns to be followed or a multi-process guideline combining several different alternative ways of working. These four cases are represented in our paradigm-based process model by four strategies: *Simple*, *Context-driven*, *Pattern-driven* and *Strategy-driven*. *Simple* and *Context-driven* process models are based on the NATURE process modelling formalism [12, 25] whereas the *Strategy-driven* process model, also called Map formalism, was proposed by [27] (see the introduction of this paper). The guidelines supporting the application of these strategies can be found in [1, 20].

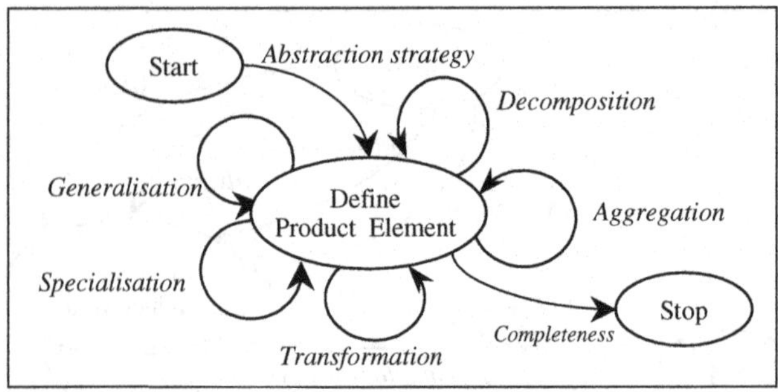

Fig. 8. Abstraction Strategy for Product Model Construction

Fig. 9 is an illustration of the use of the *Abstraction strategy* to *Construct a Product model* in the Lyee[1] industrial project. The guideline of Fig. 8 was followed for the definition of the *Lyee User Requirements Model* (*LURM*) by abstracting from the *Lyee Software Requirements Model* (*LSRM*) [24]. The latter is used by the LyeeAll CASE tool [13, 14] in order to generate programs, provided a set of well-formatted software requirements are given. These requirements are expressed in rather low-level terms such as screen layouts and database accesses. Moreover they are influenced by the LyeeALL internals such as the Lyee identification policy of program variables, the generated program structure and the Lyee program execution control mechanism. Experience with LyeeAll has shown the need to acquire software requirements from relatively high level user-centric requirements. The meta-model of the LSRM presented in the bottom part of Fig. 9 has been used as a baseline paradigm model for the more abstract LURM construction shown in the top part of Fig. 9.

The central concept in the LSRM is called a *Word*. A *Word* corresponds to a program variable: input words represent values captured from the external world whereas output words are produced by the system by applying specific formulae. The execution of formulae is controlled by the *Process Route Diagram (PRD)*. A *PRD* is composed of *Scenario Functions* (*SF*), composed of *Pallets*, which are made of *Vectors*. In order to carry out the generated program control the function generates its own *Words*, such as the *Action words* related to *Vectors* and *Routing words* to distribute the control over the various *SFs* of a *PRD*.

In order to comply with the Lyee paradigm, the LURM should be centred on a notion, which abstracts from the concept of *Word*. Obviously *Words* required by the Lyee processing mechanism are not relevant at this level. On the contrary, the concern is only with *Domain words*. Besides, there is a need to provide the requirements holder with a means to grasp a 'set of words' conceptually associated with one another. The notion of '*System interaction*' is proposed for that purpose. An interaction delineates a number of input and output data, logically assembled together. Each word of an interaction is defined as a model element called *Item* by applying the *Abstraction strategy* (Fig. 8). The concept of *Defined* is proposed as an aggregation of

---

[1] Lyee, which stands for GovernmentaL MethodologY for SoftwarE ProvidencE, is a methodology for software development used for the implementation of business software applications. Lyee was invented by Fumio Negoro.

logically related *Items* thanks to the *Aggregation strategy*. The *Specialisation strategy* is applied in order to specialise the *Item* into *Output* and *Input*. An *Output* is produced by the system whereas the *Input* is captured from the user. In the same manner, the *Input* is specialised into *Active* and *Passive*. The former triggers the system actions whereas the latter represents values captured from the user. Similarly, the concept of *Precedence Succedence Graph (PSG)* is obtained by abstraction of the *PRD* concept from the LSRM. It specifies the ordering conditions between *Defineds* as the *PRD* do it with *Words*.

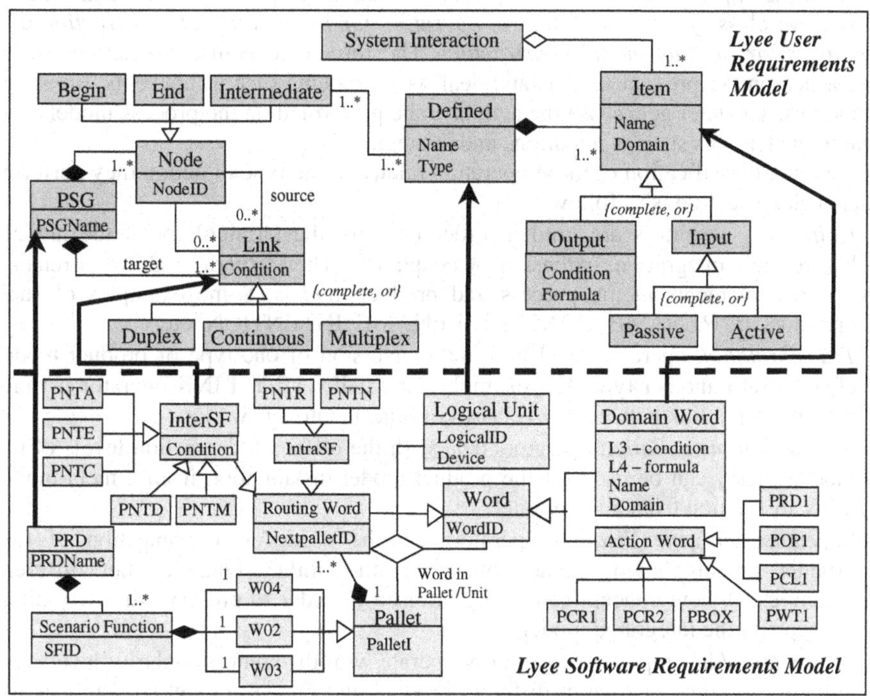

Fig. 9. Lyee Product Models for Software Requirements and for User Requirements

The process part of the LURM was defined by following the *Pattern-based strategy* (Fig. 7). A set of patterns has been defined to take into account different situations in the user requirements definition. Each pattern provides an advice to capture and formulate requirements. More about these patterns, their definition and application could be found in [24].

6 Generic Features

The paper demonstrates that *meta-modelling* remains the core technique in SME. All approaches presented above are based on meta-modelling. In the assembly-based SME approach every method chunk must be instance of a specific meta-model for modular methods [20]. The extension-based approach depends on the model of the method to extend which is itself instance of a specific meta-model, and proposes patterns to extend this model. The patterns are generated from the meta-patterns that are also defined at the meta level. The paradigm-based approach is generally based on meta-modelling.

All these approaches deal with the definition, instantiation, transformation or assembly of method models and meta-models. The corresponding method construction activities can be generalised by the means of a set of *generic operators*. As all these approaches explicitly separate the notions of product model and process model, we classify these operators in *operators for process model construction* and *operators for product model construction*. The former generalise the actions to be performed on the product models and deal with elements such as concepts, links and properties. The later generalise the actions to be performed on the process models and deal with elements such as intentions and strategies.

An other classification of these operators relates to the type of action they perform. Such a classification is as follows:

- *Unification* operators are used in order to unify the terminology of the models before their integration, extension or adaptation. They generally allow to rename different elements in the process and product models. Some examples of such operators are RENAME_CONCEPT, RENAME_INTENTION, etc.
- *Transformation* operators deal with the conversion of one type of product model element into another type. For example, the OBJECTIFY_LINK operator permits to transform a link between two classes of objects into a new class.
- *Abstraction/instantiation* operators deal with the different abstraction levels of the models. They can be used for the product model instantiation from a meta-model or its abstraction from another one.
- S*pecialisation/generalisation* operators can be used for a connection of two product models having some concepts with similar semantics but different structures. A new concept can be generalised in order to preserve the two initial concepts in the integrated model.
- Aggregation/decomposition operators operate with different granularity levels and allow to combine or to split different product and process model elements as for example AGGREGATE_CONCEPTS or DECOMPOSE_ SECTION.
- A*ddition* operators allow to add supplementary elements (concepts, links, sections) in the product and process models in order to connect or to enhance them.
- *Cancellation* operators such as REMOVE_LINK or REMOVE_STRATEGY eliminate the inadequate elements from the product or process models.

We are aware of the fact that this list of operators is not an exhaustive one and we are currently working on it.

The last point that we propose to raise in this section concerns the *requirements matching problem*. The specificity of SME approaches is that they are requirements-driven. Any method construction technique proposed by such an approach must take into account the definition of the method requirements and the selection of the solutions that satisfy them. As a consequence, the matching mechanism between the requirements model and the solution model is paramount. Our belief is that such a mechanism must include *similarity measures*. The method engineer needs to be able to measure the similarity of different elements from the process models like intentions, sections or entire maps as well as the similarity of different product models elements like concepts or links. Currently every approach integrated in our generic process model proposes its own manner to resolve the requirements matching problem. Our objective is to propose some generic process and product similarity measures that could be adapted or instantiated in different SME approaches.

7 Conclusion

In this paper we proposed a generic process model for SME. This process model allows us to capture different approaches for project specific method construction and to provide guidelines in order to assist the method engineer in the selection of the approach best fitting the project situation.

Our generic process model already contains three SME approaches that can be applied separately or combined in order to construct a new method or to adapt an existing one. As this model is defined as a map with associated guidelines it is possible to include other SME approaches in a rather simple manner. They can be integrated as different strategies to satisfy the intention *Construct a Method* (Fig. 1).

In order to provide a strong methodological support with our generic SME process model we propose a set of generic method construction operators. We are also working on different similarity measures which are necessary to evaluate the similarity between different method elements as well as for evaluating the matching conditions of a given method chunk with the method requirements.

Our future preoccupation is to complete this generic SME process model by integrating other approaches and to validate it through real projects. We will also continue refining the definition of the generic method construction operators and the metrics for process and product models similarity measurement. We will also consider the exploit of the distance measures supposing that in some cases they might be more suitable than those of similarity.

References

1. Benjamen A., *Une Approche Multi-démarches pour la modélisation des démarches méthodologiques*. PhD dissertation. University of Paris 1 – Sorbonne, 1999.
2. Böhlen M.H. *Valid time integrity constraint*. Report TR 94-30. 1994.
3. Brinkkemper S., M. Saeki, F. Harmsen, *Assembly Techniques for Method Engineering*. Proc. of CAiSE'98. Pisa Italy, 1998.
4. Cockburn A., *Writing Effective Use Cases*. Addison-Wesley, 2001.
5. Deneckere, R., *Approche d'extension de méthodes fondée sur l'utilisation de composants génériques*, PhD thesis, University of Paris 1-Sorbonne, 2001.
6. Deneckere, R., Souveyet, C., *Patterns for extending an OO model with temporal features*. Proceedings of OOIS'98 conference. Springer-Verlag, Paris (France), 1998.
7. Gehani N., Jagadish H.V. *Ode as an active database: constraints and triggers*. Proceedings of the 17th VLDB, Barcelona, Spain, pp. 327–336. 1991.
8. Grundy, J.C., J.R. Venable, *Towards an integrated environment for method engineering*, Proc. IFIP WG 8.1 Conf. on 'Method Engineering', Chapman and Hall, pp 45–62, 1996.
9. Harmsen A.F., *Situational Method Engineering*. Moret Ernst & Young , 1997.
10. Hofstede, A.H.M. Ter., *Information modelling in data intensive domains*, Dissertation, University of Nijimegen, The Netherlands 1993.

11. Jacobson I., M. Christenson, P. Jonsson, G. Oevergaard, *Object Oriented Software Engineering: a Use Case Driven Approach.* Addison-Wesley, 1992.
12. Jarke M., C. Rolland, A. Sutcliffe, R. Domges, *The NATURE requirements Engineering.* Shaker Verlag, Aachen 1999.
13. Negoro, F. *Methodology to Determine Software in a Deterministic Manner.* Proceedings of ICH, Beijing, China, 2001.
14. Negoro, F. *A proposal for Requirement Engineering*, Proceedings of ADBIS, Vilnius, Lithuania, 2001.
15. Plihon V., J. Ralyté, A. Benjamen, et al. A *Reuse-Oriented Approach for the Construction of Scenario Based Methods.* Proc. of the ICSP'98, Chicago, US, 1998.
16. Prakash, N., *On Method Statics and Dynamics. Information Systems.* Vol.34, No.8, 1999.
17. Prakash, N., M.P.S. Bhatia. *Generic Models for Engineering Methods of Diverse Domains.* Proc. of CAISE'02, Toronto, Canada, LNCS Volume 2348, pp. 612., 2002.
18. Punter H.T., K. Lemmen, *The MEMA model: Towards a new approach for Method Engineering.* Information and Software Technology, 38(4), pp.295–305, 1996.
19. Ralyté J., C. Rolland, *An Assembly Process Model for Method Engineering.* Proceedings of the 13th CAISE'01, Interlaken, Switzerland, 2001.
20. Ralyté J., C. Rolland, *An approach for method reengineering.* Proceedings of the 20th International Conference on Conceptual Modelling, ER2001, Yokohama, Japan, 2001.
21. Ralyté J., *Requirements Definition for the Situational Method Engineering*, IFIP TC8/WG8.1 Working Conference on Engineering Information Systems in the Internet Context, Kanazawa, Japan, 2002.
22. Ralyté J., C. Rolland, V. Plihon, *Method Enhancement by Scenario Based Techniques.* Proceedings of the 11th CAiSE'99, Germany, 1999.
23. Ralyté J., *Reusing Scenario Based Approaches in Requirement Engineering Methods: CREWS Method Base.* Proc. of the First Int. Workshop REP'99 (DEXA'99), Florence, Italy, September 1999.
24. Rolland, C. *A User Centric View of Lyee Requirements.* In New Trends in Software Methodologies, Tools and Techniques, H. Fujita, P. Johannesson (Eds.). IOS Press, Ohmsha, 2002.
25. Rolland, C., C. Souveyet, M. Moreno, *An Approach for Defining Ways-of-Working*, Information Systems Journal, 1995.
26. Rolland C., V. Plihon, J. Ralyté, *Specifying the reuse context of scenario method chunks.* Proc. of the 10th CAISE'98, Pisa Italy, 1998.
27. Rolland, C., N. Prakash, A. Benjamen: *A Multi-Model Vew of Process Modelling*, Requirements Engineering Journal (4)(4), pp169–187, 1999.
28. Saeki, M., K. Wen-yin, *Specifying Software Specification and Design Methods*, Proc. CAISE'94, LNCS 811, Springer Verlag, pp 353–366, Berlin, 1994.
29. Saeki M., K. Iguchi, K Wen-yin, M Shinohara, *A meta-model for representing software specification & design methods.* Proc. of the IFIP WG8.1 Conference on Information Systems Development Process, Come, pp 149–166, 1993.
30. Snodgrass, I. Ahn. A ytaxonomy of time in databases. Proceedings of ACM SIGMOD conference. 1985.

Modeling Organizational Architectural Styles in UML

Jaelson F. B. Castro[1], Carla T. L. L. Silva[1], John Mylopoulos[2]

[1] Centro de Informática, Universidade Federal de Pernambuco, Av. Prof. Luiz Freire S/N, Recife PE, Brazil 50732-970, + 55 81 32718430
{jbc,ctlls}@cin.ufpe.br

[2] Dept. of Computer Science University of Toronto, 10 King's College Road Toronto M5S3G4, Canada, +1 416 978 5180
jm@cs.toronto.edu

Abstract. Today's information systems operate within a dynamic, organizational context and consequently require flexible architectures to ensure that they remain operational and useful. The Tropos software development methodology is founded on the premise that social and intentional concepts (such as those of *actor* and *goal*) can be used throughout the development process from early requirements to implementation. Earlier work within the scope of the project has defined a number of organizational architectural styles which are suitable for cooperative, dynamic and distributed applications. In this paper, we use UML to describe these novel architectural styles. In doing so we are able to provide a detailed representation of both the structure and behaviour of the styles.

1 Introduction

Many information systems fail to properly support the organizations of which they are an integral part. This often happens due to a lack of proper understanding of the organizational context by the system developers. It can also be the result of frequent organizational changes that cannot be accommodated by existing systems (or their maintainers). In this context, requirement engineering has been recognized as the most critical phase in information systems development, because technical considerations have to be balanced against social and organizational ones. The Tropos project [1], [2] has proposed a software development methodology inspired by organizational concepts, which reduces as much as possible this impedance mismatch between an information system and its intended environment. The proposed methodology supersedes traditional development techniques, such as structured and object-oriented ones in the sense that it is tailored to systems which operate within an organizational context.

Companies are continually changing as they strive to improve their business strategies and processes. Stakeholders are demanding ever more flexible and complex systems. Hence, software has to be based on architectures that can evolve and change continually to accommodate new components and meet new requirements. Software architectures describe a software system at a macroscopic level in terms of a manageable number of subsystems/components/modules interrelated through data and control

J. Eder and M. Missikoff (Eds.): CAiSE 2003, LNCS 2681, pp. 111–126, 2003.

dependencies. However, an architecture is more than just structure, it includes rules on how system functionality is achieved in terms of the structure. A flexible architecture with loosely coupled components is much more likely to accommodate new feature requirements than one that has been highly optimized specifically for its initial set of requirements. Unfortunately, the classical architectural styles [12] and the styles for e-business applications [13],[14] do not focus on business processes nor on non-functional requirements of the application. As a result, the organizational structure is not described nor the conceptual high-level perspective of the application.

In this context, the Tropos project has defined organizational architectural styles [7],[8],[9] based on concepts and design alternatives coming from research in organization management, used to model coordination of business stakeholders – individuals, physical or social systems. From this perspective, software system is like a social organization of coordinated autonomous components that interact in order to achieve private and shared goals. The NFR framework [6] can be used to conduct the selection of the most suitable organizational architectural style, using as criteria desired qualities (non-functional requirements, or NFRs) identified during requirements analysis. Tropos relies on the i* notation [5] to describe both requirements and organizational architectural styles. Unfortunately, this notation is not widely accepted by software practitioners, since it is just beginning to be recognized as a suitable notation for representing requirements, and tool support is also limited. Moreover, it is not able to represent details that are sometimes required in architectural design, such as the exchange of signals and data between architectural components, as well as the valid sequence of these signals (protocol).

On the other hand, the Unified Modeling Language – UML [4] has been widely accepted as the industry's standard language of blueprints for software. As a graphical language for visualizing, specifying, constructing, and documenting the artifacts of a software-intensive system, UML has proven itself valuable in helping organizations to manage the complexity of their systems. UML has also been used to represent the architecture of simple and complex systems. As an architectural description language, UML can provide means for representing design decisions. It can lead to architectural models which describes the high-level design elements of the system and their connectors, supporting different viewpoints of the system under construction. Moreover, it is supported by a wide range of tool providers.

In an effort to provide a detailed representation for the architectural phase of the Tropos methodology, also to represent the organizational architectural styles in terms of a mainstream industrial notation, we propose in this paper an extension of UML to accommodate the concepts and features used for representing organizational architectures in Tropos. Such an extension is based on UML for Real-Time systems, which is tuned for real-time software systems and is being used for modeling software architectures. This proposal is an extension and improvement of an earlier attempt to represent Tropos concepts in UML [3].

The rest of this paper is organized as follows: section 2 presents the Tropos methodology. Section 3 describes how organizational architectural styles can be modeled using UML. In section 4, we discuss related work, while section 5 summarizes the results of this research and outlines future work.

2 The Tropos Methodology

Tropos proposes a software development methodology and a development framework which are founded on concepts used to model early requirements and complements proposals for agent-oriented programming platforms. This methodology is based on the premise that in order to build software that operates within a dynamic environment, one needs to analyze and model explicitly that environment in terms of "actors", their goals and dependencies on other actors. Tropos supports five phases of software development: Early Requirements, Late Requirements, Architectural Design, Detailed Design and Implementation.

Early requirements analysis focuses on the intentions of stakeholders. These intentions are modeled as goals, which through some form of analysis, eventually lead to the functional and non-functional requirements of the system-to-be [15]. Late requirements analysis results in a requirements specification, which describes all functional and non-functional requirements for the system-to-be. In *Tropos*, the information system is represented as one or more actors, along with other actors from the system's operational environment. In other words, the system comes into the picture as one or more actors who contribute to the fulfillment of stakeholder goals. Both the process to detect the relevant stakeholders and their goals as well as the method to conduct the transition among Tropos models are out of scope of this paper. For further details about *Tropos*, see [1],[2].

A system architecture constitutes a relatively small, intellectually manageable model of system structure, which describes how system components work together. Unfortunately, traditional architectural styles for e-business applications [13],[14] focus on web concepts, protocols and underlying technologies but not on business processes nor non functional requirements of the application. As a result, the organizational architecture styles are not described nor the conceptual high-level perspective of the e-business application.

Tropos has defined organizational architectural styles [7],[8],[9] for agent, cooperative, dynamic and distributed applications to guide the design of the system architecture. These architectural styles *(pyramid, joint venture* (Fig. 1), *structure in 5, takeover, arm's length, vertical integration, co-optation, bidding, …*) are based on concepts and design alternatives coming from research on organization management.

For example, the joint venture architectural style (Fig. 1) allows a decentralized architecture. The main feature of this style is that it involves an agreement between two or more principal partners/components in order to obtain the benefits derived from operating at a large scale, such as partial investment and lower maintenance costs, as well as reusing the experience and knowledge of the partners/components, since they pursue joint objectives.

To support modeling and analysis during the initial phases, Tropos adopts the concepts offered by *i** [5], a modeling framework defined in terms of concepts such as *actor* (actors can be *agents*, *positions* or *roles*), as well as social dependencies among actors, including *goal*, *softgoal*, *task* and *resource* dependencies. This means that both the system's environment and the system itself are seen as organizations of actors, each having goals to be fulfilled and each relying on other actors to help them with goal fulfillment.

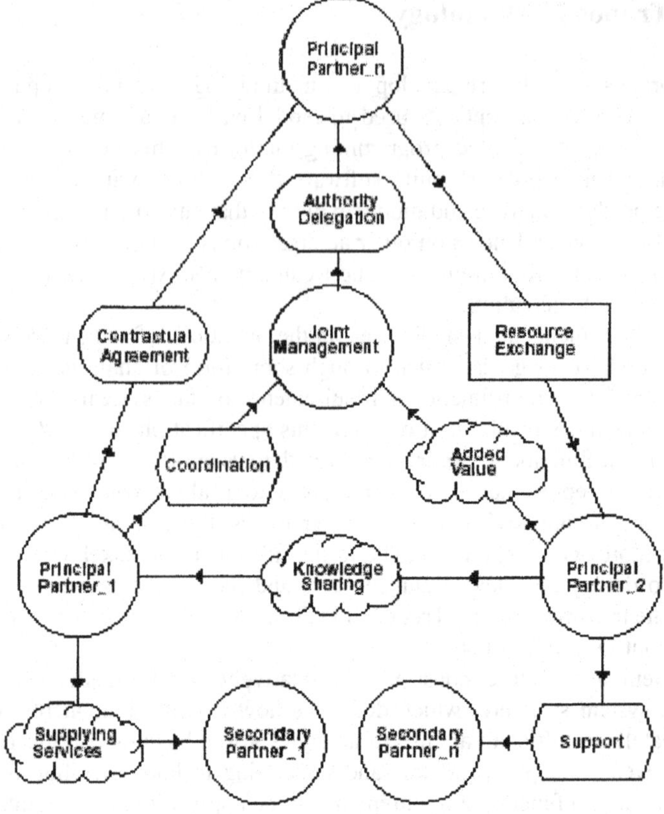

Fig. 1. Joint venture

As shown in Fig. 1, actors are represented as circles; *dependums* -- goals, softgoals, tasks and resources -- are respectively represented as ovals, clouds, hexagons and rectangles; and dependencies have the form *depender→dependum→dependee*. For further information on the nature of dependencies, please refer to [5]. Hence, in Tropos we have the following concepts:

- Actor: An actor is an active entity that carries out actions to achieve goals by exercising its know-how.
- Dependency: A dependency describes an intentional relationship between two actors, i.e., an "agreement" (called dependum) between two actors: the depender and the dependee, where one actor (depender) depends on another actor (dependee) on something (dependum).
- Depender: The depender is the depending actor.
- Dependee: The dependee is the actor who is depended upon.
- Dependum: The dependum is the type of the dependency and describes the nature of the agreement.
- Goal: A goal is a condition or state of affairs in the world that the stakeholders would like to achieve. How the goal is to be achieved is not specified, allowing al-

ternatives to be considered. Goal dependencies are used to represent delegation of responsibility for fulfilling a goal.

- Softgoal: A softgoal is a condition or state of affairs in the world that the actor would like to achieve, but unlike in the concept of (hard) goal, there are no clear-cut criteria for whether the condition is achieved, and it is up to subjective judgment and interpretation of the developer to judge whether a particular state of affairs in fact achieves sufficiently the stated softgoal. Softgoal dependencies are similar to goal dependencies, but their fulfillment cannot be defined precisely (for instance, the appreciation is subjective, or the fulfillment can occur only to a given extent).
- Resource: A resource is an (physical or informational) entity, with which the main concern is whether it is available. Resource dependencies require the dependee to provide a resource to the depender.
- Task: A task specifies a particular way of doing something. Tasks can also be seen as the solutions in the target system, which will satisfy the softgoals (operationalizations). These solutions provide operations, processes, data representations, structuring, constraints and agents in the target system to meet the needs stated in the goals and softgoals. Task dependencies are used in situations where the dependee is required to perform a given activity.

The first task during architectural design is to select among alternative architectural styles using as criteria the desired qualities identified in the previous phase (Late Requirements). They will guide the selection process of the appropriate architectural style. More details about the selection and non-functional requirements decomposition process can be found in [7],[8]. A further step in the architectural design consists in defining how the goals assigned to each actor are fulfilled by agents with respect to social patterns. Further details about social patterns can be found in [1],[2].

The detailed design phase is intended to introduce additional details for each architectural component of a system. In our case, this includes actor communication and actor behavior. To support this phase, we can propose to adopt extensions to UML [3], like AUML, the Agent Unified Modeling Language [18] proposed by the FIPA (Foundation for Physical Intelligent Agents) [16] and the OMG Agent Work group. Tropos also includes techniques for generating an implementation from a detailed design. For further details about these phases of *Tropos* methodology, see [1],[2].

In the next section, we show how architectural design can be represented by using an extension of UML. We expose our proposal for representing architectural design in the Tropos methodology using this extension of UML.

3 Modeling Organizational Architectural Styles in UML

Powerful extensibility mechanisms of UML enables us to represent new concepts in UML and a number of views are captured and sufficiently represented through the use of the UML meta-model. In this section we show how architectural constructs could be derived from more general UML concepts by using these mechanisms and also describe how the concepts and features used for representing organizational architectures into Tropos are captured and rendered using these constructs.

3.1 Representing Architectures in UML

The UMLRT [10],[11] is using UML as an architectural modeling language. Some specific architectural modeling concepts are defined as specializations of generic UML concepts. This allows us to take advantage of the notation that is widely recognized by software practitioners. These specializations, usually expressed as stereotypes, conform to the generic semantics of the corresponding UML concepts, but provide additional semantics specified by constraints [10]:

- Capsules: A capsule is a stereotype of the UML class concept with some specific features. A capsule uses its ports for all interactions with its environment. The communication with others capsule is done by one or more ports. The interconnection with other capsules is via connectors using signals. A capsule is a specialized active class and is used for modeling a self contained component of a system. For instance, a capsule may be used to capture an entire subsystem, or even a complete system.
- Ports: A port represents an interaction point between a capsule and its environment. They convey signals between the environment and the capsule. The type of signals and the order in which they may appear is defined by the protocol associated with the port. The port notation is shown as a small hollow square symbol. If the port symbol is placed overlapping the boundary of the rectangle symbol denotes a public visibility. If the port is shown inside the rectangle symbol, then the port is hidden and its visibility is private. When viewed from within the capsule, ports can be of two kinds: relay and end ports. Relay ports (Fig. 8) are ports that simply pass all signals through and end ports are the ultimate sources and sinks of all signals sent by capsules. These signals are generated by the state machines of capsules.
- Protocols: A protocol specifies a set of valid behaviors (signal exchanges) between two or more collaborating capsules. However, to make such a dynamic pattern reusable, protocols are decoupled from a particular context of collaborating capsules and are defined instead in terms of abstract entities called protocol roles (stereotype of Classifier Role in UML) (Fig. 9).
- Connectors: A connector is an abstraction of a message-passing channel that connects two or more ports. Each connector is typed by a protocol that defines the possible interactions that can take place across that connector (Fig. 8).

3.2 Organizational Architectural Styles in UML

The organizational styles are generic structures defined at a metalevel that can be instantiated to design a specific application architecture. They support non-functional requirements, represented in Tropos methodology such as softgoals, during architectural design phase. Unlike functional requirements which define what a software is expected to do, non-functional requirements specify global constraints on how the software operates or how the functionality is exhibited. NFRs are as important as the functional ones. They are not simply desired quality properties, but critical aspects of dynamic systems without which the applications cannot work and evolve properly. The need to treat non-functional properties explicitly is a critical issue when software architecture is built. Organizational architectures integrate NFR with architectural project, since NFRs are composing part of these styles.

Aiming to narrow the semantic gap between a software architecture and the requirements model from which it is derived, Tropos relies on the i* notation [5] to describe both requirements and organizational architectural styles. Unfortunately, this notation is not widely accepted by software practitioners, since it is just beginning to be recognized as a suitable notation for representing requirements and its tool support is also limited. On the other hand, the Unified Modeling Language- UML [4] has been used to represent the architecture of simple and complex systems. Using UML as an Architecture Design Language in the Tropos methodology allow us for representing detailed information which sometimes is required in architectural design, such as set of signals that are exchanged between architectural components, which are not supported by the i* notation. In the sequel we explain how the concepts of Tropos can be accommodated within UML-RT, in order to represent organizational architectures in UML.

As explained in section 2.1, in Tropos actors are active entities that carries out actions to achieve goals by exercising their know-how. In section 3.1, we explained that in UML Real-Time, capsules are specialized active classes used for modeling self contained components of a system. Hence, an actor in Tropos is represented in terms of a capsule in UML-RT (Fig. 2). Note that ports are physical parts of the implementation of a capsule that mediate the interaction of the capsule with the outside world. The motivation and reasoning for mapping these concepts to UML include those of [17].

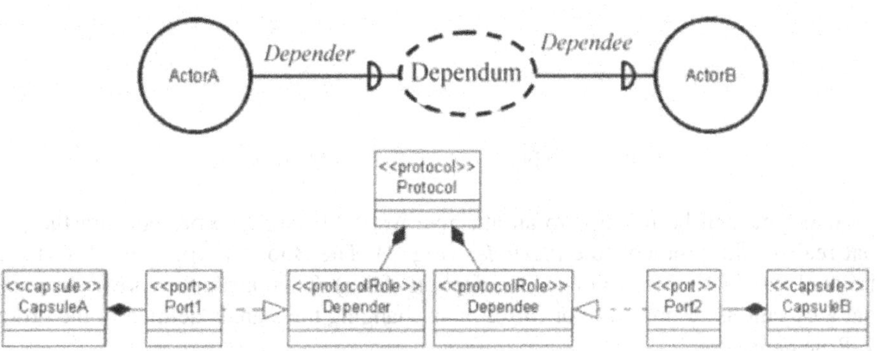

Fig. 2. Mapping a dependency between actors to UML

In Tropos a dependency describes an "agreement" (called *dependum*) between two actors playing the roles of *depender* and *dependee,* respectively. The *depender* is the depending actor, and the *dependee,* the actor who is depended upon. Dependencies have the form *depender→dependum→dependee*. In UML-RT, a protocol is an explicit specification of the contractual agreement between its participants, which plays specific roles in the protocol. In other words, a protocol captures the contractual obligations that exist between capsules. Hence, a *dependum* is mapped to a protocol and the roles of *depender* and *dependee* are mapped to protocol roles that are comprised by the protocol (Fig. 2).

The type of the dependency between two actors (called *dependum*) describes the nature of the agreement. Tropos defines four types of *dependums*: goals, softgoals, tasks and resources. Each type of *dependum* will define different features in the protocol and therefore in ports that realizes its protocol roles.

As noted earlier, protocols are defined in terms of entities called *protocol roles.* Since *protocol roles* are abstract classes and ports play a specific role in some protocol, a *protocol role* defines the *type* of a port, which simply means that the port implements the behavior specified by that *protocol role.* As defined earlier, capsules are complex, physical, possibly distributed architectural objects that interact with their surroundings through ports. Note that a port is both a composite part of the structure of the capsule and a constraint on its behavior.

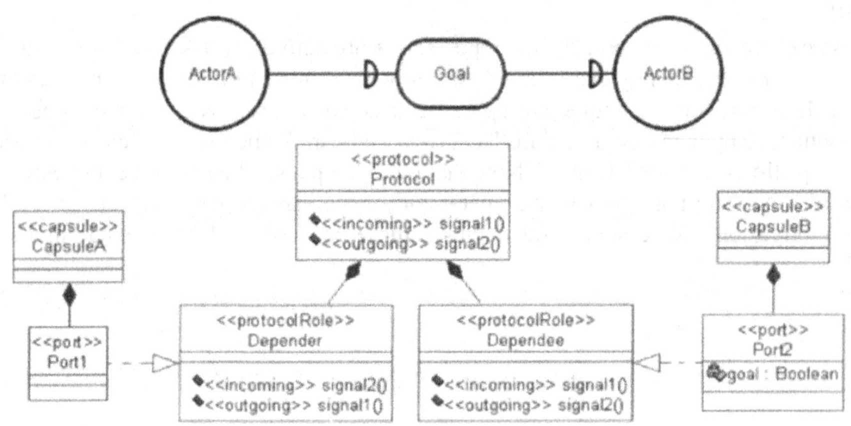

Fig. 3. Mapping a goal dependency to UML

Goal type will be mapped to an attribute with Boolean type present into the port that realizes the protocolRole *dependee* (Fig. 3). The Boolean type is used to depict the goal satisfaction (true) or no satisfaction (false). This attribute represents a goal that a capsule is responsible for fulfill by exchanging the signals defined in the protocolRole *dependee*.

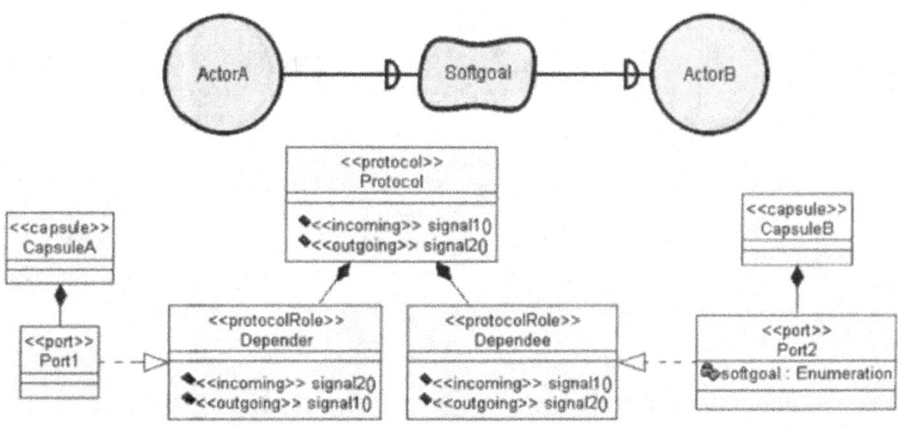

Fig. 4. Mapping a softgoal dependency to UML

Softgoal type is mapped to an attribute with enumerated type present into the port that realizes the protocolRole *dependee* (Fig. 4). The enumerated type is used to depict the degree of satisfaction of the softgoal. This attribute represents a quality goal that a capsule is responsible for fulfill to a given extent by exchanging the signals defined in the protocolRole *dependee*.

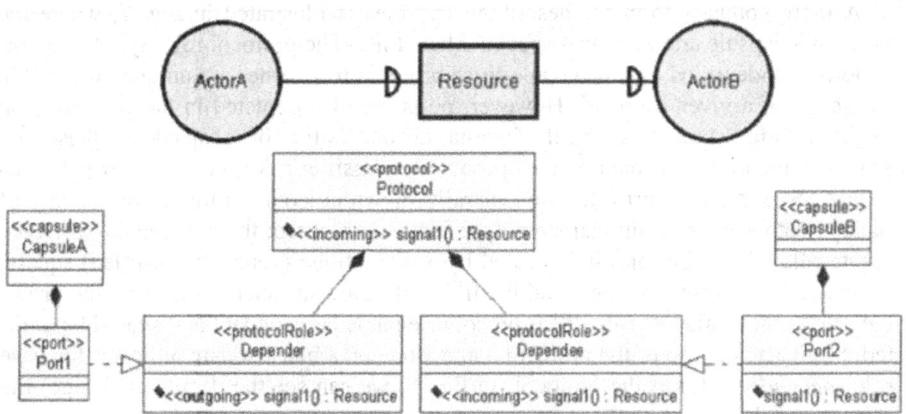

Fig. 5. Mapping a resource dependency to UML

Resource type is mapped to the return type of an abstract method placed on protocolRole *dependee* that will be realized by a port of a capsule (Fig. 5). This return type represents the type of the resulting product from an operation related to some service that the capsule is responsible to perform. This resulting product will represent a resource that a capsule is required to provide by exchanging signals defined in the protocolRole *dependee*.

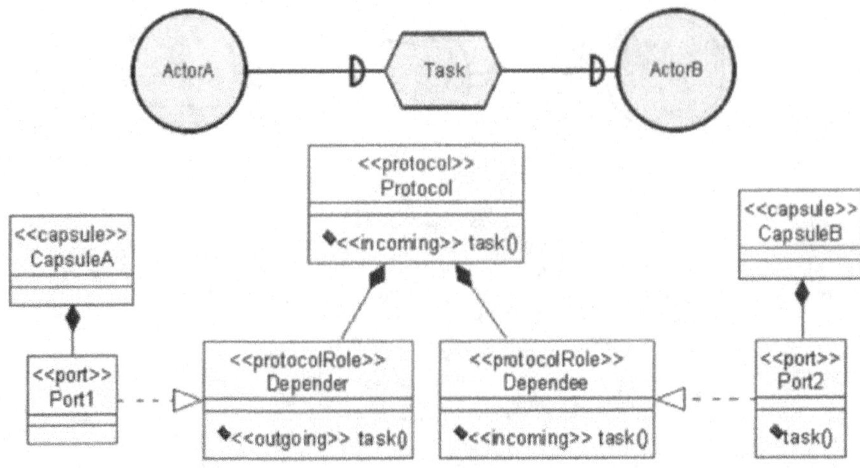

Fig. 6. Mapping a task dependency to UML

Task type is mapped to an abstract method placed on protocolRole *dependee* that will be realized by a port of a capsule (Fig. 6). This method will represent an operation related to some service that the capsule is responsible to perform by exchanging signals defined in the protocolRole *dependee*.

A more compact form for describing capsules is illustrated in Fig. 7, where the ports of a capsule are listed in a special labeled list. The protocol role (type) of a port is normally identified by a pathname since protocol role names are unique only within the scope of a given protocol. However, ports are also depicted in the collaboration diagrams (Fig. 8) that describe the internal decomposition of a capsule. In these diagrams, ports are represented by the appropriate classifier roles, i.e., the *port roles*. To reduce visual clutter, port roles are generally shown in iconified form. For the case of binary protocols, an additional stereotype icon can be used: the port playing the conjugate role (*depender* role) is indicated by a white-filled (versus black-filled) square. In that case, the protocol name and the tilde suffix are sufficient to identify the protocol role as the conjugate role; the protocol role name is redundant and should be omitted. Similarly, the use of the protocol name alone on a black square indicates the base role (*dependee* role) of the protocol. In Fig. 8, we can see the details of (inside) the capsule and the end port/relay port distinction is indicated graphically.

Fig. 7. A capsule class diagram

In UML-RT, each connector is typed by a protocol that specifies the *desired* behavior that can take place over that connector. A key feature of connectors is that they can only interconnect ports that play complementary roles in the protocol associated with the connector. In a class diagram, a connector is modeled by an association while in a capsule collaboration diagram it is declared through an association role. Hence, a dependency (*depender→dependum→dependee*) in Tropos is mapped to a connector in UML-RT (Fig. 7 and Fig. 8).

In the sequel we show how the Joint Venture organizational architectural style is modeled using UML-RT.

3.3 Joint Venture in UML

The UML notation of capsules, ports and connectors is used to model the architectural actors and their dependencies. In Fig. 8, each capsule is representing an actor of the joint venture architecture. When an actor is a *dependee* of some dependency, its corresponding capsule has an implementation port for each dependency (ex. Port1), which is used to provide services for others capsules. When an actor is a *depender* of some dependency, its corresponding capsule has an implementation port to exchange messages (ex. Port3). However, notice that there is some reasonable distance between the representation given in Figure 1 and that in Figure 8.

This architecture presents six capsules disposed according to Fig. 8:

- The capsule Joint Management is responsible for ensuring the strategic operation and coordination of such a system and its partner capsules on a global dimension. Through the delegation of authority it coordinates tasks and manages sharing of knowledge and resources.
- The two secondary partners are capsules responsible for supplying services or for supporting tasks for the organization core.
- The three principal partners are capsules responsible for managing and controlling themselves on a local dimension. They can interact directly with other principal partners to exchange, provide and receive services, data and knowledge.

From Fig. 1 you can recall the goal dependency *Authority Delegation* between *Principal Partner_n* and *Joint Management* actors. Each actor present in Fig. 1 is mapped to a capsule in Fig. 8. Each *dependum*, i.e., the "agreement" between these two actors is mapped to the protocol in Fig. 9. A protocol is an explicit specification of the contractual agreement between the participants in the protocol. In our study these participants are the two actors previously mapped to capsules. Each dependency is mapped to a connector in Fig. 8. Each connector is typed by the protocol that represents the *dependum* of its corresponding dependency. The type of the dependency describes the nature of the agreement, i.e., the connector type describes the nature of the protocol. The four types of *dependums* (Goal, Softgoal, Task and Resource) are mapped to four types of protocols (Figures 9, 10, 11 and 12).

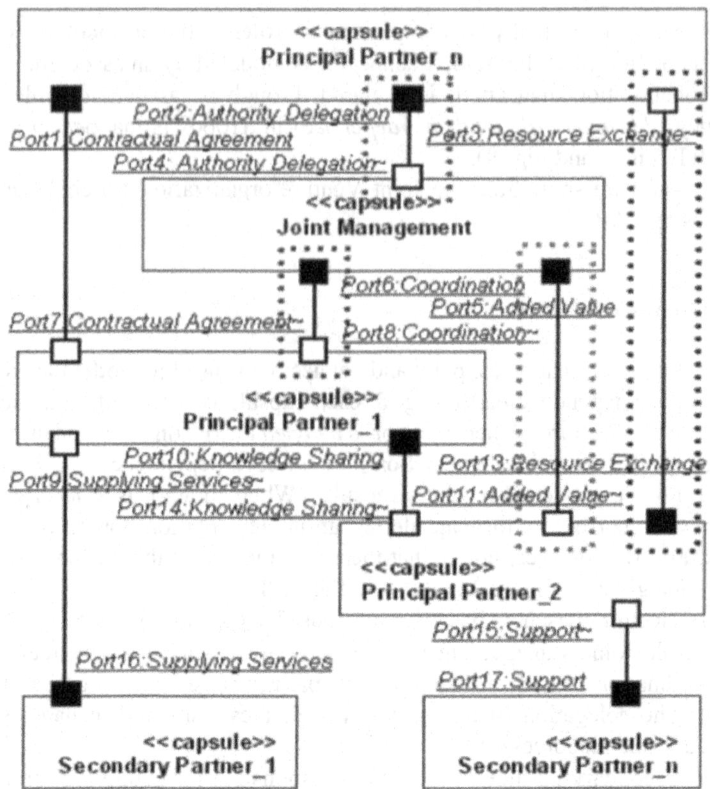

Fig. 8. Joint Venture Style in UML-RT's capsule collaboration diagram

For example, in the Goal type, the protocol *Authority Delegation* (Fig. 9) assures that this goal will be fulfilled by using the signals described in the protocolRole *dependee*. The goal will be mapped to a Boolean attribute present in the port that implements the protocolRole *dependee*. This attribute will be true if the goal has been fulfilled and false otherwise. Hence, in the dependency between *Principal Partner_n* and *Joint Management* capsules depicted in the second doted area of Fig. 8, the goal dependency will be mapped to a boolean attribute located in the port which composes the capsule *Principal Partner_n* and implements the protocolRole *dependee* of the protocol that assures the fulfillment of this goal (Fig. 9).

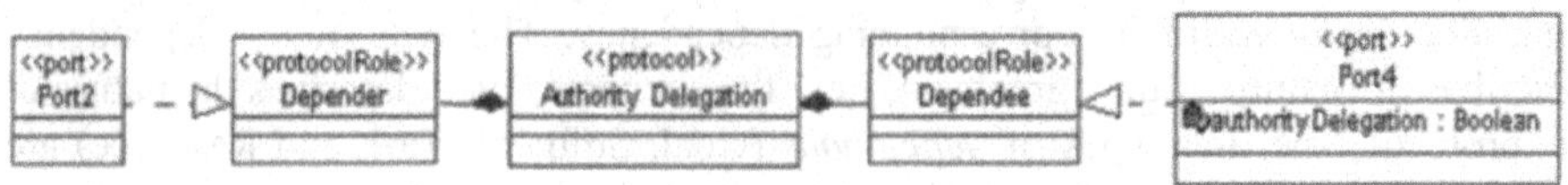

Fig. 9. Protocols and Ports representing the Joint Venture's goal dependency Authority Delegation

Now examine the softgoal dependency *Added Value* between *Principal Partner_2* and *Joint Management* actors depicted in Fig. 1. In this case, the protocol *Added*

Value (Fig. 10) assures that this softgoal will be satisfied in some extent by using the signals described in the protocolRole *dependee.* The softgoal will be mapped to a enumerated attribute present in the port that implements the protocolRole *dependee.* This attribute will represent different degrees of softgoal fulfillment. Hence, in the dependency between *Principal Partner_2* and *Joint Management* capsules depicted in the third doted area of Fig. 8, the softgoal dependency will be mapped to a enumerated attribute located in the port which composes the *Joint Management* capsule and implements the protocolRole *dependee* of the protocol that assures some degree of fulfillment of this softgoal (Fig. 10).

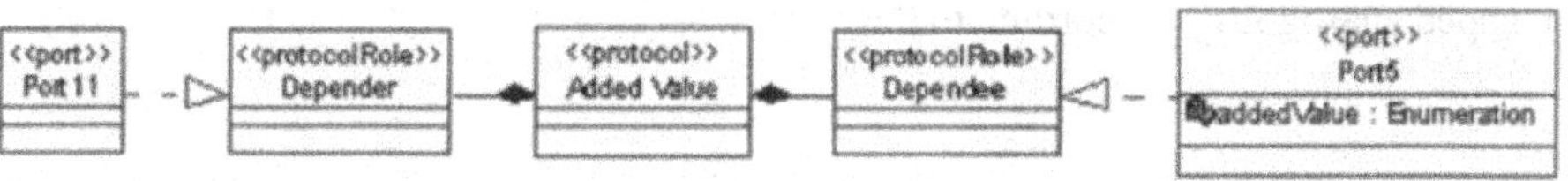

Fig. 10. Protocols and Ports representing the Joint Venture's softgoal dependency Added Value

In the sequence, look at the task dependency *Coordination* between *Principal Partner_1* and *Joint Management* actors depicted in the Fig. 1. Here, the protocol *Coordination* (Fig. 11) assures that this task will be performed by using the signals described in the protocolRole *dependee.* The task itself will be mapped to a <<incoming>> signal in the protocolRole *dependee* and the port that implements that protocolRole will be committed to realize their signals. Hence, in the dependency between *Principal Partner_1* and *Joint Management* capsules depicted in the first doted area of Fig. 8, the task dependency will be mapped to a << incoming>> signal placed in the protocolRole *dependee* of the protocol that assures the performing of this task. The *Joint Management* capsule is composed by a port which implements this protocolRole *dependee* (Fig. 11).

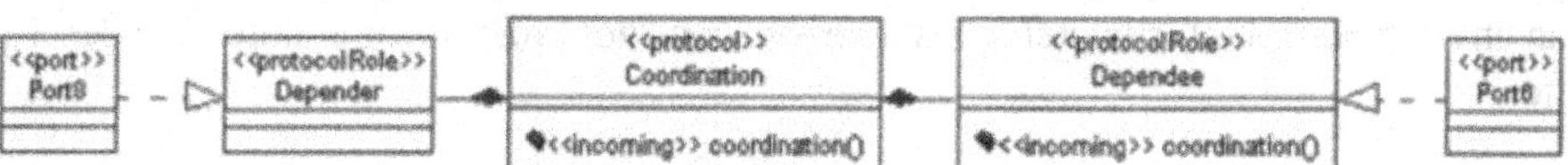

Fig. 11. Protocols and Ports representing the Joint Venture's task dependency coordination

Finally we have the resource dependency *Resource Exchange* between *Principal Partner_2* and *Principal Partner_n* depicted in the Fig. 1. Again, the protocol *Resource Exchange* (Fig. 12) assures that this resource will be provided by using the signals described as <<incoming>> signals in the protocolRole *dependee.* The resource will be mapped to a <<incoming>> signal that returns an information of type resource in the protocolRole *dependee* and the port that implements that protocolRole will be committed to realize their signals. Hence, in the dependency between *Principal Partner_2* and *Principal Partner_n* capsules depicted in the fourth doted area of Fig. 8, the resource dependency will be mapped to an <<incoming>> signal that returns an information of type resource and is placed in the protocolRole *dependee* of the protocol that assures the providing of this resource. The *Principal Partner_2* capsule is composed by a port which implements this protocolRole *dependee* (Fig. 12).

Fig. 12. Protocols and Ports representing the Joint Venture's resource dependency Resource Exchange

Although we have only detailed the mapping of four dependencies in the Joint Venture Style to their respective representation in UML-RT, the remaining ones are mapped analogously, according to their types.

4 Related Work

Social concepts have always been a source of inspiration for multi-agent research, and recently the agent community has been returning the favor by exploring the potential of agent-based models for studying social phenomena. The result of this interaction has been the formalization of a number of social and psychological concepts with important applications in engineering agent systems, concepts that are not directly supported in UML. Hence, Parunak [19] addresses an area of agent functionality that goes beyond the capabilities of current UML and presents a number of concepts, including "group", "role", "dependency," and "speech acts," into a coherent syntax for describing organizational structures, and proposes UML conventions and AUML extensions [18] to support their use in the analysis, specif ication, and design of multi-agent systems. In the case of social structures, insights from AALAADIN [20], dependency theory, and holonics can be fused into a single metamodel of groups as composed of agents occupying roles (defined as patterns of dependency and interaction) in an environment. Unfortunately, this approach was not tailored for architecture description.

5 Conclusions and Future Work

This paper proposes a set of UML extensions for representing the organizational architectural styles proposed in [7], based on UML for Real-Time systems. Use of these architectural styles allows us to build flexible architectures, with loosely coupled components, which can evolve and change continually to accommodate new feature requirements. Hence, it enables to realize stakeholders' demand for more flexible and complex systems [9]. Moreover, using organizational architectural styles in UML allow us for representing detailed information such as the communication signals exchanged by the components which compose the architecture. Currently, this additional feature isn't available in architectural design phase of Tropos methodology because it uses the i* notation in this phase. In Tropos, UML is used only in detailed design phase. Further advantages in using UML to model Tropos architectural styles include [17]:

– Unified way of cross-referencing model information: Having modeling information stored at one physical location further enables us to cross-reference that information. Cross-referencing is useful for maintaining the traceability among artifacts from architectural design and detailed design phases in Tropos.

To further develop this proposal, we plan to create a catalogue of organizational architectural styles in UML, also to extend UML to represent social patterns involving agents. Moreover, in order to evaluate our proposal, we intend to apply it to real projects.

References

1. Castro, J., Kolp, M., Mylopoulos, J.: Towards Requirements-Driven Information Systems Engineering: The Tropos Project. In Information Systems 27(6), Elsevier, Amsterdam, The Netherlands (2002) 365-389
2. Castro, J., Kolp, M., Mylopoulos, J.: Tropos: A requirements-Driven Software Development Methodology. In Proceedings oh the 13th Conf. on Advanced Information Systems Engineering, CAiSE 2001, Interlaken, Switzerland (2001). LNCS 2068, 108-123
3. Mylopoulos, J., Kolp, M., Castro, J.: UML for Agent-Oriented Software Development: the Tropos Proposal. In Proceedings of the Fourth International Conference on the Unified Modeling Language (<<UML>> 2001). Toronto, Canada (2001)
4. Rumbaugh, J., Jacobson, I., Booch, G.: The Unified Modeling Language – Reference Manual. Addison Wesley (1999)
5. Yu., E.: Modelling Strategic Relationships for Process Reengineering. Ph.D. thesis, Department of Computer Science, University of Toronto, Canada (1995)
6. Chung, L., Nixon, B. A., Yu, E., Mylopoulos, J.: Non-Functional Requirements in Software Engineering. Kluwer Publishing (2000)
7. Kolp, M., Castro, J., Mylopoulos, J.: A social organization perspective on software architectures. In Proc. of the 1st Int. Workshop From Software Requirements to Architectures. STRAW'01, Toronto, Canada (2001) 5–12
8. Kolp, M., Giorgini, P., Mylopoulos, J.: A goal-based organizational perspective on multi-agents architectures. In J.J. Ch. Meyer and Milind Tambe (Eds.) Intelligent Agents VIII: Agent Theories, Architectures, and Languages, Springer, August 2002.
9. Kolp, M., Giorgini, P., Mylopoulos, J: Information Systems Development through Social Structures, In Proc. of the 14th International Conference on Software Engineering and Knowledge Engineering (SEKE'02), Ishia, Italy, July 2002.
10. Selic, B., Rumbaugh, J.: Using UML for Modeling Complex Real-Time Systems. Rational Whitepaper (www.rational.com) (1998)
11. OMG: Unified Modeling Language 2.0. Initial submission to OMG RFP ad/00-09-01 (UML 2.0 Infrastructure RFP) and ad/00-09-02 (UML 2.0 Superstructure RFP).: Proposal version 0.63 (draft). http://www.omg.org/.
12. Shaw, M., Garlan, D.: Software Architecture: Perspectives on an Emerging Discipline. Upper Saddle River, N.J., Prentice Hall (1996)
13. Conallen, J.: Building Web Applications with UML. Addison-Wesley (2000)
14. IBM: Patterns for e-business. At http://www.ibm.com/developerworks/patterns (2001)
15. Dardenne, A., Lamsweerde, A.V., Fickas, S.: Goal-directed requirements acquisition. Science of Computer Programming, Vol. 20 (1993) 3–50
16. FIPA: The Foundation for Intelligent Physical Agents. At http://www.fipa.org (2001)

17. Medvidovic, N., Rosenblum, D.S., Robbins, J.E., Redmiles D.F.: Modeling Software Architectures in the Unified Modeling Language. Computer Science Department, University of Southern California, Los Angeles (2000)
18. Bauer, B., Muller, J., Odell., J.: Agent UML: A formalism for specifying multiagent interaction. In Proc. of the 1st Int. Workshop on Agent-Oriented Software Engineering. AOSE'00, Limerick, Ireland (2001) 91–104
19. Parunak, H.V.D., Odell., J.: Representing Social Structures in UML. Proc. of the Agent-Oriented Soft. Engineering Workshop. Agents 2001 Conference, Montreal, Canada (2001)
20. Ferber, J., Gutknecht, O.: A meta-model for the analysis and design of organizations in multi-agent systems. In Proceedings of Third International Conference on Multi-Agent Systems. ICMAS'98, IEEE Computer Society (1998) 128-135

No-redundant Metrics for UML Class Diagram Structural Complexity

Mª Esperanza Manso[1], Marcela Genero [2], and Mario Piattini [2]

[1]Department of Computer Science
University of Valladolid - Valladolid - Spain
manso@infor.uva.es
[2] Department of Computer Science
University of Castilla-La Mancha - Ciudad Real – Spain
{Marcela.Genero, Mario.Piattini}@uclm.es

Abstract. In software engineering it is widely acknowledged that the usage of metrics at the initial phases of the object oriented software life cycle can help designers to make better decisions and to predict external quality attributes, such as maintainability. Following this idea we have carried out three controlled experiments to ascertain if any correlation exists between the structural complexity and the size of UML class diagrams and their maintainability. We used 8 metrics for measuring the structural complexity of class diagrams due to the usage of UML relationships, and 3 metrics to measure their size. With the aim of determining which of these metrics are really relevant to be used as class diagrams maintainability indicators, we present in this work a study based on Principal Component Analysis. The obtained results show that the metrics related to associations, aggregations, generalizations and dependencies, are the most relevant whilst those related to size seem to be redundant.

Keywords: Class diagram structural complexity, class diagram maintainability, metrics, empirical validation, principal component analysis

1 Introduction

One of the principal goals of software engineering is to assure the quality of object oriented (OO) software from the early phases of the life-cycle, such as conceptual modelling. As class diagrams constitute a key artifact in the conceptual modelling phase, the effort spent on improving their maintainability is likely to pay off many times over in later phases.

We focus on maintainability because it has become one of the software product quality characteristics [25] that software development organizations are more concerned about, since it is the major resource consumer of the whole software life cycle [28][1]. But we are aware that maintainability is an "external quality attribute" that can only be evaluated once the product is finished or nearly finished. Therefore, it is necessary to have early indicators of such qualities based, for example, on the

[1] Maintainability is not restricted to code, it is an attribute of the different software products we hope to maintain [18], including also conceptual models.

J. Eder and M. Missikoff (Eds.): CAiSE 2003, LNCS 2681, pp. 127–142, 2003.

structural properties of class diagrams [5], such as their structural complexity and size. The theoretical basis for developing quantitative models relating structural properties and external quality attributes has been provided by Briand et al. [6] (see figure 1). It is the basis for much empirical research in the area of software artifact structural properties [16,17,30]. In this work we assume a similar representation to hold for UML class diagrams. We hypothesized that the structural properties (such as structural complexity and size) of a UML class diagram have an impact on its cognitive complexity. By cognitive complexity we mean the mental burden of the people who have to deal with the artifact (e.g. developers, testers, maintainers). High cognitive complexity leads to an artifact which reduces their understandability, and this conduces undesirable external qualities, such as decreased maintainability.

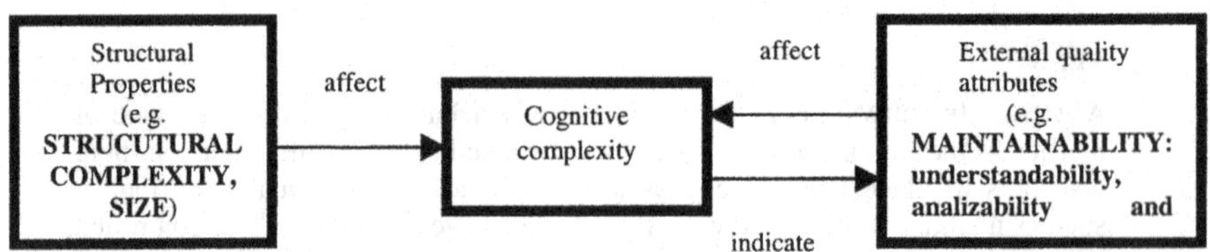

Fig. 1. Relationship between structural properties, cognitive complexity, understandability and external quality attributes [6]

In response to the great demand for measures of quality characteristics of class diagrams, and after a thorough review of some of the existing OO measures that can be applied at a high level design stage, not only to products [4,7,10,12, etc.] but also to development techniques [31], we have proposed a set of 8 measures for UML class diagram structural complexity [21][2], related to the usage of UML relationships such as, associations, dependencies, aggregations and generalizations; and we also considered traditional metrics, such as size metrics (see table 1).

Part of the information that these metrics provide might be redundant, which in statistical terms is equivalent to saying that metrics might be very correlated. This justifies the interest of analyzing the information that each metric captures to eliminate such redundancy. In the experimental research in software engineering [3,7,9], like in the other disciplines, this problem is solved by using the Principal Component Analysis (PCA) [15]. In this case, through the PCA, the purpose is to reduce the space of 11 metric dimensions that contain the initial information, in order to later study the correlation among these new dimensions, and the dependant variables of interest, in our case of maintainability.

With the aim of ascertaining if any correlation exists between the metrics we presented in table 1, and the class diagram maintainability characteristics, such as

[2] We focused on UML because it is considered a standard in OO modelling.

Table 1. Metrics for UML class diagram structural complexity

Type of Metrics	Metric definition
Size metrics	Number of Classes (NC). The total number of classes.
	Number of Attributes (NA). The total number of attributes.
	Number of Methods (NM). The total number of methods
Structural complexity metrics	Number of Associations (NAssoc).The total number of associations
	Number of Aggregations (NAgg). The total number of aggregation relationships within a class diagram (each whole-part pair in an aggregation relationship)
	Number of Dependencies (NDep). The total number of dependency relationships
	Number of Generalisations (NGen). The total number of generalization relationships within a class diagram (each parent-child pair in a generalization relationship)
	Number of Generalization hierarchies (NGenH). The total number of generalization hierarchies in a class diagram
	Maximum DIT (MaxDIT). It is the maximum DIT value obtained for each class of the class diagram. The DIT value for a class within a generalization hierarchy is the longest path from the class to the root of the hierarchy.
	Maximum HAgg (MaxHAgg). It is the maximum HAgg value obtained for each class of the class diagram. The HAgg value for a class within an aggregation hierarchy is the longest path from the class to the leaves.

understandability and analizability [25][3], we have carried out a familiy of three experiments [20,22,23]. The metric values calculated within the class diagrams used in these three experiments, is the data used in the PCA.

Summarising, and using the Goal-Question-Metric template (GQM) [1] for goal definition, the goals of this work are the following:

- First goal: Perform an *exploratory study of the UML class diagrams* to *characterize them* with respect to *a set of metrics,* from the point of view of *the software designers,* in the context of *students and professors in the Department of Computer Science at the University of Castilla-La Mancha, in Spain.*
- Second goal: Analize *the structural complexity and the size the UML class diagrams, to evaluate* them with respect to *their correlation with class diagram maintainability*, from the point of view of *the software designers* in the context of *students and professors in the Department of Computer Science at the University of Castilla-La Mancha, Spain.*

---

[3] Even though understandability has not been considered as a maintainability sub-characteristic by the ISO 9126 [25], we include it because there exists a lot of work related to software measurement, that considers understandability to be a factor that influences maintainability [8,18,24].

The rest of this paper is organized as follows: Section 2 briefly describes the PCA. The description of the data used in this study is presented in section 3, and the data analysis for obtaining no-redundant metrics for UML class diagrams comes in section 4. Finally, the last section presents some concluding remarks, and identifies further work related to OO metrics applied at early phases of OO software development.

2 Principal Component Analysis

If a group of variables in a data set are strongly correlated, these variables are likely to measure the same underlying dimensions (i.e., class internal quality attribute) of the object to be measured. PCA is a standard technique used to identify the underlying, orthogonal dimensions that explain relations between the variables in the data set.

Principal components (PCs) are linear combinations of the standarized independent variables. The sum of the square of the coefficients in each linear combination is equal to one. PCs are calculated as follows: The first PC is the linear combination of all standarized variables that explain a maximum amount of variance not explained in the data set. The second and subsequent PCs are linear combinations of all standarized variables, where each new PC is orthogonal to all previously calculated PCs, and captures a maximum variance under these conditions. Usually, only a subset of all variables have large coefficients –also called the *loading* of the variable– and therefore, contributes significantly to the variance of each PC. The variables with high loadings help identify the dimensions the PC is capturing, but this usually requires some degree of interpretation.

In order to identify these variables and interpret the PCs, we consider the rotated components. This is a technique where PCs are subjected to an orthogonal rotation. As a result, the rotated components show a clearer pattern of loadings, where the variables either have a very low or high impact on the PC. Several strategies exist to perform such a rotation. We used the *varimax* rotation, which is the most frequently used strategy in the literature.

For a set of n measures, there are at most, n orthogonal PCs, which are calculated in decreasing order of variance they explain in the data set. Associated with each PC is its *eigenvalue*, which is a measure of the explained variance by the PC. Usually, only a subset of the PCs is selected for further analysis (interpretation, rotated components, etc.). A typical stopping rule that we also use in this study, is that only PCs whose eigenvalue is larger than 1.0 are selected.

Regarding replicated studies, it is interesting to see which dimensions are also observable in other systems, and find possible explanations for differences in the results. We would expect to see consistent trends across systems for the strong PCs, which explain a large percentage of the data set variance, and can be readily interpreted. From such observations, we can also derive recommendations regarding which measures appear to be redundant, and need not be collected, without losing a significant amount of design information.

3 Data Description

The data used in this research was obtained through three controlled experiments carried out by professors and students of the Department of Computer Science at the University of Castilla-La Mancha, in Spain[4] [20,22,23]. We have followed some suggestions provided by Wohlin et al. [36], Perry et al. [27], [5] and Kitchenham et al. [26] on how to perform controlled experiments.

The common characteristics of the three experiments are the following:

- The independent variables are the structural complexity and the size of UML class diagrams, measured via the 11 metrics shown in table 1. The dependent variables are maintainability sub-characteristics of class diagrams, measured in each experiment in a different way.
- We selected a within-subject design experiment, i.e., all the tests (experimental tasks) had to be solved by each of the subjects. The tests were put in a different order for each subject.
- Subjects were given an intensive training session before the experiments took place. However, the subjects were not aware of what aspects we intended to study. Neither were they aware of the actual hypothesis stated.
- We wanted to test the hypothesis that exists correlation between the metrics we presented in table 1 and the class diagram maintainability characteristics, such as understandability, analyzability and modifiability.

In the next subsections the main characteristics of each experiment are described.

3.1 First Experiment Description

- The subjects were seven professors and ten students enrolled on the final-year of Computer Science at the Department of Computer Science at the University of Castilla-La Mancha in Spain. The professors belong to the Software Engineering area.
- The material we handed to the subjects consisted of twenty eight UML class diagrams of the same universe of discourse, related to Bank Information Systems.
- Each diagram had a test enclosed which included the description of three maintainability sub-characteristics: understandability, analyzability and modifiability.
- Each subject had to rate each sub-characteristic using a scale consisting of seven linguistic labels. For example for understandability we proposed seven linguistic labels ranging from, extremely difficult to understand, to extremely easy to understand.
- The subjects were given all the materials and we explained to the to them how to carry out the tests.
- We allowed one week for them to do the experiment, i.e., each subject had to carry out the test alone, and could have unlimited time to solve it.
- We summarised the empirical data in a table consisting of 28 rows and 14 columns. The 28 rows represent each one of the 28 UML class diagrams given

[4] The experimental material can be found in http://alarcos.inf-cr.uclm.es

out to the subjects. The first 11 columns represent the values of the dependent variables (metrics), and the final three, the median of the subjects´ ratings for understandability, analysability and modifiability.

3.2 Second Experiment Description

- The subjects were ten professors and twenty students enrolled on the final-year of Computer Science at the Department of Computer Science at the University of Castilla-La Mancha in Spain. All of the professors belong to the Software Engineering area.
- The dependent variable was measured by the time the subjects spent carrying out the tasks required in the experiment. We called this time "maintenance time". Maintenance time is comprised of the time taken to comprehend the class diagram, to analyse the required changes and to implement them. Our assumption here is that, for the same modification task, the faster a class diagram can be modified, the easier it is to maintain.
- The material we gave to the subjects consisted of nine UML class diagrams of different application domains.
- Each diagram had an enclosed test that included a brief description of what the diagram represented, and two new requirements for the class diagram. Each subject had to modify the class diagrams according to the new requirements, and specify the start and end time. The difference between the two is what we call maintenance time (expressed in minutes and seconds). The modifications to each class diagram were similar, including adding attributes, methods, classes, etc.
- The subjects were given all the materials described in the previous paragraph. We explained to them how to carry out the tests. We allowed one week for them to do the experiment, i.e., each subject had to carry out the test alone, and could use unlimited time to solve it.
- Once the data was collected, we controlled if the tests were complete, and if the modifications had been done correctly. We discarded the tests of seven subjects, which included a required modification that was done incorrectly. Therefore, we took into account the responses of 23 subjects.
- We summarised the empirical data in a table consisting of 9 rows and 12 columns. The 9 rows represent each one of the 9 UML class diagrams given out to the subjects. The first 11 columns represent the values of the measures of the independent variables (the metrics presented in table 1), and the last column represents the mean of the maintenance time for each diagram.

3.3 Third Experiment Description

- The data of this sample are very similar to the second experiment's ones. The only difference is that 9 different UML class of diagrams were taken, which implies that the values of the metrics are also different.

- The modifiability and understandability time (expressed in seconds) were considered as measures of the dependent variables.
- The subjects had to answer a questionnaire (5 questions) that reflected whether or not they had understood each diagram and they also had to write down how long it took to answer the questions. The understandability time was obtained from that.
- The maintenance time was obtained in the same way as in the second experiment. The subjects were 30 undergraduate students enrolled on the third-year of Computer Science, but we also used the empirical data obtained from the responses of 23 subjects, because the other results were incomplete.

3.4 Threats to Validity of the Empirical Data

We will discuss the various issues that threaten the validity of the empirical studies and how we attempted to alleviate them:

- **Threats to conclusion validity.** The conclusion validity defines the extent to which conclusions are statistically valid. The only issue that could affect the statistical validity of this study is the size of the sample data. We are aware of this, but it is wel acknowledged that Empirical Software Engineering suffer form the lack of enough data.
- **Threats to Construct Validity.** The construct validity is the degree to which the independent and the dependent variables are accurately measured by the measurement instruments used in the studies. The construct validity of the measures used for the independent variables is guaranteed by Poels and Dedene´s framework [21] used for their theoretical validation [29]. The measures we used for the dependent variable are different in each experiment but in all cases we used measures that really measure what we purpose to measure: the subjects´rating (first experiment), the maintenace time (second experiment), the understandability and modifiability time (third experiment), so we consider these measures constructively valid.
- **Threats to Internal Validity.** The internal validity defines the degree of confidence in a cause-effect relationship between factors of interest and the observed results. Seeing the results of the experiment we can conclude that empirical evidence of the existing relationship between the independent and the dependent variables exists. The analysis performed here is correlational in nature. We have demonstrated that several of the metrics investigated had a statistically and practically significant relationship with maintainability sub-characteristics. Such statistical relationship do not demonstrate per se a causal relationship. They only provide empirical evidence of it. Only controlled experiments, where the metrics would be varied in a controlled manner and all other factors would be held constant, could really demonstrate causality. However, such a controlled experiment would be difficult to run since varying structural complexity in a system, while preserving its functionality, is difficult in practice. On the other hand, it is difficult to imagine what could be alternative explanations for our results besides a relationship between structural complexity and maintainability sub-characteristics. We have tackled different aspects that could threaten the internal validity of the study, such as: differences among subjects, knowledge of

the universe of discourse among class diagrams, precision in the time values, learning effects, fatigue effects, persistence effects and subject motivation.

- **Threats to External Validity.** External validity is the degree to which the research results can be generalised to the population under study (UML diagrams used as design artifacts for developing OO software) and to other research settings. The greater the external validity, the more the results of an empirical study can be generalised to actual software engineering practice. Two threats to validity have been identified which limit the ability to apply any such generalisation, and we tried to alleviate them:
  - Materials and tasks used. In the experiments we tried to use class diagrams which can be representative of real cases. Related to the tasks, the judgement of the subjects (in the first experiment) is to some extent subjective, and does not represent a real task. But we improved this aspect considering more real tasks in the second and third experiment.
  - Subjects. To solve the difficulty of obtaining professional subjects, we used professors and advanced students from software engineering courses. We are aware that more experiments with practitioners and professionals must be carried out in order to be able to generalise these results. However, in this case, the tasks to be performed do not require high levels of industrial experience, so, experiments with students could be appropriate [2].

For the sake of brevity we do not explain in detail the experimental process for each experiment. Further details for each experiment can be found in [20,22,23].

4 Data Analysis and Interpretation

First, we used PCA[5] [5] to reduce the initial space of 11 metric dimensions, in which the structural complexity and the size of UML class diagrams are represented, which were the first goal of this study; eliminating redundant information (in this case metrics). In this PCA we have worked with rotated components, in order to reduce the dimension so that each one of the new components is going to be very correlated with very few of the old metrics or dimensions, which will ease the comprehension.

Later on, we used a Pearson or Spearman correlation analysis [34], depending on the type of variables of the research, with the aim of studying the correlation of the new dimensions given by the PCA with the dependant variables related to the maintainability, which is the second goal of this study.

[5] The 11.0 version of SPSS has been used [35] to analyse the samples of data described in the previous section.

4.1 Analysis of the Data of the First Experiment

4.1.1 Dimensions reduction (PCA). Three rotated PCs were obtained (see table 2), with the constraint that the eigenvalue is larger than 1.0. With these PCs 93.76% (see table 3) of the total variability is explained.

As you can observe while observing table 2:

- The PC1 picks out information of the structural complexity relative to the aggregation.
- The PC2 picks out information of the structural complexity given by the generalization.
- The PC3 refers to the structural complexity given by the relations of association and dependencies among classes.

The metrics NA, NGenH, NM and NC seem not to be relevant in the PCA. Because the correlation with the metrics that do appear in the PCA is high (see table 4), we can think that the information that they contain has already been transmitted through the metrics that are relevant in the PCA.

Table 2. Rotated Components

	PCs		
Metrics	**PC1**	**PC2**	**PC3**
MaxHAgg	**0.911**	0.231	0.126
NAggH	**0.879**	0.141	0.349
NAgg	**0.873**	0.382	0.185
NA	0.669	0.539	0.492
NGenH	0.586	0.494	0.513
MaxDIT	0.187	**0.962**	0.408
NGen	0.263	**0.893**	0.300
NM	0.567	0.675	0.429
NC	0.560	0.648	0.501
NDep	0.123	0.136	**0.943**
NAssoc	0.450	0.265	**0.817**

Table 3. Total Variation Explained by the PCs

PCs	**Eigenvalue**	**Percentage**	**Accumulated Percentage**
PC1	4.112	37.383	37.383
PC2	3.441	31.278	68.661
PC3	2.761	25.101	**93.763**

4.1.2 Correlation between the structural complexity and the PCs. The correlation of the new components with dependent variables, understandability, analyzability and modifyability has been studied by using the Spearman correlation coefficient (see table 5). The three components of each class diagram in the new space were previously calculated with the Anderson-Rubi method.

Table 4. Correlation between metrics

	NAssoc	NAagg	NAggH	NDep	NGen	NGH	MaxHAgg	MaxDIT
NC	**0.843**	**0.817**	**0.761**	**0.607**	**0.893**	**0.928**	**0.717**	**0.728**
NA	**0.830**	**0.884**	**0.841**	**0.627**	**0.802**	**0.897**	**0.784**	**0.659**
NM	**0.776**	**0.851**	**0.728**	**0.591**	**0.856**	**0.843**	**0.732**	**0.786**
NGH	**0.849**	**0.759**	**0.723**	**0.548**	**0.753**	**1.000**	**0.712**	**0.568**

Table 5. Spearman's correlation coefficient

	PC1	PC2	PC3
Understandability	**0.520 - (p=0.005)**	**0.679- (p=0.000)**	0.312 (p=0.106)
Analizability	**0.544 - (p=0.003)**	**0.702 (p=0.000)**	0.265 (p=0.174)
Modificability	**0.502 - (p=0.006)**	**0.747 (p=0.000)**	0.268 (p=0.168)

The observed results were the following:

- Understandability is highly correlated with PC2 (generalizations) (0.679 p=0.000) and less with PC1 (aggregations (0.520 p= 0.005)
- Analizability is highly correlated with PC2 (generalizations) (0.702 p=0.000) and less with PC1 (aggregations) (0.544 p= 0.003)
- Modifiability is highly corelated with PC2 (generalizations) (0.747 p=0.000) and less with PC1 (aggregations) (0.502 p= 0.006)

In conclusion, it seems that PC3, that refers to dependencies and associations, is not correlated with none of the studied dependent variables. This fact might have been produced because, after analyzing the class diagrams that were used in the experiment, it was observed that mostly they had very few associations and even less dependencies. From that comes the necessity of making a next experiment in which more emphasis is put on this type of relations. Definitively, after analyzing the data obtained in the first experiment, we can say that apparently the metrics that have to do with the aggregation and the generalization, influence the maintainability of class diagrams. Although these results are partial, they are similar to the ones found in different empirical researches made to evaluate the effect of the relation of generalization about the OO software maintainability [3,12,13,24,31]. Otherwise, as Deligiannis et al. [14] affirm, the relations of aggregation have been less studied from an empirical point of view. That is why they insist on the necessity to deepen on this subject, now that there exists the suspicion that the usage of the aggregation might complement the design of more extensive and reusable products.

4.2 Second Experiment Analysis

4.2.1 Dimensions Reduction (PCA). The solution obtained in the PCA after the rotation of the components, with an eigenvalue larger than 1 (see table 6), explains 79,151% of the total variability (see table 7).

Table 6. Rotated components

	PCs	
Metrics	**PC1**	**PC2**
NC	0.796	0.561
NA	0.359	**0.862**
NM	0.683	0.686
NAssoc	-0.08817	**0.911**
NAgg	0.729	0.239
NDep	0.728	-0.248
NGen	**0.927**	**0.00895**
NAggH	0.632	0.348
NGenH	**0.870**	0.399
MaxHAgg	**0.872**	0.269
MaxDIT	**0.832**	0.330

Table 7. Total Variation Explained by the PCs

PCs	Eigenvalue	Percentage	Accumulated Percentage
PC1	5.768	52.440	52.440
PC2	2.938	26.711	**79.151**

Table 8. Correlation between metrics

	NA	NGen	NGenH	MaxHAgg	MaxDIT
NC	**0.775**	**0.794**	**0.886**	**0.833**	**0.822**
NM	**0.900**	**0.651**	**0.887**	**0.760**	**0.827**
NAggH	0.341	0.570	**0.710**	**0.634**	**0.607**
NAgg	0.338	0.501	**0.651**	**0.928**	0.536
NDEP	0.148	**0.684**	0.438	**0.610**	0.406

In this case the conclusions that can be extracted are the following:

- The PC1 is determined because of the complexity given by the generalization.
- The PC2 otherwise, picks out the complexity of the associations and the number of attributes.

In this research the metrics that allows elimination because of having redundant information, are NC, NM, NAgg, NDep and NAggH (see table 6). The information they contain will be picked out through the metrics with the correlated ones (see table 8) that intervene in the principal components.

4.2.2 Correlation between the structural complexity and the PCs. The correlation of the new PCs has been studied (see table 8) with the dependent variable and the maintenance time, using the Pearson´s correlation coefficient (see table 9). For that, the coefficients for the factorial punctuations were previously calculated with the Anderson-Rubi method. These are the two components of the class diagrams in the new space of two dimensions.

The correlation between maintenance time and the PCs shown in the table, is only significant for the PC2 (see table 9) that corresponds to associations and attributes.

Table 9. Pearson's correlation coefficient

	PC1	PC2
Maintenance time	0.485 - (p=0.185)	**0.853 - (p=0.003)**

4.3 Analysis of the Third Experiment

4.3.1 Dimensions reduction (PCA). While studying the table of correlations among the metrics, it was observed that NM was not correlated with any of the others, that is why the PCA was made without including it, because it constitutes a dimension.

After the rotation, the PCA presented the results of table 10, with the same restriction as in the previous cases (autovalues that are bigger than one), and explained 92.075% of the total variability (see table 11).

Table 10. Rotated components

Metrics	PCs	
	PC1	PC2
NC	0.643	0.753
NA	0.423	**0.859**
NAssoc	0.667	0.579
NAgg	0.397	**0.901**
NDep	**0.855**	0.414
NGen	**0.956**	0.221
NAggH	-0.247	**0.955**
NGenH	**0.961**	0.044
HAggMax	0.741	0.591
MaxDIT	**0.941**	0.111

Table 11. Total Variation Explained by the PCs

PCs	Eigenvalue	Percentage	Accumulated Percentage
PC1	5.260	52.596	52.596
PC2	3.948	34.480	**92.075**

Table 12. Correlation between metrics

	NC	NAssoc	NA	NAgg	NDep	NGen	MaxHAgg	MaxDIT
NC	1.000	0.819	0.928	0.953	0.863	0.778	0.909	0.714
NM	0.214	0.509	0.281	0.133	0.342	0.394	0.314	0.176
NAssoc	0.819	1.000	0.763	0.714	0.862	0.714	0.828	0.654
HAggMax	0.909	0.828	0.748	0.834	0.926	0.858	1.000	0.688

From the PCs shown in table 10 the following can be concluded:

- The PC1 picks out the information related to dependencies and generalizations.
- The PC2 picks out the information related to aggregations and attributes.

In this research, the metrics that allow elimination because of having redundant information are NC, NAssoc and MaxHAgg. As seen in table 12, they are very correlated among themselves, besides others being part of the selected PCs. In this way, NC is very correlated with metrics that determine the PC2, meanwhile, NAssoc y MaxHAgg are very correlated with metrics of the PC1.

4.3.2 Correlation between the structural complexity and the PCs. Correlation of new PCs (see table 10) and NM with the dependent variables, the understandability and maintenance time have been studied, using Pearson´s correlation coefficient (see table 13).

For that, the coefficients for factorial punctuations were previously calculated with the Anderson-Rubi method, which are the two components of the class diagrams in the new space of two dimensions.

Table 13. Pearson's correlation coefficients

	PC1	PC2	NM
Understandability time	0.355 (p=0.348)	**0.769 (p=0.016)**	0.401 (p=0.285)
Maintenance time	0.472 (p=0.199)	0.365 (p=0.376)	0.146 (p=0.709)

Analyzing the obtained results in table 13, it can be observed that:

- The understandability time is highly correlated with PC2, which is related with aggregations and attributes.
- The maintenance time is not correlated with the PCs.
- Besides, the third dimension that NM represents is not related to any of the two dependent variables.

Given that in the previous experiment the maintainance time has been evaluated without making the difference between understandability and maintenance time, it is considered to be a new dependent variable in this case, Total Maintenance Time, that measures the maintenance time as the sum of both of them. In this way the results of both experiments can be better compared (see table 14).

Table 14. Pearson's correlation coefficients

	PC1	PC2	NM
Total maintenance time	0.472 (p=0.199)	**0.669 (p=0.049)**	0.146 (p=0.709)

In table 14 the results can be observed. Only the component PC2, that picks out the information of the aggregations and the number of attributes, is positively correlated with the maintainance time. As expected, the sum of the two times reduces the correlation grade, from 0.769 to 0.669, and the level of signification gets worse, from 0.016 to 0.049, although the result keeps being significant at the level 0.05.

5 Conclusions and Future Work

It is well known that software product metrics are very useful to evaluate the different characteristics that affect the quality of OO software, for example the maintainability [18]. With this idea in mind, we have carried out three controlled experiments to test if the metrics we had defined for class diagram structural complexity, and other traditional metrics related to class diagram size, could be really used as class diagram maintainability indicators at the early phases of the OO software life-cycle. With the aim to discover which of the used metrics might not be redundant in these empirical studies, we have used PCA in this work.

After performing the PCA we managed to observe in the three samples of data, that the PCs containing non-redundant information present well known characteristics of the OO design, which have to be with the usage of relations, associations, dependencies, aggregations and generalizations.

The metrics related to the size do not seem to be relevant, like NC and NM, but NA is. Although it is reasonable to think that the more classes there are in a diagram the more dependencies and associations can exist, in this research it is declared that these last ones could influence the maintainability.

If we examine the correlation among the maintainability and/or the understandibility and the PCs in the two experiments where they are measured objectively using the maintenance time (see table 9 and 14), it is clear that it is correlated in the first experiment with the PC that picks out the structural complexity of class diagrams due to the number of associations together with the number of attributes. In the second experiment it is correlated with the PC that picks out the number of aggregations and the number of attributes.

When separating the maintenance time considering the modifiability and the understandability time, the grade of dependence and the signification improve, so it would seem correct to make this difference, unless in the dependent variables.

The results of the first experiment deserve a separate comment, for the dependent variables are subjective measures. No size metric appears to be relevant in the PCA. The PC1 and PC2, that pick out the information of the aggregration and the generalization, are the ones being significantly correlated with dependent variables.

These results confirm what is already known [3,9], that the results obtained in the PCA are dependent on the data, for that even though in the three data samples the results obtained are in a certain way similar, it will be necessary to keep on making empirical researches that for one part allow people to explore the obtained results, building prediction models for the class diagram maintainability. On the other hand, it is necessary to make a family of experiments that allow the extension of conclusions as much as possible to increase the external validity of the results, including experiments with professionals and also data about real projects. Besides we are conscious of the necessity to make laboratory packages with the information of the empirical studies, to encourage their external replication and obtain a body of knowledge about the utility of metrics [2,11,33]. This can contribute to metrics being useful for OO software designers to make better decisions in the early phases of OO software development, which is the most important goal for any measurement proposal to pursue if it aims to be useful [19].

Acknowledgements. This research is part of the DOLMEN (TIC 2000-1673-C06-06) and the CALDEA (TIC 2000-1673-C06-06) projects, financed by Subdirección General de Proyectos de Investigación - Ministerio de Ciencia y Tecnología.

References

1. Basili, V., Rombach, H.: The TAME project: Towards improvement-oriented software environments. IEEE Transactions of Software Engineering, Vol. 14 Nº 16 1998 728-738
2. Basili, V., Shull, F., Lanubile, F.: Building Knowledge Through Families of Experiments. IEEE Transactions on Software Engineering, Vol. 25 Nº 4 , (1999) 435–437
3. Briand, L., Wüst, J., Lounis, H.: Replicated Case Studies for Investigating Quality Factors in Object-oriented Designs. Technical report ISERN 98-29 (version 3), International Software Engineering Research Network, (1998)
4. Briand, L., Morasca, S., Basili, V.: Defining and validating measures for object-based high level design. IEEE Transactions on Software Engineering, Vol. 25 Nº 5, (1999) 722–743
5. Briand, L., Arisholm, S., Counsell, F., Houdek, F., Thévenod-Fosse, P.: Empirical Studies of Object-Oriented Artifacts, Methods, and Processes: State of the Art and Future Directions. Empirical Software Engineering, Vol. 4 No. 4, (1999) 387–404
6. Briand, L., Wüst, J., Lounis, H.: A Comprehensive Investigation of Quality Factors in Object-Oriented Designs: an Industrial Case Study. 21st Int'l Conference on Software Engineering, Los Angeles, (1999) 345–354
7. Briand, L., Melo, W., Wüst, J.: Assessing the applicability of fault-proneness models across object-oriented software projects. IEEE Transactions of Software Engineering, Vol 28 Nº 7, (2001) 706–720
8. Briand, L., Bunse, C., Daly, J.: A Controlled Experiment for evaluating Quality Guidelines on the Maintainability of Object-Oriented Designs. IEEE Transactions on Software Engineering, Vol. 27 No. 6, (2001) 513–530.
9. Briand, L., Wüst, J.: Empirical studies of quality models. Advances in Computers Academic Press, Zelkowitz (ed), Vol. 59, (2002) 97–166
10. Brito e Abreu, F., Melo, W.: Evaluating the impact of object-oriented design on software quality. Proceedings of 3rd International Metric Symposium, (1996) 90–99
11. Brooks, A., Daly, J., Miller, J., Roper, M., Wood, M.: Replication of experimental results in software engineering. Technical Report ISERN-96-10, International Software Engineering Research Network, (1996)
12. Cartwright, M.: An Empirical view of inheritance. Information and Software Technology, Vol. 40 Nº 14, (1998) 795–799.
13. Daly, J., Brooks, A., Miller, J., Roper, M., Wood, M.: An Empirical Study Evaluating Depth of Inheritance on Maintainability of Object-Oriented Software. Empirical Software Engineering, Vol. 1 Nº 2, (1996) 109–132
14. Deligiannis, I., Shepperd, M., Webster, S., Roumeliotis, M.: A Review of Experimental into Investigations into Object-Oriented Technology, Empirical Software Engineering, Vol. 7 Nº 3, (2002) 193–231
15. Dunteman, G.: Principal Component Analysis. Sage University Paper 07-69, Thousand Oaks, CA, (1989)

16. El-Emam, K.: The Prediction of Faulty Classes Using Object-Oriented Design Metrics, NRC/ERB1064, National Research Council Canada, (1999)
17. El-Emam, K.: Object-Oriented Metrics: A Review on Theory and Practice, NRC/ERB 1085, National Research Council Canada, (2001)
18. Fenton, N., Pfleeger, S.: Software Metrics. A Rigorous and Practical Approach. Second edition. International Thomson Publishing Inc., (1997)
19. Fenton, N., Neil, M.: Software Metrics: a Roadmap. Future of Software Engineering, Ed. Anthony Finkelstein, ACM, (2000) 359–370
20. Genero, M., Olivas, J., Piattini, M., Romero, F.: Using metrics to predict OO information systems maintainability. CAISE 2001, LNCS 2068, Interlaken, Switzerland, (2001) 388–401
21. Genero, M.: Defining and validating metrics for conceptual models. Ph.D. Thesis Department of Computer Science, University of Castilla-La Mancha, (2002)
22. Genero, M., Olivas, J., Romero, F., Piattini, M.: Assessing OO Conceptual Models Maintainability. 1st International Workshop on Conceptual Modeling Quality (IWCMQ´02), within the ER 2002, LNCS (to appear) (2002)
23. Genero, M., Piattini, M., Calero, C.: Empirical Validation of Class Diagram Metrics. International Symposium on Empirical Software Engineering (ISESE 2002), Nara, Japan, IEEE Computer Society, (2002) 195–203
24. Harrison, R., Counsell, S., Nithi, R.: Experimental Assessment of the Effect of Inheritance on the Maintainability of Object-Oriented Systems. The Journal of Systems and Software, 52, (2000) 173–179.
25. ISO 9126.: Software Product Evaluation-Quality Characteristics and Guidelines for their Use, ISO/IEC Standard 9126, Geneva, (2001)
26. Kitchenham, B., Pflegger, S., Pickard, L., Jones, P., Hoaglin, D., El-Emam, K., Rosenberg, J.: Preliminary Guidelines for Empirical Research in Software Engineering. IEEE Transactions of Software Engineering, Vol. 28 No. 8, 721–734
27. Perry, D., Porter, A., Votta, L.: Empirical Studies of Software Engineering: A Roadmap, Future of Software Engineering, ACM, Ed. Anthony Finkelstein, (2000) 345–355.
28. Pigoski, T.: Practical Software Maintenance. Wiley Computer Publishing, New York, USA, (1997)
29. Poels, G., Dedene, G.: Distance-based software measurement: necessary and sufficient properties for software measures, Information and Software Technology, Vol. 42 No. 1, (2000) 35–46
30. Poels, G., Dedene, G.: Measures for Assessing Dynamic Complexity Aspects of Object-Oriented Conceptual Schemes. 19th International Conference on Conceptual Modelling (ER 2000). Salt Lake City, USA, (2000) 499–512
31. Poels, G., Dedene, G.: Evaluating the Effect of Inheritance on the Modifiability of Object-Oriented Business Domain Models. 5th European Conference on Software Maintenance and Reengineering (CSMR 2001), Lisbon, Portugal, (2000) 20–29
32. Rossi,, M., Brinkkemper, S.: Complexity Metrics for Systems Development Methods and Techniques. Information Systems,Vol. 21 No. 2, (1996) 209–227
33. Shull, F., Basili, V., Carver, J., Maldonado, J.: Replicating Software Engineering Experiments: Addressing the Tacit Knowledge Problem. 2002 International Symposium on Empirical Software Engineering (ISESE 2002), Nara, Japan, IEEE Computer Society, (2002) 7–16
34. Snedecor, G., Cochran, W.: Statistical Methods, 8 [a] ed., Iowa State University Press
35. SPSS 11.0. 2001. Syntax Reference Guide, Chicago, SPSS Inc, (1989)
36. Wohlin, C., Runeson, P., Höst, M., Ohlson, M., Regnell, B., Wesslén, A.: Experimentation in Software Engineering: An Introduction, Kluwer Academic Publishers, (2000)

Implementing UML Association, Aggregation, and Composition. A Particular Interpretation Based on a Multidimensional Framework*

Manoli Albert, Vicente Pelechano, Joan Fons, Marta Ruiz, and Oscar Pastor

Department of Information Systems and Computation
Valencia University of Technology
Camí de Vera s/n (46022) Valencia (Spain)
{malbert,pele,jjfons,mruiz,opastor}@dsic.upv.es

Abstract. This work presents a code generation process that systematically obtains the implementation of the UML association, aggregation and composition concepts in the context of the OO-Method (an OO automated software production method). A multidimensional framework, which identifies a set of basic properties, allows us to characterize association relationships in the OO conceptual modelling. By applying this framework, we provide a particular interpretation of the UML association, aggregation and composition concepts for the OO-Method. Once we have defined a clear semantics for these concepts, we introduce a code generation strategy that obtains the implementation of these abstractions depending on the value of the framework dimensions. This strategy can be applied to current OO development methods in order to systematize the software production process in model-driven approaches.

1 Introduction

Structural approaches to OO Conceptual Modeling propose two main steps for the construction of a conceptual schema: (1) finding classes, their attributes and operations and (2) identifying relationships between these classes. It is generally agreed in OO conceptual modeling [3] that relationships can be classified in three types: classification, generalization and association/aggregation. The association/aggregation is one of the most relevant and useful relationships. However, its semantics differs among the OO conceptual modeling approaches. The UML standard [4] does not solve this problem since the semantics that provides for association and aggregation concepts is ambiguous. This is discussed in [5] and is recognized in the RFP (OMGs Request For Proposals) to propose the new UML version 2.0 [7]. Due to this ambiguity, several approaches ([1], [2], [6], [8], [9], [12], [13], [14], [15]) have arisen in the last few years trying to define precise models for the association/aggregation relationship. But currently, a consensus for defining the semantics of these abstractions does not exist. Due to this lack

* The work reported in this paper has been funded by the CICYT project under grant TIC2001- 3530-C02-01 and the Valencia University of Technology, Spain.

J. Eder and M. Missikoff (Eds.): CAiSE 2003, LNCS 2681, pp. 143–158, 2003.

of consensus, if we attempt to define a process for implementing abstractions of this kind in a model-driven software production method (as our OO-Method [10] approach does), we must define a precise semantics for these abstractions.

This work discusses a particular semantic interpretation of the UML association, aggregation and composition concepts. This interpretation is obtained by applying a multidimensional framework that identifies a set of structural and functional properties (what we call dimensions) that allows us to unambiguously characterize the association/aggregation relationships. Once we have defined these conceptual abstractions, we propose a systematic method for implementing them. This method determines the OO software representation of the association/aggregation relationships according to the values of the dimensions. Our main contribution is an attempt to cover the need for improving OO methods providing systematic transformation to the design.

The paper is organized as follows: section 2 presents the multidimensional framework that we have built for identifying the properties that allow us to characterize every kind of association/aggregation relationship. Section 3 proposes a particular interpretation of the semantics of the UML association, aggregation and composition concepts. This interpretation uses the multidimensional framework presented in section 2 to define its properties. Section 4 presents a systematic approach to the implementation of the proposed association, aggregation and composition relationships. This section clearly states how the values of the dimensions presented in the framework directly influence the implementation (structure and functionality) of the relationship. Finally, we present some conclusions and further work.

2 A Multidimensional Framework

In this section, we present a multidimensional framework that identifies a set of properties which are adapted from different OO modeling methods. These properties (or dimensions) allow us to characterize association/aggregation[1] relationships in a conceptual schema.

The framework is based on an analysis process in which we have studied different approaches that analyze the association/aggregation relationships ([1], [2], [6], [8], [12], [13]). We have selected some properties from these approaches that are simple (to build an intuitive model), precise (to avoid ambiguities) and that have some influence on the software representation of the relationship (to avoid superexpressiveness). These properties should be expressive enough to ensure that the relevant characteristics of the association/aggregation relationships can be captured at the conceptual level. Some of these dimensions are used by other authors with different terms. For instance, the dimensions "delete propagation" along with the "multiplicity" defined in this work, have an interpretation which is similar to the "existence dependency" from [11]. Also, the dimension

[1] The association/aggregation relationship includes composition, which is considered a type of aggregation.

"multiplicity" that we define (similar to the way UML [4] does) is used for representing the same semantics as the property "mandatory/optional" from other approaches [6], [13].

This framework identifies the structural and behavioural properties of the the association/aggregation relationships. Thus, it provides a set of dimensions through which different kinds of association/aggregation relationships (present in current OO Models) can be categorized. This framework helps us to understand the essential characteristics and the semantics of the association/aggregation relationships, independently of the terms used for naming them.

The following subsections briefly introduce the framework dimensions. For each one, we define its intended semantics in an intuitive way, provide a nomenclature for referring to it throughout the paper, identify the element of the association that the dimension is applied to, introduce its possible values, and show the UML attributes that have close semantics to our proposed dimensions.

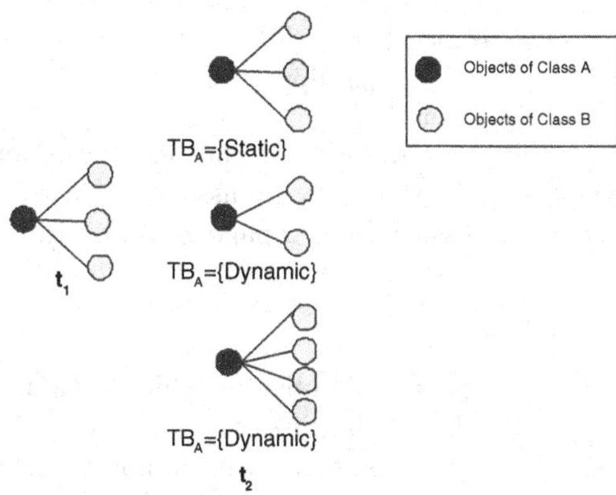

Fig. 1. A graphical example of the *temporal behaviour* dimension.

2.1 Temporal Behaviour

- `Definition`: Temporal Behaviour specifies whether an instance of a class can be dynamically connected or disconnected (creating or destroying a link[2]) with one or more instances of a related class (through an association/aggregation relationship) during its existence. The value {*Dynamic*} indicates that creating or destroying a link is possible throughout the whole life of the object. The value {*Static*} indicates that this behaviour is not possible (it is only possible during its creation process).
- `Defined over`: *association-end* (following the definition introduced on page 3-71 of the UML Standard [4]).

[2] A link is an instance of the association/aggregation relationship.

– `Nomenclature`: $\mathtt{TB}_{association-end}$[3].
– `Values`: *Static* | *Dynamic.*
– `UML Related`: attribute *changeability* of the association-end: "specifies whether an instance of the Association may be modified by an instance of the class on the other end (the source end)." (page 2-22 in [4]).

Figure 1 shows an example of the *temporal behaviour* dimension. Class A is related to class B. If the value of the TB dimension defined over class[4] A is {*Dynamic*}, adding or deleting links from an object of class A to objects of class B is possible. However, if the value of the dimension is {*Static*}, adding or deleting links is not possible.

2.2 Multiplicity

– `Definition`: Multiplicity specifies the lower(`Low`)/upper(`Upp`) number of objects of a class that must/can be connected to only one object of its associated class.
– `Defined over`: *association-end.*
– `Nomenclature`: $\mathtt{Low}_{association-end}$, $\mathtt{Upp}_{association-end}$.
– `Values`: nonnegative integers.
– `UML Related`: attribute *multiplicity* of the association-end: "specifies the number of target instances that may be associated with a single source instance across the given Association." (page 2-23 in [4]).

2.3 Delete Propagation

– `Definition`: Delete Propagation indicates which actions must be achieved when an object is deleted (over its links and its associated objects).
  - {*Restrictive*}: if the object has links, it cannot be deleted.
  - {*Cascade*}: if the object has links, the links and the associated objects must be deleted.
  - {*Link*}: if the object has links, the links must be deleted (not the associated objects).
– `Defined over`: *association-end.*
– `Nomenclature`: $\mathtt{DP}_{association-end}$.
– `Values`: *Restrictive* | *Cascade* | *Link.*
– `UML Related`: *propagation semantics.* "A consequence of these rules is that a composite implies propagation semantics; that is, some of the dynamic semantics of the whole is propagated to its parts. For example, if the whole is copied or destroyed, then the parts so are (because a part may belong to at most one composite)." (page 2-66 in [4]).

---

[3] If the name of the association-end (rolename) is not defined and its related class has only one relationship, we will use the name of the class as the name of the association-end.

[4] In order to simplify, throughout the paper we use the expression "defined over the class .." in place of "defined over the association-end related to the class.. "

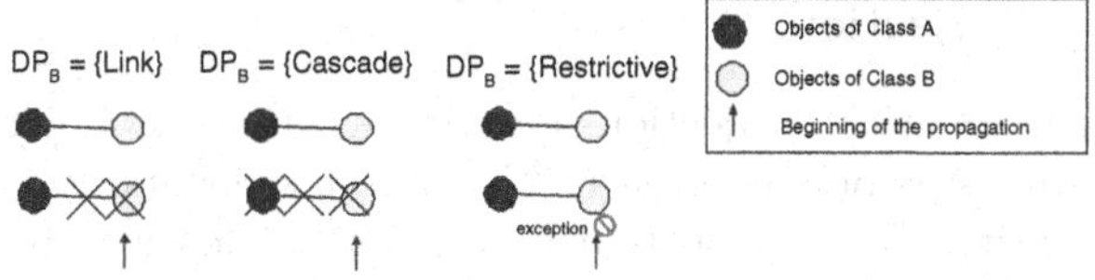

Fig. 2. A graphical example of the *delete propagation* dimension.

Figure 2 shows a graphical example of the *delete propagation* dimension. Class A is related to class B. The figure shows the different actions achieved when an object of the class B is deleted depending on the value of the dimension *delete propagation* defined over this class.

2.4 Visibility

- `Definition`: Visibility specifies whether an object can be accessed only by its associated object/s. The value {*Not Visible*} indicates that the object can be accessed only by its associated object/s. The value {*Visible*} specifies that the object can be accessed by all system objects.
- `Defined over`: *association-end.*
- `Nomenclature`: $V_{association-end}$.
- `Values`: *Visible* | *Not Visible.*
- `UML Related`: attribute *visibility* of the association-end: "specifies the visibility of the association end from the viewpoint of the classifier on the other end." (page 2-23 in [4]).

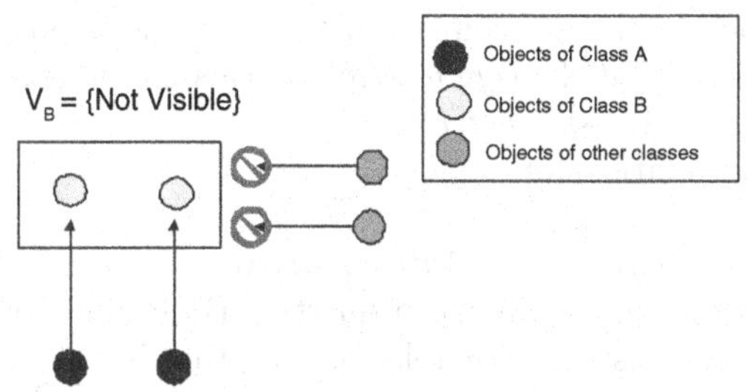

Fig. 3. A graphical example of the *visibility* dimension.

Figure 3 shows a graphical example of the *visibility* dimension. Class A is related to class B. The *visibility* dimension of class B has the value {*Not Visible*}, then objects of class B can only be accessed by their associated objects.

2.5 Identity Projection

- `Definition`: Identity Projection specifies whether an object projects its identity onto its associated object. The object keeps its own identity as its primary identity. The point is that it can also be identified by its associated object. The value {*Projected*} indicates that the object projects its identity and {*Not Projected*} indicates the contrary.
- `Defined over`: *association-end.*
- `Nomenclature`: $\mathtt{IP}_{association-end}$.
- `Values`: *Projected* | *Not Projected.*
- `UML Related`: the *identity projection* of a composite: "composite [...] projects its identity onto the parts in the relationship. In other words, each part in an object model can be identified with a unique composite object. It keeps its own identity as its primary identity. The point is that it can also be identified as being part of a unique composite." (page 3-81 in [4]).

2.6 Reflexivity

- `Definition`: Reflexivity specifies whether an object can be connected to itself. The value {*Reflexive*} indicates that this is possible and {*Not Reflexive*} indicates the contrary.
- `Defined over`: relationship.
- `Nomenclature`: $\mathtt{RF}_{relationship}$.
- `Values`: *Reflexive* | *Not Reflexive.*
- `UML Related`: a characteristic of aggregation and composition relationships. "[...] the instances form a directed, non-cyclic graph." (page 2-67 in [4]).

2.7 Antisymmetry

- `Definition`: Antisymmetry specifies whether an object can be connected to an object which is already connected to it. If this is possible, the value of the dimension is {*Not Antisymmetric*}. If this is not possible, the value of the dimension is {*Antisymmetric*}.
- `Defined over`: relationship.
- `Nomenclature`: $\mathtt{AS}_{relationship}$.
- `Values`: *Antisymmetric* | *Not Antisymmetric.*
- `UML Related`: the *antisymmetry* property. "Both kinds of aggregations define a transitive, antisymmetric relationship; that is, the instances form a directed, non-cyclic graph. Composition instances form a strict tree (or rather a forest)." (page 2-67 in [4]).

Figure 4 shows an example of the *antisymmetry* dimension. Class A is related to class B through the `rA_B` relationship. If the *antisymmetry* dimension has the value {*Not Antisymmetric*}, then creating a link from an object of class A or B to an object of the associated class that has already a link to the former is possible. However if the value of the dimension is

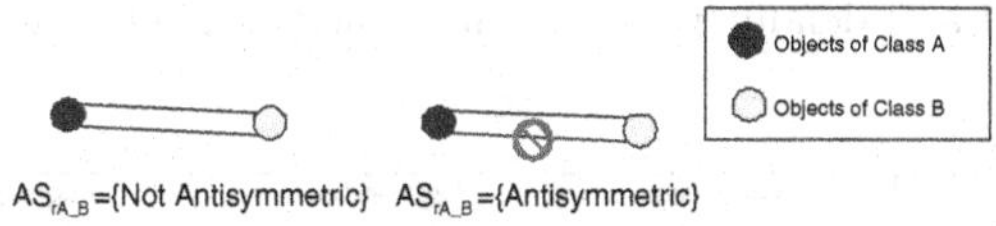

Fig. 4. A graphical example of the *antisymmetry* dimension.

{*Antisymmetric*}, the creation of a link from an object of class A or B to any object of the associated class that has already a link to the former is not possible.

The presented dimensions are used in the next section for defining a particular semantics of the UML association, aggregation and composition.

3 A Particular Semantic Interpretation

Due to the lack of a precise and clear semantics for the association/aggregation relationship, we have proposed a particular semantic interpretation for the association, aggregation and composition UML concepts in the context of the OO-Method. In order to define this semantics, we adopt only the subset of the semantics for the UML concepts that have an "unambiguous" interpretation, completing it with our own definitions. The following assertions are adopted:

- Association: "An association declares a connection (link) between instances of the associated classifiers (e.g., classes). It consists of at least two association ends, each specifying a connected classifier and a set of properties that must be fulfilled for the relationship to be valid." (page 2-65 in [4]).
- Aggregation: An aggregation is "a whole/part relationship. In this case, the association-end attached to the whole element is designated, and the other association-end of the association represents the parts of the aggregation. Only binary associations may be aggregations." (page in 2-66 [4]).
- Composition: A Composite aggregation is "a strong form of aggregation." (page in 2-66 [4]).

Although we adopt these assertions, we must fix the semantics of these concepts to avoid the ambiguity introduced by the UML standard. One way to define the precise semantics of these concepts is to determine the value of the dimensions that characterize each concept, allocating each concept in our multidimensional framework in a correct way.

The values of the dimensions for association, aggregation and composition concepts are presented in table 1, where the UML notation is used for representing the concepts. For each concept (columns) this table shows the value of the proposed dimensions[5]. In addition, the rows of the table show the default

[5] We use the symbol $\forall$ to show that a dimension can be set to any of its possible values.

Table 1. The fixed and default values of the dimensions for association, aggregation and composition.

Dimension / Concept	Association A —— B	Aggregation A ◇—— B	Composition A ◆—— B
Temporal Behaviour	$\forall$ ($TB_A = TB_B$ = Dynamic)	$\forall$ ($TB_A = TB_B$ = Dynamic)	**$TB_A = \forall$** **TB_B = Static** (TB_A = Dynamic)
Multiplicity	$\forall$	$\forall$	**$Low_A = Upp_A = 1$** **$Low_B = \forall$, $Upp_B = \forall$**
Delete Propagation	$\forall$ ($DP_A = DP_B$ = Link)	$\forall$ ($DP_A = DP_B$ = Link)	**DP_A = Cascade** **$DP_B = \forall$** (DP_B = Link)
Visibility	$\forall$ ($V_A = V_B$ = Visible)	$\forall$ ($V_A = V_B$ = Visible)	**V_A = Visible** **V_B = Not Visible**
Identity Projection	$\forall$ ($IP_A = IP_B$ = Not Projected)	$\forall$ ($IP_A = IP_B$ = Not Projected)	**IP_A = Projected** **IP_B = Not Projected**
Reflexivity	$\forall$ (Reflexive)	**Not Reflexive**	**Not Reflexive**
Antisymmetry	$\forall$ (Not Antisymmetric)	**Antisymmetric**	**Antisymmetric**

values (presented in brackets) of the dimensions for each concept. The notation used for association, aggregation and composition implies the assumption of the default values.

In this table we observe that `Association` has not fixed dimensions. This is because there are no constraints in the relationship between the related classes. `Aggregation` has two fixed dimensions: *reflexivity* fixed to {*Not Reflexive* } and *antisymmetry* fixed to {*Antisymmetric*}. These values are required because in our interpretation of the whole/part relationship a given object cannot be whole and part at the same time and if an object is a part of a whole then that same whole cannot be part of its own part [6]. `Composition` has a fixed value for each dimension since: the part has to be included in one and only one composite (thus, lower and upper *multiplicity* of the composite are 1); the part cannot change its composite (thus, *temporal behaviour* of the part is {*Static*}); when a composite is deleted, its parts are deleted too (thus, *delete propagation* of the composite is {*Cascade*}); the part can only be accessed by its composite (thus, *visibility* of the part is {*Not Visible*}); a composite projects its identity onto its parts (thus, *identity projection* of the composite is {*Projected*}); as a type of aggregation, composition fulfills the constraints of aggregation (thus, *reflexivity* is {*Not Reflexive* } and *antisymmetry* is {*Antisymmetric*}).

Figure 5 shows an example of the graphical notation used for representing the values of the dimensions. The non-default values are represented at the association-end or at the relationship that they qualify using UML stereotypes following the notation introduced on pag. 3-31 [4].

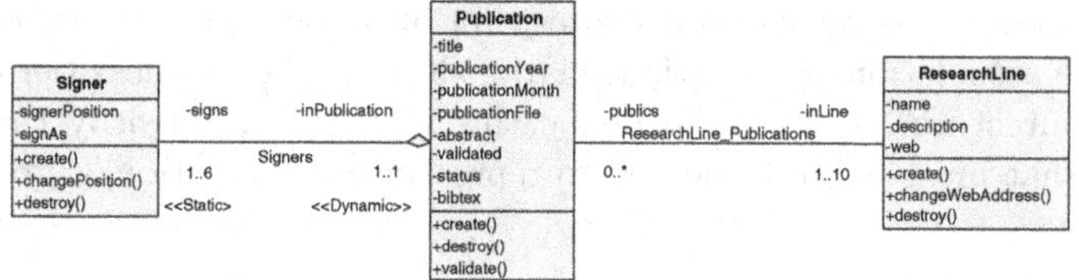

Fig. 5. Class Diagram Example

3.1 Modeling Issues

In this section we discuss the implication of the provided semantic for the conceptual modeling step. There are two issues influenced by the semantics:

- The $\{Dynamic\}$ value of the temporal behaviour dimension defined over a class implies the existence of two operations in this class for 'connecting' and 'disconnecting' the objects of the class to objects of its related class/es. These operations are the link insertion and deletion services.
- Due to the non-orthogonality of the framework dimensions, the semantic of some dimensions constrains the possible values of others. When association/aggregation relationships are modeled, the values of some dimensions imply that other dimensions have to be set to a fixed value:
  - $\mathrm{TB}_A = \{Static\}$ implies $\mathrm{DP}_A <> \{Link\}$
  - $\mathrm{Low}_A = 1$ implies $\mathrm{DP}_A <> \{Link\}$
  - $\mathrm{IP}_A = \{Projected\}$ implies $\mathrm{Upp}_A = 1$

This knowledge can be applied to build better graphical modeling tools which include semantic checking that helps the software engineer in the construction of conceptual schemas.

Once we have proposed an interpretation for the association, aggregation and composition concepts, we are going to discuss a systematic method that obtains the software representation from an association/aggregation relationship in the conceptual schema that is characterized by the framework dimensions.

4 Code Generation Process

In this section, we define the mapping between the specification of an association/aggregation relationship in the conceptual schema and its software representation. This mapping must be unique, so that a specification of an association/aggregation relationship maps to only one software representation. In the OO-Method the mappings between the elements of the conceptual schema and their software representation are defined by applying a *code generation strategy* that is provided by the *Execution Model* [10] of the OO-Method.

We present a code generation strategy for obtaining the software representation of the association/aggregation relationships at the business tier of a three tiered architecture[6]. In order to define this strategy, we identify the software elements that must be implemented to represent an association/aggregation relationship:

- Class Structure (in terms of attributes and methods).
- Instance Creation and Destruction Services.
- Link Insertion and Deletion Services.
- *Other Services* (services that do not create or destroy instances, or insert or delete links).

In this section, we present the implementation of the elements that are influenced by the dimensions of an association/aggregation relationship. These elements are the Class Structure, the Instance Creation and Destruction Services and the Link Insertion and Deletion Services. The implementation of *Other Services* is not presented because it is independent of the dimension values.

We use the example in Figure 5 to present the implementation. This figure shows a part of an UML class diagram with three classes and two relationships. The `Publication` class is related to the `Signer` class through the *signers* relationship. This relationship is a whole/part relationship, i.e., an aggregation relationship ({*Not Reflexive*} and {*Antisymmetric*}), since a signer is part of a publication. The dimensions of the relationship have the default values for each one, except for *Temporal Behaviour* over the class `Signer`, that is set to {*Static*} (because a signer cannot add or delete a link to a publication during its existence), and *Delete Propagation* over the class `Publication`, that is set to {*Cascade*} (because when a publication is deleted, the signers associated to this publication must be deleted). Also, the `ResearchLine` class is related to the `Publication` class through the *researchline_publications* relationship. This relationship is not a whole/part relationship because it does not exist a class that is part of a composite class. Then, the relationship is an association, which does not have constraints. This relationship has the default values for all dimensions.

4.1 Class Structure

In this subsection, we present the structure of classes that implement the semantics of an association/aggregation relationship. We analyze how the values of the dimensions influence the structural definition.

Classes. Given an association/aggregation relationship between two classes A and B, we generate the implementation class C_A that implements the domain class A and the implementation class C_B that implements the domain class B. If the *visibility* dimension has the value {*Visible*} defined over one of the classes, then this class must be hidden to all classes of the system except for its associated class/es.

[6] The architectural style that the OO-Method uses to implement a system is a three-tiered architecture: presentation tier, business tier and persistence tier.

Attributes. For each implementation class we define:

- An attribute for each specified attribute in its domain class[7].
- An object-valued attribute for each association/aggregation relationship of its domain class. According to the *upper multiplicity* this attribute stores an associated object (if the value is 1) or a collection of associated objects (if the value is >1).
- If the *identity projection* dimension defined over the associated class has the value {*Projected*}, the class has as identity mechanism its identity attributes and those of its associated class.

Methods. For each implementation class we define a method for each service specified in its domain class.

Following this strategy, the class structure for the relationships in the Figure 5 is (we use the C# language to document the implementation):

```
// constants representing multiplicity values
const int UpperInLine = 10;
const int UpperSigns = 6;
const int LowInLine = 1;
const int LowSigns = 1;
...
public class Signer () {
    //...attributes
    Publication SignersObj;
    // reference to the associated publication of a signer
    //...methods
}
public class Publication () {
    //... attributes
    ResearchLine[UpperInLine] ResearchLine_PublicationsCol;
    // reference to the associated researchlines of a publication
    Signer[UpperSigns] SignersCol;
    // reference to the associated signers of a publication
    //... methods
}
public class ResearchLine () {
    //... attributes
    Publication[] ResearchLine_PublicationsCol;
    // reference to the associated publications of a researchline
    //... methods
}
```

[7] The expression "its domain class" refers to "its corresponding class in the conceptual schema".

4.2 Instance Creation and Destruction

In this subsection, we present the implementation of the instance creation and destruction methods in terms of the actions that these methods should carry out according to the values of the dimensions.

Creation Services. Each creation service, specified in a class of the conceptual schema, maps to a public method (MCreate) of its own implementation class. The MCreate method of the C_A class has to create an instance of the class A and depending on the *lower multiplicity* (if $Low_B > 0$) to connect this created instance to the necessary instances of C_B class (through an Insertion Service that is presented in the next subsection).

In our example, the *creation method* of the Publication class is implemented as follows:

```
public static Publication MCreate( ) {
    Publication p = new Publication();
    // Create a publication instance
    for (int i=1 ; i < LowSigns; i++)
        p.MInsertSigners();
        // Connect the created publication to its signer/s
    for (int i=1 ; i < LowInLine; i++)
        p.MInsertResearchLine_Publications();
        // Connect the created publication to its researchline/s
    return p;
}
```

Destruction Services. Each destruction service, specified in a class of the conceptual schema, maps to a public method (MDestroy) of its own implementation class. The MDestroy method has to destroy an instance and carry out some actions depending on the value of the *Delete Propagation* dimension:

- If $DP_A = \{Restrictive\}$: destroy the object if it does not have any link, else throw an exception.
- If $DP_A = \{Link\}$: (1) check if any associated object violates the *Lower Multiplicity* when it is > 0, (2) disconnect the associated objects to the object that is going to be destroyed and (3) destroy the object.
- If $DP_A = \{Cascade\}$: (1) destroy the associated objects and (2) destroy the object.

The *destruction method* of the Publication class is implemented as follows:

```
public int MDestroy ( ) {
    for (int i=0 ; i < SignersCol.Length ; i++)
        SignersCol[i].MDestroy();
        // Destroy the associated signers because DP_inPublication =
{Cascade}
```

```
        for (int i=0;i<ResearchLine_PublicationsCol.Length;i++)
            ResearchLine_PublicationsCol[i].MDisconnectResearchLine_
Publications(this);
            // Disconnect the associated researchlines to the publication
            // because DP_publics = {Link}
        MDestroyInstance( );
        // Destroy a publication instance
        return 0;
    }
```

4.3 Insertion and Deletion Services

Classes that have {Dynamic} *Temporal Behaviour*[8] must implement insertion and deletion services. Thus these classes are responsible of adding/deleting links.

Insertion Services. They create a link to an associated object. Each insertion service specified in a class of the conceptual schema maps to a public method (`MInsertRelationshipName`) in its own implementation class. The strategy for implementing the insertion method of the C_A class is the following:

1. Check if the instance of C_A that is going to be connected by the link violates the *Upper Multiplicity* when Upp_B is $<>$ n.
2. `Create` or `Select` an instance of C_B class (that is going to be connected to the instance of the class C_A) depending on the value of the *Temporal Behaviour* and *Multiplicity* dimensions. If TB_B = {*Static*} or $Low_A = Upp_A$ the instance is *created* (through an `Indirect Creation` method). If TB_B = {*Dynamic*} and $Low_A <> Upp_A$ the instance is *selected* (through a `Selection` method). The implementation of these methods is presented throughout this section.
3. Connect the *created* or *selected* instance and the instance of the C_A class.

In our example, the `MInsertSigners` *insertion method* of the `Publication` class is implemented as follows:

```
    private int MInsertSigners( ) {
        if (SignersCol.Length < UpperSigns) {
        // (1) Check the Upper Multiplicity
            Signer sg = Signer.MCreateIndirect ();
            // (2) Create a signer to be connected to the publication
            // (Low_inPublication =Upp inPublication and TB_signs = {Static})
            sg.MConnectSigners(this);
            MConnectSigners(sg);
            // (3) Connect the created signer(sg) to the publication (this)
            return 0;
```

[8] It implies that their instances can add or delete links during their life time.

```
    } else throw new ViolatedMultiplicityException;
}
```

The MInsertResearchLine_Publications *insertion method* of the Publication class is implemented as follows:

```
private int MInsertResearchLine_Publications( ) {
    if (ResearchLine_PublicationsCol.Length< UpperinLine) {
    // (1) Checks the Upper Multiplicity
        ResearchLine rl = MSelectResearchLine_Publications();
        // (2) Select a researchline to be connected to the publication
        // (Low_publics <> Upp publics and TB_inLine = {Dynamic})
        rl.MConnectResearchLine_Publications(this);
        MConnectResearchLine_Publications(rl);
        // (3) Connect the selected researchline(rl) to the publication(this)
        return 0;
    } else throw new ViolatedMultiplicityException;
}
```

Next, we present the strategy for implementing the auxiliary methods used in the insertion method, and that have been mentioned above.

Indirect Creation Method. This is a private method (MCreateIndirect) which creates instances of an associated class due to the insertion of a link between related objects. The MCreateIndirect method of the class C_A has to create an instance of the class A and depending on the value of the *lower multiplicity* (if $Low_B > 1$) to connect the created instance to the necessary instances of the C_B class.

Selection Method. This is a private method (MSelectRelationshipName) which selects an instance of the associated class to be connected with another instance. The strategy for implementing the selection method of the C_A class is the following:

1. Select an instance of the C_B class.
2. Check if the selected instance violates the *Upper Multiplicity* when Upp_A is $<> n$.
3. Check that the selected instance is not the same as the one to which it is going to be connected if the value of the *Reflexivity* dimension is {*Reflexive* }.
4. Check that the selected instance it is not yet connected to the one to which it is going to be connected if the value of the *Antisymmetry* dimension is {*Antisymmetric*}.

Deletion Services. They delete a link to an associated object. Each deletion service specified in a class of the conceptual schema maps to a public method (`MDeleteRelationshipName`) in its implementation class. The strategy for implementing the deletion method of the C_A class is the following:

1. Check if the associated objects violate the *Lower Multiplicity* when Low>0.
2. Disconnect the associated objects (i.e., delete the link).

The *deletion method* of the `ResearchLine` class is implemented as follows:

```
public int MDeleteResearchLine_Publication(Publication pb){
    if (pb.ResearchLine_PublicationsCol.Length>LowInLine){
    // (1) Check the Lower Multiplicity of the publication
    // The researchline Lower Multiplicity is not checked because is 0
        MDisconnectResearchLine_Publications(pb);
        pb.MDisconnectResearchLine_Publications(this);
        // (2) Disconnect the reserachline and the publication
        return 0;
    } else throw new ViolatedMultiplicityException;
}
```

Note that due to the fact that the implementation of the relationship is bidirectional (i.e., the two associated classes refer to each other) we need that the insertion and deletion methods behave as a transaction. In this way we can maintain the integrity of the references.

5 Conclusions and Further Work

In this work, we have presented a particular characterization for the association, aggregation and composition concepts introduced by the UML Standard. For the definition of this characterization we have built a multidimensional framework. This framework has been based on a study of different approaches that deal with association/aggregation relationships in OO conceptual modeling. The framework identifies the relevant properties ("dimensions") of association/aggregation relationships and allows us to give precise interpretations of the association, aggregation and composition abstractions giving specific values to the dimensions of the framework. Once we have defined the semantics of these abstractions, we propose a method for implementing the newly characterized abstractions. This method determines the mappings between the dimensions of the framework and the software elements of the Solution Space.

This approach is being incorporated to the OO-Method CASE tool, the software automatic production environment that gives support to the OO-Method.

We are developing a wizard that helps the analyst to automatically determine the kind of relationship: association, aggregation and composition by asking for modeling information through questions. These questions are oriented to determine the values of the dimensions. We are attempting to improve our proposal by identifying possible structural and behavioural patterns. Finally, in order to improve the code generation process we are studying existing design patterns in order to select those that could be applied to the implementation of the association/aggregation relationships.

References

1. F. Civello. Roles for composite objects in object-oriented analysis and design. In ACM Press, editor, *OOPSLA'93*, pages 376–393, 1993. ISBN: 0-89791-587-9.
2. M. Dahchour. *Integrating Generic Relationships into Object Models Using Metaclasses.* PhD thesis, Dept. Computing Science and Eng., Université Catholique de Louvian, Belgium, March 1999.
3. R.C. Goldstein and V.C. Storey. Data Abstractions: Why and How? *Data and Knowledge Engineering*, 29:293–311, 1999.
4. Object Management Group. Unified modeling language specification version 1.4. Technical report, 2001.
5. B. Henderson-Sellers and F. Barbier. Black and white diamonds. In R. France and B.Rumpe, editors, In *Proceedings UML'99. The Unified Modeling Language Beyond the Standard*, pages 550–565. Springer-Verlag, 1999.
6. B. Henderson-Sellers and F. Barbier. What Is This Thing Called Aggregation? In J. Bosch R. Mitchell, A.C. Wills and B. Meyer, editors, *Proceedings of TOOLS 29*, pages 216–230, Los Alamitos, CA, USA, 1999. IEEE Computer Society.
7. J. Miller. What UML should be. *Communications of the ACM*, 45(11):67–69, November 2002.
8. J.J. Odell. Six different kinds of composition. *Journal of Object Oriented Programming (JOOP)*, 5(8):10–15, January 1994.
9. A.L. Opdahl, B. Henderson-Sellers, and F. Barbier. Ontological Analysis of Whole-Part Relationships in OO-models. *Information and Software Technology*, 43:387–399, 2001.
10. O. Pastor, J. Gómez, E. Insfrán, and V. Pelechano. The OO-Method Approach for Information Systems Modelling: From Object-Oriented Conceptual Modeling to Automated Programming. *Information Systems*, 26(7):507–534, 2001.
11. A. Pirotte, E. Zimányi, and M. Dahchour. Generic Relationships in Information Modeling. Technical report, YEROSS TR-98/09 Université Catholique de Louvain, Belgium, December 1998.
12. M. Saksena, R.B. France, and M.M. Larrondo-Petrie. A Characterization of Aggregation. In Springer, editor, *Proceedings of OOIS'98*, pages 11–19. C. Rolland and G. Grosz, 1998.
13. M. Snoeck and G. Dedene. Core Modelling Concepts to Define Aggregation. *L'Objet*, 7(1), February 2001.
14. Y. Wand, V.C. Storey, and R. Weber. An Ontological Analysis of the Relationship Construct in Conceptual Modeling. *ACM Transactions on Database Systems*, 24(4):494–528, December 1999.
15. M. Winston, R. Chaffin, and D. Herrmann. A Taxonomy of Part-Whole Relations. *Cognitive Science*, 11:417–444, 1987.

Exploring Web-Based Information System Design: A Discrete-Stage Methodology and the Corresponding Model

Mara Nikolaidou [1] and Dimosthenis Anagnostopoulos [2]

[1] Department of Informatics and Telecommunications, University of Athens, Panepistimiopolis, 15771, Athens, Greece
mara@di.uoa.gr

[2] Department of Geography, Harokopio University
70 El. Venizelou Str, 17671 Athens, Greece
dimosthe@hua.gr

Abstract. After the enormous success of WWW platform, a great number of enterprise systems have web-based components. Although they are built using current technological treads, they often fail to provide the desired performance. A potential cause is that, design related problems, as application modeling, resource allocation and replication, network configuration and performance evaluation, although interrelated are solved in isolation. We, thus, argue that a concise methodology for effectively designing web-based information systems offers considerable capabilities. Four discrete stages, each of them addressing a specific issue, and their dependencies are identified. We also propose a common model for the representation of system entities throughout all design stages. UML-like notation was used as a visual tool for graphical representation of model components. Since the modelling scheme is extendable, the adaptation of UML constructs simplifies the process of extending or customizing the model. A case study where the proposed methodology was used for the design a complex enterprise system and the experience obtained are also presented.

1 Introduction

The World Wide Web (WWW) platform is often characterized as the middleware providing a common platform for Intranet-based and Internet-based application development [15]. Using a Web browser is possible to download that part of any application that consists of its user interface from both the Internet and the organization's Intranet. Such applications are considered as *web-based applications*, and are built based on the multi-tiered client-server model [12]. The first and second tiers, e.g. the user interface and the application service, is built using the WWW platform, while the other tiers implement the specific application logic that may be based on different architectures, as discussed in [14]. A *web-based enterprise system* can be described as a set of web-based applications and the underlying infrastructure (both at Internet and Intranet level). Most enterprise information systems built to support current technological treads are based on this architecture. Although significant vendors, as Oracle and IBM promote web-based software platforms during

J. Eder and M. Missikoff (Eds.): CAiSE 2003, LNCS 2681, pp. 159–174, 2003.

the last decade, the proposed solutions, although expensive, often do not provide the desired performance [13]. A potential cause is that, as most enterprise systems expand gradually, system extensions are performed without ensuring overall system performance. Furthermore, web-based applications are characterized by their internal complexity, the impact of which cannot be determined using a trivial mathematics. We, thus, argue that a systematic approach for effectively designing and evaluating web-based enterprise systems offers considerable capabilities [8].

Complete and accurate description of web-based applications is a critical factor in system design, since it ensures the accurate estimation of the Quality of Service (QoS) needed from the network infrastructure, the efficient allocation of resources and the efficient performance evaluation of the overall system. When configuring or evaluating network systems, applications are usually modeled as a series of discrete requests for processing, network transfer, etc., using predefined primitives [3, 9, 11]. We consider that such approaches lack efficiency to accurately describe web-based applications, since intermediate layers are required to support application decomposition in terms of multi-tiered client-server models and permit the accurate estimation of application load. The provision of higher-level primitives to easily describe standard web-based application tiers, as the user service implemented using the WWW platform, is also required. Extendibility of the model to facilitate the description of specific products must also be explored.

In the following, we present a methodology for web-based enterprise system design. It aims at providing decision making support to the system designer to ensure system efficiency when building a new system or extending an existing one. It includes web-based application package description, resource allocation and replication, network configuration (network topology design) and performance evaluation of the proposed architectures. Four discrete stages, each of them addressing a specific issue, and their dependencies are identified. When configuring web-based enterprise systems, each of these problems is usually handled in isolation, resulting in poor performance. It is important to note the significance of a common model for the representation of system entities throughout all design stages. We propose a meta-model supporting all stages incorporating the specific characteristics of web-based enterprise systems. This meta-model enables the exploration of dependencies between design stages even if they aren't obvious, since it is used as the reference framework to estimate application requirements, apply resource allocation and replication policies and construct network topology. Although the techniques explored may be generally applied for large scale systems, we emphasize web-based enterprise system design, as the application description model is introduced to efficiently describe web-based application functionality, while the resource allocation algorithms applied provide solutions taken into account the specific characteristics of web-based architectures. The proposed approach is supported by a set of software tools. The system designer interacts with them through a Java platform, named *Web-based enterprise system Modeler,* facilitating the graphical description of web-based architectures using the proposed meta-model.

Web-based enterprise system modeling is performed using UML constructs. The Unified Modeling Language (UML) is a graphically based object-oriented notation developed by Object Management Group (OMG) as a standard for describing software architectures, which gained widespread acceptance in the software industry [2]. In [4, 7], the UML language is used to model complex system functionality, while mathematical modeling, specifically queuing networks, is adopted to estimate application performance. Using UML sequence diagrams facilitates the complete description of client-server architectures, the triggering of processes and the information exchange between them [7]. However, the detailed description of process functionality is not facilitated. UML wide acceptance was the main reason why we chose to adopt it. UML-like notation was used as a visual tool for the graphical representation of web-based architectures. Since the modeling scheme is extendable, the adaptation of UML constructs to describe the web-based enterprise system meta-model helps the *Web-based System Modeler* user when extending or customizing the model.

The rest of the paper is organized as follows: In section 2, a design methodology for web-based enterprise systems is proposed. In section 3, the web-based enterprise system modeling approach is introduced and the benefits obtained during system configuration and performance evaluation are presented. In section 4, a case study employing the proposed approach and the experience obtained is presented, while conclusions reside in section 5.

2 Design Methodology

The configuration of web-based applications is performed based on the multi-tiered services. As described in [15], a typical web-based application architecture employed in numerous commercial solutions consists of the following:

a) Web client, i. e. the first tier, which facilitates a standard user interface allowing the user to retrieve information (in the form of HTML/XML pages) or activate applications (through HTML/XML page fields).

b) Web server, i. e. the second tier, which processes and redirects user requests, gathers results and sends them to the client in the form of HTML/XML pages. Thus, it provides a middleware platform integrating the desired functionality into the HTML/XML documents.

c) External application servers implementing specific application logic. Old-fashioned applications can be incorporated within the web environment using wrapping techniques. External application services can be activated through *CGI* programs at the web server site. The concept of a *context file* may be used at the server side, in order to temporary store the results of a CGI program before gradually presenting them to the user through the Web client. An alternative solution is the provision of a direct interface allowing the connection to an already active external program associated with a URL used for its invocation.

An alternative web-based architecture is the one based on intelligent web clients that support program execution. In this case, an *applet* may be downloaded from the Web server and be executed on the client machine to activate other tiers. The aforementioned functionality is depicted in figure 1.

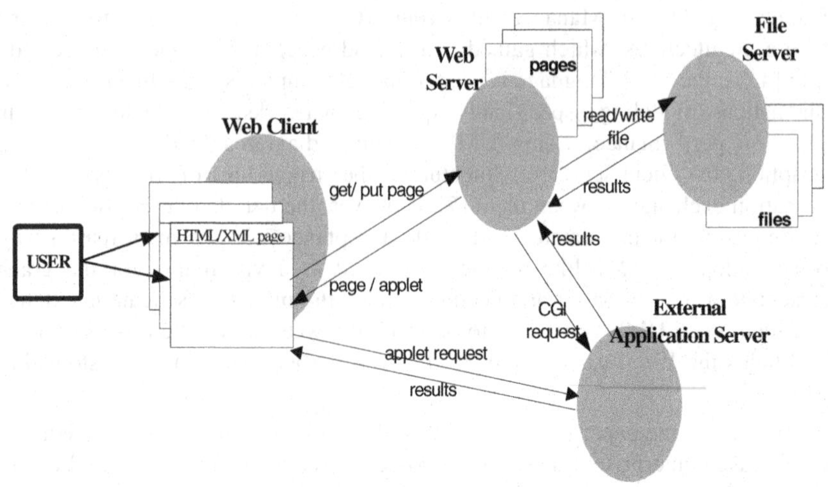

Fig. 1. Widely-adopted Web-based Application Architecture

Web-based enterprise systems have the following specific characteristics:

- The first and second application tiers are implemented using Web technology. Since the first tier is only responsible for user interaction, application functionality is implemented as a set of services distributed on different servers. This reflects on service allocation policies, since a substantial part of application services must be close to the user.
- Replication techniques are employed to increase performance and availability especially over the Internet. To achieve the required application performance, the *principle of locality* (i.e. keeping servers and data as close as possible to user) is widely applied. Replica synchronization is usually performed using asynchronous policies.
- Web-based applications usually operate on workstations. Users have their own workstation (diskless or not). Server processes are executed on dedicated servers machines. Application performance is greatly influenced by individual server machine performance.
- The communication between user-related tiers (web-based tiers) is based in HTTP protocol. Thus, identification of resources is accomplished using URLs or URIs. The network infrastructure consists of private intranets and Internet connections usually supporting TCP/IP protocol stack.

Based on aforementioned characteristics, we introduce a concise methodology for web-based enterprise system design. Four discrete stages and the dependencies between them are identified, as indicated in figure 2. Each of them addresses a specific issue explored during system configuration. All the stages are supported by a common meta-model used for web-based enterprise system description to ensure consistency.

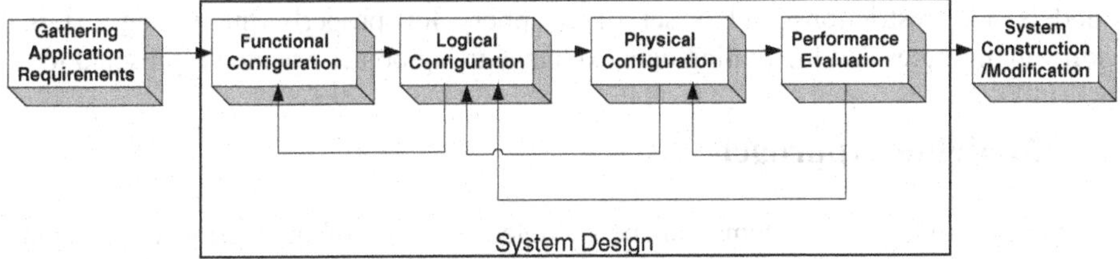

Fig. 2. Web-based Enterprise System Design Methodology

Functional configuration (stage 1) corresponds to the description of system requirements (*functional specifications*). *Logical and physical configuration* (stage 2, 3) deal with process/data allocation and replication policies and network topology design respectively. Resource allocation and network configuration problems cannot be solved independently. Thus, stages (2) and (3) are invoked interactively until an acceptable solution is reached (*physical specifications*). It is important to note the significance of a common modeling scheme for the representation of web-based enterprise system entities throughout all configuration stages. Both logical and physical configuration stages are accomplished by properly instantiating specific properties of model entities, already defined during functional configuration. System configuration phase must facilitate the *performance evaluation* (stage 4) of the proposed solution prior implementation. If the system requirements are not satisfied, logical and physical configuration must be repeatedly invoked.

To support design stages, we have implemented a software platform written in Java. It is named *Web-based System Modeler* and facilitates a) the graphical interaction with the system designer for describing the functional specifications and exploring the proposed solutions using UML-like notation, b) the instantiation of the configuration stages and c) the interaction with specific software tools supporting each stage. Functional configuration is performed using the Modeler. Logical and physical configurations are accomplished using heuristics. IDIS [10] is a knowledge-based system facilitating the representation and exploration of resource allocation and network topology design algorithms using rules of thumb. IDIS knowledge bases were extended to support web-based application functionality and the proper interfaces were developed, so that the Web-based System Modeler may use IDIS to explore resource allocation and network design problems. To evaluate system performance, a discrete event simulation tool was used [9]. Object-oriented modeling and pre-construction of model components were employed to ensure efficiency [1]. System performance cannot be partially estimated, e.g. even if only a small part of the overall architecture is altered, the entire system must be simulated again to accurately estimate performance measurements. The completion of the simulation phase is the most time consuming part of the overall design phase. Thus, redesigning an inefficient architecture imposes the all possible changes are made before the simulation process is reactivated.

Web-based System Modeler consists of a graphical interface facilitating web-based enterprise system description using UML constructs, a dictionary containing models and restrictions and a set of wrappers for properly initializing external software modules and facilitating data exchange using object-oriented representation.

3 Modeling Approach

Web-based enterprise systems can be modeled as a set of interacting components, composite or not, suited to describe specific system functionality [5]. The level of detail in component description must ensure its accuracy and completeness. Thus, a multi-level modeling schema must be introduced providing: a. high-level composite models enabling the designer to go through configuration stages and b. a consistent method for the analysis of composite models in to elementary ones depicting simple network-based operations. Since the proposed approach is focused on web-based enterprise system design, high-level models must explicitly depict standard web-based application functionality, allowing the designer to describe the system under study even if not being aware of specific implementation details, such as HTTP operation.

We argue that it is efficient to use a common model to depict the desired functionality through all the stages of web-system configuration, since it significantly contributes to simplifying the overall process. The model must enable the description of both the *functional specifications* (e.g. application logic and user behavior) and the *physical specifications* (hardware infrastructure). The functional specification and parts of the physical specifications (if pieces of the hardware or network infrastructure are already available during system configuration) are defined during functional configuration stage. The logical configuration consists of defining the relationships between functional and physical specifications, since resource allocation and replication policies result in the allocation of processes and data instances to hardware components. Physical configuration results in the creation of physical specifications. The meta-model introduced to define web-based enterprise system functionality is presented in figure 3 using UML notation. Gray rectangles represent first level entities. It identifies a basic set of object types to describe functional and physical specifications and the relations between them. Further object types may be added by the designer to describe additional functionality by extending or restricting existing object behavior. Meta-model extension is essential in order to enrich the model capability to describe custom applications.

The physical specification consists of a multi-level network architecture. Each *network* either consists of other *networks* and an *internetwork,* describing the way they are connected to each other, or represents a simple LAN or WAN connection. Network *nodes* are either *workstations* allocated to users or *server* stations, where server processes operate. Networks and internetworks also include *relay nodes* depicting routing/switching functionality. Each network/internetwork also includes a *channel* element representing the communication link. Processing and relay nodes consist of individual *elements* corresponding to the three *elementary operations* supported in a network environment: *processing*, *storing* and *transferring* data [5]. Processing nodes consists of a *processing*, *storage* and *communication* element, while *relay nodes* consist of a *processing* and many *communication elements*, one for each network they relay. Since network modeling is widely explored in both research and commercial tools, we do not further discuss this issue [6]. The approach used for modeling network, relay node and communication element entities in our model is the one presented in [1]. Each node element is responsible for serving a corresponding elementary operation. Consequently, application functionality should be internally translated into *elementary operations*. Based on elementary operation characteristics, we can determine the QoS provided by the physical specifications.

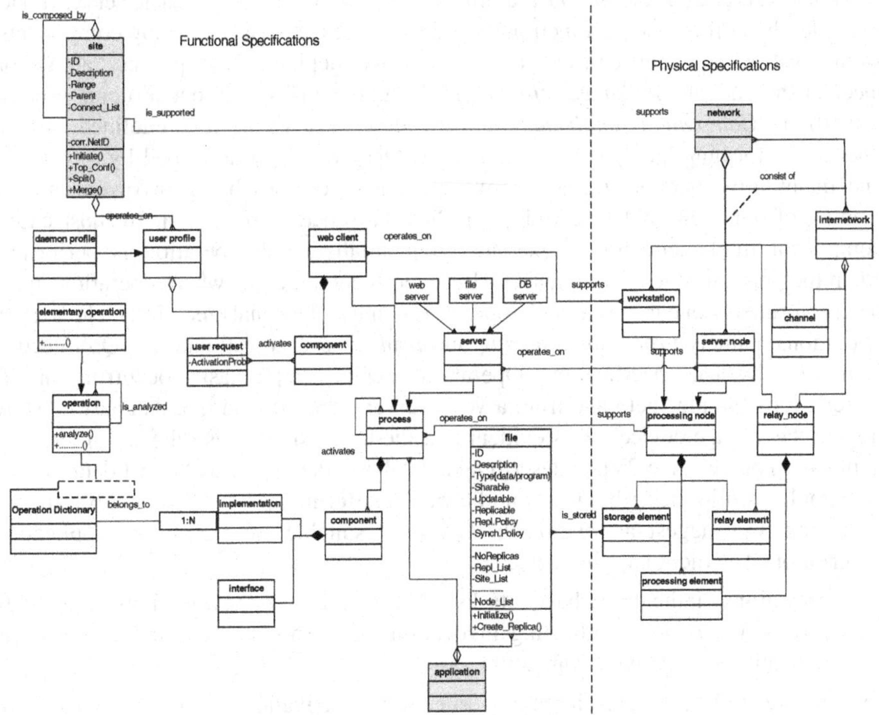

Fig. 3. System Description Meta-model

The functional specification consists of web-based application and user behavior description. Web-based applications are presented as sets of interacting *processes* and *files* accessed by them. User behavior is described through *user profiles* activating *web clients*. Each profile includes *user requests* resulting in application invocation through the web interface, e.g. by invoking specific *components* of a *web client* operating on the user workstation. Each *user request* is characterized by an *activation probability* attribute indicating how often the user activates the specific application to perform a specific task modeled as *component*. The user profile concept may efficiently depict the behavior of a specific user if this can be predetermined. The behavior of Intranet users usually acquires such characteristics. Internet user behavior is more stochastic. In this case, the user profile concept may be used to depict the behavior of user groups regarding specific services, as for example, the user profile "remote client", which can be used to represent the behavior of clients paying their credit card using a web banking system. Daemon profile models indicate the automated activation of processes. Daemon profiles operate on the same processing node as the process they activate.

The services composing application functionality can be described using the *process component* concept. Each component corresponds to the set of tasks completed when activated in a certain manner. Besides the *web client process* model, *server process* models are also supported. Specific models as the *Web Server, Database Server* and *File Server* are introduced as ancestors of the basic server model to depict the corresponding functionality. Each process consists of many components, while each component consists of an *interface* depicting the process activation mechanism and an *implementation* comprising the tasks that occur upon process activation. *Component implementation* is described using a predefined set of *operations* forming the *operation dictionary*. Operations are described by qualitative and quantitative parameters, as for example, the processes being involved and the amount of data sent and received in an "invoke process" operation. In most cases, component implementation is executed sequentially (each operation is performed when the previous one is completed). However, there are cases where operations must be performed concurrently. All operations must be analyzed into elementary operations, namely *processing, storing* and *transferring*, to estimate the QoS needed from the physical specification. Operations depict simple tasks occurring in the system, for example "get page from a Web Server", "insert data in a database", "store data in the storage device". It is evident that the term "simple" is relevant in terms of application perspective. When describing a database, the operation "insert data" seems as simple, while describing a middleware platform seems as complex. In the following, we suggest an *operation dictionary* suitable for web-based application description. The dictionary includes:

a. operations indicating basic tasks. These are *processing,* indicating data processing, *request,* indicating invocation of a server process and *synchronize,* indicating replica synchronization.

b. file related operations involving File Server activation. These are: *write/read* indicating data storage/retrieval. While *processing* is an elementary operation, *write* can be expressed through simpler ones, i.e. a *process* and a *request* sent to a *File Server.*

c. database operations depicting database functionality. There are: *insert, delete, update, select* and *activate_store_procedure*. They provide transparency when defining application functionality.

d. web-related operations used to describe web server and web client functionality. They include:
   - *Get/put page*: indicating retrieving/storing an HTML/XML page
   - *Post:* indicating form/field passing on an HTML/XML page
   - *Get applet:* indicating applet download
   - *Applet:* indicating applet activation
   - *CGI*: indicating CGI program activation
   - *Invoke Program:* indicating active program invocation

- *Handle/Retrieve context file*: indicating context file creation or modification/retrieval of context file data
- *HTTP request*: indicating send request/reply protocol implemented to support HTTP protocol

These *operations* are used to easily describe *component implementation* corresponding to Web server and Web client functionality in the model depicted in figure 1. When a *get page* request is sent to the *Web server*, the proper functions are initiated and a *HTML file* is retrieved from the *File Server* through a *read* request. Based on HTML page content, the Web server may send the *HTML page*, as a reply, back to the client, or initiate a CGI script or an active program to communicate with any *external application server*. The *get page* request is also used to download an *applet* from the *Web server* and communicate with the *external application server*.

Operations can be either elementary or of higher layer. In the latter case, they are analyzed into elementary ones. Operation decomposition is performed through intermediate stages to simplify the overall process and maintain relative data. Operation decomposition hierarchy ensures consistency, reduces complexity and enables following a common predefined decomposition mechanism. The most promising feature of this scheme is that the operation hierarchy can be further extended to include new operation, placed at the highest layer. Definition of new operations is based on existing ones to ensure consistency. Web related operation hierarchy is depicted in figure 4 using UML class diagram notation (only the decomposition of web-related operations is presented in the figure).

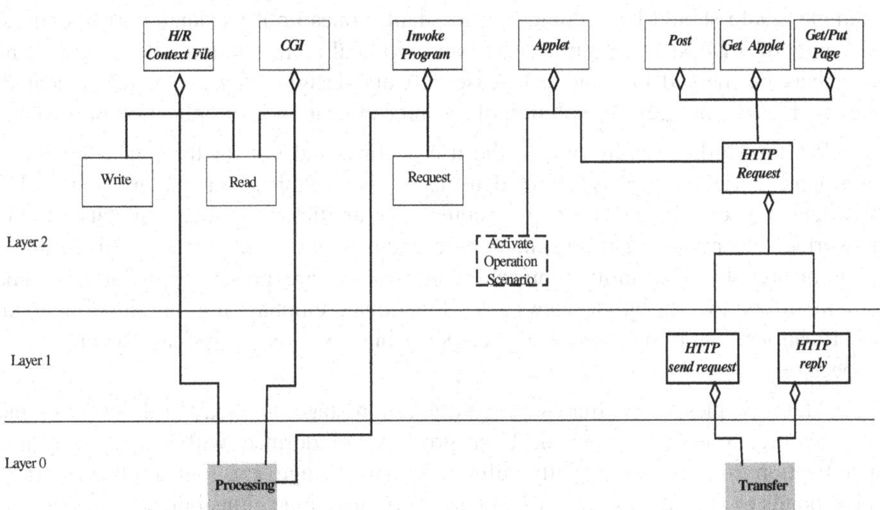

Fig. 4. Web-related Operation Decomposition Model

Dotted rectangles represent *intermediate* actions, while gray rectangles represent *elementary* ones. Although not indicated in the figure, the *activate operation scenario* operation may result in the invocation of any operation included in application description. The *http request* operation depicts the request functionality as it is implemented by HTTP protocol and it is used in the decomposition of application operations describing *Web client* functionality. Many application operations, such as *get/put page*, actually represent the invocation of the corresponding server interface, and are decomposed into *http request* operation. These types of operations are supported to simplify the description of operation scenarios, since they are described using less parameters than the corresponding request operations. Furthermore, they make server invocation transparent to the user, when describing client operation.

Using *Web-based enterprise system Modeler*, the user may further extend the operation hierarchy to describe specific application functionality by properly extending the corresponding UML diagram. When defining a new operation, the user must specify its parameters and the operation used to describe it. In order to avoid model inconsistency, the user ability to add operations is restricted. The meta-model of figure 3 can be extended in a similar manner. We decided to adopt UML notation to describe the meta-model, as a. it is a wide acceptable standard and most designers are familiar with it, b. it allows the graphical representation of specifications and c. it facilitates the automated implementation of existing model extensions.

Site concept is introduced to define the access points of the system. Definition of *sites* is retrospective. Specification of their size is performed with respect to the user's view. At the first level of detail, sites are defined as Internet access points. At the next levels of detail, each *site* is further refined, allowing the user to adjust the description of the system according to the application scale. Since each site must be supported by a network, the *site* definition is restricted by the same rules as network definition; for example, a site should be decomposed to smaller ones until its range corresponds to the limits of a LAN. During the logical and physical configuration, sites of the same level may be merged or divided to ease network design. Progressive refinement of sites enables the progressive solution of resource allocation and replication problems.

Within Modeler environment, the user defines the system through a graphical environment. Each entity is depicted using a UML symbol, for example, the *UML package* symbol is used to depict composite entities as sites, applications and networks. All entities regarding their representation obtain attributes filled manually or automatically. The entity representation symbols are presented in table 1. The system offers two different views: the functional, emphasizing on the functional specifications, and the physical, emphasizing on the physical specification, respectively.

After completing the functional configuration stage, application description and site specification are completed. User profiles are defined within sites. Physical specification may also be partially defined. The next stage, e.g. logical configuration, corresponds to allocating processes and data forming applications into sites.

Table 1. Model Entity Visual Representation using UML Symbols

Model Entity	UML Representation
Functional Specification	
Site	⇒ Package
User/Daemon Profile	⇒ Component in Component Diagram
User Request	⇒ Interface of component
Process	⇒ Component in Component Diagram (site view) or Object in Sequence Diagram (application view)
Component	⇒ Interface of component or Object Activation (site view) in Sequence Diagram (application view)
Component Interface	⇒ Class
Component Implementation	⇒ Parameterized Class
Application	⇒ Package
Physical Specification	
Network/Internetwork	⇒ Package
Node	⇒ Nodes in Deployment Diagram
Element	⇒ Node within Node in Deployment Diagram
Channel	⇒ Arc between Nodes in Deployment Diagram

4 Case Study

The proposed design methodology was tested during the configuration stage of the enterprise information system of the *Greek National Diabetes Network (GNDN)*, which consists of the National Diabetes Institute and 128 Medical Centers hosted in public hospitals allover the country. The National Diabetes Institute received a grant for building an integrated information system supporting the following services: a) medical record maintenance regarding diabetic patients, b) provision of statistical information concerning the diabetes disease, c) everyday life patient support and d) educating the public regarding the Diabetes disease. The system should be accessed through the Internet in order to provide information to different categories of users (public, patients, researchers) with different privileges, while it is maintained by physicians working in diabetes medical centers and the National Diabetes Institute.

Application design and implementation was performed using the Oracle product suite, while all applications should be web-based. Medical records are private, thus records belonging to a specific Medical Center should be only accessed from the personnel employed in it, while specific fields regarding clinical measurements can be widely accessed and statistically processed. The system supports almost 1.000.000 patient records. The size of medical centers differs according to the size of the hospital hosting it. There are three categories of medical centers regarding information system support, as indicating in table 2. As none of the applications is considered as time- critical, the required response time is 15-20 sec for all transactions. The National Diabetes Institute and medical centers are interconnected through the National Health Network, a private TCP/IP based network, interconnecting public hospitals. Network connection speed varies from 128 Kbps to 2 Mbps. In the following, we discuss detailed experience using the web-based enterprise system meta-model presented in section 3 through all the system configuration stages.

Table 2. Medical Center Requirements

Category	Avg. Number of patients per day	Max. Number of Users	Number
Small	<10	1	60
Medium	25	3	76
Lange	>45	7	32
Total	*4000*	*512*	*168*

Functional Configuration

We focus on *Medical Record* and *Statistics Provision* applications, to indicate the advantages of the application modeling scheme. The Medical Record application is based on the "typical" Oracle web-based architecture, where application interface is implemented using JAVA servlets executed in the *Oracle Application Server.* Database-related application logic is implemented using stored procedures. Since medical records are private, two different database servers had to be modeled (each one belonging to a different application), the *Medical DS* maintaining medical records and *Informational DS* maintaining specific record fields subjected to statistical processing. It is evident that the two databases had to be synchronized.

OracleApplSrv was added in the metamodel depicted in figure 3 as an ancestor of *Web Server* entity to model Oracle Application Server functionality. *OracleApplSrv* mainly consists of the invocation of forms, the management of fields and the completion of transactions consisting of stored procedures. Since a Web Server is incorporated within Oracle Application Server, it is able to accept and process HTTP requests produced by the Web clients used by the users. Two new operations were added in the operation hierarchy (figure 4) to integrate web-based functionality and ease *OracleApplSrv* description. The *Form_access (form_name, numbers_of_fields, avg_field_size, processing)* was added in the operation hierarchy to depict accessing, activating and processing of a form. This operation is further decomposed into *get page, post* and *processing* operations to depict the invocation of Oracle forms as HTML pages and the filling of specific fields. The *activate_transaction(LocalDb, sp_number, [sp_list], processing)* operation is used to depict the activation of stored procedures corresponding to each transaction. It is further decomposed into *invoke program, processing* and *post* operations. The *invoke_ program(MedicalDS, call_stored_procedure, [sp_number, sp_list])* operation depictes the invocation of *MedicalDS* to execute a specific stored procedure, while the *post* operation is used to pass stored procedure parameter values. The *invoke_program(MedicalDS, insert, [512, 128])* operation represented recording the specific user performing medical record update and is included as the last operation of the 6 components of *OracleApplSrv* built to represent *Medical Record* application modules.

Extending operation hierarchy is an important feature to ensure the detailed application description. If only predefined operations could be used, the same description would have to be repeatedly given a) within the same application component and b) in different components, to represent the same functionality. Although only up to 15 operations are needed to describe an application module, each one of the 6 components of *OracleApplSrv* is decomposed to a large number of elementary operations varying form 97 to 245.

A new action called *call_stored_procedure_step (preprocessing, data_accessed, postprocessing)* was also added in the action hierarchy to easily describe store procedure functionality. Each stored procedure consists of one to five steps. The *call_stored_procedure_step* action includes the activation of *processing*, *read* and *write* actions. Since the *Informational DS* is updated only through database replication, *synchronize* operation scenario had to be implemented according to Oracle replication mechanisms. This operation scenario is invoked whenever *synchronize* action is invoked. An instance of Application Package View describing the discussed applications is depicted in figure 5.

As indicated in table 1, in the *application view* of functional specification, process functionality is depicted as sequence diagrams. Processes are represented as objects and components as object activations. When the user clicks on an activation icon, a popup window facilitates the description of its interface and implementation. Message icons are added automatically between process activations to represent process interaction. Messages are labeled using the name of the operation initiating process activation.

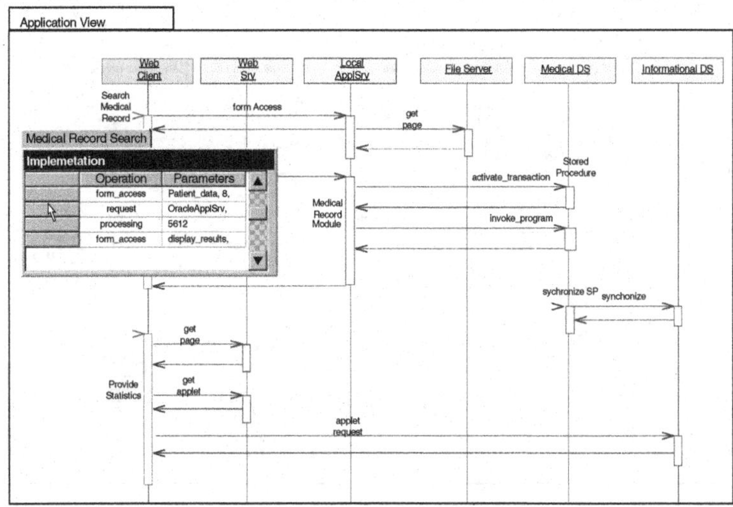

Fig. 5. Application Package View – Medical Record and Statistics Provision Application Models

As indicated in figure 5, the *Process Statistics* component invokes the WebSrv through *get_page* and *get_applet* actions and *InformationalDS* through *applet* action. It implements *Statistics Provision* application, a typical Internet application, where, after the user is identified, an applet is downloaded and executed in his/her workstation allowing the provision of specific statistics concerning the values of medical variables of patients fulfilling predetermined constraints.

Logical Configuration

The users invoke application modules through forms executed on the *Oracle Application Server* using a web browser, thus a replica of Oracle Application Server and related files were placed in all medical centers. The implementation of an Oracle Database in small-sized Medical Centers is costly. Alternative *Medical DS* allocation scenarios were studied in order to ensure the requested response time and reduce cost. After evaluating different alternatives, it was decided to keep *Medical DS* replicas in all Medical Centers except for the small ones directly connected with another one with a network connection faster than 512Kbps. It was decided to place one copy of the *Informational DS* in the National Diabetes Institute, since the Internet access of the system is supported through this specific site.

Within functional specifications, site description was conducted using two levels and the entire medical centers where placed in the second one. During logical configuration site decomposition hierarchy was modified to depict the structure of the WAN network interconnecting hospitals, thus it was feasible to consider the network topology when placing database replicas. An instance of the site view of functional specifications after completing logical configuration is depicted in figure 6.

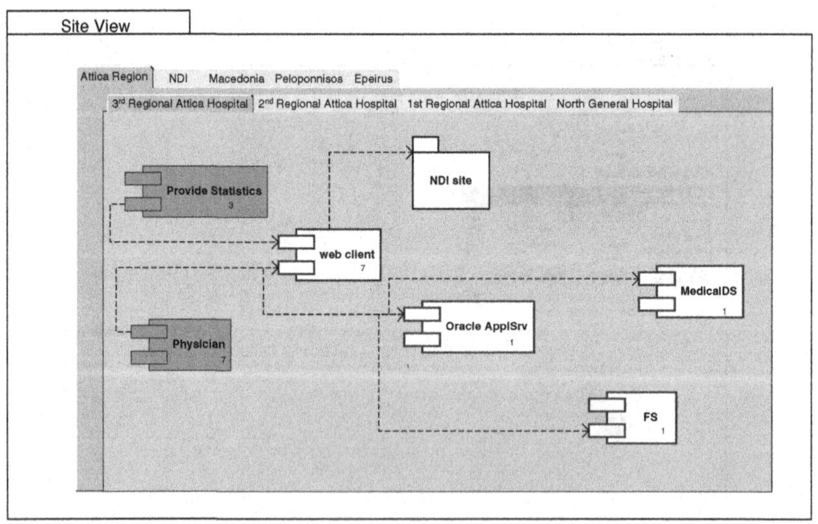

Fig. 6. Site Package View – 3rd Attica Regional Hospital

As indicated in figure 6, site decomposition is depicted using package icons. Component icons are used to represent user profiles, daemon profiles and process (they are distinguished by their color). Interfaces represent user_requests, daemon_requests and components, respectively. The number in the down right side of each component represents the number of profile or process instances operating in the specific site.

Physical Configuration

Since the system uses the National Health network, the network topology was predefined. The physical configuration focused on the design of the National Diabetes Institute site. The performance evaluation of the system indicated that the processing power of the hardware supporting Database functionality was not adequate to execute client transactions within the predefined response time. This was mainly due to the lack of statistics preventing the estimation of Internet traffic characteristics.

The underlying network and database architecture could be modeled and studied using various commercial simulation tools. However, in order to accurately estimate the network load generated and study alternative database replication scenarios, there is a need for the detailed description of the applications. Due to the increased complexity of application functionality, e.g. Oracle Application Server operation, the direct mapping of application description into low-level primitives was not feasible. The extendable *operation dictionary* concept provided a set of common high-level constructs, conforming to web-based application specifications, which enable accurate application package description and the direct mapping of this description into QoS parameters that the physical configuration must satisfy. This is the main advantage of the proposed meta-model.

Site redefinition process illustrates the ability of the proposed model to depict the impact of technological boundaries (physical specification) and resource allocation policies to application functionality (functional specification). When configuring web-based enterprise systems, each of these problems is usually handled in isolation, resulting in poor system performance. The proposed model enables the exploration of dependencies between configuration stages even if they aren't obvious, as functional specifications are corrected or filled, as physical specifications are progressively defined.

5 Conclusions

We proposed a concise methodology for the design of web-based enterprise information systems considering their specific characteristics. Four discrete stages, each of them addressing a specific issue, and the dependencies between them were identified. They include application package description, process/data replica allocation, network/hardware configuration and performance evaluation of the proposed architectures. When configuring web-based enterprise systems, each of these problems is usually handled in isolation, resulting in poor performance. The common meta-model proposed for system description through all stages promotes consistency, since all the stages are performed by properly instantiating model entity properties. As indicated in the case study using the site concept, the model was able to represent how network/hardware technological boundaries effect functional specifications and system architecture even if they are not obvious.

The proposed meta-model facilitates the accurate and detailed description of web-based applications and the estimation of QoS parameters. Extending the meta-model was proven to be an essential feature in order to describe complex application functionality, such as the one supported by Oracle Application Server. UML-like representation of meta-model entities helped through model extension/customization, since Web-based System Modeler users are usually familiar with UML constructs.

References

[1] Anagnostopoulos, D.: An Object-Oriented Modeling Methodology for Dynamic Computer Network Simulation. International Journal of Modeling and Simulation **21** (2001)

[2] Booch, G., Rumbaugh, J., Jacobson, I.: The Unified Modeling Language User Guide. Addison Wesley (1999)

[3] Cruz, J., Park, K.: Towards performance-driven system support for distributed computing in clustered environments. Journal of Parallel and Distributed Computing **59** (1999)

[4] Kaehkipuro, P.: UML-Based Performance Modeling Framework for Component-Based Distributed Systems. In: Performance Engineering, Lecture Notes in Computer Science 2047, Springer-Verlag (2001) 167–154

[5] Kramer, J.: Configuration Programming – A Framework for the Development of Distributed Systems. In: Proceedings of the International Conference on Computer Systems and Software Engineering, Israel, IEEE Computer Press (1990)

[6] Law, A.M., McComas, M. G.: Simulation Software of Communications Networks: The State of the Art. IEEE Communications Magazine **4** (1994)

[7] Mirandola, R, Cortellessa, V.: UML Based Performance Modeling in Distributed Systems. In: UML2000, Lecture Notes in Computer Science 1939, Springer-Verlag (2000) 178–193

[8] Nezlek, G.S., Hemant, K.J., Nazareth, D.L.: An Integrated Approach to Enterprise Computing Architectures. Communications of the ACM **42** (1999)

[9] Nikolaidou, M., Anagnostopoulos, D.: An Application-Oriented Approach for Distributed System Modeling. In: Proceedings of International Conference on Distributed Computing Systems, Phoenix, Arizona, US, IEEE Computer Press (2001)

[10] Nikolaidou, M., Lelis, D., et. al: A Discipline Approach towards the Design of Distributed Systems. IEE Distributed System Engineering Journal **2** (1995)

[11] Ramesh, S., Perros, H.G.: A multi-layer client-server queuing network model with non-hierarchical synchronous and asynchronous messages. Performance Evaluation **45** (2001)

[12] Reeser, R., Hariharan, R.: Analytic Model of Web Servers in Distributed Environments. In Proceeding of the International Workshop on Software and Performance, Ottawa, Canada, ACM Press (2000)

[13] Savino-Vázquez, N.N., et al.: Predicting the behavior of three-tiered applications: dealing with distributed-object technology and databases. Performance Evaluation **39** (2000)

[14] Shedletsky, J., Rofrano, J.: Application Reference Designs for Distributed Systems. IBM System Journal **32** (1993)

[15] Serain, D.: Middleware. Springer-Verlag London, Great Britain (1999)

Analysing the Impact of Adding Integrity Constraints to Information Systems

Suzanne M. Embury[1] and Jianhua Shao[2]

[1] Department of Computer Science, University of Manchester, Oxford Road, Manchester, M13 9PL, England, United Kingdom
SEmbury@cs.man.ac.uk

[2] Department of Computer Science, Cardiff University, P.O. Box 916, Cardiff, CF24 3XF, Wales, United Kingdom
J.Shao@cs.cf.ac.uk

Abstract. The ability of a business to change its working practices, in order to gain or retain competitive edge, is closely aligned to its ability to change the business rules implemented by its information systems. Unfortunately, adding a new business rule to an existing system is both time-consuming and error-prone. It is all too easy, for example, for the programmer to overlook some program elements that are affected by the addition of the new rule, with the result that it is not enforced uniformly by the system as a whole. When this happens, the information system can begin to behave in confusing and anomalous ways.

In this paper, we describe an impact analysis technique that aims to support the programmer in the difficult task of implementing an important class of business rules, namely, integrity constraints. We have adapted techniques from database integrity maintenance to allow us to identify whether a program is likely to be affected by the addition of a new constraint, and to pinpoint the specific program statements that must be guarded against the possibility of constraint violation. Our technique can also be used to provide guidance to the programmer as to the conditions that must be included in any new guards.

1 Introduction

The ability of a business to gain and retain competitive edge is closely aligned to its ability to change the *business rules* which govern its day-to-day behaviour. A business rule is a statement that "defines or constrains some aspect of a business" [10]. For example, one such rule might define the criteria that make a customer eligible for a certain kind of discount; another might state the circumstances under which credit can be given. Such rules are typically very volatile. New business rules are regularly imposed on organisations by changes to statutory regulations, government policy and economic/market conditions. However, in addition to these enforced changes, many businesses also choose to modify their business rules frequently as they fight to maximise revenues, minimise churn and capture new market share.

J. Eder and M. Missikoff (Eds.): CAiSE 2003, LNCS 2681, pp. 175–192, 2003.

One of the key costs for any organisation wishing to make changes to its business rules arises from the need to evolve the supporting information systems so that they too enforce the new rules. Adding new business rules to a software system (or modifying existing ones) is typically both time-consuming and error-prone. The reason for this is that there is no obvious correspondence between a business rule and the collection of software artefacts that implement it. Real world information systems typically consist of a great many programs, each of which has a slightly different effect on the system state and each of which may potentially have a role in enforcing a new business rule. Deciding which programs (or which parts of a program) might violate the new rule, and exactly what changes have to be made to them to prevent the violations, is an extremely challenging task.

Current software maintenance tools offer little help with this task, and it is usually necessary to manually inspect a significant proportion of the program code. Not only is this costly in terms of programmer time, but it is also highly error prone. It is extremely easy to overlook some programs that really ought to be modified or to add redundant checks to programs that cannot in fact cause a violation of the rule. And yet much of this inspection work is highly repetitive and mundane, and is therefore amenable to automation.

In this paper, we present a technique that partially automates the process of adding a particular kind of business rule to an existing information system. The business rules that we focus on are those that act as database integrity constraints [14]. Of course, evolution is straightforward for those integrity constraints that are simple enough to be implemented centrally by the database management system (DBMS). However, it is still the case that many of the more complex forms of business rule must be implemented in the application programs, either because of limitations in the capabilities of the DBMS or because of the need for better performance than can be achieved using a centralised approach. Tool support for such modifications is therefore still required, even though DBMS facilities have improved significantly over the last decade.

In the remainder of this paper, we describe our technique for determining the impact of adding a new integrity constraint to a software system. We begin (Section 2) by outlining the steps involved in implementing a new integrity constraint, and consider how far existing software tools can support each of these steps. We then go on to show how techniques from the field of database integrity maintenance (Section 3) can be adapted to provide key elements of the information necessary for performing a detailed impact analysis for this form of software maintenance (Section 4). Finally, we illustrate the behaviour of our technique on some examples (Section 5) and conclude (Section 6).

2 Implementing New Integrity Constraints

Constraint-style business rules begin life as high-level conditions that the organisational state must adhere to [10]. These conditions can typically be violated by several different actions. Consider, for example, the following constraint:

All customers with a negative balance must have a valid authorisation for their overdraft.

This rule can potentially be broken by several different operations: lowering the balance of a customer's account, or cancelling an overdraft authorisation for some customer, for example. The supporting software systems must ensure that, whenever one of these "dangerous" actions occurs, the constraint is not violated by the action. The exact processing steps required to detect a specific type of violation will, in general, depend on the action which causes it. For example, if the customer's balance is lowered, then we need to check whether it has fallen below zero and if so whether an overdraft authorisation exists. If, on the other hand, a program results in the cancellation of an overdraft request, it is only necessary to check whether that customer's balance is above zero at the time of the cancellation.

To the best of our knowledge, there is no widely accepted methodology for the implementation of business rules[1]. However, by examining the requirements for the accurate and complete implementation of constraint-type rules, we can infer something about what is involved in this evolution task and derive from it the potential for automation.

The first requirement is to understand how the new constraint may be invalidated by various forms of state change. Since we are focussing on business rules that are equivalent to constraints over a database state, each such rule can be expressed as a first order logic expression over predicates corresponding to the schema elements in the database (and the standard inequality predicates). For example, the informal constraint given earlier can be expressed in first order logic (FOL) as follows:

$$(\forall x, y, z)\ \mathit{customer}(x, y, z) \wedge z < 0 \Rightarrow \mathit{overdraftAuth}(x)$$

For any finite FOL expression, there is a finite set of atomic updates that can violate it. For example, the insertion of a new record into the *customer* table might invalidate our example constraint, but deletion of a *customer* record can never have this effect. The full set of violating updates can be discovered through analysis of the form of the constraint (as we shall describe in Section 3).

Once we know which updates can trigger a constraint violation, the next requirement is to examine each of the programs within the system, to see which of them have the capacity to effect one of these dangerous state changes. Each such program must be modified in order to prevent (or flag) violations of the rule. The most common strategy is to insert a pre- or post-condition into the program, as a guard on the offending update or any associated transaction commit operations.

[1] The nearest approximation to such a methodology is perhaps the externalisation of business rules using rule engine technology, such as that provided by ILOG JRules [11]. However, rule engines are not a universal solution to the problem of business rule implementation and they cannot easily be grafted onto an existing information system. In this paper, therefore, we concentrate on the problems faced by the maintainers of systems which have been implemented in a more traditional manner, and where the rules are internalised within the code of the application programs.

From these basic requirements, we can derive the following skeleton process for modifying an information system so that it enforces a new constraint:

1. Analyse the new constraint and determine from it which state change operations can potentially cause it to be violated.
2. Locate the set of program statements which perform the state change operations identified in step 1. From this, we can also identify the set of programs which are affected by the new constraint.
3. For each potentially dangerous program statement identified in step 2, determine whether it really does have the capability to violate the constraint (i.e. check that it does not occur under conditions which would make a violation of the rule impossible).
4. For each program statement remaining after step 3, determine how we will detect whether it violates the constraint and how such violations will be prevented (i.e. choose a pre- or post-condition approach).
5. For each program statement remaining after step 3, determine the condition that must be checked by the program in order to prevent violations in the manner selected in step 4.

Each of these steps presents a potential challenge to the maintenance programmer, either because of the complexity of the reasoning task involved or because of the sheer volume of cases that must be considered. Despite this, few software tools exist which can support the programmer in this task. Step 1, for example, must be carried out manually at present, although (as we shall later demonstrate) techniques do exist for assisting in this task.

Step 2 corresponds closely to the traditional notion of impact analysis, in that it essentially involves the identification of the set of software components (in this case, programs) that are affected by the proposed change. However, most current impact analysis tools [1] discover impacts by tracking *dependencies* of various kinds between software artefacts. While certain forms of dependencies (e.g. data dependencies) might be of use in determining which programs are impacted by the addition of a new constraint, they do not provide us with a complete solution to the problem. In fact, the kind of functionality required to support step 2 is provided to a large extent by modern data dictionary systems. For example, Predict (a data dictionary for use with the ADABAS/NATURAL development environment [17]) maintains links to program statements which contain database update commands, and thus allows easy identification of the (super)set of programs which can potentially violate a given constraint.

For steps 3 to 5, we require a tool which is able to reason over both the semantics of the programming language *and* the semantics of the data manipulation commands. Presently, very few impact analysis techniques incorporate knowledge of database semantics. There are a few commercial tools (e.g. CAST Envision [16] and Quest's SQL Impact [13]) and some limited research proposals [4,15] which perform impact analysis for database schema evolution. However, their scope is limited to changes to table and attribute structure, and they cannot identify the impacts of more complex forms of schema evolution (such as changes to integrity constraints).

3 Identifying Potentially Violating Updates

The key to automating the process of constraint implementation lies in the first of the steps mentioned in the previous section. If we can discover which updates can potentially violate the new constraint, then we can use this information, alongside conventional source code analysis techniques, to provide support for all of the remaining steps (i.e. steps 2 to 5).

As it happens, this is a problem that has been well-studied for many decades, and a variety of solutions have been proposed in the literature [12,3,9]. In general, these solutions are derived from the notion that, given any arbitrary database update, we can classify its effect on the truth value of a condition over the database state as belonging to one of the following three categories [5]:

- The update has no effect on the validity of the constraint, regardless of the circumstances under which it occurs. In this case, the update is said to be *trivially satisfying.*
- The update will always result in a violation of the constraint, regardless of the circumstances under which it occurs. In this case, the update is said to be *trivially violating.*
- The update will cause a violation of the constraint in some circumstances but not in others. Updates of this kind are said to be *potentially violating.*

As an illustration of these three categories, consider the following simple constraint:

$$ic_1 \equiv (\forall c, a, b)\ cust(c, a, b) \wedge managed(c) \Rightarrow gold(c)$$

Informally, this rule expresses the company policy that, for the purposes of the company's reward programme, all managed customers are considered automatically to have "gold" status. We will now present some example updates, and classify them according to their effect on this constraint. We will use the notation $+tablename(x_1, \ldots, x_n)$ to indicate the insertion of a new tuple $< x_1, \ldots, x_n >$ into the table called *tablename*, and the notation $-tablename(x_1, \ldots, x_n)$ to indicate the deletion of the tuple $< x_1, \ldots, x_n >$ from *tablename.* Modifications to existing tuples are expressed as combination of a deletion and an insertion.

We illustrate the different categories of update using the following examples:

- Since our example constraint is range-restricted [12], any update to a schema element which does not appear in the constraint expression can be classified as being trivially satisfying. For instance, the update

  $$-account(x, y, z)$$

  is trivially satisfying relative to our example constraint for any value of x, y and z.
- Some updates involving schema elements which *do* appear in a constraint may also be trivially satisfying, as in the case of the following update:

  $$-cust(x, y, z)$$

Deleting a customer from the database can never violate constraint ic_1. Such an update can only have the effect of falsifying the left hand side of the implication for a given set of values, and thus the implication must remain true for those values.

- There is only one update that is trivially violating for constraint ic_1. It is the composite update:

$$+cust(x, y, z),\ +managed(x),\ -gold(x)$$

Since all these updates refer to the same customer identifier (x), we know that a violation must always result if all three are executed successfully.

- Finally, we present an example of an update that is potentially violating for our example constraint:

$$-gold(x)$$

In this case, we cannot tell from the form of the update whether it will cause a violation or not. In order to make this decision, we need to interrogate the database to discover more about the context of the update. For instance, in this case, we need to know whether the customer whose gold status is being deleted is a managed customer or not. If he or she is, then this update *will* cause a violation, but if the customer is a normal domestic customer then we can freely delete his or her gold status without breaching this particular business rule.

When we add a new integrity constraint to an information system, we need to identify the set of all updates which are trivially or potentially violating for that constraint[2]. Any program capable of effecting a state change that includes such an update is potentially impacted by the addition of the new constraint.

To identify this set of updates, we can make use of techniques from the field of database integrity checking [12,2,5,9]. Various approaches have been proposed, each of which operates on a slightly different class of constraints. Here, we will describe the method we have implemented in our prototype impact analysis tool, which is adapted from a technique proposed for use in identifying database repairs [8]. Due to space restrictions, we will present a cut-down version of the method that operates over universally quantified expressions only. The reader is referred to the literature on integrity maintenance for details of techniques which can operate on constraints involving existentially quantified variables [9].

The method we describe here uses a truth table representation of the constraint to derive the different kinds of update that can cause it to become false. For example, consider the following truth table for constraint ic_1:

[2] For brevity, in the remainder of this paper, we will use the term *potentially violating updates* to indicate the set of both trivially *and* potentially violating updates.

	$cust(c,a,b)$	$managed(c)$	$gold(c)$	ic_1
1	F	F	F	T
2	F	F	T	T
3	F	T	F	T
4	F	T	T	T
5	T	F	F	T
6	T	F	T	T
7	T	T	F	F
8	T	T	T	T

The truth table shows us that a violation of ic_1 occurs iff a substitution θ_1 of values for the variables a, b and c exists, such that:

$$cust(c/\theta_1, a/\theta_1, b/\theta_1) \wedge managed(c/\theta_1) \wedge \neg gold(c/\theta_1)$$

is satisfied by the database state[3]. By examining the differences between pairs of true and false rows in the truth table, we can discover what state changes could cause such a substitution to be brought into existence. For example, consider the differences between rows 1 and 7 of the table. Suppose we have a database state ds which satisfies the row 1 expression, i.e. some substitution θ_2 exists for which the expression:

$$\neg cust(c/\theta_2, a/\theta_2, b/\theta_2) \wedge \neg managed(c/\theta_2) \wedge \neg gold(c/\theta_2)$$

is true in ds. The columns which have a different value in the two rows being compared tell us what changes we need to make to ds in order to cause it to satisfy the false row expression for θ_2 — that is, to cause a violation to be introduced. These changes are:

$$+cust(c/\theta_2, a/\theta_2, b/\theta_2), +managed(c/\theta_2)$$

The columns where the value is the same in both rows indicate the necessary and sufficient condition for determining whether a violation will definitely occur as a result of these updates. In the case of our example, the condition to be tested is: $gold(c/\theta_2)$. In other words, if we are adding a new managed customer to the database, we need to check whether that customer has gold status or not, in order to determine whether a violation with result from the update.

By considering the differences between all possible pairs of true and false rows in this way, we can extract the complete set of potentially violating updates (and their associated conditions) for this rule:

$1 \to 7$	$+cust(c, a, b), +managed(c)$	$if\ \neg gold(c)$
$2 \to 7$	$+cust(c, a, b), +managed(c), -gold(c)$	$if\ true$
$3 \to 7$	$+cust(c, a, b)$	$if\ managed(c) \wedge \neg gold(c)$
$4 \to 7$	$+cust(c, a, b), -gold(c)$	$if\ managed(c)$
$5 \to 7$	$+managed(c)$	$if\ (\exists a, b)\ cust(c, a, b) \wedge \neg gold(c)$
$6 \to 7$	$+managed(c), -gold(c)$	$if\ cust(c, a, b)$
$8 \to 7$	$-gold(c)$	$if\ cust(c, a, b) \wedge managed(c)$

[3] The proof of this is given elsewhere [8]

Any program fragment which has the potential to bring about one of these state changes can also potentially violate the constraint. For example, the state change described by the transition between row 5 and row 7 can be effected by insertion of a new *cust* tuple, or by updating an existing one.

By analysing the form of the constraint that we wish to add to the system, therefore, we can identify the set of "symptoms" that indicate where a change to source code might be required. In the following section, we will describe how we can make use of this information in analysing the impact of adding new integrity constraints to existing software systems.

4 Impact Analysis for the Addition of Constraints

The ability to determine the complete set of updates that can violate a constraint opens up a number of possibilities for developing techniques to support programmers in maintaining and evolving integrity constraints. For example, if we consider the steps involved in implementing a new constraint (as outlined in Section 2), the following forms of support can be envisaged:

1. If we know which state changes can potentially cause a violation of the new constraint, we can use this information to identify those programs which have the potential to bring such state changes about (i.e. to support steps 2 and 3). This corresponds to the set of programs which need to be modified in order to implement the new constraint. In theory, it should be possible to identify this set exactly; in practice, a more efficient technique which identifies a close superset may be just as useful. It is important, however, that any more efficient but less accurate technique returns a true superset of the actual results. We can live with the programmer having to examine a handful of programs unnecessarily, but we want to be confident that no potentially violating programs have been omitted.
2. Once we have determined that a particular program requires modification, it should be possible for a software tool to indicate to the programmer exactly which of the database update statements need to be guarded against violation of the constraint (i.e. to support step 4). Again, in practice, we can be satisfied with a technique which occasionally points out update statements that cannot violate the constraint, provided that it does not omit any statements that can.
3. Since we can derive the necessary and sufficient condition for violation along with each potentially violating update, we can also provide some guidance to the programmer as to the form of the guard condition that is required in each case (i.e. to support step 5). Of course, the actual changes to the code must be chosen by the programmer, but the advice provided by the software tool could at least help to ensure that awkward and complex cases are not overlooked or interpreted incorrectly.

Each of the above cases involves the use of information derived by the analysis of a constraint in determining the impact of adding that constraint to a given set of programs. Such impacts can be identified at a variety of granularities, ranging from identification of impacted programs (point 1 in the above list), through identification of impacted program statements (point 2), to guidance as to the form of the new code that is required (point 3).

Given the capability to determine impacted program statements, it might be thought that the ability to determine impacted programs is unnecessary. After all, the set of impacted programs should be exactly the set of programs which contain impacted statements. However, since analysis of a program to discover the set of impacted statements is a potentially expensive task, there is still some value in a "quick and dirty" filtering step, which can remove programs which are not impacted from further consideration. Only programs which pass through this filtering step are subjected to the more comprehensive impact analysis step.

Before we describe the operation of these two steps in more detail, we first present some definitions and assumptions. We use the name ic_n to refer to the integrity constraint that is to be added to the system, while Ps denotes the set of programs that are to be analysed for the impacts of this change. We assume the existence of a function called *gcu* which maps constraints onto the set of guarded complex updates which can potentially violate them. A *guarded complex update* is a pair $< Us, C >$, where Us is a set of database updates and C is the necessary and sufficient condition (i.e. the guard) that determines whether the updates in Us result in a rule violation or not. For example, at the end of Section 3, we listed the seven GCUs that are potentially violating for constraint ic_1.

Each member of Us is a triple $< UT, TN, V >$, where UT is the update type ($UT \in \{`i', `d', `m'\}$, representing the standard "insert", "delete" and "modify" update types), TN is the name of the table that is updated and V is a tuple of variables representing the updated tuple in the named table.

We further assume the existence of a function called *dbs*, which maps a program p ($p \in Ps$) onto a set of triples $< UT, TN, S >$, where UT is the update type (as defined earlier), TN is the name of the table that is updated, and S is the identifier of a statement in the program that corresponds to an update of the given type to the given table. This function provides us with a convenient means of locating program statements that correspond to particular database update commands.

4.1 Identifying Programs Likely to Be Impacted

Once the set of potentially violating updates (PVUs) has been identified for the new constraint, we can use this information to quickly determine which of the application programs are likely to be capable of violating it. Informally, we can state the criterion used to filter the set of programs as follows:

> A program is potentially impacted by the addition of the new constraint iff there is some PVU for that constraint such that every component update of the PVU is performed by some part of the program.

In the case of example constraint ic_1, this criterion implies that any program which performs a deletion from the *gold* table is impacted by the addition of ic_1.

Programs which contain no deletion or modification operations on the *gold* table and no insertions or modifications to either *cust* or *managed* are not impacted.

More formally, for a new constraint ic_n, we can define the set of potentially impacted programs IP ($IP \subseteq Ps$) as:

$$IP = \{\, p \mid (\exists u, c)\; p \in Ps \wedge < u, c > \in gcu(ic_n) \wedge$$

$$((\forall ut, tn, v) < ut, tn, v > \in u \;\Rightarrow\; (\exists s) < ut, tn, s > \in p) \,\}$$

The advantage of this filtering criterion is that it is relatively cheap to compute (especially if an index has been created that provides quick access to the database update statements performed by the program [17]). It also meets our requirements in that it can eliminate a high proportion of the non-impacted programs without eliminating any impacted programs.

It is not, however, a completely accurate determiner of impact, and some non-impacted programs will pass successfully through our filter. This can happen when the updates within a PVU all occur in a program but in such a way that it is impossible for them to be executed together in one run of the program.

Another situation in which the filter will give inaccurate results is when the PVU updates occurring in the program do so within a context where the guard condition can never be satisfied. For example, if we have the following PVU:

$$+cust(c, a, b) \;\; if \; b \leq 0$$

then a COBOL program p containing the following fragment would be considered to be potentially violating according to our filtering criterion:

```
IF WS-BALANCE > 0
   MOVE WS-CNO TO DB-CUST-CNO
   MOVE WS-CUST-ADDR TO DB-CUST-ADDR
   MOVE WS-BALANCE TO DB-CUST-BAL
   STORE CUST.
```

However, if this is the only update to the *cust* table in p, then p should not be included in the set of impacted programs. This is because the update specified in the PVU occurs in a context in which the associated condition can never be satisfied; the enclosing if-statement is already guarding the update against this particular kind of violation.

4.2 Identifying the Impacts within a Program

Having determined that a particular program is likely to be impacted by the addition of a new constraint, the next step is to perform a more detailed analysis of that program, to discover the ways in which it is impacted more precisely. In order to do this, we must identify the subset of the PVUs of the new constraint that may be performed by the program being analysed. This allows us to pinpoint the exact source code statements which are involved in each PVU, so that the programmer can be given some guidance on where new guard conditions must

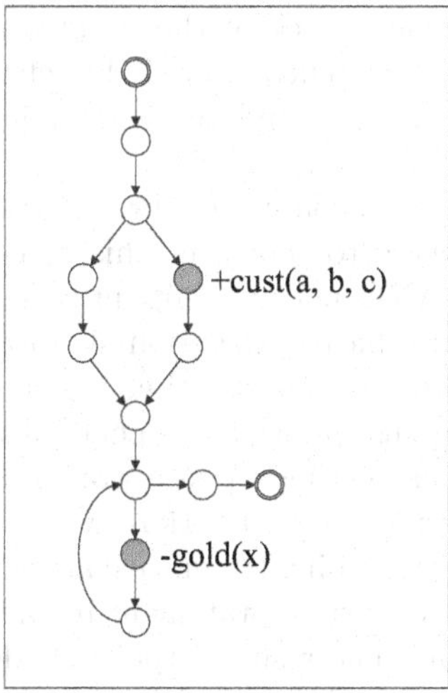

Fig. 1. Example CFG with update nodes distinguished

be added to the program. In general, of course, a given program will be capable of performing several different PVUs, and may even be able to perform the same PVU in several different ways.

Conceptually, the problem of identifying the set of program statements that can perform a PVU corresponds to the identification of subgraphs in the program's control flow graph (CFG) which contain all the updates in the PVU in sequence. For example, Figure 1 shows the basic structure of a control flow graph for a very simple program. The nodes of the graph correspond to the statements of the program and the edges between the nodes indicate the control flow paths that are possible between statements. Nodes corresponding to database update commands are shown in grey and are labelled with a description of the state change operation the command performs.

If we match this example control flow graph against the PVU set identified from constraint ic_1 then we discover that the following three PVUs can be performed by this program:

$$\begin{array}{lll} +cust(c, a, b) & \textit{if } managed(c) & \wedge \neg\, gold(c) \\ +cust(c, a, b),\ -gold(c) & \textit{if } managed(c) & \\ -gold(c) & \textit{if } cust(c, a, b) & \wedge\ managed(c) \end{array}$$

In order to compute such matches, we first construct a "trace" of the database update commands that can be performed by the program being analysed, and then match each PVU update set against this trace[4]. The trace is computed

[4] In our prototype implementation, we actually compute the trace and perform the matching at the same time, as this is more efficient than computing the trace separately from matching. However, we present them as two separate steps here, in order to simplify the presentation.

by walking the abstract syntax tree of the program, adding the identifiers of update statements as they are encountered. Effectively, it provides a (finite) representation of the sequences of update commands that may be executed by the program.

Since programs may contain conditional branches and loops, it is not possible to use a simple list structure to represent this trace. Instead, we use a form of AND-OR tree, where AND nodes represent sequential execution of traces and OR nodes represent alternative execution of traces. Traces formed from the bodies of loops are tagged with a special label, which indicates that the updates in the trace may match against multiple elements of the PVU set.

The algorithm for constructing update traces follows the usual syntax-directed pattern for analysing programs. Here, we give its definition for several representative kinds of programming language construct. In each case, the inputs to the *trace* function are the current statement in the abstract syntax tree, and the trace constructed so far. The result is the trace describing the behaviour of the program immediately after the execution of the statement given as input.

A sequence of statements: in this case, the resulting trace is that produced by execution of the second part of the sequence, in the context of the trace produced by the first.

$$\text{trace}([\![S1 \; ; \; S2]\!], \text{tr}) = \text{trace}(S2, \text{trace}(S1, \text{tr}))$$

A conditional statement: for this kind of statement, we process each branch of the conditional in the context of the given trace, and then combine the resulting traces together using an OR node.

$$\text{trace}([\![\mathit{if}\ C\ \mathit{then}\ S1\ \mathit{else}\ S2]\!], \text{tr}) = \text{or}(\text{trace}(S1, \text{tr}), \text{trace}(S2, \text{tr}))$$

A loop statement: most loop constructs actually include a conditional element, representing the exit condition. For example, consider the definition of the *trace* function for a standard *while-do* loop:

$$\text{trace}([\![\mathit{while}\ C\ \mathit{do}\ S]\!], \text{tr}) = \text{or}(\text{tr}, \text{tag}(\text{trace}(S, \text{tr}))$$

If the loop condition C is false, then this loop will execute zero times, in which case the resulting trace is simply that produced after execution of the preceding statement (i.e. the input trace). Otherwise, the final trace is that produced by executing the loop body an arbitrary number of times.

How do we produce a trace representing the effects of an arbitrary (and possibly infinite) number of iterations of the loop body? In fact, if we could be sure that every update type to every database table would appear at most once in each PVU, the answer to this question would be exceedingly straightforward, since we would obtain the same set of matches from the trace of a single execution of the loop body as we would from an arbitrary number of executions. Unfortunately, there is no reason why a PVU cannot contain multiple examples of the same kind of update. For example:

$\mathit{insert}(A, B, C), \mathit{insert}(B, D, E)\ \mathit{if}\ \ldots$

This example PVU matches with a program that contains a single insertion to the *cust* table only if the insertion command appears within the body of a loop. This is because, effectively, updates which occur with loops may match with updates in a PVU an arbitrary number of times, while updates which do not occur within a loop may be matched with only one PVU update. We can therefore model the behaviour of loops by means of the simple expedient of tagging updates which occur within loops, so that the matching algorithm is aware that they can be treated specially.

A simple non-update command: simple commands which are not database updates are essentially ignored by the trace generation algorithm, e.g.

$$\text{trace}([\![\textit{print } T]\!], \text{tr}) = \text{tr}$$

A database update command: if we encounter an update command, we must add the details of the update (represented as a triple of update type, table name and statement identifier) to the current trace. For example:

$$\text{trace}(\ [\![\ \textit{store tn}\ ]\!], \text{tr}) = \text{and}(\ \text{tr}, < `i', tn, s >\ )$$
$$\text{where s} = \text{the identifier of the current statement}$$

Having computed the trace of updates produced by a program, we can then attempt to match each of the PVUs against it. Informally, we say that a PVU $< us, c >$ matches a trace t iff all the updates in the set us occur as a sequence somewhere within t. More formally, a set of updates us matches t in the following cases:

- If $us = \emptyset$ then us matches t.
- If $us \neq \emptyset$ and $t = and(t_1, t_2)$ then us matches t iff us can be partitioned into two disjoint subsets u_1 and u_2, such that u_1 matches t_1 and u_2 matches t_2.
- If $us \neq \emptyset$ and $t = or(t_1, t_2)$ then us matches t iff us matches t_1 or t_2.
- If $us \neq \emptyset$ and $t = tagged(and(t_1, t_2))$ then us matches t iff us can be partitioned into two disjoint subsets u_1 and u_2, such that u_1 matches $and(t_1, t_2)$ and u_2 matches t.
- If $us \neq \emptyset$ and $t = tagged(or(t_1, t_2))$ then us matches t iff us can be partitioned into two disjoint subsets u_1 and u_2 such that:
  - u_1 matches t_1 and u_2 matches t, or
  - u_2 matches t_2 and u_1 matches t.
- If $us = \{< `i', tn, v >\}$ then $us$ matches $t$ iff $t = \{< `i', tn, s >\}$ or $t = < `m', tn, s >$.
- If $us = \{<' d', tn, v >\}$ then us matches t iff $t = \{< `d', tn, s >\}$ or $t = \{< `m', tn, s >\}$.

For each match against a given trace, we record the identifier of the PVU which has been matched and a list of the update statements responsible for it. We also store a "contextualised" form of the necessary and sufficient condition associated with the matched PVU. A contextualised condition is one in which some of the original variables have been replaced with variables from the program code. It describes a constraint over the program variables that are involved in the update commands, rather than over the "disembodied" logical variables of the original integrity constraint.

Details of all possible matches are recorded (and shown to the programmer), since each one represents a potential cause of violations within the program that must be guarded against. In some cases, this may mean that a single program statement matches with several different PVUs. It is important that the programmer is aware of all the ways in which a program statement may lead to a violation, before he or she decides on the guard conditions that will be added to the program.

5 An Illustrative Example

In order to illustrate our impact analysis technique in action, we will present a small (and rather artificial) example of the kinds of result it can produce. Assume that we have an information system which consists of a customer database (*db*) and three applications programs (p_1, p_2 and p_3). We wish to add constraint ic_1 to the system. Recall that ic_1 is defined as follows:

$$ic_1 \equiv (\forall c, a, b)\ cust(c, a, b) \land managed(c) \Rightarrow gold(c)$$

Program p_1 performs a query over the database and produces a report. It does not make any updates to the database, and would therefore be filtered out by our program during phase 1 of the analysis.

Program p_2, on the other hand, is used to delete customers and their associated records. All the database update commands it contains are included in the following fragment of code, which appears in the program immediately after a section of code which attempts to retrieve the customer record to be deleted. The variable `DB-CUST-CNO` identifies this record.

```
100 IF DB-REC-EXISTS
        ...
160     MOVE DB-CUST-CNO TO DB-GOLD-CNO
170     DELETE GOLD
        ...
230     MOVE DB-CUST-CNO TO DB-MANAGED-CNO
240     DELETE MANAGED
250     DELETE CUST
260     COMMIT.
```

This program meets our criterion for impacted programs, since it contains all the updates included within one of the PVUs derived from ic_1:

$$8 \rightarrow 7 \qquad -gold(c) \quad \textit{if}\ cust(c, a, b) \land managed(c)$$

During the second phase of impact analysis, the PVUs are matched against the structure of the program in more detail, and statement 170 is found to match with the PVU shown above. The contextualised condition that is attached to the record of this match is:

$$(\exists a, b)\ cust(DB\text{-}CUST\text{-}CNO,\ a,\ b) \wedge managed(DB\text{-}CUST\text{-}CNO)$$

The programmer browses the set of matches, and the statements to which they are attached, and attempts to determine how much of the contextualised condition is already implemented by the program. In fact, since the programmer knows that the *customer number* attribute is a key attribute of all three of the tables updated by this program, he or she can also deduce that the PVU condition can never be satisfied at the point when the `COMMIT` operation is invoked (line 260). This is because any *cust* and *managed* tuples which join with the deleted *gold* tuple are also deleted by the program, before the effect of this PVU is committed to the database. The programmer therefore decides that no change is required to program p_2 (except perhaps for the addition of a comment to explain why the constraint cannot be violated by this sequence of updates).

Program p_3 contains a more complex sequence of updates. The parts of the program that are relevant to our analysis (i.e. those that involve database updates) are shown below:

```
    ...
120 IF NOT DB-REC-EXISTS
130     MOVE WS-CNO TO DB-CUST-CNO
140     MOVE WS-ADDR TO DB-CUST-ADDR
150     MOVE WS-BALANCE TO DB-CUST-BAL
160     STORE CUST
170 ELSE
    ...
210 END-IF.
    ...
340 IF WS-CTYPE = "M"
350     MOVE WS-CNO TO DB-MANAGED-CNO
360     STORE MANAGED
370 ELSE
    ...
420 END-IF.
    ...
780 COMMIT.
    ...
```

This program passes successfully through the phase 1 filter, and is then matched against the PVUs. As a result, three records are created, to record the following PVU matches:

- The program may execute PVU 1 $\rightarrow$ 7, through update statements [160, 360]. The contextualised condition is:

$$\neg\ gold(DB\text{-}CUST\text{-}CNO)$$

- The program may execute PVU $3 \rightarrow 7$, through update statement [160]. The contextualised condition for determining violation is:

$$\mathit{managed}(DB\_CUST\_NO) \quad \wedge \neg\ \mathit{gold}(DB\_CUST\_NO)$$

- The program may execute PVU $5 \rightarrow 7$, through update statement [360]. The contextualised condition is:

$$(\exists a, b)\ \mathit{cust}(DB\_CUST\_NO, a, b) \quad \wedge \neg\ \mathit{gold}(DB\_CUST\_NO)$$

At first sight, the first and third of these matches might be thought to be redundant, as their update sequences are both subsets of that of the second match. However, since it is possible for the flow of control to pass through one of the identified statements (i.e. 160 and 360) without necessarily passing through them both, the program actually has the capability to violate the constraint in all these three ways. The programmer must be made aware of all these possibilities, so that the most appropriate guard (or guards) can be designed and inserted into the program.

In our example, since the conditions of the first and third matches are both stronger than the condition associated with the second, the programmer might decide to add pre-condition guards to each of the individual updates. Alternatively, he or she might decide to place a single, more complex guard before the commit operation, that tests for all three of the contextualised conditions at once.

6 Conclusions

Modifying an information system so that it enforces new business rules is a challenging and error prone task. If any of the necessary modifications are omitted or carried out incorrectly, then the business rule will only be enforced by part of the system and inconsistent behaviour will result [6]. In this paper, we have described how techniques from database integrity maintenance can be used as the basis of a technique which can help make the implementation of certain kinds of business rule a less painful and risky procedure. The technique, which has been prototyped in Prolog, helps the programmer by identifying the set of programs which have the potential to cause violations and by indicating which lines of code are responsible for this ability. It is also able to provide guidance as to the form of guard that should be inserted into the program to prevent violations from occurring at run-time.

We expect that the principal practical benefits of our technique will be in reducing the amount of time programmers have to spend examining program code that is not related to the new constraint; and in reducing the chance of errors of omission by helping to ensure that all the possibilities for violations, however complex or obscure, are considered by the programmer. It is also possible that this technique might have a role in validation of software, i.e. in helping to determine whether a software system correctly implements a given set of database constraints, or whether it has the capacity to violate some of them. In addition, knowledge of the source code statements implicated in the implementation of a constraint can also help in generating white-box test cases aimed at detecting defects in the implementation, or for use in regression testing.

However, further evaluation of the technique is required before these claims can be verified. In particular, we need to discover whether the algorithms described in this paper are capable of processing real-scale constraints and programs in realistic timescales. The time required to compute impacts by our method is dependent on two factors: the number of potentially violating updates that are derived from the new constraint, and the number of distinct sequences of database update commands that can be performed by the programs being analysed.

Unfortunately, the number of PVUs derivable from a constraint is 2^n in the average case and 2^{2n-2} in the worst case, where n is the number of distinct atomic predicates appearing in the rule. Similarly, a program containing m database update statements will be capable of performing up to $2^m - 1$ distinct update sequences, all of which must be matched against the set of PVUs. The efficiency of this technique in practice is therefore clearly a matter of concern. Our experience with extraction of business rules from legacy systems suggests that, for many rules, n will be small (less than 10, for example) [7]. We cannot be so sanguine in the case of database update statements - it does not seem unreasonable to expect a typical database application program to contain tens of update statements. However, we can reasonably expect the average number of update sequences to be much lower than that predicted by our worst case analysis.

The next stage in our research, therefore, will be to test our technique on some real application programs, for the implementation of constraints of realistic complexity. If the tool is efficient enough to be practically usable, then we can attempt to gauge its success in reducing effort and errors in integrity constraint implementation. If the algorithm's complexity is found to be a stumbling block to exploitation of the tool, we shall seek a less accurate but more efficient version of the algorithms that can at least give some help to the programmer in dealing with the complexity of the rule implementation task.

References

1. R. Arnold and S. Bohner, editors. *Software Change Impact Analysis.* IEEE Computer Society Press, 1996.
2. S. Ceri and J. Widom. Deriving Production Rules for Incremental View Maintenance. In G. Lohman, A. Sernadas, and R. Camps, editors, *Proceedings of 17th International Conference on Very Large Databases*, pages 577–589, Barcelona, 1991. Morgan Kaufmann Publishers, Inc.
3. S. Ceri and J. Widom. Production Rules in Parallel and Distributed Database Environments. In L.-Y. Yuan, editor, *Proceedings of 18th International Conference on Very Large Databases*, pages 339–351, Vancouver, August 1992. Morgan Kaufmann Publishers, Inc.

4. L. Deruelle, M. Bouneffa, N. Melab, and H. Basson. A change propagation model and platform for multi-database applications. In *Proceedings of IEEE International Conference on Software Maintenance*, pages 42–51, Florence, Italy, November 2001. IEEE Computer Society Press.
5. O. Díaz. Deriving Rules for Constraint Maintenance in an Object-Oriented Database. In A.M. Toja and I. Ramos, editors, *DEXA 92 Conference*, pages 332–337. Springer-Verlag, 1992.
6. A.B. Earls, S.M. Embury, and N.J. Turner. A Method for the Manual Extraction of Business Rules from Legacy Source Code. *BT Technology Journal*, 2002. To Appear.
7. Andrew B. Earls. A Method to Extract the Business Rules from a Large Legacy System. Master's thesis, Dept. of Computer Science, Cardiff University, 2001.
8. S.M. Embury, S.M. Brandt, J.S. Robinson, I. Sutherland, F.A. Bisby, W.A. Gray, A.C. Jones, and R.J. White. Adapting Integrity Enforcement Techniques for Data Reconciliation. *Information Systems*, 26(8):657–689, December 2001.
9. S.M. Embury and P.M.D. Gray. Compiling a Declarative, High-Level Language for Semantic Integrity Constraints. In R. Meersman and L. Mark, editors, *Proceedings of 6th IFIP TC-2 Working Conference on Data Semantics*, pages 188–226, Atlanta, USA, May 1997. Chapman and Hall.
10. D. Hay and K.A. Healy. Defining Business Rules — What are they Really? Technical report, The Business Rules Group, Revision 1.3, July 2000. Available on-line at `http://www.essentialstrategies.com/ publications/businessrules/`.
11. ILOG, Inc. JRules Business Rule Engine. `http://www.ilog.com/products/rules/ engines/jrules/`, 2002.
12. J.-M. Nicolas. Logic for Improving Integrity Checking in Relational Databases. *Acta Informatica*, 18:227–253, 1982.
13. Quest Software. Effective Application Source Code SQL Analysis for Change Impact, Performance and Quality. White paper, available at `http://www.quest.com/whitepapers/`, 2002.
14. J. Shao and C. Pound. Reverse Engineering Business Rules from Legacy Systems. *BT Technology Journal*, 17(4):179–186, 1999.
15. D.I.K. Sjöberg. Quantifying Schema Evolution. *Information and Software Technology*, 35(1):35–44, 1993.
16. CAST Software. Envision, October 2002. `http://www.castsoftware.com/`.
17. Software AG. Adabase High Performance Database System. `http://www.softwareag.com/adabas/`, 2002.

- Zhang [24] notes that current object-relational databases fail to support relationships that contain extended semantics. As a solution, she proposes an extension to SQL called Orient-SQL to allow precise specification of relationship's additional *structural* and *operational* properties. For example, relationship's participants, their superordinated or subordinated roles in the relationships and their cardinalities can be defined using structural properties. Behavior at the events of selecting, inserting, and deleting the relationship's participants in the database can be defined using operational properties.
- SQL:1999 fails to fully support modular implementation of database schemas [13] that would enable reuse of schema parts, assembly of off-the-shelf schema modules and increase schema quality by encouraging unit tests on interrelated structural (type and table definitions) and behavioral (triggers, user-defined routines) elements of a module.
- Preference queries [12] that have to be answered cooperatively by treating preferences as soft constraints are not supported in SQL:1999.

Motivated by the above examples, this paper presents our *X-Translate system*, which allows the users to extend SQL:1999 with general as well as domain-specific language constructs. The extensions defining the constructs are delivered in form of packages which can be imported into the system. The system comes with a translator that invokes methods defined by the extensions to translate statements containing custom language constructs onto SQL:1999 statements.

Sect. 2 will focus on the example of extending SQL:1999 to support modular schema implementation in detail. Sect. 3 presents the X-Translate system architecture. A list of open issues is discussed in Sect. 4, while Sect. 5 gives an overview of related work. In Sect. 6, we conclude our work and present some ideas for future work related to our approach.

2 Modularity in Schema Design

Even though a modular or even component-based design is state-of-the-art in application development ([1], [5]), there is a lack of such concepts in SQL:1999. In SQL:1999, there are only flat schemas and server modules [8], which mainly contain user-defined functions and do not deal with other schema elements. Both concepts do not offer interfaces or explicitly defined relationships between them (see [13], [15] for details). Although concepts like DataBlades or Cartridges offered by some ORDBMS vendors can be used to group schema elements, these concepts serve merely as initialization units that place their elements in a schema. Nevertheless, grouping schema elements together in nestable modules, offering interfaces to these modules and supporting relationships between the modules would make the benefits common to component-based application design also possible at the database schema level. Particularly w.r.t. the object-relational features of SQL:1999, like user-defined routines (UDR) and user-defined types (UDT), this would be extremely beneficial. The object-relational features of SQL:1999 allow to map much more functionality to the database schema which, in turn, leads to a more complex and time-consuming schema design. The main advantages of a modular schema design are in detail:

- *Reuse of parts of the schema.* By grouping semantically interrelated schema elements in modules, the elements can easily be reused in other schemas. For example, developing an XML data type and UDRs for managing XML documents inside the database, is a cost- and time-intensive task. Moreover, this functionality is probably needed by many different schemas. By grouping the schema elements for managing XML documents in a single schema module, they can easily be reused by other schemas. Without the concept of modularity, different schema elements, like UDTs and UDRs, are hidden in the schema making it unclear which elements are actually needed for a given functionality.
- *Easy and rapid schema design by assembling off-the-shelf modules.* If there is a sufficient number of (off-the-shelf) schema modules, new schemas can be developed mainly by combining existing schema modules. This does not only reduce development costs, but also decreases time-to-market.
- *Quality and robustness of a schema.* By (re)using high-quality, well-tested schema modules, both quality and robustness of a schema increase. Because most testing can be done on a small excerpt of a schema (the schema module), testing is much simpler compared to testing the whole schema at a time. The complexity of object-relational technology, especially when considering UDRs, makes testing necessary.
- *Exchange and extension of parts of the schema.* Using interfaces and, thereby, achieving *information hiding*, schema modules implementing the same interface can be replaced in a schema. This allows the optimization of schema parts and the inclusion of new code into an existing schema. Furthermore, the schema can be extended with new functionality by replacing an old schema module with a new one offering more functionality, but still complying with the old interface. We have to mention that most schema modules have a persistent state, that is, represented by tuples of a table. Exchanging stateful schema modules in a running system requires that the state of the old schema module is transferred to the new one. Nevertheless, exchanging schema modules seems to be a promising way to handle schema evolution.
- *Structural and distributed schema design.* Modularity allows structural design by dividing different tasks of the schema in separate schema modules and only define interfaces and relationships between them. The schema modules can be developed independently of each other by distributed groups of programmers.
- *Continued, component-based design.* Nowadays, a component-based development of applications is often blurred as far as the data storage component is concerned. The application components are separated at the application layer, but use a global database schema for their persistent data with overlapping parts. If each application component offers its own schema module and only well-defined relationships between the schema modules are used, the separation and isolation continues at the schema level.

The main objective of schema modularity is to control the dependencies between schema elements of separate schema modules. By schema elements we mean the modeling elements offered by SQL:1999, like tables, triggers, UDRs, UDTs, etc. The dependencies may emerge from a foreign key definition between two tables, but also a

UDR call or a trigger definition can lead to a dependency. In [15], a description and classification of the different dependencies is given. Using narrow interfaces and defining relationships between separate schema modules, the number of possible dependencies is restricted and other dependencies (unknown to the DBMS) are prohibited.

In [13], a framework for a modular schema design is introduced. We do not want to present the framework in detail, an excerpt of this framework may illustrate the idea of modular extensions of SQL:1999. The framework consists of different kinds of schema modules. In this paper, we will focus on one kind, the schema component. A schema component can contain all kinds of schema elements and can exist independently of other schema modules. It is important to know that, unlike the DDL statements of SQL:1999, there has to be a declaration of a schema component apart from the creation of a schema component. This is necessary, because a schema component may be used more than once in a schema, e.g., there may be several instances of a user management schema component, managing different kinds of users. A schema component can implement several interfaces as well as use interfaces of other schema components. Of course, only schema elements defined at the interface are visible outside the schema component. The *schema component declaration* specifies which interfaces are implemented by the schema component and which interfaces are required by the component. Concrete schema components used behind the interfaces are specified at the deployment of a component.

```
DECLARE INTERFACE BookManagementInterface
  TYPE bookT AS ( title CHARACTER(20),
                  ...)
  NOT FINAL
    METHOD getTOC() RETURNS CLOB,
    METHOD addChapter(chap Chapter, number INTEGER)
    ...;
  TYPE ChapterT AS (...) NOT FINAL;
  TABLE book OF bookT;
END INTERFACE;

DECLARE COMPONENT BookManagement
  IMPLEMENTING BookManagementInterface;
  DECLARE TYPE bookT AS ( title CHARACTER(20) NOT NULL,
                          ...)
      NOT FINAL
      METHOD getTOC() RETURNS CLOB,
      METHOD addChapter(chap Chapter, number INTEGER)
      ...;
  DECLARE TYPE chapterT AS ...;
  DECLARE TABLE book OF bookT
      title WITH OPTIONS NOT NULL;
  DECLARE TABLE chapter OF chapterT;
  ...
  DECLARE METHOD addChapter(chap Chapter, number INTEGER)
      FOR bookT
      BEGIN INSERT INTO chapter ....;
      END;
END COMPONENT;

CREATE COMPONENT bm OF BookManagement;
```

Fig. 1. Extended SQL for schema modularity

In Fig. 1, a small example for a DDL statement of a schema component declaration, called `BookManagement`, is given (lines 12-29). Line 13 defines which interfaces are implemented by `BookManagement` (in this example, there is only one interface, called `BookManagementInterface`, declared by lines 1-10). Note that in the example no interfaces and, as a consequence, no other schema modules are needed. Since `BookManagement` implements `BookManagementInterface`, all elements of the interface have to be part of `BookManagement`, like the structured types `chapterT` and `bookT`, supplemented with a constraint (`NOT NULL` in line 14). In addition to the typed table `book`, specified at the interface, `BookManagement` contains another table `chapter` and the implementations of the methods defined in the structured type (lines 25-28). After the schema component is instantiated (line 31), only the elements offered by the interface are accessible outside the schema component. That is, the table `chapter` is not accessible from outside the schema component, it can only be manipulated by method calls (e.g. `addChapter` of the `bookT`). The schema component has its own namespace and the elements are accessible only via this namespace.

3 X-Translate System Architecture

In this section, we introduce our approach to supporting different language extensions for SQL:1999, called the *X-Translate System*. The main goal of such a system is that different language extensions can be integrated into the system and, thereby, a new language containing the extensions is provided. Such an extended language is called *XSQL* (eXtended SQL). Note that XSQL does not mean a fixed combination of language extensions, but the combination specified by the currently installed language extensions of the system. Of course, not all language extensions can work together, e.g., if they use overlapping keywords. The system should be open to define new language extensions; it should be easy to define them and they should not invalidate existing legacy code that already contains SQL statements.

Certainly, we do not want to build a new DBMS from scratch, but translate XSQL to SQL:1999 and use it with an existing ORDBMS. We are quite sure that using query translation and the large expressive power of SQL:1999, most language extensions can be mapped to SQL:1999. Due to the fact that no ORDBMS vendor directly supports the exact syntax of SQL:1999, we also need a mapping from SQL:1999 to different SQL dialects. Because there is no big gap between SQL:1999 and the functionality offered by the ORDBMS vendors, this can easily be done. There are already approaches addressing this problem (see [25] for example), however, it proves possible to apply our approach successively to translate a SQL:1999 statement to a certain SQL dialect.

In Fig. 2, we illustrate the general architecture of the X-Translate system. It consists of a *translator*, an *extension directory* and an *extended system catalog*. Language extensions are defined in form of *extension packages*. Several extension packages can be imported into the system simultaneously. Each of them contains *grammar extensions*, *metamodel extensions* (to manage the metadata of the language extension), and *translation rules*, which describe how the extended grammar should be translated. The system manages the information related to the extensions within a single *extension direc-*

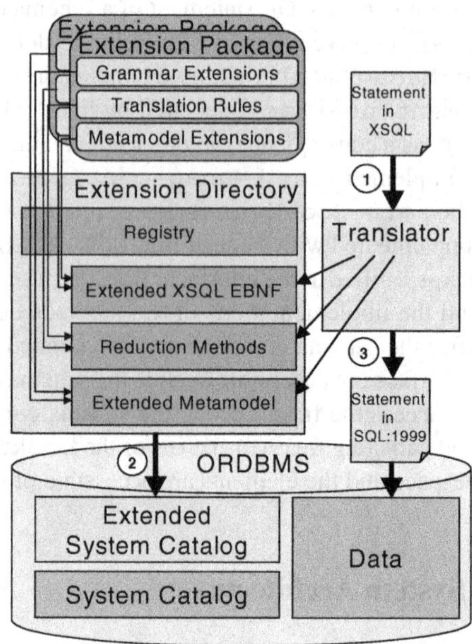

Fig. 2. General architecture of X-Translate

tory. This directory uses a *registry* to keep track of the imported packages. The grammar extensions are included in the *extended XSQL EBNF* (Extended Backus-Naur Form) and the metamodel extensions in the *extended metamodel.* The translation rules are used to generate the *reduction methods* of the system. To store the data of the extended metamodel, an *extended system catalog* is built on top of the SQL:1999 information schema. It is able to include the metadata of the extension packages and additional functionality to manage this metadata. For example, using schema modularity requires metadata for the declared schema modules and functionality to instantiate a schema module.

To translate an XSQL statement, the system works in the following way: The translator takes the XSQL statement as input (1). The statement is parsed utilizing the extended XSQL EBNF. The reduction methods are used to transform the XSQL statement to an SQL:1999 statement (3). Applying the reduction methods often requires accessing metadata stored in the extended system catalog (2). The translated statement itself can also access or manipulate data in the extended system catalog. The following sections will describe the architecture of the X-Translate system in detail.

3.1 Extension Packages

Extension packages are used to provide information needed by the system to support the use of new language constructs. This information comes in form of *metamodel extensions*, *grammar extensions*, and *definitions of translation rules*. A major challenge for extension packages is that they have to define the information in a generic way. This

```
1. <SQL schema definition statement> ::= !! All alternatives from SQL:1999
2.                                         | <SQL component declaration>
3.
4. <SQL component declaration> ::= DECLARE COMPONENT <component declaration name>
5.                                 .....
6.                                 END COMPONENT
```

EBNF extensions

```
7. <SQL component declaration> =>
8. CALL declareComponent(<component declaration name>, ...);
9. ...
10. CALL addToComponentDeclaration(
11.                  <component declaration name>,<component declaration element>)
```

Translation rules

```
12. MAP class schema component TO TABLE schema_component;
13. CREATE TYPE namespace (.....);
14. CREATE INTERNAL TABLE namemapping(realname SQL_IDENTIFIER NOT NULL,
15.                                    namesp namespace NOT NULL);
16. CREATE INTERNAL FUNCTION declareComponent(name ...)
17.   BEGIN ...
18.     ... INSERT INTO schema_component VALUES (name, ....); ...
19.   END;
```

Metamodel extensions (extended system catalog hints)

Fig. 3. Excerpt of an extension package introducing schema modularity to SQL:1999

means that the user should be given the possibility of tailoring the extensions during the import process to avoid possible conflicts with already imported packages:

- Metamodel extensions: These extensions are used to add additional constructs to the metamodel. During the import the user has to decide where in the metamodel a construct is to be inserted and what its relationships to other constructs are.
- Grammar extensions: Class implementations for new EBNF symbols are inserted into the existing class hierarchy.
- Definitions of translation rules: The rules are used to obtain the default implementation of the reduction method which reduces a high-level XSQL language construct to lower level constructs that are either directly supported by SQL:1999 or need to pass additional reduction steps. The default implementation of the reduction method as generated from the rules can afterwards be tailored by the user.

In Fig. 3, an excerpt from the extension package that introduces schema modularity extensions (as described in Sect. 2) to SQL:1999 is shown. The grammar extensions are embedded into the SQL:1999 EBNF (see lines 1-6). Translation rules have to be specified for DDL (lines 7-11) and DML statements. It is useful to encapsulate DDL statements into UDR calls to get adequate error messages. Translating a component declaration statement directly into an insert statement for the corresponding extended system catalog table would lead to an incomprehensible error message. DML statements, in contrast, are directly translated to modified DML statements. The metamodel extensions consist of information of how to upgrade the original metamodel and the extended system catalog, storing the data of the metamodel. We use the XML-based Metadata Interchange (XMI) to specify transformations on the metamodel [10] (not shown in Fig. 3 due to space restrictions, the transformed metamodel is shown in Fig. 4). The extended system catalog is modified either by hints based on the metamodel (line 12, simply mapping a class of the metamodel to a table), or by concrete DDL statements (lines 13-19). Most of the constructs are marked as `INTERNAL`, as they have no corresponding class in the metamodel. For example, to support schema modularity, a table containing the mapping information of a virtual schema element with a namespace to the internal schema element without namespace (lines 14-15) is needed.

3.2 Extension Directory

Although language extensions originate from various independent packages, they are merged to form a single-level *extension directory*. Thus, the packages can be viewed as a means for gradually extending the directory. It is the extension directory that is used by the translator and not the packages. Using the packages directly in the translation process would lead to the following problems.

- Extensions introduced from separate packages may (i) define overlapping semantics, but use distinct syntactical notation or (ii) define distinct semantics, but use overlapping syntactical notation.
- In case the extension packages are not aware of each other, how to make translation rules in one package aware of rules in the other package, e. g., to be able to define *schema modules* containing *relationships* with extended semantics (see Sect. 1)?
- How would the translator recognize the package where the translation process has to be initiated? For this purpose, at least a basic global registry system for extensions is required in any case.

As extensions are merged to a single-level directory, we force the user to make decisions on the above issues prior to using the extensions, so that these problems can be avoided at translation time. The *registry* is the simplest part of the extension directory. It is used to uniquely identify the packages that have been imported in the directory. The following sections describe the remaining parts of the directory.

Extended Metamodel. There is a set of (object-relational) constructs present in SQL:1999 that are commonly used for organizing, storing and querying data: complex structured types, typed tables, user-defined routines, etc. Imported language extensions introduce additional constructs, e.g., a table inheriting from more than one table, a relationship with extended semantics or a schema module. The extension directory uses an *extended metamodel* to organize the constructs defined in imported extension packages and thereby available in XSQL (including those already provided by SQL:1999). Instead of building the SQL:1999 part of the metamodel from scratch, we decided to use the OMG's Common Warehouse Metamodel (CWM) [18]. CWM is a metamodel based on Meta Object Facility (MOF) [16] designed to enable easy interchange of warehouse and business intelligence metadata between warehouse tools, warehouse platforms and warehouse metadata repositories. Choosing an already present and accepted OMG metamodel, the users of extension packages might already be familiar with, alleviates the tasks of importing new packages that require user assistance. The extended metamodel is stored in a dedicated repository that provides a GUI for interactive and an API

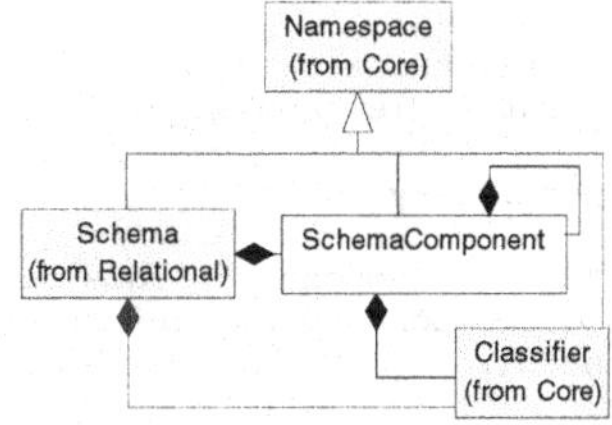

Fig. 4. Excerpt of an extended metamodel

for programmatic manipulation of the extended metamodel. Fig. 4 shows a part of the CWM extended to support schema components.

Extended XSQL EBNF. The syntax of XSQL statements is defined by the XSQL EBNF. The EBNF is extensible, meaning that at import time an extension package will attempt to apply rules that upgrade the current EBNF with new constructs. In a similar fashion as with the extensible metamodel, this process is user-mediated: The user can accept or reject the application of a specific production rule contained by the EBNF upgrade or modify the production rule to avoid possible inconsistencies with other packages and assure compliance with the metamodel. In certain cases, the system is capable of suggesting multiple alternative production rules for the EBNF upgrade. The suggested rules are constructed by exploiting the information in the metamodel and existing XSQL EBNF.

There is a mapping of XSQL EBNF symbols onto class implementations. A class implementation of an EBNF symbol will be instantiated to represent a node in the XSQL syntax tree. For this reason, the class implementation of non-terminal symbols defines associations to implementations representing other symbols, which facilitates the traversal of the syntax tree. Most importantly, a class implementation provides reduction methods used by the translator to transform XSQL statements.

Reduction Methods for Producing SQL:1999 Statements. Reduction methods implement operations used to transform nodes in the syntax tree of the XSQL statement to produce the reduced syntax tree(s) of the SQL:1999-compliant statement(s) – in most cases, a single statement in XSQL is transformed into more than one SQL:1999 statements. Class implementations for the EBNF symbols are organized into an inheritance hierarchy. For example, the class implementation for a table capable of multiple inheritance would extend the implementation for the common table construct. As the translator parses the XSQL statement to build an initial syntax tree, it uses information in the extended system catalog (see Sect. 3.3) to select the class implementation that needs to be instantiated to represent a given node in the syntax tree. Reduction methods defined by class implementations are polymorphic in the following sense:

- A reduction method in the subclass may extend or completely override the default implementation of the reduction method implemented in the superclass.

```
public class SQLComponentDeclaration implements NonTerminalSymbol {

  protected ComponentDeclarationName     name;
  protected ComponentDeclarationElements elems;

  public void reduce( SyntaxTreeSymbol caller, SyntaxTree tree ) {
    this.addReduction(
      new CallFunction( "declareComponent", this.name.getValue() ) );
    Enumeration e = this.getComponentDeclarationElements().elements();
    while( e.hasMoreElements() ) {
      this.addReduction(
        new CallFunction( "addToComponentDeclaration",
                          this.name.getValue(),
                          e.nextElement().getValue() ) );
    }
    // Store additional reduction information into the transformed tree.
  }
  ...
}
```

Fig. 5. An automatically generated reduction method

- The behavior of the reduction method (the generation of nodes for the SQL:1999-compliant syntax tree) depends on the pattern the node resides in, meaning that in order to complete the reduction process, the method may need to gather information from the neighboring nodes.

Fig. 5 shows a reduction method for transforming the declaration of a schema component into routine calls that will insert the declaration (including the component elements) to the extended system catalog. The method has been automatically generated from translation rules illustrated in Fig. 3. For a detailed overview of reduction methods and reduction pattern concepts, we refer to [3].

3.3 Extended System Catalog

The imported packages introduce constructs initially not present in the SQL:1999 or in the SQL dialect of the target database system. Because of this, the database system catalog (i.e., system tables) no longer suffices for storing database metadata (e.g., it does not allow us to store which tables and complex structured types are combined in a schema component). To support complete organization and storage of metadata needed for translating and executing XSQL statements, we introduce an *extended system catalog*. The tables in this catalog are instantiated from the constructs defined in the extended metamodel that is a part of the extension directory using the extended system catalog hints. For example, for the metamodel illustrated in Fig. 4, using the hints in Fig. 3 we obtain a table used to store schema components, a table to map the names, etc. To avoid replication of metadata, relational views are defined on DB-proprietary system tables so that these can be directly reused as part of the extended catalog. View definitions are supplied within the extension package in a specific form for each DBMS product supported by the vendor. However, the definitions can be customized by the user during the import of the package to allow the use of the extended system catalog with further DBMS products initially not supported by the vendor.

```
CALL declareComponent('BookManagement', ...);
CALL addToComponentDeclaration('bookT', ROW(ARRAY(ROW('title',...)...));
CALL addToComponentDeclaration('chapterT',...);
CALL addToComponentDeclaration('book', ...);
CALL addToComponentDeclaration('chapter', ...);
CALL addToComponentDeclaration('addChapter', ...);
...
```

Fig. 6. Excerpt of a translated statement in SQL:1999

When familiar with tables and views contained in the extended system catalog, the user may query the catalog to explore metadata for the database. Manual updates to the catalog by the user are not recommended, since the consistency of the catalog may be jeopardized. However, the translator is aware of any consistency constraints related to the catalog, so that after their execution the translated DML statements that manipulate the catalog will always leave it in a consistent state.

3.4 Translator

The translator accepts a statement in XSQL and constructs a corresponding syntax tree using the XSQL EBNF included in the extension directory. Afterwards, it invokes the reduction method of the root node in the syntax tree. The method delivers one or more reduced syntax trees that represent the translated statements in SQL:1999.

A method may access the extended metamodel and the extended system catalog via a set of dedicated APIs to gather information needed in the course of reduction. In addition, the execution of the reduction method of a node may require information related to the reduction of other nodes residing in remote parts of the XSQL syntax tree. We call constellations of nodes that require uni-directional or mutual information on each other's reduction outcomes *node patterns*. A single XSQL syntax tree may contain multiple (possibly overlapping) node patterns.

The translator exposes the functionality for initiating remote reductions and delivering the results in form of an API. In this way, all reductions in the XSQL syntax tree are initiated by the translator, which maintains a reduction log and makes sure the process does not contain any cycles and will eventually terminate.

Obtaining the second statement of Fig. 1 (line 12-29) as input, the translator would produce an SQL:1999-compliant statement as shown in Fig. 6. Encapsulated in the UDRs, these statements insert data into the extended system catalog.

4 Open Issues

This section attempts to address a set of important issues that assist us in assessing the pros and cons of the approach.

SQL serves its purpose well and the capabilities of language extensions can be simulated by providing an API in a general-purpose language (GPL), such as Java. So why introduce custom extensions?

SQL serves its purpose well as long as you downgrade your problem domain so that it fits the limits of the object-relational model. By doing this, you are losing design information and higher-level abstractions that would ideally be present in your schema. Unfortunately, both of these are key issues for effective schema reuse, matching, reengineering and reverse engineering. How can you be sure that a trigger in a schema was initially meant (a) as a pure trigger, or (b) is the result of downgrading a higher-level abstraction, such as a relationship with extended semantics, so that someone could have expressed it in the object-relational model? How can you be sure that a table in the schema was (a) meant to exist at the same level with other tables or (b) initially originated from a modular and replaceable schema part (i.e., schema module), but has been flattened out of the module to this level, since there was no effective way to represent the module in the object-relational model?

Leaving SQL unadorned and simulating its extensibility in a GPL does not solve the problem either, since the syntax and semantics of such a language may prove too limiting as well and less natural as to extend the syntax of SQL:1999 at any place convenient. In this aspect, by offering the extensions in form of an API, we don't really avoid the problem, but rather migrate it to another level: In the same manner as the syntax of SQL:1999 limits us in efficiently expressing higher-level abstractions, the syntax of the GPL might be a similar obstacle.

Object-relational databases are bloated with features we don't really need [2], [20]. Won't relationships with extended semantics, schema modules and other extensions make things look even worse?

For Date and Darwen [4], orthogonality of language concepts is a key issue: A language is orthogonal, if independent concepts are kept independent and not mixed together in confusing ways. Pitfalls in the orthogonality increase the complexity of the language and reduce its expressive power. In our opinion, careful selection of language extensions to SQL:1999 does not necessarily implicate the loss of orthogonality, but rather allows developers to retain complex high-level abstractions directly in their schema implementations and queries embedded in application code.

Customers will define own extensions and purchase off-the-shelf extension packages, which will lead to the incompatibility of extensions, cause notational havoc, prevent exchange of schema design and burden reengineering of database applications.

This is the same problem Czarnecki and Eisenecker [3] mention as they discuss the role of off-the-shelf active libraries in the context of Intentional Programming [22] (see Section 5). They claim that in the same manner as conventional libraries emerge in different domains today, standard domain-specific language extensions will emerge. Once a market for off-the-shelf extensions will be present, developers will have access to high-quality extensions provided by vendors, which will decrease the need to implement own extensions. For a detailed classification of problems related to interactions among language abstractions originating from different active libraries, we refer to [3]. In X-Translate, we cope with these problems by using a global metamodel for extension constructs, a global system catalog and a global XSQL EBNF with reduction methods. To resolve possible conflicts, the import of extension packages is user-mediated.

The reduction process impedes processing and thereby has an impact on overall performance of database applications. Therefore, language extensions introduce benefits not for customers, but mostly for developers, which can now easily design and maintain database applications.

The outcome of reducing XSQL statements are multiple statements that conform to SQL:1999. XSQL statements cannot be completely translated at compile time of the application, since in most cases the outcome will depend on the state of the system catalog at runtime. To reduce the impact of translation delay, we implemented an approach supporting *pre-compilation*. In X-Translate, the reduced statements in SQL:1999 contain empty placeholders that are filled by values fetched at runtime from the system catalog using a user-defined routine. Thereby, excessive invocations of reduction methods at run-time are avoided.

The execution time of statements once fully translated is another issue: This time can be improved by assuring that reduction methods produce efficient translations of proprietary SQL statements for a given language extension.

To a certain extent, we admit that performance drawbacks are an issue that has to be accepted if language extensions are used. However, it would be interesting to examine the trade-offs related to the total cost of ownership of applications that are easier to maintain, but on this account demonstrate minor performance disadvantages due to language extensions used.

5 Related Work

The idea of an extensible programming and metaprogramming environment is materialized in the Simonyi's work [22] on *Intentional Programming* (IP). As a programming environment, IP supports developers in the programming tasks by allowing them to load extension libraries in order to extend the programming language with general-purpose and domain-specific abstractions [3]. Among other components, the environment includes dedicated *editor and browsing tools*, allowing the developers to browse the program source in form of a syntax tree and a *reduction engine* that is used to generate an implementation based on a set of primitive abstractions. Our X-Translate system can be seen as an attempt to examine how the idea of extensible programming environment concepts applies to SQL:1999.

An early paper on query language translators by Howells et al. [6] does not discuss the notion of introducing and translating custom extensions, but rather focuses on language-to-language translation. The approach uses a common internal relational algebra tree with input language translation schemes specified as sets of extendible PROLOG clauses.

A substantial amount of work is done on transforming schemas and translating queries in one query language into SQL. For example, Keim et al. [11] describe the translation of Structured Object Query Language (SOQL) into SQL, arguing that SOQL queries are shorter, easier to write and understand and more intuitive than corresponding SQL queries. Shanmugasundaram et al. [21] present the XPERANTO system that involves the evaluation of XML queries over XML views of relational data. It supports processing arbitrary complex queries specified using the XQuery query language. Most computation is pushed to the relational engine to increase the efficiency of the system.

Query translation proves important for accessing heterogeneous information sources via a single application interface. Queries posed to this interface have to be translated to source-specific (sometimes called native) queries or commands [19]. Since SQL:1999 was chosen as a target platform, which already includes an approach for integrating heterogeneous data sources (see SQL/MED [9]), considering diverse mappings to multiple native query languages would be superfluous in our case. Instead of tackling the problems that arise from translating a single common query language to diverse native languages, our approach focuses on problems that arise on behalf of extensibility of the common language.

6 Conclusion and Future Work

In this paper, we presented X-Translate, a system supporting the definition of custom language extensions to SQL:1999. Language extensions allow the formation of complex data definition and manipulation statements as well as queries that involve custom language constructs. The main purpose of these constructs (which can be general purpose as well as domain specific) is to allow developers the expression of high-level abstractions that exist at the time the database application is developed, but usually get lost in the mapping to the limited set of original SQL:1999 constructs. We believe the loss of these abstractions is a major obstacle for efficient schema reuse and database application reengineering.

The paper has shown that the idea of extensible programming language environment (resembling the one described by Simonyi [22]) can prove useful for the implementation of schemas and the development of database applications. It is possible to support the introduction of language extensions in form of packages that are imported into the system and to semi-automatically extend the corresponding metamodel and XSQL EBNF (which are shared among different extensions). The process of importing extension packages has to be user-mediated to assist the system in resolving possible conflicts.

In the course of our future work we intend to:

- Consider further language extensions that might be useful for developers. As our first goal, we attempt to focus on version management of table data.
- Consider a number of interactive tools that would alleviate the import of extension packages into X-Translate, such as visualization and interactive editing of the extended metamodel and XSQL EBNF as well as dedicated browser tools for the extended system catalog. In addition, especially when importing new language packages, visualization of applied reductions of a statement plays an important role for discovering inconsistencies with existing language extensions. In our opinion, a dedicated debugging tool capable of tracking and visualizing successive reduction phases as well as accesses to the extended system catalog would prove useful. We will try to integrate the mentioned tools in a single visual environment to be used with the X-Translate system.

- Explore techniques for improving overall performance of the system.
- Empirically evaluate the scope in which SQL:1999 extensions alleviate the development, maintenance, and reengineering of database applications using a large set of selected sample applications.

References

[1] Atkinson, C., Bayer, J., Bunse, C., Kamsties, E., Laitenberger, O., Laqua, R., Muthig, D., Peach, B., Wust, J., Zettel, J.: Component-Based Product Line Engineering with UML. Addison Wesley, 2002.

[2] Carey, M., Hellerstein, J., Stonebraker, M.: A Sketch of Regres, Seminar presentation, UC Berkeley, 1999, http://db.cs.berkeley.edu/postmodern/stonebraker-final.ppt

[3] Czarnecki, K., Eisenecker, U.W.: Generative Programming, Methods, Tools and Applications, Addison-Wesley, 2000.

[4] Date, C.J., Darwen, H.: A Guide to SQL Standard, Addison-Wesley, 1996.

[5] D'Souza, D.F., Wills, A.C.: Objects, Components, and Frameworks with UML - The Catalysis Approach. Addison Wesley, 1998.

[6] Howells, D.I., Fiddian, N.J., Gray, W.A.: A Source-to-Source Meta-Translation System for Relational Query Languages, in: Proc. VLDB 1987, Brighton, Sept. 1987, pp. 227-234.

[7] ANSI/ISO/IEC 9075-1:1999, Information technology - Database languages - SQL - Part 1: Framework (SQL/Framework), ISO, 1999.

[8] ANSI/ISO/IEC 9075-2:1999, Information technology - Database languages - SQL - Part 4: Persistent Stored Modules (SQL/PSM), ISO, 1999.

[9] ANSI/ISO/IEC 9075-9:2000, Information technology - Database languages - SQL - Part 9: Management of External Data (SQL/MED), ISO, 2000.

[10] Kovse, J., Härder, T.: Generic XMI-Based UML Model Transformations, in: Proc. 8th Int. Conf. on Object-Oriented Information Systems (OOIS'02), Montpellier, Sept. 2002, pp. 192-198.

[11] Keim, D.A., Kriegel, H.-P., Miethsam, A.: Object-Oriented Querying of Existing Relational Databases, Technical Report 93-08, Dept. of Computer Science, Ludwig-Maximilian University, Munich, Germany.

[12] Kießling, W.: Foundations of Preferences in Database Systems, in: Proc. VLDB 2002, Hong Kong, Aug. 2002, pp. 311-322.

[13] Mahnke, W.: Towards a modular, object-relational schema design, in: Proc. 9th Doctoral Consortium at CAiSE'2002, Toronto, May, 2002, pp. 61-71.

[14] Meyer, B.: Harnessing multiple inheritance, in: Journal of Object-Oriented Programming 1:4, 1988, pp. 48-51.

[15] Mahnke, W., Steiert, H.-P.: Modularity in ORDBMSs - A new Challenge, in: Proc. 13. Workshop "Grundlagen von Datenbanken", GI-FG 2.5.1, Magdeburg, Juni 2001, pp. 83-87.

[16] OMG: Meta Object Facility Specification, Version 1.4, April 2002, http://www.omg.org/.

[17] OMG: Unified Modeling Language Specification, Version 1.4, Sept. 2001, http://www.omg.org/.

[18] OMG: Common Warehouse Metamodel Specifications, Version 1.0, Oct. 2001, http://www.omg.org/.

[19] Papakonstantinou, Y., Gupta, A., Garcia-Molina, H., Ullman, J.: A Query Translation Scheme for Rapid Implementation of Wrappers, in: Proc. DOOD 1995, Singapore, Dec. 1995, pp. 161-186.

[20] Schek, H.-J.: Panel: Future Directions of Database Research - The VLDB Broadening Strategy, Part 1, in: Proc. VLDB 2000, Cairo, Sept. 2000, pp. 663-664.

[21] Shanmugasundaram, J, Kiernan, J., Shekita, E.J., Fan C., Funderburk J.: Querying XML Views of Relational Data, in: Proc. VLDB 2001, Rome, Sept. 2001, pp. 261-270.

[22] Simonyi, C.: The Death of Computer Languages, the Birth of Intentional Programming, Tech. Report MSR-TR-95-52, Microsoft Research, Sept. 1995.

[23] Viega, J., Tutt, B., Behrends, R.: Automated Delegation is a Viable Alternative to Multiple Inheritance in Class Based Languages, Technical Report CS-98-03, University of Virginia, 1998.

[24] Zhang, N., Ritter, N., Härder, T.: Enriched Relationship Processing in Object-Relational Database Management Systems, in: Proc. 3rd Int. Symposium on Cooperative Database Systems for Advanced Applications (CODAS'01), Bejing, Apr. 2001, pp. 53-62.

[25] ZsqlML: XML Markup Language for SQL http://zsqlml.sourceforge.net

Aligning Application Architecture to the Business Context

Roel J. Wieringa, H.M. Blanken, M.M. Fokkinga, and P.W.P.J. Grefen

Center for Telematics and Information Technology, University of Twente,
The Netherlands
{roelw,blanken,fokkinga,grefen}@cs.utwente.nl

Abstract. Alignment of application architecture to business architecture is a central problem in the design, acquisition and implementation of information systems in current large-scale information-processing organizations. Current research in architecture alignment is either too strategic or too software implementation-oriented to be of use to the practicing information systems architect. This paper presents a framework to analyze the alignment problem and operationalizes this as an approach to application architecture design given a business context. We summarize guidelines for application architecture design and illustrate our approach and guidelines with an example.

1 Introduction

Alignment of application architecture to business architecture is a central problem in the design, acquisition and implementation of information systems in current large-scale information-processing organizations. Current research in software architecture [1,2,3] focuses on the architecture problem for the software engineer rather than for the architect of large-scale information systems. These large-scale systems contain components that are bought rather than programmed. Their architecture problem exists on a higher aggregation level than that studied in software engineering. At this higher level architects are interested not only in the extent to which an architecture supports quality attributes, but also the extent to which the application architecture fits within the business context—the architecture alignment problem.

The business-IT alignment problem has been studied at a rather strategic level that is hard to operationalize for the practicing application architect [4]. There is a need for body of operational concepts and guidelines that encompasses business architecture as well as application architecture. In this paper we present such a framework. Its first version was the result of an extensive analysis of design methods and frameworks in software engineering, product engineering and systems engineering [5,6]. We tested, simplified and elaborated the framework in a number of standard examples from the literature and then applied it to a large number of M.Sc. projects. Next, we applied it to real-life projects. Currently, we are using it in an empirical study to collect and analyze best practices in architecture alignment in banks, insurance companies and government organizations.

J. Eder and M. Missikoff (Eds.): CAiSE 2003, LNCS 2681, pp. 209–225, 2003.

One contribution of this paper lies in the definition of an integrated and unified framework for business process design and application architecture design, in which both the business and its application software are viewed as reactive systems, i.e. as systems that respond to events in their environment. Our framework refines and operationalizes a number of other frameworks, such as that of Henderson and Venkatraman [4] and of Zachman [7]. The second contribution is that we collected and validated a comprehensive set of guidelines for defining an application architecture.

In section 2 we present a our view on architecture and in section 3 we present our framework. Section 4 describes our architecture design approach. Section 5 gives an example and section 6 summarizes the architectural alignment guidelines we have collected. Section 7 discusses the results achieved so far and presents some directions for further work.

2 A Systems View on Architectures

The most widely used definition of architecture is that it is the structure, or a set of structures, of a system, consisting of elements and relations between these [1]. We add to this the requirement that the collection of elements as a whole has an added value for its environment, that the elements do not have if taken separately. So our definition of architecture is as follows.

> The **architecture** of a system is the structure, or a set of structures, of a system, consisting of elements and relations between these, *such that the relations between the elements create an overall coherent system with an added value for its environment.*

This adds a systems view to the definition, where a "system" is any coherent collection of elements whose interaction produces an added value for its environment. This includes information systems and workflow management systems, but also businesses and other kinds of organizations.

A systems view of architectures allows us to apply the definition to business systems as well as software systems. It also makes clear that in order to design a system architecture, we must study the desired added value for its environment first.

3 The Framework

3.1 System Aspects

An important part of our framework consists of a classification of system properties or *aspects* as they are also called. Borrowing from a rich set of frameworks developed in systems engineering and industrial product design, we propose the classification of information processing system properties shown in figure 1 [8],

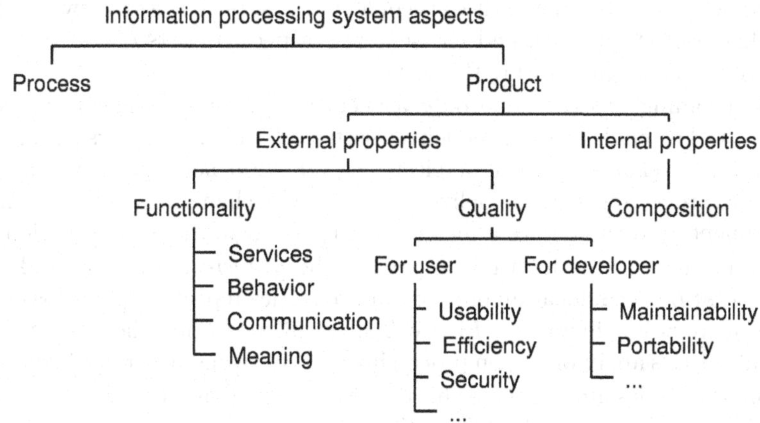

Fig. 1. Process aspects and product aspects.

[9], [5]. Each of the nodes in the tree represents an aspect of an information processing system, in other words a possible point of view from which to consider the system. The rationale behind this framework is as follows.

We start from the classic distinction between *process* on the one hand, and the *product* that results from this process on the other. The process of developing and exploiting an information processing system has an architecture, just as the result of this process, an information processing system, has an architecture. These architectures are related, because for example the composition of an information system determines the work breakdown structure of the development and exploitation process. However, the process architecture and product architecture are distinct because they are architectures of different things.

Our interest is in product architecture, where the product may be an information system, a business, or any other information processing system. (An information processing system is any system that manipulates symbols.)

The top-level distinction of product properties is between *external* and *internal* properties. External properties in turn are classified according another well-accepted partition, namely between *functional properties* and *quality properties.* Functional properties are services offered to the environment, and quality properties characterize the value that the system has for stakeholders. For example, usability, efficiency and security are aspects of the value that system services have for for users of the system, and maintainability and portability are aspects of the value of the system for developers.

The basic aspect of functionality is the *service* that the system has for its environment. (The word "function" in this paper is synonymous with "service". The word "functionality" in this paper means roughly "what a product does".) The system exists to deliver certain services to its environment. System services in turn are characterized by three functional properties. The *behavior* aspect consists of the ordering of services over time. The *communication* aspect consists of the interactions with other entities (people, devices, businesses, software) during the delivery of the service, and the semantic aspect consists of the *meaning* of the symbols exchanged during the service.

The meaning aspect is the only aspect typical for information processing systems. Other kinds of systems deliver services by means of physical processes such as the exchange of heat or electricity, that do not have a meaning. Information processing systems deliver services by exchanging symbols with their environment, and these have a meaning (usually documented in a dictionary).

Turning now to the internal properties, the *composition* of the product, we observe that our classification of external properties repeats itself at lower levels in the aggregation hierarchy. Figure 2 illustrates this for the case where all external entities are information processing entities (whose interface is symbolic).

Note that a designer does not have control over all aspects of a system. This depends upon the design charter as discussed in section 4.

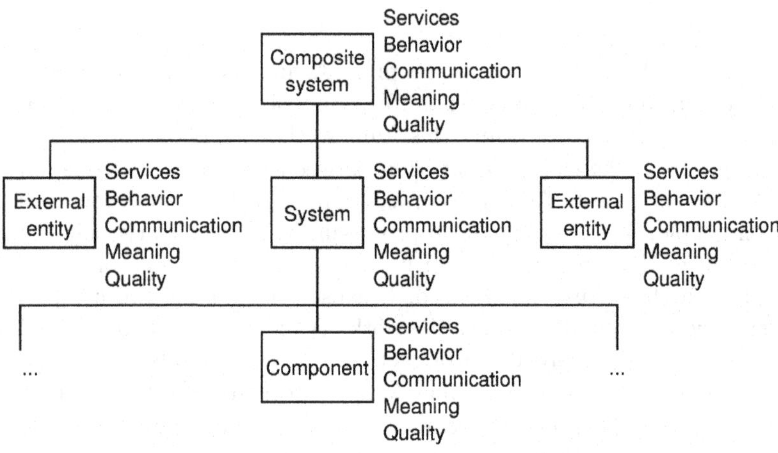

Fig. 2. Repetition of aspects at all levels of the aggregation hierarchy.

3.2 Service Levels and Refinement Levels

Information system architects must deal with three worlds, namely the physical, social and linguistic worlds (figure 3). The physical world is the world of entities that have weight, consume energy and produce heat and noise. The social world is the world of business processes, needs, added value, needs, money, norms, values etc. Part of the social world is the linguistic world of symbol manipulation. We treat this separately because it is the world of software and documents. Note that software exists only in the linguistic world; computers exist only in the physical world; and people exist in all three worlds.

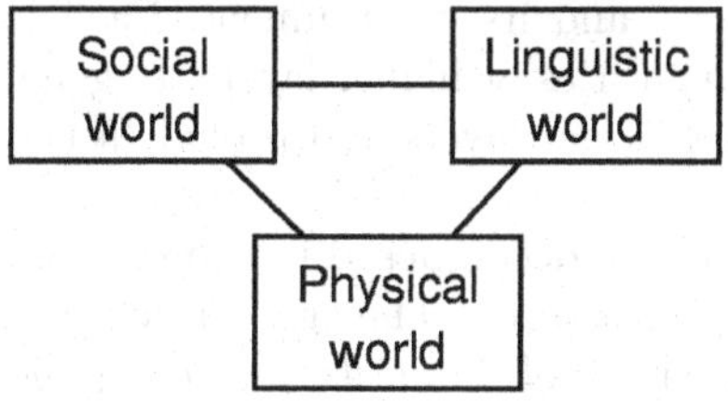

Fig. 3. Three alignment problems.

As suggested by figure 3, there are three alignment problems, not one. For example, to align software (in the linguistic world) to people (in the social world), we must ensure that the meaning attached by people to the symbols at the software interface agree with the manipulations of these symbols by the software, and that these manipulations have value for the people. To align software to the physical world, we must allocate it to processing devices with a location in the physical world, and to align this in turn to the social world we must align information processing devices to business processes. None of these alignment problems is trivial.

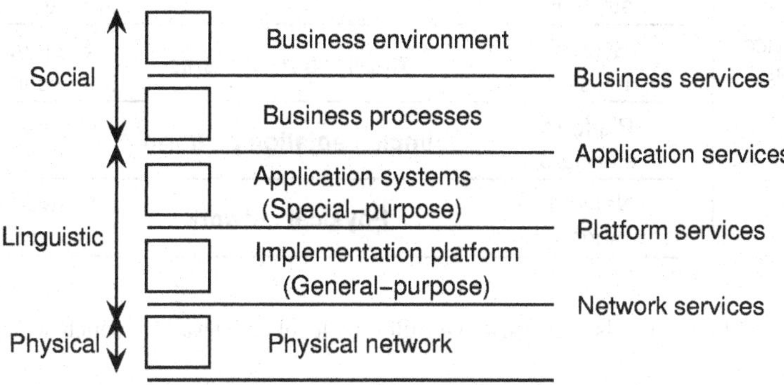

Fig. 4. Systems exist at all layers. At each layer, systems have the product aspects listed in figure 1.

A useful view on these alignment problems is to structure them in layers of service provision. Different situations will call for different layering structures, but we found that the one shown in figure 4 is a useful starting point in many cases. Each particular project may feel a need to add or delete particular service provision layers. In figure 4, we partitioned the linguistic layer into two, one of general-purpose software entities, that are usually bought and not built by a business, and another of special purpose software entities, that typically are customized or built from components. The social layer is also partitioned into two, namely the business and its environment. Each layer consists of entities that provide services to entities at higher layers. In general, entities at one layer use services of entities at lower layers and provide services to entities at higher layers.

Each entity may itself be decomposed in components not accessible to other entities. We call this *encapsulation*. The aggregation hierarchy shown in figure 2 represents the decomposition of an entity into components encapsulated by it. Each of the entities at any layer, and each of its internal components, has the aspects described earlier.

Each horizontal line in figure 4 between two layers represents service provision. The diagram represents a service-provision hierarchy, but hides the fact that the social world also interacts with the physical world directly. At each layer, entities exist that have all the properties listed in figure 1, except at the physical layer, where interactions of entities do not have a meaning.

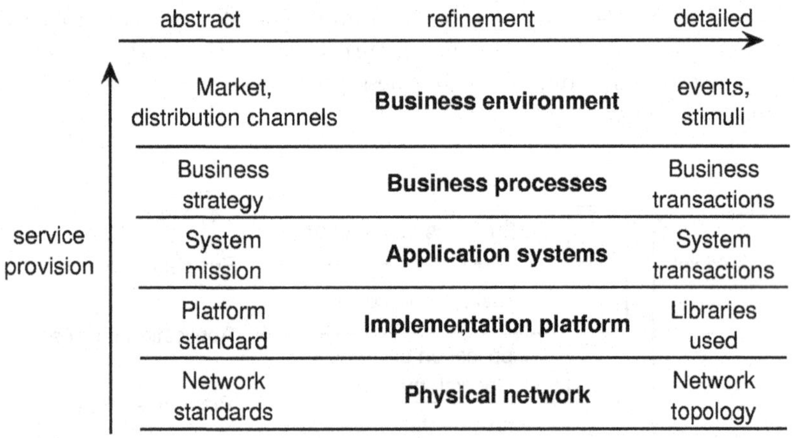

service provision ↑ / refinement →	abstract		detailed
	Market, distribution channels	**Business environment**	events, stimuli
	Business strategy	**Business processes**	Business transactions
	System mission	**Application systems**	System transactions
	Platform standard	**Implementation platform**	Libraries used
	Network standards	**Physical network**	Network topology

Fig. 5. At different levels, we can have different levels of detail in which we are interested.

Finally, we add the refinement dimension (figure 5). The refinement dimension does not classify systems, but it classifies *descriptions* of systems. Entities at each service level can be described at a high level of abstraction (few details) or at a high level of refinement (many details). Figure 5 shows some illustrative properties at different refinement levels.

To summarize, our architecture framework consists of

1. a structuring of systems into service provision layers (figure 5), where
2. at each layer, entities exist with properties that can be classified as shown in figure 1, and where
3. these properties can be described at many different levels of refinement (figure 5).

3.3 Comparison with Other Frameworks

Our framework refines the alignment framework of Henderson and Venkatraman [4]. They distinguish two dimensions, the service provision dimension (IT infrastructure level and business level) and a refinement dimension (strategic and operational levels).

Most frameworks for software system development distinguish three views, namely the function view, the behavioral view, and the data view of the system (e.g. [10]). These views correspond to our service, behavior and meaning aspects. Harel and Pnueli add to this the architecture dimension, which corresponds to our composition dimension [11].

Kruchten's 4+1 model [12] defines the logical and process views of a software system, that correspond roughly to our decomposition dimension and behavior view, respectively. His physical and development view correspond roughly to two implementation platform descriptions, namely allocation and module architecture. These are discussed in the next section.

Zachman distinguishes three kinds of descriptions, the data, process, and network description [13,7], which correspond, roughly, to our meaning, behavior and communication aspects. These descriptions can be used according to Zachman to describe the system from a great number of perspectives, namely the scope of the system, the business view, the system model, the technology model, the component model, people, external business events, and business goals. This seemingly unrelated and arbirary list of perspectives can be systematized by placing them at various levels of service provision and refinement on our framework figure 5. Details of this and other comparisons can be found elsewhere ([5, pages 329–330], [6]).

4 Our Design Approach

Figure 6 illustrates our design approach. Compared to the layers in figure 4, the business service interface and the application service interface have both been expanded to a separate layer in figure 6. The figure lists a number of architecture descriptions typically found in business modeling and information systems design. We explain these descriptions in section 5. We should point out immediately that we do not claim that all these descriptions must be produced for all software systems. Rather, each particular project will produce a few of these descriptions. The problem which descriptions to choose in which circumstances is a topic of current research. The diagram is intended to illustrate an apparent contradictory dependency among design decisions.

We give two examples, that support seemingly contradictory conclusions.

- To make a list of business activities (third description along the diagonal), we need a stimulus-response list of the business first; and to make that list, we need a list of relevant events in the environment of the business first. So in order to write a description of a lower-level entity, we need descriptions of higher-level entities first.

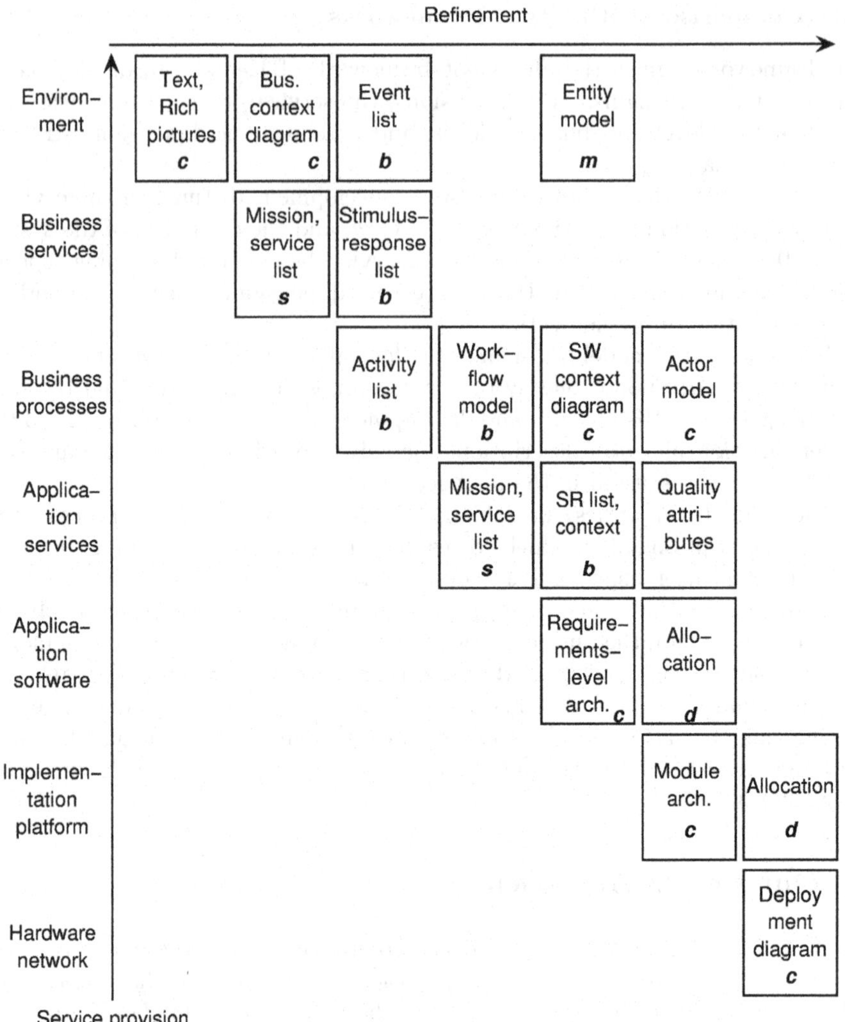

Fig. 6. Overview of some descriptions. ***s*** = service view, ***b*** = behavior view, ***c*** = communication view, ***m*** = semantic view (meaning), ***d*** = decomposition view.

– Once we have described the market and distribution channels of the business at a high level of abstraction by a piece of narrative text supplemented by a rich picture (top-left description), then it is not useful to add detail to this environment description by making a business context diagram and a business event list, because at this point, we do not know which part of the context is relevant and which events are relevant. We know which part of the context is relevant, after we have a list of business services (second description along the diagonal) and we know which events are relevant once we know which stimuli can arrive at the business boundary. So to refine a description of a higher-level entity, we need descriptions of lower-level entities first.

The paradox is resolved if (1) we develop descriptions in one column of the table together and (2) develop a refinement of a description only after we know which lower-layer service descriptions we need this refinement for.

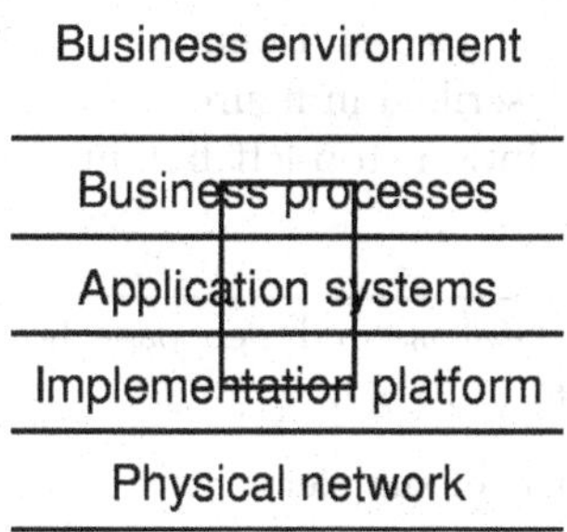

Fig. 7. The design charter. The area in the box is what the designer can change. The box circumscribes design freedom.

The second element of our design approach is that we start from an identification of the design charter, which is the circumscription of the area that the designer is allowed to change. Figure 7 gives an example. Outside the box, entities are given to the designer as they are, whether she likes it or not. Inside the box, entities may be changed withing the limits set by the design charter. Figure 7 illustrates that the design charter may span several service layers but need not include all entities at any layer. In practice, the situation is not so neat, because the charter may be spread out over many layers and skip other layers; indeed, the designer may have difficulty finding a crisp boundary of the design charter at all, and in addition, during the project, a boundary thought to be clear may change after all. This makes it all the more important to make negotiations about the boundaries of the design charter an integrated part of the system design project.

In passing, we note that the overview of descriptions in figure 6 indicates for each description which viewpoint is described. For each viewpoint, there are well-known description techniques available. For example, behavior can be described by event lists, state transition tables and state transition diagrams; communication can be described by various box-and-arrow diagrams; and decomposition can be represented by traceability tables. Notations are not the subject of this paper. A thorough survey of available techniques and guidelines for their use is given elsewhere [14].

5 Example

We illustrate our alignment approach with a case study we did for a small company, that we will call Global Travel International (GTI). GTI provides database and web-page hosting services to the travel business in a small country in North-Western Europe. Our design charter says that we may design an application to support the primary processes of GTI, but we must not change business processes nor can we change the implementation platform or underlying hardware network. To make application architecture design decisions, we start with a number of descriptions of the business environment and business processes.

The market of GTI is described in figure 8. This is an example of a top-level business environment description (top-left box in figure 6).

The market of GTI is database and web page hosting to facilitate on-line renting of holiday homes.

- **Customers** are sellers or suppliers.
- **Sellers** of GTI are private or corporate individuals seeking to rent out holiday homes. Examples are travel agencies, call centers, travel portals. One seller can act on behalf of many home owners.
- **Suppliers** are private or corporate entities that own homes that they offer for rent by travelers, either directly or through sellers. Examples are private home owners, tour operators and national tourist bureaus.
- **Travelers** are private individuals seeking to rent holiday homes.

Current threats are the dip in the travel industry and in Internet business. The largest opportunity is that GTI has the software to help other companies take the next large step in e-business.

Fig. 8. Market of GTI.

Descending to the business service layer in figure 6, we give the business mission of GTI in figure 9. This allows us to focus on the relevant part of the context. The context diagram in figure 10 adds detail to the market description of figure 8 and at the same time provides the context in which to interpret the mission statement. Conversely, the mission statement explains why this part of the context is relevant.

Having identified the business context, we can go on to identify business services. Since we are not designing the business but describing it, this is a knowledge problem. Let us assume that the list of business services is known. From the list of business services we go on to make a coarse activity model of the business (third box along the diagonal). We identify a business activity by (1) the business event that triggers it and (2) the service delivered by it. This requires us to make a list of relevant business events and, if necessary, the list of stimuli at the business interface that each event may cause. For example, a

Mission:

- to host databases and transactional web pages on behalf of customers, so that travelers can search for houses and perform on-line booking.

Services provided:

- Customer services:
  - Initialize web site and database
  - Update web site and database
  - Provide access and sales statistics
- Traveler services:
  - Provide information about holiday homes.
  - Offer reservation capability.
  - Offer payment capability.
  - Offer feedback capability.

The major services acquired from other parties are:

- Payment handling
- Authentication services

Fig. 9. Mission and external functions (services) of GTI.

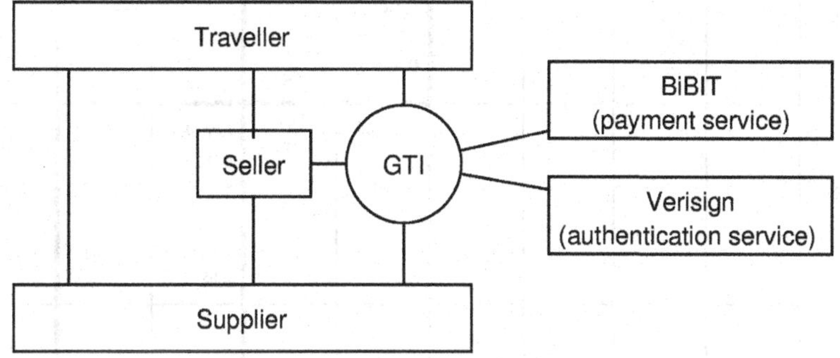

Fig. 10. The business context diagram of GTI.

customer's desire to rent a holiday home may be communicated to the business by telephone, fax, email or web page, so that one event (the creation of the wish to rent a holiday home) may be communicated to the business through four possible stimuli. Due to lack of space we abstract from multichanneling and restrict ourselves to business events only. Figure 11 summarizes the service list, event list and activity list of GTI.

So far, we have collected information about the business and summarized this in a number of descriptions. Now we approach the area within our design charter and we perform our first design activity, which is to gather activities into

Event / Service	Traveller requests booking	Traveller pays	Final payment too late	Traveller cancels booking	Traveller complains	Traveller provides experiences	New customer acquired	Customer changes products	Time to provide supplier with occupation data
Booking	Compose, Check, Reserve booking.		Release booking.	Release booking.					
Payment	Accept payment	Accept payment. Clear payment	Send reminder. Reimburse.	Reimburse					
Feedback					Treat complaint	Collect feedback.			
Initialize customer web site							Create database and web site		
Maintain web site								Update	
Provide statistics									Derive data

Fig. 11. GTI processes. The upper row lists events in the business environment. The leftmost column lists GTI services. The entries lists the activities in the business process triggered by events and delivering services.

groups that contribute to related business services. We call these groups *business responsibilities*. Each business responsibility is an aggregate of a number of business services offered to the business environment. The business responsibilities we identified for GTI are indicated by the fat rectangles in figure 11. From left to right along the diagonal, these are Booking, Traveler feedback, Web site maintenance and Information provision to customers. The business services within one business responsibility are related because they serve one process in the business environment. As we will see in the next section, this satisfies several design guidelines and we therefore have good reason to believe this is a stable structure.

Grouping business activities into business responsibilities does not change the business processes, but it defines a structure that we can use to define our application architecture. The general design principle is that we must structure the system according to those elements in the business that are expected to remain stable during the life of the system.

Our grouping of business activities into responsibilities leads us to our first design decision about the application architecture: We decide to define one application for each business responsibility. In addition, we decide to introduce a component that deals with the web interface and some databases to contain data about the subject domain. The guidelines behind these decompositions are discussed in section 6. Applying these guidelines, we get the requirements-level architecture of figure 12. This is called a requirements-level architecture because it is defined in terms of the functional requirements and business context, but not in terms of the available implementation platform. This architecture is also called conceptual architecture [1], [2] and an old term for it is essential systems model [15].

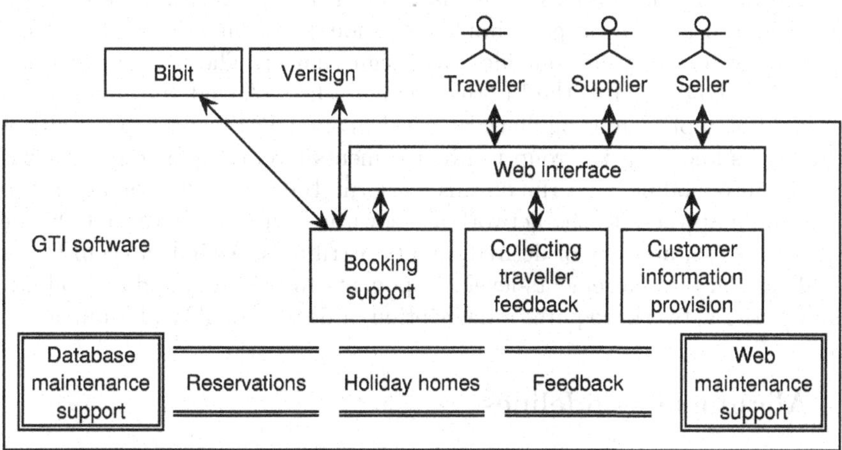

Fig. 12. Requirements-level application-architecture. Components with double borders have interfaces to all other components.

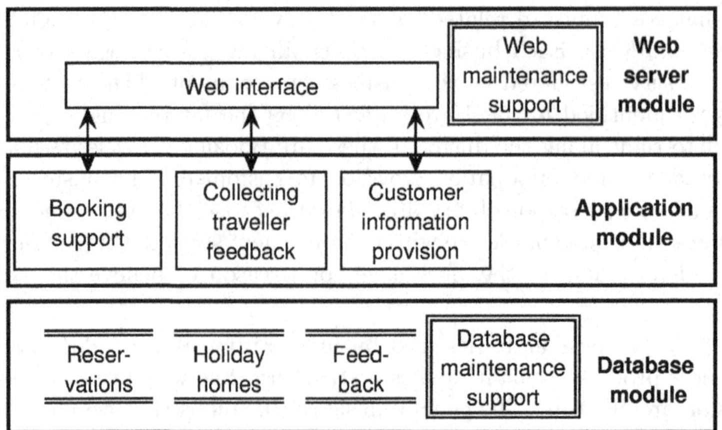

Fig. 13. Implementation-level modules.

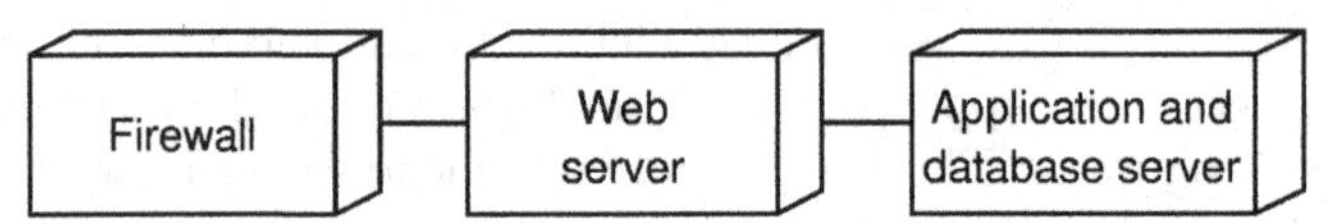

Fig. 14. Allocation of modules to nodes in the deployment network.

To transform this into an implementation architecture, we must define modules and map these to nodes in the hardware network. Both the hardware network and the general-purpose implementation platform are given to us, not designed by us. They fall outside our design charter. The network consists of several PCs connected to the Internet behind a firewall that runs on a separate PC, and the implementation platform consists of a DBMS with a 4GL and a web server. This allows us to group the requirements-level components as shown in figure 13 into modules that run on this platform. Balancing PC load against data traffic, we map these to the network as shown in figure 14. Note that this decision requires an analysis of desired quality attributes. As indicated in figure 6, the allocation of requirements-level components to modules, and of modules to nodes in the network, requires a description of desired quality attributes.

6 Alignment Guidelines

So far, we have presented an architecture framework that includes both the business and the supporting information technology, we defined a design appropach in terms of this framework, and we illustrated this by means of an example. How does this help us to improve alignment of application architecture to business architecture?

Our framework helps solving the alignment problem because it yields us a number of simple architecture design guidelines. We discuss these guidelines here, explaining how we used them in our example.

- **Functional decomposition.** For each service to be delivered, a component is defined. For GTI, this would lead to one software component for each of the business services listed in figure 11. If services can be changed independently from each other, this leads to a modular structure. Since the services in one business responsibility of GTI are not independent from each other, functional decomposition would not lead to a modular architecture.
- **Communication-oriented decomposition.** For each communication with external entities, define one component. There are three variants of this guideline.
  - ***Device-oriented.*** For each device to be communicated with, define a component that handles this communication. One uses this guideline to hide the peculiarities of a device from the rest of the software and to restrict changes in devices to one component. Since devices often can be changed independently from each other, this leads to a modular structure. The identification of a web interface component in our example is device orientation.
  - ***Actor-oriented.*** For each actor to be communicated with, define a component that handles this communication. For example, one may encapsulate the dialog with this actor in a separate component. If dialogs are independent from each other, this leads to a modular structure. The web interface in our example may be internally structured by actor.
  - ***Event-oriented.*** For each event to be responded to, define a separate component. This is called event-partitioning by McMenamin and Palmer [15]. If events can be recognized independently from each other, this leads to a modular architecture. In the case of GTI, event-orientation would lead to the definition of one component for each column in figure 11. Since the events handled in one business responsibility are not independent from each other, this would not lead to a modular architecture. In a multi-channeling architecture, where one event can be communicated to the system in a variety of ways, event-partitioning leads the idea of a front-office in which stimuli are analyzed to identify the underlying event.
- **Behavior-oriented decomposition.** For each process in the environment to be monitored or controlled, define one system component. If different processes are independent from each other, this leads to a modular architecture. We used this guideline for GTI because each business responsibility contains one business process and it is mapped to one application architecture component.
- **Subject-oriented decomposition.** For each part of the world about which data must be maintained, define one system component. This is the standard

guideline in databases and also an important guideline in object-oriented architecture design. In GTI, we used this to partition the databases into three parts, that deal with reservations, holiday homes and feedback, respectively.

As illustrated by the GTI example, we can use several guidelines to design an architecture. Different parts of an architecture may be identified by different guidelines.

These guidelines have been known in the literature for some time but they have not yet been systematized. Our contribution is to expose their underlying system: Each of these guidelines corresponds to one of the functional system aspects of our architecture framework (figure 1). Each of these guidelines map some aspect of the environment to some part of the system architecture. This transfers the modularity, or lack of it, of the environment to the system architecture. For example, if functions are independent from each other, then functional decomposition leads to a modular architecture; but if functions are dependent on each other, so that a change in one leads to a change in another, then functional decomposition does not lead to a modular architecture. And so on for the list of architecture design guidelines. The role of these guidelines with respect to other architectural concerns, such as maintanability and flexibility, remains a topic for further research.

7 Discussion and Conclusions

Our design approach picks up some ideas of Information Engineering [16] but replaces data-orientation by event-orientation. We view the business and its supporting software system as reactive systems that respond to signals and changes in conditions in their environment and to significant moments in time. Where IE maps business processes to information systems, we map business events to business services, some of which will be realized as application services.

Our approach refines that of Henderson and Venkatraman [4] by providing operationalized guidelines for aligning a requirements-level application architecture to the business architecture. We believe that it is the first comprehensive framework and design approach that links business requirements to application architecture.

Current work includes the use of the framework to collect and analyze architecture design practices in large information-processing organizations such as banks, insurance companies and government organizations. Another topic for further research is the impact of architectural guidelines on architectural concerns such as maintainability and flexibility.

Acknowledgements. Thanks are due to the company where we performed the GTI case study for their cooperation. This paper benefitted from comments by Pascal van Eck and by the anonymous reviewers on an earlier version.

References

1. Bass, L., Clements, P., Kazman, R.: Software Architecture in Practice. Addison-Wesley (1998)
2. Hofmeister, C., Nord, R., Soni, D.: Applied Software Architecture. Addison-Wesley (2000)
3. Shaw, M., Garlan, D.: Software Architecture: Perspective on an Emerging Discipline. Prentice Hall (1996)
4. Henderson, J., Venkatraman, N.: Strategic alignment: leveraging information technology for transforming operations. IBM Systems Journal **32** (1993) 4–16
5. Wieringa, R.: Requirements Engineering: Frameworks for Understanding. Wiley (1996)
6. Wieringa, R.: A survey of structured and object-oriented software specification methods and techniques. ACM Computing Surveys **30** (1998) 459–527
7. Zachman, J.: A framework for information systems architecture. IBM Systems Journal (1987) 276–292
8. Hall, A.: Three-dimensional morphology of systems engineering. IEEE Transactions on System Science and Cybernetics **SSC-5** (1969) 156–160
9. Roozenburg, N., Eekels, J.: Product design: Fundamentals and Methods. Wiley (1995)
10. Olle, T., Hagelstein, J., Macdonald, I., Rolland, C., Sol, H., van Assche, F., Verrijn-Stuart, A.: Information Systems Methodologies: A Framework for Understanding. Addison-Wesley (1988)
11. Harel, D., Pnueli, A.: On the development of reactive systems. In Apt, K., ed.: Logics and Models of Concurrent Systems. Springer (1985) 477–498 NATO ASI Series.
12. Kruchten, P.: The 4+1 view model of architecture. IEEE Software **12** (1995) 42–50
13. Sowa, J., Zachman, J.: Extending and formalizing the framework for information systems architecture. IBM Systems Journal **31** (1992) 590–616
14. Wieringa, R.: Design Methods for Reactive Systems: Yourdon, Statemate and the UML. Morgan Kaufmann (2003)
15. McMenamin, S.M., Palmer, J.F.: Essential Systems Analysis. Yourdon Press/ Prentice Hall (1984)
16. Martin, J.: Information Engineering. Prentice-Hall (1989) Three volumes.

A Three-Tier View-Based Methodology for Adapting Human-Agent Collaboration Systems*

Dickson K.W. Chiu [1], S.C. Cheung [2], and Ho-fung Leung [1]

[1] Department of Computer Science and Engineering, The Chinese University of Hong Kong, Shatin, Hong Kong, China.
kwchiu@acm.org, lhf@cse.cuhk.edu.hk
[2] Department of Computer Science, Hong Kong University of Science and Technology, Clear Water Bay, Hong Kong, China.
scc@cs.ust.hk

Abstract. With recent advances in mobile technologies and infrastructures, there are increasing demands for mobile users to connect to existing collaboration systems. This requires extending supports from web browsers on personal computers to SMS, WAP, and PDAs. However, in general, the capabilities and bandwidth of these mobile devices are significantly inferior to desktop computers over wired connections, which have been assumed by most collaboration systems. Instead of redesigning or adapting collaboration systems in an ad-hoc manner for different platforms in a connected society, we propose a methodology of such adaptation based on three tiers of views: user interface views, data views and process views. These views provide customization and help balance security and trust. User interface views provide alternative presentations of inputs and outputs. Data views summarize data over limited bandwidth and display them in different forms. Furthermore, we introduce a novel approach of applying process views to mobile collaboration process adaptation, where mobile users may execute a more concise version or modified procedures. The process view also serves as the centric mechanism for integrating user interface views and data views. This methodology also discusses ways to support external mobile users who have no agent support, customizable degree of agent delegation and the employment of constraint technology for negotiation. We demonstrate the feasibility of our methodology by extending a web-based meeting scheduler into a distributed mobile one.

1 Introduction

Recent advances in hardware and software technologies have created a plethora of mobile devices [21] with a wide range of communication, computing, and storage capabilities. The Internet is quickly evolving towards a connected society. New mobile applications running on these devices provide users easy access to remote services regardless of where they are, and will soon take advantage of the ubiquity of wireless

* This work was partially supported by the Hong Kong Research Grant Council with an Earmarked Research Grant (HKUST6187/02E).

J. Eder and M. Missikoff (Eds.): CAiSE 2003, LNCS 2681, pp. 226–241, 2003.

networking to create new virtual worlds. Moreover, as mobile devices become more powerful, peer-to-peer mobile computing will become an increasingly important computation paradigm. These trends in mobile devices and applications have profound implications for application designs in the coming years. However, this connected society will not be a simple add-on to the wired Internet. New challenging problems arise from the handling of mobility, handsets with reduced screens and varying bandwidth. As such, there are increasing demands for the support of collaboration systems across multiple platforms to connect people working together. Research issues for such adaptation involve not only user interface but also collaboration processes as well as enhanced logic within agents.

We have done some work on applying *process views* in [7] for adapting e-service enactment in a cross-organizational process environment. These views are further refined into an architecture of three tiers, viz., *user-interface views*, *process views*, and *data views*. User interface views provide alternative presentations of inputs and outputs. Data views summarize data over limited bandwidth and display them in different forms. Furthermore, we introduce a novel approach of applying process views to mobile collaboration process adaptation, where mobile users may execute a more concise version or modified procedures. The process view also serves as the centric mechanism for integrating user interface views and data views. Mobile collaboration systems typically involve the support of users with different roles and mobile devices with diverse capabilities. Our views approach presents a flexible mechanism to address this issue. Furthermore, this approach supports both mobile manual human users and different degrees of user delegation to agents in the collaboration system. As such, external users without agent support can also participate in the collaboration system. Our approach can be applied to collaboration systems related to the problems of planning, negotiation and resource allocation. These systems typically involve human users, to be assisted by agents. As an example to demonstrate the feasibility of our approach, we extend an agent-based meeting scheduler to a mobile one.

The contribution and coverage of this paper are as follows: (i) a three-tier view-based methodology for adapting applications to support mobile platforms, (ii) a novel approach of applying process views in adapting collaboration systems to a mobile environment, (iii) details on the technologies for supporting such adaptations, (iv) support for both human users and user delegated autonomous agents in a collaboration system, (v) use of constraints to limit data exchange in a collaboration system to reduce bandwidth consumption for mobile users, (vi) demonstration of the applicability of our methodology in supporting flexible mobile collaboration systems through these features. The rest of our paper is organized as follows. Section 2 presents the application requirement of the distributed mobile meeting scheduler with respect to mobile platforms, together with related work. Section 3 summarizes our three-tier view-based framework and architecture for mobile collaboration, supporting both manual human users and agents. Section 4, 5, and 6 discusses customization through these views one by one. Section 7 presents the internal architecture of these distributed mobile agents and how we adapt them. We conclude this paper with our plans for further research in Section 8.

2 Motivating Example and Related Work

Meeting scheduling is a common collaboration task that is time-consuming and tedious. It involves negotiation between two persons or among several persons, taking into account many factors or constraints. In our daily life, meeting scheduling is often performed by ourselves or by our secretaries via telephone or e-mail. Most of the time, each attendee has some uncertain and incomplete knowledge about the preferences and calendar of the other attendees. Thus a meeting scheduler is a very useful tool for group collaborations. Meeting scheduling is one of the classic problems in artificial intelligence and multi-agent systems. There are some commercial products but they are just calendars with special features, such as availability checkers, meeting reminders [15]. Shitani [31] highlighted a negotiation approach among agents for a distributed meeting scheduler based on the multi-attribute utility theory. Van Lamsweerde [2221] discussed goal-directed elaboration of requirements for a meeting scheduler, but did not discuss any implementation frameworks. Sandip [30] summarized an agent-based system for automated distribution meeting scheduler, but was not based on BDI agent architecture. However, these systems cannot support manual interactions in the decision process or any mobile support issues. Therefore we use this application as an example for our methodology.

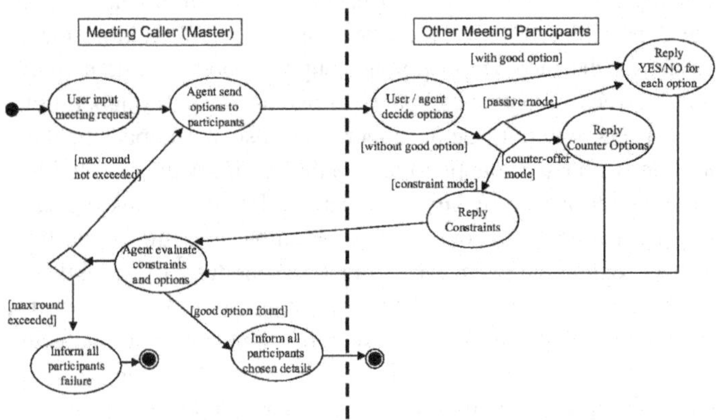

Fig. 1. Activity Diagram for Agent-based Meeting Scheduler

Fig. 1 depicts the activity diagram of an agent-based meeting scheduler. The user who proposes a meeting (or meeting proposer) enters his/her requirements and suggestions (or options) and delegates the agent to schedule the meeting. The delegated agent then contacts the other meeting participants or their delegated meeting scheduler. Each of the participants or agents then determines if any options are good. If so, the decision can simply be passed back to the proposer's agent. Otherwise, depending on the platform (cf. Fig. 2), a participant might reply in the following three respond modes: (i) *Passive mode* – the participant (or his agent) just reply that all the proposed schedules are bad, without any counter proposals. (ii) *Counter-offer mode* – the participant (or his agent) suggests other counter proposals. (iii) *Constraint mode* – the participant (or his agent) gives some of the constraints representing the participant's preference and availability. After gathering the feedback, the proposer's agent evaluates it for a common feasible solution for all participants. If this is successful, all participants will be informed of the result. Otherwise, the proposer's agent will attempt another round of proposals, with the consideration of the options already rejected by the participants and their constraints (if any). However, if the maximum round is exceeded, the proposer's agent will consider the scheduling failed and inform all participants.

Platforms / Features	PDA	WAP	SMS
Meeting requestor	Program interface	WAP interface	SMS
Agent delegation	Agent run on PDA	Agent run on server	
Alerts	ICQ, email (or SMS if user also accessible)	SMS	
Exception handling or manual mode for participants	Web interface	WAP interface	SMS
Participant response mode	Passive, Counter-offer, Constraint	Passive, Counter-offer	Passive

Fig. 2. Different Features for Users of Meeting Scheduler on Different Platforms

This approach is quite ad-hoc and cannot describe customization in other activities of this process in an orderly manner. In case we model a mobile e-service process using the existing process definition infrastructure, we can use branches to represent existing alternatives because of the different platforms that a user might use. If the representation ends there, then we are unable to differentiate between branches that represent alternative execution paths from those represent different actions due to the use of mobile devices. In the later case, the designer has to specify the tasks to be executed, based on the constraints imposed by the platform and also has to associate the corresponding data that restrict the information to be displayed and to specify the interface that defines how to present the data based on the capabilities of the displaying device. Therefore, we need to augment the specification process such that the designer can customize the process definition in an orderly and consistent way taking into account all the above aspects. We propose to address this problem using views.

Our ideas in process views for cross-organizational business interaction and e-contract enactment have been presented in [7]. This approach has been motivated by views in object-oriented data models, which can be dated back to [11], and in particular by imaginary objects in [1], which introduced the concept of inheritance of a public process from a private process to achieve interoperability in a cross-organizational e-commerce environment. Gardarin [14] discussed federated OODBMS and views for objects in a distributed environment. Liu and Shen [24] presented an algorithm for process view construction and verification, but did not discuss any of its applications. Most ongoing efforts are however target at user interface views only, such as the W3C initiative on device independence [35], Oracle's Wireless Edition [29], and IBM's Websphere Transcoding Publisher [17].

Advanced workflow management systems are now web-enabled, but only very recently researchers in process technologies are exploring mobile process support. The WHAM (process enhancement for mobility) prototype [19] supports mobile workforce and applications in a process environment, with a focus on network connectivity and the mobility of process resources. Tjao [34] introduced a Java Border Service Architecture, which is an abstract layer between presentation and application logic of an application, to handle mainly user interface issues of mobile devices, using process as an example. As for commercial products, Staffware [32] has recently introduced, WAP Business Process Server. However, all of them do not support platform specific process adaptation or integrated platform independent solution. Neither do they support view mechanisms. We are now extending our web-enabled WFMS, E-ADOME [7][8][9], to ME-ADOME [5] in order to support mobile users effectively (via SMS, WAP, and PDA browsers) with a three-tier view-based mechanism.

In summary, the three-tier view approach presented in this paper is a novel approach to adapting mobile collaboration systems. Other meeting scheduling systems cannot support manual interactions in the decision process or does not adequately address mobile support issues. Comparing with the systems close to us, our meeting scheduling system has the most features and can support both mobile agents and manual human users on the Internet.

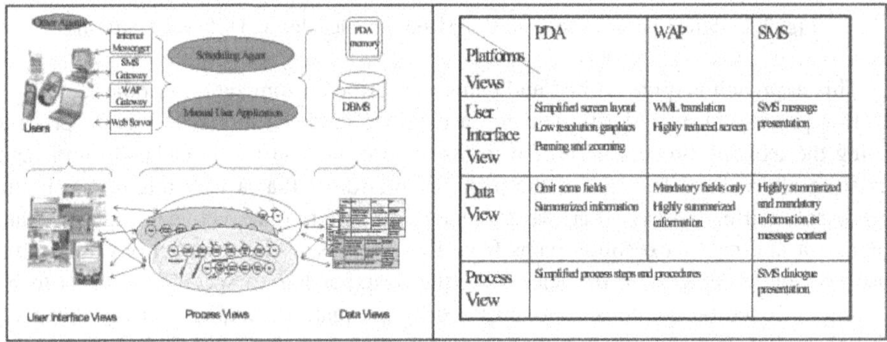

Platforms / Views	PDA	WAP	SMS
User Interface View	Simplified screen layout Low resolution graphics Panning and zooming	WML translation Highly reduced screen	SMS message presentation
Data View	Omit some fields Summarized information	Mandatory fields only Highly summarized information	Highly summarized and mandatory information as message content
Process View	Simplified process steps and procedures		SMS dialogue presentation

Fig. 3. Three-Tier Architecture and Three-Tier Views

3 Multiple-Platform Adaptation with a Three-Tier View-Based Methodology

Internet applications are generally developed with a three-tier architecture comprising front ends, application servers and back end databases. Each of these tiers hosts a set of views as shown in **Fig. 3**, which also depicts our implementation architecture. It also summarizes the contribution of different types of views to users on these mobile platforms respectively, addressing the technological limitations of different mobile platforms, viz. PDA, WAP and SMS, with reference to mobile E-service requirements.

Views help balance trust and security, that is, only information necessary for the process enactment, enforcement and monitoring of the contract is made available to the concerned parties, in a fully control and understandable manner. At the front-end tier, user interface views provide mobile users with alternative presentations and interfaces to interact with the process views hosted at the application servers tier. User interface views can be developed based on the technology of XML Style Language (XSL) [36]. A user interface view consists of multiple screens and forms based on the capabilities of the front end devices. For example, Fig. 9(a) and (b) give the screens in two user interface views for devices with and without graphical capabilities, respectively. A process view is a projection of an E-service process that concerns a user and his/her front-end device. Process views are synchronized and enacted by application servers. A data view consists of multiple tables that collectively represent a projection of data that are required in the enactment of an E-service.

We separate user alerts from user sessions to improve the flexibility [9]. Online users will be alerted by ICQ [18], with the task summary and reply URL as the message content. If a user is not online or does not reply within a pre-defined period, the application server will send the alert by email. At the same time, another alert may be sent via SMS to the user's mobile phone. Whatever the alert channel has been, the user need not connect to application server on the same device, or even on the same platform. For example, after receiving a SMS alert, the user may use a handset to connect to the application server via WAP, or reply with an SMS message. Alternatively, the user may find a PC with Internet connection or use a PDA to connect to the application server.

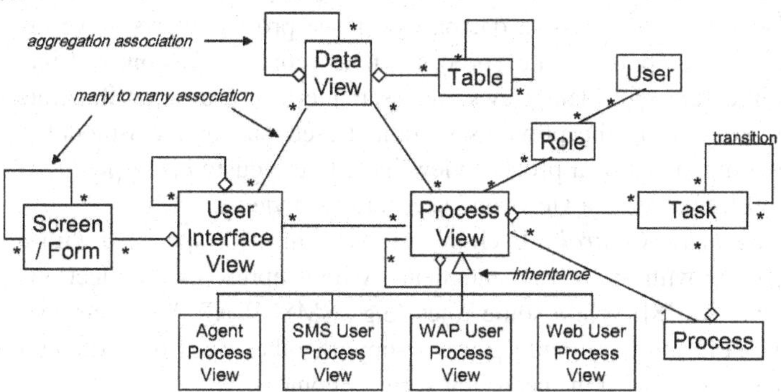

Fig. 4. Meta-model of Three-tier Views in UML Class Diagram

Fig. 4 presents our meta-model of the three-tier views. User interface, process and data views are related by many-to-many relations. In other words, a user interface view may provide the interface to multiple process views, each of which may in turn supports multiple user interface views. The scenario of extending an existing web-based application to support mobile users is usually more typical than designing a multi-platform application from scratch. In addition, the following discussion is also applicable to phased projects in which usually standard web-based application are developed as the first phase, and supporting mobile users as subsequent phases. We propose the design of the views in three tiers to be carried out in the following major steps:

1. Consider the new use cases (corresponding to the new platforms) to be added and their requirements.
2. For each new user case, consider the impact of these new requirements on existing processes. Do we need to adapt the processes? Design process views accordingly.
3. Design data views based on the requirement of the process views.
4. Design user interface views based on platform dependent restrictions.
5. Update the logic in the agents to accommodate the above changes.

4 Adaptation with Process Views

Motivated by views in federated object databases [14], we propose the use of process views as a fundamental mechanism for flexible collaboration adaptation. A process view is a structurally correct subset of a process definition (as defined in [7], [16]). We develop integrity criteria concerning the consistency between workflow views and their parent workflows, and correctness criteria concerning the consistency between workflow views and their target communication scenarios [6]. In this paper, we further propose to use the concept of process views to let different users (on different platforms) access different customized version of the same process. Within an organization, process views are also useful for security applications, such as to restrict accesses (like the use of views in databases). Thus, process views serve as the centric mechanism in our approach, i.e., process views represent customized business processes that integrate with data views and user interface views, as illustrated with our motivating example in the previous section. Based on our meta-model presented in Fig. 4, the components of a process view include the customized process flow graph, access control, related data views and user interface views:

Access (Security) Control – Each process view must be specified with one or more accessible *roles* with an *access* statement. A role represents a collection of users of similar properties [8]. While some roles (e.g., SMS, WAP, Web) are used to distinguish user platforms for mobile process support, other roles (e.g. director, manager, officer) may also be used in specifying security context.

Process Flow Graph – Most contemporary WFMSs use a hierarchical composition approach, i.e., a process is composed of sub-processes and so on down to leaf-nodes of atomic activities. This provides a good granularity for providing views of the process flow graph. If a process view is to be made available, a fundamental provision is the topmost level process flow graph. However, the detailed composition of individual sub-process may be concealed. Thus a process in the flow graph can be presented in one of the following ways: (i) a white-box sub-process is specified with a sub-process view by a statement "process p1 view v1" (i.e., the details of the sub-process is further visible and subject to the restriction of a sub-process view); (ii) a black-box sub-process (is limited from further details of its further internal composition[1]; (iii) a gray box where some sub-processes are visible while other sub-processes are concealed. Similarly, we can define customized parts the process flow graph for different parts of

[1] Unless a view is specified for the sub-process, it is a black box.

a composite process. Transitions among processes are specified with the *transition* statement with optional guard conditions.

Data views associated with a process instance – Data tables associated with a process need not be presented completely in a process view. Some fields may be hidden from the views, some may be read only, while some may be presented with write access. Data views are specified with the *dataview* statement. We omit further details of data views as they can be specified with standard Structure Query Language (SQL) statements 12. Further examples are given in Section 5.

User interface views associated with a process instance – User interface views (further specified in XSL) associated with a process specify different user interfaces for users on different platforms. Further details and examples are given in the next sub-section.

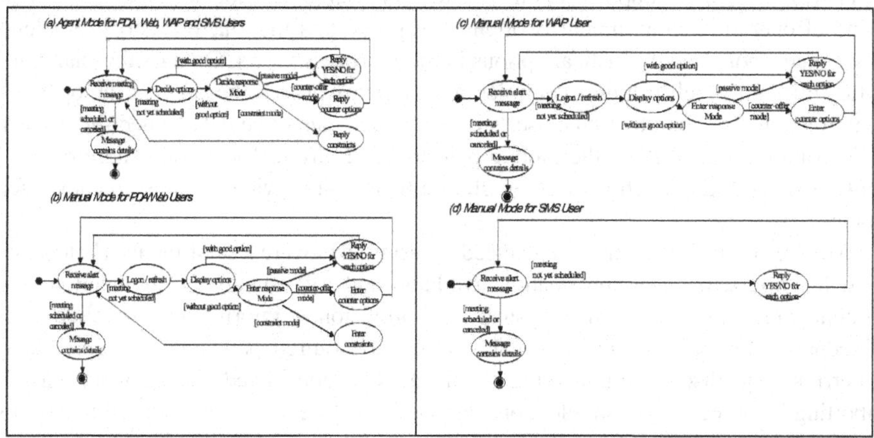

Fig. 5. Different Process Views for Participants on Different Platforms

Fig. 5 summarizes the details of the process views that take place at the meeting participants other than the meeting proposer, i.e., these process views address the differences among the agent-delegated process (Fig. 5a) and customized processes for users on different platforms (Fig. 5b-d). After receiving an alert via ICQ or email, a PDA user (or other users on a web browser) or WAP user in manual mode log on the *manual user application* on a web server to review the detailed information of the meeting proposal. In addition, the user may also access his timetable from the application or as a separate task (e.g., a separate program in his PDA or phone) whichever appropriate. The user then determines if any options are good. If so, the decision can be passed back to the proposer's agent through the web or WAP interface respectively. Otherwise, a PDA user might reply in any of these three respond mode described in the previous subsection. However, the *constraint mode* is too complicated to be supported through a WAP interface and is therefore not provided to WAP users. As for a SMS user, the only practical option is to reply with a SMS message, as other ways of responding is far too complicated.

In general, there is no universal recipe for designing process views, as this process is analogous to designing a piece of customized software. In order to capture the requirements for users of a mobile platform, a commonly adopted approach from object-oriented design is to carry out use case analysis. We should concentrate on the difference of the requirements for the mobile users from those under standard browsers. These differences are compared with the standard processes to formulate views. We should identify similar or identical tasks to maximize reuse, and in particular, consider the possibility of customizing them with data views and user interface views instead of rewriting them.

Usually, a complete detailed business process is too complicated for a mobile environment. Therefore, typical requirements are simplification of the process, reordering of work steps, delegation of tasks (work steps) to other personal, etc. For example, a user with only SMS support can only make very simple decisions or feedback. As this kind of operating environment is often error prone and may have security problems, we suggest not allowing critical options in these process views. On the other hand, it is often difficult to tell if a user can tolerate a complex process because of the operating environment or even due to the user's mood, which cannot be determined merely with observation facts, such as the mobile platform and physical location. Therefore, it is always a good idea to allow users to choose their desired view options whenever feasible.

Mobile applications may be enhanced by using the awareness of the user's location, and location dependent information available and relevant to the application, e.g., mobile workforce management systems and provision of information to mobile users. Exception handling due to unavailability of the required personnel, network delay, interrupts and disconnections, etc., should also be considered. In the worst case of aborting a process, we should consider additional requirements for compensation processes (e.g., an order cancellation) under a mobile environment.

5 Adaptation with Data Views

A data view is a set of tables comprising a projection of the enterprise data that are required for the enactment of some process views. Fig. 6 presents visually the schema of a data view in UML Class Diagram for the *Display options* process view. Note that a class or an association in the diagram maps to a data table with columns representing the class attributes [4]. The main table in this data view is the *Proposal* table, which consists of a number of proposals made by different proposers. A proposal can be a counter-offer of a previous proposal. Each proposal contains a description and the time when the proposal was made. A proposal consists of constraints in venue and time. Multiple available time slots can be suggested in an option.

The data view for *Display option* process view is a projection and selection of the entire data set for the meeting scheduler. Fig. 7 presents the entire schema for the mobile meeting scheduler example. As shown in the figure, the data view in Fig. 6 is a selected subset of data objects as well as a projection of some data object fields.

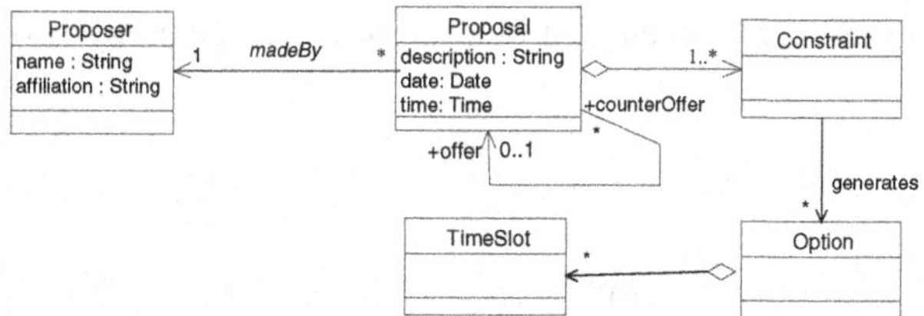

Fig. 6. The UML Schema of a Data View for WAP Manual Mode Process View

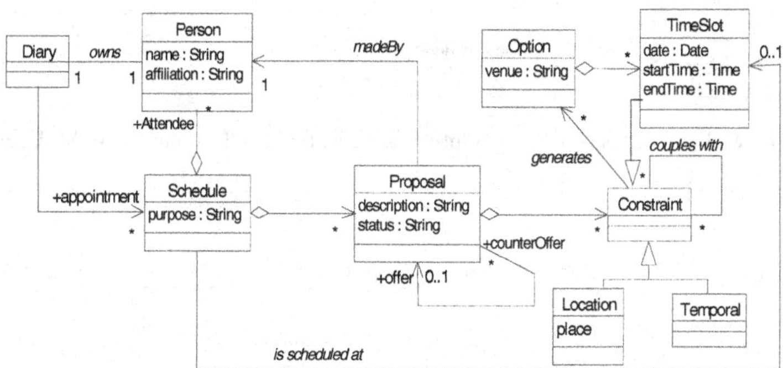

Fig. 7. The UML Schema for the Mobile Meeting Scheduler System

With a process view defined, we can proceed to analyze its data requirement. Each work step requires data from the database in some form. In particular, we should identify mandatory fields, optional fields and fields that are to be skipped in the view, in order to cope with the simplification required for mobile users. However, additional fields those have to be computed for summarizing information and knowledge may be required. In case that the mobile user cannot provide mandatory information or input them effectively, we may need to modify the process so that the mandatory information can be provided later or by someone else. Therefore, like designing software, the process is not a linear one. In addition, security requirements should also be considered, e.g., sensitive information may have to be restricted to users within the office or to those of pre-approved locations. *Data views* may also be employed to hide less important data field or to show alternate summary columns.

6 Adaptation with User Interface Views

User interface views provide users with appropriate interfaces to interact with process views within the capabilities of front end devices. This means the user interface views for a web user can be different from that for a WAP user. Fig. 8 presents two possible user interface views that support the *Display options* task in the process views depicted in Fig. 5 for web users and WAP users, respectively. Both Fig. 8(a) and (b) correspond to the same XML document object, but are rendered by two different XSL style sheets.

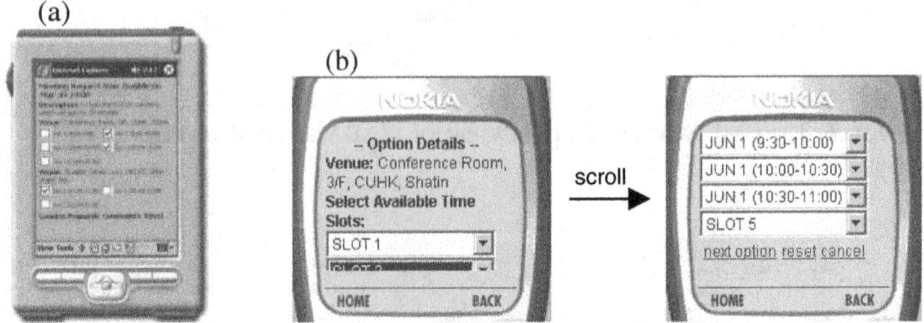

Fig. 8. Two Types of Display Option Screens for (a) PDA and (b) WAP Users

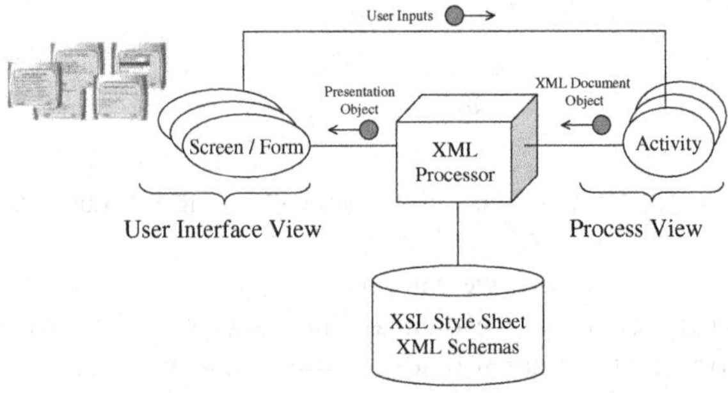

Fig. 9. Implementation Framework for User Interface Views

The differences between the *process views* for the PDA user and those for the WAP user are minor. However, these two processes need to be customized at the *user interface tier* instead, i.e., the appearance of the screens and input is different while they are referring to the same set of information items. *User interface views* can be facilitated by contemporary XML technologies augmented with XSL in elegantly, as further explained in the next section. Similarly, users on PDAs and PCs may also prefer different user interface views to cater for the difference in screen size.

Fig. 9 presents the implementation framework for user interface views using XSL technology [36]. Information to be presented at a user interface view is structured as XML document objects by a process view, such as the WAP based process view in Fig. 5(b). For example, an XML document object of a meeting proposal is generated by the *Display Option* activity. XML document objects are then transformed by an XML processor into presentation objects based on specified XML schemas and XSL style sheets. The presentation objects for a WAP user interface view are decks and cards in the Wireless Markup Language (WML).

We usually need to remove graphics or reduce the resolution, provide panning and zooming, shorten fields or provide summarized ones instead, break one web page into several screens, etc. For user input, we should consider the difficulties in entering data (especially typing) on mobile devices, and provide menu selections as far as possible. For PDA interface, the main problem is just a smaller screen, some of which may be black-and-white. If the original full-function user interface is too complicated (e.g., too many unnecessary features or high resolution screen layout), another simplified *user interface view* is probably required. Pictures and documents may require to be shown in lower resolution and documents may be outlined and level-structured. Panning and zooming (supported by most browsers) should also help. For users on a WAP interface connecting to the application server via a WAP gateway, the screen is extremely small. A *user interface view* is mandatory to map the original one into WML.

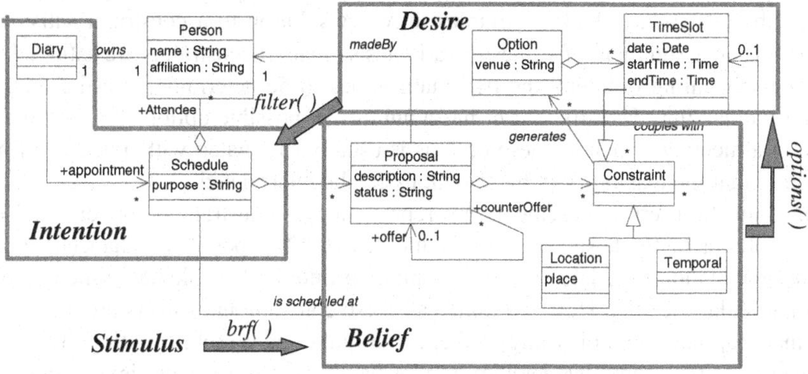

Fig. 10. Mapping Between Data Schema in Fig. 7 and BDI Architecture

7 Adapting the Decision Agent

After presenting our three-tier view-based approach and the application environment, we proceed to discuss the architecture of the agents for human-agent collaboration and how we adapt them to a mobile environment in this section. Fig. 10 summarizes the implementation of the data schema using Belief-Desire-Intention (BDI) agent architecture. Our BDI architecture is composed of three main data sets: belief, desire, and intention. Information or data are passed from one data set to another through the application of some functions. Once the percepts are sensed as input, the *belief revision function* (*brf*) converts it to a belief. The *desire* set is updated by generating some options based on the data in belief set. Options in desire set are then filtered to new intentions of the agent, and a corresponding action is then outputted. In our meeting scheduler, a BDI agent simulates a secretary for arranging appointments on behalf of a human user. Thick arrows indicate update operations. Here, we have not explicitly elaborated the *plan* in the mapping because it is outside the scope of the scheduler. For instance, the plan to attend a meeting may consist of taking a bus and then change for a train. In general, a plan of an agent involves proper resource allocation so as to realize its intentions.

Constraint satisfaction [25][33][26] is one of the major research areas in Artificial Intelligence. Many real life problems, which cannot be easily modeled in specific mathematical forms and solved by conventional Operations Research methods, may be expressed as constraint satisfaction problems. In its basic form, a constraint satisfaction problem consists of a finite number of variables, each ranging over its own finite domain of discrete values, and a finite number of constraints. Each constraint is a relation over a subset of the variables, restricting the combinations of values these variables that they can take. Formally, a *Constraint Satisfaction Problem* is a tuple $<X, D, C>$, where X is a finite set of variables, D a function mapping a variable to its domain, and C a finite set of constraints. For any variable x in X, we require that $D(x)$ is a finite set of discrete constants. A constraint $c(y_1,y_2,\ldots,y_n)$ in C is a relation over a finite subset $\{y_1,y_2,\ldots,y_n\}$ of n variables in X. A solution to a constraint satisfaction problem is an assignment of values to variables so that all constraints are satisfied. In a meeting-scheduling problem, the two main issues to be determined are the time and place of a meeting. Usually, a user has a number of possible options for the time and place of a meeting. Each of these options is usually associated with a degree of preference so that the feasibility of these options can be interrelated.

Once all the users requirements are represented as constraints, conventional constraint solving method, such as systematic search [21], possibly enhanced by constraint propagation [3][21][27], can be applied to find the feasible day, time and place for a particular meeting. However, since all these conventional solvers are centralized, it is inappropriate to employ any of them in a multi-agent mobile setting. This is because employing a centralized solver implies having to require every involved agent to send all or part of personal calendars to a designated agent, which is supposed to find out a feasible solution to the meeting-scheduling problem. Obviously, this is inappropriate in multi-agent systems, in which all agents are supposed to enjoy privacy protection and autonomy. Moreover, there is no way to avoid the designated agent's selfish yet rational behavior of arranging the meeting at a day, time and place that is most convenient to itself only.

We observe that any meeting scheduling protocol involves a trade-off between privacy protection, message exchange costs, and computational efficiency of scheduling. The protocol we describe in the previous paragraph, which commonly known as *open-calendar protocol* is computational efficient yet provides no privacy protection. Another problem is that too much unnecessary data is sent. Therefore this approach wastes bandwidth and is not suitable for mobile users or agents. On the other extreme, the most privacy-protected protocol is to require, say, Mary, to make a sequence of specific suggestions to Franklin. Each of these suggestions consists of a specific day, a specific time on that day, and a specific place. Franklin considers each of them and decides whether or not to accept the suggestion. This protocol, which we call the *passive mode*, is a simple, inefficient protocol (may be causing too many exchanges of short messages) that provides high degree of privacy protection. We can see that there is a spectrum of protocols in between these two extremes, which require the agents to exchange their private information to a certain degree. For example, in the *counter-offer* mode implemented, the meeting proposing agent first sends several options to other participants, who are expected to indicate the feasibility of each of these individual options. Each participant may also counter-propose by replying with a set of his/her own constraints. As such, a balance among privacy protection, message exchange costs, and computational efficiency can be achieved.

Another issue concerning meeting scheduling is the recognition of users' preferences. In our implementation, user preferences are recognized by associating a solution evaluation function defined according to the user's preferences, and enhance the tree search to a branch-and-bound search strategy [21]. In adaptation towards mobility, the agent should be aware of the current locations of all the participants, i.e., the stimulus should include this information. This information is used for ensuring that the participants can arrive at the meeting place on time. We also need to extend the *belief*, *intention*, and *desire* data sets to accommodate for this information, as well as to extend the *brf*, *options*, and *filter* functions accordingly.

Our origin project aimed at exploring the feasibility of implementing agents on PDA platforms. We implemented them in Microsoft embedded Visual C++. We found that the mobile agents can run a good speed on a PDA over a wireless local area network (LAN), i.e., they can solve the constraints in a few seconds. As such, this distributed architecture does not need a centralized server and therefore can be highly scalable, especially noting that there may be many concurrent negotiations but the participants involving in a single negotiation are usually few.

8 Conclusions and Further Work

This paper has presented a pragmatic three-tier view-based methodology in adapting various types of users and agents, in particular wireless mobile ones, in a connected society for collaboration systems. This paper has also introduced a three-tier view-based architecture (viz., *process view*, *user interface view* and *data view*) to provide such support. We have demonstrated the feasibility of our methodology by showing how a meeting scheduler can be adapted to accomplish such objectives. Compared with other researches on this topic, our methodology employs an improved environment through standard state-of-the-art technologies, which can adapt to changing requirements of mobile users and devices, with extensive support for reuse. Further note that, specification of process views is based on standard UML activity diagram, many of the techniques presented in this paper can thus be applicable to other systems. In addition, the concepts of *user interface view* and *data view* should be widely applicable to a wide range of mobile applications.

In our current project, we aim at extending the system to support mobile users in a connected society. Currently, we implement the agents on PC-based server platforms in Java as well. We further include location information to these scheduling agents. On the other hand, we implement the applications to support manual user decisions with our three-tier view methodology. The next phase of our project is to port the Java agents from PC platforms to PDAs by using J2EE to test whether newer PDAs can support agent implementation effectively when we can acquire them later.

For process views, we are working on further details of formal definitions, construction and verification algorithms, more detailed taxonomy, view update mechanisms, and more operations support. In addition, we are interested in the application of our three-tier view-based approach in various advanced real-life e-commerce environments, such as procurement, finance, stock trading and insurance. In particular, we are looking into location depend application, such as mobile workforce management and mobile customer relationship management (CRM) applications. For agent-based application, we are investigating exceptions and their automatic handling, such as cancellations and rescheduling.

References

1. S. Abiteboul and A. Bonner. Objects and Views. In Proceedings of ACM SIGMOD Conference, pp. 238–247, 1991.
2. G. Alonso, et al. Exotica/FMDC: a Process Management System for Mobile and Disconnected clients. Distributed & Parallel Databases, **4**(3):229-247, 1996.
3. Bessière, C. and Cordier, M. Arc-consistency and Arc-consistency again. In Proceedings AAAI-93, pp. 108–113, 1993.
4. D. Carlson. Modeling XML Applications with UML, Addison-Wesley, 2001.
5. D.K.W. Chiu, S.C. Cheung and E. Kafeza. View-based Support for Mobile Workflow. In Proceedings of 1st International Conference on Mobile Business, CDROM, Athens, Greece, July 2002.
6. D.K.W. Chiu, S.C. Cheung, Sven Till, K. Karlapalem, Q. Li, and E. Kafeza. Workflow View Driven Cross-Organizational Interoperability in a Web Service Environment. Information Technology and Management, Kluwer Academic Publishers, 2003 (to appear).
7. D.K.W. Chiu, K. Karlapalem, Q. Li and E. Kafeza. Process Views Based E-Contracts in a Cross-Organization E-Service Environment. Distributed and Parallel Databases, Kluwer Academic Publishers, 12(2-3):193–216, 2002.
8. D.K.W. Chiu, Q. Li and K. Karlapalem. A Meta Modeling Approach for Process Management System Supporting Exception Handling. Information Systems, 24(2):159–184, 1999.
9. D.K.W. Chiu, Q. Li and K. Karlapalem. Web Interface-Driven Cooperative Exception Handling in ADOME Process Management System. Information Systems, Pergamon Press, Elservier Science, 26(2):93–120, 2001.
10. V. Chopra, et. al. Professional XML Web Services. Wrox Press, 2001.
11. U. Dayal. Queries and Views in an Object-Oriented Data Model. In Proceedings 2nd International Workshop on Database Programming Languages, 1989.
12. R. A. Elmasri and S. B. Navathe. Fundamentals of Database Systems. Addison-Wesley, 3rd edition, 2000.
13. H. Evans and P. Ashworth. Getting Started with WAP and WML. Sybex, 2001.
14. G. Gardarin, B. Finance and P. Fankhauser. Federating object-oriented and relational databases: the IRO-DB experience. In Proceedings of the 2nd IFCIS International Conference on Cooperative Information Systems (CoopIS '97), pp. 2–13, 1997.

15. L. Garrido, R. Brena and K. Sycara. Cognitive Modeling and Group Adaptation in Intelligent Multi-Agent Meeting Scheduling. In Proceedings of First Iberoamerican Workshop on Distributed Artificial Intelligence and Multi-Agent Systems, pp. 55–72, 1996.
16. A. ter Hofstede, M. Orlowska and J. Rajapakse. Verification Problems in Conceptual Process Specifications. Data & Knowledge Engineering, Pergamon Press, Elservier Science, 24(3) 239–256, 1998.
17. IBM Redbooks. New Capabilities in IBM Websphere Transcoding Publisher Version 3.5 Extending Web Applications to the Pervasive World. IBM Corp., 2001.
18. ICQ. http://www.icq.com
19. J. Jing, K. Huff, B. Hurwitz, H. Sinha, B. Robinson and M. Feblowitz. WHAM: Supporting Mobile Workforce and Applications in Process Environments. In Proceedings of 10th International Workshop on Research Issues in Data Engineering, San Diego, California, IEEE Press, pp. 31–38, 2000.
20. G. Kappel, B. Pröll, W. Retschitzegger and W. Schwinger. Customization for Ubiquitous Web Applications – A Comparison of Approaches. Int. Journal of Web Engineering and Technology (IJWET), Inaugural Volume, Inderscience Publishers 2003.
21. V. Kumar. Algorithms for Constraint-Satisfaction Problems: A Survey. AI Magazine, **13**(1)32–44, 1998.
22. A. van Lamsweerde, R. Darimont and P. Massonet. Goal-Directed Elaboration of Requirements for a Meeting Scheduler: Problems and Lessons Learnt. In Proceedings of Second IEEE International Symposium on Requirements Engineering (RE '95), pp. 194–203, 1995.
23. Y.-B. Lin and I. Chlamtac. Wireless and Mobile Network Architectures. John Wiley & Sons, 2000.
24. D.-R. Liu and M. Shen. Modeling Processs with a Process-View Approach. In Proceedings of 7th International Conference on Database Systems for Advanced Applications (DASFAA 2001), April 2001, Hong Kong, IEEE Computer Society, pp. 260–267
25. Mackworth, A. K. Consistency in Networks of Relations. Artificial Intelligence, **8**(1) 99–118, 1977.
26. Marriott, K. and Stuckey, P. J. Programming with Constraints: an Introduction. The MIT Press, 1998.
27. Mohr, R. and Henderson, T. C. Arc and Path Consistency Revisited. Artificial Intelligence, **28**:225–233, 1986.
28. Object Management Group. Foreword UML specification 1.4, September 2001.
29. Oracle Inc. Oracle9iAS Wireless. http://www.oracle.com/ip/deploy/ias/index.html?wireless.html
30. Sandip, S. Developing an Automated Distributed Meeting Scheduler. IEEE Expert, pp. 41–45, 7/8–1997.
31. T. Shitani, T. Ito and K. Sycara. Multiple Negotiations among Agents for a Distributed Meeting Scheduler. In Proceedings of 4th International Conference on MultiAgent Systems, July, 2000, pp. 435–436.
32. Staffware Corporation. Staffware Global – Staffware's Opportunity to Dominate Intranet based Process Automation, 2000, http://www.staffware.com
33. Tsang, E. Foundations of Constraint Satisfaction. Academic Press, 1993.
34. A. M. Tjoa, R. R. Wagner and A. Al-Zobaidie. On Integrating Mobile Devices into a Process Management Scenario. In Proceedings of 11th International Workshop on Database and Expert Systems Applications (DEXA 2000), IEEE Press, pp. 186–192, 2000.
35. W3C. Device Independence Activity. http://www.w3.org/2001/di/
36. http://www.w3.org/XML/

Deliberation in a Modeling and Simulation Environment for Inter-organizational Networks

Günter Gans[1], Matthias Jarke[1,2], Gerhard Lakemeyer[1], and Dominik Schmitz[1]

[1] RWTH Aachen, Informatik V, Ahornstr. 55, 52056 Aachen, Germany
[2] Fraunhofer FIT, Schloss Birlinghoven, 53754 Sankt Augustin, Germany
{gans,jarke,lakemeyer,schmitz}@cs.rwth-aachen.de

Abstract. Inter-organizational networks of people, information and communication systems are often described by the interplay between individual goals and actions and the strategic dependencies among individuals and subgroups. Our research aims at improving requirements engineering for such networks by not just representing these goals and dependencies statically, but also by studying the dynamic interactions between both. In previous work, we proposed the prototype environment SNet for the representation and dynamic evaluation of agent-based designs for inter-organizational networks. A key feature of SNet was the automatic translation of extended i* models into the action language ConGolog. While this allowed the simulation of agent networks specified in i*, the resulting agents were purely reactive, which limits the usefulness of the system, in particular as a decision-support tool for network members, who need to evaluate the utility of different courses of action. In this paper we propose to remedy the situation by explicitly incorporating deliberation into the agent design of SNet. At the level of i*, deliberation is represented in terms of goals which are satisfiable by different tasks or agents. Utilities are modeled, in part, using the existing concept of softgoals, which are given a quantitative interpretation. At the level of ConGolog, decision-theoretic features are built into the interpreter, which drives the simulations, and the process of delegating tasks to other agents is explicitly represented.

1 Introduction

Given the need to understand and evaluate business processes, a number of formal approaches have been proposed over the years. Some of these [Sch94],[OSS94], and [PJ96] support the simulation of such processes thus enabling the assessment of the effects of different business strategies.

It has been argued that these methods do not suffice to adequately model inter-organizational networks, which are comprised of human, organizational, and technological actors. A crucial aspect of these networks are the interdependencies among the various actors, which result, for example, from the need to delegate certain activities, which in turn requires a certain level of trust between the (human) members of the network. The graphical modeling language i* [Yu95],

J. Eder and M. Missikoff (Eds.): CAiSE 2003, LNCS 2681, pp. 242–257, 2003.

which was developed for early requirements engineering, has proven to be particularly suitable as a modeling tool in this context because it explicitly deals with dependency relations, besides other notions like actors, goals, resources, and tasks. To capture the dynamic aspects of agent networks, i* was recently extended to include a linear time logic, which together with a model checker allows to verify whether certain states of a network are reachable [FPMT01]. While this approach is perhaps best suited for debugging purposes, it seems desirable to include mechanisms which allow simulations of different scenarios within a network, which would be useful in analyzing its properties and could serve as a decision-support tool for network members. For this purpose we [GJK+01, GJLV02] and Wang and Lespérance [WL01] independently proposed to amalgamate i* and the action formalism ConGolog [dGLL00]. In our system called SNet, extended i* diagrams are automatically translated into executable ConGolog programs, supported by the metadata manager ConceptBase [JEG+95].

One major drawback of the existing approaches, including our own, is that the agents themselves are limited in the kinds of choices they are able to make during a simulation. In our case, these are essentially determined by the values of certain parameters supplied before and during a simulation. In other words, during a particular simulation run, the agents simply commit reactively to the choices required by the design of the agent network and do not themselves engage in deliberation about what the most appropriate course of action might be.[1] Including such a facility in the agents has a number of advantages. For one, it allows for more flexibility in agent design. For another and perhaps more importantly, the decision-making process itself seems to be a crucial aspect of human actors, which should be reflected in the model so that its effects can be studied formally. Finally, such an approach promises to lead to more intelligent designs of technological agents within inter-organizational networks.

In order to achieve deliberation, we make use of the fact that i* already supports the notion that a goal can be achieved by more than one task. While in the old version of SNet, a goal was treated merely as postcondition of the tasks that achieve them, we now focus on the *intentional* force of a goal in that it triggers the process of finding the currently best way or plan of achieving it.

As we already mentioned, an important aspect of inter-organizational networks is that agents depend on each other in performing certain tasks or subtasks, which gives rise to *delegation.* Moreover, there are often a number of possible alternatives for delegation which are often best resolved by some form of *bidding* or *negotiations* between a delegator and candidate delegatees. Our framework includes an explicit model of bidding and delegation.

In order to decide among different courses of action, it is important to rank them according to some measure of *utility.* To this end we make use of another construct offered by i*, *softgoals.* Roughly, softgoals can be thought of as desirable properties such as the level of comfort of car seats produced by a company. While in Yu's original work, softgoals were treated in a rather vague way, we

[1] Strictly speaking, [WL01] allow choices using ConGolog's notion of nondeterministic actions. However, this results in a commitment to the first choice that works, which may not be the most reasonable one to take.

have chosen to give them a precise quantitative interpretation so that they can be used as criteria from which utility measures can be derived. For example, when two car seat producers assign different values to the comfort level they offer for their seats, this can be used by the car manufacturer in deciding who to work with. Based on earlier work on trust and distrust in agent networks [GJK+01], we also take into account the level of trust between agents when computing utilities, which is particularly important when deciding among different possibilities for delegation.

Roughly, our overall approach then is this: taking our previous work on SNet as the starting point, we provide a new mapping between i* diagrams and the action language ConGolog; when goals can be achieved in more than one way, this will lead to ConGolog programs with nondeterministic choices. During execution, these choices will first be evaluated and compared, resulting in a plan with highest utility ready for execution. During evaluation, bidding may occur, which itself may trigger plan evaluations and bidding by other agents such as subcontractors.

The rest of the paper is organized as follows. In Section 2, we briefly introduce the foundations of SNet, i*, Congolog, and the mapping between the two. In Section 3, we present our approach to deliberation by mapping i*-models into suitable programs of ConGolog, whose evaluation includes a form of decision-theoretic planning. In Section 4, we consider implementation issues and we end the paper with a brief discussion and an outlook on future work.

2 The Modeling and Simulation Environment SNet

In this section, we very briefly go over those parts of SNet which are relevant to this paper. The reader is referred to [GJLV02] for a more comprehensive account. Before we begin, let us introduce a simplified fragment of an inter-organizational network taken from the automobile industry, which we use as a running example. We consider a car producer together with subcontractors producing seats, rims, or headlights. We are interested in scenarios where, for example, the car producer wants to build a new car and thus needs seats and has to decide which subcontractor to appoint. The appointment possibly depends on the type of car the car producer wants to build, say a sportive car or a limousine.

2.1 An Extended Version of i*

The i* framework is a graphical language and includes the *strategic dependency (SD)* model for describing the network of relationships among actors and the *strategic rationale (SR)* model, which, roughly, describes the internal structure of an agent in terms of tasks, goals, resources, etc. Compared to Yu's original formulation we added a few new features to SR models such as task preconditions. Figure 1 shows part of an extended SR model of the *SeatProducerA* car seat producer with a focus on the tasks (denoted as hexagons) to be carried out.

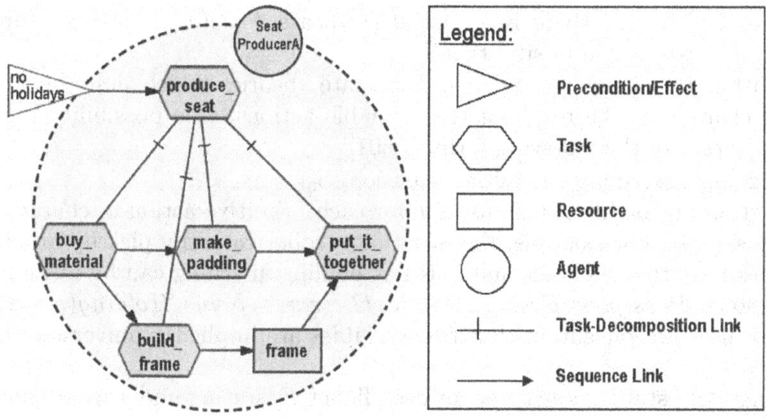

Fig. 1. Modeling in i*/SNet

The main task *produce_seat* is decomposed into four subtasks, which are partially ordered using *sequence links*.[2] Resources (denoted as rectangles) are entities which can be created, handed over between tasks and consumed. In the example, the resource *frame* is produced by the task *build_frame* and afterwards consumed by the task *put_it_together*, which depends on the existence of frames. Tasks can have preconditions and effects (both denoted as triangles). In Figure 1, the precondition *no_holidays* restricts the execution of *produce_seat* to regular working days.

2.2 Introduction to ConGolog

We can only present a very short overview over the logic-based high-level language ConGolog. ConGolog is based on the situation calculus, an increasingly popular language for representing and reasoning about the preconditions and effects of actions [McC63]. It is a variant of first-order logic,[3] enriched with special function and predicate symbols to describe and reason about dynamic domains. We will not go over the language in detail except to note the following features: all terms in the language are one of three sorts, ordinary objects, actions or situations; there is a special constant S_0 used to denote the *initial situation*, namely that situation in which no actions have yet occurred; there is a distinguished binary function symbol *do* where $do(a, s)$ denotes the successor situation to s resulting from performing the action a; relations whose truth values vary from situation to situation are called *relational fluents* , and are denoted by predicate symbols taking a situation term as their last argument; similarly, functions varying across situations are called *functional fluents* and are denoted

[2] Sequence links were not present in the original SNet, but were since added for convenience (see also [WL01] for a similar construct).

[3] Strictly speaking, a small dose of second-order logic is required as well, an issue which should not concern us here.

analogously; finally, there is a special predicate $Poss(a, s)$ used to state that action a is executable in situation s.

Within this language, we can formulate theories which describe how the world changes as the result of the available actions. One possibility is a *basic action theory* of the following form [Rei01]:

- Axioms describing the initial situation, S_0.
- Action precondition axioms, one for each primitive action a, characterizing $Poss(a, s)$. For example, the fact that a robot can only pick up an object if it is next to the object and it is not holding anything can be formalized as follows: $Poss(pickup(r, x), s) \equiv NextTo(r, x, s) \wedge \forall y.\neg Holding(r, y, s)$.
  We use the convention that free variables are implicitly universally quantified.
- Successor state axioms, one for each fluent F, stating under what conditions $F(x, do(a, s))$ holds as a function of what holds in situation s. These take the place of the so-called effect axioms, but also provide a solution to the frame problem. As an example, consider a simple model of time which progresses in a discrete fashion by 1 unit as a result of a special action *clocktick*. The time of a situation can then be specified with the help of a fluent $time(s)$ and the following successor state axiom:

  $$\begin{aligned} time(do(a, s)) = t \;\equiv\; & a = clocktick \wedge t = time(s) + 1 \\ & \vee\, a \neq clocktick \wedge t = time(s) \end{aligned}$$

  We remark already here that we are using a temporal version of the situation calculus with discrete linear time, where time advances as specified by this axiom.
- Domain closure and unique-name axioms for actions.

ConGolog [dGLL00], an extension of Golog [LRL+97], is a language for specifying complex actions (high-level plans). It comes equipped with an interpreter which maps these plans into sequences of atomic actions assuming a description of the initial state of the world, action precondition axioms and successor state axioms for each fluent.

α	primitive action
$\phi?$	test action
$[\sigma_1, \sigma_2, \ldots, \sigma_n]$	sequence
if ϕ then σ_1 else σ_2	conditional
while ϕ do σ	loop
$ndet(\sigma_1, \sigma_2)$	nondeterministic choice of actions
$pi(x, \sigma)$	nondeterministic choice of arguments
$star(\sigma)$	nondeterministic iteration
$conc(\sigma_1, \sigma_2)$	concurrent execution
$pconc(\sigma_1, \sigma_2)$	prioritized concurrent execution
$interrupt(\phi, \sigma)$	triggers σ whenever ϕ holds
$proc(\beta(\vec{x}), \sigma)$	procedure definition

We will not go over the formal semantics of ConGolog here except to note that it uses a conventional transition semantics defining single steps of computation and where concurrency is interpreted as an interleaving of primitive actions and test actions. For details see [dGLL00].

2.3 Mapping the i* Model to a ConGolog Program

The mapping of the i* elements considered so far results in a purely reactive program. A complex task is transformed into a procedure whereby the body is derived from the subelements. The sequential relations between the subelements are reflected via the use of sequence and `conc`. There are primitive actions preceding and following the body, so that the preconditions to and effects of this element can be reflected in the program. In this simple model all primitive tasks have the same duration (1) and are thus mapped directly to primitive actions. Resources are reflected by fluents. Sequence links, precondition/effect and resource elements are mapped to precondition axioms and effect axioms respectively.

Here is an excerpt of the transformation into ConGolog of the *SeatProducerA*.

```
proc(produce_seats(seatProducerA),
     [pre_produce_seats(seatProducerA),
      conc([buy_material(seatProducerA),
            make_padding(seatProducerA)],
           build_frame(seatProducerA)),
      put_it_together(seatProducerA),
      post_produce_seats(seatProducerA)]).

causes_val(build_frame(seatProducerA), frame, seatProducerA, true).
poss(put_it_together(seatProducerA), and(frame=seatProducerA,
                             executed(make_padding(seatProducerA)))).
```

The main task *produce_seat* is turned into a ConGolog procedure which first checks whether its preconditions are satisfied (*pre_produce_seat*), then calls its subtasks, using concurrency whenever possible, and finally handles effects that are specific to the main task (*post_produce_seat*). (Sub-)Tasks which are not decomposed further are turned into primitive actions such as *build_frame* or *put_it_together*, for which precondition axioms (*poss*) and effect axioms (*causes_val*) need to be specified. For example, the effect axiom for *build_frame(seatProducerA)* simply sets the value of *frame* to *seatProducerA* unconditionally.

When given three agents *CarProducer*, *SeatProducerA*, and another seat producer *SeatProducerB*, the main program of the simulation would simply be the following.

```
proc(main,
     conc(interrupt(true, carProducer_proc),
          conc(interrupt(true, seatProducerA_proc),
               interrupt(true, seatProducerB_proc)))).
```

Here we concurrently start all three agent programs. The interrupt mechanism makes sure that the programs are restarted immediately after termination. The termination of a simulation is achieved by disabling the interrupts.

3 Modeling Deliberative Agents in Inter-organizational Networks

The agents we introduced in the previous section are purely reactive. They neither have the opportunity to choose between different ways to pursue their goals nor to decide in which way, or if at all, to execute certain tasks other agents expect them to do. In this section we show how this can be included by taking a particular stance on interpreting goals and softgoals in i*, by adding an explicit account of delegation, and by incorporating a form of decision-theoretic planning into the formalism.

3.1 The Use of Goals and Softgoals for Deliberation

Goals in i* can be viewed in two ways. One view is forward-directed where goals are simply postconditions of those tasks that fulfill them. This is how the original SNet interprets them. The other is backward-directed or intentional, that is, starting from the goal, one asks what would be the best way of achieving a goal given a number of possible alternatives. This is the view we will follow in this paper.[4]

To illustrate our approach, let us consider an SR model for the actor *CarProducer* (Figure 2), focusing on tasks, goals (denoted as ovals), and so-called *softgoals*, which are also part of Yu's original i*.

Here the goal *engage_a_seat_supplier* can be achieved in two ways. On one hand, the agent *SeatProducerA* is able to fulfill the goal by executing the action *produce_seats*. On the other hand the agent *SeatProducerB* could execute a task with the same name to achieve the goal, too. Therefore the agent *CarProducer* has the choice between these two alternatives.

Since agents ultimately need to choose among the possible alternatives, we need criteria which the agent can use to distinguish among them. For this purpose we use *softgoals* such as *sportivity* or *comfort*. In i*, the semantics of softgoals is left somewhat vague, but the intuition is that these, like goals, are desirable properties, but that, unlike goals, their satisfaction is a matter of degree. For example, there usually is no clear-cut definition of when a seat is comfortable. Here we keep this intuition, but also provide an unambiguous quantitative interpretation, that is, a softgoal takes a numeric value. Moreover, this value reflects the utility of the property represented by this softgoal.

To see how we arrive at the utility, consider the *contribution links* in Figure 2 that are drawn between the *produce_seats* task of the two seat producers and the softgoals *sportivity* and *comfort*. The idea is that the seat producers supply their respective values for those softgoals. The car producer will then compute, separately for each seat producer, a *utility* value in the range between 0 and 1 using a utility function attached as an attribute to the softgoals (not shown in

[4] Note that i* itself does not commit itself to a particular view.

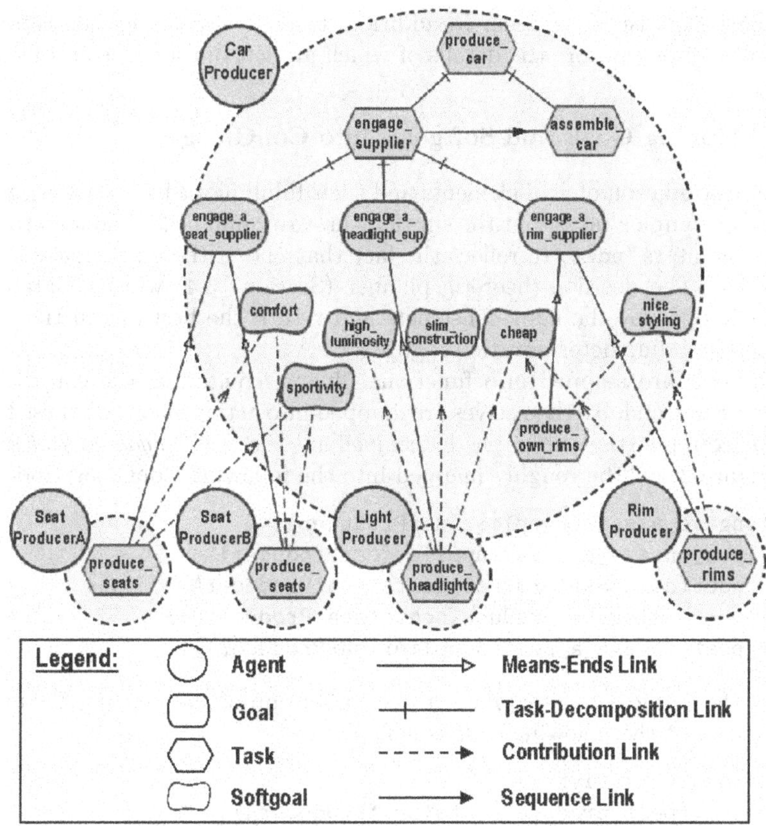

Fig. 2. Modeling Deliberation in i*/SNet

the figure). Finally, the utilities are combined using some weighting scheme,[5] which may differ depending on the type of car, say a sports car versus a sedan, and the seat producer with highest overall utility is chosen for the task. For more details on how utilities are computed and compared see the description of the planning component in Section 3.4.

We end this section with a brief remark on the role of *trust* in inter-organizational networks. Clearly, trust has an impact on whether and how agents interact with each other. Based on our previous work [GJK+01], the original SNet already includes basic mechanisms to model and update trust between two agents with respect to a task. In particular, trust is interpreted as a subjective probability and hence can be quantified.[6] In the current version of SNet, this

[5] We remark that our weighted-sum model for decision making is only one possibility among a large number of other multi-criteria decision making methods (see, for example, [Tri00]).

[6] Note that, in contrast to [YL00], we do not model trust in terms of softgoals and contribution links. See [GJK+01] for the reasons why.

treatment of trust is retained. In addition, trust is also used when computing the utility of delegation, the details of which are left out for reasons of space.

3.2 Mapping Goals and Softgoals into ConGolog

The transformation of goal elements and their fulfilling tasks is rather similar to the one of complex tasks, but the subelements are combined by nondeterministic choice operators (`ndet`) to reflect the fact that one of these alternatives has to be chosen. The decision-theoretic planner (Section 3.4) will evaluate all the choices implied by the `ndet`-constructs and return the best one in the form of the corresponding deterministic program.

Softgoals are mapped into functional fluents containing the contributions. The contribution links themselves are mapped into action effects on these fluents.

For example, the subgraph determined by the goal *engage_a_seat_supplier* (see Figure 2) will be roughly mapped into the following ConGolog-Code:

```
proc(engage_a_seat_supplier(carProducer),
     [pre_engage_a_seat_supplier(carProducer),
      ndet(delegate(produce_seats(seatProducerA)),
           delegate(produce_seats(seatProducerB))),
      post_engage_a_seat_supplier(carProducer)]).
```

For the softgoal *sportivity* and the contribution of the *produce_seats* task of *seatProducerA* the following code is generated:

```
prim_fluent(sportivity).
causes_val(post_produce_seats(seatProducerA),
           sportivity,
           150,
           true).
```

Here the value 150 is taken from a given scale, say 0 to 200. The planner will take this value and convert it to a utility in the range 0 to 1.

3.3 Delegation

The delegation process is modeled using a simple communication protocol.[7] The protocol consists of three steps: In the first step, the agent who wants to delegate a task (the delegator) sends a request to the agent whom he wants to perform the task (delegatee). This request includes the delegator's preferences by mentioning relevant criteria (softgoals) with a suitable weighting and the earliest possible starting time (EPST) when the delegatee can start this job. The delegatee then answers with an offer specifying to what extent the softgoals will be fulfilled and when the job will be finished. Finally the delegator must inform the delegatee

[7] For more sophisticated scenarios, other protocols involving several rounds of negotiations may be more suitable (see [SQ01] for example). We leave this for future work.

whether in fact he is given the job or not, thus sending a confirmation respectively cancellation message.

So if the car producer wants to produce a new sports car it could start a request towards *SeatProducerA* for sportive seats:

```
send_mail(carProducer,     /* From:    */
          seatProducerA,   /* To:      */
          produce_seats,   /* Subject: */
          ask((sportivity, 0.8), (comfort, 0.2), 10))
                 /* (criteria, weights) and EPST */
```

SeatProducerA might answer as follows:

```
send_mail(seatProducerA,   /* From:    */
          carProducer,     /* To:      */
          produce_seats,   /* Subject: */
          answer((sportivity, 150), (comfort, 100), 14))
                 /* contributions and end time */
```

Then the car producer could confirm this delegation by sending:

```
send_mail(carProducer,     /* From:    */
          seatProducerA,   /* To:      */
          produce_seats,   /* Subject: */
          confirm)
```

3.4 Decision-Theoretic Planning

The need to reason about how to perform a job results either from the agent's own initiative like producing a car[8] or from a newly received delegation request such as the request from the car producer to *SeatProducerA* for the production of car seats.

Since the description of how to do a job may contain several alternatives to choose from, the agent must be given the ability to decide on them. For that purpose we already introduced criteria and a utility model to evaluate the alternatives. Here we propose a planner that completely evaluates all possibilities leading to a globally optimal decision for the given utility functions. Roughly, the planner does the following. For each possible course of actions specified by a nondeterministic program, it generates the deterministic program corresponding to this course of actions. The utility of this program is computed and compared with all the other alternatives. Finally, the program representing the best alternative is returned.

Given that we only need to deal with ConGolog programs that are the result of a mapping from an i* model, the planning component can be restricted to cope with a small set of ConGolog elements: primitive actions, non-recursive

[8] In our simulations the *initiative* to perform a task is itself simulated using so-called exogenous events provided by ConGolog.

procedures, ; (sequence), **conc**, **ndet**, and **delegate** (as a special mark for tasks to be delegated).

As a simple example, one of the deterministic alternatives of the ConGolog procedure for the goal *engage_a_seat_supplier* (see page 250) is the following:

```
[pre_engage_a_seat_supplier(carProducer),
 delegate(produce_seats(seatProducerA)),
 post_engage_a_seat_supplier(carProducer)]
```

To compute the utilities and the duration of the job the resulting deterministic program is then processed. Attention must only be paid to handle delegate. Once the planning process meets such an element, a message is sent to the agent containing a weighting of relevant criteria and an earliest possible starting time for the delegated task resulting from the planning so far. The answer of the agent, i.e. alleged criteria contributions and finishing time, can be modified according to the trust the agent has in his partner. The planning process is continued with this (possibly) modified information taken into account.

After processing an alternative completely the utility can be computed by applying utility functions to the corresponding fluents representing the relevant criteria. The agents involved in the loser of the comparison with the up to now best solution are immediately informed about the cancellation of their jobs (see the delegation protocol).

Once all alternatives are processed the best one is known. Since the non-determinisms are eliminated in advance the processed alternative itself can be used as the policy of how to proceed. The instantiation of the time parameter resulting from the processing is used in the plan monitoring component which checks for delays during execution of this job (see also Section 4.1). Allowing for conc elements in the policy is also important because of possibly occurring delays. A pure sequence of primitive actions would be too restrictive, since a delayed execution of a delegated task could then block the agent's own actions.

If planning results from an agent's own initiative, it can commit to the chosen alternative by sending confirmation messages to all agents involved and adding the policy to its schedule. If planning results from a delegation request the computed data can be used to answer this request. In this case the agent has to wait for a final confirmation before adding the job to its schedule. Both cancellation or confirmation are propagated towards the agents involved in the chosen alternative.

Returning to our example (see Figure 2) and assuming that the chosen alternative reflects that for fulfilling the goal *engage_a_seat_supplier SeatProducerA* has proven to be best and for *engage_a_rim_supplier* it occurs that the car producer should do it himself the following policy is created for the task *produce_car* of the car producer:

```
[pre_produce_car(carProducer),
 pre_engage_supplier(carProducer),
 conc([pre_engage_a_seat_supplier(carProducer),
       delegate(produce_seats(seatProducerA)),
       post_engage_a_seat_supplier(carProducer)],
```

```
        conc([pre_engage_a_headlight_supplier(carProducer),
              delegate(produce_headlights(lightProducer)),
              post_engage_a_headlight_supplier(carProducer)],
             [pre_engage_a_rim_supplier(carProducer),
              produce_own_rims(carProducer),
              post_engage_a_rim_supplier(carProducer)])),
   post_engage_supplier(carProducer),
   assemble_car(carProducer),
   post_produce_car(carProducer)]
```

In [BRST00], a related decision-theoretic variant of Golog (DTGolog) was proposed. Our planning component differs in that it is a special purpose planner which does not allow for all Golog actions or stochastic actions. On the other hand, we consider concurrency which DTGolog does not.

4 Modifications in SNet: Implementation Aspects

4.1 Realization of Autonomous Agents in ConGolog

Since we focus on deliberative autonomous agents as representatives for members of an inter-organizational network, this autonomy of an agent has to be reflected in the implementation. We implemented this multi agent framework within Golog itself:

```
proc(agent_simulator(Agents),
     while(true, [/* deliberative phase */
                  check_delay(Agents),
                  check_mails(Agents),
                  /* acting phase */
                  start_actions(Agents),
                  clock_tick(system),
                  end_actions(Agents),
                  reset_phase(system)])).
```

The parameter to this main program is a list of all agents in the simulation. In every time unit two phases can be identified: First a *deliberative* phase where all agents check their current job for unexpected delays. If an unacceptable delay occurs an agent might decide to cancel the execution to prevent future jobs from being affected.[9] Handling mails leads to the use of the planning component and might add future jobs to the agent's schedule (fluent `schedule(Agent)`).[10] An agent starts a new planning process whenever he detects a new `ask` message in his mailbox. Within this planning process the agent can send requests to other agents, if he depends on a delegation, thus activating their planning process. Planning and so handling mails is finished as soon as every planning process of

[9] We do not provide a general recovery mechanism like re-planning yet. Only the agent who initiates this task has the obligation to re-initiate it.

[10] Since exogenous actions are masked as mails to the agent itself, these actions initiate the planning rounds.

every agent is finished and none of the agents has got a mail in its inbox any more.

During the *acting* phase each agent is allowed to execute its current job which is stored in the fluent `prog_in_execution(Agent)`. This phase is subdivided into two phases (starting and finishing phase[11]) by `clock_tick`, which also increases the `time` by 1. To realize the execution of an agent's current job, a special primitive action `execute(Agent)` is introduced, after which the history is not only extended by this action but also by an action taken by the given agent.

Executing the primitive action `reset_phase` allows for the starting phase again and finishes the run for the current time unit. The program then loops back to start with the deliberative phase for the next time unit.

In comparison to the old implementation (especially the old main program see page 247) the following observations can be made:

- Providing a *deliberative* phase is completely new. The old agents were reactively waiting for the preconditions of their tasks to become true to be able to execute them.
- The agents now can communicate with each other about delegations.
- The sub-division of the *acting* phase corrects the old implementation.
- In the old version we need not store agent programs in fluents but resulting from this the agent itself is given more control over his jobs e.g. cancellation of the current job, adding new jobs (from delegations).

Communication is realized just as in [LLL+95] via primitive (system) actions `send_mail`, `sense_mail`, and `remove_mail`. The four types of messages can be derived from the delegation protocol: ask, answer, confirm, cancel. We could not adopt the model provided as a successor to this one by [SLL97] because of its different approach towards delegation. In contrast to our approach in their model already a request adds a non-removable goal to the asked agent to fulfill the request.

4.2 Architecture of the SNet Tool

The extension towards more deliberative agents has no impact on the software architecture of the original SNet (see Figure 3) as a whole. We use OME3 (Object Modeling Environment) [LY] to build up the static extended i* model (.tel file). The plugins for OME are modified to reflect the new semantics of the revised goal and softgoal elements and to provide the correct transformation to ConGolog code (.pl file).

ConceptBase [JEG+95] as the database in which the model is stored and which is used for static analysis and the translation process is not affected at all.

The implementation of the ConGolog interpreter (IndiGolog) in which the simulation runs is also adapted for example to the process model, the planning

---

[11] The sub-division is due to a technical reason resulting from the process model for primitive tasks in combination with the simple interleaved concurrency model.

component, and the new agent model, e.g. the handling of the special primitive action `execute(Agent)`.

The simulator uses ConceptBase to retrieve the graphical representation of a model, shows a step by step view of the simulation run and provides access to control the simulation for example via exogenous actions. Thus it must accomodate the changes in the IndiGolog interpreter and the ConGolog code resulting from the transformation.

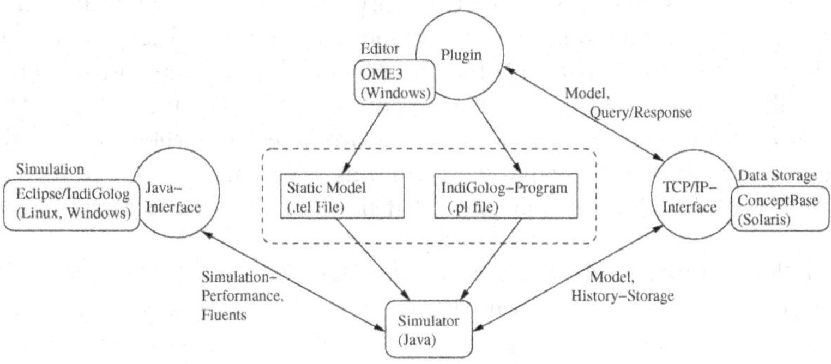

Fig. 3. SNet Software Architecture

5 Discussion

The usefulness of the approach proposed here can be discussed using an analogy with static and dynamic simulation techniques in engineering systems. For example, in chemical engineering, static equilibrium analysis tells you how a chemical plant will behave in steady state. Unfortunately, history knows several plants where such steady-state simulations showed beautiful results but the desired steady state could never be reached after actually building the plant (or, even worse, could not be shut down once started, without major damage).

Similarly, many failures of business process reorganizations or attempts to set up inter-organizational information and cooperation systems demonstrate that brittle social forms such as inter-organizational networks or inter-organizational information systems may work beautifully in a stable state, but there might be no way to get them started or significantly changed from an actual state. SNet aims at simulating such dynamic settings. Currently, several application domains are under investigation. For example, we have made a comparative static analysis of high-tech entrepreneurship networks in a German and an American region and will try to formally reconstruct these results using our approach, with the aim of evaluating different strategies for improving the entrepreneurship situation in Germany [FM03,JKM03]. As another example, we have developed negotiation support technology for eCommerce, and will apply our approach to forecast the impact of this technology on the regional architecture and construction industry network where this technology is being tried out [Sch02]. As a third example, a collaborative research center in Aachen is studying the optimization of innovation chains in chemical engineering across organizational boundaries. This requires information sharing across organizational boundaries without losing the key trade secrets of the involved partners [JM02]. Again, it will be interesting to analyze the goal settings, dependencies, and inter-organizational cooperation and information exchange rules under which such a cross-organizational business innovation can be successfully set up and maintained.

From the point of view of SNet itself, many further extensions seem desirable. For example, as was argued in [GJK+01], distrust between agents plays an important role in that it leads to an increased level of monitoring of the activities of distrusted partners. We would like to incorporate an appropriate model of such behavior in SNet. As a simplification for modeling big (realistic) models we plan to make use of i*'s *role concept.* Instead of modeling similar agents separately, agents will be assembled during transformation by assigning roles to them. In this regard agent properties become important since they then provide the only differences between agents capable of fulfilling the same role. Of course, equally important is an in-depth evaluation of our methodology in a real-world scenario.

Acknowledgment. This work was supported in part by the Deutsche Forschungsgemeinschaft in its Priority Program on Socionics, and its SFB 476 (IMPROVE).

References

[BRST00] C. Boutilier, R. Reiter, M. Soutchanski, and S. Thrun. Decision-theoretic, high-level agent programming in the situation calculus. In *AAAI-2000, 17th National Conference on Artificial Intelligence, Austin, Texas*, 2000.

[dGLL00] G. de Giacomo, Y. Lespérance, and H.J. Levesque. ConGolog, a concurrent programming language based on the situation calculus. *Artificial Intelligence*, 121(1-2):109–169, 2000.

[FM03] C. Funken and M. Meister. Netzwerke als Single Bars, affinity groups und interorganisationales Regime. Freiburg, 2003.

[FPMT01] A. Fuxman, M. Pistore, J. Mylopoulos, and P. Traverso. Model checking early requirements specifications in Tropos. In *Proceedings Fifth IEEE International Symposium on Requirements Engineering (RE01), Toronto, Canada*, August 27–31 2001.

[GJK+01] G. Gans, M. Jarke, S. Kethers, G. Lakemeyer, L. Ellrich, C. Funken, and M. Meister. Requirements modeling for organization networks: A (dis-)trust-based approach. In *Proceedings of the 5th IEEE International Symposium on Requirements Engineering (RE01)*, pages 154–163, Toronto, Canada, August 2001.

[GJLV02] G. Gans, M. Jarke, G. Lakemeyer, and T. Vits. SNet: A modeling and simulation environment for agent networks based on i* and ConGolog. In *Proceedings of the 14th International Conference on Advanced Information Systems Engineering (CAiSE02)*, LNCS 2348, pages 328–343, Toronto, Canada, May 2002.

[JEG+95] M. Jarke, S. Eherer, R. Gallersdörfer, M. A. Jeusfeld, and M. Staudt. ConceptBase - a deductive object base for meta data management. *Journal of Intelligent Information Systems, Special Issue on Advances in Deductive Object-Oriented Databases*, 4(2):167–192, 1995.

[JKM03] M. Jarke, R. Klamma, and J. Marock. *Zu den Wirkungen des regionalen Kontexts auf Unternehmensgründungen*, chapter Gründerausbildung und Gründernetze im Umfeld technischer Hochschulen: ein wirtschaftsinformatischer Versuch, pages 115–154. EUL-Verlag, 2003.

[JM02] M. Jarke and H. C. Mayr. Mediengestütztes Anforderungsmanagement. *Informatik Spektrum*, 25(6):452–464, 2002.

[LLL+95] Y. Lespérance, H. J. Levesque, F. Lin, D. Marcu, R. Reiter, and R. B. Scherl. Foundations of a logical approach to agent programming. In *ATAL-95, Intelligent Agents II. Workshop on Agent Theories, Architectures, and Languages*, 1995.

[LRL+97] H.J. Levesque, R. Reiter, Y. Lespérance, F. Lin, and R. Scherl. Golog: A logic programming language for dynamic domains. *Journal of Logic Programming*, 31(1):59–84, 1997.

[LY] L. Liu and E. Yu. Object Modeling Environment (OME). http://www.cs.toronto.edu/km/ome.

[McC63] John McCarthy. Situations, actions and causal laws. Technical report, Stanford University, 1963. Reprinted 1968 in Minsky, M.(ed.): Semantic Information Processing, MIT Press.

[OSS94] A. Oberweis, G. Scherrer, and W. Stucky. INCOME/STAR: Methodology and tools for the development of distributed information systems. *Information Systems*, 19(8):643–660, 1994.

[PJ96] P. Peters and M. Jarke. Simulating the impact of information flows on networked organizations. In *Proceedings of the 17th International Conference on Information Systems, Cleveland, Ohio, USA*, pages 421–439, December 1996.

[Rei01] Raymond Reiter. *Knowledge in Action: Logical Foundations for Specifying and Implementing Dynamical Systems.* MIT Press, 2001.

[Sch94] A.-W. Scheer. *Business Process Engineering - Reference Models for Industrial Companies.* Springer Verlag, Berlin, 2 edition, 1994.

[Sch02] M. Schoop. Electronic markets for architects - the architecture of electronic markets. *Information Systems Frontiers*, 4(3):285–302, 2002.

[SLL97] S. Shapiro, Y. Lespérance, and H. J. Levesque. Specifying communicative multi-agent systems with congolog. In *Working Notes of the AAAI Fall 1997 Symposium on Communicative Action in Humans and Machines*, pages 72–82, Cambridge, MA, Novemeber 1997. AAAI Press.

[SQ01] M. Schoop and C. Quix. Doc.com: a framework for effective negotiation support in electronic marketplaces. *Computer Networks*, 37(2):153–170, 2001.

[Tri00] E. Triantaphyllou. *Multi-Criteria Decision Making Methods: A Comparative Study.* Kluwer Academic Publishers, 2000.

[WL01] Xiyun Wang and Yves Lespérance. Agent-oriented requirements engineering using ConGolog and i*. In *Working Notes of the Agent-Oriented Information Systems (AOIS-2001) Workshop, Montreal, QC*, May 2001.

[YL00] E. Yu and L. Liu. Modelling trust in the i* strategic actors framework. In *Proceedings of the 3rd Workshop on Deception, Fraud and Trust in Agent Societies, Barcelona, Catalonia, Spain (at Agents2000)*, June 3–4 2000.

[Yu95] E. Yu. *Modelling Strategic Relationships for Process Reengineering.* PhD thesis, University of Toronto, 1995.

Information Integration in Schema-Based Peer-To-Peer Networks

Alexander Löser[1], Wolf Siberski, Martin Wolpers, and Wolfgang Nejdl[2]

[1] CIS, Technical University Berlin, 10587 Berlin, Germany
aloeser@cs.tu-berlin.de

[2] Learning Lab Lower Saxony, University of Hannover, 30167 Hannover, Germany
{siberski,wolpers,nejdl}@learninglab.de

Abstract. Peer-to-peer (P2P) networks have become an important infrastructure during the last years. Using P2P networks for distributed information systems allows us to shift the focus from centrally organized to distributed information systems where all peers can provide and have access to information.

In previous papers, we have described an RDF-based P2P infrastructure called Edutella which is a specific example of a more advanced approach to P2P networks called schema-based peer-to-peer networks. Schema-based P2P networks have a number of advantages compared with simpler P2P networks such as Napster or Gnutella. Instead of prescribing one global schema to describe content, they support arbitrary metadata schemas and ontologies (crucial for the Semantic Web). Thereby they allow complex and extendable descriptions of resources thus introducing dynamic behavior to the former fixed and limited descriptions, and can provide complex query facilities against these metadata instead of simple keyword-based searches.

In this paper we will elaborate topologies, indices and query routing strategies for efficient query distribution in such networks. Our work is based on the concept of super-peer networks which provide better scalability compared to traditional P2P networks. By adapting existing concepts of mediator-based information systems to super-peer based networks, as we will show in this paper, they are able to support sophisticated routing, clustering and mediation strategies based on the metadata schemas and attributes. The resulting routing indices can be built using local clustering policies and support local mediation and transformation rules between heterogeneous schemas, and we sketch some first ideas for implementing these advanced functionalities as well.

1 Introduction

Recently information systems that use peer-to-peer (P2P) networks as infrastructure evolved from simple P2P-based systems like Napster and Gnutella to more sophisticated ones based on distributed indices (e.g. distributed hash tables) such as CAN [19] and CHORD [21]). Using P2P-topologies for information systems enables us to shift the focus from centrally organized to distributed information systems where all peers can provide and have access to information in the network. These approaches provide the advantages of P2P topologies, e.g. robustness and flexibility. At the same time some new problems arise, e.g. fast and reliable data retrieval or efficient search. In this paper we

J. Eder and M. Missikoff (Eds.): CAiSE 2003, LNCS 2681, pp. 258–272, 2003.

address some of the problems associated with web content management and distribution, focusing on the handling of complex metadata[1] sets for data description and the support of complex queries for data retrieval.

We assume that these queries are expressed based on the schemas used for annotation. In order to query only those peers capable of answering we obviously must investigate more advanced routing algorithms than simple query broadcast. Therefore, based on information about schemas used by each peer, we create and maintain explicit query routing indices which facilitates more sophisticated routing approaches. The query is still evaluated by the peers holding the metadata sets, but only peers having annotations based on the schema elements used in the query will receive it. The routing indices do not rely on a single schema but can contain information about arbitrary schemas used in the network.

Allocating these routing indices together with clustering and mediation functionality at every peer would require a considerable amount of processing power at each peer. Also, because peers tend to join and leave the network unpredictably, the topology would be subject to constant inefficient reorganization. Therefore, we use a super-peer topology for these schema-based networks, where designated super-peers with high availability, processing power and bandwidth form a network backbone, and each peer connects to one super-peer only (see [25] for the general characteristics of super-peer networks; Kazaa, Grokster and Morpheus are examples of such super-peer systems). The super-peers are responsible for construction and maintenance of routing indices and for query routing. To support reorganization within the network each super-peer uses a so called clustering-policy. Such a policy constrains the set of peers accepted by a particular super-peer. For example, a super-peer may use a policy to accept only peers which use the Dublin Core schema. We use these policies 1) to induce network clustering based on content with the goal of reducing the amount of query broadcast and 2) to restrict the set of schemas for a particular super-peer. Restricting schemas allow us to define local mapping rules -correspondences- between schemas of a particular super-peer. Since clustering rules restrict the amount of schemas and attributes for each super-peer, we introduce a global schema at each super-peer and map peer schemas to it. We show how such a mapping is done within a particular super-peer.

There are only a few research groups that have investigated these schema-based P2P networks so far. In our group we have been working on a schema-based network called Edutella [15][16] (see http://edutella.jxta.org for the source code), which aims at providing access to distributed collections of digital resources through a P2P network. Resources in the Edutella network are not described using ad hoc metadata fields (like Napster & Co), but use RDF schemas and RDF metadata for their description. In order to retrieve information stored on the Edutella network we use the query language RDF-QEL. RDF-QEL is based on Datalog semantics and thus compatible with all existing query languages, supporting query functionalities which extend the usual relationally complete query languages.

Two other interesting approaches are the ones investigated by Bernstein et al. and Aberer et al. Bernstein et.al. [5] propose the Local Relational Model (LRM) enabling general queries to be translated into local queries with respect to the schema supported

[1] We use the terms metadata and annotations synonymously.

at the respective peer, using the concept of local translation/coordination formulas to translate between different schemas. Aberer et.al. [2,1] propose schema-based peers and local translations to accommodate more sophisticated information providers connected by a Gnutella-like P2P topology.

In section 2 we will describe the general topology of our schema-based super-peer network and the indices used to route queries. We will then discuss clustering and mediation algorithms in such networks in section 3.

2 Schema-Based Routing in P2P Networks

P2P networks that broadcast all queries to all peers don't scale. We therefore propose a super-peer topology for these networks and the use of indices at these super-peers to address scalability requirements. These indices are built using schema information from their associated peers. The super-peer network constitutes the "backbone" of the P2P network which takes care of message routing and integration / mediation of metadata.

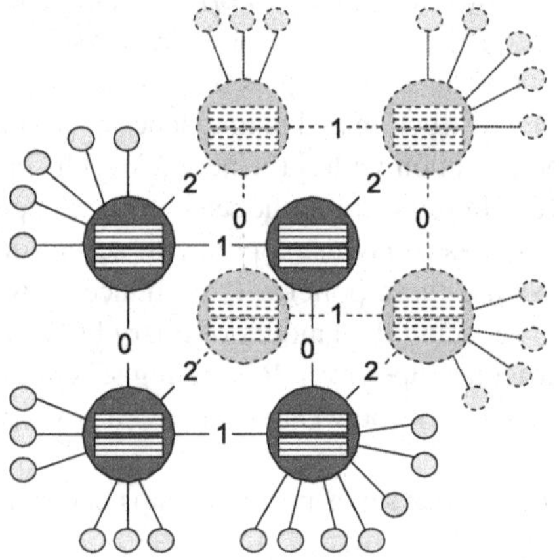

Fig. 1. Peers connected to the super-peer "backbone"

We will assume that the super-peers in our network are arranged in the HyperCuP topology [20]. Most solutions we propose in this paper could be realized with other super-peer topologies, too, which would actually lead to interesting extensions derived from the ideas in this paper. We focus on HyperCuP, because first, it is the topology we have implemented in our super-peer network, and second, it is very efficient for broadcasts and partitioning which makes it quite suitable as a super-peer topology.

In HyperCuP, the super-peers from a hyper cube (or, more generally, a Cayley graph), thus enabling efficient query broadcasts with guaranteed non-redundancy. Each node issuing a broadcast can be thought of as the root of a specific spanning tree through the P2P network. The topology allows for $\log_2 N$ path length and $\log_2 N$ number of neighbors, where N is the total number of nodes in the network (i.e. the number of super-peers in our case). Also, a path of $\log_2 N$ length exists between any two super-peers, thus any two distinct schemas can be reached within a short number of hops from each other. See [20] for detailed information about this topology.

Peers connect to the super-peers in a star-like fashion, providing content and content metadata (see Figure 1 for a small HyperCuP topology).

The introduction of super-peers in combination with routing indices reduces the workload of peers significantly by distributing queries only to the appropriate subset of all possible peers (see also [7] who discusses routing indices based on various aggregation strategies of content indices). In our approach, we have introduced two different kinds of routing indices, based on schema information. In the next sections we will discuss these routing indices in detail.

2.1 Routing Super-Peer/Peer Queries and Responses

The first kind of indices needed in super-peers are so-called super-peer/peer routing indices (SP/P-RIs). In these indices each super-peer stores information about metadata usage at each directly connected peer.

On registration the peer provides the super-peer with its metadata information by publishing an advertisement. This advertisement encapsulates a metadata based description of the most significant properties of the peer. As this may involve quite a large amount of metadata, we build upon the schema-based approaches which have successfully been used in the context of mediator-based information systems (e.g. [24]).

To ensure that the indices are always up-to-date, peers notify super-peers when their content changes in ways that trigger an update of the index. If a peer leaves the network, all references to this peer are removed from the indices. In contrast to some other approaches (e.g. Gnutella [10], CAN [19], Tapestry [26]), our indices do not refer to individual content elements but to whole peers (as in CHORD [21]).

At each super-peer, elements used in a query are matched against the SP/P-RIs in order to determine local peers which are able to answer the query (see also [2] for a related approach). A match means that a peer understands and can answer a specific query, but does not guarantee a non-empty answer set. The indices can contain the information about peers (or other super-peers, see 2.2) at different granularities: schema identifiers, schema properties, property value ranges, and individual property values.

To illustrate index usage, we will use the following sample query: *find lectures in German language from the area of software engineering suitable for undergraduates.* In the Semantic Web context this query would probably be formalized using the Dublin Core schema (DC, [4]) for document specific properties (e.g. title, creator, subject) and the Learning Object Metadata schema (LOM, [11]) which provides learning material specific properties, in combination with classification hierarchies (like the ACM Computing Classification System, ACM CCS) in the subject field. In line with RDF conventions citels01, we identify properties by their name and their schema (expressed by a namespace shorthand). "dc:subject" therefore denotes the property "subject" of the DC schema. So, written in a more formal manner, the query becomes:

> *Find any resource where the property* dc:subject *is equal to* ccs:softwareengineering, dc:language *is equal to "de" and* lom:context *is equal to "undergrad".*

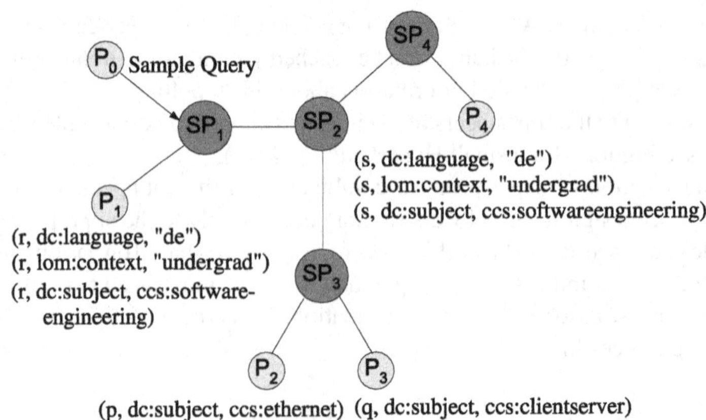

Fig. 2. Routing example network

Table 1 shows the values requested in the query at the different granularities; e.g. the query asks for DC and LOM at the schema level, while it requests a lom:context value of "undergrad" at the property value level, etc.

In order to further clarify things we consider the scenario shown in Figure 2. In this network, various resources are described on different peers, which in turn are attached to super-peers.

Peer P_0 sends the sample query mentioned above to its super-peer SP_1. In our example, this query could be answered by the peers P_1 and P_4, attached to SP_1 and SP_4, respectively. These contain metadata about resources r and s which match the query.

The following paragraphs will explain how the routing indices at the different granularities facilitate routing the query to the right peers.

Schema Index. We assume that different peers will support different schemas and that these schemas can be uniquely identified (e.g. the dc and lom namespaces are uniquely identified by an URI). The routing index contains the schema identifier as well as the peers supporting this schema. Queries are forwarded only to peers which support the schemas used in the query. Super-peer SP_1 will forward the sample query to attached peers which use DC and LOM to annotate resources.

Table 1. Contents of the sample query at different granularities

Granularity	Query	
Schema	dc, lom	
Property	dc:subject, dc:language, lom:context	
Property Value Range	dc:subject	ccs:sw'engineering
Property Value	lom:context dc:language	"undergrad" "de"

Property/Sets of Properties Index. Peers might choose to use only parts of (one or more) schemas, i.e. certain properties, to describe their content. While this is unusual in conventional database systems, it is more often used for data stores using semi-structured data, and very common for RDF-based systems. In this kind of index, super-peers use the properties (uniquely identified by namespace/schema ID plus property name) or sets of properties to describe their peers. Our sample query will be sent to peers using at least dc:subject, dc:language and lom:context (e.g. SP_1 will send the query to P_1, as P_1 contains all of these properties). Sets of properties can be useful to characterize queries (i.e. we might use a "sets-of-properties index" to characterize and route the most common queries).

Property Value Range Index. For properties which contain values from a predefined hierarchical vocabulary we can use an index which specifies taxonomies or part of a taxonomy for properties. This is a common case in Edutella, because in the context of the semantic web quite a few applications use standard vocabularies or ontologies. In our example, peers could be characterized by their possible values in the dc:subject field, and the query would not be forwarded to peers managing "ccs:networks" or "ccs:artificial_intelligence" content (as these sub-hierarchies are disjoint from the ccs:software_engineering sub-hierarchy), and will not be forwarded to peers which use the MeSH vocabulary (because these peers manage medical content).

Note that the subsumption hierarchy in a taxonomy such as ACM CCS can be used to aggregate routing information in order to reduce index size.

Property Value Index. For some properties it may also be advantageous to create value indices to reduce network traffic. This case is identical to a classical database index with the exception that the index entries do not refer to the resource, but the peer providing it. This index contains only properties that are used very often compared to the rest of the data stored at the peers. It would be very interesting to investigate how these indices could be combined with the value mapping approach described in [12].

In the example, this is used to index string valued properties such as dc:language or lom:context.

2.2 Routing among Super-Peers Based on Routing Indices

As with peers, we want to avoid broadcasting queries to all super-peers. To achieve this goal we introduce super-peer/super-peer routing indices to route among the super-peers. These SP/SP indices are essentially extracts and summaries (possibly also approximations) from the local SP/P indices. They contain the same kind of information as SP/P indices, but refer to the (direct) neighbors of a super-peer. Queries are forwarded to super-peer neighbors based on the SP/SP indices, and sent to connected peers based on the SP/P indices.

Table 2 gives a full example of the SP/SP routing index of SP_2 at the different granularities. For example, SP_2 knows at the schema level that all of its neighbors (SP_1, SP_3, SP_4) use the DC namespace, but only SP_1 and SP_4 contain information described in the LOM schema. Thus, the sample query will not be routed to SP_3, as it requires both DC and LOM.

The same applies for the other levels of granularity. A special case is the Property Value Range level; note that ccs:networks is a common super concept of ccs:ethernet and ccs:clientserver in the ACM CCS taxonomy. Making use of the topic hierarchy, the routing index can contain aggregate information like this in order to reduce index size.

Update of SP/SP indices is based on the registration (or update) messages from connected peers. We assume for the moment that a peer can connect to an arbitrary super-peer and define the index update procedure as follows: when a new peer registers with a super-peer, it announces the necessary schema (and possibly content) information to the super-peer. The super-peer matches this information against the entries in its SP/P index. If new elements have to be added in order to include the peer into the SP/P index, the super-peer broadcasts an announcement of the new peer to the super-peer network (according to the HyperCuP protocol, so that it reaches each super-peer exactly once). The other super-peers update their SP/SP indices accordingly. [20] describes the algorithms for joining and leaving of super-peers.

Although such a broadcast is not optimal, it is not too costly either. First, the number of super-peers is much less than the number of all peers. Second, if peers join the super-peer frequently, we can send a summary announcement containing all new elements only in pre-specified intervals instead of sending a separate announcement for each new peer. Third, an announcement is necessary only if the SP/P index changes because of the integration of the new peer. As soon as the super-peer has collected a significant amount of peers (hopefully with similar characteristics, see our discussion on clustering in the next section), the announcements will rather be an exception. We are planning simulations as part of our further work to validate these assumptions quantitatively.

Further work will include simulations to collect data on performance characteristics of the approach.

3 Adaptive Clustering and Mediation in Peer-to-Peer Networks

In the last section we described how queries can be routed using schema-based routing indices. This routing still has the problem that most queries must be broadcast if the peer distribution is arbitrary. In this section we discuss concepts how peers can be

Table 2. SP/SP index of SP_2 at different granularities

Granularity	**Index of SP_2**		
Schema	dc		SP_1, SP_3, SP_4
	lom		SP_1, SP_4
Property	dc:subject		SP_1, SP_3, SP_4
	dc:language		SP_1, SP_4
	lom:context		SP_1, SP_4
Property Value Range	dc:subject	ccs:networks	SP_3
	dc:subject	ccs:software-engineering	SP_1, SP_4
Property Value	lom:context	"undergrad"	SP_1, SP_4
	dc:language	"de"	SP_1, SP_4

smartly clustered in order to avoid unnecessary broadcasting. Furthermore, we propose ideas for mediating information provider peers and consumer peers dynamically by using schema based clustering techniques and for using mediation correspondences to transform between different schemas.

3.1 Rule-Based Clustering of Peers

Obviously, we still have to define what kind of similarity measures we want to use for our partitions. In [20] we have discussed how to partition a HyperCuP-based P2P network based on a topic ontology shared by all peers. Here, we present a new approach called *rule based clustering*. The main idea is to group and register peers in *subject specific clusters (SSC)* via cluster specific rules. Each super-peer represents such a cluster. A typical cluster may group peers with equal properties, e.g. more static properties like specific query and result schemas, specific domain/IP address ranges, or more dynamic properties, like a minimum number of resources at a peer, average answer time or average number of results[2]. Every cluster provides its own *rules*, expressing which peers are allowed to join the cluster and which peers are denied to enter the cluster. We will call a complete set of such rules a *subject specific cluster policy*. Typically the super-peer's administrator will define such a policy[3]. Each rule consists of an event, a constraint and an action. This approach has already been widely used in database systems[23][8]. We distinguish between three different *events*:

Enter A peer likes to join an super-peer.
Leave A peer leaves a super-peer.
Check A super-peer checks the current status of an already connected peer.

An event can be connected to one or many constraints. A typical *constraint* is defined by a property, an operator (=,!=, INCLUDE, EXCLUDE[4]) and a value, e.g.

```
Peer.Advertisement.Property query_schema = "LOM"
```

When checking a constraint, the result can either be "TRUE" or "FALSE". Constraints can be combined using conjunction (AND) and disjunction (OR). As long as a constraint meets our schema, we allow the formulation of arbitrary constraints using arbitrary property sets, since most super-peer administrators will use their own context specific set. If a super-peer receives a peer advertisement consisting of an unknown property, the property is ignored by the super-peer. If a super-peer misses a property in a peer's advertisement while checking the value of a constraint, the result of the constraint is assumed as "FALSE".

[2] Further properties for peers and information sources are discussed in [9][14][22]

[3] We assume that a small number of participants of our P2P network will be competent enough and interested in defining such rules while most of users are only interested in providing and retrieving information from the network. This assumption is supported by the fact that some existing single schema P2P networks, typically only used for file sharing purpose like *Direct Connect* [17] and *E-Donkey*, already use simple administrator based rules for clustering peers successfully.

[4] Further work will include the investigation of more operators, in particular operators which will express fuzzy similarity.

Depending on events and constraints *actions* will be triggered. For instance, the above mentioned event "Enter" will trigger one of the following actions:

Approve (Peer) A peer will be approved to join the super-peer.
Reject (Peer) A peer will be rejected from the super-peer.
Redirect (Peer) A peer will be forwarded to another super peer. Note that this action may occur after approving or rejecting a peer.

In the following example we assume that a super-peer is only interested in peers providing materials by using the LOM or DC schemas and that possible peers have to be member of the domain "cs.tu-berlin.de". The corresponding policy of the super-peer can be expressed by defining one rule[5]:

```
ON (Event) Enter IF (
   ((Peer.Advertisement.Property query_schema="LOM") OR
   (Peer.Advertisement.Property query_schema="DC")
   )
   AND
   (Peer.Advertisement.Property peer_name
         INCLUDE "cs.tu-berlin.de")
)
DO (Action) Approve(Peer)
ELSE (Action) Reject(Peer)
```

Having defined the super-peers clustering policy, the super-peer administrator may be interested in some specific peers which provide relevant information. An approach would be just to wait until peer advertisements occur, denoting peers wishing to join his super-peer. We will also investigate techniques to invite specific peers joining the super peer and to examine automatically advertisements of peers connecting to other super-peers. This includes concepts as broadcasting such invitations periodically to attract matching peers.

Using the proposed clustering approach several problems remain open. One problem is to realize an overall sound clustering. Since rules are specified by local administrators, some peers may not be accepted by neither super-peer at all. This may occur if the peer does not provide a suitable advertisement for a cluster. This may be especially the case when the peer does not meet the minimum requirements of the cluster, e.g. provides only a few results for a query, does not include a specific query schema, does not use a specific ip-address and so on. In our network we explicitly allow a super-peer administrator narrowing its super-peer policy to reject poor information sources. For this reason some peers may not be accepted by any super-peer at all. To avoid 1) dropping to many peers, which maybe are relevant for other super-peers, and 2) help "new peers" to discover a suitable super-peer when entering the network we will investigate in our further research two promising approaches:

[5] The above mentioned examples are described by using a non-existent pseudo language. We will investigate, how existing languages used in the context of the semantic web are feasible to express our semantics.

Meta Data Annotation Current Super-Peer based peer-to-peer applications for music sharing technologies use meta data to describe the policy of each super-peer.[6] Although we did not explicitly specify a model for such annotations yet we believe that such annotations using a dedicated model will help peers identifying a suitable super-peer.

Redirects between Super-Peers Super-Peer administrators may define "links or redirects" between selected super peers. Such links will redirect peers from one super-peer to another if they had been rejected from one super-peer.[7].

3.2 Correspondences-Based Mediation between Different Schemas

Using the criteria of [18] and [3] the super-peer network described in the last sections may be classified as a federated information system (FIS) without a global schema, a so called loosely coupled system. Such systems offer a uniform multi database query language to access data in different sources, but do not have a global schema. Data sources in such systems must be structured and support unrestricted query access. In tightly coupled systems, for instance mediator-based systems [24], users see only one schema and do not have to bother with different sources and their structures. Hence, a tightly coupled FIS inherently offers location, language, and schema transparency. In contrast, loosely coupled systems usually only offer language transparency: a user does not need to learn the query language of each source, but he still has to know their schemas.

In this section we will describe how mediation services may provide schema transparency in our system. We assume that each super-peer will cluster peers for a specific domain using an appropriate clustering policy. Further each peer of the cluster will provide at least one query schema. Unfortunately we cannot assume that every peer will use the same term in its query schema for the same meaning. To resolve this heterogeneity we will introduce in this section local correspondences between different schemas of peers registered at a super-peer. Such correspondences incorporate a local domain mapping logic between schemas of the peers and a global schema of one super-peer. Each super-peer may consist of several correspondences expressing different semantics to correspondences used in other super-peers. Such local correspondences therefore will only resolve heterogeneity within its super-peer.

This new setting might surprise, since in comparison to the setting described in the last sections, where only local schemas are used directly, we now use at least one global schema for each super-peer. We believe that by introducing a local schema in a loosely coupled information system advantages of both strategies, loosely bound information sources and mediation services of tight coupled information systems may be used. Further, clustering peers for a specific domain by query schemas of peers might help to narrow the amount of integration work, in particular formulating correspondences between peer and super-peer schemas for a with a given set of query schemas.

[6] For instance *Direct Connect* provides a list with every super-peer available to join in the network consisting its policy (min of open Slots, min available GB amount of data, allowed IP address range, name of the peer-mostly includes information about its shared music styles...).

[7] We are aware of only one super-peer network, Direct Connect, which uses this approach to redirect between different hubs.

In our further research we will investigate how such a tight integration of clustering and mediation concepts may be used in our peer-to-peer infrastructure providing richer queries.

For our mediation service we assume that every peer will provide information about its query schema in an advertisement. Typically a super-peer will collect several advertisements related to its peers.[8] If a super receives a query from a consumer it tries to identify relevant advertisements matching the schema of the query. We distinguish between the following three cases:

1. A query exactly matches the advertisement of one potential peer.
2. A query exactly matches advertisement of many peers, all using the same schema.
3. A query could be resolved combining results from many peers using different schemas.

Case one and two may occur when a super-peer's clustering policy forces its peers to use only one schema. Since we allow heterogeneous schemas in our super-peer network we are mainly interested in case three which includes case one and two already. This implies we have to investigate methods to transform schemas between different peers, so different query schemas can be integrated with each other.

Consider the example where a super-peer has defined *subject specific clustering rules (SSCRs)* (see also section3.1) and now accepts only peers using either LOM or DC schema. When receiving queries consisting of LOM and DC specific attributes the super-peer has to translate between the attributes of LOM and DC. To resolve these heterogeneities, we investigated concepts for transformation rules between different schemas, so called *correspondences*, already used in mediator-based information systems (MBIS) [24]. We identified *Query Correspondence Assertions (QCA)*[13] and *model correspondences (MOCA)*[6] as a flexible mechanisms to express such correspondences between heterogeneous schemas. With QCAs, a human administrator defines the intentional equivalence of two views, where one is defined as a query against the mediator schema and the other is defined as a query against one source schema. In contrast to MBIS where correspondences are used as rules to translate between global and local schemas, in super-peer networks typically translations exist between different local schemas only. Such MBIS-based correspondences can also be used as rules to describe such translations. We will adapt the existing concepts of MOCAs and QCAs as a possible way to define schema correspondences in peer-to-peer networks and describe their use in our network by an example.

In the following example the super-peer administrator defines a query schema *lectures(lecture:identifier, lecture:language, lecture:subject, lecture:educationalcontext)* which returns documents identified by its URL. First we define correspondences between attributes of the peer schemas and the corresponding attributes of the *lectures* schema[9]:

1. lectures:Identifier = dc:identifier
   lectures:language=dc:lang
   lectures:subject=dc:subject

[8] Depending on the super-peer's policy, peer advertisements may contain many different schemas.

[9] The correspondences are based on existing LOM-DC mappings, see *http://kmr.nada.kth.se/el/ims/md-lomrdf.html*.

2. lectures:Identifier = lom:general.identifier
   lectures:language=lom:general.language
   lectures:context=lom:educational.context

Using the above mentioned correspondences we now create views on the peer specific schemas:

1. lecturesViewDC(lectures:Identifier,lectures:language,lectures:subject)
   ← DC(dc:Identifier, dc:lang, dc:subject)
2. lecturesViewLOM(lectures:Identifier, lectures:language, lectures:context)
   ← LOM(lom:general.identifier,lom:general.language, lom:educational.context)

Then we describe, which attributes of the super-peers lectures schema could be answered by the local peer schemas:

1. lectures(lectures:identifier,lectures:language,lectures:subject,-)
   ← lecturesViewDC(lectures:Identifier,lectures:Language,lectures:subject)
2. lectures(lecture:identifier,lecture:language,-, lecture:context)
   ← (lectures:Identifier,lectures:Language,lectures:context)

Combining all correspondences results in two main schema correspondences bridging the heterogeneity between the peers P1 and P2:

Peer1:Correspondence1 lectures(lectures:identifier,lectures:language,-,lectures:edu...context)
← v(lectures:Identifier,lectures:language,lectures:context)
← LOM(lom:general.identifier,lom:general.language,lom:educational.context)
Peer2:Correspondence2 lectures(lectures:identifier,lectures:language,lectures:subject,-)
← v(lectures:Identifier,lectures:language,lectures:subject)
← DC(dc:identifier,dc:subject,dc:lang)

A super-peer stores relations between correspondences and peers in his indices. When a super-peer receives a query *lecture (lecture:identifier, lecture:language, lecture:subject, lecture:educationalcontext)* the super-peer identifies P1:Correspondence1 and P2:Correspondence2 as a combination of relevant correspondences that are semantically included in the user query and will probably compute correct results. The query is forwarded to the relating information provider peers Peer 1 and Peer 2, then the results have to be collected and combined by the super-peer. Integrating these concepts in our super-peer network allows us to build up subject and context specific super-peers in our network. Consider the example where a super-peer administrator is interested in clustering e-learning content providers (see Figure 3). By defining the super-peer's policy using rule based clustering he allows peers connecting to his super-peer only when they provide LOM or DC schema metadata. Next the administrator defines which complex query schemas his super-peer supports and defines the correspondences between these schemas. Finally he invites a first set of relevant information provider peers to join his super-peer. Now the super-peer is ready to receive queries related to learning materials. Other provider peers may join the super-peer later and increase the content mediated through this super-peer.

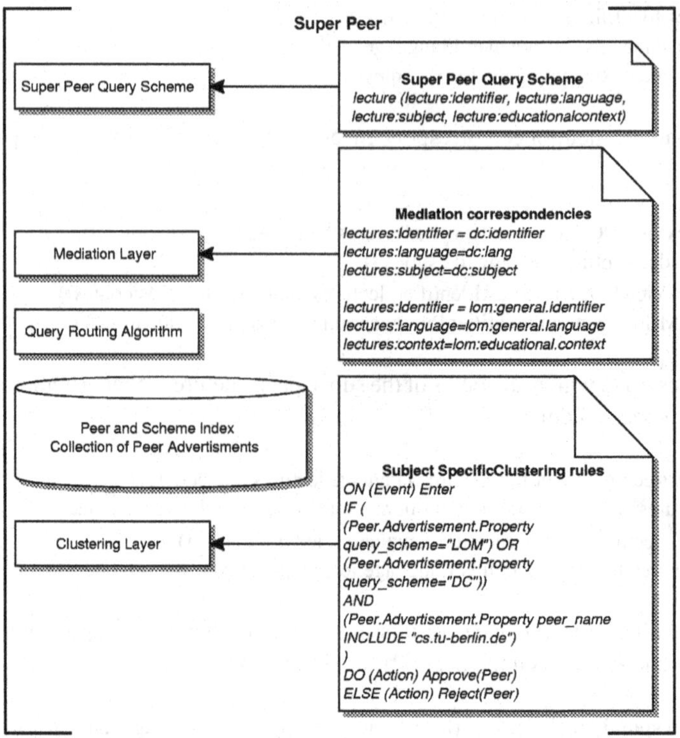

Fig. 3. Context specific Super Peer for E-Learning Materials

4 Conclusion

Schema-based P2P networks have a number of important advantages over previous simpler P2P networks. Peers in these networks provide and use explicit (possibly heterogeneous) schema descriptions of their content, thus allowing us to build up an infrastructure ideally suited to connect heterogeneous information providers.

We proposed a super-peer topology as a suitable topology for these schema-based P2P networks and discussed how the schema information can be used for routing and clustering in such a network. In our approach super-peer indices exploit the RDF ability to uniquely identify schemas, schema attributes and ontologies, and are used for routing between super-peers and peers as well as within the super-peer backbone network.

Combining rule based clustering and correspondences between different schemas is used to adaptively collect and filter heterogeneous information sources and to integrate them in a context specific way mediated through super-peers. This approach combines the dynamic self organizing behavior of peer-to-peer networks with existing information integration concepts of mediator-based information systems. In comparison to traditional mediator-based information systems, information consumers and information providers can connect dynamically and schema usage can be extended dynamically.

Rule based clustering in large heterogeneous super-peer networks can cluster peers efficiently to avoid broadcasting and flooding the network with queries. Subject specific clustering techniques can create peer based ontologies of information consumers and information providers for a specific context.

References

1. K. Aberer, P. Cudré-Mauroux, and M. Hauswirth. The chatty web: Emergent semantics through gossiping. In *Proceedings of the Twelfth International World Wide Web Conference (WWW2003)*, Budapest, Hungary, May 2003.
2. K. Aberer and M. Hauswirth. Semantic gossiping. In *Database and Information Systems Research for Semantic Web and Enterprises, Invitational Workshop*, University of Georgia, Amicalola Falls and State Park, Georgia, April 2002.
3. A.Sheth and J. Larson. Federated database systems for managing distributed, heterogeneous, and autonomous databases. *ACM Computing Surveys*, 22(3):183–236, 1990.
4. D. Beckett, E. Miller, and D. Brickley. Expressing simple dublin core in RDF/XML. Technical report, Dublin Core Metadata Initiative, 2002. `http://dublincore.org/documents/2002/07/31/dcmes-xml/`.
5. P. A. Bernstein, F. Giunchiglia, A. Kementsietsidis, J. Mylopoulos, L. Serafini, and I. Zaihrayeu. Data management for peer-to-peer computing: A vision. In *Proceedings of the Fifth International Workshop on the Web and Databases*, Madison, Wisconsin, June 2002.
6. S. Busse. *Model Correspondences in Continuous Engineering of MBIS - doctorial thesis.* Logos Verlag, September 2002.
7. A. Crespo and H. Garcia-Molina. Routing indices for peer-to-peer systems. In *Proceedings International Conference on Distributed Computing Systems*, July 2002.
8. U. Dayal, E. N. Hanson, and J. Widom. Active database systems. In *Modern Database Systems*, pages 434–456. ACM SIGMOD International Conference on Management of Data, 1995.
9. H. Garcia-Molina and B. Yang. Efficient search in peer-to-peer networks. In *Proceedings of ICDCS*, 2002.
10. Gnutella.
11. IEEE P1484.12 Learning Object Metadata Working Group. Draft standard for learning object metadata. Technical report, IEEE Learning Technology Standards Committee (LTSC), 2002. `http://ltsc.ieee.org/doc/wg12/LOM_1484_12_1_v1_Final_Draft.pdf`.
12. A. Kementsietsidis, M. Arenas, and R. J. Miller. Mapping data in peer-to-peer systems: Semantics and algorithmic issues. In *Proceedings of the ACM SIGMOD International Conference on Management of Data)*, June 2003.
13. U. Leser. *Query Planning in Mediator Based Information Systems – doctorial thesis.* TU Berlin, June 2000.
14. F. Naumann. *Quality-Driven Query Answering for Integrated Information Systems - doctorial thesis.* Springer Verlag, lecture notes in computer science, 2261 edition, July 2002.
15. W. Nejdl, B. Wolf, C. Qu, S. Decker, M. Sintek, A. Naeve, M. Nilsson, M. Palmér, and T. Risch. EDUTELLA: a P2P Networking Infrastructure based on RDF. In *WWW 11 Conference Proceedings*, Hawaii, USA, May 2002.
16. W. Nejdl, M. Wolpers, W. Siberski, A. Löser, I. Bruckhorst, M. Schlosser, and C. Schmitz. Super-Peer-Based Routing and Clustering Strategies for RDF-Based Peer-To-Peer Networks. In *Proceedings of the Twelfth International World Wide Web Conference (WWW2003)*, Budapest, Hungary, May 2003.
17. Neo-Modus. Direct Connect Homepage. http://www.neo-modus.com/.

18. M. Oezsu and P. Valduriez. *Principles of distributed database systems*. Prentice Hall, 2nd edition edition, 1999.
19. S. Ratnasamy, P. Francis, M. Handley, R. Karp, and S. Shenker. A scalable content addressable network. In *Proceedings of the 2001 Conference on applications, technologies, architectures, and protocols for computer communications*. ACM Press New York, NY, USA, 2001.
20. M. Schlosser, M. Sintek, S. Decker, and W. Nejdl. HyperCuP—Hypercubes, Ontologies and Efficient Search on P2P Networks. In *International Workshop on Agents and Peer-to-Peer Computing*, Bologna, Italy, July 2002.
21. I. Stoica, R. Morris, D. Karger, M. F. Kaashoek, and H. Balakrishnan. Chord: A scalable peer-to-peer lookup service for internet applications. In *Proceedings of the 2001 Conference on applications, technologies, architectures, and protocols for computer communications*. ACM Press New York, NY, USA, 2001.
22. D. M. Strong, Y. W. Lee, and R. Y. Wang. Data quality in context. *Communications of the ACM*, 40(5):103–110, 1997.
23. J. Widom and U. Dayal. *A Guide To Active Databases*. Morgan-Kaufmann, 1993.
24. G. Wiederhold. Mediators in the architecture of future information systems. *IEEE Computer*, 25(3):38–49, 1992.
25. B. Yang and H. Garcia-Molina. Designing a super-peer network. `http://dbpubs.stanford.edu:8090/pub/2002-13`, 2002.
26. B. Y. Zhao, J. D. Kubiatowicz, and A. D. Joseph. Tapestry: An infrastructure for fault-tolerant wide-area location and routing. Technical Report UCB/CSD-01-1141, UC Berkeley, EECS, 2001.

Processing Queries in a Large Peer-to-Peer System

Leonidas Galanis, Yuan Wang, Shawn R. Jeffery, and David J. DeWitt

University of Wisconsin-Madison Computer Sciences Department
1210 West Dayton Street, Madison, WI 53706, USA
{lgalanis, yuanwang, jeffery, dewitt}@cs.wisc.edu

Abstract. While current search engines seem to easily handle the size of the data available on the Internet, they cannot provide fresh results. The most up-to-date data always resides on the data sources. Efficiently interconnecting data providers, however, is not an easy problem. Peer-to-peer computing is the latest technology to address this problem. However, efficient query processing in peer-to-peer networks remains an open research area. In this paper, we present a performance study of a system that facilitates efficient searches of large numbers of independent data providers on the Internet. In our scenario, each data provider becomes an autonomous node in a large peer-to-peer system. Using small indices on each node, we can efficiently direct queries submitted on any node to the relevant sources. Experiments with a large peer-to-peer network demonstrate the feasibility of our approach.

1 Introduction

Information on the Internet is constantly growing and changing. Search engines and current web repositories ([9], [10] and [16]) can efficiently handle the amount of data on the web and provide fast searches over the data they have crawled and indexed. Nevertheless, they cannot provide the most up-to-date results or search the data storage back-ends of sites that dynamically generate web pages. The only way to access the most recent versions of available data is to directly submit searches to each data source. Therefore, it is not surprising that most content publishers provide their own search service.

A single web query may require a very large number of sites to provide results. Hence, a system is needed that is able to efficiently identify the relevant data sources. A candidate approach would be to organize all the data sources in a large peer-to-peer (P2P) network where queries are answered by the relevant sites. Such a distributed system has several advantages. There is no central point of failure and no central repository necessary to facilitate searches. The absence of a global authority allows sites to enter and leave the system at will, as well as independently manage their data. Finally, each query will always retrieve the most up-to-date results.

Deployment of such a P2P system allows efficient searches across the entire content of a large number of sites. To achieve this, the system must exhibit certain qualities. For each query, it is necessary to efficiently locate all the relevant data sources. Additionally, the entire system must scale to a large number of sites without compromising site independence or performance.

Motivated by the emerging need to query data distributed across many independent data sources, we have built a prototype distributed query processing system for que-

J. Eder and M. Missikoff (Eds.): CAiSE 2003, LNCS 2681, pp. 273–288, 2003.

ries on XML data. Our system makes use of data items that change infrequently and often appear in queries, such as metadata and words characteristic of a specific site. Indices over these data items map this data to the corresponding sites and use these indices to direct queries. When sites join the system, they exchange information that allows for the construction of these indices. Thus, query content drives selection of promising data sources.

Our prototype distributed search engine, the low-level layer of the query processing system, was used to run experiments using real data on a test bed consisting of up to 200 peers. We studied system performance with various levels of information exchanged among nodes in the system. The amounts of exchanged information ranged from no information, which is similar to a Gnutella-like ([8]) processing strategy, to full summary information replicated on each node. Our experiments show a larger than expected performance increase as the number of messages passed at query time is reduced. As more information about peers in the network is stored on each node, network bandwidth usage is reduced due to a large reduction in the number of messages exchanged. Consequently, when each node stores complete summary information about all peers in the P2P network, the average query response time drops by a factor of as much as 75 and query throughput improves by as much as a factor of 20 over a Gnutella-like approach. Our approach efficiently connects data providers, allows queries to retrieve the most up-to-date data, preserves site autonomy, and puts reasonable demands on the bandwidth of the network.

This paper is organized as follows: In Section 2, we present the system architecture of our approach. Section 3 describes the join policies for peers. Section 4 outlines the methods for selecting peers relevant to queries. Section 5 describes our experimental setup. We present the results of our experiments in Section 6. Section 7 reviews related work and Section 8 draws conclusions and presents future research directions.

2 System Architecture

Each node in the peer-to-peer system consists of an XML search engine and a communication infrastructure that allows communication among peers. The local XML search engine [29] enables document searches based on both structure and content. Along with the local indices, each node maintains additional indices that facilitate the forwarding of queries to data providers that have relevant data. When peers join the peer-to-peer system, they exchange information with peers already in the network for two main reasons: a) They need to make their presence known to the system and advertise their data and b) they want to obtain index information about other peers in the system from the peers to which they are directly connected.

Advertising a node's data to other nodes in the system requires a meaningful summarization of gigabytes of data. Fortunately, XML provides mark-up tags that describe a data collection. Usually, a large XML data collection has a relatively small set of descriptive XML elements. Furthermore, a data collection at a node may have text words that are characteristic of that node. We will refer to XML elements and text words collectively as *keywords*. For example, an art auction site can be distinguished by the fact that it stores elements called *item*, *price*, or *current_bid* and contains text words such as "painting" or "sculpture". The elements for an online retailer could be *item*, *price*, and *brand*. It would also have different characteristic text words such as "electronics" or "books". XML metadata and classification techniques such as [12] and [3] provide further ways to summarize the content of peers. Throughout this paper it is assumed that the XML tags provided by the participating nodes have-system wide defined semantics. The system does not try to compensate for semantic heterogeneity, which is an orthogonal problem. Section 4 outlines why our design is still valid even in the presence of semantic heterogeneity.

2.1 XML Search Engine

Our search engine framework supports the execution of *containment queries* that fully exploit the structure in XML documents. For example, the query (in XPath notation [25]) *//book//author//name="John Smith"* returns all documents that contain books by John Smith. Each search engine indexes its local data using inverted lists, which map keywords to documents. These indices enable the processing of containment queries as in the Niagara system [14]. Our version uses B+-Trees to implement inverted lists and employs an improved version of the Multi-Predicate Merge Join algorithm presented in [29]. A search engine that facilitates complex queries over structured data distinguishes our system from file-sharing systems.

2.2 Peer Indices

In addition to its local inverted indices, each node maintains indices containing information residing at other peers in the network. The *peer index* (PI) is a simple inverted list that maps keywords to peers in the network and is used for selecting peers based on query content. Each peer stores in its PI all keywords published by other peers during joining. Using the PI, a query can be sent directly to nodes that are likely to have results. Section 4 presents how our prototype system uses the peer indices.

The number of keywords in the PI, and thus the size of the PI, depends on how many keywords each peer decides to publish when it joins the system and how many keywords each peer decides to retain in its PI. We expect a node to only publish a small subset of its keywords, such as words that are often found in queries or that are especially representative of its local data. XML tags are especially good candidate keywords since they are regarded as being descriptive of the actual data. PI entries for tags can also contain structural information which allows the system to further distinguish among data sources.

The simplicity and generality of the PI concept makes it applicable to data collections other than XML. We chose XML for our prototype system because it seems to be the emerging standard for information exchange and data integration. In general, any distributed data collection that can be queried using some query language can benefit from PIs. The rough guideline is as follows: Items that appear in queries and are characteristic of a data collection should be put in the PI. For example in the context of relational data one could put attribute and table names in the PI in order to facilitate query routing given a SQL query. Furthermore, selected data values (such as names of cities) can also be incorporated into the PI.

2.3 Horizons

Knowledge of all the peers in the system may seem limiting for scaling the system to a very large number of peers. By introducing a *horizon*, a node can bound the number of peer IDs that it stores in its PI.

Definition 1: A node N enforces a *horizon* if it stores in its PI only a subset of the peers in the network. IDs of peers outside of N's horizon are substituted with IDs of peers within N's horizon. Queries that need to be sent to peers outside N's horizon are relayed by nodes within N's horizon.

When a peer joins the P2P network, it starts with an initial PI obtained from another peer and then modifies its PI based on local storage constraints and query workload characteristics, evicting infrequently used keywords and nodes. Thus, a peer's horizon evolves to contain information about frequently queried keywords and nodes that usually return relevant results. The evolution of a PI horizon is depicted in Fig. 1. The size and shape of the horizon is dependent on N's storage constraints and query workload. The tradeoff is that a small horizon will result in more messages for a query that retrieves data outside the horizon, whereas a large horizon will require more storage space for peer information.

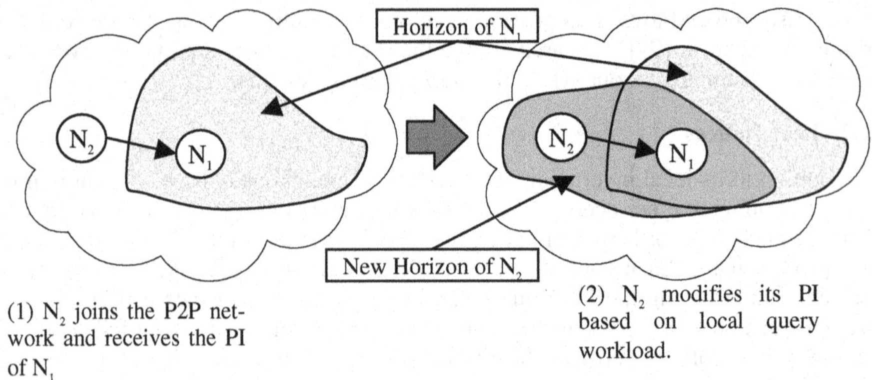
Horizon of N1
N2
N1
N2
N1
New Horizon of N2
(1) N2 joins the P2P network and receives the PI of N1
(2) N2 modifies its PI based on local query workload.

Fig. 1. The evolution of a peer index

3 System Evolution

A peer becomes part of the P2P network by *joining*. The general case of a join between two nodes, shown in Fig. 2, arises when node N_1 contacts node N_2 by sending a *join request*. Both nodes have already joined with other nodes and belong to existing join graphs.

Definition 2: A *Join Graph* is a non-directed graph $G(V, E)$ where $V = \{N_i \mid \text{node } N_i$ has joined with at least one $N_j \neq N_i\}$ and $E = \{(N_i, N_j) \mid \text{node } N_i \text{ has joined with } N_j\}$.

Definition 3: The *Distance* of two nodes N_i and N_j ($d(N_i, N_j)$) is the number of hops on the shortest path from N_i to N_j in the Join Graph.

The join graph represents a logical overlay network and illustrates how nodes joined with one another. It does not correspond to the underlying network topology. Thus, the distance between two nodes does not necessarily reflect the communication cost between them. The system uses the join graph for every message that has to flow to others peers in the system, such as join update messages and update messages that nodes create when their data changes.

When peers join the system, they receive information about already existing peers. Thus, a newly joined node ends up with a PI that contains information about all exchanged keywords in the system and all the peers in its initial horizon. Joining starts when a peer N_1 contacts another peer N_2 and requests to join the P2P network. The joining nodes exchange messages containing information about their local data and their peer index. This new information is then sent to each node's neighbors. The resulting messages flow throughout the join graph and are processed exactly once on each node. Thus, a join between two peers creates a wave of messages that eventually reaches all the peers in the system. The result is a peer-to-peer network in which each node has a summary of the data on all other peers.

Propagating information to every node in the network whenever a new node joins may seem limiting for the network's scalability. We, however, expect our system to be used by data repositories that want to make their data available as long as possible with only short down-times, rather than by individual users that share media files. It is expected that a peer may go down for a short time. When it comes back up, however, only an update containing the returning node's changed data, if any, needs to be propagated through the network.

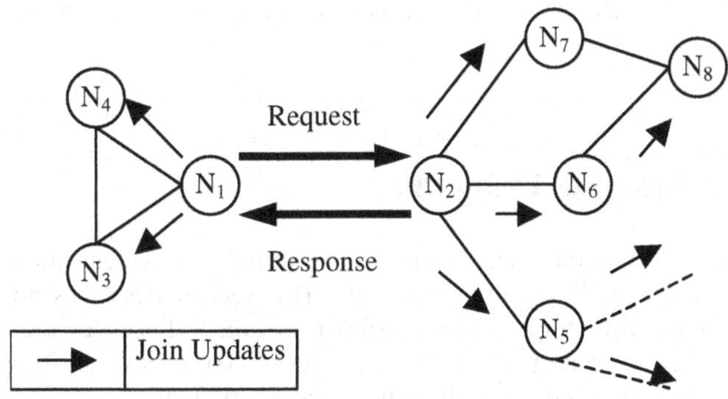

Fig. 2. Node N_1 joins with node N_2

We employ a simple network join algorithm that guarantees all nodes eventually obtain a summary of the data on all other peers. However, if nodes do join and leave frequently, alternative methods of joining can be employed. One such approach would be to use an *incremental join.* As with the simple join algorithm, the incremental join begins with a newly arriving peer receiving a PI from a directly connected peer. However, update messages about the new peer are not propagated to all neighbors. As the new peer issues queries, it piggybacks selected keyword data on its query messages. The data that is attached to the message is based on factors such as the content of the query, the length of time the node has been connected, and the size of the message. Through this process, the new peer informs other peers incrementally. Conversely, when other peers' queries arrive at the new node, it receives information about the rest of the network. Thus, the system gradually evolves to a state which is the result of the global query workload. The dynamic evolution of the PIs is an open issue left as future work.

Based on the premise that each node chooses a set of keywords that is characteristic of its data, one can argue that this set will remain fairly stable over time. Periodically or when triggered by update events, a node may decide to inform its peers about new or modified local data. It constructs an update message and propagates this throughout the system along the edges of the join graph. When a peer receives an update, it processes it, replacing old entries in the PI or removing obsolete ones.

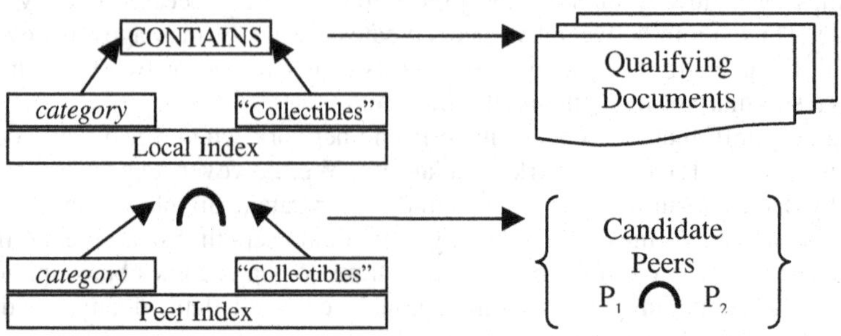

Fig. 3. Peer selection example for the query *//category*[*text*() *contains "Collectibles"*]"

4 Efficient Searches Using PIs

Using the peer indices constructed during node joining, nodes can direct searches to the nodes that are most likely to have results. This section describes how the system uses those indices. The simple example shown in Fig. 3 illustrates the basic mechanism of selecting candidate peers for a given query. To retrieve all XML documents that contain a category element that contains the word "Collectibles", one would use the query Q = *//category*[*text*() *contains "Collectibles"*]. Executing Q on the local inverted index, the system retrieves a collection of local documents that satisfy Q. Querying the PI yields two sets of peers, P_1 and P_2, for the element *category* and the word "Collectibles," respectively. Each peer in P_1 has *category* elements in its index and each peer in P_2 has "Collectibles" words in its index. The set $P_1 \cap P_2$ contains peers that are likely to have results, while it is reasonably certain, assuming all updates have been received, that peers in $(P_1 - P_2) \cup (P_2 - P_1)$ will not have any qualifying documents. Thus, if the system sends the query to peers in $P_1 \cap P_2$, we will get all possible results and at the same time will not take up resources of peers in $(P_1 - P_2) \cup (P_2 - P_1)$. Note that if either of the inputs of the intersection does not have any peers associated with it, the system reverts to a union, expanding the set of candidate peers in hope of finding results. For example, if P_2 were empty, the system would send the query to all or some of the *category* peers in case they return any results. Due to space limitations and the fact that our experimental data does not benefit from structural information in the PIs we do not present the structural details in this paper.

The semantic meaning of the tag *category* and the word "Collectibles" may not be uniform across the nodes that will receive the query. Hence, the results may contain documents that will not match what the user had in mind but will definitely match the query correctly. A post-processing step on the results based on *themes* as proposed in [2] can achieve semantic correctness. In any case, the goal of contacting only a small subset of the nodes in the system will have been achieved. Section 5 shows how important it is to reduce the number of nodes contacted given a query.

5 Experimental Setup

We have compared several strategies for P2P query propagation on a 100-node cluster of PCs, which was used to stage 100-node and 200-node peer-to-peer networks. We create a scenario where a large number of data providers publish frequently changing data and desire to make it searchable by their peers. Four aspects make up our methodology: the scenario, the data, the peer-to-peer system set-up, and the simulation of users submitting queries to nodes in the system.

5.1 Scenario

Our scenario considers a large distributed auctioning system. Nodes are independent auction sites with subscribers who sell their items and bid on ongoing auctions. Each auction site specializes in specific categories of items. Users at each site would like to be able to pose queries that will be answered by all peers in the peer-to-peer system that may have relevant data. Sites may join the system by contacting any peer they choose. The result is a system that has a large number of nodes in a logical network similar to those in existing peer-to-peer systems.

```
<Item id="1045782232">
        <Name>US Navy Flag Cards</Name>
        <Category>Collectibles</Category>
        <Category>Cards</Category>
        <Currently>$24.00</Currently>
        <Quantity>1</Quantity>
        <Number_of_Bids>0</Number_of_Bids>
```

Fig. 4. XML document excerpt

5.2 Data

Since we wanted to evaluate these strategies on real and not synthetic data, we crawled eBay's US site ([7]) and downloaded data for 6,500,000 items on auction at that time. This data was then used to feed a modified version of the XMark [20] benchmark data generator to augment the synthetic data it creates. This process produced about 45GB of XML data. Fig. 4 shows an excerpt of the item data.

We use the category hierarchy of eBay to divide the data among the peers. The category spectrum is divided into chunks that contain approximately the same number of items. Sets of chunks are assigned to each peer, which in turn, creates local inverted indices on elements and text words. We believe that this set-up represents a realistic environment of independent, interconnected, specialized auction sites.

Table 1. Linux cluster properties

System Property	Value
CPU	PIII 1GHz Dual Processor
Physical Nodes	100
Number of CPUs	200
RAM	1GB
Disk	IDE
OS	Linux 6.2 Kernel 2.2.19
Interconnection Network	100 Base-T
Java VM	IBM VM 1.3.0

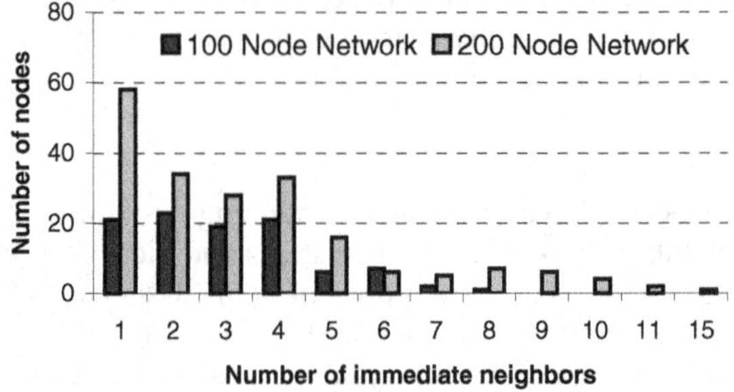

	100 Nodes	200 Nodes
Mean fan-out	3	3.5
Diameter	9	10

Fig. 5. Distribution of join edges in the 100 and 200-node networks

Table 2. Experimental system parameters

Parameter	Value
Unique Element Tags	41
Unique Category Words	4081
Total Categories	5828
Categories Per Node	109 ($\pm$65)
Category Words Per Node	128($\pm$81)
Documents Per Node	60,000-70,000
Keywords Per Node	~110,000
Average Local Index Size	~450 MB
Search Engine Buffer Pool Size	100 MB
Number of Users Per Node	12
User Think Time	15 seconds
User Type Time	9 seconds
Query Processing Threads Per Node	60
Result Collector Timeout	3 Minutes

Table 3. Correspondence of horizon size to query processing strategy

Fixed Radius Horizon Size	Query Processing Strategy
1	Routing indices (*H1*)
2-7	Intermediate levels of system information stored on each node (*H2-H7*)
Infinite	Full Summary Information (*FSI*)

5.3 System Set-Up

A 100-node dual-CPU cluster of PCs running Linux 6.2 (see Table 1) was used to emulate the nodes of a peer-to-peer system. For each peer-to-peer network, we create a join graph. Fig. 5 shows the basic characteristics of the networks used. Before running queries, nodes join with each other in order to produce the pre-defined network. While running, the nodes simulate wide area network delays (60ms exponentially distributed). A list of system parameters is shown in Table 2. Our prototype is implemented in Java with BerkeleyDB [1] used as the storage manager.

The experiments used *fixed radius horizons*. This allowed the study of various levels of peer information on each node and their impact on overall system performance. *Definition 4:* A node *N* has a *fixed-radius horizon* of *h* if it stores peer IDs only for nodes N_i for which the distance $d(N, N_i) \leq h$. The value *h* is the radius of the horizon. With a fixed-radius horizon, a peer only stores information about peers nearby in the join graph and maps the remaining peers to nodes on the horizon boundary. The correspondence of fixed-radius horizon size to query propagation strategy is shown in Table 3.

5.4 Queries and User Simulation

Users in our scenario submit search queries in order to retrieve relevant documents from the system. Those queries can be arbitrarily complex, but contain predicates that allow the selection of candidate peers. Because nodes in our scenario specialize in auction item categories, we use the *category* element content to guide the selection of peers that receive queries. For example, the following query asks for all open auctions that contain an item named "Silver Dollar" that belongs to the "Collectibles" category: *//open_auction//item*[*category.text*() *contains "Collectibles"* AND *name.text*() *contains "Silver Dollar"*]. The peer selection predicate in this case is: *category.text*() *contains "Collectibles"*. For the experiments presented in this paper, queries with only category selection predicates were used. To generate the peer selection predicates for our queries, conjunctions of category words were used to generate a large pool of queries (about 200,000). Each node is assigned a number of queries and a number of users that randomly submit queries from the node's pool. The users work in cycles thinking and typing as described in [22] before submitting a query. Each user waits a specific time T after submitting a query for the network to return results. T is proportional to the moving average M of the response times of the last 100 queries. We set T = 15×M. This feedback mechanism allows the query rate to converge to a value the system can handle and models user behavior. Users adapt their waiting time to the system's performance.

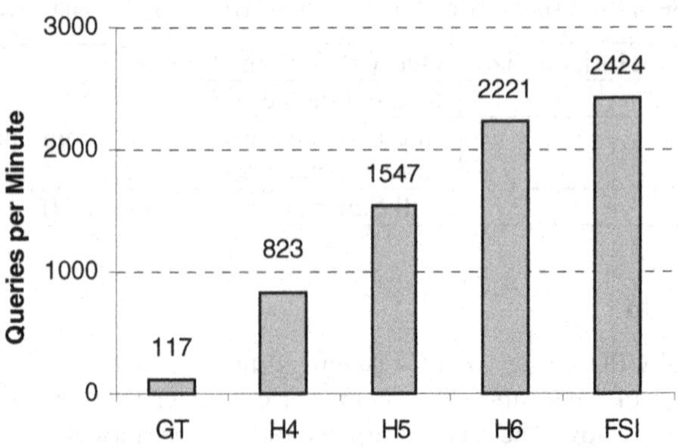

Fig. 6. 100 Nodes, throughput

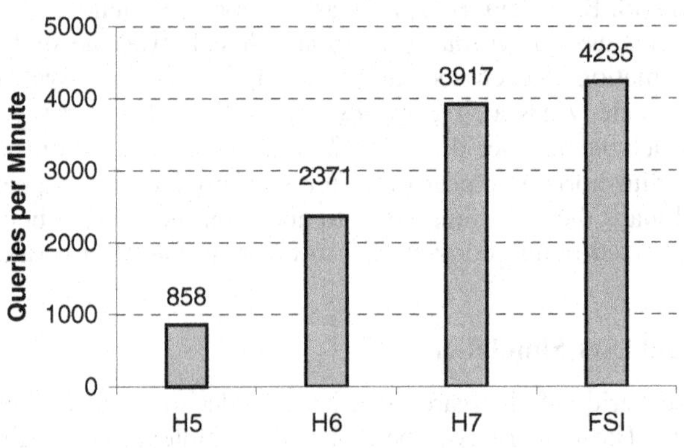

Fig. 7. 200 Nodes, throughput

6 Experiments

The experiments evaluate system performance for two network sizes (100 and 200 nodes) with various fixed radius horizon sizes and full summary information. Results from the naïve case of sending each query to every immediate neighbor (Gnutella-like) are also presented as the baseline approach. Before running experiments, a simulator was used to calculate the expected number of messages that peers would exchange during query processing. The inputs to the simulator are the indices created during joining. The results of the simulation were used to help verify the system experiments.

To take measurements, we used a time window *W*, usually 20-30 minutes long, during which all users in the system were submitting queries. For each configuration, the average query response time over all the queries within the time window *W* was computed along with the overall average query throughput. Query response time was defined to be the time to the first result. The average number of messages per query was also computed by normalizing the number of actual messages exchanged by the total number of queries executed during the time window. All 95% confidence intervals of the measurements are within at most ±7% of the corresponding mean values.

The data for the 200-node network was obtained by cloning the data and indices from the 100-node network instead of redistributing and re-indexing. This approach allows us to alter only the size of the network. The node selectivity of queries, the size of the local inverted indices, and the number of keywords that nodes exchange remain constant.

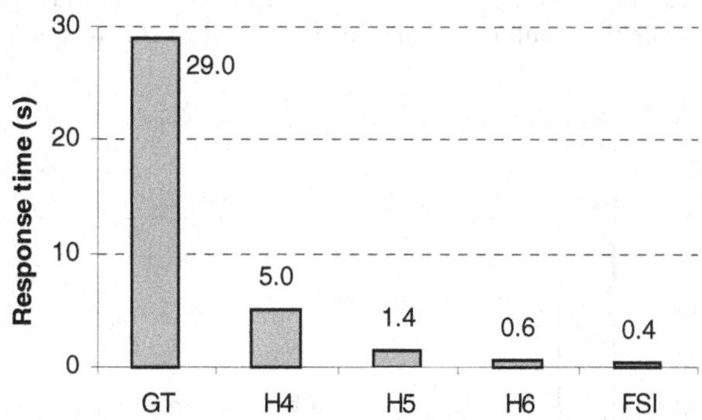

Fig. 8. 100 nodes, response time

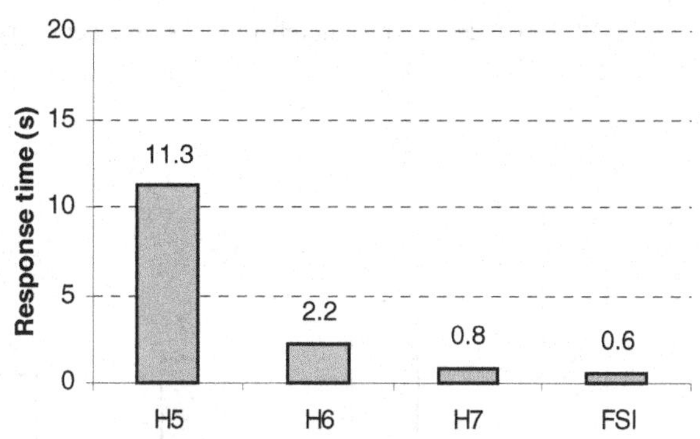

Fig. 9. 200 nodes, response time

6.1 Throughput and Response Time

We performed experiments with a number of different configurations, including the full summary index case (*FSI*), configurations with fixed width horizon sizes of 4 (*H4*), 5 (*H5*), 6 (*H6*), and 7 (*H7*), and a Gnutella-like configuration (*GT*) without any PIs. The results obtained are presented in Figs. 6, 7, 8, and 9. These results clearly indicate that the best performance is obtained by maintaining full summary information about each node in the system: In the 100-Node network the average throughput and query response times are 2,420 queries/min and 0.4 seconds, respectively. In the

200-Node network the corresponding values are 4,240 queries/min and 0.6 seconds respectively. The improvement in query throughput in the 100-node case is 2,071% over the Gnutella-like configuration *GT*. The response time is 72 times better. Note also that query messages in *GT* travel only for 5 hops in the network and thus retrieve only 55% of the results found by the *FSI* configuration. To retrieve all possible results, messages in *GT* would need to travel for even more hops, which would make the performance of this approach even worse. We also observed degrading performance as the radius of the horizon decreased, which is a result of the total number of messages processed by the system as discussed below. Note that *GT* is not reported for 200 nodes since the result of the queries were useless due to system overload.

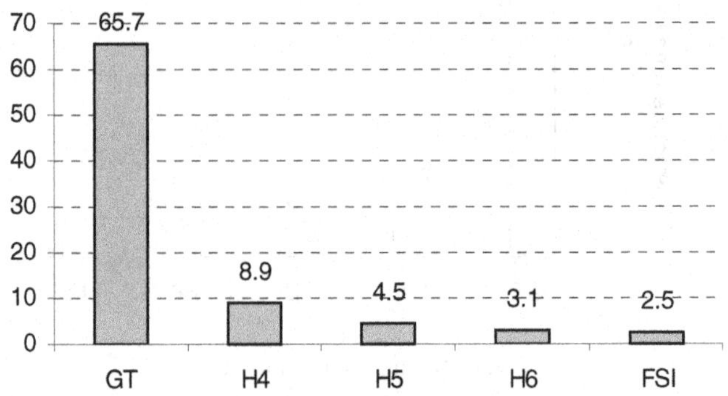

Fig. 10. 100 nodes, average number of messages per query

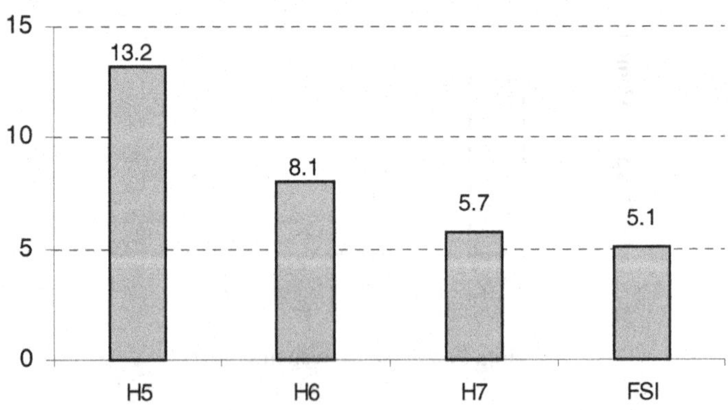

Fig. 11. 200 nodes, average number of messages per query

6.2 Analysis

The average number of messages per query that the system processed during the time window while measurements were being collected is presented in Figs. 10 and 11. The observed message counts fairly closely match the results obtained from the simulation. As expected, the overall performance of the system and the number of query messages exchanged are strongly correlated with one another. The significantly large number of messages the system processes in the case of *GT* explains its unacceptable performance. In our experimental set-up, smaller horizons lead to as many as four times more messages (e.g. *H4* vs. *FSI* on 100 nodes).

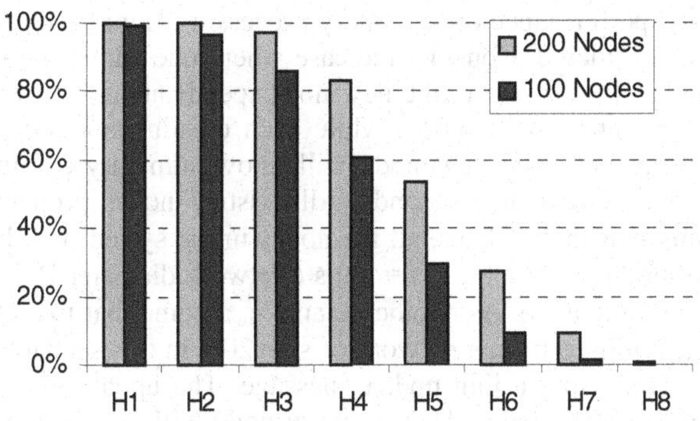

Fig. 12. Percentage of queries out of horizon

To explain the observed number of messages, we calculated the percentage of queries that left their origin horizon, shown in Fig. 12. These results suggest that the increase in the number of messages in smaller horizons is a consequence of the fact that more queries need to exit their respective horizons. Each time a query goes beyond the horizon of its originating node it incurs at least one extra message because it must be relayed to at least one node before reaching the destination. In our experiments, the performance of *H6* with 100 nodes and *H7* with 200 nodes is very close to *FSI* because only a small percentage of the queries leave the horizons of their originating nodes. Thus, the goal should be a system in which at least 90% of the queries stay within their origin horizon. Only *FSI* can guarantee this. If, however, *FSI* is not feasible due to large PI sizes, the system should evolve in a way that decreases the probability of a query going out of a horizon.

Table 4. Average number of messages per query

	GT	*H1*	*H3*	*H4*
100 Nodes	123	30	16	9
200 Nodes	279	110	66	31

Our experiments demonstrate significant performance increases when the number of messages passed at query time is reduced. While it is expected that a naïve query propagation strategy would be inefficient, it is surprising how poorly any strategy that routes queries through other peers performs compared to the *FSI*. Recent efforts ([5]) have focused on efficiently routing queries to the best neighbor. In our scenario, routing, which is essentially *H1*, performs much better than *GT* as can be seen in Table 4. We, however, feel that its use is not justified for two reasons: a) It attempts to replicate functionality already found in current Internet protocols and b) the number of messages it incurs is much higher than that using other small horizons as Table 4 demonstrates. *H1* is significantly better than *GT*, but at the same time much worse than *H3* and *H4*. Additionally, our experimental results demonstrate that *H4* does not perform as well as *FSI*. In order to achieve satisfactory query performance, we believe it is worth allocating the necessary resources needed for *FSI*.

6.3 Join Processing Times

Even though best performance during query processing is our main focus, the cost of joining must be considered. Consider the case where one additional node joins a network of 199 nodes. In our set-up, the new node spends about 4 seconds processing a join response from an existing node, while each existing node spends 0.3 seconds processing join updates. The new node will know summary information about all other nodes in the system in 4 seconds. All existing nodes propagate join updates prior to updating their index. Thus, all the nodes in the system will become aware of the new node after about D·d + 0.3 s = 0.9 s (Network diameter D = 10, average network delay d = .06 seconds). As another example, assume that two existing networks of 100 nodes each join to form a network of size 200. In this scenario, each node will spend about 2s processing a join update message. The update message will contain peer information for 100 nodes. Hence, every node will have summary information about all other nodes in the new network after about 2.6s (D = 9, d = .06). It is clear that in an environment in which nodes do not exhibit the volatile behavior of users sharing music files performing the join we propose is essential for achieving better query throughput.

7 Related Work

Current research efforts with peer-to-peer systems can be largely attributed to the widespread use of file-sharing systems such as Napster [15] and Gnutella [8]. Napster is used for searching collections of media files using centralized indices to which clients connect and upload their file lists and search other users' lists. However, Napster is a hybrid peer-to-peer solution since it employs a centralized index for searches. OpenNap servers [17] work as Napster index servers, but forward queries they cannot answer themselves to a neighbor. A comprehensive study of an OpenNap network appears in [27]. They propose a mathematical model, which they validate on a network of 5 servers. Gnutella is a pure peer-to-peer application that allows searches to flow through a network of interconnected peers. In Gnutella, each peer forwards a search to all its immediate neighbors in a breadth first manner. This simple way of executing searches has been widely criticized for its abuse of network bandwidth. Our study quantifies how wasteful the flooding strategy can be. Recently, support for super-peers has been added to the Gnutella protocol. A study of super-peer networks appears in [28]. In both cases no query content based node selection is performed.

The attempt to reduce wasted bandwidth in the Gnutella network has prompted several research efforts. A simulation study of routing indices is presented in [5]. The goal is to choose the best neighbor of a node to forward the search until the desired number of results is reached. This approach only evaluates routing and does not explore directly contacting relevant peers. Techniques for improving Gnutella performance are presented [26]. Among them is a technique that indexes content of nodes in the neighborhood. The index is not used for routing but for answering queries on behalf of other nodes.

Distributed lookup services have been investigated in [6], [13], [19] and [21]. Supported queries are restricted to object lookups by their keys. In addition, identifiers help route lookups to the relevant data pools. In contrast, our focus is on complex queries on data content. Distributed database systems ([18], [24]) have addressed query processing in a wide area environment, but usually assume full control over all the nodes in the system and the existence of detailed catalogs, and thus do not allow ad-hoc formation of peer-to-peer networks.

Sun's JXTA Search [23] provides searches of data sources that actively produce data, such as news sites. The goal is to retrieve the most up-to-date data, which is not possible using a fully centralized index like Google. At the same time, they try to avoid flooding those data sources with queries, by building indices on the queries a data source can answer. The indices reside on index servers (called hubs), to which affiliated data sources connect. There is no strategy for forwarding queries to other hubs, as they anticipate that nodes of similar topics will connect to the same hubs and that a small number of hubs is sufficient to index large numbers of information providers. However, they have not evaluated their approach on a large number of hubs.

8 Conclusions and Future Work

We have presented a performance study of a peer-to-peer system of autonomous XML search engines with a variety of strategies for P2P query processing. In essence, the join mechanisms pre-compute query destinations and store them in the peer indices. The intended use of our research prototype is as a low-level layer for our distributed query processing system that needs to discover all relevant XML documents for a given query in the philosophy of the Niagara System. Results from large-scale experiments on a pure peer-to-peer system demonstrate significantly improved query throughput and response time over current peer-to-peer architectures. The prototype we have implemented will be used as a test bed for future research into join algorithms, as well as various query processing techniques.

References

[1] BerkeleyDB. http://www.sleepycat.com.

[2] R. Braumandl, M. Keidl, A. Kemper, D. Kossmann, A. Kreutz, S. Seltzsam, K. Stocker. ObjectGlobe: Ubiquitous query processing on the Internet. VLDB Journal 10(1): 48-71 (2001)

[3] J. Callan, M. Connell, A. Du. Automatic Discovery of Language Models for Text Databases. SIGMOD 1999 Conference.

[4] J. Chen, D. J. DeWitt, F. Tian, Y. Wang. NiagaraCQ: A Scalable Continuous Query System for Internet Databases. SIGMOD 2000 Conference.

[5] A. Crespo, H. Garcia-Molina. Routing Indices For Peer-to-Peer Systems. Tech Report http://dbpubs.stanford.edu:8090/pub/2001-48

[6] F. Dabek, M. F. Kaashoek, D. Karger, R. Morris, I. Stoica. Wide-area cooperative storage with CFS. SOSP 2001

[7] eBay. http://www.ebay.com

[8] Gnutella Resources. http://gnutella.wego.com/.

[9] GoXML. http://www.goxml.com
[10] Google. http://www.google.com
[11] S. Gribble, A. Halevy, Z. Ives, M. Rodrig, D. Suciu. What Can Databases Do for Peer-to-Peer. WebDB Workshop 2001.
[12] P.G. Ipeirotis, L. Gravano, M. Sahami. Probe, Count, and Classify: Categorizing Hidden-Web Databases. SIGMOD 2001 Conference.
[13] J. Kubiatowicz et al. OceanStore: An Architecture for Global-Scale Persistent Storage. In Proc. ASPLOS 2000.
[14] J.F. Naughton, D.J. DeWitt et al. The Niagara Internet Query System. IEEE Data Engineering Bulletin 24(2): 27–33(2001)
[15] Napster. http://www.napster.com
[16] B. Nguyen, S. Abiteboul, G. Cobena, M. Preda. Monitoring XML Data on the Web. SIGMOD 2001 Conference
[17] OpenNap Project. http://opennap.sourceforge.net
[18] M. T. Özsu, P. Valduriez. Principles of Distributed Database Systems, Second Edition. Prentice-Hall 1999
[19] A. Rowstron, P. Druschel. Storage management and caching in PAST, a large-scale, persistent peer-to-peer storage utility. SOSP 2001
[20] A. R. Schmidt, F. Waas, M. L. Kersten, D. Florescu, I. Manolescu, M. J. Carey, R. Busse. The XML Benchmark Project. Technical Report INS-R0103, CWI, Amsterdam, The Netherlands, April 2001.
[21] I. Stoica, R. Morris, D. Karger, M.F. Kaashoek, H. Balakrishnan. Chord: A Scalable Peer-to-Peer Lookup Service for Internet Applications. In Proc. SIGCOMM 2001.
[22] TPC-C Benchmark Standard Specification Revision 5.0.
[23] S. Waterhouse. JXTA Search: Distributed Search for Distributed Networks. White Paper http://search.jxta.org
[24] R. Williams, D. Daniels, L. Haas, G. Lapis, B. Linsey, P. Ng, R. Obermarck, P. Selinger, A. Walker, P. Wilms, R. Yost. R*: An Overview of the Architecture. IBM Research Report RJ3325.
[25] XML Path Language (XPath) 2.0 http://www.w3.org/TR/xpath20/
[26] B. Yang, H. Garcia-Molina. Efficient Search in peer-to-peer networks. In Proc. ICDCS 2002.
[27] B. Yang, H. Garcia-Molina. Comparing Hybrid Peer-to-Peer Systems. In Proc. VLDB 2001.
[28] B. Yang, H. Garcia-Molina. Designing a Super-Peer Network, In Proc. ICDE 2003.
[29] C. Zhang, J.F. Naughton, D.J. DeWitt, Q. Luo, G. Lohman. On Supporting Containment Queries in Relational Database Management Systems. SIGMOD 2001 Conference.

Consistent Process Execution in Peer-to-Peer Information Systems

Klaus Haller and Heiko Schuldt

Database Research Group, Institute of Information Systems
Swiss Federal Institute of Technology (ETH Zürich)
CH-8092 Zürich, Switzerland {haller,schuldt}@inf.ethz.ch

Abstract. The proliferation of Internet technology resulted in a high connectivity between individuals and companies all over the world. This technology facilitates interactions within and between enterprises, organizations, etc. and allows for data and information exchange. Automating business interactions on this platform requires the execution of processes. This process execution has to be reliable, i.e., guarantees for correct concurrent and fault tolerant execution are vital. A strategy enforcing these properties must take into consideration that large-scale networks like the Internet are not always reliable. We deal with this by encapsulating applications within mobile agents. Essentially, this allows users to be temporary disconnected from the network while their application is executing. To stress the aspect of guarantees, we use the term *transactional agents*. They invoke services provided by resources, which are responsible for logging and conflict detection. In contrast, it is the transactional agents' task to ensure globally correct concurrent interactions by means of communication. The used communication pattern is a sample implementation of our newly developed protocol. It is, to our best knowledge, the first distributed protocol that addresses the global problem of concurrency control and recovery in a truly distributed way and that, at the same time, jointly solves both problems in a single framework. Because (i) processes are long running transactions requiring optimistic techniques and (ii) large networks require decentralized approaches, this protocol meets the demands of process-based applications in large scale networks.

1 Introduction

The proliferation of Internet technology in the recent years resulted in a high connectivity between individuals and companies all over the world. Together, they form a unique world-wide platform for business interactions, or – more general – for data and information exchange. Hence, this technology facilitates interactions within and between enterprises, organizations, etc. This offers new opportunities for automating business interactions, because a wide variety of services – like booking flights and hotels or registering for conferences – are today supported by computers and can be invoked over the network, e.g., the Internet. Application development in this context requires to combine different invocations of such services into a coherent whole. This is done by using *processes*. Each activity of a process corresponds to a service invocation or, in case of intra-process parallelism, to the invocation of a set of semantically equivalent services.

J. Eder and M. Missikoff (Eds.): CAiSE 2003, LNCS 2681, pp. 289–307, 2003.

Vital to such process-based applications in large-scale dynamic networks like the Internet is to have sophisticated system support guaranteeing that executions are reliable. Essentially, process executions have to be shielded from unreliable network connections. However, several problems resulting from this kind of environment have to be solved in order to provide a holistic solution for reliable process execution.

First, the dynamics of the network has to be taken into account. This means that the location of services to be invoked as process activities is not known at built-time when processes are specified (*dynamic service providers*). Hence, it is not possible to hard-code this information. Consequently, the services corresponding to process activities have to be specified by using predicates. In a travel planning process, for instance, an activity should rather be specified like 'Go to all European airlines and search for flights from Zürich to Klagenfurt' instead of coding this in the traditional way 'Go to `www.swissair.com` and `www.aua.com` and invoke appropriate services (whose names have also to be known at built-time) there'. Obviously the second approach has disadvantages in a dynamic world where certain airlines stop operation or, more importantly, new low-price airlines start operation.

Second, the characteristics of the underlying network have to be considered. Essentially, when the *network is unreliable*, e.g., when network partitioning takes place or when bottlenecks occur, this has severe effects on the execution of processes. If, for instance, the travel planning process is executed on a mobile device like a PDA, this device has to be connected to the network as long as the process is executing. Otherwise, process execution would stop since remote services could no longer be invoked. The same problem arises in case of network partitioning if a process wants to invoke a service that belongs to a different partition. To cope with this problem, both process descriptions and their execution states have to be brought to the hosts on which the services reside. To do this, we use the concept of mobile agents [Whi97]. Processes are encapsulated in a single mobile agent which migrates through the network for the purpose of process execution. In the case of intra-process parallelism, the mobile agent clones such that these clones are able to invoke different services at the same time even at different hosts. In terms of the travel planning application started on a PDA, this paradigm gives the user the freedom to disconnect from the network after her application is launched. For all these reasons, mobile agents seamlessly provide support to problems related to unreliable network connections.

Third, since service providers are autonomous, they can unilaterally decide to revoke their services. This might have severe consequences on process executions when among these services a particular service has been unique in the network (i.e., when there is no semantically equivalent service left). Essentially, all processes in which this service is to be used cannot continue their execution. However, in order to reliably execute processes, each process has to terminate in a well-defined state, even in the case of failures of the underlying network, in the case services disappear, or when run-time failures of process instances occur. Yet, all these failures have to be handled in a flexible way. Essentially, failure handling for processes must not be realized with an "all-or-nothing" semantics meaning that all effects of a process are undone after a failure occurs. Rather, following the idea of transactional processes [SABS02] which support semantic atomicity [GM83], appropriate alternative execution strategies should be considered. These alternative strategies have to be specified at built-time. Most importantly, they allow for flexible failure handling by forward recovery [Tay86]. In the travel planning example, such a contingency strategy could be to search for a train connection when no appropriate flight is offered or when all seats are already booked.

Finally, different processes may concurrently access shared data, wrapped by services. In this case, appropriate mechanisms are required to protect processes to interfere with each other in an undesired way. Obviously, this *isolation* property requires that flow of information between independent processes via shared services is controlled such that a consistent view of the overall system is guaranteed. Therefore, the system is responsible for controlling the concurrent access to shared services and, as a consequence, to correctly synchronize parallel processes. The latter two problems, i.e., (semantic) atomicity and isolation, are well understood in traditional database systems. However, the first two aspects mentioned above – unreliable network connections and dynamically evolving networks– require to re-think the solutions that have been proposed so far. Conventionally, transaction management supporting atomic and isolated executions relies on a centralized coordinator, i.e., a transaction manager.

However, such a centralized approach is not suitable in large-scale, unreliable and dynamic networks. First, having a dedicated place for controlling all applications within the overall network might soon become a bottleneck when the number of processes increases. Second and more importantly, processes are not able to execute correctly in case the coordinator cannot be contacted due to some network failure. For all these reasons, a solution for the problems related to failure handling and synchronization has to be combined with mobile agents we use as operational environment for process execution. Support for flexible failure handling requires that alternative execution strategies are made available to these agents as parts of the process specification such that these alternatives can be effected in case of failures. While this can be seamlessly solved locally within each agent, support for the global problem of synchronizing concurrent process executions requires a more radical shift of paradigm. The synchronization of concurrent applications is shifted to the individual agents. Hence, the global problem is solved by distributing meta information needed for synchronization purposes to the individual agents. This meta information is then kept consistent by means of communication. In particular, it allows to locally decide whether multi-agent executions are correct.

The combination of all these aspects leads to a framework supporting *information processing in peer-to-peer environments*. We ensure that processes – which not only search for and retrieve data, but also manipulate data – are executed in peer-to-peer networks with transactional guarantees. The main contribution of this paper is a decentralized approach to process synchronization. This approach is embedded into an operational environment in which mobile agents flexibly execute processes in dynamic peer-to-peer networks. Within the AMOR project (Agents, MObility, tRansactions) of ETH Zürich, we have built a prototype system that accounts for all different aspects.

The paper is organized as follows: We start with an overview of the AMOR system (Section 2), followed by a discussion of the decentralized transaction processing architecture in Section 3. Section 4 discusses the main ideas underlying the AMOR protocol. The latter will be presented in detail in Section 5. We discuss the AMOR-prototype in Section 6. Section 7 provides a survey of related work. Section 8 concludes.

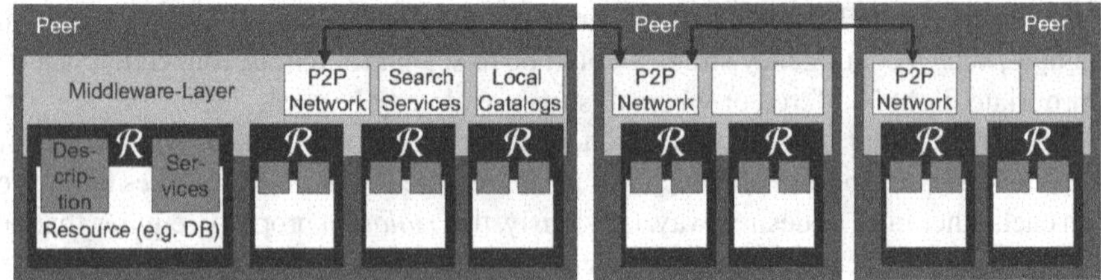

Fig. 1. The AMOR System Model

2 The AMOR System

The bottom layer of the AMOR system encompasses a set of distributed and autonomous *resources*, e.g., database systems or flat files (Figure 1). Such resources are wrapped by so-called *resource agents* ($\mathcal{R}$). Each resource provides a certain set of services to the outside world. This allows to hide the details of the type of resources and the implementation of services. Thus, by using a service-oriented interface, data access and manipulation takes place at a semantically higher level of abstraction compared to traditional read/write operations in databases. However, in order to make these services available, each resource agent has to provide metadata describing its type and the semantics of its resource, e.g., whether it manages flights or databases. More formally, we denote by $\mathcal{S}^*$ the universe of all services offered and, accordingly, the universe of all resource agents in our system by $\mathcal{R}^*$. We assume the resources wrapped by all $\mathcal{R}_i, \mathcal{R}_k \in \mathcal{R}^*$ to be pairwise disjoint. With this, we demand that the services of a resource agent only operate on local resources and are not redirected to remote resources.

All resources and therefore also the resource agents reside on *peers*[1]. Hosts may accommodate more than one resource agent. Also, the number of resource agents may differ between peers. Peers communicate with each other via the AMOR middleware layer (Figure 1). This layer forms a peer-to-peer (P2P) network out of the single peers. Each of them can unilaterally and spontaneously decide to join or leave the network such that the network configuration continuously evolves.

On top of this peer-to-peer network, mobile *transactional agents* execute processes. Each transactional agent corresponds to a process instance. Processes consist of a set of partially ordered activities. Activities, in turn, correspond to service invocations wrapped by some $\mathcal{R}_i$. When specifying a process, a programmer has to describe the type of services that are to be invoked as process activities. In addition, certain activities allow for several semantically equivalent services to be invoked in parallel. For example, finding the cheapest flight to some destination may take place by contacting several resources concurrently. Hence, it is the task of the programmer to set the level of concurrency for individual activities. All this information is the input for an agent generator which assembles a mobile transactional agent (Figure 2). This agent executes the process by migrating from peer to peer within the network and by locally invoking services. More formally, a transactional agent $\mathcal{T}_i$ is a pair $(S_i, <_i)$ where $S_i \subseteq \mathcal{S}^*$ is a set of services

[1] In the mobile agents terminology, they are also called *places*.

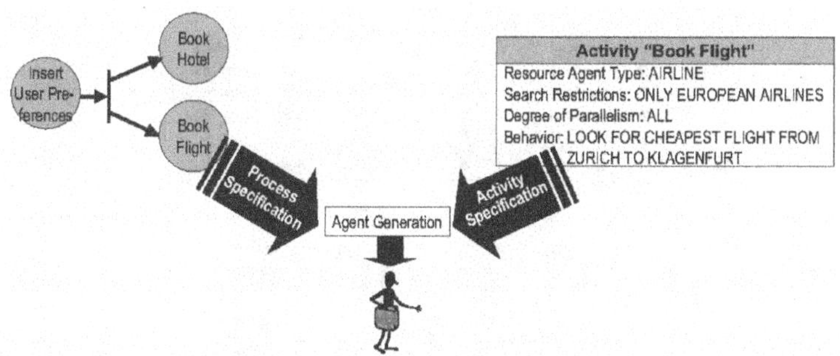

Fig. 2. Agent Generation Process

invoked by $\mathcal{T}_i$ and $<_i \subseteq S_i \times S_i$ is the (partial) invocation order of the services of S_i with c_i (commit) or a_i (abort) as terminal elements.

The invocation of services requires that services which meet the specified semantics can be found dynamically. Hence, the run-time environment has to support the search for particular services by providing service repositories where services are described for example by WSDL. This search functionality is incorporated into the peer-to-peer middleware layer. This layer evaluates the specification of an activity (Figure 2) to be executed next and returns the location of appropiate $\mathcal{R}$s. Then – if parallelism is desired – the agent clones and each clone migrates to a dedicated $\mathcal{R}$. After all prallel service invocations have succeeded, the next activity, according to the process specification, is executed. Again, the agent searches for potential peers (possibly clones) and migrates to the peer where the service invocaction takes place. In case of a failure, the system should be brought back to a consistent state. Additionally – to enforce consistency – also the flow of information between processes has to be controlled in order to enforce consistency.

3 The AMOR Approach for Decentralized Transaction Processing

In this section, we present the basic concepts of the AMOR decentralized approach to transaction management. This includes a comparison with the conventional transaction management architecture. Thereby, we focus on how to enforce the isolation property in AMOR. In AMOR, each $\mathcal{T}_i$ represents an individual, independent, and distributed transaction. In such environments, transaction management is typically provided by a dedicated coordinator, e.g., a TP Monitor [BN97]. The coordinator's task is to orchestrate the execution of distributed transactions, in particular, to enforce not only their atomic commitment but also their isolated execution by using a 2PC/2PL-protocol [GR93]. This requires all transactions of the system to register with the coordinator such that the latter one is equipped with global knowledge.

Such a centralized approach is highly appropriate for small, well-delimited environments with a fixed number of peers, but it cannot be applied to large-scale networks with a large number of distributed, heterogeneous, and autonomous peers (e.g., the intranet of an international company, not to speak about globally distributed networks like the

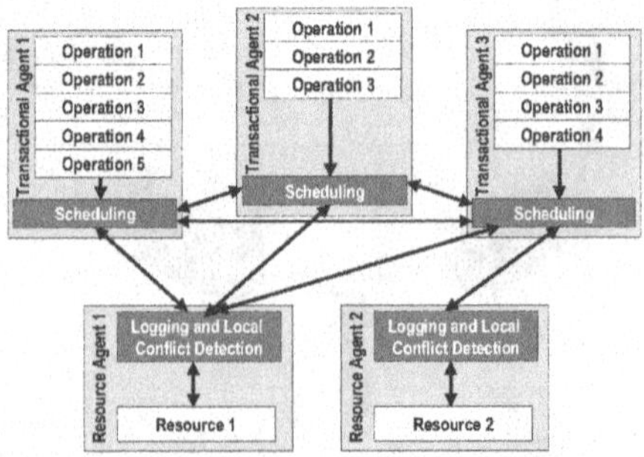

Fig. 3. Decentralized AMOR Approach to Transaction Processing

semantic web). In addition, also administrative aspects (i.e., peers might dynamically join or leave the system) prohibit centralized approaches to be used efficiently.

Hence, we must strive for a *distributed implementation* of the functionality of a coordinator. Following the unified theory of concurrency control and recovery [VHBS98], this coordinator jointly enforces both atomicity and isolation. In terms of recovery, each failure of some $\mathcal{T}_i$ has to be handled properly, either by an alternatvie execution or by undoing the effects of all services it has invoked so far (semantic atomicity). If $\mathcal{T}_i$ wants to undo activities, it has to know where they have been executed. Consequently – because there is no centralized component to which all requests are submitted – $\mathcal{T}_i$ itself has to log all its service invocations. Using this log information, a $\mathcal{T}_i$ can undo the effects of its regular services in reverse order (or, if specified in the process model, sets of entities can be undone by additional compensation activities). Hence, the abort of a $\mathcal{T}_i$ is followed by service invocations compensating the previous, regular invocations and finally by the commit of c_i. By this, we can enforce the atomicity property. In addition, the concurrent invocation of services has to be controlled such that each $\mathcal{T}_i$ is correctly shielded from other transactional agents. Shielding means in this context that there is no cyclic flow of information between different transactional agents.

Such a flow of information emerges if different $\mathcal{T}_i$s invoke non-commuting services. Two services do not commute (are in conflict) if their order matters, i.e., if the return values of the two service invocations or those of any succeeding activities change when the conflicting activities were ordered differently. More formally, the invocations of two services $s_{k,j}$ and $s_{k,m}$ provided by resource agent $\mathcal{R}_k$ commute if the return values of all services in the sequence $S' < s_{k,j} < s_{k,m} < S''$ are the same than those in the sequence $S' < s_{k,m} < s_{k,j} < S''$ where S' and S'' are arbitrary sequences of service invocations from $\mathcal{S}^*$ [Aea94]. This conflict behavior belongs to the knowledge of each $\mathcal{R}$. So each $\mathcal{R}$ can reason about its local conflicts. The union of all local conflicts of $\mathcal{R}$ comprises – due to the independence of the resources – all the conflicts of the system.

Conflict information is needed for reasoning about global correctness. This reasoning is based on the notion of schedule. Such a schedule $\mathbf{S}$ is a tuple $\mathbf{S} = (\mathcal{T}_S, <_S)$ reflecting the concurrent execution of a set of transactions $\mathcal{T}_s$ where $<_S$ is the order in which the services of the $\mathcal{T}_i \in \mathcal{T}_S$ are invoked (with $<_i \subseteq <_S$ for all $\mathcal{T}_i$ of $\mathcal{T}_S$).

Using a serialization graph for reasoning about the correctness of a schedule requires global information to be available at a central coordinator — the transaction manager.

However, due to the absence of such a transaction manager in AMOR, conflict information on local service invocations has to be communicated from a resource agent to the corresponding $\mathcal{T}_i$. Then, scheduling can be enforced by distributing this conflict information between transactional agents, thereby replicating meta information needed for synchronization purposes. In Figure 3, this distributed AMOR approach to transaction management is illustrated.

Yet, an important aspect of the AMOR protocol is to bridge the gap between the available, local view of transactional agents and the global knowledge needed to enforce the correctness criteria of the unified theory of concurrency control and recovery. Given the absence of a global coordinator, the challenge is to nevertheless enforce global correctness, although transactional agents are acting autonomously and in parallel while not necessarily having up-to-date information on the services invoked by other transactional agents.

4 Concepts and Data Structures for Decentralized Transaction Processing in AMOR

4.1 Ensuring Correctness at Commit-Time: Requirements and Limitations

The applications implemented by mobile transactional agents are considered to be highly distributed and long-running, thereby far exceeding the complexity and duration of conventional funds transfer transactions. Hence, traditional locking-based protocols, e.g., strict two phase locking, cannot be applied. The reason is that these protocols would – especially when combined with two phase commit protocols – unnecessarily block the access to the underlying resources. In contrast, due to the independence of resources, conflicts may only occur when two transactional agents invoke services on the same resource. Business processes are often characterized as applications for which conflicts are rare. AMOR is supporting this characterization, although it is not a vital requirement for the AMOR protocol.

For all these reasons, we follow an optimistic approach in AMOR. This means that each $\mathcal{T}_i$ executes a service invocation of $\mathcal{T}_i$ on the spot without determining whether is allowed or not. However, prior to the commit of $\mathcal{T}_i$, a validation is required which checks whether it has executed correctly (based on the correctness criteria of the unified theory) and is therefore allowed to commit. This is closely related to well-established optimistic concurrency control protocols like backward-oriented concurrency control, BOCC [KR81]. Following this optimistic protocol, a $\mathcal{T}_i$ is allowed to commit if it does not depend on some active (uncommitted) $\mathcal{T}_j$. In here, dependency means that $\mathcal{T}_i$ and $\mathcal{T}_j$ are in conflict at some resource $\mathcal{R}_k$ by services $s_{k,i}$ invoked by $\mathcal{T}_i$ and $s_{k,j}$ invoked by $\mathcal{T}_j$ with $s_{k,j} < s_{k,i}$. In order to guarantee that no such dependencies exist, each $\mathcal{T}_i$ has to query 'its' resource agents at commit time (i.e, the resource agents where it has invoked services). Then, the latter determine – based on their local log – all local conflicts with active transactional agents in which $\mathcal{T}_i$ is involved. Hence, a transactional agent is allowed to commit correctly i.) when it has queried all resource agents where it has invoked services, ii.) when all have responded to this query, and iii.) when there is no dependency to an uncommitted transactional agent.

While this approach enforces correct concurrency control, it features an important drawback. Essentially, cyclic conflicts and therefore non-serializable executions are not detected until commit time, even when these cyclic conflicts have been imposed much earlier in the work of some $\mathcal{T}_i$. Yet, detecting such cyclic conflicts at an earlier stage, i.e., when they actually appear, would allow for much less redundancy.

4.2 Region Concept

In order to overcome the drawback of enforcing correctness at commit time, we have to detect cycles as early as possible. Thus, we equip each $\mathcal{T}_i$ with metadata reflecting a multi-agent execution. Such metadata – in a first approach – could be a copy of the global serialization graph. This, on the one side, allows each transactional agent to detect cyclic conflicts early. But on the other side, maintaining a copy of the complete serialization graph with each $\mathcal{T}_i$ is not practical since it would impose considerable communication overhead.

However, an important observation is that in the type of system we are addressing, more or less closed –albeit not static– communities exist. These communities are sets of closely related resources accessed by the same transactional agents, i.e., agents which aim at addressing the same or similar tasks. Hence, conflicts are only possible between agents invoking services within the same community. We denote the set of transactional agents executing in such a community as *region*. In terms of the data structures maintained for concurrency control purposes, a region corresponds to the nodes of a connected subgraph of the global serialization graph. Consequently, only this connected subgraph (termed *region serialization graph*) has to be replicated among all $\mathcal{T}_i$ of the same region. Obviously, if all region serialization graphs are free of cycles, so is the global serialization graph. Thus, reasoning about system-wide correctness can be safely shifted to the universe of region serialization graphs. By making use of the partitioning of the system in disjoint regions, AMOR uses replicas of region serialization graphs maintained by each transactional agent to enforce correct multi-agent executions. This requires that i.) conflicts are communicated from resource agents to the corresponding transactional agents and ii.) the replica of region serialization graphs are kept consistent among all $\mathcal{T}_i$ of the same region.

However, regions are not static. Rather, the composition of regions is affected by the services invoked by the transactional agents of a region. For example if a service invocation of $\mathcal{T}_i$ imposes a conflict with a service invocation of a $\mathcal{T}_j$ of another region – as a consequence of this conflict – the two originally independent regions have to be merged.[2] Hence, as an additional requirement for consistent metadata management in AMOR, the two region serialization graphs have to be consolidated and finally distributed among all transactional agents of the new region. Similarly, by correctly committing a transactional agent or in case of a rollback, regions may split and so does the corresponding region serialization graph.

[2] In worst case, when all $\mathcal{T}_i$ conflict, there is only one region and the complete serialization graph has to be replicated.

4.3 Region Serialization Graphs

The task of guaranteeing consistency of replicated region serialization graphs is shifted to the transactional agents of the corresponding region. The information needed for this purpose is provided by the resource agents (such that each $\mathcal{T}_i$ is able to update its local copy of the region serialization graph after a service invocation) and is exchanged between transactional agents by means of asynchronous messages so as to keep the local replica consistent. Every time the local region serialization graph of some $\mathcal{T}_i$ changes due to a service invocation, the complete graph is propagated to all other $\mathcal{T}_j$ of the same region. Essentially, communication between transactional agents has to consider delays in the delivery of messages leading to message overtaking. Therefore, certain extensions to the data structure of region serialization graphs are required.

Consistently with the traditional notion of serialization graph, the nodes of the region serialization graph correspond to transactional agents and the directed edges to conflicts between them. However, the edges are marked with the pairs of service invocations that have caused the edge (note that several such pairs might exist for the same edge). In addition, *each edge* is extended by a version number. However, changes of the serialization graph are communicated by messages. So message overtaking has to be taken into account for instance when messages are delivered along different paths. Then, it is essential to know which information is more up to date, when region serialization graphs are merged after a new graph has been received from another transactional agent.

5 A Protocol for Decentralized Optimistic Transaction Processing

The aim of the AMOR protocol is to enforce correct concurrent and fault tolerant agent execution. This requires communication between transactional agents in order to exchange meta-data regarding the order of conflicting service invocations. The latter is derived from the resource agents. In order to let the transactional agents know about these conflicts, the resource agents have to report local conflicts to them after services have been invoked.

5.1 Service Invocation

Processes are executed by transactional agents $\mathcal{T}_i$. Therefore, they contact resource agents $\mathcal{R}_k$ in order to invoke services $s_{k,i}$ on them. Such services are – due to the optimistic approach followed in AMOR – executed immediately. At the same time, not only each transactional agent logs where it has executed a service, but also the resource agents make a corresponding log entry. Using the local log and the local commutativity relation, each resource agent determines if and which new conflicts have emerged.

In case of new conflicts, $\mathcal{R}_k$ returns information about these conflicts to $\mathcal{T}_i$. This notification contains information on all $\mathcal{T}_m$ this service invocation is in conflict with and the services of these $\mathcal{T}_m$. Then, $\mathcal{T}_i$ – as the receiver of this information – first updates its local region serialization graph: If the graph does not contain a newly emerged edge up to now, meaning that the represented dependency is not known, it is inserted in the graph and the version number (see Section 4.3) is set to one. Otherwise, if the edge

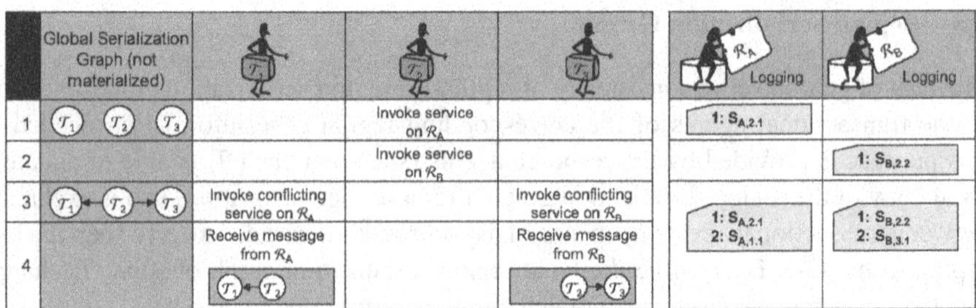

Fig. 4. Example: Service invocation

is marked as removed, it means that such a conflict has existed at least once before. However, it disappeared later because of a partial rollback. Consequently, now, the edge is marked as valid and the version counter increased by one. After $\mathcal{T}_i$ has updated its local graph, it must share this information with the other transactional agents. Therefore, the serialization graph is distributed (see below), before the next service is invoked.

We want illustrate the service invocation procedure with a small sample scenario. In this scenario, we assume two resource agents, $\mathcal{R}_A$ and $\mathcal{R}_B$. On top of them, three transactional agents, $\mathcal{T}_1, \mathcal{T}_2$, and $\mathcal{T}_3$ operate. This execution (and the side-effects on the system state) are illustrated in Figure 4. The left column of this figure depicts the global system information, i.e., the global serialization graph. This information is, however, not permanently materialized by any agent of the system. The other columns contain knowledge materialized in the different agents and the activities performed by the transactional agents.

In the first two steps, $\mathcal{T}_2$ invokes a service on $\mathcal{R}_A$ and one on $\mathcal{R}_B$, respectively. In the third step, the two other transactional agents $\mathcal{T}_1$ and $\mathcal{T}_3$ concurrently invoke services on $\mathcal{R}_A$ and $\mathcal{R}_B$, respectively, which both conflict which the ones of $\mathcal{T}_2$. This is detected by $\mathcal{R}_A$ and $\mathcal{R}_B$. Following the AMOR coordination protocol, they notify $\mathcal{T}_1$ and $\mathcal{T}_3$ about these local conflicts such that $\mathcal{T}_1$ and $\mathcal{T}_3$ can maintain their local region serialization graphs (step 3). Nevertheless, none of the local serialization graphs contains the full knowledge of the (not materialized) global serialization graph: While $\mathcal{T}_2$ is not aware of any conflict, both other transactional agents only know about the conflicts they are involved in. Consequently, the transactional agents have to exchange their information.

5.2 Messaging: Distribution of Metadata

Enforcing consistency between local serialization graphs and the global graph requires that the transactional agents exchange messages. For this, an agent $\mathcal{T}_i$ which has caused a new edge by some service invocation (or any other change of the graph) is responsible for distributing this information within its region, since $\mathcal{T}_i$ is the only one being immediately informed about this by the underlying resource agent.

When a $\mathcal{T}_p$ receives a message from $\mathcal{T}_i$ containing the extended region serialization graph of $\mathcal{T}_i$, it updates its local version of the graph. Thus, $\mathcal{T}_p$ not just replaces its copy with the newly arrived one, but it has to merge the two versions. This is due to the fact that different transactional agents may concurrently invoke services. Consequently, they concurrently update their local copy of the serialization graph. A second reason is that it has to be ensured that newly arrived, yet older data does not overwrite formerly received, newer data during the process of merging. In case an edge appears in both graphs, the one with the higher version number is chosen. Afterwards – to prevent the graph from uncontrolled enlargement – it is checked for nodes that do not belong the region anymore. Such edges can be safely removed.

After merging, $\mathcal{T}_p$ propagates the merged graph to all transactional agents which have been in its local copy but not in the one received from $\mathcal{T}_i$. So they also receive the new information. Hence, also $\mathcal{T}_i$ may be a receiver in case $\mathcal{T}_p$ has knowledge not known to $\mathcal{T}_i$ (e.g., in case of the consolidation of two different regions). The recipients of the message originating from $\mathcal{T}_p$, in turn, merge the new graph with their local replica and again forward it, if needed.[3]

This forwarding and graph merging is the subject of the continuation of our example in Figure 5. After the update of the local serialization graphs, the propagation process is started. Since both $\mathcal{T}_1$ and $\mathcal{T}_3$ have caused changes to their region serialization graph, they have to inform all other transactional agents of the same region (step 5). For this, they depend on their local knowledge about the region. So $\mathcal{T}_1$ and $\mathcal{T}_3$ both only send a message to $\mathcal{T}_2$ encompassing their updated region serialization graph, but not to each other, because both do not know that the other agent also belongs to the same region. In the following step 6, we assume that the message from $\mathcal{T}_1$ arrives at $\mathcal{T}_2$. So $\mathcal{T}_2$ is able to update its graph with the new information. Because $\mathcal{T}_2$ does not have any new information, there is no need to send any message back to $\mathcal{T}_1$. Note that $\mathcal{T}_2$ cannot propagate its graph to $\mathcal{T}_3$, because it does not know about it up to now.

This changes in step 7, when $\mathcal{T}_2$ receives the message of $\mathcal{T}_3$. So $\mathcal{T}_2$ merges the newly received graph from $\mathcal{T}_3$ with its local one. Obviously, simply overwriting the local copy of $\mathcal{T}_2$ is not the correct solution, because information about the conflict between $\mathcal{T}_2$ and $\mathcal{T}_1$ would be lost. But if $\mathcal{T}_2$ merges both graphs, this results in a region serialization graph which now encompasses information on all conflicts of the region.

Afterwards, $\mathcal{T}_2$ has to figure out whether or not it has to propagate its region graph. Because the message sent by $\mathcal{T}_3$ did not contain any edge between $\mathcal{T}_1$ and $\mathcal{T}_2$, $\mathcal{T}_3$ obviously has less information than $\mathcal{T}_2$ and has to be a receiver. The same is true for $\mathcal{T}_1$. So $\mathcal{T}_2$ assumes that $\mathcal{T}_1$ has the same knowledge. Consequently, $\mathcal{T}_2$ reasons that $\mathcal{T}_1$ does not know about the edge between $\mathcal{T}_2$ and $\mathcal{T}_3$. This results in the situation in step 8, in which $\mathcal{T}_2$ forwards its merged graph to $\mathcal{T}_1$ and $\mathcal{T}_3$. Again, these messages contain the complete region serialization graph of the sender ($\mathcal{T}_2$). After the receivers $\mathcal{T}_1$ and $\mathcal{T}_3$ have merged their local graphs with the received graph, all transactional agents have up-to-date region serialization graphs.

5.3 Commit Processing

When a $\mathcal{T}_i$ wants to commit, it first has to check whether an incoming edge to $\mathcal{T}_i$'s node exists in its local replica of the region serialization graph (checking this with the

[3] To reduce the number of messages, it is possible to collect messages going to the same receiver. This does no effect the basic properties of the protocol, if eventually each message is sent to its receiver as described in this section.

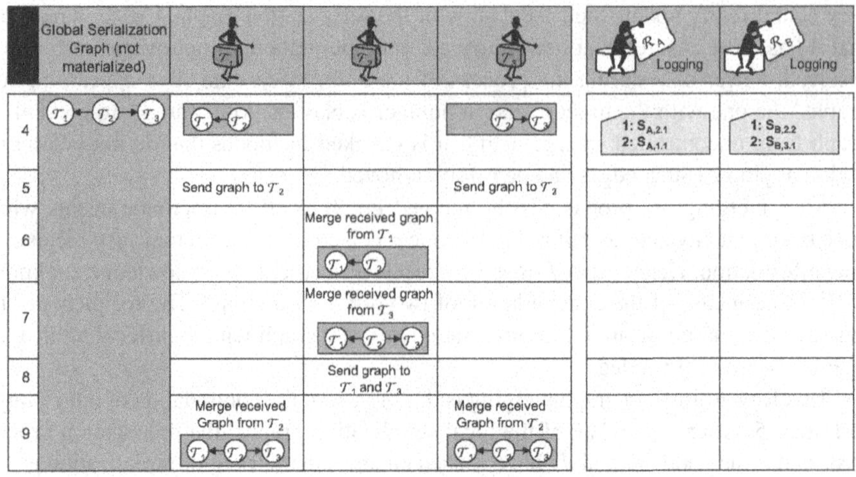

Fig. 5. Example: Messaging for keeping replica consistent

local copy is sufficient since all conflicts in which $\mathcal{T}_i$ is ordered after other transactional agents – i.e., all incoming edges to $\mathcal{T}_i$ – are immediately communicated to $\mathcal{T}_i$ after each service invocation). If this is the case, $\mathcal{T}_i$ has to wait until this edge disappears in order to correctly commit. Otherwise, $\mathcal{T}_i$ notifies all other $\mathcal{T}_j$ of its region to mark all edges it is involved in as removed and finally to remove the node corresponding to $\mathcal{T}_i$. $\mathcal{T}_i$ can be safely removed after its commit, since it does not have any incoming edge in the serialization graph. Then, this updated graph is also distributed by messages among all nodes having formed the region prior to the commit of $\mathcal{T}_i$. Hence, in certain cases, this might have the consequence that a region splits into two or even more independent regions.

5.4 Cycle Resolution

Due to the replication of metadata, each transactional agent of a region is able to locally check for cyclic conflicts. In case a cycle is detected, the associated transactional agents have to agree on one agent $\mathcal{T}_j$ to abort (this is orthogonal to the AMOR protocol and may be for instance the agent having caused the cycle or the one having invoked the least number of services so far). Then, the recovery process is started by $\mathcal{T}_j$ but might affect, due to cascading aborts, also other transactional agents. Due to the optimistic protocol where service invocations are executed (and committed) immediately although having side effects, cycle resolution may lead to a cascading abort of several active transactional agents.

5.5 Recovery

When a $\mathcal{T}_i$ aborts, it has to undo the effects of all regular services it has invoked so far in reverse order (or by invoking a service that jointly removes the effects of a set

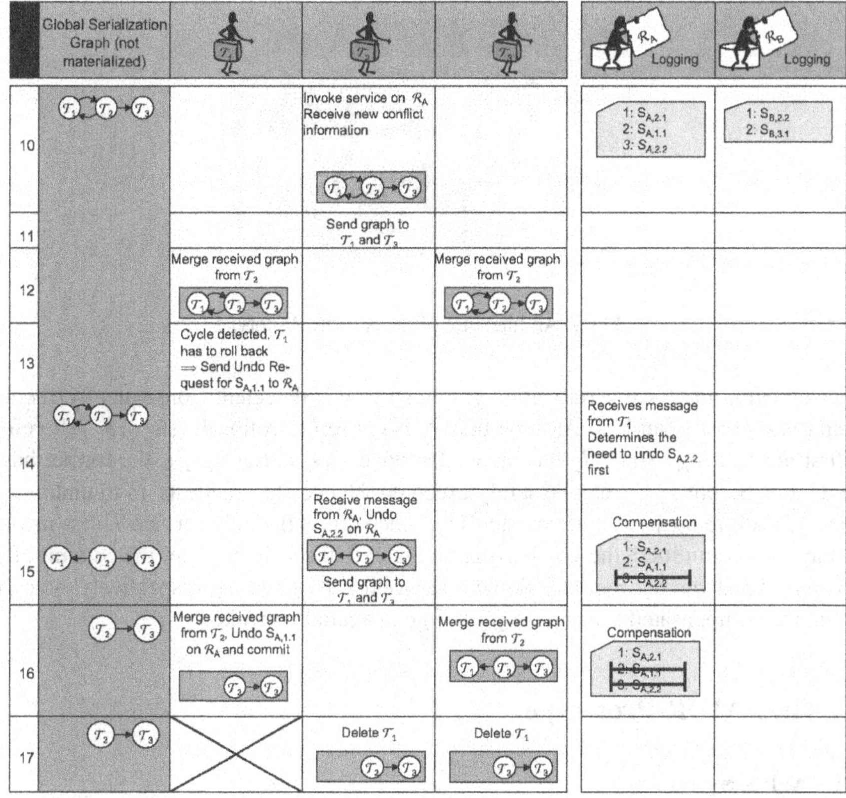

Fig. 6. Example: Cycle Resolution and Rollback

of regular service invocations). To do this correctly and efficiently, in a first step $\mathcal{T}_i$ sends a notification to all $\mathcal{R}_k$ where it has invoked regular services. In case no other conflicting service invocation $s_{k,j}$ of some $\mathcal{T}_j$ has occurred after $s_{k,i}$, the resource agent can immediately correctly undo the service. Otherwise, first all these $\mathcal{T}_j$ have to abort before $s_{k,i}^{-1}$ can be safely invoked by $\mathcal{T}_i$. To enforce this prerequisite, the corresponding abort request for $\mathcal{T}_j$ is generated by $\mathcal{R}_k$. This abort, in turn, may cascadingly lead to the abort of other transactional agents. In addition to determining whether other agents have to be aborted due to the abort request of $\mathcal{T}_i$, each $\mathcal{R}_k$ guarantees that it rejects service invocations which are in conflict with $s_{k,j}$, the service which effects are to be undone, until $s_{k,i}^{-1}$ has been invoked. When $\mathcal{R}_k$ is prepared (and when all cascading aborts are effected correctly), $\mathcal{T}_i$ is able to migrate to $\mathcal{R}_k$ and to invoke $s_{k,i}^{-1}$. As a consequence, all edges of the region serialization graph in which $s_{k,i}$ is involved are marked as removed. Finally – after all regular service invocations of $\mathcal{T}_i$ have been undone this way – $\mathcal{T}_i$ is able to commit.

We conclude our example by discussing the production, detection, and resolution of a cycle in the (region) serialization graph: In step 10, $\mathcal{T}_2$ invokes another service on $\mathcal{R}_A$. This invocation is assumed to be in conflict with $s_{A,1.1}$ invoked before by $\mathcal{T}_1$. So

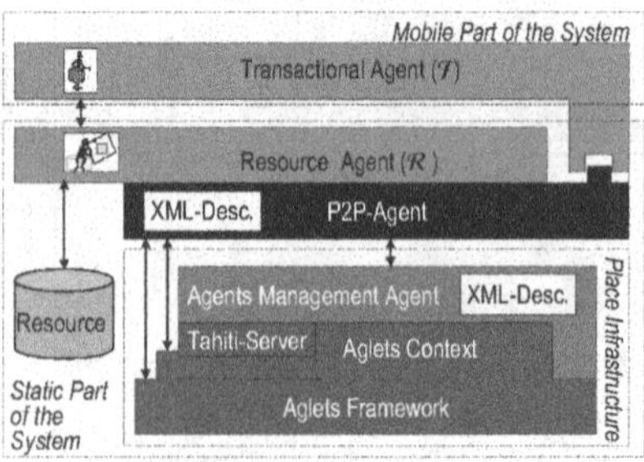

Fig. 7. Architecture of the AMOR Prototype

after updating the local serialization graph, a cycle is detected. Consequently, the new graph is sent to $\mathcal{T}_1$ and $\mathcal{T}_3$. Assume that $\mathcal{T}_1$ is chosen to rollback (step 13). Therefore, it first notifies $\mathcal{R}_A$. Since $\mathcal{T}_2$ has invoked service $s_{A,2.2}$ after $s_{A,1.1}$, the former has to be undone before $s_{A,1.1}^{-1}$ can be safely executed. Hence, $\mathcal{R}_A$ requests $\mathcal{T}_2$ to undo $s_{A,2.2}$ (step 14) before $s_{A,1.1}$ is undone (step 15). Since this is the only service $\mathcal{T}_1$ has invoked so far, $\mathcal{T}_1$ is committed, thereby leaving no effect to the system. After the commit of $\mathcal{T}_1$, it is removed from the region serialization graphs of $\mathcal{T}_2$ and $\mathcal{T}_3$, respectively (step 16). Then, the compensated service $s_{A,2.2}$ of $\mathcal{T}_2$ can again be invoked.

6 The AMOR-Prototype

6.1 Aglets System

We have implemented the AMOR prototype (Figure 7) on top of the Aglets framework [LO98]. This framework implements basic migration and communication functionality. The limitation of the basic Aglets framework is that an agent has to know the concrete address of other agents for means of communiaction, and, in case of migration, the address of the destination. This is realized in a run-time environment which is called Aglet Context. Each context can be understood as a peer in the network. On top of each peer, the framework provides a graphical user interface termed Tahiti Server. This GUI allows to easily start and stop agents resp. see which agents are currently running on a certain context.

6.2 Peer-to-Peer Agents

In a first step of our AMOR project, our aim was to overcome the restrictions of the Aglets System regarding migration and messaging, i.e., that the targets have to be hard-coded at build-time time. Instead, we have realized a higher level of abstraction called Peer-to-Peer Agents. These agents not only allow to find others with a certain name, they even allow to use predicates to specify agents (in case of messaging) and peers/places (in case of migration). Consequently, we equip the agents and places with descriptions. For example, the property 'type' is attached to agents allowing to differentiate for instance

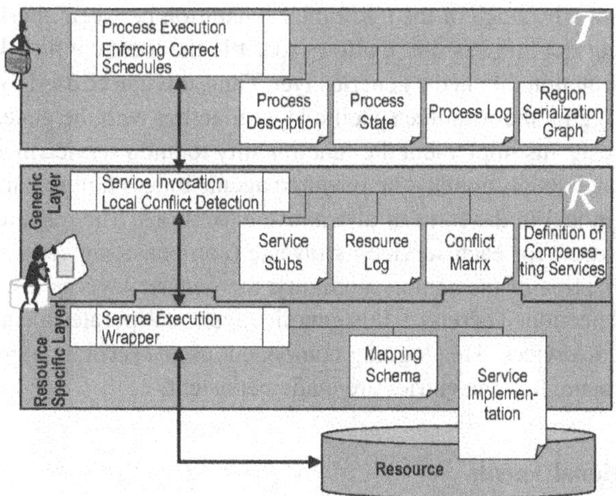

Fig. 8. Implementation Details of the AMOR Prototype

between agents providing weather forecasts (type='WeatherRA') and agents representing flight databases (type='FlightDatabaseRA').[4] Agents Management Agents (AMAs) bring these descriptions and the queries together [HS01]. They are transparent to the agent programmer, because they belong to the place infrastructure. On each place, exactly one AMA resides and works as a bookkeeper for the agents running locally. To connect a peer with the rest of the world, the AMA additionally manages the information about other peers. By this, the AMAs form a peer-to-peer network. This network is then used to propagate queries and evaluate them over the whole network or subparts of it. Thus, the P2P-Agents (together with the AMAs) realize a new mechanisms for migration and messaging on a higher level of abstraction.

6.3 Resource Agents

Resource Agents have two main tasks: i) they support transaction processing functionality and ii) they provide a uniform service interface. The second aspect deals with the problem of heterogeneity that emerges if we include existing resources into our system. This problem requires a solution which is tailored to the individual resource, whereas the first aspect can be realized in a general way.

This separation of resource-dependent and resource-independent aspects is reflected by a two layered implementation of the resource agent (Fig. 8). The upper, generic layer provides the interface to the transactional agents by offering the functionality to invoke services. Therefore, it has a general description of the services provided by a resource (service stubs). The service execution itself is implemented by the resource specific layer. This layer knows the mapping of the service stubs to the resource specific implementation of services.

[4] We assume a common terminology. By this, we can abstract in our work from the problem of defining and applying an appropriate ontology.

An important advantage of the traditional separation between interfaces and implementations of service stubs is that it allows to settle the local conflict detection and the compensation functionality in the generic layer. Thus, this can be used for any underlying resource by plugging the resource specific layer together with the generic one.

All resource agents implement the functionality to undo service invocations. Therefore, transactional agents contact the resource agents unless failure handling is not part of the process model in the form of alternative executions. The resource agents (in the generic layer) know for each service its inverse (compensating service). Whereas this allows the realization of (semantic) atomicity, the generic layer is also responsible for local conflict detection. Therefore, this generic layer incorporates a conflict matrix and logs the invoked services. This logging component uses a separate logging database on each place to ensure that the entries are made persistent.

6.4 Transactional Agents

Transactional Agents operate on top of these resource agents. They contain their process descriptions for example encompassing that we look for a flight from Zürich to Klagenfurt. Also, they contain the process state, e.g., that we have an offer for this flight for 299,- EUR has been discovered. But, additionally, each transactional agent also has to have a process log. This log memorizes which service has been invoked on which resource agent. If the transactional agent wants or is asked to rollback, it can determine which resource agents it has to contact to compensate its previously invoked services.

7 Related Work

The overall goal of the AMOR project is to provide a decentralized implementation for concurrency control and recovery. This is closely related to distributed deadlock detection [KKG99], which – together with a locking based protocol – can solve the same problem. However, such approaches are optimized for short-living transactions. Following an optimistic approach, AMOR also addresses long-running transactions.

For the same kind of environment, also timestamp ordering protocols [Tho79] can be applied, if global timestamps are available. In such approaches, serialization orders are not derived dynamically but are rather predefined by the timestamps assigned to each transaction. However, the risk of violating timestamp orders increases with the duration of transactions and finally leads to a large number of rollbacks induced by the violation of timestamp orders. Hence, also these protocols are rather suitable for short living transactions. Some approaches aim at weakening the strictness of the timestamp orders, e.g., dynamic timestamp allocation and validation [BEHR82], or multidimensional timestamp protocols [LB87]. These protocols dynamically assign timestamps. However, like all timestamp approaches, these protocols only address correct concurrency control and neglect recovery. Similar to traditional timestamp ordering, validation-based, optimistic concurrency control protocols such as BOCC [KR81] potentially come along with a large number of rollbacks when the duration of transactions and thus the number of conflicts increases. Essentially, these protocols check for the correctness of schedules not before commit time.

To support atomic applications in large-scale environments, the Transaction Internet Protocol (TIP) has been proposed. [LE98] Essentially, TIP implements a 2PC protocol. Recent extensions like Web Service Transactions (WS-Transactions) [Cea01] also support 'Business Activities', which are based on an optimistic service execution model with compensations. However, both, TIP and WS-Transactions, do not consider isolation.

Important related work regarding agents in general has been done by Chen and Dayal [CD00] and by Pitoura and Bhargava [PB95]. The latter provide an introductory discussion on using agents for accessing databases. The first discuss how multiple (non-mobile) agents can cooperate in order to guarantee atomic (but not necessarily isolated) workflow execution.

Focusing more on mobile agents, valuable work has been done in the context of transactions and workflow execution. The idea of mobile agents executing workflows – first published in [CGN96] – is similar to our approach to build transactional agent applications on top of services made available by different resource agents. Other approaches even address the intersection of mobile agent technology and transaction management. First results were achieved by enforcing atomicity and fault tolerance based on the concept of replication [SP98]. More recent approaches like [SAE01], albeit still concentrating on the atomicity aspect, also provide support for concurrency control. This is achieved by combining timestamp-ordering and 2PC [GR93], hence with a rather limited degree of concurrency. However, all these approaches aim not at combining optimistic transaction processing techniques with the isolation property. Therefore, they focus on short living transactions. Hence, they do not consider isolation and therefore lack support for reliable workflow resp. process execution in large, complex systems.

Finally, the underlying network model of the AMOR project is a peer-to-peer network. Recently, research in this direction has attracted quite some attention. This work was mainly driven by file sharing systems like Gnutella [Gnu]. Research concentrated very much on novel access methods, e.g. [Abe01]. However, such access methods are orthogonal to ARMOR and can therefore easily be integrated into our system.

8 Summary and Outlook

In this paper, we have presented the ideas of the AMOR project which allows for a novel decentralized implementation of transaction management in a peer-to-peer environment. Our approach is based on mobile transactional agents manipulating data provided by (non-mobile) resource agents. The resource agents are responsible for logging and (local) conflict detection. In contrast, it is the transactional agents' duty to ensure globally correct schedules by communication.

To this end, sophisticated replication management of metadata needed for synchronization purposes is applied. Each transactional agent receives information about local conflicts when it invokes a service. This information is used to update the local view on the relevant portion of global metadata, i.e., the region serialization graph. The different local replica of these graphs are kept consistent by means of communication at the agent level. To this end, we have introduced a new protocol that defines which information has to be transferred such that each transactional agent has sufficient information to decide whether a multi-agent execution is correct. For reasoning about correctness, we apply the unified theory of concurrency control and recovery that jointly addresses the problems imposed by atomicity and isolation.

The two significant features of AMOR — the protocol allowing for decentralized transaction management, thus providing dedicated transactional execution guarantees for mobile agents and the support for location transparent migration and messaging — make the project a powerful effort towards transactional location transparent peer-to-peer information processing.

In our future work, we aim extending the existing AMOR framework by providing support for shielding unreliable network connections. To this end, we are working on a cost model by which the effects of disconnections and, more general, of different network latencies and bandwidths can be modeled. The goal is to extend the AMOR transaction model by these costs as dedicated quality-of-service parameters and to make use of this cost information for scheduling purposes. By this, we will build a sophisticated framework realizing our vision of reliable process execution in peer-to-peer networks.

References

[Abe01] K. Aberer. P-Grid: A Self-Organizing Access Structure for P2P Information Systems. In *9th Int. Conf. on Cooperative Information Systems, Trento, Italy*, 2001.

[Aea94] G. Alonso et al. Unifying Cconcurrency Control and Recovery of Transactions. In *Information Systems*, 1994.

[BEHR82] R. Bayer, K. Elhardt, J. Heigert, and A. Reiser. Dynamic Timestamp Allocation for Transactions in Database Systems. In *Proc. of the 2nd Int'l Symposium on Distributed Data Bases, Berlin*, 1982.

[BN97] P. Bernstein and E. Newcomer. *Principles of Transaction Processing*. Morgan Kaufmann, 1997.

[CD00] Q. Chen and U. Dayal. Multi-agent cooperative transactions for e-commerce. In *7th Int. Conference on Cooperative Information Systems, Eilat, Israel*, 2000.

[Cea01] F. Cabrera et al. Web services transaction, 2001. BEA Systems, IBM, Microsoft.

[CGN96] T. Cai, P. Gloor, and S. Nog. Dartflow: A Workflow Management System on the Web using Transportable Agents. Technical Report TR96-283, Dartmouth College, 1996.

[GM83] H. Garcia-Molina. Using Semantic Knowledge for Transaction Processing in a Distributed Database. *ACM Transactions on Database Systems (TODS)*, 8(2):186–213, June 1983.

[Gnu] Gnutella. `http://www.gnutella.com`.

[GR93] J. Gray and A. Reuter. *Transaction Processing: Concepts and Techniques*. Morgan Kaufmann, 1993.

[HS01] K. Haller and H. Schuldt. Using Predicates for Specifying Targets of Migration and Messages in a Peer-to-Peer Mobile Agent Environment. In *5th Int. Conf. on Mobile Agents (MA), Atlanta, GA*, 2001.

[KKG99] N. Krivokapic, A. Kemper, and E. Gudes. Deadlock Detection in Distributed Database Systems: A New Algorithm and a Comparative Performance Analysis. *VLDB Journal*, 8(2):79–100, 1999.

[KR81] H. Kung and J. Robinson. On optimistic Methods for Concurrency Control. *ACM Transactions on Database Systems*, 6(2), 1981.

[LB87] P. Leu and B. Bhargava. Multidimensional Timestamp Protocols for Concurrency Control. *IEEE Transactions on Software Engineering (TSE)*, 13(12):1238–1253, 1987.

[LE98] J. Lyon L. Evans, J. Klein. Transaction Internet Protocol Version 3.0. http://www.ietf.org/rfc/rfc2371.txt, 1998. IETF RFC 2371.

[LO98] D. Lange and M. Oshima. *Programming and Deploying Java Mobile Agents with Aglets*. Addison Wesley Longman, 1998.

[PB95] E. Pitoura and B. Bhargava. A framework for providing consistent and recoverable agent-based access to heterogeneous mobile databases. *SIGMOD Record*, 24(3):44–49, 1995.

[SABS02] H. Schuldt, G. Alonso, C. Beeri, and H.-J. Schek. Atomicity and isolation for transactional processes. *ACM Transactions on Database Systems (TODS)*, 27(1), 2002.

[SAE01] R. Sher, Y. Aridor, and O. Etzion. Mobile Transactional Agents. In *21st Int. Conf. on Distributed Computing Systems, Phoenix, AZ*, 2001.

[SP98] A. Silva and R. Popescu-Zeletin. An Approach for Providing Mobile Agent Fault Tolerance. In *2d Int. Workshop on Mobile Agents, Stuttgart, Germany*, 1998.

[Tay86] D. Taylor. Concurrency and Forward Recovery in Atomic Actions. *IEEE Transactions on Software Engineering*, SE-12(1):69–78, January 1986.

[Tho79] R. Thomas. A Majority Consensus Approach to Concurrency Control for Multiple Copy Databases. *ACM Transactions on Database Systems (TODS)*, 4(2):180–209, June 1979.

[VHBS98] R. Vingralek, H. Hasse-Ye, Y. Breitbart, and H.-J. Schek. Unifying Concurrency Control and Recovery of Transactions with Semantically Rich Operations. *Theoretical Computer Science*, 190(2), 1998.

[Whi97] J. E. White. Telescript. In W. Cockayne and M. Zyda, editors, *Mobile Agents: Explanations and Examples*, 1997.

Translating and Searching Service Descriptions Using Ontologies

Daniela Damm[1], Farshad Hakimpour[2,4], and Andreas Geppert[3,5]

[1]Department of Information Technology, University of Zurich, Switzerland
damm@ifi.unizh.ch

[2]Department of Geography, University of Zurich, Switzerland
farshad@geo.unizh.ch

[3]Credit Suisse, Zurich, Switzerland
geppert@acm.org

Abstract. Web services offer a promising approach to accomplish a loose coupling of processes across organizational boundaries. Several industry standards have been developed to describe process or service related information. Although these standards capture similar concepts, they nonetheless rely on diverging interpretations of processes and their components. In this paper, we present an approach to facilitate the search for services, where services and requests can be described using heterogeneous standards. To enable the mapping of a request to different service description standards, formal ontologies are used. Ontologies are related on the basis of similarity relations in order to translate between elements of different service descriptions. The resulting translation is used to process a request and find an adequate service. We present a top-down and a bottom-up method to implement this kind of request processing.

1 Introduction

Development and evolution of web services allow an enterprise to loosely couple its internal processes with business activities of its suppliers or other partners. Based on common standards, web services enable an interaction between the applications of involved parties without the time-consuming and expensive integration of the involved information systems. Web service-related standards focus mainly on technical aspects of the interaction between two applications [7]. More business process-related aspects of a product or service (like business activities, document exchange, role descriptions) are not addressed.

For this purpose several industry standards (like RosettaNet, ebXML, XPDL) can be applied.[6] Although these standards capture similar concepts, they nonetheless rely on diverging interpretations of processes and their components. Moreover, the B2B-

4. The work of Farshad Hakimpour is funded by Swiss National Science Foundation (Project Number: 2100-053995).

5. Work done while with the University of Zurich

6. We will refer to such standards as service description standards or languages.

J. Eder and M. Missikoff (Eds.): CAiSE 2003, LNCS 2681, pp. 308–323, 2003.

standards often lack unambiguous specifications of the meaning of their constituent terms.

To enhance its processes by integrating external web services, an enterprise must be able to locate the services that meet its requirements. In contrast to traditional process design, the expected number of available web services on the Internet is ever increasing [4]. Manual service detection is no longer possible and efficient service detection mechanisms must be provided.

We present an ontology-based approach to facilitate the resolution of heterogeneity of different service description standards. We use a higher-level ontology that is based on existing service description standards. This ontology is used to match service requests and descriptions formulated in different description languages. While issuing a request, the service consumer can search for services independent of the service description language. We assume that every standard relies on a formalized ontology (called lower-level ontology here) and that a service description specified in a standard is based on its lower-level ontology. We use the lower-level ontologies to detect semantic similarities between different standards that can be applied to translate service descriptions or requests.

The remainder of this paper is organized as following. In section 2, we give a brief overview of web service-related concepts. Section 3 discusses related research approaches. In section 4, we present an overview of our approach. The subsequent sections present different aspects of our work in more detail. In section 5 we discuss the detection of semantic similarities between different standards. Based on the similarity relations, a transformation structure for the translation between two standards is built. Section 6 describes the generation of the transformation structure. In section 7 we show the application of the transformation structure to translate a service description document. In section 8 a top-down and a bottom-up approach to implement the service request processing are introduced and compared. Finally, section 9 concludes the paper and discusses future work.

2 Web Services in a Nutshell

Web services provide concepts and methods to implement dynamic and flexible interaction between companies and their respective business processes. Standards and systems allow an enterprise to offer its products and services via the Internet to its customers and partners. The use of standardized technologies enables the coupling of enterprises' activities without the need for expensive and time-consuming integration with the partner's information systems [7]. Web service technologies are mainly based on WSDL[7], UDDI[8] and SOAP[9].

WSDL is used to describe the interface of a service as an XML document. It contains the minimal necessary information to enable interaction between web service ap-

7. Web Service Description Language (http://www.w3.org/TR/wsdl).
8. Universal Description, Discovery, and Integration (http:// www.uddi.org/).
9. Simple Object Access Protocol (http://www.w3.org/tr/soap/).

plications (such as data formats, messages, port types, etc.). In order to offer his services, a service provider generates a WSDL document and publishes it either directly or to a service registry. UDDI is a standard defining the interface of such service registries. Web services are stored in the form of business registrations which are XML files used to describe business entities and their services. A UDDI service registry entry captures general information (e.g. provider name, contact information), taxonomy references and technical aspects of a service. SOAP is used to implement the interaction between service providers and consumers. Based on a service description, a service consumer generates a SOAP request to invoke the corresponding web service. WSDL focuses on the basic, technical description of service enactment [1]. In order to implement interactions between companies, additional information about a service must be provided (e.g. descriptions of involved business partners, their role, provided activities) [7]. For this purpose several existing industry standards can be used.

We distinguish two different kinds of standardization efforts: *interaction-oriented* and *process-oriented* standards. Interaction-oriented standards focus on the cooperation between business partners and provide concepts to model the information exchange and an abstract description of activities between them. A detailed specification of enterprise internal processes is not in the scope of such standards. An example is *RosettaNet*, which proposes partner interface processes (PIP) in order to describe interaction along the whole supply chain between two processes executing in different enterprises [16]. ebXML offers a framework for the modelling of interactions between business partners and the exchange of business-related information (*business documents*) [8]. The flow of business activities and the involved business document exchange is specified in a process specification. (Other examples of interaction-oriented standards are cXML [6], EDI or OBI).

In contrast to interaction-oriented standards, process-oriented standards support detailed process descriptions, involved activities and their dependencies. Examples of process-oriented standards are XPDL or BPML [19,2]. XPDL relies on the process meta model of the Workflow Management Coalition and is intended to provide a standardized workflow model in order to enable the exchange of workflow specifications between business partners. It provides concepts for a detailed representation of activities, actors and data related to a workflow. Another example of a process-oriented standard is BPML, also intended to support the exchange of process-related specifications between partners.

Although each of these standards contains the same or similar concepts, they often use different names for these concepts (for example: sequence [16] and choreography [8] are semantically equivalent). Likewise, the same term can be used in different standards to denote more or less different concepts. For example, the term "transaction" means business transaction in [8], while in [16] it refers to a database transaction.

3 Related Work

Two projects supporting integration of heterogeneous service description standards are Meteor and PSL. Meteor is using a common taxonomy of service-related terms to resolve semantic heterogeneity which is used to detect similar terms in different service descriptions in order to enhance the detection of services as well as the mapping of the interfaces of services during their combination [4]. If two service descriptions contain the same attribute, the similarity of their values is quantified by calculating their distance within the taxonomy tree. The detection of similarity is limited to the attribute values and only a mapping of homogenous service requests and descriptions is supported.

The Process Specification Language (PSL) project which defines a specification language for process-related information as a base for the implementation of common gateways to exchange data among different process-related applications [17]. PSL is not concerned with existing process-related standardization efforts, but relies on a proprietary process meta model. PSL provides a formal ontology which defines the semantics of the terminology of PSL [5]. To exchange process data between two applications, the underlying semantics of their specification languages has to be mapped to the overlapping part of the PSL ontology, and the applications' syntax has to be translated into the KIF syntax applied in PSL. Only if the semantics of all three ontologies (that is both ontologies underlying the involved applications and the PSL ontology) have common terms and concepts, information can be exchanged.

Another line of research aims at enhancing existing web service related standards in order to improve their modeling capabilities and to describe complex services [1,3,13]. In [13] a process ontology developed by the MIT Process Handbook project is used to support the discovery of services. Depending on the activities a web service contains, indexes are added to its description based on the process taxonomy defined in the ontology. These indexes can be used to query service repositories more precisely.

The DAML-S project provides a description language for services based on semantic web enabling technologies [1]. DAML-S allows the description of business related aspects of services, and can thus be used to complement existing web service related standards. Two specific elements for the service description are provided. A SERVICE PROFILE allows a high-level description of a service and its provider, while a SERVICE MODEL expresses usage-oriented information. By enhancing a service description with this information (e.g. description, quality aspects, service categories) the service discovery, invocation and combination can be supported. Another approach based on technologies related to the semantic web is the Web Service Modeling Framework (WSMF) [3]. It extends the modeling capabilities of DAML-S in order to provide a flexible framework for the description of various aspects related to web services.

4 The Proposed Solution – An Overview

To avoid semantic heterogeneity, we should guarantee a unique interpretation for every term used in the communication between partners. While relating service descriptions, we face semantic obstacles at two different levels:

1. different service descriptions from different communities presented in the same structural standard
2. different service descriptions prepared in two different standards

The main concern of this work is the second issue. We aim at finding an approach for the automatic or semiautomatic communication between a service consumer and a provider using different standards while resolving semantic conflicts. A unique and explicit definition for every term in an ontology can serve our purpose to avoid semantic heterogeneity [14]. The major advantage of using ontologies is to avoid misinterpretations by detecting the differences and similarities in the meaning of terms.

In our work, we use a formal higher-level ontology for service description languages (SDL-ontology) to support the detection of services specified in heterogeneous service description standards. We assume that the underlying semantics of each particular service description standard are captured in a formal ontology and service descriptions or requests written in this language are referring to the underlying ontology. The translation between two different service description languages is done by merging their underlying ontologies with respect to the SDL-ontology. Note that the building of ontologies is not within the scope of this paper. Methodologies for this can be found in [9,10,18,11].

The SDL-ontology specifies the meaning of common terms in the involved description service languages. It is built by integrating low-level ontologies of different available service description languages. If another description language has to be added to the solution, in a first step, it has to commit to the SDL-ontology. This process cannot be automated, but needs human intervention. Good knowledge of the low-level language ontology as well as the SDL-ontology is required.

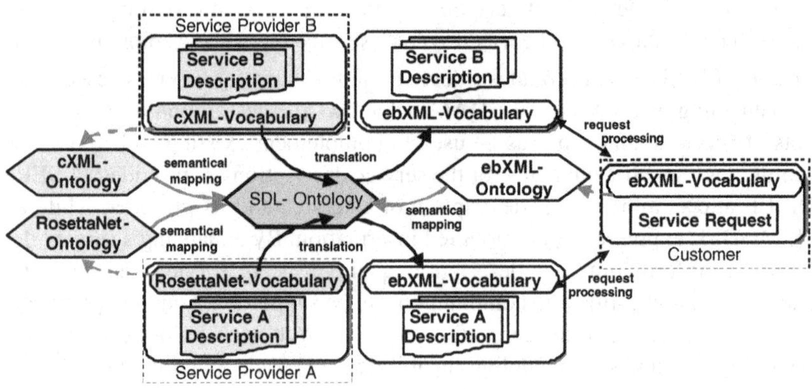

Fig. 1. Ontology-based Service Search (bottom-up)

Once a language is fully added (that is, its low-level ontology is imported and commits to the SDL-ontology), based on the similarity relations introduced in [12] a reasoning system can be used to detect similarities between the low-level ontologies. The result is then used to implement the mapping of a service request with existing service descriptions written in different languages. To allow a mapping of heterogeneous service request and descriptions, similarity relations detected during the merging of the underlying ontologies are used to translate either service descriptions or service requests.

Generally, two approaches for the translation can be distinguished. Applying a top-down procedure, a service request is translated into other available languages. A translated service request is then transferred to the service sources (e.g., a service registry) in order to search for matching service descriptions. Alternatively, in the bottom-up approach service descriptions are translated into one of the available languages and mapped to a service request that is also specified in one specific language. Figure 1 shows the bottom-up approach.

Scenario: E-Parking Service. In the following we consider an e-parking service as an example to illustrate our approach. It is taken from a current European research project[10] at our department[11] implementing an e-parking platform that offers the possibility for customers to reserve parking lots electronically. It combines services offered by different car park providers. Several devices such as computer, PDAs or mobile phones can be used to access the e-parking services. Figure 2 shows a part of the e-parking service description.

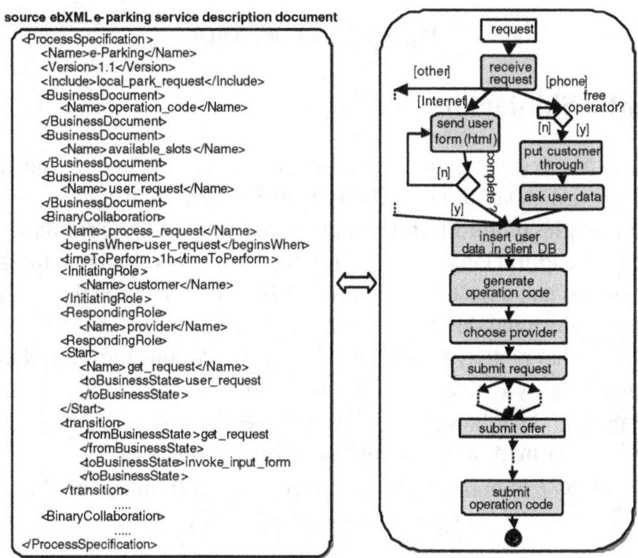

Fig. 2. E-Parking Service

In order to request a parking lot, a registered customer sends a message specifying the desired date, time and location as well as the type of vehicle. In return, he receives a list with available parking slots matching his requirements. The customer selects one of the offers and (if the request can be processed successfully) receives an operation code as parking slot token in return.

We assume that the e-parking service is defined in ebXML and that a service consumer uses XPDL to specify his request (see Figure 3) [8,19].

To process the XPDL request, a translation between ebXML and XPDL has to be provided. In the following we will use the e-parking service to illustrate our approach.

10. E-parking: User-Friendly e-Commerce to Optimise Parking Space (IST-2000-25392)

11. Department of Information Technology, University of Zurich.

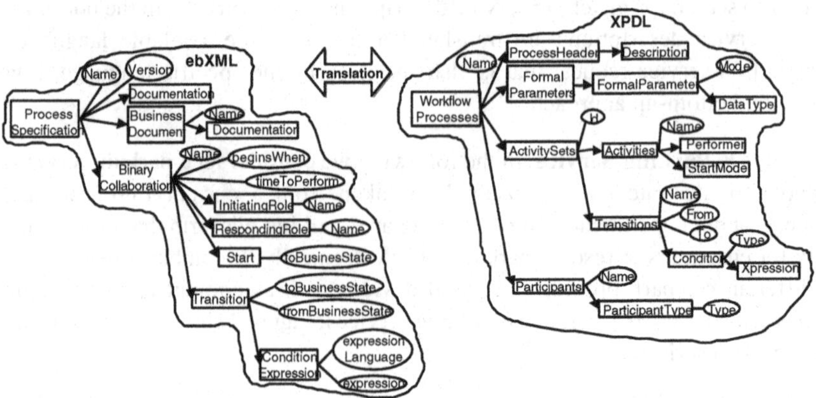

Fig. 3. ebXML and XPDL

5 Semantic Similarities

The translation of a service request or description specified in one standard to another description standard is based on similarity between terms and concepts captured in the underlying ontologies of the different languages. To obtain these similarity relations between service description languages, we use the ontologies available for the service description languages and detect similarities or differences between them. This is done by *matching* their intensional definitions (i.e., definitions of the meaning of terms by logical axioms). For that matter, we use the similarity relations introduced in [12]. There, four levels of similarity between two terms ${}^pT_i$ and ${}^qT_j$ defined in formal ontologies p and q are proposed. The relations *equal, specializes (generalizes), disjoint, overlaps* are defined as follows (ι maps a term to its intensional definition):

- ${}^pT_i$ is equal to ${}^qT_j$ if and only if both intensional definitions are the same:
$$({}^pT_i = {}^qT_j) \Leftrightarrow (\iota[{}^pT_i] \equiv \iota[{}^qT_j]) .$$
- ${}^pT_i$ specializes ${}^qT_j$ if and only if the conjunction of the two intensional definitions is the same as the definition of ${}^pT_i$:
$$({}^pT_i \leq {}^qT_j) \Leftrightarrow (\iota[{}^pT_i] \wedge \iota[{}^qT_j]) \equiv \iota[{}^pT_i] .$$
- ${}^pT_i$ overlaps ${}^qT_j$ if and only if the conjunction of the two intensional definitions is not false:
$$({}^pT_i \sim {}^qT_j) \Leftrightarrow (((\iota[{}^pT_i] \wedge \iota[{}^qT_j]) \equiv \iota[T_k]) \wedge \neg(\iota[T_k] = False)) .$$
- ${}^pT_i$ and ${}^qT_j$ are disjoint if and only if the conjunction of the two intensional definitions is false:
$$({}^pT_i \neq {}^qT_j) \Leftrightarrow ((\iota[{}^pT_i] \wedge \iota[{}^qT_j]) \equiv False) .$$

Matching in this phase requires both ontologies to commit to the SDL-ontology. A reasoning system uses this higher-level ontology as a common reference of the two ontologies for matching.The results of the merging is stored and used for the translation between different service description languages.

similarity relations between ebXML and XPDL

equal (ProcessSpecification, WorkflowProcesses)	overlap (BusinessDocument, FormalParameter)
specialize (BinaryCollaboration, ActivitySets)	specialize (Xpression, expression)
equal (Documentation, Description)	specialize (Start, Transition)
equal (Transition, Transition)	specialize (InitiatingRole, Participants)
specialize ((RespondingRole, Participants)	equal (ConditionExpression, Condition)
equal (Name, Name)	specialize (Id, Name)
specialize (fromBusinessState, From)	specialze (toBusinessState, To)

Fig. 4. Similarity Relations between ebXML and XPDL

Figure 4 shows parts of the similarity relations that can be detected between the terms of ebXML and XPDL.

6 Generating a Transformation Structure

In this section we apply the similarity relations between the ontologies to generate a transformation structure between two description standards. Based on the similarities between elements (and their intensional definitions) of description standards, we build a transformation structure. This transformation structure is then used to translate a service description into another service description language. It is not possible to translate the terms of a source (S) and a target service description standard (T) without regarding the structural differences of both. The purpose of a transformation structure is to preserve the structural aspects of T while translating a document. The transformation structure captures not only the semantic similarities of the terms in S and T, but maps the terms in S to the structure of T. It thus offers a way to relate the elements in a particular service document written in S according to their semantics (defined in the underlying ontology of S) to both, the terms and the structure of T. Once a transformation structure is generated, it can be used to translate any document in S to a document in T.

One main objective while generating a transformation structure is to prevent hierarchical relations that are not part of the specification of the elements in S from being included in the translation document. For example, if the specification of an activity contains an application, it can have different interpretations: the activity uses the application, or the activity is enacted by the application. Thus, while relating elements of S and T, we cannot simply change the hierarchical dependencies. Due to the hierarchical structure of XML, we do not have further knowledge about the semantics of a relation between two elements s_1 and s_2 (e.g. s_2 is a subelement of s_1) in S. Thus, the transformation structure is built in a way that the hierarchical dependencies between elements in S are reflected by their counterparts in T (that is, if s_2 is a subelement of s_1 in S, its corresponding element t_2 is a subelement of t_1 in T), but not their inversion (t_1 is a subelement of t_2). Although this can result in empty elements in the translated service description, it avoids the translation of relations between elements in S to different relations in T without knowing for sure whether the intensional definitions of the relations are semantically similar.

If a term s in S generalizes a term t in T, instances of s are not necessarily classified in the extension of t. Therefore, we cannot provide an automatic translation in such a case. The same applies for a term s in S that overlaps with a term t in T. As the main objective of this work is the matching of service requests with provided services, we aim to keep all the available information of a service during the translation processing. Although such additional information cannot be expressed by the standard T, it can still contain useful information for the decision process of a consumer to select a service or not. In order to generate a translation document that is consistent with T and can be processed by an application relying on T, we add such extensions only as comment to service descriptions. A user can take them into account, but applications do not have to cope with them. In order to avoid information loss, we also keep information about disjoint terms of S and T (that is, a term s in S has a minimum semantic similarity to any term in T) as comments in the translation document.

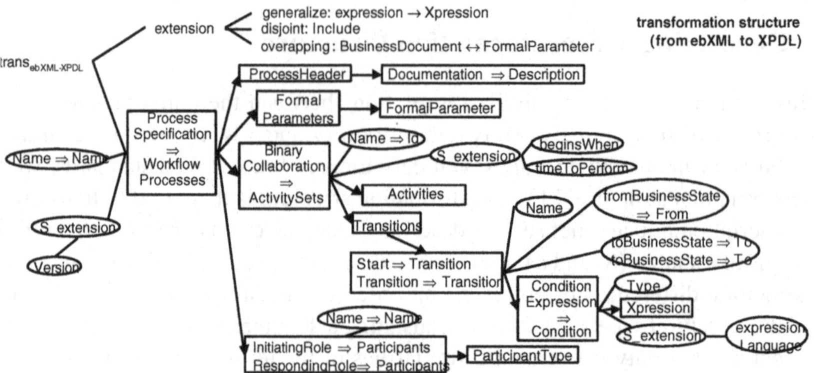

Fig. 5. Transformation structure from ebXML to XPDL

Figure 5 shows the transformation structure for the translation from ebXML to XPDL that is based on the similarity relations between both description standards (see figure 4). In the following we will describe the different steps of generating a transformation structure between S and T. The transformation structure $trans_{S\text{-}T}$ from S to T is generated, starting at the root element of S. First, the similarity relations between elements in S and T, and second, similarity relations between attributes of these elements are processed to generate the transformation structure.

Relating elements of S to those of T

- Generalization, overlapping and disjoint elements:
  If a term *s* in S generalizes or overlaps a term *t* in T, we add *s* as a comment to the translation document. We also include information about the similarity between *s* and *t* (generalize, overlap). During the generation of the transformation structure, we copy the term *s* to a special element in the $trans_{S\text{-}T}$ extension (e.g., $expression_{ebXML}$ is a generalization of $Xpression_{XPDL}$). During the translation, the values of extension are transformed to comments (see section 7.). Disjoint elements in S are included to $trans_{S\text{-}T}$ in the same way (e.g., $Include_{ebXML}$).
- Equal or specialization:
  In case a term *s* in S is equal to or specializes a term *t* in T, we copy the whole subtree $subtree_t$ of T that contains *t* to $trans_{S\text{-}T}$ and include a link from *s* to *t'* (copy of

t) in $subtree_{t'}$. (For example, $ProcessSpecification_{ebXML}$ and $WorkflowProcesses_{XPDL}$ refer to the same concept, thus we include the subtree of *WorkflowProcesses* of the XPDL schema to the translation structure and add an link from *ProcessSpecification* to *WorkflowProcess*.) In the next step we try to resolve semantic relations between the subelements of *s* and the subelements of *t'* in the $subtree_{t'}$ in $trans_{S\text{-}T}$:

- Common hierarchical relation between elements:
  If a subelement s_n of *s* is equal to or specializes a subsequent element t_n' of *t'* in $subtree_{t'}$, we simply include a link between s_n and t_n' to $subtree_{t'}$. This is done to keep common hierarchical dependencies between corresponding elements of S and T and thus, to transform the hierarchical structure of S to the hierarchical structure of T.
- Avoid inversion of hierarchical relations:
  If a subelement s_n of *s* cannot be related to any subelement of *t'* in $subtree_{t'}$, we do not map it to an element that is a superelement of *t'* (which corresponds to *s*). This would change the hierarchical dependency between *s* and s_n during the translation of a document. To avoid the inclusion of an inverted relation, we add a copy $subtree_{tn''}$ of the $subtree_{tn}$ to $trans_{S\text{-}T}$, include a link between s_n and t_n'', and then try to map the subelements of s_n to subtree t_n'' correspondingly.

Relating attributes of elements of S to T

After generating the transformation structure for every element in S, we add the semantic relations between attributes of two equivalent terms *s* and *t*. For every element *t'* in the transformation structure that contains a link to a term *s* in S (e.g. *ProcessSpecification*, *BinaryCollaboration*, *Start*), we consider the similarity relations between the attributes s.attr and t.attr of *s* and *t*.

- If an attribute *s.attr* is equal to *t.attr* and the type of *s.attr* can be converted to the type *t.attr*, we include *t'.attr* to $trans_{S\text{-}T}$ and add a link to *s.attr*. (For example, both $ProcessSpecification_{ebXML}$ and $WorkflowProcesses_{XPDL}$ have an attribute *Name* that addresses the same concept and both are of the same type, thus we add this attribute to the translation structure.) In case an *s.attr* is a specialization of *t.attr*, we proceed in the same way.
- During the translation, we copy information of an attribute *s.attr* that cannot be related to any attribute t.attr to $trans_{S\text{-}T}$ in form of a comment to the translation document. Therefore, we add an additional attribute *S_extension* to every element in the transformation structure that has a link to a term in S. For every attribute *s.attr* that cannot be related (that is equal or specializes) to any attribute *t.attr* in T, we add a reference to *S_extension* (e.g. XPDL does not contain an equivalent to the attribute *Version* of the *ProcessSpecification* in ebXML). While generating the translation service document these references in *S_extension* are transformed into a comment of *t*.

We exemplify the generation of a translation structure with a simple example shown in figure 6. In the first step, all terms in S that generalize or overlap a term in T or are disjoint to them are copied to *extension* of $trans_{S\text{-}T}$. For example, we include an entry for *c* (generalizing *z*), *b* (overlapping *y*) and *w* which is disjoint to *T* in *extension.* Then, we process terms of *S* that are equal to or are specializations of terms in *T*. Starting at the root *a* (that is equal to *x*), we include to $trans_{S\text{-}T}$ the corresponding $subtree_{x'}$. Then we add the semantic relations of the subelements of *a* that can be mapped directly to the hierarchical structure of *T*. In our example, only *d* and its subelement *l* have the same hierarchical dependencies as their corresponding elements *m* and *k* in *T*.

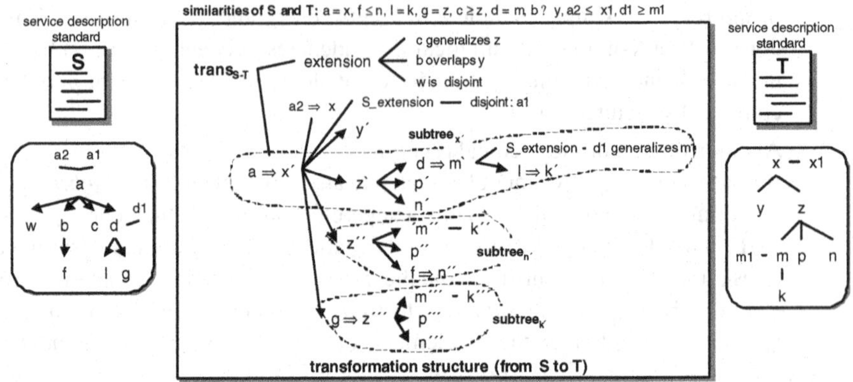

Fig. 6. Generating a transformation structure

Now, the remaining elements *f* and *g* have to be included to $trans_{S\text{-}T}$. For *f* that specializes *n*, we add the copy $subtree_{n'}$ of the subtree in *T* (up to the root *x*) that contains *n* to $trans_{S\text{-}T}$. In the same manner, $subtree_{z'}$ is added for *g* to $trans_{S\text{-}T}$. Finally, the semantic similarities of the attributes of the elements of *S* that are equal or are a specialization of the elements in *T* and therefore are not captured in the extension of $trans_{S\text{-}T}$ are included to the transformation structure.

7 Translation of Service Description Documents

In this section we will show how the transformation structure between the description languages can be used to translate a service request or description from one service description standard to another. In the following, we will focus on the translation of service descriptions (a service request can be translated analogously). The translation of a service description is done in two steps. First, the elements in the service description document are associated with the transformation structure. Then, based on these associations the translated service description document is generated.

To translate the source document we use the semantic links in the transformation structure. Every element in the source document is associated with its corresponding element in the transformation structure. To do this, we process the source document and the elements specified there, starting with the root elements in the document. If a (root) element s_r in the source document has a corresponding element $s_{r'}$ in the transformation structure, we create an instance of the $subtree_{sr'}$ and relate the attributes of s_r to $s_{r'}$ in $subtree_{sr'}$. Attributes, that do not have a semantic link in the transformation structure are added to the *S_extension* attribute of $s_{r'}$. In the same way, we copy subsequent elements *s1,..., sn* of s_r to $subtree_{sr'}$ and create an instance of the particular $subtree_{sx'}$ in $subtree_{s'}$. Figure 7 shows the result of the association of the element in the e-parking service description document (see Figure 2) to the transformation structure $trans_{e\text{-}bXML\text{-}XPDL}$ presented in Figure 5.

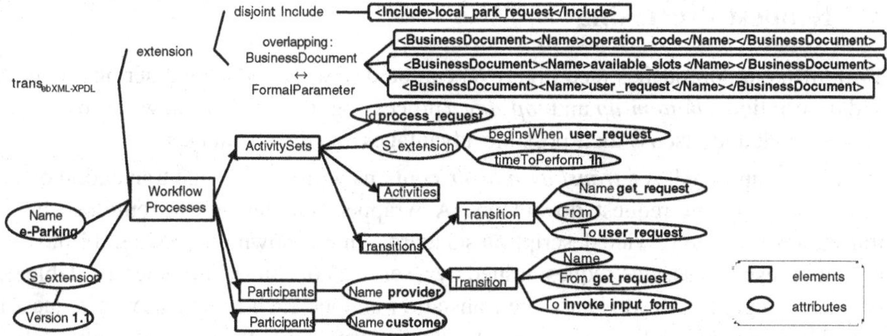

Fig. 7. Association of e-parking service description document

Once every element in the source document has been copied to the transformation structure, the translated service description document can be generated. In a backtracking-oriented method we process the transformation structure and if an element or its sub-elements in the structure have been instantiated, we include the XML specification of the element, its attributes and sub-elements to the translation document (see figure 8). The values of an attributes S_extension of an element s are included as a comment in form of *<!--S extension: <attr*$_S$*> value </attr*$_S$*> -->* to the specification of s. For example, for the attribute *Version* of ebXML the comment *<!-- ebXML extension: <Version>1.1</Version> -->* is added to the specification of *WorkflowProcess.*

Every reference in *extension* (elements of S that cannot be translated automatically) is added as a comment to the translated service document: *<!—ebXML extension: (relation: reference)* -->*. For example, the comment for the element *Include* is *<!—ebXML extension: disjoint: <Include>local_park_request</Include> -->*.

```
<WorkflowProcesses>                                              resulting XPDL e-parking
   <!– ebXML extension: <Version>1.1</Version> –>                service description document
   < Name >e-Parking</ Name >
   < ActivitySets >
      < Id >process_request</ Id >
      < Transitions>
         < Transition ><Name>get_request</Name> <to>user_request</to></ Transition >
         < Transition ><from>get_request</from> <to>invoke_input_form</to></ Transition >
      .....</Transitions>
   .....</ ActivitySets >.....
   < Participants ><Name>customer </Name></ Participants >
   < Participants ><Name>provider</Name>< Participants >
<!—ebXML extension:
   disjoint: < Include>local_park_request</Include >
   overlapping FormalParameter:<BusinessDocument><Name>operation_code </Name></BusinessDocument>
   overlapping FormalParameter:<BusinessDocument><Name>available_slots</Name></BusinessDocument>
   overlapping FormalParameter:<BusinessDocument><Name>user_request </Name></BusinessDocument> -->
</ WorkflowProcesses >
```

Fig. 8. Translation of the e-parking service document

If elements in the transformation structure have not been instantiated during the association, but have instantiated sub-elements, they are included as blank XML elements. These empty elements serve as containers for their sub-elements in the translation document. Figure 8 illustrates the generation of the translated description document by means of the e-parking example.

8 Request Processing

Two different approaches (see Figure 9) can be devised for mapping service requests and descriptions: *bottom-up* and *top-down* processing. In this section, we give an overview of both and discuss their possible advantages and disadvantages.

In both approaches a *translation layer* contains wrappers for the translation of service description or request documents. A wrapper implements the ontology-based translation between service description standards. In top-down processing, this layer is used to translate a service request issued by a service consumer into other available description languages. In this case the translation is done each time a service request is issued by a consumer. The source registry that is responsible for managing information about service providers transfers the translated services to the particular service sources. In this approach, the actual matching of a service request with the available descriptions is done by the service provider systems. Using the translated service request, available service descriptions are compared to the consumer's requirements. If a service fits the request, the provider transfers it back to the translation layer, where it is then translated into the language used by the consumer. As a result, the consumer receives a list with service descriptions translated into his service description language.

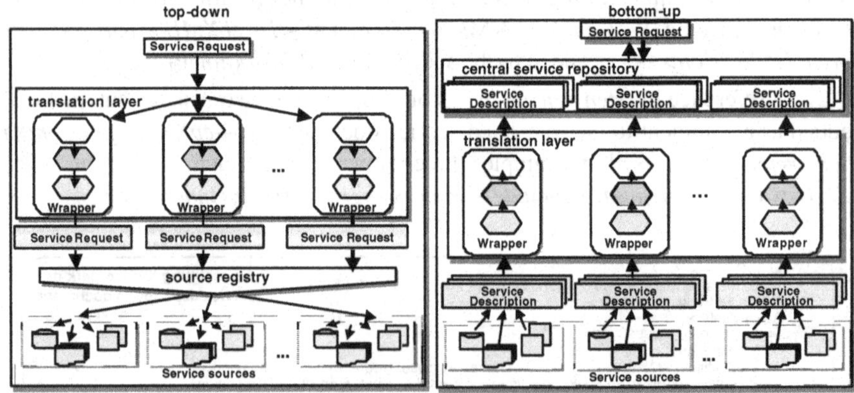

Fig. 9. top-down vs. bottom-up service request processing

In contrast, in the bottom-up approach one central service description language (CSDL) is used to store homogenous service description in a central service repository. This service description language is used to formulate service requests. A consumer can access the central repository with a corresponding interface (e.g. a web form) where he can issue his request.[12] The input of the consumer is then transformed into a CSDL-document that is transferred to the central service repository. Afterwards, it is mapped to the stored service descriptions. Descriptions which are satisfying the request's requirements are then delivered to the consumer.

To publish his services, a provider sends the descriptions of the services he offers to the translation layer, where they are translated into CSDL and stored in the central service repository. Thus, each time a new service is added or an existing one is changed, it has to be translated.

Advantages and disadvantages are summarized in Table 1. Their influence on the application of the two kinds of processing a request are discussed in the following.

One disadvantage of the bottom-up request processing is the necessity of storing translated service descriptions centrally. Validation and consistency checking of service descriptions, support of service migration as well as request processing have to be provided centrally. Thus, bottom-up approach leads to a higher central administrative workload than the top-down approach where service descriptions are maintained locally and requests are processed at the service sources. In addition, in a top-down architecture, a consumer can use his own description language to post a request to the platform, while the bottom-up processing requires a fixed central language and special support for the formulation of requests must be offered.[13]

Table 1. Comparison of bottom-up and top-down request processing

Criteria	Bottom-up	Top-down
workload during build-time	very high	no
workload for processing one request	little	high
translation quality	high	low
support of language variety	medium	high
central maintained functionality	high	little
workload changing service descriptions	high	no
workload for adding new descriptions	high	low

As mentioned, in case of the bottom-up processing every service description must be translated in advance without knowing if it ever will be requested by a consumer. However, the translation of a service description is necessary only when a service is published to the platform or a service change requires an update of its description. Once the translation has been done, a request does not require an additional translation.

In the top-down approach, each request as well as the received service descriptions must be translated on the fly. Note, however, that only the service description satisfying the requirements have to be translated and thus, the overall translation workload will be limited.

Summarizing, a bottom-up approach requires much effort during build-time but offers a more efficient and accurate request processing at runtime. It can be used for ap-

12. To offer an interface which is as much as possible independent of a specific language and therefore understandable for a broad range of consumer, it should be based on the common concepts and terms captured in the SDL-ontology.

13. Beside special interfaces, it is also possible to add another translation layer in order to translate heterogeneous service request, which would increase the work necessary to process one request.

plications where the service offers are rather stable. Furthermore, in order to avoid unnecessary translations, the range of services published should be limited to a specific area. Accordingly, a bottom-up architecture can provide best support for closed, long-term enterprise networks (e.g. to enable inter-organizational cooperation), whereas the top-down architecture can better handle dynamic scenarios where service offerings change frequently. Furthermore, the support of different service request languages is more convenient for applications with a wider, non-limited range of service consumers and providers (e.g. for common service directories).

9 Conclusion

In this paper we have introduced an approach for a semantically correct translation of service descriptions between existing description standards. Our focus is on resolving semantic heterogeneity during the processing of service requests. We advocate formal ontologies to reslove semantic heterogeneity during the translation process.

Two major approaches for an architecture of a system for searching and translating services are presented: bottom-up and top-down. While both of them are generally suited to fit the requirements presented, we argue that each of them has its own advantages and disadvantages for specific application scenarios.

At the moment we focus only a translation of hierarchical relations of elements that are common in the regarded standards. However, XML does not provide semantical information about the nature of the relations between elements of a standard. A model that allows the descriptions of the underlying semantics of such relations (e.g. ER or UML diagrams) has to be used. Therefore, in order to cover also other relations between the elements or concepts (e.g., the inversion of a relation), we will extend our approach and consider conceptual schemas as base for building a translation structure.

References

1. Ankolekar, A.; et al.: DAML-S: Web Service Description for the Semantic Web, in: Proceedings of ISWC 2002, Sardinia, Italy, June 9-12, Springer (2002) 348-363
2. Arkin, A.: Business Process Modeling Language (BPML). BPMI.org Business management initiative. November (2002) http://www.bpmi.org/
3. Bussler, C.; Fensel, D.; Maedche, A.: A Conceptual Architecture for Semantic Web Enabled Web Services, In: SIGMOD Record, Special Issue Semantic Web and Databases (2002)
4. Cardoso, J., Sheth, A.: Semantic e-Workflow Composition. Technical Report LSDIS Lab, Computer Science Department, University of Georgia (2002) http://lsdis.cs.uga.edu/lib/2002.html
5. Ciocoiu, M., Nau D.: "Ontology-Based Semantics". Proceedings of KR'2000, Breckenbridge, Colorado, April 12-17 (2000)
6. cXML, http://www.cxml.org
7. Deitel, H.M., Deitel, P. J., DuWaldt, B., Trees, L. K.: Web Services - A Technical Introduction. Prentice Hall, New Jersey (2002)
8. ebXML, http://www.ebxml.org/specs/index.htm

9. Fernandez, M., Gomez-Perez, A., Juristo, N.: METHONTOLOGY: from ontological art to ontological engineering. In: Workshop on Ontological Engineering AAAI'97, Stanford USA (1997)
10. Guarino, N. and Welty, C.: Identity, unity, and individuality: Towards a formal toolkit for ontological analysis. In: Horn, W. (eds.): Proceedings of ECAI-2000 The European Conference on Artificial Intelligence, Amsterdam. IOS Press (2000)
11. Gruninger, M., Fox, M.: Methodology for the Design and Evaluation of Ontologies. Proceedings of IJCAI'95, Workshop on Basic Ontological Issues in Knowledge Sharing, April 13 (1995)
12. Hakimpour, F., Geppert, A.: Resolving Semantic Heterogeneity in Schema Integration: An Ontology Based Approach. In: Welty, C.; Smith, B. (eds.): Proceedings of International conference on Formal Ontologies in Information Systems FOIS'01. ACM Press (2001) 296-308
13. Klein, M.; Bernstein, A.: Searching for services on the semantic web using process ontologies, in: Proceedings of The First Semantic Web Working Symposium. Stanford (2001)
14. Obrst, L., Wray, R. E., Liu, H.: Ontological Engineering for B2B E-Commerce. In: Welty, C., Smith, C. (eds.): Proceedings of International conference on Formal Ontologies in Information Systems FOIS'01. ACM Press (2001) 117-126
15. Singh M. P., Cannata P. E., Huhns M. N., Jacobs N., Ksiezyk T., Ong K., Sheth A. P., Tomlinson C., Woelk, D.: The Carnot heterogeneous Database Project: Implemented Applications. Distributed and Paralled Databases, Vol. 5, No. 2 (1997) 207-225
16. RosettaNet consortium, http://www.rosettanet.org
17. Schlenoff, C., Ciocoiu, M., Libes, D., Gruninger, M.: Process Specification Language: Results of the First Pilot Implementation. In: Proceedings of the International Mechanical Engineering Congress and Exposition, Nashville, Tennessee, November (1999)
18. Uschold, M., King, M., Moralee, S., Zorgios, Y.: The Enterprise Ontology (1995), http://www.aiai.ed.ac.uk/~entprise/enterprise/ontology.htm
19. Workflow Process Definition Interface - XML Process Definition Language (XPDL). WFMC Document Number WFMC-TC-1025, Hampshire (2002)

On the Query Refinement in the Ontology-Based Searching for Information

Nenad Stojanovic

Institute AIFB,
University of Karlsruhe,
76128 Karlsruhe, Germany
nst@aifb.uni-karlsruhe.de

Abstract. One of the main problems in the (web) information retrieval is the ambiguity of the users' queries, since the users tend to post very short queries. This seems to be valid for the ontology-based information retrieval in which the domain ontology is used as the backbone of the searching process. In this paper we present a novel approach for determining the possible refinements of an ontology-based query. The approach is based on measuring the ambiguity of a query with respect to the original user information need. We defined several types of the ambiguities concerning the structure of the underlying ontology and the content of the information repository. For each of these ambiguities we defined the set of refinements/explanations, which help in more efficient searching for information in an ontology-based information repository.

1 Introduction

The basic problem in the searching for knowledge provided by traditional IR systems is that it only partially reflects the process which humans use in searching for goods in the bricks-and-mortar environment. Briefly, in the non-virtual search, there exist a shop assistant, who helps a user to express his need more clearly and guides the user through the searching space. It means that a user refines his query incrementally according the suggestion made by a shop assistant. In [1] we present the conceptual architecture of the Librarian Agent which simulates the role a human librarian plays in the searching for information resources in a library. The Librarian Agent analyses a user's query based on: (i) the structure of the used vocabulary, (ii) the capacity of the information repository and (iii) the information about the users' past activities in the portal. Based on these analyses, the agent, through an interactive dialogue, guides the users in more efficient searching for information. Particularly, for a query given by a user, the agent measures its ambiguity. In case of high ambiguity, the agent suggests the user the most effective reformulation of the query, considering the underlying vocabulary, the information repository and the agents' experience (based on the past behaviour of users). Last, the agent analyses the users' requests off-line and compares the users' interests with the capacity of the information repository, in order to find which "new titles" should be obtained or which topics are no more interesting for users. The approach assumes the existence of a common vocabulary which is used for creating the queries as well as for providing meta-information about the content of information resources. In this case the problem of merging query's and document's

J. Eder and M. Missikoff (Eds.): CAiSE 2003, LNCS 2681, pp. 324–339, 2003.

term space is resolved on the semantic level, by using synonyms – very similarly to the solution a human librarian uses in resolving the meaning of a term. Moreover, in order to simulate background knowledge which a human librarian uses in searching, we extend the vocabulary to the conceptual model of the given domain, i.e. an ontology. Therefore, we consider ontology-based searching for information [2].

In this paper we focus more on the problem of determining the ambiguity in a user' request and providing corresponding refinements. We define the concept ambiguity, provide a categorization of the ambiguities of users queries and develop methods for measuring and resolving these ambiguities. The approach is based on the analysis of the structure of the underlying vocabulary (ontology) and the content of the information repository. For the analysis of the content of an information repository we use the formal concept analysis (FCA) [3], a mathematic theory about order sets. FCA clusters given data very efficiently and the analysis of the concept lattice formed around a query, discovers many interesting properties of that query, including its ambiguity and possible refinements. Moreover, the additional source for the query's ambiguity resolution (i.e. query refinement) is the query-transaction-log, which is analysed in order to discover frequently used query sequences (so called query patterns).

The paper is organised as follows: In the second section we give the basic terminology we use in this paper, whereas the section 3 presents our Librarian Agent scenario. In the section 4 we give a motivating example for the proposed approach, which is described in the section 5. In the section 6 we discuss some of the related works, whereas section 7 contains conclusion remarks.

2 Background

In this section we give the basic terminology we use in this paper. The presentation is arranged as a sequence of definitions so that the reader, if necessary, can come back to this section in order to clarify statements in the subsequent sections of the paper.

Let $\Re$ and $\aleph$ denote real and natural numbers, respectively. All subscripts are in $\aleph$, unless otherwise specified. If S is a set, 2^S denotes its power set, i.e., the set of all subsets of S, and $|S|$ denotes its cardinality.

Definition 1: Ontology
A core ontology is a structure $O := (C, \leq_c, R, \sigma, \leq_r)$ consisting of

- two disjoint sets C and R whose elements are called concept identifiers and relation identifiers, respectively,
- a partial order $\leq_c$ on C, called concept hierarchy or taxonomy
- a function $\sigma : R \rightarrow C^+$, called signature
- a partial order $\leq_r$ on R called relation hierarchy, where $r_1 \leq_r r_2$ implies $|\sigma(r_1)| = |\sigma(r_2)|$ and $\pi_i(\sigma(r_i)) \leq_c \pi_i(\sigma(r_i))$ for each $1 \leq i \leq |\sigma(r_i)|$

Often we call concept identifiers and relation identifiers, respectively, for the sake of simplicity.

Definition 2: Domain and Range
For a relation $r \in R$ with $|\sigma(r)| = 2$, we define its domain and its range by $dom(r) := \pi_1(\sigma(r))$ and $range(r) := \pi_2(\sigma(r))$.

Definition 3: Axioms
Let *L* be a logical language. A *L*-axiom system for an ontology $O := (C, \leq_c, R, \sigma, \leq_r)$ is a pair $A := (AI, \alpha)$, where

- *AI* is a set whose elements are called axiom identifiers and
- $\alpha : AI \rightarrow L$ is a mapping.
  The elements of $A := \alpha(AI)$ are called axioms.

An ontology with *L*-axioms is a pair *(O, A)*, where *O* is an ontology and *A* is an *L*-axiom system for *O*.

In the FOL notation axioms (or rules) are written as " $p \leftarrow q_1,...,q_n$.". This is read declaratively as q_1 and ... and q_n implies *p*. Each of p (the head) and the q_i's (the symbols of the body) are atomic formula (also referred to as literals), consisting of a predicate (relation) applied to terms, which are either constant or variables. A literal is an atom or a negated atom. In our research, we use F-Logic [4] as the logical language.

Definition 4: Relation properties
We define three properties of the relations: reflexivity, symmetry and transitivity, which are defined by functions r_r, r_s, r_t respectively, in the following manner: $r_t : R \rightarrow R_t$.

Definition 5: Knowledge Base
A Knowledge Base is a structure $KB := (C_{KB}, R_{KB}, I, l_c, l_r)$ consisting of

- two sets C_{KB} and R_{KB}
- a set *I* whose elements are called instance identifiers (or instances or objects in brief)
- a function $l_C : C_{KB} \rightarrow I$ called concept instantiation
- a function $l_r : R_{KB} \rightarrow I^+$ called relation instantiation

A relation instance can be depicted as $r(I_1, I_2,..., I_n)$, where $r \in R_{KB}, I_i \in I$. *r* is called predicate and I_i is a term.

Definition 6: (ontology-based) Query
A (conjunctive) query is of the form or can be rewritten into the form:

$$\forall \overline{X} \ \overline{P}(\overline{X}, \overline{k}) \ \wedge not(\overline{N}(\overline{X}, \overline{k})) \ ,$$

with $\overline{X}$ being a vector of variables $(X_1,..., X_n)$, $\overline{k}$ being a vector of constants (concept instances), $\overline{P}$ being a vector of conjoined predicates (relations) and $\overline{N}$ a vector of disjoined predicates (relations).

For example, for the query "*forall x worksIn(x, KM) and researchIn(x, KMsystems)*" we have $\overline{X} := (x)$, $k := (KM, KMsysteme)$, $\overline{P} := (P_1, P_2)$, $P_1(a,b,c) := worksIn(a,b)$, $P_2(a,b,c) := researchIn(a,c)$.

Each part of a query that can be treated as a regular ontology-based query is called *sub-query* of that query. A query can be viewed as an axiom without a head.
Note: in this paper we consider only conjunctive queries. Since a disjunctive query can be represented as a disjunction of several conjunctive queries our approach can be very easily extended to the disjunctive queries.

3 The Librarian Agent

The role of the Librarian Agent is (i) to support the disambiguation of the queries posted by users (query management) and (ii) to enable the changes in the knowledge repository regarding the users' information needs (collection management).

Fig.1. sketches the application scenario for the Librarian Agent. A user posts the query (cf. 1 in the Fig.1.) which is first processed by the Librarian Agent. The Agent measures the ambiguity of the query (cf. 2 in the Fig.1.) by considering the capacity of the information repository (knowledge base) and the domain vocabulary - ontology. The user is provided by the explanation what is ambiguous in the query and how this ambiguity can influence the result of the querying. Moreover, the agent recommends the user some changes (refinements) in the query (cf. 3 in the Fig.1.). The Agent receives the feedback information about how many (and which) refinements' steps a user performed (cf. 4, 5 in the Figure 1), and it uses this information to refine its own strategies for creating recommendations.

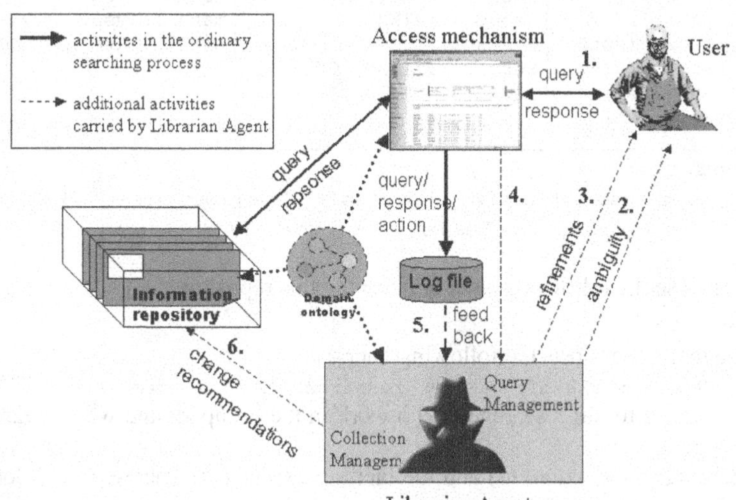

Fig. 1. The roles of the Librarian Agent in the process of searching for knowledge

As the result of the querying, the access mechanism retrieves a list of resources, which is analyzed (cf. 5 in the Fig.1.) by the Librarian Agent in order to make recommendations for the changes in the collection (cf. 6 in the Fig.1.). This recommendation takes into account the analysis of the queries posted by users and the used vocabulary, as well. In order to avoid disturbing the users by additional questioning, the feedback information is collected implicitly by analyzing the activities of the users captured in the log file of the system (cf. 5 in the Fig.1.).

The conceptual model of the given domain – the domain ontology, supports the processing of each step in this approach.

In the rest of this paper we focus on the Query Management component of the Librarian Agent. More information about Collection Management can be found in the [5].

4 Motivating Example

In order to make the description of our approach more understandable we give here an example of the problems which can occur in the ontology-based searching.

Let us consider the following example related to the activities of an institute, referred as the *Research ontology* in the rest of the text:

knowledge base:

Researcher(rst) [1] Researcher(nst) Researcher(ysu) Researcher(jan) Researcher(meh) isA(PhD_student, Researcher) [2] isA(Professor, Researcher), PhD_student(nst) PhD_student(ysu) Professor(rst) Professor(jan)	workIn(rst, KM) [3] workIn(nst, KM) workIn(ysu, KM) workIn(jan, KM) workIn(meh, KM) research_group(KM) researchArea(KMsystem) researchArea(CBR) group_Area(KM, KMsystem) [4] researchIn(rst, CBR) [5] lecture(Ontology)	teaches(rst, Ontology) [6] teaches(nst, Ontology) teaches(ysu, Ontology) teaches(jan, Ontology) teaches(meh, Ontology) teaches(meh, DM) project(OntoWeb) head(rst,OntoWeb) manages(ysu,OntoWeb) participate(meh,OntoWeb)

axioms:

$$\forall\ x, y, z\ \mathtt{researchIn(x,z)} \leftarrow \mathtt{workIn(x,y)} \wedge \mathtt{group\_Area(y,z)} \quad (1)$$

$$\forall\ x, y\ \mathtt{Professor(x)} \leftarrow \mathtt{head(x,y)} \wedge \mathtt{project(y)} \quad (2)$$

Let analyse the following cases of querying this repository:

1. Case

Suppose that a user posts the following query:

$$\forall\ x \leftarrow \mathtt{worksIn(x,\ KM)} \wedge \mathtt{researchIn(x,\ KMsystems)},$$

which searches for all researchers who work in the group KM and who research in the KMsystems.

According to the axiom (1) and the fact group_Area(KM, KMsystem) it follows that all researchers who work in the group KM, research in the KMsystems as well. It means

[1] it means that rst is a Researcher

[2] it means that PhD_student is a subtype Researcher

[3] it means that rst works in the group KM

[4] it means that KM group is focused on research in KMsystems

[5] it means that rst researches in the CBR

[6] it means that rst teaches course about Ontology

that the constraints in the query are redundant (`worksIn(x, KM)` and `researchIn(x, KMsystems)`) and the user should be informed that one of constraints provides no effects on the searching. This information should help the user to understand how his information need is interpreted in the query-system and probably he will refine the query. Moreover, the system should analyse the ontology and the information repository in order to recommend some refinements. For example, the user might be interested in researchers who research in a sub-area of `KM` and not in the whole `KM`.

2. Case

Suppose that a user makes the query:

$\forall$ x $\leftarrow$ `worksIn(x, KM)` $\wedge$ `not researchIn(x, KMsystems).`

Similar to the previous example, this query will be expanded with the information `researchIn(x, KMsystems)`, i.e. that researcher x researches in the area `KMsystems`. However, this information is contradictory with a constraint posted originally by the user. The user should be informed that such a query will never return a result, i.e. that a researcher, who works in the group `KM` and does not research in the `KMsystems` cannot exist. The system should recommend a suitable refinement automatically (by analysing ontology and content).

3. Case

Suppose the query:

$\forall$ x $\leftarrow$ `researcher(x)` $\wedge$ `head(x, Ontoweb).`

According to the axiom (2) only a `Professor` can be the `head` of a `project`. It means that the query will consider only a special sub-type of `researchers` (i.e. `Professor`) and the user should be informed about this new constraints. Probably, the predicate `head` has not been properly used regarding the user information need - his information need can be to find all `researcher` who manage `project OntoWeb`. The system should discover this potential refinement automatically and suggest the user such query modification (predicate `head` -> `manages`), which does not implies new constraints in the query.

4. Case

Suppose the following query:

$\forall$ x $\leftarrow$ `worksIn(X,KM)` $\wedge$ `teaches(X, Ontology).`

Although there are no additional constraints implied by the ontological structure (i.e. rules), the system should discover that in the underlying information repository, all `researchers` who work in the `KM group` are included in the `Ontology lecture`. Therefore, the constraints posted by the user are redundant and he should be informed and guided how to resolve that problem, similarly as in the case 1.

It is clear that the resolving of these situations requires a careful analyse of the underlying ontology and knowledge base regarding the user's query in order to suggest the most suitable refinements of that query. In the next section we present an approach for such a query management.

5 Query Management Component of the Librarian Agent

5.1 The Ambiguity of a Query

The goal of the query management system is to discover ambiguities in queries and to recommend corresponding refinements. We treat a query as an ambiguous one, when the user's information need cannot be uniquely determined from that query[7]. Practically, it means that the same list of results can be obtained for at least one query, which is different from the given one.

The users often estimate the ambiguity of a query through the number of results: a lot of results can be an indicator that there are some irrelevant results, i.e. that some other information needs are covered by that query. In most of the existing IR system, the user gets only this information, the number of results, as the characterisation of the ambiguity. However, the ambiguity of a query is a more complex category and it requires handling by using a more formalised approach.

We have found two main factors, which affect an ambiguity of a query:

1. used vocabulary (i.e. ontology)

(i) e.g. the query for all researchers has a different ambiguity in two vocabularies in which the concept Researcher is modelled through, for example, five and ten subconcepts, respectively (this is called *Clarity*), or

(ii) e.g. the query for "researcher and project" has different ambiguity in a vocabulary where just one relation between the concepts Researcher and Project exists (e.g. participates), than in the vocabulary where two relations between these concepts exist (e.g. participates and headOf) (it is called *Context Clarity*) and

2. the information repository

e.g. the query for a Professor in a repository related to an academic institution will result in much more results than the same query in a repository related to an industry organisation;

Consequently, in order to handle these situations we define two types of the ambiguity of a query:

- the *semantic ambiguity*, as the characteristic of the used vocabulary (i.e. how many interpretations can be assigned to the given query);
- the *content-related ambiguity*, as the characteristics of the information repository (i.e. how a query is related to its "neighbour's" queries).

In the next two subsections we elaborate more on these two types of ambiguities.

The Semantic Ambiguity

A term from the query can be interpreted in various ways depending on the relation between that term and other terms from the vocabulary. For example, the term `Researcher` from the *Researcher ontology* in motivating example, can be interpreted as `Professor` or `PhD_Student`. The possibility to measure this ambiguity increases with the representation power of the vocabulary. In the case of an ontology-based query we define following four types of the *semantic ambiguity*, based on the definition of an ontology given in the section 2:

---

[7] This statement reflects the distinction between the user's unarticulated information need and the query which results from that [6]. One of the common pitfalls in modern IR approaches is the ignorance of this distinction.

1. Incompleteness

The query contains incomplete information about the used concepts/relations. It means that the query can be *automatically* expanded in order to clear the meaning of the query. For the *Research ontology* the query "`forall x,y,z researcher(x) and project(y) and lecture(z) and head(x,y)`" is incomplete because there is a relation between concept `researcher` and `lecture`, namely `teaches`, which can be used to specify the query more precisely.

Regarding the definition of a query given in the section 2, we give the following formalisation of the incompleteness of a query Q which contains subquery $p_1(\overline{X},k) \wedge p_2(\overline{X},k)$:

$$\forall p_1, p_2 \in \overline{P}, y, z \in \overline{X}, C_1, C_2 \in \overline{C}, \exists \; r_1, r_2 \in R \wedge (p_1(\overline{X},k) = l_c(C_1, y)) \wedge$$
$$(p_2(\overline{X},k) = l_c(C_2, z)) \wedge (dom(r_1) = C_1) \wedge range(r_1) = C_2 \wedge \neg\exists p_x \in \overline{P}| \; (p_x = r_1)$$
$$\rightarrow the \;\; query \;\; Q \;\; is \;\; incomplete$$

2. Clarity

A query is incompact or redundant if it contains more terms than are needed and desired to express the same "idea". Concept hierarchy and property hierarchy from the domain ontology are used to check this criterion. The important source of the unclarity are the transitive relation, in general. For example, for the query "`forall x researcher(x) and PhD_Student(x)`" is not clear whether the user is interested in all researchers or only in PhD students. Another example is the case 3 in motivating example.

The formalisation of a query Q which contains predicates $p_1(\overline{X},k) \wedge p_2(\overline{X},k)$:

$$\forall p_1, p_2 \in \overline{P}, y \in \overline{X}, C_1, C_2 \in \overline{C}, \exists \; r_1, r_2 \in R \wedge (p_1(\overline{X},k) = l_c(C_1, y)) \wedge$$
$$(p_2(\overline{X},k) = l_c(C_2, z)) \wedge (C_1 \le c C_2) \rightarrow the \;\; query \;\; Q \;\; is \;\; unclear$$

or in general case for any transitive relation:

$$\forall p_1, p_2 \in \overline{P}, y \in \overline{X}, C_1, C_2 \in \overline{C}, \exists \; r_1 \in R_t \wedge i_1, i_2 \in I \wedge p_1(\overline{X},k) = r_1(y, i_1) \wedge$$
$$p_2(\overline{X},k) = r_1(y, i_2) \wedge r_1(y, i_1) \le_t r_1(y, i_2) \rightarrow the \;\; query \;\; Q \;\; is \;\; unclear$$

3. Redundancy

The query is redundant when it contains the same constraints. We define two types of the redundancy:

1) redundant constraints in the query (case 1 in the motivating example)
2) redundancy in the information repository (case 4 in the motivating example)

The formalisation of a query Q which contains sub-query $p_1(\overline{X},k) \wedge p_{21}(\overline{X},k) \wedge ... \wedge p_{2f}(\overline{X},k)$:

$$\forall p_1, p_{21}, ..., p_{2f} \in \overline{P}, y \in \overline{X}, C_1, C_2 \in \overline{C}, \exists \; r_1 \in R \wedge i_1, i_2 \in I \wedge p_1(\overline{X},k) = r_1(y, i_1)$$
$$\wedge \, p_{21}(\overline{X},k) = r_{21}(y, i_2) \wedge ... \wedge p_{2f}(\overline{X},k) = r_{2f}(y, i_2) \wedge derive(r_1, r_{21}, ..., r_{2f})$$
$$\rightarrow the \;\; query \;\; Q \;\; is \;\; redundant$$

Predicate *derive(a, b,..., l)* depicts the existence of the axiom $a \leftarrow b \wedge ... \wedge l$.

4. Un-satisfiable query

When a query produces no results we treat it as unsatisfable. Similar to the redundancy we define two types of this criterion:

1) contradictory constraints in the query (example 2 in the motivating example)

2) gap in the information repository

The formalisation of the first type for a query Q which contains predicates $p_1(\overline{X},k) \wedge p_{21}(\overline{X},k) \wedge ... \wedge p_{2f}(\overline{X},k)$:

$$\forall p_1 \in \overline{N}, p_{21},..., p_{2f} \in \overline{P},, y \in \overline{X}, \exists \ r_1 \in R \wedge i_1, i_2 \in I \wedge p_1(\overline{X},k) = r_1(y,i_1) \wedge$$

$$\wedge\, p_{21}(\overline{X},k) = r_{21}(y,i_2) \wedge ... \wedge p_{2f}(\overline{X},k) = r_{2f}(y,i_2) \wedge derive(r_1, r_{21},..., r_{2f})$$

$$\rightarrow the \ \ query \ \ Q \ \ is \ \ contradictor$$

In [5] we have defined measures for estimating first two types the semantic ambiguity of an ontology-based query: *ContextClarity* and *Clarity*, respectively. Very briefly, *ContextClarity* is inversely proportional to the number of relations between two concepts, whereas, the *Clarity* is inversely proportional to the number of subconcepts of a concept. Due to lack of space we omit here the formal definitions which can be found in the original paper.

The Content-Related Ambiguity

The *content-related ambiguity* of a query depends on the capacity of the information repository (i.e. which resources are stored in the repository). Since this capacity determines the list of results of a query, the content-related ambiguity of a query can be defined by comparing the results of the given query with the results of another queries. In the rest of this subsection, we define several relations between queries in order to estimate this type of the ambiguity of a query.

Let $Q = (M,O)$ be the query-answering pair, whereas M is an ontology-based query (i.e. metadata) and O is the list of results (i.e. objects) on the query Q. M and O are called query_terms and query_objects respectively.

Definition 7: Structural equivalence (=) by:

$(M_1,O_1) = (M_2,O_2) \leftrightarrow O_1 = O_2$, which can be written as $Q_1 = Q_2 \leftrightarrow O_1 = O_2$

Two queries are structurally equivalent if their result sets are the same.

Definition 8: Structural subsumption (parent-child) (<) by:

$(M_1,O_1) < (M_2,O_2) \leftrightarrow O_1 \subset O_2$.

A query-answering pair (M_2,O_2) subsumes another pair (M_1,O_1) if the result set of the second query-answering pair subsumes the results of the first one. For a query-answering pair Q_1 we define two subsumption relations:

– direct parent ($<_{dir}$): If $Q_1 < Q_2 \wedge \neg\exists Q_i, Q_1 < Q_i < Q_2$, Q_2 is direct_parent of the Q_1;

– direct child ($>_{dir}$): If $Q_2 < Q_1 \wedge \neg\exists Q_i, Q_2 < Q_i < Q_1$, Q_2 is direct_child of the Q_1.

For a query Q_a we define five properties which characterise its structural ambiguity: *Largest equivalent query, Smallest equivalent query Uniquness, Covering* and *CoveringTerms.*

The largest equivalent query for the query Q_a is its equivalent query with the maximal query_terms. It is calculated in the following way: $Q_{a\max} = (\bigcup_{Q_i <_{dir} Q_a} M_i, O_a)$. It means that the largest equivalent query contains the union of query_term of all direct_child.

The smallest equivalent query for the query Q_a is its equivalent query with minimal query_terms. There can be several such queries. They are calculated in the following way: $Q_{a\min} \in \{(\times(M_i \cap M_a), O_a) | \; Q_a <_{dir} Q_i, i = 1,..n\}$

For a query Q_a it is possible to define a subset of objects, which are unique for that query, i.e. they cannot be obtained for any direct_child query. We call that the *Uniqueness* of the query and it is calculated in the following way.

$Uniquness(Q_a) = \{O_a / \{\cup O_i\} | Q_i <_{dir} Q_a, i = 1..n\}$

Covering and *CoveringTerms* are measures which define the percent of identical answers and query_terms, respectively, in two queries. More formally, for two queries Q_a and Q_b we define:

$Covering(Q_a, Q_b) = |O_a \cap O_b| / \max\{|O_a|, |O_b|\}$

$CoveringTerms(Q_a, Q_b) = |M_a \cap M_b| / \max\{|M_a|, |M_b|\}$

It is clear that the calculation of the above mentioned parameters could be time-consuming. In order to make this calculation more effective we use formal concept analysis (FCA) for organising data in the so-called concept lattices, which correspond to the multi-inheritance hierarchical clusters. Each of these clusters can be considered as a query posted to the repository and consequently, the lattice represents the query clustering. By analysing such lattices many interesting relation between queries can be discovered and used for measuring query ambiguity and/or for the query refinement.

Due to the lack of space we omit here the detailed introduction of the FCA which can be found in [3]. We mention only the main concepts needed for the understanding of our approach.

Formal Concept Analysis (FCA) is a technique derived from the lattice theory that has been successfully used for various analysis purposes. Organization over the data is achieved via a mathematical entity called a formal context. A formal context is a triple (G, M, I) where G is a set of objects, M is a set of attributes, and I is a binary relation between the objects and the attributes. A **formal concept** of a formal context (G, M, I) is a pair (A, B) where $A \subseteq G$, $B \subseteq M$, $A = B' = \{g \in G \mid \forall m \in B: (g,m) \in I\}$ and $B = A' = \{m \in M \mid \forall g \in A: (g,m) \in I\}$. For a formal concept (A, B), A is called extent and is the set of all objects that have all the attributes defined in B. Similarly, B is called the intent and is the set of all attributes possessed in common by all the objects in A. As the number of attributes in B increases, the concept becomes more specific, i.e. a specialization ordering is defined over the concepts of a formal context by: $(A_1, B_1) \le (A_2, B_2) \Leftrightarrow B_2 \subseteq B_1$.

In this representation more specific concepts have larger intents and are considered "less than" (<) concepts with smaller intents. The same partial ordering is achieved by considering extents, in which case more specific concepts have smaller extents. The partial ordering over concepts is always a lattice.

In the Fig.2. we present an example of the concept lattice generated (partially) for the example given in the section 2.

Table 1. A part of the *Research ontology*

Attributes / Objects	Researcher	Prof.	workIn ->>KM	researchIn ->>CBR	researchIn->>KMsystems	teaches->>Ontology
rst	x	x	x	x	x	x
nst	x		x	x	x	x
ysu	x		x	x	x	x
jan	x	x	x		x	x
meh	x		x		x	x

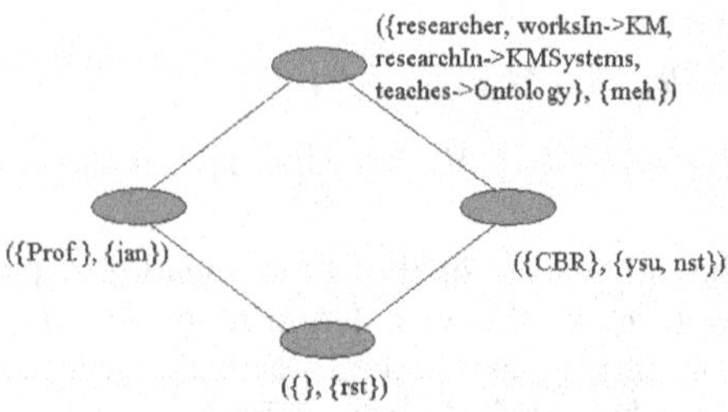

Fig. 2. Example showing the process of generating a derived concept lattice from a set of data given in the table 1. The concepts represented in the lattice should be read as in the following example: foremost left formal concept, (`{Prof.}, {jan}`), corresponds to the objects (`jan, rst`) and attributes (`Researcher, Prof., workIn->>KM, researchIn->>KMSystems, teaches->>Ontology`)

Such a representation enables very intuitive interpretation of a query: one can see a formal concept as a representation of a query state, where the intent of the concept represents the query itself and the extent represents all resources that match the query. For example, the query "`forall x Prof(x) and researchIn(x, KMSystem)`" will be mapped onto the formal concept (`{Prof.}, {jan}`) (note that a concept encompasses all objects from its subconcepts).
Such an ordering in the query space enables very easily interpretation of query results regarding their ambiguity. For example, in the case 4 in the motivating example, the query "`forall x worksIn(X,KM) and teaches(X, Ontology)`" is mapped onto the formal concept (`{Researcher, worksIn->KM, researchIn->KMSystems, teaches->Ontology}, {meh}`). By analysing the properties of this formal concept we reason about the ambiguities of the query:

1) the query contains redundant constraints: all `Researcher` which work in `KM group`, teach the `Ontology lecture`
2) this query is semantically equivalent to the queries

```
forall x Researcher(x)
forall x researchIn(x, KMSystems)
forall x teaches(x, Ontology)
```

In other words, by reading the attributes of the formal concept which corresponds to the query, we can estimate the proposed ambiguity parameters directly. The formal expression of the query's ambiguities using FCA is out of the scope of this paper. In the next subsection we give more details about the possibilities to use FCA as a query refinement mechanism.

5.2 Refinement

Our approach for query refinement tries to reflect the refinement model which a human librarian (or shop assistant) uses in his daily work. It means that we use three sources of information in suggesting query refinement:

1. the structure of the underlying ontology (vocabulary)
2. the content of the knowledge repository
3. the users' behaviour (how users refine their queries on their own)

Since all of our ambiguity measures are formally defined, it is very easily to determine which part of the given query is ambiguous and to focus user's attention on these "ambiguous" constraints. For example, by using the definition of the *incompleteness* in the section 4.1.1, in the case of such an ambiguity in his query, the user should be provided with the recommendation to add a relation (r_1) in the query, in order to clarify the meaning of the query.

Moreover, using the quantification of the ambiguities we can determine which of the ambiguities should be resolved firstly. For example, for the case 1 from the motivating example, `forall x worksIn(x, KM) and researchIn(x, KMsystems)`, the system suggests the refinement of the second predicate (`researchIn(x, KMsystems)`) because its clarity according to the *Clarity* factor, presented in the previous subsection, is greater than the clarity of the first one. Moreover, the approach uses the FCA to determine the possible refinements with respect to the content of the knowledge repository. For example, by considering concept lattice presented in Figure 3 the system will suggest refinement `researchIn(x, CBR)` for the case 1 in the motivating example.

Hence, our approach tries to combine semantics of the domain model (1. source) with the capacity of the information repository (2. source) in order to provide recommendations for the most relevant refinements, by assuming that the user will refine its query linearly (not to change the whole query).

The third source for making the query's refinement recommendation (i.e. user's behaviour) requires an analysis of the users activities in an ontology-based application. In [7] we presented a framework for capturing user's activities in a semantic query log file. This query log is "mined" in order to discovery so called query patterns, which describes regularities in the behaviour of the users during searching a portal. That analysis is out of the scope of this paper.

Discussion

In the following we present briefly how the concept lattice[8] can be used in supporting these types of the refinement. Due to lack of space the approach is described quite informally.

The first interesting feature that can be found in the lattice structure is that adding additional attributes into a query will always move the query state to some formal concept below the current state, which maps mathematically to the definition of the

[8] we consider that concept lattice represents all implicit information which can be derived from the domain axioms

sub-concept relation. To find all query states that model such extensions of the current query we have to find all subconcepts of the current position.

By comparing the intents of the concepts along the edges we can map the attributes that can be added to the new position in the lattice. In the example given in Figure 3 the possible refinements for the query `forall x researchIn(x, CBR)` will be adding the constraint "`Prof.`", pointing to the concept with objects `rst` in the extent. From the concept lattice it is clear that all other refinements, e.g. "`workIn->>KM`", "`Researcher`" etc will not change the list of results, since all these attributes are related to the concepts above the concept (`{CBR},{rst, ysu, nst}`).

The same discussion can be applied for the deleting attributes from a query, which will always move the query state to some concept above the current state, which maps mathematically to the definition of the superconcept relation. To find all query states that model such reduction of the current query we have to find all superconcepts of the current position. For example, for the query `forall x worksIn(x, KM) and researcher(x) and researchIn(x, CBR)`, which corresponds to the concept (`{CBR},{rst, ysu, nst}`), the reduction of the constraints "`Researcher(x)`" or "`worksIn(x, KM)`" will not provide any new results. From the structure of the concept lattice it is clear that only the reduction of the constraint "`researchIn(x, CBR)`" effects the query results.

However, the concept lattice does not provide explicit specification of the generalisation and specialisation of an attribute, because all concepts which are below a concept in the lattice have more attributes than that concept. The trivial case is when a concept X has only one parent concept in the lattice: then one of the attributes associated to the parent concept is the "real" generalisation of the "new" attribute in the concept X. For example, the concept (`{Prof.}, {rst, sst}`) has only one parent which contains the generalisation of the attribute "`Prof.`" (attribute "`Researcher`"). For the case of more parent concept, the semantic of the attributes has to be processed.

The next case is the query that contains some contradiction, i.e. query for something that does not exist in the data set. Such a query will point to a bottom element with an empty extent and we can avoid offering these refinements easily. Moreover, by using the properties of the concept lattice, it is possible to determine ideal position of an *unsatisfiable* query in the lattice and by moving along the edges in order to determine:

1) which constraints should be relaxed from the original query in order to get results and

2) what is the first approximation of the result of that unsatisfiable query

Such a query relaxation can be very useful mechanism to cope with the uncertainties in the queries or gap in the knowledge repository. For example, in a skill management application an unsatisfiable query for an expert in several research areas, will result in the nearest real neighbour of that ideal request.

Another useful feature when finding query refinements this way is that once we found the states that are possible refinements we have the size of the new result set which is the size of the extent of the concept that will be reached. Using this feature of the lattice we can give the user the information of the size of the next result set before she chooses a refinement, a front-end can allow sorting or filtering the refinements by this size.

6 Related Work

Query Ambiguity

The determination of an ambiguity in a query, as well as the sources of such an ambiguity is the prerequest for the efficient searching for information. Although some recent work is done in quantifying the query ambiguity based on the language model of the knowledge repository [8], [9], the IR research community did not explore the problem of using rich domain model in modelling the querying. Some very important results in the query analysis can be found in the deductive database community [10], namely semantic query optimisation. That approach, although revolutionary for using domain knowledge for the optimal compilation of the queries, does not consider the ambiguity of the query regarding user's information need at all.

Query Refinement

There is a lot of research devoted to the query refinement in the Web IR community. In general, we see two directions of the modifying queries or query results to the need of a users: query expansion and recommendation systems respectively. *The query expansion* is aimed at helping the users make a better query, i.e. it attempts to improve retrieval effectiveness by replacing or adding extra terms to an initial query. The *interactive query expansion* supports such an expansion task by suggesting candidate expansion terms to users, based usually on hyper-index [11] or concept-hierarchies [12] automatically constructed from the document repository. In [13] the model of the query-document space is used for the interactive query expansion. *Recommendation systems* [14] try to recommend items similar to those a given user has liked in the past (content-based recommendation) or try to identify users whose tastes are similar to those of the given user, and recommend items they have liked (collaborative recommendation). Personalised web agents, e.g. WebWatcher [15] track the users browsing and formulate user profiles which are used in suggesting which links are worth following from the current web page.

However, none of these approaches uses rich domain model for the refinement of a query, i.e. the reasons for doing a refinement are not based on the deeply understanding of the structure of a query or the deeply exploring of the interrelationships in the information repository. Moreover, none of them tries to determine (measure) the ambiguity in a query and to suggest a refinement which will decrease such an ambiguity.

Formal Concept Analaysis

In [16], the authors described an approach, named REFINER, to combine Boolean information retrieval and content-based navigation with concept lattices. For a Boolean query REFINER builds and displays a portion of the concept lattice associated with the documents being searched centred around the user's query. The cluster network displayed by the system shows the result of the query along with a set of minimal query refinements/enlargements. A similar approach is proposed in [17], by adding the size of the query result as an additional factor of the navigation. Moreover, the distance between queries in the lattice is used for similarity ranking.

The main drawback in these approaches is that both start from the characteristics of the concept lattice and try to map these characteristics into the query refinement process. In that way, practically, they constrain the queries which are analysed to the set of queries which correspond to the formal concepts in a formal context (i.e. a query is treated only when it is the largest query of an other queries in the repository). Thus, they do not model the query refinement process and miss some very important properties for the refinement (such as a set of equivalent queries, max_Equality, min_Equality, uniquness). Another problem is that they do not consider the partial ordering of the metadata into a vocabulary, losing the possibilities to find a real specialisation/generalisation of a query, which is one of the very frequently used refinements. Moreover, the ambiguity of the query, as the crucial reason for the query refinement process, is not treated at all.

7 Conclusion

In this paper, we presented an approach for the query management in ontology-based IR systems. The system treats a library scenario in which users query the repository for knowledge resources. Consequently, the so-called Librarian Agent plays the role of the human librarian in the traditional library – it uses all possible information, about the domain vocabulary, the behaviour of previous users and the capacity of the knowledge repository, in order to help users to find the resources they are interested in. Based on various analyses, the agent, through an interactive dialogue, guides the users in more efficient searching for information. Particularly, for a query given by a user, the agent measures its ambiguity, regarding the underlying vocabulary (i.e. ontology), as well as the content (capacity) of the information repository. In case of high ambiguity, the agent suggests the user the most effective reformulation of the query. The recommendation can be based on the query-patterns, found by analysing users' past behaviour in the given application.

We find that our approach represents a very important step in simulating the brick-and-mortar environment and benefiting from applying the practical results obtained in that area in the searching for information in the virtual world. Moreover, this approach leads to the self-adaptive knowledge portals, which can discover some changes from the user's interactions with the system automatically and evolve their structure correspondingly.

One of the very important benefits we did not elaborate in this paper is the optimisation of an ontology-based query using presented approach. Indeed, a query can be translated in several semantically equivalent forms and one with the minimal cost will be evaluated. It will be the part of our future works.

Acknowledgement. The research presented in this paper would not have been possible without our colleagues and students at the Institute AIFB, University of Karlsruhe. Research for this paper was partially financed by BMBF in the project "SemiPort" (08C5939).

References

1. Stojanovic, N.: On the role of a Librarian Agent in Ontology-based Knowledge Management Systems, Workshop Ontologiebasiertes Wissensmanagement, 2. Konferenz Professionalles Wissensmanagement, Luzern, April 2003

2. N. Guarino, C. Masolo, and G. Vetere, "OntoSeek: Content-Based Access to the Web", *IEEE Intelligent Systems*, 14(3), pp. 70–80, (May 1999).
3. Ganter, B and Wille, R: *Formal Concept Analysis: Mathematical Foundations.* Springer Verlag, 1999.
4. Kifer, M., Lausen, G., Wu, J.: Logical Foundations of Object-Oriented and Frame-Based Languages, Journal ACM, 42:741–843, 1995
5. Stojanovic, N., Stojanovic, L: Usage-oriented Evolution of Ontology-based Knowledge Management Systems, *Proceedings of the 1st Int'l Conf. on Ontologies, Databases and Application of Semantics (ODBASE-2002)*, Irvine, CA, 2002.
6. Saracevic, T.: Relevance: A Review of and a framework for the thinking on the notion in information science. Journal of the American Society for Information Science, 26, (6), 321–343, 1975
7. Stojanovic, N., Stojanovic, L., Gonzalez, J: More efficient searching in a knowledge portal – an approach based on the analysis of users' queries, Fourth International Conference on Practical Aspects of Knowledge Management (PAKM 2002), Vienna, 2002, Springer LCNS/LNAI
8. Ponte, J. and Croft, W.B.: A language modeling approach to information retrieval, Proceedings of ACM SIGIR'98, 275–28, 1998.
9. Cronen-Townsend, S. and Croft, W.B.: Quantifying Query Ambiguity, in the Proceedings of HLT 2002,pp. 94–98.
10. Chakravarthy, U., Grant, J. and Minker, J: *Logic-based approach to semantic query optimization.* ACM Transactions on Database Systems, 15(2):162–207, 1990.
11. Bruza PD and Dennis S. Query Reformulation on the Internet: Empirical Data and the Hyperindex Search Engine. In: Proceedings of RIAO97, Computer-Assisted Information Searching on Internet, Montreal, June 1997
12. Joho, H., Coverson, C., Sanderson, M., Beaulieu, M.: Hierarchical presentation of expansion terms, ACM SAC, 2002
13. Wen, J.-R., Nie, J.-Y. and Zhang, H.-J. Clustering User Queries of a Search Engine. WWW10, May 1–5, 2001, Hong Kong.
14. Balabanovic, M., Shoham, Y.: Content-Based, Collaborative Recommendation. CACM 40 (3): 66–72 (1997)
15. Joachims, T.; Freitag, D.; and Mitchell, T. 1997. Webwatcher: A tour guide for the World Wide Web. In Proc. IJCAI-97.
16. Carpineto, C., Romano, G. Effective re formulation of boolean queries with concept lattices. *In Flexible Query Answering Systems FQAS'98*, pp. 277{291, Berlin Heidelberg, Springer-Verlag, 1998.
17. Becker, P., Eklund, P., Prospects for Document Retrieval using Formal Concept Analysis, *Proceedings of the Sixth Australasian Document Computing Symposium*, Coffs Harbour, Australia, December 7, 2001.

An Ontology-Driven Framework for the Management of Semantic Metadata Describing Audiovisual Information

Chrisa Tsinaraki, Eleni Fatourou, and Stavros Christodoulakis

MUSIC/TUC, Technical University of Crete Campus, 73100 Kounoupidiana, Crete, Greece
{chrisa, eleni, stavros}@ced.tuc.gr

Abstract. In this paper, we describe a framework for the management of semantic metadata that describe audiovisual content. The main objectives of this work are to provide a framework allowing enhanced retrieval performance and better user interfaces for audiovisual data, based on extensions of the well accepted international standards for the digital media, digital broadcasting and TV-Anytime domains like TV-Anytime and MPEG-7, as well as to provide an interoperability framework between TV-Anytime and MPEG-7 for the rapidly expanding set of interoperating digital library and interactive TV applications. The framework was developed in the context of the UP-TV project, which investigates TV-Anytime architectures and services. Our approach is ontology-driven, in the sense that we provide ontology based domain-specific extensions of the standards for describing multimedia content. Several aspects of the framework are based on the existence of ontologies. Our framework allows the creation of more efficient user interfaces for accessing content, better retrieval performance and better support in the indexing phase. It also provides compatibility in indexing between the two standards and interoperability for TV-Anytime and digital library applications supported by TV-Anytime servers. We have developed a domain-specific ontology (football games) to test our framework ideas and implementation. The developed ontology uses as primitive modelling elements those provided by the MPEG-7 metadata model. The mapping of the ontology to TV-Anytime metadata primitives is straightforward. We show in detail the concrete implementation of the framework on top of relational databases and its interfaces with the other system components.

1 Introduction

We are witnessing the last few years increasing cooperation (and sometimes merging) of computer, home electronics, software, broadcasting and audiovisual information provision industries. Some of the more popular scenarios offered to users include digital audiovisual libraries [8], [11], [6], video on demand services [3] [16] [17] [19] and recently TV-Anytime services [15]. The simpler TV-Anytime scenario foresees that future TVs will be equipped with a processor and large, inexpensive disk storage devices that will be capable of selecting on a continuous basis broadcasted digital TV programs for the user to see on his spare time, according to his personal interests (profile). More recently, the TV-Anytime consortium emphasizes also an open home TV platform with Internet connection capabilities, as well as high-speed access to

J. Eder and M. Missikoff (Eds.): CAiSE 2003, LNCS 2681, pp. 340–356, 2003.

TV-Anytime Servers, which have expanded program-capturing capabilities. The server may also offer additional digital library services, thus integrating TV-Anytime, digital library and video on demand services.

As we move from the simpler traditional multimedia services to the more advanced ones, content-based retrieval, either directly from the user or in a way transparent to him, becomes a dominant factor for the success of such services, as it is needed in the different levels of interaction of the service provision system with the end-users. For example, a sports reporter might search among football match videos in a video library in order to retrieve videos of football matches where a certain player, e.g. Ronaldo, scores. On the other hand, an end-user might denote in his preference profile in a personalized TV environment that he would like all the goals of a football match to be recorded for him. While viewing them he may request to see some extracts of the goals of Ronaldo against the same team two years ago from the digital library of the server, as well as articles, comments, critics from reporters, pictures or other audiovisual material about him. In those cases, appropriate retrieval capabilities on the content of the audiovisual information are needed.

The requirements of the above use cases can be satisfied in a system, which stores semantic descriptions for the audiovisual information and provides semantic-based search capabilities on the information content. The semantic descriptions are in fact semantic metadata for the content of the audiovisual information – that is, data describing the content of the audiovisual information. The descriptors may refer to the whole multimedia content or to parts of the content (segments). To guarantee interoperability in complex application environments as the ones above, it is of outmost importance to adhere to international standards.

Widely accepted standards for audiovisual applications and content descriptions include *MPEG-7* [18] and *TV-Anytime* [22]. MPEG-7 is a standard used for the description of multimedia and video metadata that defines a set of *Description Schemes (DSs),* essentially complex data types, which will be used to describe audiovisual content. MPEG-7 provides a set of description schemes rooted on the *SemanticBase DS*, which contain all the constructs needed for semantic content description. The TV-Anytime forum on the other hand, works on the specification of advanced TV broadcasting servers and TV clients that support personalized ubiquitous services. The TV-Anytime forum has been working on a metadata series, where the most visible parts of metadata are the attractors/descriptors or hyperlinks used in electronic program guides, or in Web pages. This information will be used from the end-users in order to decide whether or not to acquire a particular piece of content. In complex application environments as the above, the content of specific multimedia segments may have been described in either standard.

Before the establishment of standards, research on the semantic description of audiovisual data has been carried out in several models [1] [2] [9] [14] [6] some of which have been implemented in either prototype or real-world systems. During standard definition some research groups used the draft standards and fed their experience back to the standard definition process [20] [21] [12]. Some other systems have been based on specific standards, but there exists no interoperability support [13] [15]. It is very important that we base our research and development efforts on top of the existing standardization efforts (MPEG-7 and TV-Anytime) and that we seek to expand the retrieval functionality of these frameworks for application specific areas providing at the same time for the compatibility of the enhanced functionality.

Our approach to providing enhanced content-based retrieval in advanced audiovisual applications as the above is ontology[1]-driven. The modelling of the metadata for the description of audiovisual information is based on domain-specific ontologies and several aspects of the framework are based on these ontologies. The use of domain-specific ontologies significantly enhances retrieval performance in an open environment, since it guides the users on what is the language they can use to specify their content preferences, and it also guides the indexers and/or the automatic indexing mechanisms to provide legal content descriptions for specific content. The specification of the legal content descriptions in specific domains not only enhances the retrieval performance in the recall/precision sense, but also allows for better interactive interfaces between naive users and the system. It also enables the use of a better user interface metaphor for interactive TV which is based on selection from a list of allowed constructs and values, instead of inserting text with the help of the remote control. The systematic definition of domain-specific ontologies and their integration to MPEG-7 and TV-Anytime frameworks provides a standardized way of enhancing the functionality of those frameworks.

Newer Interactive TV trends as outlined also in the TV-Anytime forum foresee that the TV sets will be equipped not only with a large disk, but they will also have Internet connections which will allow enhanced TV-Anytime functionality through the connection of home TV-Anytime servers with last mile connections and also allow functionality for users on the move. This expanded TV-Anytime functionality imposes interoperability requirements for TV-Anytime with other audiovisual and digital library standards, like MPEG-7. For example, last mile servers may provide additional archival audiovisual information in MPEG-7, which has been produced by other information providers (Web etc.). In our framework, compatibility and interoperability between the standards is maintained since the same ontology is mapped to be used for the extension of both standards. The retrieval or filtering mechanisms can easily map the preferences of the user (which are also described using the ontology) to both the MPEG-7 and the TV-Anytime metadata representations and achieve enhanced retrieval.

In this paper we describe the framework we have developed for the management of semantic metadata used for the content-based description of audiovisual information. The design of the framework is based on existing, widely accepted standards in the Digital TV and TV broadcasting domains, namely MPEG-7 and TV-Anytime. The framework provides "dual" support, in the sense that it provides pure TV-Anytime functionality as well as pure MPEG-7 functionality, on top of two different repositories, populated consistently using the same annotation tool. This work has been done in the context of the UP-TV project[2]. The proposed approach can be used in any environment where the need for a detailed description of audiovisual material exists.

---

[1] An *ontology* is a set of entities and relationships among them that capture the knowledge on a specific application domain [10].

[2] UP-TV (Ubiquitous & Personalized TV Services) is a European IST project, in which MUSIC takes part and is responsible for its metadata management system.

The rest of this paper is organized as follows: In section 2 we provide an outline of our framework, while in section 3 we refer to our model for the representation of content-description metadata and the ontology we have developed for the annotation of football match videos. The semantic base, where semantic metadata are stored, is described in section 4, while the metadata annotation component we have developed and the API for the support of advanced semantic-based queries are described in sections 5 and 6 respectively. In section 7 we present the conclusions of our work and a brief description of our future research in this area.

2 Framework Description

In this section we provide an outline of the framework we developed for the management of semantic metadata for audiovisual information. The architecture of our framework is depicted in Fig. 1.

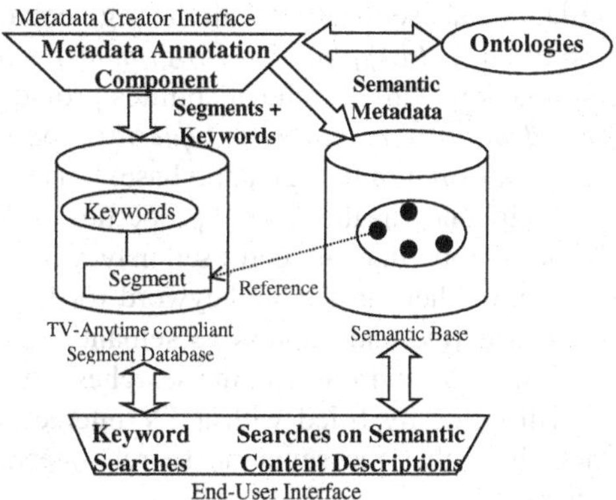

Fig. 1. Framework Architecture

The framework includes two different repositories: A *TV-Anytime compliant Segment Database* containing segmentation metadata represented as TV-Anytime segments, and an *MPEG-7 compliant Semantic Base* where semantic metadata are stored. Capabilities for the population of the Semantic Base are provided, as well as advanced information retrieval capabilities based on the semantic metadata. The framework development includes:

1. The establishment of *a two-layered model for the annotation of audiovisual content*: A set of core metadata entities defined in the Semantic part of MPEG-7 that can be used for the annotation of any video program comprise the first layer of our model, while for specific categories of video content appropriate ontologies are defined. The ontology entities and the relationships among them comprise the second layer of our model [20], [21].
2. The definition of *ontologies for specific subject domains* that implement the second layer of our model. The ontologies are represented using MPEG-7 syntax and constructs. We have developed and integrated an ontology for football matches in

order to test our framework ideas. We will expand the capabilities of our system with other domain-specific ontologies in the future (e.g. news).

3. The implementation of a *Semantic Base* (on top of a relational database) for the metadata information management. The database schema encapsulates our core model as well as the supported ontologies. In fact, the database schema is MPEG-7 compliant.
4. The implementation of a *Metadata Annotation Component* for the population of the semantic base. The component has been integrated with the segmentation tool developed by MUSIC/TUC in the context of the UP-TV project. For each video program, as well as for the video segments defined in a video program, the annotation component is used for the definition of the corresponding metadata items. Then, the metadata items are stored in the semantic base. The semantic base also stores references from the metadata items to the corresponding programs and/or segments. In addition, sets of keywords that are automatically inferred from the metadata items are produced. These keywords are used for the annotation of the video programs and the video segments defined as their parts and are stored in a TV-Anytime compliant database together with the segmentation metadata.
5. The implementation of an *API (Application Programmer's Interface)* that permits, in addition to the simple keyword search capabilities provided by the TV-Anytime compliant database, *advanced semantic-based queries*. The API methods make use of the semantic metadata stored in the semantic base, thus the queries posed can be more accurate as far as it concerns the desired properties of the query results.

From the above, it is obvious that the end-user may search among the programs and segments in our system either via simple keyword (or keyword phrase) searches or using more complex, accurate and expressive semantic searches. As the later is difficult to be supported in a TV environment, the searches will be posed using certain search templates that will be easily filled with a TV interaction device (e.g. remote control). We must note here that the semantic search interfaces are based on the ontologies present in the system.

All the framework components have been implemented in the Linux OS environment, using the MySQL database for the Semantic Base and the TV-Anytime compliant database. The Semantic Annotation Component has been implemented in java.swing. The ontology for the description of football matches is expressed using MPEG-7 syntax and constructs. The advanced search functions made available through the search API are implemented using JDBC on top of a relational database.

3 Semantic Metadata Model

In this section, we describe the model for the representation of content-description metadata for audiovisual information. As we have already mentioned it is compatible with the MPEG-7 and TV-Anytime standards. Both standards provide syntax and constructs for the definition of metadata items for the description of audiovisual content. We will provide an overview of the metadata models for both standards next.

In MPEG-7 a set of description schemes provides the complex data types needed for the semantic description of audiovisual content. The more important among the description schemes are:

- *SemanticBase DS:* The abstract type *SemanticBaseType* is defined here. SemanticBaseType is the base type extended by other description schemes according to the needs for the description of semantic entities of specific types in a narrative world.
- *SemanticBag DS* and *Semantic DS:* Description schemes used for the description of collections of semantic entities. *SemanticBagType* is an abstract type, defined in the SemanticBag DS, extending SemanticBaseType, while *SemanticType* is defined in Semantic DS. SemanticType is concrete type, thus its instances are used for the representation of semantic entity collections.
- *AgentObject DS:* The actors that appear in an audiovisual segment are described here using the extensions of the abstract type *AgentObjectType* that extends SemanticBaseType. Actors in general are represented using the *AgentType*, an abstract type extending AgentObjectType defined in the *Agent DS*. *PersonType*, *OrganizationType* and *PersonGroupType* extend AgentType, are defined correspondingly in the *Person DS*, the *Organization DS* and the *PersonGroup DS* and are used for the representation of persons (e.g. a football player), organizations (e.g. a football team) and groups of persons.
- *Object DS:* The *ObjectType* defined here extends SemanticBaseType and is used for the description of objects and object abstractions in the material world (e.g. the ball in a football match).
- *Event DS:* The *EventType* defined here extends SemanticBaseType and is used for the description of events that take place in a semantic world (e.g. a goal).
- *ConceptDS:* The *ConceptType* defined here extends SemanticBaseType and is used for the description of concepts present in an audiovisual segment (e.g. co-operation).
- *SemanticState DS:* The *SemanticStateType* defined here extends SemanticBaseType and is used for the description of a state of the world described in an audiovisual segment and the parametric description of its features (e.g. the score in a football match before and after a goal).
- *SemanticPlace DS:* The *SemanticPlaceType* defined here extends SemanticBaseType and is used for the description of a place in a semantic world (e.g. Athens).
- *SemanticTime DS:* The *SemanticTimeType* defined here extends SemanticBaseType and is used for the description of semantic time (e.g. Easter).

An important attribute, useful for the support of ontologies, is defined in SemanticBaseType and is inherited in all its extensions: *AbstractionLevel*. AbstractionLevel is of type *AbstractionLevelType*. It has only one attribute, Dimension, of non-negative integer type. When AbstractionLevel is not present in a semantic description, the description refers to specific audiovisual material. When AbstractionLevel is present, abstraction exists in the description. When the Dimension of AbstractionLevel is 0, there exists a description of a semantic entity (e.g. the football player Ronaldo) that is related to every audiovisual segment where the entity appears. When AbstractionLevel has a non-zero Dimension, it specifies classes for the description of abstract semantic entities. The bigger the Dimension of AbstractionLevel, the more extended the abstraction in the description (e.g. Ronaldo is an instance of the "football player" class with AbstractionLevel.Dimension=1, while "football player" is an instance of the "person" class with AbstractionLevel.Dimension=2).

The TV-Anytime standard provides, through the TV-Anytime metadata series, the TV-Anytime metadata system for enabling the consumer to find, navigate and manage content from a variety of internal and external sources including, for example, enhanced broadcast, interactive TV, Internet and local storage. It defines a standard way to describe consumer profiles including search preferences to facilitate automatic filtering and acquisition of content by agents on behalf of the consumer.

As far as it concerns semantic metadata describing audiovisual programs and segments, they are related to the types BasicContentDescriptionType and BasicSegmentDescriptionType respectively. These types include the following common description elements:

- *Title*: A title given to the segment or program. There can be multiple titles for a segment or program.
- *Synopsis*: A textual description of the segment or program content.
- *Keywords*: Important words or phrases, describing the content of the segment or program.
- *RelatedMaterial*: References to external material, related to the content of the segment or program.

It is obvious from the above that the main mechanism in the TV-Anytime metadata system that could be used for semantic content description is the use of keywords or keyword phrases. Taking advantage of this mechanism, it would be possible to support a keyword-based information retrieval mechanism, similar to a Web search engine. The experience from the search engines shows that such a mechanism has limited performance (precision/recall).

In the digital TV environment we have additional problems due to the interface limitations (lack of keyboard, limited resolution). Instead of an interface that allows the user to select letters to form keywords, an interface that provides a set of application-specific search templates has been implemented.

In our framework we define domain-specific ontologies compatible with the standards. We integrate these ontologies in our databases. The indexers (people responsible for providing metadata for indexing the segments of the audiovisual content) use terms and relationships from the controlled vocabulary with the precise semantics that the ontology contains to do the indexing. In this work they may use the PC interfaces. The users on the other hand, utilize TV-based interfaces. However these interfaces guide the users to select from an existing set of items and relationships through templates and selection mechanisms that guarantee faster interaction and better retrieval performance.

We have dual support, for both MPEG-7 and TV-Anytime in our framework:

- We maintain a Semantic Base where semantic metadata for the description of the content of audiovisual information are stored. We have chosen to define the core entities as restrictions of the corresponding MPEG-7 entities, as the MPEG-7 definitions cannot be fully exploited in a TV-Anytime like environment, while they make the system much more complicated. Thus, the Semantic Base is MPEG-7 compliant. The Semantic Base is described in detail in section 4.
- A TV-Anytime compliant database is used for the storage of segmentation information annotated with keywords that describe the segment contents. The

keywords in the TV-Anytime database have been inferred from the semantic metadata stored in the Semantic Base. The inference is based on the knowledge encapsulated in domain-specific ontologies and a set of rules stored in the Semantic Base. Each rule is a template, which produces a keyword phrase for each relationship (e.g. for a goal scored by Ronaldo is produced the keyword phrase "Ronaldo scores"). In addition, independent keywords corresponding to the metadata items related to the video segment are stored in the TV-Anytime database (e.g. "Ronaldo" and "goal" for a goal scored by Ronaldo).

This approach is compliant with the TV-Anytime forum policies, as the forum moves to the support of servers that provide added value services together with the standard TV-Anytime functionality.

3.1 Ontology for the Description of Football Matches

In order to evaluate our framework, we have defined an ontology for the description of football matches. The entities of the ontology and the relationships among them comprise the second layer of our video metadata model. The definition of the ontology is based on the rules of FIFA (the international organization responsible for the definition of football rules) [7].

We defined our ontology using MPEG-7 syntax and constructs. Thus, we use the mechanism provided by MPEG-7 for the definition of abstract semantic entities, the use of AbstractionLevel. An MPEG-7 compliant XML document contains the entities of interest that have been defined.

In the following paragraphs, the representation of time periods, places, actor roles and events in a football match are described.

Time. Abstract time entities, referring to the time periods in a football match are defined in our ontology. The part-of hierarchy of the ontology terms for the time periods of a football match is shown in Fig. 3.

As shown in Fig. 3, there exist the *Pre–game Time*, the *Arbiter*, the *First half*, the *Halftime*, the *Second half*, the *Extra time*, the *Time lost* and the *Penalty period.* The *Start Time Point* is the beginning of the First half, while the *End Time Point* is the end of the Second half.

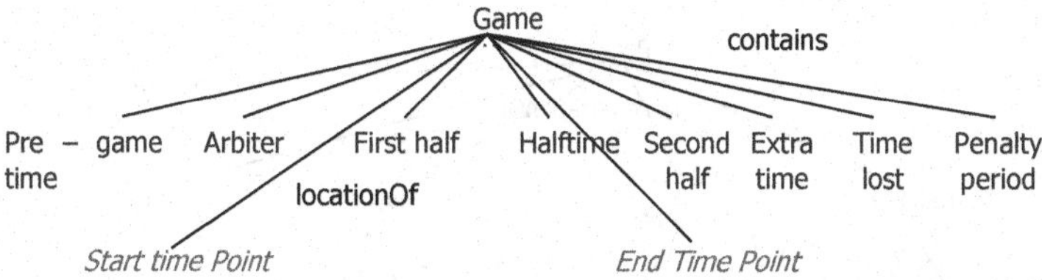

Fig. 2. The ontology terms for time periods in a football match

Places. Football matches usually take place in a stadium. In order to make possible the support of more accurate queries (e.g. events near the halfway line), we have defined a part-of hierarchy of the ontology terms for the stadium regions, as shown in Fig 2. According to Fig. 2, the ontology terms for the stadium regions are:

1. The *Area of Play*. It contains the *Field* and the *Goal Posts*. The field's *Boundaries* are the *Goal Line* and the *Touch Line*. There exist the team *Territories* and their *Attacking Halves* (the territory of a team is the opponent's attacking half). In the field exist the *Center Circle* (that contains the *Center Mark*), the *Penalty Areas* (attached to the *Penalty Arcs*) and the *Corner Arcs* (where the *Corner Flags* are located).
2. The *Technical Area*.
3. The *Spectator's Seats*, including the fans' *Gates*.
4. The *Speaker's Seats*.
5. The *Dressing Rooms*.

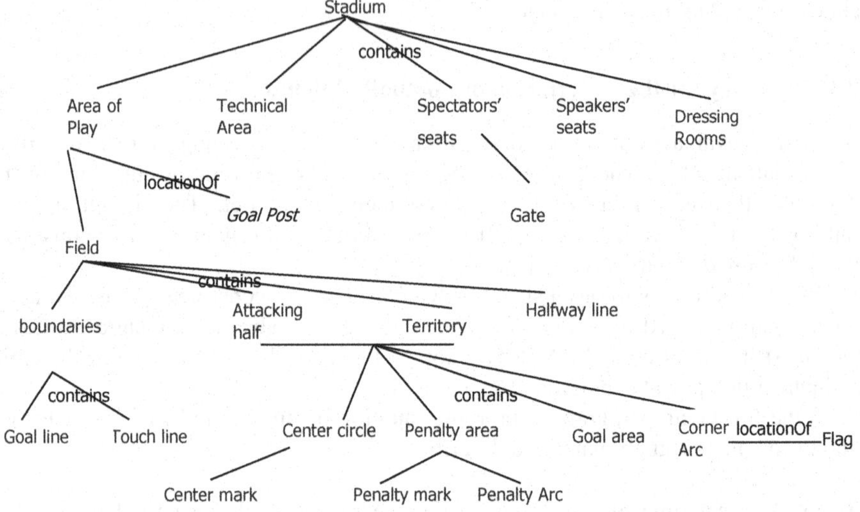

Fig. 3. The part-of hierarchy of the ontology terms for regions of the stadium

Actor Roles. The roles of the football match actors (e.g. teams, players etc.) are abstract semantic entities contained in our ontology. The ontology entities for the representation of person roles in a football match are shown in Fig. 4, while the entities and relationships for the description of teams are depicted in Fig. 5.

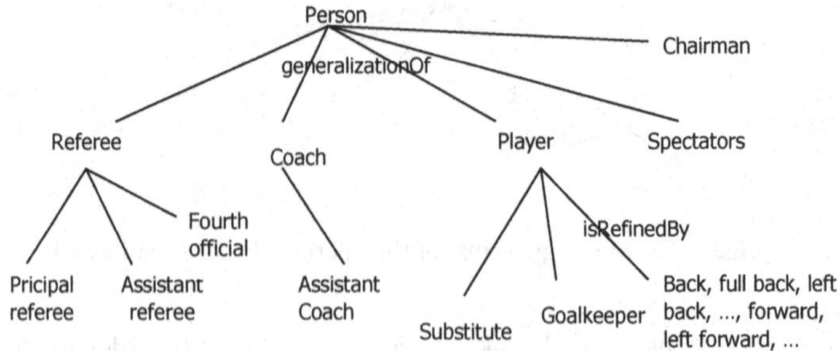

Fig. 4. The ontology terms for person roles in a football match

According to Fig. 4, the roles in a football match are *Referee*, *Coach*, *Player*, *Spectator* and *Chairman*. A referee instance may be the *Principal referee*, an *Assistant referee* or a *Fourth official*. A Player instance may be a *Goalkeeper*, a *Substitute* or may be in a specific place (e.g. *Left Forward*), which refines his role. The roles are represented by abstract MPEG-7 Person entities (AbstractionLevel=2).

As shown in Fig. 5, a team, resented as an MPEG-7 Organization instance, may be *Visiting Team* or *Home Team*. Team players comprise PersonGroups.

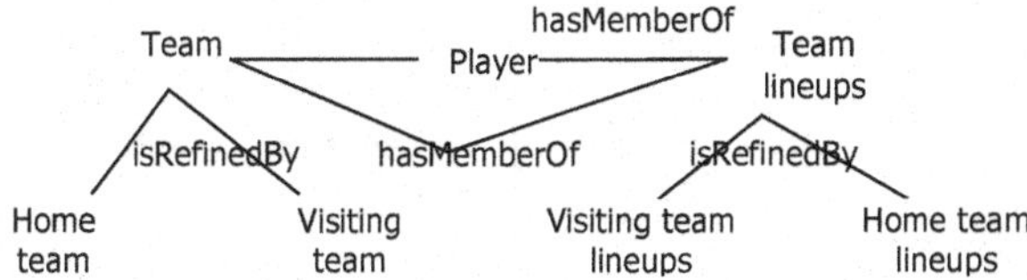

Fig. 5. The ontology terms for the teams participating in a football match

Events. The events that take place in a football match are specified in the FIFA rules [7]. An event may fall in one of 3 categories: *Referee Actions*, *Game Actions* and *Miscellaneous*. We implement them in our model as MPEG-7 Event instances (AbstractionLevel=2). As the events are too many (123) to fit in a diagram, their names and the category that each one falls are listed in Table 1.

Table 1. The ontology terms for the events taking place in a football match

Referee Action	Principal Referee Action, Whistle, Red Card, Book a player, Yellow Card, Advantage Rule, Warning, Assistant Referee Action, Raise flag, Fourth Official Action
Game action	Interact with a player, Hit the ball, Pass, Shoot, Trap, Player action, Ball action, Clear, Illegal Action, Foul, Off-side, Dangerous play, Half volley, Heel, Toed Ball, Juggling, Deadening the ball, Trap, chest, Trap, foot, Kick, Trap, thigh, Diving, First time, Flick, Bicycle kick, Scissor kick, Backswing, Chip shot, Banana kick, In swinger, Out Swinger, Missile, Pass, back, Pass, front, Power kick, Outlet, Assist, Cross, Through Ball, Pass, drop, Early Service, Pass, forward, Pass, hospital, 50/50 ball, Pass, lead, Nutmeg, Pass, push, Send, Hacking, Hand-to-ball, Obstruction, Carrying the ball, Header, Instep drive, Volley, Pass, square, Pass, hopped, Goal, Golden goal, Sudden death, Clinical goal, Substitution, Switch, Fake, Feint, Close down, Re-start, kick-off, Penalty kick, Free kick, Dropped Ball, Indirect free kick, Direct free kick, Corner kick, Goal kick, Throw-in, Retake, Injury, Jump, Fall, Ball to Hand, Reflection
Miscella-neous	Reaction of the spectators, Applause, Boo, Encourage, Sing, Wave flags, Throw items, Give instructions, Medical treatment, Talk, Fight, Hit, Shake hands, Cheer

4 Semantic Base

In this section we describe the Semantic Base maintained in our framework for the storage of the metadata describing audiovisual information. The Semantic Base is implemented on top of a MySQL relational database. The schema of the underlying database depicts our core model and is MPEG-7 compliant. Thus, the entities represented in the Semantic Base are the MPEG-7 types described in section 3. The database tables that represent these entities are shown in Fig. 6.

In addition, in the Semantic Base information related to the audiovisual segments but not contained in them (e.g. the age of a player) is stored. This information is stored in the tables Person, Organization, PersonGroup, State, Place and Time. These tables are shown in brief in Fig. 7.

Due to its semantic content, the Semantic Base can support much more powerful queries than those supported by a keyword only based annotation system.

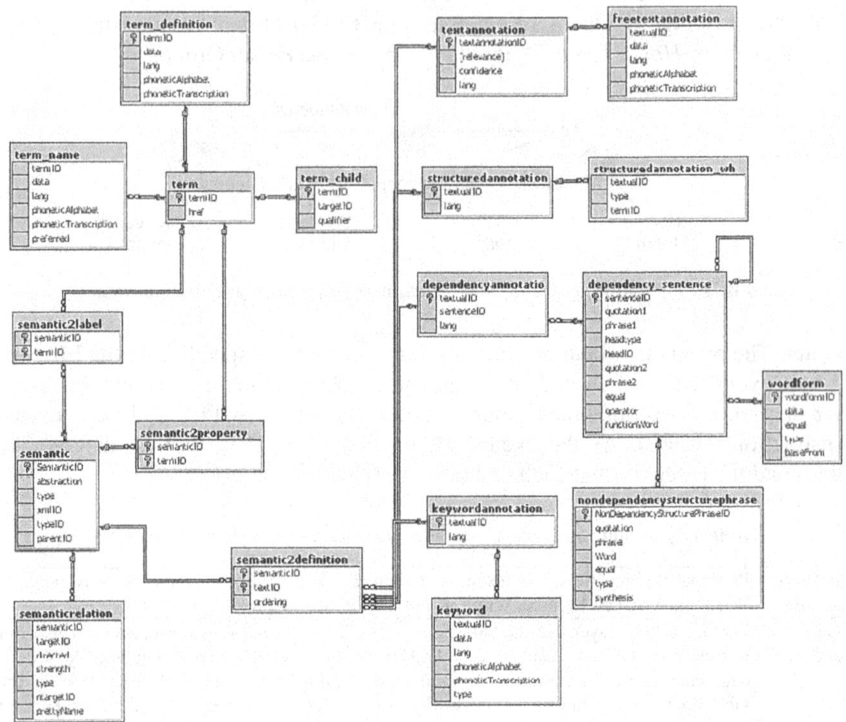

Fig. 6. The MPEG-7 compliant part of the Semantic Base schema

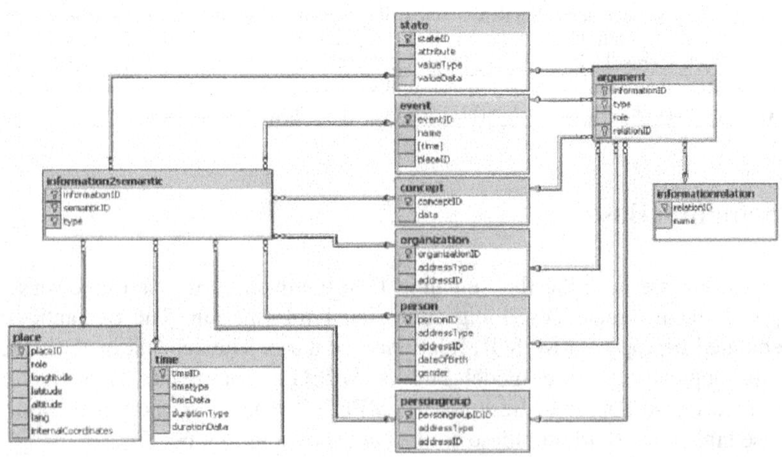

Fig. 7. Representation of the additional information

5 Semantic Annotation Component

The semantic metadata stored in the Semantic Base are created during the segmentation process and are related to certain audiovisual programs and segments. Thus, the segmentation process includes a *metadata creation process*. For this reason, we have implemented in java.swing the *Semantic Annotation Component*, which is used, as a component of a segmentation tool, by the metadata creators, who are responsible for the appropriate (manual or semiautomatic) segmentation and metadata description of the programs.

When the metadata creation finishes, a set of segments, annotated with appropriate keywords or keyword phrases is inserted in the TV-Anytime compliant segment base and a set of metadata items describing them is inserted in the semantic base. The metadata items in the Semantic Base reference the corresponding programs and/or segments. The keywords and the keyword phrases for a segment are produced in an automated way from the metadata that correspond to the segment in order to achieve TV-Anytime compatibility. The metadata creation process is guided, for each kind of audiovisual program, by the appropriate ontology.

The use case diagram of Fig. 8 depicts the usage scenario of the semantic annotation component for the annotation of football match audiovisual programs and segments. As is shown there, the person responsible for the segmentation process (Segmenter) uses a segmentation tool in order to define the video program segments. Segment definition includes segment annotation, thus the semantic annotation component is used as part of the segmentation tool[3].

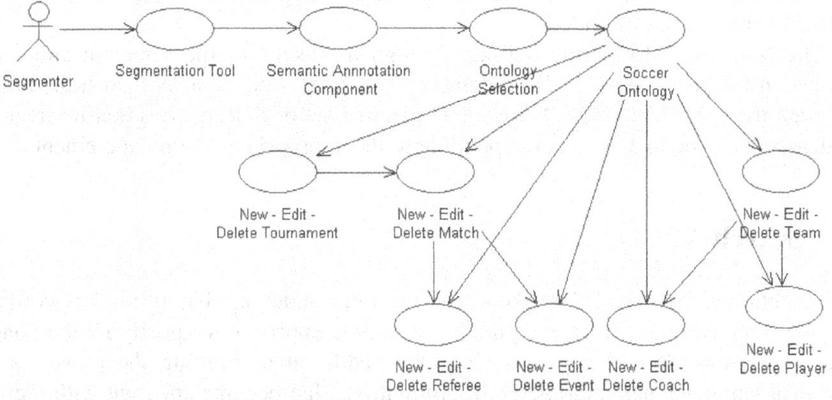

Fig. 8. Use Case diagram of the Semantic Annotation Component

The first task of the segmenter is the selection of the appropriate ontology for the segment annotation (the "soccer ontology" is selected for football matches). Then, the tournament to which the current match belongs is selected. If the tournament doesn't

[3] The metadata items defined for each audiovisual segment have their own Semantic Time that allows the expression of the game time of the event. This permits the support of multiple cameras, as video time may be different from the game time (e.g. 40th video minute may correspond to the 36th game minute, as a goal has been shown 4 times of duration 1 minute).

exist, a new tournament is defined and selected. After tournament selection, the football match is selected. Again, if the match doesn't exist it is first defined. The match is associated with the participating teams and each team is associated with its coach. All the non-existent entities are defined. Then, for each notable event in the segment an appropriate event instance is created. The event is associated with the appropriate metadata items (e.g. a goal is associated with the scorer and the goalkeeper) after instantiating the non-existent ones. In Fig. 9 a goal event is defined.

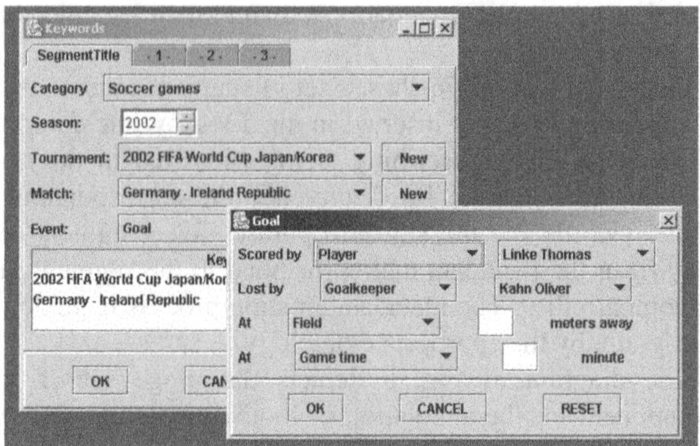

Fig. 9. Goal definition

The semantic annotation component also permits the definition of semantic information for time points contained in a segment, thus enhancing the information retrieval capabilities provided.

The semantic information defined through the usage of the semantic annotation tool is in the form of an XML document. The XML document is then transformed, through the usage of an XSLT document [5], in a set of SQL queries that insert in the semantic base the instances corresponding to the appropriate document elements.

6 Search API

As mentioned above, TV-Anytime allows only indexing based on keywords or keyword phrases. However, the pure TV-Anytime approach to specifying the content utilizing keywords and keyword phrases in addition to limiting the power of the retrieval language, has interoperability limitations that become apparent with the new evolutions in technology, standards and business models. The use of domain specific ontologies to limit the possible values of keywords in conjunction with the TV-Anytime metadata alleviates two significant problems:

- New TV-Anytime Forum trends emphasize the existence of servers that are connected with high capacity lines with homes and provide additional digital audiovisual channels, but also digital library functionality with multimedia content. This content may be structured according to the MPEG-7 standard to give high discriminatory power to users.
- It is highly possible that digital audiovisual information stored in the TV-Anytime server will also be used by other consumption channels, for example PCs or mobile

devices (the later is a scenario also supported by the TV-Anytime Forum). It is also possible that digital audiovisual content will be transferred between servers to support users during travelling. In all the above scenarios high precision and recall of the retrieval mechanism is needed and the limitations of the TV interface do not exist. A more powerful than keyword based retrieval mechanism presents advantages.

To overcome these limitations, we have developed a search API containing functions that allow the user to pose powerful MPEG-7 queries if he wishes (simple keyword queries to support also TV-Anytime queries are a special case).

The API does not make any assumptions on the kind of the end-user equipment and interaction capabilities. The application through which the end-user interacts with the rest of the system uses a set of SQL queries that retrieve the IDs of the entities specified in the interface (e.g. retrieve the ID of the Person named "Ronaldo"). Thus, the search API can be used in different environments (e.g. TV, Web), with different user interaction capabilities (e.g. remote control vs. mouse and keyboard): In a TV interface a search template is presented, where only the missing words need to be filled from a list presented in the TV. In this case, the proper items are selected using the remote control. On the other hand, in the Web, a Java application that permits full user interaction will be provided.

The same API and set of interfaces can be used to interact and retrieve audiovisual contents described in both the database which supports the MPEG-7 standard and the database that supports the TV-Anytime standard, taking into account that both databases are based on domain-specific extensions of the standards which use the same ontology.

The API has been implemented in Java, using JDBC on top of a relational database. It is comprised of two functions that are capable of supporting queries that contain one or more criteria combined with the logical operators AND and OR. More specifically, the API functions are:

1. *GetSegmentA((AND|OR)? (informationID informationType semanticID)+)*, where:
   - The first argument denotes the operator (AND/OR) used for the combination of the different criteria expressed in the rest of the query. The argument can appear at most once and may be omitted if there is only one criterion.
   - The second argument is a set of triplets that describe the query terms, that is the metadata items that must be related to the query results: *informationID* is the id of the item, *informationType* is the type of the item and *semanticID* is the role of the item. There must appear at least one triplet in a query. The "null" value should be used when we don't want to set a criterion for any part of the triplet.

   This function permits queries that retrieve audiovisual segments related to specific metadata items. No relationships among the metadata can be defined, while the query terms may be combined using the AND and OR logical operators.

   In Table 2 we present examples of queries expressed using GetSegmentA, where we assume that the informationID of the person named "Ronaldo" is 1 and the informationID of the person named "Rivaldo" is 2.
2. *GetSegmentB(informationID informationType semanticID (AND|OR) (informationID informationType semanticID relationType)*)*, where:

Table 2. Examples of queries expressed using GetSegmentA

Query	Description in Free Text
`GetSegmentA(1 Person null)`	"Give me the segments where Ronaldo appears" (not only as a player!)
`GetSegmentA(1 Person player-obj)`	"Give me the segments where the player Ronaldo appears"
`GetSegmentA(AND, (1 Person player-obj) (null Event goal-event))`	"Give me the segments where the player Ronaldo appears and a goal is scored" (the scorer may be any player)
`GetSegmentA(OR, (1 Person player-obj) (2 Person player-obj))`	"Give me the segments where the players Ronaldo or Rivaldo appear"

- The first argument is a triplet that describes the main query term that is a metadata item related to the other ones: *informationID* is the id of the item, *informationType* is the type of the item and *semanticID* is the role of the item.
- The second argument denotes the operator (AND/OR) used for the combination of the query terms expressed in the rest of the query. The argument can appear at most once and may be omitted if no query terms follow.
- The third argument is a set of quadruplets that describe the query terms that are related to the main query term: *informationID* is the id of the item, *informationType* is the type of the item, *semanticID* is the role of the item and *relationType* is the type of the relationship of the current item with the main query term. There can appear any number of quadruplets in a query. The "null" value should be used when we don't want to set a criterion for any part of the quadruplet.

This function permits queries that retrieve audiovisual segments that relate to a specific metadata item that is the main query term. The main query term may be related, through specific relationships, to the other metadata items (including the information related to them that is not present in the described audiovisual segment, a feature of special interest in Digital Library environments).

In Table 3 we present examples of queries expressed using GetSegmentA, where we assume that the informationID of the person named "Ronaldo" is 1 and the informationID of the person named "Kahn" is 3. We also assume that the Greek citizenship has citizenshipID 1.

Table 3. Examples of queries expressed using GetSegmentB

Query	Description in Free Text
`GetSegmentB(null null goal-event AND 1 Person player-obj hasCauserOf)`	"Give me the segments where the player Ronaldo scores"
`GetSegmentB(null null goal-event AND (1 Person player-obj hasCauserOf) (3 Person player-obj hasPatientOf))`	"Give me the segments where the player Ronaldo scores against the goalkeeper Kahn"
`GetSegmentB((null Person player-obj hasCauserOf) AND (1 citizenship person2citizenship))`	"Give me the segments where a player with Greek citizenship appears"

The combination of the above functions (through the union or intersection of the results of more than one queries) can support even more complex queries. Thus, powerful queries in several platforms can be supported. The integration of the API to the end-user applications remains a challenge, especially in the Digital TV environment.

7 Conclusions – Future Work

We have described a framework for the management of semantic metadata used for the description of audiovisual information. Metadata modelling is based on domain-specific ontologies and several aspects of the framework are based on these ontologies. Our framework provides interoperability and "dual" support for both MPEG-7 and TV-Anytime in order to capture the needs of the evolving digital multimedia applications and architectures. This support is provided through the maintenance of two information repositories, an MPEG-7 compliant Semantic Base and a TV-Anytime compliant database.

The Semantic Base maintenance permits the support of advanced queries based on the semantic base contents, which allows better content description and retrieval performance. In addition, it allows better user interfaces, especially user interfaces based on list selection, which are more appropriate for interactive TV. This support can be exploited, through the Search API that we have implemented. The API can facilitate retrieval in TV-Anytime, digital video libraries, video on demand and integrated application environments.

Our current work in this area includes:

- Investigation of system performance and automatic adaptation oriented aspects in the ontology-driven framework.
- The deployment of the framework in order to provide automatic (or semi-automatic) abstractions of the audiovisual content, based on the corresponding semantic information stored in the semantic base and the domain specific ontologies.
- Experimentation with the retrieval performance (precision vs. recall) of queries aiming to retrieve the same audiovisual content on top of both the TV-Anytime compliant database and the Semantic Base.
- Investigation of domain specific fuzzy query and user interface aspects.
- Methodology and system development for semi-automatic creation of MPEG-7 metadata descriptions from the TV-Anytime descriptions. Since MPEG-7 descriptions encode more semantics, a single TV-Anytime description may correspond to more than one MPEG-7 descriptions.
- The definition of ontologies for other application domains (e.g. news) and the adaptation of existing ones in order to enhance the capabilities of our system. Complexity and cost for these tasks will be investigated.

Acknowledgments. Our thanks to the staff of MUSIC/TUC, especially Fotis Kazasis and Nektarios Moumoutzis, for their comments and suggestions during the design of the framework presented in this paper. This work was financially supported by the UP-TV project.

References

1. Al-Khatib Q., Day F., Ghafoor A., Berra B., *Semantic Modelling and Knowledge Representation in Multimedia Databases*, IEEE Transactions on Knowledge and Data Engineering, Vol. 11, No. 1, January/February 1999
2. Analyti A., Christodoulakis S., *Multimedia Object Modeling and Content-Based Querying*, Proceedings of Advanced Course – Multimedia databases in Perspective, Netherlands 1995.
3. Christodoulakis S., Pappas N., Kyriakaki G., Maragoudakis Y., Mavraganis Y., Tsinaraki C., *The KYDONIA multimedia information server*, Proceedings of the European Conference on Multimedia Applications Services and Techniques – ECMAST 97, Milan, May 1997
4. Carnegie Mellon University, *Informedia project*, http://www.informedia.cs.cmu.edu
5. Clark J., *XSL Transformations (XSLT) Specification Version 1.0*, W3C Recommendation, http://www.w3.org/TR/xslt, November 1999
6. de Jong F., Westerveld T., *MUMIS: Multimedia Indexing and Searching*, Proceedings of the CBMI 2001 Workshop, pp. 423–425
7. Federation Internationale de Football (FIFA), *Football Game Rules*, www.fifa.org, 2002
8. Gemmell D.J., Han J., Beaton R., Christodoulakis S., *Delay-Sensitive Multimedia on Disks*, IEEE Multimedia 1.3, Fall 1994.
9. Grosky W., *Managing Multimedia Information in Database Systems*, Communications of the ACM, Vol. 40, No. 12, December 1997
10. Guarino N, *Formal Ontology and Information Systems*, pp. 3-15, Proceedings of the first International Conference Formal Ontology in Information Systems (FOIS '98), June 6–8 1998, Trento, Italy, Ed. Guarino N., IOS Press
11. Hacid M-S., Decleir C., Kouloumdjian J., *A Database Approach for Modeling and Querying Video Data*, IEEE Transactions on Knowledge and Data Engineering, Vol. 12, No. 5, September/October 2000
12. IBM Japan, *Video Enrichment project*, http://www.tri.ibm.com/projects/video/index_e.htm
13. Jaimes A., Echigo T., Teraguchi M., Satoh F., *Learning Personalized Video Highlights from Detailed MPEG-7 Metadata*, in Proceedings of the IEEE International Conference on Image Processing, ICIP 2002, Sept 22–25, Rochester, NY, USA
14. Jiang H., Elmagarmid A. K., *WVTDB – A Semantic Content-Based Database System on the World Wide Web*, IEEE Transactions on Knowledge and Data Engineering, Vol. 10, No. 6, November/December 1998
15. Kazasis F., Moumoutzis N., Pappas N., *Informative Annex: Generic Architecture for handling TVA Metadata using relational database technologies*, contribution TV-Anytime Forum/Metadata WG, 2nd Implementer's workshop, Geneva July 2002
16. Kyriakaki G., *MPEG Information Management Services for Audiovisual Applications*, Master Thesis, Technical University of Crete, March 2000
17. Mavraganis Y., Maragoudakis Y., Pappas N., Kyriakaki G., *The SICMA multimedia server and the virtual museum application*, Proceedings of the European Conference on Multimedia Applications Services and Techniques – ECMAST 98, Berlin, March 1998.
18. MPEG Group, *MPEG-7 (Multimedia Content Description Interface)*, http://mpeg.telecomitalialab.com/standards/mpeg-7/mpeg-7.htm
19. Pappas N., Christodoulakis S., *Design & Development of a Stream Service in a Heterogeneous Client Environment*, Proceedings VLDB 2000.
20. Tsinaraki C., Papadomanolakis S., Christodoulakis S., *A Video Metadata Model supporting Personalization & Recommendation in Video-based Services*, Proceedings of the MDDE Workshop 2001 (in conjunction with ReTIS 2001), pp 104-109, Lyon (France), July 2001
21. Tsinaraki C., Papadomanolakis S., Christodoulakis S., *Towards a two-layered Video Metadata Model*, Proccedings of the DEXA Workshop 2001 – DLib, pp 937–941, 3–7 September 2001, Munich
22. TV-Anytime Forum, http://www.tv-anytime.org/

Designing a Federated Multimedia Information System on the Semantic Web

Richard Vdovjak, Peter Barna, and Geert-Jan Houben

Eindhoven University of Technology,
POBox 513, 5600 MB Eindhoven,
The Netherlands
{r.vdovjak, p.barna, g.j.houben}@tue.nl

Abstract. A federated Web-based multimedia information system on one hand gathers its data from various Web sources, on the other hand offers the end-user a rich semantics describing its content and a user-friendly environment for expressing queries over its data. There are three essential ingredients to successfully deploy such a system. First, one needs a design methodology identifying different design phases and their underlying models which serve as a framework for the designer. Second, there must be a set of tools that are able to execute the design, i.e. they serve as the back-end of the information system instantiating the models with data coming from various Web sources. Third, there also must be an entry point for the end-user, where he is able to explore what the system can do for him and where he can formulate his queries. This paper is a follow-up of our previous work describing the Hera design methodology and contributes to all three issues above. In particular, it refines the existing methodology by presenting an explicit RDFS-based integration model and explains how the mediator uses this model to obtain query results. The issue of a user-friendly front-end is addressed by introducing our interface for browsing and querying RDFS-based ontologies.

1 Introduction

Designing a Web-based federated information system (IS) that deals with multimedia items requires the consideration of both the IS back-end that integrates various Web sources, and the IS front-end that serves as an entry point for the user query. If this query is issued not only against text-like data but also against multimedia data, the semantic issues become crucial. Consider for instance the following user query: *"Give me all pictures of Niagara Falls taken from the Falls Avenue in Niagara Falls, Canada with a telelens"*. The first part of the query denotes the subject (waterfalls) being photographed. The second identifies the position of the photographer. Note the ambiguity of the "Niagara Falls" collocation, first denoting the waterfalls, and then being a part of the position description as a town name. Moreover, there is the third part of the query, imposing an additional lens constraint which basically says that we are only interested in those images that provide enough details and a narrow perspective achievable

J. Eder and M. Missikoff (Eds.): CAiSE 2003, LNCS 2681, pp. 357–373, 2003.

only by using a lens of that focal length. It is evident that queries of this kind are not likely to be satisfactorily answered by keyword based search engines. By translating this query into a set of keywords and trying a keyword based search engine we either obtained an empty set of results (e.g. Google Image Search) or a countless number of irrelevant pictures featuring big photo lenses (e.g. AltaVista Image Search retrieved over 1.4 million images and the top scored ones were indeed mostly showing long lenses and other photo equipment). Examples like this show a clear need for something more powerful than keywords. The use of ontologies, taxonomies of classes within a certain domain linked by properties indicating different relations among those classes, would enable to enhance queries and improve both the precision and the recall. Ontologies are becoming the essence of Web portals offering integrated views over various domains.

There are three important ingredients to successfully deploy such systems. First, one needs a design methodology identifying different design phases and their underlying models/ontologies which serve as a framework for the designer. Second, there must be a set of tools that are able to execute the design, instantiating the models with data coming from various Web sources. Third, there also must be an entry point for the end-user, where he is able to explore what the system can do for him and where he can formulate his queries. This paper is a follow-up of our previous work describing the Hera design methodology [1] and [2]. It contributes to all three issues above. In particular, it refines the existing methodology by presenting an explicit RDFS-based integration model, and explains how the mediator uses this model to obtain query results. The issue of a user-friendly front-end is addressed by introducing our interface for browsing and querying RDFS-based ontologies. A design of a Web-based photo portal is used as our case example for illustrating our ideas.

2 Hera Methodology

A primary focus of the Hera project is to support Web-based information system (WIS) design and implementation. A WIS generates a hypermedia presentation for data that in response to a user query is retrieved from the data storage. This entire process of retrieving data and presenting it in hypermedia format needs to be specified during the design of the WIS.

The typical structure of the WIS design in the Hera perspective consists of three layers:

- Semantic Layer: defines the content that is managed in the WIS in terms of a conceptual model; this layer includes the definition of the process of integration needed to gather the data from different sources; if the data is made available from outside the WIS, a search agent or information retrieval engine could be the interface to the WIS.
- Application Layer: defines the abstract hypermedia (navigation) view on the data in terms of an application model, which represents the structure shown to the user in the hypermedia presentation; this layer includes the definition

of the adaptation in the hypermedia generation, e.g. based on a user model and user/platform profile.
- Presentation Layer: defines those details that together with the definitions from the Application Layer are needed to generate a presentation for a concrete browsing platform, e.g. HTML, WML or SMIL.

In this paper we focus mainly on the integration and data retrieval process of the Hera methodology. This combined phase helps to make the data available from different sources, such that in response to a *user query* a *conceptual model instance* is generated that contains the data for which the application is going to generate a presentation: see Figure 1[1].

The integration is in principle performed before querying, as opposed to the retrieval and presentation generation that are performed for every query. It represents the data stored and therefore uses an integration model to map the data from the different sources into concepts of the conceptual model. From a mapping at schema (ontology) level a mapping at instance level is derived. This mapping is needed whenever for a given query the instances that compose the query result are to be retrieved. These instances need to be extracted by the mediator from the different *source ontology instances*. The role of the integration is to make these source ontology instances available(on-demand).

The data retrieval handles the reception of the *user query* , and in response produces a *conceptual model instance* for the query result. It starts with the translation of the query formulated by the user into a query that can act as a retrieval request on the data stored. This translation takes into account that while the user is allowed to formulate a query by mentioning items from the conceptual model or application model, the application model defines exactly which concepts need to be retrieved in connection with the items mentioned: this is known as query extension. Subsequently, using the query engine, the mediator retrieves the data from the sources and provides the query result. Finally, this query result needs to be transformed into the conceptual model instance that is passed on to the phase of presentation generation[2] .

2.1 Related Work

Most of the web engineering approaches (e.g. UWE [3] or XWMF [4]) do not explicitly consider integration and neither the user support for the query generation process, as opposed to what is the case in Hera. Given its RDF-based nature we address XWMF here in more detail. The eXtensible Web Modeling Framework (XWMF) [4] consists of an extensible set of RDF schemas and descriptions to model web applications. The core of the framework is the Web Object Composition Model (WOCM), a formal object-oriented language used

[1] The ellipses denote the transformations (in XSLT or Java) and the rectangles denote models or data. The shapes in grey denote application-independent items, the shapes with bold lines are query independent, while the others are query-dependent items.

[2] Details of this phase are beyond the scope of the paper, interested reader is referred to [2].

to define the structure and content of a web application. WOCM is a directed acyclic graph with complexons as nodes and simplexons as leaves. Complexons define the application's structure while simplexons define the application's content. Simplexons are refined using the subclassing mechanism in different variants corresponding to different implementation platforms. While Hera provides both a modeling framework and a methodology for developing web applications, XWMF appears to be only a modeling framework.

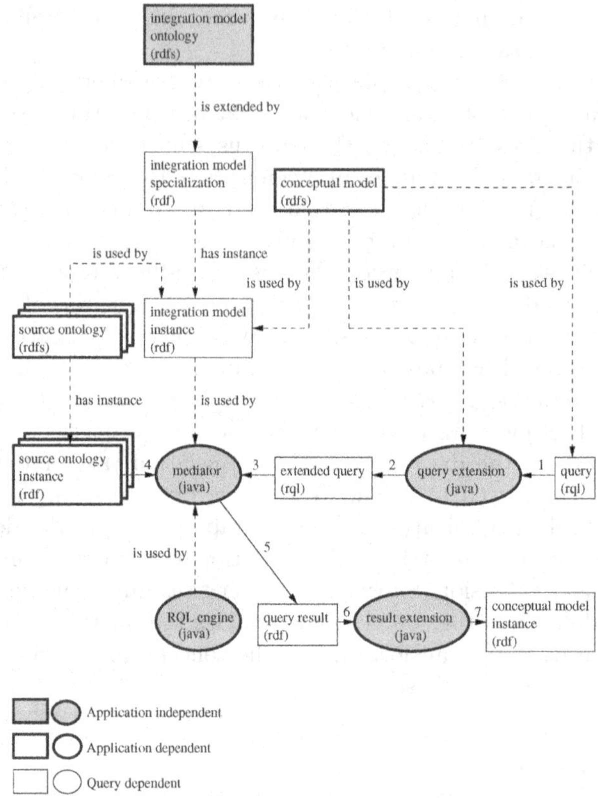

Fig. 1. Integration and data retrieval

3 RDF, RDFS, RQL and Their Role in Hera

The Resource Description Framework (RDF) [5] is a general-purpose data language issued as a W3C standard. An RDF model consists of resources, named properties, and property values. RDF Schema (RDFS) [6], an extension to RDF which is itself expressed in RDF terms, provides a support for creating vocabularies at the type (schema) level. RDFS defines a modeling language by assigning a special semantics to several (system) resources and properties amongst which *rdfs:Class* , *rdfs:Property* , *rdfs:subClassOf* , *rdfs:subPropertyOf* .

In Hera, RDF(S) is the main format used for the different models in the design phases. One of the reasons for choosing RDF(S) is that it is flexible (supporting schema refinement and description enrichment) and extensible (allowing the definition of new resources/properties) Moreover, it is coming with the promise of web application interoperability. Hera model instances are represented in plain RDF validated against their associated models (schemas) represented in RDFS.

Since RDF(S) is used as our vehicle for capturing semantics of different domains within the IS being designed, we also need a query language that would enable us to retrieve the information of interest from these knowledge bases. The most advanced RDF(S) query language to date is RQL [7]. It covers both queries over RDF schemas and RDF instances. RQL queries that we will consider consist, similarly to SQL quires, of `SELECT-FROM-WHERE` clauses. The `SELECT` clause specifies resources (variables) which are of interest. The `FROM` part is the core of the query and specifies one or more path expressions (i.e. subgraphs of the entire schema graph) where the variables are being bound. Finally, the `WHERE` clause contains filtering conditions that are being applied on the variables bound in the `FROM` statement.

```
SELECT PHOTO
FROM   {PHOTO:GeoPhoto}depictsTheme{THEME:Universe},
       {PHOTO}takenFromPlace{PLACE:AddressablePlace}.country{COUNTRY},
       {PLACE}town{TOWN},{PLACE}street{STREET},
       {PHOTO}takenWithSettings.usedLens{LENS:TeleLens}
WHERE THEME like "*Niagara Falls" and
      COUNTRY like "Can*" and
      TOWN like "Niagara*" and
      STREET like "Falls Av*"
```

Fig. 2. User query in RQL

Despite its relative intuitiveness, RQL is still too low-level for an average end-user who wants to formulate queries over RDFS-based ontologies. It would be unreasonable to expect the end-user to type in a query like the one depicted in Figure 2, which is the RQL syntax of the “Niagara picture request” presented in the introduction. We address this issue later in section 5.2 by introducing our visual interface that enables the user to generate such RQL queries in a point-and-click manner.

RQL in combination with its java-based interpreter called Sesame [8] proved to be useful when building our retrieval engine, which in fact acts (with some limitations) as a distributed RQL query engine.

4 Integration and Data Retrieval

The main task of this design phase is to connect the application's conceptual model with several autonomous sources by creating channels through which the data will populate on request the concepts from the conceptual model. This involves identifying the right concepts occurring in the source ontologies and relating them to their counterparts in the conceptual model. Note that as opposed to classical database schema integration we do not aim at integrating all source concepts, but rather select only those that are relevant with respect to the defined conceptual model.

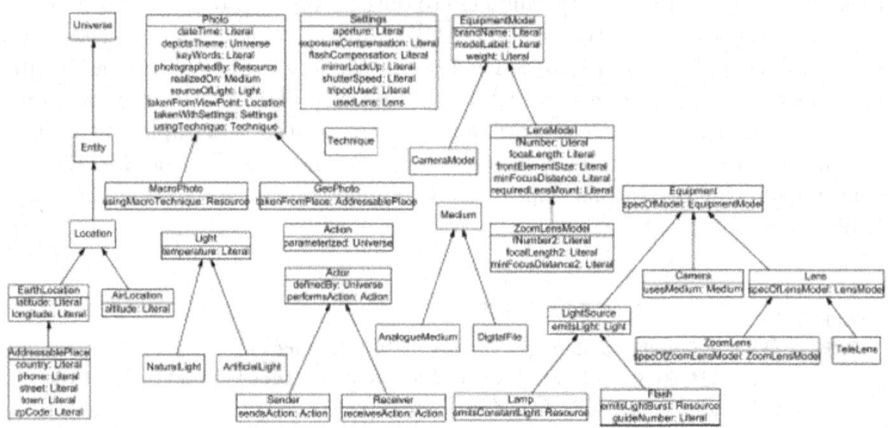

Fig. 3. Conceptual model

4.1 Conceptual Model

The conceptual model (CM) provides a uniform semantic view over multiple data sources. The CM serves as an interface between data retrieval and presentation generation. The CM is composed of concepts and concept properties that together define the domain ontology. There are two types of concept properties: concept attributes which associate media items to the concepts and concept relationships that define associations between concepts.

The running example used throughout the paper describes the design of a federated multimedia information system (MIS) implementing a photo library portal that allows the user to create on-the-fly photo exhibitions (browseable presentations of images of interest), study the photo technique behind these images and help him to rent or buy the necessary photo equipment in order to be able to achieve similar results.

The data is assembled on demand, based on the visitor's query, from the photos coming from different (online) photostock agencies, annotated with relevant descriptions. The photo equipment data is gathered from (online) catalogues and matched with (online) photo rental offers. All this data is accessible from a single entry point, semantically represented by the CM. Figure 3 presents an excerpt of this CM which is composed of several sub-ontologies covering the semantics of different sub-domains:

- The `photo` sub-ontology consists of terms coming from the photo domain. It describes things like different kinds of `Light`, various photo `Techniques`, different camera `Settings` etc. The cornerstone of this ontology is the class `Photo` which is linked by its properties with the aforementioned classes. There is also a property called `depictsTheme` that connects the `Photo` class from the photo ontology with the `Entity` class from the general ontology.
- The `equipment` sub-ontology focuses on the photo hardware, describing and classifying different kinds of lenses, cameras and other related accessories.
- The general sub-ontology consists of all terms one can possible take a picture of, the most general term being the `Entity` class.
- The ternary sub-ontology serves as a means to describe a story captured on the photograph, where there are two or more actors that perform (either send or receive) an action. For instance a photo depicting a man biting a dog is certainly a different story than that depicting a dog biting a man.

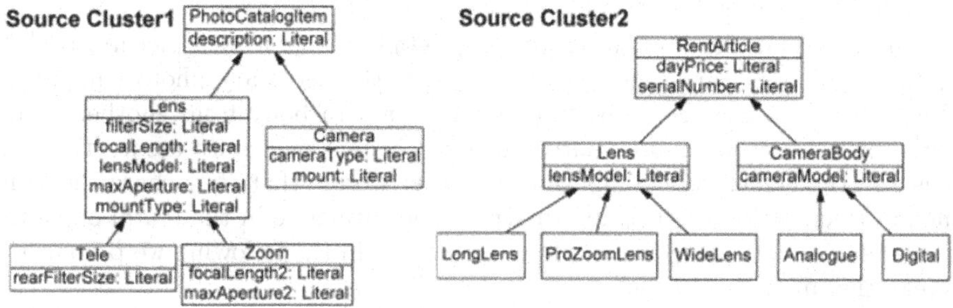

Fig. 4. Integrated sources: Photo Equipment Catalogue, Photo Equipment Rental

4.2 Sources

In our previous research [1] [9] we discussed how to overcome the syntactic heterogeneity of different source formats by introducing a layered approach starting with a layer of wrappers. In this paper we focus on the issues regarding the semantic heterogeneity. We consider for integration only those sources that are capable of exporting their schema in an RDFS based ontology and their data upon request (an RQL query) in RDF. In other words, we assume that each source offers its data on the Semantic Web platform providing RQL query services.

It is often the case on the Web that the information is duplicated and offered (possibly with a different flavor) from several sources. We group such sources into semantically close clusters and provide a means to order them dynamically within a cluster, based on several notions of quality introduced by the designer. Sources within a cluster do not necessarily have the same structure but should provide approximately the same semantic content. Sometimes for the sake of simplicity we abuse the word source when in fact we mean a whole cluster represented by that source.

As already mentioned, the data in our photo portal is coming from three sources/clusters: an online photo catalogue, rental offers, and online photostock agenicies. The abbreviated ontologies describing schemas of the first two clusters are depicted in Figure 4. The third kind of sources describing photostock agencies is omitted due to space limitations and we will consider it hereafter identical with the relevant parts of the CM.

The photo catalogue source (Figure 4 cluster 1) captures specifications of two sorts of catalogue items: lenses and cameras together with their respective subclasses. A seemingly similar class hierarchy featuring lenses and camera bodies exists also in the second source representing rental offers (Figure 4 cluster 2). There is, however, a considerable semantic gap between the two sources. The first source considers lenses or cameras as models, i.e. a virtual set of features and specifications. The second source refers to lenses and cameras as physical entities, i.e. concrete lenses and cameras (including their serial number) that are available for renting.

Suppose that the user, after reading details about a nice picture, decides to take similar pictures and he wants to rent the necessary photo equipment. When renting a lens from one source and a camera body from another source (remember there are more sources in one cluster) one must assure that the lens and the camera are compatible. In other words, that they share the same mount specification. As this information is not available in the rental offers the system has to look it up in the photo catalogue. In the following we present the integration model which helps to resolve such issues.

4.3 Integration Model

The integration model (IM) addresses the problem of relating concepts form the source ontologies to those from the CM. This problem can also be seen as the problem of merging or aligning ontologies. The approaches to automate the solution to this problem are usually based on lexical matches, relying mostly on dictionaries to determine synonyms and hyponyms; this is however often not enough to yield good results. Even when the structure of ontologies is taken into account the results are often not satisfactory especially in the case of uncoordinated development of ontologies across the Web [10]. For this reason and for the fact that every mistake in the integration phase will propagate and get magnified in all the subsequent phases, we currently rely on the designer or a domain expert to articulate CM concepts in the semantic language of sources.

What we offer the designer, is an integration ontology by the instantiation of which he specifies the links between the CM and the sources.

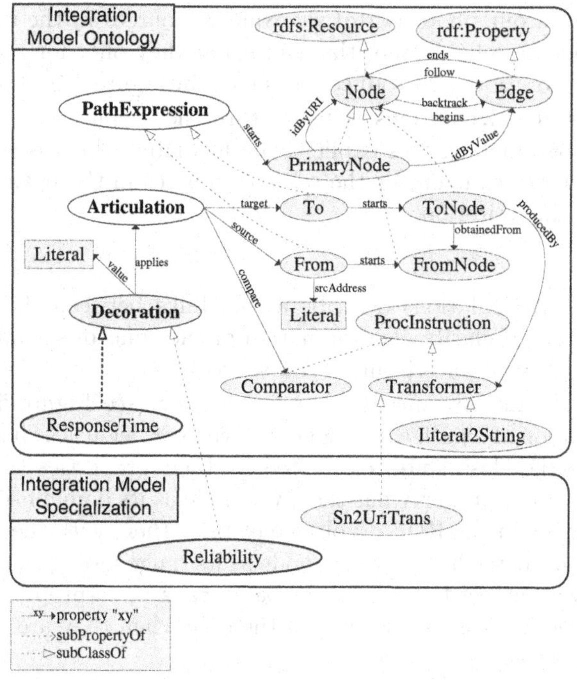

Fig. 5. Integration model ontology and its specialization

Integration Model Ontology. The integration model ontology (IMO) depicted in Figure 5 is a meta-ontology[3] describing integration primitives that are used both for ranking the sources within a cluster and for specifying links between them and the CM. The IMO is expressed in RDFS allowing the designer to tailor it for a particular application. The main concepts in the IMO are `Decoration` and `Articulation`.

Decorations. Decorations serve as a means to label "appropriateness" of different sources (and their concepts) grouped within one semantically close cluster. By having a literal property `value` they offer a simple way of ranking otherwise equivalent sources from several different points of view. There are some general decoration classes that are predefined in the framework (e.g. `ResponseTime`).

[3] IMO is a meta-ontology in the sense that its instances are dealing with concepts from other ontologies (source ontologies and the CM).

However, which ordering criteria are of interest depends mostly on the application. That is why the concept of `Decoration` is meant to be extended (specialized) by the designer. In this way we allow the designer to capture in the IM his (mostly background) knowledge regarding the sources.

For instance in our photo portal we example sources in the `Cluster 2` are graded based on the reliability of the equipment they offer for rent. Hence the `Reliability` decoration is introduced as shown in Figure 5 bottom.

The idea behind decorations is to capture the "reputation" of sources in different areas. By making this explicit, the mediator which is responsible for evaluation of queries can consult the relevant sources in the optimal way w.r.t. the chosen ordering criterion.

Articulations. Articulations describe actual links between the CM and the source ontologies and clarify also the notion of the concept's uniqueness which is necessary to perform joins from several sources.

Before we explain the concept of `Articulation` (see Figure 5) we need to introduce the notion of a path expression. A path expression is a chain of concepts (represented by the class `Node`) connected by their properties (represented by the class `Edge`). If the property has the given node as its domain (in other words we follow the arrow in the RDF graph) we connect them with the `follow` meta-property. If the property has the given node as its range (going against the arrow in the graph), we connect the two by the `backtrack` meta-property. This allows us to define inverse relationships even in the case when they are not present in the source ontologies.

Each path expression starts with a link to `PrimaryNode` which is a special node that can be uniquely identified either by a URI (`idByURI`) or by value (`idByValue`). The first points to a resource whose URI serves as an ID, the second points to a property (the `Edge` type) the value[4] of which serves as an ID.

In our example we chose to identify source concepts with identification-by-value due to the simpler way of deciding whether two resources describe the same thing. In the case of URI identification the decision whether two URIs refer to the same real-life object would require some sort of a web institution that normalizes several URIs to a canonical URI. This is in our opinion rather restrictive and a value-based identification is likely to work better when looking at the data coming from the Web source. The only exception where we chose to use `idByURI` is the local (mediator's) CM instance of the Equipment concept; this URI is generated from the `pr:serialNumber`.

An articulation contains two path expressions: the target path expression `To` pointing into the CM and the path expression called `From` pointing to a source (note the `srcAddress` property, value of which is the source URL). The target path expression contains nodes of type `ToNode`[5] that extends the `Node` with two

[4] By a value of a property we mean the object in RDF terminology.

[5] The ToEdge property is defined in a similar way but was omitted in order to simplify the figure.

properties: `obtainedFrom` and `producedBy`. The first links this node to its counterpart in the `From` path expression, the second points to a converting processing instruction called `Transformer`, which is called by the mediator to transform the source into the target. Processing instructions are resources containing a piece of Java code, an XSLT transformation, an RQL query or a combination of those. They are used by the mediator for changing and comparing values. Some general processing instructions are provided by the framework (e.g. the `Literal2String` transformer); those that are application-dependent are introduced in the specialization of IMO by the designer (e.g. the `Sn2UriTrans` transformer).

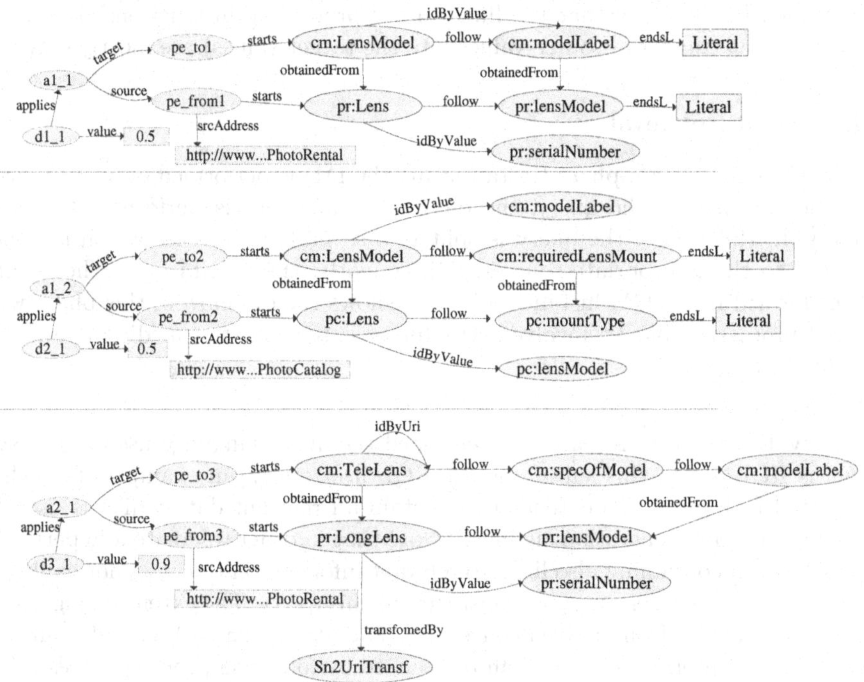

Fig. 6. Articulations, integration model instance

4.4 Integration Model Instance

The integration model instance is produced by the designer by instantiating the IMO[6]. Even though it is an ontology instance, it deals with the sources and the CM at the schema level, i.e. it makes statements about their concepts, not about instances. The choice of using RDF(S) as our underlying format proved to be

[6] Currently we are involved in building tools that allow the designer to specify the links and generate the articulations in the RDF(S) format automatically.

very useful since it is easy in its distributed fashion to make statements about other resources. Figure 6 shows three articulation examples.

The first is a simple articulation linking the `cm:LensModel` and its property `cm:modelLabel` with their counterparts from the photo rental source. The prime nodes are defined by the value of the properties: `cm:modelLabel` and `pr:serialNumber`.

The second articulation defines the lens property `cm:requiredLensMount` by linking it to the property `pc:mountType` from the catalogue source. Note the match between the identifying properties both referring to the model label.

The third articulation maps the concept `cm:TeleLens` into its counterpart `pr:LongLens` from the photo rental source. Note that these articulations were simplified in the sense that the links to the processing instructions (i.e. transformers that transform source values into the target values) are mostly omitted.

4.5 Data Retrieval

While the integration phase (instantiating the IM) is performed only once, prior to the user asking the query, the data retrieval phase is performed for every query. In this phase, the query is split into several sub-queries which are then routed to the appropriate sources. Subsequently, the results are gathered and transformed into a CM instance. Figure 1 shows the dataflow of this phase with three processing blocks involved: the query extension, the mediator, and the result extension.

Query Extension. As already mentioned the query language used in our system is RQL [7]. In this sub-phase the RQL user query, an example of which is depicted in Figure 2, is extended to contain all relevant data which is used by the presentation generation engine[2]. Note that in order to create a hypermedia presentation containing also links to relevant information that was not explicitly mentioned in the user query we must extend this query. The extension algorithm traverses the CM from a given concept(s) (`PHOTO: GeoPhoto`) and adds all concepts and/or literal types that can be reached by following property edges in the CM graph.

Mediator. The mediator is responsible for finding the answer to the query by consulting the available sources based on the integration model instance. As shown in Figure 1 the mediator takes the extended query as its input. Then it proceeds as follows: for every variable occurring in the `select` clause of this query it locates an articulation(s) which contains this variable. From this articulation the mediator determines the name of the concept occurring in the source and also the way how to obtain that concept, i.e. the necessary transformer(s) for the concept values, the address of the source, and the path expression to the concept of interest within the source schema. This path expression can be seen as a query executed on a particular source. Hence, consulting articulations in the IM instance in fact means query unfolding as it is known in the GAV approach.

The acknowledged disadvantage of the GAV approach is that in principle it requires changing the definition of the global schema (in our case the CM) each time a new source is added. This is however clearly not the case in our framework, since the only thing which changes when a new source is added or removed is the IM instance (new articulations are added or removed). From this point of view, we keep the CM independent from the sources, similarly to the LAV approach. Details concerning these approaches are beyond the scope of the paper, for details see [11]. If there are more articulations found for a given variable, that means there are several competing sources offering values for this variable. In this case the decorations attached to each articulation are used to decide the order in which the sources will be consulted.

After the sources are consulted, i.e. appropriate RQL queries are routed to them, the mediator waits for the response. Subsequently, it collects the results and assembles them into an answer which consists of a collection of tuples (in RDF terminology a bag of lists).

Result Extension. The answer provided by the mediator is a valid response to the RQL query that was asked, however it is not yet a CM instance. The result extension module transforms the "flat" collection of tuples by adding the appropriate properties into a valid RDF graph which adheres to the CM. This (query-dependent) CM instance serves as a basis for the presentation generation phase.

5 Hera Front-End

In the above sections we discussed how to design a data retrieval back-end for a multimedia information system. Here we focus on the front-end, the part of the system that interacts with the end-user. To bring an existing MIS to the end-user, two prerequisites are essential. Firstly, the users have to become familiar with the structure of the CM, i.e. to explore the ontology that captures the semantics of the MIS. Secondly, the system should help the users in generating the queries over this ontology, and visualize the results.

5.1 Visualizing the CM

As already mentioned, the CM is expressed in RDF(S). The problem of visualizing RDF(S) lies in the fact that it is difficult to show the whole expressive power of RDF(S) and at the same time to keep the user interface (UI) still comprehensible, easy to use, browse and navigate.

The two main approaches currently used: the tree-based approachand the graph-based approach, do not in our opinion address the above issues completely. The tree metaphor, though very familiar as UI, does not help the user in grasping other concept relationships than that used to construct the tree structure (most of the time being the rdfs:subClassOf relationship). The graph metaphor, on the other hand, displays all concept relationships but as a result introduces the

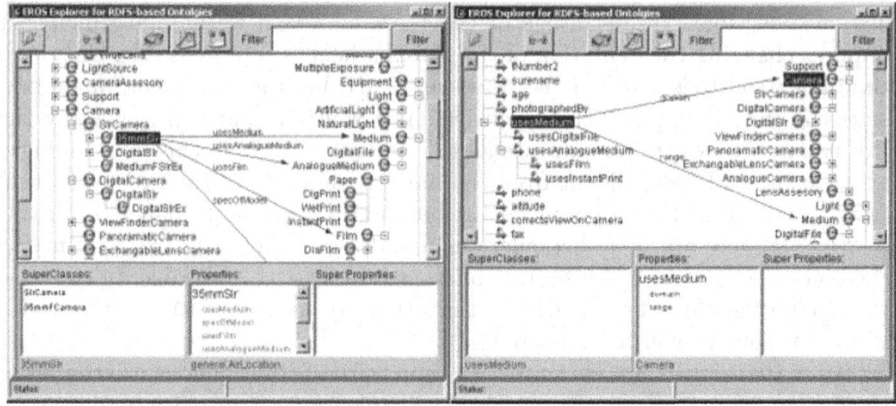

Fig. 7. The EROS interface: Class-centric view, Property-centric view

full complexity of a directed labeled graph in which is very difficult to spot the hierarchical structure of the ontology "hidden" behind the special edges and not reflected by the position of the class nodes.

Combining the advantages of the two mentioned UI metaphors, one would desire the simplicity of a browsable tree and at least a part of the expressiveness of the graph based approach. This is exactly what we tried to achieve by the EROS[7] interface.

5.2 The EROS Interface

The main idea behind this interface is to consider properties as partial mappings that map (some) elements (classes) from the class hierarchy into other (possibly identical) elements within the same hierarchy. Note that the set of all elements from the hierarchy serves two purposes: firstly as a (potential) domain of all properties and later as their (potential) range. This double purpose inspired us to have two (almost) identical hierarchy trees in our interface, the left tree being the domain ("from") tree, and the right tree being the range ("to") tree. Properties themselves are depicted as arrows connecting the classes from the left / domain tree with the classes from the right / range tree. Note that this approach makes it possible to display for a certain property at the same time both the context (the neighboring class hierarchy) of the domain class and the context of the range class. Cases of multiple inheritance are handled by displaying a list of super classes for the currently selected class. This approach, illustrated in Figure 7(left) can be considered as "class-centric" since the key transitive property on which both trees are built is the *subClassOf* relation.

As already mentioned in section 3 properties in RDF(S) are first-order citizens. So, if the user prefers to view the ontology with the "property-centric

[7] Explorer for Rdfs-based OntologieS

optics" and desires to explore the tree hierarchy based on the relation *subPropertyOf* the EROS interface can easily accommodate this demand by imposing that the left tree hierarchy is built based on the *subPropertyOf* relation and the right tree (still hierarchically based on *subClassOf*) represents the domains and ranges of the properties from the left tree as depicted in Figure 7(right).

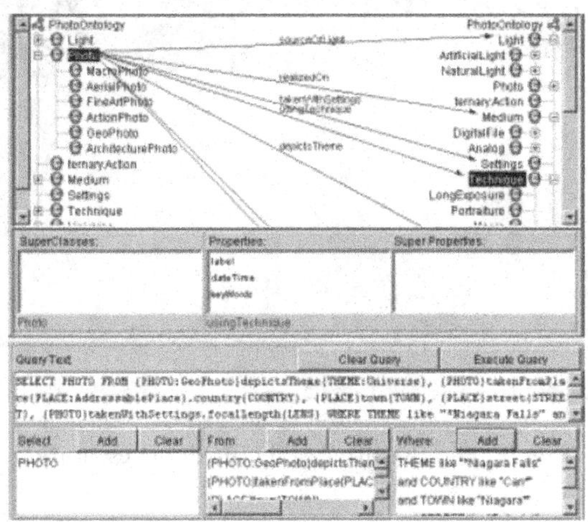

Fig. 8. The EROS interface: Query Building Mode

5.3 Query Generation Support

When in query mode, the EROS interface, guides the user in building RQL queries, i.e. specifying the `SELECT-FROM-WHERE` clauses. As the most tricky clause to build is the `FROM` part, the EROS interface starts by assisting the user in the formulation of a single path expression of the form: $\{VAR_i : DC_i\}p_i\{VAR_j : RC_j \mid L\},\ldots$ This expression can be combined in a so-called chained expression which takes the following form: $\{VAR_i : DC_i\}p_i\{VAR_j : RC_j \mid L\}.p_j\{VAR_m : RC_m \mid L\}\ldots$ Where $VAR_x : Y$ denotes that a variable of type Y, p_x represents a property, DC_i and RC_j denote classes serving as a domain and range respectively; L represents a literal.

EROS allows the user to generate such expressions by selecting a node in the graph (a variable of a certain type), then selecting a property (p_I) of the chosen node that navigates the user to the destination node (again a variable). If the destination node is not of a literal type, the user can choose another property of that node traversing the graph further (building a chained path expression) or he can create a new path expression concatenating it with the previous ones.

Filling in the `SELECT` clause consists of choosing variables that are of interest from the list of variables introduced in the `FROM` clause. Similarly to the `SELECT` clause, the `WHERE` clause starts by selecting variables bound in the `FROM` clause

Fig. 9. The Resulting Hypermedia Presentation

and then building a Boolean expression by utilizing an offered list of appropriate operators. The queries that can be built in this way represent a large class of practical queries for ontology exploration and data retrieval as illustrated in Figure 2. However, we acknowledge that we do not cover the complete expressive power of RQL (e.g. nested queries nor implicit schema queries are not supported). Figure 8 depicts the query building part of the EROS interface. Note that the built query is that presented in Figure 2 and after its execution, the Hera system offers the query results in the form of a multimedia presentation depicted in Figure 9.

6 Conclusions and Future Work

As the nature of applications changes under the influence of the Semantic Web (SW) initiative, the need to capture the semantics of the application data increases. In the typical application representing SW ideas, the semantic annotation of Web resources is crucial. As the illustrative example we showed how the Hera methodology addresses this issue and how RDF(S) can help to improve the querying multimedia information systems. We presented an RDF(S)-based integration model and illustrated its use in a multimedia federated IS.

Essential in the use of RDF(S) are the ontologies. They help to organize the resources in terms of their semantics, and thus offer a nice specification of the semantics of the entire application. However, for many applications this specification in terms of ontologies needs to be used by humans. The end-users use such an ontology to find or search for terms and to mentally reason about these terms. Before they are constructing actual queries on the RDF metadata they need to familiarize with the ontology. For this purpose an effective visual representation of ontologies is vital. We addressed this issue providing a visual interface in which the user is able to view the ontology both from the viewpoint of classes and that of properties. This interface also assists in the generation of RQL queries.

In the future we plan to help also the designer by turning this interface into an authoring tool which would allow for specification of the models used in the Hera methodology. From the integration perspective we intend to address the issue of query relaxation which would allow to retrieve approximate results in the case when the exact query does not succeed to find an answer.

References

1. Richard Vdovjak and Geert Jan Houben. Providing the semantic layer for wis design. In *Advanced Information Systems Engineering, 14th International Conference, CAiSE 2002*, volume 2348 of *Lecture Notes in Computer Science*, pages 584–599. Springer, 2002.
2. Flavius Frasincar, Geert Jan Houben, and Richard Vdovjak. Specification framework for engineering adaptive web applications. In *The Eleventh International World Wide Web Conference, Web Engineering Track*, 2002. `http://www2002.org/CDROM/alternate/682/`.
3. Nora Koch, Andreas Kraus, and Rolf Hennicker. The authoring process of the uml-based web engineering approach. In *First International Workshop on Web-Oriented Software Technology*, 2001.
4. Reinhold Klapsing and Gustaf Neumann. Applying the resource description framework to web engineering. In *Electronic Commerce and Web Technologies, First International Conference, EC-Web 2000*, volume 1875 of *Lecture Notes in Computer Science*, pages 229–238. Springer, 2000.
5. Ora Lassila and Ralph R. Swick. Resource description framework (rdf) model and syntax specification. W3C Recommendation 22 February 1999.
6. Dan Brickley and R.V. Guha. Rdf vocabulary description language 1.0: Rdf schema. W3C Working Draft 30 April 2002.
7. Gregory Karvounarakis, Vassilis Christophides, Dimitris Dimitris Plexousakis, and Sofia Alexaki. Querying rdf descriptions for community web portals. In *17iemes Journees Bases de Donnees Avancees*, pages 133–144, 2001.
8. J. Broekstra and A. Kampman. Sesame: A generic architecture for storing and querying rdf and rdf schema. Aidministrator Nederland b.v. October 2001.
9. Richard Vdovjak and Geert Jan Houben. Rdf-based architecture for semantic integration of heterogeneous information sources. In *International Workshop on Information Integration on the Web*, 2001.
10. Natalya F. Noy and Mark A. Musen. Anchor-prompt: Using non-local context for semantic matching. In *Workshop on Ontologies and Information Sharing at the Seventeenth International Joint Conference on Artificial Intelligence*, 2001.
11. Jeffrey D. Ulman. Information integration using logical views. In *Proceedings of the 6th Int. Conference on Database Theory, ICDT'97*, volume 1186 of *Lecture Notes in Computer Science*, pages 19–40. Springer, 1997.

Embedding Metrics into Information Systems Development Methods: An Application of Method Engineering Technique

Motoshi Saeki

Dept. of Computer Science, Tokyo Institute of Technology
Ookayama 2-12-1, Meguro-ku, Tokyo 152, Japan
saeki@cs.titech.ac.jp

Abstract. Many methods for information systems development such as object oriented analysis and design (OOA & OOD) support the activities to construct artifacts, but do not include the activities to measure the quality of the artifacts or to improve them based on the results of their measurement. In this paper, by using a meta modeling technique, we propose a general framework of extending an existing method into the method which includes the activities for attaching semantic information to the artifacts and for measuring their quality using this information. Embedding this information into a method can be considered as a method assembly of the meta model of the method and the metrics model. We can formally represent this process with Method Engineering Language (MEL). We show an example that our technique is applied to; the extended version of a use case modeling method.

1 Introduction

Various methods for information systems development such as object oriented methods[10] have been proposed in this decade and are being put into practice. These methods only support the human activities to construct artifacts, but do not include the activities to measure the quality of the artifacts and/or to improve them based on the results of their measurement. Since there are wide varieties of artifacts for methods, we should have different metrics to measure the quality for the methods and it is necessary to define the metrics according to the methods. For example, in the method where we develop a class diagram, we can use the CK metrics[8] and improve artifacts based on the values of CK metrics. The technique of Cyclomatic number[13] can be applied to the construction of an activity diagram of UML (Unified Modeling Language)[15] in order to measure its complexity, so that we can avoid constructing complicated activity diagrams. These examples show that effective metrics vary on a method.

The existing metrics such as CK metrics and Cyclomatic number are for expressing the structural and syntactical characteristics of artifacts only, but do not reflect their semantic aspects. Suppose two class diagrams of Elevator Control System, which are the same except for the name of a class; one includes the

J. Eder and M. Missikoff (Eds.): CAiSE 2003, LNCS 2681, pp. 374–389, 2003.

class named "A" and in the other one the class is named "Elevator". Although these diagrams are completely the same in graph structural view, the latter diagram has higher quality rather than the former, because the latter uses the domain-specific word "Elevator" and every reader can easily understand what this class denotes. However, the existing metrics provides the same value for these two diagrams. This example shows that the metrics expressing semantic aspects allows us to measure the quality of artifacts more correctly and precisely. It is difficult to extract automatically semantic information from the complete artifacts, thus a developer can and should attach this semantic information to the artifacts (including intermediate ones) by manual during his development activities. That is to say, the method that the developer adopts should include the supports of attaching semantic information. And the method should also suggest how to calculate the measures from the attached semantic information. In the above example of the class diagrams of "Elevator", the example method should support the human activity of measuring the occurrences of domain specific words in a class diagram and suggest how to improve the quality of the diagram based on this measurement. The measure of the occurrences of domain specific words is specific to this method. To embed the function of measuring artifact quality into methods, we should explore the techniques how to build the methods supporting the metrics of artifacts, including the definition of the metrics.

Method engineering is a discipline for exploring techniques to build project-specific methods[4], and meta modeling techniques to specify methods semi-formally or formally have been developed to manipulate the methods by computer. It provides the technique called method assembly to compose a new project-specific method from a set of meaningful parts of the existing methods[5, 14,17]. Meaningful parts of methods are called method fragments or method chunks. A method assembly technique can be used to embed metrics models into the existing methods and to get a new method that has the function to measure the quality of artifacts. In the above example of "Elevator" class diagram, we have two method fragments; 1) a meta model of class diagram method as a base, and 2) a metric model based on the occurrences of domain-specific words in class diagrams. When we assemble these two method fragments, we can get a new method that can measure the quality of class diagrams based on the occurrences of domain-specific words. Thus a meta modeling technique is used to define metrics model according to a method, and the assembly technique provides a general framework how to tailor an existing method into a new method that can measure the quality of artifacts.

In this paper, by using a meta modeling technique and a method assembly one, we propose a general framework of extending an existing method into the method which includes the activities for attaching semantic information to the artifacts and for measuring their quality. Semantic information and the definition of the measures are formally defined on a meta model, and they are embedded into a meta model of an original method by performing a method assembly. We use the formal language Method Engineering Language (shortened to MEL), since it provides a unified framework to describe both of method fragments and method assembly processes. Furthermore, we present an example that our technique is applied to; the extended version of a use case modeling method. In the example, we get the use case modeling method where the quality of a use case diagram can be calculated. It can be formalized as method assembly processes and be defined in MEL. In this sense, this paper shows the expressive power of MEL through the application to the example.

In the next section, we introduce how to describe method fragments, i.e. a meta modeling technique. Section 3 presents a general framework how to extend methods on its meta model. We call this extended version of a method a measurable method. Section 4 presents the example of defining the metrics for use case diagrams, and we show how to get the measurable method by using method assembly.

2 Meta Modeling Technique and MEL

Although the textbooks and manuals of a development method such as object oriented methods contain narrative texts written in natural language, figures and examples for ease of understanding, there are several techniques to model a method formally or semi-formally in order to manipulate the method by computer, e.g. to generate CASE tools based on it[12]. These techniques are called meta modeling techniques. Roughly speaking, methods consist of two facets; one is artifact and the other is activity. The artifact facet specifies what artifacts are developed following a method, e.g. class diagrams, while the activity one specifies the processes to develop the artifacts, e.g. "Identify objects and classes at first" in object oriented methods. Figure 1 shows a simplified example of a meta model for the method of constructing a use case diagram of UML diagrams[15]. In the figure, the structure of the artifact is defined in a class diagram, while the activities and their execution order are specified in an activity diagram. Dotted arrows (object flows) stand for the artifacts that are produced by an activity. For example, the second activity "Identify Use Cases" produces a set of the identified "Use Cases" and their relationships to "Actors".

Although we use a class diagram and an activity one of UML on account of the easiness to understand, we describe the meta models in more formal style by using Method Engineering Language (MEL)[6]. Figure 2 shows the MEL descriptions of Figure 1. In MEL, method fragments are classified into two types ; product fragment and process one. The description of a product fragment in MEL can be considered as a textual representation of a class diagram which defines the structure of the products shown in Figure 1 (a). The description that begins with the reserved word "PRODUCT" defines the concept of product elements included in a method and corresponds to a class of Figure 1(a). On the other hand, the word "ASSOCIATION" declares the relationship between concepts, i.e. an association between the classes. The description of a process fragment corresponds to a textual representation of an activity diagram. MEL has syntactic constructs for composing more complicated activities from the

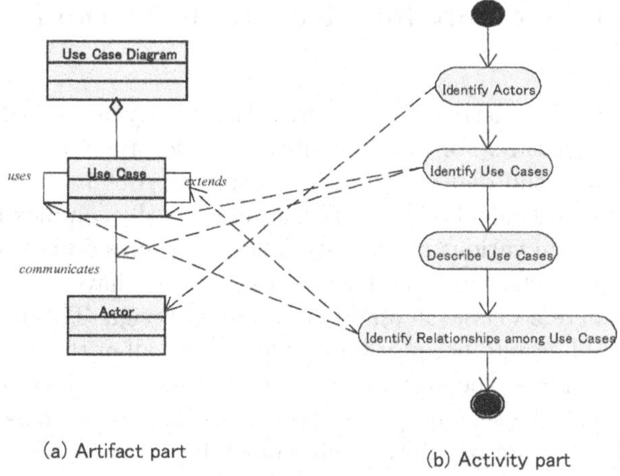

Fig. 1. An Example of A Meta Model

activities, e.g. sequential execution, conditional branch, iteration and parallel execution including fork and join, etc. Readers can find the activity "Construct a use case diagram" is composed as a sequential execution of the four activities, as shown in Figure 2(b). The reserved word "REQUIRED" specifies the input products for the process.

PRODUCT Use Case Model;
ID Use Case Model;
IS_A Diagram, Structured Text;
LAYER Diagram;
PART OF Analysis Model;
NAME TEXT;

PRODUCT Use Case:
LAYER Concept;
PART OF Use Case Model;
SYMBOL Oval;
NAME TEXT;
ASSOCIATED WITH {(uses,), (extends,), (hasUseCase,), (communicates,)}.

ASSOCIATION hasUseCase:
ASSOCIATES (Use Case Diagram, Use Case);
CARDINALITY (1..n; 1..1).

(a) Product Fragment

PROCESS Construct a Use Case Diagram:
LAYER Diagram;
TYPE Creation;
PART OF Create an Analysis Model;
REQUIRED {Interview results};
REQUIRED OPTIONAL
Current Information system;
(- Identify Actors ;
- Identify Use Cases ;
- Describe Use Cases ;
- Identify Relationships among Use Cases ;
)
DELIVERABLES {Use Case Diagram}.

(b) Process Fragment

Fig. 2. An Example of MEL Descriptions

3 Method Assembly for Measurable Methods

Almost of all existing metrics for measuring the quality of an artifact is based on its syntactical structure. For example, in CK metrics, the number of operations[1] per class (WMC), the depth of an a class from a root in an inheritance tree (DIT) and so on are calculated, in order to express the complexity of an object oriented design from various viewpoints. These measures do not reflect semantic aspects of the artifacts. Suppose that many operations having the same function occur in the different classes in an object oriented design. This design cannot be said to be a good design, because we should modify all of the occurrences of the operations if we change the function, i.e. it has low modifiability. To quantify this situation, we need the semantic information on which operations have the same function, and this type of information cannot be automatically obtained from the syntactic characteristics of the design document. A developer should add this information by manual during his development activities. More concretely, he investigates which operations have the same function and attach this information as attributes of the artifacts. And he also defines how to calculate the metrics from the attached attributes. It greatly depends on development methods what attributes to attach and how to quantify quality characteristics.

Furthermore McCall et. al. proposed that a quality characteristic such as completeness could be quantified by a weighted arithmetic average of the metrics [7], and these weight factors also depend on the methods. In this sense, we extend the existing method into a new one whose meta model has 1) attributes in its artifact part, 2) activities for investigating the attribute values of the artifact, 3) expressions for calculating metrics from the attribute values, and 4) mathematical expressions such as weighted arithmetic average for quantifying quality characteristics based on the metrics. Figure 3 shows a general framework for extending an existing method on its meta model. The upper left part Meta Model (Method Description) of the figure shows a general description in an existing method, where the activity "Identify Artifact Elements" produces the elements of the artifacts. On the other hand, in the lower left part Metrics Model Definition, we define attributes, metrics, weighted factors. It also includes the activity of attaching the semantic information of artifacts as attribute values ("Describing Attribute Values") and the activity of using quality characteristics for artifact improvement ("Considering Quality Characteristics"). The classes "Metrics" and "Quality Characteristics" specify the measures using "Attribute" and the expressions for calculating quality characteristics from the metrics respectively. By assembling these two parts to a new method, we can get the right part of the figure. We call it a measurable method of the existing method. This assembly process can be formally specified with specific manipulation operators of MEL on the meta models as mentioned in [6,9].

[1] We should have used the term "methods" instead of "operation". To avoid the confusion to a development method, however we use the word "operation" in this paper.

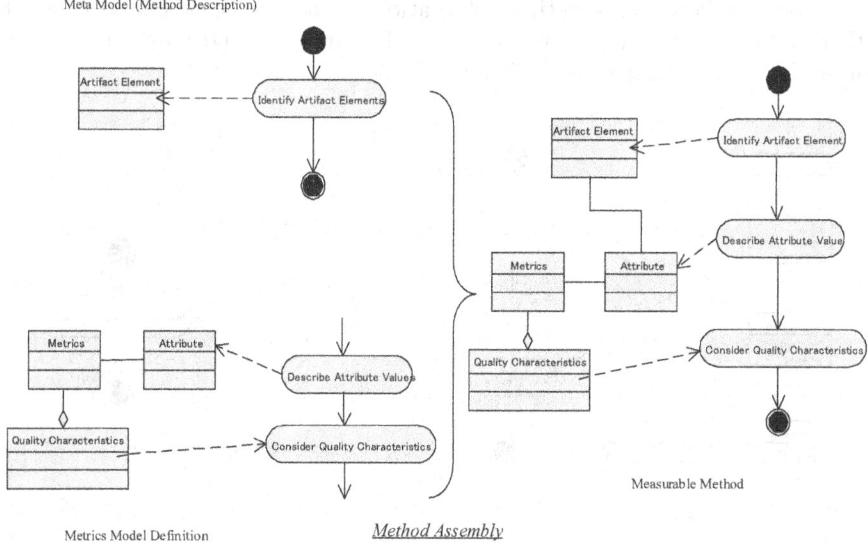

Fig. 3. Method Assembly for Measurable Methods

The above is a very simple but general framework for producing measurable methods. The point is that we can produce measurable methods by means of applying method assembly to the existing, non-measurable methods. Let's consider another but also general example to get measurable methods by using method assembly.

GQM (Goal-Question-Metric) model has been proposed in [3] as a framework for defining and interpreting software measurement. Its model includes three basic concepts; 1) Goal: the purposes of the measurement, in more detail, a goal specifies what objects are measured for what purposes from which viewpoints with respect to which focuses, 2) Question: Questions are for clarifying the attainment of the Goal and for assessing the Goal, and 3) Metric: a set of data to quantitatively answer the corresponding Questions. A class diagram of the upper left part GQM Meta Model in Figure 4 illustrates a meta model of GQM products, while an activity diagram in the part shows the process to enact GQM framework for measurement. At first, developers define a GQM model, i.e. define Goals, generate Questions for each Goal and define Metric for the Goals, and then collect the data according the specification of the Metric. After that, they interpret the data to evaluate the Questions and the Goals.

The application of GQM framework to measure the quality of artifacts can also be considered as the method assembly of a GQM and non-measurable methods, as shown in Figure 4. Metric is connected to artifact elements through its "Attribute" values, and the activities of GQM are embedded in the form of parallel composition to the activities of the non-measurable method. In [11], GQM approach was applied to meta data management in data warehouses, and the GQM meta model was adapted to schemas of data warehouses. In this sense, it can be considered as a method adaptation in an artifact aspect only. On the other hand, our technique includes method adaptation and assembly not only for artifact parts but also activity parts.

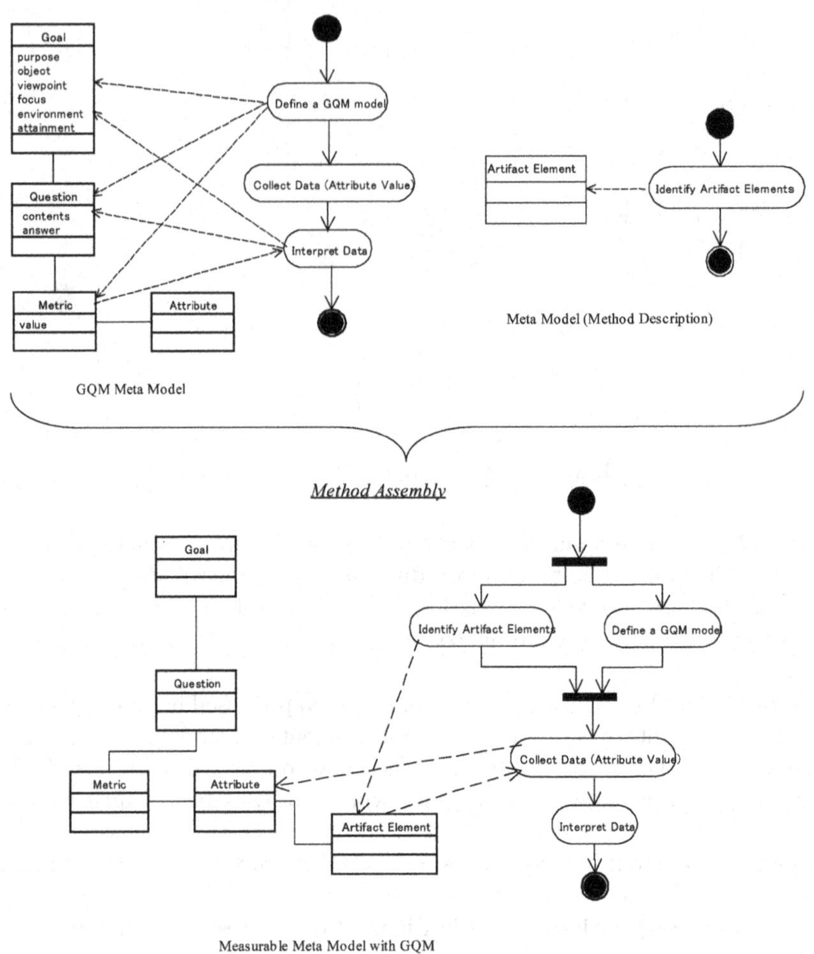

Fig. 4. GQM Meta Model and Its Method Assembly

4 Defining Metrics with MEL: An Example of Measurable Use Case Modeling Method

4.1 Modifiability on Use Case Diagrams

Quality characteristics for requirements specifications are listed up in IEEE830 standards[1], e.g. completeness, correctness, modifiability etc. One of the typical metrics on a use case diagram is the number of the use cases appearing in the diagram, and it is based on syntactical features of the diagram. Since it is insufficient to quantify the quality characteristics of IEEE 830, we should consider the metrics relevant to the meaning of use cases. For simplicity, we focus on the metrics relevant to modifiability. If we modify a use case, its modification can propagate to the use cases that are connected to it with "<<extends>>" or "<<uses>>" relationships. The number of the occurrences of these relationships among use cases can be a measure denoting modifiability. This measure can be calculated directly from the structural characteristics of a use case diagram. Let's consider other measures that are more relevant to the meaning of use cases. Based on [16], we adopt two additional dependency relationships among the use cases; data dependency and control dependency, and the concept of basic types of use cases called use case types. An analyst identifies both of them during his activities for constructing a use case diagram, and it means that he should perform additional activities, e.g. "Identify Control Dependencies", "Identify Data Dependencies" and "Identify Use Case Types" after finishing the activity "Identify Use Cases".

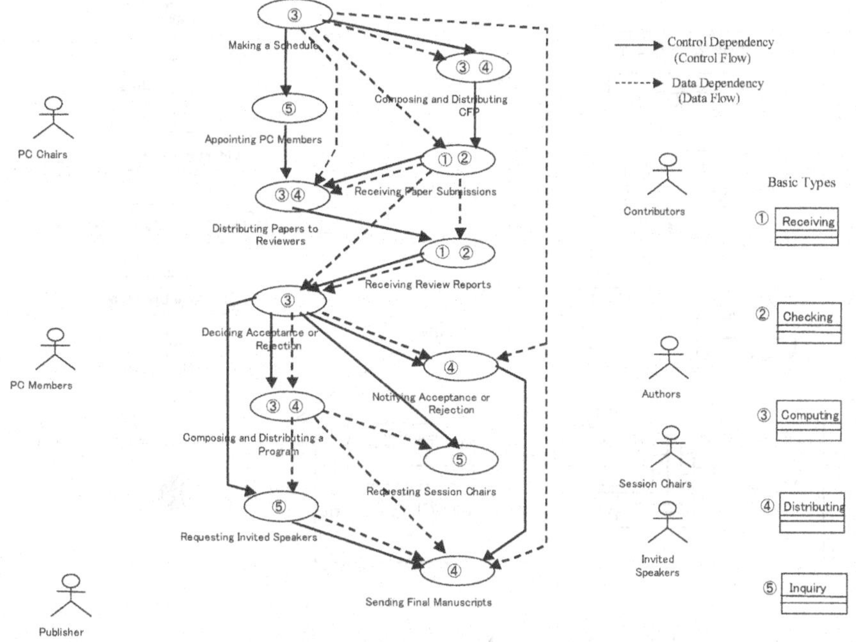

Fig. 5. An Example of Use Case Diagrams

Figure 5 illustrates a use case diagram together with dependency relationships and the information on use case types. For simplicity, we omit the interactions between the actors and the use cases in the figure. This example is a tool for supporting tasks that program committee chairs (PC chairs) of academic international conferences have to perform. The PC chairs should compose the CALL FOR PAPER (CFP) and organize the committee. They receive paper submissions and distribute them to the reviewers, normally PC members. After getting the review reports from the reviewers and summarizing them ("Receiving review reports" in the figure), they have PC meetings to decide which papers will be accepted or rejected. The authors of the papers are notified of their acceptance or rejection by the PC chairs.

A control dependency expresses the execution order on use cases. For example, after the use case "Notifying acceptance or rejection" is performed, "Sending final manuscripts" should be done. A data dependency relationship represents which use cases consume the data that another use case produces, and is also significant to identify the use cases that we should modify. The modifications on a use case can propagate the different use cases that have control or data dependencies to it, so these occurrences has an influence on the difficulty in the modifications. The more they occur in the diagram, the more difficult its modification is.

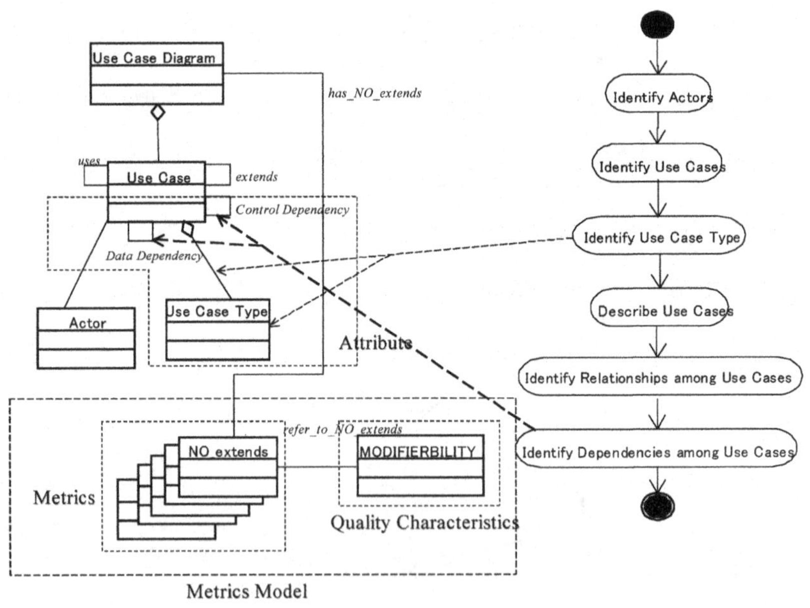

Fig. 6. A Meta Model of Measurable Use Case Modeling Method

A use case type is a kind of an abstraction or a semantic category, which stands for abstract meaning of a use case, and a set of the use case types depends on an application domain. In the domain of the example like a data processing system, we use five use case types "Receiving", "Checking", "Computing", "Distributing" and "Inquiry", all of which are the manipulation on data. Considering the purpose of executing a use case, an analyst attaches these types to the identified use cases. The circled numbers in a use case in the figure shows the use case types that are attached to it. For example, the use case "Receiving Paper Submission" has the purposes of receiving paper submissions as data and of checking if the submitted papers meet a certain format or not. That is to say, the two types "Receiving" and "Checking" are attached to it. In this case, it has the two roles, i.e. compounded meaning and its modifications can be complicated because we should consider both of these two roles simultaneously during the modification process. Thus we can use the number of attached use case types to each use case as a measure of modifiability.

Figure 6 depicts a meta model, and it is the result of embedding these attributes for quantifying modifiability to the existing meta model, according to the general framework in Figure 3. For example, readers can find that the concept "Use Case Type", the associations "Control Dependency" and "Data Dependency" are added as attributes to the product part of the meta model (product fragment). As for a process part of the meta model (process fragment), two activities for the metrics are added. For example, the activity "Identify Use Cases Types" is for finding the types of the identified use cases. The activity for control and data dependencies "Identify Dependencies among Use Cases" is also added in the process part. We call this extended version of use case modeling method a measurable use case method.

As mentioned above, we have two types of metrics from which the modifiability can be indirectly measured; one is NOD (Number of Dependencies) for denoting the ratio of how many relationships occur among use cases and the other one NUCT (Number of Use Case Types) is the multiplicity ratio of multiplicity of use case types attached to use cases. The definition of the metrics can be defined by using the meta model as follows;

$$\text{NOD} = \frac{\mathit{AllDependencies} - \#\mathit{Dependency}}{\mathit{AllDependencies}}$$

$$\text{where } \mathit{AllDependencies} = (\#UseCase \times (\#UseCase - 1))/2.$$

$$\text{NUCT} = \frac{1}{AVE_{u \in UseCase}\{\#\{ut \in UseCaseType \mid aggregates(u, ut)\}\}}$$

Note that *AllDependencies* denotes the number of all possible dependencies on a use case diagram from graph theoretic view, i.e. combinations between arbitrary two use cases. We should explain conventional notation appearing in the above expressions. The name of each class and the name of each association denote a set and a predicate respectively. For instance, $UseCase$ and $u \in UseCase$ denote a set of the identified use cases and a use case u respectively. We use "*aggregates*" as the predicate name of an object aggregation relationship. For instance, $aggregates(u, ut)$ denotes that the use case u has a use case type ut. $\#S$ stands for the number of the elements of the set S. $AVE_{p(x)}\{s(x)\}$ means the average value of a set of the numbers $s(x)$ constructed from x such that $p(x)$. *Dependency* appearing in NOD is either *extends*, *uses*, *Control Dependency* or

Data Dependency. Thus we have four variations of the metrics related to a kind of dependency among use cases, and we call them NO_extends, NO_uses, NO_CD and NO_DD in order. In the example, these values are 1, 1, $(66 - 13)/66 = 0.8$ and $(66 - 15)/66 = 0.77$ because $AllDependencies = (12 \times (12 - 1))/2 = 66$. Since NUCT is the reciprocal number of an average of attached use case types for each use case, we can get NUCT$= 12/17 = 0.71$.

Finally, as McCall did, we adopt weighted arithmetic average to quantify modifiability from these five metrics values and we can get it as follows;

$$MODIFIABLITY =$$

$$w_1 \times \text{NO\_extends} + w_2 \times \text{NO\_uses} + w_3 \times \text{NO\_CD} + w_4 \times \text{NO\_DD} + w_5 \times \text{NUCT}$$

$$\text{where } w_1 + w_2 + w_3 + w_4 + w_5 = 1 \text{ and } 0 \leq w_i \leq 1 (i = 1, ...5).$$

This expression and the weighting factors are specified in an instance of class "Quality Characteristics" as shown in Figure 3, and much experience can determine their values. In this paper, taking the same value, i.e. 0.2 for each, as an example, we get the value $0.2 \times 1 + 0.2 \times 1 + 0.2 \times 0.8 + 0.2 \times 0.77 + 0.2 \times 0.71 = 0.2 + 0.2 + 0.16 + 0.15 + 0.14 = 0.85$ as MODIFIABILITY quality. By using this technique, we can quantify the other quality characteristics of a use case diagram as a requirement specification.

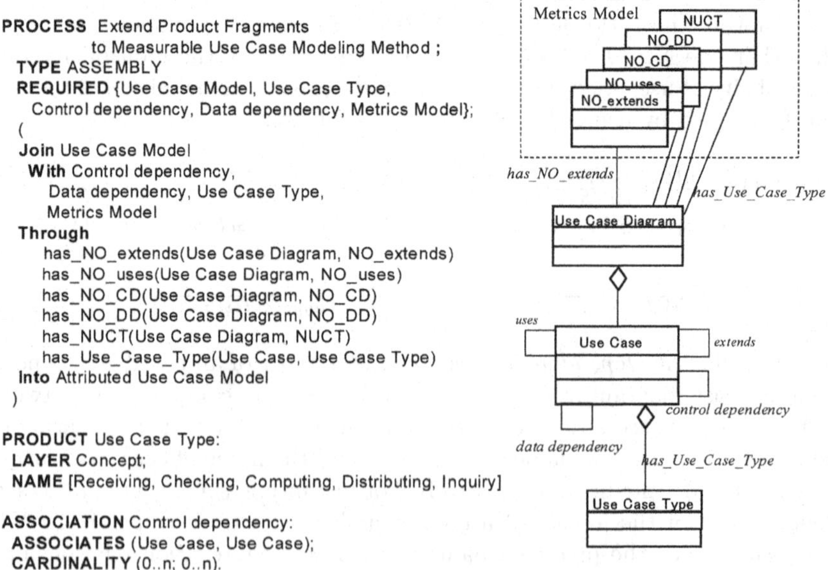

Fig. 7. Method Assembly for Product Fragments of Measurable Use Case Modeling Method

Figure 6 shows a meta model of the measurable use case modeling method that can quantify the modifiability of a produced use case diagram, by using above technique. Each class whose category is "Metrics" in the figure denotes a metrics such as No_extends and No_uses. The class "MODIFIABILITY" defines how to calculate the modifiability from the metrics. The details how to calculate quality characteristics will be mentioned in the next subsection.

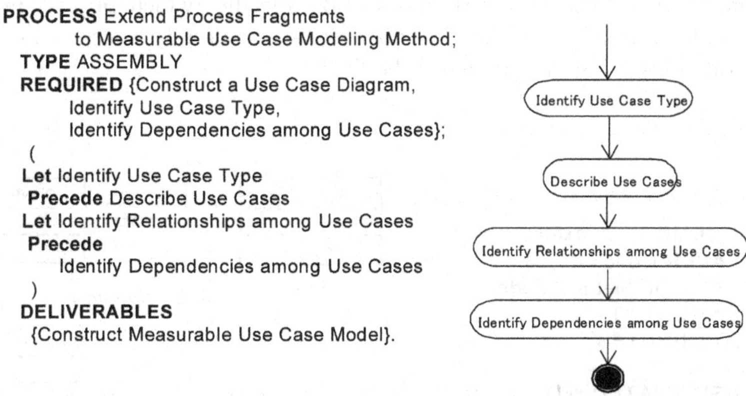

Fig. 8. Method Assembly for Process Fragments of Measurable Use Case Modeling Method

4.2 Defining Measurable Methods by Method Assembly

As shown in Figure 6, the measurable use case modeling method is an extension of a use case modeling method and we can get it by assembling some product fragments and process ones. In MEL, we can define a method assembly process as a set of the process fragments that specify how to add new fragments. It consists of two fragments; one is for assembling product fragments and another is for process ones.

Figure 7 illustrates a part of a method assembly process of Use Case Model and Metrics Model, in order to get a product fragment of the measurable use case modeling method. The readers can find that a concept as a class "Use Case Type" and two associations, e.g. Control Dependency and Data Dependency are newly added to the original method, by using "Join ... With ... Through ... Into" statement of MEL. "Join F1 with F2 Through A1 into F3" is an operation to assemble a product fragment F1 and a fragment set F2 by using associations A1, and the fragment F3 is a result of the operation. In this figure, additional six associations, e.g. "*has_NO_extends*" and "*has_Use _Case_Type*" are adopted to connect Use Case Type and Metrics Model to Use Case Model. A part of the assembled fragments like Metrics Model will be shown later in Figure 9, and Metrics Model is a meta model which consists of Metrics concepts (NO_extends,

NO_uses, NO_CD, NO_DD, NUCT) and Quality Characteristics concept (Modifiability).

Figure 8 shows an assembly process for process fragments of the measurable use case modeling method. Two new process fragments as activities “Identify Use Case Types” and “Identify Dependencies among Use Cases” are added to the original process fragment of use case modeling method. The assembly operation “Let P1 Precede P2” creates an execution order between the process fragments P1 and P2. Note that REQUIRED section specifies which process fragments are assembled as inputs of the assembly process “Extend Process Fragments to Measurable Use Case Modeling Method”.

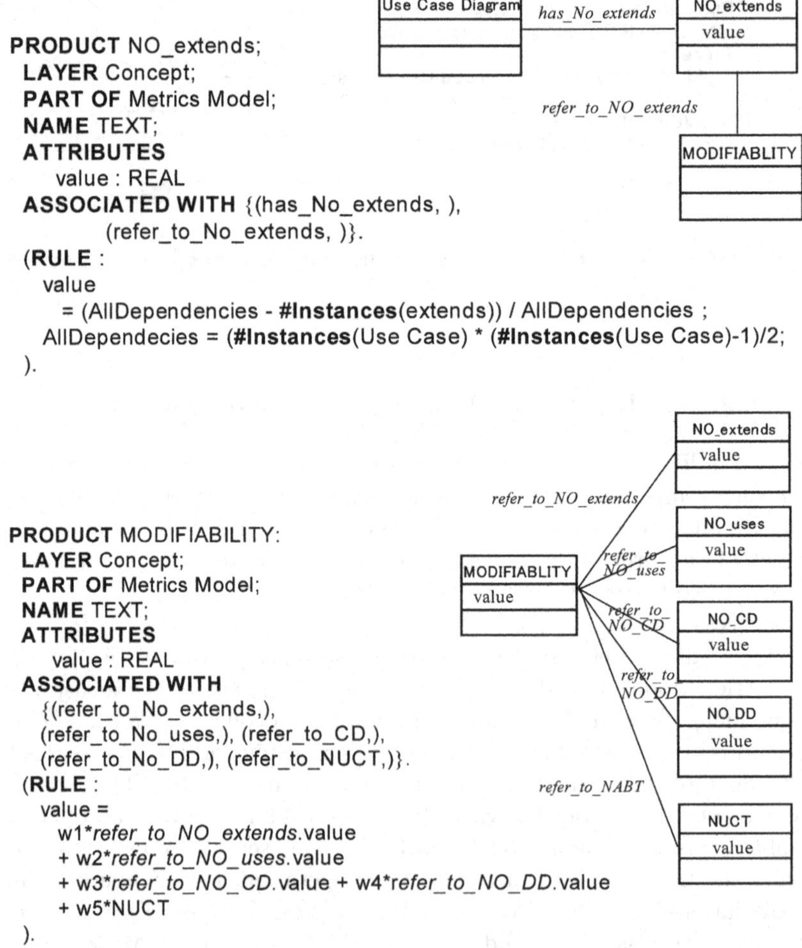

Use Case Diagram
has_No_extends
NO_extends
value
refer_to_NO_extends
MODIFIABLITY
PRODUCT NO_extends;
LAYER Concept;
PART OF Metrics Model;
NAME TEXT;
ATTRIBUTES
value : REAL
ASSOCIATED WITH {(has_No_extends,),
(refer_to_No_extends,)}.
(RULE :
value
= (AllDependencies - #Instances(extends)) / AllDependencies ;
AllDependecies = (#Instances(Use Case) * (#Instances(Use Case)-1)/2;
).
PRODUCT MODIFIABILITY:
LAYER Concept;
PART OF Metrics Model;
NAME TEXT;
ATTRIBUTES
value : REAL
ASSOCIATED WITH
{(refer_to_No_extends,),
(refer_to_No_uses,), (refer_to_CD,),
(refer_to_No_DD,), (refer_to_NUCT,)}.
(RULE :
value =
w1*refer_to_NO_extends.value
+ w2*refer_to_NO_uses.value
+ w3*refer_to_NO_CD.value + w4*refer_to_NO_DD.value
+ w5*NUCT
).
NO_extends
value
refer_to_NO_extends
NO_uses
value
refer_to_NO_uses
MODIFIABLITY
value
refer_to_NO_CD
NO_CD
value
refer_to_NO_DD
NO_DD
value
refer_to_NABT
NUCT
value

Fig. 9. Definitions of Metrics and Quality Characteristics with MEL

Finally, we need to define product fragments which have the functions to calculate quality characteristics like MODIFIABILITY. Figure 9 illustrates the definitions of the metrics NO_extends and the quality characteristics MODIFIABILITY. These definitions include their calculating expressions and weighting factors in "rule" section of MEL. The rule section also specifies invariants which hold on attribute values. For example, the attribute "value" in NO_extends is calculated by means of an equation of the rule section.

Figure 10 shows how to calculate the modifiability of a use case diagram according to the definitions of Figs 6, 7, 8 and 9. It is written in UML object diagram, because it can be considered as an instance of the meta model of Figure 6.

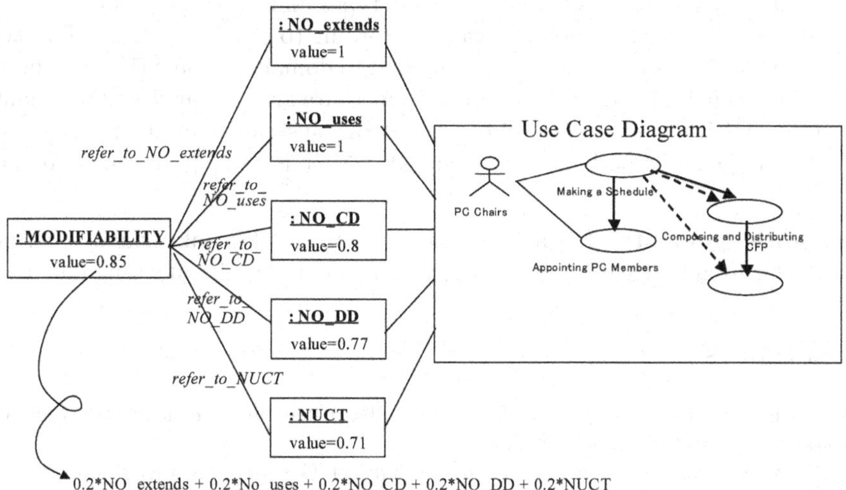

Fig. 10. Calculating Quality Characteristics

5 Conclusion and Research Agenda

This paper presented a general framework how to embed quantification techniques to the existing development methods by using method engineering techniques. The meta models of a measurable method allows us to generate (semi-) automatically CASE tools supporting measurement activities and the improvement of product quality, by means of a CAME (Computer-Aided Method Engineering) tool such as Decamerone[9], Mentor[18] and MetaEdit+[12].

Research agenda for the future directions can be summarized as follows;

1. Refining a technique for modeling and defining metrics. In this paper, we use usual mathematical expressions to define the metrics. Like [2], the usage of Object Constraint Language (OCL)[20] is one of the promising approaches to express wide varieties of metrics easily and to interchange their definitions among different development organizations.

2. Collecting metrics definitions. To assess our technique, we need various kinds of metrics and apply our technique to them. We are exploring the metrics for quantifying different quality characteristics on wide varieties of artifacts and are trying to formalize both of metrics and methods.
3. Usage of metrics. Since our technique includes defining development methods, we should consider how to use the defined metrics in order to improve the quality of artifacts during development processes. More concretely, we should clarify what activities improve the artifacts by using the metrics in the method, like GQM[3].
4. Support of activities for identifying semantic information (attributes). To get the precise quality characteristics, a developer identifies semantic information of product elements. In the example of the measurable use case modeling method, a developer identifies use case types and it is a problem how to set up a set of use case types in advance according to problem domain. This type of semantic information is closely related to domain ontology[19] and the ontology is helpful to develop metrics to measure artifact quality in a semantic level. MEL has another level of an ontology system for method concepts[9]. The usage of method ontology included in MEL is also a promising approach.

Acknowledgements. The author would like to thank Sjaak Brinkkemper and Frank Harmsen for their insightful suggestions to Method Engineering Language.

References

1. IEEE Recommended Practice for Software Requirements Specifications. Technical report, IEEE Std. 830-1998, 1998.
2. F. B. Abreu. Using OCL to Formalize Object Oriented Metrics Definitions. In *Tutorial in 5th International ECOOP Workshop on Quantitative Approaches in Object-Oriented Software Engineering (QAOOSE 2001)*, 2001.
3. V. Basili. Software Modeling and Measurement: The Goal/Question/Metric Paradigm. Technical Report UMIACS-TR-92-96, University of Maryland, 1992.
4. S. Brinkkemper. Method Engineering: Engineering of Information Systems Development Methods and Tools. *Information and Software Technology*, 37(11), 1995.
5. S. Brinkkemper, M. Saeki, and F. Harmsen. Meta-Modelling Based Assembly Techniques for Situational Method Engineering. *Information Systems*, 24(3):209 –228, 1999.
6. S. Brinkkemper, M. Saeki, and F. Harmsen. A Method Engineering Language for the Description of Systems Development Methods (Extended Abstract). In *Lecture Notes in Computer Science (Proc. of CAiSE'2001)*, volume 2068, pages 473–476, 2001.
7. J.P. Cavano and J.A. McCall. A Framework for the Measurement of Software Quality. In *Proc. of ACM Software Quality Assurance Workshop*, pages 133–139, 1978.
8. S. Chidamber and C. Kemerer. A Metrics Suite for Object-Oriented Design. *IEEE Trans. on Software Engineering*, 20(6):476–492, 1994.
9. F. Harmsen. *Situational Method Engineering.* Moret Ernst & Young Management Consultants, 1997.

10. I. Jacobson, G. Booch, and J. Rumbaugh. *The Unified Software Development Process*. Addison Wesley, 1999.
11. M. Jarke, M. Jeusfeld, C. Quix, and P. Vassiliadis. Architecture and Quality in Data Warehouses. In *Lecture Notes in Computer Science (CAiSE'98)*, pages 93–113. Springer-Verlag, 1998.
12. S. Kelly, K. Lyytinen, and M. Rossi. MetaEdit+ : A Fully Configurable Multi-User and Multi-Tool CASE and CAME Environment. In *Lecture Notes in Computer Science (CAiSE'96)*, volume 1080, pages 1–21, 1996.
13. T. McCabe and C. Butler. Design Complexity Measurement and Testing. *CACM*, 32(12):1415–1425, 1989.
14. J. Ralyte and C. Rolland. An Assembly Process Model for Method Engineering. In *Lecture Notes in Computer Science (Proc. of CAiSE'2001)*, volume 2068, pages 267–283, 2001.
15. J. Rumbaugh, I. Jacobson, and G. Booch. *The Unified Modeling Language Reference Manual*. Addison Wesley, 1999.
16. M. Saeki. Reusing Use Case Descriptions for Requirements Specification : Towards Use Case Patterns. In *Proc. of 6th Aisa-Pacific Softwrae Engineering Conference (APSEC'99)*, pages 309–316, 1999.
17. M. Saeki. Role of Model Transformation in Method Engineering. In *Lecture Notes in Computer Science (Proc. of CAiSE'2002)*, volume 2348, pages 626–642, 2002.
18. S. Si-Said, Rolland C., and G. Grosz. MENTOR : A Computer Aided Requirements Engineering Environment. In *Lecture Notes in Comupter Science (CAiSE'96)*, volume 1080, pages 22–43, 1996.
19. Y. Wand. Ontology as a Foundation for Meta-Modelling and Method Engineering. *Information and Software Technology*, 38(4):281–288, 1996.
20. J. Warmer and A. Kleppe. *The Object Constraint Language*. Addison Wesley, 1999.

A Value-Oriented Approach to E-business Process Design

Jaap Gordijn[1]* and Roel J. Wieringa[2]

[1] Department of Computer Science, Vrije Universiteit, De Boelelaan 1081, 1081 HV Amsterdam, The Netherlands. gordijn@cs.vu.nl
[2] Department of Computer Science, University of Twente, P.O. Box 217, 7500 AE, The Netherlands. roelw@cs.utwente.nl

Abstract. Innovative e-commerce ideas have often floundered on an inadequate analysis of the expenses and benefits of the idea and an inadequate integration of the required e-business processes with other business processes. We present a requirements analysis and business process design approach that focuses on the analysis of the expenses and benefits of the e-commerce idea to all actors involved. We map this value viewpoint to the available business processes of the actors and show how to derive an economically feasible cross-organizational business process design.

1 Introduction

The implementation of an innovative e-commerce idea has to surmount several obstacles, each of which may cause an implementation failure. First, an innovative idea is, by definition, an idea that has not yet been implemented before. It is difficult to estimate the profitability of the idea before it is implemented. This indicates a need for techniques that allow us to estimate the profitability of an e-commerce implementation as early as possible. Second, e-commerce, again by definition, is the exchange of goods or services by means of computer software and networks. The profitability of an implementation of the idea must therefore discussed by business managers *and* software application architects. This requires specification and analysis techniques that can be understood by both groups of stakeholders. Third, any implementation of the idea must be integrated with the business processes and IT infrastructure available in the participating business actors. We define e-business as the implementation of business processes in computer networks. Implementation of an e-commerce idea requires the design of e-business processes that minimize the expenses for the business actors while at the same time maintaining the estimated profitability. This requires business process design techniques that incorporate techniques for the estimation of expenses and benefits.

* Partly sponsored by the *Stichting voor Technische Wetenschappen (STW)*, project VWI 4949 and by EU-IST project IST-2001-33144 Obelix, and EU-EESD project NNE5-2001-00256 BusMod.

J. Eder and M. Missikoff (Eds.): CAiSE 2003, LNCS 2681, pp. 390–403, 2003.

In this paper, we further develop an approach to explore an innovative e-commerce idea and to estimate its benefits, called e^3-*value* [5]. We use simple notations that require no more than a few minutes explanation in order to be understood. At the same time, these notations are sufficiently precise for application architects to make design decisions. We also introduce a method to map the e-commerce idea to a cross-organizational business process, maintaining the orientation on expenses and benefits. Finally, we briefly discuss the problem of mapping this cross-organizational process to the processes and information systems available in each business actor.

The ideas presented in this paper have been developed and tested in four consultancy projects (see [5]) in the field of advertizing, news and internet service provisioning, and music. Additionally, tool support is currently developed by the EC-IST project Obelix on ontologies for e-business. The contribution of this paper lies in the integration of the commercial and technical viewpoints in e-commerce implementation. We think that the neglect of the commercial viewpoint has been a frequent cause of failure in business process design and information system development. This paper argues that we should include this viewpoint in our scope.

In section 2, we introduce the viewpoints that we use in this paper. In section 3, we elaborate the commercial viewpoint, which focuses on value, and in section 4 we elaborate the business process viewpoint, which acts as an intermediary between the commercial and technical viewpoints. Section 5 summarizes the results and discusses topics for further research.

2 Viewpoints in E-business Process Design

The task of the e-business requirements engineer is to match business processes of a set of business actors to consumer needs in a market. (A consumer can be a business (i.e. a legal person) or it can be a natural person.) This problem can be structured by distinguishing four different viewpoints.

- Taking the **value viewpoint,** we produce three descriptions of the e-commerce idea.
  - The *value hierarchy* identifies the top-level consumer need and allocates this to objects of economic value to be produced by the business actors.
  - The *value exchange graph* refines this by identifying the activities in which these value objects are created or exchanged by the business actors. This graph can be seen as a shared discussion object, and can be used to generate profitability sheets.
  - *Profitability sheets* quantify the value exchanges for each business actor.
- Taking the **business process viewpoint**, we describe inter-organizational business processes and intra-business tasks.
  - A *process hierarchy* describes the transactions among businesses that realize the desired value objects.
  - A *task hierarchy* decomposes each process into tasks to be performed by business actors.

– Taking the **information systems viewpoint**, we describe an allocation of tasks to information systems and applications available in the business actors.

In this paper we focus on the first two viewpoints and briefly discuss the third.

We present no fixed sequence of writing the different descriptions listed above. However, there are two orientations associated with two viewpoints.

– *Divergence.* Taking the value viewpoint, we explore possible value activities and value exchanges that could realize the e-commerce idea. The focus is on creating new possibilities for value creation.
– *Convergence.* Taking the business process viewpoint, we identify the realistic means to realize the value proposition identified from the value viewpoint. The focus is on reducing expenses. Convergence, and expense reduction, is also the focus in the information system viewpoint.

In practice, these activities are intertwined.

We illustrate our approach using the case of the *Amsterdam Times*, which publishes a newspaper. The *Amsterdam Times* has a subscriber base. The initial e-commerce idea is to offer subscribers web services, such as accessing news articles on-line on a pay-per-view basis, surfing on the Internet and email. In this paper we focus on the idea to offer subscribers an on-line news article archive only.

During exploration of this idea, it became apparent that its commercial basis is the use of a *termination* fee to finance the on-line article service. In this context, *termination* is picking up the phone when someone calls. When a caller calls a callee, the telecommunication network sets up a connection path from caller to callee. When the callee picks up the phone, the termination point of this connection is realized. If an actor is willing to cause termination of a large quantity of telephone calls, most telecommunication operators are willing to pay the actor for that. This price paid by the telecommunication operator per realized termination is called the *termination fee.* Because the *Amsterdam Times* has a large subscriber base, it is capable of generating a large number of terminations. The stakeholders involved in exploring the e-commerce idea were not capable of articulating the idea this way initially. The elaboration process presented below helped them in doing this.

3 The Value Viewpoint

3.1 Value Hierarchy

One of the lessons learned from the *Amsterdam Times* project is that easily understandable description techniques are needed for the exploration of an e-commerce idea. Persons are involved with no background knowledge in conceptual modeling techniques at all and with no time nor inclination to learn these techniques. Hence, all our notations are simple.

We start elaborating an e-commerce idea with the elicitation of a **value hierarchy.** Figure 1 shows a value hierarchy for the on-line article idea. The numbers are used to be able to refer to parts of the hierarchy later on. They are not part of the notation. The value hierarchy says that to satisfy the need

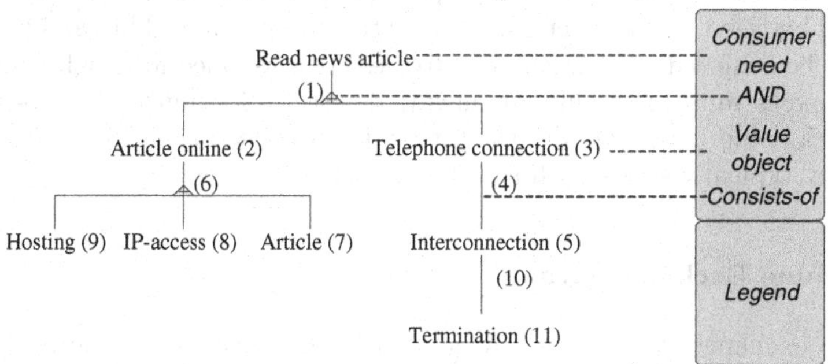

Fig. 1. Value hierarchy showing the objects satisfying a consumer need.

to read a news article, we need an online article and a telephone connection. The on-line article can be provided if there is an article, a hosting service that stores the article, and IP access to the stored article. A telephone connection can be provided if we have a number of interconnections and a termination at the consumer. Note that the further we elaborate the hierarchy, the more design choices we make. Such design choices occured during the execution of the online article project. For instance, the hierarchy proposed in this paper supposes that a *read news article* need can be decomposed into an *article online* object and a *telephone connection*, each to be delivered by a separate actor. Telecommunication companies refer to this as call termination. Another possible hierarchy supposes that the *telephone connection* is deeper into the hierarchy, as a sub-part of the *article online.* This is refered to as call origination (see [5]). Then delivery of an *article online* by a specific actor consists of the article itself, and the telephone connection needed to deliver the article.

In general, a value hierarchy is a rooted a-cyclic directed graph whose root represents a consumer need. Starting with a consumer need increases the chance that a product is really wanted by a consumer [12]. Children of a node represent value objects used to satisfy this need. A **value object** is a good or service of economic value to some actor.

The edges of a value hierarchy represent the *contributes-to* relationship. The reverse relationship is called *consists-of.* An AND-node represents the fact that all children are needed for the higher-level one and an OR-node represents that fact that only one of the children is needed.

The leafs of the value hierarchy are the boundary of our value descriptions. We know that one or more actors can produce these leaf objects against known expenses, so in order to elaborate the e-commerce idea, we do not need to decompose these leaf objects further. The value hierarchy is an important tool to relate the satisfaction of a consumer need (the intended benefit) to activities already performed by the business actors (expenses made to create the benefit).

Value hierarchies are similar to goal hierarchies known from requirements engineering (RE) [15,1,3]). Both are means-end hierarchies. The difference is that the nodes in a value hierarchy represent value objects to be produced or exchanged between business actors, whereas the nodes in a goal hierarchy represent goals to be achieved. Often, goal hierarchies are developed for single business actors, whereas value hierarchies are always developed for multiple business actors. Finally, a value hierarchy always starts with a consumer need, whereas a goal hierarchy typically starts with a business mission.

3.2 Value Exchange Graph

A value exchange graph shows which actors are involved in the creation and exchange of the value objects shown in the value hierarchy. The constructs which make up such a graph and their semantics have been defined extensively in [5].

Figure 2 shows a value exchange graph for our running example.

Like a value hierarchy, the value exchange graph represents a number of design decisions. The graph of figure 2 shows that there is a set of consumers called *Readers*, and that these exchange value objects with the *Amsterdam Times* and with an actor called the *Last Mile*. These in turn exchange value objects with a complex actor, a *Telecommunication consortium*, which consists of two actors, *Data Runner* and *Hoster*. Inside each actor node, one of more value activities are shown as rounded rectangles. Some of the exchanged value objects are numbered. This is not part of the notation. The numbers correspond with the numbers in the value hierarchy. We now explain the value exchange graph in more detail.

An **actor** is an entity perceived by itself and by its environment as an independent economic (and often also legal) entity. An actor makes a profit or increases its utility by performing activities. In a sound, sustainable, value exchange model *each* actor should be capable of making a profit. Actors are represented by rectangles with sharp corners. Sets of actors with similar properties, called markets, are represented by stacked rectangles.

To satisfy a consumer need, or to produce a value object for others, an actor should perform a value activity, for which it may be necessary to exchange value objects with other actors. A **value activity** is an operation that can be performed in an economically profitable way by at least one actor. It is depicted by a rounded rectangle. An important design decision represented by a value exchange graph is the decision whether a value object is to be obtained from other actors by means of a value exchange, or to be produced by means of a value activity by the actor itself. This e.g. reflects decisions on out-sourcing, and decisions about the optimal size of an enterprise [14].

A **value exchange**, depicted by an arrow, shows that actors are willing to exchange objects of value with each other. Value exchanges are between actors,

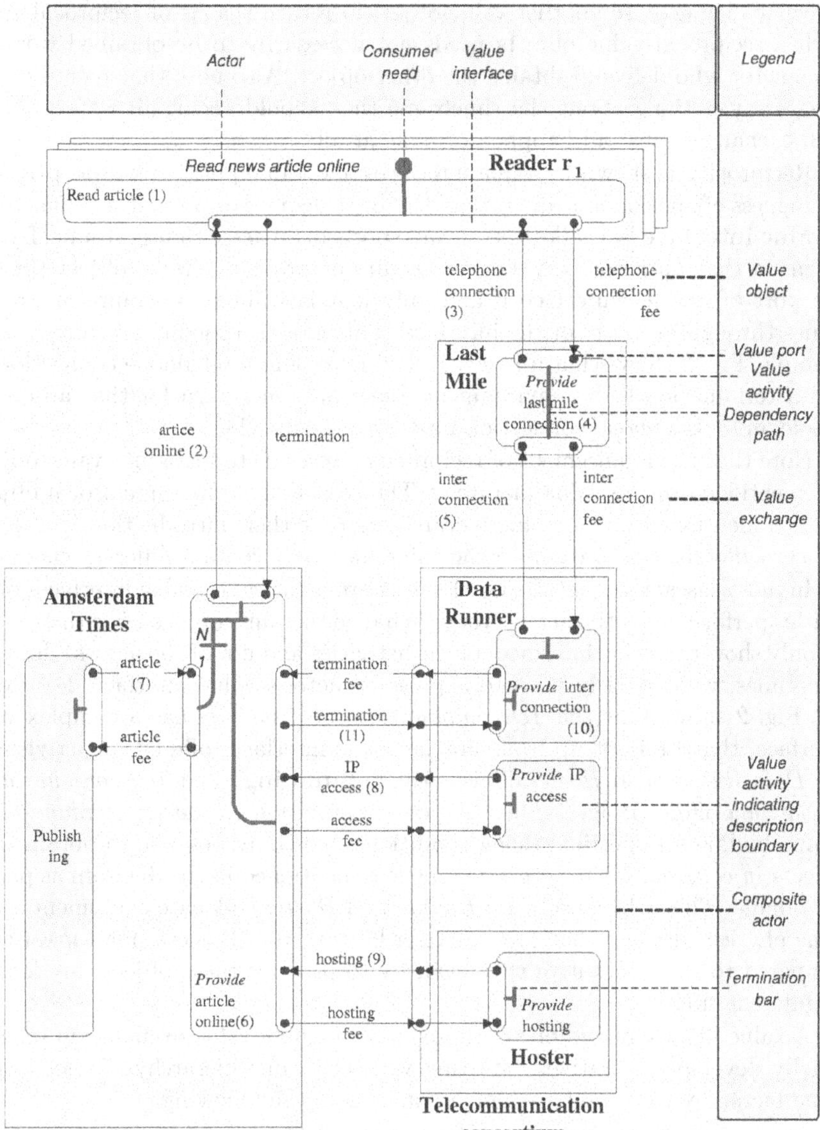

Fig. 2. The on-line article service offered by *Amsterdam Times* is funded by termination fees to be paid by the *Telecommunication consortium.*

or between value activities performed by actors. So in the example, a telephone connection is exchanged between the *Last Mile*, and a *reader*.

Each value exchange graph expresses economic reciprocity. We assume that our actors are rational economic entities that are only willing to offer a value object if they acquire another value object in return that is of reciprocal value. Such a reciprocal value objects needs not necessarily to be obtained from the same actor who delivers/obtains the other object. Also note that reciprocal exhanges say nothing about the timeframe they should occur; all we say is that such exchanges must all happpen or none at all .

Reciprocity is shown by value interfaces and value ports. A **value port** is a willingness of an economically rational actor to acquire or provide a value object. A **value interface** is a collection of value ports of an actor that is atomic. By this we mean that an actor is willing to acquire or provide a value object through one port of a value interface if and only if it is willing to acquire or provide values through all ports of the interface. This models economic reciprocity. For example, Fig. 2 shows that a *reader* is willing to offer a telephone connection fee and a termination to its environment, but wants in return for that an on-line article and a telephone connection to deliver the article.

Note that the requirement of reciprocity causes us to introduce value objects not mentioned in the value hierarchy. The reason that these reciprocal objects are not mentioned in the value hierarchy is that their introduction is a design choice. Different elaborations of the value hierarchy contain different choices.

In most cases, value interfaces of actors are identical to value interfaces of activities performed by the actors: they exchange the same objects. For these cases, we only show the value interfaces of the activities and not of the actors. However, sometimes, we explicitly need to express an actor's value interface. For example, Fig. 2 shows that the *Telecommunication consortium* has a complex value interface, that iss built up from simpler value interfaces offered by activities in the *Data Runner* and *Hoster*. This is called **bundling.** The *Telecommunication consortium* offers IP access, hosting and termination to the *Amsterdam Times* as one bundle for specific pricing conditions. It is only possible to obtain these objects *in combination* in return for the fees mentioned in the diagram as part of the bundle. This is because *Data Runner* and *Hoster* co-locate equipment at the same physical site and therefore can offer hosting and IP-access for a lower tariff compared to the alternative that facilities to produce these objects are located at different sites.

A value hierarchy and one or more corresponding value exchange graphs are usually developed iteratively, starting with the value hierarchy. To get from a value hierarchy to a value exchange graph, note the following.

- The value objects in the hierarchy are the input or output of a value activity.
- The consists-of relationships between value objects in the hierarchy indicate a value activity in the graph. This activity produces a value object by using other value objects. An AND-node in the value hierarchy indicates that several value objects are needed to produce the output value object, and so the corresponding value activity at least aggregates and possibly transforms value objects into the desired output object.

For instance, the AND construct labeled (1) in Fig. 1 results in a value activity called Read article labeled (1) in Fig. 2, to be performed by a *reader*. The graph shows that the *reader* needs to aggregate an article online and a telephone connection to be able to satisfy his need. The graph also shows that the *Amsterdam Times* produces the article itself by the value activity Publishing, and obtains IP access and Hosting from others.

We observed earlier that the leafs of a value hierarchy represent a system boundary. We know that other objects are needed to produce these leaf objects, but we do not describe these other objects because the business actors already know how to do this, and moreover, they already have activities in place by which they do it. The value exchange graph shows these activities as well as the value objects they produce. These activities are greyed in Fig. 2. We assume that these activities are profitable for the performing actor. This assumption must be validated by the business managers participating in the analysis.

Note that the development of a value hierarchy and a related value exchange graph is a process of step-wise refinement. It is common to start with a more course-grained hierarchy, which results in a value exchange graph with a few actors and value activities. To find more fine grained value hierarchies and value exchange graphs, we have proposed a deconstruction process which breaks down a hierarchy and graph into smaller parts [4].

3.3 Profitability Sheets

To estimate the profitability of the value activities and exchanges, we have to estimate the number of actual value exchanges in a time period (e.g. a month). For each actor, the results are summarized on a **profitability sheet**, which shows our best estimate whether the e-commerce idea could be profitable (see Table 1 for an example).

To create the profitability sheet, we first express the occurrence of a consumer need by a black dot in the consumer activity (Fig. 2). Each such occurrence will lead to an exchange across the consumer value interface, as indicated by the dependency path connecting the dot with the interface symbol.

A **dependency path**, depicted by grey lines, shows via which value interfaces an actor should exchange objects when triggered. Each dependency path connects two or more interfaces of a value activity by means of AND nodes (represented by a bar) and OR-nodes (represented by a split). It defines a Boolean combination of interfaces that must be valid for each activation of the activity. The dependency path defines the business logic of the activity, because it says that each conjunction of interface activivation compatible with it, is profitable. Dependency paths are used to assemble the data on profitability sheets.

When we do not care about the path of an activity (e.g. because the activity is already performed by the actor according to a known and profitable business model), we indicate this with a termination bar. In our example, the activities that produce leaf value objects of the value hierarchy are greyed.

The value exchange graph in Fig. 2 shows that each activation of the consumer value interface leads to an exchange with the *Amsterdam Times* and of the *Data Runner*, and this in turn leads to the activation of the value interface of these actors. The paths show the following information.

- The *Last Mile* exchanges a telephone connection for a telephone connection fee if and only if it exchanges an interconnection for an interconnection fee.
- The *Amsterdam Times* needs to obtains a termination fee, IP access and hosting service from the *Telecommunication consortium* to offer an article online. Also, it shows that a number (*N*) of *online* articles can be produced by using only *one* article *written by a journalist*. This shows that the marginal expense of generating a copy of a same article is zero.

Dependency paths have been inspired by Buhr's use case maps [2] but differ from them because they do not carry any scenario information. They do not represent business processes but are instructions to assemble the profitability sheets.

To construct the profitability sheet, we start at the consumer need and follow the paths and value exchanges, until we have reached all termination bars. Each time value objects are exchanged between actors, we update the profitability sheets for these actors.

A next step is to calculate the economic value of objects in terms of a monetary unit (e.g. Euros). How to do so depends on the kind of actor. *End consumer* actors want to maximize their consumer value, defined by [16] as the receipts experienced by consuming the object divided by the sacrifices to obtain the object. Holbrook's consumer value framework can be used to elicit factors which determine the valuation by consumers [6]. Table 1 presents a profitability sheet for an *enterprise actor*. Such an actor wants to maximize its profit and net cash flow, or at least wants to play break even. According to enterprise investment theory [7], cash flows are considered only for an investment evaluation. Consequently, Table 1 shows objects representing goods, services or intangibles (in short, objects other than fees) in parentheses, because we do not consider these objects for profitability analysis. Then for fees, the sheet shows how these fees are calculated, and a best estimate on the profitability for actors (not given here due to confidential project data). The profitability sheet for each actor gives the information for business managers to decide whether it makes business sense to go ahead to the next stage of elaborating this e-commerce idea, which is the definition of business processes required to produce the desired value objects.

4 Inter-organizational Business Process Viewpoint

The value exchange viewpoint elaborates the e-commerce idea for the strategic manager. It does not represent processes but the *willingness* of an economically rational actor to create and exchange value. It represents a steady state that exists when as yet to be identified technology and people do their work. Taking the process viewpoint, we describe

- which inter-organizational processes must exist to be able to satisfy the consumer need, and
- which tasks each actor must perform to realize within these processes.

This elaborates the value viewpoint for the operational manager. It shows which activities have to performed by whom or what, and in which order, to produce which result. We discuss each of these hierarchies in turn.

Table 1. Profitability sheet for the *Amsterdam Times*

Actor	Amsterdam Times	
Consumer need	Read news article online	
	Value Object In	*Value Object Out*
Exchanges with readers:	(*termination*)	(*online article*)
Exchanges with telco:	*termination fee* = *telephone connection fee* × *revenue sharing factor*	(*termination*)
	IP (*access*)	*IP access fee* = *fee per second* × *duration*
	(*hosting*)	*hosting fee* = *fee per pageview* × *page views*

4.1 Business Process Hierarchy

To find the required inter-organizational business process, we ask which processes must be performed to create the steady-state situation as represented by the value exchange graph.

Inter-organizational business processes are on-going activities that involve at least two actors. To identify the required processes, we use the following three types of processes, which are well known from both business science [9] and business process / requirements engineering [10,13] literature:

- *Primary processes,* which directly contribute to the satisfaction of consumer needs. This includes processes performed in the steady state, as well as ex-ante processes such as supplier selection and service subscription, and ex-post processes such as dispute resolution or service unsubscription.
- *Support processes,* which enable execution of primary processes and provide a suitable working environment.
- *Management process,* which organize, staff, direct, and monitor primary and support processes.

Fig. 3 shows inter-organizational processes needed for satisfying the consumer need to read an online article. The leafs represent processes; the other nodes classify the processes according to the taxonomy above.

Primary processes contribute directly to consumer satisfaction. The primary process consists of article delivery, which is the steady state of value activities and exchanges represented by the value exchange graph, and the subscription

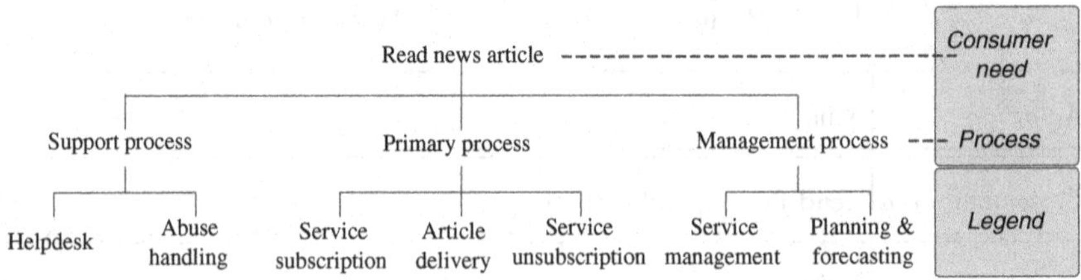

Fig. 3. Process hierarchy for on-line news article delivery.

and unsubscription processes, which represent the entry and exit of a consumer to and from this steady state. Each of these processes involves several actors and is therefore cross-organizational. This requires careful integration of the information systems and business processes of the participating actors.

Support processes contribute indirectly to consumer need satisfaction. Here we identify two of such processes. The helpdesk process handles complaints and solves problems of end-customers. Because in this specific case service provisioning is partitioned over a number of actors, it is an inter-organizational process too. The same holds for abuse management: *Readers* can for instance use the offered IP-access for unintended and sometimes illegal purposes. This may result in blocking reader's access to the service.

Cross-organizational management processes organize, staff, direct and monitor the other processes. An important management process in this case is planning and forecasting. To make the article online business case successful it is important that precisely sufficient resources (e.g. modem ports to dial in, webserver capacity) are available to serve the *Readers*. A shortage in resources (e.g. modem ports) immediately results in a decrease in revenues because revenues are based on the total duration of telephone connections. On the other hand, unused resources, representing a substantial investment, result in a loss, especially for *Data Runner* and *Hoster* since these parties have invested in theses resources. Another process is service management itself. Service management consists of managing the quality of service (e.g. measuring the percentage of *Readers* who get a service denial, for instance caused by shortage in modem resources), developing the service from a content point of view (broader selection of articles, search for related articles, etc), and negotiating between parties about service delivery (e.g. between *Amsterdam Times* and the *Telecommunication consortium*).

4.2 Task Hierarchy

Whereas business processes are on-going inter-organizational activities, task are terminating activities with input and output, assigned to a specific actor and therefore intra-organizational. For each process identified, we decompose the process into tasks which can be assigned to value activities of an actor. We try to reuse as much as possible of existing processes and information technology.

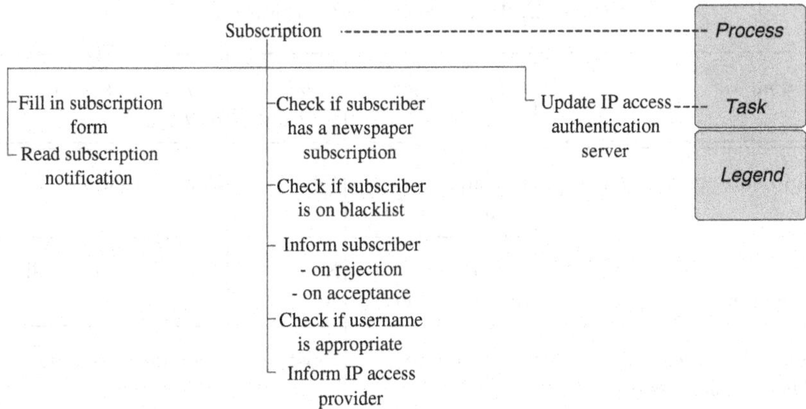

Fig. 4. Tasks for the subscription process

Fig. 4 shows the tasks for the subscription process as a task hierarchy. To identify the tasks, we constructed a UML activity diagram of the service subscription process, with a swimlane for each actor, identifying the tasks of each actor that are already in place and those that must be invented. This is however not a deliverable to be shown to management. The task hierarchy provides sufficient detail for a description of an e-commerce idea and does not require stakeholders more than two minutes to understand. A task hierarchy is used for the following purposes.

- To understand the tasks needed to fulfill consumer need;
- To understand which tasks must be performed by an actor to realize a value activity;
- To identify whether tasks are new for an actor, or whether tasks performed anyway can be used or changed;
- To gain insight in operational expenses of processes and tasks, which can then be compared to the estimations expressed in the profitability sheets;
- To identify information systems that can support the tasks. Linking tasks to information systems is part of the information system viewpoint, not discussed here.

To this end, we annotate the task hierarchy with a **task expenses estimation table** (see table 2). To assess the profitability of an e-commerce idea, it is important to discover substantial labor resulting in high expenses which may inhibit the business idea. Additionally, it is important to recognize whether tasks should be newly developed or existing tasks can be used for building the process.

5 Discussion and Conclusions

To sum up, the value viewpoint identifies actors, value activities and exchanges needed to satisfy the top-level consumer need. The process viewpoint identifies

Table 2. Task expenses estimation table.

Task name	*Estimated labor*	*Existing/new*	*Implements value activity*
Fill in subscription form	10 minutes / form	New	Read article
Check if a subscriber has a newspaper subscription	1 minute /subscription	New	Provide article online
Update IP access authentication server	0 (automated)	Existing	Provide IP access
...	...	...	...

all the tasks needed to perform these activities and exchanges. The value viewpoint indicates revenues and expenses, whereas the process viewpoint indicates expenses only.

What we have achieved so far is a conceptual framework of three viewpoints that integrates the commercial and technical views, and we introduced a number of simple description techniques that can be understood by all stakeholders and are yet precise enough to analyze commercial and technical feasibility of the idea. The proposed process can be viewed as a kind of commercial-technical co-design of e-business systems. The approach has been validated in a number of consultancy projects in the field of internet service provisioning, news, ads, energy, music and banking.

Guidelines for the transition from the value viewpoint to the process viewpoint are currently lacking. Guidelines for business process modeling [10] concentrate on the single-actor case and do not relate business process design decisions to a commercial value viewpoint. For the allocation of tasks to information systems (part of the information system viewpoint) there are some practical guidelines [11], some of which date back to Information Engineering [8], but again the integration with the process and commercial viewpoints is weak or non-existing. Our future research will focus on providing guidelines for these transitions, and validating these in additional consultancy projects.

Acknowledgment. We wish to thank the consortium working on the *Amsterdam Times* project for their cooperation.

References

1. Annie I. Antón. *Goal Identification and Refinement in the Specification of Information Systems.* PhD thesis, Georgia Institute of Technology, Raleigh, NC, 1997.

2. R. J. A. Buhr. Use case maps as architectural entities for complex systems. *IEEE Transactions on Software Engineering*, 24(12):1131–1155, 1998.
3. A. Dardenne, A. van Lamsweerde, and S. Fickas. Goal-directed requirements acquisition. *Science of Computer Programming*, 20:3–50, 1993.
4. J. Gordijn and J. M. Akkermans. Ontology-based operators for e-Business model de- and reconstruction. In Yolanda Gil, Mark Musen, and Jude Shavlik, editors, *Proceedings of the First International Conference on Knowledge Capture*, pages 60–67, New York, NY, oct 2001. ACM-Press. Also available from http://www.cs.vu.nl/~gordijn/.
5. Jaap Gordijn. *Value-based Requirements Engineering – Exploring Innovative e-Commerce Ideas.* PhD thesis, Vrije Universiteit, Amsterdam, NL, 2002. Also available from http://www.cs.vu.nl/~gordijn/.
6. Morris B. Holbrook. *Consumer Value: A Framework for Analysis and Research.* Routledge, New York, NY, 1999.
7. Charles T. Horngren and George Foster. *Cost Accounting: A Managerial Emphasis, sixth edition.* Prentice-Hall, Englewood Cliffs, NJ, 1987.
8. J. Martin. *Strategic Data-Planning Methodologies.* Prentice-Hall, 1982.
9. Henry Mintzberg. *Structures in Fives: Designing Effective Organizations.* Prentice Hall, Englewood Cliffs, NJ, 1983.
10. Martyn A. Ould. *Business Processes – Modelling and Analysis for Re-engineering and Improvement.* John Wiley & Sons, Chichester, UK, 1995.
11. R. Tagg and C. Freyberg. *Designing Distributed and Cooperative Information Systems.* International Thomson Computer Press, 1997.
12. Don Tapscott, David Ticoll, and Alex Lowy. *Digital Capital – Harnessing the Power of Business Webs.* Nicholas Brealy Publishing, London, UK, 2000.
13. R.J. Wieringa. *Requirements Engineering: Frameworks for Understanding.* John Wiley & Sons, New York, NY, 1996.
14. Oliver E. Williamson. *The Economic Institutions of Capitalism: Firms, Markets, Relational Contracting.* The Free Press, New York, NY, 1985.
15. E. S. K. Yu and J. Mylopoulos. Why goal-oriented requirements engineering. In E. Dubois, A. L. Opdahl, and K. Pohl, editors, *Proceedings of the 4th International Workshop on Requirements Engineering: Foundation for Software Quality (RESFQ 1998)*, Namur, B, 1998. Presses Universitaires de Namur.
16. V. A. Zeithaml. Consumer perceptions of price, quality, and value: A means-end model and synthesis of evidence. *Journal of Marketing*, (52):2–22, jul 1988.

Derivation Rules in Object-Oriented Conceptual Modeling Languages

Antoni Olivé

Dept. Llenguatges i Sistemes Informàtics
Universitat Politècnica de Catalunya
08034 Barcelona (Catalonia)
olive@lsi.upc.es

Abstract. We propose three new methods for the definition of derivation rules in O-O conceptual modeling languages. The first method applies to static rules, and associates each derived element with a defining operation. The specification of this operation is then the definition of the corresponding derivation rule. The second method applies to constant relationship types whose instances can be derived when the instances of one of its participant entity types are created. We propose a variant of the previous method to deal with these types. The third method deals with hybrid types, and suggests a simple way to define their partial derivation rules. We propose an adaptation of the three methods to the UML.

1 Introduction

Derived types and derivation rules have been considered fundamental components of conceptual schemas of information systems since the early eighties [17]. The rationale is that derivation rules are domain knowledge that an information system needs to know in order to be able to derive some facts and, according to the 100% (or completeness) principle [18], that knowledge must be described in the conceptual schema. The importance of derivation rules is also recognized in industry, where they are sometimes classified as a kind of business rule [6].

Many conceptual modeling languages provide specific constructs for defining derived types and derivation rules. Among the early languages we mention SDM [16], which provides a detailed analysis of derivation kinds and the constructs supporting them; and CIAM [13], which puts a strong emphasis on derived types and the temporal perspective. Among the recent languages, we mention the family of languages descendants of KL-ONE [5], called Description Logics, which provide a specific formal syntax for defining derived entity and relationship types, and a strong reasoning support [4, 8]; Chimera [9], which includes deductive rules for data derivation, and a set of mappings for the implementation of these rules in commercial database systems (triggers, views, etc.); and ORM [14], which allows informal and formal [2] versions of derivation rules. Finally, we mention the standard language UML [24], which also allows defining derived types and derivation rules.

J. Eder and M. Missikoff (Eds.): CAiSE 2003, LNCS 2681, pp. 404–420, 2003.

The approaches taken by the above languages for defining derivation rules are diverse. This fact poses naturally the question of which is the best approach, if it exists. This paper tries to provide an answer to that question in the context of object-oriented languages [22] and, in particular, in the context of the UML.

We have analyzed the possible methods for defining derivation rules in object-oriented languages, and we recommend one of them as the probably most appropriate in many practical situations. The recommended method consists in defining a query function for each derived type. The derivation rule is then the postcondition assertion of the corresponding function. We adapt the method to the case of the UML. In this language, the query functions are the query operations, and their postconditions can be specified formally in the OCL language [24, ch. 6]. We show that the recommended method simplifies the languages.

Many derivation rules are static, in the sense that they derive facts that hold in a state of the information base from other facts holding in the same state. We believe that the above results can be adapted to temporal derivation rules, although this will not be explored in this paper. However, we have identified a special kind of derivation rule which lies in between the static and the temporal ones. We call them creation-time rules, because they are evaluated when objects are created. These rules derive constant relationship types, whose value is established at the time an object is created. We have found, surprisingly, that many relationship types are derived in this way. In the paper, we characterize these rules, show how they can be defined in object-oriented languages and, in particular, in the UML.

We study also the approaches for defining hybrid entity and relationship types. A type is hybrid when it is partially base and partially derived [23]. Hybrid types can always be transformed into derived ones [1, 15], and this may explain why they have received very little attention in the conceptual modeling literature (one notable exception is [20]). However, the transformation may not be always convenient. This paper proposes a method for defining hybrid types in object-oriented languages and, in particular, in the UML.

This paper is structured as follows. The next Section reviews the basic concepts, presents the method we propose for the definition of derived types and derivation rules in object-oriented languages, and suggests an adaptation to the UML. Section 3 extends the above method to creation-time rules. Section 4 deals with hybrid types, and presents the method we propose for their definition in object-oriented languages. Section 5 summarizes the conclusions and points out future research. Throughout the paper, we include examples taken from the EU-Rent (a car rental company) case study described in [6].

2 Language Constructs for Defining Derivation Rules

In this Section, we start by reviewing the concepts of derivability and derivation rules. Then, we propose a new method for the definition of derivation rules in O-O languages. We suggest also an adaptation of the method to the UML.

2.1 Derivability and Derivation Rules

The derivability of an entity or relationship type is the way how the information system knows its population at any instant [23]. According to derivability, a type may be base, derived or hybrid. We give below a few comments on each of them. We adopt here a logical and temporal view of the information base, and assume that entities and relationships are instances of their types at particular time points. In the information base, we represent by $E(e,t)$ the fact that e is instance of entity type E at time t, and by $R(e_1,\dots,e_n,t)$ the fact that entities $e_1,\dots,e_n$ participate in a relationship instance of R at time t. We denote by $R(p_1{:}E_1, \dots, p_n{:}E_n)$ the schema of a relationship type named R with entity type participants $E_1, \dots, E_n$, playing roles $p_1, \dots, p_n$, respectively. When the role name is omitted, it is assumed to be the same as the corresponding entity type. In the logical representation, attributes will be considered as ordinary binary relationship types.

An entity type is *base* when its population is given directly or indirectly by the users by means of insertion and deletion events. Similarly, a relationship type is base when its instances are given directly or indirectly by the users by means of insertion, update and deletion events.

An entity type E is *derived* when its population at time t can be obtained from the facts in the information base, using a derivation rule. The general form of the rule is[1]:

$$E\,(e,t) \leftrightarrow \phi\,(e,t)$$

The expression $\phi\,(e,t)$ defines the necessary and sufficient conditions for e to be an instance of E at t. The information system may know the population at time t by using the above rule. Derived entity types can be classified into several categories. One of them, that we will use later on, is specialization. We say that E is derived by *specialization* of entity types $E_1, \dots, E_n$ when the population of E at t is a subset of the intersection of the populations of $E_1, \dots, E_n$ at t [23].

Derived relationship types are defined similarly. A relationship type $R(p_1{:}E_1, \dots, p_n{:}E_n)$ is derived when its instances at time t can be obtained from the facts in the information base, using a derivation rule. The general form of the rule is:

$$R\,(e_1,\dots,e_n,t) \leftrightarrow \varphi(e_1,\dots,e_n,t)$$

The information system may know the population at time t by using the above rule. We also say that R is derived by specialization of relationship types $R_1, \dots, R_m$ when the instances of R at t are a subset of the intersection of the instances of $R_1, \dots, R_m$ at t.

Derivation rules may be static or temporal. A static derivation rule derives a fact ($E(e,t)$ or $R(e_1,\dots,e_n,t)$) holding at t from other facts holding at the same time t. A temporal derivation rule derives a fact holding at t from one or more facts that may hold at previous times t' ($t' \le t$). In this paper, we deal almost exclusively with static derivation rules; the only exception is Section 3.

An entity or relationship type is *hybrid* when its population is given partially by the users (insertion, update and deletion events) and partially by a derivation rule. We deal with hybrid types in Section 4.

One of the derived entity types that may be defined in the case study is *CarToBeServiced*. Cars must be serviced every three months or 10,000 miles, whichever occurs first. In logic, its derivation rule could be:

CarToBeServiced (car, t) $\leftrightarrow$ Car (car,t) $\wedge$ MileageNow (car,mNow,t) $\wedge$

[1] The free variables are assumed to be universally quantified in the front of the formula.

LastService (car,dateLast,t) ∧ MileageLastService (car,mLast,t) ∧
(t – dateLast > 3Months ∨ mNow – mLast > 10000m)

Note that *CarToBeServiced* is a specialization of *Car*. On the other hand, the above rule is static because the cars to be serviced at *t* can be determined from the existing cars, and their properties, at time *t*.

An example of derived relationship type is: CarRentalRate (Car, Money). The rental rate of a car is defined as the rate for the group that car's model belongs to. Thus, the derivation rule in logic is:

CarRentalRate (car,rentRate,t) ↔
Car (car,t) ∧ ModelOfCar (car,cModel,t) ∧
CarGroupOfModel (cModel,cGroup,t) ∧
GroupRentalRate (cGroup,rentRate,t)

Note that this rule is also static.

2.2 Defining Derivation Rules in Object-Oriented Languages

Now, we focus on how to define derivation rules in O-O conceptual modeling languages. In general, the elements of the structural parts of these languages are entity types, attributes and relationship types. These elements may be base or derived.

Structurally, we propose to define the derived elements like the base ones, with the addition of some mark to indicate that they are derived. In this way, derived elements can (and must) be referred to in any part of a conceptual schema (constraints, derivation rules, etc.) like the base ones.

We propose to define derivation rules by means of operations. All O-O languages and data models include the concept of operation [22, 7]. Our operations will be query operations (also called query functions), which return a value but do not alter the information base.

The key point of our method consists in associating each derived element with a query operation, called the *defining* operation. The only purpose of a defining operation is to specify the corresponding derivation rule. The defining operations are purely conceptual; they may or may not be part of the implementation. The defining operations are not visible to the rest of the schema and, therefore, they should not be invoked in any part of the schema.

The signature of a defining operation depends on the derived element. For a derived entity type *E*, the defining operation is a class operation of *E* without arguments:

population (): Set (E)

The intended result of the operation is the set of entities which are instance of *E*. The exact name of the operation (*population*) must be decided in the adaptation of the method to a particular language; normally it will be a predefined name.

In the case study, the defining operation corresponding to entity type *CarToBeServiced* would be a class operation of that entity type with signature:

population () : Set (CarToBeServiced)

For an attribute *A* of entity type *E* with values of type E_1, the defining operation is an instance operation in *E* without arguments:

op_A (): [E_1 | Set (E_1)]

where the result is E_1 or *Set* (E_1) depending on whether *A* is single valued or multivalued, respectively. The result of the operation is the value of attribute *A* for the corresponding instance entity. The exact name of the operation (*op_A*) must be decided in the adaptation of the method; normally it will be just *A* or based on *A*.

In the case study, the derived relationship type *CarRentalRate* would probably be defined as a single valued attribute *rentalRate* of *Car*. The defining operation is an instance operation of *Car* with signature:

rentalRate (): Money

For a binary relationship type $R(p_1{:}E_1, p_2{:}E_2)$ the defining operation may take one of the four following forms (the exact name of the operation must be decided in the adaptation of the method):

- Instance operation of E_1 with signature op_p_2 (): [E_2 | *Set* (E_2)]. The result is E_2 or *Set* (E_2) depending on the cardinalities of *R*. The result of the operation is the instance, or the set of instances, of E_2 related to an instance of E_1.
- Instance operation of E_2 with signature op_p_1 (): [E_1 | *Set* (E_1)]. Similar to the above.
- Instance operation of E_1 with signature op_p_2 ($e_2{:}E_2$): *Boolean*. The result is *true* if there is a relationship between *self* and the instance given in the parameter, and *false* otherwise.
- Instance operation of E_2 with signature op_p_1 ($e_1{:}E_1$): *Boolean*. Similar to the above.

From a conceptual point of view, the four options are equivalent. The place (E_1 or E_2) where the operation is defined does not imply any navigability. Conceptually, relationship types are navigable in all directions. The designer may choose the place (s)he thinks is more natural or easier to specify. A factor that may influence the decision is the possibility of redefinition, which we explain below.

In the case study, one of the derived relationship types is:

AvailableNextDay (branchWhereAvailable:Branch, carAvailable:Car)

A car is available to a branch the next day if it is owned by that branch and currently it is in the parking lot, or it is due today from rental to that branch. In general, a branch has several cars available next day, but a car may be available next day at most to one branch. The defining operation could be defined in *Branch* with one of the signatures:

carAvailable (): Set (Car)
carAvailable (c:Car): Boolean

Or, alternatively, defined in *Car* with one of the signatures:

branchWhereAvailable (): Branch
branchWhereAvailable (b:Branch): Boolean

We proceed similarly for an *n*-ary relationship type $R(p_1{:}E_1,\ldots, p_n{:}E_n)$, with $n > 2$. Now we have a choice of $n(n\text{-}1)$ defining operations, each of which:

- is an instance operation of some E_i, $i \in \{1,..,n\}$,
- has $n - 2$ arguments, and
- has a return result of type E_j, $j \neq i$, $j \in \{1,..,n\}$

For $i = 1$ and $j = 2$, the general form of the instance operation is:

op_p_2 ($p_3{:}E_3$, …, $p_n{:}E_n$): [E_2 | Set (E_2)]

where again the result is E_2 or *Set* (E_2) depending on the cardinalities of *R*. The result of the operation is the set of instances of E_2 related to an instance of E_1 and to the instances of E_3, …, E_n given in the arguments. The exact name of the operation (*op_p2*) must be decided in the adaptation of the method. Normally, if one of the participants is a data type, we would not define the operation in it.

In the case study, we have the derived ternary relationship type:

CarsAvailableNextDay

(branchWhereAvailable:Branch, CarGroup, numberOfCars: Natural)

It is defined as the number of cars of a given car group available the next day to a given branch. In this case, it seems natural to define the defining operation in *Branch*, with signature:

numberOfCarsAvailableNextDay (cg: CarGroup): Natural

The above operations are specified formally in the style and the (sub)language most appropriate to the corresponding O-O language. In general, the preferred style could be the use of postconditions. For query operations, postconditions specify the value of the result. Note that postconditions of query operations do no have the frame problem [3].

In all O-O languages, instance operations may be redefined in subtypes. This applies also to the query operations we have defined above for the derivation rules of attributes and relationship types. The important implication of this is that, in our method, derivation rules of attributes and relationship types can be redefined.

In the case study, we have an example of redefinition in attribute:

TotalCost (ReturnedRental, amount:Money)

This attribute gives the amount to be paid by a customer when a rental is returned. That amount is defined as the sum of the insurance and rental amounts. In an O-O language, the defining operation of this attribute would be an operation in *ReturnedRental*, with signature:

totalCost (): Money

However, for *LateRental*, a subtype of *ReturnedRental* corresponding to the rentals returned after their due time, the total cost includes a late charge. We then redefine the defining operation:

totalCost (): Money

in *LateRental*. The specification of this operation will define the derivation rule of total cost for the particular case of a late rental.

2.3 Adaptation to the UML

The above method is easily adaptable to any O-O conceptual modeling language. The main decisions to be made are:

- How to specify the defining operations.
- The language of the above specification.
- How to relate a derived element with its defining operation.

We suggest here an adaptation to the UML. We have chosen to specify the defining operations by means of postconditions, using the OCL language. The relationship between a derived element and its defining operation is basically by naming conventions. We illustrate the adaptation with some examples from the EU-Rent case study.

In the UML, derived elements are marked with a slash (/) placed in front of their name. Figure 1 shows five derived elements: the entity type *CarToBeServiced*, the

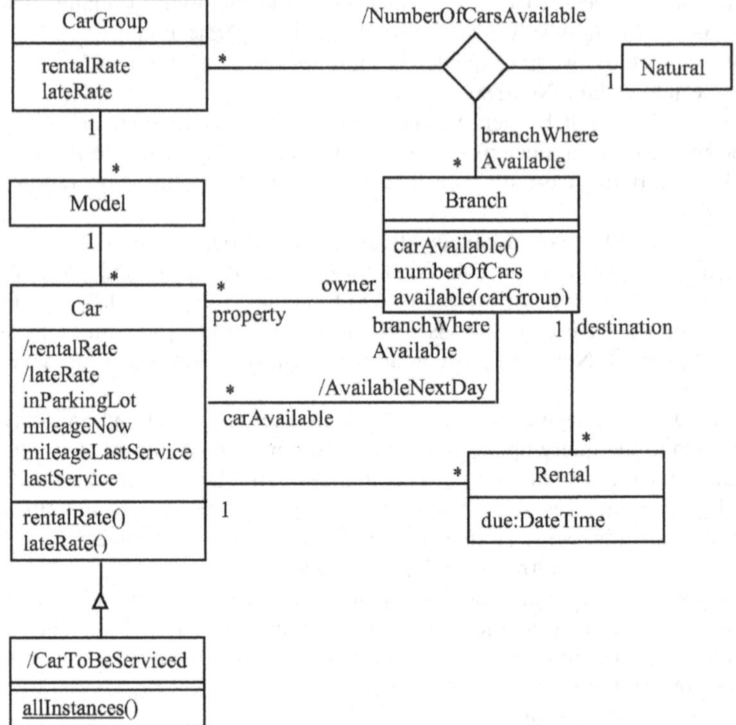

Fig. 1. Fragment of the EU-Rent case study with derived types, in the UML.

attributes *RentalRate* and *lateRate* of *Car*, the binary association (relationship type) *AvailableNextDay* and the ternary association *NumberOfCarsAvailable*.

Figure 1 shows also the defining operations corresponding to the five derived elements. Normally, these operations would not appear in the class diagrams of conceptual schemas, because they cannot be invoked. We have included them here only for illustration purposes.

In the UML, operations have, among others, the boolean attribute *isQuery* [24, p.2-27]. The value of this attribute for our defining operations is *true* (indicating that the operation leaves the state unchanged).

The OCL includes, for each entity type *E*, the predefined class operation of *E*:

```
allInstances () : Set (E)
```

which gives the set of all instances of *E*, and all its subtypes, at the time the operation is evaluated [24, p.6-30]. This operation must not be specified by the designer, because its meaning is predefined. We propose, however, to use this same operation as the defining operation of derived entity types. In these cases, the designer should specify the postcondition of the operation, using the OCL.

In the case study, the OCL specification of the defining operation of *CarToBeServiced* is:

```
context CarToBeServiced :: allInstances ():
                                    Set(CarToBeServiced)
```

```
post result = car.allInstances() -> select
              (mileageNow - mileageLastService > 10000 or
               Now - lastService > 3Months)
```

In the postcondition, we have used a special variable, *Now*, which we assume gives the current time. In Figure 1, the name of the operation *allInstances* is underlined to indicate that it is a class operation. For space reasons we do not show the return type in the diagram.

Note that in the above example we have used the expression `car.allInstances()` and, therefore, we have invoked the operation *allInstances*. This is the only way we have in the OCL to know the population of an entity type. This operation is the only exception to the general rule that the defining operations should not be invoked in the OCL expressions corresponding to constraints or derivation rules (postconditions).

For attributes, the name of the defining operation is the same as the name of the attribute. The specification of the defining operation corresponding to attribute *rentalRate* is then:

```
context Car :: rentalRate () : Money
  post result = model.carGroup.rentalRate
```

A similar example is attribute *lateRate*, which gives the rate to be paid by rentals returned late. It is defined similarly to the *rentalRate*. The specification of its defining operation is:

```
context Car :: lateRate () : Money
  post result = model.carGroup.lateRate
```

For binary relationship types, we propose that the name of their defining operation be the same as the name of the corresponding role. In the example of Figure 1, a possible specification of the defining operation in *Branch* corresponding to association *AvailableNextDay* could be:

```
context Branch :: carAvailable () : Set (Car)
  post result = property -> select (inParkingLot = True)
           -> union (rental -> select (due = Today).car)
```

It is difficult to establish a general convention regarding the name of the defining operation for *n*-ary associations. It may be preferable to let the designer give the name (s)he thinks is more adequate. In such a case, it will be necessary to document with a note or otherwise that the operation is a defining operation of a derived association.

In the example of ternary association *NumberOfCarsAvailable*, Figure 1, we have defined an operation with the same name in *Branch*. The OCL specification would be:

```
context Branch ::
  numberOfCarsAvailable (inCarGroup : CarGroup) : Natural
  post result = carAvailable ->
             select (c: Car | c.model.carGroup =
             inCarGroup) -> size ()
```

Note the reference to *carAvailable* in this postcondition. This is an example of a derived association used like a base one in an OCL expression.

Figure 2 provides an example of derivation rule redefinition. Attribute *totalCost* of a returned rental is defined as:

```
context ReturnedRental :: totalCost () : Money
  post result = insuranceAmount + rentalAmount
```

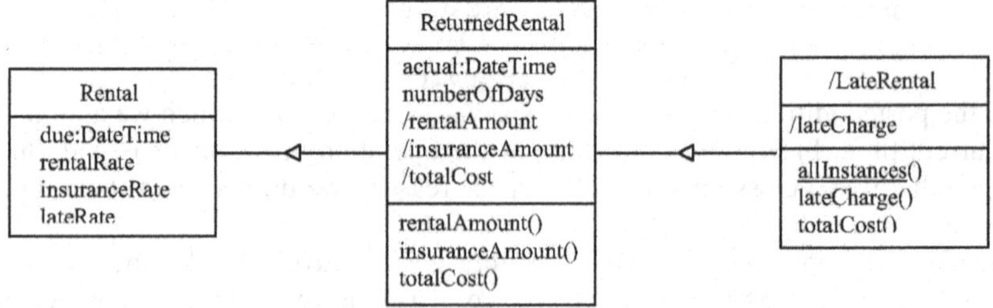

Fig. 2. Fragment of the EU-Rent case study with derived types, in the UML. (*Rental* is extended in Figure 3)

but this derivation rule is redefined in *LateRental.* This is shown by redefining the operation *totalCost*() in this type. Here, the derivation rule could be:

```
context LateRental :: totalCost () : Money
  post result = insuranceAmount + RentalAmount +
                lateCharge
```

Note that *LateRental* is a derived entity type. The specification of its defining operation could be:

```
context LateRental :: allInstances () : Set(LateRental)
  post result = ReturnedRental.allInstances() ->
                                         select(actual > due)
```

Therefore, *LateRental* is a specialization of *ReturnedRental.*

2.4 Comparison with Other Methods

We now compare our method with the methods used by other languages. Given that the focus of this paper is on the definition of derivation rules in O-O languages, here we only compare with languages that may be considered more or less object-oriented and that include, in particular, the concept of redefinable (query) operation, or similar. This explains why we do not include in the comparison other conceptual modeling languages such as Telos [9], Syntropy [10], Description Logics [8], or ORM [14].

We start the comparison with the UML. In this language, derivation rules are represented by abstraction dependencies with the stereotype <<derive>>. A dependency relates the derived element (the client) with the elements (the suppliers) from which it can be computed. The details of the computation are specified by a mapping expression written in some language, possibly the OCL [24, p. 2-19]. Graphically, the dependency is shown as a dashed arrow between those elements [24, p. 3-90+].

We believe that our method has two main advantages over the UML method. The first is the economy. We draw on a standard construct already provided by the language (operation), instead of requiring a new, specific construct (dependencies with the stereotype <<derive>>). Our approach makes the language and its supporting tools simpler, which is important in many respects. In particular, in the framework of the Model Driven Architecture (MDA) [25], our approach eases the development of mappings from conceptual schemas to platform specific models, because now derivation rules become just a particular case of operations.

The second advantage is obtained by the use of the standard mechanism of operation redefinition, with its well defined semantics. As we have seen, this mechanism may simplify the definition of some complex derivation rules. Redefinition does not apply to UML dependencies.

In Chimera [9, 12], the derived elements may be entity types, attributes and relationship types (views). In the three cases, the corresponding derivation rules are defined by means of deductive rules. The derivation rules of attributes may be redefined, but not those of relationship types. On the other hand, entity types may have operations, which in particular can be accessor operations. The difference between derived attributes and accessor operations is very small [9, p. 199]. In the first case, the attribute can be referred to as any other (base) attribute; in the latter, it can be referred to by means of an explicit operation invocation.

Our method can be adapted to the Chimera. We would associate to each derived element an accessor operation with some predefined name. In this way, the deductive rules for data derivation would not be needed, thus making the language simpler. On the other hand, using our method the derivation rules of relationship types could be redefined.

Finally, we point out the similarity between our method and the one used by the language for deductive object-oriented databases proposed recently in [19]. In this language, derived information is defined by a method type and a method rule. Roughly, a method type defines an attribute or a relationship type. A method rule corresponds to a query operation, although defined as a deductive rule. Methods are declared within class declarations, and the methods are invoked trough instances of the classes. Like in our proposal, method rules may be redefined in subclasses.

3 Derivation Rules for Constant Relationship Types

The method described in the previous section can be extended easily to deal with a frequently used particular class of derived relationship types. These are the constant relationship types whose instances can be derived when the instances of one of its participant entity types are created. In this section, we characterize this class of relationship types and explain how they can be defined in our method.

A relationship type $R\ (p_1{:}E_1,\ \ldots,\ p_i{:}E_i,\ \ldots,\ p_n{:}E_n)$ is constant with respect to p_i if the set of instances of R in which participates an instance e_i of E_i is determined when e_i is created, and remains fixed during its lifetime [11]. For example,

RentalRate (Rental, Money)

is constant with respect to *Rental*, because the rate to be paid by a rental is determined at creation time (when a rental is created), and cannot be changed later.
All the attributes shown in Figure 2 are constant relationship types with respect to *Rental*, *ReturnedRental* or *LateRental*. The only exception is attribute *due* of *Rental*, because rentals can be extended.

Formally, $R\ (p_1{:}E_1,\ \ldots,\ p_i{:}E_i,\ \ldots,\ p_n{:}E_n)$ is constant with respect to p_i if:

$$\mathrm{R}\ (e_1,\ldots,e_i,\ldots,e_n,t)\ \rightarrow \forall t'\ (E_i\,(e_i,t') \rightarrow \mathrm{R}\ (e_1,\ldots,e_i,\ldots,e_n,t'))$$

That is, if $R\ (e_1,\ldots,e_i,\ldots,e_n,t)$ holds at time t then it must also hold at all times t' at which e_i is instance of E_i. The adaptation to the example is:

$$\mathrm{RentalRate\ (r,rentRate,t)} \rightarrow \forall t'\ (\mathrm{Rental\ (r,t')} \rightarrow \mathrm{RentalRate\ (r,rentRate,t')})$$

Like any other, constant relationship types can be derived, and their derivation rule can be static or temporal. An example with a static rule is (Figure 2):

InsuranceAmount (ReturnedRental,Money)

which is defined as the insurance rate of the rental multiplied by the number of days of the rental. In logic:

InsuranceAmount (rr,insAmt,t) $\leftrightarrow$
ReturnedRental (rr,t) $\wedge$ InsuranceRate (rr,iRate,t) $\wedge$
NumberOfDays (rr,nd,t) $\wedge$ insAmt = nd * iRate

There are some derived constant relationship types whose derivation rule is temporal and, in principle, they cannot be defined in non-temporal languages. However, in many cases these rules have a particular form that allows their definition, even in non-temporal languages. We call them *creation-time* rules. An example is:

RentalRate (Rental,Money)

The rate of a rental is the rental rate of its car at the time *when the rental is created.* The following static derivation rule would be incorrect:

RentalRate (r,rentRate,t) $\leftrightarrow$ Rental (r,t) $\wedge$
CarOfRental (r,rentedCar,t) $\wedge$ CarRentalRate (rentedCar,rentRate,t)

This rule is incorrect because the rental rate of the car *rentedCar* can change after the rental is created, but this does not imply that the rental rates of the previous rentals of that car must be changed. The correct form of the rule must define that the rental rate is determined from the rental rate of the car when the rental is created. Assuming a predicate *CreatedAt* (*Rental,Time*) that gives the instant when a rental is created, the rule would then be:

RentalRate (r,rentRate,t) $\leftrightarrow$ Rental (r,t) $\wedge$ CreatedAt (r,t_0) $\wedge$
CarOfRental (r,rentedCar,t_0) $\wedge$ CarRentalRate (rentedCar,rentRate,t_0)

Let R $(p_1{:}E_1, \ldots, p_i{:}E_i, \ldots, p_n{:}E_n)$ be constant with respect to p_i. We say that R is derived with a creation-time rule if its derivation rule has the form:

$$\mathrm{R}\ (e_1,\ldots,e_i,\ldots,e_n,t) \leftrightarrow \mathrm{E}_i\ (e_i,t) \wedge \mathrm{CreatedAt}\ (e_i,t_0) \wedge \varphi\,(e_1,\ldots,e_n,\ t_0)$$

where the literals in $\varphi\,(e_1,\ldots,e_n,\ t_0)$ can be evaluated at time t_0 with facts holding at that time. In the example above, we have:

$\varphi\,(e_1,\ldots,e_n,\ t_0) \equiv$
CarOfRental (r,rentedCar,t_0) $\wedge$ CarRentalRate (rentedCar,rentRate,t_0)

It can be shown that all derived constant relationship types whose derivation rule is static, can be defined as derived with a creation-time rule.

Now, we focus on how to define creation-time rules in O-O languages. Most non-temporal O-O languages use a concept, *object creation*, which we will use too to define creation-time derivation rules. That concept is used, among other things, to define the initial value for attributes, which is the value an attribute takes when an object is created, if no explicit value is given. In the UML, such initial value is, in general, an expression that is meant to be evaluated at the time the object is initialized [24, p. 2–26].

There is an analogy between initial values for attributes and creation-time derivation rules, because both are meant to be evaluated when an object is created. The analogy justifies the method we propose to define creation-time rules. If a relationship type R $(p_1{:}E_1, \ldots, p_i{:}E_i, \ldots, p_n{:}E_n)$ is constant with respect to p_i, and is derived by a creation-time derivation rule, then we define this rule as an operation of

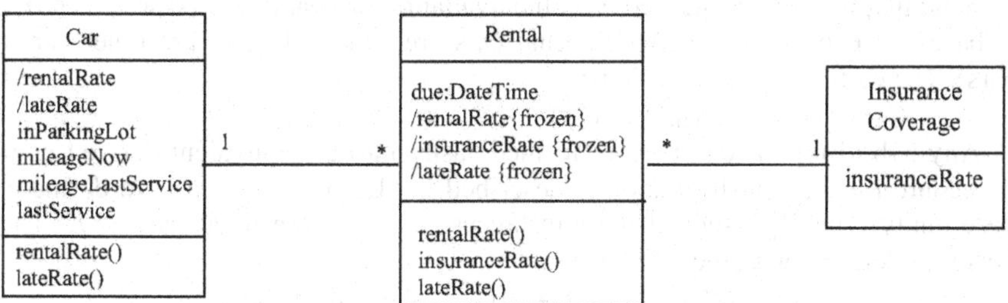

Fig. 3. Attributes *rentalRate*, *insuranceRate* and *lateRate* of *Rental* are derived with a creation-time derivation rule.

E_i, with the understanding that the rule is meant to be evaluated when the instances of E_i are created. In the example of *RentalRate*, we would define the operation in *Rental*.

Figure 3 illustrates the adaptation of our method to the UML with three examples. In this language, a constant attribute is defined with the keyword *frozen*. The same keyword is used for constant binary associations. The figure defines that *rentalRate*, *insuranceRate* and *lateRate* are constant attributes of *Rental*. The three attributes are derived. The creation-time rule for *rentalRate* is:

```
context Rental :: rentalRate () : Money
  post result = car.rentalRate
```

The rule for *lateRate* is similar:

```
context Rental :: lateRate () : Money
  post result = car.lateRate
```

The insurance rate of a rental is given by the insurance coverage of that rental. The rule, then is:

```
context Rental :: insuranceRate () : Money
  post result = insuranceCoverage.insuranceRate
```

4 Hybrid Types

In this section, we review the concept of hybrid entity and relationship types, and then we propose a method for their definition in O-O languages. We suggest also an adaptation of the method to the UML.

4.1 Definition

An entity type *E* is *hybrid* when its population is given partially by the users (insertion and deletion events) and partially by a derivation rule, which has the general form:

$$E(e,t) \leftarrow \phi(e,t)$$

Such derivation rules are partial because they define only part of the population of *E*. A hybrid entity type has an extensional part (given by the users) and an intensional one (given by the derivation rule). We will assume that these parts are disjoint, as is normally the case.

In the case study, the conceptual schema includes entity types *Car* and *ExternalCar*. An external car is a car a branch rents from a competitor to satisfy a demand that cannot be satisfied with the available own cars. In this case, *ExternalCar* is base and *Car* is hybrid. All external cars are cars, but there are other cars (own cars). The partial derivation rule is:

Car (c,t) $\leftarrow$ ExternalCar (c,t)

Any hybrid type *E* can be transformed easily into an equivalent derived one. The procedure for the transformation is described in [1, 15]. The idea is to define a new base entity type E_{base}, such that its instances are the extensional part of *E*. Then, *E* becomes derived, with the derivation rule:

$$E\ (e,t) \leftrightarrow \phi\ (e,t) \vee E_{base}\ (e,t)$$

In the example, we would have:

Car (c,t) $\leftrightarrow$ ExternalCar (c,t) $\vee$ Car_{base} (e,t)

Similarly, a relationship type *R* is *hybrid* when its population is given partially by the users (insertion, update and deletion events) and partially by a derivation rule, which has the general form:

$$R\ (e_1,...,e_n,t) \leftarrow \varphi\ (e_1,...,e_n,t)$$

As before, any hybrid relationship type can be transformed into an equivalent derived one.

In the case study, when a customer picks up a car (s)he must sign a contract and declare the additional drivers, if any. The drivers of a car are the signer of the contract and the declared additional drivers. Thus, we could have the relationship types:

SignerOfContract (Rental, Customer)

Driver (Rental, Customer)

In this case, *Driver* is hybrid, with the partial derivation rule:

Driver (r,cust,t) $\leftarrow$ SignerOfContract (r,cust,t)

4.2 Defining Hybrid Types in Object-Oriented Languages

Most O-O languages (including the UML) ignore the hybrid types. The obvious solution is, then, to transform these types into their derived equivalents. Unfortunately, as we have seen, this requires the definition of a new type (E_{base} or R_{base}), which in some cases may be considered artificial.

However, we have found that the *IsA* construct (generalization or specialization links), present in all O-O languages, allows a simple method for the definition of hybrid types.

In the method we propose, we require that the partial derivation rule of an entity type *E* have the general form ($n \geq 1$):

$$E\ (e,t) \leftarrow E_1\ (e,t) \vee ... \vee E_n\ (e,t)$$

That is, the intensional population of *E* is given by the union of the populations of E_1, ..., E_n. We call these types the intensional types of *E*. To avoid circularity, an intensional type of *E* cannot be derived by specialization of *E*. The example above follows this form, with $n = 1$ and E_1 = *ExternalCar*.

All partial derivation rules ($E\ (e,t) \leftarrow \phi\ (e,t)$) can be transformed into this form by defining, if needed, a new derived entity type E_1 with derivation rule ($E_1\ (e,t) \leftrightarrow \phi\ (e,t)$), and then we have ($E\ (e,t) \leftarrow E_1\ (e,t)$). However, our method provides the best results when the original derivation rule has already the form:

$$\phi\ (e,t) \equiv E_1\ (e,t) \vee ... \vee E_n\ (e,t)$$

so that no transformation is needed.

We then propose to define a hybrid entity type *E* with intensional entity types E_1, ..., E_n by:

- defining the *n IsA* relationships: E_1 *IsA E*, ..., E_n *IsA E*.
- defining that E_1,..., E_n are the intensional types of *E*. The exact form of this definition will depend on the particular O-O language.

Note that we use the semantics of *IsA* to define implicitly that:

$$E(e,t) \leftarrow E_1(e,t) \vee ... \vee E_n(e,t)$$

In the example, we would just define:

ExternalCar IsA Car

and that *ExternalCar* is the intensional type of *Car*.

Similarly, we propose to define a hybrid relationship type *R* with intensional relationship types R_1, ..., R_n by:

- defining the *n IsA* relationships: R_1 *IsA R*, ..., R_n *IsA R*. We require that the language allows defining *IsA* relationships between relationship types.
- defining that R_1,..., R_n are the intensional types of *R*. The exact form of this definition will depend on the particular O-O language.

In the example, we would just define:

SignerOfContract IsA Driver

and that *SignerOfContract* is the intensional type of *Driver*.

If the O-O language allows *IsA* relationships between attributes, then hybrid attributes can be defined in the same way as hybrid relationship types. If this is not the case, then the attribute must be transformed first into an equivalent relationship type.

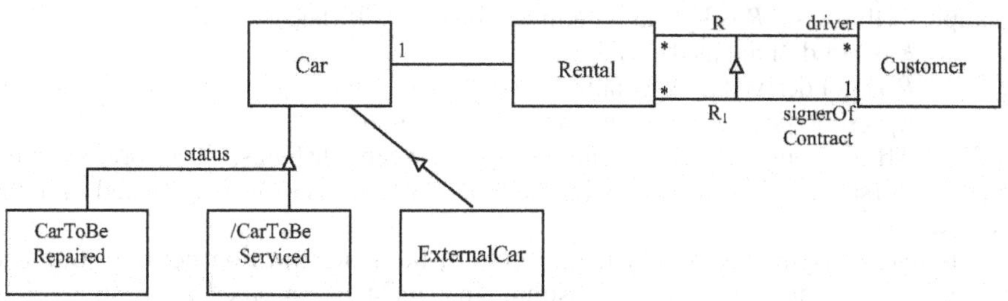

Fig. 4. Examples of hybrid entity (*Car*) and relationship (*R*) types.

4.3 Adaptation to the UML

The above method is easily adaptable to any O-O conceptual modeling language. We suggest here a possible adaptation to the UML.

The adaptation of the above definition of hybrid entity types is almost trivial. The only problem is how to define that E_1, ..., E_n are the intensional entity types of *E*. We assume multiple classification and, therefore, in the general case *E* may be also a supertype of other types.

The solution we propose is to use the discriminator attribute that UML defines in generalization links [24, p. 2-45]. The discriminator is a string (including the empty string) that allows grouping a set of generalizations with the same supertype. In the general case, the same entity type may be the supertype of several sets of generalizations. We propose then to use a particular name as the discriminator that groups the generalizations links of the intensional entity types. Here we will use the empty string. Naturally, other names are possible.

Therefore, in our method an entity type *E* is hybrid with intensional types E_1, ..., E_n if:

- *E* is not defined as derived.
- E_1, ..., E_n are not derived by specialization of *E*.
- E_1, ..., E_n are subtypes of *E* with the empty discriminator.

Figure 4 shows the example in the UML. *Car* is hybrid with intensional type *ExternalCar* because:

- *Car* is not defined as derived.
- *ExternalCar* is not derived by specialization of *Car*.
- *ExternalCar* is subtype of *Car* with the empty discriminator.

CarToBeRepaired and *CarToBeServiced* are not intensional types of *Car* because their generalization links have discriminator *status*. On the other hand, *CarToBeServiced* is derived by specialization of *Car*. In this example, we assume that external cars may also be cars to be repaired and/or serviced.

Note that the set of generalization links defining the intensional types of *E* cannot be subjected to the constraint {complete}[24, p. 2-45] because then *E* would not be hybrid, but derived. That set must have the constraint {incomplete}, which we assume as default.

The same adaptation applies to hybrid relationship types. UML allows generalization links between relationship types (associations). Figure 4 shows also an example of this case. *R* is hybrid with intensional type R_1 because:

- *R* is not defined as derived.
- R_1 is not derived by specialization of *R*.
- R_1 is subtype of *R* with the empty discriminator.

The UML does not allow *IsA* relationships between attributes. Therefore, we must transform first the hybrid attributes into hybrid associations and then proceed as in the previous case.

It is interesting to observe that, in Figure 4, the generalization between *Car* and *ExternalCar* is not a taxonomic constraint that must be enforced at run-time [23]. According to the usual interpretation, the constraint is automatically enforced by the schema. Analogously, the same interpretation applies to the generalization between *R* and R_1.

4.4 Comparison with Other Approaches

To the best of our knowledge, only [20, p. 57] has made a proposal for the definition of hybrid relationship types in conceptual schemas. The proposal consists in using a special graphical symbol to denote a hybrid relationship type, and to attach to it the partial derivation rule (written in some unspecified language).

The main advantages of our method are that we do not require a new symbol, we draw on the semantics of the *IsA* relationship to define the intensional population of a hybrid type, and we do not need to write the partial derivation rule. On the other hand, we deal also with hybrid entity types.

5 Conclusions

We have proposed three related methods for the definition of derivation rules in O-O conceptual modeling languages. The first method applies to static rules, and associates each derived element with a defining operation. The specification of this operation is then the definition of the corresponding derivation rule. The second method applies to constant relationship types whose instances can be derived when the instances of one of its participant entity types are created. We have seen that the derivation rules of these types have usually a common form, that we have called creation-time rule. We have described a variant of the previous method to deal with these rules. The third method deals with hybrid types, and suggests a simple way to define their partial derivation rules.

The three methods have been formalized in logic and described independently of any particular O-O language. We have proposed also adaptations of the three methods to the UML. The methods are fully compatible with the UML-based CASE tools, and thus they can be adopted in industrial projects, if it is felt appropriate.

We hope that our methods will ease the definition of derivation rules. The need of including derived types and their (formal) derivation rules in conceptual schemas has always been considered important, but nowadays, in the framework of the emerging Model Driven Architecture, it is becoming mandatory. On the other hand, we hope that our methods will ease the implementation of derivation rules.

Our work can be continued in several directions. We mention two of them here. The first is the adaptation of our methods to other languages. The second direction is to develop mappings for transforming derived types and our derivation rules to the appropriate constructs of other platform independent and/or platform specific models. The mappings should take into account whether derived types are materialized or computed when needed and, in many aspects, could draw upon the available knowledge [9, 27].

Acknowledgements. I would like to thank Jordi Cabot, Dolors Costal, Cristina Gómez, Maria Ribera Sancho and Ernest Teniente for their many useful comments to previous drafts of this paper. This work has been partially supported by the Ministerio de Ciencia y Tecnologia and FEDER under project TIC2002-00744.

References

1. Bancilhon, F.; Ramakrishnan, R. "An Amateur's Introduction to Recursive Query Processing Strategies". Proc. ACM SIGMOD Int. Conf. On Management of Data, May 1986, pp. 16–52.
2. Bloesch, A.C.; Halpin, T.A. "Conceptual Queries Using ConQuer-II". Proc. ER'97, LNCS 1331, pp. 113–126.
3. Borgida, A.; Mylopoulos, J.; Reiter, R. "...And Nothing Else Changes: The Frame Problem in Procedure Specifications". Proc. ICSE 1993, pp. 303–314.
4. Borgida, A. "Description Logics in Data Management". IEEE Transactions on Knowledge and Data Engineering, 7(5), 1995, pp. 671–682.
5. Brachman, R.J.; Schmolze, J.G. "An Overview of the KL-ONE Knowledge Representation System". Cognitive Science 9, 1985, pp. 171–216.

6. Business Rules Group. "Defining Business Rules – What Are They Really?". Final Report, July 2000, http://www.businessrulesgroup.org/first_paper/br01c0.htm
7. Cattell, R.G.G.; Barry, D.K. (Eds) The Object Data Standard: ODMG 3.0. Morgan Kaufmann Pubs., 280 p.
8. Calvanese, D.; Lenzerini, M.; Nardi, D. "Description Logics for Conceptual Data Modeling". In Chomicki, J.; Saake, G. (eds). Logics for Databases and Information Systems, Kluwer, 1998, pp. 229–263.
9. Ceri, S.; Fraternali, P. Designing Database Applications with Objects and Rules. The IDEA Methodology. Addison-Wesley, 1997, 579 p.
10. Cook, S.; Daniels, J. Designing Object Systems. Object-Oriented Modelling with Syntropy. Prentice Hall, 389 p.
11. Costal, D.; Olivé, A.; Sancho, M-R. "Temporal Features of Class Populations and Attributes in Conceptual Models". Proc. ER 1997, LNCS 1331, pp. 57–70
12. Guerrini, G.; Bertino, E.; Bal, R. "A Formal Definition of the Chimera Object-Oriented Data Model". Journal of Intelligent Information Systems, 11(1), pp. 5–40.
13. Gustaffsson, M.R.; Karlsson, T.; Bubenko, J.A. jr. "A Declarative Approach to Conceptual Information Modelling". In Olle, T.W.; Sol, H.G.; Verrijn-Stuart, A.A. (eds.) Information systems design methodologies: A Comparative Review. North-Holland, 1982, pp. 93–142.
14. Halpin, T. Information Modeling and Relational Databases. From Conceptual Analysis to Logical Design. Morgan Kaufmann Pub., 2001, 761 p.
15. Halpin, T. "UML Data Models from an ORM Perspective (Part 9)". Journal of Conceptual Modeling, June 1999, Issue 9.
16. Hammer, M.; McLeod, D. "Database Description with SDM: A Semantic Database Model", ACM TODS, 6(3), 1981, pp. 351–386.
17. Hull, R.; King, R. "Semantic Database Modeling: Survey, Applications, and Research Issues", ACM Computing Surveys, 19(3), 1987, pp. 201–260.
18. ISO/TC97/SC5/WG3. "Concepts and Terminology for the Conceptual Schema and the Information Base", J.J. van Griethuysen (ed.), March 1982.
19. Liu, M.; Dobbie, G; Ling, T.W. "A Logical Foundation for Deductive Object-Oriented Databases", ACM TODS 27(1), pp. 117–151.
20. Martin, J. Odell, J. Object-Oriented Methods: A Foundation. Prentice Hall, 1995, 412p.
21. Mylopoulos, J.; Borgida, A.; Jarke, M.; Koubarakis, M. "Telos: a language for representing knowledge about information systems". ACM TOIS, 8(4), pp. 327–362.
22. Meyer, B. Object-Oriented Software Construction. Prentice Hall, 1997, 1254 p.
23. Olivé, A. Teniente, E. "Derived types and taxonomic constraints in conceptual modeling", Information Systems 27 (2002), pp. 391–409.
24. OMG. "Unified Modeling Language Specification", Version 1.4, September 2001, http://www.omg.org/technology/documents/formal/uml.htm.
25. OMG. "Model Driven Architecture (MDA)", Doc. number ORMSC/2001-07-01, http://cgi.omg.org/docs/ormsc/01-07-01.pdf
26. OMG. "Meta-Object Facility ((MOF™))". Version 1.4, April 2002, http://www.omg.org/technology/documents/formal/mof.htm
27. Winter, R. "Design and implementation of derivation rules in information systems". Data & Knowledge Eng., 26, 1998, pp. 225–241.

Issues of Information Semantics and Granularity in Cross-Media Publishing

Moira C. Norrie and Beat Signer

Institute for Information Systems, ETH Zurich
CH-8092 Zurich, Switzerland
{norrie,signer}@inf.ethz.ch

Abstract. While there have been dramatic increases in the use of digital technologies for the storage and processing of information, the affordances of paper have ensured its retention as a key information medium. Recent developments in digitally augmented paper provide the potential to embed active links within printed documents, thereby turning paper into an interactive medium. In this paper, we address the issues of information granularity and semantics that arise in integrating paper as a first-class interactive information medium in hypermedia systems and show that the information server is vital in realising the true potential of this vision. Further, we discuss the authoring issues of cross-media information environments and the forms of tools required to support the various categories of authoring activity.

1 Introduction

Earlier predictions of the paperless office in which paper documents would be replaced entirely by digital documents no longer seem realistic [19,23]. Paper as a medium has many advantages over digital media in terms of how people can work with it, both individually and in groups. It is portable, cheap and robust. It is much more convenient to scan through a book by rapidly flicking through pages than to browse a digital document. Paper also supports forms of collaboration and interaction that are difficult to mimic in current digital worlds. Whereas the focus in the past has been to replace paper, increasingly, the trend is towards integrating printed and digital media, thereby achieving the best of both worlds.

Integration of printed and digital media can be achieved through technologies for encoding active links on paper in such a way that special reader devices can detect and activate these links. There have been various technical solutions proposed to achieve this aim and it is beyond the scope of this paper to discuss these in detail. Generally, we refer to these solutions as coming under the heading of *digitally augmented paper* and would recommend the following references to readers interested in more detail of the various technologies [2,7,10,11,15].

While the paper, printing and reader technologies required to fully support digitally augmented paper are still in their infancy, various forms of reader devices are now emerging in the marketplace. For example, Sony Ericsson's Chatpen uses a camera to track movement on a page based on a special printed grid

J. Eder and M. Missikoff (Eds.): CAiSE 2003, LNCS 2681, pp. 421–436, 2003.

pattern of tiny dots developed and licensed by the company Anoto [1]. Expected developments in the near future for invisibly encoding document positions on paper and cheaper reading devices will surely have a dramatic effect on the spread and use of digitally augmented paper.

The question remains as to the potential uses and models of interaction afforded by digitally augmented paper. How can we fully exploit the potential of paper as a client device and integrate it seamlessly into hypermedia systems? While a number of research projects have proposed different variations of digitally augmented paper and presented their visions for its use, none have really addressed the issue of making paper a *first-class medium* in the context of a hypermedia system. This means that it should be possible to link not only from paper to digital resources, but also from digital resources to paper and even from paper to paper.

The key to incorporating paper into hypermedia systems as a first-class medium lies primarily with the server rather than the client technologies. The server must be capable of dynamically mapping document positions to information objects and vice versa. It must manage not only the links, but also their semantics and have flexible means of classifying and associating both digital and printed resources. We argue therefore that the potential functionality and flexibility of the system will be determined by the underlying information model and architecture.

In this paper, we show how issues of information semantics and granularity impact on the richness of the resulting interactive information environment. However, everything comes at a price, and we discuss the consequences for the content provider in terms of complexity and cost. Indeed, we discuss how it could require a major shift away from the traditional practices of publishers towards the content management solutions that have been adopted in the web publishing world.

To explain the issues and possible solutions, we develop in a stepwise manner an information model for an application server for digitally augmented paper. This model is the basis for the information server that we have developed within the European project Paper^{++} [18] which is investigating concepts and technologies aimed at enriching the use of paper in everyday settings. A detailed description of the Paper^{++} server component can be found in [15].

We begin in Sect. 2 with an introduction to cross-media publishing and simple solutions that have been proposed to link printed material to digital resources. Section 3 then discusses issues of granularity and examines in more detail the means of embedding active links within printed documents to arrive at a highly-interactive environment. In Sect. 4, we address the issue of information semantics and how to provide richer information environments. Section 5 deals with the general issues of the authoring of cross-media material and the different categories of system and publishing tools to support them. Concluding remarks are given in Sect. 6.

2 Cross-Media Publishing

It is common nowadays for publishers to produce a package of related materials on different media. For example, the BBC (British Broadcasting Corporation) often produces books and also websites to accompany television documentaries. As a specific example, for their series on ocean life called *Blue Planet*, they have an associated book and a website with games, quizzes and a fact file on different species [3]. In addition, this series was adopted by the Open University [17] in a course on oceanography and a course text book was published to be used in conjunction with the TV programmes which are also available on video and DVD. We will use this example as a small case study to examine the issues of information granularity and semantics that arise in developing a system that could link these various forms of printed and digital materials together through the use of digitally augmented paper. We first note however that such cross-media publishing is not just something of concern to the large commercial content publishers. It is something that most of us do in producing teaching materials such as lecture slides, handouts, manuals, tutorials, exercises, demonstrator applications and course websites.

How is linking across media currently done? As a first remark, it is important to note that, in many cases, it is not done at all. What might at first appear to be a package of related materials, is often actually a set of quite independently produced materials. For example, we used a children's nature encyclopaedia as a basis for a first demonstrator and user studies experiment since both a book and a CD-ROM were available from the same publisher. However, discussions with the publisher and examination of the material revealed that both were not only marketed as independent products, but also designed and developed by separate departments with little or no cooperation and had different content. The Paper^{++} nature encyclopaedia prototype running on a Tablet PC (a) and on a Pocket PC (b) is shown in Fig. 1. For further information about the user studies see [8].

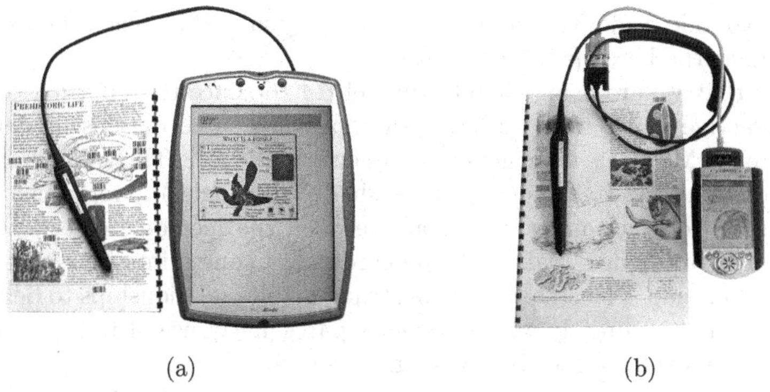

(a) (b)

Fig. 1. Nature encyclopaedia application

Where linking from printed documents is provided, it is usually done through a printed reference either to another printed document or to a digital resource by means of a URL. In the electronic version of the document, URLs may be converted automatically to active hypermedia links based on recognised formats.

In the case of the Blue Planet material, the main linking occurs between the Open University course book and the TV programmes (on VHS or DVD). At the end of a section of text, there is a recommendation to view all or part of a programme. These recommendations are indicated by a video cassette symbol placed alongside the text as shown in Fig. 2.

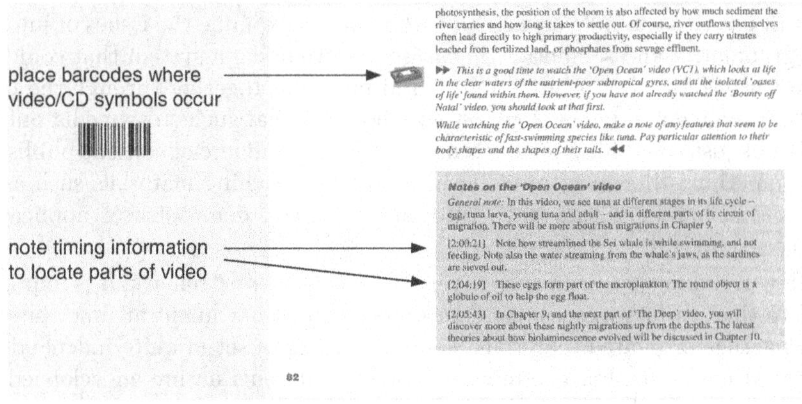

Fig. 2. Page of Open University course book

As a first means of creating an active link from the course book to the video material, we could add a barcode alongside the video symbol as indicated in Fig. 2. The barcode is an encoding of a unique digital resource identifier (ID) and a simple mapping table on the server could be used to map this ID to a multimedia file. In Fig. 3, we show such a mapping and model this as an association `Binds` between a set of `ResourceIds` and a set of `Resources`. Using normal barcode reader technology, we could play video files when the user swipes or points at the barcode with the reader.

Note that we are using the OM model [14,16] since the information servers for interactive paper that we have developed are based on this model and its associated OMS data management frameworks [12,24]. The OM model has a collection construct (represented by the shaded rectangles) to represent semantic groupings of objects and associations between the members of collections are represented by shaded ovals with the cardinality constraints over participation written alongside. The association construct enables relationships to be classified and manipulated directly which becomes particularly useful in supporting link management for hypermedia browsing.

What comments can we make to such a simple linking scheme? The first is that the links are unidirectional, only supporting links from the printed doc-

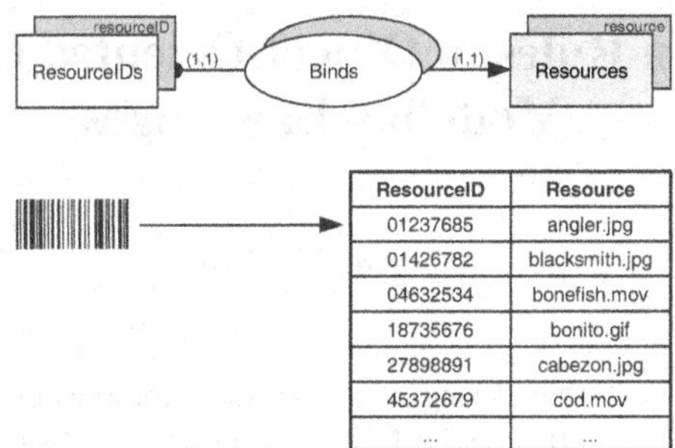

Fig. 3. Simple mapping of IDs to resources

ument to digital resources. Secondly, the link paths are restricted to length 1. The activation of a link causes a file to be displayed using the appropriate application, but there is no way to link to further digital resources or to link back to the printed document, or even other printed documents. For example, in the case of the Blue Planet material, it might be useful to have a link to a video and then to be able to follow links to related video clips, entries in the fact file of the website or relevant on-line quizzes and also to images in the Blue Planet book.

These limitations are in many ways due to the over-simplistic information model which simply binds IDs to files. A much richer information model can lead to much richer and more flexible interactive information environments and this is what we want to develop in the remainder of this paper. However, it is important to emphasise that most systems linking printed documents, or indeed other physical objects, to digital resources are based on such a basic mapping model [5,6,13,22]. The focus has tended to be on the hardware and communication technologies and their uses, rather than on the information models. What we want to show is that approaching the problem from an information point of view can take us a step further in realising the potential of *interactive paper*.

3 Interactive Paper

Our goal is to, not only provide links between printed and digital materials, but also support highly-interactive systems that enable the reader to easily move back and forth between the printed and digital worlds.

"Highly-interactive" implies a fine level of granularity of information objects in both the printed and digital worlds. However, most of the Blue Planet material is produced as relatively large chunks of information such as 45 minute TV programmes, sections of text, complete quizzes etc. As described in the last section, the course textbook links entire sections of text to TV programmes. Since the publishers are aware that this level of granularity for video material is too coarse, they do provide timing information to enable readers to locate parts of a TV programme related to a section of the text or specific themes addressed within the section. To create a richer information environment, a much finer level

Derivation Rules in Object-Oriented Conceptual Modeling Languages

Antoni Olivé

Dept. Llenguatges i Sistemes Informàtics
Universitat Politècnica de Catalunya
08034 Barcelona (Catalonia)
olive@lsi.upc.es

Abstract. We propose three new methods for the definition of derivation rules in O-O conceptual modeling languages. The first method applies to static rules, and associates each derived element with a defining operation. The specification of this operation is then the definition of the corresponding derivation rule. The second method applies to constant relationship types whose instances can be derived when the instances of one of its participant entity types are created. We propose a variant of the previous method to deal with these types. The third method deals with hybrid types, and suggests a simple way to define their partial derivation rules. We propose an adaptation of the three methods to the UML.

1 Introduction

Derived types and derivation rules have been considered fundamental components of conceptual schemas of information systems since the early eighties [17]. The rationale is that derivation rules are domain knowledge that an information system needs to know in order to be able to derive some facts and, according to the 100% (or completeness) principle [18], that knowledge must be described in the conceptual schema. The importance of derivation rules is also recognized in industry, where they are sometimes classified as a kind of business rule [6].

Many conceptual modeling languages provide specific constructs for defining derived types and derivation rules. Among the early languages we mention SDM [16], which provides a detailed analysis of derivation kinds and the constructs supporting them; and CIAM [13], which puts a strong emphasis on derived types and the temporal perspective. Among the recent languages, we mention the family of languages descendants of KL-ONE [5], called Description Logics, which provide a specific formal syntax for defining derived entity and relationship types, and a strong reasoning support [4, 8]; Chimera [9], which includes deductive rules for data derivation, and a set of mappings for the implementation of these rules in commercial database systems (triggers, views, etc.); and ORM [14], which allows informal and formal [2] versions of derivation rules. Finally, we mention the standard language UML [24], which also allows defining derived types and derivation rules.

J. Eder and M. Missikoff (Eds.): CAiSE 2003, LNCS 2681, pp. 404–420, 2003.

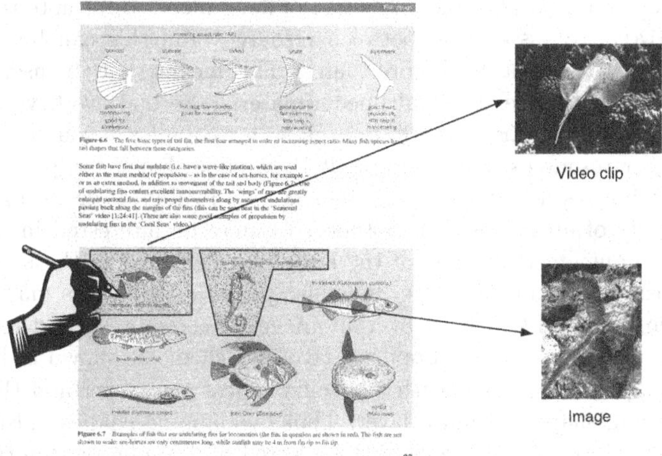

Fig. 4. Active areas

for example using a specially designed grid of barcodes printed using invisible inductive ink. Again, a number of technical solutions have been proposed to enable this.

The active areas can be defined as one of a number of simple geometrical shapes or as a complex shape composed from other shapes. In Fig. 5, we show the corresponding part of the information server's schema.

We have replaced the notion of `ResourceIDs` with a general notion of `Anchors` that are bound to `Resources`. As a specialisation of `Anchors`, we have a sub-collection `Shapes` which may in turn be a simple shape or a complex shape (`CompShapes`) consisting of two or more shapes.

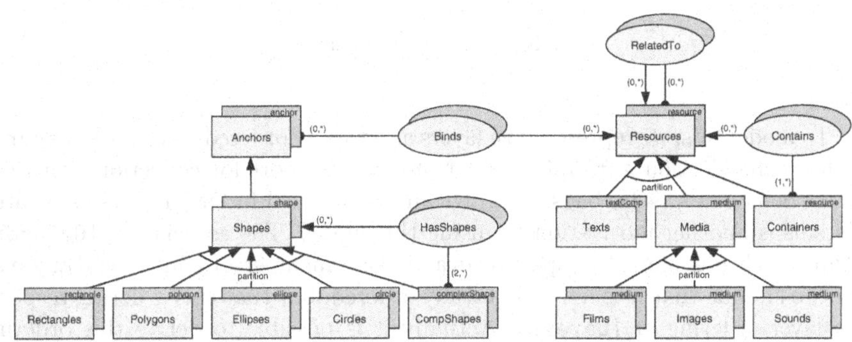

Fig. 5. Linking areas to digital resources

We have also expanded the modelling of `Resources`. First note that we now have a `RelatedTo` association between resources and this can be used to increase the link path length to more than 1. This means that the user can follow further links to other related multimedia material. Second, we have categorised `Resources` as `Texts`, `Images` etc. and allow for complex resources which may contain other resources. For example, it is possible that a complex image contains other images as indicated by the example in Fig. 4, or we may want to activate parts of an image. For instance, we may be interested in detailed information about a certain part of the body of a fish such as the fin, or a word concept printed within an image. It is also possible that areas may overlap as arises when a printed text flows over an image. This requires a further extension to the information model to support a layering scheme as shown in Fig. 6.

Each shape is associated with a specific logical page layer and there can be no overlapping shapes within a layer. Thus overlapping shapes must belong to different layers and in the case that the selected position lies within two or more shapes, the shape within the uppermost layer is selected. In addition, specific layers may be activated and deactivated and this enables us to generate context dependent results by binding a particular position on a page to different resources according to the current set of active layers. For example, this could be used to provide a "zoom in" effect on images if we were to define the shapes and layers such that repeated selection of a position on a page caused the uppermost layers to be deactivated in turn, thereby moving down to smaller image parts defined on the lower levels. The zoom in/out functionality enables a whole range of new interaction and user interface possibilities in working with static paper, where the digital media can be used to give feedback about the context (current layer) within an image.

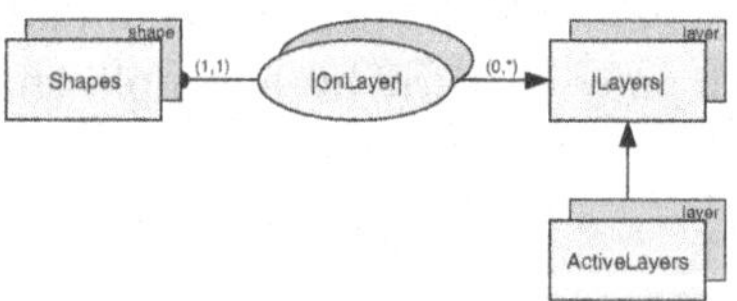

Fig. 6. Layers and shapes

To model this, we represent the layers as a totally ordered collection `|Layers|` with a subcollection `ActiveLayers`. Note that support for collections with different behaviours (sets, bags, rankings and sequences) in OM and its associated systems is another motivation for using this model. The association `|OnLayer|` relates each member of `Shapes` to exactly one member of collection `|Layers|` and we assume that it is not only totally ordered, but that this ordering respects the layer ordering of `|Layers|`. Actually it is possible to derive this ordering automatically within the system, but we model it explicitly here for the sake of simplicity.

OM is object-oriented and has a full algebra over objects, collections and associations. Without going into detail of the OM query language AQL, we show below a query that, given a point (x, y), will return the uppermost shape of the active layer set that contains that point.

```
first(domain((OnLayer rr ActiveLayers)
              dr (all S in Shapes having S.contains(x,y))
            )
      )
```

First, two selections are applied to the association `OnLayer`: we select pairs where the second element belongs to `ActiveLayers` and, in a second step, we further select those pairs where the first element is a member of `Shapes` where the method `contains` returns `true` for the input parameters x and y. Having carried out this reduction of the `OnLayer` association, we then take the `domain` which gives the collection of shapes containing the point (x, y) and belonging to an active layer. Since `OnLayer` is a total ordering that respects the ordering of `Layers`, the `domain` operation will maintain that ordering and `first` will select the uppermost shape as required. Details of the algebra and query language are given in [24].

So far we have achieved a mapping of elements of a printed document to digital resources, but we still do not have the capability to perform an inverse mapping from the digital world to the printed world. The problem is that we have insufficient information about the context of an embedded link within a document. It is not enough to know the coordinates within a page that define an active area. We must also know the page and the document that contains that area. We therefore extend the model with document and page information as shown in Fig. 7.

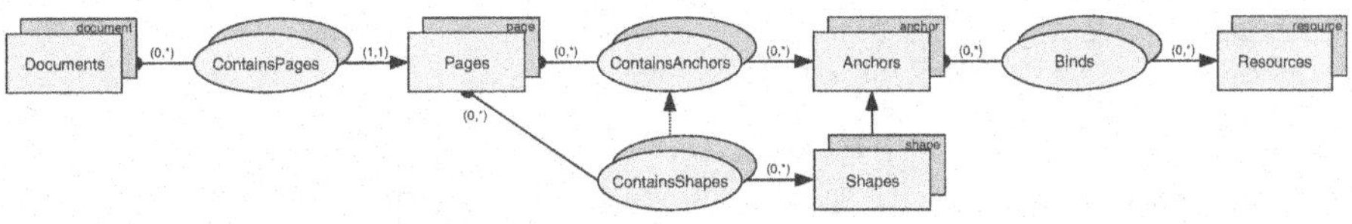

Fig. 7. Context of links within documents

While this is simple to model, we must think about what this means in terms of the underlying technologies. The encoding system must be amended to include information about the document and page number. With current encoding schemes, it would be difficult to include globally unique document IDs within a grid-based page position encoding scheme. Within the Paper^{++} project, we have encoded page and coordinate information within the page encoding scheme and handle document IDs separately through either the use of RFID tags or special printed document encodings on the cover page.

With the additional contextual information of document and page, we are able to map digital resources to active areas within documents. For example, we could easily find where a given video or term (printed word or phrase) is used within a document set. This now gives us a basic mapping back and forth between printed and digital media. Note that these back references to printed documents are not just another piece of text within the database giving, for example, a document title and a page number. In fact, the links back to physical paper are built dynamically based on meta information about other documents bound to the same information object. This meta information is already present in the information model (bidirectional associations) and therefore no additional authoring is required. In the following sections, we shall see how this can be extended with the use of derived links and link sharing.

4 Enriched Information Environments

At this point we have achieved a relatively simple two-way linking of printed and digital resources. But can we really say that we have achieved an integration of printed and digital information? The answer is "no" since there is no information about the semantic content of these resources. On the printed side, our objects of interest are simply areas of a page. On the digital side, we simply have content such as texts, images, audio and video without these being related to any conceptual information about the application domain such as oceanography in the case of the Blue Planet example.

To provide a richer information environment, we could introduce information concepts into the server by extending the schema to cover concepts about the application domain as shown in Fig. 8.

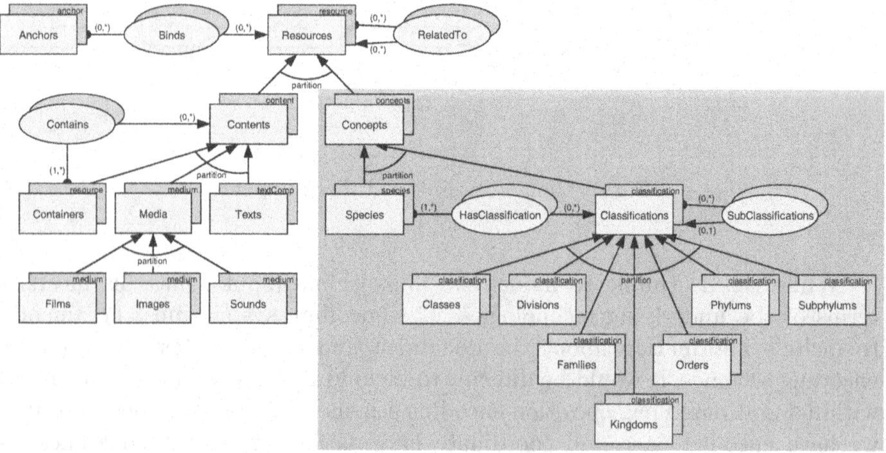

Fig. 8. Adding concepts as resources

We have now partitioned `Resources` into `Contents` to represent the basic text and media files as before and a new collection `Concepts` to cover the representation of application specific information. Essentially, `Concepts` is a way of integrating an application database into the information server of the cross-media publishing framework.

The application concepts part of the schema shown in Fig. 8 actually more or less corresponds to the information currently available in the facts file on the Blue Planet website. Users can select a classification and then one of a list of species in that classification and a simple fact file with basic information about the species including physical description, statistics, habitat, diet and distribution will be displayed. There are no links within this information to maps, images etc. or to related species such as predators. Since OMS supports attributes of type `mime`, it would be an easy matter to include links to multimedia files within the species objects and in this way already achieve a more highly-linked system than is currently available on the Blue Planet website, as well as having links between the printed and digital material. Note that we have extended the basic schema to include general forms of classifications that appear in biological databases.

Extending the application part of the schema to include further information such as geographical locations and with appropriate associations as shown in Fig. 9 would clearly further enrich the information environment.

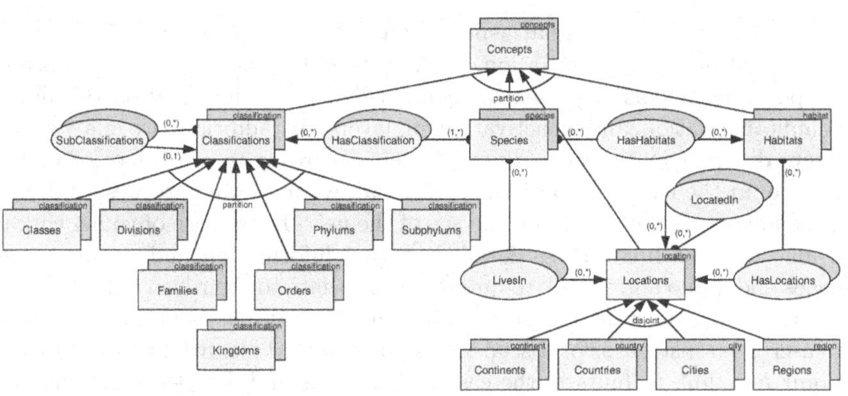

Fig. 9. Extended application model

While the introduction of an application database can potentially provide readers of printed material with access to a wealth of related digital materials, like all database development projects, it needs significant investment to do it well. Developing a full application database requires domain expertise and lots of data input. Therefore this may not be the solution for all forms of cross-media publishing. However, it is important to point out the potential long-term rewards of such an investment, especially when one considers reusability. Even within the Paper^{++} project, we found that we could reuse all or part of application models.

As mentioned previously, our first demonstrator application was based on a nature encyclopaedia [8]. When we came to examine the Blue Planet material, we found of course that the core application schema remained much the same and the difference lay in the data.

The BBC are well-known for the high standard of their nature documentary series and over the years there have been many. Such a nature database could be used for all of these programmes and, of course, would provide a rich source of material that the BBC itself could use in the planning and development of their programmes. In fact, according to our sources, they are in the process of developing such a database and this could provide a valuable source of material if integrated into their cross-media publishing activities in the future.

With the introduction of an application schema which effectively links different concepts of the application domain, note that we can also introduce more powerful forms of derived linking of printed materials. Assume that there is a link from an element of one document to a particular species object. Further assume a link from a second document such as an atlas to a location object. Then through the associations `HasHabitats` and `HasLocations`, a user interested in that species and its habitat can be directed to one or more places within the atlas. Derived linking may be particularly powerful in the case of open authoring systems where users may dynamically add their own links from printed documents to digital resources and links can be shared within user communities.

This leads us to the final aspects that we want to consider here, namely personalisation and customisation. We have already alluded to the use of layering as a potential means of presenting context-dependent information through the dynamic activation and deactivation of layers. In addition, we may want to present different materials to different users according to preference or role. For example, in the case of Blue Planet material, we may want to present different links and content dependent on the age of the user. In the case of young children, we may want to link to less detailed textual information and rather to more images and audio and to link to quizzes appropriate to their age. For educational scenarios, we may want to present different information according to whether the user is an instructor or a student. In particular, links from an exercise sheet or quiz may link to hints in the case of a student and detailed solutions in the case of an instructor.

For this reason, it is important to model users within the system and for that we introduce into the Paper^{++} server a special user concept. Note however that the user information may be shared across applications and hence we show it as a separate component in Fig. 10.

Here we show the main components of the information server that we developed for the nature encyclopaedia application. For each application domain, there is a *Transformation Component* that defines the active areas and their binding to resources, an *Application Component* that is the domain-specific database and also a *Presentation Component* which manages templates to enable client-dependent delivery of content. For example, we have implemented

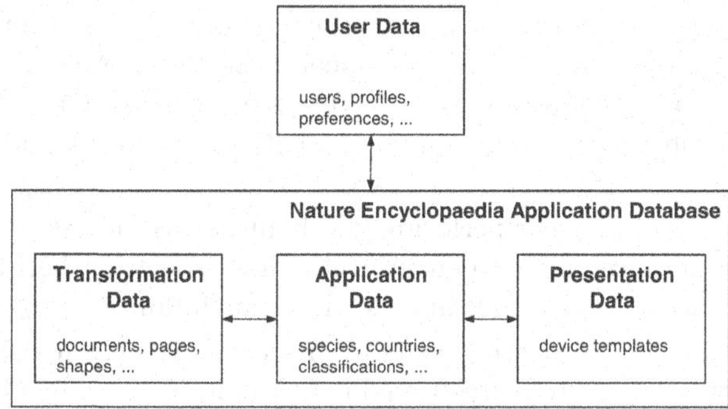

Fig. 10. Information server

this application for access from a range of devices including standard desktop browsers and PDAs as described in [15].

The *User Component* may be shared by a number of applications. Note however that it is also possible as discussed above that the *Application Component* could be shared by applications.

5 Authoring and Publishing Tools

When considering the activity of authoring cross-media material, there are a number of fundamental factors to take into account. These factors deal with issues such as the intended usage of the system and the source of materials and they will greatly influence the types of authoring to be supported and hence the approaches and tools to be used. While it is beyond the scope of this paper to describe any particular authoring tool or publishing framework in detail, we want at least to indicate some of the approaches that we are investigating.

The first factor to consider is whether the content is already available in the form of digital and printed materials. If so, the main authoring activity is *link authoring* and a tool is required to support the creation of links between the existing content elements. The second factor is then whether only the publishers can author links or also the users of the material in which case *dynamic link authoring* must be supported. If users can author their own links, the next question is whether there is an *open link authoring* scheme, in which users can link arbitrary materials and not only those provided by a single publisher. For example, a student may wish to link concepts in a set of lecture notes to text books or to websites. Clearly, the ability to freely create links between arbitrary printed materials implies a major shift to a future world of interactive paper.

All link authoring tools require some means of linking positions within a document to resources in the information server. Two problems arise. How can links be marked so that the user is aware of them and how can we ensure the stability of the association between document positions and elements of the document? Any changes to document content will alter the physical position of elements. Dynamic authoring of links by users across existing printed documents is technically simpler in that the document is static. However, in this case, a solution needs to be found to inform the users of link positions. One possibility is to consider combining a highlighter pen with the reader device as described in [2].

In the case of a publisher performing link authoring, access to the document rendering system is required to ensure that the association between document elements and physical page coordinates will be maintained.

First experiences within the Paper^{++} project have shown that existing authoring "solutions" tend to be restricted in flexibility (e.g. by handling only rectangular shapes) and often lack support for context-sensitive information such as user-dependent anchors or personalised links [21]. The authoring tool we are developing is flexible by supporting any kind of shapes and multi-layer authoring for complex figures. Further, it enables the authoring of multi-user documents. These multi-user documents contain anchors (shapes) linking to different resources based on the user currently working with the document. Finally, we are investigating a better integration of the reading device into the overall authoring process. The user should not only be able to define the active page areas (anchors) by marking them on screen but rather generating them directly on the physical paper by using the reader to draw a shape's outline.

The explicit authoring of links can certainly be time-consuming and it may be based on the knowledge or experience of a single individual. Especially in the case of open, dynamic link authoring systems, it is desirable to share links among communities of users, thereby enabling users to benefit from the knowledge of others. In addition, user profiling and access paths can be used to generate virtual trails, suggesting links to users based either on their own or the community's experiences similar to the ideas described in [4]. These are topics that we have partly addressed in the context of other projects (e.g. a personal assistant for access to web databases [20]) and we are currently integrating these ideas into the Paper^{++} information server.

So far, we have considered only link authoring. If the content does not already exist, then the authoring activity will consist of both *content authoring* and *link authoring*. In this case, the content can be developed with the resulting hypermedia system in mind and tools can be used that generate both printed and digital documents along with the links between them. In such a case, instead of using traditional authoring tools such as a word processor, a content management approach of the form now prevalent in website engineering could be employed. For example, within our research group, we are developing flexible and powerful content management solutions that manage content, structure, layout and view objects and dynamically create device and context dependent delivery of information using an XML/XSLT framework [9]. We are now exploiting these systems to generate, not only digital documents such as HTML for web browsers, but also printed documents with embedded active links.

We have briefly outlined the various forms of authoring activity that need to be supported and indicated the sorts of tools and technologies that are required.

However, it is clear that, in many cases, the different forms may all be required within a single application domain. For example, in a university learning environment, the instructors may want to generate on-line and printed material which is linked together, but additionally students will want to add and share links both within this set of materials and also to external sources.

6 Concluding Remarks

A study of the literature on digitally augmented paper, reveals that the "information" aspect often tends to be ignored or underplayed. This shows itself in terms of the very basic, over-simplistic models that are often used on the server side to implement the mapping between the printed documents and digital resources. However, the information model of the server has a major role to play in facilitating the integration of printed and digital materials.

We have presented a case study in cross-media publishing to show how a range of extensions to the information model of the server can lead to more flexible, customisable systems that in turn yield much richer information environments. This provides the potential for paper to be integrated as a first-class medium into hypermedia systems.

The information model presented forms the basis of the server that has been implemented for interactive paper in the context of the European project Paper^{++}. Using the server and various prototypes of the reader and printing technologies, we have already been able to demonstrate the potential uses of interactive paper and to carry out preliminary user studies. We are now in the process of developing various authoring tools both for open, dynamically linked systems and also for major content providers.

Acknowledgements. The work reported in this paper is part of the European project Paper^{++}, under the Disappearing Computer Programme (IST-2000-26130). We thank the other members of the project for their contributions and feedback on our work.

References

1. Anoto AB, http://www.anoto.com.
2. T. Arai, D. Aust, and S. Hudson. PaperLink: A Technique for Hyperlinking from Real Paper to Electronic Content. In *Proceedings of ACM CHI'97, Conference on Human Factors in Computing Systems*, March 1997.
3. The Blue Planet Website, BBC, http://www.bbc.co.uk/nature/blueplanet/.
4. V. Bush. As We May Think. *Atlantic Monthly*, July 1945.
5. PaperLink, code-it AG, http://www.code-it.ch/.
6. CueCat, DigitalConvergence, http://www.crq.com/.
7. M. Dymetman and M. Copperman. Intelligent Paper. In *Proceedings of EP'98, 7th International Conference on Electronic Publishing, Document Manipulation, and Typography*, April 1998.

8. D. Frohlich, E. Tallyn, N. Linketscher, B. Signer, and G. Adams. Reading Augmented Paper: Children's Experiences from a Simulation Study. Technical Report HPL-2001-308, HP Labs, 2001.
9. M. Grossniklaus and M. C. Norrie. Information Concepts for Content Management. In *Proceedings of DASWIS 2002, International Workshop on Data Semantics in Web Information Systems*, Singapore, Republic of Singapore, December 2002.
10. D. L. Hecht. Printed Embedded Data Graphical User Interfaces. *IEEE Computer*, March 2001.
11. C. Kafka. DataGlyphs Bridge Paper and Digital Worlds. *Docu World*, 1998.
12. A. Kobler, M. C. Norrie, B. Signer, and M. Grossniklaus. OMS Java: Providing Information, Storage and Access Abstractions in an Object-Oriented Framework. In *Proceedings of OOIS'2001, 7th International Conference on Object-Oriented Information Systems*, Calgary, Canada, August 2001.
13. P. Ljungstrand, J. Redström, and L. E. Holmquist. WebStickers: Using Physical Tokens to Access, Manage and Share Bookmarks to the Web. In *Proceedings of DARE'2000, Designing Augmented Reality Environments*, Elsinore, Denmark, April 2000.
14. M. C. Norrie. An Extended Entity-Relationship Approach to Data Management in Object-Oriented Systems. In *Proceedings of ER'93, 12th International Conference on the Entity-Relationship Approach*, Arlington, USA, December 1993.
15. M. C. Norrie and B. Signer. Web-Based Integration of Printed and Digital Information. In *Proceedings of DIWeb'02, 2nd Workshop on Data Integration over the Web*, Toronto, Canada, May 2002.
16. M. C. Norrie, A. Steiner, A. Würgler, and M. Wunderli. A Model for Classification Structures with Evolution Control. In *Proceedings of ER'96, 15th International Conference on Conceptual Modelling*, Cottbus, Germany, October 1996.
17. The Open University, http://www.open.ac.uk/.
18. Paper^{++}, IST-2000-26130, http://www.paperplusplus.net.
19. A. J. Sellen and R. Harper. *The Myth of the Paperless Office.* MIT Press, November 2001.
20. B. Signer, A. Erni, and M. C. Norrie. A Personal Assistant for Web Database Caching. In *Proceedings of CAiSE'2000, 12th International Conference on Advanced Information Systems Engineering*, Stockholm, Sweden, June 2000.
21. I. Siio, T. Masui, and K. Fukuchi. Real-world Interaction using the FieldMouse. In *Proceedings of UIST'99, 12th Annual ACM Symposium on User Interface Software and Technology*, November 1999.
22. NeoMedia Technologies. IDOCs Linking the Worlds of Print and Electronic Media. Technical report, NeoMedia Technologies, September 1998.
23. S. Whittaker and J. Hirschberg. The Character, Value, and Management of Personal Paper Archives. *ACM Transactions on Computer-Human Interaction*, June 2001.
24. A. Würgler. *OMS Development Framework : Rapid Prototyping for Object-Oriented Databases.* PhD thesis, ETH Zurich, 2000.

Ranking Web Documents with Dynamic Evaluation by Expert Groups

Sea Woo Kim[1] and Chin-Wan Chung[2]

[1] Division of Information and Communication Engineering,
373-1, Kusong-Dong, Yusong-Gu, Taejon 305-701, Korea
seawoo@islab.kaist.ac.kr

[2] Division of Computer Science,
373-1, Kusong-Dong, Yusong-Gu, Taejon 305-701, Korea
chungcw@islab.kaist.ac.kr

Abstract. In spite of the wide use of the Internet, it is difficult to develop desirable web documents evaluation that reflects users' needs. Many automatic ranking systems have used this citation system to measure the relative importance of consumer products or documents. However, the automatic citation analysis has a limitation in that it does not truly reflect the importance of the varying viewpoints of human evaluation. Therefore, human evaluations of web documents are very helpful in finding relevant information in a specific domain. Currently, human evaluation is done by a single expert or general users without considering the degree of domain knowledge of evaluators. In this paper, we suggest that a dynamic group of experts for a certain web document be automatically created among users to evaluate domain specific web documents. The experts have dynamic authority weights depending on their performance of the ranking evaluation. In addition, we develop an evaluation effectiveness measure for ranking processes. This evaluation by a group of experts provides more accurate search results and can be a good measure of user preferences when the size of users' feedback is small. Also, dynamic change of authority weight provides the evaluation effectiveness of experts. Furthermore, dynamic change of authority weight provides the evaluation effectiveness of experts.

1 Introduction

Together with the development of the Internet and the popularity of WWW, Web document recommendation systems have drawn significant attention. Many Web document comparison search engines have been introduced and developed, but still have difficulty in providing completely relevant answers to the general subject of queries. The main reason is not due to the lack of data but rather an excess of data. This data has a variety of characteristics and information that is not specific to users. This is what led to the necessity of web document rankings. For the time being, the web documents are listed by using a ranking measure called connectivity analysis. This improves the quality of search results. An example of this method is the IBM HITS system. This method works on the assumption that a document that is cited

J. Eder and M. Missikoff (Eds.): CAiSE 2003, LNCS 2681, pp. 437–448, 2003.

many times is popular and important. The hub scores of its parent pages are summed into its authority score and the authority scores of its children pages are summed into its hub score [4][5]. By iteration, it determines highly referenced pages.

Another ranking method is called Page Rank. This method works in two phases. First, it computes a ranking for every document based on the web connectivity graph [2] with a random walk traversal. Second, it considers the relative importance of the document by checking ranks of back link pages. When the document has back links to pages with high authority such as www.yahoo.com, it is ranked as highly important.

However, even these methods have a limitation. They do not truly reflect the importance of the varying viewpoints of human evaluation. There are many cases where simple citation counting does not reflect our common sense concept of importance [2]. Also documents, products and academic publication papers are significantly different in terms of citation analysis. Some search engines employ the method based on textual similarity [1][8]. Normally they count the frequency of terms in a domain to decide lexical affinities instead of using advanced natural language processing techniques. And yet even textual similarity analysis has its limitations.

While the above approaches consider topological links of the web, a combination of a broad search of the entire web with domain-specific textual and topological scoring of results is suggested [1]. Aridor has specialized knowledge agents for specific domains to extract the most relevant documents. Similarly we are interested in ranking Web documents in a specific domain. In our approach, the search engine goes through the process of a domain-specific web search and shows the list of popular documents for each specialized subject.

In this paper we use a method to evaluate web documents by a group of human agents[21], and we call it an expert group. We believe that the importance and level of authority of consumer products or documents should be determined by interactions between human and consumer products or documents. Furthermore, domain groups should be responsible for document ranking for each category. This domain group should have authorities to evaluate documents. This approach will overcome the disadvantages of the automatic ranking method through incomplete information processing based on citation authority or lexical affinities, which ignore the content of web documents. Another benefit is that when the size of evaluation feedback of general users is not big enough, this method can give the initial measurement of users' preferences.

2 Methodologies

2.1 Model of Recommending Documents

We define a group of people with high authority as an expert group. This expert group is automatically promoted from the general users to evaluate web documents on a specific category. There are three groups in three levels for each category, the general user group, the expert candidate group, and the expert group as shown in Figure 1. The expert candidates are chosen among active users. The access count of web documents are recorded, and user participation is measured and classified. Access count to important products and the participation level of a user determine the activity of a user. This activity is the major factor to decide experts and their potential for future activity. An expert candidate will be given a test to measure his/her knowledge about a certain domain. Then the results of the test are calculated to decide if he/she can be an expert. If a candidate is qualified for the expert-pool, then he/she will be allowed to score and rank web documents that are to be evaluated.

Similar to the three user groups, we have three groups of web documents in three levels for each category, the general document group, the candidate document group, and the recommended document group as shown in figure 1. A pool of candidates for the expert groups are nominated and to be upgraded for the expert group for each category. A category is created considering subjects and it can be subsequently refined into many categories when the access to it exceeds a threshold. Each web document contains the information of how many search engines being utilized in our search engine are referring to the document, and keeps a record of how many times online users have accessed the web document using our search engine.

If a web document is referred to many times in many search engines under a given category, then it can be highly ranked. This kind of web document is considered as a candidate document that needs to be evaluated by an expert group. If a web document is accessed many times by users recently, then it can be highly ranked. This web documents one of the candidate documents to be evaluated by an expert group. This approach is likely to produce more fine-grained and reliable results to a new environment of web patterns. For every category there is a list of recommended documents evaluated by an expert group, which are sorted by score. Human experts decide which of the candidate document are to be promoted for the recommended documents.

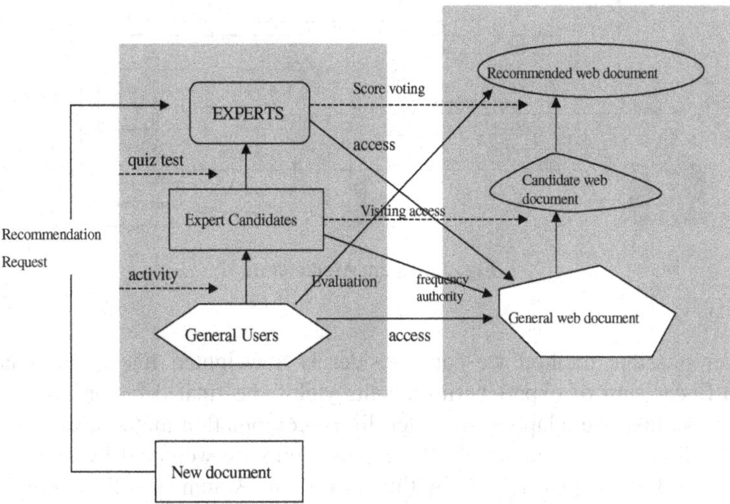

Fig. 1. Diagram of user group and documents group

2.2 Dynamic Evaluation by Expert Group

A meta-search engine that is run to collect addresses of cited web document from conventional search engines as shown in Figure 2. List of web documents are collected from the each search engine directory. Web crawler automatically performs this process. At the time of the query, the ranking by the number of citations from shopping malls and expert ranking are combined. The combined rank documents are shown to the users. The visiting log of users are recorded and monitored. The method of employing an expert group is based on the idea that for a given decision task requiring expert knowledge, many experts may be better than one if their individual judgments are properly combined.

In our system, experts decide whether a document should be classified into a top ranked list for a given category. A simple way is the majority voting, where each expert has a binary vote for a document and then the document obtaining equal to or greater than half of the votes are classified into a top ranked list [7]. The result of the decision for documents is stored along with their addresses.

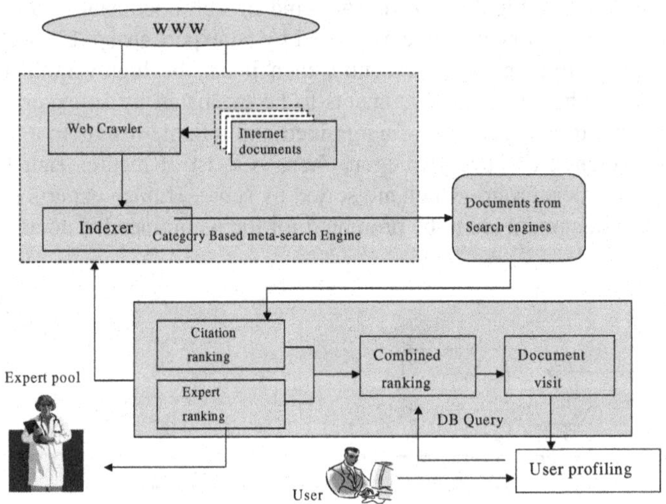

Fig. 2. System Architecture

Another possible method we can consider is a weighted linear combination. A weighted linear sum of expert voting results yields the final decision documents. In this paper, we take the adaptive weighted linear combination method, where the individual contributions of members in the expert group are weighted by their judgment performance. The evaluations of all the experts are summed with weighted linear combinations. The expert-voted results will dynamically change depending on each expert's performance and effectiveness. Our approach of expert group decision is similar to a classifier committee concept in automatic text categorization [9]. Their methods use classifiers based on various statistical or learning techniques instead of

human interaction and decision. The explanation of choosing group members and determining authority i.e. effectiveness for each expert is as follows.:
We have a visiting access matrix C=[C_{ij}] between users and Web documents, which is given by

$$C_{ij} = \begin{cases} 1 & \text{If a user } u_i \text{ visits a search engine } d_p \\ 0 & \text{otherwise} \end{cases}$$

C_{ij} is binary to prevent spam effects. Since it is binary one user's frequent vote dose not influence the visiting access matrix. From this information, we define an activity measure $I_a(u_i)$ for a user u_i and a visiting access measure $I_v(\ \beta dj\ )$ for a web document dj as follows :

$$I_a(u_i) = \sum_{j=1}^{Nd} Cij \ , \ I_v(\ dj\ ) = \sum_{i=1}^{Nu} Cij$$

where N_d is the number of documents and N_u is the number of users registered in the meta-search engine.

Our meta-search engine extracts web documents from $N_{s,}$ -existing search engines, which are denoted as s_i, i=1,...., N_s. Then we define a frequency authority measure $I_f(d_j)$ based on the search engines over a web document d_j as follows :

$$I_f(d_i) = \sum_{j=1}^{Ns} \delta_j m_{ij}$$

where δ_i is a weight for each search engine, initially set to 1.

The frequency authority measure represents the frequency of a document in a meta-search engine.
If this measure $I_f(\ dj\ )$ is larger than a threshold, then we can assume that the document p_j is of good quality and importance. Using the visiting access matrix C=[c_{ij}] and the consumer product matrix M=[m_{ij}], we can calculate the popularity and performance of each search engine used in the meta-search engine. Search engine frequency matrix Y=[y_{ij}] is defined as $Y = C \cdot M^T$ then weight δ_k for each search engine can be updated as follows:

$$\delta_k = \frac{\sum_{i=1}^{Nu} y_{ik}}{\sum_{j=1}^{Ns}\sum_{i=1}^{Nu} y_{ij}}$$

The candidate users that are to be promoted to experts for a category can be determined by checking the measure I_a calculated during a given period. Every week or so, this activity measure is updated. Candidates are required to pass a test to become an expert. The web documents of good quality or importance are determined by checking the frequency authority measure I_f and visiting access measure I_v over web documents. Thus, we can decide candidate document among general documents using the following measure:

$$Ic = \alpha I_f + \beta I_v + \gamma$$

where α, β, γ are scaling factors. If Ic is larger than a threshold τ, the corresponding document will be accepted as a candidate document. The selected documents wait for an evaluation by experts for a given category. For each candidate document, experts are required to evaluate the document and give them scores. An evaluation score matrix is defined as $X = [\ \chi_{ij}\ ]$ when the i-th expert evaluates a consumer product pj with a voting score χ_{ij}. We have a weighted importance or authority over experts for each category. The evaluation score matrix shows a relation between experts and candidate documents. The weight is determined by their activity measure *Ia*, test score, and other factors. Experts are assigned the same weight at the initial stage as experts are not differentiated at this moment.

The weight is dynamically changed by their activity and feedback from online users about recommended documents through voting results.

This weighted measure is useful even when the number of expert members is not fixed. Thus, for each document *dj* listed as a candidate document the weighted authority voting score is defined as follows:

$$V(d_j) = \sum_{k=1}^{Ne} \frac{w_k}{\sum_{i=1}^{Ne} w_i} \chi_{kj} \qquad w_k = EI_a(u_k) + H$$

where N_e is the number of experts for a given category, and r_k is the relative authority for the k-th expert in the expert pool, and w_k is the weight calculated using activity measure, test scores and other career factors for the k-th expert member. And E,H are scaling factors.

The weight w_k is a dynamic factor, and it discriminates bad experts from good experts in terms of their activity and users' voting results. When some experts show little participation in voting or evaluate incorrectly, their authority weight w_k becomes smaller. For example, when an expert voting score is larger than the weighted average voting score and the average score is smaller than the desirable rank score, the expert status is rewarded, otherwise penalized. Therefore, some experts receive rewards and others receive penalties depending on the weighted average voting score of experts. All experts receive penalties or rewards in our application. It is possible that some experts with too many penalties are excluded from the expert group and new experts are added to the group.

We define an error measure *E* as a squared sum of differences between desired voting scores and actual voting scores as follows:

$$E = \frac{1}{2}\sum_{j=1}^{n} (V(d_j) - V'(d_j))^2 = \frac{1}{2}\sum_{j=1}^{n}(\sum_{k=1}^{N_e} \frac{w_k}{\sum_{i=1}^{Ne} w_i}\chi_{kj} - V'(d_j))^2$$

where n is the number of documents evaluated by users, $V'(d_j)$ is the desired voting score for an expert-voting document d_j. We assume $V'(d_j)$ is the average score evaluated by all users, but in reality it is rarely possible to receive the feedback from all users.

We chose the coefficient 1/2 to make its gradient formula simpler, which will be shown later. We assumed this value could be determined by the feedback from general on-line users. Voting scores of the experts should reflect common ideas of users about ranking and satisfy desires of many users to find proper relative appropriate information, because an expert is a representative of general users and has a extensive expect knowledge in a specific domain.

Now we use a gradient-descent method over error measure *E* with respect to a weight w_k and the gradient is given by

$$\frac{\partial E}{\partial \omega i} = \frac{\partial}{\partial \omega i}(\frac{1}{2}\sum_{j=1}^{n}[V(d_j) - V'(d_j)^2)$$

$$=\frac{1}{2}\bullet 2\sum_{j=1}^{n}[V(d_j)-V'(d_j)]\frac{\partial V(d_j)}{\partial \omega i}$$

$$=\sum_{j=1}^{n}\Delta_j\frac{\partial V(d_j)}{\partial \omega_i}=\sum_{j=1}^{n}[\chi ij-V(d_j)]\frac{\Delta_j}{S}$$

where $s=\sum_{k=1}^{N_e} w_k$ is the sum of weights, and $\Delta_j=[v(d_j)-V'(d_j)]$ is the difference between the predicted voting score and the users evaluation score for a document d_j.

If we update weights of experts for ranking by feedback from users about a document d_j , the weight is changed by the following dynamic equation

$$\omega_i(t+1)=\omega_i(t)-\eta[\chi_{ij}-V(d_j)]\frac{\Delta_j}{S}$$

2.3 Evaluation Effectiveness

User effectiveness is measured by calculating how close the evaluation of the general users and experts. In this paper we use four measures for calculating user effectiveness.

1. Rank Order Window Measure. Given a sample query or category, we can represent the effectiveness as the percentage of top-ranked list of user ratings which rank in the same or very close position as an expert group does. A window is defined as a cluster of a certain group. Given top-ranked products P={$p_1,p_2,\ldots,p_n$}, we can define effectiveness Λ_δ of rank-order window δ (p_k) where p_k is the k-th web document from the test set for a given category, and $\delta(d_k)$ is the width of the window centered in the rank $\delta(p_k)$ assigned by the ratings of experts for d_k .

$$S(p_k)=1-\frac{1}{\delta(d_k)}\min(\delta(d_k),|\sum_{i=\mu(p_k)-\delta(d_k)}^{\mu(p_k)+\delta(d_k)}\frac{\mu(d_k)-Q(d_i)}{2\delta(d_k)+1}|)$$

$$\Lambda_\delta=\frac{\sum_{k=1}^{n}S(d_k)}{n}$$

where $Q(d_i)$ is the rank position of the average rating score of users for a document d_i. $S(d_k)$ calculates the rank order difference in the window $[\mu(d_k)-\delta(d_k),\mu(d_k)+\delta(d_k)]$. In the window the evaluation difference between the expert and general user can be bigger than the size of window. In that case $\delta(d_k)$ is the minimum value. In the equation, we added 1 to $2\delta(d_k)$ in denominator. We added 1 because we need non-zero denominator at any time.

2. $F\gamma$ measure with Rank Order Partition. Evaluation effectiveness also can be described in terms of precision and recall widely used in information retrieval. Precision is the conditional probability that when a document is predicted to be in a positive class, it truly belongs to this class. Recall is the conditional probability that a document belonging to positive class is truly classified into this class [10,11]. We partition recommended documents by their rank order and make classes. We define a positive class i as top [(i -1)*10+1~ i *10] ranked documents by expert voting and a negative class as the others. For Example, class 2 documents are top [11~20] ranked documents.

The precision probability Pi and recall probability Ri for ranking site class i may be estimated using the contingency relations between expert rating and user rating, and those probabilities in our application can be calculated with transition instances between classes. A transition instance pij is define as the number of instances that are predicted to be in class i by user ratings.

$$Pi = \frac{pij}{\sum_{j=1}^{m} pij \cdot |i-j+1|}, \qquad Ri = \frac{pij}{\sum_{j=1}^{m} pij \cdot |i-j+1|}$$

where m is the number of classes, and $\overline{P}, \overline{R}$ are the average precision and recall probabilities, respectively. The distance between classes is considered to calculate Pi, Ri. Then effectiveness can be computed using the value of F_β for $0 \le \beta \le \infty$ [3,14,20].

$$F_\beta = \frac{(\beta^2+1)\cdot \overline{P} \cdot \overline{R}}{\beta^2 \cdot \overline{P} + \overline{R}}$$

To balance precision and recall, a value $\beta = 1$ is used in our experiments. If F_β is close to zero, then the current documents ranked in a class through expert voting result can be seen to have many false responses from feedback of general online users or many new documents positioned to the top ranks. If F_β is close to one, then top-ranked sites have good feedback from general users and little change occurs on the top ranked lists.

2.4 Expert Group Evaluation Algorithms

The general users do evaluations of consumer product ranking and it can be calculated by two methods. First, the user can use the same scale as a user does to evaluate the web documents. In this paper, we define the method which use the same scale of evaluation for expert group and general users as "absolute method", and define the method which use the same scale of evaluation for expert group and general users as "relative method". Table 1 shows the absolute method.

The evaluation of web documents and its ranking process for a search engine is shown in Table 2. It shows the algorithm for the growth of top ranked documents and the dynamic change of authority weights of experts. Table 2 shows the relative method.

3 Experiments

Actual experiment is performed using two different methods: user's absolute feedback and relative feedback. Then four effectiveness measures are used such as rank order window, rank function, spearman's correlations and F_β measure. There are 200 web documents. We used movie category with 100 users and 5 experts.

Table 1. Algorithm for an absolute feedback ranking

Repeat
– choose candidate members among users with the measure I_a
– choose expert members among candidates using I_a and quiz test
– decide authority weight for each expert,
$w_k = \alpha I_a + \gamma$
– choose candidate documents among general documents with the measure $\alpha I_v + \beta I_f + \gamma > \tau$
- list the ranked documents.
–when a user evaluates each ranked document the authority weight for each expert is updated by
$w_k(t+1) = w_k(t) + \eta H_{\varepsilon}(V(d_i), V^l(d_i)) \chi_{ki}$
– create classes for ranking documents.
– calculate precision P_i and recall R_i for every class I.
– calculate the evaluation effectiveness with the measure f_β.
– If F_β is close to 1, then it reaches desirable status
Until performance is satisfiable

Table 2. Algorithm for a relative feedback ranking

Repeat
– The same as absolute method
- when a user evaluates each ranked document the authority weight for each expert is updated using the equation

$$H_e(a,b) = \begin{Bmatrix} 1 \text{ if } a-b \geq e \\ -1 \text{ if } a-b \leq -e \\ 0 \text{ otherwise} \end{Bmatrix}$$

– The same as absolute method

Figure 3 shows the experiment using the absolute feedback algorithm. The result is similar to that of the simulation. Figure 3 also shows the experiment using user effectiveness evaluation methods using the absolute feedback method. The general users just express their preference by scale of 10 to 30 regarding a certain web document's quality. This feedback influences the weight of each expert for next session. As time passes, all the measurements converge to a certain value. Therefore after we found no significant change the evaluation of expert is stabilized and can be trusted by the general users.

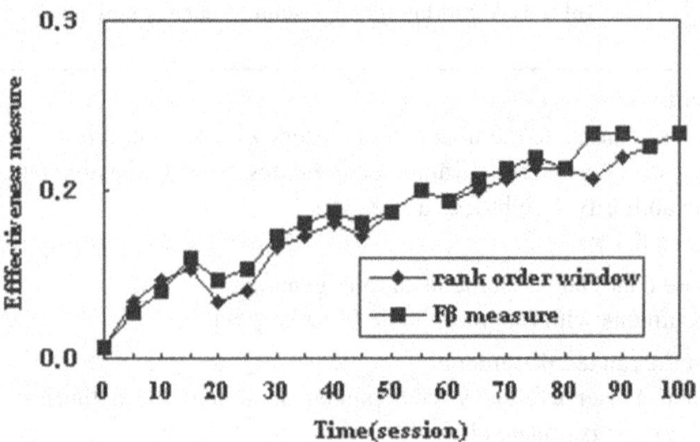

Fig. 3. User's Absolute Feedback

After the feedback of general users, an expert with low score is excluded from the expert group. In many cases, the users are not in the same scale as the expert group. Therefore, it is not easy to compare the two groups scores to figure out the correlation. This leads to the introduction of relative feedback by the general user.

Figure 4 shows the user's relative feedback method. The general users just express their preference by three categories; good, neutral, or bad regarding a certain product's quality. This feedback influences the weight of each expert for next session. After the feedback of general consumers, an expert with a low score is excluded from the expert group. For both absolute feedback and relative feedback methods the weight for each expert converges as session increases. Also we found that the product evaluation results of experts and general users are getting close to each other. This increases the user effectiveness as this paper defined in section 2.

4 Conclusion and Future Works

In this paper, we have shown a dynamic evaluation for consumer product ranking through human interaction. Expert group is automatically formed among users. Each expert has his own authority to evaluate web documents. This authority is dynamically changed using feedback of users. Expert group evaluation is more attractive compared to other search engines because it can receive more human feedback.

Our search engine is very domain-specific to improve the performance of search results and show the top ranked products. We have clustered top rank documents by their rank order, and thus we applied expert evaluation effectiveness to those clusters to test if our ranking list is reliable. Thus, we achieve the early web document recommendation system when responses of general users are small. Evaluation effectiveness measures show that our system satisfies the general users.

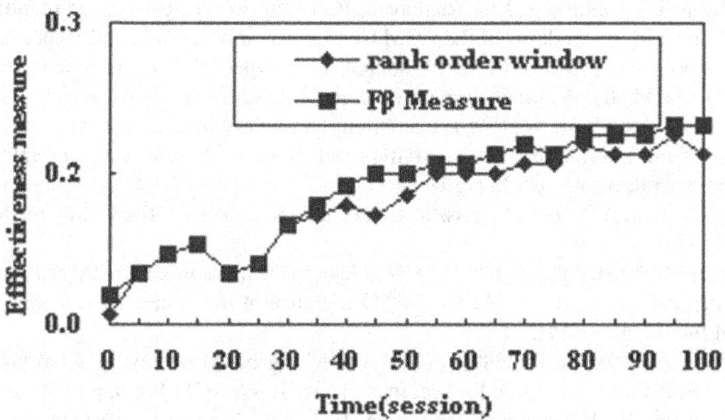

Fig. 4. User's Relative feedback

Future works include applying this idea to design a meta-search engine for specific domain: movies, music, and shopping mall documents. In addition, all documents should be classified in advance before the proposed system is applied. Currently, our categorization of all documents into specific domains is user-defined but not automatic. This is one of the text categorization problems [20]. We plan to develop a text categorization process to filter out documents irrelevant to a domain for a given query.

Also, comparison with PageRank or other methods should be included. Using the user effectiveness measures as we suggested, a search engine of web documents or web products will be prototyped [22][23].

Furthermore, users will evaluate using the mobile Short Message Service(SMS) that will improve higher response rate. Currently, web documents are evaluated on the web and we found the users feels more comfortable to evaluate them through the SMS service. Web service ranking is another area that can be expanded from our ranking model.

Acknowledgement. This work was supported in part by the Ministry of Information & Communications, Korea, under the Information Technology Research Center (ITRC) Support Program.

References

[1] Aridor, Y., Carmel, D., Lempel, R., Soffer, A. & Maarek, Y.(2000), Knowledge Agents on the Web, in Fourth International Workshop on cooperative Information Agents.

[2] Brin, S. & Page, L.(1998), The anatomy of a large-scale hypertextual web search engine, in proceedings of the Seventh International World Wide Web Conference.

[3] Cohen, W.&Singer, Y(1999),"Context-sensitive learning methods for text categorization", ACM transactions on Information Systems 17(2), 141–173.

[4] Gibson, D., Kleinberg, J. & Raghavan, R.(1998), Inferring Web communities from link topology, in Proceedings of the ACM Conference on Hypertext and Hypermedia.
[5] Kleinberg, J.(1998), Authoritative sources un a hyperlinked environment, In Proceedings of the ACM-SIAM Symposium on Discrete Algorithms.
[6] Larkey, L. & Croft, W.(1996). Combining classifiers in text categorization, in Proceedings of the International ACM SIGIR Conference on Research and Development in Information Retrieval, pp.289–297
[7] Li, Y.& Jain, A. (1998), "Classification of text documents", The Computer Journal 41(8), 537–546
[8] Liere, R & Tadepalli, P.(1997), Active learning with committees for text categorization, in Proceedings of the AAAI-97, 14th Conference of the American Association for Artificial Intelligence,k PP.591–596.
[9] Maarek, Y&Smdja, F.(1989), Full text indexing based on lexical relations, an application: Software libraries, in Proceedings of SIGIR 89, ACM Press, pp.198–206
[10] Raghavan, V., Bollmann, P. and Jung, G.(1989)."A critical investigation of recall and precision as measures of retrieval system performance", ACM transactions on Information Systems, 7(3):205–229
[11] Sebastiani, F.(1999), Machine learning in automated text categorization: a survey, Technical Report, IEI-B4-31-1999, Istituto di Elaborazione dell'Informazione, C.N.R, Pisa, IT.
[12] Van Rijsbergen, c.(1979), Information Retrieval, Butterworths, London.
[13] Yang, Y.(1994), Expert network: Effective and efficient learning from human decisions in text categorization and retrieval, in Proceedings of the International ACM SIGIR Conference on Research and Development in Information Retrieval, pp. 13–22.,1994
[14] Yang, Y.(2000),"An evaluation of statistical approaches to text categorization", Information Retrieval 1(1-2),69–90., 2000
[15] W. Hill, L. Stead, M. Rosenstein, and G. Furnas. Recommending and evaluating choices in a virtual community of use. In Proceedings of ACM CHI'95, pages 194–201,1995.
[16] P. Resnick, N. Iacovou, M. Sushak, P. Bergstrom, and J. Riedl. Grouplens: an open architecture for collaborative filtering of netnews. In Proceedings of Computer Supported Cooperative Work Confernce, pages 175–186, 1994.
[17] S.M. Ross. Introduction to Probability Models. Academic Press, London, 7th edition, 2000. U.Shardanand and P.Maes. Social information filtering: algorithms for automating word of mouth'. In proceedings of ACM CHI95,1995.
[18] I. Soboroff, C. Nicholas, and editors M. Pazzani Web Aocument Selection. In Proceedings of the SIGIR-99 Workshop on Recommender Systems, Berkeley, California, 1999.
[19] H.M. Taylor and S. Karlin. An Introduction to Stochastic Modeling. Academic Press, London, 3rd edition, 1998.
[20] C.J van Rijsbergen. Information Retrieval. Butterworths, London, 1979.
[21] S.W. Kim and C.W.Chung, "Web Document Ranking by Differentiated Expert Group Evaluation," HCI International 2001, pp.415–419, Aug. 2001
[22] Anil L. Norri, E-business Architectures and Standards, Tutorial, VLDB'02, HongKong, China ,2002.
[23] B. Benatallah and F. Casati, editors. Special Issue on Web Services. Distributed and Parallel Databases, An International journal 12(2-3), Sep. 2002.

Conceptual Modeling of Web Service Conversations

Boualem Benatallah[1], Fabio Casati[2], Farouk Toumani[3], and Rachid Hamadi[1]

[1] School of Computer Science and Engineering
The University of New South Wales, Sydney NSW 2052, Australia
{boualem,rhamadi}@cse.unsw.edu.au
[2] Hewlett-Packard Laboratories
Palo Alto, CA, 94304 USA
casati@hpl.hp.com
[3] Laboratoire LIMOS, ISIMA, Campus des Cezeaux
BP 125, 63173 Aubiere Cedex, France
ftoumani@isima.fr

Abstract. Web services are emerging as a promising technology for the effective automation of inter-organizational interactions. Several standards that aim at providing infrastructure to support Web services description, discovery, and composition have recently emerged including WSDL, UDDI, and BPEL4WS. Indeed, advances in this area promise to take cross-organizational application integration a step further by facilitating the automatic discovery and invocation of relevant services. However, despite the growing interest in Web services, several issues still need to be addressed to provide similar benefits to what traditional middleware brings to intra-organizational application integration (e.g., transaction support). In this paper, we identify a framework for defining extended service models to enable the definition of richer Web service abstractions. We also identify and define specific abstractions based on an analysis of existing e-commerce Web portals. Finally, we show how the model and the abstractions are supported by a conversation manager implemented on top of the SELF-SERV platform.

1 Introduction

Web services are emerging as the technology of choice for application integration across wide area networks and across companies [1,2,3,4]. The essential benefit they bring to application integration is standardization. In fact, Web service technology builds on top of Web standards and extends them with additional languages and protocols (e.g., WSDL, UDDI, and SOAP [5]) that enable service description, discovery, and interaction. Standardization is important in Enterprise Application Integration (EAI) [6,3], but is critical in the Web where the interaction occurs without a central coordinator and without a central authority.

However, despite the growing interest in Web services, several issues still need to be addressed to provide similar benefits to what traditional middleware

J. Eder and M. Missikoff (Eds.): CAiSE 2003, LNCS 2681, pp. 449–467, 2003.

brings to intra-organizational application integration. Indeed, EAI middleware provides much more than basic features such as service description, discovery, and invocation. For example, it supports *transactions*, a very useful abstraction when it comes to developing reliable distributed applications. Having a shared understanding of this abstraction makes it easier to describe the properties of a system. In addition, automated tools can support, manage, and enforce transactions, without the developer having to worry about writing ad-hoc code for this purpose. Without the help of transactional middleware, the development of reliable applications would be quite hard.

Abstractions provided by EAI middleware can be beneficial for modeling and implementing Web services as well, although their notion needs to be reinterpreted in this new context. For example, a notion of transactions for Web service operations may define whether from a users' perspective, an operation can be aborted at any time without effect. A more complex transaction model may also allow for operation or conversation description languages that specify that an operation can only be rolled back within a specified time or with the payment of a fee. Just like for EAI middleware, this abstraction has the potential of simplifying the interpretation of service behaviors and allowing the development of tools that support the definition of transactional services and enforce transactional properties, without the application developers having to worry about it. Indeed, it is not surprising that proposals in this direction are emerging [7,8].

Endowing Web services with abstractions analogous to those of traditional application integration is not, however, sufficient to support many of the requirements posed by application integration over the Web, since the problem is more complex in this domain. In fact, in EAI many of the properties and semantics of the services are assumed to be known a priori. Very often, clients and servers are deployed by the same project team. This is why the service interface (for example specified in terms of CORBA-IDL) is often all that is available in terms of service description. Properties and semantics are discussed face to face, and are either documented informally or not at all.

In Web services this is not the case (or, at least, this scenario is not the one Web services are targeting). The idea here is to enable developers to discover (at development time) service descriptions on the Web and, by reading these descriptions, be able to code client applications that can (at run time) bind to and interact with services of a specific type (i.e., compliant to a certain interface and protocol). As such, richer service descriptions and richer description models are needed, so that users can better understand the service execution semantics and how to interact with the service. In addition, richer service description model also allows the development of tools that better support Web service deployment, execution, monitoring, and management, as the transaction example demonstrate. Finally, it enables a more sophisticated dynamic binding, as clients can be more selective on the properties of the services they bind to when they search for a service. Referring again to the transactional example, clients can for instance require that the service supports transactions. The ultimate goal is that a service description includes all that is needed for developers to understand how to write clients that interact with the service and for automated tools to dynamically bind to a service, based on the specified characteristics. This is essential especially as the number of services to be integrated grows and the environment becomes more dynamic. This is the scenario that Web services eventually aim at addressing, despite the many hard challenges it presents.

In this paper we identify a framework for defining extended service models, to enable the definition and description of richer abstractions and achieve the above-mentioned benefits. The main goal that guided us in the design of the framework is that of enabling the definition of service properties in a way that can support: (i) humans in understanding the service properties, (ii) clients in searching services based on these properties, and (iii) applications in automating the enforcement of the properties, much like transactional middleware supports transactional abstractions.

In addition to the framework, we identify and specify a set of abstractions that we have found useful and commonly needed in many practical situations. We observe that defining framework and properties that cover many different aspects of Web services is relatively easy. Indeed, there are tons of service description models around, developed in many different fields of computer science, and trying to extend service descriptions with functional and non-functional properties (we discuss some of them in Sect. 5). The problem, often overlooked, is that adding abstractions to models and primitives to languages is a delicate issue. In fact, while in general new abstractions may provide the benefits described above, they also make the service model more complex. Complexity severely compromises the usability (and therefore the adoption) of models and languages. Indeed, simple things are always the ones that work best, because they are both easier for users to understand and for developers to implement. Therefore, the hard part lies in striking a balance between expressive power and simplicity. As a consequence, another goal that guided our work is exactly that of striking this balance and "right-sizing" the model, while providing room for it to evolve as the need arises. In order to achieve this goal, we tried to understand what is the minimal set of features and abstractions that are useful and needed in practice to describe a Web service. This required an analysis of existing e-commerce applications and of their behaviors so that we could:

- determine a set of abstractions that could adequately model most or even all of them, and
- avoid the artificial introduction of complex abstractions that we could have thought useful, and that may even be needed in some occasion, but that are rarely used in practice.

In the following, we describe in detail how we approached the problem (Sect. 2), what are the resulting frameworks and models that we have developed (Sect. 3), and how they are supported by extending the SELF-SERV service development platform [9] (Sect. 4). Finally, in Sect. 5, we review some related work and give concluding remarks.

2 Web Portal Interaction Analysis: In Search of Real Needs

This section describes the rationale that guided the analysis of existing Web applications to identify the abstractions needed in real scenarios.

2.1 Web Portals versus Web Services

When starting the research described in this paper, our original intent was that of analyzing existing Web services to understand their characteristics and requirements in terms of description languages. However, we quickly recognized that a better approach was to analyze e-commerce Web portals rather than Web services. There are two main reasons for this choice. The first is that the Web services area is still rather immature. Only few Web services are available on the Internet, and they typically provide very simple functionalities (such as conversions from postscript to PDF), without any commitment required on either the client or the service side (e.g., no guarantees and no payments). There are indeed a few contexts in which Web services are available and are used for e-commerce transactions, but this mostly happens within a closed community of business partners, so that these services (and, most of all, the description of their interface and conversation) are not publicly available.

On the other hand, Web-based commerce is now a mature area. There is a huge number of Web portals that enable B2B, B2C, and C2C business transactions. In particular, e-commerce Web portals often include "terms and conditions" documents that describe the semantics of many operations (in particular those that involve some form of commitment on the client's or provider's side). However, Web portals are oriented to humans, while Web services are oriented to applications. Nonetheless, we believe that by analyzing a Web portal it is possible to extrapolate what would be the behavior of an "equivalent" Web service. For example, by analyzing a Web site (such as `Travelocity.com`) and by understanding the operations it makes available via a browser as well as the semantics of such operations, we can extrapolate what would be the behavior of its dual "Web service".

2.2 An Embryonic Conversation Model

To perform this kind of reverse engineering analysis we needed a Web service description model, so that we could use it to abstract the Web service characteristics of a Web portal. However, we intentionally wanted a model that was very simple, so that it could help us start from a minimal base and progressively extend it as needed, as opposed to start from a rich model that included many possibly unnecessary features, thereby defeating our purpose of determining a "right-sized" Web service description model. A key ingredient of any service model is the interface definition language. For this, we simply use WSDL as a base, as it is now an accepted standard. Besides, WSDL is quite simple, and as such it suits our purposes. Another important aspect of a service is the *conversation* it supports, i.e., the set of acceptable message exchanges and the order in which they should occur. For this, we defined a very simple conversation model, with the idea of progressively extending it according to the requirements derived from the analysis of real applications.

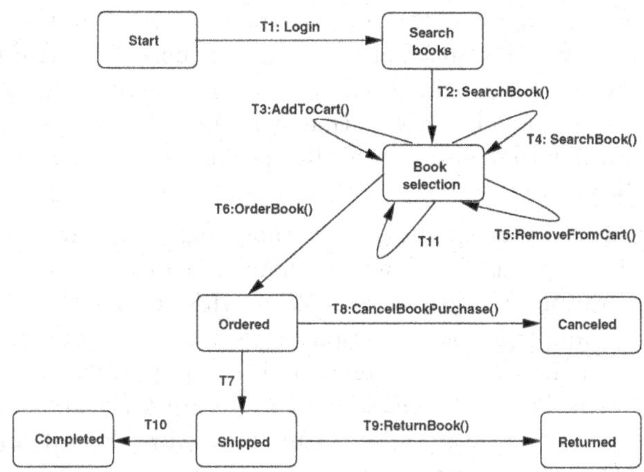

Fig. 1. The behaviour of `Amazon.com` as a Web service

The proposed embryonic conversation description model is based on the traditional state machine formalism, since it is simple, well known, and suited to describe reactive behaviors, which is the most relevant one as far as conversations are concerned (although, as we will see, other aspects of conversation behaviors need to be modeled as well). We assume that a conversation a Web service supports is modeled by a set of states and state transitions. States are labeled with a logical name, such as `logged_in`, `seat_reserved`, or `conversation_completed`. Transitions are labeled by service operations. When an operation `op` is invoked within a conversation that is in state `src`, then:

- if `src` has an output transition `tr` labeled with operation `op`, then the conversation moves into the destination state of `tr`,
- if `src` has no output transition labeled with operation `op`, then the conversation remains in state `src`.

This model is analogous to that of WSCL [10], although it is expressed through a state machine rather than a simplified version of UML activity diagrams, since we believe that state machines are better suited, for the reasons described above. In the following, we will use the term *conversation schema* to denote the specification of a conversation, while the term *conversation instance* will refer to an individual execution of a conversation between a service and a client. Figure 1 presents an example of a conversation schema supported by Web portal, namely `Amazon.com`, modeled with the formalism described above. Some transitions are unlabeled as they are not caused by explicit operation invocations. This is one of the indicators that this simple model is not enough, as anticipated, and that extensions are needed. The figure shows a slightly simplified version of the actual interfaces and conversations supported by the site, but this is solely for ease of presentation.

2.3 Discussions and Observations

In this section, we discuss the main lessons learned during the analysis of about twenty Web portals including `Amazon.com`, `Travelocity.com`, and `Expedia.com`. They will provide the basis for progressively extending the Web service conversation model in a way that it retains the same simplicity (to the possible extent), but that also allows the specification of the features that are really needed in practice.

Implicit and timed transitions. Most transitions between states occur due to explicit operation invocations. However, there are cases in which transitions occur without operation invocations, or at least without an explicit invocation by requesters. An example is the transition between states `Ordered` and `Shipped`. This transition occurs when the ordered books are physically shipped to the customer. An important type of *implicit transitions* are *timed transitions*. A timed transition occurs automatically after a time interval is elapsed since the transition is *enabled* (i.e., the conversation state is the transition's source state), or as a certain date and time is reached. As an example, flights on `Travelocity.com` can be put on hold for a period of time, or until midnight of the next day.

Compensation. In several Web portals we found operations (called *compensating* operations in the following) whose purpose is to semantically cancel the effects of other operations (called *forward* operations). For example, there are operations to cancel the purchase of a book or the reservation of a flight. Note that, unlike rollback in database transactions, "cancel the effects" here is meant from the perspective of the client. On the provider's side, executing forward operations and subsequently compensating them may indeed be very expensive in terms of money, time, and other resources. The execution of a compensation operation is typically allowed only within a certain time period. For example, this is how most online booksellers handle returns. Compensation may also have an associated cost (e.g., cancellation fee). Cost and time constraints are sometimes combined, so that the fee is charged only after a certain date and time, or after some time has elapsed from the execution of the forward (i.e., compensated) operation.

Resource locking. The execution of some operations seems to acquire (or, using database terminology, lock) some resources for the client. For example, flight reservation Web portals allow customers to hold seats on a plane. Analogously to compensations, resource reservation may be associated to a cost, and may have a validity limited in time, after which the resource is released.

Conditions and instance-specific properties. In some conversations, transitions may require that certain conditions be verified in order to be enabled. For example, some operations may only be available to "premium" customers. As another example, `Amazon.com` has the concept of "gold box", where special one-day discounts are offered to certain customers. Other aspects of a conversation may also be instance-specific. For example, the cancellation fee and the time constraint may vary depending on the client or on the kind of goods being purchased.

Multi-state enabled operations. Many operations can be executed in more than one state. In particular, most conversations have a subset of operations that can be executed at any time. For example, it is always possible to search for books or flights, without "loosing" previously done work (e.g., the content of the shopping cart). Another related observation is that, in many cases, the execution of such operations does not cause a state change.

3 Modeling Multiple Aspects of Web Service Conversations

The previous section has outlined many aspects to be included when specifying Web services, thereby paving the road for extending the embryonic model according to what appear to be the needs of service developers. We focus specifically on conversations, both because conversation modeling is one of the most interesting (and innovative) aspects of service descriptions, and because the discussion in the previous chapter has emphasized that many service properties are defined in the context of a conversation. In particular, we intend to provide two different contributions in this section: the first is to define an extensible conversation meta-model that enables the definition of conversation properties. The second is to identify specific properties, based on the analysis of the previous section. We observe that this analysis, being driven by and extrapolated from Web portal analysis, may be polarized towards certain classes of Web services and may not fully account for the requirements of applications that are more cross-organizational and loosely coupled in nature. A more comprehensive analysis will be possible only when the requirements of such Web services applications become better known.

3.1 Requirements for a Conversation Model

We start the description of the conversation model by characterizing the requirements for such a model, based on the findings discussed in the previous section as well as on the intended usage of the model.

Genericity: The model should provide a set of *horizontal* properties that can be used to expose the semantics of a service, so that the concepts and the supporting tools are generally applicable. As such, the semantics of the defined properties should go across domains. Transactionality is one such example. We are not interested in defining vertical (domain-specific) properties: this is the job of standardization consortia, and besides we do not have the required knowledge and expertise.

Automated support: While a main goal of the model is to provide human readable description of a service, our aim is also that of enabling the development of tools that provide automated conversation support. This also means that, although at the conceptual level the semantics of properties should be independent of any particular representation language, an agreed upon notation for representing properties is also essential. We will propose one such notation, which is also the one supported by the conversation management tool presented in Sect. 4.

Extensibility: While we have tried to identify the main properties in our Web portal analysis, there are other properties that we failed to recognize, or that may become relevant in the future. In addition, each vertical domain may recognize the need for adding more properties. Therefore, the model should be extensible in that it should allow the use of any identified property to describe a specific abstraction.

Relevance: As mentioned before, adding abstractions to models and primitives to languages is a delicate issue. In fact, while in general new abstractions may provide the benefits described above, they also make the model more complex. Therefore, the model should not contain artificial and complex abstractions that could have been thought as useful, and that may even be needed in some very rare occasion, but that are not actually used in practice. Indeed, we argue that the identification of properties should be based on the analysis of existing Web and business to business applications. The identified properties should provide the basis for an effective reasoning paradigm for understanding the behavior of service conversations (e.g., a composite service can reason about the transactional effect of one of its components on the overall service). Their use should benefit several automation activities of the service life cycle including services selection, composition, monitoring and management.

Compliance with Web services standards: The model should build upon the building blocks of XML and Web service concepts and standards (e.g., XML Schema, SOAP, WSDL, and UDDI).

3.2 Conversation Meta-model

The "skeleton" on which we base the proposed conversation model is essentially a state machine, just like in the embryonic model presented above. We have motivated earlier why state machines are an appropriate paradigm for defining the set of conversation supported by a service (although other analogous approaches are possible). State and transitions have the same meaning as those described earlier. However, we generalize the approach by enabling the association of several *descriptive properties* with transitions, to characterize when the transition should occur and what are its implications (e.g., transactional semantics). In addition to transition properties, we also characterize properties of the conversations as a whole. In particular, we have identified the following characterizations as being useful for both conceptually describing a conversation and for automatically supporting its execution:

Conversation objects. Service objects refer to service main information such as product sold by an e-commerce portal. In our model, we consider service requests (i.e., operation names and input parameters) and responses (i.e., output parameters) as conversation objects. This is compatible with the Web services model where users submit requests, whose structure (e.g., SOAP message) is represented according to service interfaces. As illustrated below, among other usages, service objects can be referenced in the pre-conditions of operation invocations (i.e., state transitions). In addition to service requests and responses, a service object may consist of an internal variable. Internal variables can represent service data items such as service-log (i.e., a variable that keeps a reference to the logged service invocations). They can also represent conversation-specific data items such as conversation instance identifier or the maximum number of operation invocations in a conversation instance.

Requester profiles. Requester profiles characterise users invoking operations. A requester profile consists of a set of attributes such as identity of user, purchase history, membership of a user to group(s) (e.g., `premier_member`), etc. Similarly to conversation objects, requester profiles may be used in the description of conversations (e.g., in pre-conditions of operation invocations).

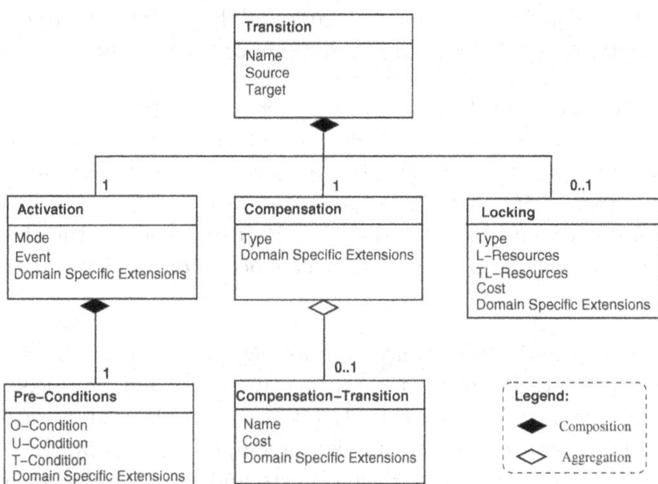

Fig. 2. UML Conceptual Model for Transition Properties

3.3 Transitions with Multiple Properties

In this section, we will describe transitions using our conversation description model. We discuss a list of properties that can be used to capture abstractions identified in Sect. 2.3. These properties consist of an initial set of abstractions that we have found to be useful and commonly needed in many practical situations, namely *description*, *activation*, *compensation*, and *locking* properties. The model is extensible in the sense that other properties may be defined and used.

The description property provides human-understandable description (e.g., textual or HTML document) about the Web service conversation. It also contains any information that is not easily formalized and can not be interpreted by an automated tool such as a conversation controller.

The conceptual model shown in Fig. 2 represents a UML static model for the different components that constitute the properties of a transition. Each property is described using a set of attributes. The model is also open to the extension of definitions of properties by adding new domain-specific attributes[1]. The remainder of this section gives details about the identified transition properties, namely *activation*, *compensation*, and *locking*.

Activation Property. This property allows to describe the triggering features of a transition. Besides the fact that a transition is activated by invoking an operation, an activation property specifies an *activation mode*, the *activation event* and *pre-conditions*. The activation mode indicates whether the triggering of the transition is *explicit* (`mode="user"`) or *implicit* (`mode="provider"`). When the activation mode is explicit, the transition is activated by explicitly invoking a service operation. In this case, the value of the attribute `event` is the name of the corresponding operation. When the activation mode is implicit, the value of the attribute event is a specification of a temporal event (i.e., the transition will occur automatically after the occurrence of this event). A pre-condition is a triple `(O-condition`, `U-condition`, and `T-condition)`, where:

- An `O-condition` specifies conditions on service objects.
- A `U-condition` specifies conditions on user profiles. It is used to specify the fact that an operation can be invoked by certain users (e.g., an operation is only available to `"premium"` customers).
- A `T-condition` specifies *temporal constraints* to allow the description of *timed* transitions (e.g., a transition can occur only within a certain time period).

A part of a pre-condition may be missing, in which case, the associated condition is `True`. An `O-condition` (respectively, `U-condition`) is a predicate or query over service objects (respectively, user profiles). It is satisfied if the predicate is `True` or the query result is not empty. We adopt XPath [11] as a language to express queries as service objects and user profiles are represented using XML.

The definitions of temporal constrains use XPath time functions (e.g., current time) and some pre-defined time functions in our model. A complete description of the temporal model, we use to specify temporal constraints, is outside the scope of this paper. In this section, we describe the constructs that are used to model timed transitions.

To keep track of beginning dates, termination dates, and number of invocations of transitions, we introduce the following functions: `beginT` and `endT`. `beginT(T)` (resp., `endT(T)`) denotes the beginning (resp., termination) date of

[1] Attributes named in Fig. 2 are cross-domain attributes.

the last invocation of the transition T within the same conversation instance. The conversation model features also the following temporal predicates:

- M-Invoke prescribes when an implicit transition must be automatically fired.
- C-Invoke prescribes a deadline or a time window within which a transition can be fired.
- L-Invoke prescribes the maximum number of invocations of a given transition within a time window.

M-Invoke is used to specify temporal events. C-Invoke and L-invoke are used to specify temporal pre-conditions of a transition. For the sake of simplicity, we assume that all temporal values (time instants, durations, and intervals) are expressed at the same level of granularity. Formally, a temporal constraint is specified as either Pred(op,d), where Pred $\in$ {M-Invoke, C-Invoke}, or L-Invoke(op,n,d1,d2). op is a comparison operator (e.g., $=$, $\leq$, and between) and d (resp., d1, and d2) is either an absolute time or a relative time (e.g., beginT(T)). The constraint M-Invoke(op,d) is only authorized for implicit transitions and means that the transition is automatically fired when the condition current-date op d is evaluated to True. Here, current-date denotes the system time. The constraint C-Invoke(op,d) means that the transition can be triggered only if the condition current-date op d is evaluated to True. The constraint L-Invoke(op,n,d1,d2) means that the transition can be invoked n times within the time interval [d1,d2]. In all the previous predicates, a time value can be expressed as a function on service object or user profiles attributes. This allows to cater for requirements such as the time constraint may vary depending on the client or on the kind of goods being purchased.

Let us consider the descriptions of the activation properties of the transitions T9 and T10 of Amazon.com example (see Fig. 1). The following XML code represents the descriptions of the respective activation properties.

```
<transition  name="T9"  source="Shipped"  target="Returned">
  <activation  mode="user"  event="ReturnBook">
    <pre-conditions  O-condition="True"
                     U-condition ="boolean(/user[@membership='gold'])"
                     T-condition="C-Invoke(<,end(T7) + 30 days)"/>
  </activation>
</transition>
<transition  name="T10"  source="Shipped"  target="Completed">
  <activation  mode="provider"  event="M-Invoke(>=, end(T7) + 30 days)">
    <pre-conditions  O-condition="True"  U-condition = "True"
                     T-condition="True"/>
  </activation>
</transition>
```

The transition T9 can be explicitly performed (mode="user") by invoking the operation ReturnBook within 30 days after the completion of the transition T7 by only "gold" customers. After this period of time, the transition T9 cannot be performed (constraint C-Invoke). However, the transition T10 is implicit (mode="provider"). This transition is automatically performed 30 days after the completion of the transition T7 (constraint M-Invoke).

Compensation Property. This property specifies the effect of a transition on the client state. With regard to this property, we distinguish the following types of transitions:

- *Effect-less* to denote a transition which has no effect on the client state. Cancelling this kind of transition does not require the execution of any particular operation. For example, the transition T2, carried out during the execution of the operation SearchBook(), do not have any effect on the client state. The cancellation of these transitions is implicit and does not require the execution of any particular operation.
- *Credential-disclosure* to denote a transition which has no effect on the client state from transactional point of view (e.g., the client is not going to make a payment), but client may be required to reveal certain credentials (e.g., postal address, credit card number) to the provider. In general, the release of these credentials is governed by privacy policies. We do not consider further this aspect as it is a challenging topic by its own. We assume here that cancellation of these kind of transitions is implicit and does not require the execution of any particular operation.
- *Definite* to denote a transition whose transactional effects are permanent (i.e., are not compensatable). For example, after the delivery of the purchased items, the Amazon.com service remains in the state shipping during 30 days, corresponding to the period of time where the user can, under certain conditions, returns the purchased items. After this period of time, the transition cannot be undone. This abstraction is conveyed by labeling the transition T10, for instance, as definite transition.
- *Compensatable* to denote a transition which has some effect on the client state but this effect can be undone by explicitly invoking a compensation operation. A compensatable transition is characterized by giving the name of the corresponding compensation transition and its cancellation cost. Similarly to time values in T-condition, values of cost attribute can be expressed as functions on service objects and user profiles. Consider, for instance, the transition T7. The effect of this transition consists of transferring money from the client bank account to the provider account. However, the effect of this transition can be (partially) undone (i.e., the client can be refunded) if the client decides to return the purchased items (operation ReturnBook()). The transition T8:CancelBookPurchase() can be used to compensate the transition T6:OrderBook().

The examples below illustrate the transactional properties of the transitions T6, T7, and T10 of Amazon.com example (see Fig. 1).

```
<transition  name="T6"  source="BookSelection"  target="Ordered">
  <transaction  type="Compensatable">
```

```
    <compensation-transition  name="T8"  cost="0"/>
  </transaction>
</transition>
<transition  name="T7"  source="Ordered"  target="Shipped">
  <transaction  type="Compensatable">
    <compensation-transition  name="T9"  cost="/books/book/price * 0.1"/>
  </transaction>
</transition>
<transition name="T10"  source="Shipped"  target="Completed">
  <transaction  type="Definite"/>
</transition>
```

The transitions `T6` and `T7` are `compensatable` and their effects can be respectively undone using the compensation transitions `T8` and `T9`. The effects of the transition `T10` cannot be undone (i.e., it is a `definite` transition).

Resource Locking Property. This property specifies temporary reservation of provider resources for a client when invoking a transition. We distinguish the following types of resource locking:

- *Lock* to denote that certain resources are locked for the client. A resource is a service object. The list of locked objects is specified by means of an XPath query.
- *Tentative-Lock* to denote that there is a tentative non-blocking reservation on certain resources. In fact, this kind of transitions is similar to the lightweight reservations in the *Tentative Hold Protocol*[2]. It allows several clients to place locks on the same item, and then once one client completes the purchase of the item the other clients receive notifications that their locks are no longer valid. An example of *Tentative-Lock* can be found in the travel arrangements domain. Some airlines companies allow travel agents to make flight reservations without effectively locking the seats until the tickets are paid. When the number of available seats in a given flight decreases, a warning is sent to the agents that have reservations in that flight. Whenever one flight becomes fully booked, the agents are notified that their reservations are no longer valid.

Information about the status of the resources is conveyed by the attribute `type` of the element `locking`. The locking type indicates whether some resources are locked (`type="L"`), some resources are on tentative lock (`type="TL"`), or both (`type="mixed"`), i.e., some resources are locked and others are on tentative lock. The attribute `L-resources` (respectively, `TL-resources`) is a query that specifies the resources to be locked (respectively, on tentative lock). Finally, the attribute `cost` indicates the cost of resources locking.

Assume that, in the example of Fig. 1, the transition `T7` locks the items that are in the shopping cart (i.e., purchased books) for which the price is above $100 at a cost of $10. In this case, the locking property is specified as follows:

[2] http://www.w3.org/TR/tenthold-1.

```
<transition name="T7" source="Ordered" target="Shipped">
  <locking type="L" L-resources="/books/book/price > 100"
           TL-resources="" cost="10"/>
</transition>
```

4 Automated Support for Conversation Management

In this section, we present the design and implementation of a tool called *conversation manager.* This tool is used to facilitate the creation, monitoring, and control of conversation life cycle operations. It is implemented as an extension of the SELF-SERV service development platform. A description of SELF-SERV prototype can be found in [9]. The prototype architecture (see Fig. 3) features a *service manager* and a *conversation manager.* These modules have been implemented using Java and the IBM Web Services Toolkit (WSTK) [12]. WSTK provides several components and tools for Web service development (e.g., UDDI, WSDL, and SOAP). Services communicate via (SOAP) messages. The implementation of the conversation manager is an ongoing effort. Here we describe an initial design and implementation of the conversation manager. The conversation manager consists of two modules, namely, *conversation builder* and *conversation controller.* Section 4.1 overviews the design of the conversation controller. Section 4.2 describes the creation and management of conversations using the conversation builder and conversation controller.

4.1 Conversation Controller: Overview

The conversation controller is essentially an extensible object attached to a service. It contains operational knowledge (e.g., conversation states). It also provides operations for monitoring conversations (e.g., triggering a transition). At run-time, a conversation controller is responsible for:

- Receiving service requests (i.e., SOAP request messages), determining if new conversation instances should be created, and removing conversation instances when they are no longer valid.
- Checking whether messages received and sent are in accordance with conversation definitions.
- Triggering transitions whenever all their pre-conditions are met.
- Tracing service executions.

The information required by a conversation controller to conduct the above tasks is extracted from the conversation definition and represented in the form of *control tables.* Control tables are associated to states. A control table of a state `S` is a set of rules of the form `E[C]/A` such that:

- `E` is an event of the form : (i) `explicit(op)`, meaning that an invocation of an operation `op` has been received, or (ii) `implicit(t)`, meaning that a temporal event `t` has occurred.

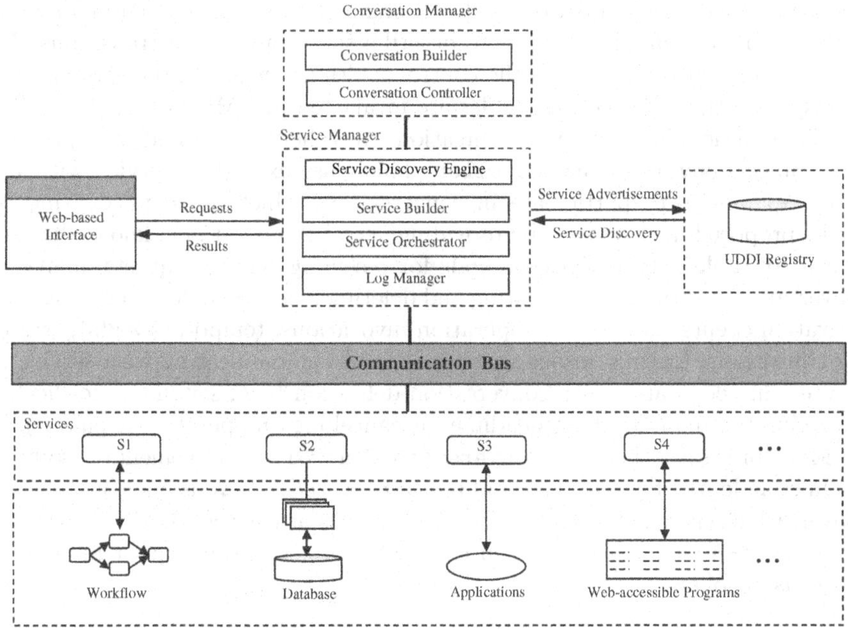

Fig. 3. Prototype Architecture

- `C` is a conjunction of conditions appearing in the pre-conditions clause of a transition (i.e., `O-condition`, `U-condition`, and `T-condition`).
- `A` is an action of the form `trigger(T)`, meaning that the transition `T` of the state `S` needs to be triggered. The triggering of a transition causes: (i) a state transition, meaning that the conversation controller marks the conversation instance as moved from the source state into the target state of the transition, and (ii) the invocation of the corresponding Web service operation[3].

Briefly, the basic semantics of a control table, is as follows: While at state `S` (i.e., state S is active), when one of the elements (i.e., one of the event) of the table is triggered, if its condition evaluates to true, the corresponding transition is activated. The control tables of a conversation are statically derived by analysing the activation properties of transitions. The detailed description of the generation algorithm is outside the scope of this paper due to space reasons.

4.2 Creating and Managing Conversations

The conversation builder assists providers to create conversation definitions and generate control tables. A conversation definition is edited through a visual interface and translated into an XML document for subsequent processing. The

[3] In the case of an implicit transition, the corresponding operation is an internal service operation.

visual interface offers an editor for describing a state machine diagram of a conversation. It also provides means to describe the properties of transitions. The conversation builder generates the control tables using the XML representation of a conversation. The control tables are formatted in XML as well.

The functionalities of the conversation controller are realised by a pre-built class called `ConversationController`. This class extends a service with pre-built capabilities to participate in conversations which are defined using the model proposed in this paper by providing access to operational knowledge such as control tables. It provides methods for receiving service requests, managing conversation instances (i.e., creating and deleting instances), detecting transition activation events (i.e., explicit operation invocations, temporal events), triggering transitions, tracing service executions, and communicating with service requesters in accordance with conversation definition (e.g., sending a notification informing the requester that deadline for cancelling an operation is passed).

More precisely, the class `ConversationController` implements a software module made up of a *container* and a *pool of objects*. There is one container per conversation schema. The container is a process that runs continuously, listening to service request messages. When the container receives a request message, it proceeds as follows[4]:

- If the message does not carry an existing conversation instance identifier (i.e., the conversation instance is unknown to the container because it is a new or expired conversation), a new controller object is created, and this object is given access to the conversation control tables. The task of handling the request message is delegated to this newly created object by invoking a method called `process_request` on it. The newly created object is temporarily added to the pool of objects so that it can handle subsequent messages related to the same conversation as they arrive.
- If on the other hand the container has previous knowledge about the conversation instance to which the request message relates, the message is forwarded to the controller object that was created when the first message related to that instance was received. This object is retrieved and the method `process_request` is invoked on it.

A service may participate in several conversations simultaneously. Each controller object in the pool is dedicated to a particular conversation instance, and processes all the incoming and outgoing messages related to that instance. By keeping track of the status of these requests and by having access to the relevant control tables, the controller object is able to check whether messages received and sent are in accordance with conversation definition and detect when should a given transition of the conversation be activated. When a controller object detects that a given transition needs to be activated, it sends an invocation message to the related service. Once the corresponding completion message is received, the object sends the response to the requester. The lifespan of a controller object

[4] Conversations are tracked in a similar manner as in WS-Coordination, i.e., we assume that SOAP Messages carry identifier of conversations in their headers.

is bound to the life span of the associated conversation. This means that, once the conversation expires (e.g., because of timeout), the associated controller object is no longer needed. The container removes the object from the pool and destroys it. It is worth-noting that the conversation controller relies on the log manager to trace conversation executions and interactions.

It should be noted that controller objects are different from service instances. Controller objects are responsible for managing conversation instances. Service instances are responsible for processing invocations to the service, initiating the service, collecting the outputs, and returning them back to controller objects that initiated the invocations. The messages exchanged between a controller object and a service instance are SOAP request/response messages. The `controller class` is provided by our system. A service provider only needs to download and install the class `ConversationController` in order to support the functionalities of the conversation controller (i.e., message correlation, conversation/messages conformance checking, etc). In fact, a service creator needs to provides only the business logic of the service. The class `ConversationController` shields the service creator from the implementation details of the functionalities of the conversation controller.

5 Related Work and Conclusions

In this paper, we argue that abstracting Web services in terms of generic properties that describe conversation behaviors (e.g., transactional semantics and temporal constraints), will benefit several automation activities in cross-organizational application integration.

Several ongoing efforts recognize the need to extend the current technological infrastructure for Web services in order to effectively support cross-organization application integration [8]. Emerging standards such as BPEL4WS [13], WSCI [14], WS-Coordination [15], and WS-Transaction [7], layer up functionality related to composition and transactions on top of the basic Web service standards such as SOAP, WSDL, and UDDI [5]. BPEL4WS is particularly related to the work presented in this paper since, in addition to proposing a model for composing Web services, it also presents a way for defining the conversations that a Web service supports. However, the conversation functionality provided by BPEL4WS is essentially driven from its composition nature: in other words, BPEL4WS has been primarily designed as a composition language, in which the same formalism used for composition (a process) can also be used for defining conversations. As such, many of the properties needed for defining conversations (such as activation and compensation properties) are missing from BPEL4WS. WS-Coordination and WS-Transaction are also related to the work presented in this paper since they deal with conversations, and in particular with transactional conversations. However, their goal is that of providing a framework through which conversation properties can be enforced, rather than providing a conversation model. Other efforts which aim at addressing issues related to reliable coordination and transactional execution of integrated services include the OASIS Business Transaction Protocol (BTP)[16]. In general, the focus in this area is on extending traditional transaction techniques to provide reliable and dependable execution of integrated services. In the context of Web service conversations,WSCL [10] builds upon WSDL to describe valid interactions that a service can support, but focuses only on choreography aspects (i.e., acceptable message exchanges and the order in which they should occur). Within the research community, a Web service middleware which is based on the notion of *transactional attitudes* was proposed in [17]. The middleware monitors and controls client transactions according to transactional capabilities of provider services. Finally, we mention that other complementary proposals such as [18, 19] focus on enhancing the descriptions of services with non-functional properties (e.g., quality of service).

Our work makes complementary contributions to the efforts mentioned above. Our approach builds upon the building blocks of Web standards and provide a framework for defining extensible conversation meta-model, to enable the description of generic abstractions such as temporal constraints and implications of service conversations. We presented a conceptual model for the identified abstractions. We derived most of the concepts of abstractions from the analysis of real e-commerce Web portals. We presented a conversation management tool that supports the identified abstractions.

References

1. Aissi, S., Malu, P., Srinivasan, K.: E-Business Process Modeling: The Next Big Step. IEEE Computer **35** (2002) 55–62
2. Benatallah, B., Casati, F., eds.: Special Issue on Web Services. Volume 12 of Distributed and Parallel Databases., Kluwer Academic Publishers (2002)
3. Bussler, C.: B2B Protocol Standards and their Role in Semantic B2B Integration Engines. IEEE Data Engineering Bulletin **24** (2001) 3–11
4. Weikum, G., ed.: Special Issue on Infrastructure for Advanced E-Services. Volume 24 of IEEE Data Engineering Bulletin., IEEE Computer Society (2001)
5. Curbera, F., Duftler, M., Khalaf, R., Nagy, W., Mukhi, N., Weerawarana, S.: Unraveling the Web Services Web: An Introduction to SOAP, WSDL, and UDDI. IEEE Internet Computing **6** (2002) 86–93
6. Cobb, E.E.: The Evolution of Distributed Component Architectures. In: Proceedings of the 9th International Conference on Cooperative Information Systems (CoopIS'01), Trento, Italy (2001)
7. Cabrera, F., Copeland, G., Cox, B., Freund, T., Klein, J., Storey, T., Thatte, S.: Web Services Transaction (WS-Transaction). `http://dev2dev.bea.com/techtrack/ws-transaction.jsp` (2002)
8. Papazoglou, M.P.: The World of e-Business: Web Services, Workflows, and Business Transactions. In: Proceedings of the CAiSE'02 International Workshop on Web Services, e-Business, and the Semantic Web (WES'02), Toronto, Canada (2002)
9. Sheng, Q.Z., Benatallah, B., Dumas, M., Mak, E.: SELF-SERV: A Platform for Rapid Composition of Web Services in a Peer-to-Peer Environment. In: Proceedings of the 28th Very Large Data Base Conference (VLDB'02), Hong Kong, China (2002)

10. Banerji, A., Bartolini, C., Beringer, D., Chopella, V., Govindarajan, K., Karp, A., Kuno, H., Lemon, M., Pogossiants, G., Sharma, S., Williams, S.: Web Services Conversation Language (WSCL). Note, W3C (2002) http://www.w3.org/TR/wscl10.
11. Clark, J., DeRose, S.: XML Path Language (XPath) Version 1.0. http://www.w3.org/TR/xpath (1999)
12. IBM WSTK Toolkit. (http://alphaworks.ibm.com/tech/webservicestoolkit)
13. Curbera, F., Goland, Y., Klein, J., Leymann, F., Roller, D., Thatte, S., Weerawarana, S.: Business Process Execution Language for Web Services (BPEL4WS). http://dev2dev.bea.com/techtrack/BPEL4WS.jsp (2002)
14. Arkin, A., Askary, S., Fordin, S., Jekeli, W., Kawaguchi, K., Orchard, D., Pogliani, S., Riemer, K., Struble, S., Takacsi-Nagy, P., Trickovic, I., Zimek, S.: Web Service Choreography Interface (WSCI). Note, W3C (2002) http://www.w3.org/TR/wsci.
15. Cabrera, F., Copeland, G., Freund, T., Klein, J., Langworthy, D., Orchard, D., Shewchuk, J., Storey, T.: Web Services Coordination (WS-Coordination). http://dev2dev.bea.com/techtrack/ws-coordination.jsp (2002)
16. OASIS Committee Specification: Business Transaction Protocol, version 1.0 (2002)
17. Mikalsen, T., Tai, S., Rouvellou, I.: Transactional Attitudes: Reliable Composition of Autonomous Web Services. In: Workshop on Dependable Middleware-based Systems (WDMS'02), Washington DC (2002)
18. Maximilien, E.M., Singh, M.P.: Conceptual Model of Web Service Reputation. SIGMOD Record **31** (2002)
19. O'Sullivan, J., Edmond, D., ter Hofstede, A.: What's in a Service? Distributed and Parallel Databases **12** (2002) 117–133

Management Applications of the Web Service Offerings Language (WSOL)

Vladimir Tosic, Bernard Pagurek, Kruti Patel, Babak Esfandiari, and Wei Ma

Department of Systems and Computer Engineering, Carleton University,
1125 Colonel By Drive, Ottawa, Ontario, K1S 5B6, Canada
{vladimir, bernie, kpatel, babak, weima} @ sce.carleton.ca

Abstract. We discuss possible Web Service Management (WSM) and Web Service Composition Management (WSCM) applications of the Web Service Offerings Language (WSOL) and how the language supports these applications. WSOL is a novel language for the formal specification of classes of service, various constraints (functional constraints, Quality of Service – QoS, and access rights), and management statements (subscription and pay-per-use prices, monetary penalties, and management responsibilities) for Web Services. Describing a Web Service in WSOL, in addition to the Web Services Description Language (WSDL), enables monitoring, metering, and management of Web Services. Metering of QoS metrics and evaluation of constraints can be the responsibility of the provider Web Service, the consumer, and/or one or more mutually trusted third parties (SOAP intermediaries or probes). Further, manipulation of classes of service (switching, deactivation/reactivation, and dynamic creation) can be used for dynamic (i.e., run-time) adaptation and management of Web Service compositions.

1 Introduction

The World Wide Web Consortium (W3C) defines a **Web Service** as "a software application identified by a URI, whose interfaces and binding are capable of being defined, described and discovered by XML artifacts and supports direct interactions with other software applications using XML based messages via Internet-based protocols" [1]. Here, URI means 'Uniform Resource Identifier' and XML means 'Extensible Markup Language'. The three main Web Service technologies are the SOAP protocol for XML messaging, the WSDL (Web Service Description Language) language, and the UDDI (Universal Description, Discovery, and Integration) directory.

When SOAP, WSDL, and UDDI were first published, we examined them to see how they support management activities. It was easy to conclude that these technologies needed significant additions to better support the management of Web Services and Web Service compositions. In particular, WSDL does not support specification of various constraints, management statements, classes of service, Service Level Agreements (SLAs) and other contracts between Web Services. Explicit, precise, and unam-

J. Eder and M. Missikoff (Eds.): CAiSE 2003, LNCS 2681, pp. 468–484, 2003.

biguous specification of such information is crucial for management activities [2, 3, 4]. Therefore, we have decided to develop our own XML language for this purpose and named this language the '**Web Service Offerings Language (WSOL)**'.

WSOL can be used for several purposes. For example, it can be used for selecting Web Services that are best for particular circumstances [2]. However, we are particularly interested in applications in the **Web Service Management (WSM)** and the **Web Service Composition Management (WSCM)**. WSM is the management of a particular Web Service or a group of Web Services within the same domain of management responsibility. On the other hand, WSCM is the management of Web Service compositions (a.k.a. orchestrations, choreographies, flows, networks). While there are important differences between WSM and WSCM [5], WSOL supports both WSM and WSCM. In this paper, we discuss possible WSM and WSCM applications of WSOL and how the language supports these applications.

In this section, we have introduced the general area of our research. In the next, we describe the main constructs and concepts of WSOL. In Section 3, we discuss applications of WSOL in the management of Web Services and how the language supports these applications. In Section 4, we examine how manipulation of WSOL service offerings can be used for dynamic adaptation and management of Web Service compositions. A brief overview of some recent related works is presented in Section 5. We summarize the conclusions and directions for future work in Section 6.

2 The Web Service Offerings Language (WSOL)

WSOL is a language for the formal specification of classes of service, various constraints, and management statements for Web Services. It is an XML-based language compatible with WSDL version 1.1. The syntax of WSOL is defined using XML Schema. In this section, we describe the main characteristics of WSOL, emphasizing those that are crucial for WSM and WSCM applications of WSOL.

The main **categories of constructs** in WSOL are:

1. service offerings,
2. constraints,
3. management statements,
4. reusability constructs, and
5. dynamic relationships between service offerings.

We summarize the main characteristics of these categories of constructs in the following five subsections. Precise syntax, illustrative examples, and discussion of the WSOL language constructs are given in [6] and, partially, in [2].

To verify the WSOL syntax, we have developed a **WSOL parser** called 'Premier' [6]. Its implementation is based on the Apache Xerces XML Java parser. This parser produces a DOM (Document Object Model) tree representation of WSOL files and reports eventual syntax errors and some semantic errors. We have also designed Java classes that will be the results of the compilation of WSOL files. We have not yet finished a code generator that creates the designed Java classes from DOM trees produced by our WSOL parser. A prototype WSOL compiler would then be a combination of the 'Premier' WSOL parser and this code generator.

2.1 Classes of Service and Service Offerings

When described in WSOL, a provider (supplier) Web Service can offer multiple classes of service to its consumers (requesters). By a '**class of service**' we mean a discrete variation of the complete service and quality of service (QoS) provided by one Web Service. Classes of service of one Web Service refer to the same functionality (i.e., the WSDL description), but differ in constraints and management statements. For example, they can differ in usage privileges, service priorities, response times guaranteed to consumers, verbosity of response information. The benefits of multiple classes of service per one Web Service are advocated in detail in [7].

We define a '**service offering**' in WSOL as a formal representation of a single class of service of one Web Service. Consequently, a service offering is a combination of formal representations of various constraints and management statements that determine the corresponding class of service. It can also be viewed as one contract or one SLA between the provider Web Service, the consumer, and eventual management third parties. A Web Service can offer multiple service offerings to its consumers, but a consumer can use only one of them at a time. WSOL service offerings are specified separately from the WSDL description of the Web Service. This enables dynamic creation, deactivation, and/or reactivation of service offerings without any modification of the underlying WSDL file. Figure 1 shows an example WSOL service offering. Descriptions of service offerings are usually long and complex, so we have shown in Figure 1 only example parts that will be discussed later in this paper.

2.2 Constraints and Expressions

In WSOL, every **constraint** is a Boolean expression that states some condition to be evaluated. The constraints can be evaluated before and/or after invocation of operations or at particular date/time instances. WSOL enables the formal specification of:

1. **Functional constraints**. These constraints define conditions that a functionally correct operation invocation must satisfy. They usually check some characteristics of message parts of the invoked operation. WSOL enables specification of pre-, post-, and future-conditions, as well as invariants. The novel concept of a future-condition [2], [5] is introduced to model conditions evaluated some time after the provider finishes execution of the requested operation and sends results to the consumer. It enables specification of operation effects that cannot be easily expressed with post-conditions. An example is delivery confirmation for goods bought using Web Services.
2. **QoS (non-functional, extra-functional) constraints**. These constraints describe properties such as performance, reliability, and availability. They check whether the monitored QoS metrics are within specified limits. They can be checked for a particular operation invocation or periodically, at specified times. For the specification

of QoS constraints, WSOL needs external ontologies of QoS metrics and measurement units. We have summarized requirements for such ontologies in [8]. In our current implementation of WSOL, we have simply assumed that ontologies of QoS metrics are collections of names with information about appropriate data types and measurement units. Similarly, ontologies of measurement units are simple collections of names without any additional information. A more appropriate definition of ontologies of QoS metrics, measurement units, as well as monetary units for price/penalty statements is planned for a future version of WSOL.

3. **Access rights**. An access right specifies conditions under which any consumer using the current service offering has the right to invoke a particular operation. If access is not explicitly allowed, it is forbidden. Access rights are used in WSOL for service differentiation. On the other hand, specification of conditions under which a particular consumer (or a class of consumers) may use a service offering and other security issues are outside the scope of WSOL.

```
<wsol:serviceOffering name= "SO1" service = "buyStock:
buyStockService" accountingParty = "WSOL-SUPPLIERWS" >
  <wsol:constraint name= "QoScons2" service = "WSOL-ANY"
portOrPortType = "WSOL-EVERY" operation = "WSOL-EVERY" >
    <expressionSchema:booleanExpression>
      <expressionSchema:arithmeticExpression>
        <expressionSchema:QoSmetric metricType=
"QoSMetricOntology:ResponseTime" service = "WSOL-ANY"
portOrPortType = "WSOL-ANY" operation = "WSOL-ANY"
measuredBy = "WSOL_INTERNAL" />
      </expressionSchema:arithmeticExpression>
      <expressionSchema:arithmeticComparator type= "&lt;" />
      <expressionSchema:arithmeticExpression>
        <wsol:numberWithUnitConstant>
          <wsol:value>0.3</wsol:value>
          <wsol:unit type= "QoSMeasOntology:second " />
        </wsol:numberWithUnitConstant>
      </expressionSchema:arithmeticExpression>
    </expressionSchema:booleanExpression>
  </wsol:constraint>
  ...
  <wsol:managementResponsibility  name= "MangResp1" >
    <wsol:supplierResponsibility scope= "tns:AccRght1" />
    <wsol:consumerResponsibility scope= "tns:Precond3" />
    <wsol:independentResponsibility scope= "tns:QoScons2"
entity = "http://www.someThirdParty.com" />
  </wsol:managementResponsibility>
</wsol:serviceOffering>
```

Fig. 1. Parts of an Example WSOL Service Offering

WSOL constraints are defined using the <*constraint*> element, which is independent of particular types of constraint. The *type* attribute of the <*constraint*> element refers to the XML schema defining a particular type of constraint. We have defined XML schemas for the above-mentioned types of constraint. Using the XML Schema mechanisms, additional types of constraint can be defined. An example WSOL constraint, the QoS constraint '*QoScons2*', is shown in Figure 1. This QoS constraint contains a comparison of a measured QoS metric '*ResponseTime*' and the constant '*0.3 second*'. It is evaluated for every operation of the '*buyStockService*' Web Service. The '*measuredBy*' attribute states that the QoS metric is measured by the same entity that evaluates this QoS constraint.

Boolean expressions in constraints can contain standard Boolean operators (AND, OR, NOT, IMPLIES, EQUIVALENT), references to operation message parts of type Boolean, and comparisons of arithmetic, string, date/time, or duration expressions. WSOL also supports checking operation message parts that are arrays (of any data type) using quantifiers ForAll and Exists. Arithmetic expressions can contain standard arithmetic operators (+, -, unary -, *, /, **), arithmetic constants, and references to operation message parts of numeric data types. WSOL provides only basic built-in support for string and date/time/duration expressions. In addition, it is possible to perform external operation calls in any expression. Here, 'external' means 'outside the Web Service for which the constraint is specified'. These external operations can be implemented by other Web Services or they can be implemented by the management entities evaluating the given constraint. In the latter case, although these external operations are described with WSDL, they are invoked using internal mechanisms, without any SOAP call.

2.3 Management Statements

A WSOL **statement** is any construct, other than a constraint, that states some important management information about the represented class of service. WSOL enables formal specification of several management statements:

1. subscription price statements,
2. pay-per-use price statements,
3. monetary penalty statements, and
4. management responsibility statements.

In addition, WSOL has the general <*statement*> element for the specification of additional statements. It is analogous to the general <*constraint*> element.

Price statements specify the price that a consumer using the particular service offering has to pay for successful use of the Web Service. A service offering can contain subscription price statements and/or pay-per-use price statements. A **subscription price statement** specifies the monetary amount a consumer pays for using this service offering during some period. A **pay-per-use price statement** states the monetary amount a consumer pays for invoking particular operation. **Penalty statements** specify the monetary amount that the Web Service has to pay to a consumer if the consumer invokes some operation and the Web Service does not fulfil all constraints in the service offering. A **management responsibility statement** specifies what entity has the responsibility for checking a particular constraint, a constraint group, or the complete service offering. A management entity can be the provider Web Service, the consumer, or an independent third party trusted by both the provider and the consumer [9]. Figure 1 shows an example WSOL management responsibility statement, '*MangResp1*'. In this example, the provider (supplier) Web Service evaluates the access right *'AccRght1'*, the consumer evaluates the pre-condition *'Precond3'*, and a third party evaluates the QoS constraint *'QoScons2'*.

2.4 Reusability Constructs and the Syntax of Service Offerings

The WSOL reusability constructs enable easier specification of new service offerings, constraints, or management statements from existing ones. WSOL has a number of reusability constructs:
1. constraint groups (CGs),
2. inclusion statements,
3. constraint group templates (CGTs),
4. template instantiation statements, and
5. declarations of external operation calls.

A **constraint group (CG)** is a named set of constraints and/or statements. Arbitrary levels of nesting of CGs are allowed. When a new CG is defined and some of the contained constraints, statements, and CGs have been already defined elsewhere, there is no need to define them again. They can simply be included into the new containing CG using the WSOL **inclusion statements**. On the other hand, new constraints, statements, and CGs can also be defined inside a containing CG. A new CG can be defined as an extension of an existing CG, inheriting all constraints, statements, and nested CGs and defining some additional ones. A **constraint group template (CGT)** is a parameterized CG. At the beginning of a CGT, one defines one or more abstract CGT parameters, each of which has a name and a type. Definition of parameters is followed by definition or inclusion of constraints, statements, and nested CGs in the same way as for CGs. Constraints inside a CGT can contain expressions with CGT parameters. A CGT is instantiated when concrete values are supplied for all CGT parameters in a **template instantiation statement**. One CGT can be instantiated many times with different parameter values. The result of every such instantiation is a new CG. The concept of a CGT in WSOL is a very powerful specification mechanism. Many classes of service contain constraints with the same structure, but with different constant values. In our opinion, it is an even more important specification concept than the extension (single inheritance) of CGs, CGTs, and service offerings. A **declaration of an external operation call** is used to enable referencing results of the same external operation call in several related constraints.

Syntactically, a WSOL **service offering** is similar to a CG. It is a set of defined or included constraints, statements, and CGs (including instantiations of CGTs) that all refer to the same Web Service. WSOL supports extension (single inheritance) of service offerings, similarly to the extension of CGs and CGTs. However, service offerings must not be nested. Another syntactic difference is that every service offering has exactly one accounting party, specified in a special attribute, *'accountingParty'*, of the *<serviceOffering>* element and not in management responsibility statements. The accounting party is a special management party responsible for keeping track of the use of the provider Web Service and management third parties, as well as what constraints were satisfied and what were not. While it is syntactically similar to a CG, a service offering has special run-time characteristics. For example, consumers can choose and use service offerings, not CGs. In addition, dynamic relationships can be specified only for service offerings, not for CGs. Figure 1 shows an example WSOL service offering. Its parts were discussed in subsections 2.2 and 2.3.

2.5 Dynamic Relationships between Service Offerings (SODRs)

Dynamic relationships between service offerings (a.k.a. **service offerings dynamic relationships – SODRs**) are those that can change during run-time, e.g., after dynamic creation of a new class of service. For example, one **SODR** can state what class of service could be an appropriate replacement if a particular constraint from some other class of service cannot be met. Such relationships should not be built into definitions of service offerings, to avoid frequent modification of these definitions. On the other hand, **static relationships between service offerings** are those that are built into definitions of service offerings and do not change during run-time. Two important examples of such relationships are inheritance of service offerings and instantiation of the same CGT with different parameter values. Both static and dynamic relationships between service offerings are useful for easier selection and negotiation of service offerings. In addition, dynamic relationships are very useful for dynamic adaptation of Web Service compositions discussed in Section 4.

After researching several alternatives, we have decided to represent SODRs as triples <*SO1, S, SO2*> where:

1. *SO1* is the used service offering,
2. *S* is the set of constraints and/or CGs from SO1 that are not satisfied (a CG is not satisfied if at least one of its constraints or nested CGs is not satisfied); and
3. *SO2* is the appropriate replacement service offering.

These triples are specified in a special XML format outside definitions of service offerings (often in special files) to make their evolution independent from the evolution of other characteristics of a service offering. However, the XML format for the specification of these triples is an integral part of the WSOL language. It is built upon the WSOL concepts of a constraint and a CG, as well as WSOL solutions for naming of constraints, CGs, and service offerings. We are also considering an extension of this XML format so that *S* could also contain arbitrary WSOL Boolean expressions. This would enable specification of complex relationships between the unsatisfied constraints and CGs, as well as using external operation calls.

3 Applications of WSOL for Web Service Management

In addition to the WSOL language, we are developing the corresponding management infrastructure and management algorithms. Appropriate specification of management information, such as WSOL constraints and management statements, is the key for successful management activities. Functional constraints can help in determining whether a Web Service behaves correctly. Consequently, they are useful in fault man-

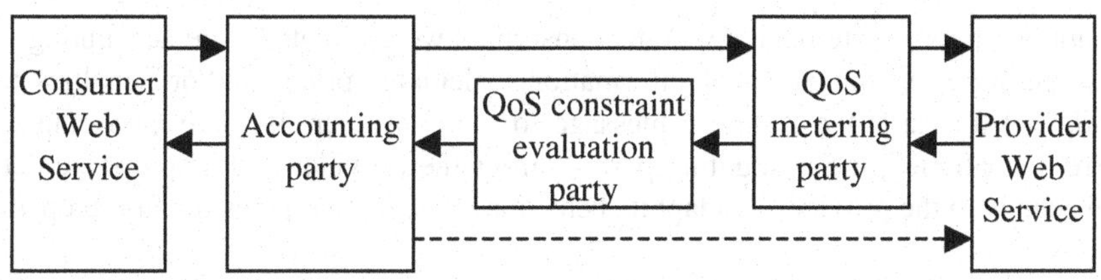

Fig. 2. An example configuration of management third parties as SOAP intermediaries

agement. Formal and precise specification of QoS constraints is the basis for monitoring and metering of QoS metrics. It prescribes which QoS metrics to monitor, where and how to do this monitoring, how to eventually calculate aggregate QoS metrics, what the expected values of QoS metrics are. Consequently, formal and precise specification of QoS constraints is particularly useful in performance management. Access rights limit access to operations and ports of a Web Service. While WSOL access rights are used primarily for service differentiation, they could also be a part of a comprehensive security management solution for Web Services. Statements about prices and monetary penalties are invaluable in accounting management. WSOL service offerings are precise and complete enough to serve as simple contracts or SLAs for Web Service monitoring, metering, control, accounting, and billing. Further, dynamic (i.e., run-time) manipulation of service offerings, discussed in the next section, is a useful tool for both Web Service Management (WSM) and Web Service Composition Management (WSCM).

Figure 2 shows an example configuration of management third parties as **SOAP intermediaries**. In this example, only QoS constraints are evaluated and distinction is made between the accounting party, the QoS metering party, and the QoS constraint evaluation party. When a consumer submits a request for executing a provider's operation, the management third parties are organized as SOAP intermediaries for the request, as well as the eventual response message. The request from the consumer to the provider first goes through the accounting party, which logs that the request has been made. The request is then forwarded to the QoS metering party, which performs necessary activities. For example, for metering response time the QoS metering party logs the time that will be considered as the beginning time of the operation invocation. Next, the request message is forwarded to the provider Web Service, which performs the requested operation and sends the response message. The response message first goes through the QoS metering party. In the response time measurement example, the QoS metering party logs the time that will be considered as the ending time of the operation invocation and subtracts from it the logged beginning time. The information about the measured QoS metrics can be transferred to the QoS constraint evaluation party along with the original response message from the provider. One way to piggyback this information is to use SOAP headers. The QoS constraint evaluation party receives the response message and the information about the measured QoS metrics and evaluates appropriate constraints. It forwards to the accounting party the response message together with the information whether the evaluated constraints were satisfied or not and appropriate details if some constraints were violated. The accounting party logs the received management information, calculates prices and/or penalties to be paid, and forwards the response message to the consumer. If some QoS constraints were not satisfied, the accounting party notifies the provider with appropriate details. This can help the provider to adapt its behavior to meet guarantees for future operation requests.

Note that the discussed example is only one possible way to use WSOL for WSM. There are other management scenarios that can be accommodated with WSOL. For example, some QoS metrics, such as availability, can be measured using probing instead of message interception. WSOL supports this by modeling **probing entities** as separate Web Services that provide results of their measurements through operations of some agreed-upon interfaces. These operations can be invoked in appropriate QoS constraints in WSOL service offerings, using the WSOL external operation call mechanism. Further, to reduce overhead, some QoS constraints can be evaluated **periodically**, either for randomly selected operation invocations (on average: 1 in n) or at particular date/time instances. Also note that often there is no need to have a large number of specialized third parties. The overhead can in the above example is reduced when instead of three separate parties for accounting, QoS metering, and evaluation of QoS constraints, only one third party with all these functions is used. It is also possible to put all these functions into the provider Web Service, reducing the overhead further. However, in such a case, the consumer has to trust the provider.

We have designed a WSOL management infrastructure supporting evaluation of WSOL constraints, metering and calculation of used QoS metrics, and accounting of executed operations and evaluated WSOL constraints. The design of this infrastructure and, particularly, its proof-of-concept prototype implementation are based on extensions of Apache Axis (Apache eXtensible Interaction System) [10], a popular open-source SOAP engine. A SOAP engine is an application that receives, processes, and sends SOAP messages. Axis has several good features that we found crucial for our WSOL management infrastructure. Here we emphasize the two most important. First, Axis has a modular, flexible, and extensible architecture based on configurable chains of pluggable SOAP message processing components, called handlers. Such architecture enables implementing our WSOL management infrastructure as a set of additional handlers and handler chains plugged into Axis easily. Second, Axis defines a SOAP message processing node that can be used for provider Web Services, consumer Web Services, and SOAP intermediaries. Consequently, it can be used for all WSOL management parties.

The design and prototype implementation of our WSOL management infrastructure will be discussed in detail in a forthcoming publication. Here we outline the main concepts. An Axis handler [10] can process the input, the output, or the fault SOAP message. It can alter the SOAP message—e.g., add/remove headers—or perform some other message processing—e.g., measurement of QoS metrics. Consequently, we implement metering and calculation of QoS metrics, evaluation of WSOL constraints, and accounting inside specialized Axis handlers that we have developed. We have designed these handlers so that a WSOL compiler can generate them automatically from WSOL files. However, since our prototype WSOL compiler is not yet fully im-

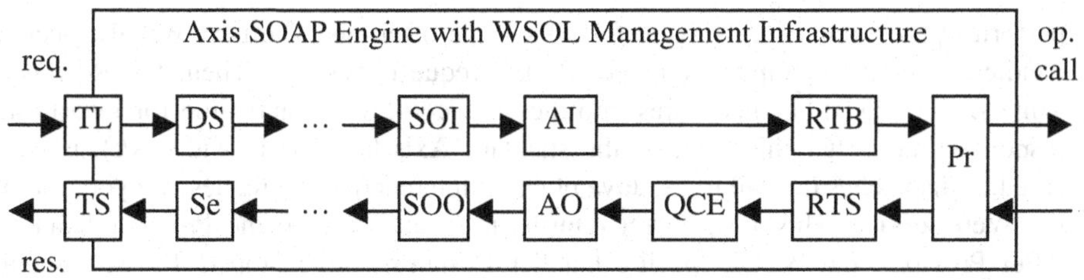

Fig. 3. An Example Configuration of Handlers inside the Provider-side Axis SOAP Engine with WSOL Management Infrastructure

plemented, we have manually implemented some of these handlers in our prototype WSOL management infrastructure.

The crucial Axis data structure passed between handlers is the message context [10]. It contains information about the request message, the response message, and a bag of properties. The message context properties determine how handlers process the message and can be modified by handlers. We transport WSOL information between WSOL-specific Axis handlers in special properties of the message context. For WSOL information transported in SOAP headers between management parties, translation between SOAP headers and Axis message context properties is provided. In addition to the special message context properties, we have also developed data structures for storing descriptions of WSOL constructs and the actual measured or computed data. Examples of stored data are values of QoS metrics and the information whether a constraint is satisfied or not. We use this data for accounting and for determining whether dynamic adaptation, discussed in the next section, is needed.

An Axis chain [10] is an ordered, pipelined collection of handlers. There are tree types of chain in Axis. A transport chain performs processing related to the transport of SOAP messages. A global chain performs other processing applicable to all Web Services. A service chain performs processing characteristic for a particular Web Service. Since processing of WSOL constraints and management statements differs between service offerings of the same Web Service, we could have introduced the fourth type of chain – a 'service offering chain'. For simplicity, we have put all WSOL-related handlers into service chains, but added some program code deciding what handlers are executed in particular cases.

In Figure 3, we have shown an example configuration of handlers inside the provider-side Axis SOAP engine extended with WSOL management infrastructure. The example is analogous to the example in Figure 2, but in Figure 3 all shown modules are parts of the provider Web Service. In other words, the provider Web Service measures response time, evaluates a QoS constraint limiting response time, and performs accounting. The Transport Listener (TL) component of Axis receives the request SOAP message and passes it to the standard Axis handler called Deserializer (DS), which creates a message context instance used by other handlers. After Deserializer, several other standard Axis handlers are executed, not shown in Figure 3. The first WSOL-specific handler in the input flow is Service Offering Input (SOI), which performs processing characteristic for all service offerings. The next WSOL-specific handler, Accounting Input (AI), records the request message. Then, the Response Time Begin (RTB) handler stores into message context the start time for measuring response time. After this handler, the standard Axis handler, Provider (Pr), is executed. It dispatches the call to the Java object implementing the requested operation of the Web Service. This Java object returns its results back to the Provider handler. After Provider, the WSOL-specific handler Response Time Stop (RTS) stores into message context the stop time for measuring response time, as well as the difference between this stop time and the start time stored by RTB. The QoS constraint limiting response time is evaluated in the WSOL-specific handler QoS Constraint Evaluation (QCE). This handler stores its results into the message context. The Accounting Output (AO) handler uses the information from the message context to calculate prices and eventual penalties to be paid. The last WSOL-specific handler in the output flow is Service Offering Output (SOO), which performs characteristic for all service offerings. After this handler, some standard Axis handlers, not shown in Figure 3, are executed. The last of these handlers is Serializer (Se), which packs information from the message context instance into SOAP. The Transport Sender (TS) component of Axis sends the response SOAP message to the consumer. The information about the measured response time, the evaluated constraint, and eventual prices or penalties to be paid is in the SOAP header.

While the evaluation of periodic constraints differs from the example illustrated in Figure 3, it is also supported by our WSOL management infrastructure. Timer, a special active object in our infrastructure, initiates evaluation of periodic constraints and measurement or calculation of periodic QoS metrics. The processing is done in one or more modules, similar to Axis handlers. The results of such evaluation, measurement, or calculation can be stored locally for future processing. They can also be reported to other management parties in a special notification SOAP message.

4 Applications of WSOL for Web Service Composition Management

We are also investigating management and dynamic adaptation of Web Service compositions without breaking an existing relationship between a provider Web service and its consumer. To achieve this goal we are exploring management and dynamic adaptation mechanisms that are based on the manipulation of service offerings in WSOL. Our dynamic adaptation mechanisms include switching between service offerings, deactivation/reactivation of existing service offerings, and creation of new service offerings. These mechanisms can be used between operation invocations that are part of the same transactions or session. The crucial language support for these mechanisms is the specification of dynamic relationships between service offerings (SODRs), discussed in Subsection 2.6.

Dynamic switching between service offerings can be initiated by a provider Web Service or its consumer. The consumer can initiate it to dynamically adapt the service it receives without finding another Web service. The provider Web Services can initiate it to gracefully upgrade or degrade its service and/or QoS in case of changes.

Deactivation and reactivation of service offerings is used by a Web service in cases when changes in operational circumstances affect what service offerings it can provide to consumers. When a change of circumstances occurs, a Web service can dynamically and automatically deactivate service offerings that cannot be supported in the new circumstances. The affected consumers are switched to an appropriate replacement service offering and notified about the change. If there is no appropriate replacement service offering, an alternative provider Web Service has to be sought. The deactivated service offering may be reactivated automatically at a later time after another change of circumstances and, eventually, the consumers can be automatically switched back to their original service offering and notified about the change.

Dynamic creation of new service offerings can be used when there has been a change in the Web Services implementation (e.g., in case of dynamic versioning/evolution) or the execution environment. To some limited extent, it can also be performed on demand of important consumers. It then becomes a substitute for negotiation of a custom-made contract or SLA between Web Services. Note that dynamic creation of new service offerings can be non-trivial and incur non-negligible overhead. Therefore, we use it only in exceptional circumstances.

Deactivation, reactivation, and dynamic creation of service offerings can be followed by appropriate deactivation, reactivation, or creation of SODRs.

Compared to finding alternative Web Services (i.e., rebinding of Web Service compositions), these three dynamic adaptation mechanisms enable faster and simpler adaptation and enhance robustness of the relationship between a Web Service and its consumer. These capabilities are relatively simple and incur relatively low overhead, while providing additional flexibility. (Dynamic composition of new service offerings can be an exception for the previous statement.) However, compared to finding alternative Web Services, these dynamic adaptation mechanisms have limitations. Service offerings of one Web Service differ only in constraints and management statements, which might not be enough for adaptation. Further, appropriate alternative service offerings cannot always be found or created. Therefore, manipulation of service offerings is a complement to, and not a complete replacement for, finding alternative Web Services. The first step in dynamic adaptation of a Web Service composition should be to try to find a replacement service offering from the same Web Service. If this is not possible, only the second step should be to try to find a replacement Web Service and perform re-composition. In some cases, the used provider Web Service can provision a temporary replacement service offering while the consumer searches for another, more appropriate, Web Service.

We have integrated the support for these dynamic adaptation mechanisms into our WSOL management infrastructure, discussed in the previous section. Hereafter, we denote the parts of our WSOL management infrastructure that support dynamic adaptation mechanisms as 'WSCM modules'. WSCM modules are usually parts of the provider-side WSOL management infrastructure, but some can also be used in consumers and third parties. While our WSCM modules are not based on the functionality provided in Apache Axis, they use the same data structures as our extensions for accounting of executed operations and evaluated WSOL constraints. These data structures store information such as which constraints or CGs were satisfied or unsatisfied. This information is used in determining whether the provider Web Service should switch a consumer to a more appropriate service offering and maybe even deactivate a service offering that can no longer be fulfilled. In addition, data structures in our WSCM modules store descriptions of SODRs and supplementary information, such as what service offerings are active or deactivated and what consumers use particular service offerings. This information is used in determining what service offering is the best candidate for switching to and in handling of affected consumers.

We have designed algorithms for autonomous (i.e., without external intervention) provider-side switching, deactivation, and reactivation of service offerings, and deactivation and reactivation of SODRs. These algorithms are executed in a provider-side WSOL management infrastructure when certain conditions are met. They use the data structures mentioned above. Currently, we have only rudimentary support for dynamic creation of service offerings and SODRs.

On the other hand, consumers can also initiate switching of service offerings and, in theory, creation of service offerings. Further, it is useful to enable that selected external WSCM entities (human administrators or specialized software) can have access to our dynamic adaptation mechanisms. Therefore, we expose these mechanisms as operations of the special 'service offering management (SOM)' port of every Web Service. While we suggest that every WSOL-enabled Web Service provide the SOM port, some or all Web Services of the same vendor (e.g., Web Services using the same SOAP engine instance) can share the actual implementation of its operations. The SOM port contains operations for switching, activation, deactivation, and creation of service offerings and for activation, deactivation, and creation of SODRs. However, it also contains some other operations that are crucial for WSOL-enabled Web Services. One example is the operation that returns a WSOL file with descriptions of all service offering available to a particular consumer. A similar operation returns a WSOL file with descriptions of all relevant SODRs. Another example is the input-only operation that a third-party accounting party uses to inform the provider Web Service about the values of metered or calculated QoS metrics, evaluated WSOL constraints, and their monetary consequences. Note again that only selected external entities are allowed access to the majority of operations in the SOM port. We will discuss the SOM port in detail in a forthcoming publication.

5 Related Work

Our work on WSOL draws from the considerable previous work on differentiated classes of service and formal representation of various constraints in other areas (e.g., [11]). At the beginning of our research, there was no relevant work of this kind for Web Services. In parallel with our research, several related works emerged.

The most important related works to WSOL are the two recent languages for formal XML-based specification of custom-made SLAs for Web Service: the **Web Service Level Agreements (WSLA)** [4, 9] from IBM and the HP work on the formal specification of Web Service SLAs [3, 12]. The latter work seems to be part of the HP's **Web Service Management Language (WSML)**. SLAs in these two languages contain QoS constraints and management information. Both WSLA and WSML are oriented towards management applications in inter-enterprise scenarios. It seems that they assume existence of some measurement and management infrastructure at both ends. This is a different assumption from the one that we have adopted for WSOL. Further, these languages specify more detail for QoS constraints than WSOL and specify custom-made SLAs, not classes of service. In these aspects, they are more powerful than WSOL. It seems that this results in higher run-time overhead than the overhead of the simpler WSOL. These languages are accompanied by appropriate management infrastructures [9, 12]. These infrastructures are more powerful, but also more complex, than the infrastructure we are developing for WSOL. Both WSLA and WSML have some support for templates, but only at the level of an SLA, not its parts. They do not have support for inheritance and the other reusability constructs present in WSOL. Contrary to WSOL, these languages do not address formal specification of functional constraints, access rights, and other constraints. To conclude, while both WSLA and WSML are very good languages for their domain and purpose, they do not address all the issues that WSOL does.

Another recent related work is **WS-Policy** [13] – a general framework for the specification of policies for Web Services. A policy can be any property of a Web Service or its parts, so it corresponds to WSOL concepts of a constraint and a management statement. WS-Policy is only a general framework, while the details of the specification of particular categories of policies will be defined in specialized languages. The only such specialized language currently developed is WS-SecurityPolicy. WS-PolicyAssertions can be used for the formal specification of functional constraints, but the contained expressions can be specified in any language. It is not clear whether and when some specialized languages for the specification of QoS policies, prices/penalties, and other management issues will be developed. Another set of issues is where, when, and how are WS-Policy policies monitored and evaluated. WS-Policy has a number of good features, such as flexibility, extensibility, and reusability. However, some of the advantages of WSOL are the explicit support for management applications, built-in support for various constraints and management statements, unified representation of expressions, wider range of reusability constructs, and specification of classes of service and relationships between them.

Further, the **DAML-S (DAML-Services)** [14] community works on semantic descriptions of Web Services, including specification of some functional and some QoS constraints. However, constraints in DAML-S are not currently specified in a precise, formal, and detailed notation, as in WSOL. They are only placeholders for the future description of rules. In addition, they are specified for a more comprehensive service description, not for the actual control and management. These are two major differences between DAML-S and WSOL. While DAML-S has the concept of a service profile, there is no concept of a class of service and no specification of dynamic relationships. Consequently, we find that WSOL has a clear advantage in Web Service Management and Web Service Composition Management.

Apart from these recent works that partially address similar issues to WSOL, there are several other resent works that recognize the importance of the formal specification of various constraints, SLAs, and contracts for Web Services and special types of Web Service (such as Grid Services and Semantic Web enabled Web Services). In [2], we concluded that the unique characteristics of WSOL, compared to the recent related works, are its **expressive power**, **mechanisms for reduction of run-time overhead**, and **support for management applications**.

6 Conclusions and Future Work

WSOL supports management applications with:

1. the formal and unambiguous specification of various constraints, statements about prices and monetary penalties, and management responsibility statements;
2. the possibility to specify management third parties in management responsibility statements, in the '*measuredBy*' attribute of QoS metrics, and in external operation calls to management third parties that act as probes;
3. the explicit specification of accounting parties (specific management parties); and
4. the built-in format for the specification of dynamic relationships between service offerings (SODRs).

WSOL can be used for both Web Service Management (WSM) and Web Service Composition Management (WSCM). WSOL service offerings can serve as simple contracts or SLAs for Web Service monitoring, metering, control, accounting, and billing. They can be metered and evaluated by the provider Web Service, the consumer, and/or one or more mutually trusted third parties (SOAP intermediaries or probes). Manipulation of service offerings can be used as a lightweight complement and addition to rebinding of Web Service compositions.

Several recent related works—WSLA, WSML, and WS-Policy—address issues that partially overlap with WSOL. In some aspects, they are more powerful than WSOL. However, WSOL also has its advantages, such as classes of service, SODRs, reusability constructs, and relative simplicity and lightweightness. An integration of WSLA, WSML, WS-Policy, and WSOL would benefit WSM and WSCM.

While WSOL can be improved in several ways, we consider the language relatively complete and stable. We direct our research efforts mainly towards the further development of the WSOL management infrastructure, its prototype implementation, and the research of WSOL applications in WSCM. We have set up an experimental computer network on which we run in parallel multiple Web Service compositions. In this environment, we are experimenting with WSCM both with and without WSOL. For example, in some experiments we compare switching of service offerings with replacing a deactivated Web Service with its equivalent found in a local UDDI directory. We want to gain more precise understanding of the management applicability and boundaries of WSOL. We also trying to uncover and clarify the most important issues for the future management-related research using WSOL. We will describe the results of such experiments in a forthcoming publication, along with further details about the WSOL management infrastructure and its prototype.

We have left some important areas for future work. One of them is discovery and selection of WSOL service offerings. We have to address the integration of WSOL into UDDI to enable discovery of WSOL service offerings. Further, we believe that static and dynamic relationships between service offerings can be very useful for comparing similar service offerings in the process of negotiation and selection. More research in this area is needed. Another important area is security. WSOL could be used with security technologies for Web Services. For example, different keys could be used for encryption of the message body and various QoS measurements and constraint evaluation results, so that only relevant management parties would see them.

References

1. World Wide Web Consortium (W3C): Web Services Description Requirements. W3C Working Draft 28 October 2002. On-line at: http://www.w3.org/TR/2002/WD-ws-desc-reqs-20021028/ (2002)
2. Tosic, V., Pagurek, B., Patel, K.: WSOL – A Language for the Formal Specification of Various Constraints and Classes of Service for Web Services. Res. Rep. OCIECE-02-06. Ottawa-Carleton Institute for Electrical and Computer Engineering. Nov. 15, 2002. On-line at: http://www.sce.carleton.ca/netmanage/papers/TosicEtAlResRepNov2002.pdf (2002)
3. Sahai, A., Durante, A., Machiraju, V.: Towards Automated SLA Management for Web Services. Research Report HPL-2001-310 (R.1), Hewlett-Packard (HP) Laboratories Palo Alto. July 26, 2002. On-line at: http://www.hpl.hp.com/techreports/2001/HPL-2001-310R1.pdf (2002)
4. Keller, A., Ludwig, H.: The WSLA Framework: Specifying and Monitoring Service Level Agreements for Web Services. Journal of Network and Systems Management, Vol. 11, No 1 (Mar. 2003) Plenum Publishing (2003)
5. Tosic, V., Pagurek, B., Esfandiari, B., Patel, K., Ma, W.: Web Service Offerings Language (WSOL) and Web Service Composition Management (WSCM). In Proc. of the OOWS'02 (Object-Oriented Web Services) workshop at OOPSLA 2002 (Seattle, USA, Nov. 2002) On-line at: http://www.research.ibm.com/people/b/bth/OOWS2002/tosic.zip (2002)
6. Patel, K.: XML Grammar and Parser for the Web Service Offerings Language. M.A.Sc. thesis, Carleton University, Ottawa, Canada. Jan. 30, 2003. On-line at: http://www.sce.carleton.ca/netmanage/papers/KrutiPatelThesisFinal.pdf (2003)
7. Tosic, V., Patel, K., Pagurek, B.: WSOL – Web Service Offerings Language. In Proc. of the Workshop on Web Services, e-Business, and the Semantic Web at CAiSE'02 (Toronto, Canada, May 2002). Lecture Notes in Computer Science (LNCS), No. 2512. Springer-Verlag (2002) 57–67
8. Tosic, V., Esfandiari, B., Pagurek, B., Patel, K.: On Requirements for Ontologies in Management of Web Services. In Proc. of the Workshop on Web Services, e-Business, and the Semantic Web at CAiSE'02 (Toronto, Canada, May 2002). Lecture Notes in Computer Science (LNCS), No. 2512. Springer-Verlag (2002) 237–247
9. Dan, A., Franck, R., Keller, A., King, R., Ludwig, H.: Web Service Level Agreement (WSLA) Language Specification. In Documentation for the Web Services Toolkit, Version 3.2.1. Aug. 9, 2002. International Business Machines Corporation (IBM) (2002)

10. The Axis Development Team: Axis Architecture Guide, Version 1.0. Apache Axis WWW page. On-line at: http://cvs.apache.org/viewcvs.cgi/~checkout~/xml-axis/java/docs/architecture-guide.html (2003)
11. Beugnard, A., Jezequel, J.-M., Plouzeau, N., Watkins, D.: Making Components Contract Aware. Computer, Vol. 32, No. 7 (July 1999) IEEE (1999) 38–45
12. Sahai, A., Machiraju, V., Sayal, M., van Moorsel, A., Casati, F.: Automated SLA Monitoring for Web Services. In Proc. of the 13th IFIP/IEEE International Workshop on Distributed Systems: Operations and Management, DSOM 2002 (Montreal, Canada, Oct. 2002). Lecture Notes in Computer Science (LNCS), No. 2506. Springer-Verlag (2002) 28–41
13. Hondo, M., Kaler, C. (eds.): Web Services Policy Framework (WS-Policy), Version 1.0. Dec. 18, 2002. BEA/IBM/Microsoft/SAP. On-line at: ftp://www6.software.ibm.com/software/developer/library/ws-policy.pdf (2002)
14. The DAML Services Coalition: DAML-S: Semantic Markup for Web Services. WWW page for DAML-S version 0.7. Oct. 2, 2002. On-line at: http://www.daml.org/services/daml-s/0.7/daml-s.html (2002)

Leveraging Web-Services and Peer-to-Peer Networks

Mike P. Papazoglou[1], Bernd J. Krämer[2], and Jian Yang[1]

[1] INFOLAB — Tilburg University, PO Box 90153,
NL-5000 LE Tilburg, The Netherlands
{mikep,jian}@uvt.nl,
[2] FernUniversität Hagen,
D-58084 Hagen, Germany
bernd.kraemer@fernuni-hagen.de

Abstract. Peer-oriented computing is an attempt to weave interconnected machines into the fabric of the Internet. Service-oriented computing (exemplified by web-services), on the other hand, is an attempt to provide a loosely coupled paradigm for distributed processing. In this paper we present an event-notification based architecture and formal framework towards unifying these two computing paradigms to provide essential functions required for automating e-business applications and facilitating service publication, discovery and exchange.

1 Introduction

A large number of enterprises nowadays is implementing a SOAP/WSDL/UDDI layer on top of existing applications or components and is assembling applications by consuming web-services. The manifestation of web-services for such applications is through widely accepted industry standards such as XML, SOAP, WSDL (Web-Services Definition Language) and UDDI (Universal Description, Discovery and Integration protocol). Interactions of web-services occur as SOAP calls carrying XML data content and the service definitions of the web-services are expressed using WSDL as the common (XML-based) standard. WSDL is used to publish a web service in terms of its *ports* (addresses implementing this service), *port types* (the abstract definition of operations and exchanges of messages), and *bindings* (the concrete definition of which packaging and transportation protocols such as SOAP are used to inter-connect two conversing end points). The UDDI standard is a directory service that contains service publications and enables web-service clients to locate candidate services and discover their details.

The characterization of the web-service operation is the classic client/server model. The service provider (server) will register with the UDDI registry and the requester (client) will contact the registry to discover the server location so that it can interact with it. This is a straightforward approach to distributed computing that provides the advantage that clients are coupled to the servers only via a contract mechanism. Since this contract is fully described by using WSDL, developers can construct clients using the contract information. All providers

J. Eder and M. Missikoff (Eds.): CAiSE 2003, LNCS 2681, pp. 485–501, 2003.

must make their services available by publishing their contract and advertising their service.

Peer-to-Peer (P2P) computing is the sharing of computer resources and services through direct communication between systems. Each functional unit in the network, called a peer, is behaviourally similar and is logically capable of both providing and consuming information. True P2P networks are vastly distributed and do not require a centralized directory for indexing purposes. When a peer decides that data hosted on another peer is useful, it visits directly this peer in order to obtain that data. The P2P network is usually fluctuating and dynamic with peer neighbour relationships breaking and reforming as the load or infrastructure stability changes.

When comparing P2P networks with web-services functionality, we observe that peer-to-peer systems also leverage a service-oriented architecture but have their own idiosyncrasies. Unlike web-services, the determination of who is a provider, a requester or a registrar (of a resource) is much looser. Typically, a peer is all three of the aforementioned roles. However, like web-services, peers must also publish a resource (allowing it to be found and accessed by other peers) with efficient precision for the other peers to be able to broadcast their needs and receive meaningful responses. Publication and discovery are paramount for both paradigms, however, the two approaches diverge on lookup services. Peers use decentralized discovery while web-services use larger centralized directories such as UDDI. Lastly, another similarity is that both web-services and P2P networks have heavy emphasis on distributed computing and on using XML as a means to describe information.

Fortunately, the standards and frameworks used to create web-services can also be utilized to develop P2P applications. This is because both sets of architectures fundamentally coordinate interactions between loosely coupled systems. Utilizing a common framework based on current web-service technologies would enable P2P developers with elementary building blocks for building applications. In fact, JXTA, the P2P framework initiated by Sun Microsystems [10], i s making adjustments to its core platform to make peers interoperate with web-services using protocols like SOAP and WSDL.

This paper examines key intersect points that enable web-services and P2P networks to work together and in particular, looks at ways in which web-services discovery can benefit from P2P decentralization. Our contribution concentrates on an architectural approach and formal framework towards unifying web-services and P2P networks to provide essential functions required for automating e-business applications and facilitating service publication, discovery and exchange.

2 Problems with Web-Service Directories

To open new markets and find new sources of supply enterprises use a common service registry (UDDI) for identifying potential trading partners and for cataloguing their business functions and characteristics. UDDI specification provides two main types of interfaces (APIs): one for describing services and registering service entries in the directory and one for enquiring about service entries and provider characteristics. This allows the services to be dynamically discovered and composed into more complex (value-added) services.

It is expected that vertical sectors will have a variety of specialised UDDI directories that serve their community as a whole offering business functionality on the Web. In fact some *vertical* e-marketplaces, such as semiconductors, travel industry, and automotive industry already provide to their members a unified view of sets of UDDI-based products and services to enable them to transact business using diverse mechanisms, such as web-services. And this is already happening to a large extend. With these vertical e-marketplaces services can be published and hosted throughout the e-marketplace network and used on demand. The goal of web-services when used within the context of e-marketplaces is to enable business solutions by composing and programming web-services, e.g., using the Business Process Execution Language for Web Services (BPEL4WS) [3]. This allows companies to conduct electronic business, by invoking web-services, with all partners in a marketplace rather than with just the ones with whom they have collaborative business agreements. Service offers are described in such a way, e.g., WSDL over UDDI, that they allow automated discovery to take place and offer request matching on functional and non-functional service capabilities.

One of the major problems with the centralized indexing scheme provided by UDDI is that it does not scale well because the number and physical distribution of the UDDI clients can quickly overwhelm this centralized configuration and can lead to serious performance bottlenecks. Adding more servers or implementing load-balancing strategies does not constitute a practical solution as they may prove to be costly and disruptive. In contrast to UDDI, P2P networks content is normally described and indexed locally to each peer and search queries are propagated across the network. In this model no central index is required to span the network.

One of the major points of intersection between P2P and web-service technologies involves bringing the decentralization aspect of P2P networks to the central service discovery mechanisms of web-services provided by UDDI. It is not difficult to envision a P2P network architecture that promotes a logically decentralized arrangement of registered service descriptions and that also provides web-service descriptions much in the same way that UDDI does.

3 A Federated Architecture for P2P Web-Services

To enable the fusion of web services and P2P computing we can employ a federation of UDDI-enabled peer registries that operate in a decentralized fashio rather than requiring each peer to publish their own service descriptors locally or centrally (on the UDDI). Such federations may represent common interest groups of peers that band together to ensure that they provide added-value syndicated services to their customers. A *peer (service) syndication* seeks to promote in-demand services by offering sets of related services throughout the federation rather than on a single UDDI location, see Figure 1.

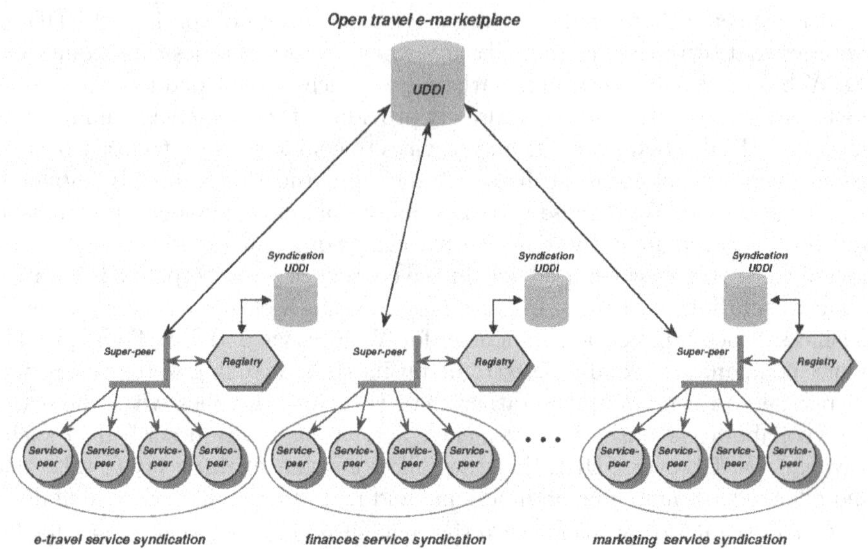

Fig. 1. Conceptual architecture of the P2P service network.

Two of the key concepts in a peer service syndication are the notions of *publication* and *subscription*. Publications are simple XML documents that name, describe and publish the existence of peers that act as service providers, while subscriptions also name, describe and publish the service requirements of peers that act as service requesters within a service syndication. Discovery within a service syndication becomes an issue of matching service subscriptions against service publications.

A peer syndication is formed for specific specialised areas of interest within an e-marketplace, e.g., e-travel, finances, marketing and so on. Service providers (peers) first publish their services on the e-marketplace UDDI and then they may join a service syndication. When joining the P2P web-service network, a peer first registers itself by publishing services it wishes to offer to other peers. Secondly, it may subscribe to services that it is interested in from other peers in the syndication. For each syndication a specific peer acts as *super-peer* by providing directory services to the peer syndication, see Figure 1. The registry of the super-peer contains among other things a syndication UDDI sub-directory. Whenever a peer joins a syndication the syndication UDDI receives a mirror copy its service publication from the e-marketplace UDDI.

The super-peer acts as an event-notification service that receives and stores the publications and subscriptions of the entire peer-syndication. To achieve this a super-peer manages a select set of meta-operations for peers, such as joining/leaving the network, publishing service publications, and service subscriptions.

Event-notification is a concept used for asynchronous coordination of distributed systems. The event notification service (super-peer) can carry out a *selection process* (on the basis of subscription/publication matching) to determine which of the published notifications are of interest to which of its peers, thus routing and delivering notification only to those peers that are interested.

To exemplify these points we introduce a service syndication scenario in the domain of e-travelling based on specifications of the open travel agency (OTA) [13]. OTA has specified a set of standard business processes, which use XML for structured data messages, for searching for availability and booking a reservation in the airline, hotel and car rental industry, as well as the purchase of travel insurance in conjunction with these services.

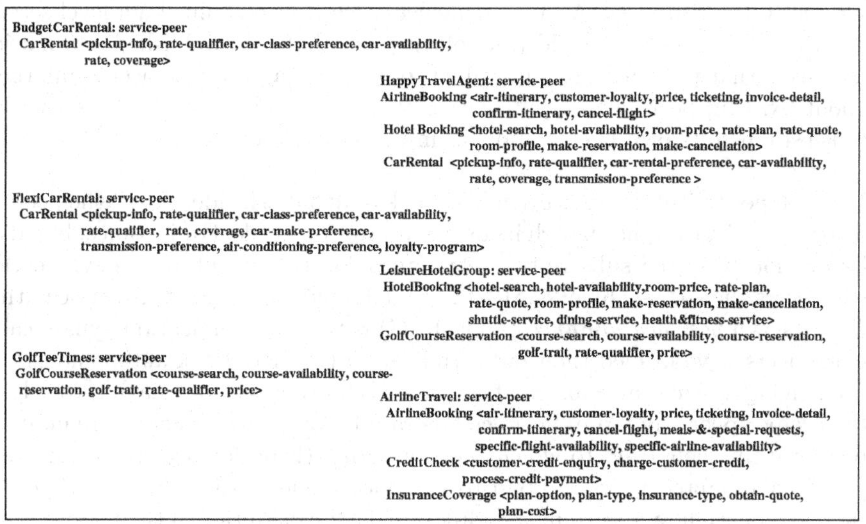

Fig. 2. Sample publications in the e-travel service syndication.

Figure 2 illustrates possible publications made by airline associations, car rental agencies, hotel corporations and leisure operators that have published their services as part of an e-travel service syndication. For reasons of brevity we show only six service peers in this figure. Each publication consists of three parts: the peer's (service provider's) name, e.g., `BudgetCarRental`, its WSDL `portType` name, e.g., CarRental, and the name of the operations contained in it. WSDL `portTypes` contain the abstract definition of operations. All service providers in the marketplace (and syndication) use standard (unique) names for their port types and associated operations.

The goal of each super-peer is to send an update to its syndication to notify all potential subscribers about new publications (registrations) and deletions of registrations it receives. When a super-peer receives a new publish/subscribe event from a peer that wishes to join the network, e.g., `BudgetCarRental`, it performs two kinds of matching operations. The first matching operation matches the new peer's publication against all subscriptions that are relevant to it. If, for instance, `BudgetCarRental` has published information about CarRental rate qualifiers (rq), and car class preferences (ccp) then it could be matched with the subscriptions of the peers `HappyTravelAgent` and `FlexiCarRental` - assuming that these have subscribed to such information. The second matching operation matches all previous publications against the service subscriptions of this new peer. If, for instance, `BudgetCarRental` has subscribed to information relating to HotelBooking it can be matched with peers such as `LeisureHotelGroup` and `HappyTravelAgent` assuming that these two peers have published the information in which `BudgetCarRental` is interested. Whenever a match is detected, the super-peer forwards the peer publication information such as the services offered, their matching peers and their addresses to all the peers that have subscribed to their services. As a consequence, each peer contains high-level service descriptions as well as the addresses of the peers that have published information (services) that this peer has subscribed to. In this way the new peer is informed about existing peers whose publications match its subscription needs and can thus establish its own peer group within the syndication.

Each peer within a service syndication knows only the identity of the peers in its own syndication that match its own subscription needs. For instance, based on its previously stated subscriptions `BudgetCarRental` would form a syndication with peers such as `LeisureHotelGroup` and `HappyTravelAgent`. A peer can thus form its own *peer-acquaintance group* (PAG) within the syndication dynamically. Once peers have formed their own syndication they can work autonomously by exchanging services and information with each other without having to rely to their super-peer any more. Peers collaborate by propagating service requests to peers within their PAG to which they subscribe (henceforth named *acquainted peers*). Acquainted peers respond to a service request issued by a *local peer* in their syndication by returning a high-level UDDI description of their service content such as their `BusinessKey`, `Tmodel` structure and `bindindTemplate`. After receiving this information, the local peer invokes the `get_detail()` operations of the syndication UDDI API to retrieve more detailed information about the service port-types, elements and bindings of the services offered by its acquainted peers, see Figure 1.

The above P2P service network combines aspects of the directory services P2P model exemplified by Napster [12] and the "pure" P2P architecture exemplified by Gnutella and Freenet [9,6]. It follows a federated approach where a relatively small number of super-peers provide directory services to peer groups managed by a super-peer. The super-peer is used only for notification purposes when peers attempt to locate or communicate with each other. Each peer in the P2P service network builds up a (constantly changing) peer-group of other peers and stores locally some minimal information about them. Whenever a peer receives a request for service that it cannot fully satisfy it routes segments of it to appropriate peers within its peer-group for execution.

4 Publish/Subscribe in the P2P Web-Services Network

The publish/subscribe mechanism used in this paper is a *P2P communication protocol* that enables an exchange of asynchronous notifications between loosely coupled peers in a P2P network of web-services. This mechanism is partially based on an event notification scheme proposed for wide-area networks [2].

4.1 Service Publication and Subscription Matching

A peer publishes a set of WSDL port-types, each having a set of operations characterizing the service it offers. For a given service syndication we assume that the set of all possible port-type and operation names **PN** and **OP**, respectively, are well-defined. All publications are maintained by a super-peer known to all peers in the peer set **P**. The sets **PN**, **OP**, and **P** contain all permissible port type, operation, and peer names, respectively.

Organizing and manipulating publication contexts. A *port-type* is a pair (n, O) with $n \in \mathbf{PN}$ and $O \subseteq \mathbf{OP}$ and a *publication* can be expressed as a set of port-types. The information about publications and their publishing peers can be maintained in a matrix relating a set of peers with all their publications known in a specific service syndication at a particular time. We call this matrix a *publication context.* The peer names are represented by rows in the matrix, while the port-types are represented by its columns. A cross in row p and column (pt, O) indicates that peer p has published port-type (pt, O). Table 1 illustrates a publication context for the port-types and peers used in the example in Figure 2[1].

Publication contexts and the matching of a peer's subscription against a given publication context can be modelled mathematically in terms of formal concept analysis [8], which relies on the theory of ordered sets and complete lattices. Formally, a publication context $C := (P, Pt, I)$ consists of a set $P \subseteq \mathbf{P}$ of peer names, a publication, i.e., a set of port-types, $Pt \subseteq \{(n, O) \mid n \in \mathbf{PN} \wedge O \subseteq \mathbf{OP}\}$, and an incidence relation $I \subseteq P \times Pt$. The fact that a peer p has published a certain port-type (n, O) is expressed as $(p, (n, O)) \in I$.

For a set of peers in $Q \subseteq P$ the expression:

$$[Q] := \{pt \in Pt \mid (p, pt) \in I \text{ for all } p \in Q\} \tag{1}$$

computes the set of *port-types belonging to the peers in* Q. For instance, [`LeisureHotelGroup`] = {`GolfCourseRes(cs,ca,cr,gt,rq,p)`, `HotelBk(hs,ha,rpr,rp,rq,rpf,mr,mc,ss,ds,hfs)`}

A publication context can be extended or modified incrementally by means of only a few operations provided by each super-peer as follows:

[1] Due to space limitations, we henceforth represent in all tables and figures operations corresponding to the constructs in Figure 2 by their initial letters only.

Table 1. Example of a publication context for the travel syndication service depicted in Fig. 2

	AirlineBk(ai,cl,p,t,id,ci,cf)	AirlineBk(ai,cl,p,t,id,ci,cf,msr,sfa,saa)	CarRental(pi,rq,ccp,ca,r,c)	CarRental(pi,rq,crp,ca,r,c,tp)	CarRental(pi,rq,ccp,ca,r,c,tp,cmp,acp,lp)	CreditCheck(cce,ccc,pcp)	GolfCourseRes(cs,ca,cr,gt,rq,p)	HotelBk(hs,ha,rpr,rp,rq,rpf,mr,mc)	HotelBk(hs,ha,rpr,rp,rq,rpf,mr,mc,ss,ds,hfs)	InsuranceCov(po,pt,it,oq,pc)
AirlineTravel		×				×				×
BudgetCarRental			×							
FlexiCarRental					×					
GolfTeeTimes							×			
HappyTravelAgent	×			×				×		
LeisureHotelGroup							×		×	

`void addPeer(peer` p`)`: The effect of this operation on a given publication context (P, Pt, I) is an extended context $(P \cup \{p\}, Pt, I)$. The corresponding matrix is extended by a new row labelled p, provided that a row labelled p does not exist already.

`void addPortType(peer` p`, portType` pt`)`: The current publication context (P, Pt, I) is extended to yield $(P, Pt \cup \{pt\}, I \cup \{(p, pt)\})$ if $p \in P$, otherwise it remains unchanged. If a row labelled p exists in the matrix, the matrix will then be extended by a new column pt (if not already available) while a cross is introduced at the intersection of row p and column pt (provided that it does not exist).

`void addOperation(peer` p`, portTypeName` n`, opName` o`)`: The effect of this operation on the current context (P, Pt, I) is a new context (P, Pt', I') with $Pt' := Pt \cup \{(n, O \cup \{o\}) \mid (n, O) \in Pt \wedge o \notin O \wedge (p, (n, O)) \in I\}$ and $I' := I \cup \{(p, (n, O \cup \{o\})) \mid (n, O) \in Pt \wedge o \notin O \wedge (p, (n, O)) \in I\}$. The matrix is extended by a new column labelled $n(o_1, \ldots, o_n, o)$ for the column $n(o_1, \ldots, o_n)$ related to row p, provided that o is different from $o_1, \ldots, o_n$. In addition, a cross is introduced at the intersection of row p and the new column $n(o_1, \ldots, o_n, o)$.

`void addPublication(peer` p`, portType` pt`)`: This operation is defined by combining the operations `addPeer(peer` p`)` and `addPortType(peer` p`, portType` pt`)`.

`void deletePeer(peer p)`: If $p \in P$ of the current context (P, Pt, I), the result is the context $(P - \{p\}, Pt', I')$ with $Pt - \{pt \mid (p, pt) \in I \wedge \not\exists (p', pt) \in I \text{ with } p \neq p'\}$ and $I' := I - \{(p, pt)\}$.

In the matrix we just delete row p and all columns pt that are related only to p.

`void deletePortType(peer p, portType pt):` The intended meaning of this operation is that peer p no longer publishes port-type pt. The modified contex is defined by (P, Pt', I') with

$$Pt' := \begin{cases} Pt - \{pt\} \text{ if } \nexists (p', pt) \in I \text{with } p \neq p' \\ \text{otherwise } Pt \end{cases}$$

and $I' := I - (p, pt)$.

`void deleteOperation(peer p, portTypeName n, opName o):` The effect of this operation is a context in which operation o is removed from port-type pt published by peer p. More precisely, we obtain the new context (P, PT', I') defined as follows: $Pt' := Pt - \{(n, O) \mid (n, O) \in Pt \wedge o \in O \wedge \nexists (p', (n, O)) \in I \text{with } p \neq p'\} \cup \{(n, O - \{o\}) \mid (p, (n, O)) \in I \wedge o \in O\}$ and $I' := I - \{(p, (n, O)) \mid o \in O\} \cup \{(p, (n, O - \{o\})) \mid (p, (n, O)) \in I \wedge o \in O\}$ under the condition that p exists and p is related to any port-type $pt \in Pt$ that contains operation o. Otherwise the context remains unchanged.
This operation has the following effect on the matrix. The column that is labelled $n(op_1, \dots, o, \dots o_n)$ and has a cross at its intersection with row p is removed. A new column labelled $n(op_1, \dots, o_n)$ is added and a new cross is added in the newly inserted column $n(op_1, \dots, o_n)$.

Service searching and subscription. A search for services is typically triggered by a requester indicating the port-type and the associated set of operations that it is interested in. That is, a service request $r = (n, \{o_1, \dots, o_n\})$ is a port-type name and a set of operation names. A peer p matches a service request r in a given publication context (P, Pt, I) if p publishes a port-type (n, O) that includes at least the operations contained in the request. Accordingly, we define a function $match(p, r) \equiv \exists (n, O) \in [\{p\}]$ such that $\{o_1, \dots, o_n\} \subseteq O$ (see Definition 1 for the meaning of the symbol [ ]). All publishing peers that satisfy a request r form the *peer-acquaintences* $acq(r)$ group of the peer that issues a service request. Consequently, $acq(r) := \{p \in P \mid match(p, r)\}$.

In general, a peer seeks other peers that publish a coherent set of port-types and not just a single port-type. Consequently, we extend the above definitions to what we call a *subscription.* A subscription S is defined, just like a publication, as a set of pairs $(s, O))$ with $s \in \mathbf{PN}$ and $O \subseteq \mathbf{OP}$. We say that a peer p *matches a subscription* S if it matches all requests in S, i.e., $match(p, S) \equiv \forall r \in S : match(p, r)$. The *peer-acquaintances* $acq(S)$ of a subscription S with respect to a publication context (P, Pt, I) and a subscription request r are defined as:

$$acq(S) := \bigcap_{r \in S} acq(r). \tag{2}$$

Table 2 shows simple examples of peer-subscriptions and their resulting peer-acquaintances. This table shows that subscription 2 extends Subscription 1 by

Table 2. Examples of peer-subscriptions and their acquaintances.

Example	*Subscription*	*Acquaintances*
Subscription1	{CarRental(rq,ccp,r,c}	{BudgetCarRental, FlexiCarRental }
Subscription2	{CarRental(rq,ccp,r,c,tp,cmp,acp}	{FlexiCarRental}
Subscription3	{HotelBk(hs,ha,rpr,rp,rq,mr), GolfCourseRes(cs,ca,rq,p)}	{LeisureHotelGroup}
Subscription4	∅	P
Subscription5	{CarRental(pi,ccp), HotelBk(hs,ha)}	∅
Subscription6	{AirlineBk() }	{AirlineTravel, HappyTravelAgent}

requesting additional operations to be matched. These additional operations are found only in the `CarRental` port-type published by peer `FlexiCarRental`, i.e., a subset of the acquaintances of subscription 1. We also observe that the port-type of Subscription 2 is a subtype of the port-type of Subscription 1. Therefore, we define a *subtype relationship* "$\leq$" between port-types $pt = (n, O)$ and $pt' = (n', O')$ with $n, n' \in \mathbf{PN}$ and $O, O' \in \mathbf{OP}$ that is induced by the subset relationship among the operations as follows:

$$pt' \leq pt \equiv (O \subseteq O' \wedge n = n')$$

We also notice that an empty subscription like Subscription 4 is matched by all peers, and Subscription 5 yields an empty set of acquaintances because the requested combination of port-types is not supported by any peer in the syndication. Subscription 6 is matched by all peers advertising the port-type named `AirlineBk` as it contains no operations. This signifies that the subscriber is obviously satisfied with any possible operation included in the requested port-type.

The above considerations imply that subtyping relationships between logically associated port-types should be first introduced at the publication context and then be used to match potential subscriptions. We can extend a given publication context (P, Pt, I) to the context $(P, \overline{Pt}, \overline{I})$, by taking all possible subtype relationship between port-types carrying the same port-type name into account. This is defined as:

$$\overline{Pt} = Pt \cup \{(n, Q) \mid (n, O) \in Pt \wedge Q \subseteq O\} \tag{3}$$

and

$$\overline{I} = I \cup \{(p, (n, Q)) \mid (p, (n, O)) \in I \wedge Q \subseteq O\} \tag{4}$$

In the matrix representation of a publication contexts this means to add: (1) all necessary columns (n, Q) for each published port-type (n, O) such that $(n, O) \leq (n, Q)$ and (2) a cross at the intersection of row p with each new column (n, Q) provided that a cross exists at the intersection of row p with column (n, O), for each $(n, O) \leq (n, Q)$. Table 3 is the extended table constructed from Table 1 by adding all appropriate port-type subtype relationships. Additional columns (not all of which are shown) are marked in a light grey colour.

Table 3. Example of a supplemented publication context for the travel domain depicted in Fig. 2.

	AirlineBk()	AirlineBk(ai)	...	AirlineBk(ai,cl,p,t,id,ci,cf)	AirlineBk(ai,cl,p,t,id,ci,cf,msr)	...	AirlineBk(ai,cl,p,t,id,ci,cf,msr,sfa,saa)	CarRental()	...	CarRental(pi,rq,ca,r,c)	CarRental(pi,rq,ccp,ca,r,c)	CarRental(pi,rq,crp,ca,r,c)	CarRental(pi,rq,ca,r,c,tp)	CarRental(pi,rq,crp,ca,r,c,tp)	CarRental(pi,rq,ccp,ca,r,c,tp)	...	CarRental(pi,rq,ccp,ca,r,c,tp,cmp,acp,lp)	...
AirlineTravel	×	×	×	×	×	×	×											
BudgetCarRental								×	×	×	×							
FlexiCarRental								×	×	×	×		×		×	×	×	
GolfTeeTimes																		
HappyTravelAgent	×	×	×	×				×	×	×		×	×	×				
LeisureHotelGroup																		

We can simplify our definition of the acquaintances of a subscription $S \subseteq \overline{Pt}$ by using the extended publication context and matrix $(P, \overline{Pt}, \overline{I})$ as follows:

$$acq(S) = [S] := \{p \in P \mid (p, pt) \in \overline{I} \text{ for all } pt \in S\}. \quad (5)$$

where $[S]$ determines the set of all peers that publish all port-types in S. We shall henceforth always refer to the extended form of a publication context.

Subscriptions are maintained the same way as publications are maintained. In addition, any change to a peer's publication context must be automatically mirrored against the set of known subscriptions which are maintained in a subscriber's table. Subscribers provide a call-back method that is invoked from the super-peer to inform them when they are affected from any changes that invalidate or extend a subscription that they made. A subscription is invalidated, for instance, if:

- an operation that a subscriber requested from a port-type is deleted from that port-type,
- the peer to which the subscription was bound is deleted, or
- a port-type that is a subtype of a requested port-type is deleted.

A subscription is extended if a new subtype of a subscribed port-type is added or a new operation is added to a super-type of requested port-type such that the extended port-type now matches the requested port-type.

Structural organisation of publications and subscriptions. The acquaintances of a subscription can be computed by traversing the extended matrix and selecting all the peers that satisfy a subscription. A more elegant way to organize publication contexts and subscriptions and determine matching acquaintances is by means of a *concept lattice* $\mathbf{C}(P, Pt, I)$. This lattice is derived automatically from a given publication context (P, Pt, I) using an efficient algorithm described in [7]. This algorithm relies on the notion of a *formal concept* of a context (P, Pt, I), which is defined as a pair (Q, T) with $Q \subseteq P, T \subseteq Pt, [Q] = T$ and $[T] = Q$ (see definition 1 and peer-publish-all-relations, respectively.). Q is called the *extent* and T is the *intent* of the concept (Q, T). If two concepts such as (Q_1, T_1) and (Q_2, T_2) are two concepts of a given context, then (Q_1, T_1) is called a *subconcept* of (Q_2, T_2) if $Q_1 \subseteq Q_2$ or, equivalently, if $T_2 \subseteq T_1$.

Figure 3 illustrates the concept lattice of the complete sample publication in Table 1. This figure includes all missing port-types and operations found in Figure 2. The super-peer organises the publication space around this type of concept lattice and stores it in its own local registry.

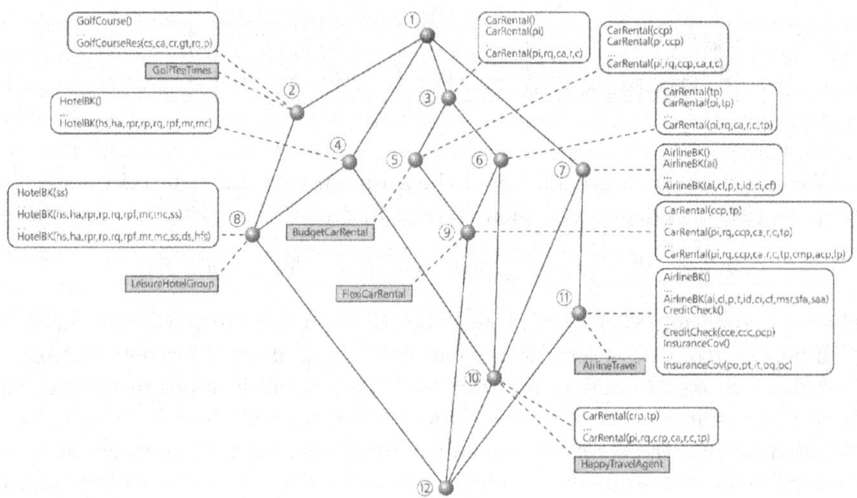

Fig. 3. Concept lattice including subtype relationships among published services.

There are two types of labels attached to the nodes in this publication lattice: port-types and peer names (shaded rectangles). Each node represents a formal concept relating its extent, i.e., a set of peer names, with its intent, i.e., a set of port-types published by all peers in its extent. All port-types reachable via upwards paths from a node in the lattice determine the node's intent. For instance, the intent of node 10 is the sum of the port-types listed in nodes 1, 3, 4, 6, and 7. Conversely, all peers reachable downwards from a node in the lattice form the extent of that node. The peers in the extent of a given node are those peers that have published the port-types associated with its intent. Consider, for instance, node 6: the port-types `CarRental()`,`CarRental(pi)`, ..., `CarRental(pi,rq,cq,r,c,tp)`, which form the intent of node 6, are published by the peers associated with node 9 and 10, i.e, `FlexiCarRental` and `HappyTravelAgent`, which form its intent. The top node of the lattice represents the concept relates all the peers in a given publication context with the port-types they all share in common (in our example there are none therefore the concept is $(P, \emptyset)$). The bottom node of the lattice relates the sum of all port-types in a publication context with those peers that publish this sum (in our example there are none, therefore the concept associated with the bottom node is $(\emptyset, Pt)$).

The collection of subscriptions in a syndication are organised in a similar fashion in a subscription lattice. In this way we can use a uniform mechanism to determine subscription/publication matches and which subscribers are affected by a change to the publication lattice.

4.2 Peer Group Formation

A peer group is formed by applying the *match* function on a peer's subscription against a publication context C. Suppose that the very first subscription of the peer `BudgetCarRental` is: $S := \{\texttt{CarRental(tp)}, \texttt{HotelBooking(hs,..,mc)}\}$. A *matched-subscription lattice* for `BudgetCarRental`'s subscription, shown in Figure 4, is generated by matching subscription S against the complete publication lattice of the super-peer, shown in Figure 3. The matched-subscription lattice is a true subset of the extended publication lattice stored at the super-peer and indicates the peers and matching concepts that conform to `BudgetCarRental`'s subscription. This figure shows that `BudgetCarRental`'s subscription has resulted in forming a lattice with the peeers: `HappyTravelAgent`, `LeisureHotelGroup` and `FlexiCarRental`. In this matched subscription lattice `LeisureHotelGroup` provides the additional hotel functionality requested but not the car rental functionality, `FlexiCarRental` provides the additional car rental functionality requested but not the hotel functionality, while `HappyTravelAgent` provides both requested functionalities. In the first instance when a peer has made its initial subscription, the matched-subscription lattice is stored locally at this peer's site and its forms its *local subscription lattice.* This local subscription lattice can be used in the future to locate relevant peer acquaintances when attempting to process a service request without having to resort to the super-peer any more. A local subscription lattice grows as a peer gets notified of new subscriptions.

A peer's publication lattice is thus fluctuating with peer relationships breaking and reforming dynamically based on the peer's interests and the number of peers entering or leaving its group as a result of this.

Whenever a *service request* is posed at a local peer, its set of subscriptions needs to be evaluated to determine whether it can support this new request. In case that execution of the new request is not fully supported locally, then a new subscription (for this peer) reflecting the missing information will be generated from the service request and will be sent to the super-peer.

When a peer decides to leave the P2P network, a notification will be sent from the super-peer to all relevant peers, which in turn will update their lo-

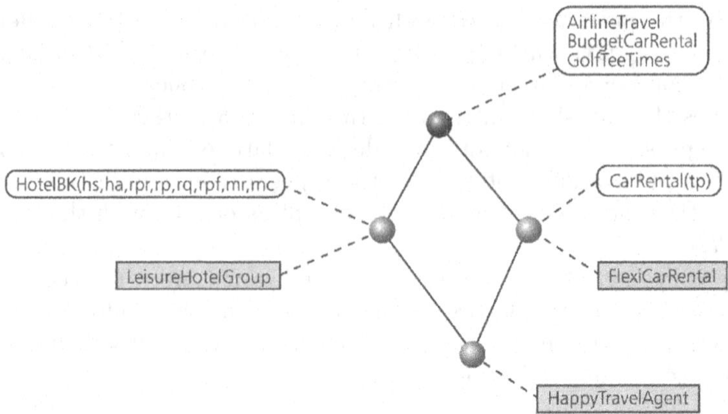

Fig. 4. A matched-subscription lattice for `BudgetCarRental`

cal subscription lattices. This happens in accordance with the lattice updating operations defined in the previous subsection.

5 Service Request Processing

When a service request arrives, the local peer will use its local subscription lattice as a point of reference to resolve a set of acquainted peers in its PAG to which the request should be routed. The response to a request includes descriptions of the service content that the acquainted peers provide in connection to the sub-request they receive.

To understand how service requests are processed assume that `BudgetCarRental` that has formed a PAG with peers `HappyTravelAgent`, `LeisureHotelGroup` and `FlexiCarRental`. Further assume that this peer needs to handle a sub-request that requires hotel booking functionality, e.g., search for a particular type of hotel that is not supported locally. After receiving this request `BudgetCarRental` determines (on the basis of its local subscription lattice, shown in Figure 4) that its acquainted peers `HappyTravelAgent` and `LeisureHotelGroup` can handle this type of request. Subsequently, the peer `BudgetCarRental` requests technical information about its two acquainted peers from the UDDI using the `get_Detail` operations of the UDDI enquiry API. The `get_Detail` operations are used to retrieve technical details such as access information required to invoke a service. This technical information describes the format input messages should be sent in, what protocols are appropriate, what security is required, and what form of a response will result after sending input messages. More specifically, the `get_ServiceDetail`, `get_bindingDetail`, and `get_tModelDetail` functions of the UDDI API are invoked to retrieve the above technical details that are required to interact with a service endpoint.

Now assume that after receiving this technical information the local peer `BudgetCarRental` has decided to invoke one (or both) of its two acquainted peers `HappyTravelAgent` and `LeisureHotelGroup`. Also assume that the service requester is interested in hotels within 5 kms North West of Schiphol airport. This request can be expressed as shown in Figure 5 on the basis of the standard Hotel Search Request message provided by the OTA specifications for hotel industry messages (see section-5 of OTA 2001 Message specifications). This message provides the ability to search for a list of hotel properties that meet certain criteria, and supply information in return that is related to the specific request. Geographic data, such as proximity to a specific location, landmark, attraction or destination point, could also be used to constrain the summary response to a limited number of hotels.

```
<Request HotelSearchRQ xmlns="http://www.opentravel.org/OTA"
        xmlns:xsi="http://www.w3.org/2001/XMLSchemainstance"
        xsi:noNamespaceSchemaLocation="OTA_HotelSearchRQ.xsd">

        <HotelSearchCriterion Type="Area" MatchType="Exact"
                                          ImportanceType=="Mandatory" >
          <HotelSearchValue>
              <RefPoint Distance="5" DistanceMeasure="km"
               Direction="NW">Schiphol Airport </RefPoint>
         </HotelSearchValue>
       </HotelSearchCriterion>
</Request>
```

Fig. 5. Sample service request.

In Figure 5 the statement < HotelSearchRQ > identifies the request as targeting hotel property data. This statement may have one to many < HotelSearchCriterion > child elements that identify a single search criterion by means of criteria types. A < MatchType > attribute indicates whether the match to a string value must be exact or only partial. The < ImportanceType > attribute is used to allow the responding web-service implementation to search for appropriate hotels and respond to preference criteria in the order of importance to the service client. This construct indicates whether the input criterion is mandatory, of high, medium or low priority. The < HotelSearchValue > element is a required child element of < HotelSearchCriterion > that contains the values expected by the `Type` attribute.

The response to the request in Figure 5 returns a list of hotel properties that meet the criteria of the request. A sample response to the request of Figure 5 is found in Figure 6.

6 Related Work

Recent work in content-based search include *content-addressable networks* – where the content of queries is used to efficiently route messages to the most relevant peers – such as CAN [14], Chord [4], and Pastry [5] as well as some variations of publish/subscribe networks [11]. These content-based P2P networks place emphasis on discovery of content rather than on a logical organization of the information space and on establishing relationships between constructs in

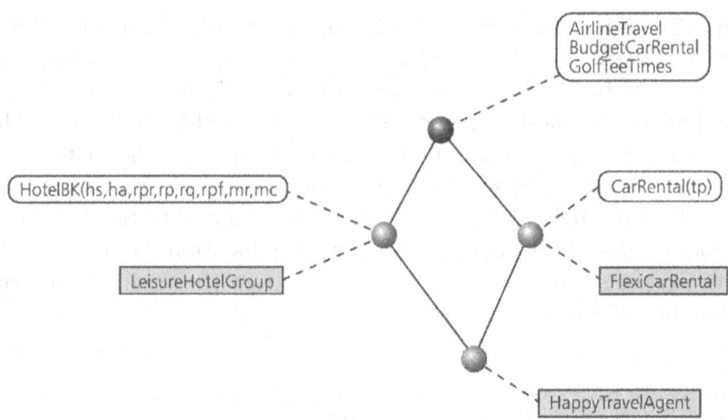

Fig. 4. A matched-subscription lattice for `BudgetCarRental`

cal subscription lattices. This happens in accordance with the lattice updating operations defined in the previous subsection.

5 Service Request Processing

When a service request arrives, the local peer will use its local subscription lattice as a point of reference to resolve a set of acquainted peers in its PAG to which the request should be routed. The response to a request includes descriptions of the service content that the acquainted peers provide in connection to the sub-request they receive.

To understand how service requests are processed assume that `BudgetCarRental` that has formed a PAG with peers `HappyTravelAgent`, `LeisureHotelGroup` and `FlexiCarRental`. Further assume that this peer needs to handle a sub-request that requires hotel booking functionality, e.g., search for a particular type of hotel that is not supported locally. After receiving this request `BudgetCarRental` determines (on the basis of its local subscription lattice, shown in Figure 4) that its acquainted peers `HappyTravelAgent` and `LeisureHotelGroup` can handle this type of request. Subsequently, the peer `BudgetCarRental` requests technical information about its two acquainted peers from the UDDI using the `get_Detail` operations of the UDDI enquiry API. The `get_Detail` operations are used to retrieve technical details such as access information required to invoke a service. This technical information describes the format input messages should be sent in, what protocols are appropriate, what security is required, and what form of a response will result after sending input messages. More specifically, the `get_ServiceDetail`, `get_bindingDetail`, and `get_tModelDetail` functions of the UDDI API are invoked to retrieve the above technical details that are required to interact with a service endpoint.

Now assume that after receiving this technical information the local peer `BudgetCarRental` has decided to invoke one (or both) of its two acquainted

```
<?xml version="1.0" encoding="UTF-8"?>
<OTA_HotelSearchRS xmlns:xsi="http://www.w3.org/2001/XMLSchema-instance"
xsi:noNamespaceSchemaLocation="OTA_HotelSearchRS.xsd" xmlns="http://www.opentravel.org/OTA">
<Success/>

<HotelSearchRecord HotelName="Hilton Hotel" Relevance="100">
     <HotelReference ChainCode="HH" BrandCode=".." HotelCode=".."/>
      <LocationDescription> 3.5 kms NW of Schiphol Airport</LocationDescription>
      <SearchValueMatch Match="true">Deluxe</SearchValueMatch>
      <MarketingText>Pool, Spa, and Health Club on premises</MarketingText>
</HotelSearchRecord>
   ... ... ...
<TotalReturns> 5 </TotalReturns>
</OTA_HotelSearchRS>
```

Fig. 6. Sample service response.

the publication space. A major difference between our approach and these activities is that our approach structures the publication and subscription space in concepts lattices that logically organize the publication/publication content by establishing semantic links and relationships between content concepts such as port-type and operation names.

On the industrial research side, work that comes closer to the research reported herein is Sun Microsystem's Project Juxtapose (http://www.jxta.org) – usually referred to as JXTA [15]. JXTA is not based on a publish/subscribe and event notification scheme. Its search peers act as hubs and can register with other hubs as information providers to field queries from other peers based on arbitrary content description registrations. JXTA tends to centralize registration/subscription information and control in hubs, whereas in our approach peers register only high-level information about themselves, such as their name, address and names of the service elements they are willing to share with other peers, with a super-peer. Moreover, unlike JXTA peers do not use the super-peer to locate each other or communicate with one another. Instead, each peer builds up a (constantly changing) peer-group of other peers and stores some minimal information about them.

7 Summary

In this paper we highlighted key intersect points that enable using service-oriented and peer-to-peer-computing technologies together and presented an architectural approach and formal framework towards unifying them.

We introduced a federation of UDDI-enabled peer registries, which operate in a decentralized fashion, rather than requiring each peer to publish their own service descriptors locally or centrally (on the UDDI). Federations are collections of behaviourally similar cooperating peers that provide a common set of circumstances and that band together to ensure that they provide added-value syndicated-services to their customers. Peer federations use a publish/subscribe model that enables the loosely coupled exchange of asynchronous notifications and an efficient mechanism based on concept-lattices to match notifications to subscribers and route notifications from publishers to interested subscribers.

There are several advantages that the publish/subscribe model for P2P networks of web-services offers. These include simplicity and ease of use, openness, extensibility, scalability, and semantic-based request routing.

References

1. S. Botros and S. Waterhouse, "Search in JXTA and other Distributed Networks," Proc. 2001 Int'l Conf. Peer-to-Peer Computing, 2001; available online at http://people.jxta.org/stevew/BotrosWaterhouse2001.pdf.
2. A. Carzaniga, D. Rosenblum, and A. Wolf, "Design and Evaluation of a Wide-Area Event Notification Service", in ACM Trans on Computer Systems, Vol. 19, No. 3, pp. 332–383, 2001.
3. Curbera, F., Goland, Y., Klein, J., Leyman, F., Roller, D., Thatte, S., and Weerawarana, S., "Business Process Execution Language for Web Services(BPEL4WS) 1.0," August 2002, available at http://www.ibm.com/developerworks/library/ws-bpel.
4. F. Dabek, et. al. "Building Peer-to-Peer Systems with Chord, a Distributed Lookup Service", http://pdos.lcs.mit.edu/chord2001.
5. P. Druschel and A. Rowstron "Pastry: Scalable Distributed Object Location and Routing for Large Scale Peer-to-Peer Systems", ACM SIGCOMM, 2001.
6. Freenet Home Page. http://freenet.sourceforge.com
7. Algorithmen zur formalen Begriffsanalyse. In: B. Ganter, R. Wille, and K.E. Wolff (eds), *Beiträge zur Begriffsanalyse.* B.I.-Wissenschaftsverlag, Mannheim, 1987, pp. 241–254
8. B. Ganter, R. Wille. *Formal Concept Analysis.* Springer 1999
9. Gnutella Development Home Page. http://gnutella.wego.com
10. L. Gong. "Project JXTA: A Technology Overview", available at http://www.jxta.org/project/www/white_papers.html.
11. D. Heimbigner "Adapting Publish/Subscribe Middleware to Achieve Gnutella-like Functionality", ACM Symposium on Advanced Computing (SAC), 2001.
12. www.napster.com, 2001.
13. Open Travel Alliance (OTA), "Document 2001C Specifications", available at http://www.opentravel.org, 2001.
14. S. Ratnasamy, et. al. "A Scalable Content Addressable Network", ACM SIGCOMM, 2001.
15. S. R. Waterhouse, D. M. Doolin, G. Kan and Y. Faybishenko, "JXTA Search: a Distributed Search Framework for Peer-to-Peer Networks" in IEEE Internet Computing, vol. 6, pp. 68–73, 2002.

View Materialization vs. Indexing: Balancing Space Constraints in Data Warehouse Design

Stefano Rizzi and Ettore Saltarelli

DEIS – University of Bologna
Viale Risorgimento, 2
40136 Bologna – Italy
{srizzi, esaltarelli}@deis.unibo.it

Abstract. View materialization and indexing are the most effective techniques adopted in data warehouses to improve query performance. Since both materialization and indexing algorithms are driven by a constraint on the disk space made available for each, the designer would greatly benefit from being enabled to determine a priori which fractions of the global space available must be devoted to views and indexes, respectively, in order to optimally tune performances. In this paper we first present a comparative evaluation of the benefit (saving per disk page) brought by view materialization and indexing for a single query expressed on a star scheme. Then, we face the problem of determining an effective trade-off between the two space fractions for the core workload of the warehouse. Some experimental results are reported, which prove that the estimated trade-off is satisfactorily near to the optimal one.

1 Introduction

Among the techniques adopted in relational implementations of data warehouses (DW's) to improve query performance, view materialization and indexing are surely the most effective ones.

View materialization consists in precomputing and storing a set of partial aggregates useful to solve, with decreased cost, frequent and/or crucial queries within the workload. Several approaches to view materialization were devised in the literature (see [16] for a survey and a general statement of the problem), mostly aimed at determining the subset of views which allows to minimize the execution cost of a given workload under a given space constraint.

The other technique universally adopted to reduce query execution costs is, of course, indexing. Though a number of papers were devoted to proposing or adapting indexing techniques for DW's [12,13,14], only a few works focus on the selection of indexes for DW's. Since indexes may be built on any view materialized, in order to reduce the problem complexity materialization and indexing are often faced separately, meaning that the optimal indexing scheme is chosen, under a space constraint, *after* the set of views to be materialized has been determined [4].

J. Eder and M. Missikoff (Eds.): CAiSE 2003, LNCS 2681, pp. 502–519, 2003.

It is apparent that, in most approaches, both materialization and indexing are driven by a rough indication of the disk space made available for each. Since the warehouse administrator can reasonably constrain only the *global* space available, S, as stated in [1] the designer must be capable of estimating which fractions of S should be devoted to views and indexes, S_V and S_X respectively, in order to optimally tune performances. Due to the high computation complexity of the algorithms for selecting the optimal sets of views and indexes, it is highly desirable that a good balancing of S_V and S_X is decided a priori, since a trial-and-error approach would require to execute the optimization algorithms several times under different space constraints. To this end, since the benefit of both materialization and indexing strongly depends on the characteristics of the queries formulated on the DW, we believe that the workload must be necessarily taken into account.

Let the workload be composed of GPSJ queries, typical of OLAP applications: essentially, queries consisting of a selection and an aggregation operated over a join. The key factors which impact the optimization benefit for a GPSJ query are its aggregation level (defined by its grouping set) and its selectivity (defined by the HAVING/WHERE clause). It is reasonable to expect that materialization will offer great advantage for queries with coarse aggregation, which compute a few groups out of a huge number of tuples, since accessing a small view is much cheaper than accessing a huge table. On the other hand, indexes will give their best when solving queries with high selectivity, which select only a few tuples, since accessing lots of useless tuples will be avoided. Thus, intuitively, queries with fine aggregation and high selectivity encourage indexing, while queries with coarse aggregation and low selectivity encourage materialization. On the other hand, as sketched in Figure 1, it is difficult to predict even qualitatively which of the two optimization techniques will fit best for queries falling outside these two regions.

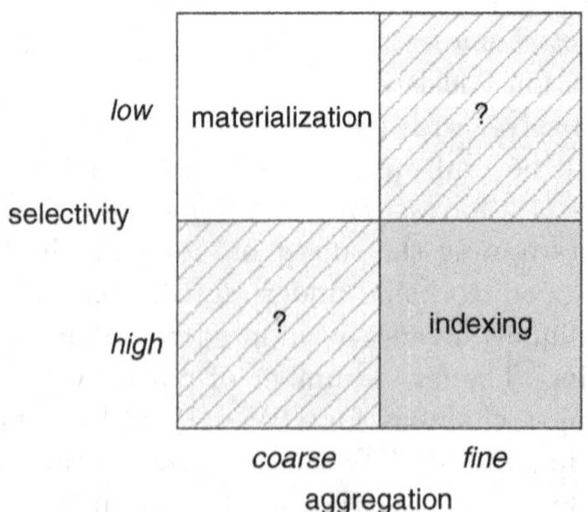

Fig. 1. Recommended optimization techniques depending on the query selectivity and aggregation level

models, besides a dimension, a *hierarchy* of attributes functionally determined by the dimension itself: thus, it includes non-key attributes for the dimension and for the other attributes of the hierarchy; the key is typically a surrogate generated by the DBMS.

Example 1 *The working example adopted in this paper is derived from the well-known TPC-H benchmark [15]; its star scheme is as follows:*

PART (<u>PartId</u>, Part, Brand, MFGR, Type, Container, Size)
SUPPLIER (<u>SupplierId</u>, Supplier, SNation, SRegion)
ORDER (<u>OrderId</u>, Order, ODate, OMonth, OYear, Customer)
LINEITEM (<u>PartId</u>, <u>SupplierId</u>, <u>OrderId</u>,
Qty, ExtPrice, Discount, DiscPrice, UnitPrice, Tax)

where LINEITEM is the fact table and the others are dimension tables. Note that dimension tables are denormalized: for instance, in SUPPLIER, the supplier nation SNation functionally determines his region SRegion. □

3.2 The Workload

The workloads we consider are sets of GPSJ queries. A GPSJ (Generalized Projection-Selection-Join) query q is a generalized projection over a selection over a join [5]; as such, it may be expressed in relational algebra over a star scheme as follows:

$$q = \pi_{G,M} \sigma_{Pred}(FT^{(0)} \bowtie DT_1^{(0)} \bowtie \ldots \bowtie DT_n^{(0)})$$

where $Pred$ is a conjunction of simple range predicates on dimension table attributes, G is a set of dimension table attributes (*grouping set*), and M is a set of aggregated measures each defined by applying an aggregation operator to a measure in $FT^{(0)}$. Generalized projection $\pi_{G,M}$ is an extension of duplicate eliminating projection [5]; from the SQL point of view, it corresponds to grouping by the attributes in G and inserting G, M in the selection clause.

Example 2 *A possible GPSJ query on the LINEITEM scheme is the one which returns the total quantity ordered during 2001 and the average unit price for each type of product and each supplier nation in the western region:*

$$\pi_{\mathsf{Type,SNation,OYear},SUM(\mathsf{Qty}),AVG(\mathsf{UnitPrice})}\ \sigma_{\mathsf{SRegion}='West'\ AND\ \mathsf{OYear}='2001'}\ (R)$$

where R = PART $\bowtie$ SUPPLIER $\bowtie$ ORDER $\bowtie$ LINEITEM. *The equivalent SQL formulation is as follows:*

```
SELECT P.Type, S.SNation, O.OYear, SUM(L.Qty), AVG(L.UnitPrice)
FROM LINEITEM AS L, PART AS P, SUPPLIER AS S, ORDER AS O
WHERE L.PartId=P.PartId
AND   L.SupplierId=S.SupplierId
AND   L.OrderId=O.OrderId
AND   S.SRegion='West' AND O.OYear='2001'
GROUP BY P.Type, S.SNation, O.OYear
```
□

We will assume that all selection predicates are *external*, i.e. that they are formulated on attributes functionally determined by an attribute in the grouping set G.[1] Besides, we will assume for simplicity that at most one selection predicate is formulated on each dimension table. A dimension table (or, equivalently, a hierarchy) on which q formulates a predicate is said to be *conditioned* in q.

3.3 Views

Materializing a view from the base fact table $FT^{(0)}$ may be seen as consolidating the result of a query. Here we will only consider views consolidated from GPSJ queries in which no selection predicate is formulated and the measures returned are all those in $FT^{(0)}$, each aggregated by the most appropriate aggregation operator. Thus, each view is fully characterized by its grouping set; the base fact table $FT^{(0)}$ can be seen as a particular case of a view, whose grouping set G_0 is the set of the dimensions of analysis (G_0 ={Part,Supplier,Order} in the LINEITEM example).

View materialization obviously involves a modification of the DW logical schema. Among the different alternatives proposed in the literature and in the practice, in this paper we adopt the variant of the classic star scheme in which one separate fact table is created for each materialized view and a separate dimension table is created for each attribute belonging to the grouping set of at least one view. Thus, view $FT^{(G)}$ with grouping set $G = \{a_1, \ldots, a_{|G|}\}$ will be associated to dimension tables $DT_1^{(G)}, \ldots, DT_{|G|}^{(G)}$ where $DT_i^{(G)}$ contains one surrogate key and a field for each attribute functionally dependent on a_i, including a_i itself.

Example 3 *Materializing the view with grouping set {Part,OMonth} means enriching the LINEITEM scheme with the following tables:*

OMONTH (OMonthId, OMonth, OYear, Customer)
LINEITEM1 (PartId, OMonthId, SumQty, SumExtPrice, SumDiscount, SumDiscPrice, AvgUnitPrice, SumTax) □

Materializing view $FT^{(G)}$ brings benefit to all the queries whose grouping set is "coarser" or equal to G: in fact, they all can be solved with reduced costs by rewriting them on $FT^{(G)}$ instead of $FT^{(0)}$. The notion of "coarseness" of a grouping set is formally described as a partial ordering over the (exponential) set of possible grouping sets, represented by the well-known *multidimensional lattice* proposed in [9].

4 Modeling Query Execution Plans

Evaluating the benefit of materializing a view or creating an index for a single query requires to estimate the costs for executing that query when the

[1] A predicate which does not satisfy this requirement can be easily made external by refining the grouping set of the query.

view/index is absent and when it is present. Thus, a reference model for query execution plans must be considered. The execution plans considered in this work are derived from the rule-based optimizer model described in [4], which was determined by carrying out a black-box analysis on the optimizer of Red Brick 6.0 [10].

Relational DBMSs necessarily require that an index is built at least on the primary key of each table; thus we will assume that, for each view materialized (including the base fact table), indexes are always built on the primary key of both the fact table and the dimension tables. Besides these primary indexes, other secondary indexes may optionally be built, if it is convenient, on non-key attributes of dimension/fact tables. In this work, indexes built on numerical measures of the fact table are not considered for simplicity.

A query execution plan is a sequence of elementary operators, each modeling a function carried out by the DBMS on either tables or indexes. According to the rule-based model adopted in [4], the execution plan for query q in presence of B^+-tree and bitmap indexes is mainly determined by the number c of dimension tables conditioned in q:

- If $c = 0$, the fact table is sequentially scanned then joined with all the dimension tables involved in q through a nested-loop on their primary key indexes.
- If $c = 1$, the conditioned dimension table is accessed by the index on the conditioned attribute if such index has been created, by sequential scan otherwise. The join with the fact table is based on nested-loop if the fact table is indexed on the corresponding foreign key, on hybrid hash otherwise. The result of the join is then joined with all the other dimension tables requested in output.
- If $c > 1$, each conditioned dimension table is joined separately with the fact table. A conditioned dimension table is accessed by the index on the conditioned attribute if such index has been created, by sequential scan otherwise. The join with the fact table is based on nested-loop if the fact table is indexed on the corresponding foreign key, on hybrid hash otherwise. The tid sets obtained from the different conditioned dimension tables are then intersected, and the corresponding tuples of the fact table are accessed. Finally, the result is joined with all the dimension tables requested in output.

Of course, after the join has been completed, the grouping is executed.

Example 4 *The graphical representation of two possible execution plans on the base fact table* LINEITEM *for the query in Example 2 are depicted in Figure 2 (the group-by operator is not reported). In the first one (top of figure), only primary indexes have been created; thus, conditioned dimension tables are accessed by sequential scan and joined with the fact table by hybrid hash. In the second plan (bottom of figure), indexes on the conditioned attribute* SUPPLIER.SRegion *and* ORDER.OYear*, as well as indexes on the foreign keys* LINEITEM.SupplierId *and* LINEITEM.OrderId*, have been built; thus, conditioned dimension tables are* *accessed via index and joined by nested loop with the fact table, accessed via index as well. The rest of the plan does not change in the two cases.* □

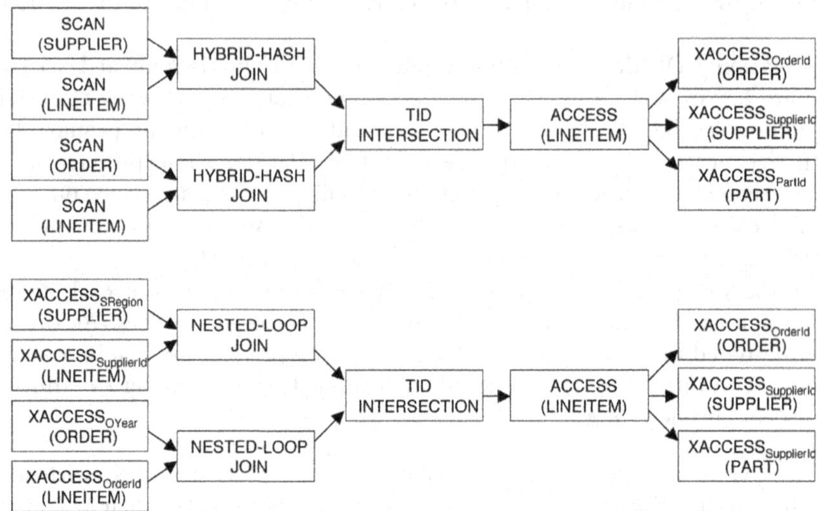

Fig. 2. Execution plans for the query in Example 2 (ACCESS denotes accessing a table via tuple identifiers, XACCESS via an index)

5 The Cost Model

Let q be a query over the star scheme composed of tables $FT^{(0)}$, $DT_1^{(0)}$, ..., $DT_n^{(0)}$, and let G and G_0 be, respectively, the grouping sets of q and $FT^{(0)}$ ($|G_0| = n$). As detailed in Section 6, our approach to evaluate the benefits of materialization and indexing for q is based on the comparison between the costs for executing q over three notable configurations of the logical/physical scheme:

1. No view is materialized and only primary indexes are built on the base fact table $FT^{(0)}$ and on each $DT_i^{(0)}$. In this case q is solved by hybrid-hash join on $FT^{(0)}$ (*reference plan*);
2. The view $FT^{(G)}$ yielding the least cost for q, i.e. the view having grouping set G, is materialized; only primary indexes are built on $FT^{(G)}$ and on each $DT_i^{(G)}$. In this case q is solved by hybrid-hash join on $FT^{(G)}$ (*view plan*);
3. No view is materialized but, besides primary indexes, also all potentially useful secondary indexes on $FT^{(0)}$ (those on foreign keys) and on each $DT_i^{(0)}$ (those on conditioned attributes) are built. In this case q is solved by nested-loop join on $FT^{(0)}$ (*index plan*).

Note that reference and view plans are structured as in Figure 2 at the top, while index plans are structured as in Figure 2 at the bottom.

The notation used in defining the cost model for these plans is summarized in Table 1; the simple formulae adopted for estimating the numbers of table pages and index leaves are omitted for brevity. According to the execution model described in Section 4 and assuming that hierarchies are ordered in such a way that the conditioned ones come first, the cost in disk pages of the reference, view, and index plans for q (*not* comprising the cost of group-by) may be estimated respectively as follows:

$$cost_{ref}(q) = \begin{cases} NPF(G_0)+ \\ \quad \sum_{i=1}^{|G|}(NPD(a_i^{(G_0)}) + NLD(a_i^{(G_0)})) & \text{if } c = 0 \\ NPF(G_0) + NPD(a_1^{(G_0)})+ \\ \quad f \cdot \sum_{i=2}^{|G|}(NPD(a_i^{(G_0)}) + NLD(a_i^{(G_0)})) & \text{if } c = 1 \\ (c+f) \cdot NPF(G_0) + \sum_{i=1}^{c} NPD(a_i^{(G_0)})+ \\ \quad f \cdot \sum_{i=1}^{|G|}(NPD(a_i^{(G_0)}) + NLD(a_i^{(G_0)})) & \text{if } c > 1 \end{cases} \tag{1}$$

$$cost_{view}(q) = \begin{cases} NPF(G)+ \\ \quad \sum_{i=1}^{|G|}(NPD(a_i^{(G)}) + NLD(a_i^{(G)})) & \text{if } c = 0 \\ NPF(G) + NPD(a_1^{(G)})+ \\ \quad f \cdot \sum_{i=2}^{|G|}(NPD(a_i^{(G)}) + NLD(a_i^{(G)})) & \text{if } c = 1 \\ (c+f) \cdot NPF(G) + \sum_{i=1}^{c} NPD(a_i^{(G)})+ \\ \quad f \cdot \sum_{i=1}^{|G|}(NPD(a_i^{(G)}) + NLD(a_i^{(G)})) & \text{if } c > 1 \end{cases} \tag{2}$$

$$cost_{ix}(q) = \begin{cases} cost_{ref}(q) & \text{if } c = 0 \\ f \cdot (NL(a_1^{(cond)}) + NPD(a_1^{(G_0)}) + NLS + NPF(G_0)+ \\ \quad \sum_{i=2}^{|G|}(NPD(a_i^{(G_0)}) + NLD(a_i^{(G_0)}))) & \text{if } c = 1 \\ \sum_{i=1}^{c} f_i \cdot (NL(a_i^{(cond)}) + NPD(a_i^{(G_0)}) + NLS)+ \\ \quad f_1 \cdot NPF(G_0)+ \\ \quad f \cdot \sum_{i=1}^{|G|}(NPD(a_i^{(G_0)}) + NLD(a_i^{(G_0)})) & \text{if } c > 1 \end{cases} \tag{3}$$

Some considerations on the assumptions and approximations introduced:

- All fact and dimension tables are assumed to be ordered on their primary keys.
- All selection predicates are assumed to select a continuous range of values.
- The cost for tid-intersection is neglected; when estimating the cost of an index access, the cost for descending the tree is neglected. The cost of group-by is not considered here: the reason for this will be made clear in Section 6.
- For simplicity, when estimating the number of accesses to the fact table in the presence of selection predicates, we assume that the tuples to be read are adjacent; a more precise evaluation would require to use the Cardenas formula [3].

These formulae have been validated by comparing the costs they estimate with the corresponding costs measured on Red Brick for different values of the parameters; the error is always less then 10%.

Table 1. Notation for the cost model

Query	
G	grouping set
$\|G\|$	number of attributes in G
$a_i^{(G)}$	attribute of the i-th hierarchy in G, $1 \leq i \leq \|G\|$
$a_i^{(G_0)}$	attribute of the i-th hierarchy in G_0, $1 \leq i \leq \|G\|$
c	number of conditioned hierarchies ($0 \leq c \leq \|G\|$)
$a_i^{(cond)}$	conditioned attribute in the i-th hierarchy, $1 \leq i \leq c$
f_i	selectivity of the selection predicate on the i-th hierarchy, $1 \leq i \leq c$ ($0 \leq f_i \leq 1$, $f_i = 1$ if not conditioned)
f	global selectivity ($f = \prod_{i=1}^{c} f_i$)
Tables	
$card(G)$	cardinality of $FT^{(G)}$
$NPF(G)$	number of pages of $FT^{(G)}$
$NPD(a_i^{(G)})$	number of pages of $DT_i^{(G)}$
Indexes	
$NL(a_i^{(cond)})$	number of leaves of index on attribute $a_i^{(cond)}$ over $DT_i^{(G_0)}$
$NLD(a_i^{(G)})$	number of leaves of primary index on $DT_i^{(G)}$
$NLF(G)$	number of leaves of primary index of $FT^{(G)}$
NLS	number of leaves of secondary index on a foreign key of $FT^{(0)}$

The results presented in this section are computed on a star scheme including 3 equal hierarchies of 10 attributes each; the domain cardinality is 1000. The base fact table includes 10^6 tuples with 8 measures. Each measure and attributes takes, respectively, 8 and 20 bytes. Each disk page is 8 KB. Figure 3 shows how $cost_{view}(q)$ depends on the grouping set G and on the global selectivity f of q for $c = 2$; the cost of the reference plan is very similar to $cost_{view}(q)$ for $G = G_0$. The cost of the view plan is linear in both $card(G)$ and f; this is due to the fact that its most significant term is $(c + f) \cdot NPF(G)$.

Figure 4 shows how $cost_{ix}(q)$ depends on G and f for $c = 2$. The cost does not significatively depend on $card(G)$, since q is executed on $FT^{(0)}$; the dependence on f is slightly parabolic.

6 Benefit Evaluation

In this section we will discuss and compare the benefits, meant as savings per disk page, of view materialization and indexing for different classes of queries.

We define the *benefit of materialization* for q as the difference between the total costs for executing q on $FT^{(0)}$ and on $FT^{(G)}$ with only primary indexes built, divided by the space overhead of materialization:

$$bf_V(q) = \frac{cost_{ref}(q) + costGB_{ref}(q) - (cost_{view}(q) + costGB_{view}(q))}{space_{view}(q)} \quad (4)$$

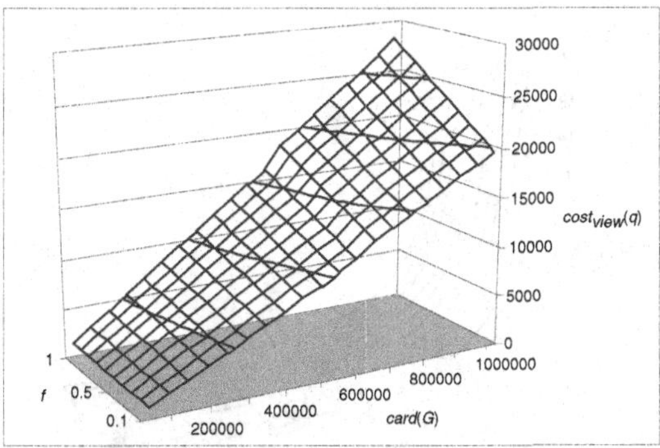

Fig. 3. Cost of the view plan for $c = 2$ (expressed in disk pages)

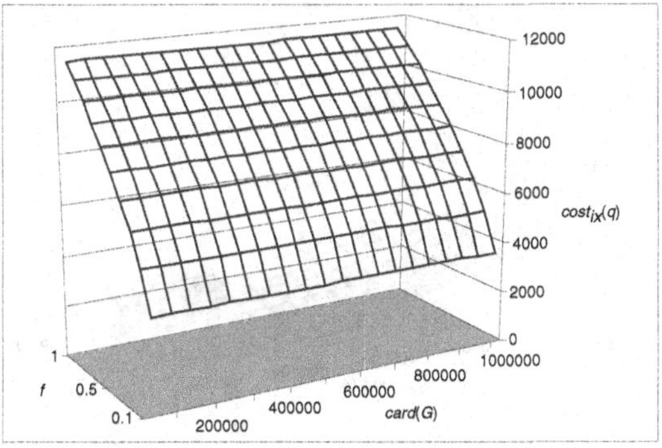

Fig. 4. Cost of the index plan for $c = 2$

where $costGB_{ref}(q)$ and $costGB_{view}(q)$ are the costs of grouping for the reference and the view plans, while

$$space_{view}(q) = NPF(G) + NLF(G) + \sum_{a \in G}(NPD(a) + NLD(a)) \qquad (5)$$

By definition, for a query q whose grouping set is $G^{(0)}$ it is $space_{view}(q) = 0$ and $bf_V(q) = 0$.

As to grouping, consistently with the Red Brick implementation, we assume that a hash-based algorithm is used. The experimental tests revealed that, while the cost of grouping depends substantially on the number of groups in output, it depends only marginally on the number of tuples to be grouped. Thus, since the number of groups is the same for both plans (it only depends on the grouping set and on the selectivity of q), we will assume for simplicity that $costGB_{ref}(q) = costGB_{view}(q)$. [2]

[2] The error introduced is obviously higher for low values of $card(G)$, since the difference between the number of tuples to be grouped in the reference and the view plans

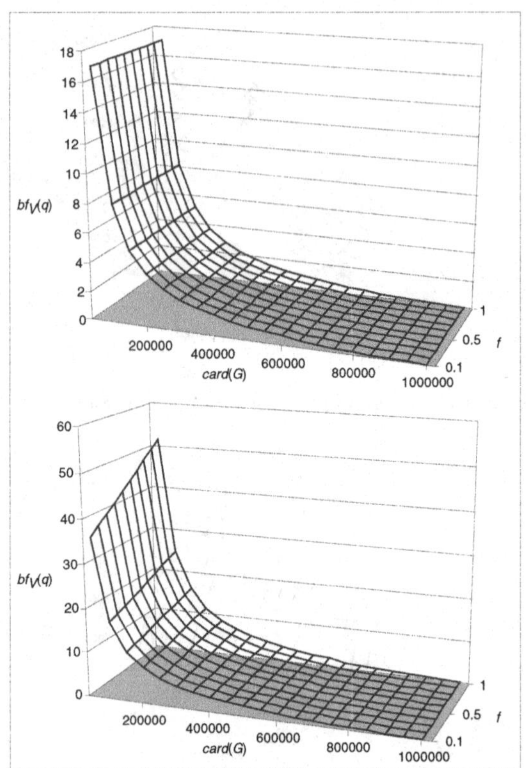

Fig. 5. Benefit of materialization for $c = 1$ (top) and $c = 2$ (bottom)

Figure 5 shows the benefit of materialization for $c = 1$ and $c = 2$ (case $c = 0$ is not shown since very similar to $c = 1$). While in the first case the benefit is largely independent of f [3], in the second it varies linearly with it. The dependence on $card(G)$ is always hyperbolic (roughly, it is $bf_V(q) = O(card(G_0)/card(G))$).

We define the *benefit of indexing* for q as the difference between the costs for executing q on $FT^{(0)}$ when only primary indexes are built and when all potentially useful indexes are built, divided by the space overhead of indexing; the group-by cost is not considered since it is the same for both the reference and the index plans (both the tuples in input and the groups in output are the same for the two plans):

is more relevant. On the other hand, in this case the benefit is high since the view on G is very small. Thus, a possible way of taking the group-by cost into account would be to multiply the benefit of materialization by a corrective factor greater than 1.

[3] This is due to the fact that no indexes are built and hybrid-hash join is used. The main term determining the cost is that related to the sequential scan of the fact table, which is independent of f.

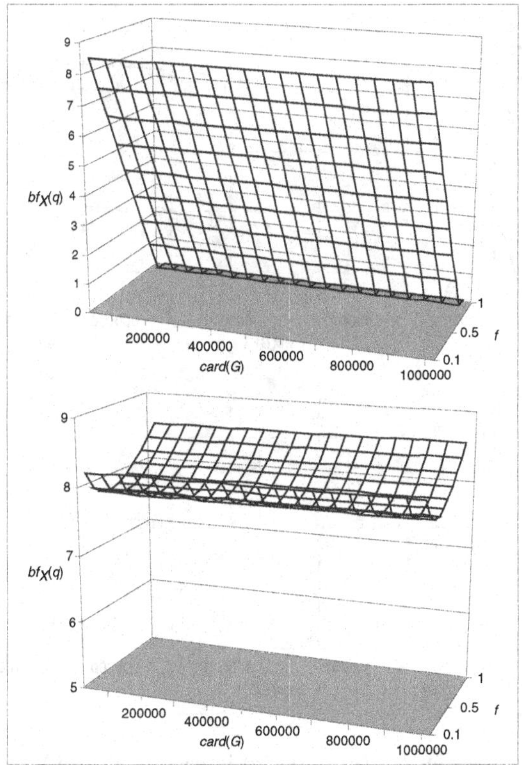

Fig. 6. Benefit of indexing for $c = 1$ (top) and $c = 2$ (bottom)

$$bf_X(q) = \frac{cost_{ref}(q) - cost_{ix}(q)}{space_{ix}(q)} \tag{6}$$

where [4]

$$space_{ix}(q) = \sum_{i=1}^{c} NL(a_i^{(cond)}) + c \cdot NLS \tag{7}$$

Figure 6 shows the benefit of indexing for $c = 1$ and $c = 2$ (for $c = 0$ it is obviously $bf_X(q) = 0$). While in the first case the benefit is linear in f, in the second it is nearly constant; in both cases it does not depend on $card(G)$.

It is now very interesting to compare the two benefits. Figure 7 shows the contour lines of the surface representing $bf_V(q) - bf_X(q)$ in function of $card(G)$ and f; the white and the grey areas correspond, respectively, to $bf_V(q) > bf_X(q)$ and $bf_V(q) < bf_X(q)$. Compare this diagram with the qualitative one sketched in Figure 1: the influence of selectivity is less relevant than we expected; besides, though the benefit of materialization reaches higher values than indexing, the convenience area for indexing is much larger.

[4] Assuming that, for indexing foreign keys of fact tables, B^+-trees are always used.

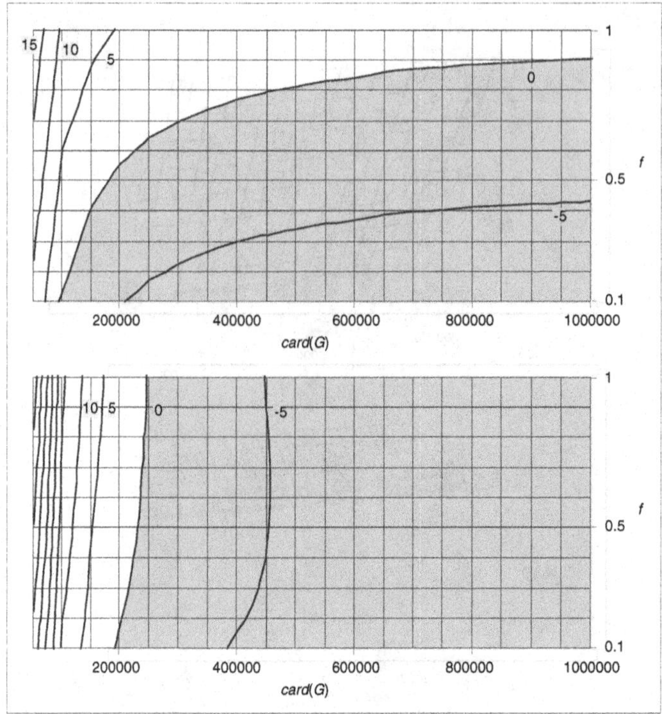

Fig. 7. Contour lines for $bf_V(q) - bf_X(q)$ in case $c = 1$ (top) and $c = 2$ (bottom)

7 Balancing Space Constraints

Given a constraint S (expressed in disk pages) on the total disk space available for optimization, in this section we propose an approach to estimate the fractions of S to be devoted to materialization and indexing, S_V and S_X respectively, with reference to a given workload W. We will assume that the space $S_V^{(0)}$, required to store the base fact table $FT^{(0)}$ together with its dimension tables and primary indexes, is *not* included in S; thus, even case $S = 0$ corresponds to a feasible constraint (no optimization at all). On the other hand, S_V and S_X are to be meant, respectively, as the space to be allocated for views (not including the base fact table) plus their related dimension tables and primary indexes, and the space to be allocated for indexes on foreign keys of fact tables (including the base one) and non-key attributes of dimension tables.

We will first introduce two extreme optimization situations, which we will call full materialization and full indexing:

- Given a workload W, *full materialization* occurs when, for each query $q \in W$, an ad hoc view $FT^{(G)}$ (where G is the grouping set of q) is materialized. Letting $S_V^{full} = \sum_{q \in W} space_{view}(q)$, the total disk space required for full materialization is $S_V^{(0)} + S_V^{full}$.

- A materialized view is *fully indexed* when, for each $q \in W$ to be executed on it, all the useful indexes have been created. Given a set of views taking space S_V, we will denote with $(S_V)_X^{full}$ the total space for full indexing all of them plus the base fact table; thus, $(0)_X^{full}$ is the space to fully index the base fact table only, while $(S_V^{full})_X^{full}$ is the space to fully index also all the views in case of full materialization. We estimate $(S_V)_X^{full}$ by assuming that

$$\frac{S_V + S_V^{(0)}}{(S_V)_X^{full}} \approxeq \frac{S_V^{full} + S_V^{(0)}}{(S_V^{full})_X^{full}} \tag{8}$$

$$\Rightarrow \quad (S_V)_X^{full} \approxeq \frac{S_V + S_V^{(0)}}{S_V^{full} + S_V^{(0)}} \cdot (S_V^{full})_X^{full} \tag{9}$$

In the remainder we will assume that $S \leq S_V^{full} + (S_V^{full})_X^{full}$; if not, the space constraint is redundant and the space trade-off can be easily found.

As a first observation, an index may only be built on a view which has been materialized: thus, for a set of materialized views taking space S_V, $(S_V)_X^{full}$ is an upper bound to the space which can be realistically filled with indexes. For instance, given $S = 10000$ disk pages, let $S_V = 6000$ and $S_X = 4000$ define the space trade-off for a workload which encourages indexing. Now, suppose that fully indexing the views materialized within S_V plus the base fact table requires only 1000 pages: 3000 pages uselessly reserved to indexes will be wasted, while they could have been more profitably used for materialization.

As a second observation, the space reserved for materialization should not overcome S_V^{full}. For instance, let $S = 10000$, $S_V = 8000$, and $S_X = 2000$ for a workload which encourages materialization. Now, suppose that full materialization requires only 6000 pages besides the base fact table: 2000 pages uselessly reserved to views will be wasted, while they could have been more profitably used for indexing.

As depicted in Figure 8, this situation can be summarized by constraining the feasible trade-off solutions, for each value of S, as follows:

$$S_V + S_X = S \tag{10}$$

$$0 \leq S_X \leq (S_V)_X^{full} \tag{11}$$

$$0 \leq S_V \leq S_V^{full} \tag{12}$$

Thus the grey area shown in Figure 8, delimited by

$$S_X^{upper} = \min\left\{(S_V)_X^{full}, S\right\} = \min\left\{\frac{(S_V^{full})_X^{full} \cdot (S + S_V^{(0)})}{S_V^{full} + (S_V^{full})_X^{full} + S_V^{(0)}}, S\right\} \tag{13}$$

$$S_X^{lower} = \max\{0, S - S_V^{full}\} \tag{14}$$

represents the space of the feasible solutions ($S_X^{lower} \leq S_X^{upper}$ when $0 \leq S \leq S_V^{full} + (S_V^{full})_X^{full}$). Within such space, the optimal values for S_V and S_X are

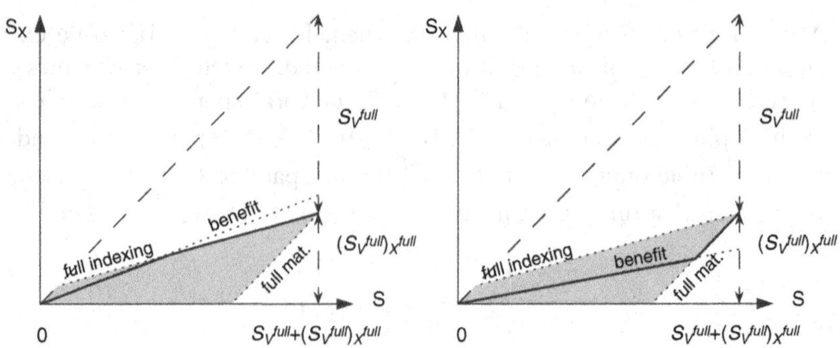

Fig. 8. Estimated values for S_X in function of S when the workload encourages indexing (left) and materialization (right)

estimated by considering the ratio between the benefits of materialization and indexing, computed on the whole workload. For a given global constraint S and with reference to workload $W = \{q_1, \dots, q_p\}$, let

$$S_X^{bf} = \frac{S}{1 + \frac{\sum_{q_i \in W} bf_V(q_i)}{\sum_{q_i \in W} bf_X(q_i)}} \tag{15}$$

Then, the estimate for the optimal space trade-off is defined as follows:

$$S_X = \begin{cases} S_X^{lower}, & \text{if } S_X^{bf} < S_X^{lower} \\ S_X^{bf}, & \text{if } S_X^{lower} \leq S_X^{bf} \leq S_X^{lower} \\ S_X^{upper}, & \text{if } S_X^{bf} > S_X^{upper} \end{cases} \tag{16}$$

$$S_V = S - S_X \tag{17}$$

8 Experimental Tests and Conclusions

In this paper we have presented a comparative evaluation of the benefits brought by view materialization and indexing in DW's in function of the query characteristics. Then, we have proposed a heuristic approach to estimate, for a given workload and a global space constraint, the optimal trade-off between the space devoted to view materialization and that devoted to indexing.

The experimental tests presented in this section were conducted on the same star scheme used in Section 5. Three different workloads were considered, each including 25 queries: W_1, which encourages indexing, W_2, which encourages materialization, and W_3 in which queries are uniformly distributed in the space of $card(G)$ and f.

Figure 9 shows how the global cost of workload W_3 (expressed in disk pages) varies depending on the relative space amount devoted to materialization and indexing, for different values of S. Since each disk page takes 8 KB, the space

Table 2. Percentage difference between the workload costs for the optimal and the estimated solutions. In parentheses the situations in which the space constraint is redundant

S	W_1	W_2	W_3
12800	0.0%	0.1%	0.0%
25600	0.6%	1.4%	1.7%
38400	0.5%	0.2%	1.0%
51200	0.4%	1.5%	0.3%
64000	0.0%	(0.0%)	0.0%
76800	0.0%	(0.0%)	2.5%
89600	0.0%	(0.0%)	0.0%
102400	0.0%	(0.0%)	0.0%
115200	0.0%	(0.0%)	(0.0%)
128000	0.0%	(0.0%)	(0.0%)

constraint ranges approximatively between 100 MB and 1 GB. The algorithms used for view materialization and indexing are those proposed, respectively, in [2] and [4]. The cost for a non-optimal space trade-off may even be three times that of the optimal trade-off; the irregular shape of the curves is due to the sub-optimality introduced by the heuristic approaches to materialization and indexing.

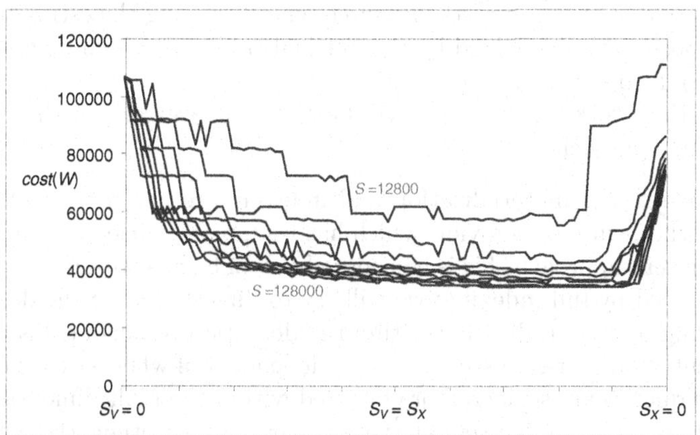

Fig. 9. Cost of workload W_3, as a function of the relative space amount devoted to materialization and indexing, for increasing values of S

Figure 10 compares the estimated and optimal values for S_X in function of S for all three workloads, emphasizing the relative position of the full indexing and the full materialization lines, as well as the values of S_X^{bf} suggested by the ratio between the materialization and the indexing benefits.

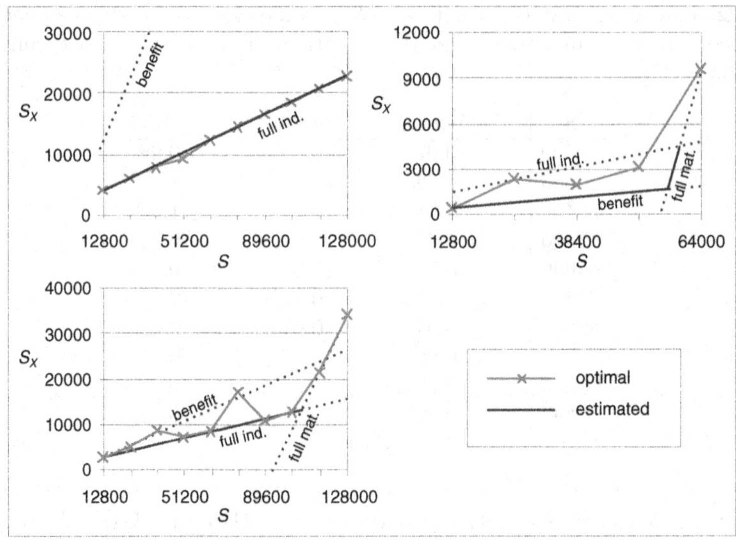

Fig. 10. Estimated and optimal values for S_X in function of S for W_1 (top left), W_2 (top right), and W_3 (bottom)

Finally, Table 2 reports the percentage difference between the workload costs for the optimal solution and for the solution estimated by our approach.

It is apparent that the costs measured when applying the estimated trade-off are very close to those yielded by the optimal trade-off, which demonstrates the utility of our approach.

Our future work on this topic will be aimed at overcoming the main limitations of our approach:

- The benefits of materialization and indexing are not really independent of each other, since only a view which has been materialized can be indexed. In our present approach this is considered through the thresholding mechanism introduced by full indexing; we will try to directly model the dependence of indexing on materialization within the definition of benefit, instead.
- Presently, our benefit estimates are independent of whether the grouping sets of the queries are scattered or clustered within the multidimensional lattice. Intuitively, if grouping sets are very "near" to each other, the actual benefit of materialization is higher than our estimate, since one common view may dramatically decrease the cost for several queries.
- Rule-based optimizers present some well-known drawbacks due to the fact that they do not take query costs into account. Developing and adopting a detailed cost model also for a cost-based optimizer will widen the usability of our approach.
- In this approach we considered only the workload cost as an indicator of the quality of optimization, while also the maintenance costs of both views and indexes should be considered.

Another interesting evolution of our approach is related to the absence of a specific workload. In this case, S_X^{bf} could be estimated by considering a uniform distribution of queries, i.e. by computing the integrals of $bf_V(q)$ and $bf_X(q)$ over the $card(G) \times f$ space.

References

1. S. Agrawal, S. Chaudhuri, and V. Narasayya. Automated selection of materialized views and indexes for SQL databases. In *Proc. 26th VLDB*, pages 496–501, Cairo, Egypt, 2000.
2. E. Baralis, S. Paraboschi, and E. Teniente. Materialized view selection in multidimensional database. In *Proc. 23rd VLDB*, pages 156–165, Athens, 1997.
3. A.F. Cardenas. Analysis and performance of inverted database structures. *Communications of the ACM*, 18(5):253–263, 1975.
4. M. Golfarelli, S. Rizzi, and E. Saltarelli. Index selection for data warehousing. In *Proc. DMDW*, Toronto, 2002.
5. A. Gupta, V. Harinarayan, and D. Quass. Aggregate-query processing in data warehousing environments. In *Proc. 21st VLDB*, Zurich, 1995.
6. H. Gupta. Selection of views to materialize in a data warehouse. In *Proc. ICDT*, pages 98–112, 1997.
7. H. Gupta, V. Harinarayan, A. Rajaraman, and J.D. Ullman. Index selection for OLAP. In *Proc. ICDE*, pages 208–219, 1997.
8. H. Gupta and I.S. Mumick. Selection of views to materialize under a maintenance cost constraint. In *Proc. ICDT*, Jerusalem, Israel, 1999.
9. V. Harinarayan, A. Rajaraman, and J. Ullman. Implementing data cubes efficiently. In *Proc. ACM SIGMOD Conf.*, Montreal, 1996.
10. Informix. *Informix Red Brick Decision Server administrator's guide, Version 6.0*, November 1999.
11. W.J. Labio, D. Quass, and B. Adelberg. Physical database design for data warehouses. In *Proc. ICDE*, pages 277–288, 1997.
12. V. Markl, F. Ramsak, and R. Pieringer. The TransBase HyperCube RDBMS: multi-dimensional indexing of relational tables. In *Proc. 17th ICDE*, Heidelberg, Germany, 2001.
13. P. O'Neil and G. Graefe. Multi-table joins through bitmapped join indices. *SIGMOD Record*, 24(3):8–11, 1995.
14. P. O'Neil and D. Quass. Improved query performance with variant indexes. In *Proc. ACM SIGMOD Int. Conf. on Management of Data*, Tucson, AZ, 1997.
15. M. Poess and C. Floyd. New tpc benchmarks for decision support and web commerce. *ACM SIGMOD Record*, 29(4), 2000.
16. D. Theodoratos and M. Bouzeghoub. A general framework for the view selection problem for data warehouse design and evolution. In *Proc. DOLAP*, McLean, 2000.

A Framework for the Design of ETL Scenarios

Panos Vassiliadis[1], Alkis Simitsis[2], Panos Georgantas[2], and Manolis Terrovitis[2]

[1] University of Ioannina,
Dept. of Computer Science,
Ioannina, Greece
pvassil@cs.uoi.gr
[2] National Technical University of Athens,
Dept. of Electrical and Computer Eng.,
Athens, Greece
{asimi, pgeor, mter}@dbnet.ece.ntua.gr

Abstract. Extraction-Transformation-Loading (ETL) tools are pieces of software responsible for the extraction of data from several sources, their cleansing, customization and insertion into a data warehouse. In this paper, we delve into the logical design of ETL scenarios. We describe a framework for the declarative specification of ETL scenarios with two main characteristics: genericity and customization. Moreover, we present a palette of several templates, representing frequently used ETL activities along with their semantics and their interconnection. Finally, we discuss implementation issues and we present a graphical tool, ARKTOS II that facilitates the design of ETL scenarios, based on our model.

1 Introduction

Data warehouse operational processes normally compose a labor intensive workflow, involving data extraction, transformation, integration, cleaning and transport. To deal with this workflow, specialized tools are already available in the market [3,4,6,8], under the general title *Extraction-Transformation-Loading* (ETL) tools. To give a general idea of the functionality of these tools we mention their most prominent tasks, which include (a) the identification of relevant information at the source side; (b) the extraction of this information; (c) the customization and integration of the information coming from multiple sources into a common format; (d) the cleaning of the resulting data set, on the basis of database and business rules, and (e) the propagation of the data to the data warehouse and/or data marts. In the sequel, we will not discriminate between the tasks of ETL and Data Cleaning and adopt the name ETL for both these kinds of activities.

If we treat an ETL scenario as a composite workflow, in a traditional way, its designer is obliged to define several of its parameters (Fig. 1). First, the designer is responsible for defining an *Execution Plan* for the scenario. The definition of an execution plan can be seen from various perspectives. The *Execution Sequence* involves the specification of which activity runs first, second, and so on, which activities run in parallel, or when a semaphore is defined so that several activities are synchronized at a rendezvous point. ETL activities normally run in batch, so the

J. Eder and M. Missikoff (Eds.): CAiSE 2003, LNCS 2681, pp. 520–535, 2003.

designer needs to specify an *Execution Schedule*, i.e., the time points or events that trigger the execution of the scenario as a whole. Finally, due to system crashes, it is imperative that there exists a *Recovery Plan*, specifying the sequence of steps to be taken in the case of failure for a certain activity (e.g., retry to execute the activity, or undo any intermediate results produced so far). At the same time, an *Administration Plan* should be specified, involving the notification of the administrator either on-line (monitoring) or off-line (logging) for the status of an executed activity, as well as the security and authentication management for the ETL environment.

We find that research has not dealt with the definition of data-centric workflows to the entirety of its extent. In the ETL case, for example, due to the data centric nature of the process, the designer must deal with the *relationship of the involved activities with the underlying data*. This involves the definition of a *Primary Data Flow* that describes the route of data from the sources towards their final destination in the data warehouse, as they pass through the activities of the scenario. Also, due to possible quality problems of the processed data, the designer is obliged to define a flow for the problematic data, i.e., the rows that violate integrity or business rules. It is the combination of the execution sequence and the data flow that generates the semantics of the ETL workflow: the data flow defines what each activity does and the execution plan defines in which order and combination.

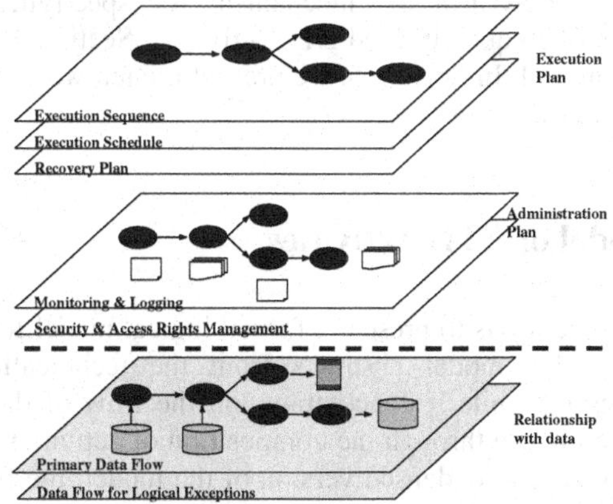

Fig. 1. Different perspectives for an ETL workflow

In this paper we work in the internals of the primary data flow of ETL scenarios. We present a generic metamodel for the definition of the data-centric part of ETL activities. Particular attention is paid to the declarative specification of the data semantics of activities. In the pursuit of higher reusability and flexibility, we specialize the set of our generic metamodel constructs with a palette of frequently-used ETL activities, which we call *templates*. Moreover, in order to achieve a uniform extensibility mechanism for this library of built-ins, we have to deal with specific language issues: thus, we also discuss the mechanics of template instantiation to concrete activities. The design concepts that we introduce have been implemented in a tool, ARKTOS II, which is also presented.

Our contributions can be listed as follows:

- First, *we define a formal logical Metamodel as a logical abstraction of ETL processes.* The data stores, activities and their constituent parts are formally defined. An activity is defined as an entity with (possibly more than one) input schema(ta), an output schema and a parameter schema, so that the activity is populated each time with its proper parameter values. The flow of data from producers towards their consumers is achieved through the usage of *provider relationships* that map the attributes of the former to the respective attributes of the latter. A serializable combination of ETL activities, provider relationships and data stores constitutes an ETL scenario.
- Second, *we provide a reusability framework* that complements the genericity of the Metamodel. Practically, this is achieved from a set of "built-in" specializations of the entities of the Metamodel layer, specifically tailored for the most frequent elements of ETL scenarios. This palette of template activities will be referred to as *Template layer* and it is characterized by its extensibility; in fact, due to language considerations, we provide the details of the mechanism that instantiates templates to specific activities.
- Finally, we discuss *implementation* issues and we present a graphical tool, ARKTOS II that facilitates the design of ETL scenarios, based on our model.

This paper is organized as follows. In Section 2 we present a generic model of ETL activities. Section 3 describes the mechanism for specifying and materializing template definitions of frequently used ETL activities. Section 4 presents ARKTOS II, a prototype graphical tool. In Section 5, we present related work. Finally, in Section 6 we conclude our results.

2 Generic Model of ETL Activities

The purpose of this section is to present a formal logical model for the activities of an ETL environment. This model abstracts from the technicalities of monitoring, scheduling and logging while it concentrates on the flow of data from the sources towards the data warehouse through the composition of activities and data stores. For lack of space we present a condensed version of the model; the full-blown version of the model can be found in [10].

- *Data types.* Each data type `T` is characterized by a name and a domain, i.e., a countable set of values. The values of the domains are also referred to as *constants.*
- *Attributes.* Attributes are characterized by their name and data type. Attributes and constants are uniformly referred to as *terms.*
- A *Schema* is a finite list of attributes. Each entity that is characterized by one or more schemata will be called *Structured Entity.*
- *RecordSets.* A recordset is characterized by its name, its (logical) schema and its (physical) extension (i.e., a finite set of records under the recordset schema). We can treat any data structure as a "record set" provided that there are the means to logically restructure it into a flat, typed record schema. In the rest of this paper, we will mainly deal with the two most popular types of recordsets, namely *relational tables* and *record files.*

- *Functions*. A *Function Type* comprises a name, a finite list of *parameter data types*, and a single *return data type*. A *function* is an instance of a function type.
- *Elementary Activities*. In our framework, activities are logical abstractions representing parts, or full modules of code. We employ an abstraction of the source code of an activity, in the form of a LDL statement, in order to avoid dealing with the peculiarities of a particular programming language. An *Elementary Activity* is formally described by the following elements:
    - *Name*: a unique identifier for the activity.
    - *Input Schemata*: a finite set of one or more input schemata that receive data from the data providers of the activity.
    - *Output Schema*: a finite set of one or more schemata that describe the placeholders for the rows that are processed by the elementary activity.
    - *Parameter List*: a set of pairs which act as regulators for the functionality of the activity (the target attribute of a foreign key check, for example). The first component of the pair is the name of the parameter and the second is its value, i.e., a schema, an attribute, a function or a constant.
    - *Output Operational Semantics*: a declarative statement describing the content passed to each of the output of the operation, with respect to its input. This statement defines (a) the operation performed on the rows that pass through the activity towards its corresponding output schema and (b) a mapping between the attributes of the input schema(ta) and the respective attributes of the output schema. In this paper, we focus on LDL [7,13] as the formalism for the expression of this statement.
    - *Priority*: the order of execution of the activity within the particular scenario. In our approach we simplify the complexity of the Execution Plan (which includes conditional paths, parallel executions, rendezvous, etc.) through a total order of execution for the activities of the scenario.
- *Provider* relationships. These are `1:N` relationships that involve attributes with a provider-consumer relationship. The flow of data from the data sources towards the data warehouse is performed through the composition of activities in a larger scenario. In this context, the input for an activity can be either a persistent data store, or another activity, i.e., any structured entity under a specific schema. Provider relationships capture the mapping between the attributes of the schemata of the involved entities. Note that a consumer attribute can also be populated by a constant, in certain cases.
- *Part_of* relationships. These relationships involve attributes and parameters and relate them to their respective activity, recordset or function to which they belong.
- *Instance-of* relationships. These relationships are defined among a data/function type and its instances.
- *Regulator* relationships. These relationships are defined among the parameters of activities and the terms that populate these activities.
- *Derived provider relationships*. A derived provider relationship is another form of provider relationship that occurs through the composition of provider and regulator relationships. Formally, assume that `source` is a node in the architecture graph, `target` is an attribute of the output schema of an activity `A` and `x,y` are parameters in the parameter list of `A`. The parameters `x` and `y` need not necessarily be different. Then, a derived provider relationship

pr(source,target) exists iff the following regulator relationships (i.e., edges) exist: rr1(source,x) and rr2(y,target). Intuitively, the case of derived relationships models the situation where the activity computes a new attribute in its output. In this case, the produced output depends on all the attributes that populate the parameters of the activity, resulting in the definition of the corresponding derived relationship.

For each of the aforementioned entities, we assume an infinitely countable, mutually disjoint set of names (i.e., a domain) and its respective scenario-specific finite subset, which we list in the following: **D** for Data Types, **F** for Function Types, **C** for Constants, Ω for Attributes, Φ for Functions, **S** for Schemata, **RS** for RecordSets, **A** for Activities, **Pr** for Provider Relationships, **Po** for Part-Of Relationships, **Io** for Instance-Of Relationships, **Rr** for Regulator Relationships, **Dr** for Derived Provider Relationships. The full layout of an ETL scenario, involving activities, recordsets and functions can be deployed along a graph in an execution sequence that can be linearly serialized. We call this graph, the *Architecture Graph*. The involved data types, function types, constants, attributes, activities, recordsets and functions constitute the nodes of the graph. We model the different kinds of relationships of these nodes (i.e., part-of, instance-of, provider, regulator and derived provider relationships) as the edges of the graph. Formally, let **G(V,E)** be the Architecture Graph of an ETL scenario. Then, $\mathbf{V} = \mathbf{D} \cup \mathbf{F} \cup \mathbf{C} \cup \Omega \cup \Phi \cup \mathbf{S} \cup \mathbf{RS} \cup \mathbf{A}$ and $\mathbf{E} = \mathbf{Pr} \cup \mathbf{Po} \cup \mathbf{Io} \cup \mathbf{Rr} \cup \mathbf{Dr}$.

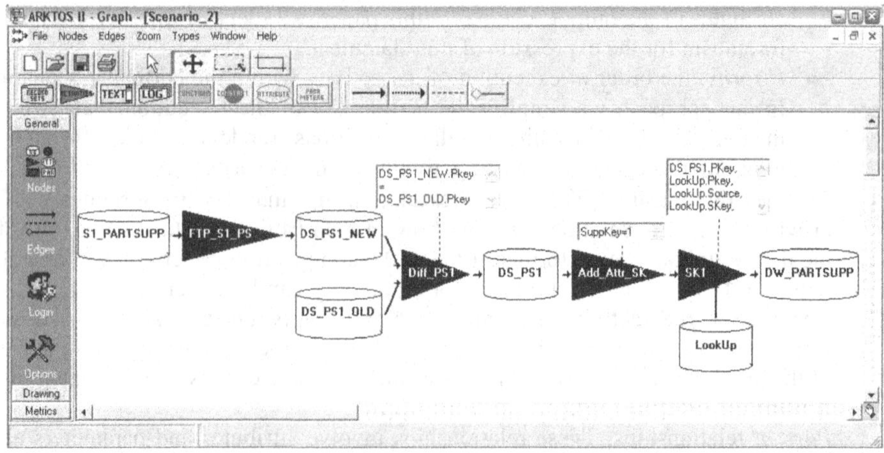

Fig. 2. Bird's-eye view of the motivating example

Motivating Example. To motivate our discussion we will present an example involving the propagation of data from a certain source S1, towards a data warehouse DW through intermediate recordsets belonging to a Data Staging Area (DSA) DS, where all the transformations take place. The scenario involves the propagation of data from the table PARTSUPP of source S_1 to the data warehouse DW. Table DW.PARTSUPP(PKEY,SUPPKEY,DATE,QTY,COST) stores information for the available quantity (QTY) and cost (COST) of parts (PKEY) per supplier (SUPPKEY). The data source S_1.PARTSUPP(PKEY,DATE,QTY,COST) records the supplies from a specific geographical region, e.g., Europe. All the attributes, except for the dates are instances of the `Integer` type. The scenario is graphically depicted in Fig. 2 and involves the following transformations.

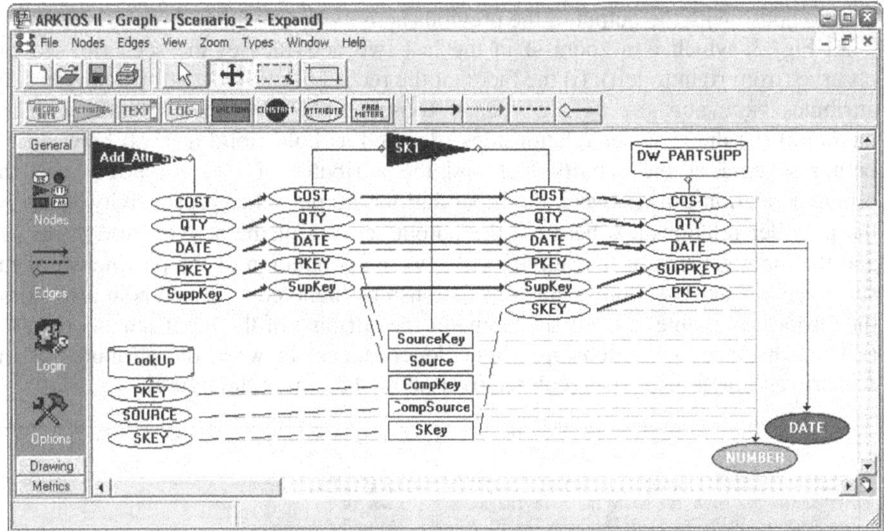

Fig. 3. Architecture graph of a part of the motivating example

1. First, we transfer via `ftp` the snapshot from the source S_1.PARTSUPP to the file DS.PS1_NEW and of the DSA.
2. In the DSA we maintain locally two copies of the snapshot of the source. The recordset DS.PS1_NEW(PKEY,DATE,QTY,COST) stands for the last transferred snapshot of S_1.PARTSUPP. By detecting the difference of this snapshot with the respective version of the previous loading, DS.PS1_OLD(PKEY,DATE,QTY,COST), we can derive the newly inserted rows in source S_1.PARTSUPP. We store these rows in the file DS.PS_1(PKEY,DATE,QTY,COST). Note that the difference activity that we employ, namely `Diff_PS1`, checks for differences only on the primary key of the recordsets; thus we ignore any possible deletions or updates for the attributes COST, QTY of existing rows.
3. In order to keep track of the supplier of each row, we need to add a 'flag' attribute, namely SUPPKEY, indicating 1 for the respective supplier. This is achieved through the activity `Add_Attr_SK`.
4. Next, we assign a surrogate key on PKEY. In the data warehouse context, it is common tactics to replace the keys of the production systems with a uniform key, which we call a *surrogate key* [5]. The basic reasons for this replacement are performance and semantic homogeneity. Textual attributes are not the best candidates for indexed keys and thus need to be replaced by integer keys. At the same time, different production systems might use different keys for the same object, or the same key for different objects, resulting in the need for a global replacement of these values in the data warehouse. This replacement is performed through a lookup table of the form L(PRODKEY,SOURCE,SKEY). The SOURCE column is due to the fact that there can be synonyms in the different sources, which

are mapped to different objects in the data warehouse. In our case, the activity that performs the surrogate key assignment for the attribute PKEY is SK1. It uses the lookup table LOOKUP(PKEY,SOURCE,SKEY). Finally, we populate the data warehouse with the output of the previous activity.

In Fig. 3, which is a zoom-in in the last two activities of the scenario, we can observe (from right to left): (i) the fact that the recordset DW.PARTSUPP comprises the attributes PKEY,SUPPKEY,DATE,QTY,COST (observe the UML-like notation with the diamond) (ii) the provider relationships (denoted as bold, solid arrows) between the output schema of the activity SK1 and the attributes of DW.PARTSUPP; (iii) the provider relationships between the input and the output schema of activity SK1; (iv) the provider relationships between the output schema of the activity Add_Attr_SK and the input schema of the activity SK1; (v) the population of the parameters of the surrogate key activity from regulator relationships (denoted as dotted bold arrows) by the attributes of table LOOKUP and some of the attribute of the input schema of SK1; (vi) the instance-of relationships (light dotted edges) between the attributes of the scenario and their data types (colored ovals at the bottom of the figure).

```
a1_in1(A_IN1_A1,A_IN1_A2,A_IN1_A3,A_IN1_A4)
<- ds_ps1_new(A_IN1_A1,A_IN1_A2,A_IN1_A3,
        A_IN1_A4).

a1_in2(A_IN2_A1,A_IN2_A2,A_IN2_A3,A_IN2_A4)
<- ds_ps1_old(A_IN2_A1,A_IN2_A2,A_IN2_A3,
        A_IN2_A4).

semi_join(A_OUT_A1,A_OUT_A2,A_OUT_A3,
                         A_OUT_A4) <-
a1_in1(A_IN1_A1,A_IN1_A2,A_IN1_A3,A_IN1_A4),
  a1_in2(A_IN2_A1,_,_,_),
  A_OUT_A1=A_IN1_A1,
  A_OUT_A1=A_IN2_A1,
  A_OUT_A2=A_IN1_A2,
  A_OUT_A3=A_IN1_A3,
  A_OUT_A4=A_IN1_A4.

a1_out(A_OUT_A1,A_OUT_A2,A_OUT_A3,A_OUT_A4)
<-
a1_in1(A_IN1_A1,A_IN1_A2,A_IN1_A3,A_IN1_A4),
~semi_join(A_IN1_A1,A_IN1_A2,A_IN1_A3,A_IN1_
A4),
  A_OUT_A1=A_IN1_A1,
  A_OUT_A2=A_IN1_A2,
  A_OUT_A3=A_IN1_A3,
  A_OUT_A4=A_IN1_A4.

ds_ps1(X1,X2,X3,X4) <-
a_out(A_OUT_A1,A_OUT_A2,A_OUT_A3,A_OUT_A4),
  X1=A_OUT_A1,
  X2=A_OUT_A2,
  X3=A_OUT_A3,
  X4=A_OUT_A4.

a2_in(A_IN_A1,A_IN_A2,A_IN_A3,A_IN_A4)<-
  ds_ps1(X1,X2,X3,X4),
  X1=A_IN_A1,
  X2=A_IN_A2,
  X3=A_IN_A3,
  X4=A_IN_A4.

a2_out(A_OUT_A1,A_OUT_A2,A_OUT_A3,
                    A_OUT_A4,A_OUT_A5) <-
  a2_in(A_IN_A1,A_IN_A2,A_IN_A3,A_IN_A4),
  A_OUT_A1=A_IN_A1,
  A_OUT_A2=A_IN_A2,
  A_OUT_A3=A_IN_A3,
  A_OUT_A4=A_IN_A4,
  A_OUT_A5='SOURCE1'.

a3_in(A_IN_A1,A_IN_A2,A_IN_A3,A_IN_A4,A_IN_A5) <-
a2_out(A_OUT_A1,A_OUT_A2,A_OUT_A3,A_OUT_A4,
                                  A_OUT_A5),
  A_OUT_A1=A_IN_A1,
  A_OUT_A2=A_IN_A2,
  A_OUT_A3=A_IN_A3,
  A_OUT_A4=A_IN_A4,
  A_OUT_A5=A_IN_A5.

a3_out(A_OUT_A1,A_OUT_A2,A_OUT_A3,A_OUT_A4,
                         A_OUT_A5,A_OUT_A6)<-
  a3_in(A_IN_A1,A_IN_A2,A_IN_A3,A_IN_A4,A_IN_A5),
  lookup(A_IN_A5,A_IN_A1,A_OUT_A6),
  A_OUT_A1=A_IN_A1,
  A_OUT_A2=A_IN_A2,
  A_OUT_A3=A_IN_A3,
  A_OUT_A4=A_IN_A4,
  A_OUT_A5=A_IN_A5.

dw_partsupp(X1,X2,X3,X4,X5,X6) <-
  a3_out(A_OUT_A1,A_OUT_A2,A_OUT_A3,A_OUT_A4,
  A_OUT_A5,A_OUT_A6).

LEGEND: a1: Diff_PS1  a2: Add_Attr_SK  a3: SK1
```

Fig. 4. LDL specification of the motivating example

Language Issues. Originally, we used to specify the semantics of activities with SQL statements. Still, although clear and easy to write and understand, SQL is rather hard to use if one is to perform rewriting and composition of statements. Thus, we have supplemented SQL with LDL [7], a logic-programming, declarative language as the basis of our scenario definition. LDL is a Datalog variant based on a Horn-clause logic that supports recursion, complex objects and negation. In the context of its implementation in an actual deductive database management system, LDL++ [13], the language has been extended to support external functions, choice, aggregation (and even, user-defined aggregation), updates and several other features.

In general, there is a simple rule for constructing valid ETL scenarios in our setting. For each activity, the designer must provide three kinds of provider relationships: (a) a mapping of the activity's data provider(s) to the activity's input schema(ta); (b) a mapping of the activity's input schema(ta) to the activity's output, along with a specification of the semantics of the activity (i.e., the check / cleaning / transformation / value production that the activity performs), and (c) a mapping from the activity's output schema towards the data consumer of the activity. Several integrity constraints come along with this simple guideline; for lack of space we refer the interested reader to [10] for further insight. Fig. 4 shows the LDL program for our motivating example.

3 Templates for ETL Activities

In this section, we will present the mechanism for exploiting template definitions of frequently used ETL activities. The general framework for the exploitation of these templates will be accompanied with the presentation of the language-related issues for template management and appropriate examples.

3.1 General Framework

Our philosophy during the construction of our metamodel was based on two pillars: (a) *genericity*, i.e., the derivation of a simple model, powerful to capture ideally all the cases of ETL activities and (b) *extensibility*, i.e., the possibility of extending the built-in functionality of the system with new, user-specific templates.

The genericity doctrine was pursued through the definition of a rather simple activity metamodel, as described in Section 2. Still, providing a single metaclass for all the possible activities of an ETL environment is not really enough for the designer of the overall process. A richer "language" should be available, in order to describe the structure of the process and facilitate its construction. To this end, we provide a palette of *template* activities, which are specializations of the generic metamodel class.

Observe Fig. 5 for a further explanation of our framework. The lower layer of Fig. 5, namely *Schema Layer*, involves a specific ETL scenario. All the entities of the Schema layer are *instances* of the classes `Data Type`, `Function Type`, `Elementary Activity`, `RecordSet` and `Relationship`. Thus, as one can see on the upper part of Fig. 5, we introduce a meta-class layer, namely *Metamodel Layer* involving the aforementioned classes. The linkage between the Metamodel and the Schema layers is achieved through instantiation ("`InstanceOf`") relationships. The Metamodel layer implements the aforementioned genericity desideratum: the classes which are involved in the Metamodel layer are generic enough to model any ETL scenario, through the appropriate instantiation.

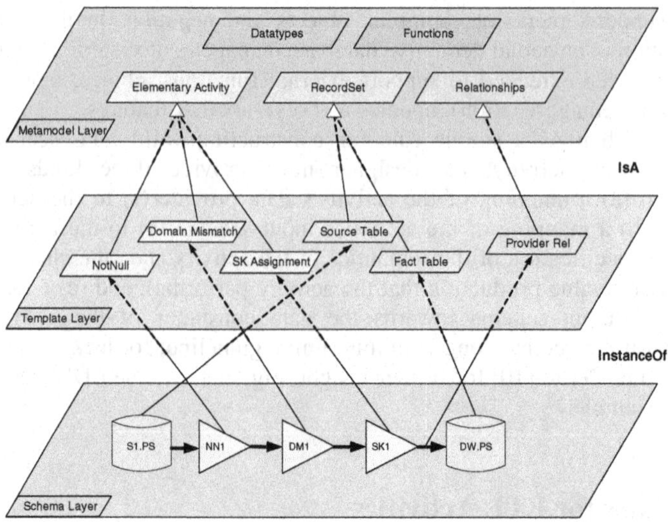

Fig. 5. The metamodel for the logical entities of the ETL environment

Still, we can do better than the simple provision of a meta- and an instance layer. In order to make our metamodel truly useful for practical cases of ETL activities, we enrich it with a set of ETL-specific constructs, which constitute a subset of the larger metamodel layer, namely the *Template Layer*. The constructs in the Template layer are also meta-classes, but they are quite customized for the regular cases of ETL activities. Thus, the classes of the Template layer as specializations (i.e., subclasses) of the generic classes of the Metamodel layer (depicted as "`IsA`" relationships in Fig. 5). Through this customization mechanism, the designer can pick the instances of the Schema layer from a much richer palette of constructs; in this setting, the entities of the Schema layer are instantiations, not only of the respective classes of the Metamodel layer, but also of their subclasses in the Template layer.

In the example of Fig. 5 the concept `DW.PS` must be populated from a certain source S_1`.PS`. Several operations must intervene during the propagation: for example, checks for null values and domain violations, as well as a surrogate key assignment take place in the scenario. As one can observe, the recordsets that take part in this scenario are instances of class `RecordSet` (belonging to the metamodel layer) and specifically of its subclasses `Source Table` and `Fact Table`. Instances and encompassing classes are related through links of type `InstanceOf`. The same mechanism applies to all the activities of the scenario, which are (a) instances of class `Elementary Activity` and (b) instances of one of its subclasses, depicted in Fig. 5. Relationships do not escape the rule either: observe how the provider links from the concept `S1.PS` towards the concept `DW.PS` are related to class `Provider Relationship` through the appropriate `InstanceOf` links.

As far as the class `Recordset` is concerned, in the Template layer we can specialize it to several subclasses, based on orthogonal characteristics, such as whether it is a file or RDBMS table, or whether it is a source or target data store (as in Fig. 5). In the case of the class `Relationship`, there is a clear specialization in terms of the five classes of relationships which have already been mentioned in Section 2: `Provider`, `Part-Of`, `Instance-Of`, `Regulator` and `Derived Provider`.

Following the same framework, class `Elementary Activity` is further specialized to an extensible set of reoccurring patterns of ETL activities, depicted in Fig. 6. We now present each of the aforementioned classes in more detail. As one can see on the top side of Fig. 5, we group the template activities in five major logical groups. We do not depict the grouping of activities in subclasses in Fig. 5, in order to avoid overloading the figure; instead, we depict the specialization of class `Elementary Activity` to three of its subclasses whose instances appear in the employed scenario of the Schema layer.

The first group, named *Filters*, provides checks for the satisfaction (or not) of a certain condition. The semantics of these filters are the obvious (starting from a generic `selection` condition and proceeding to the check for `null values`, `primary` or `foreign key violation`, etc.). The second group of template activities is called *Unary Operations* and except for the most generic `push` activity (which simply propagates data from the provider to the consumer), consists of the classical `aggregation` and `function application` operations along with three data warehouse specific transformations (`surrogate key assignment`, `normalization` and `denormalization`). The third group consists of classical *Binary Operations*, such as `union`, `join` and `difference` of recordsets/activities as well as with a special case of difference involving the `detection of updates`. Except for the aforementioned template activities, which mainly refer to logical transformations, we can also consider the case of physical operators that refer to the application of physical transformations to whole files/tables. In the ETL context, we are mainly interested in operations like *Transfer Operations* (`ftp`, `compress/decompress`, `encrypt/decrypt`) and *File Operations* (`EBCDIC to ASCII`, `sort file`).

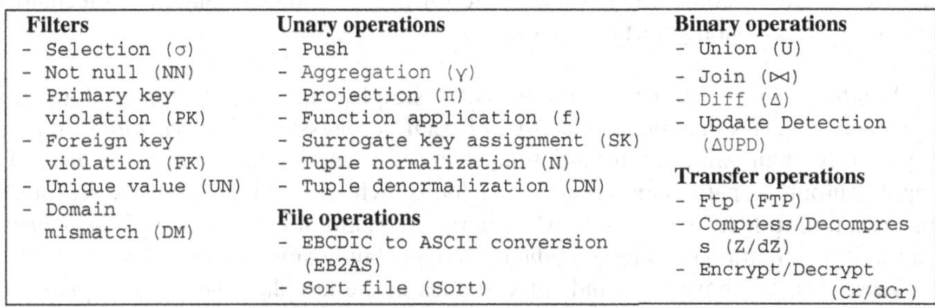

Filters	Unary operations	Binary operations
- Selection (σ)	- Push	- Union (U)
- Not null (NN)	- Aggregation (γ)	- Join (⋈)
- Primary key violation (PK)	- Projection (π)	- Diff (Δ)
- Foreign key violation (FK)	- Function application (f)	- Update Detection (ΔUPD)
- Unique value (UN)	- Surrogate key assignment (SK)	**Transfer operations**
- Domain mismatch (DM)	- Tuple normalization (N)	- Ftp (FTP)
	- Tuple denormalization (DN)	- Compress/Decompres s (Z/dZ)
	File operations	- Encrypt/Decrypt (Cr/dCr)
	- EBCDIC to ASCII conversion (EB2AS)	
	- Sort file (Sort)	

Fig. 6. Template activities, along with their graphical notation symbols, grouped by category

Summarizing, the Metamodel layer is a set of generic entities, able to represent any ETL scenario. At the same time, the genericity of the Metamodel layer is complemented with the extensibility of the Template layer, which is a set of "built-in" specializations of the entities of the Metamodel layer, specifically tailored for the most frequent elements of ETL scenarios. Moreover, apart from this "built-in", ETL-specific extension of the generic metamodel, if the designer decides that several 'patterns', not included in the palette of the Template layer, occur repeatedly in his data warehousing projects, he can easily fit them into the customizable Template layer through a specialization mechanism.

3.2 Formal Definition and Usage of Template Activities

Once the template layer has been introduced, the obvious issue that is raised is its linkage with the employed declarative language of our framework. In general, the broader issue is the usage of the template mechanism from the user; to this end, we will explain the substitution mechanism for templates in this subsection and refer the interested reader to [12] for a presentation of the specific templates that we have constructed.

A *Template Activity* is formally defined as follows:

- *Name*: a unique identifier for the template activity.
- *Parameter List*: a set of names which act as regulators in the expression of the semantics of the template activity. For example, the parameters are used to assign values to constants, create dynamic mapping at instantiation time, etc.
- *Expression*: a declarative statement describing the operation performed by the instances of the template activity. As with elementary activities, our model supports LDL as the formalism for the expression of this statement.
- *Mapping*: a set of bindings, mapping input to output attributes, possibly through intermediate placeholders. In general, mappings at the template level try to capture a default way of propagating incoming values from the input towards the output schema. These default bindings are easily refined and possibly rearranged at instantiation time.

The template mechanism we use is a substitution mechanism, based on macros, that facilitates the automatic creation of LDL code. This simple notation and instantiation mechanism permits the easy and fast registration of LDL templates. In the rest of this section, we will elaborate on the notation, instantiation mechanisms and template taxonomy particularities.

Notation. Our template notation is a simple language featuring four main mechanisms for dynamic production of LDL expressions: (a) *variables* that are replaced by their values at instantiation time; (b) a function that returns the *arity* of an input, output or parameter schema; (c) *loops*, where the loop body is repeated at instantiation time as many times as the iterator constraint defines, and (d) *keywords* to simplify the creation of unique predicate and attribute names.

Variables. We have two kinds of variables in the template mechanism: *parameter variables* and *loop iterators*. Parameter variables are marked with a `@` symbol at their beginning and they are replaced by user-defined values at instantiation time. A list of an arbitrary length of parameters can be defined with the notation `@<parameter name>[]`. For such lists the user has to explicitly or implicitly provide their length at instantiation time. Loop iterators, on the other hand, are implicitly defined in the loop constraint. During each loop iteration, all the properly marked appearances of the iterator in the loop body are replaced by its current value (similarly to the way the C preprocessor treats `#DEFINE` statements). Iterators that appear marked in loop body are instantiated even when they are a part of another string or of a variable name. We mark such appearances by enclosing them with `$`. This functionality enables referencing all the values of a parameter list and facilitates the creation an arbitrary number of pre-formatted strings.

Functions. We employ a built-in function, arityOf(<input/output/parameter schema>), which returns the arity of the respective schema, mainly in order to define upper bounds in loop iterators.

Loops. Loops are a powerful mechanism that enhances the genericity of the templates by allowing the designer to handle templates with unknown number of variables and with unknown arity for the input/output schemata. The general form of loops is [<simple constraint>] { <loop body> } where simple constraint has the form <lower bound> <comparison operator> <iterator> <comparison operator> <upper bound>. Upper bound and lower bound can be arithmetic expressions involving arityOf() function calls, variables and constants. Valid arithmetic operators are +,-,/,* and valid comparison operators are <,>,=, all with their usual semantics. If lower bound is omitted, 0 is assumed. During each iteration, the loop body will be reproduced and the same time all the marked appearances of the loop iterator will be replaced by its current value, as described before. Loop nesting is permitted.

Keyword	Usage	Example
a_out a_in	A unique name for the output/input schema of the activity. The predicate that is produced when this template is instantiated has the form: <unique_pred_name>_out (or, _in respectively)	difference3_out difference3_in
A_OUT A_IN	A_OUT/A_IN is used for constructing the names of the a_out/a_in attributes. The names produced have the form: <predicate unique name in upper case>_OUT (or, _IN respectively)	DIFFERENCE3_OUT DIFFERENCE3_IN

Fig. 7. Keywords for templates

Keywords. Keywords are used in order to refer to input and output schemas. They provide two main functionalities: (a) they simplify the reference to the input output/schema by using standard names for the predicates and their attributes, and (b) they allow their renaming at instantiation time. This is done in such a way that no different predicates with the same name will appear in the same program, and no different attributes with the same name will appear in the same rule. Keywords are recognized even if they are parts of another string, without a special notation. This facilitates a homogenous renaming of multiple distinct input schemas at template level, to multiple distinct schemas at instantiation, with all of them having unique names in the LDL program scope. For example, if the template is expressed in terms of two different input schemata a_in1 and a_in2, at instantiation time they will be renamed to dm1_in1 and dm1_in2 (as specified by the user) so that the produced names will be unique throughout the scenario program. In Fig. 7 we depict the way the renaming is performed at instantiation time.

Instantiation Mechanism. Template instantiation is the process where the user decides to pick a certain template and create a concrete activity out of it. This procedure requires that the user specifies the schemata of the activity and gives concrete values to the template parameters. Then, the process of producing the respective LDL description of the activity is easily automated. Instantiation order is important in our template creation mechanism, since, as it can easily been seen from the notation definitions, different orders can lead to different results. The instantiation order is as follows:

1. `arityOf()` functions and parameter variables appearing in loop boundaries are calculated first;
2. loop productions are done by instantiating the appearances of the iterators; this leads to intermediate results without any loops;
3. all the rest parameter variables are instantiated;
4. keywords are recognized and renamed.

A simple example of template instantiation for the *function application* activity is presented in Fig. 8. To understand the overall process better, first observe the outcome of it, i.e., the specific activity which is produced, as depicted in the final row, labeled *Keyword renaming*. The output schema of the activity, `fa12_out`, is the head of the LDL rule that specifies the activity. The body of the rule says that the output records are specified by the conjunction of the following clauses: (a) the input schema `fa1_in`; (b) the application of function `f1` over the attributes `FA12_IN_1`, `FA12_IN_2` and the production of a value `OUTFIELD`, and (c) the mapping of the input to the respective output attributes as specified in the last three conjuncts of the rule.

The first row, *Template*, shows the initial template as it has been registered by the designer. `@FUNCTION` holds the name of the function to be used, `f1` in our case, and the `@PARAM[]` holds the inputs of the function, which in our case are the two attributes of the input schema. The attributes of the output schema are specified by the expression `[i<arityOf(a_in)+1]{A_OUT_$i$,}OUTFIELD`. In a similar fashion, the attributes of the input schema and the parameters of the function are also specified; note that the expression for the last attribute in the list is different (to avoid repeating an erroneous comma). The mappings between the input and the output attributes are also shown in the last two lines of the template. In the second row, *Parameter instantiation*, we can see how the parameter variables were materialized by the user at instantiation. In the third row, *Loop productions*, we can see the intermediate results after the loop expansions are done. As it can easily be seen these expansions must be done before `@PARAM[]` variables are replaced by their values. In the fourth row, *Variable instantiation*, the parameter variables have been instantiated creating a default mapping between the input, the output and the function attributes. Finally, in the last row, *Keyword renaming*, the output LDL code is presented after the keywords are renamed. Keyword instantiation is done on the basis of the schemata and the respective attributes of the activity that the user chooses.

Taxonomy. Most commonly used activities can be easily expressed by a single predicate template; it is obvious, though, that it would be very inconvenient to restrict activity templates to single predicate ones. Thus, we separate template activities in two categories, *Simple Templates*, which cover single-predicate templates and *Program-Based Templates* where many predicates are used in the template definition.

Template
```
  a_out([i<arityOf(a_in)+1]{A_OUT_$i$,} OUTFIELD) <-
    a_in([i<arityOf(a_in)]{A_IN_$i$,}[i=
arityOf(a_in)]{A_IN_$i$}),
    @FUNCTION([i< arityOf(@PARAM[$i$])+1]{@PARAM[$i$],} OUTFIELD),
    [i<arityOf(a_in)] {A_OUT_$i$=A_IN_$i$,}
    [i=arityOf(a_in)] {A_OUT_$i$=A_IN_$i$}.
```
Parameter Instantiation
```
  @FUNCTION =f1
  @PARAM[1]=A_IN_2
  @PARAM[2]=A_IN_3
```
Loop productions
```
  a_out(A_OUT_1, A_OUT_2, A_OUT_3, OUTFIELD)<-
    a_in(A_IN_1, A_IN_2, A_IN_3),
    @FUNCTION(@PARAM[1],@PARAM[2],OUTFIELD),
    A_OUT_1=A_IN_1,A_OUT_2=A_IN_2,A_OUT_3=A_IN_3.
```
Variable Instantiation
```
  a_out(A_OUT_1, A_OUT_2, A_OUT_3, OUTFIELD)<-
    a_in(A_IN_1, A_IN_2, A_IN_3),
    f1(A_IN_2, A_IN_3,OUTFIELD),
    A_OUT_1=A_IN_1, A_OUT_2=A_IN_2, A_OUT_3=A_IN_3.
```
Keyword Renaming
```
  fa12_out(FA12_OUT_1, FA12_OUT_2, FA12_OUT_3, OUTFIELD)<-
    fa12_in(FA12_IN_1, FA12_IN_2, FA12_IN_3),
    f1(FA12_IN_2, FA12_IN_3,OUTFIELD),
    FA12_OUT_1=FA12_IN_1, FA12_OUT_2=FA12_IN_2,
                                        FA12_OUT_3=FA12_IN_3.
```

Fig. 8. Instantiation procedure

In the case of Simple Templates, the output predicate is bound to the input through a mapping and an expression. Each of the rules for obtaining the output is expressed in terms of the input schemata and the parameters of the activity. In the case of Program-Based Templates the output of the activity is expressed in terms of its intermediate predicate schemata, as well as its input schemata and its parameters. Program-Based Templates are used to define activities that employ constraints like *does-not-belong*, or *does-not-exist*, which need an intermediate negated predicate to be expressed intuitively. This predicate usually describes the conjunction of properties we want to avoid, and then it appears negated in the output predicate. Thus, in general, we allow the construction of a LDL program, with intermediate predicates, in order to enhance intuition. This classification is orthogonal to logical one of Section 3.1. For more details we refer the reader to the long version of this paper [12].

4 Implementation

In the context of the aforementioned framework, we have prototypically implemented a graphical tool, ARKTOS II, with the goal of facilitating the design of ETL scenarios, based on our model. The task of the user is to define the activities of the scenario; in this job, he/she is greatly assisted (a) by a friendly GUI (where all the details are captured though forms and point-and-click operations), and (b) by a set of reusability 'templates'. Whereas the *genericity* principle is supported by the fact that any activity of our model can be tailored by the user, the *customization* principle is supported by the reusability templates. The notion of 'template' is in the heart of ARKTOS II, and there are templates for practically every aspect of the model: data types, functions and activities. Templates are extensible, thus providing the user with the possibility of customizing the environment according to his/her own needs. Especially for activities, which form the core of our model, we provide a specific menu with a set of frequently used ETL Activities. Moreover, the system assists the user in several ways: apart from the friendly GUI (Fig. 2), ARKTOS II offers zoom-in/zoom-out capabilities (a particularly useful feature in the construction of the data flow of the scenario through inter-attribute 'provider' mappings –see also Fig. 2 and 3) and automatic consistency checks for the completeness and integrity of the design. A distinctive feature of ARKTOS II is the computation of the scenario's design quality by employing a set of metrics [10] either for the whole scenario or for each activity of it.

The scenarios are stored in ARKTOS II repository (implemented in a relational DBMS); the system allows the user to store, retrieve and reuse existing scenarios. All the metadata of the system involving the scenario configuration, the employed templates and their constituents are stored in the repository. The choice of a relational DBMS for our metadata repository allows its efficient querying as well as the smooth integration with external systems and/or future extensions of ARKTOS II.

We have implemented ARKTOS II with Oracle 8.1.7 as basis for our repository and Ms Visual Basic (Release 6) for developing our GUI. The connectivity to source and target data stores is achieved through ODBC connections and the tool offers an automatic reverse engineering of their schemata.

5 Related Work

There is a variety of ETL tools in the market; we mention a recent review [1] and several commercial tools [3,4,6,8]. Research prototypes include the AJAX data cleaning tool [2] and the Potter's Wheel system [9]. These two research prototypes are based on algebras, which we find specifically tailored for the case of homogenizing web data. Clearly, ARKTOS II is a design tool; still, with respect to the design capabilities of the aforementioned approaches, our technique contributes (a) by offering an extensible framework though a uniform extensibility mechanism, and (b) by providing formal foundations to allow the reasoning over the constructed ETL scenarios. Finally, we should refer the interested reader to [10] for a detailed presentation of ARKTOS II model. The model is accompanied by a set of *importance metrics* where we exploit the graph structure to measure the degree to which activities/recordsets/attributes are bound to their data providers or consumers. In [11] we propose a complementary conceptual model for ETL scenarios.

6 Conclusions

In this paper, we have focused on the data-centric part of logical design of the ETL scenario of a data warehouse. First, we have defined a formal logical Metamodel as a logical abstraction of ETL processes. The data stores, activities and their constituent parts, as well as the provider relationships that map data producers to data consumers have formally been defined. Then, we have provided a reusability framework that complements the genericity of the aforementioned Metamodel. Practically, this is achieved from an extensible set of specializations of the entities of the Metamodel layer, specifically tailored for the most frequent elements of ETL scenarios, which we call template activities. Finally, we have presented a graphical design tool, ARKTOS II, with the goal of facilitating the design of ETL scenarios, based on our model.

As future work, we already have preliminary results for the optimization of ETL scenario under certain time and throughput constraints. A set of loosely coupled tools is also under construction for the purposes of optimization of the execution of ETL scenarios.

References

[1] Gartner. ETL Magic Quadrant Update: Market Pressure Increases. Available at http://www.gartner.com/reprints/informatica/112769.html

[2] H. Galhardas, D. Florescu, D. Shasha and E. Simon. Ajax: An Extensible Data Cleaning Tool. In Proc. ACM SIGMOD Intl. Conf. On the Management of Data, pp. 590, Dallas, Texas, (2000).

[3] IBM. IBM Data Warehouse Manager. Available at http://www-3.ibm.com/software/data/db2/datawarehouse/

[4] Informatica. PowerCenter. Available at http://www.informatica.com/products/data+integration/powercenter/default.htm

[5] R. Kimbal, L. Reeves, M. Ross, W. Thornthwaite. The Data Warehouse Lifecycle Toolkit: Expert Methods for Designing, Developing, and Deploying Data Warehouses. John Wiley & Sons, February 1998.

[6] Microsoft. Data Transformation Services. Available at www.microsoft.com

[7] S. Naqvi, S. Tsur. A Logical Language for Data and Knowledge Bases. Computer Science Press 1989.

[8] Oracle. Oracle Warehouse Builder Product Page. Available at http://otn.oracle.com/products/warehouse/content.html

[9] V. Raman, J. Hellerstein. Potter's Wheel: An Interactive Data Cleaning System. In *Proceedings of 27th International Conference on Very Large Data Bases (VLDB)*, pp. 381–390, Roma, Italy, (2001).

[10] P. Vassiliadis, A. Simitsis, S. Skiadopoulos. Modeling ETL Activities as Graphs. In Proc. 4th Intl. Workshop on Design and Management of Data Warehouses (DMDW), pp. 52–61, Toronto, Canada, (2002).

[11] P. Vassiliadis, A. Simitsis, S. Skiadopoulos. Conceptual Modeling for ETL Processes. In Proc. 5th ACM Intl. Workshop on Data Warehousing and OLAP (DOLAP), pp. 14–21, McLean, Virginia, USA (2002).

[12] P. Vassiliadis, A. Simitsis, P. Georgantas, M. Terrovitis. A Framework for the design of ETL scenarios (long version). Available at http://cs.uoi.gr/~pvassil/publications/caise03_long.pdf

[13] C. Zaniolo. LDL++ Tutorial. UCLA. http://pike.cs.ucla.edu/ldl/, Dec. 1998.

Context Comparison for Object Fusion

Fabrice Jouanot[1], Nadine Cullot[2], and Kokou Yétongnon[2]

[1] EPFL, Database Laboratory
Fabrice.Jouanot@epfl.ch
[2] University of Burgundy, LE2I
{Nadine.Cullot,Kokou.Yetongnon}@u-bourgogne.fr

Abstract. We propose a solution to help the integration of heterogeneous sources based on the fusion of objects according to their context. New requirements for information exchange have emerged with all the developments around Internet. Information consumers want to access and combine data from remote and heterogeneous sources in a transparent and dynamic way. To achieve this level of interoperation is yet a real challenge. We present a model to define local data as informative objects with a contextual representation associated to them. A semantic context comparison mechanism, based on a semantic distance, reconciles context of applications and constructs virtual objects in which rules make the fusion of informative objects. Virtual objects play the role of interface for transparent user access.

1 Introduction

Cooperation of information systems is greatly influenced by the development of the World Wide Web. Models, methodologies and tools have to be adapted to the new requirements of the cooperation end-users. Help them to find their way in the jungle of the knowledge providing by the Web is really suitable. To reach this major aim, it is necessary to deal with the different kinds of heterogeneities that can be encountered in a cooperation of information systems. We agree that syntactic and structural heterogeneities which concern model and data structure differences can be solved using translator tools, pivot models or other solutions proposed in the literature. The real challenge is now to take into account data semantics to find relevant information. In IS cooperation, different approaches have been developed based on federated or mediator/wrapper architectures. Mediation approaches are well adapted to dynamic environments. In schema mediation, the mediator localizes and integrates relevant data to construct a mediation schema which can be queried by end-users. Projects such as DIOM [1], DISCO [2], DOK [3] are schema mediation solutions. In context mediation, the mediator dynamically integrates information to answer a end-user query. SemWeb [4], On2Broker [5,6], Observer [7], WebFindit [8] or InfoSleuth [9,10] are context mediation solutions. These projects propose different solutions to modelize data semantics. On2Broker is interested in the semantics of Web documents which can be in different formats (RDF, XML-like, ...). The solution includes four basic engines (query engine, info agent, inference engine, and database manager)

J. Eder and M. Missikoff (Eds.): CAiSE 2003, LNCS 2681, pp. 536–551, 2003.

which are all relied on ontologies. WebFindIt defines a complete architecture to access to different databases by browsering their application domain using their associated metadata (co-databases). Metadata, ontologies and contexts are tools to modelize data semantics. Metadata describe intrinsic properties of data. The Dublin Core [11] is an example of metadata about document exchange. Ontologies are more and more recognized as a promising solution to modelize data semantics. Ontologies can be viewed as the formal modelization of shared concepts. Projects such as DOGMA [12] or KAON [13] propose formal models to modelize ontologies. Nicolas Guarino [14] classifies ontologies according to their task and point of view. Top-level ontologies (1) describe very general concepts. Domain ontologies (2) describe a vocabulary related to a generic domain. Task ontologies (3) describe a task or an activity. And application ontologies describe concepts depending on a particular domain and a task. They can be viewed as a specialization of task and domain ontologies. Contexts are used to describe semantics of data relied to one or more application in a specific domain. With the Guarino's classification, contexts can be compared to application ontologies. The development of metadata, contexts or ontologies leads to other related requirements which are needs to compare these ontologies or contexts, to be able to communicate in a large way. Some recent works focus on the definition of measures to compare terms [15], concepts or ontologies [16].

The DILEMMA (Dynamic and Interoperable Logical Extended Mediation Model Architecture) [17] project described in this paper is an hybrid approach of schema and context mediation which allows information system (IS) cooperation using contexts to modelize data semantics. The main idea is to provide tools to build a cooperation which can be updated in an incremental manner according to end-user requirements. DILEMMA proposes a model to describe data with their meanings and a semantic reconciliation method which is based on the definition of a semantic distance to compare contexts. In this approach, a cooperation between two IS can be summarized in four steps. In the first one, provider and consumer systems have to describe their own application domain to make the meaning of their data or requirements understandable and unambiguous. This is done using a model (section 2) which allows the definition of information via Informative Objects (I-Objects) and the description of a context for these I-Objects via the definition of concepts. The second step is a context comparison between two contexts which aims to identify their similar concepts using a semantic distance (section 3). The third step considers the results of this comparison to choose relevant I-Objects which can be interpreted in a consumer context (section 4.1). The last step consists in an object fusion process (section 4.2) which integrates semantically related I-Objects into virtual I-Objects to access to all the data of the cooperation in a transparent way.

2 Objects and Contexts

The data description is made up of three layers with a progression in the semantic granularity from high level terminological concepts to value understanding. The first layer consists in mapping the local data (if exist) into a pivot model to structure information and to simplify exchanges. This layer defines I-Objects as interface to access data. The second layer is the definition of a local context to deal with the semantics of the application domain. It is built using a set of terminological concepts and roles. The third layer clarifies the I-Object meanings on the defined context. Interpretation rules allow to interpret I-Objects on the context and characterization rules allow to explicit intrinsic properties of data values (as unit, scale, precision).

2.1 Definition of I-Objects

An I-Object class definition is composed of a profile and may be a deductive rule description. A profile $Classname[Method_1 => Type_1; ...; Method_n => Type_n]$ defines a set of attributes called methods which can be mono-valued $Method =>$ $Type$, multi-valued $Method \gg Type$ or parameterized $Method(Parameter->$ $Type) => Type$. Access rights (*public, private and shared*) can be added to control importation, exportation and reuse of the I-Object class. All defined I-Objects inherit from a basic class called Very First Object (*vfo*) which provides four common methods : *repository* to precise the URL of the source, *description* to give a literal definition of the class, *version* number to find right I-Objects and *Mproperty* a method used for the characterization of data values. An I-Object is an instance of an I-Object class. The term I-Object is sometimes used instead of I-Object class by misuse of language. If the I-Object class is a virtual I-Object class then a deductive rule completes the definition of the class. The rule allows to define how to combine I-Object instances of existing classes to build this new virtual one.

The first example below shows the definition of an I-Object class *person*. It inherits from vfo, has a parameterized method *firstName* and has a complex method *address*.

```
class person::vfo[ repository -> '192.52.237.1';
                   description -> 'A person is a human described by ...';
                   version -> 1].
class person[ name => string; firstName@(num => integer) => string;
              ssn => string; address => Address; tel =>> string ].
class Address::vfo[ repository -> '192.52.237.1'; ... ]
```

The second example below shows the definition of a virtual I-Object class *lausannois* which inherits from the class *person* and describes the inhabitants of the city of Lausanne.

```
lausannois::person.
rule(X,A) X:lausannois :- X:person[ address -> A ],
                          A:Address[ city -> 'Lausanne' ].
```

In addition to these I-Objects, the model defines function libraries where specific transformation functions can be stored. These functions are useful to resolve semantic mismatch of method values between different I-Objects and they play an important role in the object fusion process. The example below shows the definition of a library *DateConverter*. It contains one function *age2date* which returns a date of birth from an age. A class *student* is also defined. It inherits from a class *person* and has a method *ybirth*. This method is calculated from the value of the method *age* using a deductive rule. The rule gives the value of the method *ybirth* for a *student* using the function *age2date*.

```
library DateConverter[ age2date@(age -> integer)=> date ].
class student::person[ age => integer; Netud => string;
                       inscrip =>> Inscription; ybirth => integer].
rule{A, AN, X} X[ ybirth -> AN ] :- X:student[ age -> A ],
               DateConverter[ age2date@(age -> A) -> AN ].
```

2.2 Definition of a Local Context

A context is composed of concepts called conceptual classes. A conceptual class is defined by its name and a list of its roles. They describe the roles played by the other classes for this conceptual class. If $\Phi_{\mathcal{D}}$ the set of conceptual classes on a domain $\mathcal{D}$, $Cc \in \Phi_{\mathcal{D}}$ is defined by :

$$\mathbf{Cc} = \mathbf{concept\ name}\{+\mathbf{synonym\_list}, -\mathbf{antonym\_list}\}[\ \mathbf{role\_list}\ ].$$

- **name** the name of the conceptual class. It represents a terminological definition of the concept and it depends on the language;
- **role_list** describes the semantic surrounding of a concept. A role defines a semantic relation between the concept which owns it and concepts which play this role. The set of roles played by other classes for Cc is noted $\mathcal{R}_{Cc}$. If $r_i \in \mathcal{R}_{Cc}$, r_i is defined as below :
  - $\mathbf{r_i}\{+\mathbf{synonym\_list}, -\mathbf{antonym\_list}\} => \mathbf{Cc_{r_i}}$ with $Cc_{r_i} \in \Phi_{\mathcal{D}}$ describes that Cc_{r_i} plays the role r_i for Cc.
  - $\mathbf{r_i}\{+\mathbf{synonym\_list}, -\mathbf{antonym\_list}\} => \{\mathbf{Cc_{r_ij}}\}$ with $\forall j = 1..n, Cc_{r_ij} \in \Phi_{\mathcal{D}}$ describes that Cc_{r_ij} plays the role r_i for Cc.
- **synonym_list** defines a set of terms which are synonyms of a concept or a role. It allows to enlarge the meaning of an entity and can optimize the comparison between two entities.
- **antonym_list** defines a set of terms which could be consider as synonyms but have an opposite meaning in this context.

Finally conceptual classes can be organized in inheritance hierarchies which allow role inheritance with some constraints. The example below depicts a part of a context definition. The concepts *life form, human, individual, etc.* are introduced. They are linked togother with roles. For example, the concept *birth date* plays the role *birth* for the concept *life_form*. The context can be viewed as a local ontology of the application domain.

```
concept life form[ birth => birth date; death => decease date; age => Age ].
concept human{+man}::life form.
```

```
concept individual{+person,+guy}::human
               [ identifier => identity; home{+house} => address ].
concept address{+place,+localization}
               [ component => {number, street, post code, town} ].
concept identity[ identifier => social number;
                  name => {first name, last name} ].
concept christian name::first name.
```

2.3 Definition of Interpretation Rules

Rules allow to interpret the profile of an I-Object class i.e. to describe its meaning. Three categories of rules can be distinguished : simple rules, method rules and rules with constraints.

A simple rule specifies that the meaning of an I-Object class can be found in a particular concept. It links an I-Object class to a conceptual class. For example, the class *person* can be interpreted on the concept *individual* as follows.

```
inter person:::individual.
```

A method rule specifies the meaning of the values returned by a method. It links a method of an I-Object to a conceptual class. For example, the methods *name* and *ssn* of the class *person* can be interpreted on the conceptual classes *last name* and *social number*. Parameters of a method have also to be interpreted in a similar way. The example below lists some interpretations of methods.

```
inter person.name:::last name.
inter person.ssn:::social number.
inter address.cp:::post code.
```

An interpretation rule with constraints allows to interpret any sub-set instances of an I-Object class. The example below specifies that the first name of a person can be interpreted as a Christian name.

```
inter{X,Y} X{Y:person[firstName@(num->1)->X]}:::christian name.
```

Moreover, interpretation rules can be completed by an interpretation path which can avoid ambiguities of interpretation in complex contexts. This expression below specifies that the method *name* of the class *person* is interpreted on the concept *last name* when it plays the role *name* for the concept *identity*, which itself plays the role *identifier* for the concept *individual.*

```
inter person.name:::last name <= identity (<= individual.identifier).name
```

2.4 Definition of Characterization Rules

The model provides some metadata which represent the most used types of data in usual information systems. Metadata are represented with meta conceptual classes, called MCc. Two hierarchies of MCc are pre-defined : one for spatial data representation and another for classical data representation such as time, geometry, mass, electricity and many more-sub types of numerical values. Part of the hierarchy for classical data is presented in the figure 1. The meta conceptual classes Geometry, Mass, Time, etc. inherit the roles and semantic surrounding from the root MCc Numerical Datum Reference Information.

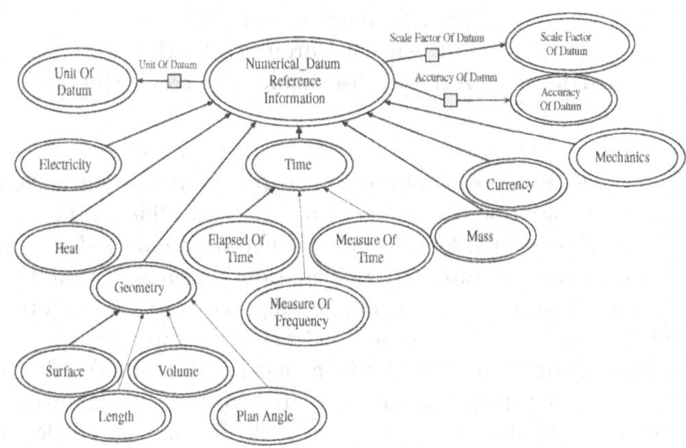

Fig. 1. Part of the hierarchy of classic meta conceptual classes.

This root MCc is relied using roles to three MCcs Unit Of Datum, Scale Factor Of Datum and Accuracy Of Datum to define the intrinsic properties of a numeric value which are respectively its unit, scale and precision. These MCcs are called terminal classes and have got a list of values, terms or expressions which can be used to parameterize the characterization of the I-Objects values .

The figure 2 presents the characterization of the values of the method *age* of the class *student* upon these metadata. The method *age* is interpreted on the conceptual class *Age* which derives from the from MCc *Elapsed Of Time*. The MCc *Elapsed Of Time* inherits from *Time* which inherits from *Numerical Datum Reference Information*. The method *age* is characterized specifying its unit *year*, scale *1* and precision *0* which means that the value is exact.

Formally, the characterization of a method is achieved giving the characterization of its values on each terminal meta-class (property) which plays a role for the MCc on which this method is indirectly interpreted. The example below gives the formal definition of the method *age* of the I-Object class *student* as described graphically in figure 2. The method *MProperty*, inherited from *vfo*, allows the characterization of the method *age* of the class *student* on its unit (1), scale (2) and precision (3). Each characterization is done with the method Mproperty, giving the name of the method, the terminal class considered and the characterization value.

```
concept Age::Elapsed Of Time.
inter student.age:::Age.
(1)  class student[ MProperty('age','Unit Of Datum') -> 'year' ].
```

Context Comparison for Object Fusion

Fabrice Jouanot[1], Nadine Cullot[2], and Kokou Yétongnon[2]

[1] EPFL, Database Laboratory
Fabrice.Jouanot@epfl.ch
[2] University of Burgundy, LE2I
{Nadine.Cullot,Kokou.Yetongnon}@u-bourgogne.fr

Abstract. We propose a solution to help the integration of heterogeneous sources based on the fusion of objects according to their context. New requirements for information exchange have emerged with all the developments around Internet. Information consumers want to access and combine data from remote and heterogeneous sources in a transparent and dynamic way. To achieve this level of interoperation is yet a real challenge. We present a model to define local data as informative objects with a contextual representation associated to them. A semantic context comparison mechanism, based on a semantic distance, reconciles context of applications and constructs virtual objects in which rules make the fusion of informative objects. Virtual objects play the role of interface for transparent user access.

1 Introduction

Cooperation of information systems is greatly influenced by the development of the World Wide Web. Models, methodologies and tools have to be adapted to the new requirements of the cooperation end-users. Help them to find their way in the jungle of the knowledge providing by the Web is really suitable. To reach this major aim, it is necessary to deal with the different kinds of heterogeneities that can be encountered in a cooperation of information systems. We agree that syntactic and structural heterogeneities which concern model and data structure differences can be solved using translator tools, pivot models or other solutions proposed in the literature. The real challenge is now to take into account data semantics to find relevant information. In IS cooperation, different approaches have been developed based on federated or mediator/wrapper architectures. Mediation approaches are well adapted to dynamic environments. In schema mediation, the mediator localizes and integrates relevant data to construct a mediation schema which can be queried by end-users. Projects such as DIOM [1], DISCO [2], DOK [3] are schema mediation solutions. In context mediation, the mediator dynamically integrates information to answer a end-user query. SemWeb [4], On2Broker [5,6], Observer [7], WebFindit [8] or InfoSleuth [9,10] are context mediation solutions. These projects propose different solutions to modelize data semantics. On2Broker is interested in the semantics of Web documents which can be in different formats (RDF, XML-like, ...). The solution includes four basic engines (query engine, info agent, inference engine, and database manager)

J. Eder and M. Missikoff (Eds.): CAiSE 2003, LNCS 2681, pp. 536–551, 2003.

- **case 1,** if $D_{cc}(Cc, Cc') = 0$ then $D(Cc, Cc') = 0$
- **case 2,** if exists a set of conceptual classes playing roles for Cc and Cc', if exists a set of conceptual classes for which Cc and Cc' played roles for, then

$$D(Cc, Cc') = \frac{1}{2}D_{Cc}(Cc, CC') + \frac{1}{2}(\alpha \times \frac{\sum\limits_{i=1..n} \boldsymbol{R}_{Cc,Cc'}(i)}{n} + \beta \times D_{rj}(Cc, Cc'))$$

$with\ 0 < \alpha < 1,\ 0 < \beta < 1\ and\ \alpha + \beta = 1.$

α and β allow to weight the two parts of the semantic expression to give more or less importance between both surrounding parts.

- **case 3 and 4,** if one of the set of conceptual classes "roles played for Cc and Cc'" or "roles played by Cc and Cc'" does not exist, then $D(Cc, Cc')$ is defined respectively as

$$D(Cc, Cc') = \frac{1}{2}D_{Cc}(Cc, CC') + \frac{1}{2}(\frac{\sum\limits_{i=1..n} \boldsymbol{R}_{Cc,Cc'}(i)}{n})$$

or

$$D(Cc, Cc') = \frac{1}{2}D_{Cc}(Cc, CC') + \frac{1}{2}(D_{rj}(Cc, Cc'))$$

- **case 5,** if no set of conceptual classes "roles played for Cc and Cc'" or "roles played by Cc and Cc'" exists, then $D(Cc, Cc')$ is defined as

$$D(Cc, Cc') = D_{cc}(Cc, Cc')$$

This global distance $D(Cc, Cc')$ uses other specific distances to calculate the distance between two concepts. We briefly present all these distances. First $D_{MCc}(Cc, Cc')$ (used in the calculation of D_{cc}) is a basic distance which evaluates the semantic distance between two conceptual classes Cc and Cc' according only to their relationships with meta conceptual classes. In fact, $D_{MCc}(Cc, Cc')$ is true if the meta conceptual classes, from which the compared concepts derived, are semantically compatible, and false if not.

If Cc_1, Cc_2 two concepts from a context, Cc'_1, Cc'_2 two concepts from another context, MCc and MCc' two meta conceptual classes, the distance D_{MCc} between Cc_1 and Cc'_1, noted $D_{MCc}(Cc_1, Cc'_1)$, is defined as follows :

$$\begin{cases}
D_{MCc}(Cc_1, Cc'_1) = 1 \\
\quad if\ Cc_1 :: MCc\ (direct)\ or \\
\qquad Cc_1 :: .. :: Cc_2 :: MCc\ (indirect) \\
\quad and\ Cc'_1 :: MCc\ (direct)\ or \\
\qquad Cc'_1 :: .. :: Cc'_2 :: MCc\ (indirect) \\
D_{MCc}(Cc_1, Cc'_1) = 0 \\
\quad if\ Cc_1 :: MCc\ ou\ Cc_1 :: .. :: Cc_2 :: MCc \\
\quad and\ Cc'_1 :: MCc\ ou\ Cc'_1 :: .. :: Cc'_2 :: MCc' \\
\quad and\ MCc \neq MCc' \\
else \\
D_{MCc}(Cc_1, Cc'_1) = v\ with\ v = 0\ or\ v = 1
\end{cases}$$

The values of the variable v depend on the particular cases shown in figure 3: this value resolves the uncertainty which appears in these conciliation cases.

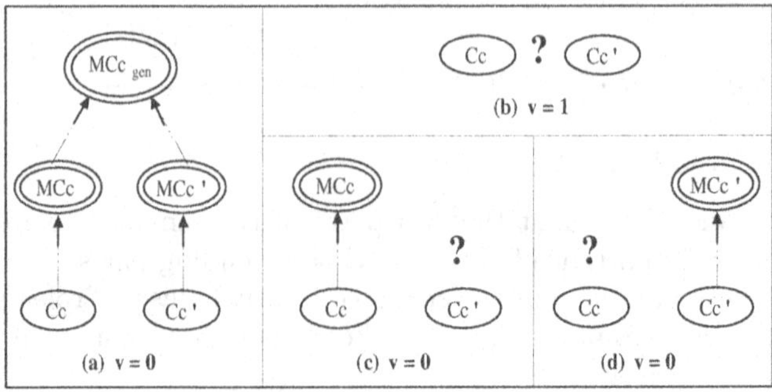

Fig. 3. Particular conciliation cases for D_{MCc} basic distance.

The distance $D_{cc}(Cc, Cc')$ focuses on the taxonomic aspects of concepts Cc and Cc'. Its calculation takes into account three semantic features of a concept: its name with its synonymy and antonymy relationships, its position into the inheritance hierarchy of concepts and its meta-conceptual relationships. In the formal definition below, we consider the general case where the both concepts are placed in a hierarchy. Other definitions exist according to the fact that one of the concepts (or both) is placed or not into a hierarchy. The distance $D_{cc}(Cc, Cc')$ is equal to the previous distance $D_{MCc}(Cc, Cc')$ when all comparison criteria success, and equal to zero if not. In fact the value of $D_{MCc}(Cc, Cc')$ determines the possibility of a similarity between concepts.

If Cc a concept from the consumer context, Cc' a concept from a provider context, $\mathcal{N}(Cc)$ the name of Cc, $\mathcal{S}(Cc)$ the synonyms of Cc and $\mathcal{A}(Cc)$ the antonyms of Cc, then $D_{cc}(Cc, Cc')$ can be formally defined as follows :

$$
\begin{cases}
D_{Cc}(Cc, Cc') = D_{MCc}(Cc, Cc')\ if \\
\qquad card((\mathcal{N}(Cc) \cup \mathcal{S}(Cc)) \cap \mathcal{N}(Cc') \cup \mathcal{S}(Cc'))) > 0 \\
\qquad and\ \forall Cc'_j \in \Phi'_{\mathcal{D}},\ Cc'_j :: .. :: Cc' \\
\qquad\quad card((\mathcal{N}(Cc) \cup \mathcal{S}(Cc)) \cap \mathcal{N}(Cc') \cup \mathcal{S}(Cc'))) \geq \\
\qquad\quad card((\mathcal{N}(Cc) \cup \mathcal{S}(Cc)) \cap \mathcal{N}(Cc'_j) \cup \mathcal{S}(Cc'_j))) \\
\qquad and\ \forall Cc_j \in \Phi_{\mathcal{D}},\ Cc_j :: .. :: Cc \\
\qquad\quad card((\mathcal{N}(Cc) \cup \mathcal{S}(Cc)) \cap \mathcal{N}(Cc') \cup \mathcal{S}(Cc'))) \geq \\
\qquad\quad card((\mathcal{N}(Cc_j) \cup \mathcal{S}(Cc_j)) \cap \mathcal{N}(Cc') \cup \mathcal{S}(Cc'))) \\
\qquad and\ \forall Cc_i \in \Phi_{\mathcal{D}},\ Cc :: .. :: Cc_i \\
\qquad\quad card((\mathcal{N}(Cc) \cup \mathcal{S}(Cc)) \cap \mathcal{N}(Cc') \cup \mathcal{S}(Cc'))) > \\
\qquad\quad card((\mathcal{N}(Cc_i) \cup \mathcal{S}(Cc_i)) \cap \mathcal{N}(Cc') \cup \mathcal{S}(Cc'))) \\
\qquad and\ if\ card(\mathcal{S}(Cc) \cap \mathcal{A}(Cc')) = 0 \\
\qquad and\ card(\mathcal{S}(Cc') \cap \mathcal{A}(Cc)) = 0 \\
else \\
D_{Cc}(Cc, Cc') = 0
\end{cases}
$$

The criteria of this definition precise that a better distance between Cc and a concept inherited from Cc' must not exist, and a better distance between Cc' and a concept inherited from Cc must also not exist.

However the semantics of a concept is contained in its roles : roles played by other concepts for this one, and roles played by this concept to the others. To evaluate this neighborhood similarity, an important operation is the distance between roles D_r. The distance D_r measures the similarity of two roles based on its taxonomy only. If Cc a concept from the consumer context, Cc' a concept from a provider context, r a role of Cc and r' a role of Cc', $D_r(Cc.r, Cc'.r')$ is defined as follows :

$$\begin{cases} D_r(Cc.r, Cc'.r') = 1 \ if \ D_{Cc}(Cc, Cc') = 1 \\ \qquad\qquad and \ card((\mathcal{N}(r) \cup \mathcal{S}(r)) \cap (\mathcal{N}(r') \cup \mathcal{S}(r'))) > 0 \\ \qquad\qquad and \ card(\mathcal{S}(r) \cap \mathcal{A}(r')) = 0 \\ \quad else \\ D_r(Cc.r, Cc'.r') = 0 \end{cases}$$

We will not detail moreover the calculation of the semantic distance. All the information about the calculation of the semantic distance can be found in [17].

4 Object Fusion

We assume that the context comparison process has selected some relevant conceptual classes in the provider context equivalent to some other classes in the consumer context. They have to be imported and interpreted on this consumer context.

4.1 Re-interpretation Problematic

To construct a coherent interpretation of the imported I-Object classes with their profiles and associated function libraries on the consumer context, it may be necessary, to avoid ambiguities, to use interpretation paths. The figure 4 illustrates this problem. The concept *individual* from the consumer context has been evaluated as similar to the concept *person* from the provider context. The interpretation of the method *name* of the class *student* which is *lastname <= person.identity* on the provider context cannot be directly imported in the consumer context. A new interpretation path is built using the results of the context comparison. In the example, the method *name* of the class *student* is re-interpreted on the consumer context using the interpretation path *lastname <= identity(<= individual.identifier).name*.

The very first part of a re-interpretation path is given by the step of importation. We suppose the importation of an interpretation on a conceptual class Cc' on Cc (consumer context). The following levels of re-interpretation are constructed in an incremental way, comparing conceptual classes Cc'_j, which appear in the interpretation path of a conceptual class Cc', with conceptual classes Cc_i which appear in the interpretation path of a conceptual class Cc similar to Cc'.

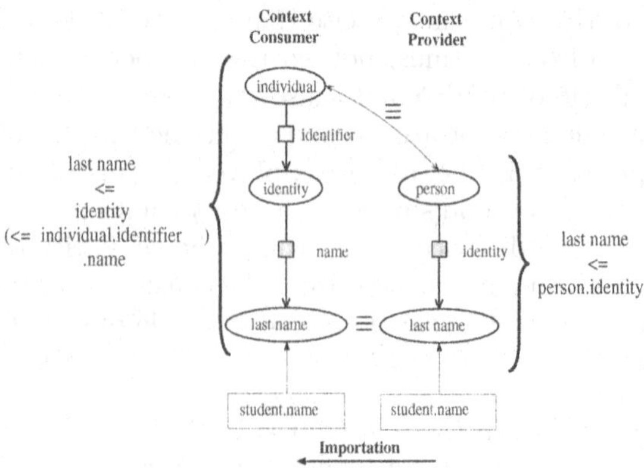

Fig. 4. An example of re-interpretation mechanism.

For each level, we consider two similar conceptual classes Cc_i and Cc'_j, helped with similarities of Cc_{i+1} and Cc'_{j+1} for which Cc_i and Cc'_j play a role. To decide the re-interpretation form, five cases of similarities are considered:

- **case 1 :** conceptual classes for which Cc_i and Cc'_j play a role are similar ($Cc_{i+1} \equiv Cc'_{j+1}$). The level of provider interpretation path $Cc'_j(<= Cc'_{j+1}(...).r'_{j+1}).r'_j$ becomes $Cc_i(<= Cc_{i+1}(...).r_{i+1}).r_i$ in the consumer context.
- **case 2 :** conceptual classes for which Cc_i and Cc'_j play a role are not similar but a unique interpretation path exists in the consumer context which carries out to a conceptual class Cc_{i+n} similar to Cc'_{j+1}. This level of interpretation adds the successive steps to find Cc_{i+n}. The level of provider interpretation path $Cc'_j(<= Cc'_{j+1}(...).r'_{j+1}).r'_j$ becomes $Cc_i(<= Cc_{i+1}(<= ...(<= Cc_{i+n}.r_{i+n})...).r_{i+1}).r_i$ in the consumer context.
- **case 3 :** conceptual classes for which Cc_i and Cc'_j play a role are not similar but a unique interpretation path exists in the provider context which carries out to a conceptual class Cc'_{j+m} similar to Cc_{i+1}. This level of interpretation deletes the successive steps to find Cc'_{j+m}. The level of provider interpretation path $Cc'_j(<= Cc'_{j+1}(...(<= Cc'_{j.m}.r'_{j+m})...).r'_{j+1}).r'_j$ becomes $Cc_i(<= Cc_{i+1}(...).r_{i+1}).r_i$ in the consumer context.
- **case 4 :** conceptual classes for which Cc_i and Cc'_j play a role are similar but two possible roles exist $r1_{i+1}$ and $r2_{i+1}$ which are played by these classes for Cc_{i+1}. The interpretation rule on the provider context is $Cc'_j(<= Cc'_{j+1}.r'_{j+1}).r'_j$. This state gives several possible re-interpretation paths and requires a human decision to define the relevant path.
- **case 5 :** similar classes for which Cc_i and Cc'_j play a role don't exist. The re-interpretation is stopped and the re-interpretation discovered until this case happens is considered as a correct interpretation path on the consumer context. This interpretation can be completed by a user or a domain specialist if needed.

4.2 I-Objects Fusion

With all information correctly interpreted on the consumer context, it is now possible to define virtual I-Objects. This is a semi-automatic process where user has to define its interface by giving the profile of a virtual I-Object class, by interpreting this class, characterizing it and applying a fusion operator to create integration rules. Two kinds of operator exist : the merging operator (Operation $\oplus$), which is detailed below, and the joining operator (Operation $\otimes$).

When **Operation** $\oplus$ is applied to a virtual I-Object, rules are generated to merge instances of all similar classes into the virtual one. All these instances can be accessed using the virtual class. This rule generation is composed of two steps. The first one finds equivalent classes and builds skeleton of rules. Formally, if C_G is a virtual class to group equivalent objects which have an interpretation on the concept Cc and, $C_{i=1..n}$ are classes all having the same interpretation on Cc as on C_G, then the following grouping rules are generated :

$$\mathbf{X : C_G : -X : C_i}$$
$$with\ X\ being\ a\ variable\ for\ unification\ process.$$

The second step finds relevant methods which are equivalent to methods of virtual class and enriches rules from the first step. Formally, if C_G and each equivalent C_i own a method, respectively m_G and m_i, having a compatible interpretation path, then grouping rules can be completed as follows :

$$\mathbf{X : C_G[m_G- > Y] : -X : C_i[m_i- > Y]}$$
$$with\ X\ and\ Y\ two\ variables\ for\ unification\ process.$$

If C_G and each equivalent C_j own a method, respectively m'_G and $m"_j$, having an indirect compatible interpretation path – i.e. $m"_j$ return objects which belong to classes C_k which own a method m'_k with the same interpretation path than m'_G –,then grouping rules can be completed as follows :

$$\mathbf{X : C_G[m_G- > Y] : -X : C_j[m"_j- > Z], Z : C_k[m'_k- > Y]}$$
$$with\ X,\ Y\ and\ Z\ three\ variables\ useful\ for\ unification\ process.$$

The **Operation** $\otimes$ is more complex than $\oplus$. When it is applied to a virtual class, user has to specify a join criteria and rules are generated to join a similar class (to virtual class) with other classes which have the join criteria as a method and some methods equivalent to methods of the virtual class.

The fusion is user-driven and the example below shows how an interface can be defined to exploit the semantics expressed in this contextual approach. For example, we consider a user-consumer who wants to create an interface to access information about names and sizes of students. We suppose that the context of this consumer is given and that a context comparison has been initiated with two provider sources *source1* and *source2*. This consumer context depicts only concepts that characterize a student : A student is a person who studies at the university, with a first name, a name as identity and a height as characteristic (*height* derives from a MCc *Length*).

The user creates its interface as an I-Object definition and interprets it on its local context. Interpretation rules in this example are simplified and no interpretation path is defined. The user clarifies the semantics of its data defining the characterization of the method *size* specifying that its values has to be expressed in foot (only).

```
concept individual{+person,+human}
                [ identifier => identity, characteristic => height ].
concept height::Length.
concept identity[ name => {first name, last name} ].
concept christian_name::first name.
concept student::individual [ study => university ].

class student[ lname => string; cname => string; size => real ].
class student[ MProperty@('size','Unit Of Datum') -> 'foot' ].
inter student:::student.
inter student.lname:::last name.
inter student.cname:::christian name.
inter student.size:::height.
inter{X,Y} X{Y:student[ MProperty@('size','Unit Of Datum') -> X ]}
          :::Unit Of Datum <= Length.Unit Of Datum.
```

The figure 5 presents the interpretation of the class *student* defined by the consumer and the result of the context comparison between the two providers *source1* and *source2*. Similarities in the structure of I-Objects appear clearly in this simple graph. For example, *student.cname*, *student1.firstname@(1)* and *etudiant2.prenom* (source2 is french) are identified as similar.

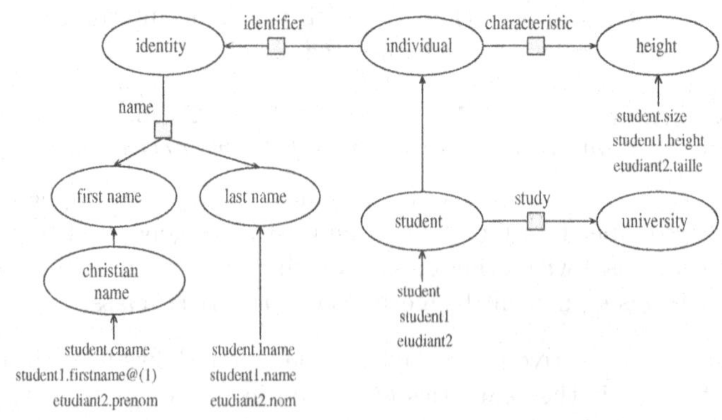

Fig. 5. Reconciliation of different sources on a consumer context

The application of the operation $\oplus$, noted $\oplus$(student),gives the two rules below in the first step. Each I-Object class similar with *student* is unified in a rule which maps I-Objects of *student1* and *etudiant2* to I-Objects of *student.*

Similar methods from each unified class have to be mapped to the profile of *student* in a second step.

```
X:student :- X:student1[ repository -> "source1.fr" ].
X:student :- X:etudiant2[ repository -> "source2.fr" ].
```

The result of this second step of $\oplus$ on this example updates the rules as follows :

```
(1) X:student[ lname -> NF; cname -> NB; size -> SZ ]:-
    X:student1[ repository -> "source1.fr"; name -> NF;
                firstname@(1) -> NB; height -> SZ ].

(2) X:student[ lname -> NF; cname -> NB; size -> SZ ]:-
    X:etudiant2[ repository -> "source2.fr"; nom -> NF; prenom -> NB;
                 taille -> SZ ].
```

The I-Object class *student* is now a well defined virtual I-Object which can plays the role of interface to access data from different sources. A problem keeps unsolved if data from sources are expressed in a different format, for example if *source2* uses the meter unit to express the height of students rather than foot. This problem can be resolved by comparing the characterization of the unified methods and is taken into account with another automatic operation called adaptation operation.

An adaptive operation is automatically applied on the rules which define virtual I-Objects built with $\oplus$ or $\otimes$. This operation is composed of four steps :

- A comparison of the characterization rules for methods which are unified in the virtual I-Object definition rule. Characterization mismatch is retained for the following step.
- A template function is built for each type of mismatch characterization. This function is created in a specific library called *MODEL_LIBRARY*. This template is interpreted and characterized on the local context.
- Calls to these templates are inserted in the rule definition of the virtual I-Object.
- Search for relevant functions in the local context which match with the interpretation of templates and replace these ones by functions if exist.

In the example above, if the characterization of the method *taille* shows that the unit for these data values is *meter*, a characterization mismatch appears between *student.size* and *etudiant.taille*. The adaptation operation generates the template function *template1* in library *MODEL_LIBRARY*. This templates gives a model of function to transform meter value into foot value. The adaptation operation provides a correct characterization for parameter and results of this function as presented below :

```
library MODEL_LIBRARY[ template1@(parameter->real)->real ].
inter MODEL_LIBRARY.template1(parameter:::height):::height
library MODEL_LIBRARY[ MProperty('template1','Unit_Of_Datum') -> 'foot' ].
library MODEL_LIBRARY[ MProperty('template1@parameter','Unit_Of_Datum')
                       -> 'meter' ].
```

The example below shows how a template is inserted in the body of a virtual I-Object definition. The variable which unifies directly methods with mismatch characterization is replaced by a template call.

```
(2bis) X:student[ lname -> NF; cname -> NB; size -> SZ ]:-
            X:etudiant2[ repository -> "source2.fr"; nom -> NF;
                         prenom -> NB; taille -> TA ],
             MODEL_LIBRARY[ template1@( parameter -> TA)-> SZ ].
```

This virtual I-Object can now be used to access student data from two heterogeneous sources in a transparent way.

5 Conclusion and Future Works

DILEMMA proposes three important features to enhance cooperation of information systems : (1) a semantic mediation model for the definition of I-Objects and their meanings on a local context, (2) a reconciliation method which assures the comparison of contexts using the definition of a semantic distance, (3) a mechanism of object fusion to construct virtual I-Object classes which allows a transparent access to the cooperation. In this approach, information do not depend on domain or universal ontologies and the comparison mechanism is always possible. Some recent works also focus on the definition of similarity distances to compare concepts described using ontologies and inter-ontologies mapping may be necessary to assure a complete comparison process. The mechanism of object fusion is based on the results of the context comparison. It allows to group I-Objects which are interpreted on similar concepts. The discovery of relevant I-Objects over the cooperation depends on the quality of the context. Thus, a promising way may be to construct local contexts by specializing and adapting some pre-defined top-level ontologies.

References

1. Lee, Y., Liu, L., Pu, C.: Towards interoperable heterogeneous information systems: An experiment using the diom approach. In: Proceesings of the 12th ACM Symposium on Applied Computing (ACM SAC'97) Special track on Database Technology, San Jose, California, USA (1997)
2. Tomasic, A., Raschid, L., Valduriez, P.: Scaling heterogeneous databases and the design of disco. In: Proceedings of the 16th International Conference on Distributed Computing Systems (ICDCS'96), Hong Kong, IEEE Computer Society Press (1996) 449–457
3. Tari, Z., Cheng, W., Yetongnon, K., Savnik, I.: Towards cooperative databases: The distributed object kernel approach. In Yétongnon, K., Hairi, S., eds.: Proceedings of Conference on Parallel and Distributed Computing Systems (PDCS'96), Dijon, France, The International Sociaty for Computers and their Applications (ISCA), isbn 1880843-16-1 (1996) 595–600

4. Bishr, Y., Radwan, M., Pandayaal, J.: Semweb - a prototype for seamless sharing of geoinformation on the world wide web in a client/server architectures. In: Third Joint European Conference and exhibition on Geographical Information. (1997) 145–154
5. Fensel, A.D., Decker, S., Erdmann, M., Studer, R.: Ontobroker: The very high idea. In: Proceedings of the 11th International Flairs Conference (FLAIRS-98), Sanibal Island, Florida (1998)
6. Goi, A., Fensel, A.D., Angele, J., Decker, S., Erdmann, M., Schnurr, H.P., Studer, R., Witt, A.: On2broker: Lessons learned from applying ai to the web. Technical Report 383, Institue AIFB (1998)
7. Mena, E., Illarramendi, A., Kashyap, V., Sheth, A.: Observer: An approach for query processing in global information systems based on interoperation across pre-existing ontologies. International Journal of Distributed and Parallel Databases (DAPD) (2000) 223–271
8. Ouzzani, M., Benatallah, B., Bouguettaya, A.: Ontological approach for information discovery in internet databases. Journal of Distributed and Parallel Databases **8** (2000) 367–392
9. Jr., R.J.B., Bohrer, B., Brice, R.S., Cichocki, A., Fowler, J., Helal, A., Kashyap, V., Ksiezyk, T., Martin, G., Nodine, M.H., Rashid, M., Rusinkiewicz, M., Shea, R., Unnikrishnan, C., Unruh, A., Woelk, D.: Infosleuth: Semantic integration of information in open and dynamic environments (experience paper). In Peckham, J., ed.: Proceedings ACM SIGMOD International Conference on Management of Data (SIGMOD'97), Tucson, Arizona, USA, ACM Press (1997) 195–206
10. Nodine, M., Bohrer, W., Ngu, A.H.H.: Semantic brokering over dynamic heterogeneous data sources in infosleuth. In: Proceedings of the 15th International Conference on Data Engineering (ICDE'99), Sydney, Austrialia, IEEE Computer Society (1999) 358–365
11. Weibel, S., Kunze, J., Lagoze, C., Wolf, M.: Dublin core metadata for resource discovery. Technical Report IETF 2413, The Internet Society (1998)
12. Jarrar, M., Meersman, R.: Formal ontology engineering in the dogma approach. In R. Meersman, Z., ed.: CooPIS/DOA/ODBASE 2002, Springer, Lecture Notes in Computer Science vol. 2519 (2002) 1238–1254
13. Motik, B., Maedche, A., Volz, R.: A conceptual modeling approach for semantic-driven enterprise applications. In R. Meersman, Z.T., ed.: Proceedings of the First Inetrnational Conference on Ontologies, Databases and Applications of Semantics (ODBASE), Springer, Lecture Notes in Artificial Intelligence , vol. 2519 (2002) 1082–1099
14. Guarino, N.: Semantic matching: Formal ontological distinctions for information organization, extraction, and integration. In Pazienza, .T., ed.: International Summer School (SCIE'97), Frascati, Italy, Lecture Notes in Computer Science, Vol. 1299, Springer, ISBN 3-540-63438-X (1997) 139–170
15. Resnik, P.: Semantic similarity in a taxonomy: An information-based measure and its application to problems of ambiguity in natural language. In: Journal of Artificial Intelligence Research (JAIR), vol. 11. (1999) 95–130
16. Maedche, A., Staab, S.: Measuring similarity between ontologies. In: 13th International Conference on Knowledge Engineering and Knowledge Management (EKAW02), Madrid, Spain (2002)
17. Jouanot, F.: DILEMMA : vers une coopération de systèmes d'informations basée sur la médiation sémantique et la fusion d'objets. PhD thesis, Burgundy University - France (2001)

A Methodology for *e*-Service Substitutability in a Virtual District Environment

Valeria De Antonellis[1], Michele Melchiori[1], Barbara Pernici[2], and Pierluigi Plebani[2]

[1] *Università di Brescia*
Via Branze, 38 – 25123 Brescia, Italy
{deantone,melchior}@ing.unibs.it
[2] *Politecnico di Milano*
Piazza Leonardo da Vinci, 32 – 20133 Milano, Italy
{pernici,plebani}@elet.polimi.it

Abstract. A virtual district is defined as a consortium of independent member enterprises which operate in an integrated and organic way to exploit business opportunities. Such enterprises cooperate to achieve common goals following agreed upon *cooperative processes.*
Considering a cooperative process as a set of activities performed by *e*-Services provided by the different enterprises, this work studies the compatibility among *e*-Services to support the dynamic substitution of failed or modified *e*-Services.
The methodology takes into account both syntactic and semantic analysis, using a domain ontology to match the different terminology used by the different *e*-Service providers.

Keywords: *e*-Service, dynamic substitution, compatibility, virtual districts

1 Introduction

The last few years have witnessed several efforts for the development of service oriented environments with the purpose of supporting the retrieval, composition, and execution of e-Services over the Internet. Research work [1,2,3] has recently focused on methods and tools for presenting an abstract view of internal processes to hide internal details of process execution inside organizations and for service composition [4]. Several research issues are still to be solved concerning service composition using web services [5].

Within the Italian VISPO (Virtual district Internet-based Service PlatfOrm) Project, started in 2001, we aim at developing an environment for cooperative processes based on e-Services composition mechanisms. In particular, the goal is to support the dynamic composition of e-Services considering not only the design of complex e-Services starting from simple e-Services, but also the dynamic substitution of failed or modified e-Services.

This work proposes a methodology to support the dynamic substitution of available *e*-Services in a virtual district. Such methodology is composed by four

J. Eder and M. Missikoff (Eds.): CAiSE 2003, LNCS 2681, pp. 552–567, 2003.

phases devoted to the clustering of *e*-Services in compatibility classes for possible substitution.

The paper is organized as follows: Section 2 briefly presents the VISPO project, Section 3 the actors and tools involved in our approach. Section 4 presents the main steps that compose our methodology, followed by Section 5 where a running example used for further illustration of our approach is introduced. Finally, Sections 6, 7, and 8 illustrate in detail the methodological phases.

2 VISPO Project

A virtual district is defined as a consortium of independent member enterprises which operate in an integrated and organic way to exploit business opportunities. From a technological standpoint the information systems of such enterprises have to communicate following a process called *cooperative process*.

Within the Italian VISPO project we aim at developing a flexible environment to support the design of service-based cooperative processes and the composition of *e*-Services, by considering not only the design of complex *e*-Services starting from simple ones, but also the dynamic substitution of failed or modified *e*-Services. The structure of the cooperative processes and the modalities of interaction are designed according to the nature of interactions in a virtual district, ranging from completely hierarchical structures to open markets [6].

In VISPO the following models are defined:

- e-*Service Model* (target of this work): characteristics of *e*-Services are specified in their syntactic and semantic aspects;
- *Orchestration Model*: interactions between *e*-Services and their coordination are specified;
- *Business Transaction Model*: the orchestration is defined on the basis of predefined business transaction patterns, which specify the characteristics of interactions between organizations and provided *e*-Services.

In the *e*-Service Model, according to [7], we consider an *e*-Service as a black box that exports a set of methods (operations) to be invoked in a precise order. In particular, an *e*-Service can be defined in terms of:

- **Interface**: specifying the provided operations and exchanged information.
- **Behavior**: specifying the effects in terms of pre- and post-conditions and the order in which the provided operations have to be invoked.
- **Quality of service**: defining *e*-Service features like availability, performance level, and cost.

In this paper we will consider the models for representing interface and behavior of *e*-Services in terms of pre- and post-conditions, which will be presented in subsection 6.1 and 6.2 respectively.

Several languages are available to describe *e*-Services. WSDL [8] is the de facto standard language to describe a Web Service interface. BPEL4WS [9] can be used to describe the behavior of the *e*-Services and the conversation among them. As for the quality, WSOL [10] is currently available. Furthermore, DAML-S [11] can be used to create a service ontology, also specifying the pre- and post-condition, whereas the UDDI Registry can be used to store references to existing *e*-Services.

Once the *e*-Services that compose a cooperative process are identified, one or more of them could be substituted after being selected, due to one of the following events:

- during execution, the *e*-Service fails or cannot be reached;
- a better service, with respect to quality of service parameters, could be provided by a new *e*-Service;
- a new version of a selected *e*-Service, offered by the same provider is available.

The proposed methodology aims at supporting such substitution cases during the execution time of a cooperative process and without affecting the process behavior.

3 The Approach

Since two *e*-Services can be substituted each other only if the two are compatible, our substitutability approach is based on the idea that the *e*-Service specifications have to be classified in order to track the relationships among them in terms of compatibility. In such a way, given an *e*-Service and using this relationships we can, in a semi-automated way, search for the compatible *e*-Service

Figure 1 shows the reference VISPO architecture of the proposed approach. Two main sets of *e*-Services are considered:

- `District specific e-Services`: oriented to the cooperative processes in the district and provided by the organizations belonging to the virtual district.
- `General purpose e-Services`: realized to be used in several environments and published in UDDI Registry [12].

In particular, we perform *e*-Service identification on the basis of semantic relationships. Such distinction derives from the difficulty to collect both the syntactic and semantic aspects of the *e*-Service not directly managed inside the districts.

For the district specific *e*-Services an enhanced version of UDDI, called VISPO Registry and described later in this work, is mainly used to maintain *e*-Service specifications. Semantic knowledge about services and information contents is organized in the the Domain Service Ontology and Domain Knowledge Ontology.

Two main actors are involved during the design and execution time of the cooperative process: the `Application programmer` and the `Domain Expert`.

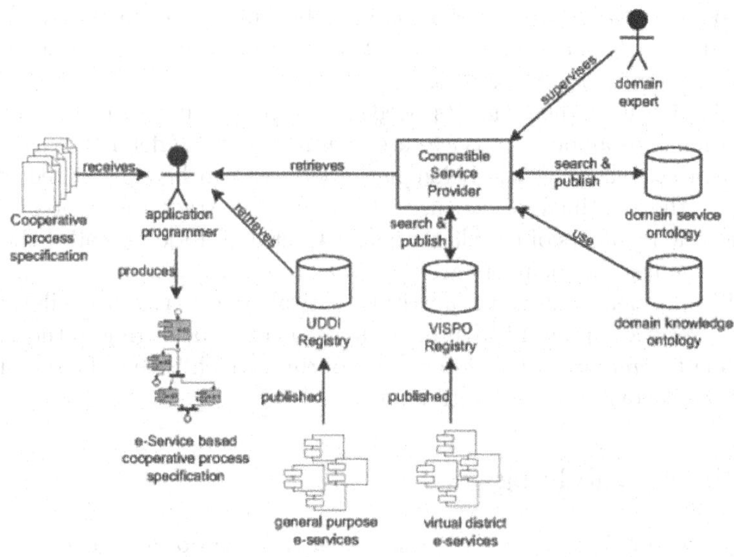

Fig. 1. Reference VISPO architecture

Given a cooperative process specification, the Application Programmer composes the available *e*-Services, in order to satisfy given requirements for a cooperative process. Considering the *e*-Services as black boxes, two different behaviors are to be considered for the cooperative process:

- *Non-observable* behavior: related to the behavior of the composing *e*-Services. Since an *e*-Service is considered as a black box, we cannot modify its internal structure, but only use the provided methods, following its specifications.
- *Observable* behavior: related to the existing cooperation among the organizations which participate in the process.

The objective is to be able to substitute an *e*-Service, when necessary, without affecting the observable behavior of the cooperative process [13].

For this purpose, the Application Programmer is supported by the Compatible Service Provider (CSP). The CSP is a module of the VISPO architecture which, under the supervision of the Domain Expert:

- Allows to publish *e*-Services maintaining the needed classification of *e*-Service specifications in the VISPO Registry and in the Domain Service Ontology.
- Given an *e*-Service specification, allows to retrieve a compatible *e*-Service.

Moreover, the CSP refers to a `Domain Knowledge Ontology` to discover relationships, as for example homonymy or hyperonymy, between terms used in the organizations belonging to the district.

In our approach, two *e*-Services can substitute each other only if they are compatible. In such a way, given an *e*-Service we can, in a semi-automated way, search the compatible *e*-Services.

Once identified the elements needed to discover and store the compatibility relationships among *e*-Services are identified, we can define the *compatibility class* as a set where all the belonging *e*-Services can be substituted with each other. All the identified services are related to an abstract description that represents all the members of the class: this abstract description is called the *abstract service* whereas the members are the *concrete services*.

When problems related to substitutability arise (e.g. a service fails), the failed concrete service can be substituted with another one belonging to the same class according to *mapping information*, a set of rules which have to be satisfied when we substitute one *e*-Service with another.

4 The Methodology

In order to provide to the CSP the needed information to create and use the compatibility classes, using the data sources and tools, four main steps compose our methodology from *e*-Services publication to their invocation:

- *Publication*: the service provider publishes its *e*-Service in a repository. In case of district specific *e*-Services the VISPO Registry is used, instead, in case of general purpose *e*-Services any available UDDI Registry can be used.
- *Classification* : under supervision of the Domain Expert control, a compatibility analysis is performed on *e*-Services stored in the VISPO Registry in order to construct a Domain Service Ontology that classifies *e*-Services according to semantic relationships. The classification is is not performed on general purpose *e*-Services classification because is not feasible to collect syntactic and semantic information of all the *e*-Service published in all the available UDDI Registries.
- *Retrieval*: for district specific *e*-Services we analyze the relationship with the other *e*-Services described into the Domain Service Ontology defined in the previous step. For general purpose *e*-Services, we look for a similar *e*-Service querying the existing UDDI Registry and using a subset of the techniques adopted for the classification of the other kind of *e*-Services.
- *Substitution*: using the mapping information, and under the supervision of the Domain Expert, we substitute the failed service with another one belonging to the same class.

5 A Running Example

The activity diagram in Figure 2 represents a sofa manifacturing process schema, where the `fabric cutting`, `frame creation`, and `sewing and stapling` phases represent the strategic activities that mark the quality of the sofa.

The rest of the activities can be performed by services provided by external organizations, where the procurement service can be used to acquire the basic material and the selected delivery service will have to be able to transport huge elements.

Let us assume that inside the virtual district several e-Service providers exist. For example:

- The organizations A and B provide a procurement service.
- The organizations A, C, and D provide a warehousing service.
- The organization E provides a delivery service.

Nearby, a set of general purpose e-Services can be used in order to support activities like the procurement of water, or a cleaning service. In our example, the organization F provides a cleaning service that can be used for cleaning of the sofa after assembling and for the enterprise office cleaning.

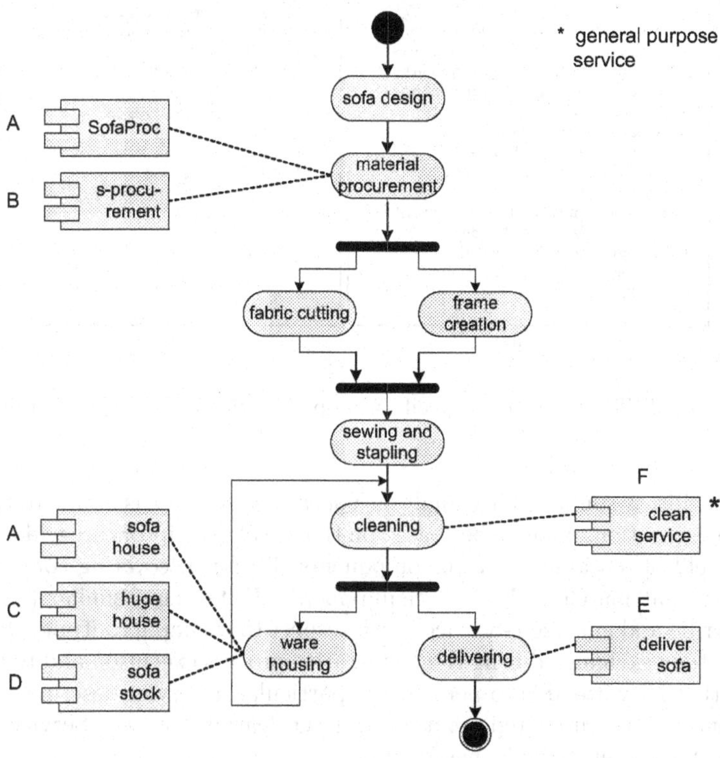

Fig. 2. Activity diagram of the sofa realization process and relationships with available e-Services

6 Publication

In order to perform compatibility analysis, we describe an *e*-Service in terms of its interface and behavior with pre- and post-condition. The descriptions are stored in the VISPO Registry.

6.1 *e*-Service Interface

For interface specification, we use WSDL to represent provided operations and corresponding input and output messages. Figure 3(a) illustrates a portion of the WSDL file that represents the `DeliverSofa` *e*-Service provided by the organization E.

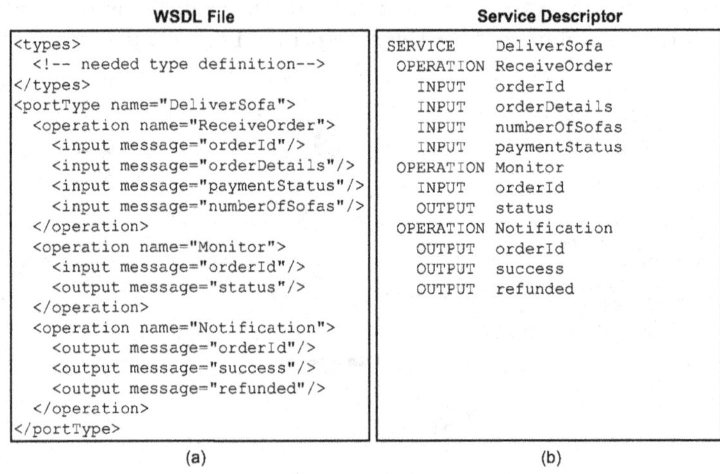

Fig. 3. WSDL example specification part of the *deliver sofa* e-Service

To facilitate compatibility analysis a *service descriptor* is added to the previous representation. Approaches based on the use of descriptors are widely studied in the field of reusable software components [14] for discovering components in a library that match with given requirements. Following a similar perspective, we describe and analyze *e*-Services with respect to the input/output information entities they exchange during the cooperative process execution and to the operations that they are able to perform. In particular, a service descriptor provides a summary, structured representation of the features of an *e*-Service that are relevant for a compatibility based analysis.
A descriptor is formally described as a set of triplets:

$$\langle \text{ operation } (OP), \text{ input entities } (IN), \text{ output entities } (OUT) \rangle$$

to provide the following information about an *e*-Service:

- a set OP of the operations that the *e*-Service can perform;
- a set IN of the input information entities;
- a set OUT of the output information entities.

Descriptors can be automatically extracted from the WSDL file, obtaining for each `portType` the structure depicted in Figure 3(b). This figure presents a possible descriptor of a `DeliverSofa` *e*-Service.

6.2 *e*-Service Behavior with Pre- and Post-conditions

Specification of *e*-Service behavior is obtained through a pre- and post-condition pair that gives a characterization of the *e*-Service semantics and in particular, provides complementary information with respect to the *e*-Service descriptor.

Pre- and post-conditions are logical statements on the input/output parameters of services and constitute a well known means to specify formally the behavior of a piece of software [13]. In our case the pre-condition is the statement to be verified before the execution of the service, whereas the post-condition must be satisfied after the service execution.

As a simple example, for the `DeliverSofa` service it can be required, as a pre-condition, that at least a sofa is available and that the payment for the delivery is valid before initiating its execution. In this case, the pre-condition can be written as: $(numberOfSofas \geq 1 \wedge paymentStatus = OK)$. The post-condition may state the successful delivery or that in the case of failed delivery a refund is required: $(success = YES \wedge refund = NO) \vee success = NO \wedge refund = YES)$.

Since pre- and post-conditions may not always available or specified for a given service, our approach allows analysis of service compatibility also when the descriptor is the only information available on *e*-Services.

According to the service description proposed in DAML-S, pre- and post-conditions can be associated both to the whole service and to the single operations of the service. Currently, we define the service compatibility on the basis of single operation pre- and post-conditions. Future work will extend the model to take into account also the possible orders in which operations of a service can be performed, to obtain more information for the compatibility analysis.

6.3 The VISPO Registry

Since the publication of the general purpose *e*-Services can be performed using a typical UDDI Registry [15], in this section we consider only the district specific *e*-Services.

To store *e*-Service specifications and descriptors, an augmented version of UDDI Registry called VISPO Registry is introduced in the VISPO Project. Figure 4 represents the internal structure of the VISPO Registry where, beside the WSDL references, there is a database that stores the descriptors.

As suggested in [16] the specification of an *e*-Service can be composed by two different WSDL documents linked to the respective `tModel`:

- *WSDL Service Interface Document* which presents only the `type`, `message`, and `portType` elements which define the interface of the *e*-Service without any reference about the protocol used for the invocation.
- *WSDL Service Implementation Document* which specializes the `portType`, through the `binding` element, specifying the protocol used.

In order to cluster *e*-Services in compatibility classes, a WSDL file that represents the abstract service is introduced. Under the supervision of the `Domain Expert` any UDDI entry which represents the *e*-Service can be linked, through the `tModel`, to the abstract service specification.

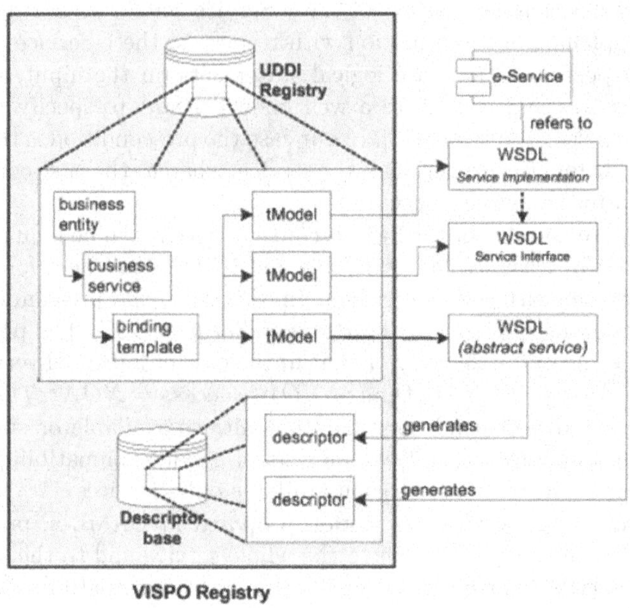

Fig. 4. VISPO Registry architecture

7 Classification

In this section we describe the process of *e*-Service classification and service ontology construction in VISPO, that is based on the analysis of compatibility between services. As noted above, the classification is required to permit the evaluation of *e*-Services compatibility and to facilitate their dynamic substitution in the cooperative process.

To the purposes of describing, maintaining and allowing the access to the classified *e*-Services, we introduce the Domain Service Ontology that organizes *e*-Services according to semantic relationships. We also propose an approach to construct the Domain Service Ontology in a disciplined way, based on the the available information about the e-Services enriched with knowledge provided by the Domain Expert, and to represent the ontology according to DAML-S model.

We think this aspect of our approach is particular relevant since there are several models for service ontologies but there is a little work on how to actually construct them.

In our framework, the Domain Expert designs the Domain Service Ontology on the basis of service descriptions composed of: (i) the service descriptor, that we assume available for each e-Service, (ii) the documentation associated with each e-Service, and (iii) further characterization of e-Services, provided by the Domain Expert, as pre- and post-conditions.

The e-Services are organized in the ontology according to three semantic relationships: `equivalent-to`, `is-a` and `similar-to`. These relationships are exploited to permit the browsing of ontology and to support the search for a compatible e-Service of a given abstract service. In fact, if we consider two e-Services described and semantically related in the ontology, and we need to substitute the first one with the second one in a cooperative process, then the existence of specific semantic relationships between the e-Services gives us information about their degree of compatibility.

7.1 Construction of the Domain Service Ontology

Behavior-Based Analysis and Classification

`Equivalent-to` and `is-a` relationships are established between pairs of e-Services on the basis of analysis of their pre- and post-conditions and of their descriptors. Description of this analysis is based on the ideas and the terminology of [13] for the software component specification and matching, but introducing some modification and adaptation to make concepts suitable to our context.

First of all, we define "matching properties" between operations. Given two e-Services S_i and S_j, we say that operation o_{ik} of S_i has an *OP-exact-match* with o_{jh} of S_j, if: (i) pre-conditions (resp. post-conditions) of o_{ik} and o_{jh} are logically equivalent, (ii) o_{ik} and o_{jh} have the same name and the same parameters. That is, the two operations are equivalent.

Exact match is a strict requirement, so a weaker relation is introduced. Operation o_{ik} of S_i has an *OP-partial-match* with o_{jh} of S_j, if: (i) pre-condition of o_{ik} implies pre-condition of o_{jh}, (ii) post-condition of o_{jh} implies post-condition of o_{ik}, (iii) o_{ik} and o_{jh} have the same name and the same parameters. That is, o_{ik} can be substituted with o_{jh}. Here the rationale is that o_{jh} can substitute o_{ik} in a process since, before the operation execution, satisfaction of o_{ik} pre-condition implies the satisfaction of o_{jh} pre-condition. After o_{jh} executed, the o_{jh} post-condition is true and therefore o_{ik} post-condition is satisfied, as expected by the process logic.

We now can extend the definitions of the exact match and the partial match properties to e-Service.

A service S_i has *SERV-exact-match* with S_j (S_i *SERV-EM* S_j) if: (i) they have identical descriptors (that is, they provide the same set of operations with the same parameters), (ii) each operation o_{ik} in S_i has an *OP-exact-match* with an operation o_{jh} in S_j and viceversa. The meaning is that there is a strong indication that service S_i can substitute S_j and viceversa.

Furthermore, we say that S_i has *SERV-partial-match* with S_j (S_i *SERV-PM* S_j), if: (i) the descriptor of S_j includes the descriptor of S_i (or equivalently, the interface of S_j provides at least the operations described in the interface of S_i), (ii) for each operation o_{ik} in S_i, there is a corresponding operation o_{jh} in S_j, such that o_{ik} has OP-exact-match/OP-partial-match with o_{jh}. That is, for each operation o_{ik}, there is corresponding operation o_{jh} that can replace o_{ik} and this conditions gives an indication that S_i can be substituted by S_j.

The existence of a *SERV-partial-match* among two e-Services S_i and S_j gives an indication that we can substitute e-Service S_i with e-Service S_j but possibly with an adaptation effort because of the not exact match between their corresponding operations. The contribution given to the ontology construction by the behavior-based analysis is the following.

If a *SERV-exact-match* among S_i and S_j is established, a relationship S_i `equivalent-to` S_j is added to the Domain Service Ontology to denote their equivalence according to behavior and interface.

If a *SERV-partial-match* among S_i and S_j is established and there is no *service exact match*, a relationship S_j `is-a` S_i is added to the Domain Service Ontology to denote can substitute e-Service S_i with service S_j according to their interface and behavior.

Interface Similarity-Based Analysis and Classification

We describe now a different analysis, called *Interface similarity-based analysis*, that permits to establish further semantic relationships among e-Services and that is based on descriptors, and therefore on interface information only. This kind of analysis is particular suitable in the case where pre- and post-conditions are not available at all or are missing for some of the e-Services.

In the *Interface similarity-based analysis* starting from the descriptors, e-Services are classified according to similarity criteria with respect to information entities and performed operations.

In particular, the e-Service classification is based on the computation of the following similarity coefficients performed by the ARTEMIS tool environment [17].

- *Entity-based similarity coefficient*. The Entity-based similarity coefficient of two e-Services S_i and S_j, denoted by $ESim(S_i, S_j)$, is evaluated by comparing the input/output information entities in their corresponding descriptors.
  In particular, names of input and output entities are compared to evaluate their degree of affinity $A()$ (with $A() \in [0,1]$). The affinity A() between names is computed exploiting a thesaurus of weighted terminological relationships (e.g., synonymy, hyperonymy). To cover the terminology used in the descriptors two different alternatives are possible in ARTEMIS: to use a pre-existing, domain independent basic ontology, such as WordNet, or to use an hybrid ontology that is a thesaurus containing both terminological relationships extracted from WordNet and terminological relationships supplied by the domain expert.

Two names n and n' of entities have affinity if there exists at least one path of terminological relationships in the thesaurus between n and n' and the strength of path is greater or equal to a given threshold.
The higher the number of pairs of entities, one from the first service and one from the second, with affinity, the higher the value of $ESim$ for the considered e-Services.

– *Functionality-based similarity coefficient*. The Functionality-based similarity coefficient of two e-Services S_i and S_j, denoted by $FSim(S_i, S_j)$, is evaluated by comparing the operations in their corresponding descriptors. Also in this case, the comparison is based on the affinity $A()$ function.
Two operations are similar if their names, their input information entities and output information entities have affinity in the thesaurus. The similarity value of two operations is obtained by summing up the affinity values of their corresponding elements in the descriptors.
The value of $FSim$ coefficient is such that the higher the number of pairs of operations, one from the first service and one from the second, with similarity, the higher its value for the considered e-Services.

Finally, a global similarity coefficient $GSim$ for each pair of services S_i and S_j is evaluated by taking a weighed sum of $ESim(S_i, S_j)$ and $FSim(S_i, S_j)$, that is a measure of their level of overall similarity.

The result of similarity-based classification are clusters of similar e-Services with defined similarity relationships. A hierarchical clustering algorithm [18] is used to determine clusters based on the strength of global similarity established among e-Services. In particular, similarity thresholds can be properly set and experimented in the ARTEMIS tool environment to provide different levels of compatibility under different perspectives.

The contribution given to the ontology construction by the Interface similarity-based is the following.

If S_i and S_j are in the same cluster according to the similarity-based classification, and there is no SERV-exact-match or SERV-partial-match between them, the S_i `similar-to` S_j relationship maintained in the cluster is referred in the ontology.

A particular case of `is-a` relationship is given by two e-Services which have in common the same WSDL Service Interface Document. In such situation the e-Services will have an high $GSim$ value because they probably differ only for the protocol adopted during the transmission.

Description of the ontology. e-Service descriptions and semantic relationships in Domain Service Ontology are formally represented in the DAML-S, that provides a model and a representation language for Web service ontologies. The formal specification of the ontology permits, for example, the access of ontology by DAML-S-enabled agents and the consistency checking. In particular, the DAML-S language is a markup language that extends DAML+OIL [19] with a set of classes and properties for describing services. In particular, a service is described according to different perspectives: (i) a declarative perspective, called

`Service Profile`, for giving information on the service provider, on what functionalities the service provides, and on quality rating information; (ii) an operational perspective, called `Process Model`, where the service is described in terms of operations, parameters, pre- and post-conditions and flow control; (iii) a `Service Grounding` perspective that specifies details, such as protocols and message formats, addressing, etc., on how to access a concrete service.

To the purpose of giving DAML-S representation of our Service Ontology, we notice that descriptions of *e*-Services, in particular descriptors and pre- and post conditions, fit directly in the `Process Model` in DAML-S. Further information can be provided by the Domain Expert to cover also the `Service Profile` and the `Service Grounding` of the service to the purpose of giving a more complete service characterization. The semantic relationships can be easily represented: the `is-a` are naturally mapped into the `subClassOf` construct of DAML-S, while the `equivalent-to` and `similar-to` are not basically included in DAML-S and we need to introduce them explicitly in DAML-S representations of our ontology.

7.2 Definition of Mapping Information

Often a perfect and transparent substitution of a *e*-Service with another *e*-Service is practically impossible; in fact, different *e*-Services use different technologies and the exchanged messages are different in syntax and semantics. So, besides the construction of the compatibility class, it is necessary to define the information, here called *mapping information*, necessary to actually substitute the service with a compatible one.

Mapping information is used to define the transformations needed to pass from the abstract service to the concrete service.

For each operation defined in the abstract service we still use ARTEMIS to identify a corresponding operation into the concrete service. This identification is based on the degree of affinity between the names used in the WSDL descriptions.

It is important to note after this analysis, it can occur that a compatible concrete service provides an operation not requested by the abstract service, or that a compatible concrete service does not provide an operation requested by the abstract service. Whereas in the former case the concrete service can be chosen even if there is an operation that will be never invoked, in the latter one even if the previous analysis does not discover any compatibility, the *e*-Service has to be discarded because we assume that the minimal substitutable element is the *e*-Service and not the operation.

Given two operations with name affinity, the correspondences between their parameters are analyzed. Moreover, for each matching pair of parameters, their data types are matched.

All the information about the correspondence between the operations, parameters and data types constitutes the mapping information used by the VISPO platform for wrapping the *e*-Service after the invocation.

8 Retrieval and Substitution

The relationships defined in the Service Ontology and in the VISPO Registry described above allow to determine the compatibility degree only for district specific *e*-Services and to individuate the compatibility class of an abstract service. The compatibility and substitutability among general purpose *e*-Service is established only on the basis of similarity-based analysis.

Substitutability among district specific e-Services. This analysis is strongly based on the Domain Service Ontology. According to the three relationship described in the Service Ontology, different efforts in substitutions are required:

- *equivalent-to* or *is-a* relationships: the matching is exact, so the substitution can be performed automatically but should be validated by the Domain Expert. Each of the methods defined for the substituted *e*-Service has a corresponding method in the substituting *e*-Service. Given a service described in the ontology the compatibility class corresponds to all the services that are equivalent to, or that are descendant in the is-a hierarchy, of the considered service.
- *similar-to* relationship: here the domain expert holds a central role in order to substitute the two compatible *e*-Service. Definition of mapping information is required to facilitate the wrapping of the substituting *e*-Service. The compatibility class of a service is formed in this case of all the service that are related to the given one by *similar-to* relationship.

Substitutability among general purpose e-Services. For this set of *e*-Services the a-priori knowledge about their syntactic and semantic aspects is less than the specific district *e*-Services. For this reason the compatibility evaluation can be performed during the substitution time.

After a typical retrieval in the available UDDI Registries, a possible approach can use a subset of the technics described above. In particular, once a possible compatible *e*-Service is found, the descriptors for both, the failed and candidate *e*-Service, are automatically generated. Using the Interface similarity-based approach discussed in the Section 7, we can also identify the semantic affinity and the mapping information.

In the VISPO architecture when substitution problems arise, the Compatible Service Provider, given an abstract service, queries the VISPO Registry and, based on the available compatibility classes, creates a list of compatible services ordered by their compatibility degrees. In such a list, besides the name of the *e*-Services, the mapping information are present.

A second module, called *Invocation Module*, gives in input such list. The Invocation Module selects the best available *e*-Service in the list and wraps it using the mapping information in order to invoke it in the cooperative process. In future research work, such selection will take into consideration also quality of service characteristics for each *e*-Service.

9 Conclusion

In the present work we propose methods and techniques to study the compatibility of services in order to support their dynamic composition inside a virtual district. The *e*-Service interface is analyzed and the behavior is studied focusing on its representation provided by pre-conditions and effects.

Future work will extend the current approach considering the quality of service aspects and also the behavior in terms of execution status. Automatic or semi-automatic adaptation of *e*-Service to the requirements of a given process will be studied, extending the mapping information approach. *e*-Service substitutability in mobile information systems will be studied, with the goal of dynamically selecting the best available *e*-Services at any moment during process execution.

Acknowledgments. The authors thank Enrico Mussi for his thesis work on the realization of the Compatible Service Provider.

This work is supported by Italian MIUR-MURST under the VISPO and MAIS contracts.

Pierluigi Plebani is supported by a grant from Fondazione Silvio Tronchetti Provera.

References

1. Casati, F., Georgakopoulos, D., Shan, M.C., eds.: Technologies for E-Services, Second International Workshop, TES 2001, Rome, Italy, September 14–15, 2001, Proceedings. Volume 2193 of Lecture Notes in Computer Science. Springer (2001)
2. Buchmann, A.P., Casati, F., Fiege, L., Hsu, M.C., Shan, M.C., eds.: Technologies for E-Services, Third International Workshop, TES 2002, Hong Kong, China, August 23–24, 2002, Proceedings. Volume 2444 of Lecture Notes in Computer Science. Springer (2002)
3. Bussler, C., Hull, R., McIlraith, S.A., Orlowska, M.E., Pernici, B., Yang, J., eds.: Web Services, E-Business, and the Semantic Web, CAiSE 2002 International Workshop, WES 2002, Toronto, Canada, May 27–28, 2002, Revised Papers. Volume 2512 of Lecture Notes in Computer Science. Springer (2002)
4. Yang, J., Heuvel, W., Papazoglou, M.: Tackling the Challenges of Service Composition in e-Marketplaces. In: 12th International Workshop on Research Issues on Data Engineering (RIDE-2EC 2002), San Jose, CA, USA, February 25–26, 2002, Proocedings. (2002)
5. Hansen, M., Madnick, S., Siegel, M.: Process Aggregation using Web Services. In: Technologies for E-Services, Third International Workshop, TES 2002, Hong Kong, China, August 23–24, 2002, Proceedings. (2002)
6. Colombo, E., Francalanci, C., Pernici, B.: Modeling Coordination and Control in Cross-organizational Workflows. In: On the Move to Meaningful Internet Systems, 2002 – DOA/CoopIS/ODBASE 2002 Confederated International Conferences DOA, CoopIS and ODBASE 2002 Irvine, California, USA, October 30–November 1, 2002, Proceedings. Volume 2519 of Lecture Notes in Computer Science. Springer (2002)

7. Mohan, C.: Dynamic E-business: Trends in Web Services. In: Technologies for E-Services, Third International Workshop, TES 2002, Hong Kong, China, August 23–24, 2002, Proceedings. (2002)
8. Christensen, E., Curbera, F., Meredith, G., Weerawarana, S.: Web Services Description Language (WSDL) 1.1. `http://www.w3.org/TR/wsdl` (2001)
9. Curbera, F., Goland, Y., Klein, J., Leymann, F., Roller, D., Thatte, S., Weerawarana, S.: Business Process Execution Language for Web Services, version 1.0. `http://www.ibm.com/developerworks/library/ws-bpel/` (2002)
10. Tosic, V., Patel, K., Pagurek, B.: WSOL - Web Service Offerings Language. In: Web Services, E-Business, and the Semantic Web, CAiSE 2002 International Workshop, WES 2002, Toronto, Canada, May 27–28, 2002, Revised Papers. (2002)
11. DAML Service Coalition: DAML-S: Semantic Markup For Web Services. `http://www.daml.org/services/daml-s/0.7/daml-s.html` (2002)
12. ARIBA, IBM, Microsoft: Uddi Executive White Paper. `http://www.uddi.org/pubs/UDDI_Executive_White_Paper.pdf` (2001)
13. Zaremski, A.M., Wing, J.M.: Specification matching of software components. In: Proceedings of the 3rd ACM SIGSOFT symposium on Foundations of software engineering. ACM Press (1995) 6–17
14. Damiani, E., Fugini, M.G.: Fuzzy Identification of Distributed Components. In: Computational Intelligence, Theory and Applications, International Conference, 5th Fuzzy Days, Dortmund, Germany, April 28-30, 1997, Proceedings. Volume 1226 of Lecture Notes in Computer Science. Springer (1997)
15. McKee, B., Ehnebuske, D., Rogers, D.: Uddi Version 2.0 API Specification. `http://www.uddi.org/pubs/ProgrammersAPI-V2.00-Open-20010608.pdf` (2001)
16. Brittenham, P., Cubera, F., Ehnebuske, D., Graham, S.: Understanding WSDL in a UDDI Registry. `http://www-106.ibm.com/developerworks/webservices/library/ws-wsdl/` (2002)
17. Castano, S., de Antonellis, V.: A Schema Analysis and Reconciliation Tool Environment for Heterogeneous Databases. In: International Database Engineering and Applications Symposium, IDEAS 1999, 2–4 August, 1999, Montreal, Canada, Proceedings, Montreal, Canada (1999)
18. Jain, A., Dubes, R.: Algorithms for Clustering Data. Prentice-Hall, Englewood Cliffs, N.J. (1988)
19. van Harmelen, F., Patel-Schneider, P.F., Ian Horrocks, E.: Reference description of the DAML+OIL ontology markup language. `http://www.daml.org/2001/03/reference (2001)`

Coordinating Web-Service Enabled Business Transactions with Contracts

Willem-Jan van den Heuvel and Hans Weigand

INFOLAB, Tilburg University, PO Box 90153,
Tilburg 5000 LE, The Netherlands
{wjheuvel,weigand}@uvt.nl

Abstract. The main contribution of this paper is the development of a contract-based framework for coordinating web-services that are engaged in long-running, cohesive business transactions. The proposed framework offers an amplification to both traditional and reinvented flavors of E-Business ACIDity for statically ensuring e-business transaction robustness and reliability by introducing agreement (atomicity). In addition, this framework provides an agreement-driven model for dynamically coordinating web-service orchestrations.

1 Introduction

Web Services (WSs) are touted as a contemporary paradigm for the development of distributed, Internet-based and platform-agnostic business applications [1]. Their prime appeal to the business community lies in their capability to facilitate interaction between complex, heterogeneous and highly distributed, enterprise information systems using standards for virtually all interoperation aspects.

Last years, we have witnessed the emergence of plethora standardization initiatives covering web-service description-, discovery- and orchestration languages. From a conceptual perspective, web-service descriptions extend "traditional" object interfaces by extending the list of signatures (named port types) with (1) binding information, (2) meta-data about non-functional attributes for security, performance etc., (3) knowledge about the web-service in terms of a standard supplier/product taxonomy, and lastly, (4) contact information of the service provider. Prominent examples of state-of-the-art web-service description standards include WSDL [2], and OASIS's ebXML Services [3].

Web-services are implemented with web-service components that can be composed and deployed dynamically to support business transactions. A business transaction can be loosely defined as a sequence of actions that are performed by trading partners, and aim at accomplishing a predefined goal [9]. In contrast to traditional production workflows, the execution paths of aggregated web-services can not be computed in advance, which means that a priori it is not know with which other web-services they will collaborate. This makes it rather cumbersome to design, develop and enact, robust and dependable web-service compositions that implement business transactions.

To overcome these problems, web-service choreography languages typically provide some support for two categories of transactions: simple (atomic) or aggregated (cohesive) transactions. Atomic transactions are typically considered as holistic "all-or-nothing" entities whose internal logic is to be either fully completed (committed) or aborted. This type of atomicity assumes that there exists a high-level of trust between trading partners, and that the transaction has a relatively short duration involving

J. Eder and M. Missikoff (Eds.): CAiSE 2003, LNCS 2681, pp. 568–583, 2003.

a limited number of resources. Cohesive transactions on the other side, are longer in duration and typically require management of a large number of resources across trusted domains. In contract to atomic transactions, roll-backs are not desired by their cohesive counterparts. Instead, compensation mechanisms are applied to reverse the effect of the actions that take place within a transaction.

From our perspective, a key predicament of existing web-service conversation and coordination languages is their predominant focus on interface interactions, while ignoring the essence of coordination: communication. Proposed conversation languages typically encompass message-level support mechanisms, e.g., request and response operators that are geared towards orchestrating complex web-services for enabling business transactions.

However, *what* actually is communicated, and the *effect* of the communication in terms of what is being achieved in terms of mutual commitments is kept implicit. By capturing mutual commitments that result from pairs of message exchanges in e-contracts [1], business transactions can be designed and enacted in a transparent way, while respecting essential design parameters of service oriented computing like autonomy and loose-coupling. In this article, we will argue that contracts are the most natural vehicles to prescribe the coordination between two or more web-services. Contracts are used to make explicit the (legally binding) commitments that the partners make, and in which future commitments to performs actions are laid down [6], [8]. Contracts can be used to check upon completeness and consistency of business transactions, and might serve as a design- and run-time container for preserving semantic and syntactic interoperation, e.g., specifying semantic ontological mappings and syntactic gateways (wrapper mediators) between the orchestrated web-service interfaces. Due to reasons of simplicity, the latter two aspects will not be investigated any further here; instead we refer to [4] and [5].

In this article, we further investigate *transactional e-contracts* as an alternative to existing transaction models. In particular, we consider communication as an alternative and more flexible coordination mechanism than traditional coordination protocols. Before introducing the notion contracts, we will firstly present an overview of important standardization initiatives and indicate their shortcomings.

2 The Standardization Tower of Babylon

The past two years, many standards for composing web-services have been suggested by both academia and industry. Here, we will focus at the following four web-service orchestration standards for designing and enabling business transactions: (1) the Business Process Execution Language for Web-Services (BPEL4WS) [11] (Microsoft, IBM and BEA), (2) the Business Process Modeling Language (BPML) [20] (BPMI.org), (3) the Web Services Choreography Interface (WSCI) language [19](BEA Systems, Intalio, SAP AG, and Sun Microsystems), and lastly, (4) the Web Service Conversation Language (WSCL) [16] (W3C). Related initiatives stem from respectively the domain of E-Business message interaction standardization for enabling global marketplaces (whose predecessor was EDI), and workflow design and enactment. Notably, the first category of standardization initiatives is embodied by ebXML's Business Process Specification Schema (BPSS) [21], RosettaNet's Partner-Interface-Processes (PIPS) and OASIS's Business Transaction Protocol (BTP) [14]. The XML Processing Description Language (XPDL), entails a prominent representative of the latter (standardization) category and

[1] Please note that in this article we will use the term contracts and e-contract interchangeably.

is promoted by the Workflow Management Coalition. In the below, we will briefly describe the most influential representatives of these three domains.

BPEL4WS [11] comprises a language for representing and implementing executable business processes between multiple trading partners by synthesizing web-service definitions (in WSDL). In addition, business protocols are employed to model exchanged messages while regarding the process dynamics of involved parties as a black box. BPEL4WS is complemented with three specifications: WS-Coordination [13], WS-Transactions [12], and, Conversation Support (CS)-WS [10]. WS-Coordination provides an extensible framework to synchronize the operations (port types) of orchestrated web-services that are involved in a business process. WS-Transactions defines transaction mechanisms for both atomic and cohesive transactions and builds forward on the coordination framework that is delineated in WS-Coordination. Lastly, CS-WS serves to govern message exchanges between trading partners by allowing them to specify both low-level plumbing messaging as well as "business-level" conversation policies for enforcing sequencing constraints and timing constraints.

Another initiative in the realm of web-service orchestration languages constitutes W3C's WSCL [16]. WSCL may be defined on top of web-service representation languages such as WSDL, and caters the specification of conversations between web-services of two business partners as a sequence of allowed document exchanges between their abstract "business-level" and externally visible interfaces. Basically, WSCL allows the following types of interactions: a-symmetric (one-way) and symmetric (two-way). A-symmetric interactions can be defined with two categories of communication primitives: `Send` (reflecting a web-service sending a request to a recipient), `Receive` (a web-service receiving a request from a sending party). Symmetric interactions can be constructed using the following two intertwined communication primitives: `SendReceive` and `ReceiveSend`.

ebXML entails a joint initiative by UN/CEFACT and OASIS, that has its roots in the EDI domain, and is designed for developing a horizontal, "one-ring-to-rule-them-all" XML-based collaboration infrastructure for integrating business processes between multiple vendors. ebXML's collaboration structure comprises the following three main building blocks: Collaboration Protocol Profiles (CPPs), Collaboration Protocol Agreements (CPAs), and lastly, Business Process Specification (BPSs) schemas. Due to reasons of space, we refer to ebXML.org for an in depth discussion of these standardized elements for modeling and enacting collaborations. An initiative that can be used in conjunction with ebXML embodies OASIS' Business Transaction Protocol (BTP) [14]. BTP provides mechanisms for facilitating both atomic and cohesive transactions that are defined using a comprehensive framework encompassing actors, roles and obligations.

RosettaNet is committed to support interoperability in electronic business by providing a dictionary of terms and by standardizing Partner Interface Process (PIP) (see: $http://www.rosettanet.org$). The PIP is materialized as a model that depicts the activities, decisions and Partner Role interactions that make up an E-business transaction between two partners. Each partner must fulfill all obligations that are stipulated in the PIP. Therefor, the PIPs encompass sequences of messages with transactional characteristics, corresponding to the level of communicative agreement in our framework. A fundamental problem with PIPs is however that it is not explicitly stated how the reliability and robustness of transactions can be guaranteed. In addition, RosettaNet does not address the integration of PIPs in order to enact cohesive web-services. To extend the PIP framework in that direction, it would be necessary to describe the effects of a

PIP in terms of obligations, authorizations etc. These extensions would then serve as the foundation of an agreement-based coordination model.

Both BTP and WS-Transaction provide a widely accepted foundation on top of which we will design e-contracts that coordinate cohesive business transactions. We will further consider their internal operations and advantages, but also their deficiencies to support communication and resulting agreements in the next section.

3 Achieving Business Transaction Atomicity with BPEL4WS/BTP

Atomicity of transaction embodies the substantial particle of modern transaction theory ([22], [23]). The atomicity property of transactions assumes "all-or-nothing" behavior of a block of state-changing operations. This property is especially critical for highly distributed systems with multiple concurrently running web-services, as it ensures that systems will remain in an ambiguous state both in the case a block of operations succeeds or fails. Atomic distributed transactions are supported by (variants of) the two-phase commit protocol. As expressed in its name, this protocol is basically organized in two rounds of message exchanges. During the first round, the coordinating transaction manager requests all cohorts to prepare for commit. Once all resources have positively responded to the resource manager and durably stored intermediate results, the coordinator initiates the binding transaction by issuing a commit message. After all cohorts have successfully concluded their operations, they report this to the coordinator. In case of failure, e.g., time-out, roll-back or compensation mechanisms can be invoked by the coordinator. To overcome the potential blocking problem with the 2-PC protocol between the coordinator sending a preparation message to the cohorts and the decision making process before sending the final message to them, the slightly more costing three phase commit (3-PC) protocol has been suggested [26].

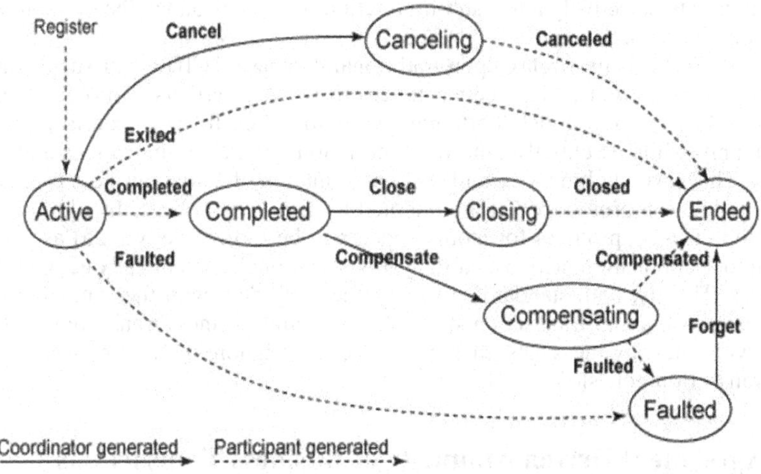

Fig. 1. BusinessAgreement Protocol State Diagram (From:[12])

State-of-the-art transaction languages for web-services, such as WS-Transactions (that is part of BPEL4WS) and BTP, implement variants of the 2-PC.

In particular, WS-Transaction predefines two coordination protocols that relax upon the standard atomicity and isolation requirements: the `BusinessAgreement` and the `BusinessAgreementWithComplete` protocols. These protocols are heavily inspired by Sagas [22] and open nested transaction protocols. Figure-1 depicts the two-party `BusinessAgreement` protocol. This protocol is organized as follows. Firstly, the participants in a business transaction need to register themselves for establishing a coordination-context, moving the protocol to the `Active` state. Subsequently, the following scenarios might occur. In case the participant's involvement is no longer required in the context of the transaction, it may issue an `Exited` message changing the protocol's state into `Ended`. If the participant has concluded his work item and intends to collaborate further on in the transaction, it sends a `Completed` message to its parent (the coordinator). The coordinator then decides on compensation or completion of the participant's task. After `Completion` the protocol moves to the `Ended` state, whereas the `Compensation` state might also yield into a `Faulted` message, moving the participant to the `Faulted` state. The coordinator then submits a `Forget` message, forging the protocol in the `Ended` state. Lastly, the coordinator can order the participant to abandon its task by sending a `Cancel` message, whereafter the participant might respond with a `Cancelled` message, putting the protocol again in the `Ended` state.

A competitive standardization initiative for ensuring reliability and robustness of business transactions is BTP (see section-2). BTP deals with atomic transactions (called atoms) and cohesive transactions (cohesions) in the following way. Atomic transactions are equipped with a variant to all-or-nothing behavior and are coordinated using the 2-PC protocol. In particular, it relaxes requirements for isolation of atomic transactions by introducing the notion of confirm sets and counter effects. Therefore, the BTP defines a dominant "super"-coordinator for deciding about whether or not to have a veto-decision that forces all involved web-services to cancel, in the case that any subordinate web-service is not capable of committing. Cohesions also do not comply fully to traditional requirements for ACIDity. At the level of the coordination protocol, the coordinator may choose to selectively allow sub-transactions to cancel, and at the same time permit other ones to commit.

Both standards thus relax upon traditional database ACIDity for supporting long-running business transactions between various trading partners. However, these standards do have some critical shortcomings. Firstly, they focus at interface-level operations only while essentially ignoring transaction-level communications and commitments. This severely hinders seamless transformation of actual business protocols into the coordination protocols that are adopted by the web-services. In addition, the application of 2-PC protocol for atoms appears to be too restrictive [25] as it does not take into account alternative execution paths of optional, semantically equivalent, web-services. Thirdly, both standards do not sufficiently deal with the synchronization of business process and transaction states. By allowing business transaction to be modelled with one-way messages, they clearly seem to ignore the link between message- and transaction-cohesions.

4 Agreement Driven Atomicity of Business Transactions

In [15], Tygar states that the "traditional" notion of atomicity is not suitable for e-business transactions and suggests the following three levels of atomicity: goods-, payment- and certified delivery atomicity. Money atomicity should ensure that money (e.g., for payments) can not be destructed or created while transferring it from the sender to the recipient. Money atomicity, he furthermore argues, is a prerequisite for goods atomicity, stating that before goods can be delivered, money should be handed over. Obviously, in case of tangible goods or money (payment) the exact identification of artifacts can, and has not, to be guaranteed. However, in some cases with low-levels of trust between trading partners, this identification might in fact be a requirement. This is an additional level of security achieved by the third e-business atomicity property: certified-delivery. Certified-delivery atomicity allows trading partners to exactly determine which goods and money aretransacted. In [18], we have suggested to categorize these levels of atomicity as *operation atomicity* requirements on the business transactions (see Figure-2). Trading parners can select one or more categories of these atomicity types, possibly according to the commitments that are laid down in the "real-world" business contract. This level of atomicity is grounded on `Request` and `Reply` atomicity, that shape the essential *infrastructure* atomicity requirements that need to be established in the pre-transaction execution phase.

To operationalize both infrastructure and operational atomicity, we will in the remainder of this paper provide the formal foundation of this taxonomy by defining them with an orthogonal concept on atomicity: *Agreements* [27]. In particular, we will argue that agreements are more effective and flexible to support sophisticated and highly volatile e-business protocols, e.g., based on the assent of parties. Moreover, we will show that they constitute a natural vehicle for capturing communication between parties that is based on mutual consensus on future actions and authorizations. The question then becomes: on what points agreement is needed, and how can this kind of agreement be established? To accomplish this, we will develop a framework that is constructed on top of the web-services stack and serves as the basis for sophisticated coordination agreement-based coordination protocols. In the following section, we will first introduce a running example that will be used in the remainder of this paper for reasons of exploration and illustration.

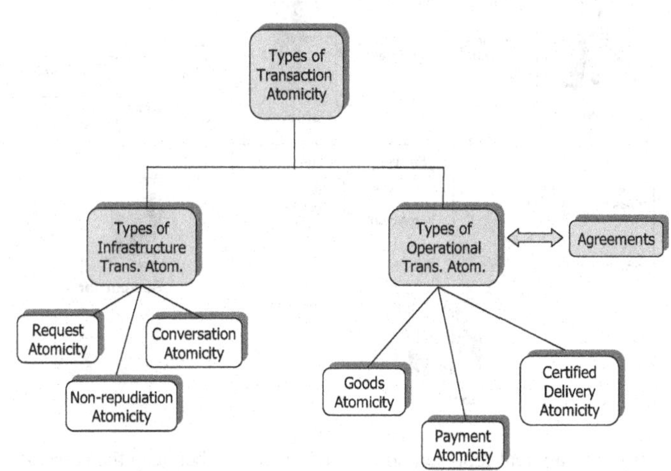

Fig. 2. Taxonomy of Transaction Atomicity Criteria

5 Running Example

The running example that we present in this paper is based on a condensed version of the case study that has been presented by Bons in [17]. Especially, we will consider the "open-account post-payment scenario" here. A global overview of the contracts and participants involved in this case has been depicted in Figure-3.

In this case we assume that the shipper produces goods for the consignee, and arranges the transportation (by sending a transport instruction to the sea-carrier) and transfers the goods to the carrier. The consignee has to pay a price for these goods and services in return. The agreement between the consignee and the shipper has been formalised in the C-terms sales contract (this indicates some terms of contract from an international standard), which assumes that the transfer of goods will be performed by a third-party agent, i.e. the sea-carrier. In other words, the transportation is an outsourced activity. The C-term sales contract states that the obligation of the shipper is to properly hire the sea-carrier; so this party is not responsible for the successful delivery of the goods. The sea-carrier is dependent on the delivery of the goods by the shipper. The shipper has to pay freight in return for the services of the sea-carrier. The payment of the freight by the shipper as well as that of the consignee, are facilitated by another third party, a bank. So, there also exist relationships between the shipper and the bank (to pay freight to the shipper) and the consignee and the bank (to pay money for the goods and transportation). The payment task of the bank also can be perceived as an outsourced activity. The bank needs a receipt of the funds to be transferred from the principal (e.g., the shipper or the consignee) and a receipt of the payment order that indicates the receiving party. To conclude the structural aspects, we assume that the shipper does not trust the consignee and vice-versa. Besides that the sea-carrier does not trust the consignee nor the shipper. However, the shipper and the consignee trust the sea-carrier, and the bank is trusted by all subjects.

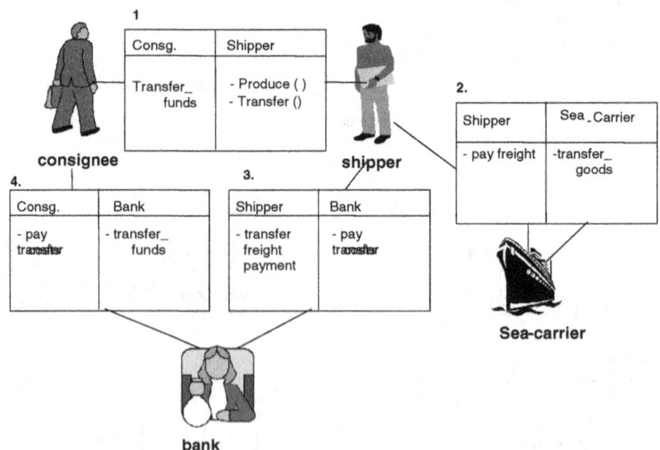

Fig. 3. Graphical representation of the contracts between the subjects

The procedural aspects of the case are as follows. The shipper manufactures the goods and subsequently organizes the transport of the goods by sending a transport instruction to the sea-carrier. Once the shipper has transferred the goods to the sea-carrier he will instruct his bank to pay the freight to the sea-carrier by sending a receipt that contains the amount of money, and another receipt that prescribes the order. Finally, the shipper waits until the consignee has paid for the goods through the consignee's bank. The sea-carrier is triggered by receiving the instruction of the shipper. Thereafter he will wait with actually transporting the goods until he has received the goods and a payment of freight through the shipper's bank. Lastly the consignee is triggered by receiving the goods from the sea-carrier. Thereafter, he will transfer the payment through his bank to the shipper.

We assume that the trading partners use web-services for supporting their part of the transaction. For reasons of space, we have omitted SOAP binding information and only included the WSDL definition of the web-service component "Transfer_Goods" that is published by a sea-carrier in the below. This web-service can be invoked by the shipper to inquire whether or not a sea-carrier is capable of transporting a product to the consignee before a specific deadline (hence, internally this may result in an order line).

```
<?xml version="1.0" encoding="utf-8"?> <definitions
  xmlns:s="http://www.w3.org/2001/XMLSchema"
  xmlns:tns="http://"infolab.uvt.nl/people/wjheuvel/wsdl/HelloService.wsdl"
  xmlns="http://schemas.xmlsoap.org/wsdl/">
  <types/>

  <message name="request_transferGoods">
      <part name="Shipper_ID" type="xsd:integer"/>
      <part name="Goods" type="xsd:string"/>
      <part name="Destination" type="xsd:string"/>
      <part name="Deadline" type="xsd:date"/>
   </message>
   <message name="request_transfer_goodsResponse">
      <part name="Notification_Sea_Carrier" type="xsd:boolean"/>
   </message>

  <portType name="Transfergoods_PortType">
      <operation name="transfer_goods">
         <input message="tns:request_transferGoods"/>
         <output message="tns:request_transfer_goodsResponse"/>
      </operation>
   </portType>

  <service name="TransferGoodService">
    <document> </document>
    <port name="Transfergoods_PortType" binding="tns:transferGSoap">
      <soap:address location="http://infolab/people/wjheuvel/wsdl"/>
    </port>
  </service>
</definitions>
```

In particular, this excerpt includes the definition of the port type `Transfergoods_PortType` that can be invoked by the shipper, and encompasses one operation `transfer_goods`. This operation includes the following four (typed) input parameters: `Shipper_Id`, `Goods`, `Destination`,and `Deadline`, and results in a notification to the shipper whether or not the goods can be actually transported.

6 Web-Services and Business Transactions: Contracts as the Binding Factor

This section outlines a unified metamodel that serves as the foundation for designing contract-driven web-service enabled business transactions. In addition, we will introduce a communication-based coordination protocol to control the execution of business transactions and deliver some degree of dependability and reliability.

6.1 The Unified Transaction-Contract Metamodel

In order to leverage contract-driven transaction management, we here propose a semi-formal metamodel that is named the "Unified Transaction-Contract Metamodel". This metamodel basically comprises two interrelated parts, see Figure-4. The left hand-side part represents business transactions that are enacted using web-service components (see section-1), whereas the right-hand side part of Figure-4 specifies the contractual substrates. These transactions are enabled by web-components which serve to implement web-service functionality. `WebComponents` can be specified with languages such as WSDL, that basically encompass a list of port type definitions and binding information, and can be orchestrated with languages such as BEPL4WS to support `BusinessTransactions`. From a formal perspective, web-components (W) can be regarded as algebraic systems: $W =< S, P_c, PR_c >$), where S represents a collection of non-empty carrier sets $\{A_s\}_s \in S$. $P_c = \{O_c^1, .., O_u^n\}$ denotes a set of port types that use A. Finally, PR_c delineate a set of predicates that works on A. The process logic of a `BusinessTransaction` is reflected as a collection of `TransactionStates`. A transaction state presents a snapshot of the progress of a `BusinessTransaction` and is defined as the (intermediate) value of one or more attributes of a collection of `WebComponents`. Transaction states can be algebraically specified using multiple-world semantics: $< P_c(I_c^1, ..., I_c^n), D > \mapsto < I_c^1, D' >$, where P_c designates a port type of web-component c, I_c^1 the return type and the remainder of the arguments input types. This formulae thus states that invoking method P_c moves a transaction state from D to D'.

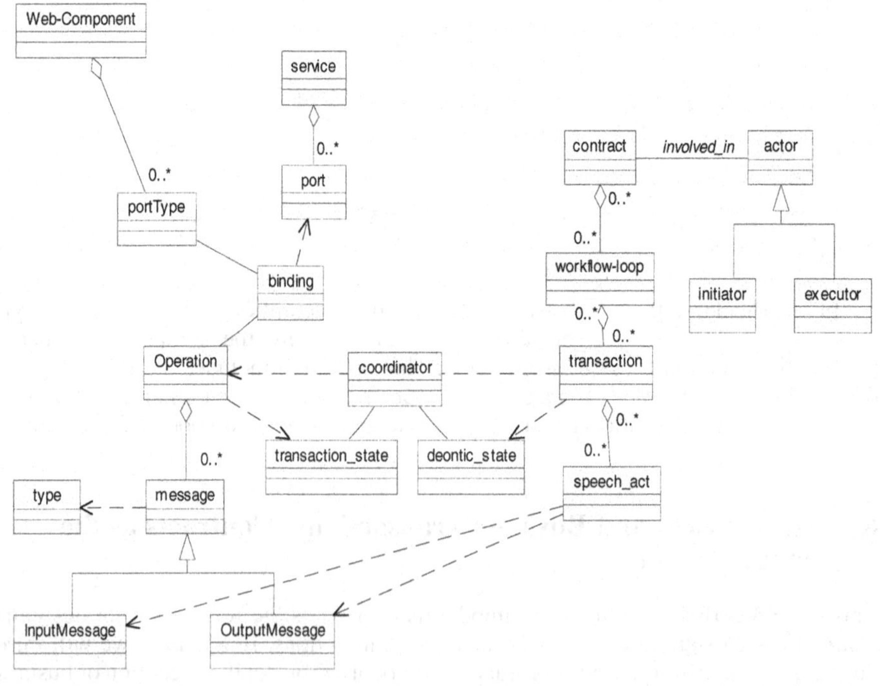

Fig. 4. Meta-model for Contract-based web-service component enabled Business Transactions.

The right-hand side of the meta-model represents four interconnected levels of constituents of a business transaction scenario. These four levels in fact reflect different levels of agreement (atomicity) that can be achieved during a business transaction. The layers are represented as extensions of the Formal Language for Business Communication (FLBC) of Kimbrough [33]. We have chosen for this language because it not only adresses the syntax but also the semantics of business messages. FLBC represents a message as a sequence of speech acts, typically assertions and declarations that form the basis of potential reasoning procedures. FLBC uses the following elements to describe the speech act: the speaker and the hearer, the illocutionary force, the content and the context. FLBC-II that is defined in [34], distinguishes between three illocutionary points, to be an assertion, a request and a query. These three atomic speech acts are used to represent a variety of message types, such as appointments (assertions), staff action messages (directives) and read/review/comment messages (directives). The context in which the communication takes place, is represented by means of either the message-ID to which is responded, the time when the message was sent, the machine-ID from which the message was sent and/or the persons to which the message is cc-ed. The machine-ID can be interpreted as being a means to ensure infrastructure atomicity, viz., request and non-repudiation atomicity.

6.2 The Communication Layers

In the following, we will outline the communication constituents from the meta-model:

Speech Acts. The lowest level we identify in our framework is that of the speech act. A speech act focuses on what people are 'doing in saying something' [28]. A speech act can be defined as an utterance that in it self is constituted of a performative act, like requesting and promising. In the speech act theory of Searle [29], a fundamental distinction is made between the propositional contents and the illocutionary force.

The message type definition in the excerpt shown below, describes the propositional content "the request to transfer goods with the name $transfer_goods on date $date on place $location", and the illocutionary force "accept".

```
MsgType accept_request_transfer_goods (sender($sea_carrier),
    receiver($shipper), product($transfer_goods), location($location), date($date) ==
    (actor($sea_carrier), actor($shipper), accept,
    TransferGoodsService.Accept_RequestTransferGoodsResponse)
```

Note that the propositional content has the following syntax: `ServiceName.MessageName`. This implies that in this way, the low-level message interaction paths for the higher-levels (transactions, workflow-loops and contracts) and the web-service component interfaces are paved (see Figure-4).

In some cases, a message combines multiple speech acts. This "bundling" provides a higher-order kind of agreement atomicity: the agents commit to the whole or not at all.

Transaction. A transaction has been defined by us as the smallest possible sequence of actions (speech acts) that leads to a certain deontic state (see Figure-4), in other words an obligation or an authorization, or an accomplishment. Deontic state transitions can be formally represented using a variant of dynamic logic: dynamic deontic logic [24]. The formal semantics of Dynamic Logic is given by means of a Kripke structure where there are accessibility relations Ra associated with each action a.

These deontic consequences of (a sequence) of speech act play an important role during the representation of the electronic commerce transaction, because collectively they define the contract between the two parties. In general, it requires a "hand-shake" of at least two messages before a communicative action is realized. For example, the combination of the request of the customer to deliver a product, together with the promise of the supplier to actually deliver it, constitutes a deontic effect, e.g. an obligation to the supplier to deliver the product, and an obligation of the customer to pay the agreed price. More in general, a transaction can be defined as a sequence of speech acts that leads to an agreement. Therefore, the transaction can be considered as the basic unit of agreement atomicity, as it is aimed at communicative agreement. A transaction can be represented by means of a set of communicating subjects, speech acts, constraints on the sequence of these actions and the goal and exit states [30].

The following excerpt indicates the transaction `request_transfer_goods` that basically coordinates the operation `transfer_goods` that was defined in the WSDL specification.

```
TransType request_transfer_goods (speaker($shipper), addressee($sea_carrier), product($goods),
         location($location), date($date) ==
      ([trading_partner(shipper), trading_partner(sea-carrier)],
      [request_transfer_goods($shipper,$sea_carrier,$location, $date,
      TransferGoodsService.request_transferGoods), accept_request_transfer_goods($sea_carrier, $shipper,
      $location, $date, TransferGoodsService.Accept_RequestTransferGoodsResponse),
      before(Accept_RequestTransferGoodsResponse, Request_TransferGoodsRequest))
```

Workflow Loop. The next level of agreement atomicity concerns workflow-loops [8]. A workflow-loop is a set of related transactions aimed at some goal. Only at this level, the obligations, authorizations and accomplishments are modelled. They are modelled as states, which are connected through transactions: for example, an initiating and evaluating transaction [31] are connected by the obligation of the executor to perform the action - the obligation is the output of the former and the input of the latter transaction. The agreement enhanced by the workflow loop can be called *service agreement*: there has to be agreement between the service that one party wants to offer and the service that the other party wants to use. This can be realized by having initiating and evaluating transactions. In that way, service agreement builds on top of communicative agreement, and can not be realized without it.

Below we have presented the workflow-loop definition of the agreement between the shipper and the sea-carrier from the perspective of the shipper. After the sea_carrier has requested a transfer_of_goods, the sea_carrier is obligated to transfer the goods.

```
WflType transfer_goods (initiator($shipper), executor($sea_carrier),
        product($transfer_goods), location($location), date($date)) ==
    ([person($shipper), person($sea-carrier)],
    /* Obligation of the sea_carrier to transfer goods after request
    /* of the shipper
    S1: OBL($sea_carrier, transfer_goods)
    in request_transfer_goods($shipper, $sea-carrier, $price, $location, $date)
    goal accept_transfer_goods ($sea-carrier, $shipper, $price)
    exit cancel (request_transfer_goods) --> Cancel_Request)
```

Contract. A business transaction is based on contractual agreement. It is what Taylor calls a symmetrical type of exchange ([35],p. 211). In this type of exchange all actors involved in the conversation, have a common interest in a particular object. In case of electronic commerce, the actors are typically the consumer, supplier and one or more third party(-is), and the common object of interest is the product. The exchange must be based on reciprocity, and this is typically implemented by the fact that the service is rewarded by a financial service. Hence we get two workflow loops. Figure 4 shows an example of a reciprocal transaction pattern. The customer requests a certain product. The supplier on the other hand, requests money for it in return. Both transaction patterns are coupled by means of an agreement on the terms of exchange. This agreement that described the mutual obligations and authorisations is often called a contract. Whenever the agreement is reached, the transaction takes place. Note that the parties may agree in advance on certain temporal constraints between the two workflows, for example, that payment is done after delivery. Such constraints have the effect of putting the risk on one side or another. At the end of a contract the mutual obligations of the partners should be fulfilled. This resembles exactly the idea of a real world contract that governs the business relation between two partners. It governs the behaviour of the two parties until the end of the contract at which time there should not be any "spurious" obligation on either side. Both parties are "free" again.

The contract specifies the workflow loops that interact, and temporal conditions between these loops. For example: the request to transfer the goods from the shipper must take place before the request to transfer the payment.

```
ContractType Shipper/Sea-Carrier (customer($shipper), supplier($sea_carrier),
        product($transfer_goods), location($location), date($date) ==
    ([person($shipper), person($sea-carrier)], transfer_goods($shipper, $sea-carrier,
    $transfer_goods, $location, $date), [person($sea-carrier), person($shipper)],
    transfer_freight($sea_carrier, $shipper, $transfer_goods, $location, $date),
    transfer_goods.request_transfer_goods BEFORE transfer_funds.request_transfer_freight)
```

The contracttype `Shipper/Sea-carrier` consists of two workflow loops: `transfer_goods` and `transfer_freight`. Furthermore, the contracttype defines constraints between (speech) acts between both workflow loops: the request to transfer goods in the `Transfer_goods` workflow, has to be preceded by the request to transfer freight in the `transfer_funds` workflow loop.

Note that for illustration purposes we have added an additional constraint to the actual casus description: the sea-carrier can only ask to transfer the freight from the shipper, after the transaction in which the shipper has requested the sea-carrier to transfer the goods is finished successfully. In the default case, no constraints are specified and the two (transactions in) the two workflows can run truly in parallel.

Any contract presupposes a third party, be it a governmental institution, law or another institutional entity. This third party may exist outside the system, but it can also an agent within the system. If there is an active third party (Contract Manager), the contract may contain a third workflow describing the deontic states in which the contract can be, and the actions connecting them. These typically include control actions from the Contract Manager.

6.3 Transaction Coordination Protocol with Contracts

In order to ensure atomicity of business transactions, coordination protocols have been incorporated in web-service composition and transaction languages (see section-3). In particular, existing transaction specification standards, e.g., BTP and WS-Transactions tend to adopt 1-PC and 2-PC coordination protocols for guaranteeing atomicity. Cohesive transactions are typically designed as variants to Sagas and open nested transactions. As outlined in section-3, BTP adopts a voting/enrollment process where the coordinator has the final vote with regard to commitment or rejection of the overall business transaction. WS-Transactions on the other hand uses two coordination protocols for supporting cohesive transactions the `BusinessAgreement` protocol, and, the `BusinessAgreementWithComplete` protocol. Both protocols assume that there exists a central coordinator. The first was already explained in the above. The latter is an extension to this protocol with a nested scope to ensure the coordinator that it has received all requests to execute a task within the context of a cohesive business transaction.

Here, we sketch an the basics of a coordination model for business transactions that are governed by agreements as laid down in contracts. This coordination model explicitly links the transaction (agreements) to the business process state, allows multiple execution paths to be determined dynamically, and is centered around communication primitives and patterns. This model comprises the following two components (see Figure-5): transaction execution and transaction control.

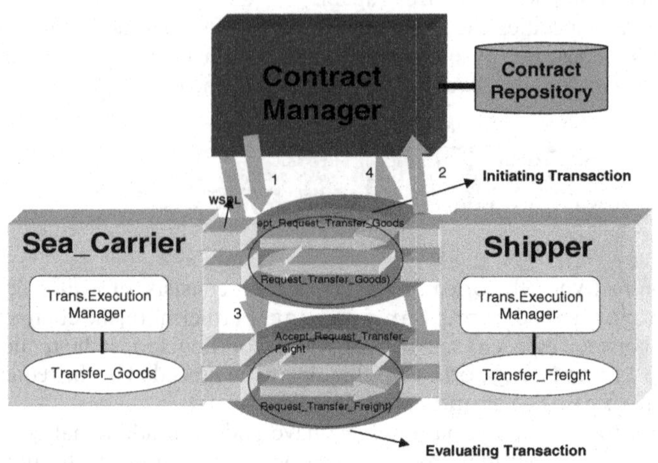

Fig. 5. Transaction Coordination with Contracts.

The transaction execution is specified using web-service descriptions languages, like WSDL. The transaction execution defines business process logic as a set of alternate and/or sequentially or parallel executing web-service port types [36]. The resulting transaction execution interface masks off internal business processes from the transaction controller in order to adhere to requirements of autonomy and loose-coupling. This is a realistic assumption as partners mostly do not want to loose autonomy in a trading relationship.

Cross-organizational transactions (hence service-driven workflows) are managed by patterns of control messages that can be specified in an e-contract. The transaction control basically comprises two parts: the initiating phase (Step-1 and -2 in Figure-5) and the evaluating control (Step-3 and -4 in Figure-5) phase. So, both phases serve to "encapsulate" the the execution transaction. The initiating control phase initiates an internal transaction execution based on his promise to deliver a service. Then the internal workflow takes over the control, allocates the resources to the scheduled tasks, and tracks the operations. The internal `transaction_state` of a participating, cohesive webservice is monitored on two levels.

The first level is the level of service control, which is performed by the initiating partner who is the customer of the service. The second level is the level of contract control, which is performed by a third party, that is, the Contract Manager. The Contract Manager has its own workflow definition; formally, this definition not different from the workflow definitions of the parties. That is, it contains a number of deontic states and how they are connected by means of transactions. The role of the Contract Manager is similar to the role of coordinator in the `BusinessAgreement` protocol mentioned above, and in fact, if this mechanism is in place, it can be used to implement the role of Contract Manager. Typically, the workflow of the Contract Manager is a subset of all the deontic states, as the Contract Manager is needed only when the parties themselves fail to come to an agreement.

The task of service control is to dynamically check that the deadlines are being met and to take action when some failure occurs. After the internal web-service process logic has been executed, control is given back to the customer and the transaction will be finalized by the assertion of the customer that the service has been delivered according to the former promise and to the satisfaction of the customer (see Figure-5). In case a web-service is unavailable or exceeds a predefined process execution load threshold, the service control manager might then automatically pursue other semantically equivalent web-services to take over the job. These alternative routes need not be defined within the contract; they can be defined in the task description or contingency plan ([32]), or searched for at run-time with a service matching agent [37]. If the contract defines alternatives or compensations, of course these are executed.

The Contract Manager executes its own workflow, as coordinator of the business transaction. When the de-central service control fails, the Contract Manager can take over and perform compensating or alternative actions. Note that the Contract Manager workflow is either implemented as a large or a fine-grained coordinator component, depending on whether tight- or loose- coupling of the orchestrated web-services is desired. Here, we repeat that although the function of Control Manager is always present somehow, it does not need to be a computerized third-party in the system. The function can be implemented on an organizational or legal level. In case of significant power asymmetry between partners (Lord of the Chain), the role of Contract Manager can be taken by the dominant partner.

7 Conclusions and Future Research

In this paper, we have reported on a contract-based framework for coordinating dependable cohesive web-services that implement business processes. This framework offers an alternative way to both traditional and modern E-business flavors of ACID-ity, and is centered around the notion of *agreements* between interacting business partners. In particular, a unified meta-model is proposed that integrates web-service definition languages that reflect behavior in the object world, with contracts, which represent the inter-subject world as a set of obligations, authorizations and permissions. In addition, we have argued how this meta-model might serve as the foundation for coordination models for ensuring agreement "atomicity" in conjunction with web-service coordination protocols such as 2- and 3-PC, and WS-Transactions's Sagas-based `BusinessAgreement` protocol.

Although the meta-model needs to be extended and formalized, we think that the initial contract definition we presented in this paper adds a valuable perspective to the "traditional" pure object-, and not subject-, oriented way of web-service orchestration modeling and design: the communication and the resulting mutual commitments.

Several similar initiatives have been launched to introduce contracts as a means to script web-services. A recent example is the CrossFlow project. The CrossFlow project aims at developing a framework to support contract based service trading [38]. However, this particular contract specification language is equipped with less business semantics, and not linked to a business object framework. In [39] an agent-based architecture is sketched to support contracts and cross-organizational business processes.

This architecture comprises a contract manager, process manager and a message manager and could be applied to support the proposed contract-based coordination model. Verharen [30] was one of the first to propose a separation between task specification and interaction specification. In his agent-oriented architecture, the interaction is also specified using contracts.

Our current results are exploratory in nature; aspects of the language in this paper are being validated in several projects. Elements of the proposed framework are incorporated in the Process-Integration for Electronic Commerce (PIEC) project that is conducted in collaboration with the Dutch Telematics Institute. As future work, we plan to fully validate and refine the framework starting with the development of a formal model. Following this, we intend to implement support for the framework with an experimental prototypes that we wish to subsequently test using case study or action research.

References

1. J. Yang and M.P. Papazoglou. *Interoperation Support for Electronic Business.* Communications of the ACM, Vol.43, No. 6, pp. 39-47, June 2000
2. E. Christensen et al. *Web Services Description Language (WSDL) 1.1* http://www.w3.org/TR/wsdl W3C Technical Report, March 2001.
3. M Rawlins et al. *ebXML Technical Architecture Specifcation, V1.4* http://www.ebxml.org/specs/ebTA.pdf ebXML.org, 2001
4. V. Kashyap and A. Sheth Semantic and Schematic Similarities Between Database Objects: A Context-Based Approach VLDB Journal, 5(4): 276-304, 1996
5. M. Vidal et al. *A Meta-Wrapper for Scaling up to Multiple Autonomous Distributed Information Sources* Proceedings of Conference on Cooperative Information Systems 148-157, New-York, USA, 1998
6. H. Weigand and W. Hasselbring *An Extensible Language for Business Communication* In: O. Etzion, P. Scheuermann (Eds), Cooperative Information Systems (COOPIS 2000), Springer-Verlag, 2000.
7. V. Kalogeraki et al. *A Peer-to-Peer Architecture for Delivering E-Services* HP Technical Report HPL-2001-181, 20010801, 2001.
8. T. Winograd *A language/action perspective on the design of cooperative work*, In: I.Greif (Ed), Computer Supported Cooperative Work: A Book of Readings, Morgan Kaufmann, 1986.
9. F. Leymann and D. Roller, *Production Workflow: Concepts and Techniques*, Prentice Hall, New Jersey, 2000.
10. J. Hanson et al. *Conversation support for Business Process Integration*, In: Proceedings 6th IEEE International Enterprise Distributed Object Computing Conference (EDOC-2002), IEEE Press, 2002, pp. 65-74.
11. F. Cubera et al. *Business Process Execution Language for Web-Services, Version 1.0*, http://www.ibm.com/developerworks/library/ws-bpel (visited: 4-9-2002), Joint BEA Systems, IBM, Microsoft Technical Report, 31 July 2002.
12. F. Cabrera et al. *Web Services Transaction (WS-Transaction)* http://www.ibm.com/developerworks/library/ws-transpec (visited: 4-9-2002) Joint BEA Systems, IBM, Microsoft Technical Report, 9 August 2002.
13. F. Cabrera et al. *Web Services Coordination (WS-Coordination)*, http://www.ibm.com/developerworks/library/ws-coor (visited: 4-9-2002), Joint BEA Systems, IBM, Microsoft Technical Report, 9 August 2002.
14. A. Ceponkus et al. *Business Transaction Protocol, Version 1.0*, http://www.oasis-open.org/committees/business-transactions/, documents/specification/2002-06-03.BTP_cttee_spec_1.0.pdf (visited: 5-9-2002) OASIS Technical Report, OASIS, 2002.
15. J.D. Tygar *Atomicity in Electronic Commerce.* netWorker, 22: 32-43, ACM-Mixed Media, 1998.

16. A. Banerij et al. *Web-Services Conversation Language (WSCL)*, http://www.w3.org/TR/wscl10/ (visited: 23-10-2002), W3C Technical Report, March 2002.
17. R. Bons, *Designing Trustworthy Trade Procedures*, Phd Thesis, Rotterdam School of Management, 1997.
18. W.J. van den Heuvel and S. Artyshchev *Developing A Three-Dimensional Transaction Model for Supporting Atomicity Spheres*, Proceedings of International Workshop on Web Services: Research, Standardization, and Deployment (WS-RSD'02), 3-9808628-1-X Erfurt, Germany, October, 2002.
19. A. Arkin et al. *Web Service Choreography Interface 1.0.* http://dev2dev.bea.com/techtrack/wsci.jsp (visited 12-10-2002), BEA Systems, Intalio, SAP, Sun Microsystems Report, 2002.
20. A. Arkin *Business Process Modeling Language.* BPMI.Org, Last Call Draft Report, 13 November 2002.
21. Business Process Project Team. *ebXML Business Process Specification Schema.* Last Call Draft Report, 13 November 2002.
22. J. Gray and A. Reuter *Transaction Processing : Concepts and Techniques*, Morgan Kaufmann, San Francisco, 1993.
23. N. Lynch et al. *Atomic Transactions* Morgan Kaufmann, 1993.
24. H. Weigand, F. Dignum and E. Verharen. *Integrated Semantics for Information and Communication Systems*, In: R. Meersman, L. Mark (Eds), Database Application Semantics. Chapman & Hall, 1997.
25. *WebTransact: A Framework for Specifying and Coordinating Realiable Web Services Compositions* Paulo de Figueiredo Pires PhD Thesis, University of Rio de Janeiro, June 17, 2002.
26. D. Skeen *Nonblocking Commit Protocols* Proc. of ACM SIGMOD, June 1982.
27. An ACID Framework for Electronic Commerce In: Proceedings of The First International Conference On Telecommunications and Electronic Commerce, Dallas, TX, USA, November 16-19, 2000.
28. J. Austin *How to do things with words*, Clarendon Press, 1962.
29. J. Searle, *An essay in the philosophy of language*, Cambridge University Press, 1969.
30. H. Weigand, E. Verharen and F. Dignum. *Interoperable Transactions in Business Models.* In P. Constantopoulos, J. Mylopoulos and Y. Vassiliou (eds.), Advanced Information Systems Engineering, pages 193-209, LNCS1080, Springer-Verlag, 1996.
31. J.L.G. Dietz. Business modelling for business redesign. In *Proc. HICSS '94*; pp. 723-732. IEEE Press, 1994.
32. H. Weigand and A. Ngu *Flexible specification of interoperable transactions* Data & Knowledge Engineering 25 (1998), pp327-345, 1998.
33. Kimbrough, S. and Lee, R., *On formal aspects of electronic commerce: examples of research issues and challenges*, In: Proceedings HICSS'96, IEEE Computer Society Press, 1996.
34. S. Kimbrough and S.A. Moore, *On automated message processing in electronic commerce and work support systems: Speech Act*, ACM Transactions on Information Systems (TOIS), 1997
35. J.R. Taylor, *Rethinking the Theory of Organizational Communication*, Ablex Publishing Company, 1993.
36. J. Yang and M.P. Papazoglou Web Component: A Substrate for Web Service Reuse and Composition. A. Banks Pidduck, J. Mylopoulos, C.C. Woo, M. Tamer Ozsu (Eds.), Proceedings of CAiSE 2002, 21-36, Springer, LNCS 2348, 2002.
37. K. Sycara at al., *Dynamic Service Matchmaking Among Agents in Open Information Environments*, SIGMOD Record, (28)1:47-53, 1999.
38. J. Vonk at al. *Cross-organizational Transaction Support for Virtual Enterprises* In: O. Etzion, P. Scheuermann (Eds), Cooperative Information Systems (COOPIS 2000). Springer-Verlag, 2000.
39. W.J. van den Heuvel and Z. Maamar Towards a Framework to Compose Intelligent Web-Services: How Intelligent Web-Service support Cross-Organizational Business Transactions. Accepted for publication in: Comunications of the ACM, 2003.

Pro-active Monitoring of Electronic Contracts

Lai Xu and Manfred A. Jeusfeld

Tilburg University, CRISM/Infolab
5000 LE, Tilburg, The Netherlands
{L.Xu, Manfred.Jeusfeld}@uvt.nl
http://infolab.uvt.nl/people/{lxu,jeusfeld}

Abstract. Contracts between multiple business partners play an increasing role in a global economy where activities along the value chain are executed by independent yet co-operating companies. Information technology to enact a value chain is now being deployed in the form of ERP systems and Web services. However, there is little known how to formally check whether such an enactment is indeed fulfilling the contract between the parties. In this paper, we investigate which parts of a contract can be formalized to be automatically monitored. Our approach not only supports the detection of actual violations but also pro-active detection of imminent contract violations.

1 Introduction

A contract between multiple business partners contains some statements about their business relationship, in particular on their physical and informational actions. One purpose of such a contract is to distinguish expected and acceptable behavior from forbidden behavior.

The introduction of workflow systems and enterprise resource planning systems increases the automation of business contract execution. To the same degree, the demand for automated monitoring increases because more information about the contract execution has to be processed by the business partners.

The business partners are interested in answers to the following questions:

1 Given the current state of contract execution, which actions are expected from a partner in the future.
2 Is a contract violation imminent, i.e. likely to happen within short time? Which partner has to be reminded to fulfill her obligation?
3 Which partner is responsible for a contract violation?

We address the problem by regarding it as a *formalization* problem: Given a paper contract, formalize it into suitable representations such that the three main questions can be answered. Essentially, we map informal requirements (the paper contract) into formal specifications that are subject to automated processing very much like system requirements are mapped into implementations. Due to lack of space, the paper shall put some emphasis on question 2, the pro-active monitoring of imminent contract violations.

J. Eder and M. Missikoff (Eds.): CAiSE 2003, LNCS 2681, pp. 584–600, 2003.

The paper uses a standard case study from the CrossFlow project [30] throughout the paper (see Section 2 for more details). Section 3 presents the formal contract model and defines key concepts like actions (any activity mentioned in a contract), commitments (a sequence of activities promised by some partner to become true in the future), and contract constraints (a statement about the well-formedness of a contract execution). The latter are used to inform business partners about which actions are expected from them in the future. The commitments are sequences of action types which some contract partner is responsible to make true during contract execution.

Finally, Section 5 presents related work and the paper concludes.

2 Case Study

The paper describes a standard multi-partner scenario [30] which outlines the manner in which a car damage claim is handled by an insurance company (AGFIL). The contract parties work together to provide a service level which facilitates efficient claim settlement. The parties involved are called Europ Assist, Lee Consulting Services, Garages and Assessors. Europ Assist offers a 24-hour emergency call answering service to policyholders. Lee C.S. coordinates and manages the operation of the emergency service on a day-to-day level on behalf of AGFIL. Garages are responsible for car repair. Assessors conduct the physical inspections of damaged vehicles and agree repair upon figures with the garages.

The general process of a car insurance case is described as following: *the policyholder phones Euro Assist using a free-phone number to notify a new claim. Euro Assist will register the information, suggest an appropriate garage, and notify AGFIL which will check whether the policy is valid and covers this claim. After AGFIL receives this claim, AGFIL sends the claim details to Lee C.S.. AGFIL will send a letter to the policyholder for a completed claim form. Lee C.S. will agree upon repair costs if an assessor is not required for small damages, otherwise an assessor will be assigned. The assessor will check the damaged vehicle and agree upon repair costs with the garage. After receiving an agreement of repairing car from Lee C.S., the garage will then commence repairs. After finishing repairs, the garage will issue an invoice to the Lee C.S., which will check the invoice against the original estimate. Lee C.S. returns all invoices to AGFIL. AGFIL processes the payment. In the whole process, if the claim is found invalid, all contractual parties will be contacted and the process will be stopped.* The case study shows a rather complex workflow between multiple partners.

3 Monitorable Contract Model

A contract is an agreement between two or more parties that is binding to those parties and that is based on mutual commitments [12]. Our monitorable contract model (in Figure 1) consists of two core components: the **Monitorable Element (ME)** and the **Monitoring Mechanism (MM)** [20]. The **ME** includes the description of the *trade process*, specifically the actions and commitments involved.

A commitment in this paper defined as a guarantee by one party towards other parties that some action sequence shall be executed completely provided that some trigger, involve and finish action happens, and the other parties fulfill their end of the bargain. **ME** also includes contract constraints for describing *logic relationships* among actions and guards of contract constraints for specifying the right order of actions which checks what obligations remain to be realized after the occurrence of the guarded action. The **MM** is a dynamic mechanism for contract monitoring, it consists of the *monitoring module* and the *reactive module*. The *monitoring module* includes the commitment graph, the maintaining guard algorithm and pro-active detection algorithm. A commitment graph is an overview of commitments between partners, so a commitment graph is the encoding of some contract clauses. The maintaining guard algorithm and pro-active detection algorithm dynamically trace which actions have occurred, which have not occurred but are expected to occur, and which may never occur, it provides a possibility for reminding and warning messages to be sent before anomalous actions occur. The *reactive module* has four submodules: reminding, warning, tracing, and compensating module. They respectively support anticipation and avoidance before anomalous actions occur, detection and compensation after anomalous actions occur. The **ME** and **MM** will be explained in the next sections.

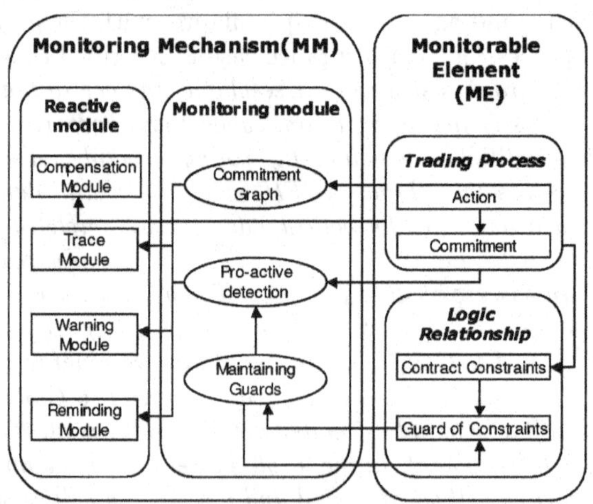

Fig. 1. The monitorable contract model

3.1 The Monitorable Element

Based on the car insurance case, actions and commitments between business partners are identified and specified. Contract constraints will be explained using all specified actions. Guards for each contract constraint scheme are calculated in following sections.

Actions. An action is an atom in our contract model. An action is specified by an action name, a sender of the action, a receiver of the action and a deadline before which the action need to perform. Because a contract party can be involved in different commitments and play the different roles, we specify the roles of a party as $\mathcal{R}$. A set of total roles of a contract denotes as $\mathbb{R}$.

Definition 1 *A party can act as the different roles in different commitments. Let ID be a domain ID,* **roles of a party** $\mathcal{R}_x$ *can be specifed as:*

$$\mathcal{R}_x = \{r_1, r_2, \ldots : r_1, r_2, \ldots \in ID\}$$

Let $\mathcal{P}$ *be a set of parties, the* **set of all roles** *is*

$$\mathbb{R} = \bigcup_{\forall x \in \mathcal{P}} \mathcal{R}_x$$

Example 2 *In car insurance, we use following abbreviations for different contractual parties: P for Policyholders; AG for AGFIL; E for Europ Assist; L for Lee Consulting Services; G for Garage; and A for Assessor. All partiers is a set* $\mathcal{P}$*:*

$$\mathcal{P} = \{P, AG, E, L, G, A\}$$

the garage (G) involved to the repair service *commitment, it acts as a repairer as role* G'*. In the* daily service *commitment, the garage is a cooperator with Lee C.S. as role* G''*. In the* pay repair cost *commitment, the garage acts as a receiver as role* G'''*. Hence the garage plays three roles* G', G'', G'''*.*
All the roles of the garage can act as is a set $\mathcal{R}_{garage}$*:*

$$\mathcal{R}_{garage} = \{G', G'', G'''\}$$

In car insurance case, a set of all roles $\mathbb{R}$ *can be specifed as:*

$$\mathbb{R} = \{P', P'', E, AG, L, A, G', G'', G'''\}$$

An action has a particular *name* from domain ID, a *sender* of the action and a *receiver* of the action from $\mathbb{R}$ and a performance *deadline* of the action from time $\mathcal{T}$. Deadlines provide the flexibility to initiate actions at a more optimal time, rather than immediately invoking operations the moment a condition occurs.

Definition 3 *Let* $\mathbb{R}$ *be a set of all roles of all parties, ID be the domain ID, and* $\mathcal{T}$ *be the time. An* **action** *is specifed as:*

$$action = (name, sender, receiver, t)$$

where $name \in ID, sender, receiver \in \mathbb{R}$ *and* $t \in \mathcal{T}$*. We require all names of actions to be unique so they can be used as identifiers.*
a set of actions $\mathbb{A}$ *for a contract can be specified as :*

$$\mathbb{A} = \bigcup_{\forall x \in \mathcal{P}} \{action\}$$

For car insurance case, all actions are specified in Appendix 2 of our research report[21]. According to contracts between partners, each action should support certain commitments. In next section, we specify commitments which are the key part of contracts.

Commitments. In this paper, a commitment is a guarantee by one party towards other parties that some action sequence shall be executed completely provided that some trigger, involve, and finish action happens, and the other parties fulfill their end of the bargain. The notion of commitment in this paper is not related to beliefs, desires, or intentions [17] [31]. In Cohen and Levesque's research, commitments are related to establishing common beliefs about a certain state of the world [31]. In our monitoring model, we do not reason about beliefs of the contractual parties involved, which Daskalopulu did in evidence-based contract performance monitoring [7]; we do not argue assessment of legal status and directives in business process automation which Abrahams did in [1]. The notion of commitment used in this paper is sufficient for the purpose for which it is used.

In a multi-party contract, for finishing a commitment, different party's actions are involved. Those actions can trigger, involve, and finish the commitment. For example, in the car repair service commitment, the garage first needs to receive the policyholder's car as a trigger of this commitment. The garage will repair the car after Lee C.S. agreed the repair cost which the garage estimated before. Actions included in a commitment have different attributes. A commitment is described by a commitment name, sender of the commitment, receiver of the commitment, and a series of actions and their attributes.

Definition 4 *Let $\mathbb{A}$ be a set of actions, for each action $a \in \mathbb{A}$ can trigger(tr), involve(in) or finish (fi) a commitment, hence, each action has its attribute,* **attributes** *of actions $\mathcal{U}$ can be specifed as:*

$$\mathcal{U} = \{tr, in, fi\}$$

Let ID be the domain ID, $\mathbb{A}$ be a set of actions, $\mathcal{P}$ be a set of parties and $\mathbb{R}$ be a set of all roles of all parties played. A **commitment** *is specified as :*

$$commitment = (name, sender, receiver, \{(a_1, u_1), (a_2, u_2), \ldots, (a_n, u_n) : a_i \in \mathbb{A}, u_i \in \mathcal{U}\})$$

where name is an identifer, $name \in ID$; sender and receiver are the contract parties, $sender, receiver \in \mathbb{R}$; $a_1, a_2, \ldots, a_n$ denotes all actions involved in the commitment and their attributes $u_1, u_2, \ldots, u_n$. We require all names of commitments to be unique so as they can be used as identifiers.
A set of commitments $\mathbb{M}$ can be specified as:

$$\mathbb{M} = \bigcup_{\forall x \in \mathcal{P}} \{commitment\}$$

Let $X = \{1, 2, 3, \ldots\}$ and $a \in \mathbb{A}$, a sequence function $f_{position} : \mathbb{A} \times \mathbb{M} \rightarrow X$,

$$f_{position}(a_i, m) = \begin{cases} i & \text{iff } i \text{ is the sequence number of action } a_i \text{ in commitment } m \\ undef & \text{otherwise} \end{cases}$$

$f_{position}(a_i, m)$ is the position of action a_i in the commitment m.

Examples of commitments of the car insurance case can be found in Appendix 3 of our research report[21].

Contract constraints. Among actions there exist logic relationships which we call contract constraints. Contract constraints show the occurrence order among actions in a business process ([29] and [28]). The formal specification of contract constraints is described as following,

Constraint 5 *Using Temporal Logic (in Appendix 1 of our research report[21]), let $\mathbb{A}$ be a set of actions, and $a, b, c \in \mathbb{A}$, $\overline{a}, \overline{b}$ and $\overline{c}$ denotes $a, b,$ and c will never occur respectively. A contract constraint is defined using the follow schemes:*

$$\overline{a} \wedge \overline{b} \vee a \cdot b \qquad \text{(scheme 1)}$$

$$((\overline{a} \vee \overline{b}) \wedge \overline{c}) \vee a \cdot b \cdot c \vee b \cdot a \cdot c \qquad \text{(scheme 2)}$$

$$a \cdot b \vee \overline{b} \qquad \text{(scheme 3)}$$

$$a \cdot b \cdot c \vee b \cdot a \cdot c \vee \overline{c} \qquad \text{(scheme 4)}$$

Constraint scheme 1 denotes an *initiation* relationship, a and b can never occur, or a and b occur in order, which means a must occur before b. *Constraint scheme 2* captures a *joint initiation* relationship, if a or b never occur, c will certainly never occur ; if c occurs, a and b both have occurred before. *Constraint scheme 3* describes an *enable* relationship, if b occurs, that means a has occurred before, otherwise b will never occur. *Constraint scheme 4* indicates a *joint enable* relationship; if c occurs, a and b have occurred before, no matter with the order of a and b's occurrence, otherwise c will never occur. The contract constraint schemes can be extended in different business applications. Examples of contract constraints can be found in Appendix 4 of our research report[21].

Guards of contract constraints. For each contract constraint scheme, the guard captures how far that scheme has progressed. After the occurrence of the guarded action, it checks what obligations remain to be realized. The guard of an action for a contract constraint regards to which actions have occurred, which have not occurred but are expected to occur, and which should not occur in the future.

Definition 6 *Let $\mathcal{L}$ be a temporal logic language (see Appedix 1), some used symbols $-, \neg, \diamond, \Box$ and $\cdot$ are introduced as following: $\overline{a}$ denotes a will never occur; $\neg a$ denotes a has not yet occurred; $\diamond a$ denotes a will eventually occur; $\Box a$ denotes a has occurred; $a \cdot b$ denotes a will occur before b. $\mathcal{W}$ be a set of contract constraints, $\mathcal{S}$ be a constraint scheme in $\mathcal{W}$, $\mathcal{S} \in \mathcal{W}$, and $\mathbb{A}$ be a set of actions. $I_1, I_2 \in \mathcal{S}$, $a_1, \ldots, a_n \in \mathbb{A}$, $\Gamma = \{a, \overline{a} : a \in \mathbb{A}\}$ is an alphabet, $\Gamma \subseteq \mathcal{L}$. A function G: $\mathcal{S} \times \Gamma \mapsto \mathcal{L}$ is the guard of contract constraints. It is inductively defined as:*

$$\mathsf{G}(I_1 \vee I_2, a) \equiv \mathsf{G}(I_1, a) \vee \mathsf{G}(I_2, a)$$

$$\mathsf{G}(I_1 \wedge I_2, a) \equiv \mathsf{G}(I_1, a) \wedge \mathsf{G}(I_2, a)$$

$$\mathsf{G}(a_1 \cdot \ldots \cdot a_n, a_i) \equiv \begin{cases} \top & (i = 1 \ \ and \ \ n = 1) \\ \Box a_1 \wedge \ldots \wedge \Box a_{i-1} \wedge (\neg a_{i+1} \wedge \ldots \wedge \neg a_n \wedge \\ \qquad \diamond(a_{i+1} \cdot \ldots \cdot a_n)) & (1 \leq i < n) \\ \diamond(a_1 \cdot \ldots \cdot a_n) & (i < 1 \ \ or \ \ i > n) \end{cases}$$

$$\mathsf{G}(\overline{a_1}\cdot\ldots\cdot\overline{a_n},a_i)\equiv\begin{cases}0 & (1\le i\le n)\\ \diamond(\overline{a_1}\cdot\ldots\cdot\overline{a_n}) & (i<1\ \ or\ \ i>n)\end{cases}$$

$$\mathsf{G}(a_1\cdot\ldots\cdot a_n,\overline{a}_i)\equiv\begin{cases}0 & (1\le i\le n)\\ \diamond(a_1\cdot\ldots\cdot a_n) & (i<1,\ \ or\ \ i>n)\end{cases}$$

$$\mathsf{G}(\overline{a_1}\cdot\ldots\cdot\overline{a_n},\overline{a}_i)\equiv\begin{cases}\top & (i=1\ \ and\ \ n=1)\\ \Box\overline{a_1}\wedge\ldots\wedge\Box\overline{a_{i-1}}\wedge(\neg\overline{a_{i+1}}\wedge\ldots\wedge\neg\overline{a_n}\wedge \\ \qquad\qquad \diamond(\overline{a_{i+1}}\cdot\ldots\cdot\overline{a_n})) & (1\le i<n)\\ \diamond(\overline{a_1}\cdot\ldots\cdot\overline{a_n}) & (i<1,\ \ or\ \ i>n)\end{cases}$$

$$\mathsf{G}(0,a)\equiv 0$$
$$\mathsf{G}(\top,a)\equiv\top$$

Example 7 *Let $\mathbb{A}$ be a set of actions, $a,b\in\mathbb{A}$, Γ be an alphabet, $a,\overline{a},b,\overline{b}\in\Gamma$, guards of constraint scheme 1 (initiate scheme) as follows:*

$$\begin{aligned}\mathsf{G}(\overline{a}\wedge\overline{b}\vee a\cdot b,a)&\equiv\mathsf{G}(\overline{a},a)\wedge\mathsf{G}(\overline{b},a)\vee\mathsf{G}(a\cdot b,a)\\ &\equiv(0\wedge\diamond\overline{b})\vee\neg b\wedge\diamond b\\ &\equiv\neg b\wedge\diamond b \qquad (1)\\ \mathsf{G}(\overline{a}\wedge\overline{b}\vee a\cdot b,\overline{a})&\equiv\diamond\overline{b} \qquad (2)\\ \mathsf{G}(\overline{a}\wedge\overline{b}\vee a\cdot b,b)&\equiv\Box a \qquad (3)\\ \mathsf{G}(\overline{a}\wedge\overline{b}\vee a\cdot b,\overline{b})&\equiv\diamond\overline{a} \qquad (4)\end{aligned}$$

The guards of contract constraint scheme 1 mean: action a can occur when b has not yet occurred and may occur in the future; action a can never occur if b can never occur; b can occur only if a has occurred; b will never occur when a may never occur as well.

We explain the meaning of guards. According to example in Appendix 4 (1) of our research report[21], for equation *Example 7(1)* , when Europ Assist has notified AGIFL about the claim, AGFIL has not yet sent a claim form to the policyholder, but AGFIL may send a claim form soon. For equation *Example 7(2)* , if Europ Assist never send any claim to AGFIL, AGFIL may never send a claim form to the policyholder neither. For equation *Example 7(3)* , if AGFIL has sent the claim to the policyholder, it means Europ Assist has sent this claim to AGFIL. For equation *Example 7(4)* , if AGFIL never sends the claim to the policyholder, it means Europ Assist never sends a claim to AGFIL.

3.2 The Monitoring Mechanism

Our monitoring mechanism includes a monitoring module and a reactive module. The monitoring module observes occurred activities and captures any relevant information that arises during the fulfillment of the contract. The reactive module receives the triggered information based on the output of the monitoring modules and the monitorable contract, and sends a relevant message (such as warning and reminding) as responses. In the following sections, we will discuss the commitment graph, maintaining guard algorithm and pro-active detection algorithm in the monitoring module respectively.

Commitment graphs. It is widely accepted that commitments are the core of contracts, commitments are an even more important concept to specify multi-party contracts. In this section, we present a commitment graph which shows complex relationships among commitments. Commitment relationships are not only about a condition commitment relationship [22][1], for example, if a contractee first ships goods to a contractor, the contractor will pay to cost of goods later, the commitment of shipping goods is a condition to activate a commitment of payment. In our car insurance case, the relationship between *repair service commitment* and *daily service commitment* is a mixed relationship: after Lee C.S. agreed the repair cost in *daily service commitment*, the garage can repair the car in *repair service commitment*; after the garage repairs the car and returns the invoice, *daily service commitment* will go on to execute its following actions. In Figure 2 presents the commitment graph for the car in-

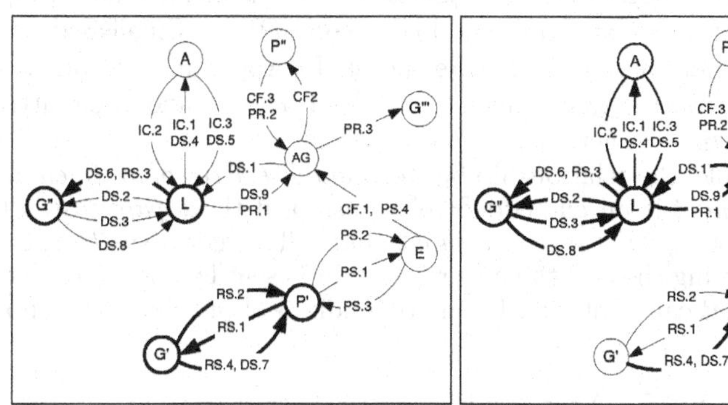

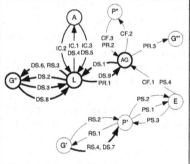

(a) Highlight repair service commitment C_repairService

(b) Highlight daily service commitment C_dailyService

Fig. 2. Commitment Graph

surance case. For all edges of this graph, we use the following abbreviations: PS for C_phoneService, RS for C_repairService, DS for C_dailyService, IC for C_inspectCar, PR for C_payRepairCost, CF for C_claimForm. In Appendix 5 of our research report[21], we summarize commitments, involved actions and their attributes and abbreviations of each action.

[1] We regard commitment orders as an integral of contracts. They shall formalized in the **Definition** 9 (page 10).

We know commitment C_repairService and commitment C_dailyService involve following actions from Appendix 3 of our research report[21].

$$\begin{aligned}(\mathsf{C\_repairService}, \mathsf{G}, \mathsf{P}, \{&(\mathsf{A\_sendCar}, tr), (\mathsf{A\_estimateRepairCost}, fi),\\ &(\boxed{\mathsf{A\_agreeRepairCar}}, tr), (\boxed{\mathsf{A\_repairCar}}, fi)\})\end{aligned}$$

$$\begin{aligned}(\mathsf{C\_dailyService}, \mathsf{L}, \mathsf{AG}, \{&(\mathsf{A\_forwardClaim}, tr), (\mathsf{A\_contactGarage}, in),\\ &(\mathsf{A\_sendRepairCost}, in), (\mathsf{A\_assignAssessor}, in),\\ &(\mathsf{A\_sendNewRepairCost}, tr), (\boxed{\mathsf{A\_agreeRepairCar}}, fi),\\ &(\boxed{\mathsf{A\_repairCar}}, tr), (\mathsf{A\_sendInvoices}, in),\\ &(\mathsf{A\_forwardInvoices}, fi)\})\end{aligned}$$

We observe action A_agreeRepairCar includes in commitment C_repairService as the 3rd action and includes in commitment C_dailyService as the 6th action. Action A_repairCar includes in commitment C_repairService as the 4th action also includes in commitment C_dailyService as the 7th action. Hence, each action is indicated as an edge in a commitment graph, information about which commitment this action is involved in and the sequence of this action for a particular commitment is recorded as edge codes. An edge for action A_agreeRepairCar has two codes: C_repairService.3 and C_dailyService.6. In our commitment graph, we use edge code RS for C_repairService and edge code DS for C_dailyService, $RS.3$ and $DS.6$ both denote action A_agreeRepairCar. In Appendix 5 of our research report[21], we summarize commitments, involved actions and their attributes and abbreviations of each action.

Another example, the relationship between *daily service commitment* and *inspect car commitment* is an embedded relationship, if the *repair cost* is higher than a certain amount, *daily service commitment* will trigger *inspect car commitment*. After inspecting the car, the new repair cost is sent by a assessor and *daily service commitment* can continue. From Appendix 3 of our research report[21], we have:

$$\begin{aligned}(\mathsf{C\_dailyService}, \mathsf{L}, \mathsf{AG}, \{&(\mathsf{A\_forwardClaim}, tr), (\mathsf{A\_contactGarage}, in),\\ &(\mathsf{A\_sendRepairCost}, in), (\boxed{\mathsf{A\_assignAssessor}}, in),\\ &(\boxed{\mathsf{A\_sendNewRepairCost}}, tr), (\mathsf{A\_agreeRepairCar}, fi),\\ &(\mathsf{A\_repairCar}, tr), (\mathsf{A\_sendInvoices}, in),\\ &(\mathsf{A\_forwardInvoices}, fi)\})\end{aligned}$$

$$\begin{aligned}(\mathsf{C\_inspectCar}, \mathsf{A}, \mathsf{L}, \{&(\boxed{\mathsf{A\_assignAssessor}}, tr), (\mathsf{A\_inspectCar}, in),\\ &(\boxed{\mathsf{A\_sendNewRepairCost}}, fi)\})\end{aligned}$$

After all actions include in commitment C_inspectCar are finished, commitment C_dailyService can continue. We use IC for C_inspectCar, then action A_assignAssessor has two edge codes$DS.4$ and $IC.1$, and action A_sendNewRepairCost has two edge codes $DS.5$ and $IC.3$.

A commitment graph is a directed graph consisting of a set of vertices corresponding to all roles $\mathbb{R}$, a set of edges corresponding to actions and their codes, and commitment orders .

Definition 8 *Let $\mathbb{A}$ be a set of actions, $a \in \mathbb{A}$, $\mathbb{M}$ be a set of commitments, $m \in \mathbb{M}$, and $X = \{1, 2, \dots\}$, a sequence function $f_{position}(a, m)$, an edge is specified as a relation from $\mathbb{A} \times \mathbb{M} \times X$:*

$$edge = \bigcup_{\forall m, a \in m} \{(a, m, f_{position}(a, m)) : a \in \mathbb{A}, m \in \mathbb{M}, f_{position}(a, m) \in X\}$$

a set of all edges is:

$$\mathbb{E} = \bigcup_{\forall a \in \mathbb{A}} \{edge\}$$

Definition 9 *Let $\mathbb{M}$ is a set of commitments. A commitment occurrence order is specified as a relation from $\mathbb{M} \times \mathbb{M}$:*

$$order\_commitment = \{(m_1 \cdot m_2) : m_1, m_2 \in \mathbb{M}\}$$

If $m_1 \cdot m_2$ is a commitment order, we inferpret it as: commitment m_2 is only active when commitment m_1 has been finished, i.e. only after the actions of m_1 has occurred in the past, the commitment m_2 can be inccoporated to trace back contract violations.
A set of commitment orders lists all relationships which a commitment occurs before than another commitment, it is specifed as:

$$\mathbb{O} = \bigcup_{\forall x \in \mathcal{P}} \{(m_1 \cdot m_2)\}$$

For the car insurance case, examples of the commitment orders inducively presented as following:

$$\begin{aligned}\mathbb{O} = \{&\mathsf{C\_phoneService} \cdot \mathsf{C\_repairService}, \mathsf{C\_phoneService} \cdot \mathsf{C\_dailyService},\\ &\mathsf{C\_phoneService} \cdot \mathsf{C\_claimForm}, \mathsf{C\_phoneService} \cdot \mathsf{C\_inspectCar},\\ &\mathsf{C\_repairService} \cdot \mathsf{C\_payRepairCost}, \mathsf{C\_dailyService} \cdot \mathsf{C\_payRepairCost},\\ &\mathsf{C\_inspectCar} \cdot \mathsf{C\_payRepairCost}, \mathsf{C\_claimForm} \cdot \mathsf{C\_payRepairCost}\}\end{aligned}$$

After we specify commitment graph notes, edges, and commitment occurrence orders, the commitment graph can be specified as following:

Definition 10 *Let $\mathbb{R}$ be a set of nodes, $\mathbb{E}$ be a set of edges, and $\mathbb{O}$ be a set of commitment order list. The commitment graph can be specifed as:*

$$G = (\mathbb{R}, \mathbb{E}, \mathbb{O})$$

When an edge has more than one edge code, it means this action is involved in different commitments. The edge codes present a complicated relationship among commitments. A commitment graph is a visual tool to show commitment relationships in a complex multi-party contract, it assists in locating the responsible parties for violations.

Using commitment graphs, action occurrence is based on the commitment order and the sequence number with in a commitment. Some actions with multi-abbreviation show that they involve in different commitments.

Algorithm for guard maintenance. Executing guards is a well-known operation with agent systems monitoring [27]. When an action a is attempted, its guard is evaluated, evaluation usually means checking if the guard evaluates to $\top$. Based on section 3.1 *contract constraints* and *guards of contract constraints*, we know actions can occur, can never occur, or have not yet occurred. If a's guard is satisfied, a is executed; if it is 0, a is rejected; else the partner of perform action a is made to wait. Whenever a occurs, a notification is sent to each pertinent partner who performs action b, whose guards are updated accordingly. If b's guard becomes $\top$, b is allowed; if it becomes 0, b is rejected; otherwise, the partner perform action b is made to wait some more and so on. In this algorithm, $\mathcal{A}$ is a set of all actions; $\Gamma = \{a, \overline{a} : a \in \mathcal{A}\}$ is set of actions and their complement, U and V are the temp set of actions and their complement, $guard[u]$ and $guard[v]$ are the temp storages of guards. We dynamically update our guards using **Algorithm 1**.Using the guard of the contract constraint scheme 1, if a

Algorithm 1 Maintaining Guards

```
U = ∅;
while Γ − U ≠ ∅ do
  take next u out of Γ − U;
  guard[u] = G(constraint, u)
  if guard[u] ≡ ⊤ then
    do(u);
    U = U ∪ {u, ū};
    V = Γ − U;
    while V ≠ ∅ do
      take any v out of V;
      guard[v] = G(guard[u], v);
      guard[v̄] = G(guard[u], v̄);
      V = V − {v, v̄};
    end while
  else if guard[u] ≡ 0 then
    reject occurrence of u;
  else
    send reminding or warning messages;
  end if
end while
```

is attempted and b has not already happened, a's guard evaluates to $\top$, consequently, a is allowed and a notification $\Box a$ is send. Upon receiption of this notification, b's guard is simplified from $\Box a$ to $\top$. Now if b is attempted, it can happen immediately. If b is attempted first, it must wait because its guard is $\Box a$. Sometime later if $\Box a$ received, which simplifies its guard to $\top$.

The maintaining guard algorithm shows how to use guards to dynamically monitor business processes. It makes it possible to send the pertinent reminding message or warning message during the fulfillment of the contract.

Pro-active detection. In our approach, guards of contract constraints are used for proactive monitoring purposes. We will explain how to use guards and deadline of action together to trigger reactive module. The pro-active detection algorithm is specified in **Algorithm 2**, w denotes a contract constraint scheme, a, b are actions, $a, b \in w$; $a.t$ indicates the deadline of action a; we use Petri Net to overview a business process[41][13][20][19], the *places* correspond to states or each party and *transitions* correspond to actions of different parties, M_0 be a initial marking of Petri Net.

When an action is attempted, if the guard of the action evaluates to $\top$, this action can occur immediately, the rest of actions will be reminded and their guards will be updated; let $f_w(a)$ be a function that gives warning time of *action* a. If $f_w(a)$ has passed and the action has not occurred yet, the warning module will be triggered and a reminding message will be send to parties involved. The time boundary between triggering reminding module and triggering warning module can be changed in different application.

Algorithm 2 Pro-active Detection

```
if G(w, a) ≡ ⊤ then
  while ¬done(a) ∧ f_w(a) < t ≤ a.t do
    warn(a)
    ∀b ∈ {w − {a}}  remind(b)
  end while
  if done(a) ≡ TRUE then
    update(M_0)
    Call Algorithm 1
    remind(b)
  end if
end if
```

In above sections, we explain our monitoring approach which include a monitorable contract model and a dynamic monitoring mechanism. Using our pro-active detection approach, the monitorability of contracts can be improved, avoidance and anticipation of violations are important features for our monitoring system. In next sections, the related work will discussed and compared.

4 Related Work

Looking at the object-oriented constraints perspective, Bertrand Meyer [3] [2] refined the assertion based approach into the design by a contract method in the Eiffel language. The basic idea is that a component and its clients have a contract with each other. The client guarantees certain preconditions before calling a method, the component guarantees certain postconditions after the call. If the pre-and postconditions are included in a form that the compiler can check, then any violation of the contract between caller and component can be detected immediately. The prime focus of the approach is to deliver reliable software, and as such does not include pro-active monitoring.

Business process flow languages, like IBM's WSFL [9] and BPEL4WS [5], Microsoft's XLANG [39], provide a comprehensive structure for describing a business process in detail and there are also the obvious place to describe assertions. BPEL4WS focuses on non functional or procedural contract. Neither provides any explicit support for the "business contract" level of abstraction.

Various authors have proposed electronic contract models or languages based on different views. Kimbrough and Moore formalize and extend *speech act theory* [18] [33] [34] as **Formal Language for Business Communication (FLBC)**[37] [38], and apply it to deontic reasoning [36] and business messaging [37] [38]. *Deontic logic* [14] [42] based contract models [12] [44] [26] [32] [43] describe obligations, permissions, and forbiddances for finishing a business process, which work in an extremely ideal process. **CrossFlow**[16] and **E-ADOME**[15] use contracts for inter-organizational workflow process integration. Contracts in CrossFlow and E-ADOME describe the agreed workflow interfaces as activities and transitions, based on WfMC's WPDL (Workflow Process Definition Language). Contracts also specify what data objects in the remote workflow are readable or updateable. They are a side effect of business automations, and as for now does not have pro-active monitoring.

Other authors have added monitoring support to electronic contracts. **Business Contract Architecture (BCA)** [24] [45] does not provide generic monitoring facilities, expecting each application to develop its own monitoring code to detect and signal non-conformance to the contract monitor; contract enforcement is limited to either signaling violation and or preventing the non-performing party from from entering further contracts. Daniel Reeves et al's **declarative language for negotiating executable contracts** can facilitate modification during negotiation [35] and include prioritized conflict handling features. However, it cannot be expected that all possible conflict scenarios throughout all business processes are recognized completely before the contract fulfillment stage. In **SeCo** (secure electronic contracts) [11], the monitoring services allow events to be triggered according to the current state of the contract and informs an enforcement service to initiate an enforcement activity. They only look at the negotiation stage. Daskalopulu et al. use **subjective logic** [40], which addresses a problem of a measurable belief, to realize **evidence-based contract monitoring** [7] [8] in the contract fulfillment stage. Unfortunately the monitoring is not pro-active. Milosevic et al. apply subjective logic to contract enforcement [25], but do not look at monitoring.

In existing e-commerce frameworks, the XML-based **Trading Partner Agreement Markup Language (tpaML)** from IBM research [6] 'trading partner agreement' are used as 'contract'. tpaML is now pursued under the **OASIS Collaboration Protocol Profile (CPP) and Agreement (CPA)** specifications [10]. tpaML and CPP/CPA capture the interoperation parameters (e.g. message formats, communication protocols, etc.), there are no provision for fulfillment monitoring. Microsoft's **BizTalk** has auditing and optional document mining function as well [23]. Their goals are to support recovering from failures, instead of prevention. Consequently, the development of contract models for contract fulfillment monitoring is relatively unexplored. Our approach provides a pro-active detection of imminent contract violations. Now we answer three questions which we address in *introduction*. Using guards of contract constraints and the guard maintenance algorithem, we answer *question 1* to trace the current state of contract execution and to show the actions we can expect from a partner in the near future. Using the algorithm for pro-active detection, we answer *question 2* to try to prevent contract violations by sending reminding and warning messages before. Using a commitment graph, we answer *question 3* to show partners relevant to the contract violation.

5 Conclusions

This paper proposes an approach to formalize electronic contracts into a set of representations that enable automatic monitoring. The execution of a contract is seen as a stream of actions that happen over time. A paper contract is mapped into two parts. The first parts are the so-called contract constraints. These conditions are tested on their validity during contract execution. The second part of the contract are the commitments which are essentially guarantees by one partner to another partner that some action sequence will occur. The commitments are used to trace back a violation of a contract constraint to the partner who has made a matching commitment.

Apart from this main result, we see further achievements of our model that enhance its suitability for electronic contract executions. Imminent contract violations may be forecasted by checking the state of the so-called guard expressions ahead of the formal deadline of an expected action. This feature allows pro-active use of formal contract representations in order to avoid real violations.

Our execution model is compatible with workflow engines for distributed execution of multi-partner contracts. The action sequences can be seen as the log of a petri net machine which controls the execution of the contract. However, we do not require such an execution engine as long as a sequence of actions is generated for monitoring. Using a workflow engine would have the advantage that the checks for guards can be integrated into the proper workflow at the right place so that a partner no longer has to decide when to execute a check for an imminent or real contract violation.

When contracts are automatically monitored, both the likelihood of violation decreases (as partners can be alerted in advance of a real violation) and opportunities for compensating violations are created. Rather than passing a violation case to a legal law suit, the failing partner can be forced to commit to a compensation that creates value for all partners. Without automatic monitoring, the detection of compensation opportunities is simply too costly to justify complete monitoring.

Further research has to be undertaken in the area of quality safeguards in electronic contracts. Lack of trust between partners may be dealt with by introducing a trusted third party which sub-divides actions into parts that are then irrevocable or provide monitoring services. An electronic contract can be analyzed prior to its execution in order to avoid incomplete commitment structures. Specifically, one may verify whether any violation of a contract constraint can be traced back to a commitment, i.e. a partner who is responsible for the violation. A prototype for algorithms 1 and 2 has been developed in prolog. We plan to test the prototype with action streams generated by a commercial execution environment for web services e.g. IBM WebSphere [4]. The test shall show in how far the message types provided there provide suitable action sequences needed for contract monitoring.

References

1. Abrahams A. An asynchronous rule-based approach for business process automation using obligations. *the 3rd ACM SIGPLAN Workshop on Rule-Based Programming (RULE'02), Pittsburgh, USA*, 2002.
2. Meyer B. Building bug-free oo software: An introduction to design by contract. *http://www.eiffel.com/doc/manuals/technology/contract/.*
3. Meyer B. *Object-Oriented Software Construction 2nd Edition.* Prentice Hall, 1997.
4. IBM Corporation. Websphere. 2002. http://www-3.ibm.com/software/info1/websphere/index.jsp.
5. Klein J. Leymann F. Roller D. Thatte S. Curbera F., Goland Y. and Weerawarana S. Business process execution language for web services.
6. Dias D.M. Parr F.N. Kearney R. Sachs M.W. Lau T.C. Dan A., Nguyen T.N. and Shaikh H.H. Business-to-business integration with tpaml and a business-to-business protocol framework. *Springer-Verlag, Lecture Notes in AI, 2000.*
7. Dimitrako T. Daskalopulu A. and Maibaum T. Evidence-based electronic contract performance monitoring. *INFORMS Journal of Group Decision and Negotiation, Special Issue: formal Modeling of Electronic Commerce*, 2002.
8. Dimitrakos T. Daskalopulu A. and Maibaum T. S. E. E-contract fulfillment and agents' attitudes. *Proceedings ERCIM WG E-Commerce Workshop on The Role of Trust in e-Business*, 2001.
9. Leymann F. Web service flow language.
10. Organization for the Advancement of Structured Information Standards (OASIS). Oasis ebxml collaboration-protocol profile and agreement specification version 2.0. 2002.
11. Schopp B Greunz M and Stanoevska-Slabeva K. Supporting market transactions through xml contracting containers. *Proceedings of the Sixth Americas Conference on Information Systems (AMCIS 2000). Long Beach, CA*, 2000.

12. Weigand H. and Xu L. Contracts in e-commerce. *9th IFIP 2.6 Working Conference on Database Semantic Issues in E-Commerce Systems (DS-9)*, 2001.
13. Desel J. and Esparza J. *Free Choice Petri Nets.* Cambridge University Press, 1995.
14. Meyer J. and Wieringa R. *Deontic Logic in Computer Science: Normative System Specification.* John Wiley and Sons, 1993.
15. Chiu D. Kafeza E. and Kafeza I. View-based contracts in an e-service cross-organizational workflow environment. *Proceedings of the second International Workshop on Technologies for E-Service(TES'01)*, 2001.
16. Grefen P Koetsier M. and Vonk. Cross-organisational/workflow: Crossflow esprite/28635 contract model, deliverable d4b. 1999.
17. Cohen P Kumar, S. Towards a fault-tolerant multi-agent system architecture. *In Proceedings of The Fourth International Conference on Autonomous Agents (Agents 2000),ACM Press, pp. 459–466.*, 2000.
18. Austin J. L. *How to do things with words. 2nd Edition.* Oxford University Press, 1976.
19. Xu L. Car insurance case. *Research Paper, Tilburg University.*
20. Xu L. Agent-based monitorable contract. *Research Paper, Tilburg University*, 2002.
21. Xu L. and Jeusfeld M. A. A concept for monitoring of electronic contracts, research paper, tilburg university. `http://infolab.uvt.nl/pub/itrs/itrs010.pdf`.
22. Venkatraman M. and Singh M. P. Verifying compliance with commitment protocols: Enabling open web-based multiagent systems. *Autonomous Agents and Multi-Agent Systems. volume 2, number 3.*
23. Andrews G.M.T. Beckman B. Klein J. Mital A. Mehta B., Levy M. Biztalk service 2000 business process orchestration. *International Conference on Data Engineering (ICDE'02).*
24. Bond A. Milosevic Z., Berry A. and Raymond K. Supporting business contracts in open distributed systems. *2nd International Workshop on Services in Distributed and Networked Environments,(SDNE'95) Whistler, Canada*, 1995.
25. Dimitrakos T. Milosevic Z., Jøsang A and Patton M.A. Discretionary enforcement of electronic contracts. *Proceedings of EDOC'2000. IEEE Comp. Soc. Press*, 2002.
26. Sierra C. Norman T.J. and Jennings N.R. Rights and commitments in multi-agent agreements. *Proceedings of the 3rd International Conference on Multi-Agent Systems (ICMAS-98). Paris, France*, 1998.
27. Singh M. P. A customizable coordination service for autonomous agents. *International Workshop on Agent Theories, Architectures, and Languages (ATAL).*
28. Singh M. P. Developing formal specifications to coordinate heterogeneous autonomous agents. *Proceedings of the International Conference on Multiagent Systems (ICMAS).*
29. Singh M. P. Synthesizing coordination requirements for heterogeneous autonomous agents. *Autonomous Agents and Multi-Agent Systems. volume 3, number 2.*
30. CrossFlow Project. Insurance requirements. *CrossFlow consortium.*
31. Cohen P. R. and Levesque H. J. Communicative actions for artificial agents. In Victor Lesser and Les Gasser, editors, *Proceedings of the First International Conference on Multi-Agent Systems (ICMAS'95)*, pages 65–72, San Francisco, CA, USA, 1995. The MIT Press: Cambridge, MA, USA.
32. Lee R. Towards open electronic contracting. *Electronic Markets, Vol. 8, No. 3, 10/98.*
33. Searle J. R. *Speech acts: An essay in the philosophy of language.* Cambridge University Press, 1969.

34. Searle J. R. and Vanderveken D. *Foundations of Illocutionary Logic.* Cambridge University Press, 1985.
35. Wellman M. P Reeves D. M., Grosof B. N. and Chan H. Toward a declarative language for negotiating executable contracts. *In Proceedings of the AAAI-99 Workshop on Artificial Intelligence in Electronic Commerce (AIEC-99), Menlo Park, CA, USA*, 1999.
36. Kimbrough S. Reasoning about the objects of attitudes and operators: Towards a disquotation theory for the representation of prepositional content. *Eight International Conference on Artificial Intelligence and the Law (ICAIL 2001)*, 2001.
37. Kimbrough S. and Moore S. On automated message processing in electronic commerce and work support systems: Speech act theory and expressive felicity. *ACM Transactions on Information Systems. 15(4). ACM Press. New York, NY. pp. 321–367*, 1997.
38. Moore S. Kqml and flbc: Contrasting agent communication languages. *International Journal of Electronic Commerce 5(1)*, 2000.
39. Thatte S. Xlang web services for business process design.
40. Jøsang A. A logic for uncertain probabilities. *International Journal of Uncertainty, Fuzziness and Knowledge-Based Systems. 9(3), pp. 279–311*, 2001.
41. Reisig V. *A primer in Petri net design.* Springer-Verlag, 1992.
42. von Wright G. Deontic logic. *Mind*, 1951.
43. Verharen E. Weigand H., Dignum F. Dynamic business models as a basis for interoperable transaction design. *Information Systems*, 1997.
44. Tan Y.H. and Thoen W. A logical model of directed obligations and permissions to support electronic contracting in electronic commerce. *International Journal of Electronic Commerce (IJEC). 3(2). pp. 87–104.*
45. Milosevic Z. *Enterprise Aspects of Open Distributed Systems. PhD Thesis, pp. 154–248.* Department of Computer Science, University of Queensland, 1995.

Goal-Oriented Requirements Engineering: A Case Study in E-government

Paolo Donzelli[1] and Paolo Bresciani[2]

[1] Department of Innovation and Technology
Italian Cabinet Office
Via Barberini 38, I-00187 Roma (Italy)
p.donzelli@governo.it
[2] ITC-irst
Via Sommarive 18, I-38050 Trento-Povo (Italy)
bresciani@itc.it

Abstract. This paper presents a requirements engineering framework based on the notions of *Actor*, *Goal*, and *Intentional Dependency*, and applies it to a case study in the field of Information Systems for e-Government.
The framework provides the analyst with a powerful tool for capturing high-level organizational needs and transforming them into system requirements in a smooth and controlled manner, and for redesigning, at the same time, the organizational structure that better exploit the new system. Organizations are modeled using *Actors*. Thus, a network of interacting actors form the organization model. These actors collaborate or conflict in their efforts to achieve individual or organizational goals. *Goals* represent relationships between actors and link organizational needs to system requirements.
In comparison with other more articulated actor- and goal-centered approaches to requirements and software engineering, the proposed framework adopts only a basic set of notational elements, and introduces a simplified, top-down, decomposition-based, analysis process. This approach greatly enhances stakeholders' acceptance and understanding, that are crucial factors for the success of real projects, especially when very diverse stakeholders, with very different skills and backgrounds, are involved, as in the case of e-Government projects.
The definition of the requirements for an Electronic Record Management System for e-Government is used to illustrate the framework.

1 Introduction

In Requirements Engineering (RE), Goal and Actor orientation has been recognized as an approach more promising than other system- and functionality-based techniques used in most of the traditional Software Engineering methodologies [7,13,1,2,17,18,6, 15]. By adopting the notions of *Actor*, *Goal*, and *Intentional Dependency*, it is in fact possible to refine high-level requirements originating from the organizational setting (i.e., stakeholders' needs and desires) into detailed descriptions of the system to be implemented (in terms of architecture, components, and functions), in a smooth and controlled manner, particularly if the target programming paradigm is an agent-oriented one [14,4,5], but not only [16].

J. Eder and M. Missikoff (Eds.): CAiSE 2003, LNCS 2681, pp. 601–616, 2003.

This paper presents a requirements engineering framework (called *REF*), by means of its sample application to a case study in e-Government.

REF is designed to deal with, and reason about, socio-technical systems. It is a powerful tool that allows the analyst to model high-level organizational needs and to transform them into system requirements, while redesigning the organizational structure to better exploit the new system. The modeling effort breaks activities down into more intellectually manageable components on the basis of common conceptual notations. To this end, REF introduces the notions of *Actor*, *Goal*, and *Intentional Dependency* as modeling elements used throughout requirements acquisition, formalization and analysis, to capture and describe both the new system and the organizational context in which the system will operate. The framework uses *Actors* (any kind of active entity, e.g., teams, humans and machines, including the target system) to model the organization [9,20]. As well, it uses *Intentional Dependencies* among actors to describe the organizational context in terms of a network of interacting actors collaborating or conflicting in their efforts to achieve both individual and organizational goals. Finally, REF uses *Goals* [9,20,7] to model actors' relationships (in terms of intentional dependencies), and, eventually, to link organizational needs to system requirements.

Describing both the requirements of the system-to-be and the encompassing organizational context by means of the same notions, not only allows us to verify the fulfillment of the organizational needs very directly, but also allows for a high stakeholders' involvement.

The paper is organized as follows. Section 2 describe the reasons for using REF in Requirements Engineering for e-Government applications. Section 3 introduces the case study. The applications of REF to the case study is then described (Section 4), including the use of interesting and novel high-level features (Section 5). Conclusions are drawn in Section 6.

2 REF and E-government Applications

E-Government means to exploit Information and Communication Technologies (ICT) to provide in a more efficient way higher quality services to the government customers (citizens and businesses), mainly through electronic delivery channels (from Internet-based channels, to digital TV, mobile phone, etc.).

E-Government is a particularly interesting and challenging sector for RE, in which it is relevant to adopt a methodology capable of taking into account different actors, their points of view, and the resulting strategic dependencies. In this context, in fact, very diverse kinds of actors (e.g., citizens, employees, administrators, politicians and decision-makers in general —both at central and local level) are involved, each of them with its objectives and goals. Some goals may be quite straightforward (as, e.g., for a citizen, to be able to require on-line a new passport), others rather complex and articulated (as, e.g., for an administrator, to be compliant to laws and norms), and sometimes they may diverge quite considerably. For example, to have a passport so easily delivered, the administration has to be able to perform cross-checks of personal data usually managed by different (possibly decentralized) units, and to enable mechanisms for secure identification (e.g., digital signature) and transmission. Thus, in general, e-Government applications have to operate in a social environment characterized by a rich tissue of actors with strong inter-dependent intents. Due to this complex network of interrelated objectives, synergies and conflicts may be present. Being able to clearly identify the set of involved actors, their objectives (i.e., goals), and the way they depends on each other in order to achieve such goals, most likely by exploiting possible synergies or trying to avoid potential conflicts, is of utmost importance to obtain a clear and complete comprehension of the organizational setting into which the new technology should be introduced. And only from such a deep comprehension of the application context the correct system requirements can be derived, and, consequently, the correct system can be designed and implemented. Thus, a RE methodology satisfying this perspective must be capable of describing both the requirements of the system and its social context. These descriptions must share a common notation, in order to be able to strictly connect the system requirements to the real organizational needs the organization has, and to easily evaluate the possible impact the system may have on the way of acting of the organization and its actors.

REF tries to provide such a capability by adopting a diagrammatic notation for describing the organizational settings: this notation immediately conveys the intentional dependencies among the different actors, and allows for a detailed analysis of the goals upon which the actors depend, through a goal decomposition process. Moreover, the notation is used to describe not only the organizational setting but also the system itself, as an (artificial) actor placed in the context of the organization. Thus, *Actors*, in REF diagrams, may represents social entities (both individuals and organizations, e.g., enterprises, departments, offices) as well as artificial elements of the organization (e.g., pre-existing systems and, of course, the target system).

Another very important notion, in the REF notation, is that of *Goal. Goals* represent states of the world that are desired by one (or more) actor(s), and for the achievement of which an actor may depend on other actors. REF adopts a semi-formal approach for describing actors and goals, based on precisely defined typed graphs, in which nodes are labeled with natural language sentences that intuitively describe their semantics. Of course, some level of common understanding, shared by the analyst and the stakeholders, is assumed.

The REF notation is widely inspired by the i* framework [19] for RE [20] and business analysis and re-engineering [21]. Moreover, REF introduces also a clear methodology to drive the process of requirements discovery, definition, refinement and reconciliation [9]. An important difference between REF and i* is that only the most basic and essential notational ingredients of i* are adopted in REF [9]. Another important simplification is introduced by imposing a strict top-down approach to the process of goal analysis. These choices, although apparently constraining, results to be quite successful in practical terms. Several case studies [10,11] demonstrate, in fact, that the simplified notation and process facilitates the acceptance of REF by the stakeholders, and contributes to a quicker introduction of the methodology in the RE process.

As in i* [19,21] and in other derived methodologies, like, e.g., Tropos [14], a distinction is made in REF between soft and hard goals [11]. *Soft-goals* are used to specify, at a qualitative level, not sharply-cut objectives, the precise definition of which require to develop further details, while *hard-goals* clearly define a state/target, an actor desires to reach. For example, "having a passport delivered" is clearly an hard-goal, while "having it delivered quickly" is a soft-goal, being the notion of "quickly" highly subjective.

3 The Case Study

The case study reports on an on-going project aiming at introducing an Electronic Record Management System (ERMS) into the administrative processes of the Italian Cabinet Office, to transform a huge repository of documents (from decrees, to tenders related documentation) into a ready available source of knowledge to be shared among all the actors acting within the organization. The impact of such a system on the common practices of the communities and the sub-communities of knowledge workers who will adopt it is quite relevant. Indeed, ERMS is at the moment used by more than 300 employees and handles a flow of about 200.000 document/year, but it is expected to reach about 2000 users and 2 million documents/year.

ERMS is based on the adoption of complex ICT solutions which allow efficient storage and retrieval of document-based unstructured information, by combining classical filing strategies (e.g., classification of documents on a multi-level directory, cross-reference between documents, etc.) with modern information retrieval techniques. Moreover, it encompasses mechanisms for facilitating routing and notification of information and documents among the users, and supporting interoperability with similar (typically remote) systems, through e-mail and XML. It represents the basic elements for a knowledge workplace, i.e., a working environment where a knowledge worker can easily access and gather information, produce knowledge and deliver results through a multitude of channels (from personal computers, to laptops, PDAs, mobile phones, etc.).

Accordingly to the REF process, a first organization diagram describing the original organizational setting before the introduction of the ERMS was produced (see Figure 1). In REF diagrams, circles represent *actors*, and dashed ovals are used to bound the internal structure of complex actors, i.e., actors containing other actors. As well, rounded boxes represent *hard-goals* and clouds represents *soft-goals*. Goals are always connected with arrows to (one or more) actors: an incoming arrow means that that goal is desired, wanted, or needed by the connected actor. An out-going arrow means that there is a dependency, on the connected actor, for the fulfillment of the goal. Thus, in the most general case in which an actor A is connected to a goal G that is connected to another actor B, we have that A (who wants G) depends on B for G to be fulfilled. In a very similar way, *resources* (rectangles), and *tasks*[1] (hexagons), may be represented. An actor is connected to a task when it wants the task to be performed; a task is linked to an actor when the actor is committed at performing the task. An actor is linked to a resource when it needs that resource; a resource is linked to an actor when the actor has to provide it. In Figure 1, the complex actor Organizational Unit corresponds to the organizational fragment into which it is planned to introduce the new ERMS, whereas the Head of Unit, the Secretary, the Employee, the Archivist, the Personal Computer and the Physical Archive are simple actors, acting within the Organizational Unit.

The Secretary receives from the enclosing context (out of the diagram scope) the input documents, which then she passes to the Head of Unit. That is, the Head of

[1] A task is a well specified prescriptive activity.

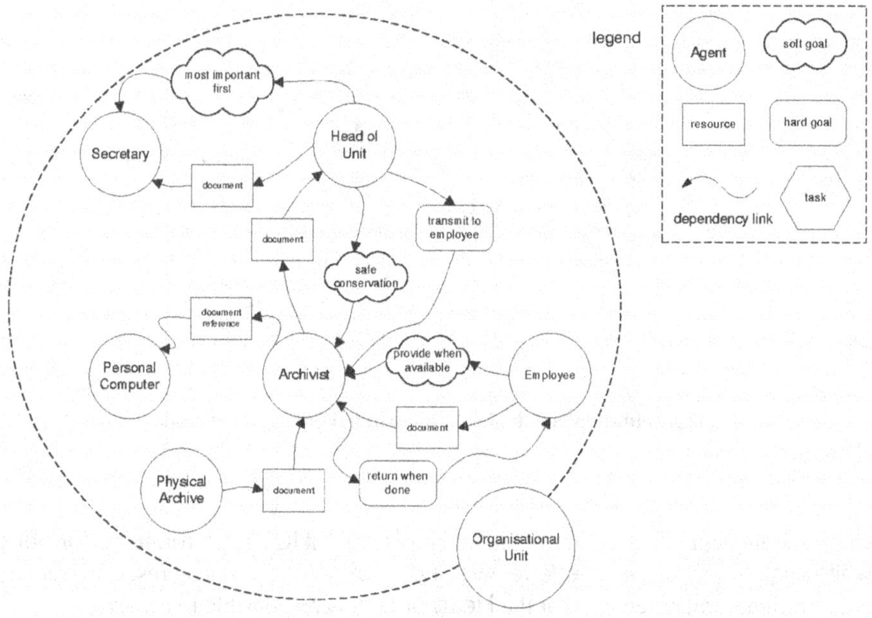

Fig. 1. The organizational context before the ERMS

Unit depends on the Secretary for receiving the document (a resource) and for the qualitative constraint: most important first (a soft-goal). It is up to the Head of Unit to decide to which employee the document has to be assigned (transmit to employee). For this, and for the safe conservation of the document, she depends upon the Archivist. On its turn, the Employee depends upon the Archivist to "provide the document as soon as available" (the soft-goal provide when available). The complete description of the diagram can be found in [11].

The organizational unit before the introduction of the ERMS works in a simple way, with a flow of documents between the actors and a set of responsibilities very well defined, as quite intuitively captured in Figure 1; nevertheless, several factors (international benchmarking studies, citizens demand, shrink budgets, etc.) called for the decision of leveraging new technologies to transform the organization's bureaucratic structure into a more creative and knowledgeable environment.

This led to the definition of ERMS requirements, as discussed next.

4 Applying REF

The first step towards the identification of the requirements for the ERMS, together with the new organizational setting suitable to exploit ERMS capabilities, is to produce a new organization diagram, capturing the motivating pushes underlying the project. Figure 2 represents again the complex actor Organizational Unit and the actor Head of Unit. As

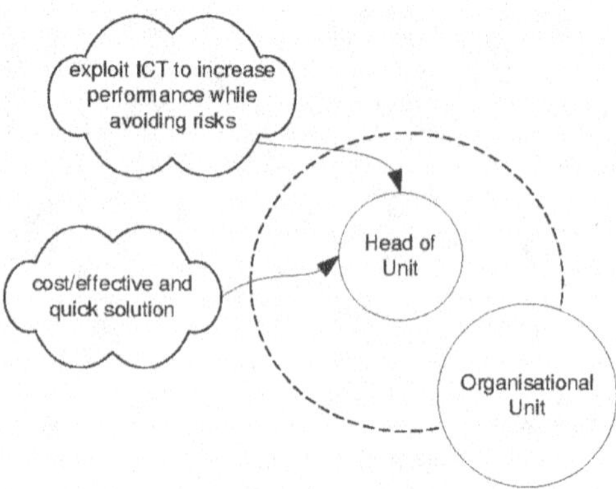

Fig. 2. Introducing the ERMS: the initial organization model

well, new elements are introduced: the soft-goals exploit ICT to increase performance while avoiding risks, and cost/effective and quick solution, that represent the required organizational improvement that the Head of Unit is responsible to achieve.

REF models are introduced and refined along an incremental and iterative analysis process, including three distinct phases: *Organization Modeling*, *Hard-Goal Modeling*, and *Soft-Goal Modeling*. This helps to reduce the complexity of the modeling effort.

During *Organization Modeling*, the organizational context is analyzed and the actors and their hard and soft goals identified. Any actor may generate its own goals, may operate to achieve goals on the behalf of some other actors, may decide to collaborate with other actors for a specific goal, or to delegate it, and might clash on some other ones. The resulting goals will then be refined, through interaction with the involved actors, by hard and soft goal modeling. The diagrams presented so far are example of output of the organization modeling phase.

The *Hard-Goal Modeling* phase seeks to determine how the actor can achieve an hard-goal placed upon it, by decomposing it into more elementary subordinate hard-goals and tasks.

The *Soft-Goal Modeling* aims at producing the operational definitions of the soft-goals that emerged during the organizational modeling, sufficient to capture and make explicit the semantics that are usually assigned implicitly by the involved actors [3,6] and to highlight the system quality issues from the start. A soft-goal is refined in terms of subordinate soft-goals, hard-goals, tasks and constraints, where *constraints* (represented by a rounded box with a line) are associated with soft-goals to specify the corresponding quality attributes. So, for example, the soft-goal "make a document easily and promptly available", beside spawning the hard-goal "make a document available", will lead also to a set of constraints (e.g., types of access channels, number of hours after which a document is available, etc.) specifying the concepts of "easy" and "prompt". Thus, soft-goals become a knowledge representation vehicle that: 1) encourages the interaction between the analysts and the stakeholders; 2) leads towards a common terminology; 3) supports reasoning about trade-offs; 4) allows freezing temporary solutions, and formalizing final decisions. Soft-goal models, in addition, allows the analysts and the stakeholders to early detect synergic as well as clashing requirements, which usually are hidden behind generic and left implicit assumptions, providing, at the same time, an operational and cooperative way to better exploit or resolve them, by coordinating or reconciling the different stakeholders' points of view.

According to the REF process, the analysts, through continuous interaction with the stakeholders, and supported by the different models, will deal first with the high level organizational structure, then will descend step by step into the details of the application context of the new system, until the focus will be placed upon the single actors and their role within the organization. In particular, once an initial model of the organization is built (as in Figure 2), the REF process evolves in a cyclic way through the phases of hard and soft goal modeling, and of organization modeling. Hard and soft goal modeling refines the goals (both hard and soft) discovered during organization modeling; as well, output from goal modeling is used to enrich and extend the initial organizational model: the new actors so introduced may lead to new hard and soft goals, triggering goal modeling again. The two activities of hard and soft modeling are, of course, tightly connected and, at least to some extent, may be developed in parallel.

Thus, on the basis of the organization model in Figure 2, the analysis may proceed by modeling the emerging soft-goals. An example of the result of a soft-goal modeling activity is presented in Figure 3. The figure describes how the soft-goal exploit ICT to increase performance while avoiding risks is iteratively top-down decomposed to finally produce a set of tasks, hard-goals, and constraints that precisely defines the meaning of the soft-goal, i.e., the way to achieve it.

Figure 3, in other terms, gives the operational elements that the Head of Unit will apply to achieve the assigned goal. Again, the arrowhead lines indicate dependency links. A soft-goal depends on a subordinate soft-goal, hard-goal, task, resource or constraint, when it requires that goal, task, resource or constraint to be achieved, performed, or implemented in order to be achieved itself. These dependency links may be seen as top-down decompositions of the soft-goal, in a similar way as introduced by i* [19, 21] and NFR [6]; yet they are different in the direction of the arrows, due to their reading as "dependencies" given above. This choice provides some advantages: first, it results to be, for the stakeholders, an acceptable and well understood simplification [11], because the same kind of link is used to describe both actor dependencies and goal and task decompositions; as well, this allows for a more intuitive reading of the diagrams and a more natural flow of the dependencies and decompositions among the different models; finally, the top-down direction of the decomposition process is evidenced. Soft-goals decompositions may be conjunctive (to satisfy the original soft-goal, all the sub-components must be satisfied), indicated by the label "A" on the dependency link, or disjunctive (it is sufficient that only one of the components is satisfied), indicated by the label "O".

5 Special Links Supporting the Analysis Process

Soft-goal modeling is usually a long and fatiguing process, during which stakeholders and analyst interact more times, according to the strategy devised by the analyst. In order

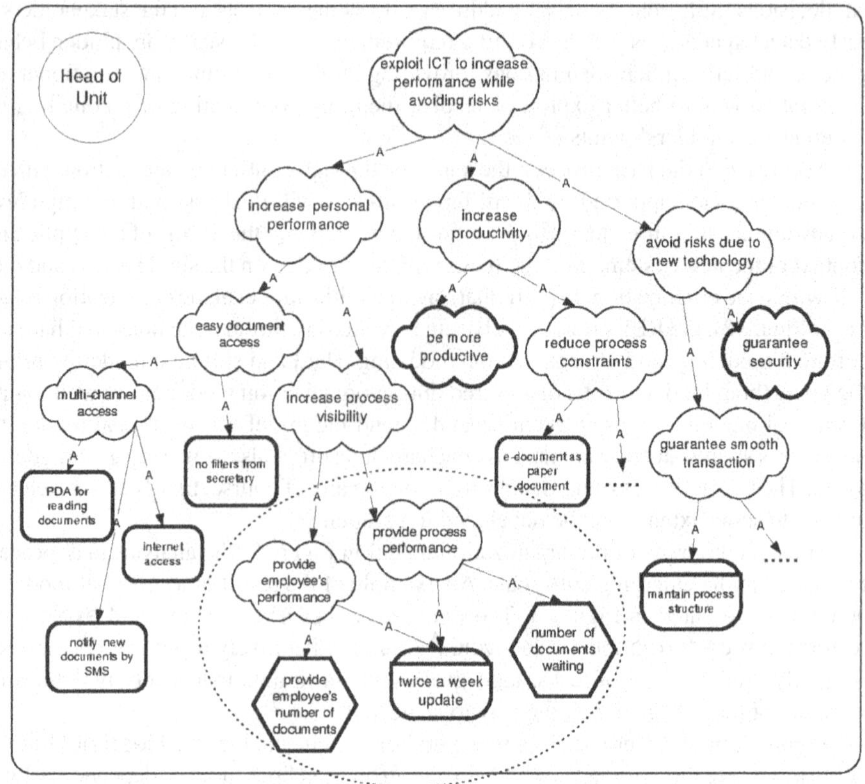

Fig. 3. The exploit ICT to increase performance while avoiding risks Soft-Goal Model

to better understand this process, let us take a step back, and analyze Figure 4, where the soft-goal model of Figure 3 is shown at an initial stage of the process.

According to Figure 4, the Head of Unit has: to increase personal Performance, to increase productivity of the whole unit, and to avoid risks due to new technology. Let us consider in details only the sub-soft-goal: increase personal performance. It spawns two subordinate soft-goals, easy document access, and increase process visibility, to take better informed decisions. In particular, the soft-goal increase process visibility will eventually lead to the identification of some information about the process that the system will have to provide (i.e., tasks, that is functionalities, that the system will have to implement), as shown in Figure 3.

As mentioned, obtaining such details is a costly process. Before venturing in it, the analyst may prefer, in order to minimize the future analysis effort, to highlight situations where she believes that some commonalities among different goals could be hidden, i.e., situations in which possible shared goals (or tasks, resources, or constraints) could be found during some of the possible alternative developments of the analysis.

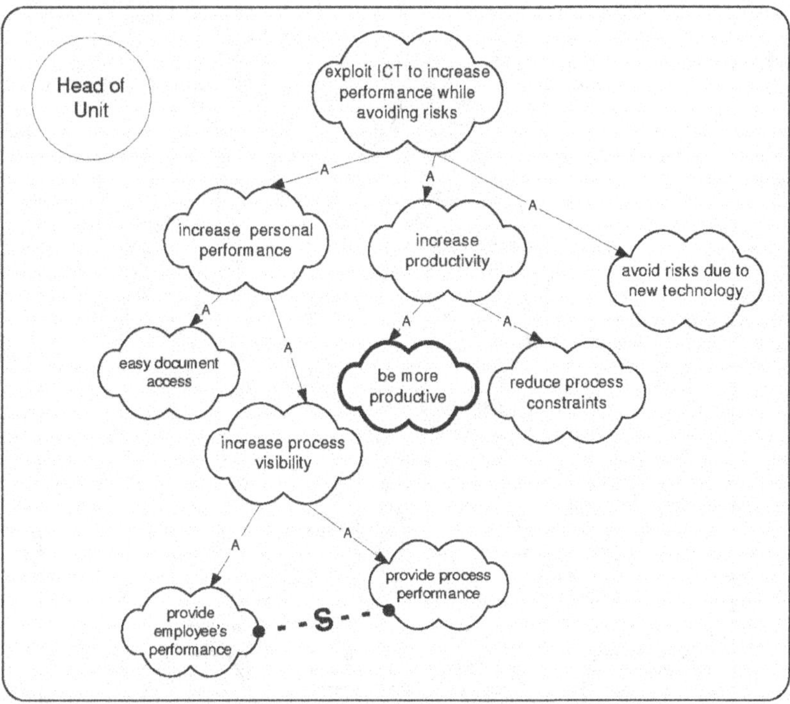

Fig. 4. The exploit ICT to increase performance while avoiding risks Soft-Goal Model under construction

Such a possibility has to be granted as soon as possible. In fact, once the sub-trees have been expanded, not only possible common aspects could easily be cluttered by the details, but, also, the two different sub-trees developments may have led to so diverging solutions that reconciliation or coordination or sharing parts become almost impossible.

In such a perspective, REF provides to the analyst a specific notation to connect two or more goals between which a possible commonality is presumed: it is a dotted line, labeled with "S" (for "Sharing") and referred to as a S-connection . It is relevant noticing that the S-connections are used only by the analysts and have to be removed once the diagram is ready to be presented to the stakeholders.

In Figure 4, the S-connection is used to connect the two soft-goals provide employee's performance and provide process performance. The S-connection may act as a high-level reasoning support tool to enable the analysts to record their intuitions while building the goals models, i.e., making notes to drive their strategies. For example, to highlight where a top-down breath-first diagram expansion may be preferable to a top-down depth-first strategy. As well, the S-Connection reminds the analyst to pay special attention in developing the two sub-trees, and to continuously verify, during the process, the presence of possible common items in the two sub-trees, by organizing more interviews with the stakeholders, and possibly joint elicitation sessions. The final soft-goal

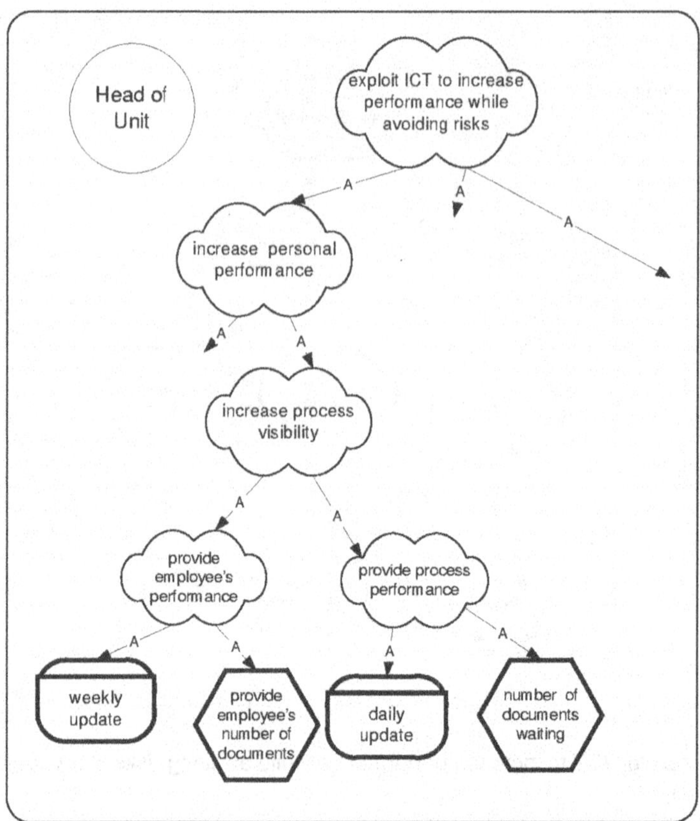

Fig. 5. The exploit ICT to increase performance while avoiding risks alternative (without sharing) Soft-Goal Model. Only the modified diagram fragment is depicted

diagram in Figure 3, where the constraint twice a week update has been identified as a common item for the two soft-goals, confirms the validity of the foreseen commonality. Clearly, this is a trivial example: the S-Connection can be better appreciated when deeper sub-trees or different actors are involved. Nevertheless, even in this simple case, the value of the S-Connection can be appreciated, by considering what would have happened without it. The two soft-goals provide employee's performance and provide process performance could have been taken into account in two very different moments and by means of independent analyses and interviews with the stakeholders, leading to two different frequency of update: daily for the process data and weekly for the employee's ones, as shown in Figure 5.

Of course, the diagram in Figure 5 is the one that more finely represent the requirements spontaneously expressed by the stakeholders (it is assumed that weekly update and daily update corresponds to the best options —from the local points of view— in the two cases, respectively). Nevertheless, the solution discovered with Figure 3 (twice a

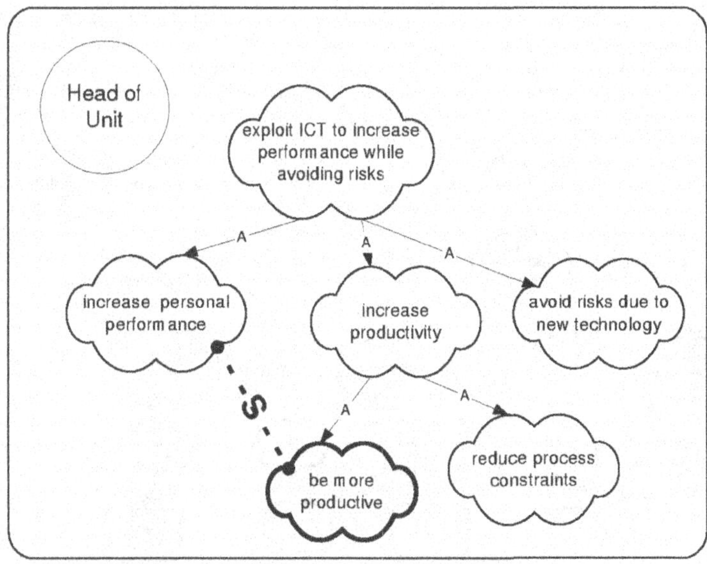

Fig. 6. A possible sharing between goals of different agents

week update) may be considered a reasonable compromise. Moreover, this acceptable (from the local points of view) trade-off corresponds to a much higher global advantage: any possibly necessary further analysis will be carried on in fact only once, rather than twice. In our example the final constraints (leafs with thick borders) correspond to well (quantitatively) characterized requirements for the system-to-be, in other terms, to functional requirements. This means that the solution of Figure 5 will lead to a faster, cheaper, and lighter systems architecture, design, and implementation.[2]

Another, and less trivial, use of the S-Connection is represented in the diagram fragment of Figure 6.

Here, the possible sharing is between the soft-goal increase personal Performance, that the Head of Unit wants to achieve, and the soft-goal be more productive, that the Head of Unit imposes, transfers, to the Employee. In this case, one part of the analysis continues inside the Head of Unit diagram, but the other part is dealt with in the employee's soft-goals analysis diagram. Thus, a possible sharing may happen among different diagrams, as in Figure 7.

Again, as in the previous case, the analysis of such a shared soft-goal immediately assume a higher relevance and priority over the analysis of other goals. Its satisfaction is desired by two actors! The analysis can be carried out only once for both the actors, exploiting the approach to better combine their needs in a synergic way, and avoiding

[2] It is relevant here to note that small advantages at requirements time are then considerably amplified during later phases of Software Engineering: saving a single constraint in REF may finally correspond to saving several lines of implemented code.

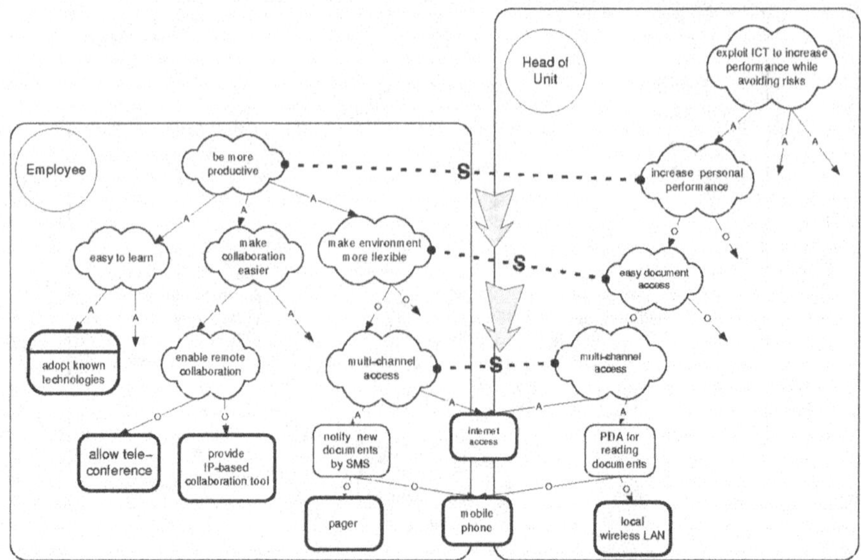

Fig. 7. S-Connection among two different actors

duplications that, although most of the times are due only to slightly different ideas, may generate over complexity in terms of system's functionalities.

Figure 7 summarizes several steps of the analysis process. First, the S-connections is placed at a very top level. The S-connection is then moved by the analyst during the goal refinement process, and better positioned to indicate more specific areas where commonalities could be hidden. At each refinement step, in both the diagrams, several options (evidenced by "O" dependencies) are possible, but the priority is given to those that allow to move the S-connection down, favoring the search of commonalities, accordingly with the opinions of both the stakeholders.

In Figure 7, such movements are evidenced with large gray arrows. Initially, the S-connection links the soft-goal increase personal performance and the soft-goal be more productive. After an initial and combined refinement of the two soft-goals, the analyst moves the S-connection down, between the soft-goals make environment more flexible and easy document access. Finally, after further refinements, the analyst finds two very similar —even with the same label— soft-goals (the multi-channel access), between which the S-connection is placed. Although very similar, these two soft-goals may in reality hide different ideas about what multi-channel access means, i.e., the Head of Unit and the Employee can have different concepts of this capability. For example, while they may agree on a classical Internet based access, the Head of Unit may also want to use a wireless communication based PDA to remotely access the ERMS, while for the Employee may be enough to be informed by a SMS when new documents have been assigned. Thus, different options of refinement of the two commonly labelled soft-goals are possible, but a preference is given to those that eventually operationalize both

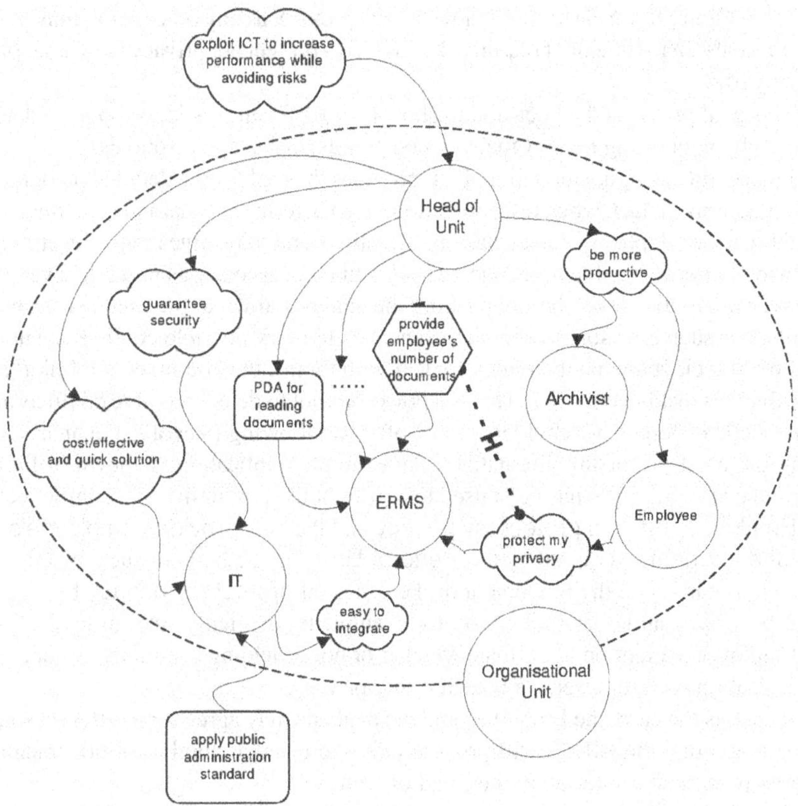

Fig. 8. The evolving organization model

the soft-goals by means of common goals, shared by both the actors. This solution is shown in Figure 7, where the common communication channel (mobile phone) has been accepted by both the actors, as viable to enable both SMS messaging and PDA remote access. Thus, the leaf nodes drawn in thick lines (meaning that they have not to be further analyzed inside the considered context, but transfered to another actor, namely, the ERMS systems) correspond to the final (possibly common) system requirements.

As a final step, let's consider how the initial organization model of Figure 2 can now be enriched, leading to the model in Figure 8 (where some details have been omitted for the sake of clarity). Some new actors have been introduced: the Archivist and the Employee, which have to be more productive, the Information Technology, which has to guarantee security and the ERMS, upon which the identified goals, tasks and constraints will be placed. From Figure 8, we can also see that the Head of Unit has decided to delegate the soft-goal cost/effective and quick solution to the actor Information Technology, which, on its turn, will have to achieve other goals coming from the external environment, such as, for example, apply public administration standards.

From Figure 8, we can also see how the Employee, as any other actor, may generate its own goals. In particular, it requires the ERMS to protect her privacy (soft-goal protect my privacy).

This goal provides the occasion to show how REF can provide support in detecting and resolving clashing needs (goals, or constraints, tasks, and resources).

Indeed, through goal modeling, REF provides the tool for the detailed recognition of such situations. In fact, when fully operationalized in terms of tasks and constraints, goals models can be adopted to detect clashing situations and to resolve them. Nevertheless, it is always better to be able to recognize such situations as early as possible, even if only at a very qualitative level, before pushing the analysis down to the final constraints and details. For such a reason, to enable the analysts to mark possible conflicting situations (and build their refinement strategy to deal with them), the H-connection link ("H" for "Hurting") is available in REF. This is a powerful tool to detect possible conflicts and try to reconcile different stakeholders points of view, allowing to evolve the analyses only along the most promising alternatives. An example application is shown in Figure 8, where the H-connection has been used to highlight the possibility of a conflict between the Employee soft-goal protect my privacy and the task provides employee's number of documents, required by the Head of Unit. On the basis of such an annotation, the analyst carries on the refinement of the soft-goal protect my privacy by bearing in mind possible conflicts with the task, for example by explicitly submitting the issue to the Employee's attention to evaluate whether or not providing the number of documents she is dealing with represents a breach of her privacy.

If such is the case, the Employee and the analysts may agree for a different solution, for example that the ERMS will provide only the average number of documents, and then propose such a solution to the Head of Unit.

Concluding, the H-connection, similarly to the S-connection, provides the analyst with a marking mechanism very useful to better drive and control the analysis process. As it happens with S-connections, also the H-connections are dropped once the final diagrams are ready to be submitted to the stakeholders In fact, S-connections, as well as H-connections, are used only to support the analyst during the development phases. Once a stable model has been produced, there is no more the need to maintain this kind of annotations in the diagrams, specially if different unexploited S-connections and H-connections are present, since one of the main aims of REF is to keep the diagrams as simpler as possible for the stakeholders.

6 Conclusions

The paper introduced REF, a requirements engineering framework explicitly designed to support the analysts in reasoning about socio-technical systems, and transform high-level organizational needs into system requirements. By adopting concepts as those of *Actors*, *Goals*, and *Intentional Dependency*, and introducing an essential graphical notation, REF results to be a very effective and easy to deal with (usable) tool, able to tackle complex real situations, while remaining simple enough to allow a concrete and effective stakeholders involvement. In addition, REF supports the analysts in dealing with complex and system/organizational design related issues, such as shared and clashing stakeholders' needs, by introducing some specific analysis-oriented notations to allow an early marking and detection of such situations.

The described application example demonstrates the feasibility of the suggested approach, and the benefits it offers during the early phases of requirements engineering, when the analyst and the stakeholders have to cooperate to understand and reason about the organizational context within which the new system has to function, in order to identify and formalize not only the system requirements, but also the organizational setting that better exploits the new system's capabilities.

Finally, although REF addresses only the early stages of the requirements engineering process, the possibility of combining its outcome with techniques more suitable for dealing with further system development phases has been investigated. For example, practical results suggest that it can be usefully applied as a forerunner to object-oriented approaches, such as those based upon UML [8], as well as to Agent-Oriented Software Engineering approaches for the development of Multi-Agent-Systems [4,14,12].

References

1. A. I. Antón. Goal-based requirements analysis. In *Proceedings of the IEEE International Conference on Requirements Engineering (ICRE '96)*, Colorado Springs, USA, Apr. 1996.
2. A. I. Antón and C. Potts. Requirements for evolving systems. In *Proceedings of the International Conference on Software Engineering (ICSE '98)*, Kyoto, Japan, Apr. 1998.
3. V. Basili, G. Caldiera, and H. Rombach. *The Goal Question Metric Approach.* Wiley&Sons Inc, 1994.
4. P. Bresciani, A. Perini, , F. Giunchiglia, P. Giorgini, and J. Mylopoulos. A Knowledge Level Software Engineering Methodology for Agent Oriented Programming. In *Proceedings of the Fifth International Conference on Autonomous Agents*, Montreal, Canada, May 2001.
5. J. Castro, M. Kolp, and J. Mylopoulos. Developing agent-oriented information systems for the enterprise. In *Proceedings Third International Conference on Enterprise Information Systems*, Stafford UK, July 2000.
6. L. K. Chung, B. A. Nixon, E. Yu, and J. Mylopoulos. *Non-Functional Requirements in Software Engineering.* Kluwer Publishing, 2000.
7. A. Dardenne, A. van Lamsweerde, and S. Fickas. Goal-directed requirements acquisition. *Science of Computer Programming*, 20(1-2):3–50, 1993.
8. P. Donzelli and M. Moulding. Application domain modelling for the verification and validation of synthetic environments: from requirements engineering to conceptual modelling. In *Proceedings of the Spring 2000 Simulation Interoperability Workshop*, Orlando, FL, Mar. 2000.
9. P. Donzelli and M. Moulding. Developments in application domain modelling for the verification and validation of synthetic environments: A formal requirements engineering framework. In *Proceedings of the Spring 99 Simulation Interoperability Workshop*, LNCS, Orlando, FL, 2000. Springer-Verlag.
10. P. Donzelli and R. Setola. Putting the customer at the center of the IT system — a case study. In *Proceedings of the Euro-Web 2001 Conference — The Web in the Public Administration*, Pisa, Italy, Dec. 2001.
11. P. Donzelli and R. Setola. Handling the knowledge acquired during the requirements engineering process. In *Proceedings of the Fourteenth International Conference on Knowledge Engineering and Software Engineering (SEKE)*, 2002.

12. P. Giorgini, A. Perini, J. Mylopoulos, F. Giunchiglia, and P. Bresciani. Agent-oriented software development: A case study. In *Proceedings of the Thirteenth International Conference on Software Engineering - Knowledge Engineering (SEKE01)*, Buenos Aires, June 2001.
13. S. Jacobs and R. Holten. Goal driven business modelling: supporting decision making within information systems development. In *Proceedings of conference on Organizational computing systems*. ACM Press, 1995.
14. J. Mylopoulos and J. Castro. Tropos: A framework for requirements-driven software development. In J. Brinkkemper and A. Solvberg, editors, *Information System Engineering: State of the Art and Research Themes*, Lecture Notes in Computer Science. Springer-Verlag, 2000.
15. J. Mylopoulos, L. Chung, S. Liao, H. Wang, and E. Yu. Exploring alternatives during requirements analysis. *IEEE Software*, 18(1):92–96, 2001.
16. A. Perini, P. Bresciani, P. Giorgini, F. Giunchiglia, and J. Mylopoulos. Towards an Agent Oriented approach to Software Engineering. In *Proceedings of WOA 2001 – Dagli oggetti agli agenti: tendenze evolutive dei sistemi software*, Modena, Sept. 2001. Pitagora Editrice Bologna.
17. C. Rolland and N. Prakash. From conceptual modelling to requirements engineering. *Annals of Software Engineering*, 10:151–176, 2000.
18. A. van Lamsweerde. Requirements Engineering in the Year 00: A Research Perspective. In *Proceedings of the 22nd International Conference on Software Engineering, Invited Paper*, ACM Press, June 2000.
19. E. Yu. *Modeling Strategic Relationships for Process Reengineering*. PhD thesis, University of Toronto, Department of Computer Science, University of Toronto, 1995.
20. E. Yu. Why agent-oriented requirements engineering. In *Proceedings of 3rd Workshop on Requirements Engineering For Software Quality*, Barcelona, Catalonia, June 1997.
21. E. Yu and J. Mylopoulos. Using goals, rules, and methods to support reasoning in business process reengineering. *International Journal of Intelligent Systems in Accounting, Finance and Management*, 1(5):1–13, Jan. 1996.

Organizational Patterns for Early Requirements Analysis

Manuel Kolp[1], Paolo Giorgini[2], and John Mylopoulos[3]

[1]IAG - Information Systems Research Unit - University of Louvain, 1 Place des Doyens, B-1348 Louvain-La-Neuve, Belgium, tel.: 32-10 47 83 95, kolp@isys.ucl.ac.be
[2]Department of Information and Communication Technology - University of Trento 4 via Sommarive, I-38100, Trento, Italy, tel.: 39-0461-88 2052, paolo.giorgini@dit.unitn.it
[3]Department of Computer Science - University of Toronto, 40 St George Street, M5S 2E4, Toronto, Canada, tel.: 1-416-978 5180, jm@cs.toronto.edu

Abstract. Early requirements analysis is concerned with modeling and understanding the organizational context within which a software system will eventually function. This paper proposes organizational patterns motivated by organizational theories intended to facilitate the construction of organizational models. These patterns are defined from real world organizational settings, modeled in *i** and formalized using the Formal Tropos language. Additionally, the paper evaluates the proposed patterns using desirable qualities such as coordinability and predictability.

1 Introduction

Modeling the organizational and intentional context within which a software system will eventually operate has been recognized as an important element of the requirements engineering process (e.g., [1, 5, 22]). Such models are founded on primitive concepts such as those of *actor* and *goal*. This paper focuses on the definition of a set of organizational patterns that can be used as building blocks for constructing such models. Our proposal is based on concepts adopted from organization theory and strategic alliances literature. Throughout the paper, we use *i** [22] as the modeling framework in terms of which the proposed patterns are presented and accounted for.

The research reported in this paper is being conducted within the context of the *Tropos* project, whose aim is to construct and validate a software development methodology for agent-based software systems. The methodology adopts ideas from multi-agent system technologies, mostly to define the implementation phase of our methodology. It also adopts ideas from Requirements Engineering, where actors and goals have been used heavily for early requirements analysis. The project is founded on that actors and goals are used as fundamental concepts for modeling and analysis during *all phases of software development*, not just early requirements, or implementation. More details about *Tropos* can be found in [3]. The present work

J. Eder and M. Missikoff (Eds.): CAiSE 2003, LNCS 2681, pp. 617–632, 2003.

continues the research in progress about social abstractions for the *Tropos* methodology. In [14], we have detailed a social ontology for *Tropos* to consider information systems as social structures all along the development life cycle. In [13, 15, 10], we have described how to use this *Tropos* social ontology to design multi-agent systems architectures. As a matter of fact, multi-agent systems can be considered structured societies of coordinated autonomous agents. In the present paper, we emphasize now the use of organizational patterns based on organization theory an strategic alliances for early requirements analysis, with the concern of modeling the organizational setting for a system-to-be in terms of abstractions that could better match its operational environment (e.g., an enterprise, a corporate alliance, …)

The paper is organized as follows. Section 2 describes organizational and strategic alliance theories, focusing on the internal and external structure of an organization. Section 3 details two organizational patterns – the structure-in-5 and the joint venture – based on real world examples of organizations. These two patterns are modeled in terms of social and intentional concepts using the *i** framework and a formal specification language (Formal Tropos) founded on *i**. Section 4 identifies a set of desirable qualities for comparing and evaluating these patterns. Finally, Section 5 summarizes the contributions of the paper and overviews related work.

2 Structuring Organizations

Since the origins of civilization, people have been designing, participating in, and sharing the burdens and rewards of organizations. The early organizations were primarily military or governmental in nature. In the *Art of War*, Sun Tzu describes the need for hierarchical structure, communications, and strategy. In the *Politics*, Aristotle wrote of governmental administration and its association with culture. To the would-be-leader, Machiavelli advocated in the *Prince* power over morality. The roots of organizational theories, then, can be traced to antiquity, including thinkers from around the world who studied alternative organizational structures. Such structures consist of stakeholders – individuals, groups, physical or social systems – that coordinate and interact with each other to achieve common goals. Today, organizational structures are primarily studied by two disciplines: *Organization Theory* (e.g., [17, 18, 19, 21]), that describes the internal structure of an organization, and *Strategic Alliances* (e.g., [6]), that model the external collaborations of independent organizations who have agreed to pursue a set of shared business goals.

2.1 Organization Theory

"An organization is a consciously coordinated social entity, with a relatively identifiable boundary, that functions on a relatively continuous basis to achieve a common goal or a set of goals" [21]. Organization theory is the discipline that studies both *structure* and *design* in such social entities. Structural issues deal with descriptive aspects while design issues address prescriptive ones. Organization theory, as far back as Adam Smith, describes how practical organizations are actually structured, offers suggestions on how new ones can be constructed, and how old ones can change to improve effectiveness. To this end, schools of organization theory have proposed patterns to try to find and formalize recurring organizational structures and behaviors.

For instance, the structure-in-5 pattern [17] consists of the typical strategic and logistic components generally present in many organizations. At the base level, the Operational Core takes care of basic tasks – the input, processing, output and direct support procedures – associated with running the organization. At the top lies the Apex, composed of executive actors. Below it, sit the Technostructure, Middle Line and Support components, which are responsible for control/standardization, management, and logistics, respectively. The Technostructure component carries out the tasks of standardizing the behavior of other components. Additionally, it is responsible for applying analytical procedures that help the organization to adapt to the environment. Actors joining the apex to the operational core make up the Middle Line. The Support component assists the operational core for non-operational services that are outside the basic flow of operational tasks and procedures. We describe and model examples of structures-in-5 in Section 3. Other proposed patterns are, for example, the matrix, the pyramid, and the lattice (see e.g. [18]). For further information about the patterns we are working on, see [13].

2.2 Strategic Alliances

A strategic alliance links specific facets of the businesses of two or more organizations. At its core, this structure is a trading partnership that enhances the effectiveness of the competitive strategies of the participant organizations by providing for the mutually beneficial trade of technologies, skills, or products based upon them. An alliance can take a variety of forms, ranging from arm's-length contracts to joint ventures, from multinational corporations to university spin-offs, from franchises to equity arrangements (see e.g. [6]. Varied interpretations of the term exist, but a strategic alliance can be defined as possessing simultaneously the following three necessary and sufficient characteristics:

- The two or more organizations that unite to pursue a set of agreed upon goals remain independent subsequent to the formation of the alliance.
- The partner organizations share the benefits of the alliances and control over the performance of assigned tasks.
- The partner organizations contribute on a continuing basis in one or more key strategic areas, e.g., technology, products, and so forth.

For instance, the joint venture pattern involves agreement between two or more intra-industry partners to obtain the benefits of larger scale, partial investment and lower maintenance costs. A specific joint management actor coordinates tasks and manages the sharing of resources between partner actors. Each partner can manage and control itself on a local dimension and interact directly with other partners to exchange resources, such as data and knowledge. However, the strategic operation and coordination of such an organization are only ensured by the joint management actor in which the original actors possess participation equity. We describe and model examples of joint ventures in Section 3. For further information about the patterns we are working on, see [13].

3 Modeling Organizational Patterns

We have overviewed our organizational patterns in [13]. To model and formalize two of them in more detail, we describe in this section four case studies. The first two examples – FoodCo and Agate Ltd – will be used to illustrate and define formally the structure-in-5, a pattern adopted from organization theory; the others – Airbus and Eurocopter – serve the same purpose for the joint-venture pattern used in strategic alliances.

3.1 Structure-in 5 Pattern

We describe first two case studies from [2]. The presented organizations are modeled in terms of the structure-in-5 pattern. We then formalize the pattern.

FoodCo. FoodCo is a food enterprise based in the East Anglian region of the UK that produces a range of perishable foods for major UK supermarket chains. Its products line ranges from extended to pre-packed vegetables and salads, includes a wide range of sauces, pickles, sandwich toppings, and almost anything made of vegetable that can be sold in jars. There are one farm with a market garden and three factories on the site as well as two warehouses.

The structure of the organization follows the structure-in-5. A *Board* of eight directors forms the *strategic apex.* It is responsible for defining the *general strategy* of the organization: five different chief managers (administration & finance, marketing, planning, operation, and distribution) are required to apply the different aspects of that general strategy in the coordination of the work in the area of their competence: *Policy and Budget* for *Planning and Administration/Finance*, *Production Management* for *Operation,* and *Customer Relationship Management* for *Marketing and Distribution.*

Operation groups production managers and, typically, *coordinates* all managerial aspects of the production. To this end, it relies on *Planning and Administration/ Finances* for dealing with *Planning and Control* aspects of the production and on *Marketing and Distribution* for *Delivery & Sales Logistics*. The *Planning and Administration/Finances* departments constitute the *technostructure* that implements work procedures and policy, management control, planning and budget of the enterprise. This includes the financial strategy, the general administration and human resources management.

The *support* involves the *Marketing and Distribution* staff. *Marketing* coordinates the *customer relationship management* (market study, sales, ...), while *Distribution* controls the work at the warehouse, and pick-up & dispatch activities.

Finally, the *operational core* groups line workers, factory and farm foremen that are under the direct supervision of production managers (*middle line*).

Figure 1 models the FoodCo structure-in-5 using the *i** strategic dependency model.

*i** is a modeling framework for early requirements analysis [22], founded on notions such as *actor*, *agent, role, position, goal, softgoal, task, resource, belief* and different kinds of social *dependency* between actors. Its strategic dependency model describes the network of social dependencies among actors. It is a graph, where each node represents an *actor*, and each link between two actors indicates that one actor depends on another for something in order that the former may attain some goal. A dependency describes an "agreement" (called *dependum*) between two actors: the *depender* and the *dependee*. The *depender* is the depending actor, and the *dependee,* the actor who is depended upon. The type of the dependency describes the nature of the agreement. *Goal* dependencies are used to represent delegation of responsibility for fulfilling a goal; *softgoal* dependencies are similar to goal dependencies, but their fulfillment cannot be defined precisely (for instance, the appreciation is subjective, or the fulfillment can occur only to a given extent); *task* dependencies are used in situations where the dependee is required to perform a given activity; and *resource* dependencies require the dependee to provide a resource to the depender. As shown in Figure 1, actors are represented as circles; dependums – goals, softgoals, tasks and resources – are respectively represented as ovals, clouds, hexagons and rectangles; and dependencies have the form *depender* $\rightarrow$ *dependum* $\rightarrow$ *dependee*. We also use later the notion of role (circle with a double line) allowing us to model the same actor assuming different roles

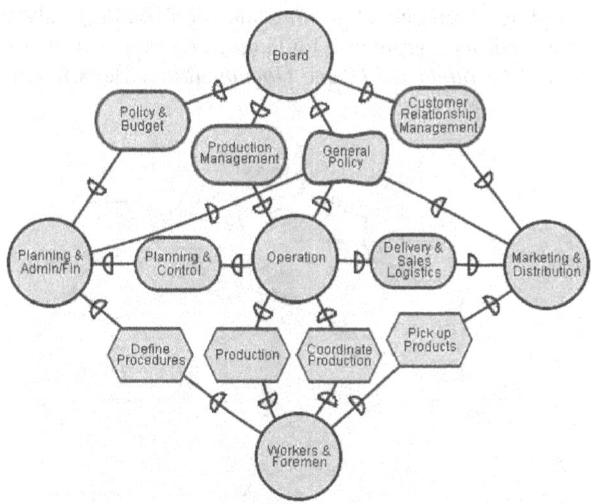

Fig. 1. FoodCo in Structure-in-5

Agate. Agate Ltd is an advertising agency in Birmingham, UK that employs more than fifty staff as described in Figure 2.

Direction
1 Campaign Director
1 Creative Director
1 Administrative Director
1 Finance Director

Edition
2 Editors
4 Copy writers

IT
1 IT manager
1 Network administrator
1 System administrator
1 Analyst
1 Computer technician

Administration
1 Office manager
3 Direction assistants
4 Manager Secretaries
2 Receptionists
2 Clerks/typists
1 Filing clerk

Accounts Edition
1 Accountant manager
1 Credit controller
2 Accounts clerks
2 Purchasing assistants

Campaigns Management
2 Campaign managers
3 Campaign marketers
1 Editor in Chief
1 Creative Manager

Graphics
6 Graphic designers
2 Photographers

Documentation
1 Media librarian
1 Resource librarian
1 Knowledge worker

Fig. 2. Organization of Agate Ltd

The *Direction* – four directors responsible for the main aspects of Agate's *Global Strategy* (advertising campaigns, creative activities, administration and finances) – forms the *strategic apex*. The *middle line* composed of the *Campaigns Management* staff is in charge of *finding* and *coordinating* advertising campaigns (marketing, sales, edition, graphics, budget, …) supported in these tasks by the *Administration and Accounts* and *IT and Documentation* departments.

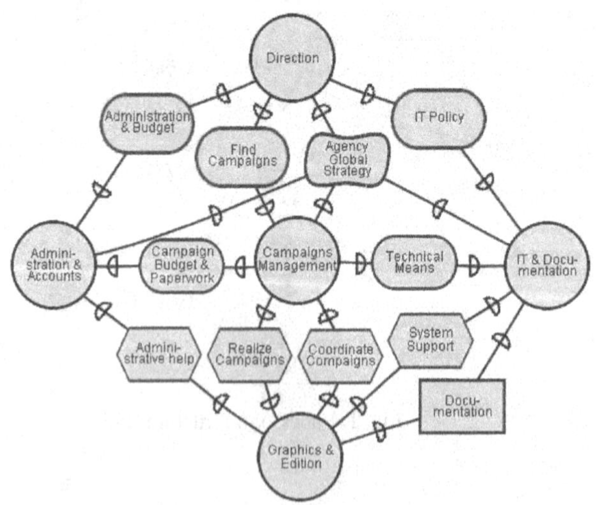

Fig. 3. Agate in Structure-in-5

The *Administration and Accounts* constitutes the *technostructure* handling administrative tasks and policy, paperwork, purchases and budgets. The *support* is constituted of the *IT and Documentation* departments. It defines the *IT policy* of Agate, provides *technical means* required for campaigns and ensures *system support* as well as information retrieval services (*documentation* resources). The *operational core* includes the *Graphics and Edition* staff in charge of the creative and artistic aspects of *realizing campaigns*: texts, photographs, drawings, layout, design, logos,…

Figure 3 models the structure-in-5 organization of Agate Ltd.

Figure 4 generalizes the structure-in-5 pattern explored in Figures 2 and 3. The pattern must be composed of five actors. Each of them assumes the responsibilities described in Section 2.

Dependencies between the *Strategic Apex* as depender and the *Technostructure*, *Middle Line* and *Support* as dependees must be goal dependencies. A softgoal dependency models the strategic dependence of the *Technostructure*, *Middle Line* and *Support* on the *Strategic Apex*. Relationships between the *Middle Line* and *Technostructure* and *Support* must be of type goal dependencies. The *Operational Core* relies on the *Technostructure* and *Support* through task and resource dependencies. Only task dependencies are permitted between the *Middle Line* (as depender or dependee) and the *Operational Core* (as dependee or depender).

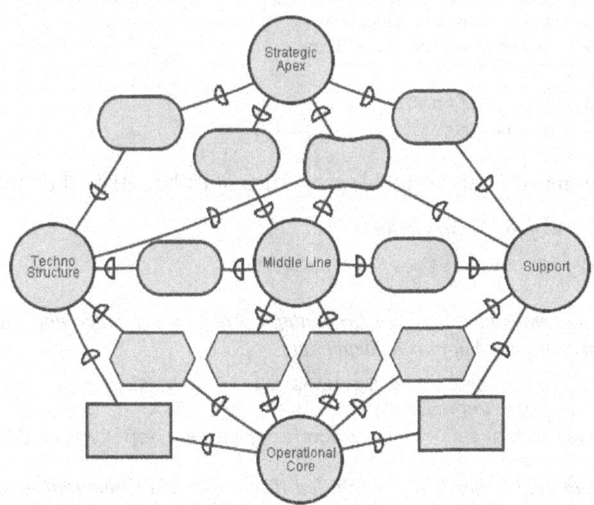

Fig. 4. The Structure-in-5 Pattern

To specify the structure and formal properties of the pattern, we use *Formal Tropos* [8] which offers the primitive concepts of *i** augmented with a rich specification language inspired by KAOS [5]. Formal Tropos offers a textual notation for *i** models and allows one to describe dynamic constraints among the different elements of the specification in a first order linear-time temporal logic. Moreover, *Formal Tropos* has a precise semantics which makes specifications amenable to formal analysis. Basically, *Formal Tropos* conceives three main types of classes: *actor, dependency, and entity*. The attributes of a *Formal Tropos* class denote relationships among different objects being modeled.

In order to express conditions about Strategic Dependency models, such as for instance our organizational patterns, we extend *Formal Tropos* with metaclasses. In particular, we have:

```
Metaclasses
  Actor := Actor name [attributes][creation-properties]
          [invar-properties][actor-goal]
   With subclasses:
     Agent (with attributes occupies: Position, play: Role)
     Position (with attribute cover: Role)
     Role
  Dependency:= Dependency name type mode Depender name Dependee name
              [attributes][creation-properties][invar-properties]
              [fulfill-properties]
  Entity:= Entity name [attribute] [creation-properties]
          [invar-properties]

Classes: Classes are instances of Metaclasses.
```

Part of the Structure-in-5 pattern specification is in the following:

```
Actor StrategicApex
       SoftGoal StrategicManagement
Actor MiddleLine
       Goal ManagementControl
       Task OperationCoordination
Actor Support
       Goal PolicyDefinition
       Goal Logistics
```

The following structural (global) properties must be satisfied by the pattern:

Only one instance of the Strategic Apex

```
∀ sa1,sa2: StrategicApex → (sa1=sa2)
```

Only softgoal dependencies between the Stategic Apex as dependee and the Middle Line, the Technostructure and the Support as dependers

```
∀ sa: StrategicApex, ml: Technostructure ∨ Middle_Agency ∨
  Support, dep: Dependency
  ((dep.dependee=sa ∧ dep.depender=ml) → (dep.type=softgoal))
```

The previous softgoal dependency is fulfilled if and only if all the goal dependencies between the Middle Agency, the Technostructure and the Support as dependers and the Stategic Apex as dependee have been achieved sometimes in the past

```
∀ sa: StrategicApex, ml: MiddleLine, dep1: Dependency
  ((dep1.type=softgoal ∧ dep1.dependee=sa ∧ dep1.depender=ml) ∧
   (∀ dep2: Dependency (dep2.type=goal ∧ (dep2.depender=sa ∧
    dep2.dependee = ml ∧ ♦Fulfilled(dep2)))) → Fulfilled(dep1))
```

Only task dependencies between the Middle Line and the Operational Core

```
∀ml: MiddleLine, oc: OperationalCore, dep: Dependency
  ((dep.depender=ml ∧ dep.dependee=oc) ∨
   (dep.depender=oc ∧ dep.dependee=ml)) → (dep.type = task))
```

Only resource or task dependencies between the Technostructure and the Operational Core

```
∀ts: Technostructure, oc: OperationalCore, dep : Dependency
  ((dep.depender=ts ∧ dep.dependee=oc) →
   (dep.type=task ∨ dep.type=resource))
```

Only resource or task dependencies between the Support and the Operational Core

```
∀ sp: Support, oc: OperationalCore, dep: Dependency
   ((dep.depender=sp ∧ dep.dependee=oc) →
    (dep.type=task ∨ dep.type=ressource )
```

3.2 Joint-Venture Pattern

We describe here two case studies from [6]. The presented organizations are modeled following the joint venture structure. We then formalize it as an organizational pattern.

Airbus. The Airbus Industrie joint venture coordinates collaborative activities between European aeronautic manufacturers to built and market airbus aircrafts. The joint venture involves four partners: Aerospatiale (France), DASA (Daimler-Benz Aerospace, Germany), British Aerospace (UK) and CASA (Construcciones Aeronauticas SA, Spain). Research, development and production tasks have been distributed among the partners, avoiding any duplication. Aerospatiale is mainly responsible for developing and manufacturing the cockpit of the aircraft and for system integration. DASA develops and manufactures the fuselage, British Aerospace the wings and CASA the tail unit. Final assembly is carried out in Toulouse (France) by Aerospatiale. Unlike production, commercial and decisional activities have not been split between partners. All strategy, marketing, sales and after-sales operations are entrusted to the Airbus Industrie joint venture, which is the only interface with external stakeholders such as customers. To buy an Airbus, or to maintain their fleet, customer airlines could not approach one or other of the partner firms directly, but has to deal with Airbus Industrie. Airbus Industrie, which is a real manufacturing company, defines the alliance's product policy and elaborates the specifications of each model of aircraft to be launched. Airbus defends the point of view and interests of the alliance as a whole, even against the partner companies themselves when the individual goals of the latter conflict with the collective goals of the alliance.

Figure 5 models the organization of the Airbus Industrie joint venture using the *i** strategic dependency model. Airbus assumes two roles: Airbus Industrie and Airbus Joint Venture. *Airbus Industrie* deals with demands from customers, *Customer* depends on it to receive airbus aircrafts or maintenance services. The *Airbus Joint Venture* role ensures the interface for the four partners (*CASA, Aerospatiale, British Aerospace* and *DASA*) with *Airbus Industrie* defining Airbus strategic policy, managing conflicts between the four Airbus partners, defending the interests of the whole alliance and defining new aircrafts specifications. *Airbus Joint Venture* coordinates the four partners ensuring that each of them assumes a specific task in the building of Airbus aircrafts: wings building for *British Aerospace*, tail unit building for *CASA*, cockpit building and aircraft assembling for *Aerospace* and fuselage building for *DASA*. Since Aerospatiale assumes two different tasks, it is modeled as two roles: *Aerospatiale Manufacturing* and *Aerospatiale Assembling*. *Aerospatiale Assembling* depends on each of the four partners to receive the parts of the planes.

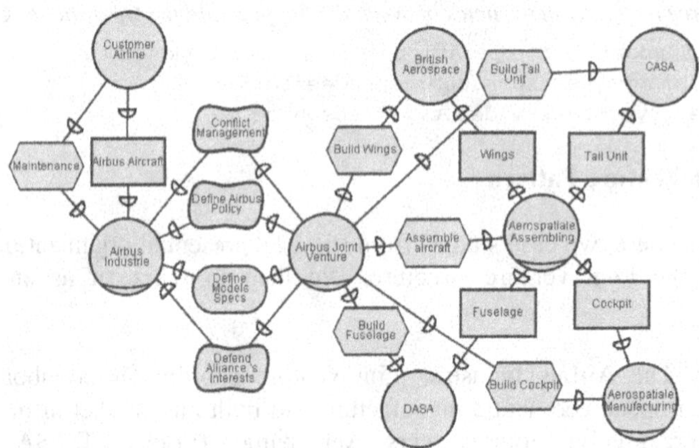

Fig. 5. The Airbus Industrie Joint Venture

Eurocopter. In 1992, Aerospatiale and DASA decided to merge all their helicopter activities within a joint venture Eurocopter. Marketing, sales, R&D, management and production strategies, policies and staff were reorganized and merged immediately; all the helicopter models, irrespective of their origin, were marketed under the Eurocopter name. Eurocopter has inherited helicopter manufacturing and engineering facilities, two in France (La Courneuve and Marignane), one in Germany (Ottobrunn). For political and social reasons, each of them has been specialized rather than closed down to group production together at a single site. The Marignane plant manufactures large helicopters, Ottobrunn produces small helicopters and La Courneuve concentrates on the manufacture of some complex components requiring a specific expertise, such as rotors and blades.

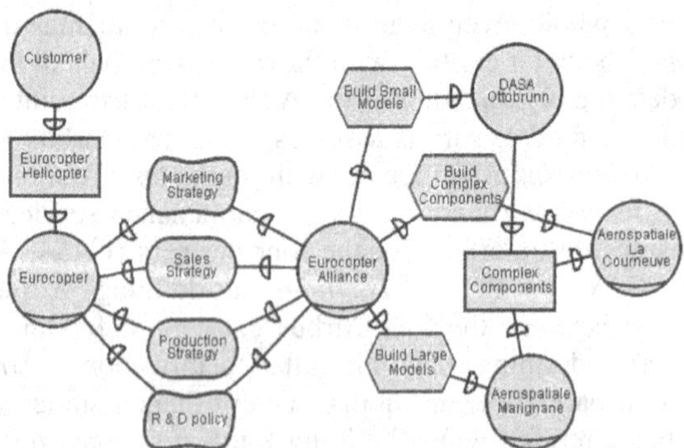

Fig. 6. The Eurocopter Joint Venture

Figure 6 models the organization of the Eurocopter joint venture in *i**. As in the Airbus joint venture, Eurocopter assumes two roles. The *Eurocopter* role handles helicopter orders from customers who depend on it to obtain the machines. It also defines marketing, sales, production and R & D strategies and policy. The *Eurocopter joint venture* role coordinates the manufacturing operations of the two partners – DASA and Aerospatiale – and depends on them for the production of small helicopters (*DASA Ottobrunn*), large ones (La Courneuve) and complex components (Marignane) such as rotors and blades. Since Aerospatiale assumes two different responsibilities, it is considered two roles: *Aerospatiale Marignane* and *Aerospatiale La Courneuve*. *DASA Ottobrunn* and *Aerospatiale Marignane* depends on *La Courneuve* to be supplied with complex helicopter parts.

Figure 7 generalizes the joint venture model explored in Figures 5 and 6. Partners depend on each other for providing and receiving resources. Operation coordination is ensured by the joint manager actor which depends on partners for the accomplishment of these assigned tasks. The joint manager actor must assume two roles: a private interface role to coordinate partners of the alliance and a public interface role to take strategic decisions, define policy for the private interface and represents the interests of the whole partnership with respect to external stakeholders.

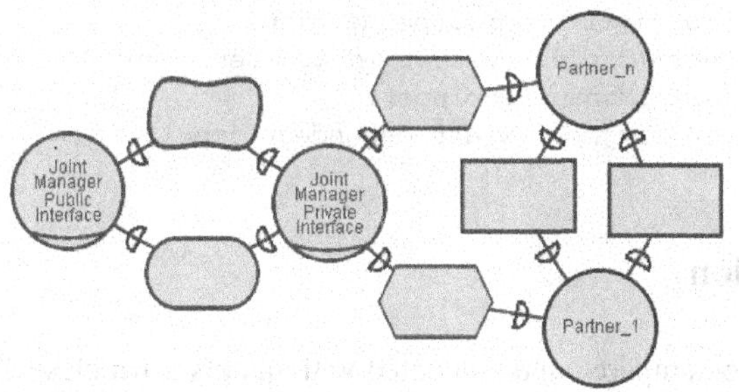

Fig. 7. The Joint Venture Pattern

Part of the Joint Venture pattern specification is in the following:

```
Role JointManagerPrivateInterface
     Goal CoordinatePatterns
Role JointManagerPublicInterface
     Goal TakeStrategicDecision
     SoftGoal RepresentPartnershipInterests
Actor Partner
```

The following structural (global) properties must be satisfied:

Only one instance of the joint manager

```
∀ jmpri1, jmpri2: JointManagerPrivateInterface (jmpri1=jmpri2)
```

Only resource dependencies between partners

```
∀ p1, p2:  Partner, dep: Dependency
 (((dep.depender=p1 ∧ dep.dependee=p2) ∨
  (dep.depender=p2 ∧ dep.dependee=p1)) → (dep.type=resource))
```

Only task dependencies between partners and joint manager, with joint manager as depender

```
∀ jmpri: JointManagerPrivateInterface, p:Partner, dep:Dependency
   ((dep.dependee=p ∧ dep.depender=jmpri) → dep.type=task)
```

Only goal or softgoal dependencies between the joint manager roles

```
∀ jmpri:JointManagerPrivInterf,  jmpui: JointManagerPubInterf,
  dep: Dependency((dep.depender=jmpri ∧ dep.dependee=jmpui) →
    (dep.type=goal ∨ dep.type=softgoal))
```

Partners only have relationships with other partners or the joint manager private interface

```
∀ dep: Dependency,  p1: Partner
 ((dep.depender=p1 ∨ dep.dependee=p1) →
  ((∃p2: Partner(p1≠p2 ∧ (dep.depender=p2 ∨ dep.dependee=p2))) ∨
   (∃jmpi: JointManagerPrivInterf
    ((dep.depender=jmpi ∨ dep.dependee= jmpi))))
```

The joint manager private interface only has relationships with the joint manager public interface or partners

```
∀ dep: Dependency,  jmpi: JointManagerPrivInterf
 ((dep.depender=jpmi ∨ dep.dependee=jpmi) →
  ((∃p: Partner((dep.depender=p∨ dep.dependee=p))) ∨
   (∃jmpui: JointManagerPubInterf (
    (dep.depender=jmpui ∨ dep.dependee= jmpui))))
```

4 Evaluation

Patterns can be compared and evaluated with quality attributes [20]. For instance, the following qualities seem particularly relevant for organizational structures [10]:

Coordinativity. Actors must be able to coordinate with other actors to achieve a common purpose or simply their local goals.

Predictability. Actors can have a high degree of autonomy in the way they undertake action and communication in their domains. It can be then difficult to predict individual characteristics as part of determining the behavior of the system-at-large.

Fallibility-Tolerance. A failure of one actor does not necessarily imply a failure of the whole structure. The structure then needs to check the completeness and the accuracy of data, information and transactions. To prevent failure, different actors can, for instance, implement replicated capabilities.

Adaptability. Actors must be able to adapt to changes in their environment. They may allow changes to the component's communication protocol, dynamic introduction of a new kind of component previously unknown or manipulations of existing actors.

The ***structure-in-5*** improves *coordinativity* among actors by differentiating the data hierarchy - the support actor – from the control hierarchy - supported by the operational core, technostructure, middle agency and strategic apex. The existence of three different levels of abstraction (1 – Operational Core; 2 – Technostructure, Middle Line and Support; 3 – Strategic Apex) addresses the need for managing *predictability*. Besides, higher levels are more abstract than lower levels: lower levels only involve resources and task dependencies while higher ones propose intentional (goals and softgoals) relationships. Checks and control mechanisms can be integrated at different levels of abstraction assuming redundancy from different perspectives and increase considerably *failability-tolerance*. Since the structure-in-5 separates data and control hierarchies, integrity of these two hierarchies can also be verified independently. The structure-in-5 separates independently the typical components of an organization, isolating them from each other and allowing then dynamic *adaptability*. But since it is restricted to no more than 5 major components, more refinement has to take place inside the components.

The ***joint venture*** supports *coordinativity* in the sense that each partner actor interacts via the joint manager for strategic decisions. Partners indicate their interest, and the joint manager either returns them the strategic information immediately or mediates the request to some other partners. However, since partners are usually heterogeneous, it could be a drawback to define a common interaction background. The central position and role of the joint manager is a means for resolving conflicts and preventing *unpredictability*. Through its joint manager, the joint-venture proposes a central communication controller. It is less clear how the joint venture style addresses *fallibility-tolerance*, notably *reliability*. However, exceptions, supervision, and monitoring can improve its overall score with respect to these qualities. Manipulation of partners can be done easily to *adapt* the structure by registering new ones to the joint manager. However, since partners can also exchange resources directly with each other, existing dependencies should be updated as well. The joint manager cannot be removed due to its central position.

Table 1 summarizes the strengths and weaknesses of the reviewed styles.

Table 1. Strengths and Weaknesses of some Organizational Patterns

	Coord.	Predict.	Failab-Tol.	Adapt.
S-in-5	+	+	++	+-
Joint-Vent.	+-	+	+-	+-

A more precise and systematic analysis of these quality attributes can be done with goal-oriented frameworks such as KAOS [5] or the NFR framework [4]. In the NFR framework, qualities are represented as *softgoals*. Analyzing them amounts to a means-ends decomposition of softgoals into more fine-grained subgoals. Each pattern contributes positively/negatively to some of the identified subgoals. The overall evaluation of a pattern with respect to a quality is arrived at by propagating contributions from bottom towards the top of a softgoal dependency graph. A partial example of such a graph is shown in Figure 8.

The analysis resulting in a softgoal dependency graph is intended to make explicit the space of alternatives for fulfilling a top-level attribute. The organizational patterns are represented as operationalized attributes (saying, roughly, "fulfilled by the pattern *structure-in-5 / joint-venture*").

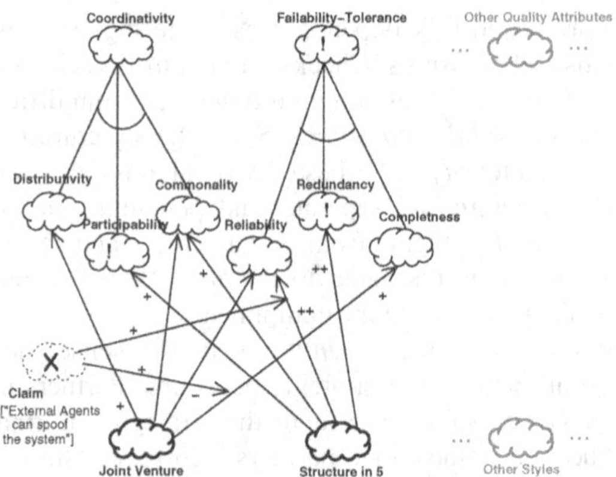

Fig. 8. Partial Evaluation for Organizational Styles

The evaluation process is defined in terms of contribution relationships from softgoals to softgoals, labeled "+", "++", "-", "--" that mean respectively *partially satisfied*, *satisfied*, *partially denied* and *denied*. Design rationale is represented by claims drawn as dashed clouds. Such features make it possible for domain characteristics such as priorities to be considered and properly reflected in the decision-making process. Exclamation marks are used to mark priority attributes while a check-mark "✓ " indicates a fulfilled softgoal and a cross " X" labels a denied one.

Relationships types (AND, OR, ++, +, -, and --) between quality attributes are formalized to offer a tractable proof procedure. To each quality attribute we associate two different variables: S for satisfiability and D for deniability. These variables can assume three possible values: *null* (–) , *partial* (*p*), and *total* (*t*). For instance, when S=*t*, an attribute is totally satisfied, when S=*p* it is partially satisfied, and when S=– there is no evidence to say something about its satisfiability (analogously for D).

S and D are not required to be logically exclusive since there may be contradictory contributions, e.g., for a particular pattern, a softgoal is satisfied and partially denied at the same time. Table 2 shows propagation rules for ++, +, -, and -- relationships with respect to satisfiability (S). Notice that the null value does not produce any effect in the propagation. A dual table is given for the deniability and the partial deniability.

Table 2. Propagation rules for Satisfiability

S	++	+	-	--
t	S=*t*	S=*p*	D=*p*	D=*t*
p	S=*p*	S=*p*	D=*p*	D=*p*

Under the assumption that $- < p < t$, we use min-value and max-value functions respectively for AND and OR relationships. The basic algorithm for the labels propagation is presented in Figure 9.

Initially, all the nodes are initialized with the available evidence, a null value is assigned to the nodes for which we do not have evidence. At each step the value of the two variables S and D of each node is calculated using the nodes' value of the previous step. The final value for D and S is given by the maximum value of all contributions of the incoming relations. The algorithm terminates when an iteration adds no new values to any the variables of any node of the graph. The use of maximum value function guarantees the termination of the algorithm. Further details about this propagation algorithm are presented in [11].

```
 Initialize NODES'
 do
 NODES ← NODES'
foreach node n_i
  foreach incoming relation A_ij
    D_j ← ComputeD(A_ij)
    S_j ← ComputeS(A_ij)
 n_i.D' ← Max_j(D_j)
 n_i.S' ← Max_j(S_j)
while(NODES≠NODES')
```

Fig. 9. Basic propagation algorithm

5 Conclusions

Modelers need to rely on patterns, styles, and idioms, to build their models, whatever the purpose. We argue that, as with other phases of software development, early requirements analysis can be facilitated by the adoption of organizational patterns. This paper focuses on two such patterns and studies them in detail, through examples, a formalization using Formal Tropos, and an evaluation with respect to desirable attributes.

There have been many proposals for software patterns since the original work on design patterns [9]. Some of this work focuses on requirements patterns. For example, [16] proposes a set of requirements patterns for embedded software systems. These patterns are represented in UML and cover both structural and behavioral aspects of a requirements specification. Along similar lines, [7] proposes some general patterns in UML. In both cases, the focus is on late requirements, and the modeling language used is UML. On a different path, [12] proposes a systematic approach for evaluating design patterns with respect to non-functional requirements (e.g., security, performance, reliability). Our approach differs from this work primarily in the fact that our proposal is founded on ideas from Organization Theory and Strategic Alliances literature. In [13, 15, 10], we have already described organizational patterns but to be used for designing multi-agent system architectures. Considering real world organizations as a metaphor, systems involving many software actors, such as multi-agent systems could benefit from the same organizational models. In the present paper, we have focused on patterns for modeling organizational settings, rather than software systems and emphasized the need for organizational abstractions to better match the operational environment of the system-to-be during early requirements analysis.

References

[1] A. I. Anton, "Goal-Based Requirements Analysis", *Proceedings of the 2nd Int. Conf. On Requirements Analysis, ICRE'96*, 1996, pp.136–144.

[2] S. Bennett, S. McRobb, and R. Farmer. *Object-Oriented Systems Analysis and Design – using UML.* McGraw Hill, 1999.

[3] J. Castro, M. Kolp and J. Mylopoulos. "Towards Requirements-Driven Information Systems Engineering: The Tropos Project". In *Information Systems* (27), Elsevier, Amsterdam, The Netherlands, 2002.

[4] L. K. Chung, B. A. Nixon, E. Yu and J. Mylopoulos. *Non-Functional Requirements in Software Engineering*, Kluwer Publishing, 2000.

[5] A. Dardenne, A. van Lamsweerde, and S. Fickas, "Goal–directed Requirements Acquisition", *Science of Computer Programming, 20*, 1993, pp. 3–50.

[6] P. Dussauge and B. Garrette, *Cooperative Strategy: Competing Successfully Through Strategic Alliances*, Wiley and Sons, 1999.

[7] Fowler, M., *Analysis Patterns: Reusable Object Models*, Addison-Wesley, 1997.

[8] A. Fuxman, M. Pistore, J. Mylopoulos, and P. Traverso. "Model Checking Early Requirements Specification in Tropos". In *Proc. of the 5th Int. Symposium on Requirements Engineering, RE'01*, Toronto, Canada, Aug. 2001.

[9] E. Gamma, R. Helm, R. Johnson, J. Vlissides, *Design Patterns: Elements of reusable Object-Oriented Software*, Addison-Wesley, 1995.

[10] P. Giorgini, M. Kolp, and J. Mylopoulos. "Multi-Agent and Software Architecture: A Comparative Case Study". In *Proceedings of the 3rd International Workshop on Agent Software Engineering* (AOSE'02), Bologna, Italy, July 2002.

[11] P. Giorgini, J. Mylopoulos, E. Nicchiarelli, and R. Sebastiani. Reasoning with Goal Models. In Proceedings of the 21st International Conference on Conceptual Modeling (ER02), LNCS 2503 Springer Verlag. Tampere, Finland, October, 2002,

[12] D. Gross and E. Yu, "From Non-Functional Requirements to Design Through Patterns", *Requirements Engineering 6(1)*, 18–36, 2002.

[13] M. Kolp, P. Giorgini and J. Mylopoulos. "A Goal-Based Organizational Perspective on Multi-Agents Architectures". In *Proc. of the 8th Int. Workshop on Intelligent Agents: Agent Theories, Architectures, and Languages* (ATAL2001), Seattle, USA, August 2001.

[14] M. Kolp, P. Giorgini, and J. Mylopoulos. "Information Systems Development through Social Structures". In *Proceedings of the 14th International Conference on Software Engineering and Knowledge Engineering* (SEKE'02), Ishia, Italy, July 2002.

[15] M. Kolp, P. Giorgini, and J. Mylopoulos. "Organizational Multi-Agent Architecture: A Mobile Robot Example". In *Proceedings of the 1st International Conference on Autonomous Agent and Multi Agent Systems* (AAMAS'02), Bologna, Italy, July 2002.

[16] Konrad, S., and Cheng, B., "Requirements Patterns for Embedded Systems", *Proceedings of the Tenth IEEE Joint International Requirements Engineering Conference* (RE'02), Essen, September 2002.

[17] H. Mintzberg, *Structure in fives:designing effective organizations*, Prentice-Hall, 1992

[18] J. Morabito, I. Sack and A. Bhate. *Organization Modeling : Innovative Architectures for the 21st Century*, Upper Saddle River, N.J., Prentice Hall PTR, 1999.

[19] W. R. Scott. *Organizations: rational, natural, and open systems*, Prentice Hall, 1998.

[20] Shaw, M., and Garlan, D. *Software Architecture: Perspectives on an Emerging Discipline*, Upper Saddle River, N.J., Prentice Hall, 1996.

[21] M.Y. Yoshino and U. Srinivasa Rangan. *Strategic alliances: an entrepreneurial approach to globalization*, Boston, Mass., Harvard Business School Press, 1995.

[22] E. Yu. Modeling *Strategic Relationships for Process Reengineering*, Ph.D. thesis, Department of Computer Science, University of Toronto, Canada, 1995.

Evolving Requirements through Coordination Contracts

Ana Moreira[1], José Luiz Fiadeiro[2], and Luís Andrade[3]

[1] Dept. Informatics, Faculty of Sciences and Technology, New University of Lisbon, 2829-516 Caparica, Portugal
amm@di.fct.unl.pt

[2] Department of Mathematics and Computer Science, University of Leicester Leicester LE1 7RH, United Kingdom
jose@fiadeiro.org

[3] ATX Software S.A., Alam. António Sérgio 7–1C, 2795-023 Linda-a-Velha, Portugal
landrade@atxsoftware.com

Abstract. Use-case driven software development processes can seriously compromise the ability of systems to evolve if a careful distinction is not made between "structure" and "use", and this distinction is not reflected immediately in the first model and carried through to the implementation. By "structure", we are referring to what derives from the nature of the application domain, i.e. to what are perceived to be the "invariants" or core concepts of the business domain, as opposed to the business rules that apply at a given moment and determine the way the system (solution) will be used.

This paper shows how the notion of coordination contract can be used to support the separation between structure and use at the level of system models, and how this separation supports the evolution of requirements on "use" based on the revision or addition of use cases, with minimal impact on the "structure" of the system.

1 Introduction

Use cases as introduced by Jacobson [11] and incorporated into the UML [3] play a fundamental role in object-oriented system development: they provide a description of the way the system is required to interact with external users. Existing proposals for a software development based on the UML are use case driven. It is not difficult to understand why. Given that the ultimate goal is to produce software that fulfils the expectations of the prospective users, driving the process based on user needs seems to make good sense.

However, our own experience in developing software using object-oriented methods has revealed that this approach is not without dangers. A use-case driven process can compromise the ability of the system to evolve if a careful distinction is not made between "structure" and "use", and this distinction is not reflected immediately in the

J. Eder and M. Missikoff (Eds.): CAiSE 2003, LNCS 2681, pp. 633–646, 2003.

first model and carried through to the implementation. By "structure", we are not referring to the architecture of the solution but what derives from the nature of the application domain, i.e. to what are perceived to be the "invariants" or core concepts of the business domain, as opposed to the business rules that apply at a given moment and determine the way the system will be used.

The high degree of volatility of most application domains makes this distinction between core concepts and business rules a fundamental one. Time-to-market, and other business constraints dictated by the fierce competition that characterise the business activities of today, require that information systems be able to accommodate new business rules with minimal impact on the core services that are already implemented.

We believe that use-cases play a fundamental role in software development. However, we must be able to separate core entities from volatile business rules in the initial requirements analysis activity, and ensure that is evolution, and not construction, that is use-case driven. Such a process will be better shaped for supporting continuity and robustness to changes in the business domain. Hence our purpose in this paper is to use a new semantic primitive – coordination contract – for structure to be separated from use, and for evolution to become use-case centred.

The rest of this paper is organised as follows. In Section 2 we set the scenes of the problem we want to discuss by modelling a case study in a traditional way. In Section 3 we initiate a discussion about evolution and show why existing object-oriented approaches are not evolutionary. In Section 4 we give a brief overview of coordination contracts as a semantic primitive. In Section 5 we illustrate how contracts can be used to cope with changes in the business rules. In Section 6 we relate coordination contracts with other work. Finally, in Section 7 we draw some conclusions.

2 Capturing Requirements through Use Cases

2.1 Use Case Driven Approach: An Overview

Use cases, together with a use case driven approach to software development, were first introduced by Jacobson [11] and then adopted by the UML [3]. Since then, use case modelling has become a popular and widely used technique for capturing and describing functional requirements of a software system. It is also used as a technique for bridging the gap between descriptions that are meaningful to software users and descriptions that contain sufficient details for modelling and constructing a software system.

A use case model is represented by a use case diagram and use case descriptions. The diagram provides an overview of actors and use cases, and their interactions. The use cases' descriptions detail the functional requirements. An actor is anything that interfaces with the system. Some examples are people, other software, hardware devices, data stores or networks. Each actor assumes a role in a given use case. A use case represents an interaction between an actor and the system, i.e. it describes the outwardly visible requirements of a system. Use cases are recommended as a primary artefact and contribute to analysis, design as well as planning, estimating, testing and documentation. In addition, a use case model will often be part of a contract between the development organization and the customer regarding the functional requirements of the system to be developed. The quality of the use case model therefore has a large impact on the quality of the rest of the project.

Identifying and describing the user requirements should be accomplished in a systematic way. After building the use case model we can then draw interaction diagrams to describe the use cases' behavioural part. As new objects are found during this process we can start constructing a class diagram.

2.2 The Toll Collection System Case Study

In order to illustrate modelling and further evolution of requirements, let us use a simplified version of the toll collection system implemented in Portugal [5].

> "In a road traffic pricing system, drivers of authorised vehicles are charged at tollgates automatically. The tolls are placed at special lanes called green lanes. For that, a driver has to install a device (a gizmo) in his/her vehicle. The registration of authorised vehicles includes the owner's personal data, bank account number and vehicle details.
>
> Gizmos are read by the tollgate sensors. The information read is stored by the system and used to debit the respective accounts.
>
> When an authorised vehicle passes through a green lane, a green light is turned on, and the amount being debited is displayed. If an unauthorised vehicle passes through it, a yellow light is turned on and a camera takes a photo of the vehicle's licence plate.
>
> There are green lanes where the same type of vehicles pay a fixed amount (e.g. at a toll bridge), and ones where the amount depends on the type of the vehicle and the distance travelled (e.g. on a motorway)."

Looking at who will get information from the system and who will provide it with information helps identifying the following actors:

- Vehicle owner: this is responsible for registering a vehicle;
- Vehicle gizmo: this comprehends the vehicle and the gizmo installed on it;
- Bank: this represents the entity that holds the vehicle owner's account;
- System clock: represents the internal clock of the system that periodically triggers the calculation of debits.

Asking what are the main tasks of each actor helps identifying use cases. For the actors identified we have the use cases listed below and depicted in Figure 1:

- Register vehicle: is triggered by "vehicle owner"; it is responsible for registering a vehicle and its owner, and communicate with the bank to guarantee a good account;
- Pass single toll: is triggered by "vehicle gizmo"; it is responsible for dealing with tolls where vehicles pay a fixed amount. It reads the vehicle gizmo and checks on whether it is a good one. If the gizmo is ok the light is turned green, and the amount to be paid is calculated and displayed. If the gizmo is not ok, the light is turned yellow and a photo is taken.

- Enter motorway: is triggered by "vehicle gizmo"; it checks the gizmo, turns on the light and registers an entrance. If the gizmo is invalid, a photo is taken.
- Exit motorway: is triggered by "vehicle gizmo"; it checks the gizmo and if the vehicle has an entrance, turns on the light accordingly, calculates the amount to be paid (as a function of the distance travelled), displays it and records this passage. If the gizmo is not ok, or if the vehicle did not enter in a green lane, the light is turned yellow and a photo is taken.
- Pay bill: is triggered periodically by "system clock"; it sums up all passages for each vehicle, issues a debit to be sent to the bank and a copy to the vehicle owner.

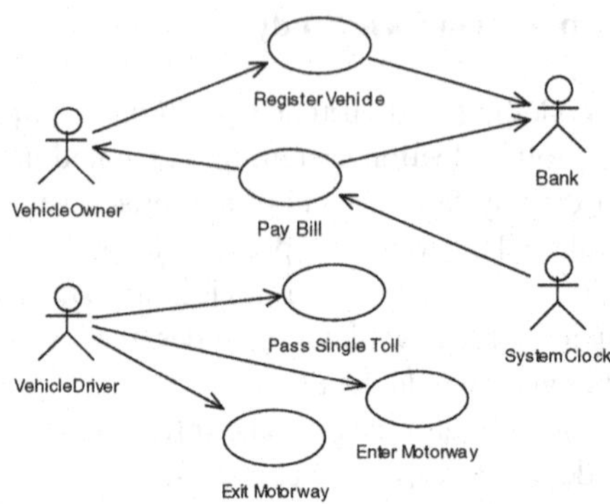

Fig. 1. The use case diagram of the road pricing system

The actors are linked to the use cases through association relationships. The arrow indicates the communication path between an actor and a use case.

The behaviour of each use case can be better defined in a set of interaction diagrams. We favour sequence diagrams, for their simplicity and because it is easier to see the temporal order of the messages. Each message on a sequence diagram corresponds to an operation on a class. So that sequence diagrams are not too complex, we build sequence diagrams to show scenarios, that is, an individual story of a transaction. For the three main use cases `PassSingleToll`, `EnterMotorway` and `ExitMotorway`, we can identify at least two scenarios for each one; one to deal with authorised vehicles and another to deal with non-authorised vehicles. Figure 2 depicts the sequence diagram for an authorised vehicle passing a single toll. (Other scenarios can be drawn in a similar way).

3 Supporting Requirements Modelling and Evolution

To promote understandability and reusability and to support requirements evolution, the models that we develop, as well as the design solutions that we derive from them, should provide mechanisms that help us to guarantee separation of concerns at different levels. This section shows what can be achieved using UML.

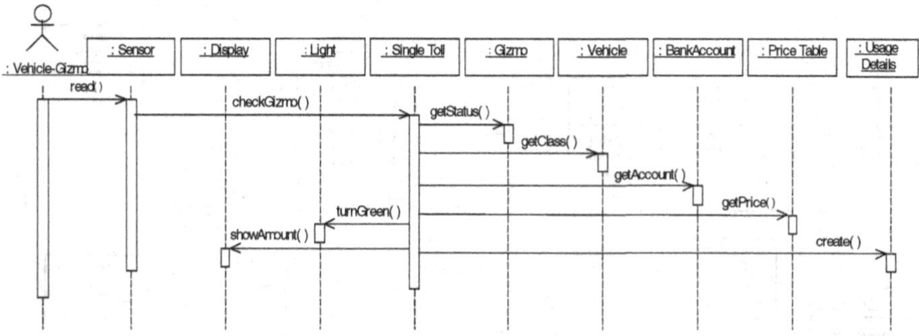

Fig. 2. A sequence diagram for the primary scenario Pass Single Toll

3.1 Building a Class Diagram

In UML we can use different kinds of objects to deal with different categories of information and behaviour. For example, an interface, or boundary, object should only be responsible for defining the structure of the interactions between the environment and the system. The interface object `SingleToll`, depicted in Figure 2, also controls the application, i.e. it is the system's decision maker. It is this object that decides what to do if the vehicle is an unauthorized one, for example. This makes the end system less reusable and understandable, compromising maintainability and making requirements evolution difficult to achieve.

Control objects, as proposed by Jacobson, can solve part of this problem [11]. They provide a means to separate interfacing responsibilities, from the basic system's entities and from functionalities that are hard to distribute among interface and entity objects. Interface objects can then be concerned only with the interactions with the outside world, while control objects drive the application, centralizing the responsibility of coordinating the set of tasks necessary to perform an use case. (And entity objects deal with the core concepts of the problem domain, of course.) Changes in the way actors interact with the system will then just affect the interfaces and the system's functionality does not need to be touched.

Control objects are transient objects that are instantiated to perform a single action, usually being the coordination of several other actions on server (entity) objects, and are destroyed when that action ends. They can be used when the functionality of the use case requires processing information from several objects and this includes decision points where the next alternative to be executed has to be chosen. Therefore, when in a sequence diagram the coordination task is being given to an interface object, as in Figure 2, a control object (in this case `SingleTollProcessor`) should be introduced between `SingleToll` and `Gizmo` to deal with that. Such an approach would result in adding five control objects to our class diagram (see Figure 3). Notice that the dashed arrows represent typical interactions needed to handle the behaviour described in the use cases.

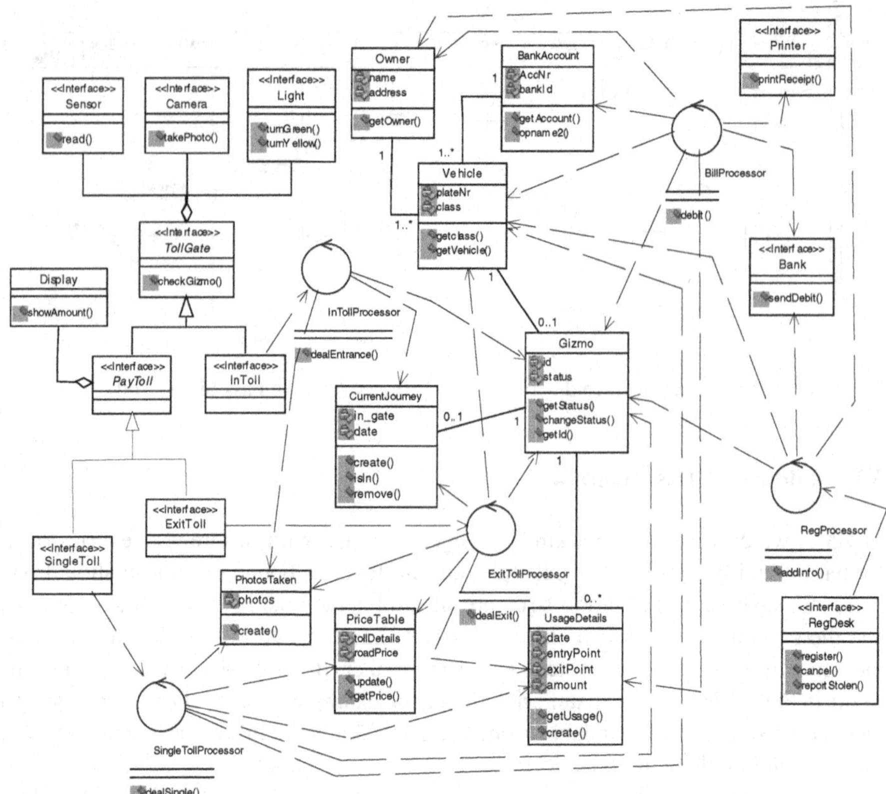

Fig. 3. Class diagram for the road pricing system

3.2 Dealing with Evolving Requirements

Control objects help to derive a good structural model for the system from the use-case analysis, but are they able to deal with the evolution of requirements that derive from new or different ways of using the system? Evolving requirements that reflect changes occurring at the level of business rules should not affect the entities that model the core concepts of the application domain. This cannot be achieved simply using control objects, as these objects are static, i.e. they cannot be reconfigured dynamically. A mechanism to support evolution should allow us to change the business rules without obliging us to change the core concepts already implemented.

To illustrate the problems raised by evolving requirements lets imagine that the owner of the system decides to offer a new set of packages to the users of the already modelled road pricing system.

"Certain public resources have physical limitations. For example, highways and bridges have a limited capacity for free-flowing traffic beyond which traffic congestion dramatically reduces the capacity for traffic flow. Several proposals for differential pricing seek to provide a monetary incentive for drivers to use such limited resources during off-peak hours so alleviating the problems of congestion. In practice, peak hour tolls or other user charges are set at a higher price than the price for off-peak usage. The larger price differential the greater the incentive for a change in driver habits. In this way the differential becomes a variable that can be changed depending on factors that influence the demand for road or bridge facilities, such as season of the year, popular holidays, weekends, etc. Additionally, a differential can be set to discriminate between users based on social factors, such as setting lower rates for health care vehicles, fire engines, handicapped drivers."

These requirements suggest two new use cases, one to deal with the special vehicles package and another to deal with the peak hour traffic package.

In a traditional approach, we must modify the already modelled classes, or even add new classes, to incorporate the new functionality into the system. Let us analyse the changes needed to handle peak hour traffic. In a typical classroom solution the condition `isPeakHour` would be declared on `PriceTable` as a precondition on `getPrice()`. Having the new business rule "hardwired" to `PriceTable` does not seem a very good strategy, for when the owner of the system comes up with a new price-package for customers, other changes will need to be made.

A naïve solution to adapt the existing system to the new business rule would be to enrich `PriceTable` with the new operation `getPeakHourPrice()`. Besides requiring obvious and direct changes to the class `PriceTable`, this solution is also intrusive on the client side because the client classes now have to decide on which operation to call. A further disadvantage of this solution is in the fact that the "business rule" is completely coded in the way the client class calls the price table and, thus, cannot be "managed" explicitly as a business notion.

The typical object-oriented solution to this new situation consists in defining a subclass `PeakHourPriceTable` with new attributes defining the peak hour periods. The operation `getPrice()` would have to be redefined so that the price is calculated according to a new rule. Nevertheless, there are two main drawbacks in this solution: (1) it introduces, in the conceptual model, classes that have no counterpart in the real problem domain (it is time of the day that may be "peak hour", not the price table); (2) this solution is still intrusive because the other classes in the system need to be made aware of the existence of the new specialised class so that links between instances can be established through the new class.

Dealing with special vehicles package would require similar changes in `PriceTable`, but also the creation of a new association class between classes `Vehicle` and `Owner` to establish the set of people driving special vehicles. In this case, the solution would affect even more the components in the system and, as before, is still intrusive as all the existing components have to be made aware that the new association class has become available.

The above two new business packages would oblige us to change the analysis models, the designs, and, of course, compile the corresponding code in an already implemented system. What would be interesting is to deal with new business rules without having to change an existing solution.

What we propose is to have two different kinds of concepts to handle evolution:

- classes of objects (e.g. Vehicle and Owner) that correspond to core business entities that are relatively stable in the sense that the organisation would normally prefer not to touch them;
- business products (e.g. special deals for off-peak usage) that may change according to the business policies of the organization.

Ideally, the business products should be added or removed from the system without requiring modifications in the core objects already implemented.

4 Coordination Contracts

Coordination contracts are the mechanism that will help achieving the dynamic evolution we have been arguing for. They provide simple modelling mechanisms, encapsulating all the design issues regarding dynamic reconfiguration of the system. Therefore the model is focused only on the rules that may change the behaviour of an existing system.

The notion of coordination contract was proposed in [1] for representing explicitly, as first class citizens, the rules that determine the way object interaction needs to be coordinated to satisfy business requirements. Our perception has been that this information is too often dispersed between the different diagrams that support models in the UML, both static and dynamic. For instance, a class diagram may contain associations whose only purpose is to provide the relationships that are necessary for given objects to be coordinated. The specific rules that enforce the required coordination may be found coded in one or more interaction diagrams, for instance in terms of message sequencing, or in state machines for controlling the operations being coordinated. The end result is that this dispersion makes it difficult for these interactions to be changed when new business requirements have to be added or old ones need to be modified.

Contracts allow for such coordination mechanisms to figure explicitly in class diagrams as special association classes whose semantics is similar to that of connectors in software architectures. A coordination contract (or, for simplicity, just "contract") consists, essentially, of a collection of role classes (the partners in the contract) and the prescription of the coordination effects (the glue in the terminology of software architectures) that will be superposed on the partners to coordinate their joint behaviour.

As a semantic primitive, coordination contracts are basically independent of any conceptual modelling approach in the same sense as, say, entities, associations or attributes are. The general form of a contract is:

```
contract <name>
   partners <list-of-participants>
   invariant <invariant properties>
   constants <local constants>
   attributes <local attributes>
   operations <local methods>
   coordination <coordination rules>
end contract
```

A contract has a name, a list of partners (the objects whose interactions we may want to coordinate), describe the invariant properties that the partners of the contract have to satisfy, a list of local constants, attributes and operations that may be useful to help specify the coordination mechanisms and, finally, the coordination section under which we describe the behaviour to be superposed. Each interaction under "coordination" has the form:

```
when <event>
  with <guard>
do <reaction>
```

The condition under "when" establishes the trigger of the interaction. Typical triggers are the occurrence of actions or state changes in the partners. The "do" clause identifies the reactions to be performed, usually in terms of actions of the partners and some of the contract's own actions. Together with the trigger, the reactions of the partners constitute what we call the synchronisation set associated with the interaction. Finally, the "with" clause puts further constraints on the actions involved in the interaction, typically further preconditions.

The intuitive semantics of contracts can be summarised as follows:

- Contracts are added to a system by identifying the instances of the partner classes to which they apply; these instances may belong to subclasses of the partners. The actual mechanism of identifying the instances that will instantiate the partners and superposing the contract is outside the scope of the paper. This can be achieved directly as in languages for reconfigurable distributed systems [13], or implicitly by declaring the conditions that define the set of those instances.
- Contracts are superposed on the partners taken as black-boxes: the partners in the contract are not even aware that they are being coordinated by a third party. In a client-supplier mode of interaction, instead of interacting with a mediator that then delegates execution on the supplier, the client calls directly the supplier; however, the contract "intercepts" the call and superposes whatever forms of behaviour are prescribed; this means that it is not possible to bypass the coordination being imposed through the contract because the calls are intercepted.
- The same transparency applies to all other clients of the same supplier: no changes are required on the other interactions that involve either partner in the contract. Hence, contracts may be added, modified or deleted without any need for the partners, or their clients, to be modified as a consequence.
- The interaction clauses in a contract identify points of rendez-vous in which actions of the partners and of the contract itself are synchronised; the resulting synchronisation set is guarded by the conjunction of the guards of the actions in the set and requires the execution of all the actions in the set.
- The effect of superposing a contract is cumulative; because the superposition of the contract consists, essentially, of synchronous interactions, different contracts may apply simultaneously to the same partners for the same trigger, which means that the synchronisation set that is going to be executed as a reaction to the trigger consists of the union of the synchronisation sets of the applicable triggers. Furthermore, the resulting synchronisation set is guarded by the conjunction of the guards of the

individual synchronisation sets. Determining which contracts should apply in which states (of a system) is another matter, one that relates to the management of the evolution of the system, not to its computational behaviour. We are currently developing a language for addressing such aspects, which relates to existing proposals for dynamic reconfiguration of distributed systems and software architectures [13].

Coordination contracts can be represented in UML as a new stereotype <<contract>> of classifier whose icon is the scroll symbol. Figure 4 shows the idea, with a simplified example taken from our case study.

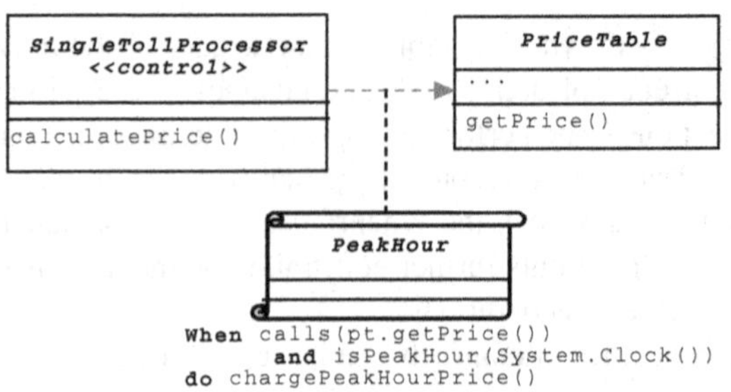

Fig. 4. PeakHour contract

A contract is a persistent entity that, through the *when* clause, intercepts interactions with the partners or detects events in the partners to which it has to react. In our example, whenever `SingleTollProcessor` calls `getPrice()` in `PriceTable` the contract `PeakHour` intercepts the call and if the time is within a peak hour period, it superposes a different way to calculate the price to be charged.

Notice that contracts do not define classes, with public properties. They do not offer services; instead, they coordinate services provided by the core classes.

5 Evolving with Coordination Contracts

The purpose of coordination contracts is to provide mechanisms that allow business rules to be added or removed from a system without affecting what is already specified and implemented. The two new use cases can be modelled through contracts, one for each use case, as shown below. As a contract details the business rules of a use case, changes in the use case only imply changes in the contract. Since contracts can be dynamically added and removed from a system, changes in the requirements are easily propagated to a solution.

The contract `PeakHour` is responsible for coordinating peak hour traffic and the contract `SpecialVehicle` coordinates the prices for special vehicles. We can complement the class diagram with a scroll symbol for each contract (and a note describing the trigger, the condition, if any, and the actions to be superposed). For example, as `PeakHour` intercepts calls to the operation `getPrice()`, we can "hang" the new symbol on the dependencies (dashed arrows) reaching PriceTable (see Fig. 4).

The full specification of `PeakHour` contract is:

```
contract PeakHour
   partners pt: PriceTable;
   constants peakCharge: Float:= 0.5;
             t1am: Time:= 7; t2am: Time:= 9;
             t1pm: Time:= 17; t2pm: Time:= 19;
   operations
      ?isPeakHour(t: Time): Bool :=
         (t>t1am and t<t2am) or (t>t1pm and t<t2pm)
   coordination
   peakHour:
      when calls(pt.getPrice(classVehicle,local)) and
            isPeakHour(System.clock())
      do {return(pt.getPrice(classVehicle,local)* (1 +
                  peakCharge))}
end contract
```

In our example, `PeakHour` defines several constants and the operation `isPeak-Hour()` that will be used in the *when* clause to select the subset of interactions to `PriceTable` that will be intercepted. If a vehicle uses a tollgate during peak hours, the contract will coordinate the behaviour superposing a different algorithm to calculate the amount to be paid. Otherwise, if the vehicle uses the system during off-peak hours, the price paid is the regular one and the contract will have no effect. Notice that the core classes previously modelled are seen as black boxes. As we said before, they do not know that their interactions are being intercepted and coordinated by a third party, which implies that they do not have to be modified.

The interactions established through contracts are atomic, i.e. the synchronisation set determined by each coordination entry of the contract is executed as a transaction. In particular, the object that calls `PriceTable` will not know what kind of coordination is being superposed. From its point of view, it is `PriceTable` that is being called.

`SpecialVehicle` contract is specified as follows:

```
contract SpecialVehicle
  partners st: SingleToll; et: ExitToll; v: Vehicle;
           g: Gizmo; pt: PriceTable;
  constants discount: Float:= 0.2;
  attributes p: Integer; special: Boolean;
  coordination
  VIVehicles:
      when(calls(st.checkGizmo(id)) or
           calls(et.checkGizmo(id) and special)
         local g:= Gizmo.getById(id);
      do
      {if g.getStatus() then
         p:= pt.getPrice(v.getClass(id),local)*
            (1-discount);
         st.Light.turnGreen();
         st.Display.showAmount(p);
         st.usageDetails.create(local,System.date(),p);
```

```
else st.Light.turnYellow();
          st.photosTaken.create(st.Camera.takePhoto());}
end contract
```

As only a subset of vehicles can benefit from a lower price, interactions are intercepted earlier than in the previous contract. Now we intercept calls, triggered by (special) vehicles, sent by pay tolls to the corresponding control objects and superpose a different behaviour. As we can see, when a contract is put "over" a control object superposing its single operation behaviour, the end result is replacing the control object in some situations. In a situation where we are developing a system for the first time, we propose to scrap control objects and use coordination contracts instead. This means that in our class diagram, each control object would be substituted by a regular coordination contract where the partners would be the classes with dependencies to that object.

We have not yet included in the specification the conditions under which a vehicle subscribes a given contract. This is left to the "coordination context" through which we can configure the system by using the services it makes available [2]. For example, for a vehicle to subscribe the `SpecialVehicle` contract the coordination context must offer the service `subscribeSpecialVehicle()`, as follows:

```
Coordination context Vehicle (v: Vehicle)
  workspace
     component types SingleToll; ExitToll; Vehicle;
                     Gizmo; PriceTable
     contract types SpecialVehicle;
      ...
     services
        subscribeSpecialVehicle(g: Gizmo, s: Special):
           pre exist v and v.owns(g)
           post exists'SpecialVehicle(any,any,v,g,any) and
              SpecialVehicle(any,any,v,g,any)'.special=s
end context
```

Each context is "anchored" to a component or set of components. In this example the anchor is a vehicle instance. The workspace section lists the component and contract types involved in that context. The services are specified in terms of their pre and post conditions. When instantiating the contract, its partners have to be instantiated as well. In our example we use the keyword **any** to signify that this contract is valid for all objects of the type of the corresponding partner. The service is available to vehicles and its parameters are the gizmo owned by the vehicle and a boolean variable that states if the vehicle is special.

As `PeakHour` contract is valid for all vehicles, this means that special vehicles using the system during off-peak hours will get both discounts, resulting in a cumulative effect. In situations where several contracts are superposing conflicting behaviour to the same trigger, we can establish priorities among contracts to define which is the one that performs the superposition.

6 Related Work

What we propose through coordination contracts is a set of modelling primitives to support the development and evolution of software systems. What distinguishes our approach and takes it beyond what object-oriented and component-based methodologies can provide is its separation between computation and coordination. The computation level is concerned with the functionalities of the core entities of the domain while the coordination level is responsible for the volatile business rules that describe how a system is to be used.

For this purpose we brought together concepts and techniques from software architectures (the notion of connector [14]), parallel program design (the notion of superposition (or superimposition) [4, 7, 12]), distributed systems (the notion of techniques for supporting dynamic reconfiguration [13]) and programming languages, which have coined the term "Coordination Languages and Models" (the idea of separating computation from coordination [9]) that are now integrated in the concept of coordination contract. The coordination contracts can be dynamically superposed on the system, i.e. at run-time. The basic idea is to model the collaborations outside the components as coordination contracts that can be applied at run time to coordinate their behaviour.

Other technologies, such as aspect-oriented programming [6] and design patterns [8], also contribute to making software more amenable to change. However, they do this at a lower level of abstraction, at the design or even at the implementation level. What we claim is that we can do that earlier in the software development life cycle, using more abstract, higher level, primitives. Coordination contracts are used at a specification level (and in this paper at a requirements level). A good design can be changed at run-time, but that is more difficult to do, and usually requires a very good understanding of the existing solution. Design patterns, for instance, offer solutions that are too low level to be able to support an evolution process that takes place at the much higher level of abstraction in which business strategies and rules are (re)defined: they are useful for providing the design infrastructure that will support the required levels of adaptability, but they cannot be used for modelling and controlling the evolution process by themselves.

7 Concluding Remarks

We illustrated how coordination contracts can be used for handling requirements evolution, by means of a case study. We started by modelling the requirements using an approach based on the UML and then introduced new requirements to illustrate how contracts can be used to deal with evolution.

Coordination contracts are just a "technology", i.e. a means to an end. How to use these means for the end purpose is another matter, and one that we have not addressed in the paper. Knowing which concepts from the application domain correspond to core entities and which correspond to volatile business rules requires a good deal of expertise that is not necessarily available to everyone. Therefore, we should also work on the requirements engineering methods in a way that this distinction becomes apparent when interacting with the clients. That is, use-case analysis needs to be in a context where the distinction between core entities and business rules is more clearly promoted. We believe that, through coordination contracts, we have the modelling primitive that will allow for this distinction to be enforced. Although we have focused only on modelling, we have already developed an implementation of coordination patterns based on design patterns that can be deployed on current platforms for component-based development like CORBA, EJB and COM [10].

Acknowledgements. We thank M. Wermelinger, J. Gouveia and G. Koutsoukos for insightful discussions during the development of this work.

References

1. Andrade, L.F. and Fiadeiro, J.L.: "Interconnecting Objects via Contracts", in UML'99 – Beyond the Standard, R.France and B.Rumpe (eds), LNCS 1723, Springer Verlag, 1999, pp. 566–583
2. Andrade, L.F., Fiadeiro, J.L. and Wermelinger, M.: "Enforcing Business Policies through Automated Reconfiguration", in 16th Int. Conf. On Automated Software Engineering, IEEE Computer Society Press 2001, 426–429.
3. Booch, G., Rumbaugh, J., and Jacobson, I.: *The Unified Modeling Language User Guide*, Addison-Wesley, 1999
4. Chandy, K. and Misra, J.: *Parallel Program Design – A Foundation*, Addison-Wesley, 1988
5. Clark, R. and Moreira, A.: "Constructing Formal Specifications from Informal Requirements", in proc. Software Technology and Engineering Practice, IEEE Computer Society, Los Alamitos, California, 1997, pp. 68–75
6. Elrad, T., Filman, R., and Bader, A.: "Theme Section on Aspect-Oriented Programming", Communications of ACM, Vol. 44, No. 10, 2001
7. Francez, N. and Forman, I.: *Interacting Processes*, Addison-Wesley, 1996
8. E., Gamma, Helm, R., Johnson, R. and Vlissides, J.: *Design Patterns: Elements of Reusable Object Oriented Software*, Addison-Wesley 1995
9. Gelernter, D. and Carriero, N.: "Coordination Languages and their Significance", Communications ACM 35(2), 1992, pp. 97–107
10. Gouveia, J., Koutsoukos, G., Andrade, L. and Fiadeiro, J., "Tool Support for Coordination-Based Software Evolution", in *Technology of Object-Oriented Languages and Systems – TOOLS 38*, W.Pree (ed), IEEE Computer Society Press 2001, 184–196
11. Jacobson, I.: *Object-Oriented Software Engineering – a Use Case Driven Approach*, Addison-Wesley, Reading Massachusetts, 1992
12. Katz, S.: "A Superimposition Control Construct for Distributed Systems", ACM TOPLAS 15(2), 1993, pp. 337–356
13. Magee, J. and Kramer, J.: "Dynamic Structure in Software Architectures", in 4th Symp. on Foundations of Software Engineering, ACM Press, 1996, pp. 3–14
14. Perry, D. and Wolf, A., "Foundations for the Study of Software Architectures", ACM SIGSOFT Software Engineering Notes, 17(4), 1992, pp. 40–52

Fitting Business Models to System Functionality Exploring the Fitness Relationship

C. Salinesi and Colette Rolland

Centre de Recherche en Informatique
Université Paris 1 – Panthéon Sorbonne
90, rue de Tolbiac 75013 Paris – France
{camille, rolland} @univ-paris1.fr

Abstract. One of the major concerns in Requirements Engineering is to establish that the 'whys' of the system to be developed fit the 'whats' of the delivered system. The aim is to ensure a 'best fit' between organisation needs (whys) and system functionality (whats). However, systems, once developed, undergo changes and it is of prime importance that the changed need and the changed system functionality continue to preserve the 'best fit'. We explore the fitness relationship to reveal its nature and its engineering process. We identify major issues that must be addressed in this process to arrive at the best fit. We also consider the preservation of this relationship in the face of change and discuss some issues specific to this scenario. The results presented are founded in our experience in about a dozen industrial and research European projects.

1 Introduction

Requirements engineering is seen as a way of establishing a relationship between the "whys" and the "whats" of the system under development [Lamsweerde01][Yu01]. The latter deals with the system functionality whereas the former provides its rationale. The "whys" are captured in the *Business Model* (*BM*) whereas the "whats" are available in the *System Functionality Model* (*SFM*). When system development starts from scratch, then establishing the relationship between the "whys" and the "whats" is a means by which requirements engineering ensures that system functionality matches organizational requirements. We refer to the relationship between *BM* and *SFM* as the **fitness relationship** [Potts97]. When the system undergoes a change then, just as there is a fitness relationship between the *As-Is BM* and the *As-Is SFM* reflecting the current state, requirements engineering must ensure the fitness relationship between the *To-Be SFM* and the *To-Be BM* expressing the future state.

In this paper we consider some of the common issues involved in the twin problems of *establishing the fitness relationship* and *preserving it in the face of change*. We will use examples extracted from four European and industrial projects that we have been involved in [Rolland00a][Rolland00b][Rolland01][Rolland03]. These projects considered change management in different change contexts, and the main problem was that of ensuring a proper fit between the *BM* and the *SFM*.

J. Eder and M. Missikoff (Eds.): CAiSE 2003, LNCS 2681, pp. 647–664, 2003.

The broad framework used in this paper is in Fig. 1. It accepts the prevalent view of change as a move from the *As-Is* to the *To-Be* situation [Jackson95]. However, it departs from the traditional view in highlighting the fitness relationship itself and its engineering through the change process.

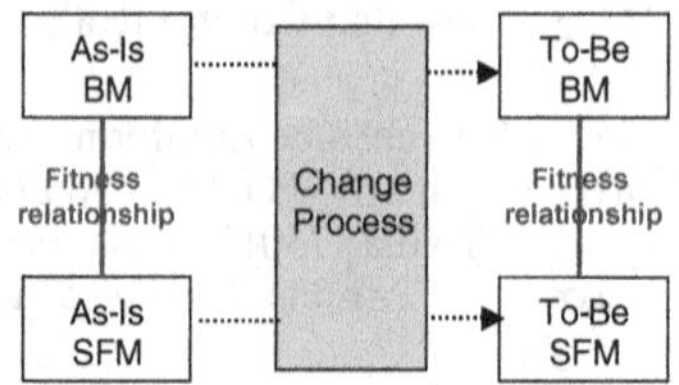

Fig. 1. The broad change framework

Thus, the framework raises two main points of interest: (a) *understanding* the fitness relationship, and (b) *engineering* the fitness relationship.
The former deals with characterizing, conceptualizing, and modeling, the fitness relationship whereas the latter deals with establishing and preserving it in the face of change. Issues relating to (a) above represent the static point of view whereas those of (b) above follow the dynamic viewpoint.

It has been recognized that there is a *conceptual mismatch* between the *SFM* and the *BM* levels [Arsajani01][Alves02]. It is considered necessary to minimize this mismatch. Since the fitness relationship deals with the system as well as the business viewpoints, *modelling the fitness relationship* should provide two faces, one for understanding the system viewpoint and the other for the business viewpoint. Thus, the representation should integrate these two viewpoints suitably. It may be inconvenient to view the fitness relationship as one monolithic flat structure. A layered approach may facilitate understanding. Therefore, in order to present the fitness relationship at different levels of detail, it is necessary to have a *refinement* mechanism as well as a means to control the *quality* of the refinement.

To sum up, it can be surmised that an understanding of the fitness relationship requires a position to be adopted on the following issues

Issue 1: Conceptual mismatch;
Issue 2: Modelling the relationship;
Issue 3: Refining the relationship;
Issue 4: Refinement Quality.

Moving to the engineering aspect, the framework suggests that there are two engineering contexts, with and without the change process. The former corresponds to the case of development from scratch where the fitness relationship has to be freshly established, and the latter which involves the production of the fitness relationship through change. This latter corresponds to the preservation of the fitness relationship. The process of establishing or preserving the fitness relationship necessarily involves the exploration of alternative ways by which elements of the *BM* can be related to one or several elements of the *SFM*. Thus, one common issue to both these contexts is the *exploration* and subsequent selection from a set of alternatives. Thus, we have the fifth issue as follows: **Issue 5**: Exploring alternatives.

Our experience in a wide range of change handling projects shows that change arises in a number of different ways. Each of these can be characterized by a specialization of the framework of Fig. 1. For example, in the case of ERP system customizing, the *As-Is BM* is an *As-Wished* model expressing the business requirements for the *To-Be* situation. The *As-Is SFM* is the *Might-Be Model* expressing the set of functionalities that could be installed in the *To-Be SF*. In this case, the production of the fitness relationship is through a matching process which aim is to find the best fit between the ERP functionality and the wished *BM*.

The next issue in engineering the fitness relationship, namely **Issue 6**, is the *identification of the different engineering classes.* Our experience, suggests that there are four classes :

- Direct change propagation;
- Customization from product family;
- Adaptation of a baseline product; and
- Component assembly.

Each class has its own engineering process. Given the body of opinion which supports modeling of engineering processes, we believe that these four processes have to be modeled and additionally, suitable *guidance* mechanisms should be developed to direct/monitor their enactment.

Despite the diversity of processes, we found some common underlying strategies. The customisation and assembly processes ask for an identification of *similarities* between the old and the new situation whereas direct propagation and adaptation highlight the *differences* between the old and the new. This leads us to believe that there are two strategies underlying these four cases, namely gap driven and match driven strategies.

Thus, we have three issues

Issue 7: Modelling and guiding the engineering process; and

Issue 8: Engineering strategies

In the rest of this paper we consider these eight issues. The next section deals with the four issues that arise in understanding the fitness relationship. Section 3 of the paper considers the four issues of engineering the fitness relationship.

2 Understanding the Fitness Relationship

In this section we consider the four first issues dealing with the understanding and characterization of the fitness relationship.

Issue 1: Conceptual Mismatch

BMs and *SFMs* are typically expressed in different languages. Business models use concepts such as goal, process, actor and role whereas system functionality models deal with objects, operations, events and the like. The distance between these two sets of concepts is referred to by [Arsajani 01] as the "*conceptual mismatch*" between the business and software models. We experienced this issue in ERP installation projects, where we found that ERP experts and organisational stakeholders had difficulty to match each other requirements [Rolland01]. Indeed, the customisation process typically focuses on the ERP functionality and on its customisation. The functionality is expressed in low level details such as data to be maintained and operations to be carried out whereas organisations think in terms of their goals and objectives. This results in a language mismatch between ERP experts and organisation stakeholders. This mismatch exposes the ERP system installation to the danger of failing to meet the requirements of organisations.

One way to obviate this issue is to leverage the functional view to a requirements view and to express both with the *same language*. This shall allow to express the fitness relationship in a more straightforward manner. Goal centred languages seem to be the most adequate to this purpose as they explicitly capture the *why* and *how* of both system functionality and business process [Yu01][Lamsweerde01]. Our experience is based on the use of the *Map* representation system for a *uniform representation of business goals and system functionalities.* A detailed description of the notion of map can be found in [Rolland01]. A brief overview is as follows:

A map is a labelled directed graph (see Fig. 2) with *goals* as nodes and *strategies* as edges between goals. The directed nature of the graph shows which goals can follow which one. An edge enters a node if its strategy can be used to achieve the corresponding goal. Since, there can be multiple edges entering a node, the map is capable of representing the many strategies that can be used for achieving an goal.

A *goal* can be achieved by the performance of a process. Each map has two special goals, *Start* and *Stop*, to start and end the process respectively.

A *strategy* is an approach, a manner to achieve an goal. The strategy S_{ij} characterizes the flow from the source goal G_i to the target goal G_j and the way G_j can be achieved once G_i has been achieved.

A *section* is the key element of a map. It is a triplet $<G_i, G_j, S_{ij}>$ and represents a way to achieve the target goal G_j from the source goal G_i following the strategy S_{ij}. Each section of the map captures the condition to achieve a goal and the specific manner in which the process associated with the target goal can be performed.

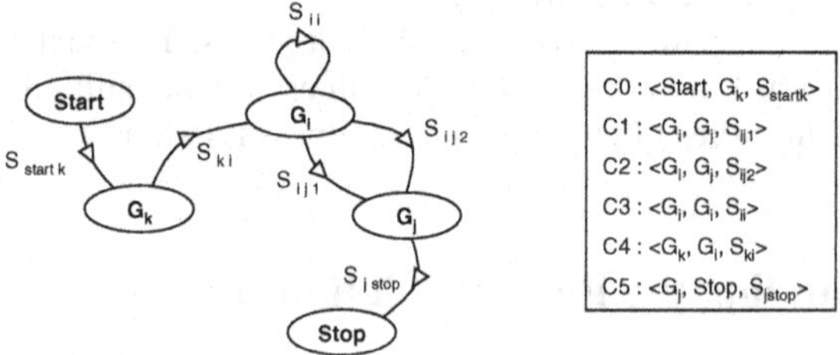

Fig. 2. A map

Sections of a map are *connected* to one another :

(a) when a given goal can be achieved with different strategies. This is represented in the map by several sections between a pair of goals. Such a map topology is called a *multi-thread.*

(b) when a task can be performed by several combinations of strategies. This is represented in the map by a pair of goals connected by several sequences of sections. Such a topology is called a *multi-path.* In general, a map from its *Start* to its *Stop* goals is a multi-path and may contain multi-threads.

As an example, the map of Fig. 2 contains six sections C0 to C5. It can be seen that C1 and C2 together constitute a multi-thread whereas {C4, C1} and {C4, C3, C2} are two paths between G_k and G_j constituting a multi-path.

All the projects which serve as the basis for discussion in this paper used the map representation system as a means to unify the business view and the system functionality view.

Issue 2: Modelling the Relationship

Despite the fact that the fitness relationship is mentioned in many approaches, it is rarely a concept per se. For example, most of recent object oriented methodologies argue in favor of relating business models to software models but adopt a process tracking approach leading to a *loose indirect, coupling* by which a business case is related to a software component through a number of development process steps. The relationship between a use case and a component in Catalysis [D'Souza99] or the RUP [Jacobson99] are examples of such loose coupling.

In contrast goal driven approaches help in establishing a more *direct coupling* as a goal is operationalised in a system functionality. For example, in a goal driven requirements engineering approach such as KAOS [Lamsweerde01] an operationalisable goal is directly related to a system constraint expressed in terms of system objects, actions and events that will contribute to this goal achievement.

Our experience is that in the current prevalent context of rapid change a *direct and strictly defined coupling* is required. This shall facilitate the propagation of a business change onto a system functionality.

This coupling is achieved in the map formalism by *simply relating each section of a map to a system functionality.* Therefore, any section can be regarded from two viewpoints : the *business viewpoint* and the *system viewpoint.* As a result, a map section expresses a direct relationship between a system function and a business process.

For example, the map in Fig. 3 shows how the SAP Material Management (MM) module can be abstracted into sections of a map [Rolland01]. Every section in the map represents both (i) a SAP's MM function, and (ii) the business goal that can be satisfied by using this function.

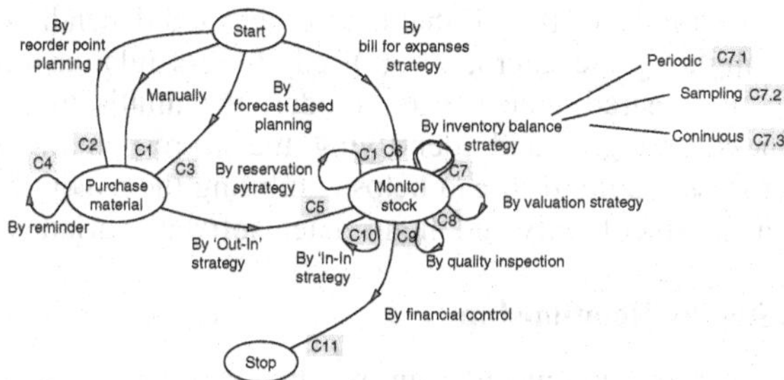

Fig. 3. Map describing how to *Satisfy material needs efficiently* with SAP's MM module

From the *business viewpoint*, material management deals with supplying materials in the right quantity, at the right place and time, and at the minimum cost. The map identifies through two goals that this involves two issues: to *Purchase material*, and to *Monitor stock.* It also make explicit the different manners by which each goal can be achieved. For example there are four strategies to *Purchase material*, namely *Manually*, *By forecast based planning*, *By reorder point planning* and *By reminder.*

From the *system viewpoint*, the map indicates which SAP function helps to achieve the *Material purchase* and *Monitor Stock* goals, and how. For example, the SAP MM module contains a "Create purchase order" function (or 'transaction' in SAP's terms). At the operational level, this function entails the identification of material requirements. The material requirements are defined by references to the needed materials, their vendors, their prices, the dates and plant at which they should be delivered, etc. At the business level, the issue is the one of purchasing material to satisfy material needs of the organization. The function contains variants depending of the purchase situation. These are referred to in the four sections C1, C2, C3, and C4, as documented in Table1. For each of the four sections, the table outlines the variant of the SAP function that is to be used.

Table 1. Documenting map sections

Code	Name	Description
C1	Purchase material	Create a purchase order based on a purchase requisition manually defined with information about the material, vendor, date, price, etc. If the information is correct the purchase order is created with a unique identification number.
C2	Purchase material based on reorder points	Automatically generate purchase requisitions any time a stock event that causes the stock of a given material to fit the reorder point criteria occurs. The purchase requisitions can then be transformed into purchase orders.
C3	Purchase material based on forecast	Automatically generate purchase requisitions at the dates defined in the forecast scheduling the purchases that shall be made for a given material. The forecast is computed based on former purchases of the material. Once generated, the purchase requisitions can be transformed into purchase orders.
C4	Purchase material by reminder	Automatically remind of a purchase order for which no delivery has been noticed within due date.

As illustrated in the SAP example above, our experience showed that the multi-thread topology of the map is useful to reasoning about alternative fitness relationships. The multi-thread (a) makes explicit the different business strategies to achieve a goal and (b) identifies the variants of the SF that can be selected depending on the situation at hand, thus highlighting the alternative (ORed) fitness relationships. We found that when eliciting the desired state (To-Be model) the multi-thread helps envisioning multiple business strategies and identifying the corresponding required SF. In a customizing process the multi-thread helps exhibiting the panel of business strategies embedded in the product family and their related software variants.

Issue 3: Refining the Relationship

Refinement is an abstraction mechanism by which a given entity is viewed as a set of interrelated entities. Refinement is known as a means to handle complexity. Our belief is that such *refinement mechanism* is required for *handling the fitness relationship* in *a systematic, controlled manner.* Indeed, it would be inconvenient to view in one shot, a fitness relationship as one monolithic, flat structure. A layered approach may help mastering progressively the complexity of the relationship. This confirms our experiences which show that the refinement ratio (see Table2) is around 20, meaning that a relationship, initially seen as a whole, finally leads to a complex organization of about 20 sub-relationships.

From our knowledge, there are very few attempts to provide a refinement mechanism of the fitness relationship ([Potts97b]). In goal driven approaches, it is known that goals can be used to capture the objectives of a system at various levels of abstraction [Lamsweerde01] and goal decomposition ([Bubenko94] [Nurcan02] [Finkelstein02]) is traditionally used to relate high level goals to low level, operationalisable goals. These are leaves of the goal graph that point out to the required functionalities of the system. One can therefore see that goal decomposition does not support a top-down reasoning about the fitness relationship. Instead goal decomposition is a mechanism leading to the establishment of the fitness relationship as the link between a system functionality and a leave of the goal graph.

In the map approach we defined a refinement mechanism in order to *refine a section* of a map at level *i* into an *entire map* at a lower level *i+1*. Therefore, a fitness relationship (captured in a section of the map) is refined as a complex graph of sections, each of them corresponding to sub-relationships between the business and the system. Therefore, what is refined by the refinement mechanism offered by maps is in fact the fitness relationship itself. We found this mechanism helpful to understanding the fitness relationship at different levels of detail.

Let us exemplify this mechanism by refining the section C5, *Monitor stock by Out-In strategy* of the SAP map presented in Fig. 3. The C5 refined map is shown in Fig. 4. From the *business viewpoint*, this map explains how the *Monitor Stock by 'Out-In' strategy* is refined as a graph of goals and associated strategies. The map tells us that stock entries shall not be permitted unless they have been checked. This is reflected in Fig. 4 by the ordering of the two goals *Accept delivery* and *Enter goods in stock*. The map also shows that there are several ways to achieve each of these two goals. For example, there are four strategies to *Accept delivery*: the *Okay* strategy (when the delivery conforms the order) and three reconciliation strategies, namely the *Reconciliation by PO recovery*, the *Reconciliation of unit difference*, and the *Reconciliation of under/over delivery*. Each of these provides a way of accepting deliveries that don't match the order but are within specified tolerances, missing order reference, unit difference, under/over quantity, respectively. From the *system viewpoint*, this map explains how the *complex function C5* is made of other functions and in which way these functions co-operate to achieve collectively the C5 goal. The map shows that there are seven sub-functions C5.1 to C5.7 of the C5 function that shall co-operate as indicated by the multi-thread and multi-path topology of the M5 refined map.

Since refinement results in a map, it produces a multi-thread, multi-path structure at level *i+1*. As a result, for a given section at level *i*, not only (1) multiple threads describe *alternative sub-sections* at level *i+1*, but also (2) the multi-path structure introduces several different *combinations of sub-sections*. Therefore, section refinement is a more complex structure than a simple composition structure such as AND/OR goal decomposition Indeed, it provides at the same time (a) several alternative decompositions of the initial fitness relationship into its constituents, and (b) different alternatives to its constituents themselves. We found this mechanism useful in practice as a means to fine tune the selection of the adequate system sub-functions in a customizing process.

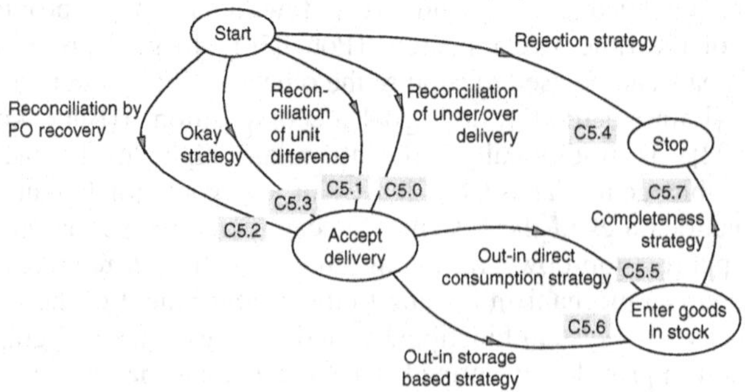

Fig. 4. Refined map M5 of section C5 of the SAP MM map shown in Fig. 3

As an example, let us consider two companies who have selected the *Out-In strategy* of the SAP map to *Monitor stock*. The refined map M5 (Fig.4) helps each of them to refine their selection in different ways. For example, while one company may want to *Accept delivery* by *reconciliation of over/under delivery*, the other may be driven by the *reconciliation by purchase order recovery* strategy. Similarly, one company may want to *Enter goods in stock* using the *Out-in direct consumption* strategy that allows one to consume goods even though they are not yet entered in stock, whereas the other company may select only the *Out in storage* strategy, i.e. systematically enter goods in stock before they are consumed. Therefore, while the two companies have the same fitness relationship at the level of abstraction of the MM map, the refinement mechanism allows us to differentiate the sub-relationships relevant for each company.

Issue 4: Refinement Quality

If refinement is necessary as a way to master complexity, it also generates its own difficulties. One is to control the *level of abstraction* in a given refinement. This has been found for example, in using refinement in use case driven approaches [Weidenhaupt98]. Cockburn reported [Cockburn00] that the application of his refinement mechanism (by which an action in a scenario can be seen as a goal attached to a new use case and associated scenarios) led to mix up of abstraction levels in the same scenario. It seems that several levels of abstraction are source of difficulty, in particular with respect to consistency of the entities belonging to the same level. This issue is related to the *black box/white box* principle [Weidenhaupt98] [BenAchour99] [Kamsties02]. According to this principle, it is useful to see an entity as a black box at a level of abstraction i and then as a white box at level $i+1$. When a system is seen as a black box, its internal properties are hidden and the emphasis is on the relationship between the system and other systems. When it is seen as a white box, the internal of the system is on the contrary apparent. The problem arises when the white box analysis shows that the content of the box covers different levels of abstraction.

We encountered this problem when applying the map refinement mechanism in projects, and we believe that complementing the *refinement mechanism* of the fitness relationship with *refinement quality assurance* is an issue.

In a project with the Renault company [Rolland03], we defined and experienced the use of a set of *refinement quality rules.* The aim was to ensure a unique level of abstraction in a given level of map refinement. In essence rules helped, given a map at a refinement level *i*: (a) to detect and move up sections into maps at level i-1; (b) to detect and move down sections into maps at level i+1 and, (c) to improve sections at the same level. We briefly illustrated (a) and (b) in Fig. 5. Rules help detecting the following in the initial map (m) :

- The goal *Evaluate risk* is a means to *Decide on the offer.* It is thus a sub-goal to *Decide on the offer*, and belongs to a lower level of abstraction. This led to the introduction of a map (c) that refines the section *<Gather offer data, Decide on the offer, by semi-automated risk evaluation>*; the goal *Evaluate the risk* was moved down.
- Map (b) as resulting of the above transformation can be abstracted into a single section of a higher level map (a). The section relates to the goal *Gain the customer*, and offers a strategy, namely *By contracting* which is an alternative to the two other strategies already identified : *By keeping customer loyalty*, and *By prospecting.*

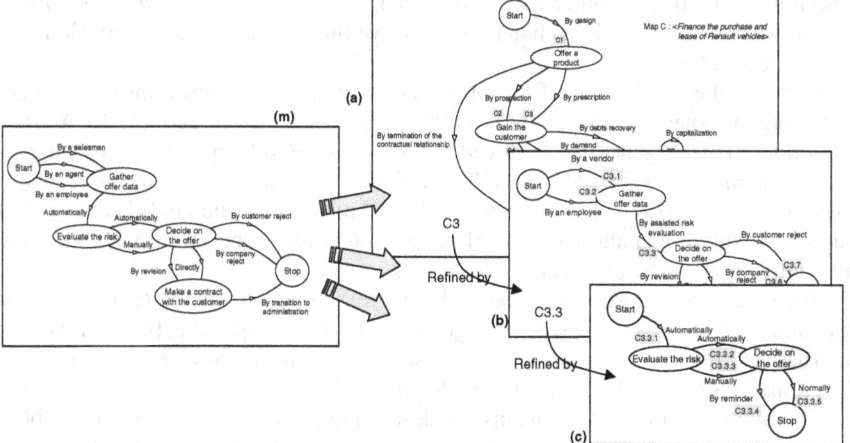

Fig. 5. Applying rules to control refinement quality

In order to reinforce the importance of the *refinement quality checking* issue, we present in Table 2 data gathered from three projects in industry [Rolland03] [Rolland01] [Rolland00b]. The table shows that a top-down approach was followed in the three cases, starting form one single map with a limited number of goals and strategies. The table also reflects the fact that systematic section refinement could rapidly lead to a combinatorial explosion of the number of maps to document. There is therefore, a need to control the refinement. It was also found necessary to identify when the refinement is needed and when it is not. In the DIAC project for example, we achieved the latter through a consensus based process : each section was subject to a vote and the refinement was considered unnecessary when the fitness between the business requirement and the selected product was agreed upon by the stakeholders.

Table 2. Practice data

	Goals in top level map	Sections in top level map	Refinement levels	Total number of maps	Number of transactions or screens
PPC	2	6	3	37	200 transactions,
DIAC	3	14	3	36	2000 screens
SAP MM	2	11	2	14	About 50

3 Issues in Engineering the Relationship

Whereas the four previous issues were dealing with understanding the fitness relationship we are now moving to the issues related to its production.

Issue 5: Exploring Alternatives

This issue relates to the exploration of the different ways to link a business goal and a system functionality; in other words to investigate the *alternative fitness relationships* for the problem at hand. In a change perspective this is crucial for the envisionment of the future system.

Most of the goal based RE approaches recognize the usefulness of goals in exploring alternative designs [Anton98] [Yu01] [Lamsweerde01] [BenAchour99] [Paech02]. This is generally achieved using AND/OR refinement where "alternative goal refinements [expressed with OR links] allow alternative system proposals to be explored." [Letier02]. Our experience with goal analysis [Rolland98] is that providing automated support to alternative goal generation is useful because manual search for alternative is far to be exhaustive [Rolland99].

However, if alternative goals help reasoning about alternative system functionalities to achieve the parent goal, the issue of exploring fitness relationship alternatives raises the question of reasoning about alternative combinations of functionalities across the entire AND/OR goal graph.

We found that maps, as a means for describing alternative complex assemblies of functionalities, can help in this exploration and in the discovery of the ones that best fit the business goals. The multi-thread topology of maps corresponds to OR structures in a goal graph. In addition, the multipath map topology helps reasoning and evaluating alternative assemblies of functionalities. Such assemblies give rise to a *payoff analysis*. The result is the selection of sections that show the combination of the functionalities required.

For example, the map shown in Fig. 6 identifies seven different functionalities for the management of electricity supply in a utility company. Each functionality is identified by a section in the map. The *<Start, Sell electricity, with credit strategy>* section identifies C4 for selling electricity in a conventional way, which provides IT support to manage the process chain of conventional meter reading, electricity consumption billing and payment collection with seven sub-component as map M4 shows it.

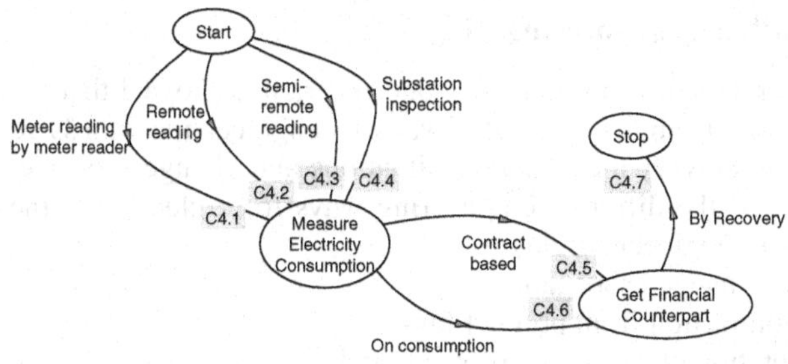

Fig. 6. *Manage electricity supply* and *Sell electricity by credit strategy* maps

Once C4 has been selected, one has to decide on how electricity should be measured and how the financial counterpart should be obtained. Each sub-component selection has however a payoff that can be analysed in the view of its combination to another component. The pay-off analysis for C4 sub-components is summarized in the Table3 below.

Table 3. Pay-off summary for the selection of C4 sub-components

<table>
<tr><th></th><th></th><th colspan="2">Get financial counterpart</th></tr>
<tr><th></th><th></th><th>Contract based</th><th>On consumption</th></tr>
<tr><td rowspan="4">Measure electricity consump-tion</td><td>Meter reading by meter reader</td><td>Can be envisaged at sustainable cost if visits are achieved at a low frequency (e.g. once or twice a year)</td><td>Excluded because too difficult to organise all visits at the required pace.</td></tr>
<tr><td>Remote reading</td><td colspan="2">Cost effective combination that can be done in real time. However, remote reading is not completely secure. A complimentary check of electricity measurement is thus needed, e.g. by meter reader, or by substation inspection.</td></tr>
<tr><td>Semi-remote reading</td><td>Cost effectiveness is a linear function of the number of contracts per cluster of semi-remote reader.</td><td>Very costly if the number of customers paying on consumption, per cluster of remote reader is low</td></tr>
<tr><td>Substation inspection</td><td>Only possible if the connected meter readers relate to single contract. Otherwise, calls for individual reading.</td><td>Cost effective way to handle the verification of consumers invoiced by remote reading clustered on the same substation.</td></tr>
</table>

Let us consider the case where it is necessary to get financial counterparts both contract based and on consumption. The table shows that remote readings are a cost effective way to handle electricity measurement in both cases. Indeed, it is real time and therefore adapted to payment on consumption. Besides, the cost of installing remote readers can be included in the contract prices and recovered in the long term. However, the payoff table also says that remote reading, as it is automated, is not fully reliable and should be double-checked, e.g. by using subsection inspection. New opportunities emerge from further analysis. For example, remote reading makes it possible to analyse consumption in real time; new types of contracts can also be proposed to automatically adapt electricity production to consumption. This would be useful when electricity provision should be reliable, e.g. for refrigeration warehouses, hospitals, telephony service, etc.

Issue 6: Identifying Engineering Classes

As already mentioned in introduction, our experience showed that there are different change situations leading to specific ways to engineer the fitness relationship. Our suggestion is to *classify* these change situations and change processes as a means to better understand the different engineering ways to produce the fitness relationship. We propose four engineering classes

- Direct change propagation;
- Customization from product family;
- Adaptation of a baseline product; and
- Component assembly.

Fig. 7 is the customized version of the generic change framework presented in Fig.1. It corresponds to the case of *direct change propagation*. In this situation, the change is led by the move from the *As-Is BM* to the *To-Be BM*. The relationship between the *As-Is BM* and the *As-Is SFM* is used to propagate the business changes onto system functionality changes and to produce the *To-Be SFM* fitting the *To-Be BM*.

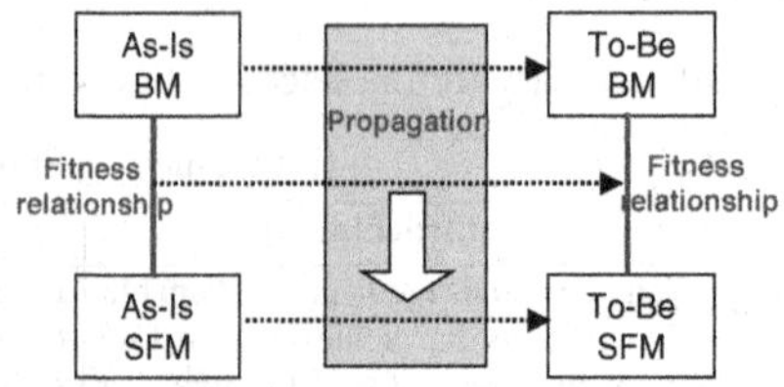

Fig. 7. Direct change propagation

This first engineering class corresponds to the traditional evolutionary change of an 'in house' system that is driven by organisational change. However today, with an increase of the 'to-buy' policy over the 'to-do', the fitness relationship is established through rather more complex engineering processes shown in Figures 8, 9, and 11 respectively.

Fig. 8 displays the case of *customising a product family*. Here, the requirements of the organisation are expressed in the *As-Wished BM*. The *Might-Be SFM* (Might-Be System Functionality Model) reflects the functional capability of the product family. The *To-Be BM* and its counterpart, the *To-Be SFM* result from a *model-match centred process* which searches for the best match between the organisational requirements (expressed in *As-Wished BM*) and what is provided by the Product Family, (*Might-Be SFM*).

The third engineering class shown in Fig. 9 corresponds to a case of *system adaptation*. Such an adaptation is caused by changes in the organizational context in which a legacy software system is now to operate. This typically occurs because of mergers/take-overs, globalisation, standardisation of practices across branches of a company etc. Several legacy software systems are already running when such events occur. In this context, it is out of question to develop a new system from scratch. However, it is possible to integrate the legacy systems or to select one of these for adaptation and uniform deployment across the organization. *The Is-Baseline FM* (Is-Baseline Functionality Model) models the functionality of the selected system

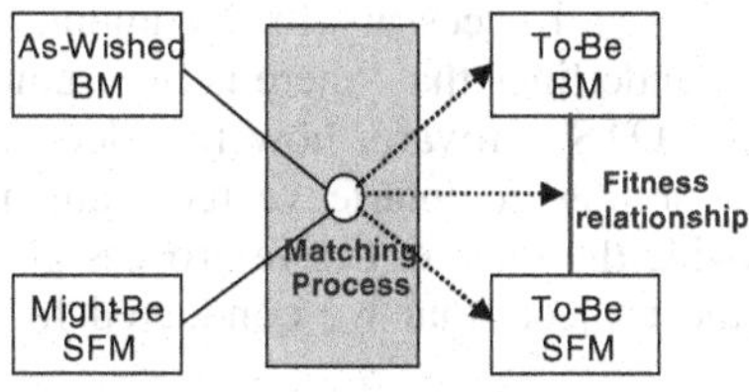

Fig. 8. Customization from product family

for uniform deployment across the organization. The *As-Wished BM* expresses the requirements of the organization who wants to adapt its requirements to the new situation at hand. The *To-Be BM* and its counterpart the *To-Be SFM* result from a gap *centred process* that focuses on eliciting the gaps between models. Indeed, eliciting the differences (or gaps) between the current baseline-functionality model and its future version seems to be the most efficient way to perform the change.

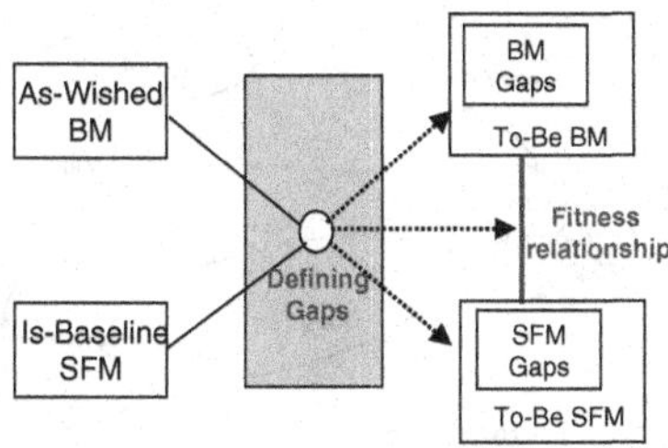

Fig. 9. Adaptation of a baseline product

Finally, Fig. 10 displays the case of *COTS based system development*. Here the process of establishing the fitness relationship is centred on the retrieval and assembly of system component matching organizational requirements. The *Might-Be SFMs* model the different available COTS components. The *As-Wished BM* reflects the organizational needs. The *To-Be BM* and its counterpart the *To-Be SFM* result of a process where component matching the organization needs are retrieved and then assembled together.

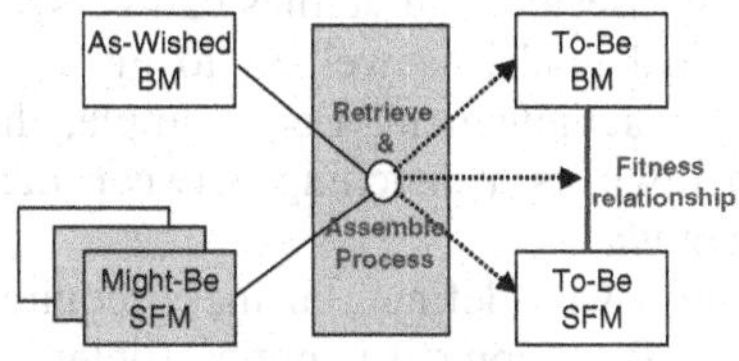

Fig. 10. Component assembly

Issue 7: Modelling and Guiding the Engineering Process

The importance of having quality engineering processes is recognized in the RE, SE and IS communities. This is also true for most recent challenges such as the ones raised by COTS selection and assembly [Maiden98] [Brons00] or [Boehm02]. In this area, modelling processes is still necessary to document, guide, and improve them. For example, [Maiden02] underlines that "there is little guidance available on how to acquire requirements for COTS software, how to select COTS software compliant with these requirements, or how to interleave requirements acquisition and COTS software selection to provide the most effective process guidance". We identified the same needs in each of the projects that we conducted for this class of engineering problem.

Our experience in these projects is that people have specific expectations and requirements about these process models. First, they are facing an issue and have a goal in mind and would like process models to let them easily situate both and to suggest different alternative paths to achieve the goal and solve the issue. Second, they want freedom and flexibility in their ways of working; one single imposed way-of-working is not acceptable. They expect to learn about the different ways by which each of their goals can be achieved and each issue can be solved. Third, they want advice on how to choose between the different alternative solutions that shall be proposed to solve a given issue.

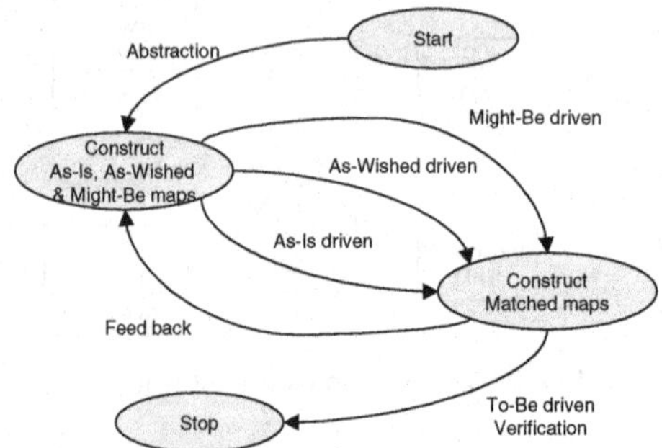

Fig. 11. The ERP customisation requirements process model

Fig. 11 shows a process model that was developed for an ERP customisation project. As the figure shows, the process model was developed under the form of a map. Indeed, our various experiences [Assar00], [Ralyte01], [Benjamen99], [Tawbi01] showed us that maps are useful to specify both methodological goals and the various strategies to achieve those. Besides, guidelines can be specified in maps to guide the selection of methodological goals, as well as to guide strategy selection, situation identification, and section achievement. For example, the process model identifies that ERP customisation involves a matching between the *BM* and *SFM* that can be achieved in three different ways:

1. If the context is that of a well-defined business requirements to which the system should fit, and in-house development is not a problem, then the As-Wished driven matching strategy can be used.
2. If on the contrary, the system is less likely to change than the business (e.g. because customising the system has become too expensive [Rolland01]), or if the system customisation is an opportunity to change the business (e.g. because it allows to generalise its associated best practice in the business) then, the matching process should be driven by the system. This is what the Might-Be driven strategy proposes.

If it is particularly important to preserve the functionality provided by the existing system in the To-Be SFM, then an As-Is driven matching is required. We encountered such functional non regression requirements when we studied the introduction of software components for selling electricity in the PPC company at the occasion of European electricity market deregulation [ISE01].

Issue 8: Engineering Strategies

Despite the diversity of processes dealing with each of the four classes of engineering problems, our reflection from experiences led us to identify two common underlying strategies. On one side of the spectrum we found that *similarities* between pairs of models are useful to support the matching process whereas at the other end of the spectrum focusing on differences or *gaps* is the most relevant technique. For example, customising (Fig.7) and component assembly processes (Fig.10) call for a matching technique whereas a gap measurement technique is more suitable for processes of the type 'adaptation from a product line' (Fig.9).

Similarity modelling and gap modelling are not easy tasks if they are not achieved in a systematic way. The challenge is to maximize the knowledge gained, while limiting the amount of effort needed to gain it. For example, we developed *Goal semantic similarity* metrics and *Goal structure similarity* metrics to automate the measurement of similarity between maps [Ralyte01]. This is typically an issue that is met in the component assembly class of engineering problem. Indeed, looking in a collection of components (specified with Might-Be SFMs) for the ones that best fit a given business (specified with As-Wished BM) necessitates a systematic measurement of similarity between each map of the collection of Might-Be SFMs and the As-Wished BM.

We also experienced in industry the importance of modelling gaps in a baseline product adaptation project. In the DIAC project [Rolland03], it was not desirable to specify the future system functionalities as would be done if they were developed from scratch. Indeed, most of them already existed in the baseline system. Rather, the project owners wanted a documentation of the transformations that should be made on the baseline system to get the future one. These were specified under the form of a collection of gaps expressed as operations to perform on the Is-Baseline SFM maps to obtain the To-Be SFM maps. In the end, 98 of the gaps identified were specified in the requirements documentation. Fig. 12 presents some of these by organising them in a table and illustrating the resulting To-Be map. For each goal, strategy and section involved in a gap, the operation achieved to define the To-Be map is quoted in a separate line (operations are named in the left column).

The table shows for example that the baseline system offered the opportunity to shift the focus from a traditional contract oriented way of dealing with customers to a more customer centric one. This is specified by the operation of replacement of the goal *Define an offer* by the goal *Prepare a contract*, and by adding of the goal *Collect a demand.*

It is very common that a baseline system also brings new technologies with it. For this reason, the business experts involved in the project required new system functions fully exploiting the Internet technology. The introduction of these new functions into the system was specified by adding the strategies *By a customer via internet* and *By pull* in the To-Be map.

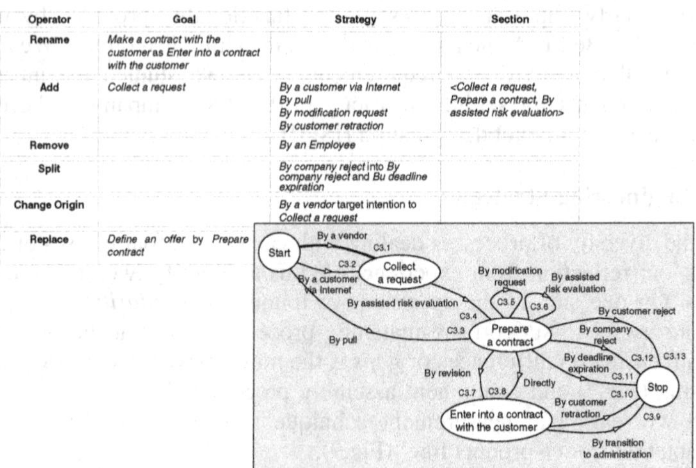

Operator	Goal	Strategy	Section
Rename	*Make a contract with the customer* as *Enter into a contract with the customer*		
Add	*Collect a request*	*By a customer via Internet* *By pull* *By modification request* *By customer retraction*	*<Collect a request, Prepare a contract, By assisted risk evaluation>*
Remove		*By an Employee*	
Split		*By company reject* into *By company reject* and *Bu deadline expiration*	
Change Origin		*By a vendor* target intention to *Collect a request*	
Replace	*Define an offer* by *Prepare contract*		

Fig. 12. Example of gaps and resulting map

The table emphasizes other gaps, such as renaming goals, splitting strategies, introducing sections, etc. Each of them is the result of a discussion about the fitness of the baseline system with the business vision. The gaps resulting from this discussion show how the Is-Baseline SFM (and sometimes the As-Wished BM) was to be transformed to get the To-Be SFM. The resulting map specifies a To-Be SFM that fits to the To-Be BM.

4 Conclusion

Our experience of Requirements Engineering and Information System Engineering stands in a number of industrial projects and European research projects. The common point we found in all these projects was the prime importance of establishing and preserving the fitness relationship between businesses and systems. A number of issues directly derive from this point. However, the prevalent view is that of a system and a business that change in a concurrent way. We depart from this traditional view by proposing to specify the fitness relationship itself and to engineer it through the change process. This entails a number of issues that were reported and discussed in this paper. Each issue was discussed individually with respect to the state of the art literature and with references to our own experiences. We believe more references should be introduced and we plan to do so in order to (i) validate/invalidate our belief that these are important issues that should be dealt with, (ii) help improve the classification of engineering processes, (iii) help us identify and/or confirm the common strategies that are used in these processes and finally, (iv) validate these strategies by comparison with the other existing ones.

References

[Alves02] C. Alves, A. Finkelstein. *Challenges in COTS-Decision Making: A Goal-Driven Requirements Engineering Perspective.* In Procs of Workshop on Software Engineering Decision Support, in conjunction with SEKE'02. Ischia, Italy, July 2002.

[Anton98] A.I. Anton C. Potts. *The Use of Goals to Surface Requirements for Evolving Systems.* In Procs IEEE International Conference on Software Engineering, IEEE Computer Soctety. 1998

[Arsanjani 01] A. Arsanjani, J. Alpigini. *Using Grammar-oriented Object Design to Seamlessly Map Business Models to Component-based Software Architectures. In Procs* of the International Symposium of Modelling and Simulation, May 16-18, 2001, Pittsburgh, PA, USA, pp 186–191.

[Assar00] S. Assar, C. Ben Achour, S. Si Said. *Un modèle pour la Spécification de Processus d'Analyse des Systèmes d'Information.* Proc. 18ème Congrès INFORSID , Lyon France, May 2000.

[BenAchour99] C. Ben Achour. *Extraction des Besoins par Analyse de Scénarios Textuels.* Phd Thesis, Univ. Paris 6 – Pierre et Marie Curie. 1999.

[BenJamen99] A. Benjamen. *Une approche multi-démarches pour la modélisation des démarches méthodologiques.* Phd thesis. Université de Paris I – Panthéon Sorbonne. 1999.

[Bubenko94] J. Bubenko. *Enterprise Modelling.* In Ingenierie de Systèmes d'Information, Vol 2, Num. 6, pp. 657–678.1994.

[Cockburn00] A. Cockburn. *Writing Effective Use Cases.* Addison-Wesley. 2000.

[D'Souza99] D. F. D'Souza, A. C. Wills. *Objects, Components, and Frameworks with UML The Catalysis Approach.* Addison-Wesley, Object Technology Series. 2001.

[Finkelstein02] D. Bush ., A. Finkelstein. *Requirements Elicitation for Complex Safety Related Systems. In Procs London Communication Symposium. London, UK, Sept. 2002*

[Jackson95] M. Jackson. *Software Requirements and Specifications.* Addison-Wesley. 1995.

[Jacobson99] I. Jacobson, G. Booch, J. Rumbaugh. *Unified Software Development Process.* Addison-Wesley, Object Technology Series. 1999.

[Kamsties 02] E. Kamsties, A. von Knethen, R. Reussner. *A Controlled Experiment on the Understandability of Different Requirements Specifications Styles.* In Procs of REFSQ'02, Essen, Germany, 2002.

[Kawalek 99] P. Kawalek, P. Kueng. *The Goal in the Organization.* In Procs of BITWorld'99, Cape Town, South Africa, July 1999.

[Lamsweerde01] A. van Lamsweerde. *Goal-Oriented Requirements Engineering: A Guided Tour.* Invited Paper for RE'01 - 5th IEEE International Symposium on Requirements Engineering, Toronto, August, 2001, pp. 249–263

[Letier02] E. Letier, A. van Lamsweerde. *Agent-Based Tactics for Goal-Oriented Requirements Elaboration. In Procs* de ICSE'02 – 24th International Conference on Software Engineering, ACM Press. May 2002.

[Nurcan02] S. Nurcan, C. Rolland. *A multi-method for defining the organizational change.* To appear in Information & Software Technology, 2002.

[Paech02] B. Paech, A.H. Dutoit, D. Kerkow, A. von Knethen. *Functional Requirements, non-Functional Requirements, and Architecture Should not Be Separated.* In Procs. of REFSQ'02. International Workshop on Requirements Engineering : Fundation for Software Quality. Essen, Germany, Sept 2002.

[Potts97a] C. Potts. *Fitness for Use: The System Quality that Matters Most.* In Procs REFSQ'97: Third Int.Workshop on Requirements Engineering: Foundation for Software Quality. Barcelona, Spain: June 16–17, 1997.

[Potts97b] C. Potts, I. His. *Abstraction and Context in Requirements Engineering: A Synthesis of Goal Refinement and Ethnography. Annals of Software Engineering, Vol. 3* pp. 23–61.1997.

[Ralyte01] J. Ralyté, C. Rolland. *An assembly process model for method engineering*. In Procs of CaiSE'01. Lecture Notes in Coputer Sciences. 2001

[Rolland00a] C. Rolland, N Prakash. Bridging the Gap Between Organisational Needs and ERP functionality. Requirtements Engineering Journal, Springer Verlag. 5:180.193. 2000.

[Rolland00b] C. Rolland. Intention Driven Component Reuse. Information Systems Engineering (S. Brinkkemper, E. Lindencrona, A. Solvberg, eds). Springer, pp. 197, 208. 2000.

[Rolland01] C. Rolland, N. Prakash. *Matching ERP System Functionality to Customer Requirements. In Procs* of the 5th IEEE International Symposium on Requirements Engineering, Toronto, Canada. August 27–31, 2001.

[Rolland03] C. Rolland, C. Salinesi. *Eliciting Gaps in Requirements Change : An Industrial Experience*. To appear in Requirements Engineering Journal. 2003.

[Rolland98] C. Rolland, C. Souveyet, C. Ben Achour. *Guiding Goal Modelling Using Scenarios*. IEEE Transactions on Software Engineering, Special Issue on Scenario Management, Vol 24, No 12, p. 1055–1071. December 1998.

[Rolland99] C. Rolland, G. Grosz, R. Kla. *Experience with Goal-Scenario Coupling in Requirements Engineering. In Procs* of the Fourth International Symposium on Requirements Engineering, RE'99. Limerick, Ireland, June 1999.

[Tawbi01] M. Tawbi. *CREWS-L'Ecritoire: un Guidage Outillé du Processus d'Ingénierie des Besoins*. PhdThesis, Université de Paris I – Panthéon Sorbonne. 2001.

[Weidenhaupt98] K. Weidenhaupt, K. Pohl, M. Jarke, P. Haumer, CREWS Team. *Scenario Usage in System Development : a Report on Current Practice*.Proceedings of ICRE'98, 3rd International Conference on Requirements Engineering, Colorado Springs USA. 6–10 April 1998.

[Yu01] E. Yu. "Agent Orientation as a Modelling Paradigm". *Wirtschaftsinformatik*. 43(2) April 2001. pp. 123–132.

Selection of Materialized Views: A Cost-Based Approach

Xavier Baril and Zohra Bellahsène

LIRMM - UMR 5506
CNRS/Université Montpellier II
161 Rue Ada
F-34392 Montpellier Cedex 5
{baril,bella}@lirmm.fr

Abstract. Recently, multi-query optimization techniques have been considered as beneficial in view selection setting. The main interest of such techniques relies in detecting common sub expressions between the different queries of workload. This feature can be exploited for sharing updates and space storage. However, due to the reuse a query change may entail an important reorganization of the multi query graph. In this paper, we present an approach that is based on multi-query optimization for view selection and that attempts to reduce the drawbacks resulting from these techniques. Finally, we present a performance study using workloads consisting of queries over the schema of the TPC-H benchmark. This study shows that our view selection provides significant benefits over the other approaches.

1 Introduction

The problem is to select a set of views to materialize that optimizes both the view maintenance and query time given some constraints. The ideal selection strategy should provide high query performance and low view maintenance cost. However, these two costs are in conflict, the issue is to find a method that ensures a balance between maintenance and query processing cost.

There are many motivations for investigating the view selection problem. At first, materialized views are increasingly being supported by commercial database systems and are used to speed up query response time. Therefore, the problem of choosing an appropriate set of views to materialize in the database is crucial in order to improve query processing cost. Another application of the view selection issue is selecting views to materialize in data warehousing systems to answer decision support queries. Furthermore, new applications of the problem of view selection arise namely in data placement in distributed databases and in peer to peer computing.

Most of the previous related approaches are more theoretical studies than pragmatic approaches and considered that the cost model is one parameter among others. In this paper, we present a pragmatic approach that is based

J. Eder and M. Missikoff (Eds.): CAiSE 2003, LNCS 2681, pp. 665–680, 2003.

on a cost model and experiments performed on a real data base system. Moreover, the processing cost of query is estimated according to the operation type. For instance, the estimated cost of a join is not the same as the cost of a selection. In related work [12], the operation cost of the query view is estimated independently of their type. We have performed experiments to quantify the effect of some parameters (query and update frequencies, number of queries, etc.) on view selection strategy. For this purpose we have compared our approach, which make use of more precise cost model than the one used in MVPP [12]. Indeed, the MVPP approach doesn't take into account the type of operations to estimate their cost.

1.1 Contribution

We make use of multi-query optimization techniques in order to detect overlapping between queries of workload. Our approach provides the following features:

- we have designed a polynomial time algorithm that select views for materialization,
- we exploit common sub expressions (with reuse factor of a view),
- the view selection is decided under space constraint,
- our approach has been implemented.

Furthermore, we present a performance study using workloads of queries over the schema of the TPC-H benchmark [11]. This study shows that our view selection provides significant benefits over the other approaches.

1.2 Outline

The rest of this paper is organized as follows. In Section 2, it is presented the problem of view selection and our formalism for graphically representing the queries of workload. Section 3 provides an overview of our approach and gives the algorithm of selecting views to be materialized. Section 4 contains the sample example. The cost model that is used in our view selection approach is described in Section 5. In Section 6, is provided the performance evaluations. Finally, Section 7 presents related work and Section 8 contains concluding remarks and future work.

2 Preliminaries

We consider Selection-Projection-Join (SPJ) views that may involve aggregation and group by clause as well. A view is a derived relation defined by a query in terms of source relations and/or other views. It is said to be materialized when its extent is computed and persistently stored. Otherwise, it is said to be virtual.

The problem addressed in this paper is similar to that of deciding which views to materialize in data warehousing [1, 2, 5, 4, 6, 10, 12]. The general problem of view selection can be formulated as follows. Given a set of source relations $R = \{R_1, \ldots, R_n\}$, a set of queries $Q = \{Q_1, \ldots, Q_k\}$, the problem is to find a set of views to materialize $M = \{V_1, \ldots, V_m\}$ under a storage space constraint, which have the best balance between view maintenance cost and query processing cost.

2.1 The Multi View Materialization Graph

In this subsection, we present the framework for representing views to materialize in order to exhibit common sub-expressions. The task of a view selection module, which is based on multi-query optimization, is (i) to recognize possibilities of shared views and (ii) to apply a strategy for selecting views to materialize. The first task involves setting up the search space by identifying common sub-expressions This task is of importance as in the multi-query optimization. But it is orthogonal to the view selection process itself.

The Multi View Materialization Graph (MVMG) is similar to the AND-OR DAG representation of queries in multi query optimization [8]. The MVMG is a bipartite Directed Acyclic Graph (DAG) composed of two types of nodes: AND-nodes and OR nodes. Each AND-node represents an algebraic expression (Select-Project-Join) with possible aggregate function. An OR node represents a set of logical expression that are equivalent (i.e., that yield the same result). The AND-nodes have only OR-nodes as children and OR-nodes have only AND-nodes as children. In fact, the MVMG represents AND-OR DAGs of several queries in a single DAG. The leaf nodes of the MVMG are equivalence nodes representing the base relations. In general, for each base relation, there is one leaf node except in case of a selfjoin. Equivalence nodes in MVMG correspond to the views that are candidate to the view selection.

We consider the equivalent query graphs of each query and provide the expression DAG derived from these graphs. Then, all the resulting graphs are merged into one Multiple View Materialization Graph (MVMG) where the common sub-expressions are represented once. We borrow the rule provided in [8] for identifying common sub-expressions. For example, equivalent nodes obtained after applying join associativity are replaced by one single equivalence node.

```
Part(partkey, name, brand, type, size, retailprice)
Supplier(suppkey, name, address, nationkey, phone, acctbal)
PartSupp(partkey, suppkey, availqty, supplycost)
Customer(custkey, name, address, nationkey, phone, acctbal)
Orders(orderkey, custkey, orderstatus, totalprice, orderdate)
Lineitem(orderkey, partkey, suppkey, linenumber, quantity)
Nation(nationkey, name, regionkey, regionkey, comment)
Region(regionkey, name, comment)
```

Fig. 1. *Tables of TPC-H benchmark*

Example The queries used in this paper are defined over a simplified version of the TPC-H schema [11] described in Figure 1. Let us consider the query Q_1, which finds the number of orders of Airbus planes ordered by different nations :

```
Select   N.name, P.brand, O.orderdate, Sum(L.quantity)
From     Part P, Customer C, Orders O, Nation N, Lineitem L
Where    P.type = 'airplane'and AND P.brand = 'Airbus' AND
         P.partkey = L.partkey AND L.orderkey = O.orderkey AND
         O.custkey = C.custkey AND C.nationkey = N.nationkey
Group by N.name P.brand, O.orderdate;
```

The AND-OR DAG representation of the query graph of query Q_1 depicted Figure 2(a) is shown in Figure 2(b). Circles represent AND nodes, i.e. operations and boxes represent OR nodes, i.e. equivalence nodes. In the transition from Figure 2(a) to Figure 2(b), new nodes are created to represent the equivalence nodes, corresponding to operation results (e.g. node labelled $A1_{12}$ represents the result of the aggregation operation).

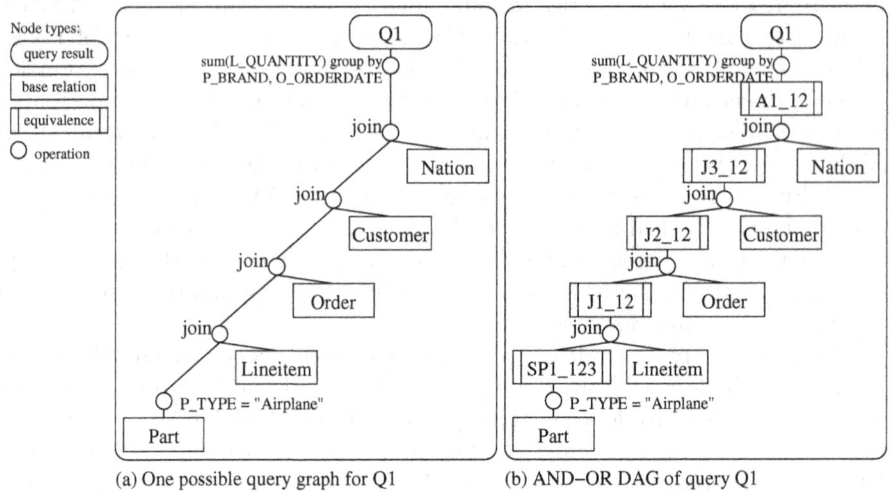

(a) One possible query graph for Q1 (b) AND–OR DAG of query Q1

Fig. 2. *Query graph and its AND-OR representation*

2.2 Notion of Level in the MVMG

Our view selection algorithm is based on the notion of level in the query tree. For this purpose, each view (equivalence node) of the query tree is associated to a level, which is defined as follows:

- $level(root) = 1$ with *root* the view representing the query result,
- $level(view) = level(parent(view)) + 1$ with *parent* a function which gives the parent of a view in the query tree.

3 Our View Selection Method

In our previous work on the view selection problem [2], only leaf nodes of the MVMG were materialized. We significantly improved our view selection strategy.

In this section, we present our strategy for selecting a set of views to be materialized. The optimal solution is the one which computes the set of equivalence nodes (i.e., views) of the MVMG such that the sum of cost of processing all the queries and maintaining all the views is minimal. However, the search space for the optimal solution is very large since it entails a great number of comparisons between all possible subsets of this set of vertices. If n is the number of nodes of a MVMG, then the number of combinations of nodes is 2^n. For this matter, we consider the sum cost of processing cost and view maintenance per query. Thus the first argument of our solution is reducing the complexity of the view selection algorithm, which selects views to materialize in the MVMG. The second argument for considering the views to materialize query by query relies in preserving the data independence whenever adding a query to the view configuration or removing one from it. Indeed, the side effect on existing queries is reduced since the view selection is applied query per query. In the related work since the view selection strategy consists in considering all equivalence nodes of the multi view query graph, the impact of adding or removing a query may lead to an important reorganization.

More precisely, we make use of the following heuristics:

- Searching the views to materialize per level and per query. This heuristic is based on the observation that the maintenance cost decreases from the root level down to the leaf level of query tree. This is true in the context when the operations of the query tree are not executed in pipeline way.
- Selecting the level, which provides the minimal sum of query processing and view maintenance cost.
- Taking the reuse of views into account. This feature allows to reduce the view maintenance cost and space storage.
- A pre-selection of beneficial views is performed as follows. A view is considered as beneficial if and only if its materialization reduces significantly the query processing cost and without increasing significantly the view maintenance. For instance, if the materialization of a view v reduces the query cost from 2 minutes to 10 sec, and increases the view maintenance cost from 1 sec to 9 sec, then view v should be materialized. View benefit is formally defined locally to a query (see 3.2) and on the entire MVMG (see 3.3).

3.1 Algorithm for View Selection

In the classical approach[1], which consists in fully materializing the view, the materialization level corresponds to the root level of the query tree. In this

[1] We refer to the approach which does not use the multi-query optimization feature by considering views separately.

approach, the query processing cost is low and the view maintenance cost may be high. The opposite solution is leaving the view virtual. Consequently, the query processing cost is high and the view maintenance cost is null. The aim of our approach is to provide a solution based on the balance between query processing and maintenance cost. For this purpose, our idea is finding an intermediary level for each query tree optimizing the sum of the query processing and the view maintenance cost.

The algorithm 1 computes, for each query, the materialization level according to the query frequency and the data update frequency of each involved relation. The complexity of the algorithm is in $O(n \times k)$ where n is the number of queries and k is the average number of levels in a query. The treatment is done in two main phases. The first one carry out a pre-selection of beneficial views. The second phase computes the total cost (query plus maintenance) for each level of the query graph and selects the one which has the minimal sum of query processing and view maintenance cost.

Due to space limitation, we don't indicate types of the variables used in the algorithms. However, we use the following syntactic convention : variables in capital letter denote sets.

```
   Data    : mvmg, q
   Result  : M // set of views to materialize for the considered query

   // set of pre-selected views;
   P = ∅;

   // pre-selection on local benefit;
   for each v of AllChildren(q) do
1      b = LocalBenefit(q, v);
       if b > 0 then
           P = P ∪ {v}
       end
   end

   // get the level having the minimum total cost;
   mlc = ∞;
   for each L of AllViewsOfLevel(q) do
2      PL = L ∩ P;
3      lc = TotalCost(q, PL);
       if lc < mlc then
           M = PL;
           mlc = lc;
       end
   end
```

Algorithm 1: Selection of a query materialization level

For each view, the pre-selection step is performed using the following formula (line 1):

$$LocalBenefit(query, view) =$$
$$QueryCost(query, \emptyset) \times frequency(query)$$
$$-(QueryCost(query, \{view\}) \times frequency(query) + \frac{MaintenanceCost(view)}{reuse(view)})$$

During the selection phase, the set of pre-selected views for the current level is computed, and stored in the variable PL (line 2): it is the intersection of the views belonging to the level (L) and the pre-selected views (P). Next, the total cost for pre-selected views of this level is computed in variable lc (line 3). The total cost is given by the following formula:

$$TotalCost(query, M) =$$
$$QueryCost(query, M) \times frequency(query) + \sum_{v \in M} \frac{MaintenanceCost(v)}{Reuse(v)}$$

Finally, the level having the minimum total cost is selected.

3.2 General Algorithm

As explained above, the algorithm 1 provided the set of candidate views for materialization. We now present the second part of the view selection method performed by the algorithm 2. It is aimed to find among the candidates views to materialize, those optimizing the global benefit under the space constraint.

The general algorithm takes into account a constraint for the storage space of the materialized views (variable s). Thus, the problem can be resumed as follows. Let us consider:

- Let C be the set of candidate views for materialization,
- Let s be the available space storage,
- Let $s(v)$ be the function giving the storage space of a view,
- Let $GlobalBenefit(v)$ be the function giving the global benefit of a view.

The first step of the general algorithm is to select the set of candidate views for materialization. For this purpose, we use the level selection algorithm for each query, and the candidates views for materialization in C.

Next, the candidate views are filtered according to their global benefit, and views having a negative benefit are removed from the set of candidate views. The formula used for the global benefit (line 2) is:

$$GlobalBenefit(view) =$$
$$QueryCost(\emptyset) - (QueryCost(\{view\}) + MaintenanceCost(view))$$

The problem is to find a set of views to materialize M, such that $\sum_{v \in M} s(v) < s$ and $\sum_{v \in M} GlobalBenefit(v)$ is maximum. This problem is similar to those of the knapsack therefore it may be solved using the dynamic programming

Data : *mvmg*, *s* // space constraint
Result : *M* // set of views to materialize
// set of candidate views for materialization;
$C = \emptyset$;
// union of candidate views for each query;
for *each q of mvmg* **do**
1 | $C = C \cup LevelSelection(mvmg, q)$
end
;
// pre-selection on global benefit;
for *each v of C* **do**
2 | **if** $GlobalBenefit(v) < 0$ **then**
| | $C = C - \{v\}$
| **end**
end
// view selection under space constraint according to global benefit;
3 $M = knapsack(C, s, s(), GlobalBenefit())$;

Algorithm 2: The general algorithm for selecting views to materialize

paradigm. For this purpose, we make use of a knapsack function (line 3). This function takes as input all the parameters described above (including the set of candidate views, the space constraint, the function given the size of a view and the function given the global benefit of a view) and returns a set of views satisfying the problem. Note that the knapsack algorithm is polynomial in $O(n \times s)$, where n is the number of candidate views for materialization ($n = |C|$) and s the available storage space. Computing benefits and costs of query and maintenance can be done in polynomial time before running the selection algorithm : it needs a traversal of the views of each queries of the MVMG. The level selection algorithm is also polynomial in the number of level of the considered query. Then, the general algorithm is polynomial because it uses only polynomial subroutines.

4 Sample Example

Let us consider four other queries in addition to Q1 presented previously in Section 2. Query Q2 finds the number of Airbus planes bought by the United States for the last 6 years.

```
Select    P.brand, O.orderdate, Sum(L.quantity)
          From Part P, Customer C, Orders O, Nation N, Lineitem L
Where     N.name = 'USA' and P.type = 'Airplane'
          and P.partkey = L.partkey
          and C.nationkey= N.nationkey
          and C.custkey = O.custkey and O.orderkey = L.orderkey
          and O.o_orderdate > 1996 and P.brand = 'Airbus'
Group By P.brand, O.orderdate;
```

Query Q3 lists the name, the brand, the price, the number and the quantity of orders of every brand of planes.

```
Select   P.name, P.brand, P.retailprice,Sum(L.quantity), Count(*) As C
From     Part P, Lineitem L
Where    p.type = 'airplane' and P.partkey = L.partkey
Group By P.name, P.brand, P.retailprice
```

Query Q4 finds the minimal and the maximal supply cost for each country and each product having the brand name 'Renault'. The associated query is as follows:

```
Select   P.partkey, N.nationkey, N.name,Min(PS.supplycost), Max(PS.supplycost)
From     Part P, Supplier S, Nation N, PartSupp PS
Where    P.brand = 'Renault'
         and P.partkey = S.partkey
         and P.partkey = PS.partkey
         and PS.suppkey = S. suppkey
         and S.nationkey = N.nationkey
Group by P.partkey, N.nationkey, N.name
```

Q5 lists the supplycosts and all the identifiers of each product having as brand name 'Peugeot' and supplied in the USA. The associated query is as follows:

```
Select   P.partkey, S.supplycost
From     Supplier S, Part P, Nation N, PartSupp PS
Where    P.P_brand = 'Peugeot'
         and N.N_name  =  'USA'
         and P.partkey = PS.partkey
         and S.nationkey = N.nationkey
         and PS.suppkey = S.suppkey
Group by P.partkey, S.supplycost
```

Figure 3 illustrates the Multi View Materialization Graph of the five queries described above. The equivalence nodes are labeled OPi_{jk} where OP is the operation type, i is a counter and jk is the list of queries sharing the node. Operation type could be A for an aggregation, J for a join and SP for a selection-projection. For example, $J1_{123}$ denotes the first join shared by queries Q_1, Q_2 and Q_3.

5 The Cost Model

5.1 Estimated Cost of the Operations

We have been inspired by the formula given in [3] for estimating the query cost of the operations: join, selection and projection. These costs are estimated according to the size of the involved relations. The formulas used for cost operations estimation are simple but sufficient : it is proven by the performances of our approach, presented in the next section.

- Estimated cost of unary operations.
  - $Cost(op) = rows$, where *op* is an aggregation operation,
  - $Cost(op) = rows$, where *op* is a selection operation,
  - $Cost(op) = rows * log(rows)$, where *op* is a projection.

  Where rows is the number of tuples of the operand.
- Estimated cost of join
  $Cost(op) = \alpha \times lrows \times rrows \times \beta \times (lrows + rrows)$, with α and β are constant, and we assume that α is relatively small. Where $lrows$ and $rrows$ are respectively the number of rows of the left and right operands.

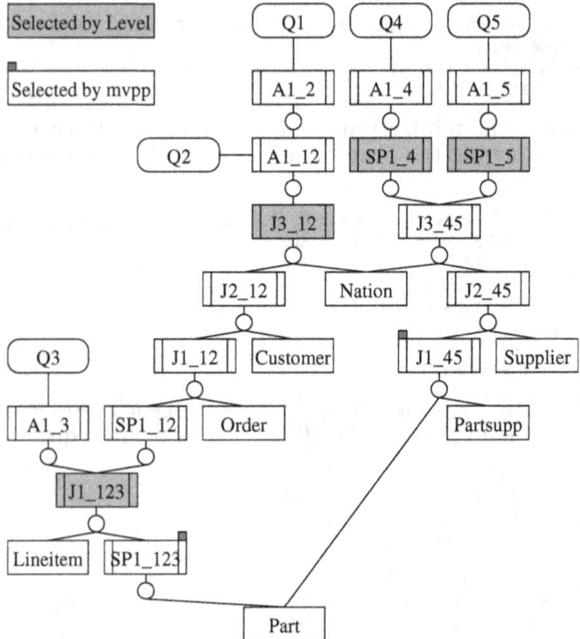

Fig. 3. *Example of MVMG Graph with five queries*

5.2 Maintenance Cost

Our view selection strategy assumes incremental maintenance. We consider two kinds of maintenance operation: add and delete. Let AddCost(view,relation) be the cost of maintaining view when a row is added to the relation and DeleteCost(view,relation) be the cost of maintaining the view when a row is deleted from the relation. To each relation is associated the frequencies of add and delete operations. Then, the maintenance cost for a view, is defined as the sum of add and delete cost for each relation, multiplied by the corresponding frequency:

$$MaintenanceCost(view) = \sum_{r \in R} AddCost(view, r) \times addF(r) + DeleteCost(view, r) \times deleteF(r)$$

Where $addF(r)$ is the frequency of adding tuples to relation r, and $deleteF(r)$ is the frequency of deleting tuples from relation r.

Reuse factor Although our method relies in selecting views per query (i.e. local optimization), it takes the reuse of views into account by merging all the queries of the workload in the same MVMG. For this purpose, we defined a reuse factor as the sum of queries frequencies using a view.

$$Reuse(view) = \sum_{q \in Q_{view}} frequency(q)$$

Where Q_{view} is the set of queries using $view$.

5.3 Query Processing Cost

In the case where there are no materialized views, the query cost is the sum of execution costs of all the operations belonging to the query graph. When there are materialized views, it is not necessary to execute operations which are descendant nodes of the views in the query graph. For that purpose, we define the query cost with to parameters: the considered query and the set of materialized views. The function *OpsToExec*$(query, M)$ returns the set of operations which are the necessary to execute to compute the result of query, given M a set of materialized views.

$$QueryCost(query, M) = \sum_{op \in OpsToExec(query,M)} Cost(op)$$

Each query is associated to a frequency giving its importance. The global query cost takes into account query frequencies. Then, the global query cost (given a set of materialized views) is the sum of each query cost multiplied by its query frequency.

$$QueryCost(M) = \sum_{q \in Q} QueryCost(q, M) * frequency(q)$$

where Q is the set of queries of the MVMG and $frequency$ a function which gives the frequency of a query.

6 Performance Study

We implemented the two algorithms presented in the section 3 for finding views for materialization. The goal of the experiments was to quantify the benefits of our view selection method. To achieve this purpose, we implemented the TPC-H database at scale of 0.01 (i.e., 10MB total size) on MySQL. We chose as workload consisting of five queries on the database schema of the TPC-H benchmark, which are presented in section 4. The experiment consists of applying the view selection method for finding the views for materialization. Once these views was known, we measured the real cost executing the queries of workload and the view maintenance cost of the materialized views.

6.1 Experiment Process

The experiments were performed on a MySQL server (version 3.23.42) through JDBC interface. The machine is a single processor (300 Mhz UltraSparc) Ultra 2, with 640 MB memory, running Solaris 5.7. Each cost has been measured three times and is expressed in millisecond (ms).

We consider several view selection strategies. The first one is our approach, called "level" approach. The "MVPP" approach [12] : we implemented the algorithm in order to achieve a comparison with our approach. In MVPP, the view maintenance is assumed to be performed by re-computing the views, according to the suggestion done in [12]. Then we consider two basic strategies : the "all" materialized approach which materializes the result of each query (this is the classical approach which does not use the multi-query optimization techniques) and the "virtual" approach which does not materialize views and always recompute queries.

We considered different scales of frequencies for access and update. Concerning update frequencies we try to extend TPC requirements which are not very accurate.

The "real" query cost is defined as the sum of the cost of executing each query of the workload on the MVMG, using materialized views as often as possible. For this purpose, we measured the execution time of each operations of the MVMG in MySQL. The query cost is the sum of all the operations used to compute the result of a query. This strategy is aimed to avoid to use the MySQL query optimizer which would modify the results. To improve query time, namely the join operation, we created indexes on the attributes involved in join conditions.

The "real" maintenance cost is defined as the sum of the cost of maintaining all materialized views. This cost includes the evaluation of cost of computing the new tuples to add (or to remove) from the view plus the cost of writing them. At first, we measured the execution time for adding or deleting a row from each view. Then, we estimated the number of rows to add to the view. Finally, the cost of writing the new added tuples is obtained by multiplying this number by the time to add a row. This cost is computed as the sum of the related operations costs, which is pondered proportionally to the number of added rows (or deleted tuples).

6.2 Experiment Results

Figure 4 presents the performance resulting from evaluating the global cost of the workload involving 1, 3, 5 and 10 queries to test scalability of the selection methods according to the number of queries. The update frequencies and access frequencies are at scale 1. This graphic shows that our approach provides the lowest global cost. The gap between our approach and the other rises according to the number of queries.

The graphic depicted in Figure 5 shows the global cost of the workload involving 10 queries while varying the access frequency. The update frequency is at scale 1. We can see, our approach outperforms the MVPP approach and the "all" materialized approach. The reason is MVPP tends to materialize views near the leaf level in the multi query graph. Therefore, the query processing is high. Note that for the MVPP strategy, the global cost decreases when the access frequency increases from 4 to 8. This is because the MVPP algorithm

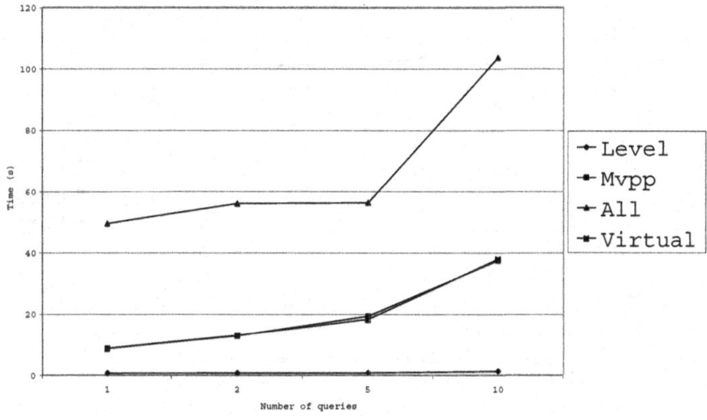

Fig. 4. *Evaluating global cost while varying the number of queries*

detects that the materialization of some views is beneficial with the increase of the access frequency.

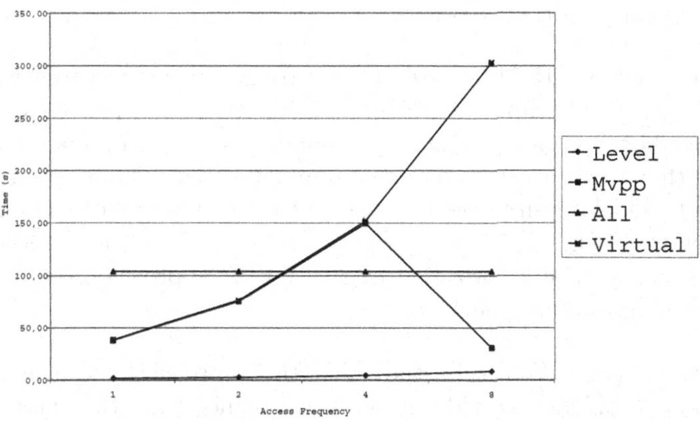

Fig. 5. *Evolving the access frequency*

Figure 6 presents the behavior of the different view selection methods while varying the update frequency for a workload involving 10 queries. The access frequency is at scale 1. We note that our approcah outperforms the others. The approach named "all" is not represented in this figure because its results are too bad and due to space limitation we don't put them on the histogram.

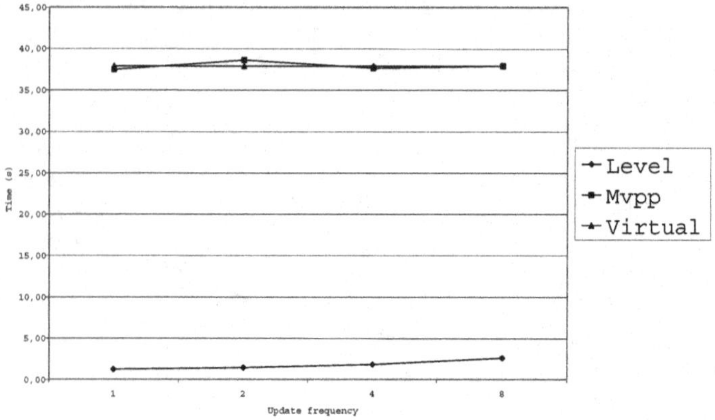

Fig. 6. *Evolving the update frequency*

6.3 Discussion

We note from the above experiments that our approach provides the better performances for global cost in all cases. Furthermore, our method supports scalability when the number of views is large (i.e., greater than 3). We have made experiments with various access and maintenance frequencies and our approach has always outperform the others.

We note that the MVPP approach tends to materialize views near the leaf level in the multi-query graph. In our opinion, there are two reasons to explain this behavior. The first one is that maintenance cost is sur-evaluated with MVPP, because they don't assume incremental maintenance. The second reason is that their cost model doesn't take into account the type of relational operations. So join operations which are very expensive are not in favor for materialization. For this reasons, the results provided by the MVPP approach often tend to be the same as the virtual approach.

Finally, we learnt from this study that the approaches using multi-query optimization techniques provide better performance than the classical approach named here "all" materialized approach.

7 Related Work

One of the key ideas of our approach is to detect common sub-expressions. This strategy has been applied in a significant number of papers in the context of multi-query optimization and also in view selection setting. The problem of the view selection and finding common sub-expressions are quite different: in the context of multi-query optimization, the problem is recognizing possibilities of shared computation whereas in our approach the problem is to find common views (corresponding to intermediary results) which will be materialized. However, the sharing feature is one parameter among several others. For instance, the strategy of choosing views to be materialized in our approach takes both the view maintenance.

Most of the previous related approaches on view selection are theoretical studies rather than pragmatic approaches and considered that the cost model is one parameter among others. The work reported in [7] is an exception since it was based on a cost model and has been implemented. However, this work focused on view maintenance problem without considering the query processing cost. Moreover, common subexpressions have been exploited for improving view maintenance cost [7].

In [10], the dynamic data warehouse design is modeled as search space problem. Rules for pruning the search space have been proposed. The first rule relies on favoring the query rewriting that uses views already materialized. The second one modifies the previous rule to favor common subexpression. However, their view selection algorithm is still in exponential time. Besides, neither implementation and/or evaluation of their method have been performed.

Our Multi View Materialization Graph is close to the Multi View Processing Plan that has been described in [12]. However, the evaluation cost of the query is not estimated according to the operation type. It seems that the estimated cost of a join is estimated as the same as the cost of a selection. "The cost of a query is the number of rows present in the table used to construct Q" [12]. DynaMat [6] is a system aimed to unify the view selection and the view maintenance problems. The principle of this system is monitoring constantly the incoming queries and materializing the set of views given the space constraint. During the update only the most beneficial subset of materialized views are refreshed within a given maintenance window. However, this approach is efficient when queries are ad hoc especially in OLAP applications. More recently, a formal study of the view selection problem focusing on its complexity has been done in [3]. It shows notably that the cost model is a parameter of importance in the view selection setting.

8 Conclusion

In this paper, we have presented a pragmatic approach of the view selection problem that combines global with local optimization. Due to the reuse a query change may entail an important reorganization of the multi query graph. Thus the data independence of the views may be compromised. In our approach, adding or removing queries can be done without great reorganization as we have shown it in this paper. While in the related work since the materialization strategy consists in considering all nodes of the multi query graph, the impact of adding or removing a query is more important. This is the counterpart of sharing and because the view selection method consider all queries together.

The view selection algorithms that we have presented in this paper have been implemented in java interfaced with a MySQL sever. We have performed several experiments and comparison with the approach reported in [12]. The experiment results have shown that our approach provides significant benefits over the all considered approaches. Furthermore, we learnt from this study that the approaches using multi-query optimization techniques provide better performance than the classical approach named here "all" materialized approach. We are planning to investigate the view selection problem in the context of a P2P Database architecture.

References

1. S. Agrawal, S. Chaudhury, and V. Narasayya. Automated Selection of Materialized Views and Indexes for SQL Databases. In *Proceedings of the 26th International Conference on Very Large Databases, VLDB'2000*, Cairo, Egypt, 2000.
2. Z. Bellahsène and P. Marot. Materializing a Set of Views: Dynamic Strategies and Performance Evaluation. In *Proceedings of International Database Engineering and Applications Symposium*, Yokohoma, Japan, September 2000. IEEE publishing.
3. R. Chirkova, A. Halevy, and D. Suciu. A formal perspective on the view selection problem. In *Proceedings of the 27th International Conference on Very Large Databases, VLDB'2001*, Roma, Italy, September 2001.
4. H. Gupta. Selection of Views to Materialize in a Data Warehouse. In *Proceedings of the International Conference on Database Theory*, Delphi, Greece, January 1997.
5. H. Gupta and I. Mumick. Selection of Views to Materialize Under a Maintenance-Time Constraint. In *Proceedings of the International Conference on Database Theory*, Jerusalem, Israel, January 1999.
6. Y. Kotidis and N. Roussopoulos. DynaMat: A Dynamic View Management System for Data Warehouses. In *Proceedings of the ACM SIGMOD Conference*, Philadelphia, USA, 1999.
7. H. Mistry, P. Roy, and K. Ramamritham. Materialized View Selection and Maintenance Using Multi-Query Optimization. In *Proceeding of the International Conference on Management of Data SIGMOD*, USA, 2001.
8. P. Roy, S Seshadri, S. Sudarshan, and B. Siddhesh. Efficient and Extensible Algorithms for Multiquery Optimization. In *Proceeding of the International Conference on Management of Data SIGMOD*, San Diego, USA, 2000.
9. D. Theodoratos and T. Sellis. Data warehouse configuration. In *In Proceedings of the 23rd International Conference on Very Large Data Bases, VLDB'1997*, 1997.
10. D. Theodoratos and T. Sellis. Incremental Design. *Journal of Intelligent Information Systems*, 15:7–27, 2000.
11. TPC-R Benchmark Standard Specification 2.01, January 1999. *http://www.tpc.org*.
12. J. Yang, K. Karlapalem, and Q. Li. Algorithm for Materialized View Design in data Warehousing Environment. In *Proceedings of the 23rd International Conference on Very Large Data Bases, VLDB'1997*, pages 136–145, Athens, Greece, 1997.

Quality Prediction and Assessment for Product Lines

Hongyu Zhang, Stan Jarzabek, and Bo Yang

Department of Computer Science
School of Computing
National University of Singapore
3 Science Drive 2, Singapore 117543
{zhanghy, stan, yangb}@comp.nus.edu.sg

Abstract. In recent years, software product lines have emerged as a promising approach to improve software development productivity in IT industry. In the product line approach, we identify both commonalities and variabilities in a domain, and build generic assets for an organization. Feature diagrams are often used to model common and variant product line requirements and can be considered part of the organizational assets. Despite their importance, quality attributes (or non-functional requirements, NFRs) such as performance and security have not been sufficiently addressed in product line development. A feature diagram alone does not tell us how to select a configuration of variants to achieve desired quality attributes of a product line member. There is a lack of an explicit model that can represent the impact of variants on quality attributes. In this paper, we propose a Bayesian Belief Network (BBN) based approach to quality prediction and assessment for a software product line. A BBN represents domain experts' knowledge and experiences accumulated from the development of similar projects. It helps us capture the impact of variants on quality attributes, and helps us predict and assess the quality of a product line member by performing quantitative analysis over it. For developing specific systems, members of a product line, we reuse the expertise captured by a BBN instead of working from scratch. We use examples from the Computer Aided Dispatch (CAD) product line project to illustrate our approach.

1 Introduction

The challenge in today's software engineering is to deliver high-quality software on time to customers [33]. Successful companies must have a focus on customer satisfaction and software quality to ensure that the desired quality is built into the software product and that customers remain loyal to the company. This is especially true for the IT industry where customers have ever-increasing expectations of software quality. Software quality has become a major concern of software organizations [43]. However, it is well known that quality is "hard to define, impossible to measure, easy to recognize [26]". A lot of research thus has been done to refine the concept of quality into a number of *quality attributes* (also known as quality characteristics, quality factors or quality criteria (see e.g., [1, 7, 15, 36]). The ISO 9126 standard for information technology [19] provides a framework for the evaluation of software quality, which defines six product quality characteristics, i.e.,

J. Eder and M. Missikoff (Eds.): CAiSE 2003, LNCS 2681, pp. 681–695, 2003.

functionality, reliability, usability, efficiency, maintainability, and portability. Nevertheless, it is a general consensus that different quality attributes can be adopted based on different users and their different intentions of the use of the software. In the software engineering context, quality attributes are also called non-functional requirements (NFRs) [9, 28, 32, 39].

Software product line (also called product family or system family) approach, initiated by Parnas [34], has attracted a lot of attention from both researchers and practitioners [11, 42]. It proves to be an effective approach to improve software development productivity [2, 29] and it has been successfully applied to the development of IS software. A product line arises from situations when we need develop multiple similar products for different clients, or from a single system over years of evolution. Members of a product line share many common requirements and characteristics. They may perform similar tasks, exhibit similar behavior, or use similar technologies. While having much in common, they still differ in certain requirements, design decisions, and implementation details. The variability stems from many sources such as customer's specific needs, mutability of the environment, system maintenance and evolution, and so on.

In the product line approach, we identify both commonalities and variabilities in a domain, and build generic assets such as domain model, product line architecture, generic components, etc. During reuse-based application engineering (the process of producing specific product line members), we reuse the product line assets instead of working from scratch. Generally speaking, there could be a large number of variants in a product line and not all configurations of the variants are valid or "good" in terms of the quality attributes of the target system. Some variants, especially design decisions, have considerable impact on system quality. Very often, we need to make tradeoffs among many "competing" decisions based on the achievable system quality and thus a systematic way of decision-making among different configurations is needed.

Feature diagrams [24] are commonly used in modeling common and variant product line requirements. Feature models appeal to many product line developers because customers and engineers usually speak of product characteristics in terms of the features the product has or delivers, so it is natural and intuitive to express any commonality or variability in terms of features [25]. A feature diagram provides a graphical tree-like notation that shows the hierarchical organization of the features. By traversing feature trees, we can find out which variants have been anticipated and accommodated in a product line. However, a feature diagram alone does not show how different configurations affect system quality attributes.

In this paper, we propose a Bayesian Belief Network (BBN) based approach to explicitly modeling the impact of variants (especially design decisions) on system quality attributes. A BBN represents domain experts' knowledge and experiences accumulated from the development of similar projects. It helps us capture the impact of variants on quality attributes, and helps us predict and assess the quality of a system by performing quantitative analysis over it. The constructed BBN is an important reusable asset in an organization. With the help of the BBN model, during reuse-based application engineering we can select a configuration of variants in a more informed and rational way.

As a representation of design knowledge, the constructed BBN could be stored and managed in an experience factory [4], which facilitates accumulation of project experiences in order to continuously improve software development practices. In this way, our approach helps companies to progress from ad hoc development towards the "rational design process".

In the remaining part of the paper, we describe our approach and illustrate it with examples from our domain-engineering project on the Computer Aided Dispatch (CAD) domain.

2 CAD Domain Overview

In this section, we give a brief overview of CAD domain. Computer Aided Dispatch (CAD) systems are mission-critical systems that are used by police, fire & rescue, health service, port operation company and many others. Figure 1 depicts a basic operational scenario and roles of a CAD system for Police.

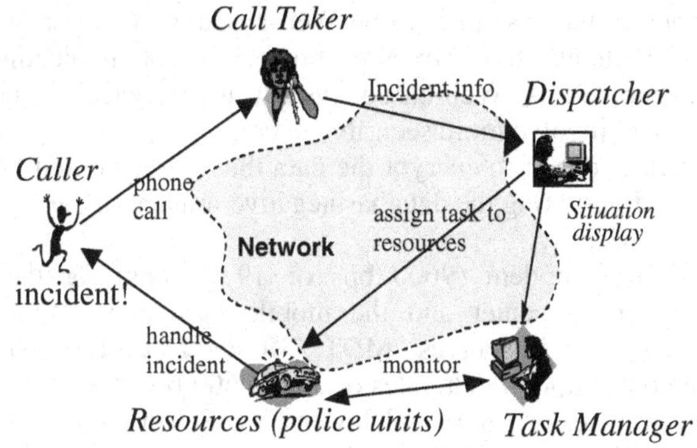

Fig. 1. The basic operational scenario in a CAD system for Police

Once a Caller reports an incident, a Call Taker in command and control center captures the details about the incident and the Caller, and creates a task for the incident. The system shows the Dispatcher a list of un-dispatched tasks. The Dispatcher examines the situation, selects suitable Resources (police units) and dispatches them to execute the task. The Resources carry out the task instructions and report to the Task Manager. The Task Manager actively monitors the situation and at the end, closes the task.

CAD systems in general shall exhibit the following quality attributes: high performance (in response time), high security, high scalability and low cost.

At the basic operational level, all CAD systems are similar - they support the dispatch of units to handle incidents. However, there are also differences across CAD systems. All these differences can be treated as variant requirements for developing a CAD product line. After domain analysis, we have identified the following variants in a CAD product line:

1. Architectural style: choosing between a three-tier one and a distributed one. In a three-tiered (client-business logic-database) system, business logic and database transactions are done in servers at control center. In a fully distributed system, the

business logic is distributed among different nodes (such as Call Taker, Dispatcher, Task Manager); each node is an active object that communicates with other nodes. A distributed system is expected to improve system performance and scalability, but may incur higher cost.

2. Database: The database can be a centralized database that is stored in a central place. Alternatively, it can also be a distributed database, which allows data to be distributed according to the organization's structure. For example, a distributed database allows the Caller Information table to be stored closer to the Call Taker site. As the distributed database allows the access of the data closer to the data usage, the communication traffic can be reduced and the performance can be improved. However, the distributed database may require more design and development effort, thus it may increase system cost. Furthermore, the selection of distributed database is dependent on the selection of architectural style – only when the distributed architectural style is selected can the distributed database be selected.
3. Deciding whether the system is to be Web-based or not. In a Web-based system, clients are web clients (based on Web browsers), communicating with server via the Internet/Intranet. A Web-based system is expected to be more scalable, however, it could involve more security concerns.
4. Deciding whether or not to encrypt the data that is transmitted between the clients and the server. Encrypting the data has negative impact on the system performance, but it improves security.
5. Selecting wireless modem (9600 bps or 19200 bps) for the communications between the control center and the mobile Resources. Wireless modems are connected to mobile Resources' MDT (Mobile Data Terminal), some wireless networks can only support data rates of up to 9600 bps. Selecting 9600 bps modem may cause lower performance and lower cost. Selecting 19200 bps modem may cause higher performance but also higher cost.
6. Validation of caller and task information. In some CAD systems, a basic validation check (i.e., checking the completeness of the Caller and Task info) is sufficient; in other CAD systems, validation includes duplicate task checking, VIP place checking, etc.; yet in other CAD systems, no validation is required at all.
7. Call Taker and Dispatcher roles (referred to as CT–DISP variant). In some CAD systems, Call Taker and Dispatcher roles are separated (played by two different people), while in other CAD systems the Call Taker and Dispatcher roles are played by the same person.
8. Dispatch Algorithm. There are different ways to dispatch Resources, using shortest distance search algorithm or location code search algorithm.

3 Modeling Variants in CAD Product Line by a Feature Diagram

Feature diagrams [24, 25] are often used to model common and variant product line requirements. Figure 2 shows a fragment of a feature diagram for CAD product line. Tools such as AmiEddi (available at www.generative-programming.org) can be used to construct feature diagrams.

Feature diagram provides a graphical tree-like notation that shows the hierarchical organization of the features. By traversing the feature trees, we can find out which variants have been anticipated during domain analysis. Features are classified as mandatory, optional and alternative (Czarnecki and Eisenecker also proposed the or-features [12]). Common requirements can be modeled as mandatory features whose ancestors are also mandatory. Variant requirements can be modeled as optional, alternative, or or-features. For example, the "Call Taker and Dispatcher roles" requirement described above has two alternative variants: "Separated" and "Merged". The optional "Validation" requirement has two or-variants: "Basic Validation" and "Advanced Validation", which means that the "Validation" requirement can be "Basic Validation", "Advanced Validation", or both or neither of them.

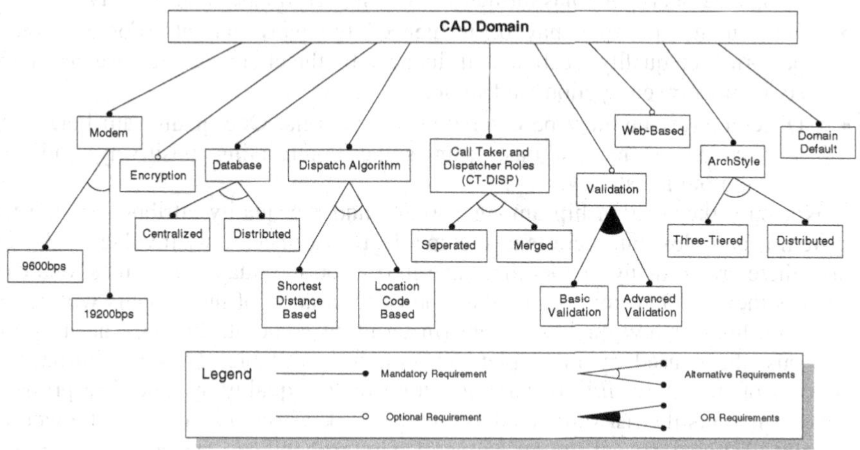

Fig. 2. CAD feature diagram (partial)

From a feature diagram, we can select a configuration of variants to construct a specific system (a product line member). For example, we can choose the following configuration of variants:

19200 bps modem, no encryption, centralized database, location code based dispatch algorithm, merged Call Taker and Dispatcher roles, basic validation, non-web based system, three-tired architecture

Obviously there exist many other configurations. Different configurations may lead to different systems that satisfy the same set of functional requirements. A natural question arises, i.e., how to choose among all possible configurations? Is there a systematical way by which we can select a "good" configuration under some criteria to construct the target system? Feature diagram alone does not give the answer or any guidelines to this question.

4 Modeling the Impact of Variants on System Quality

Generally speaking, besides the functional requirements, the customer is also very much concerned about the quality of the target system, such as performance, reliability, scalability, etc. Therefore, it is essential to assess the impact of different configurations on the system quality. If a serious negative impact of one configuration on some of the system quality attributes has been detected, we shall consider not to choose this configuration. In fact, we should aim at a target system that exhibits most desired quality attributes by choosing a "good" configuration.

Unfortunately, it is not an easy job to assess (either qualitatively or quantitatively) the impact of different configurations on the quality attributes of the target system. Basically, the difficulty results from the illusive nature of the quality and is also due to the complex interrelationships among variants (especially design decisions) and quality attributes. Taking the CAD product line as an example, we can see that:

- One variant may influence many quality attributes. For example, the choice of using data encryption has influence on both performance and security.
- One quality attribute may be influenced by many variants. For example, the performance quality attribute is influenced by the choice of database, architecture style, modem, encryption, and so on.
- Different variants may be competing or synergic. One quality attribute may be affected by many variants, with some contributing positively and others contributing negatively.

Not only the relationship among variants and the quality attributes of the target system is complex, but there is also some degree of uncertainty involved [13, 32]. In fact, there are so many factors that have impact on the quality attributes, one cannot address them all and say for sure that one configuration of the variants will certainly lead to a high or low quality system (in terms of some attributes). The uncertainty may also be caused by incomplete information available. Thus we introduce the concept of the *probability* of having a high or low quality system. The probability concept reflects the risks involved in the design decision making [6]. Littlewood and Strigini [27] also answer the questions of why probabilistic reasoning is required by software reliability engineering.

Bayesian Belief Network (BBN, also called Bayesian Network or Probabilistic Networks) is a powerful technique for reasoning under uncertainty [21, 35] and has been successfully applied to a number of domains [13, 14, 17, 18, 22]. In view of the complexity and uncertainty involved in the problem discussed above, we propose a BBN model for the prediction and assessment of the impact of variants on system quality attributes.

4.1 Bayesian Belief Network – The Graphical Model

Bayesian Belief Network (BBN) is a knowledge representation. It provides a graphical model that resembles human reasoning. A graphical model consists of a set of nodes representing variables and a set of directed edges representing causal/influential relationship among these variables. The variables and directed edges form a directed acyclic graph (DAG).

Figure 3 shows the BBN for the CAD domain. Here, nodes are variables that represent design decisions and quality attributes. A directed edge represents the influential relationship between two nodes (meaning that one has influence on the other). As described in previous section, we have identified eight variants in the CAD product line, out of which the first five (ArchStyle, Database, Web-based, Encryption, Modem) are design decisions to be made by the software developer. The last three variants (Validation, CT-DISP and Dispatch Algorithm) are functional variants that will be determined by the customer and the developer has no control over them, thus we exclude these three variants in the BBN model.

We have identified four quality attributes, namely Performance (High or Low), Security (High or Low), Scalability (High or Low), and Cost (High or Low). It should be noted that the definition of "High" or "Low" depends on specific domain's industrial norm and it varies from domain to domain. For example, for the Performance attribute of one domain, if the industry standard requires that the response time of the target system should not exceed 0.5 ms, then we may define "High" performance as one for which the response time is less than or equal to 0.5 ms, whereas the "Low" performance as one for which the response time is greater than 0.5 ms. However, based on the industrial norm for another domain, the "High" performance may be defined as one for which the response time is less than or equal to 500 ms and the "Low" performance as one for which the response time is greater than 500 ms.

The BBN model (Figure 3) captures domain experts' knowledge and experiences that are accumulated from similar projects in a domain. By studying the BBN, one can see how many design decisions and quality attributes are considered in the CAD architectural design, the design alternatives that each design decision has, and the influential relationships among design decisions and quality attributes. In this aspect, this model resembles the Softgoal Interdependency Graph (SIG) proposed by Chung et al. [9].

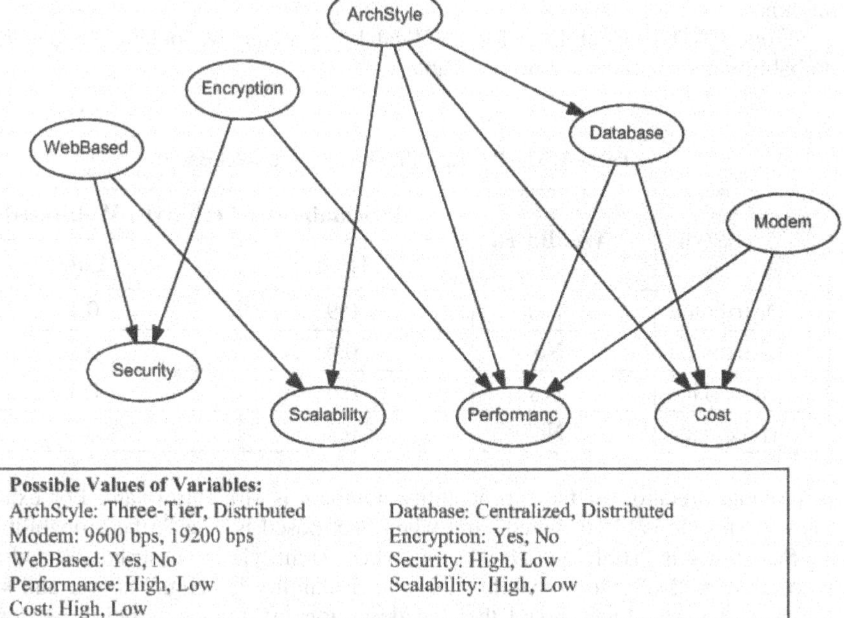

Fig. 3. The Bayesian Belief Network for CAD domain (partial)

4.2 Quantifying the Graphical Model

One advantage of the BBN is that it can not only capture the qualitative relationships among variables (denoted by nodes) but also quantify the conceptual relationships. This is done by assigning conditional probability to each node in the BBN. In a BBN, for each variable *v* with parent *Parent*(*v*), there is a corresponding conditional probability distribution *P*(*v*|*Parent*(*v*)) (If *v* has no parents, it has the prior probability *P*(*v*)). For example, in CAD domain, the probability of having high or low scalable system is conditioned by two design decisions: ArchStyle and WebBased. Thus the conditional probability is given as P(Scalability | ArchStyle, WebBased).

A probability number reflects domain expert's belief in how much a given design decision influences quality attributes. These numbers come from either objective data or the experiences of the domain expert accumulated from the development of similar projects. Group-consensus techniques can be used to assess the probabilities from a group of experts. The process of acquiring probabilities from experts is the process of knowledge engineering, in which knowledge engineers conduct interviews or surveys on experts. To assess the probability numbers, one can adapt Boehm's method used in software risk management [6]. In this method, one uses a probability-range estimation to represent the high (0.7 to1.0), medium (0.4 to 0.6) and low (0.0 to 0.3) degree of influence. Value 1.0 is logic True – if P(A=a|B=b) is 1.0, it means that given B=b, A must be a. Value 0.0 is logic False – if P(A=a|B=b) is 0.0, it means that given B=b, A shouldn't be a. Other values between 0.0 and 1.0 are in proportion to the degree of influence.

In our CAD product line, for the Scalability node, we obtain the conditional probability distribution as shown in Table 1.

Table 1. The P (Scalability | ArchStyle, WebBased)

ArchStyle	**WebBased**	**P(Scalability | ArchStyle, WebBased)**	
		High	**Low**
Distributed	Yes	0.9	0.1
Distributed	No	0.6	0.4
Three-Tier	Yes	0.6	0.4
Three-Tier	No	0.3	0.7

The interpretation of these probability numbers is straightforward. For example, when ArchStyle is "Distributed" and when WebBased is "Yes", the probability that the Scalability is "High" is 0.9; whereas when ArchStyle is "Distributed" and when WebBased is "No", the probability that the Scalability is "High" is 0.6; and so on. Again here it should be noted that the definition of "high scalability" is domain-specific.

Similarly, we can assign probabilities to other nodes in Figure 3. Due to space limitation, here we shall not list all the probability tables.

Having quantified the graphical model, we can perform quantitative analysis (e.g., predicting the quality of the target system), which will be described in detail in next section.

5 Configuring Variants in a Product Line

5.1 Reuse of Feature Diagram and BBN Model

Both the feature diagram and the BBN model we have developed so far are assets of an organization – they all capture variant requirements in a domain and can be reused in the reuse-based application engineering.

In reuse-based application engineering for CAD systems, we examine the CAD feature diagram (Figure 2) to understand how many variants are identified in the product line, and to select required variants. This is done by first analyzing customer's requirements for a specific system, and then finding a matching set of features from the feature diagram. It is important that application engineers should work with customers to select the features that the customers really want.

We also examine the BBN model (Figure 3) to understand the impact of design decisions on the quality attributes and to make decisions on adopting or rejecting a design. Not all configurations are "good" with respect to the quality requirements. Different configurations of variants may lead to different systems that satisfy the same set of functional requirements, but differ in certain quality attributes. Very often, we need to make tradeoffs among many "competing" decisions. Thus, during application engineering, we shall carefully configure variants so that the resulting system could satisfy required functional requirements and exhibit desired quality attributes.

It will certainly require extra efforts to construct the feature diagram and the BBN model for a product line. However, these efforts will pay off when the models become organizational assets and are reused for future projects. Based on these assets, one can make rational design decisions and construct target system (a member of the product line) more easily.

5.2 Quality Prediction and Assessment

In this section, we illustrate in detail how one can predict the quality of the target system and how rational design decisions can be made based on the analysis of the BBN model.

For example, if an architect designs a specific CAD system as follows (marked as configuration 1):

- ArchStyle = "Three-Tier"
- Database = "Centralized"
- Encryption = "No"
- WebBased = "No"
- Modem = "19200 bps"

We can predict the quality of the resulting CAD system by performing quantitative analysis over the CAD BBN. Assuming the above decisions have made, we can update the BBN in Figure 3 by propagating these decisions over the network and updating the probability distributions of other nodes. There are many inference algorithms available [21, 35]. In our project, we use the *junction tree* method [21], one of the efficient and scalable methods for making inferences in a BBN. The inference can be automated with the aid of BBN tools such as the Hugin tool (available at www.hugin.com). Figure 4 shows the updated BBN constructed by Hugin.

In the left frame of Figure 4, nodes that have a value of 100.00 indicate the decisions made. We can predict that the probability of having high performance is 60%, the probability of having high scalable system is 30%, the probability of having high security is 60%, and the probability of having low cost system is 60%.

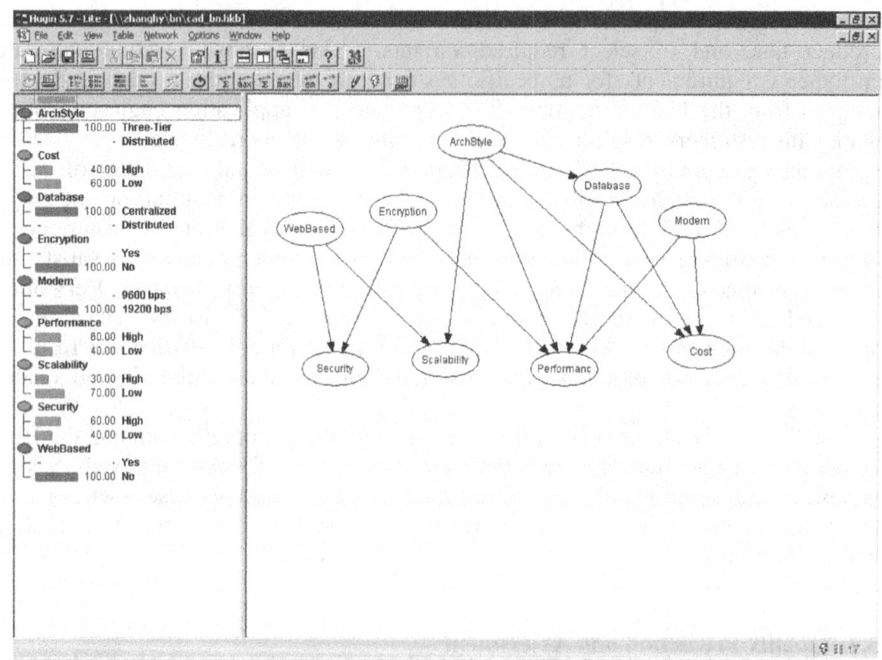

Fig. 4. The updated CAD Bayesian Belief Network (with configuration 1)

For the same CAD system, the architect may also have the following design (marked as configuration 2):

- ArchStyle = "Distributed"
- Database = "Distributed"
- Encryption = "Yes"
- WebBased = "Yes"
- Modem = "19200 bps"

We can predict from Figure 5 that this time, the probability of having high performance system is 70%, the probability of having high scalable system is 90%, the probability of having high secured system is 60%, and the probability of having low cost system is 10%.

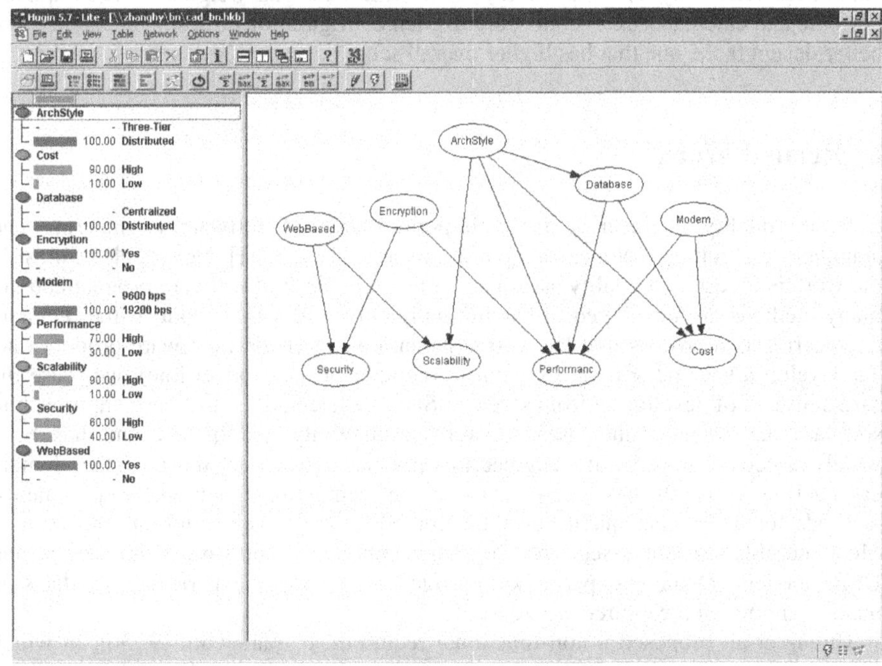

Fig. 5. The updated CAD Bayesian Belief Network (with configuration 2)

Table 2 shows the comparison between the predicted quality attributes of the target system by configuration 1 and by configuration 2. The numbers shown are the probabilities of having the desired quality attributes. The "+" sign indicates the superior configuration with respect to the quality attribute.

Table 2. The comparison between configuration 1 and configuration 2

	PERFORMANCE (High)	SCALABILITY (High)	SECURITY (High)	COST (Low)
Configuration 1	60%	30%	60%	60% (+)
Configuration 2	70% (+)	90% (+)	60%	10%

Configuration 1 is better than configuration 2 with respect to the system cost. However configuration 1 may lead to a system that is more likely to have low scalability and low performance. Configuration 2 is superior with respect to scalability and performance. However it may result in a system that is more likely to have high cost. For this specific CAD system, if the customer's preference of quality attributes is cost >> security >> performance >> scalability (where ">>" means much more important than), then the configuration 1 is preferable. If the customer's preference is performance >> security >> scalability >> cost, then the configuration 2 is preferable.

To more precisely evaluate a configuration with respects to customer's preference on multiple quality attributes, we can use more rigorous techniques such as the Analytical Hierarchy Process (AHP) [40], which assigns weights to each quality attribute and calculates an overall score to each configuration of design decisions. The better design is the one that has higher overall score.

6 Related Work

Software quality engineering is an important area of software engineering and abundant research has been carried out in this area [16, 23, 31]. Nevertheless, most of the work is focused on quality assurance of a single piece of software product and not many methods are developed to handle the quality issues in a product line. Domain engineering is a process that leads to systematic support for a software product line. To develop a specific software system (a member of the product line), we reuse the assets instead of developing from scratch. Such a systematic, reuse-based approach to software development increases software productivity and quality and has been widely accepted in software engineering practice. However, most of the domain engineering research has been focusing on achieving functional requirements; methods for addressing quality attributes or NFRs are largely informal and ad hoc. Most reusable domain assets are program components, software architectures, and UML models. Domain expert's knowledge and personal experiences in decision making are not well captured and reused.

Chung et al. proposed a non-functional requirement framework [9, 30], in which non-functional requirements are treated as soft-goals (goals that do not have a clear-cut criterion for their satisfaction) and represented graphically as softgoal interdependency graphs (SIGs). SIGs are similar to a Bayesian Belief Network in the way that they can also capture and represent design knowledge.

In last decades Bayesian Belief Network has attracted much attention from both research and industry communities. BBN provides a natural way to structure information about a domain, resembling human reasoning. BBN is based on rigorous graph theory and probability theory, over which quantitative analysis can be conducted. BBN has been successfully applied to many application domains. In software engineering area Fenton and Neil [13, 14] used BBN for software defect prediction and software quality prediction. We use BBN to represent the software design knowledge and experiences for a product line. We can perform both qualitative and quantitative analysis over the constructed BBN to understand how the design decisions influence quality attributes, and to make rational design decisions.

There are also some performance models proposed [3, 37] to establish a link between software performance and software architecture and some adopted the Layered Queuing Network (LQN) approach [38, 44]. However, these performance models do not address other quality attributes such as maintainability or security. Our proposed BBN approach considers many quality attributes and can model the interrelationship among design decisions and quality attributes.

The Architecture Tradeoff Analysis Method (ATAM) [10] and its predecessor Software Architecture Analysis Method (SAAM) [5] evaluate a software architecture mainly after the architecture is designed. These methods require a brainstorming section to generate a list of possible scenarios to test the architectures for single systems. In our approach, we explore design alternatives through careful domain analysis, and produce a BBN that is reusable in a domain.

Experience factory approach [4] defines a framework for experience management, in order to institutionalize the collective learning of an organization. The experience factory approach collects and manages a variety of experience including project data, technology reports and lessons learned, and provides repository services for this experience. As a representation of design knowledge, our BBN could be also stored and managed in an experience factory.

7 Conclusion

In software product line research, methods for handling quality attributes (NFRs) have been largely informal and ad hoc. In this paper, we propose a Bayesian Belief Network based approach to address the problem of analysis and prediction of quality attributes for a product line. We use BBN to capture the design knowledge and experiences of domain experts. Our approach improves the understanding of the impact of design decisions on quality attributes and helps the developer make more informed and rational decisions. For developing specific systems, we reuse this expertise instead of working from scratch.

We believe our approach provides a systematic way of addressing quality attributes for software product lines and helps organization achieve more matured, reuse-based software development. Clearly this research is still at early stage. In the future, we shall evaluate the effectiveness and scalability of our approach in large-scale industrial projects. Better methods and tools shall be developed to facilitate the acquisition of probabilities from experts. For some design decisions and quality attributes, the assessment of probabilities could be improved through the collection of objective data. We shall also integrate the proposed approach with frame-based product line development methods [8, 20, 41]. We hope that our approach could be an integral part of knowledge management practice in a software organization.

References

1. Anderson, B.B., Bajaj, A. and Gorr, W.: An estimation of the decision models of senior IS managers when evaluating the external quality of organizational software, The Journal of Systems and Software, 61 (2002) pp. 59–75
2. Ardis, M., Daley, N., Hoffman, D., Siy, H. and Weiss, D.: Software product lines: a case study, Software-Practice & Experience, 30 (2000) pp. 825–847
3. Aquilani, F., Balsamo, S., Inverardi, P.: Performance analysis at the software architectural design level", Performance Evaluation, 45 (2001) pp. 147–178
4. Basili, V. and Caldiera, G.: Improve software quality by reusing knowledge and experience, *Sloan Management Review*, 37 (1995) pp. 55–64.
5. Bass, L., Clements, P. and Kazman, R.: Software Architecture in Practice, Addison-Wesley (1998)
6. Boehm, B.: Software Risk Management: Principles and Practices, IEEE Software, 8 (1991) pp. 32–41.

7. Boehm, B.W., Brown, J.R., Kaspar, H., Lipow, M., MacLeod, G.J. and Merritt, M.J.: Characteristics of Software Quality. North-Holland Pub. Co., Amsterdam; American Elsevier, New York (1978)
8. Cheong, Y.C. and Jarzabek, S.: Frame-based method for customizing generic software architectures, *Proc. Symposium on Software Reusability*, SSR'99, Los Angeles (1999)
9. Chung, L., Nixon, B.A., Yu, E. and Mylopoulos, J.: *Non-Functional Requirements in Software Engineering*, Kluwer Academic, Boston (2000)
10. Clements, P., Kazman, R. and Klein, M.: *Evaluating Software Architectures – Methods and Case Studies*, Addison-Wesley (2002)
11. Clements, P. and Northrop, L.: *Software Product Lines: Practices and Patterns*. Addison-Wesley (2002)
12. Czarnecki, K. and Eisenecker, U.W.: Generative Programming: Methods, Tools, and Applications. Addison Wesley, Reading, MA, Singapore (2000)
13. Fenton, N. and Neil, M.: A critique of software defect prediction models, IEEE Transactions on Software Engineering, 25 (1999) pp. 675–689.
14. Fenton, N. and Neil, M.: Making decisions: using Bayesian nets and MCDA, Knowledge-Based Systems, 14 (2001) pp. 307–325.
15. Gillies, A.C.: Software Quality: Theory and Management. Chapman & Hall, London (1992)
16. Ginac, F.P. Customer Oriented Software Quality Assurance. Prentice Hall PTR, Upper Saddle River, N.J. (1998)
17. Heckerman, D., Horvitz, E. and Nathwani, B.: Towards normative experts systems: Part I. the Pathfinder project, *Methods of Information in Medicine*, 31 (1992) 90–105.
18. Heckerman, D., Breese, J., and Rommelse, K.: Decision-theoretic troubleshooting. *Communications of the ACM*, 38 (1995) 49-57.
19. ISO/IEC 9126: Information Technology – Software Product Evaluation: Quality Characteristics and Guidelines for their Use. (1991)
20. Jarzabek, S. and Zhang, H.: XML-based method and tool for handling variant requirements in domain models, to appear, *Proc. Fifth IEEE International Symposium on Requirements Engineering (RE'01)*, Toronto, Canada (2001)
21. Jensen, F.V.: *An Introduction to Bayesian Networks*. UCL Press, London (1996)
22. Jensen, F.V., Christensen, H.I., and Nielsen, J.: Bayesian methods for interpretation and control in multi-agent vision systems, *Proc. Applications of Artificial Intelligence*, Orlando (1992)
23. Kan, S.H.: Metrics and Models in Software Quality Engineering. Addison-Wesley, Reading, Mass. (1995)
24. Kang, K. et al.: Feature-Oriented Domain Analysis (FODA) Feasibility Study, Technical Report, CMU/SEI-90-TR-21, Software Engineering Institute, Carnegie Mellon University, Pittsburgh (1990).
25. Kang, K.C.; Lee, J. and Donohoe, P.: Feature-oriented product line engineering, *IEEE Software*, 19 (2002) pp. 58–65.
26. Kitchenham, B.: Software metrics. in Software Reliability Handbook. ed. by P. Rook. Elsevier Applied Science, London, New York (1990)
27. Littlewood B. and Strigini L.: Software reliability and dependability: a roadmap. Proceedings of the conference on The future of Software engineering. International Conference on Software Engineering (ICSE), Limerick, Ireland (2000)
28. Loucopoulos, P. and Karakostas, V.: *System Requirements Engineering*. McGraw-Hill, London, New York (1995)
29. Morisio, M.; Romano, D, and Stamelos, I.: Quality, productivity, and learning in framework-based development: an exploratory case study, IEEE Transactions on Software Engineering, 28 (2002) pp. 876–888.
30. Mylopoulos, J., Chung, L., Liao, S., Wang, H., and Yu, E.: Exploring alternatives during requirements analysis, IEEE Software, 18 (2001) pp. 92–96.
31. Nance, R.E. and Arthur, J.D.: *Managing Software Quality*. Springer, New York (2002).

32. Nixon, B.A.: Management of performance requirements for information systems, IEEE Transactions on Software Engineering, 26 (2000) pp. 1122–1146.
33. O'Regan, G.: *A Practical Approach to Software Quality*, Springer-Verlag, New York (2002)
34. Parnas, D.: On the design and development of program families, *IEEE Transactions on Software Engineering*, 2 (1976) pp. 1–9.
35. Pearl, J.: *Probabilistic Reasoning in Intelligent Systems: Networks of Plausible Inference*, Morgan Kaufmann (1988).
36. Perry, W.E.: Effective Methods of EDP Quality Assurance. QED Information Sciences, Wellesley, Mass. (1987)
37. Petriu, D. Shousha, C. and Jalnapurkar, A.: Architecture-based performance analysis applied to a telecommunication system, *IEEE Transactions on Software Engineering*, 26 (2000) pp. 1049–1065
38. Rolia, J.A. and Sevcik, K.C.: The method of layers, *IEEE Transactions on Software Engineering*, 21 (1995) pp. 689–700
39. Roman, G.C.: A taxonomy of current issues in requirements engineering. IEEE Computer, 18 (1985) pp. 14–23
40. Saaty, T.: *The Analytical Hierarchy Process*, McGraw-Hill, New York (1980).
41. Soe, M.S., Zhang, H. and Jarzabek, S.: XVCL: a tutorial, *Proc. of 14th Int. Conf. on Software Engineering and Knowledge Engineering*, SEKE'02, ACM Press, Italy, (2002) pp. 341-349.
42. Weiss, D. and Lai, C.: *Software Product-Line Engineering: A Family-Based Software Development Process*. Addison-Wesley, Reading, MA. (1999)
43. Wieczorek, M. and Meyerhoff, D. (ed.): *Software Quality: State of the Art in Management, Testing, and Tools*. Springer, New York (2001)
44. Woodside, C.M., Neilson, J.E., Petriu, D.C. and Majumdar, S.: The Stochastic Rendezvous Network Model for Performance of Synchronous Client-Server-Like Distributed Software, *IEEE Transactions on Computers*, 44 (1995) pp.20–34

User Agents in E-commerce Environments: Industry vs. Consumer Perspectives on Data Exchange

Sarah Spiekermann[1], Ian Dickinson[2], Oliver Günther[1], and Dave Reynolds[2]

[1]Institut für Wirtschaftsinformatik
Humboldt-Universität zu Berlin
Spandauer Str. 1
10178 Berlin, Germany
{sspiek, guenther}@wiwi.hu-berlin.de
[2]Hewlett-Packard Laboratories
Filton Road
Stoke Gifford
Bristol BS34 8QZ
United Kingdom
{ian.dickinson, dave.reynolds}@hp.com

Abstract. This paper focuses on the protection of user privacy in business-to-consumer (B2C) settings. In the first part of the paper we discuss today's commercially driven customer relationship management (CRM) practices and report on the results of an interview study we conducted with nine significant Internet industry players. We analyse their current practices and expectations on service and product differentiation, price discrimination, as well as data and advertisement sales. We discuss these data usage practices critically from a user as well as privacy rights perspective. In the second part of the paper we then use those insights and propose a combination of currently researched privacy technologies into one overall approach which we call "the user model". Here, we report on how a compromise could be achieved between industry's desires for one-to-one marketing and peoples' wish to maintain control over their privacy while profiting from personalization. We discuss the role of client-side profiling, identity management, and privacy metadata and propose development principles for a user-friendly interface solution.

1 Introduction

As use of the World Wide Web has grown, more and more information about individuals – their tastes, preferences, purchases and demographic details – has been codified in electronic form. Personal information has become an economic good. However, the rules of trade for such a good are still being determined. One way to describe the current situation is as follows: two opposing players, corporations (which collect personal data) and privacy rights advocates (who seek to curtail the abuse of personal data) negotiate over the terms and conditions of the personal information exchange. The third party, the consumer, generally has to abide by whatever the two parties agree upon. Corporations, in their struggle to survive in a competitive market with increasingly disloyal customers, regard customer data as a strategic asset. It

J. Eder and M. Missikoff (Eds.): CAiSE 2003, LNCS 2681, pp. 696–710, 2003.

promises them the chance to realize the vision of true one-to-one marketing of their products and services. Privacy rights advocates, on the other hand, fear "database nations" and the manipulative or discriminatory power of customer knowledge in the hands of profit-seeking corporations [Garf2000]. Consumers mostly don't know how much and what kind of data their product suppliers hold about them and what they are doing with it. There is evidence to suggest that, even knowing about such practices, individuals do not fully appreciate the consequences of misuse of their personal data. Consequently, it is hard for individuals to express their preferences for the trade-off between disclosure and access to individualized services and bonuses.

Drawing on the results of a case study of nine companies with significant Internet businesses, this paper investigates a change to the basic model of collecting and storing personal data as a basis for assisting users to gain better control of their privacy. We propose that it is essential to understand corporations, their business models, and the role of consumer data in marketing, in order to develop privacy technologies and frameworks that are acceptable to both companies and individuals. To this end, we look at the business models of two classes of online company, marketers and mediaries, and the role of customer data in them. Our analysis leads us to the conclusion that companies will not willingly give up the opportunity to identify those with whom they do business. We also recognize companies' desire to segment their customer base in order to do personalized or relationship-based marketing.

In contrast to the commercial trend towards personalization, we observe online users' stated desire to maintain their privacy. Reconciling these different views, we examine a one framework for achieving practical privacy based on client-side profiling. Specifically, we look at client-side profiling based on software agents, and show how, in principle, agent technology could provide a means for effective privacy protection. The paper is organised as follows: section 2 gives an overview of companies' data collection and usage practices and the benefits they derive from personalized marketing. It also contains a critical discussion of the benefits that users can gain from personalization practices, and why this concerns privacy advocates. Section 3 then analyses where compromise could be achieved between companies' customer relationship marketing (CRM) aspirations and privacy conscious individuals, based on client-side profiling. Section 4 concludes with a summary of findings.

2 Data Collection and Usage Practices

To evaluate companies' data collection and usage, practices, and some of their expectations for the future, we base our arguments on a) business studies literature on direct marketing, and b) on a case study based on nine extensive interviews that we developed in summer 2001. We interviewed experts in marketing and personalization at some of the most influential and well-known Internet portals, retailers and services providers in Germany and the USA. The interview study was jointly designed by research teams at Hewlett-Packard Laboratories and Humboldt University Berlin. In the following sections we primarily refer to online data collection practices and usage. However; as online and offline channels often work in parallel, and are intermingled from a company perspective, our report on data collection and usage practices is not exclusively restricted to Internet-centric practices and business models.

2.1 Internet Business and Data Collection Models

Data-mining and CRM are currently important subject on corporate agendas:

> "We need to know our customers better. That's the name of the game. Anything and everything is pretty much useful" [Net2000]

In order to understand why Internet companies regard user data as such a strategic asset, we must understand what role user and customer data plays in those companies' business models. For the purposes of this paper, we classify businesses on today's Internet into two types: marketers and mediaries.

- *Internet marketers* are organisations that derive their profit from selling goods and services to end-consumers through the on-line channel. A typical example for this type of organisation is Amazon.com. Marketers also include traditional offline retailers (e.g. WalMart) and direct marketers (e.g. Otto) that also offer their products to offline purchasers. Marketers derive their revenue from the sale of goods.
- *Internet mediaries* are organisations that offer mediating or supporting services to online users. This includes many different services, including e-mail, newsletters, information portals and referral services. These organisations, which include, for example, Yahoo! and AOL, derive their profit from selling banner advertisements, from collecting monthly user fees, and from transfer provisions.

Today, both, Internet marketers and mediaries collect and hold customer information themselves, which we term the *host model* (see Figure 1 a and b).

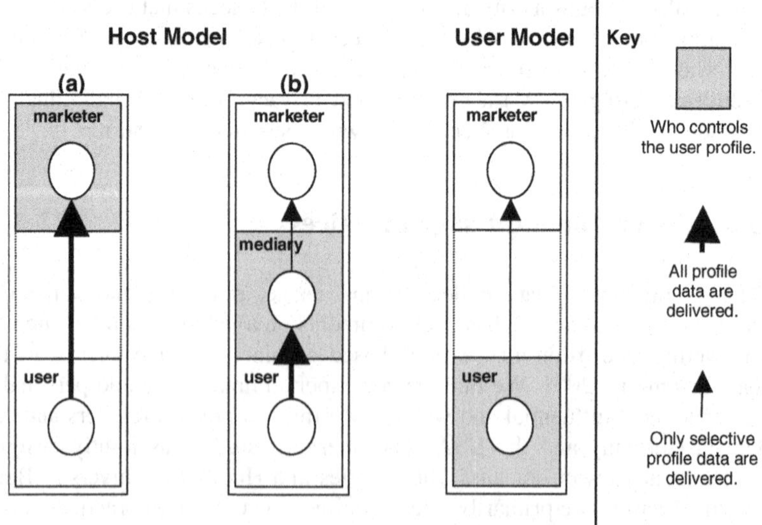

Fig. 1. The host and the user model for profile control

The host model implies that the user has no direct control over what information is stored by a given web site. As technologies such as P3P [P3P2001] achieve more widespread adoption, users will potentially gain a clearer understanding of the precise conditions under which their personal data is collected and used. However, even given this, their options are essentially limited to accepting without reservation the privacy practices of a given site, or using an alternative service. In other words Internet users in the current host model are regularly confronted with a "take it or leave it" decision: data for service (or discounts or access), or no service at all. Whether user data is then collected by a web marketer, or a mediary, once the data leaves the user's purview they cease to have control over it.Good faith or trust in the respective host is what remains as the basis for transactions. We compare this situation to an alternative in which the customer retains control of their data, and relies less on trust (see the "user model" in figure 1).

Whether this faith and trust is always justified is another question. Both marketers and mediaries use user data in many ways to their own profit and not always to the very best of all customers. The following sections will summarise how and why marketers and mediaries use customer data. For this purpose, we look at: service and product differentiation, price discrimination, targeted advertising, and data sales.

2.2 Data Usage Practices, Benefits, and Challenges

We distinguish *internal* and *external* uses of customer data. Internal data use implies that the company uses the data they collect only in order to adjust products and services to their own customers. Customer data thus serves to increase internal efficiency and/or profitability. External data use means that a company uses its user or customer data in order to derive revenue from outside the company. These revenue streams may be the result of targeted advertising or direct data sales. Figure 2 gives an overview.

2.2.1 Internal Data Usage

Our interview study revealed that four out of the five marketers we spoke to currently interact differently with different customers, depending what knowledge they have of that customer. *Service differentiation* means that companies group their customers into different value segments (e.g. A, B, C, and D customers), and then provide differing levels of service to each segment. Value in this context corresponds to the revenue a company has from, or expects to have from a customer (i.e. the number and volume of transactions), combined with the cost he or she creates. The primary reason why companies pursue service differentiation is customer retention.

Our study revealed that four out of the five marketers we spoke to segment their customers on the basis of their current value. Increasingly, however, interviewees plan to factor in the costs, and migrate to a profitability-based segmentation. Retailers in particular want to develop better models of potential future customer revenue.

From a user perspective, service differentiation can be very positively perceived. Consider the popularity of frequent flyer airline programmes. However, from a privacy perspective, we can criticize the systematic classification of people according to their financial means or spending, as it can lead to direct discrimination against those who cannot or are unwilling to spend.

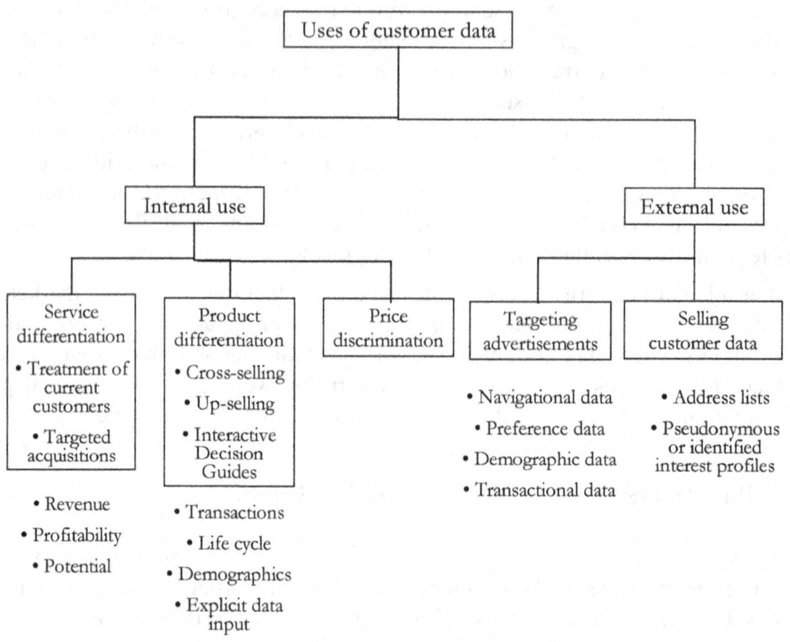

Fig. 2. How Internet companies use customer data

Product differentiation means that, based on the knowledge a company holds about its customers, it recommends products or services that it believes will suit them better. Using a customer's purchase history, demographics and clickstream (web navigation) data, companies try to derive preference and interest profiles. These profiles are then used to recommend products or services that have more functionality (at higher cost), or which enhance a product that the customer has already acquired, or which they have selected for purchase. This practice is known as *up-selling*. Alternatively, the company may recommend additional or complementary products, that might be of interest to the user according to his personal profile. This is known as *cross-selling*.

In our study, four out of five marketers we interviewed reported that they make simple personalized product offerings in the form of cross-selling or up-selling. Instead of sending bulk mails, where all customers receive the same type of offer, companies use targeted mailings or personalized websites to convince a selected group of customers of products that they believe this group to be interested in. One of our interviewees, with several million clients, claimed to offer special products and services to segments of as small as 10,000 recipients with similar profiles. As a result, the company profits from a return on marketing investment around three times higher than if it had contacted all its clients indiscriminately. The interviews confirmed that the challenge in cross-selling and up-selling is that demographic data, purchase histories, or derived preferences are not always a reliable indicator for future preferences or budget.

From a customer perspective, personalized offers based on up-selling or cross-selling practices can also be positively perceived. It allows them to save time searching for relevant information on products that are potentially of interest to them. They are made aware of offers that they would otherwise perhaps not have seen. Privacy advocates, however, fear the potentially negative effects of current product differentiation practices. Initially, systematic product differentiation has the potential of depriving people of the richness and diversity of offers. In the language of diffusion of innovation, this is called homophilous diffusion [Rog95]. Homophilous diffusion allows rapid diffusion of innovations within one socio-economic group. But diffusion throughout society requires heterophilous diffusion, where individuals seek recommendations from more advanced peers who are unlike them. This type of heterophilous diffusion can be impeded by current recommendation cross-selling and up-selling techniques.

Price discrimination refers to a seller charging buyers different prices for the same commodity. In economic literature, first and second degree price discrimination are distinguished [Ulph2000]. *First-degree* price discrimination arises when each unit of a good can be sold at a different price, while *second-degree* price discrimination occurs when different brands of the same product are sold at different prices. Price-varying markets, such as auctions, are common in online and traditional commerce. The important distinction for price discrimination in the current context is that a single seller may adjust prices according to some characteristic of the buyer while the buyer is not aware of this.

First-degree price discrimination practices for Internet trade were publicly discussed during the summer of 2000, when Amazon.com experimented with demanding different prices for the same DVD from different customers. As the subsequent uproar showed, blatantly variable pricing can cause great image and PR damage. Our interview study confirmed this. Despite its direct impact on profit, half of the participating interviewees did not believe that price discrimination would have a great influence on their profitability in the future, as image considerations would impede its systematic use as a marketing tool. Early bookings, or being the first in a queue, can reward customers as a consequence of 'open rules of the game', where everyone initially has the same chance. The problem with the type of variable prices tested by Amazon.com is of different nature: it arises when discrimination takes place based on one's personal profile, and individuals are unwitting participants with no control.

2.2.2 External Data Usage

Revenue streams from *targeted advertisement*, in particular personalized banner ads, have been the basis of many online business models. There are three main principles on which banner advertising revenues depend: the number of customers who visit a site, the conversion rate, and a website host's ability to segment users. The conversion rate is a measure of your ability to persuade your prospects to take an action. In relation to banner ads it means your ability to persuade X clients to follow a banner link out of a total number of Y clients who must have seen the ad. Whether a client has really seen a banner ad is measured with the help of webbugs in addition to cookies.

The ability to segment users strongly impacts the revenue stream a website can derive from advertising. There are two driving factors for this: first, better-targeted adverts increase the conversion rate. Secondly, offering potential advertisers a clear and well-defined market segmentation presents a better proposition, and is more likely to attract the advertisers' business, and at higher fees. The better a site knows a user, based on the segmentation, the better can it display adverts attracting the user's interest. It should also be noted that online advertising rates have fallen dramatically since the burst of the "Internet bubble", and consequently many online businesses are having great difficulty in remaining viable with fees from non-personalised advertisements. It is unclear whether even highly personalised advertisements will be sufficient to change the outlook for businesses based solely on advertising revenue.

Our interviews showed that micro-segmentation activities for advertising purposes strongly vary among companies. Thus, while one company claimed to work with around thirty segments, based on demographic data, the leading-edge company interviewed in this context claimed that they use around 700 user segments. These segments are generated by integrating historical user data, demographic data and current clickstream data into the segmentation process.

A targeting practice that benefits both companies and customers alike is facilitating users to self-customize a website. Examples of this type of service include MyCDNow, MyYahoo!, or Amazon.com's wish and recommendation lists. Typically, a user can specify his or her information preferences, and based on these, receives customized content and advertisements. However, even though this personalization service seems to offer a compelling benefit to users, the companies we interviewed reported that only about 10% of their users register to personalise their experience of the site. If the personal space on a website is enhanced with order or account tracking services, this figure rose to around 20% of customers.

Just as is the case with personalized offers, targeted advertising can certainly be seen as a benefit to consumers, as they are made aware of suitable products that they might otherwise miss. However, the problem with homophilous diffusion also arises here. Moreover, using cookies to track users' interests for advertising purposes is becoming a serious privacy problem. This is, because companies serving online advertisements, such as Doubleclick, can track users across multiple web domains. Over a period of time, doing so allows them create more comprehensive interest profiles of online users than any single service marketer or mediary can. This is done without the consent of users, and mostly unnoticed by them.

Another method of external data usage is based on *renting or selling one's data.* Privacy rights advocates fear that personal profiles are becoming a tradable good, over which the owner of the information no longer has any influence. The assumption underlying this fear is that there is a business case for corporations sharing customer data. The Electronic Frontiers Foundation states on its website:

> "Most [people] don't realize the vast information sharing chain that exists once a company or governmental agency obtains your personal information. In some cases, personal information about you that will be shared might contain only a name and an email address. Oftentimes though, personal information can include

name, address, email address, social security numbers, URLs for web sites you've visited, as well as other information that may have been built up about you in a profile." [EFF2002]

Table 1. Summary results from interviews. (Note that the meaning of > and < varies between issues considered.)

		>	no pref	<
(a) data exchange vs. profile completeness >: no exchange, but category pooled data <: exchange with others, but market basket profiles	**Aggregate**	**75%**	**0%**	**25%**
	Marketer	60%	0%	40%
	Mediary	0%	0%	100%
(b) Contact preferences >: online contact (email), <: offline contact (postal)	**Aggregate**	**56%**	**0%**	**44%**
	Marketer	40%	0%	60%
	Mediary	75%	0%	25%
(c) High-cost identified profile vs. low cost pseudonymous >: high cost, ID <: low cost, pseudonymous	**Aggregate**	**75%**	**13%**	**13%**
	Marketer	80%	20%	0%
	Mediary	67%	0%	33%
(d) Identity of user vs. quality/reliability of profile >: user identity <: profile quality (truthful and rich)	**Aggregate**	**33%**	**44%**	**22%**
	Marketer	40%	40%	20%
	Mediary	25%	50%	25%
(e) reliability/quality vs. control over profile >: quality (truthful and rich) <: control	**Aggregate**	**78%**	**0%**	**22%**
	Marketer	80%	0%	20%
	Mediary	75%	0%	25%
(f) Identified profile with 30% false data vs. pseudonymous profile, 100% accuracy >: identity, 30% error <: pseudonym, no error	**Aggregate**	**25%**	**13%**	**63%**
	Marketer	40%	20%	40%
	Mediary	0%	0%	100%

The companies we interviewed, however, all of which have a direct end-user customer base, do not have a strong interest in selling or sharing rich data on their customers. There are two major reasons for this. First, selling knowledge about customers would mean a company giving up some competitive business advantage. As described above, knowing a customer well (and, by implication, better than a competitor) has a direct impact on profitability. Secondly, selling knowledge about customers entails a strong risk to goodwill or image if customer harm, perceived or real, arises from such sales. Conversely, buying data is exposed to the risks arising from the reliability of the source. As poor promotion is regarded as detrimental, companies fear putting customers into wrong segments due to low quality data purchased externally. Consequently, we found that companies are hesitant to purchase more than address lists and socio-economic classifications from external sources. Thus, good marketing practices prohibit, at least to some extent, the sharing of enriched customer data.

In fact, none of the companies interviewed generated revenue from selling rich customer data. Only 22% said that they would sell address or mailing lists. And when asked to choose between a category-pooled profile (where only the spending of customers in one product category is known) that is not shared with others, or a market-basket profile (where the entire consumption pattern of a consumer is know) but which is shared with others, both marketers and mediaries preferred the less rich profile that they would not have to share (see Table 1 (a)).

However, concerns about the trade of customer data are not completely unfounded. All companies we interviewed also agreed that market-based profiles are more valuable than category-restricted profiles (see Figure 3). Thus, pooling is seen as a valuable profile enhancement. Also, there are scenarios in which sharing of customer data occurs beyond trading. One is where a company that owns customer data is taken over, or its assets are bought by another company. A second scenario in which customer data is pooled is when ‘friendly’ companies from different business areas, and with equally rich profiles, share data on equal terms to enhance their profiles.

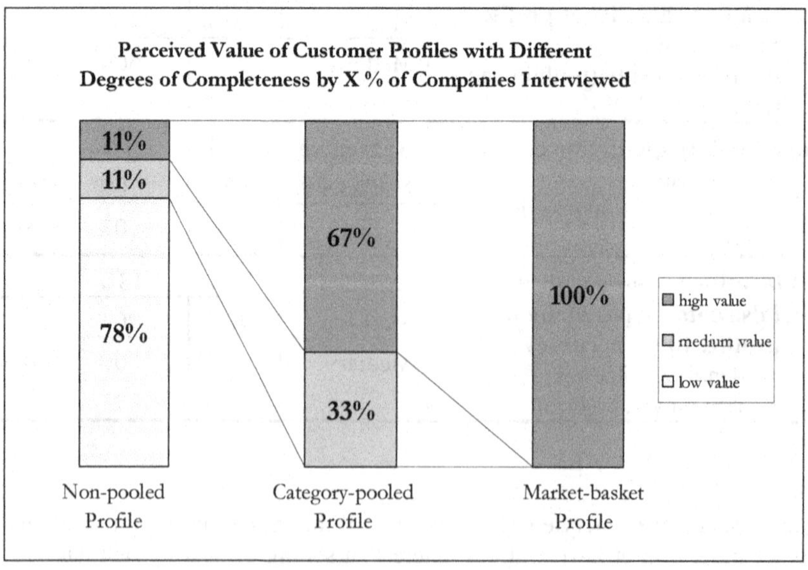

Fig. 3. Perceived value of customer profiles

3 Information System Design Implications from Data Usage Practices

3.1 Case Study Findings on Pseudonymity, Data Reliability, and Control

The above description of marketing practices and business models summarises how customer personal data is used by businesses today. Internally, marketers, particularly, use customer data to ensure higher campaign response rates and increase customer loyalty while reducing marketing expenses. Externally, customer data can be used to directly increase revenue from advertisements, or raise revenue through data rental.

Given these common business practices, developers of privacy enhancing technologies must recognize that companies view customer data as a valuable asset and will insist on having the possibility to segment customers and personalize marketing material. Moreover, as was outlined above, personalization also brings benefits for consumers that many may wish to take advantage of, or have already done so.

Against this background, it is questionable to what extent privacy enhancing technologies can be successful that lead to a default 'hiding' of users and denial of information sharing practices. Current anonymizing services such as Anonymizer.com, Freedom or JAP (Java Anon Proxy) pursue this strategy, supported by cookie management software including Junkbuster, WebWasher or CookieCooker. However, by protecting users by default from information revelation, they also deprive them of the benefits of personalization. What follows is that neither companies nor users seem to be enthused about using these software solutions; especially not to the point that they would be willing to pay for them. Given this conflict of interest between personalization and privacy, many privacy technology developers have started to propose the idea of identity management systems that protect users' privacy on the basis of transaction or relationship pseudonyms [Jend2000, Köhn2000, Libe2001]. Pseudonyms can protect a person's identity, but still allow for a personalized relationship between a customer and a company. A user can simply choose to re-use the same pseudonym to build a business relationship over time. This relationship pseudonym can then be used by the marketers or mediaries as an identifier to build up a personal profile [Köhn2000, Jend2000, Bert2000]. Marketing communications can consequently be personalized without forcing the user or customer to permanently reveal his or her true identity.

With a view to these technological advancements, we asked companies in our interviews for their views on the concept of pseudonymity in electronic business relationships. The responses revealed that, from a business perspective, there are some major challenges for the pseudonymity concept: First, companies believe that a customer profile gains in value for them, the more identified it is (Figure 4). This is because they view themselves as having an active role in commerce, which implies that they need to personally address customers and users to pro-actively market products and services. Also there is a strong belief that addressing a customer personally increases the perception of service quality [Kief2001]. And, as other authors have pointed out [Clark], there equally is an emotionally strong scepticism towards the systematic use of pseudonyms in business relations. Short-term pseudonyms or anonymous communications preclude the possibility of offering high-quality personal service, and impede the personalized marketing practices described in section 2. Relationship pseudonyms would allow for personalized marketing, but, in its current technical realization, precludes addressing the customer by their name. Finally, the use of pseudonyms presents challenges for the management of delivery or after-sales services.

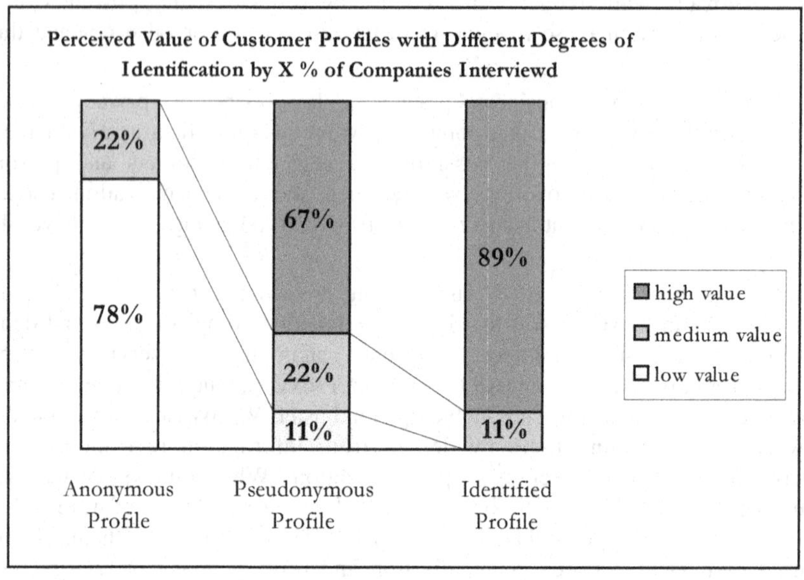

Fig. 4. Perceived value of profile identification

In addition to asking companies about the economic value of different profile types, we also asked them to express their relative preference for pairs of bipolar alternatives that would display different qualities in terms of privacy, control and reliability (Table 1, b and c). The trade-off preferences expressed by our interviewees showed that all parties are willing to invest having identified data rather than pseudonymous data (high cost identified profiles versus low cost pseudonymous profiles). Marketers in particular want to have an offline postal address from their customers, rather than just an online e-mail address.

All these arguments indicate that companies operating in the current host model will probably be opposed to implementing a privacy system on their side that supports the systematic use of pseudonyms. The profile collected would lose economic value, such at least is the current view of companies on the issue (see Figure 4).

However, as discussed above, even if companies wish to identify customers, they must still be concerned about profiles that are of low reliability. In fact, the quality and reliability of a profile, especially as far as customer preferences are concerned, were reported to be of concern for companies fearing flawed customer segmentation and flawed personalization. This is reflected in interviewees' responses when presented with a trade-off between identifying a customer, and having a reliable profile (Table 1, (d) through (f)). The results show indecision. This is a significant finding, given the arguments above where personal identification of customers appears to be a major requirement for businesses (see also the valuation of identified profile versus pseudonymous profile in figure 4). Furthermore, all companies stated a preference for a highly reliable and rich profile over actual physical profile control. And finally, interviewees also displayed a tendency to prefer 100% correct pseudonymous contact and demographic customer data than the data being identified, but with a 30% lying rate.

On the basis of these findings, we conclude that despite the high valuation of identified and rich profiles, companies are, if they are forced to make choices, willing to make some sacrifice in order to ensure the reliability of their customer data. Companies also recognize that high quality and reliable profiles are difficult to accumulate if people are afraid of losing their privacy online. Currently, they observe a high rate of false data in their databases due to people lying on their demographics and contact information. As Sheehan et al. report, 15% of individuals falsify information more than half the time they are asked to provide it. [Shee1999]. A very recent IFAK study [IFAK2002] found an even higher rate of false data provision: around 47% of 1200 Internet users interviewed stated that they sometimes lie about their e-mail address. As people become more computer and information literate, this rate could even rise, as could eventually the use of protective software.

3.2 Towards a Compromise: Client-Side Profiling and Agent Technology for Privacy Support

Given the above insights into companies' data usage practices and profiling preferences, we can essentially observe the following paradox: vendors want accurate, detailed information about their customers, which consumers often are willing to supply in order to gain access to better outcomes, but privacy advocates (and more aware consumers) worry about the misuse of identifiable, detailed personal information. Vendors want data, consumers want the benefit of the vendor having the data, but neither they nor their privacy guardians want detailed disclosure.

Two extremes of this argument are frequently advocated. At one extreme, it is suggested that full disclosure is economically necessary, and that market forces and self-regulation will curb the worst excesses. At the other extreme, it is suggested that those with a financial interest in our data can never be trusted to be responsible, and hence all possible measures should be taken to prevent disclosure. Clearly, there is scope for a middle ground.

We suggest that practical privacy means allowing a reasonable degree of disclosure, under controlled conditions, and clearly in exchange for a benefit to the user. The starting point for this practical privacy may be the fact that companies seem to be ready for compromise when it comes to the reliability and quality of the data they can receive from their customers. Moreover, data that is being provided out of free will by users, driven by the desire to receive personalized services and not apt to the risk of a backlash on privacy. For this type of highly reliable data, companies reported, marketers and mediaries alike, that they would sacrifice some control over data, meaning that the data does not have to be stored necessarily in their own databases.

From this starting point, we propose the use of a client-side software agent, profiling the user under his or her control, and managing personalized commercial relationships for the user in a privacy-friendly manner. The software agent realizes what we labelled the user model of a company-client relationship (Figure 1), because the user in this scenario would take control over data revelation and data use.

The user-model is based on a framework of mediation between users and companies (and other entities) on the WWW and includes the following key agent capabilities:

1. *Building and maintaining a rich profile under the user's control and direct sphere of influence (client-side profiling).* The central idea is that profiles are not developed exclusively by companies on the server or host side, but by software on the user's client computer. Thus the profile is built under the user's control. Parts of that personal profile can then be placed at the disposition of marketers or peer networks in order to receive appropriate and personalized recommendations.
2. *Managing multiple user identities.* Clearly it is not possible to prevent another party from observing, and hence recording, utterances (here: in the very general sense of units of interaction, such as clicking on a URL within a web site) in an interaction, since otherwise no discourse could occur. The only way in which people can prevent a decrease in their privacy despite progressive disclosure of their profiles is to manage their identities. A number of identity management systems are now being proposed by researchers [Köhn2000, Jend2000, Bert2000, Libe2001]. These tools will be able to assist online users in controlling their virtual identities, and ensure that customers revisit sites under the same virtual identity if they wish to (situational pseudonyms) but not necessarily under their true physical one.
3. *Providing an innovative user interface to assist the user to better manage their privacy settings.* Privacy, like security, is asymmetric in the sense that having it seems to have a low value, but losing it has a high cost. This leads users typically to devote little time and effort to maintaining privacy settings, or attending to privacy risks, even though the potential negative consequences are ones they wish to avoid. We therefore suggest that a key role for a privacy *agent*, in addition to being a repository for the client-side profile and identity manager, is to engage the user in an appropriate conversation around privacy preferences, and redistribute the burden of maintaining the relevant safeguards (e.g. by managing the settings of web browsers or learn by observation of the user to fine-tune his or her privacy preferences).
4. *Managing user relationships using privacy metadata.* The decision to put private information at the disposition of a third party is a choice that should be made on the basis of the sound knowledge of the reputation of the other party. This suggests an important additional privacy measure: the pro-active use of knowledge about web services and their privacy practicesas part of reputation index that indicates whether a party is trustworthy to receive ones' personal data. Such data about a service or organisation is known as *metadata*, particularly if it is machine processable. An example of such metadata is a web site's privacy

policy – a statement about that site's use of personal information. In particular, the *Platform for Privacy Preferences Project (P3P)* standard has been defined by the W3C to allow web sites to make their privacy policies machine-readable [P3P2001]. If metadata about a company's privacy (or, more particularly, lack of privacy) practices is available, a range of new services are enabled that can assist both user and vendor.

4 Conclusion

This paper has surveyed a number of aspects of protecting users' privacy in business-to-consumer (B2C) settings. In the first part of the paper we focused on the results of an interview study with nine significant Internet industry companies. We analyzed their current practices for collecting and using data on their customers, and critically discussed them from a user as well as privacy rights perspective. Based on these interview-based insights we conclude that companies fear a move to a (perceived) more passive role in commerce, a scenario in which users can choose whether or not to identify themselves. On the other hand, we also noted companies' wish for more reliable, complete and timely profile data. The wish for this type of higher quality user data may be an incentive for companies to accept and work with profiles generated on the client side. This would be a compromise between user privacy concerns and personalization benefits for both users and vendors.

Pursuing a client-side profiling strategy however, also bears some risks. Once a user reveals comprehensive data about him or herself, the circumstances under which he does so must be clearly defined. His choice must be taken on the basis of knowledge on the opposite party's reputation. Furthermore, he must have the option to shelter his identity when revealing comprehensive information. This again calls for a sophisticated identity management system operating under the user's control. Finally, all measures for privacy protection are in vain if people are not capable of using them. This means that they need not only default protection settings in their privacy tools, but also an easy to use interface supporting them in their daily privacy management tasks.

References

[Bert2000] Oliver Berthold, Hannes Federrath: Identitätsmanagement; in: Helmut Bäumler (Hg.): E-Privacy; Tagungsband zur Sommerakademie des Unabhängigen Landeszentrums für Datenschutz Schleswig-Holstein, 28. August 2000 in Kiel; Vieweg, Wiesbaden 2000; 189–204

[Bick2000] Bicknell, C., "Online Prices Not Created Equal", in: Wired News, 7th September 2000. Available from: http://www.wired.com/news/ business/0,1367,38622,00.html

[Duff2001] Duffy, D., "Get ready for the privacy backlash", Darwin B2B Network, August 2001. Available from: http://www.darwinmag.com/read/ 080101/backlash.html

[EFF2002] EFF Topics: Privacy: Marketing and Commercial. Electronic Frontier Foundation. 25th April, 2002. Available from: http://www.eff.org/ Privacy/Marketing/

[Garf2000] Garfinkel, Simon, "Database Nation – The Death of Privacy in the 21st Century", O'Reilly, 2000

[Gart2001] DeLotto, R., „Client Self-Profiling Protects Consumer Privacy", Gartner Research Note, Strategic Planning SAP-13-6930, September 2001

[Gold1997] Goldberg, Ian; Wagner, David and Brewer, Eric "Privacy-enhancing technologies for the Internet". 1997. Available from: http://www.cs.berkeley.edu/~daw/papers/privacy-compcon97-www/privacy-html.html

[Hage1997] Hagel and Rayport, "The coming battle for Customer Information", McKinsey Quarterly, no 3, pp. 64–77, 1997

[IFAK2002] IFAK study on online communication, January 2000, available at: http://www.ifak.de/about/index.php3

[Jend2000] Uwe Jendricke, Daniela Gerd tom Markotten: Usability meets Security – The Identity-Manager as your Personal Security Assistant for the Internet (PDF); in: Proceedings of the 16th Annual Computer Security Applications Conference (ACSAC 2000); New Orleans, USA; December 11–15, 2000

[Kief2001], Kiefel, Nicola, "Perspektiven von Personalisierungs-Marktmodellen und Verwendung von Kundendaten durch Unternehmen", unpublished master thesis, Berlin, September 2001

[Köhn2000] Köhntopp, M., Pfitzmann, A., "Datenschutz Next Generation", in: E-Privacy, ed. by Helmut Bäumler, Wiesbaden, 2000, pp. 316–322.

[Kotl1994] Kotler, P., Marketing Management – Analysis, Planning, Implementation, And Control, 8th edition, New Jersey, 1994

[Libe2001] The Liberty Alliance Project [Web Page]. 2001. Available from: http://www.projectliberty.org

[Lieb1996] Lieberman, Henry and Maulsby, David. Instructible agents: software that just keeps getting better. IBM Systems Journal. 1996; 35(3 - 4):539–556

[Micr2001a] Microsoft. Introducing .NET My Services [Web Page]. 2001 Sep. Available from: http://msdn.microsoft.com/library/default.asp?url=/library/en-us/Dndotnet/html/Myservintro.asp?frame=true

[Micr2001b] Microsoft Internet Explorer version 6 features. August 27, 2001. See http://www.microsoft.com/windows/ie/evaluation/features/default.asp

[Net2000] Net Genesis, "E-Metrics – Business Metrics For The New Economy", Cambride 2000

[P3P2001] World Wide Web Consortium (W3C). The Platform for Privacy Preferences Project (P3P) 1.0 Specification [Web Page]. 2001. Available from: http://www.w3.org/TR/p3p

[Pew2000] Pew Internet & American Life Project, 2000. www.pewinternet.org

[Rog95] Rogers, Everett M., Diffusions of Innovations, Fourth Edition, The Free Press, 1995

[Shea2001] Shearin, S., Liebermann, H., "Intelligent Profiling by Example", Proceedings of the Conference on Intelligent User Interfaces, IUI'01, Santa Fe, 2001

[Shee1999] Sheehan, K., Hoy, M., "Flaming, complaining, abstaining: How online users respond to privacy concerns", Journal of Advertising, Fall 1999

Pattern-Driven Design of Agent Systems: Approach and Case Study

Michael Weiss

School of Computer Science, Carleton University, Ottawa, Canada
weiss@scs.carleton.ca

Abstract. Current approaches to agent system design are generally goal-driven. An agent system is designed by iteratively decomposing system goals until they can be assigned to individual agents. However, this may lead developers to rediscover solutions to common design problems without benefiting from how they were resolved in the past. This results in duplicated effort, inconsistent design, brittle systems, and poor traceability. A more effective approach is to build an agent system incrementally from well-documented agent patterns. An agent pattern documents a proven assignment of roles to agents, and their interaction. It also documents the system qualities achieved by the application of this pattern. Individual patterns can, furthermore, be linked to each other in the form of pattern languages, which guide the designer through the design process. In this paper we describe a pattern-driven agent design process that complements goal-driven design approaches. What makes our approach different from most other pattern-based approaches is the use of softgoals for representing the system qualities affected by a pattern. We demonstrate the approach by applying it to a problem in the domain of agent-based electronic commerce.

1 Introduction

Current approaches to agent system design such as Gaia [15], and MASSIVE [11], are generally goal-driven. An agent system is designed by iteratively decomposing system goals until they can be assigned to individual agents. However, this may lead developers to rediscover solutions to common design problems without benefiting from how they were resolved in the past. This results in duplicated effort, inconsistent design, brittle systems, and poor traceability.

A more effective and less ad hoc approach is to build an agent system incrementally from well-documented agent patterns. Each agent pattern documents a proven assignment of roles to agents, and their interaction. It also documents the system qualities achieved by the application of this pattern. A pattern can therefore be considered a rule that transforms the system in such a way as to achieve certain desired non-functional requirements. Furthermore, individual patterns can be linked to each other in the form of pattern languages, which guide the designer through the design process.

J. Eder and M. Missikoff (Eds.): CAiSE 2003, LNCS 2681, pp. 711–723, 2003.

In this paper we describe a pattern-driven agent design process that complements goal-driven design approaches. This process consists of identifying the core design trade-offs for the application domain, documenting the roles agents can play, documenting patterns and their dependencies, identifying the overall system goals, and iteratively selecting and applying patterns. What makes our approach different from most other pattern-based approaches is the use of softgoals [5] for representing the system qualities affected by a pattern. We demonstrate the approach by applying it to a problem in the domain of agent-based electronic commerce.

2 Agent Patterns

Patterns are reusable solutions to recurring design problems, and provide a vocabulary for communicating these solutions to others. The documentation of a pattern goes beyond documenting a problem and its solution. It also describes the *forces* or design constraints that give rise to the proposed solution [1]. These are the undocumented and generally misunderstood features of a design. Forces can be thought of as pushing or pulling the problem towards different solutions. A good pattern balances the forces.

Patterns are not used in isolation. Although individual patterns are useful at solving specific design problems, we can benefit further from positioning them among one another to form a *pattern language*. Each pattern occupies a position in a network of related patterns, in which each pattern contributes to the completion of patterns "preceding" it in the network, and is completed by patterns "succeeding" it.

A pattern language guides developers through the process of generating a system. Beck and Johnson [4] describe this generative quality of patterns: "Describing an architecture with patterns is like the process of cell division and specialization that drives growth in biological organisms. The design starts as a fuzzy cloud representing the system to be realized. As patterns are applied to the cloud, parts of it come into focus. When no more patterns are applicable, the design is finished."

There is by now a growing literature on the use of patterns to capture common design practices for agent systems [3, 8, 7, 10]. Aridor and Lange [3] describe a set of domain-independent patterns for the design of mobile agent systems. They classify mobile agent patterns into traveling, task, and interaction patterns. Kendall et al [8] capture common building blocks for the internal architecture of agents in patterns.

Deugo and Weiss [7] identify a set of patterns for agent coordination, which are, again, domain-independent. They classify agent patterns into architectural, communication, traveling, and coordination patterns. They also describe an initial set of global forces that push and pull solutions for coordination. Kendall [9] reports on work on a domain-specific catalog of patterns developed at BT. Weiss [14] describes a pattern language for agent-based e-commerce. In related work, Kolp and Giorgini [10] document organizational styles for multi-agent systems using the Tropos framework.

The separate notion of an *agent pattern* can be justified by differences between the way agents and objects communicate, their level of autonomy, and social ability [6]. Agent patterns are documented in a similar manner as other software patterns, except for the structure of an agent pattern where we will make use of role models [13, 9] instead of collaboration diagrams. The distinction between role models and collaboration diagrams is the level of abstraction: a collaboration diagram shows the interaction of instances, whereas a role model shows the interaction of roles to be filled.

3 Pattern-Driven Agent System Design

Instead of proceeding from high-level goals and arriving at an implementation through iterative refinement, in a pattern-driven approach we start from proven solutions, and *compose* our system by systematically instantiating patterns. The goal-driven and pattern-driven approaches to design are complementary as shown in Fig. 1. Our experience building agent systems suggests that a design approach that proceeds both in a top-down and a bottom-up direction in parallel will lead to the best results

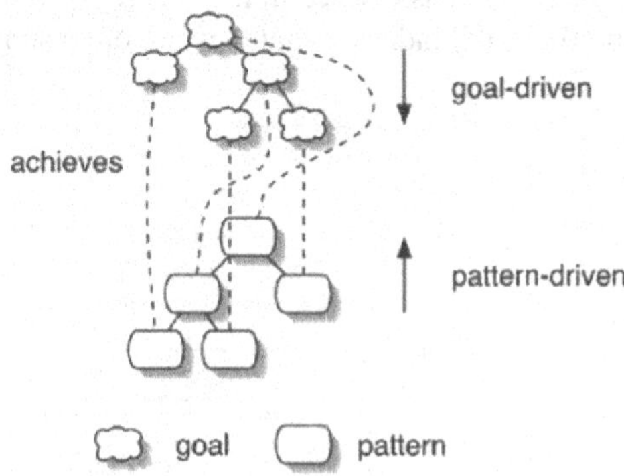

Fig. 1. Complementarity of the pattern-driven and goal-driven approaches

The implementation of the pattern-directed approach involves the steps shown in Fig. 2. The process provides two entry points, one for the pattern author, the second for the pattern user. The first three steps provide an approach for harvesting recurring design solutions and making them available as patterns. The last two steps start with a given set of patterns or pattern languages, and guide the designer through the selection of patterns appropriate to their specific application requirements.

Certain steps of this process can be supported by tools, eg the documentation of patterns, and the selection of patterns given a set of requirements. However, only partial implementations of such tools exist, for example, modeling tools that support the definition of patterns. However, the kind of tool we have in mind goes much further in supporting the designer in selecting the appropriate pattern for their needs.

Identify Domain Forces. For a given domain identify the core design trade-offs (called forces in patterns) that push and pull the design into different directions. In addition, there are forces motivating the use of agents (such as autonomy, need to interact, multiple interfaces, and adaptability) to be considered for all domains.

Document Roles. Document the roles (and their subtypes) that will be used in the patterns. Individual patterns document how these roles interact in a given design context. The task of the designer is, by selecting patterns, to assign roles to agents. Documenting the roles separately from the patterns, as does identifying the domain forces, provides a point of reference for the following description of the patterns.

Document Patterns and their Dependencies. Document the patterns and their dependencies in the form of a pattern language. Each pattern should document the forces it helps resolve, and how instantiating the pattern will change the system. This includes the resulting role model and the forces that still need to be resolved. Semi-formal methods can be used to document the forces in a pattern. For example, in [2] we have investigated the use of softgoals to document forces and their trade-offs. Here we use the concept of softgoal as defined in [5]: a softgoal represents a non-functional requirement. The prefix "soft" indicates that they are often subjective in nature.

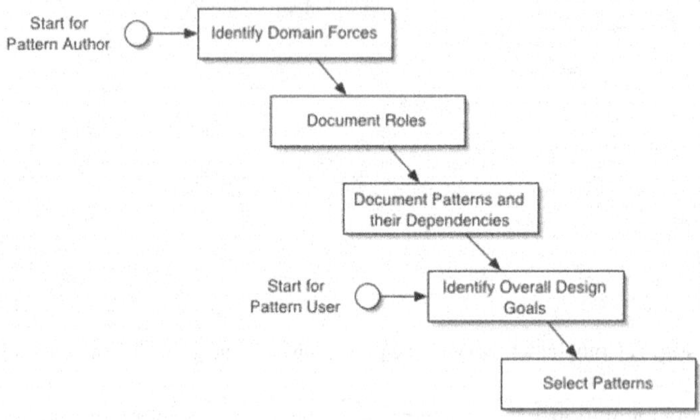

Fig. 2. Steps of the pattern-driven agent design process

Identify the Overall Design Goals. Identify the overall design goals, both functional and non-functional. Generally, the identification of patterns based on merely functional goals is rather straightforward. However, although multiple patterns may satisfy the *same* functional goals, their implications on the design in terms of non-functional goals must be carefully considered. The main thrust of our semi-formal pattern representation is geared towards matching on non-functional goals.

Select Patterns. In a first pass, select patterns based on how well they match the functional goals of the system, and then refine the selection by considering non-functional design goals. Compare the patterns and rank them on basis of their compatibility with these goals. In our tool we plan to use the algorithm described in McPhail and Deugo [12]. Repeat this step until all forces have been resolved.

4 Case Study

As a way of demonstrating the pattern-driven design approach, let us now look at a problem from the domain of agent-based electronic commerce. Consider that we want to design an *agent-based online auction* system. In an online auction system, users post items for sale, while other users place bids on those items. Users are faced with a multitude of auctions in which they can participate. Users may also need help in selecting a suitable auction, given that the number and types of items for sale often change frequently. Users also want to be informed about the status of an auction.

4.1 Identify Domain Forces

For the agent-based e-commerce domain, our analysis (see [14] for more details) identified the following forces that a design needs to trade-off. Fig. 3 shows these forces and their interactions. The label "agrees" indicates that the forces mutually support each other. The label "disagrees" means that they are in conflict, and need to be balanced.

Autonomy. An autonomous agent does not require the user's approval at every step of executing its task, but can act on its own. With agents performing autonomous actions, users are now facing the issues of trust and control over their agents.

Need to interact. Agents rely on other agents to achieve goals that are outside their scope or reach. They also need to coordinate their activities with those of other agents to ensure that their goals can be met, avoiding interference with each other.

Information overload. Users wish to find relevant information and offerings to make good deals and generate profit. The large set of traders in conjunction with their many different interfaces makes it difficult for a user to overview the market.

Multiple interfaces. One of the difficulties in finding information (eg when comparing offerings) is the number of interfaces used to present the information. One solution is to use common vocabularies, but these must also be widely adopted.

Ensuring quality. Electronic commerce lacks the immediate mechanisms for establishing trustworthiness. How can buyers trust sellers, with whom they had no previous encounter, that their order will be fulfilled satisfactorily? Even if rating mechanisms (based on the identity of the trader) are used how can we ensure that a trader cannot easily assume a new identity and start afresh with a new rating?

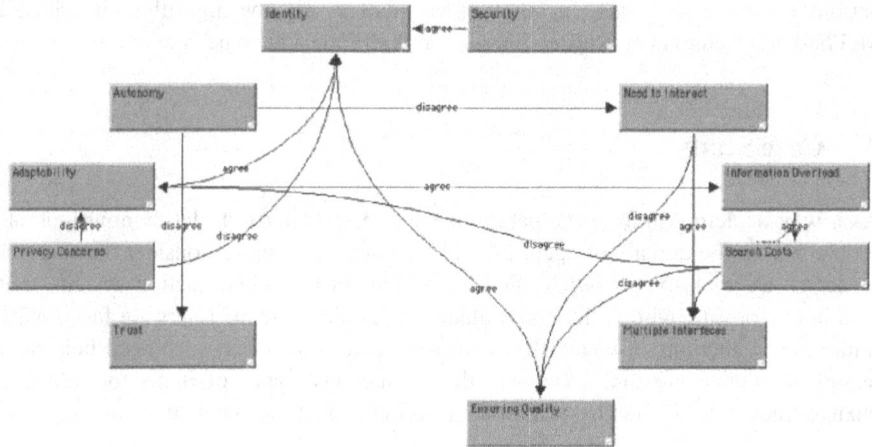

Fig. 3. Domain forces for the e-commerce domain

Adaptability. As users differ in their status, level of expertise, needs, and preferences, we need to tailor information to the features of the user, for example, by selecting the products most suitable for them from a catalog, or adapting the presentation style during the interaction with the user. Any approach to tailoring information involves creating and maintaining a user model, and thus raises privacy concerns.

Privacy concerns. Personalization requires that personal information, such as a buyer's preferences for sellers are made available to the agent providing personalized service. At the same time, users want to remain in control, and decide on an interaction-by-interaction basis which information is conveyed to another party.

Search costs. It can be expensive for traders to find each other. Electronic marketplaces are dynamic. Buyers and sellers can join and leave the marketplace, and change their needs and offerings qualitatively and quantitatively at any point in time. Thus it is difficult for market participants to keep an up-to-date list of contacts.

Identity. For various reasons, users need to be represented by unique identities. The most important are authentication (to ensure quality), repudiation, and tracking (to adapt to the user). However, tracking a user's behavior raises privacy concerns.

Trust. Trust in the sense of trusting another party with sensitive information includes storing the sensitive information (similar to privacy concerns), and trusting that proper use be made of the information (eg credit card information, age, or body measurements) are used only within the context of the current transaction.

Security. Security in the sense that the user's identity, and any sensitive information associated with it is protected. This is different from privacy concerns.

4.2 Document Roles

In our analysis, we identified four top-level roles for agent-mediate e-commerce systems as User, Task, Service, and Resource. Fig. 4 shows these roles with their subroles. The *User* role encapsulates the behavior of providing an access point for the user, managing a user's task agents, and collecting profile information about the user, among other responsibilities. *Task* roles represent users in a specific task. This is typically a long-lived, rather than a one-shot transaction. In this context, we only consider trader agents, which can represent the user either as a buyer or a seller.

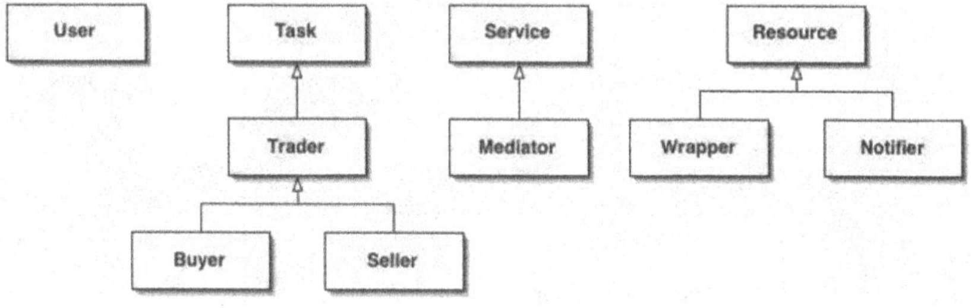

Fig. 4. Role hierarchy for e-commerce agents

Service roles typically provide a service to a group of users. They mediate the interaction between two or more agents through services. One example is a Directory role that provides a reference to an agent given its name (white pages agent), or references to agents that can provide a certain product or service (yellow pages agent). More advanced services (represented summarily by the Mediator role) facilitate more complex interactions between agents, for example, enforcing an auction protocol.

The *Resource* role abstracts from information sources. These can be legacy data sources wrapped by "glue" code that converts generic requests from other agents to the API of the data source (this glue is usually referred to as a wrapper). These can be agents that process more complex queries by first breaking them down into subqueries and then collating the results. Notifier agents, which monitor a data source for changes, and may filter for certain conditions, also belong into this category.

4.3 Document Patterns and Their Dependencies

The structure of the pattern language is shown in Fig. 5. The arrows indicate refinement links between the patterns. Each arrow in the diagram points in the direction from a "larger" pattern to a "smaller" pattern. The starting point for the language is the Agent Society pattern, which motivates the use of agents for building the application. At the next level of refinement, the diagram leads the designer to consider the patterns Agent as Delegate, Agent as Mediator, and Common Vocabulary.

Agent as Delegate and the patterns it links to deal with the design of agents that act on behalf of a single user. Agent as Mediator guides the designer through the design of agents that facilitate between a group of agents and their users. Common Vocabulary provides guidelines for defining exchange formats between agents.

The rest of Fig. 5 shows refinements of the Agent as Delegate pattern. For example, the User Agent pattern prescribes to use a single locus of interaction with the user, and represent the concurrent transactions a user participates in as buyer and seller agents. User interaction also includes profiling the user (User Profiling), and subscribing to information (eg the status of an auction) relevant to the user (Notification).

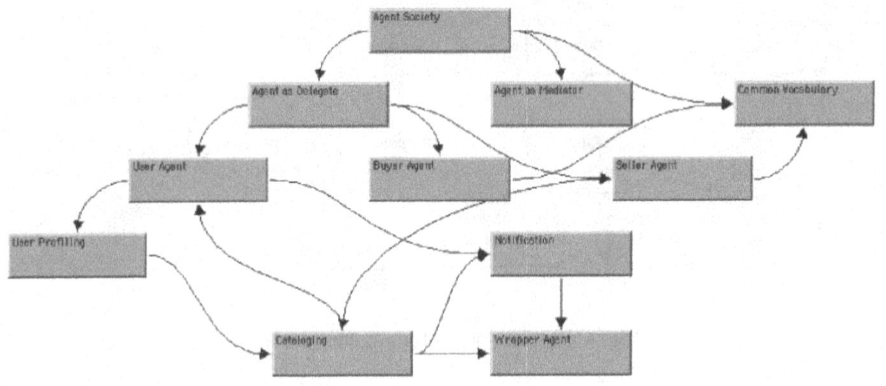

Fig. 5. Patterns for e-commerce agents and their dependencies

Each pattern is represented by its context, the problem, a discussion of the forces, and its solution. The context is represented by the dependencies between the patterns. The problem is a succinct statement on what problem the pattern addresses. The solution takes the form of a role diagram. These roles will be filled by agents.

For example, consider the User Agent pattern. It is applied after the Agent as Delegate pattern, and, in turn, refined by User Profiling, and Notification. The problem it addresses is how users instruct agents to act on their behalf (as buyers and sellers), and how they keep in control over what the agent does (eg does it have authority to complete a trade?). The role diagram for the User Agent pattern is shown in Fig. 6.

We use softgoals [5] to represent the forces a pattern helps achieve, or prevents from achieving (that is, both positive and negative contributions). A link between a pattern and a force in the softgoal graph indicates that the pattern directly contributes to its achievement. Fig. 7 shows the contributions of the User Agent pattern.

Each pattern is the result of a trade-off/balancing of forces. Representing the contributions of a pattern as a softgoal graph makes the contributions of the pattern toward achieving the domain forces explicit. It highlights the trade-offs made by a pattern, for example, if it achieves certain forces but hinders the achievement of other forces. It also makes visible the forces that remain unresolved after applying a pattern.

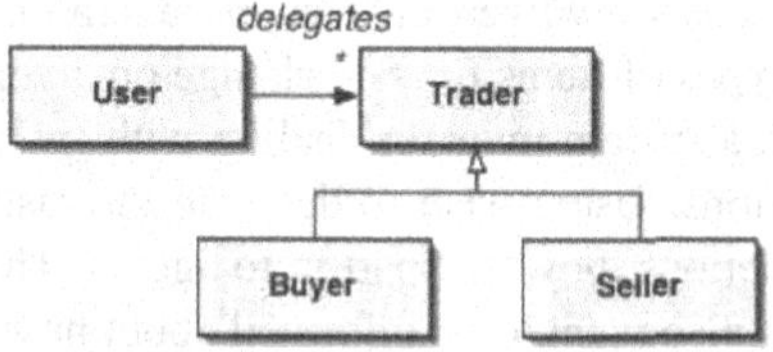

Fig. 6. Role diagram for the User Agent pattern

When we want to evaluate the effect of applying several patterns, we can combine the softgoal graphs for the individual patterns, and obtain, as a result, a softgoal graph in which the patterns are operationalizations. We can also see the result of applying alternative solutions to the same problem represented by different patterns. The choice of the pattern to use then depends on the prioritization of the forces by the designer.

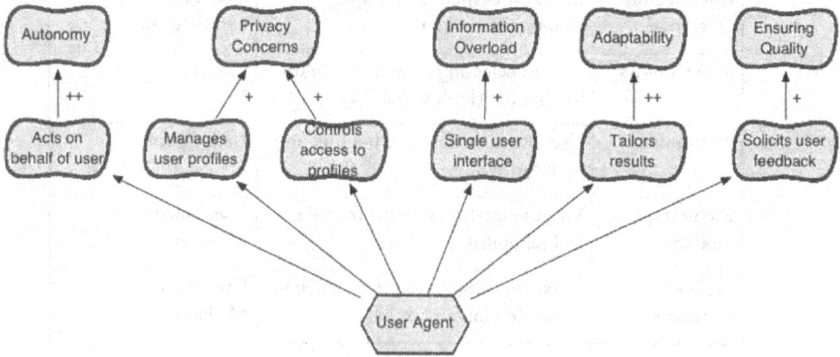

Fig. 7. A softgoal graph shows which forces the User Agent pattern helps achieve

Our notation for softgoal graphs is based on [5]. Softgoals are indicated as clouds, and patterns (that is, operationalization) are shown as hexagons. The labels on the arrows indicate the strength of the contribution, which can range from -- (breaks) and – (hurts) to + (helps) and ++ (makes the achievement of a softgoal).

In Fig. 7, the User Agent pattern helps address privacy concerns in two ways: one is by managing profiles on behalf of the user (the profile is collected at the user's end), the other is by controlling who can access those profiles, which portions of them, and to what use (in the sense of the P3P protocol for privacy protection).

4.4 Identify the Overall Design Goals

Fig. 8 lists the forces implied by the requirements of the online auction system stated earlier. Users are faced with a large number of auctions in which they can participate. Information overload is thus a driving force for the design of our system. In addition, there are high search costs involved in selecting a suitable auction for an item, given that the number and types of items for sale change on a very frequent basis.

The design of such a system involves dealing with (potentially multiple concurrent) longstanding transactions. Users wish to delegate the task of bidding and monitoring the progress of the auctions they take part in to agents. This is reflected in the force of autonomy. Users may also want to be informed about newly created auctions for items of interest. Again they would confront information overload, if they were to monitor auction sites for newly created auctions manually.

Another concern is the varying quality of the items offered and the reliability of the sellers. An auction system should provide services to ensure the quality of items and reliability of participants. Finally, as a consequence of delegating bidding and monitoring tasks to agents, the user is revealing sensitive information to the agents (such as their price preferences) that must not be revealed to other agents or misappropriated in any way. This leads us to consider the user's privacy concerns.

Information Overload	Users participate in multiple concurrent auctions	User Agent Notification
Search costs	Cost of selecting a suitable auction for an item (high variability)	Mediator
Autonomy	Users wish to delegate bidding and monitoring progress	User Agent
Ensuring quality	Varying quality of items for sale and reliability of sellers	User Agent Mediator
Privacy concerns	Sensitive information is revealed to agents (eg maximum bid)	User Agent Mediator

Fig. 8. Overall design goals for the online auction

Fig. 8 also indicates (in the right column) the pattern(s) that help address the forces identified in the left column. This is the result of the next step, selecting patterns.

4.5 Select Patterns

The last step is concerned with selecting patterns. Having identified the overall design goals, and (optionally) a prioritization among them, we now select the patterns that help achieve them. Given the softgoal representation of each pattern we can identify the patterns that best help achieve the forces implied by the requirements. Here we perform this selection manually with the help of a reverse index that lists the patterns achieving a particular force. This can be derived from the individual softgoal graphs.

For example, an inspection of the User Agent pattern shows that it contributes to four of the overall design goals: information overload (+), autonomy (++), ensuring quality (+), and privacy concerns (++). However, User Agent does not provide all the desired functionality, such as monitoring an auction, or helping find a suitable auction. Only its contribution to autonomy is strong enough that no other patterns are required to fully satisfy the non-functional design goals. For example, some of the information overload is caused by the need to monitor auctions for their current status. The Notification pattern addresses (+) this design concern. The Mediator pattern fully addresses the search cost (++) force, while raising some privacy concerns (–).

More complex schemes, for example, using a weighted distance metric (where each force is weighted by its priority to the designer), or a decision-theoretic model such as the one explored by McPhail and Deugo [12], are required if the search for matching patterns involves a larger number of patterns than were considered in this case study. Such methods are amenable to tool support, and for the future we envision that such selection algorithms can be embedded into standard object modeling tools.

Fig. 9 shows the combined softgoal graph with the contributions of each pattern. It allows us to validate that the overall design goals have been achieved. But it also points us to a potential issue wrt privacy concerns that we need to follow up on.

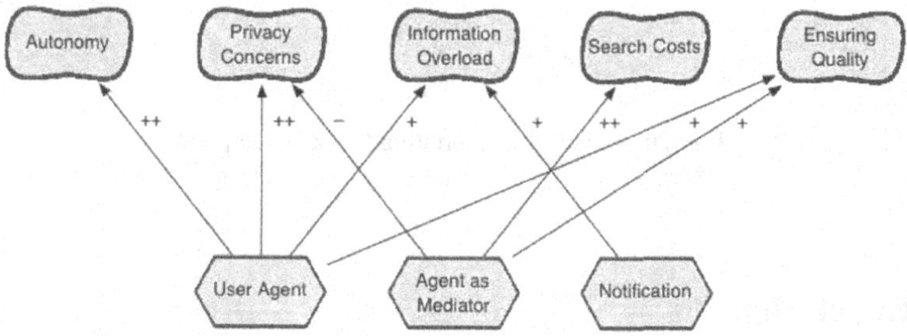

Fig. 9. Contributions of each selected pattern shown in a combined softgoal graph

Figure 10 shows how the role diagrams for the three patterns are instantiated into a concrete agent system. In the solution generated by applying the patterns of our pattern language, user agents manage trader agents that represent their users in multiple concurrent transactions (as buyers and seller). Buyer agents implement the bidding strategies of their users (characterized by parameters such as the starting price, maximum price, and rate of increase). They also inform them about important events regarding the current auction (e.g. winning or losing the auction).

While buyer agents only notify a user about the current auction, notifier agents monitor other auctions on a user's behalf. The user creates a notifier agent by initializing it with a specification of the product or service she is looking for. On receiving a notification about an auction, a user can decide to create a new buyer agent to join that auction. A mediator agent implements the auction mechanism. This agent provides a meeting place for buyers and sellers. It maintains a catalog of items for sale, and a list of auctions with administrative information for each (such as the current bid, the seller's reservation price, and the remaining duration of the auction), and oversees the execution of the auction (creating auctions, receiving bids, informing buyers/sellers).

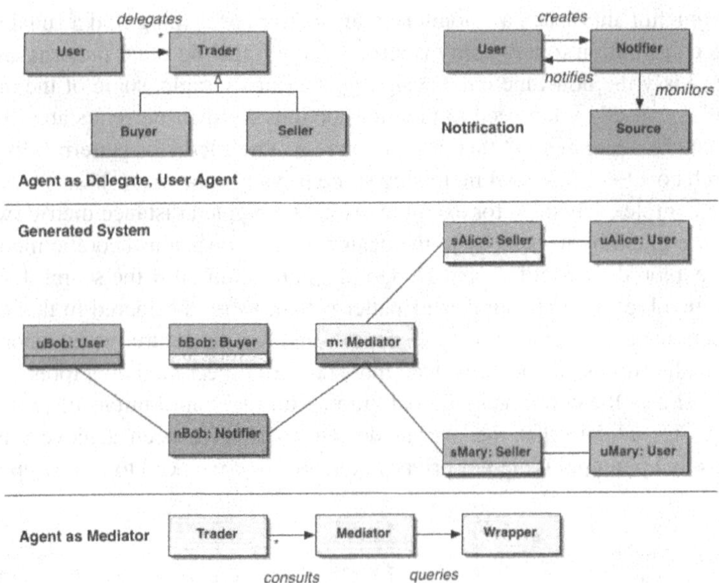

Fig. 10. Result of instantiating the selected patterns

5 Conclusion

In this paper we described a pattern-driven approach to agent system design. This approach is complementary to the goal-driven approach that most published methodologies use. The combined design approach proceeds, in parallel, in a top-down (goal-driven) and a bottom-up (pattern-driven) direction.

We illustrated the approach with a case study from the domain of agent-based electronic commerce. For space limitations we could only present the example of designing a system for online auctions. However, we have applied the approach to several other scenarios such as a yellow-pages lookup service, and customized navigation. Given our prior experience with applying a softgoal-based approach to modeling patterns in other domains such as distributed programming (see [2]), we are confident that these results can be generalized into the pattern-driven design process as described.

More work is required to document the forces that govern agent system design, and to understand their interactions. A related open problem is the selection of a pattern that is compatible with the stated functional and non-functional goals of an application. We are working on tool support to automate this task.

References

1. Alexander, C., A Pattern Language, Oxford University Press, 1977
2. Araujo, I., and Weiss, M., Using the NFR Framework for Representing Patterns, Conference on Pattern Languages of Programming (PLoP-02), 2002
3. Aridor, Y., Lange, D., Agent Design Patterns: Elements of Agent Application Design, Second Intl. Conference on Autonomous Agents, IEEE, 1998
4. Beck, K., and Johnson, R., Patterns Generate Architectures, European Conference on Object Oriented Programming (ECOOP-94), 139–149, 1994
5. Chung L., Representing and Using Non-Functional Requirements: A Process-Oriented Approach, Department of Computer Science University of Toronto, 1993
6. Deugo, D., Oppacher, F., et al, Patterns as a Means for Intelligent Software Engineering, Intl. Conference on Artificial Intelligence (IC-AI 99), 605–611, 1999
7. Deugo, D., Weiss, M., and Kendall, L., Reusable Patterns for Agent Coordination, in: Omicini, A., et al (eds.), Coordination of Internet Agents, Springer, 2001
8. Kendall, E., Murali Krishna, P., Pathak, C. et al, Patterns of Intelligent and Mobile Agents, Second Intl. Conference on Autonomous Agents, IEEE, 1998
9. Kendall, E., Role Models: Patterns of Agent System Analysis and Design, Agent Systems and Applications/Mobile Agents (ASA/MA-99), ACM, 1999
10. Kolp, M., Giorgini, P., Mylopoulos, J., A Goal-Based Organizational Perspective on Multi-Agent Architectures, Eighth Intl. Workshop on Agent Theories, Architectures, and Languages (ATAL-2001), 2001
11. Lind, J., Iterative Software Engineering for Multi-Agent Systems: The MASSIVE Method, LNCS 1994, Springer, 2001
12. McPhail, J.C., and Deugo, D., Deciding on a Pattern, 14th Intl. Conference on Industrial and Engineering Applications of Artificial Intelligence and Expert Systems (IEA/AIE-01) LNCS 2070, Springer, 2001
13. Riehle, D., and Gross, T., Role Model Based Framework Design and Integration, Conference on Object- Oriented Programs, Systems, Languages, and Applications (OOPSLA-98), 117–133, ACM, 1998
14. Weiss, M., Patterns for e-Commerce Agent Architectures: Using Agents as Delegates, Conference on Pattern Languages of Programming (PLoP-01), 2001
15. Wooldridge, M., Jennings, N., and Kinny, D., The Gaia Methodology for Agent-oriented Analysis and Design, Journal of Autonomous Agents and Multi-Agent Systems, 2002

Sharing Mobile Databases in Dynamically Configurable Environments

Angelo Brayner and José Aguiar M. Filho

University of Fortaleza (UNIFOR), Av. Washington Soares, 1321
60811-341 Fortaleza, Ceara, Brazil
{brayner, jaguiar.mia}@unifor.br

Abstract. In an environment with support for mobile computing, we may have a collection of autonomous, distributed, heterogeneous and mobile databases, denoted Mobile Database Community (MDBC), in which each database user can access databases in the community through a wireless communication infrastructure. In such an environment, new participants may join to an MDBC as they move within communication range of one or more hosts which are members of the MDBC. Furthermore, MDBC participants may transiently disconnect from the network due to communication disruptions or to save power. Therefore, an MDBC can be characterized as a dynamically configurable environment. This paper describes an agent-based architecture, denoted AMDB (Accessing Mobile Databases), which enables such communities to be formed opportunistically over mobile database hosts in ad hoc configurable environments. The AMDB architecture is fully distributed and has the capability of exploiting physical mobility of hosts and logical mobility of database queries and their results across mobile hosts.

1 Introduction

Advances in portable computing devices and wireless network technology have led to the development of a new computing paradigm, called mobile computing. This new paradigm supports that users carrying portable devices are able to access services provided through a wireless communication infrastructure, regardless of their physical location or movement patterns. Mobile computing paradigm has affected traditional models and concepts of many computer science areas. For example, in the network area, networks need to be ubiquitous, since they must guarantee user connectivity independently of the physical user location. Communication networks with such as property are called *ad hoc* networks [12]. With respect to software engineering, that new paradigm has introduced the notion of mobile code, which refers to the capability of dynamically changing the bindings between code fragments and the location where they are executed. Moreover, a mobile code needs to be "aware" about the computational environment on which it is running [10].

The database technology has also been impacted by the mobile computing paradigm. For example, in an environment with support for mobile computing, a varying number of mobile computers can be interconnected through a wireless communication infrastructure, on each of which resides a database system. In other words, a dynamic collection of autonomous mobile databases, interconnected through a wireless

J. Eder and M. Missikoff (Eds.): CAiSE 2003, LNCS 2681, pp. 724–737, 2003.

communication infrastructure, can be formed in such an environment. For now on, that collection of mobile databases will be denoted mobile database community (MDBC). Databases in an MDBC are mobile, autonomous and distributed. Moreover, they can be heterogeneous.

Therefore, sharing information among multiple heterogeneous, autonomous, distributed and mobile data sources has emerged as a strategic requirement which should be supported by the database technology. Mobility allows any time and any place data access. Accordingly, conventional concepts and techniques, used in areas, such as query processing, transaction management and data distribution, should be revisited in order to introduce the concept of mobility into the database technology. In order to illustrate this fact, consider a mobile database community M. Suppose that databases belonging to M are heterogeneous and reside in mobile computers interconnected through an ad hoc network. Now, consider a database DB which resides on a mobile computer C and it is member of M. Thus, the data of DB should be shared with the other members of the community. For this purpose, the computer C should behave as a database server belonging to M. Additionally, a user on the mobile host C may wish to query objects stored at other members of M. Of course, the heterogeneous, distributed, autonomous and mobile databases belonging to the community have to be integrated. Since the databases are mobile, a given database DB can leave the community at anytime, even though a query submitted by DB is still running in other database systems in M. Moreover, the query submitted by a user on the mobile host C can represent a distributed transaction. In this case, a protocol to guarantee the atomicity of the commit operation [1] is required. Consequently, it is necessary to address the following problems in order to make feasible the access to mobile databases in an MDBC: *(i)* heterogeneous databases integration; *(ii)* query processing over a variable number of mobile databases and; *(iii)* mobile transaction management (i.e., concurrency control and recovery for mobile and distributed transactions).

In this paper we propose an architecture, denoted Accessing Mobile Database (AMBD), for supporting database sharing in mobile database communities. The key goal of the proposed architecture is to provide access to heterogeneous, autonomous and mobile databases. The AMDB architecture is based on the concept of mobile agents and is fully distributed. Furthermore, the proposed architecture provides the necessary support for forming MDBCs opportunistically over a collection of mobile databases hosts.

It is important to note that the AMDB architecture does not require changes to the core of underlying databases systems. For that reason, we classify the AMDB approach as non-intrusive [6]. This property enables commercial DBMSs for participating in a mobile database community through the AMDB architecture. Several approaches to support mobility should be classified as intrusive, since they require that new capabilities and functionalities have to be added to the underlying database [5,7].

This paper is structured as follows. In section 2, a mobile computing environment is characterized. In section 3, the concept of mobile databases community is defined and proposed architecture is presented and analyzed. Section 4 addresses the query processing mechanism for the AMDB architecture. Mobile transaction processing issues in the MDBC context are addressed in Section 5. Section 6 concludes the paper.

2 A Mobile Computing Environment Model

In a mobile computing environment, mobile computers are grouped into components denoted cells. Each cell represents a geographical region covered by a wireless communication infrastructure. Such cells can represent a Wireless Local Area Network (WLAN), an ad hoc network, an geographical area covered by a cell phone network (called cell as well) or a combination of those communication technologies (for example, an ad hoc network inside cell of a cellular phone network).

Mobile support stations (or base stations) are components of a mobile computing platform which have a wireless interface in order to enable communication between mobile units located at different cells. Thus, each cell must be associated with one mobile support station. Communication between two base stations is made through a fixed network. In fact, mobile support stations represent fixed hosts interconnect through a high-speed wired network. From a database technology standpoint, there are two classes of database systems in a mobile computing environment: *(i)* a class consisting of database systems which reside on fixed hosts, and; *(ii)* a class of database systems which reside on mobile computers. Database systems residing on mobile hosts are denoted mobile databases

It is worthwhile to note that, when a cell in a mobile computing environment represents a WLAN or an ad hoc network, mobile computers inside the cell can communicate with each other directly. On the other hand, when a cell represents an area covered by a cell phone network, mobile units need should use the cell's base station to communicate with each other. A mobile computer can use different communication technologies. We call *vertical handoff* the fact of a mobile computer migrating from a given communication technology to another. For example a mobile computer A can use a WLAN to communicate with other mobile computer inside the same cell, and it can use a cellular phone network to communicate with mobile computers located at another cell.

From a database technology perspective, we can categorize mobility in two different types:

i. Physical Mobility: this type of mobility cope with spatial mobility of database clients and database servers through different space regions;

ii. Logical Mobility: this type of mobility is related to code migration among several mobile clients and database servers. In order to provide logical mobility, mobile computers should be able to generate database access codes (SQL expressions, stored procedures or methods), which can migrate autonomously to several databases servers. When such a code arrives at a database server, it is locally executed. After that, it returns (with the access result) to home (the host which originates the access code).

It is important to note that the AMDB architecture provides support to both of the mobility types described above.

3 Sharing Databases in Mobile Database Communities

The key goal of the proposed architecture is to enable mobile database communities to be formed opportunistically over mobile database residing on mobile hosts in environments with a wireless communication infrastructure. The proposed architecture is fully distributed (i.e. no centralized control structure is needed) and relies on existing mobile agent technology to allow transient sharing of databases. In addition, to support disconnected operations, the architecture exploits logical mobility of both database queries and their results. For the sake of clarity, we assume that mobile computers are interconnected through an ad hoc network infrastructure.

3.1 Mobile Database Communities

We characterize a database system as a mobile database, if the database system resides on a mobile unit. A Mobile Database Community (MDBC) represents a dynamic collection of autonomous mobile databases, interconnected through a wireless communication infrastructure. Observe that the notion of MDBC models the notion of a federation of databases which reside on mobile units.

A varying number of mobile computers can participate in an MDBC. In this case, MDBC members share databases available in the MDBC. The members of an MDBC can be categorized in two different classes: database server or database client. By database server, we mean that a mobile computer, which is the host of a database system (DBS). Each database system encompasses a database (DB) and a database management system (DBMS). A database represents a collection of object representing real world entities. A DBMS is the software component of the DBS. In that case, the database (or part of it) stored in a database server can be accessed by any other member of the community. The second class of MDBC members is composed by mobile hosts which participate in an MDBC as database clients. Such members can only access object stored in databases available in the MDBC. That means, either they do not have or they do not want to share an own database with the members of the community.

New participants may join to an MDBC as they move within communication range of one or more hosts which are members of the MDBC. On other hand, MDBC participants may transiently disconnect from the network due to communication disruptions or to save power. For that reason, an MDBC can be characterized as a dynamically configurable environment.

A mobile computer needs to declare to the participants of an MDBC its intention to become a member of the community. If the mobile computer is the host of a database system, it should declare that its database will be available to the members of the community. In that case, the mobile computer has to publish its database schema to the community.

It is highly likely that databases in an MDBC are heterogeneous. For example, they might be relational, native XML, oriented-object databases or any other data source (e.g., HTML pages). Thus, schemas of databases belonging to an MDBC should be represented in a common model. Since XML has been consolidated as a standard for data interchanging, we have decided to use XML as the common model for data interchanging in an MDBC. For that reason, mobile databases in an MDBC have to publish their schemas (or part of them) through XML Schema [23], a schema definition language for XML data.

Mobile users interact with mobile databases in an MDBC by means of transactions. A transaction models a sequence of operations on database objects that is executed atomically. Typically, such operations are expressed in a database query language (e.g. SQL). There are two types of transactions in an MDBC environment: local transactions and global transactions. A local transaction is submitted directly to a mobile database DB by an application running on the same host on which DB resides. A global transaction consists of database operations which should be executed on different hosts belonging to an MDBC. The notion of global transaction models distributed transactions which are composed by mobile sub-transactions. Therefore, the notion of global transaction in an MDBC generalizes the concept of distributed transaction. Since a global transaction is distributed in different mobile hosts, a protocol should enforce commit atomicity of global transactions. An example for such a protocol is the two-phase commit (2PC) protocol [1].

The correctness criterion for the execution of concurrent transactions is serializability. We assume that each mobile database in an MDBC guarantees serializability by the two-phase locking (2PL) protocol [1]. This is a quite reasonable assumption, since all existing database systems implements the 2PL to guarantee serializability.

3.2 AMDB Architecture

The AMDB architecture is based on the concept of software agent. The proposed architecture is composed by two classes of agents: stationary agents and mobile agents. The stationary-agent class is compound by two types of agents: manager agents and wrapper agents. Manager agents are responsible for managing local computational resources of a mobile computer. These resources can be used to perform tasks of mobile agents. Wrapper agents provide an interface between mobile unit users and the AMDB platform. For that reason, Wrapper agents have the following functionalities. First, they should create the execution context for mobile agents. Thus, wrapper agents behave like a middleware between a mobile agent and a database participating of an MDBC. Second, wrapper agents provide a common data representation of the stored local data at mobile computers. As already said, XML will be used as a common data representation. Additionally, a wrapper agent running on a given mobile unit is also responsible for temporarily transferring one or more services to another mobile computer of the community to improve performance or whenever a critical situation occurs (for example, temporary service unavailability such as insufficient local memory for processing a query) at its mobile computer. In this case, any mobile agent visiting the mobile unit of the wrapper agent should be redirected to the unit where the service is being provided.

Agents of the mobile-agent class are responsible for implementing the logical mobility property in the AMDB architecture. Consequently, they should be able to transport themselves from one MDBC member to another. In the proposed architecture, the basic feature of mobile agents is to carry database access code and access results, while migrating between MDBC members. There are three types of mobile agents: Runner, Loader and Broker agents. Runner agents are directly responsible for performing tasks required by mobile unit users in remote mobile databases belonging to an MDBC. Such tasks can represent data queries, data updates or schema evolution of the mobile databases. Loader agents have the functionality of carrying a database query result back to the mobile unit that has required the query. Broker agents should gather schemas of mobile databases of an MDBC, when a mobile unit joins to an

MDBC. Moreover, a broker agent can define a mobile unit as temporary storage for storing partial query results when it is necessary.

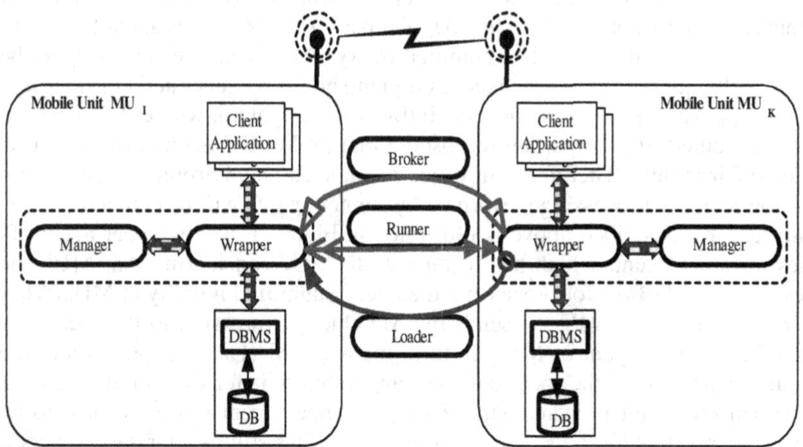

Fig. 1. Abstract Model of the AMDB Architecture.

Figure 1 depicts an abstract model of the AMDB architecture. In order to describe how the proposed architecture works, suppose that a mobile unit MU_K wants to form an MDBC. For that, it declares itself as initial coordinator of the new community to its wrapper agent. After that, the wrapper agent of MU_K sends information about the new community to all computers inside the area covered by the wireless communication network in which MU_K is connected. When news members begin to join to the new MDBC, the central coordinator role is not necessary anymore. This coordinator function will be performed local and collaboratively by the wrapper agents at each mobile unit which is member of the community.

Now, suppose that a mobile unit MU_I wants to join to the MDBC, which was initially created by MU_K. First of all, it is necessary an explicit declaration of MU_I in order to see the schemas of all databases which are member of the community. This functionality is executed by the local wrapper agent, which, in turn, creates a broker (mobile) agent and gives to it the task of querying local database schema at all mobile units, which are hosts of database systems. The broker agent will roam unit by unit and will collect the local schemas. Local database schemas will be provided by local wrapper agents. Recall that local schemas visible to the members of an MDBC are represented in XML Schema [23]. When the broker agent of MU_I returns to MU_I, it brings the schemas of the participating databases and passes them away to wrapper agent of MU_I. With the database schemas of each database of the MDBC, users or application programs at MU_I are able to access data stored at those databases through an interface provided by local wrapper agents. Therefore, users or application programs submit queries to the local wrapper agent. Such queries should be specified in an extension to the XQuery, called MXQuery [25]. The key feature of the MXQuery language is to provide mechanisms which support the capability to jointly manipulate data in heterogeneous data sources. The idea is to use the MXQuery as a multidatabase language [26] in an MDBC, making possible the integration of heterogeneous and distributed data sources. It is important to note that an MXQuery algebra has been defined based on the XML formal semantics algebraic operators (formerly XML query algebra). A global query denotes a query, which should be executed over several databases of an MDBC. When the wrapper agent of MU_I receives a global query, it creates a runner (mobile) agent at MU_L and passes to the runner agent the MXQuery expression corresponding to the submitted query. After that, the runner agent begins to process the query. The query execution plan should be generated considering optimization opportunities and the hosts (MDBC's participants), where the query will be actually executed. It is important to observe that an MDBC is characterized as a distributed environment. Therefore, most queries in such an environment are distributed. In section 5, query processing performed by runner agents will be detailed.

The scenario described above is illustrated in Figure 1. The wrapper agent of MU_I creates a runner agent, which has to migrate to $MU_{K,}$ considering that MU_K encompasses the target DBMS for processing the query submitted initially at MU_I. When the runner agent arrives at MU_K, it sends the MXQuery expression to the local wrapper agent. The wrapper agent of MU_K, in turn, maps the MXQuery expression to the native query language of the local database and submits it for execution as a common user. When the result is available, the local wrapper agent passes it back to runner agent. If the result is too huge and the runner agent has still to migrate to others units, the runner agent can create a loader agent and transfers to it the result of the query execution on MU_K. The loader agent begins a trip back to the runner-agent home unit. It is important to note that once the loader agent creation has finished, the runner agent can resume migrating to other units. Asynchronously, the loader agent takes the partial query result data back to MU_I. When the runner agent returns home, it communicates to the wrapper agent of MU_I that its task has finished. The wrapper agent unit shows the result to the user or sends the results to application program. Next agent functionalities will be described and analyzed.

4 Processing Queries in an MDBC

In section 4, we have seen that the wrapper agent is responsible for providing local database schema to all MDBC members. In existing database systems, such schemas consist of metadata and statistical data about the database such as, for example, tables' cardinality, tables' blocking factor and the height of index structures [20]. Statistical data are used for optimizing query processing. Hence, if a mobile unit wishes to participate in an MDBC, it has to send its broker agent to each mobile unit of the community providing its local schema and some statistical data. In the meanwhile, the broker agent can gather the local schemas of the visited units. Once the broker agent has returned home, the mobile unit has the necessary information for submitting queries over participant databases.

As already mentioned, users or application programs submit queries in the AMDB environment in MXQuery format. Such queries can be categorized in three classes: local, global (distributed) and remote queries. A local query only involves operations over objects of the local database. In this case, the local wrapper agent translates the MXQuery expression into the native query language of the local DMBS. After that, the wrapper agent submits the query to the local DBMS using the DBMS common user interface.

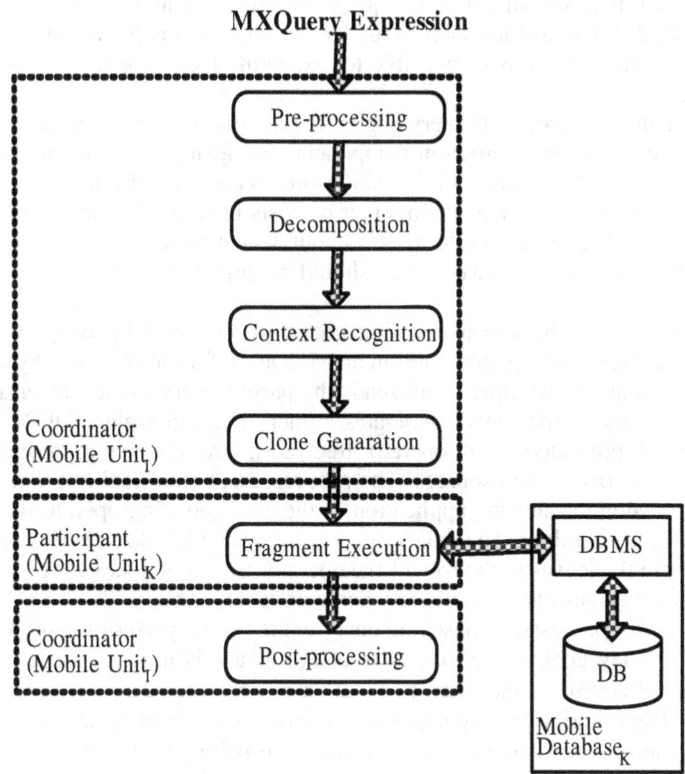

Fig. 2. Query engine architecture.

In turn, a global query may involve operations over several mobile databases of an MDBC. When a mobile computer user (or an application) submits a global query to the local wrapper agent, that agent, detecting a distributed query, creates a runner agent and delegates to it the functionality of executing the global query. It is important to observe that the runner agent receives the global query in MXQuery format. The runner agent migrates to mobile units in which the query should be executed.

Finally, a remote query encompasses operations which should be executed in a remote database belonging to an MDBC. In other words, a query submitted in MU_I should be executed over the databases of a mobile unit MU_K. Of course, those mobile units should belong to the same MDBC. A remote query is processed as follows. A user submits a remote query to the local wrapper agent, which, in turn, creates a runner agent and delegates to it the functionality of executing the remote query. For that purpose, the runner agent should migrate to the remote mobile unit in which the query should be executed.

Figure 2 depicts an abstract model of the query engine for processing global (distributed) and remote queries. According to the proposed engine, a query is processed by six distinct phases: Pre-Processing, Decomposition, Context Recognition, Clone Generation, Fragment Execution and Post-Processing phases. We denote Coordinator the origin unit that has submitted the query. The functionalities of the coordinator are executed by different agents, such as runner, loader and wrapper agents. A Participant represents a DBS, which is responsible for executing locally operations of a global or remote query.

Observe that the proposed query engine is fully distributed, since query processing activities are executed by different components (or agents) in different sites. It is important to note that the query optimization process is carried out by using metadata about local database schemas, the number of hosts in which the query should be executed and available statistics information about data at each local.

Next, we describe the phases which should be implemented by the proposed query engine.

The activities of the **Pre-processing** phase are executed by wrapper and runner agents. Initially, the query submitted in an MXQuery format is parsed by the wrapper agent. After that, the wrapper agent sends the parsed query to the runner agent. After receiving the query, the runner generates a query execution plan (QEP). The generated QEP is represented by an operator tree [2,8], whose nodes represent MXQuery algebraic operators or data sources. The root represents the final query result. An intermediate node indicates the application of the corresponding operator on the results generated by its children. The edges of a tree represent the data flow from bottom to top, i.e., from the leaves to the root of the operator tree. The nodes have also attributes like data locality, selectivity factor and name of data source.

After the Pre-processing phase, the query engine starts performing the **Decomposition** phase. They goal in the execution of this phase is to decompose a query into fragments. Of course, in the case of execution of a remote query only one fragment is produced. The criterion for decomposing a query is the locality principle. Hence, each fragment should be executed in a given database belonging to an MDBC. In fact, a query fragment represents a sub-tree of the global QEP generated by the Pre-processing module. After the Decomposition phase, the **Context Recognition** phase is processed.

Once a query has been divided into fragments, the query engine has to verify, for each fragment, whether or not a given local DBMS has resources to execute the fragment. This the main functionality of the Context Recognition phase. The context recognition phase is carried out based on information about not allowed operations for each mobile unit. That information may be provided by mobile units at moment when a mobile unit joins to an MDBC. If such information is provided, it means that local DBMS cannot perform the defined operation set. Otherwise, it means that local DBMS does not have any restriction about query operations.

If a given DBMS does not have support to execute any operation, the query engine itself is responsible for executing that operation. In fact, this should be performed by the runner agent and can be carried out either on the origin unit or on the mobile unit selected as temporary storage unit (see bellow). In this case, it is necessary a QEP reordering for bringing to high-level nodes (nodes close to the root) of the QEP the operations, which should be executed by the Runner agent.

Another functionality of the context recognition phase is to define a temporary storage unit for materializing intermediate query results. This should be done when the origin unit and other units referenced in the QEP have limited computational resources, such as main memory or disk space. In this case, such hosts do not have the necessary computational support nor to store partial result neither to execute high-level operations specified in the QEP. The step of defining a temporary storage unit is performed as follows. First, the query engine verifies whether or not the origin unit has enough resources for executing the high-level operations. If not, it verifies the other units referenced in the QEP. If none of the units can be defined as temporary storage, then an error message is sent to the user (or application program) indicating the unavailability of resources for executing the query.

Once Context Recognition phase has been finished, the **Clone Generation** phase is started. In this phase, the runner agent clones itself (cloning is supported by several agents platforms). A clone for each query fragment (generated during the Decomposing phase) is created. Each clone is responsible for executing a given query fragment. After the clones have been created, they are dispatched (carrying a query fragment) to the mobile units in order to execute the query fragments.

The **Fragment Execution** phase is started when a runner agent (or its clones) migrates to the mobile units in which query fragments of a given query should be executed. On arriving at a given mobile unit, the runner agent or a clone submits to the local wrapper agent the query fragment in MXQuery format. The wrapper agent, in turn, translates the fragment into the native query language of the local DMBS. After that, it submits the query to the local DBMS and returns the results back to the runner or clone. Obviously, local DBMSs can further optimize the processing of the query fragment it is executing.

During the execution of the Fragment Execution phase local statistical information can be gathered by the runner agent (or clone), since information about operation, cardinality of tables or of selections, for example, can be inferred while the query fragment is being executed. When the runner or clone returns to the origin unit, it sends the collected statistical data to the wrapper agent of the origin unit (coordinator) for updating statistic information about of the mobile unit in which such information was obtained.

The last phase is the **Post-processing**. This phase is initiated when the clones begin to arrive at the mobile unit, on which they were created. During this phase, the clones give to the runner agent the results of the query fragments. The runner agent, in turn, will start the execution of operations that could not be executed by local DBMSs. In this case, the runner agent performs operations corresponding to the high-level nodes of the operator tree. Once the execution has finished, the runner agent joins the result of the query fragments. After that, the runner agent passes the final result to the wrapper agent. The wrapper agent, in turn, is responsible for projecting the final result to the user or application which has submitted the query. It is important to note, that statistic information is also gathered during the execution of this phase.

5 Mobile Transaction Processing

Mobile users interact with databases in an MDBC by invoking transactions. A transaction represents a sequence of operations on database objects. There are two types of transactions in an MDBC environment: local transactions and global transactions. A local transaction is submitted directly to a mobile database DB by an application running on the same host on which DB resides. A global transaction consists of database operations which should be executed on different hosts belonging to an MDBC.

Therefore, the notion of global transaction models distributed transactions which are composed by mobile sub-transactions. In our approach, the correctness criterion for the execution of concurrent transactions is serializability. We assume that each mobile database in an MDBC guarantees serializability by the strict version of the two-phase locking (2PL) protocol [1]. This is a quite reasonable assumption, since all existing database systems implement that protocol.

In the proposed architecture, the runner agents are responsible for managing the execution of global transactions. In order to process mobile transactions, an extension to the conventional centralized version of the 2PC protocol [1] is proposed. The idea is to consider the mobility property, when processing distributed transactions over several mobile databases. The proposed extension is called mobile 2PC protocol (M2PC).

Next, we describe how the M2PC protocol works. Consider that a database system DBS_I resides on a mobile unit MU_I, which belongs to an MDBC. Suppose that a user submits a global (distributed) transaction T to MU_I. In fact, the transaction T corresponds to the execution of a query, which involves operations over several databases of the MDBC. Thus, a runner agent R is created by the wrapper agent of MU_I (see section 4). The runner agent R is responsible for managing the execution of the transaction T. For that reason, R is said to be the coordinator of T. Before starting the execution of T, the agent R creates an agent whose functionality is to play the role of a backup for the M2PC coordinator process. This is necessary because the runner agent R (coordinator) may visit a mobile unit which can disconnect from the wireless communication infrastructure or exit the mobile database community. In this case, a backup process should assume the coordination of the extended 2PC protocol.

The backup for the M2PC coordinator process is created as follows. Before starting the execution of a global transaction, the runner agent creates a broker agent and dispatches it to the MDBC members. The broker should select one of the visited mobile units to be the host of the agent, which has functionality of behaving as a backup for the M2PC coordinator. When the broker agent returns home, it passes the network address of the selected unit to the runner agent. The runner agent creates a clone, passes to it the list of units in which the operations of the global transaction have to be executed, and dispatches the clone to the select unit. That clone has the functionality of being the backup of the M2PC coordinator process. It is important to observe that the creation of that backup for the coordinator process reduces the frequency of executing a termination protocol [1] for the M2PC protocol. In the AMDB architecture, the termination protocol has to be triggered, if and only if the M2PC coordinator and its backup are unreachable.

After creating the backup for the coordinator process, the runner agent creates n–1 clones. It is important to note that each clone has the network address of the mobile unit which is the host of the backup coordinator. The clones migrate to the hosts on operations of the global transaction should be executed. The runner agent migrates to a mobile unit as well. When the clones return home, they bring the votes corresponding to the second step of the conventional 2PC protocol. They send the votes to the runner agent (coordinator for the execution of T), if it has already come back.

When a 'NO' vote is detected, the runner agent sends a message to the backup coordinator with the decision for aborting transaction. After that, the runner agent can send a message with the final decision for aborting transaction to each non-returned clone or can dispatch once more the clones to each unit already visited with the final decision for aborting transaction. If all of votes were 'YES', the runner agent sends a message to the backup coordinator with the final decision for committing the transaction. The clones are dispatched again to the MDBC units with the final decision for committing the transaction.

If the runner agent is unreachable, the backup coordinator assumes the coordination process. In this case the new coordinator decides to abort the transaction. It sends a message to the clones and dispatches them to the transaction-involved units with the decision for aborting transaction.

6 Conclusions

In this paper, we define the concept of dynamically configurable database communities in mobile computing environments. According to that concept, a dynamic collection of autonomous mobile databases, interconnected through a wireless communication infrastructure, can be opportunistically formed.

In order to provide a platform to enables such communities to be formed opportunistically over mobile database hosts in ad hoc configurable environments, an architecture is described and analyzed. The proposed architecture, denoted AMDB (Accessing Mobile Databases), supports physical mobility of hosts and logical mobility of database queries (or transactions) and their results across mobile hosts. Moreover, the proposed architecture has important additional properties for coping with database mobility, such as:

i. it does not require changes to the core of the underlying database systems;
ii. it supports opportunistic creation of database communities over a varying number of mobile and autonomous database hosts.

For query processing in mobile database communities, the proposed architecture implements a query optimizer that adapts the query plan to the execution scenario of a given query. With respect to transaction processing, the 2PC protocol was extended to take into account the mobility property. However, we are investigating other transaction models less restrictive than serializability-based model [1]. Particularly, we are interested on the semantic serializability model proposed in [3] and [4].

A prototype of the AMDB architecture is currently being developed based on IBM AGLETS platform, a Java-based platform which supports logical mobility.

References

1. Bernstein P., Hadzilacos V., and Goodman N.: Concurrency Control and Recovery in Database Systems, Addison-Wesley, 1987.
2. Bouganim L., Fabret F., Mohan C. and Valduriez P.: A Dynamic Query Processing Architecture for Data Integration Systems. IEEE Data Engineering Bulletin. Vol. 23 No. 2. June-2000.
3. Brayner A., Härder T. and Ritter N.: Semantic Serializability: A Correctness Criterion for Processing Transactions in Advanced Database Applications. DATA & KNOWLEDGE ENGINEERING, 31, 1999.
4. Brayner A. and Härder T.: Global Semantic Serializability: An Approach to Increase Concurrency in Multidatabase Systems. Cooperative Information Systems - Lecture Notes in Computer Science. 301–315. Springer-Verlag, 2001.

5. Dunham M. H. and Kumar V.: Impact of Mobility on Transaction Management. In Proceedings of the International Workshop on Data Engineering for Wireless and Mobile Access, August 1999. pp. 14–21.
6. Emerich W., Mascolo C. and Finkelstein A.: Implementing Incremental Code Migration with XML. Proceedings of the 22nd International Conference on Software Engineering. Limerick, Ireland. 2000. pp. 397–406.
7. Holliday J., Agrawal D. and A. Abbadi E.: Planned Disconnections for Mobile Databases. In Proceedings of the 11th IEEE International Workshop on Database and Expert Systems, 2001.
8. Ives Z., Florescu D., Friedman M., Levy A and Weld D. S.: An Adaptative Query Execution System for Data Integration. In Proceedings of ACM SIGMOD International Conference on Management of Data, Philadelphia, USA. 1999. pp. 299–310.
9. Kemper A. and Wiesner C.: HyperQueries: Dynamic Distributed Query Processing on the Internet. In Proceedings of 27TH International Conference on Very Large Databases, Roma, Italy. 2001. pp-551–560.
10. Lange D. B. and Oshima M.: Programming and Deploying Java Mobile Agents with Aglets. Addison-Wesley. Massachusets, USA. 1998.
11. Jing J., Helal A. and Elmagarmid A.: Client-Server Computing in Mobile Environments, ACM Computing Surveys, Vol. 31, No. 2, pp. 117–157. June 1999.
12. Macker J. P. and Corson M. S.: Mobile Ad Hoc Networks and the IETF. Internet Engineering Task Force, MANET Working Group. Online at http://www.ietf.org/html.charter/manet-charter.html.
13. Manolescu I., Florescu D., Kossman D.: Answering XML Queries over Heterogeneous Data Sources. In Proceedings of 27TH International Conference on Very Large Databases, Roma, Italy. 2001. pp. 241–250.
14. Mendonça N. C., Brayner A. and Monteiro J. M.: Mobile Database Communities: An approach for Sharing Autonomous Mobile Database in Ad Hoc Networks. Submitted for publication. 2002.
15. Murphy A. L., Pico G. P. and Roman G.-C.: Lime: A Middleware for Physical and Logical Mobility. Proceedings of the 21st International Conference on Distributed Computing Systems. April 2001. pp. 524–533.
16. Özsu M. T. and Valduriez P.: Principles of Distributed Database Systems. 2nd Edition Prentice Hall, 1999.
17. Patel J. M.: Query Processing in Mobile Environments. NFS Wokshop on Context Aware Mobile Database Management (CAMM). January 24-25, 2002, Providence, Rhode Island, USA. Online at http://www.sice.umkc.edu/nsfmobile/wshop.html/JigneshMPatel.pdf.
18. Phatak S. H., and Badrinath B. R.: An Architecture for Mobile Databases. Technical Report #DCS-TR-351. Rutgers University, Department of Computer Science. Online at ftp://www.cs.rutgers.edu/pub/technical-reports/dcs-tr-351.ps.Z.
19. Roman G.-C., Pico G. P. and Murphy A. L.: Software Engineering for Mobility: A Roadmap. In A. C. W. Finkelstein, editor: Future of Software Engineering. ACM Press, 2000.
20. Silberschatz A., Korth H. F. and Sudarshan S.: Database System Concepts. 3rd Edition McGraw Hill, 1998. ISBN 0070310866.
21. Singhal M.: Techniques for Building Large Relational Databases on Mobile Computing Systems. NFS Wokshop on Context Aware Mobile Database Management (CAMM). January 24–25, 2002. Providence, Rhode Island, USA. Online at http://www.sice.umkc.edu/nsfmobile/wshop.html/MukeshSinghal.pdf.
22. Vlach R., Lána J., Marek J. and Navarra D.: MDBAS – A Prototype of a Multidatabase Management System Based on Mobile Agents. Proceedings of the 27th Annual Conference on Current Trends in Theory and Practice of Informatics (SOFSEM), Springer-Verlag, Nov. 25 – Dec. 2, 2000. Milovy, Czech Republic.
23. XML Schema. Online at http://www.w3.org/XML/Schema.

24. XQuery 1.0 Formal Semantics. Online at http://www.w3.org/TR/query-semantics/.
25. Soares M., Brayner A.: MXQUERY: An XQuery-like Multidatabase Language. Submitted for publication. 2002.
26. Grant J., Litwin W., Roussopoulos N., Sellis T.: Query Languages for Relational Multidatabases. In Proc. of 19th VLDB Conference. 1993.

Author Index

Lecture Notes in Computer Science

For information about Vols. 1–2609

please contact your bookseller or Springer-Verlag

Vol. 2610: C. Ryan, T. Soule, M. Keijzer, E. Tsang, R. Poli, E. Costa (Eds.), Genetic Programming. Proceedings, 2003. XII, 486 pages. 2003.

Vol. 2611: S. Cagnoni, J.J. Romero Cardalda, D.W. Corne, J. Gottlieb, A. Guillot, E. Hart, C.G. Johnson, E. Marchiori, J.-A. Meyer, M. Middendorf, G.R. Raidl (Eds.), Applications of Evolutionary Computing. Proceedings, 2003. XXI, 708 pages. 2003.

Vol. 2612: M. Joye (Ed.), Topics in Cryptology – CT-RSA 2003. Proceedings, 2003. XI, 417 pages. 2003.

Vol. 2613: F.A.P. Petitcolas, H.J. Kim (Eds.), Digital Watermarking. Proceedings, 2002. XI, 265 pages. 2003.

Vol. 2614: R. Laddaga, P. Robertson, H. Shrobe (Eds.), Self-Adaptive Software: Applications. Proceedings, 2001. VIII, 291 pages. 2003.

Vol. 2615: N. Carbonell, C. Stephanidis (Eds.), Universal Access. Proceedings, 2002. XIV, 534 pages. 2003.

Vol. 2616: T. Asano, R. Klette, C. Ronse (Eds.), Geometry, Morphology, and Computational Imaging. Proceedings, 2002. X, 437 pages. 2003.

Vol. 2617: H.A. Reijers (Eds.), Design and Control of Workflow Processes. Proceedings, 2002. XV, 624 pages. 2003.

Vol. 2618: P. Degano (Ed.), Programming Languages and Systems. Proceedings, 2003. XV, 415 pages. 2003.

Vol. 2619: H. Garavel, J. Hatcliff (Eds.), Tools and Algorithms for the Construction and Analysis of Systems. Proceedings, 2003. XVI, 604 pages. 2003.

Vol. 2620: A.D. Gordon (Ed.), Foundations of Software Science and Computation Structures. Proceedings, 2003. XII, 441 pages. 2003.

Vol. 2621: M. Pezzè (Ed.), Fundamental Approaches to Software Engineering. Proceedings, 2003. XIV, 403 pages. 2003.

Vol. 2622: G. Hedin (Ed.), Compiler Construction. Proceedings, 2003. XII, 335 pages. 2003.

Vol. 2623: O. Maler, A. Pnueli (Eds.), Hybrid Systems: Computation and Control. Proceedings, 2003. XII, 558 pages. 2003.

Vol. 2624: H.G. Dietz (Ed.), Languages and Compilers for Parallel Computing. Proceedings, 2001. XI, 444 pages. 2003.

Vol. 2625: U. Meyer, P. Sanders, J. Sibeyn (Eds.), Algorithms for Memory Hierarchies. Proceedings, 2003. XVIII, 428 pages. 2003.

Vol. 2626: J.L. Crowley, J.H. Piater, M. Vincze, L. Paletta (Eds.), Computer Vision Systems. Proceedings, 2003. XIII, 546 pages. 2003.

Vol. 2627: B. O'Sullivan (Ed.), Recent Advances in Constraints. Proceedings, 2002. X, 201 pages. 2003. (Subseries LNAI).

Vol. 2627: B. O'Sullivan (Ed.), Recent Advances in Constraints. Proceedings, 2002. X, 201 pages. 2003. (Subseries LNAI).

Vol. 2628: T. Fahringer, B. Scholz, Advanced Symbolic Analysis for Compilers. XII, 129 pages. 2003.

Vol. 2631: R. Falcone, S. Barber, L. Korba, M. Singh (Eds.), Trust, Reputation, and Security: Theories and Practice. Proceedings, 2002. X, 235 pages. 2003. (Subseries LNAI).

Vol. 2632: C.M. Fonseca, P.J. Fleming, E. Zitzler, K. Deb, L. Thiele (Eds.), Evolutionary Multi-Criterion Optimization. Proceedings, 2003. XV, 812 pages. 2003.

Vol. 2633: F. Sebastiani (Ed.), Advances in Information Retrieval. Proceedings, 2003. XIII, 546 pages. 2003.

Vol. 2634: F. Zhao, L. Guibas (Eds.), Information Processing in Sensor Networks. Proceedings, 2003. XII, 692 pages. 2003.

Vol. 2636: E. Alonso, D, Kudenko, D. Kazakov (Eds.), Adaptive Agents and Multi-Agent Systems. XIV, 323 pages. 2003. (Subseries LNAI).

Vol. 2637: K.-Y. Whang, J. Jeon, K. Shim, J. Srivastava (Eds.), Advances in Knowledge Discovery and Data Mining. Proceedings, 2003. XVIII, 610 pages. 2003. (Subseries LNAI).

Vol. 2638: J. Jeuring, S. Peyton Jones (Eds.), Advanced Functional Programming. Proceedings, 2002. VII, 213 pages. 2003.

Vol. 2639: G. Wang, Q. Liu, Y. Yao, A. Skowron (Eds.), Rough Sets, Fuzzy Sets, Data Mining, and Granular Computing. Proceedings, 2003. XVII, 741 pages. 2003. (Subseries LNAI).

Vol. 2641: P.J. Nürnberg (Ed.), Metainformatics. Proceedings, 2002. VIII, 187 pages. 2003.

Vol. 2642: X. Zhou, Y. Zhang, M.E. Orlowska (Eds.), Web Technologies and Applications. Proceedings, 2003. XIII, 608 pages. 2003.

Vol. 2643: M. Fossorier, T. Høholdt, A. Poli (Eds.), Applied Algebra, Algebraic Algorithms and Error-Correcting Codes. Proceedings, 2003. X, 256 pages. 2003.

Vol. 2644: D. Hogrefe, A. Wiles (Eds.), Testing of Communicating Systems. Proceedings, 2003. XII, 311 pages. 2003.

Vol. 2645: M.A. Wimmer (Ed.), Knowledge Management in Electronic Government. Proceedings, 2003. XI, 320 pages. 2003. (Subseries LNAI).

Vol. 2646: H. Geuvers, F. Wiedijk (Eds.), Types for Proofs and Programs. Proceedings, 2002. VIII, 331 pages. 2003.

Vol. 2647: K.Jansen, M. Margraf, M. Mastrolli, J.D.P. Rolim (Eds.), Experimental and Efficient Algorithms. Proceedings, 2003. VIII, 267 pages. 2003.

Vol. 2648: T. Ball, S.K. Rajamani (Eds.), Model Checking Software. Proceedings, 2003. VIII, 241 pages. 2003.

Vol. 2649: B. Westfechtel, A. van der Hoek (Eds.), Software Configuration Management. Proceedings, 2003. VIII, 241 pages. 2003.

Vol. 2651: D. Bert, J.P. Bowen, S. King, M, Waldén (Eds.), ZB 2003: Formal Specification and Development in Z and B. Proceedings, 2003. XIII, 547 pages. 2003.

Vol. 2652: F.J. Perales, A.J.C. Campilho, N. Pérez de la Blanca, A. Sanfeliu (Eds.), Pattern Recognition and Image Analysis. Proceedings, 2003. XIX, 1142 pages. 2003.

Vol. 2653: R. Petreschi, Giuseppe Persiano, R. Silvestri (Eds.), Algorithms and Complexity. Proceedings, 2003. XI, 289 pages. 2003.

Vol. 2655: J.-P. Rosen, A. Strohmeier (Eds.), Reliable Software Technologies – Ada-Europe 2003. Proceedings, 2003. XIII, 489 pages. 2003.

Vol. 2656: E. Biham (Ed.), Advances in Cryptology – EUROCRPYT 2003. Proceedings, 2003. XIV, 429 pages. 2003.

Vol. 2657: P.M.A. Sloot, D. Abramson, A.V. Bogdanov, J.J. Dongarra, A.Y. Zomaya, Y.E. Gorbachev (Eds.), Computational Science – ICCS 2003. Proceedings, Part I. 2003. LV, 1095 pages. 2003.

Vol. 2658: P.M.A. Sloot, D. Abramson, A.V. Bogdanov, J.J. Dongarra, A.Y. Zomaya, Y.E. Gorbachev (Eds.), Computational Science – ICCS 2003. Proceedings, Part II. 2003. LV, 1129 pages. 2003.

Vol. 2659: P.M.A. Sloot, D. Abramson, A.V. Bogdanov, J.J. Dongarra, A.Y. Zomaya, Y.E. Gorbachev (Eds.), Computational Science – ICCS 2003. Proceedings, Part III. 2003. LV, 1165 pages. 2003.

Vol. 2660: P.M.A. Sloot, D. Abramson, A.V. Bogdanov, J.J. Dongarra, A.Y. Zomaya, Y.E. Gorbachev (Eds.), Computational Science – ICCS 2003. Proceedings, Part IV. 2003. LVI, 1161 pages. 2003.

Vol. 2663: E. Menasalvas, J. Segovia, P.S. Szczepaniak (Eds.), Advances in Web Intelligence. Proceedings, 2003. XII, 350 pages. 2003. (Subseries LNAI).

Vol. 2665: H. Chen, R. Miranda, D.D. Zeng, C. Demchak, J. Schroeder, T. Madhusudan (Eds.), Intelligence and Security Informatics. Proceedings, 2003. XIV, 392 pages. 2003.

Vol. 2667: V. Kumar, M.L. Gavrilova, C.J.K. Tan, P. L'Ecuyer (Eds.), Computational Science and Its Applications – ICCSA 2003. Proceedings, Part I. 2003. XXXIV, 1060 pages. 2003.

Vol. 2668: V. Kumar, M.L. Gavrilova, C.J.K. Tan, P. L'Ecuyer (Eds.), Computational Science and Its Applications – ICCSA 2003. Proceedings, Part II. 2003. XXXIV, 942 pages. 2003.

Vol. 2669: V. Kumar, M.L. Gavrilova, C.J.K. Tan, P. L'Ecuyer (Eds.), Computational Science and Its Applications – ICCSA 2003. Proceedings, Part III. 2003. XXXIV, 948 pages. 2003.

Vol. 2670: R. Peña, T. Arts (Eds.), Implementation of Functional Languages. Proceedings, 2002. X, 249 pages. 2003.

Vol. 2671: Y. Xiang, B. Chaib-draa (Eds.), Advances in Artificial Intelligence. Proceedings, 2003. XIV, 642 pages. 2003. (Subseries LNAI).

Vol. 2672: M. Endler, D. Schmidt (Eds.), Middleware 2003. Proceedings, 2003. XIII, 513 pages. 2003.

Vol. 2673: N. Ayache, H. Delingette (Eds.), Surgery Simulation and Soft Tissue Modeling. Proceedings, 2003. XII, 386 pages. 2003.

Vol. 2674: I.E. Magnin, J. Montagnat, P. Clarysse, J. Nenonen, T. Katila (Eds.), Functional Imaging and Modeling of the Heart. Proceedings, 2003. XI, 308 pages. 2003.

Vol. 2675: M. Marchesi, G. Succi (Eds.), Extreme Programming and Agile Processes in Software Engineering. Proceedings, 2003. XV, 464 pages. 2003.

Vol. 2676: R. Baeza-Yates, E. Chávez, M. Crochemore (Eds.), Combinatorial Pattern Matching. Proceedings, 2003. XI, 403 pages. 2003.

Vol. 2678: W. van der Aalst, A. ter Hofstede, M. Weske (Eds.), Business Process Management. Proceedings, 2003. XI, 391 pages. 2003.

Vol. 2679: W. van der Aalst, E. Best (Eds.), Applications and Theory of Petri Nets 2003. Proceedings, 2003. XI, 508 pages. 2003.

Vol. 2680: P. Blackburn, C. Ghidini, R.M. Turner, F. Giunchiglia (Eds.), Modeling and Using Context. Proceedings, 2003. XII, 525 pages. 2003. (Subseries LNAI).

Vol. 2681: J. Eder, M. Missikoff (Eds.), Advanced Information Systems Engineering. Proceedings, 2003. XV, 740 pages. 2003.

Vol. 2686: J. Mira, J.R. Álvarez (Eds.), Computational Methods in Neural Modeling. Proceedings, Part I. 2003. XXVII, 764 pages. 2003.

Vol. 2687: J. Mira, J.R. Álvarez (Eds.), Artificial Neural Nets Problem Solving Methods. Proceedings, Part II. 2003. XXVII, 820 pages. 2003.

Vol. 2688: J. Kittler, M.S. Nixon (Eds.), Audio- and Video-Based Biometric Person Authentication. Proceedings, 2003. XVII, 978 pages. 2003.

Vol. 2689: K.D. Ashley, D.G. Bridge (Eds.), Case-Based Reasoning Research and Development. Proceedings, 2003. XV, 734 pages. 2003. (Subseries LNAI).

Vol. 2692: P. Nixon, S. Terzis (Eds.), Trust Management. Proceedings, 2003. X, 349 pages. 2003.

Vol. 2694: R. Cousot (Ed.), Static Analysis. Proceedings, 2003. XIV, 505 pages. 2003.

Vol. 2695: L.D. Griffin, M. Lillholm (Eds.), Scale Space Methods in Computer Vision. Proceedings, 2003. XII, 816 pages. 2003.

Vol. 2701: M. Hofmann (Ed.), Typed Lambda Calculi and Applications. Proceedings, 2003. VIII, 317 pages. 2003.

Vol. 2702: P. Brusilovsky, A. Corbett, F. de Rosis (Eds.), User Modeling 2003. Proceedings, 2003. XIV, 436 pages. 2003. (Subseries LNAI).

Vol. 2704: S.-T. Huang, T. Herman (Eds.), Self-Stabilizing Systems. Proceedings, 2003. X, 215 pages. 2003.

Vol. 2706: R. Nieuwenhuis (Ed.), Rewriting Techniques and Applications. Proceedings, 2003. XI, 515 pages. 2003.

Vol. 2707: K. Jeffay, I. Stoica, K. Wehrle (Eds.), Quality of Service – IWQoS 2003. Proceedings, 2003. XI, 517 pages. 2003.

Vol. 2709: T. Windeatt, F. Roli (Eds.), Multiple Classifier Systems. Proceedings, 2003. X, 406 pages. 2003.

Vol. 2714: O. Kaynak, E. Alpaydin, E. Oja, L. Xu (Eds.), Artificial Neural Networks and Neural Information Processing – ICANN/ICONIP 2003. Proceedings, 2003. XXII, 1188 pages. 2003.

Vol. 2716: M.J. Voss (Ed.), OpenMP Shared Memory Parallel Programming. Proceedings, 2003. VIII, 271 pages. 2003.